COLONEL DAVID
[U.S. ARMY, Ret.]

ABOUT FACE

H. HACKWORTH
and JULIE SHERMAN

A TOUCHSTONE BOOK

Published by Simon & Schuster Inc.

New York London Toronto Sydney Tokyo Singapore

TOUCHSTONE

SIMON & SCHUSTER BUILDING
ROCKEFELLER CENTER
1230 AVENUE OF THE AMERICAS
NEW YORK, NEW YORK 10020

FIRST TOUCHSTONE EDITION, 1990
TOUCHSTONE AND COLOPHON ARE REGISTERED TRADEMARKS OF
SIMON & SCHUSTER INC.
DESIGNED BY KAROLINA HARRIS
MANUFACTURED IN THE UNITED STATES OF AMERICA

10 9 8 7 6 5
10 9 8 7 6 5 4 3 2 1 PBK.

LIBRARY OF CONGRESS CATALOGING IN PUBLICATION DATA

HACKWORTH, DAVID H.
    ABOUT FACE.

    BIBLIOGRAPHY: P.
    INCLUDES INDEX.
    1. HACKWORTH, DAVID H.   2. UNITED STATES. ARMY—
BIOGRAPHY.   3. SOLDIERS—UNITED STATES—BIOGRAPHY.
4. KOREAN WAR, 1950–53—PERSONAL NARRATIVES, AMERICAN.
I. SHERMAN, JULIE.   II. TITLE.
U53.H25A3   1989   355'.0092'4 [B]   88-36235
ISBN 0-671-52692-8
ISBN 0-671-69534-7 PBK.

Dedication

To Steve Prazenka, who showed us how to soldier;
To Henry Deboer, who showed us how to die;
To Glover Johns, who showed us how to lead;
And to all the doughboys, the groundpounders, the grunts—
    the American infantrymen
—past, present, and, especially, future,
to them this book is dedicated.

CONTENTS

I

II

MAPS OF KOREA
AND VIETNAM

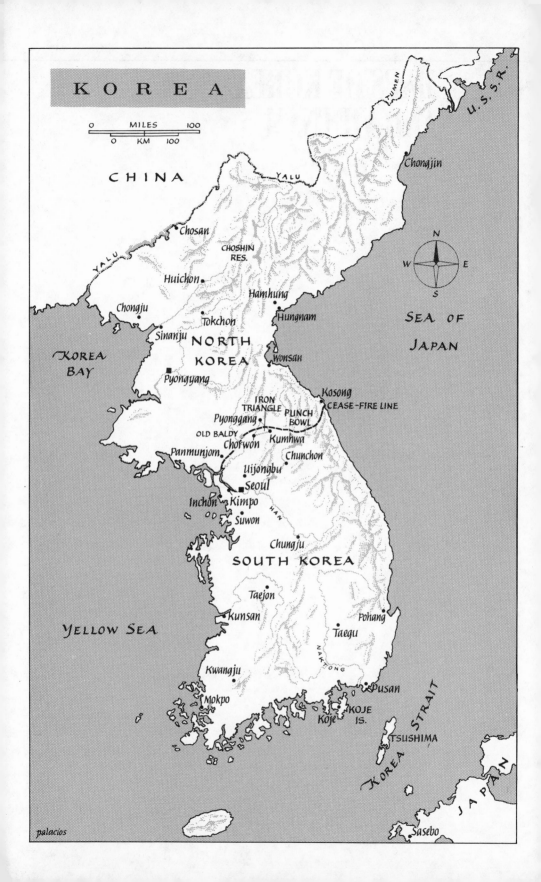

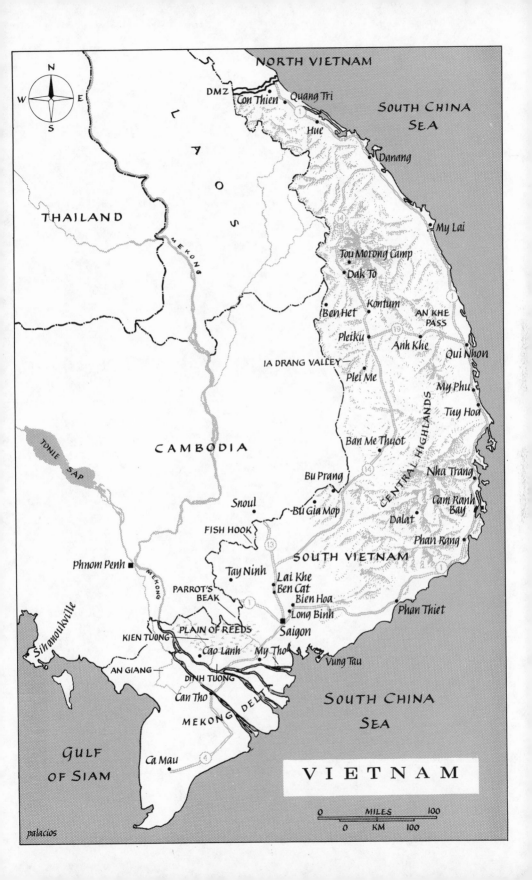

AUTHORS' NOTE

W<small>AR</small> stories present two problems to authors striving for The Truth. First of all, if you live long enough to tell them, and have enough of an audience to practice telling them *to* through the years, war stories become just that—stories. Just as time distances the storyteller from the events themselves, so do the repeated tellings. Gradually the stories are embellished in places, honed down in others until they are perfect tales, even if they bear little resemblance to what actually happened. Yet the storyteller is completely unaware of how far he may have strayed from the facts. Those countless tellings have made the stories The Truth.

The second problem with war stories is they have their genesis in the fog of war. In battle, your perception is often only as wide as your battle sights. Five participants in the same action, fighting side by side, will often tell entirely different stories of what happened, even within hours of the fight. The story each man tells might be virtually unrecognizable to the others. But that does not make it any less true.

A substantial part of the four years we worked on *About Face* was spent solving the problems that war stories create. In the earliest stage that meant, by day, regaling an audience of one with well-worn tales of youthful escapades on the battlefield, and by night beginning to dream the true and often horrible details of those "glory days," details that had been cheerfully overlooked in that day's narrative, or that perhaps had theretofore been locked away behind steel doors deep in the mind.

The next stage was finding other participants in the same events, the whereabouts of almost all of whom were unknown, usually with no clues save the single detail of a guy's hometown. (It is a curious trait in soldiers: twenty, thirty, even forty years down the track, they may not remember their buddies' first names, but they always seem to remember where they came from.) We *needed* these guys, to bring skewed-by-the-telling war stories back into focus and to fill in the blanks, to give us the view through *their* battle sights and to allow us to peer through the fog of war.

As a couple of determined civilians in the Department of the Army (DA) took up our cause and began to attach names (which we provided, many of them with fractured, phonetic spellings), ranks, and assignments long past with addresses here and now, through other DA channels and the Freedom of Information Act we began to collect after-action reports, unit journals, and thousands of pages of miscellaneous reference materials that gave us the official views of what had previously been seen only through one man's eyes (at least as far as we could prove). These documents, particularly those pertaining to the Korean War, helped enormously to round out an accurate picture of the time, and what a relief it was when the official word, abbreviated and "sanitized" as it might have been, jibed perfectly with a vague but no less strong personal recollection.

Soon, with the help of DA, lots of old friends began to check into the net. Many of them knew where other old comrades were (who in turn just happened to know how to find others still), and before long our list of contributors numbered some three hundred, covering four decades and running the gamut from four-star generals to buck privates, Regular Army men to one-hitch citizen soldiers. Through scores of interviews and thousands of pages of letters exchanged across the oceans, these men corroborated (our primary goal) and added color to the stories as we knew them. When they shared their disparate versions of "what really happened" in a battle or an event that occurred from two to four decades ago, we looked for the common thread among them (taking into account that these guys, too, had memories of varying degrees of reliability), and then, as appropriate, wove a composite picture that dovetailed with the remembered experience of Soldier David Hackworth. In this way, we hoped to give our audience a sense of the "bigger picture" that individually none of these men could have had.

Our object was honesty and accuracy; to the best of our ability and knowledge, in *About Face* we achieved both, and we apologize for any inadvertent errors or omissions on our part. To the many fine and brave soldiers who aren't mentioned by name in the pages that follow, but whose contributions to the efforts described therein were invaluable, our apologies and our respect.

We acknowledge, with boundless gratitude, the hundreds of soldiers, past and present, who took the time and, in so many cases, the great effort to help us transform *About Face* from a bunch of war stories into a broader tale of more lasting value. Our heartfelt thanks to the Department of the Army's Public Affairs Office and Valerie Sladek, who started the ball rolling to find these men; to Joyce L. Wiesner at DA's Reserve Personnel Center in St. Louis, who since mid-1985 has been an indispensable link for us between past and present; to Colonel Morris Herbert (USA, Ret.) of the U.S. Military Academy Association of Graduates, who forwarded myriads of letters on our behalf to West Point alumni all over the country; to *Infantry*, *Army*, and West Point's *Assembly* magazines, the *Army Times* and the Airborne's *Static Line* newspapers as well as to the 101st Airborne and 25th Division associations, all of which published our all-points alert requests for various people to get in touch; and a special thanks to Tim Swain (Intelligence officer, 1st Brigade, 101st Airborne Division, 1965–66) of Peoria, Illinois—our Dick Tracy, who used his Intelligence skills to track down much-needed individuals when all our other means failed.

We thank Marlys James, Louise Sherman Zemel, and David Hackworth Riggs, our Los Angeles, Washington, D.C., and Deep South liaison officers (LNOs); David Joel Hackworth, who made many journeys to the library at the University of California, Berkeley, on our request; the Public Affairs offices at Fort Benning and Fort Campbell; retired Colonels (USA) Floyd S. Gibson, Wyatt J. Mitchell, and Robert E. Macklin (Operations officer, 1st Brigade, 101st Airborne Division, 1963–64), who, along with retired Colonel Albert N. Garland, editor of *Infantry* magazine, kept us up to date on goings-on in the United States and in the U.S. Army with our own personal clipping and information service; Roy and Helen Hackworth, Jennifer Bates Jaensch, and Ward Just, all of whom saved and then so kindly shared with us the letters they'd received from the battlefield, letters that fixed names and dates and separated many a truth from the memory of it; Dina Rasor and Danielle Brian-Bland of the Project on Military Procurement; Dr. Joseph M. Siracusa, professor of history, University of Queensland (Australia), and the staff of the library there; the staff of the Mitchell Library in Sydney; and our invaluable secretaries, Jennifer Porter and Patricia Jackson.

Our thanks, too, to those Old Soldiers who read our work in progress, making suggestions, correcting errors in fact, and/or leading us back onto the path when we'd begun to wander. Chief among these men are Lieutenant Colonel Kenneth L. Eggleston (USA, Ret.), who reviewed the entire manuscript and whose enthusiasm and encouragement were no less vital to our effort than they had been almost forty years before, when as Corporal Hackworth's company commander in Italy "Captain E" said the magic words that caused the boy to re-up; Lieutenant General Henry E. Emerson (USA, Ret.) and Colonel Henrik O. Lunde (USA, Ret.), two of the great warriors of the Vietnam War, whose objective views of the second half of the book helped us add to its strength; also Colonels George Couch, Richard E. Dryer, Phillip J. Gilchrist, and Joseph B. Love, Lieutenant Colonel Dell G. Evans, Command Sergeant Majors John G. Gallagher and Robert A. Press (all USA, Ret.); Colonel George F. Mergner, Brigadier General John D. Howard, and warriors Richard R. Alexander and Jack

Speed. Finally, our thanks to Allen Peacock, our editor at Simon and Schuster, who believed passionately in the project when it was little more than an idea, and who had the tenacity and the faith in us to shut off the radio and let us get on with the job long after we'd thrown the schedule to the wind and higher headquarters was screaming for results.

For a long time during the writing of this book, we considered titling it *Line of Departure*, which is a U.S. military term that refers to an imaginary line drawn along a battle zone, the crossing of which by military units signals the start of an operation. When you cross the LD there's no turning back. So as we make ready to cross *our* LD with this book (albeit with a different title), a final word to our contributors, our readers, and especially to former Secretary of the Army Stanley Resor, who seventeen years ago so wisely cautioned one very embittered soldier to take time to cool off before going on record. The common wish among our correspondents—a wish expressed by retired, active-duty, and one-hitch personnel alike, just as it had been by Stanley Resor years ago—was that our work make a positive contribution to the U.S. Army today. While *About Face* is primarily the story of one man's military career, in recalling that career our goal throughout has been to make the present and future U.S. Army the most effective, the most efficient—the best—that it can be, for itself, and for the country it must defend.

David H. Hackworth and Julie Sherman

Queensland, Australia
October 1988

INTRODUCTION

A professional soldier's life does not fit easily into memoir unless the soldier is a senior commander, and then the memoir centers on grand strategy and not the coarse details of the battlefield; an exception, and there are not very many, is the *Personal Memoirs of U. S. Grant*. A common soldier's life seems better suited to fiction, where the author can calibrate the distance between the protagonist and the material. The novelist can assert coherence and moral balance, and it is not necessary that he or she ever heard a shot fired in anger—Stephen Crane, for example, or Olivia Manning. The personality of the author is of no consequence; the best single explication of infantry tactics that I have ever read is in Marcel Proust's *The Guermantes Way*. Of course the novelist is a writer first and foremost, comfortable on the higher slopes of irony and paradox. The novelist's reality is a written reality, forged from facts and memories, fragments of this and that, reprocessed and rewired into a narrative, a *story*.

The soldier's memory is a crowded place. More can "happen" in a minute of a soldier's wartime than in a novelist's lifetime—and happen again and again, moments of such excruciating incoherence that to shape it and balance it is to counterfeit it. One might as well try to shape a tempest. These moments are fantastic, scarcely credible, grotesque, sentimental, heartless, usually inexplicable, rarely of beauty—terrible or otherwise, though they can be noble. There is no distance between the man and the action. Nothing falls between the man and the chaotic moment except the years of training and anticipation, "a predicament of exceptional awkwardness," according to a Northern soldier at Antietam. It is never as you thought it would be. It is hard to conceive of a more demanding assignment than leading troops into battle, and keeping them there, saying to a man, "Do that," knowing that his death might result. A soldier in wartime is a law unto himself in a world unto itself, an exaggerated, exasperated world of utter disorder and misrule, the devil's paradise; it is either that or unspeakably boring, weeks and months of oceanic tedium.

Yet there are those who love it, all of it: the drill, the bivouac, the mess tent, the duty, the noise, and the silence. Probably no segment of American

society is as little known and little understood as the professional Army. It is
a nation apart, with its particular customs, laws, language, economy,
virtues, and vices. This is a state of affairs that seems to suit everyone; the
civilians can retail clichés about the soldiers, and the soldiers retail clichés
about themselves, with no one the wiser. The Army is as hierarchical as the
church and as class-conscious and snobbish as Great Britain, West Point its
Eton and the Army War College its Oxford. The Army today resembles a
great ponderous American corporation, but it was not always so. The Army
used to be filled with officers who believed their highest calling was to lead
troops into battle, not as one more Station of the Cross on their way to the
E-Ring of the Pentagon, military Gethsemane; that was why they were in
the Army instead of at General Dynamics. There were soldiers who studied
infantry tactics with the care and intelligence that Picasso devoted to the
female face, and so thoroughly that the knowledge became second nature,
almost instinct. The soldier is rarely articulate on these matters, as anyone
who has read a battle plan or an article in one of the military magazines can
attest. These documents, though far from literature, retain a coarse
authority. All soldiers know that battle is not symmetrical, it exists in its own
lawless reality, unique even as it reverberates. Verdun may have its echo in
Dien Bien Phu and Dien Bien Phu in Khe Sanh. But these are only echoes,
not the thing itself. Hemingway's scrupulously orchestrated retreat from
Caporetto is a narrative of great power. Novels and histories are wonderful
and indispensable, but they are not the thing itself.

This book is the thing itself.

I met David Hackworth in the ruins of a base camp in the Central
Highlands of South Vietnam in the summer of 1966, when he was
commanding a battalion of the 101st Airborne Division and I was a
correspondent for *The Washington Post*. He was compact, with forearms the
size of hams. His uniform was filthy and unadorned with any insignia save
the major's leaf. The base camp had been nearly overrun the night before
and now he was exhorting his troops; and they were listening, in part
because Hackworth's use of obscenity was truly inventive. Later, describing
the encounter to the writer Martha Gellhorn, I said I was struck by his
enthusiasm, his magnetism, his exuberance, his invincible cheerfulness.
Gellhorn hated the Vietnam War completely and without reservation but at
that she nodded and smiled. Yes, she said. That was the way they were in
World War II. That was the way the best of them were. It made you want
to be around them.

David Hackworth is the genuine article, a soldier's soldier, a connoisseur
of combat. He prefers the word "warrior" and is entitled to prefer it. Combat

has been his life. He enlisted in the Army at fifteen, received a battlefield commission in Korea at twenty, was four times wounded before he was twenty-one, was probably the most decorated officer in the American Army at the time of his retirement in 1971, a full colonel bound for two, conceivably three, stars had he not— But that is the subject of *About Face*, the most important soldier's memoir to emerge from the Vietnam era. This is the U.S. Army from the inside, the memoir of an infantry officer who loved the institution with the indiscriminate ardor and lavish expectations of any moonstruck Romeo. He believed the recruiting posters. He believed the legends. He believed in the Army way, as opposed to the right way or the wrong way, and he wanted to become a hero, Alvin York or Audie Murphy. The enemy would be anyone who the Army told him was the enemy. He knew that barriers of class and education would keep him from the very top of the institution, but he did not want the very top. He wanted a platoon, then he wanted a company, then he wanted a battalion, and then he wanted a brigade. Someone else could be Chief of Staff; Hackworth wanted the line.

He learned his trade, as most successful line officers do, from sergeants. The postwar peacetime Army was filled with battlewise NCOs who knew the score, not from training films but from the battleground itself. Care for your men. Maintain discipline. Always set an example. You take fewer casualties attacking than retreating: "Your job is not to die for your country but to make the other son of a bitch die for his country." Once engaged, give no quarter. Drill, drill, drill. Stay alert, stay alive. The sergeants were good teachers, but in Korea Hackworth saw the thing itself and knew he could master it. He understood the atmosphere of violence, meaning that he knew how to keep his head, to think in danger's midst. In battle, the worst thing is paralysis. He mastered his own fear, and learned how to kill. He led by example, and his men followed. This book describes all that, and the men: Deboer, Aguda, many others, many dead.

This is a world so remote from the common civilian experience that the reader must remind himself that this is not some ill-conceived movie but a man's life. Korea ended, but the career did not. Later, as captain, major, lieutenant colonel, and colonel, there were other models, the Army's fighting elite: James Gavin and Creighton Abrams from the previous generation, Hank Emerson from his own generation. By his own account, Hackworth was not an obedient protégé, and tact was never his long suit; but his heroics in Korea were a powerful credential. He made his way up on soldierly abilities alone, learning as he went. Hackworth was appalled when General Gavin resigned from the Army in protest, but by then he understood that the headquarters Army was different from the field Army, and that both had changed in the postwar fifties. "In this new Army, no one could afford to tell the truth, make an error, or admit to ignorance." When John F. Kennedy decided to commit large numbers of American advisers to South Vietnam, Hackworth volunteered at once—and was startled to be turned down. He had too much combat experience. Too *much?* Yes, he was told, the role of the American adviser was not to seek combat but to train the Vietnamese Army to seek combat, and therefore combat veterans were not needed, not *desired.* This seemed an oddly fastidious concept—war with kid gloves, let's not dirty our hands or theirs—and of course was abandoned as the Communists continued to advance and the Vietnamese Army to collapse. There were successive tours in South Vietnam—including a remarkable stint with S. L. A. Marshall, the military writer whose work must now be examined afresh—and Hackworth's disgust and pessimism grew with each tour. He found the Army lying to itself and to everyone else. The Pentagon seemed to be treating the war as the occasion for career management of its officers, every lieutenant colonel entitled to a battalion, every colonel to a brigade, and never mind the officer's qualifications. Meanwhile, the war was being lost, buried in an avalanche of bogus statistics and false promises of progress. Finally, the American command initiated the cowardly and murderous foray into Cambodia, where ARVN battalions were shredded as the frightened and ill-prepared paper tigers they were. Hackworth gave his pessimistic after-action report to senior American commanders and was told to sit down and shut up. Defeatists were not welcome. The truth was unspeakable.

His last assignment was as senior adviser to the 44th Special Tactical Zone in the South Vietnamese Delta near the Cambodian border, and it would be the final turn of the screw. On the surface, the war was being won. There were few large-scale engagements, roads were open, and terrorist activity (both sides) was down. Official reports suggested the corollary: If the Viet Cong were retreating, the ARVN must be advancing. All wrong, as Hackworth soon learned. The Communists had moved into a new phase of their struggle, and the ARVN was as ineffective as ever. But the reports were received with enthusiasm in Washington, and Hackworth was one of the first to see the grotesque irony. "It was as if the system had come full circle: these same reports, which had been in large part responsible for *escalating* the war, were now eagerly sought after by the Nixon administration as the ultimate smokescreen for their abandonment of the effort."

The last assignment, very far into no-man's-land, off the map where no rules applied, culminated in the celebrated "Issues and Answers" interview. Broadcast from the field, it was a sensation. Hackworth disclosed the bankruptcy of American training and tactics and the incapacity of the

Vietnamese Army, identified the lies and some of the liars who kept it afloat, and all but declared the war a lost cause, unwinnable. This was the simple truth, but in the pusillanimous atmosphere of 1971, Hackworth was seen as insubordinate and treacherous. But not easily dismissed. The words, after all, came not from an academic or journalist but from the man Creighton Abrams called "the best battalion commander I ever saw in the United States Army."

David Hackworth always promised to write something about his life as a soldier, something that might be believed because it was firsthand material; and because he was who he was, people might pay attention. The Army brass might read it, even though they would not like it and would try to discredit it. But they would have to account for it. *About Face* is not a pretty or orderly story, and it takes us farther into the quotidian life of the professional soldier than anything I have ever read; as a manual to the military tactics of the Vietnam War, it is without equal. Reading this life, you wonder how anyone survived it.

Ward Just
Vineyard Haven, Massachusetts
September 1988

ABOUT FACE

PART I

1   6 FEBRUARY 1951

We called him "Combat" because on training maneuvers he'd go up the goddamn hill standing up and shooting. The whole platoon harassed him for not using cover, but on the next problem he'd do the same thing. Hack was an eager guy. He did things—he didn't sit back and wait.

Captain Steve Prazenka, USA, Ret.
Intelligence and Reconnaissance Platoon Sergeant
Trieste United States Troops (TRUST), 1947–50

WHEN I first saw them, about a thousand yards to our front, the enemy looked like little black ants racing from the village toward snow-covered hills. It was a clear, cloudless morning; the temperature hovered around zero as the tanks kept rolling, closing on the ants and the hills set astride the road dead ahead.

My squad was riding piggyback on the lead tank. It was no honor being first in the grim parade; we'd already ravaged the tank's toolbox and knocked off some rations to eat on the way, and now our only comfort was the motor of the M46, which belched welcome heat over our near-frozen bodies.

The tank commander relayed Lieutenant Land's order to dismount. I got the guys off like a shot and hit the ground running as the tank rolled on beside us. But when I looked behind me, I saw that the rest of the 3d Platoon had not dismounted. Maybe I'd heard wrong. Maybe I was just overeager. But it's damn near impossible for infantrymen to reboard a moving tank, so there was no choice but to keep running, and hope I hadn't blown it too badly with the Lieutenant.

I didn't see the ants again for what seemed a lifetime, but I sure as hell knew where they were. In an instant, the familiar roar of the tanks was drowned out by the deafening sound of incoming—machine gun, mortar, artillery, and self-propelled antitank (AT) fire. Like a buzz saw, the deadly cross fire was cutting into my platoon.

There were at least a dozen enemy machine guns on the high ground on both sides of the road. My guys, still running alongside our maneuvering tank, were totally shielded; the other squads, on the exposed decks of their tanks, were hard hit. By the time we made it to the side of a rice-paddy wall and set up a base of fire, most of what was left of 3d Platoon was scattered across the frozen ground.

The tanks pulled off the road and rolled into position on line. Once there, they froze. Earlier, in the assembly area, a tank commander had told me his unit, the 64th Tank Battalion, hadn't seen much hard combat. I believed him: as soon as they were fired upon, these tankers became paralyzed. They plumb forgot all their training and just sat there in those great big armored hulls, while the enemy went on throwing everything at us but the mess-hall wok.

I jumped on the back of the platoon leader's tank, and thumped on the hatch with the butt of my rifle. The lieutenant opened the hatch a crack. "Hey, Lieutenant," I yelled, "get some fire going at the enemy! Get the big gun going! Get the machine guns going!"

The Lieutenant was not with it. It seemed as though he had no comprehension of the fix we were in. Slugs were splatting hard on the side of the tank. The self-propelled AT fire, which was screaming down the valley, dug deep furrows all around us, and yet the tanks still sat there silently, like big, fat clay ducks at a shooting gallery. "Sergeant," the Lieutenant finally said, in a shell-shocked kind of daze, "look . . . you see that out there on the ice?" Yes, I saw: it was a pile cap, a little fur ball on the ice amid my platoon's dead and wounded, the bullets and the blood. "That's my cap," he said. "Would you get it for me?"

I considered shooting the sorry son of a bitch then and there, climbing inside his tank and taking command. Fortunately, reason prevailed: I just grabbed him and shook him until he looked as if he was back to the real world. Then I instructed him to have three tanks concentrate on the self-propelled AT fire to our front, and use the others to start placing main-gun fire on the hills. To give him a bit of encouragement, I manned the tank's .50-caliber turret machine gun and blasted one of the hills myself, until I'd used up all the ammo and the commander got his men into action.

Once the 90-mm guns got going, we were on our way to gaining fire superiority. The amount of incoming decreased as the tankers started to remember why they were there. But the tank commanders stayed buttoned up inside their turrets. No one was using the .50 calibers. I just couldn't believe it—eight inches of steel between them and the chaos outside, yet they didn't have it in them to help the sun come out for the guys stopping slugs with their field jackets. I went from tank to tank, pounding on the hatches and blasting away on each of the .50s until all the ammo was exhausted. This little exercise had its effect; the tank commanders got the word and started doing what they should have been doing all along. When no further spoon-feeding was required, I returned to my platoon.

There were dead and wounded everywhere. Slugs were ricocheting off the ice; we could see sparks where they hit. Jim Parker's 2d Platoon had successfully silenced an enemy machine gun to our left, so the pressure was off enough for us to get our wounded behind the protection of the tanks and paddy walls, where they could be patched up. Our progress was hampered, though, because the tank crews kept moving their tanks. They didn't stop to think they were exposing our wounded all over again; they were too busy trying to save their own armor-coated skins. I told the tank lieutenant, whom I'd come to view—and treat accordingly—as a recruit at Fort Knox, that the next time a tank moved and exposed our guys I'd fire a 3.5 bazooka right up its ass. There was no more movement.

I saw a soldier prone on the ice. He'd been there a long time; I thought he was dead. But then I saw movement, and rushed out to get him. *My God*, I thought, *it's Deboer.*

Private Henry C. Deboer had been with George Company since early in the war. He was one of the few survivors from the original 3d Platoon, basically because in those first hard months of combat he had not seen one good firefight. He had an uncanny sixth sense: he could always tell when the platoon was in for a major bloodletting, and invariably he'd find an excuse to be somewhere else. Normally that excuse was going on sick call, which by regulation he was allowed to do, and you couldn't stop him even though you knew the only thing that was wrong with him was a chronic case of cowardice. Deboer himself even admitted he was a coward, and we hated him for it. He was an outcast from the platoon; we even had a little song about him, which we'd all sing in unison: "Out of the dark, dreary Korean countryside comes the call of the Deboer bird: *Sick call, sick call, sick call.*" He'd pulled his stunt only yesterday, as we were saddling up for this very operation. He'd sensed the bloodletting all right, but hadn't figured that the foggy overcast covering the battlefield would not lift and the attack would be postponed. He'd returned from the doc last night (with a clean bill of health) most surprised to see us; the rest of the platoon took great pleasure in the fact that his malingering little ass would be in the thick of things in the morning.

Now Deboer was ashen-faced, hit in the chest or gut—I didn't know, there was a lot of blood—and well into shock. I knew he wasn't going to make it. "Come on, Deboer, you're going to be fine! You'll be all right," I said, giving him the old pep talk as I grabbed his jacket collar and started sliding him across the ice.

But Deboer said, "No, Sarge! Just leave me . . . you're going to get hit!

Just leave me, Sarge . . ." Then suddenly he groaned: "Sarge, I shit my pants . . ." and that was it. He was gone. I left him and ran back.

Deboer, in death, became one of the great heroes of our outfit. It was true he'd never been anything in his Army life but a coward, but he'd *died* right—he died like a man. He didn't say, "Take care of me"; he said, "Leave me. Take care of yourself." And when I told the other guys the story, old Deboer became a legend in the platoon.

The road ran north–south, and we were on the east side of it. The balance of G Company was on the attack, maneuvering to secure the high ground to the north and west. My platoon, or what was left of it, was the "fix 'em" element—tying down the enemy while providing a base of fire for Parker's and Phil Gilchrist's platoons. After we got organized, I had a moment to look around. I saw my platoon leader, Lieutenant Land, sort of crouched down, leaning against the rice-paddy wall, observing the whole action. John Land was a good man; a WW II vet and former G Company NCO, he was one of the few battlefield commissions in the 27th. *Isn't he a cool customer,* I thought to myself now, *just watching this whole thing and taking it all in.* Because really that was about the only thing you could do at a time like this: stay cool, stay down, and establish fire superiority as best you could.

I examined what we had left in terms of a fighting force. "Tennessee" Mitchell, Delbert Bell, old Deboer—there were seven dead altogether, and about a dozen wounded. The platoon sergeant was gone and the assistant platoon sergeant nowhere in sight. It seemed that all that was left of 3d Platoon was the balance of my squad, bits and pieces of the other two, and a light-machine-gun team. I ran over to the Lieutenant to ask for instructions. When I got there I realized the reason Lieutenant Land was so cool was that he was dead. He'd caught a slug right between the eyes. The blood had poured down his face and chest, filled up the eyepieces of his binoculars, and frozen there. I took the binoculars and slipped the radio from his dead radio operator's back. I called Captain Michaely, our company commander, and gave him a situation report. He said I was now in charge, that we were to continue tying down the enemy and get the wounded out, in that order of priority.

Lieutenant Gilchrist's 1st Platoon was having a hell of a time. Their attack was being held up by fire from a hornet's nest of well-concealed enemy automatic-weapons positions. Just as we'd gotten the wounded under control, one of our guys who'd been doing some scouting spotted North Korean fighting positions on the other side of the dike 1st Platoon was attacking. He motioned me over to have a look. Sure enough, at least a platoon was dug in there, almost in the shadow of the tanks. They were so close that the tanks' main guns couldn't depress low enough to hit them, nor could their antitank weapons hit our tanks. It was a Mexican standoff, but not for long. "All right, who's going with me?" I asked.

"I will," said Van Mieter, our platoon medic, a stud of a guy who had as great a reputation as a fighter as he did as a doc.

While the others laid down a good base of fire, the doc and I each threw two frag grenades over the dike. When they exploded we leaped through the smoke, landing front and center of the enemy. It was eyeball-to-eyeball: the two of us facing at least thirty dazed, wounded, or dead Communists. The enemy appeared to be leaderless—they were certainly in a state of shock—and we cleaned up the position with ease, using rifles and bayonets. Then two more enemy soldiers appeared out of the smoke and confusion dragging a .57-caliber antitank "buffalo gun." We were no more than ten feet apart. I leveled my M-1 and was about to shoot when I looked down and saw that the bolt was back—my weapon was empty and it wasn't exactly the time for reloading. I lunged forward with bayonet at on guard, shouting, *"Tao zhong!"* The enemy threw up their hands.

The Chinese word for "surrender" was probably the only one I knew; I'd filed it away in my brain when we were up north. I must admit I learned it thinking that someone would be saying it to *me*, but it didn't matter now—there they stood, with burp guns still hanging around their necks, a buffalo gun at their feet, and me with an empty rifle. The funny thing was that these guys were Korean, not Chinese, and chances were they hadn't understood what I'd said anyway. On the other hand, in combination with that long, razor-sharp bayonet pointed at them, they probably would have surrendered if I'd given the order in Swahili. In any event, we took their weapons and turned the POWs over to our men on the other side of the dike. Then the doc and I continued mopping up. In numbers and in firepower, these guys certainly should have outgunned what was left of 3d Platoon; from the number of bodies, buffalo guns, and other AT weapons we found, we concluded that we'd knocked off an antitank platoon that had been as green and scared as our tankers. The only difference was, of course, that these North Koreans would never tell the story of *their* baptism of fire.

By the time we rejoined the platoon, my guys had looted the two prisoners. The only real treasure was a U.S.-made Waltham pocket watch, which the guys gave to me. It became my 6 February souvenir. None of us spoke Korean, so I tasked PFC Charles to take the POWs back to Captain Michaely for interrogation. I was really pleased we'd nailed them; prisoners are the best source of battlefield information, and with the fight still going on full tilt around us, it'd be useful to find out what the hell was happening in the enemy camp.

The 1st and 2d platoons of George were fighting hard to take the high ground. Navy Corsairs were working the enemy over with napalm and strafing runs. Cut off between mine and Gilchrist's platoons were enemy who'd been bypassed, so I took half a dozen of our guys and we went up the hill to do some hunting.

The North Koreans were in cleverly concealed, well-dug bunkers stuffed with straw for warmth. The pine-covered hill was a maze of seemingly unrelated positions, which we slowly worked through in two-man teams. "Fire in the hole!" was shouted again and again as we grenaded bunker after bunker, one man providing covering fire as the other edged close enough to flip in a frag. The enemy didn't fight back; they stayed in the bottom of their holes like trapped moles. It didn't take long before we ran out of frag grenades. A field expedient was quickly devised: we stripped tracer slugs from the machine-gun belt and clipped them for our M-1s. With one man covering, his partner would slip up to a hole and snap off a tracer or two into the position. The red-hot slugs would ignite the straw inside, and when the defender came up coughing, he'd be shot between the horns. (Gary Cooper wiped out dozens of German soldiers in *Sergeant York* by luring them out with a turkey call; if it was good enough for Sergeant York and Hollywood, it was good enough for us on 6 February 1951.) We moved from hole to hole, systematically burning the enemy out, until the hilltop above us suddenly exploded with gunfire. The Reds were counterattacking. As Gilchrist's platoon fought them off only six feet from the crest of the hill, we beat feet back to the safety of our rice-paddy wall.

Paddy walls, whose purpose in more peaceful times was irrigation control, were dirt walls about a foot thick and about three feet high— perfect cover from most direct-fire weapons. Infantrymen loved them. Now, leaning against my safe paddy wall (even as 1st Platoon fought off another counterattack with the help of the 2d, which could observe the forward slope of Gilchrist's hill and provide warning of the enemy's intention) I realized I was starving. I opened a can of C rations with my trusty P-38 and dug right in.

I started at the top of the can: big chunks of congealed fat, under which lay beef and potatoes, frozen rock-hard. About this time an enemy sniper started firing along the top of the rice-paddy wall. It was harassing fire only; no one got hurt, but it got on all our nerves far more, even, than the larger battle still raging around us. I had just gotten down to the meat and was about to take my first bite when—zzzppt!—a slug creased a furrow in the top of the wall right above my head and showered my rations with debris. I scooped it out. I was about to try another bite when—zzzppt!—another slug, same place, did the same thing. By the third time, that was it. I was pissed off. "I'm going to get that sniper. Who's going with me?" Ray Wells, an ace machine gunner and good old country boy from West Virginia, volunteered.

We followed the paddy wall to a drainage ditch that took us behind the North Korean antitank positions. The plan was simple: to get to the right rear of the sniper, shoot the son of a bitch, and go back and finish my Cs.

The ditch had an L-shaped turn. We stopped just shy of it, and I inched forward to have a quick peek: three Koreans manning a machine gun were lying in the prone about ten feet away, not looking in our direction. I slipped back to Wells, whispering that I'd take the first guy, he'd take the third, and we'd double up on the gunner in the middle. We stepped out in the ditch. The North Koreans looked up, but Wells and I were the last thing they ever saw. I knew they were dead; we were so close that I could hear the slugs thumping home through their padded jackets. We jumped over them and continued on our way.

With Wells covering my ass, I came up behind a little tree at the top of the ditch—ideal concealment for a quick look-see. After a few seconds' scan, I spotted the sniper on the hill. He was in a bunker about a hundred yards away on my left flank, and I could clearly see the side of his head and his Soviet SKS rifle. I ducked down. I didn't want to take a chance on Kentucky windage, so I adjusted my M-1 rifle sights down four clicks and got into a firing position. I had the sniper's head sitting right on top of my front sight, but just as I was about to squeeze the trigger I heard machine-gun slugs snapping over my head, and then the weapon's report. *Oh, shit,* I thought, *someone's seen me.* For all I knew it could have been one of our tankers—the slugs were coming from that direction—maybe they hadn't gotten the word we were out there. So I started to go down. But as I went down I felt the top of my head explode. I'd caught a slug.

Like most good Wolfhounds, I wasn't wearing a helmet—helmets were a pain in the ass unless there was lots of artillery and mortar fire coming in (in which case they became as essential as air). The slug ripped through my fur pile cap and propelled me from the top of the ditch as though I'd been poleaxed by Paul Bunyan. I don't know if I lost consciousness or not, but I do know I was stunned, with four-alarm sirens ringing in both ears. Wells thought I was dead and took off down the ditch. I couldn't blame him—he thought he was all alone out there behind enemy lines. Meanwhile, I tried to focus on what had happened.

Blood, really thick blood, was pumping out of my head. The first thing

I did was ask myself my name, rank, and serial number: "David Haskell Hackworth, Sergeant, RA19242907" came the automatic response, which made me decide that my head must still be okay, even if my ass was in the worst crack ever. I started crawling down the ditch. I had to crawl because the North Koreans on the high ground knew they had an intruder in their midst. I stayed low on the enemy's side; slugs were spraying the ditch fast and furious, but thumping up against the other wall. I crawled until I reached the machine-gun crew Wells and I had knocked off.

Now I was faced with a dilemma. If I jumped over them, I'd become exposed to the enemy fire coming from the hill. If I crawled over them, one of them might still be alive—and the longer I looked the more my confused head convinced me that one of them *was* alive—and he'd kill me. I couldn't shoot them because when I got hit I'd dropped my rifle. So I just stared at them, like a dumb recruit, wondering what to do. I pulled my trench knife out of my boot. Very carefully, I crawled over one of them, waiting for him to move. Crawled over the next one, waiting for him to move. Then I crawled over the third guy the same way, and slipped on, like a snake, down the ditch until it was high enough for me to crouch, then high enough to stand up and run. And the whole time, I was singing.

Whoever said there aren't any atheists on the battlefield was dead right. Often when we'd be sitting around our little fires, one of the guys in the platoon would play his guitar and we would sing. The songs were all religious ones, like "Down By the Riverside," where we'd be laying down our swords and shields, or "Please, dear Jesus, hear my plea, just a closer walk with Thee"—but they were also songs of great comradeship. And a most magic feeling would always pour out when we sang, a feeling that 3d Platoon, *our* platoon, was our family, our whole life. And somehow between God and our brothers, we were going to make it through.

So as I pounded down this ditch, I was singing "Just a Closer Walk with Thee," with deep feeling—Ella Fitzgerald, look out. To my mind I was really talking to God. I was talking to The Man. So I'm singing and running, blood's pouring out of my head—and then I remembered I didn't have my rifle. What a rotten example I had set. Good NCOs don't screw up like that; only a dumbshit of a soldier loses his rifle. So I stopped singing and started chewing my ass as I ran down that ditch.

Maybe it was because I was thinking about my lack of professionalism. Maybe it was just a second-nature thing from my training. Or maybe it was a sixth sense, I don't know. But seconds before I was home free (*Just a few feet more*, I told myself, *just around the corner*)—I stopped. "Hey, Third Platoon! It's Hackworth," I shouted. "I'm coming in!"

Then I turned the corner. I found myself looking down the throat of Corporal Wesley Morgan's mean-looking Browning automatic rifle. "Man, you were so loud coming down that ditch I thought at least a platoon of gooks was on the march! Wells told me you got it. If you hadn't called out I would have mowed you down."

2 BROWN SHOES

When I first met "The Hack," he was a fine soldier, fresh from service with TRUST—possibly our sharpest military formation, then occupying Trieste in Italy. He was the epitome of a TRUST trooper—sharp, dedicated, eager to learn, proud of the Army. Usually these young soldiers die right away. "The Hack" was a volunteer for infantry service in Korea. The rest that follows, of course, is his punishment for such stupidity.

Lieutenant Colonel Phillip J. Gilchrist, USA, Ret.
Platoon Leader/Company Commander
27th Infantry Regiment, Korea, 1950–51

ON 20 May 1946, I was on the corner of Main and Hill streets in Ocean Park, California, waiting for a bus. Al Hewitt, my best friend and childhood mentor, suddenly came running up, brandishing some magazine, which he breathlessly thrust in my face. "Look at it!" he demanded.

On the cover was an Airborne constabulary soldier in Berlin. The trooper was wearing a knockout of a uniform, complete with a very jazzy yellow scarf around his neck. His helmet had a big "C" painted on the front, and a yellow band around it, which tied in perfectly with the scarf. It was a great uniform, with the whole look made complete by the two beautiful blond fräuleins the guy had perched on his knees. Al said, "That's the army of occupation in Germany, Hack! We've got to join up!"

I didn't need any persuading; the only problem as I saw it was where to go to enlist. I'd been trying to get into one service or another for the last three years, and by now the sergeants at the Santa Monica recruiting station knew me on a first-name basis. I was still underage even if Al was not, so we hopped the first bus into Los Angeles to join up there.

Somehow we got separated on the way to the physicals. Armed with my phony ID papers (I'd gotten them the year before, when Al and I joined the merchant marine), I kept on going, and ended up in a room with an officer and a flag. I pledged allegiance to the flag, and then, kind of before I knew it, I was a soldier in the U.S. Army. The officer asked me when I wanted to start basic training, now or next week. *Now*, I said, remembering with a fifteen-year-old's lust those blond fräuleins on another trooper's knees.

There were three or four buses waiting at the ramp outside the L.A. induction center. I checked them all to see if Al had come out yet. He had not, so I got us a couple of seats and squared myself away. Recruits kept trickling out of the building and into the buses; what seemed like a very long time passed, and still Al was nowhere to be seen. He turned up just as the buses were about to pull away. I begged our driver to hold on. "Come on, Al!" I shouted. "We're leaving right now! We're going to Germany!"

"Can't go!" he called back.

"Why not?" I screamed.

"Four-F!" he yelled. "Got a punctured eardrum!"

So long, Al.

Sadly, by the time I finished training, American Airborne troops had been kicked out of Berlin; the word was that occupation U.S. paratrooper style was too much even for a country that had seen its fair share of destruction. My destination was now Italy, and when the troopship (which wasn't a troopship at all, but a freighter designed for bulk supplies) finally landed at Leghorn, twenty-four hundred troops, who'd been packed in like sardines all the way from New York, spilled onto a beach still studded with mines.

We stayed in a huge warehouse at the water's edge. It was more like an airplane hangar than anything else, and there were probably two thousand guys sleeping in there, in makeshift beds. All the windows in the place had been broken out by the troops we were replacing: the second Great War's combat men, celebrating because they were finally going home.

Wild parties, wild drinking, and whores everywhere. Whores in the barracks, whores on the beach—even if nobody else did, the whores knew where the mines were buried. And wherever you went, little kids would say, "Hey, GI, you got chewing gum? You got chocolate?" It was just like in the movies.

The outfit I was assigned to, the 752d Tank Battalion, was more of the same, including the whores. The only difference was the vets here were not quite on their way out of town. Everything was loose and everything was wild, but these vets, the majority of whom had fought from Africa to Sicily to Italy, were still lean, mean, combat-ready troops—they just didn't have time for garrison-style discipline. It was not uncommon, for example, to be awakened in the middle of the night by a drunk off-duty trooper running through the barracks firing his weapon, or to hear one of his buddies matching him, shot for shot, just for the hell of it outside. All in all, it was some violent world I found myself in—nothing like I'd expected—but with wonderful characters, veterans who could spin drunken tales until the wee hours of the morning about some little way they had beaten the system, or the signorinas they'd conquered as they fought up Italy's rugged spine. They rarely talked about combat, though, and after a very short time we new replacements stopped asking. Maybe it was just part of the role, but the old soldiers went silent on the horrors of war. It was as though they belonged to a secret fraternity, and we, the pink-cheeked unenlightened, were—in a word—outsiders.

But there were other horrors of war that we saw every day, and couldn't have gotten away from if we'd tried. Al Hewitt and I had dreamed of pretty fräuleins on our knees; Italy after World War II was dark and desperate, and unlike anything I could ever have imagined. It was like a cloudy day every day, and all the people were hurting. Even the landscape seemed to be hurting: the houses were all blown down, the bridges blown up, the fields ripped apart, and nothing was growing. There was no money and no food. Old ladies in black dresses and black scarves stood at the end of the chow line, picking through the garbage cans for enough scraps to feed their families. Young boys walked the train tracks in the hopes of scrounging the odd piece of coal to eke some warmth out of the family hearth. (When I guarded the tracks, I pretended not to hear the bits of coal clanking into empty metal buckets behind me, and made a big show of turning around to give the kids time to hide.) This grim aftermath of war would be forever etched in my fifteen-year-old mind, but, equally, I would always remember the people's will, their sheer determination to survive and start again.

Gradually most of the WW II warriors went back to the States, and the postwar wild-West feeling of lawlessness went, too. It had been great fun for a kid to be part of the hell-for-leather spirit that made up the 752d (the "Seven-Five-Deuce"), but like the tightening of a screw, one turn at a time, each day the unit became more military, the "who gives a damn" attitude of the remaining 752d combat leaders and troopers replaced by the exacting discipline of the peacetime Army.

For the next four years I learned my trade—one year with the recon company of the tank battalion in the Po Valley, and three more with Trieste United States Troops (TRUST), the illustrious unit whose five thousand handpicked members Walter Winchell called "the chrome-plated soldiers of Europe." We worked hard during those years—long, merciless days of training, repeating, repeating, repeating until we got it right—our transformation into soldiers inspired and monitored by those battle-savvy NCOs, who well knew that discipline and tactical proficiency on the battlefield were direct results of discipline and combat skills instilled on the parade and training grounds. At night it was down on our hands and knees, all of us hand-waxing the barracks floors until we had enough money to chip in and buy a buffer; you could eat off those floors (and if you couldn't, your platoon sergeant would just make you do them again), just as you could almost be blinded by the brass belt buckles and brown boots that each of us wore, polished every night to a dazzling finish. The only way out of these activities was sick call, but rarely was it used as an excuse: it took as much effort to see the doc (you had to strip your bed, cram all your perfectly pressed clothes into a duffel bag, see the supply sergeant and then the First Sergeant—not to mention the lion's share of a month's pay you'd spend having clothes re-pressed when you came back) as it did to continue on with the normal routine.

Punishment was meted out by a process known as NCO justice: for crimes such as a uniform of less than starched perfection, a bed that didn't bounce a quarter, or even a mildly insubordinate smirk, the sentence could range from fifty push-ups to double-timing around the parade field holding a 9.5-pound M-1 rifle over your head, yelling, "I'm a shithead! I'm a shithead!" until you collapsed. We rarely saw an officer above our platoon leader lieutenant (and he was seldom with the troops because of administrative duties), but no one seemed too concerned about it; above and below on the chain of command, it was well recognized that as fathers, teachers, older brothers, and chief tormentors, in Trieste the NCO corps had no equal.

Despite our spit-and-polish perfection (and the never-ending demand for same), the American soldiers occupying Trieste and the surrounding region were not just parade-ground troops. My first assignment, Company D, was the reconnaissance unit of the 752d; my last, the Intelligence and Reconnaissance (I&R) Platoon, was the eyes and ears of the TRUST (351st) Regiment. In both outfits, our job was to patrol the Italian-Yugoslavian border regularly, from the port city of Trieste to the Austrian border to the north. The reason for our vigilance was simply that although the war was over, Italy had not yet seen peace.

At the end of WW II, Yugoslavian partisans (led by Marshal Tito, who had become Yugoslavia's prime minister in March 1945) had come rushing toward Trieste as part of an attempt to regain some of the territory that had belonged to the Austrian-Hungarian empire prior to the First World War. These Communists had been thwarted by units of the U.S. 10th Mountain and 88th Infantry (Blue Devil) divisions, and by British forces, as well, who moved up to occupy the contested region along a boundary called the Morgan Line. Trieste itself, a city that had been handed over to Italy by

Austria in 1920 as a prize of war, was probably the greatest thorn in the Yugoslavs' (or "Jugs," as we called them) side, and after a two-year standoff along the Morgan Line, in 1947 the two nations signed a peace treaty that created the Free Territory of Trieste and divided it into zones. Two were occupied, respectively, by American and British troops (the third by Tito's boys), and the Jugs were less than pleased with the new arrangement. Tito felt that because Yugoslavia had fought on the right side during the war and Mussolini's Italy on the wrong, the Jugs deserved Trieste this time. Consequently, the postwar Allied troops, who'd been on a war footing in Italy from the word go, remained so. And although there were few full-on confrontations, while the Allies maintained a defensive posture in Trieste and along the Italian-Yugoslavian border, the Communists nickeled and dimed us with small-scale guerrilla operations.

The Communists were the enemy—the Cold War was already in full swing. Winston Churchill had given his famous speech at Westminster College in Fulton, Missouri, predicting that an "iron curtain" would come slamming down over all of Eastern Europe; we on the ground could see the enemy with our own eyes, as day and night we watched them watch us from tall, wooden towers along the border. What the enemy was *about* was brought home clearly at the Army's weekly Troop Information Program, where films and lectures depicted the Communists as monstrous, lumbering, savage, stupid beasts who would eat little kids if given half a chance. "Know your enemy," we were told; we learned to know them, and we knew to hate them, which I thought was all pretty good since the day might come when I'd have to kill them.

Still, the closest I ever came to chambering a round in all four years I was in Italy was on 16 September 1947—Reunification Day—the day a Yugoslav regiment marched right down a road crossing the Jug-Trieste border, intent on passing through American and British lines to reach their zone of the newly divided city.* After being told once that they could not pass through our lines, the Jugs withdrew, only to return to the same American outpost reinforced to the tune of two thousand men. West Point Lieutenant William Van Dyke Ochs, Jr., my former platoon leader (and at this time B Company's executive officer [XO] and acting CO), headed them off at the pass, firmly refusing to yield to the pressure of a Yugoslav colonel who threatened force if not allowed to proceed. The stakes were high as

* The sole purpose of the TRUST command was to protect the American zone of Trieste proper. This incident involved, first and foremost, members of B Company, 351st, a rifle company to which I'd briefly belonged (and had only just left to join the 15th Tank Company) in the first of my three TRUST assignments.

Ochs played out his bluff poker hand—his immediate force at the outpost was less than a dozen men.

Meanwhile, everyone else in the 351st had gone on alert, thinking we were about to go to war. I was with the section of tanks that raced to the scene, but Lieutenant Ochs's initial cool had prevailed, and by the time we got there and took up battle positions, the incident was well on the way to blowing over, with higher military authorities on both sides conferring about a better way to solve the problem. Ochs himself became an instant hero, and the scuttlebutt concerning his act of calm but forceful battlefield diplomacy was one that stayed in my memory for a long, long time.

My own experience in Company B had been short, basically because the minute I was assigned there I raised hell until I could get out. "I'm a recon man," I'd said again and again to anyone who would listen (and, at sixteen, I'd just say it louder if they appeared to be ignoring me), "I'm no dumb groundpounder." I was a real troublemaker, but the way I saw it was that the Army and I had a contract: I'd signed on not as an infantryman but as a recon man—Airborne recon, actually; I'd taken Armored reconnaissance basic and I'd loved my year zooming around in my little M24 light tank in the 752d. "You can't keep me here!" I'd yell at my rifle platoon sergeant, even as he gave me the worst details and most painful "close and sustained" discipline an NCO could dish out.

I think I was transferred only in order to shut me up, and even then I didn't get what I wanted. In fairness, that was only because what I wanted didn't exist; the closest thing to Armored anything in TRUST was the 15th Tank Company (the oldest tank unit in the Army, predating even WW I), and that's where I was sent. My experience in the 752d had taught me absolutely nothing about medium tanks, and the 15th's WW II Shermans (souped up with 76-mm main guns) were huge steel-monster mysteries to me. I learned quickly—of necessity—because I was assigned as assistant driver on a tank commanded by the meanest sergeant in the entire U.S. Army. Sergeant Dillard Oller of Harlan County, Kentucky, gave his gunner corrections in phrases like "down a crack" and "left a cunt hair." He was the second-best asskicker in the business (my platoon sergeant, Jesse O. Giddens, placed number one), and he kicked mine twenty-four hours a day until I loved and took care of his tank as though it were my first car. Sergeant Oller's 1947 expectations were actually those of 1930 Regular Army soldierly perfection; the style of discipline required to meet this ideal took some getting used to, however, and until I got into the swing of things I thought I was in prison. But it was the same throughout the tank company: I knew one trooper who'd spent time in the TRUST stockade, and when he came back he said that as bad as the stockade was—and it was *bad*—in terms of unrelenting discipline, high standards, and tough soldiering, the 15th was even worse.

Or better, depending on how you looked at it. Over the next eighteen months with the tank company, I became a driver and a gunner corporal—and even then, if I'd missed a fifty-five-gallon drum at twelve hundred yards on the second shot it would have been an immediate farewell to those two beautiful stripes. The rationale was simple: mistakes on the training field will be mistakes on the battlefield, and mistakes on the battlefield lead to men's deaths. The tank NCOs, many of whom were pre–WW II Horse Cav Regulars, were like gods—they were perfect, and demanded the same from us, instantly. They cut absolutely no slack as they worked overtime molding us into soldiers, in the process establishing standards that would remain with and in us for years to come. No detail escaped their eyes, and when (inevitably) one of us troops screwed up, we paid dearly for it. But the price was never as high as what we gained as a result: first, a respect and appreciation for details (the basic building blocks, which, if neglected, can foul up the works completely), and second, an incredible boost to our morale when, wonder of wonders, we got it right.

General of the Army George Catlett Marshall once said, "Morale is a state of mind. It is steadfastness and courage and hope . . . confidence and zeal and loyalty . . . élan, esprit de corps, and determination." Morale, he said, "is staying power, the spirit which endures to the end—the will to win." These words could have been the motto of the 15th Tank, and for that matter, of all of TRUST, a command that really did live twenty Regular Army years behind the times. In truth, we were probably the last bastion of the Old Army: an isolated unit on the Adriatic Sea, off by ourselves we remained untainted by the problems that were already developing in the postwar Army of a war-weary world. In TRUST, however it may have been anyplace else, every day was a new challenge, and every day brought a new achievement.

As a corporal I was assigned on temporary duty (TDY) to the regimental training unit, a provisional organization that trained new replacements right off the boat. Lieutenant Roland Carrier, commander of the Regimental Intelligence and Reconnaissance Platoon, was our provisional training officer; during the course of the program, he asked me if I'd come to his outfit as a squad leader. He said there'd be another stripe in it for me somewhere down the track; it was one of those offers I wouldn't have dreamed of refusing (I mean, I didn't even care that the I&R Platoon was a groundpounder unit), and I beat feet over there as soon as I could.

*   *   *

If TRUST troops were proud (and they were), and if TRUST troops were disciplined (and they most certainly were), then the I&R TRUST troops were the proudest of the proud, the most disciplined of the disciplined. Our platoon sergeant, Steve Prazenka, was the ultimate taskmaster; he quickly became my mentor and my hero, the one I wanted to be like when I grew up and had a whole bunch of stripes of my own. Guided by his firm hand, the I&R Platoon was an outstanding unit—without a doubt, the best in the regiment. "If you learn it right, you'll do it right the rest of your life," Prazenka would growl as the endless repetition of one thing or another began to take its toll on his charges. "If you learn it wrong, you'll do it wrong, and you'll spend the rest of your life trying to learn to do it right." Thanks to him we learned it right the first time around. We learned about weapons—ours and the enemy's—how to disassemble, assemble, and fire them. We spent days training in the woods, learning about camouflage, woodcraft, creeping, scouting, and observing; we became experts in what Prazenka called "snooping and pooping," all under his watchful eye. We had an hour's close-order drill every day, using the drills of the thirties, and if Prazenka didn't like the way we did them, he'd turn back to the old field manual (which read, "Close-order drill is the foundation of all discipline") and throw another hour's worth on top of us. Holding a 9.5-pound M-1 rifle at right shoulder arms isn't exactly a breeze at any time, and often by the time the Sergeant got through with us, our right hands would be locked stiff in the M-1 grip position for hours, somehow not getting the word that the weapon wasn't there anymore.

The importance of close-order drill could not be overestimated; the discipline it instilled was that which would maintain order on a chaotic battlefield. "You're in a life-or-death situation out there," Prazenka would say. "When you hear an order, you don't respond in ten seconds or ten minutes. You respond NOW, unless you want to get yourself or your buddy blown in half. And I don't want any 'Simon Says' shit either. When I say move, move! When I say stop, stop. When I say knock out that machine gun, you knock out that machine gun. I don't want you to think about it. Just do it."

Prazenka made out the training schedule; we marched to the tune he played and loved him for it. He commanded our respect—effortlessly, it seemed. He was twenty-two years old and to us he'd been through it all. An I&R man from basic training onward, he'd been with the 28th (Bloody Bucket) Division I&R in WW II, and was captured (after a painful cat-and-mouse game with the Nazis) deep behind the shattered U.S. lines during the Battle of the Bulge. He was just a total pro—the finest, fairest platoon sergeant who ever came down the track—who knew as much about soldiering as an Alabama Bible-bashing preacher knows about the Good Book. He could double-time ten miles first thing in the morning regardless of what he'd drunk the night before; sometimes he'd come roaring into our barracks at 0500, still loaded to the eyeballs from a wild night's partying, shouting, "Out of those sacks, boys—let go of your cocks and grab your socks, it's time to go for a run!" and off we'd go. Usually it was just five or six miles, but on special occasions (if we bugged him enough) we'd run up to the town of Prosecco—about nine miles round-trip—to try to catch a glimpse of his girlfriend Anna. The first time we'd gone up there, Anna had been out in a field tending her cows. She'd waved to us, all blond hair and big tits, shouting, " 'Ello, Stevie!" and Prazenka never heard the end of it from his envious platoon.

I&R, which was composed of the top scouts of the regiment, went out on foot and by vehicle to find the Reds. Our area of operation (AO) was a two-hundred-mile stretch fronting the Jug border. I learned plenty during these long patrols sneaking around in the woods, but the most alarming lesson was that I had no sense of direction. In recon, having no sense of direction is kind of like being a surgeon who can't stand the sight of blood. From my experience in D Company, 752d, the fact was I knew every inch of the AO by memory. Someone could give me coordinates, and just by looking at a particular curve on a road or a prominent feature in the terrain I could get within a few hundred meters of any given destination without once referring to a map. But put me on the ground within that terrain of dense bush and millions of trees and I was hopeless—I had no navigational sense whatsoever. I would have blamed Prazenka, except that he drilled us in map reading all the time—"Finding the enemy isn't worth a damn," he'd say, "if you can't give HQ an exact fix on their location"—and he was a natural at it himself. So I made a private vow: if ever I attained any rank at all, I'd always find a subordinate who was a great map reader and make him my direction man (in the I&R, this job was eventually assigned to a New Jersey–born Daniel Boone, Sylvester Wilson, a private in my squad). That way I could concentrate on the ground and the immediate situation, I wouldn't have to get all wrapped around the axle in all the details and mysteries of ground navigation and "reading right-up," and, most important, no one would ever know that I rarely even knew where I was.

But attaining rank was not easy in Trieste. Promotions were not automatic issue—you soldiered for them and you soldiered hard. The slightest infraction could lead to a bust; your platoon sergeant could (and would) pull the stripes right off your sleeve. I'd actually learned my lesson back at Fort Knox during basic, when my training sergeant mistook my well-made bed and perfectly shined shoes as signs of previous military training (I hadn't been about to tell him I'd learned it hanging around the Army base near my house in Ocean Park) and appointed me "lance sergeant" complete with three Regular Army stripes, which were sewn on a black band to be pinned to my shirtsleeves like an MP's brassard. I took my "acting jack" job most seriously, and was thought to be a shoo-in for the "best trainee" (an honor that included a promotion to PFC on completion of the course) until a week before basic was over and I had my squad out on a training recon patrol. In my fifteen-year-old judgment, the exercise we were on had no value. The other kids agreed, so I decided it was too nice a day to beat around in the bush and told everyone to take it easy. We found a pond and had a good swim; of course, we got caught by the platoon sergeant, and not only was it good-bye little black band and three Regular Army stripes, but it was hello KP, Private Hackworth, for the rest of the time I was there. It took me eighteen months in Italy to regain that lost ground, despite the fact that as early as my stint in the 752d, I'd gone to the toughest NCO preparatory school in the world, the 88th Division Leadership School near Venice, on the island of Lido.

This school was yet another torture chamber of Old Army exacting discipline. Chief instructor Lieutenant "Radar" Ryan (so called because he had eyes in the back of his head and saw *everything*) had little tolerance for the less than perfect. If you had a quarter-inch thread dangling on your fatigue jacket, he called it a "rope," burned it off with his Zippo lighter, and sentenced you to scrape out the inside of a toilet with a razor blade at midnight. If you succumbed to a blink while standing at attention, you could safely look forward to a four-hour nightly duty of scrubbing the barracks walls with a toothbrush. These activities were, of course, extracurricular; besides instilling perfection, the daily function of the school was to teach us to set the example, and, through various leadership challenges, burn into our brains the eleven principles of leadership, in action. When the course was finished, I was chomping at the bit to have a crack at the real task; little did I know that when I was finally promoted to PFC I'd stay right there for a whole year more.

Nobody wants to be a private, but being a PFC isn't much better. Anyone worth his salt wants to be at least a corporal, because then he has power: he can *give* orders, not just have to take them, and he doesn't have to pull guard nearly as much as the privates and PFCs. Long before the Leadership School, when I was about ten, I'd watched all those old sergeants stationed in Ocean Park barking at their troops; when, years later, I finally made corporal in the tank company, I called on those memories in order to become the meanest bastard of an NCO the world had ever seen. Newly, proudly perched on the first rung of the leadership ladder, it'd be fair to say I was much hated by my squad. But I didn't care. From my earliest memory, my sights had been set on a buck sergeant's stripes, like my great-uncle Roy had worn in World War I, and I'd learned enough in the Army already to know you didn't get them from being Gordon Goodguy.

I really went to town when I got my own squad in the I&R. I'd been a fanatical field-manual reader and memorizer since I'd joined the Army; now that I was "in charge" I was determined that my squad would be as well versed as I was. I'd assign them reading with the warning that anytime within the next hour, day, or week I'd come back to them and make them tell me what that manual said. Prazenka told me later he'd have a private laugh every time I assigned this homework; he'd never gone with that theory of book learning (he believed in *doing*) but didn't see anything wrong with it—if nothing else, it put the fear of God in my squad, which was good.

I just wanted my guys to be the best—at everything. The duty day began before reveille, and ended only when I was satisfied that my squad was spit-and-polish perfection. It was not unusual for me to have them scrubbing the barracks walls, washing windows, and laying out their equipment for my own personal full field inspection, which I'd carry out just before taps. The guys' gear would glisten in the dull barracks light: chrome-plated bayonet and mess gear; lacquered tent poles and pegs; the M-1's butt plate chromed, its rifle stock boned and French-waxed; the helmet liner painted, baked, and simonized to a blinding finish. Anything brass was stripped of paint and polished—the rivets on helmet liners, the eyelets and buckles on boots, the snaps on cartridge belts; even the rough leather exterior of our WW II combat boots would shine like patent leather after being smoothed over with a dog-tag chain and waxed and polished until a soldier could see his face.

I didn't make up these rules of cosmetic precision (they were just part of the basic TRUST standard, itself undoubtedly influenced by the discipline of the stockade, the large number of Old Army NCOs in our command, and the spit-and-polish elite British troops who co-located with us); I wasn't above them either (after all, my shoelaces, too, had to be washed and pressed before Prazenka made *his* full field inspection). But continuing the tank company's NCO tradition of cutting no slack was, to my mind, close to a guarantee that my squad would stand head and shoulders above all others. Still, I quietly thanked the designer of our wall lockers, who'd provided false bottoms where we could stash the field gear we *really* used, and hid away before inspection.

However hellish my nocturnal reviews seemed to the men of my squad, though, they were nothing compared to my wrath if the guys didn't measure up. All things considered, I was actually quite civilized on these occasions; generally, I'd just decide that no one was going to go on pass. "Gentlemen," I'd say, "I want you to fall out in the company street." I would then double-time them to the front gate, halt them, and have them stand at parade rest. Then I'd say, "Now, gentlemen, there is the front gate. That front gate is designed for soldiers who are good soldiers. Soldiers who deserve a pass. A pass is a privilege, not a right you have, that you get automatically. You get a pass for making me happy. For having beautiful shoes and beautiful weapons and being motivated and spirited and dedicated. I have found you to be failing in all of these areas. So, you are not going to pass through that gate. You are not going out until I consider you fit to go out, until you are soldiers who are fit to walk in the streets of Trieste. I am not proud of you men. And the reason you're not going out is *because* I am not proud of you." Then I'd double-time them back to the barracks, and open my locker where they'd see all their passes thumbtacked under the lid. "There are your passes," I'd say. "There they are and that's where they are going to stay until I'm impressed with you. Now, that may be months, gentlemen. I just don't know how long that's going to be." First Sergeant English, the topkick of Headquarters Company (to which the I&R Platoon belonged), made sure that my enthusiasm didn't keep my men off the streets of Trieste forever, but meanwhile I got and held their attention, and they shaped up.

The guys in my I&R squad liked me just about as much as my tank crew had when I'd first made corporal. Still, day by day our little band began to work together better and better, until we were bopping along like a well-oiled machine. To me the proof came on the training field, on a regimental training exercise for which the I&R was designated the aggressor force. My squad was given the mission of infiltrating behind 1st Battalion lines and capturing a prisoner, preferably an officer. I decided that if we had to get an officer, we might as well get the *commanding* officer, so we set our sights on "The Helmet," Lieutenant Colonel James Muir II, CO of the 1st Batt. We called Muir "The Helmet" because he was very small, and when he put on his steel pot it seemed to come down to the top of his boots. Capturing him would be a real coup; he was a well-liked, damn good officer who got around, saw his troops and cared a lot about their welfare, and there seemed little doubt his men would go to any lengths to protect him.

Since I knew our AO like the back of my hand, I concluded that Colonel Muir would set up his command post (CP) in one of only two places: in a hollow behind the Red Cross Club or in an orchard by Opicina. Our recon confirmed it was the Red Cross Club; we slipped behind it using side trails, and camouflaged our three recon jeeps on the side of a road nearby. In the darkness and on foot, we got to a place where we were looking down on the "enemy."

Colonel Muir's CP was hidden in a clump of trees. The sun was just rising; we could pick out tents and vehicles, and hear the sound of generators. The Colonel had a rifle company close in for security. As the I&R were the aggressors, we were wearing dark-green Russian-looking uniforms with a red triangular patch, as well as special helmets with a wooden block on top; it was winter, bitter cold, so we were also wearing heavy parkas with hoods. I instructed my men to wear their hoods over their helmets—that way, when we got into the CP area, 1st Battalion wouldn't be able to tell us from their own.

It was getting light as we infiltrated through the CP. People were getting up; I could hear mess kits clattering and guys moving through a chow line. Even though it was only a maneuver and no one could get hurt, I still had that scared feeling in the pit of my stomach, that prayer that we wouldn't get caught. My fear was wholly unjustified, though, because after we got into the CP, as far as the "enemy" could see we were indeed just some of their guys strolling through the area with our hoods on. We made our way to Colonel Muir's tent and disarmed and captured the guard outside. Then I went into the tent.

The Colonel was sleeping. I gently shook him awake. "Yes, what is it?" he asked.

"Colonel Muir, I'm Corporal Hackworth from Regimental I&R and you're a prisoner of war." Muir's eyes popped open and he reached under his pillow. He was an Old Soldier, and I knew he had a pistol there. I had my weapon pointed at him. "Sir, I have the drop on you. I hope you'll play the game. If you'll just put on your gear and come with us."

Muir withdrew his hand from under the pillow. "Fair enough, Hackworth, I'll play the game."

He could have taken his time. He could have made some noise. He could have pulled rank. But he didn't—he played the game. We left his tent and walked down the road until we got to our jeeps. I put him in the back with two guys, then hopped in the front with the driver. The windshield was down, with canvas (to prevent glare) tied over it on the hood as we drove through Muir's positions. No one suspected us. After all, we were driving *out* of 1st Batt lines, and besides, the Colonel himself was sitting calmly in the back seat. It was a perfect operation.

The main road from Muir's battalion to our regimental CP was mined with dummy antitank mines. They weren't dug in—just sitting on top of the road as window dressing for the exercise—but as we swerved around them about three miles out of Muir's CP, elements of the 1st Battalion recognized our I&R vehicles and started shooting at us with blanks. We zoomed on as fast as we could, but the windshield on my jeep hadn't been tied down properly and suddenly it flew up, the canvas cover obstructing the driver's vision. *No operation ever goes according to plan* went the old military axiom, and in my mind's eye I saw the jeep crashing into a tree, killing everyone, including the Colonel (which would have been a bit hard to explain if I'd been unlucky enough to survive). I threw myself onto the windshield and stayed there until we were beyond enemy range. Then we stopped the jeep, blindfolded Colonel Muir, turned him around nine times (by the book, so he wouldn't be able to find our CP when he was released), and drove on to a dismount point near our headquarters.

I reported in to our regimental commander, Colonel Paul W. Caraway, at his CP. Captain Kenneth Eggleston, the HQ Company CO, was there, too, and both were almost as excited as I was about the capture of Colonel Muir (whom I considered my own personal trophy). The I&R got kudos and letters of commendation from Caraway on down for our work on that maneuver. My own reward was getting my ass chewed by someone at the CP because in all the excitement I'd taken off my much-hated aggressor helmet and left it in the jeep outside. But that was TRUST for you, and I was so proud of myself and my squad that it didn't hurt much at all. And after this maneuver, Colonel Muir never forgot me; every time he saw me he'd say, "I'll get your ass, Hackworth," but good soldier that he was, he always said it with a smile.

"I'd like to tell you something, Dave," Captain Eggleston began, a few weeks before he promoted me to sergeant, "I feel that one day you will achieve a very high rank, and you are going to make a significant contribution to your country." This was a captain talking to a corporal, and I was dumbstruck. I liked Captain Eggleston. Tall and lean, with an incredible combat record from his days with the 10th Mountain Division in WW II, he was tough as they come, but he had a heart as big. He was a real leader who was never without a word of encouragement for the troops, and over the months he'd become kind of a father figure to me. Even so, his comments now, to my mind, came from out of the blue.

Once a month or so I'd catch a duty called Charge of Quarters. It was a rostered duty, and the CQ's job was basically to play high sheriff for the night, from the time the HQ Company commander went home until he or the topkick returned in the morning. There really wasn't much to do but keep things squared away and ride herd on pass control, bed check, and any unusual events—fights, arrests, breakdowns of equipment, and so forth—that occurred during the night. I was just coming off CQ when the Captain sat me down and dropped this prophetic bomb. All I could do was mumble a "thank you" and get out of there to give myself a chance to think.

Personally, I didn't expect to achieve a very high rank, and I didn't know what "Captain E" even meant by the "significant contribution" I'd make to my country. Even so, his words couldn't have come at a more opportune time: it was the eve of the end of my first hitch, and I had to decide whether to reenlist or go home. I'd been giving the matter a lot of thought recently (I was eighteen years old, and it was time to start figuring out what I was going to do with the rest of my life anyway), and the conclusion I'd kept coming to was that, in almost all ways, the Army *was* my home, that I loved it, that I belonged here. Maybe I'd already decided to make the Army my career, but I'm sure Captain Eggleston's belief in me provided the final nudge. As for the Captain's predictions, though—well, only time would tell.

Then Sergeant Prazenka went back to the States on reenlistment leave and was gone for a number of months. In his absence his replacement, Sergeant Charlie Durham, rotated home, having finished his tour, and I found myself as acting platoon sergeant, responsible for the training of the I&R. I took on my new role with great confidence and full enthusiasm, and managed to alienate most of the platoon within days. The older soldiers of the outfit, the combat vets of WW II, resented me most of all: I was playing out the role of Prazenka (and pretty well, I hoped), but with no experience to back me up. (Other than a few brushes with Red guerrillas along the border, I'd never heard a shot fired in anger, and all I really knew about war was what I'd seen in the movies and read about in manuals and books.) The guys had long been calling me "Combat"; now it became "Sergeant Combat": "Ask Sergeant Combat . . . he'll tell us how to do it," they'd say, to which I'd reply, "You're goddamned right. Field Manual 7-75, paragraph 101, says you'll do it this way and that's the way I want to see you doing it, right NOW!" I was determined not to let them get to me, but it was hard. I'd been in the Army now for more than three years, yet when it was all shaken out, I was still a greenhorn.

Prazenka came back from leave then, and I went back to my squad. I had no regrets about my decision to re-up, but I was antsy. The guys in the platoon still called me Sergeant Combat, and it frustrated the hell out of me because, after all, it wasn't my fault there wasn't a war going on. But out of the blue all that changed when, on 25 June 1950, North Korea crossed the border into the South. U.S. troops around the world went on full alert; we moved to our battle positions, because the word was that the Communists weren't going to stop at South Korea—they were going to bust out all over the globe.

We were ready for them at Trieste. The regiment moved to the border, to await the marching Red Army. Day followed day and they never came. My adrenaline was running fast and I wanted to be where the action was. I couldn't stop talking about it. Every day I'd warn Prazenka to treat me nice—I was going to Korea and I might just give him all my medals when I came back. I was ready to try out my warrior wings. I wanted to prove myself, I wanted to win that Combat Infantryman's Badge (CIB), I just wanted to *go*—so badly it hurt.

During the alert, in that the I&R manned the critical regimental observation posts (OPs), we were frequently visited by regimental commander Colonel Caraway. The Colonel was a stern, no-nonsense, often seemingly unapproachable man, but on one of his visits I got up enough nerve to ask him to help me get over to Korea. He said he'd see what he could do, and within a few weeks I got my orders. Colonel Caraway had even arranged it so that I was to be flown back to the States, unheard of at a time when most all troop transport out of TRUST was by ship.

I said good-bye to my buddies and hopped on the plane, the first NCO from Trieste on the way to Korea. Many more soon followed, of course, and about 75 percent of the TRUST NCOs who went and lived were destined to be either battlefield commissioned to lieutenant or to receive high awards, proving that "the chrome-plated soldiers of Europe," of TRUST, trained in the spirit and with the dedication of what was probably an anachronism of an army, were indeed soldiers of the highest caliber.

But in September 1950, on that plane from Italy to the States, I didn't really know that; nor did I know, in general, how much I didn't know—especially in matters of life and death. But I did know that I was hot to trot and ready for whatever came my way, and that if nothing else, I wasn't going to be Sergeant Combat ever again. A month later I was in Korea.

And a month after that, so were the Chinese.

3 HIT AND RUN

The thing that bothered me worse than anything that winter was
the cold. I'd always gone through my life bitching about it being
too hot or too cold; during the pullback from the Yalu, I decided
I would never complain about the heat again if I could only just
get warm. And the thing you had to realize, with life expectancy
what it was on the battlefield, was that chances were you weren't
going to live until spring anyway. You had to realize that you
might never get warm again.

Colonel Allan D. Bell, Jr., USA, Ret.
G/27th Artillery Forward Observer
Korea, 1950–51

THE course of the Korean War had changed dramatically since its
lightning-fast beginning. At the start, U.S. forces, hopelessly outnumbered,
outgunned, and undertrained, had been driven back by the North Koreans
into the tiniest corner of South Korea, beyond the Naktong River. There the
Eighth Army dug in its heels, determinedly holding what was known as the
Pusan Perimeter until September, when MacArthur's daring amphibious
invasion at Inchon severed the North Korean Army's lines of communications and chopped its legs out from under it. No longer was the enemy an
effective fighting force, and our certain defeat along the lines of Dunkirk in
1940 suddenly appeared to be surefire victory. Units of the Eighth Army
smashed out of the Naktong perimeter; spirits were high as we raced north,
beyond the 38th parallel, beyond the North Korean capital of Pyongyang to
within spitting distance of the Yalu River, the dividing line between North
Korea and Manchuria. Fighting was sporadic, but as units moved farther
north the weather worsened and enemy resistance increased. It was like
compressing a spring.

The night the Chinese came, I was in a foxhole in the center of my scout
section's defensive position. The sector was densely covered with screw pines
and scrub oaks; my foxhole buddy and I were sitting on the edges of our hole

when we saw—and it was like right out of a cartoon—a row of the small trees moving toward us. We chopped them down (along with the little Chinaman creeping along behind each one) with hand grenades, but that was just the beginning. The next thing I saw was what I could only describe as a wave—a human wave—of Chinese crashing over us.

For the next three hours they came: wall-to-wall Chinamen, many of whom did not even have rifles, only long lances tipped with bayonets. Others were armed with U.S. Thompson submachine guns or Russian drum-fed assault rifles. For the main, they were sorry shots, with no understanding of basic infantry tactics, but what the Chinese lacked in proficiency they made up for in numbers, and their presence heralded the start of the largest and most bitter retreat in U.S. Army history.

Upon my arrival in Korea, I'd been assigned to the 25th Recon Company as a replacement scout section leader. It was an Army mistake—my Military Occupational Specialty (MOS) was infantry, not armored, recon—and it had upset me no end, because 25th Recon guys were not eligible for the CIB regardless of how much infantry combat they saw. Add to that MacArthur's brilliant stroke at Inchon (the war had seemed over save for the victory parade), and I'd been sick that after all I'd gone through to get here, I'd missed the guts of the whole damn show. I hadn't wanted to end up in another occupation force—still Sergeant Combat, only in a new theater; in my heart I'd secretly wished the war would continue long enough to let me get involved in at least one good fight. My wish came true, only too well.

My first real firefight had occurred just before the Chinese came, on a dull, overcast day. The scout section had set up near a secondary road; we spotted a squad of North Korean soldiers, weapons at sling arms, coming out of the tree line. They were good-looking troops, but asleep at the switch—they didn't see us. It was amazing the sense of power I'd felt—ultimate power, I suppose—just watching them come and holding that weapon in my hands. We let them get within about thirty yards before we cut loose; I dropped four guys point-blank with my M-1, each dead with a six-o'clock-sight picture in the chest, just like the good book said. I felt no guilt—few of us did; I'd been trained too well, and besides, the enemy had been utterly dehumanized throughout my training. *They aren't men, they're just gooks,* * I thought, as the four enemy fell and a fierce firefight began—we'd knocked off the point element of a much larger enemy force and stirred up a hornet's nest.

Following the lead of a lot of the older veterans, earlier in the day I'd placed several clips of ammo on my rifle sling. I liked the look—it was kind

* The term "gook" is derived from the Korean word *han-guk*, which means Korean person.

of John Wayneish—and it seemed to make sense, a new clip only seconds away. But when I'd taken up my prone firing position, the sling had flopped on the rain-soaked ground. Now, as the firefight got going, I grabbed for a clip only to discover that it and the rest of them were clogged with mud. Bullets were flying and my brain stalled out. I vaguely remembered an old tale about how well the M-1 worked under any battlefield condition; quickly knocking off the bigger pieces of mud, I oozed the clip into my rifle. I got one round off. The weapon jammed, and for the next few minutes I sat in the ditch, fieldstripping, cleaning, and reassembling the thing, while my first real combat went on without me. Our artillery (arty) fire took the starch out of the North Korean advance, and we were able to scoot ass with no friendly casualties—other, that is, than Sergeant Combat's bruised pride.

My first fight had been my first screwup. I didn't know until much later that you generally don't walk away from that one.

A few days later, five of us had been on a reconnaissance patrol. It was a black night, save for the U.S. flares that hung eerily over the battlefield; very quiet but for the occasional whine of artillery fire and the odd burst of an automatic weapon. We had moved about a mile into enemy territory when we heard motors. Leaving the patrol, I crawled to a mound near the edge of the road for a firsthand look.

Through the darkness, silhouetted by the artillery flares, I could see four enemy vehicles. A file of infantry was walking on each side of the motor column, with more infantry walking in front. They were so close that I was sure only the vehicles' engines prevented them from hearing my pounding heart. They passed by. I was about to return to the patrol when I saw a lone North Korean soldier, his weapon slung, tracing a telephone wire. As he passed my position, I parted his hair with a submachine-gun magazine and dragged him back to the patrol.

Daylight wasn't far off when we headed home. Progress was slow. Initially we had to pack our zonked-out prize; later he awoke and stumbled along belligerently, but at least under his own steam. Just when we thought we had it made, we ran into a large enemy force moving down the road in formation. They were jabbering excitedly and dragging machine guns behind them on squeaky wheels. We were about six yards from the road; I lay on top of the prisoner, covered his mouth with my hand, and pressed my trench knife hard against his throat. I thought the cold steel would be enough to convince him to be good, but it wasn't—old habits die hard. He started squirming around. My hand was muffling his cries to his comrades; when he tried to bite it, I had no choice—I slit his throat, and lay there on top of him for what seemed like a bloody eternity, until the road was clear and we could hotfoot it back to the U.S. lines.

I hadn't wanted to kill him. I would rather have captured the guy—a live prisoner is worth a thousand dead hombres. But I was probably as scared as he was, and in a millionth of a second, I'd had to decide—and it was either him or my patrol.

Killing that guy and one other incident probably hammered home most that Korea was not some training maneuver, that I was really in a war, boots and all. The other occurred when we were digging in on a small knob overlooking a main north-south road. Digging in was a task a frontline trooper performed at least once a day when on the move; usually you spent the time cursing your commander for always choosing the hardest ground in town, and then moving the line just when you've finished your hole. Some of us thought it was an Army plot to keep us in shape; for myself, I'd rather have done a million push-ups. But on this particular occasion we'd gotten some great dirt. It was soft and loose, a breeze to dig, and I was about two feet down in no time. Then my shovel hit something mushy. A few quick scrapes revealed olive-drab (OD) green material; a few more uncovered the decaying corpse of a man with bright-red hair and a 24th Division patch on his moldy fatigue jacket. The soldier's hands had been tied behind him with communication (commo) wire, and he'd been shot in the back of the head. Three more bodies were found by other troopers on our little knob, all killed and buried the same way.

Company was notified; they said the men probably had been killed at the beginning of the war—that was when the 24th Division (the 25th's sister division from the pre–WW II Hawaii days) had fought along this road. We were instructed to dig out the dog tags and provide eight-digit coordinates where each body was found. The atrocity did little for morale but a lot for fighting spirit; there would be little love lost for an enemy as savage as the North Korean Reds. *So much for the "Korean Police Action,"* I and my friends all thought. This was all-out war, with no quarter given.

Now that the Chinese were in the conflict, the Recon Company's mission was to provide a reconnaissance screen in front of the 25th Infantry Division's withdrawal—in other words, to "delay, deceive, and disorganize" the undeniable Communist advance. The Chinese had struck Eighth Army like a giant steamroller, crushing many units and mauling most others. Eighth Army's commander, Lieutenant General Walton Walker, who had said in July of 1950 (as the first reel southward began), "There will be no Dunkirk, there will be no Bataan, a retreat to Pusan would be one of the greatest butcheries in history. We must fight until the end," now found himself directing yet another brave but bloody withdrawal to the south.[1] Only seven years before, General Eisenhower's forces were similarly surprised and smashed, but that time we'd had Patton to save the day; in my heart of hearts, I kind of wished someone would get the idea to use our recon company as the "Spearhead to Bastogne" for the Korean conflict. But it was not to be, and it was just as well. Unlike the 752d Recon, which had had seventeen M24 light tanks, we were a light-skinned force with only six M24s in the whole company. Divide these up among three identical platoons* (which were normally attached one to each regiment) and it wasn't exactly the punch Lieutenant Colonel Creighton Abrams had had in 1944.

Still, we had plenty to do to keep us occupied. Exchanging ground for time, the drill went that we would hold a position until the enemy was breathing hot and heavy down our necks; then we would break contact and run like hell, leapfrogging through another recon platoon or a rifle unit that was set up behind us in the same way. It was a dangerous game with no room for error, and we found ourselves playing it day after day after day.

They were strange dudes, the Chinese, seemingly with no sense of personal peril. It was not unusual to see them jump on a U.S. tank, holding grenades, and then scramble around looking for some opening to toss them in. Of course, if the tank was buttoned up, this was impossible, and the tank commander inside would simply call another tank nearby to "scratch my back," at which point the second tank would spray the first with .30-caliber coaxial machine-gun fire and wash the hitchhikers off. But there were always other Chinamen to take the dead ones' places; it was a grim fact we were constantly reminded of as we kept moving south.

Morale dropped with every rearward step of the humiliating retreat. We kept falling back—away from the Yalu, beyond Pyongyang—until soon we'd recrossed the 38th parallel and were back in South Korea. The only things I think running faster than the Eighth Army were the rumors: the Marines were cut off at a place called Chosan Reservoir in the north and were being zeroed out; the U.S. Army's X Corps had surrendered; boats were waiting at Pusan harbor to take us to Japan. Meanwhile, winter had arrived, but winter gear had not. MacArthur had said we'd be home before Christmas; I guess his supply people believed him, because the Chinese had caught us with our pants down and they were summer trousers. Feet in leather boots froze; gloves and mittens were as scarce as good-looking girls; our field jackets were as thin and protective as page one of a newspaper. We were slowly freezing to death in the bitter below-zero weather while the Chinese, like Genghis Khan's mighty hordes, marched on, seemingly unstoppable.

Food was in short supply. All spare time was spent scrounging; one of the most modern armies in the world became an army of days past, foraging and living off the land. We kicked in walls of houses, searching for rice and

---

* Each platoon was composed of two M24 tanks, a rifle squad, a scout section, and an 81-mm mortar squad.

kimchi (fermented cabbage, a Korean staple) hidden in false walls and secret caches; we cooked what we found in our steel pots. When nothing else was available we'd take the C-ration packets of sugar, powdered coffee, powdered milk, and chocolate we'd stored for days (like squirrels) in the pockets of our fatigues, mash it all together with snow in our helmets, and trick ourselves into believing it was ice cream.

Trying to beat the elements became a war in itself. It was so bitterly cold you couldn't sleep. You had to keep moving, stomping feet and flexing fingers twenty-four hours a day. Those who didn't were saying good-bye to their hands and feet (and in some cases their lives); for a while every day a couple of men were evacuated because of frostbite—black toes and fingers to be cut off at the hospital. Grenades, knives, and ammo would freeze fast to the foxhole brim. Weapons froze, too—you'd have to kick the bolts of the M-1s and Browning automatic rifles (BARs) to get them back. We seldom had rifle patches to clean our weapons; most of us cut little squares out of our shirts or trousers to do the best we could. Gun oil was a luxury usually beyond our reach; we lubricated our weapons with motor oil or the frozen lard of C rations, and took to keeping them with us in our fart sacks at night. Staying alive became our only concern, and we did. Man is most adaptable. When we passed through the villages, if a house had lots of wood—doors, window frames, even the most beautiful hand-carved furniture—we'd burn it, one piece at a time, finishing off the job by throwing a thermite grenade on the thatch roof and standing by until the whole structure was burned to the ground. Our orders were to destroy anything the enemy could use; *Gladly*, we thought to ourselves, and we could stay warm while we did it. At night, we would carefully—obsessively—bundle, stack, and restack kindling wood, while waiting for daybreak when we could light our fires. The thought of those friendly flames allowed us to make it through the night; instantaneously, at first light thousands of tiny fires would spring up across the front, and around each huddled a cluster of shivering men. It was probably as bad in the Chinese camp, except at least the Chinks were prepared with winter gear—down trousers and jackets, long overcoats that blended in with the snow, and down mittens that we liberated and wore until our own supply people came through.

It was a frigid, brutal, soul-destroying time; I knew then how the Wehrmacht must have felt during World War II, or how Napolean's army must have suffered years and years before that, when each made their horrible winter retreat from Russia.

By the time we reached Seoul, the South Korean capital—once a bustling city of millions—was virtually deserted, an empty, gray tomb. Most of its inhabitants, and those of the northern villages on its outskirts, had left and headed south with the few possessions they could carry, clogging the roads with wall-to-wall human misery. On one occasion, American fighter planes must have concluded that the hordes of desperate civilians were Chinese columns moving south; P-51s had strafed the refugees, and for at least a mile there were dead littered across the road. Retreating vehicles had to push the bodies out of the way. It was here that I realized it was only the guys on the ground who saw and understood the real horrors of war. To Air Force pilots, war is a remote thing. They make their kills from hundreds or thousands of feet in the air. Even the guys who fly on the deck do so in a flash, dropping their loads and flying away without seeing the results: the way homes and people are blown to smithereens, or the effects of napalm. At night they didn't have to listen, as we did in the winter of 1950, to "the wail of the gooks"—cries of civilian refugees begging to be let through American lines—or see in the morning, when they were allowed to pass through, the dead they'd left behind, those who'd frozen to death in open rice paddies overnight. The pilot, when he finishes his day's work, flies back to his base, lands, goes to the club, has a big steak, and if he wants to forget the day's "combat," he can drink himself into a stupor. The frontline fighter can't do that. He lives with death and the horror of the battlefield every day and every night. It's his cross to bear.

We continued retreating. Gray, rotting bodies, the unforgettable smell of death, rats feasting on the dead and growing bolder by the day—this, the flotsam and jetsam of war, led us through Seoul.

Our unit's mission was to fight a rear-guard action in the center of the city. The scout section and rifle squad set up at a downtown intersection; we took over a bank, a drugstore, and two other corner buildings. For my "command post" I used the bank manager's plush office (*Moving uptown,* I thought), which was a welcome diversion from the cold and snow. The bank vault was locked tight; as the self-appointed new bank manager I authorized the guys to open it with their 3.5 antitank bazooka. Two rounds later, the door swung open as easily as a C-ration can in the hands of a hungry trooper.

The vault contained thousands of dollars in small Korean notes—all the big stuff was gone. I told everyone to cash in, "No withdrawal forms needed," I said, and they did. We had to laugh at the propaganda leaflets that the Chinese mortared down upon us from the hills they occupied on the high ground around Seoul: "American capitalists, running dogs of Wall Street!" they accused. *How right they are,* I thought, as we stuffed pockets and packs, and even made hobo sacks to carry our spoils of war.

It was strange watching the Chinese brazenly looking down from those hills about six or eight hundred yards away. Our infantry weapons were out of range, preventing a little selective sniping, but we were able to put some effective fire on them with the M24's main gun, and had great fun taking potshots with the turret's .50 caliber. The Chinese went to ground, and shy of a cheerless Christmas we slipped out of sad, near-deserted Seoul. My section's newfound wealth was the first thing to be tossed on the side of the road; bulky dollars meant little to worn-out troopers, and it had just been a game anyway.

South of Seoul we found ourselves caught in a *friendly* battle zone, a railway yard being blasted to kingdom come by demolition-toting engineers and Air Force bombers. Railroad flatcars complete with brand-new vehicles and tanks (which would have been distributed to the front had it not collapsed) were being blown sky-high to keep them out of enemy hands; to us in the middle, the challenge of this Army obstacle course was not only to avoid our own flying debris but also the enemy incoming, which was pouring in throughout the operation.

We came upon a number of freight cars with sealed doors. One of the guys pried one open to reveal an entire carload of PX supplies—soap, cigarettes, after-shave lotion—obviously goodies needed by our rear-echelon comrades (I mean, they seldom found their way to the front), and we decided to help ourselves. Someone drove a brand-new three-quarter-ton truck off a nearby flatcar so we had a way to carry out the loot; it fell about four feet and crashed to the ground—springs breaking, fenders collapsing— but it still ran. We loaded our spoils onto the truck even as telephone poles (uprooted by our explosives) and large chunks of steel rained down around us; then we jumped aboard ourselves and unassed the place—eight recon men bouncing along in a truck right out of *The Grapes of Wrath*. We motored by a battalion of infantry hiking south down the road; "Hey, how you fixed for cigarettes?" we called, and "Aqua Velva, anyone?" as we threw all the troopers a little something. We ran out of goodies about the same time our mobile PX ran out of gas, and we reluctantly returned to the backs of our tanks with the rest of our platoon.

We were young: sometimes the war was great fun, like a game of cops and robbers, or cowboys and Indians, that you played as kids. The politics or purpose of the war was not our concern. We didn't understand or care about the big picture any more than we really understood the risks of combat—of being killed, or going home without a leg. After a while you stopped worrying if the next minute you were going to "get it." Instead you just prayed for a clean wound to get you out of there, a million-dollar wound to get you home.

After we retreated across the Han River, my platoon was given the mission to outpost a long, lonely stretch of the south bank. It was Christmas Day, and although no Chinese were in sight, it wasn't a particularly jolly time: General Walker had been killed two days before in a freak jeep-truck accident very similar to the one that had killed his World War II boss, General Patton. Still, paratroop general Matt Ridgway had taken over as the new commander of Eighth Army, and the word was we would retreat no farther. It was a good word, but my platoon had a more immediate concern: we were starving. A personal recon of the area revealed a village nearby whose only occupants were half a dozen scroungy-looking chickens; one long burst from my borrowed M-2 carbine gave us Christmas dinner in the form of three decisively dead birds that we plucked and threw on an open fire. We ate them unseasoned and undercooked—they were very, very raw, in fact—but wonderful to us, and we gobbled them down and huddled closer to the fire, thinking how lucky we were.

No sooner had we finished than a Recon Company jeep and trailer bounced across the field to our positions. Christmas dinner—turkey, cranberry sauce, and all the trimmings—had arrived. Only the American Army could do that. Unfortunately, our chicken appetizer had left all of us with roaring gut aches (making the second feast a little hard to swallow), but we wolfed it down anyway, because it was good, because it was there—and because none of us knew if this meal would be the last.

The enemy took Seoul just after the New Year. The bridge across the Han had been blown, but a few days later the Chinks got a bridgehead across and we once again headed south, in zero-degree weather, with our tails between our legs. So much for no more retreats. I began to think about all the generals' proclamations concerning this war: that we'd be home before Christmas, that the Chinese would not intervene, that we'd hold here or hold there. All of it was bullshit, and I started to wonder how they could possibly make so many dumb statements when each, invariably, fell apart when put to the test. Then I thought, *Well, maybe they just don't know*—we never saw a general on the front. We seldom saw a colonel, a lieutenant colonel, or a major either. And at squad level, we only on the rarest occasion saw a captain. So how *could* the brass know how defeated its army was if they weren't there to see an exhausted guy lie down on the road and just give up? How could they know how cold and ill equipped we were if they weren't there to see blue, gloveless hands stick to the frozen metal of weapons? How could they know how steep and rugged the terrain was if they never climbed a hill?

Still, we kept retreating, exchanging ground for time. We were always cold. Always hungry. Always tired. We were also filthy—it was too cold to even consider washing—so when we got to Suwon and found ourselves with a few days to rest, we decided to take that abandoned city by storm.

As in Seoul, everyone had left Suwon in a great hurry, so we could pretty well help ourselves to whatever we wanted. My section took over a house. We scrounged around and found an old-fashioned Korean bath, one of those stand-up jobs about chest high, with a wood furnace underneath. We filled the tub, built a roaring fire, and one by one jumped in, each of us skimming the other guy's dirt off the top of the water. I was last. The water was almost black by then, with all kinds of crud floating around, but I didn't care—I might not have gotten clean, but for the first time in weeks, I was warm.

Just after we left Suwon, my platoon was ordered to establish a night blocking position astride a north-south road that paralleled a railroad track. The scout section and rifle squad were set up in a defensive line that ran from the road through a rice paddy and onto a railroad trestle. Our machine gun was set up on the trestle pointing straight down the tracks, where it could put plunging fire directly in front of the deployed troops and flanking fire on the road fifty yards away. Our platoon leader stayed with the two M24 tanks on the road; behind him was the 81-mm mortar squad.

It was late at night. All was quiet. We were locked and cocked and pros at this deadly delaying game by now. I moved between the positions having whispered conversations with the guys; it was a habit I had, to keep myself awake and make sure the men stayed awake, too. I was at the machine gun, which was manned by a stud of a Hawaiian trooper named Sheldon, when we saw the enemy coming. There was at least a company and maybe more behind, four abreast, double-timing quietly down the railroad track. When they were no more than thirty yards from the machine gun, Sheldon let loose a long burst that cut a wide swath into their unsuspecting ranks. A burst of machine-gun fire was the signal for the infantry, tanks, and mortars to join in the fray; the scout section and rifle squad immediately poured fire into the enemy formation.

The enemy panicked; they did not fire one round in return. Instead, they broke ranks and hightailed it to the rice paddy, running right into the rifle squad's grazing fire. It was great to see—we were cleaning the clock of an enemy force at least ten times our size. *Like young Rommel did*, I thought, in 1914, when he ambushed and destroyed almost a complete British rifle company with a handful of soldiers, simply by using initiative and surprise, two of the key elements in battle.

The mortar was plopping in rounds of high explosives right on top of the confused Reds. Meanwhile, our tanks' main guns, which were loaded with antipersonnel grapeshot, hadn't fired anything at all. A white star-cluster flare popped and hovered over our positions; this was the signal to "beat feet in retreat," and we didn't need a second invitation. We scrambled to waiting vehicles and moved quickly to, and through, the U.S. lines. We'd taken no casualties, but I still couldn't understand why the tanks' guns hadn't fired. The enemy had been hurt badly, but not destroyed; if those guns had been employed we'd have completely wiped them out.

The sun was coming up as the platoon pulled into the abandoned Chonan school yard that served as the base for the Recon Company. I went over to our platoon sergeant and asked him why the tanks hadn't been used. He looked away and sort of bowed his head as if he was embarrassed, which was very strange behavior for this rugged, highly decorated warrior. "Better see the Lieutenant, young sergeant."

"Why didn't the tanks fire?" I asked my Regular Army platoon leader moments later.

"I didn't want to give our positions away," he replied.

I couldn't believe it. "Give away your positions, bullshit!" I cried. Sergeants didn't talk to officers like that, but I didn't care. We'd had the closest thing to a glorious victory that I'd seen since the Chinks stuck their noses into the goddamn war, and now this piss-weak lieutenant . . . "You were just too yellow to do your job," I shouted, and stormed back to my scout section in a rage. I grabbed my pack and my rifle. "I'm leaving this outfit right now!" I told my platoon sergeant. "I'm not waiting for orders—I'm going AWOL. I came here to fight, not to play hide-and-seek, and where I come from, officers like you've got here would have been drummed right out of the officers' corps." And with that I headed for the road.

4 THE WOLFHOUNDS

He had a unique trait of courage about him which was kind of amazing to us. I'm not saying there weren't others, too, but Hack just exhibited this day after day. And we were in a pretty tough situation. There was a lot of confusion—we were fighting the Chinese, the North Koreans, *and* the elements—so it was important to have Hack around to give everyone the spark that was needed to keep going, and add a little humor, too, when we needed that. Sometimes he did things that *I* would consider crazy—but it always sparked us, it really did. He was a fearless-type individual, but I think the reason was he always felt that Lady Luck was riding on his side, and that she always would.

Sergeant Major Walter Schroeder, USA, Ret.
Squad Leader, Platoon Sergeant, Platoon Leader
G/27th Infantry, Korea, 1950–51

"ANY man who's wild enough to go AWOL to fight is just the kind of man we want in our outfit," said Captain John Paul Vann, when I stopped at his 8th Ranger camp fresh from my breakout from the 25th Recon Company. The 8th Rangers was a great, spirited unit, recently rebuilt after being decimated the night the Chinese entered the war. After I'd explained my situation the whole outfit accepted me with open arms.

The Rangers were elite troops, forerunners of the Special Forces (Green Berets). Their mission was raids, long reconnaissance patrols, ambushes, and other special jobs that conventional troops were not trained to handle. Their history went back to Rogers' Rangers, before the Revolutionary War; during World War II there'd been six Ranger battalions whose brave and daring feats are unmatched to this day. Historically, such all-volunteer, specially trained units had been misused, tasked either with impossible missions for organizations their size, or with "palace guard" combat duties well beneath their skill and ability. When I arrived at the 8th Ranger camp, the unit was chasing guerrillas behind the main lines. Morale was high and the guys were spoiling for a good fight, but during the time I was there nothing much—to my way of thinking anyway—seemed to be happening. I was impatient to get into the thick of it, and as proud as I was to be a Ranger, guerrilla hunting was not my idea of infantry combat. (Little did I know then the starring roles that guerrilla hunting *and* Ranger CO John Paul Vann would have later in my life.) Besides, the word was that the 8th Rangers was going to be broken up soon, and something in me said to move on. So I did, until I saw a sign by the road that proclaimed "Wolfhound White Rear." *Well, if that's not a guarantee for a good fight, I don't know what is,* I thought, and hightailed it to the battalion CP.

The 27th Infantry (Wolfhound) Regiment was a colorful unit itself. The outfit had gotten its name during its stint fighting Communists in Siberia during the Russian Revolution. In Korea the Wolfhounds were known as the "Fire Brigade," because whenever there was trouble they were sent in to save the day. They weren't a special unit—just a group of guys who *thought* they were good, so they *were* good. I'd seen members of the outfit regularly over the last months, whenever the 25th Recon had been sent to their portion of the divisional front, and I'd always been knocked out because these guys acted more like pirates on the high seas than as a Regular Army regiment. To begin with, the Wolfhounds wore their regimental crest on their fatigues like the Medal of Honor—their spirit was just incredible. They were also totally nonmilitary in terms of what I was accustomed to: they seldom wore steel pots; they modified their gear to make it more functional and simply got rid of things that weighed them down unnecessarily. The long wooden handle of the entrenching tool, for example, was cut off so it wouldn't rub against your leg. Packs were thrown away and you carried a tramp's roll, which was quickly grounded when you got into a fight. BARs were stripped of bipods and carrying handles, and scabbards were tossed, with the bayonet living permanently at the end of the rifle. Grenades were carried in canteen covers (you could fit in five), and if you wanted to carry a captured weapon, go for it.

This renegade kind of soldiering was not only sanctioned but *encouraged* by the 27th's regimental commander and "Fire Chief," WW II paratrooper Colonel John "Iron Mike" Michaelis. Michaelis (who would go on to four stars) understood what made men fight. He was known for morale-boosting slogans like "You're lean, you're mean; you're rough, you're tough; you're professional killers," and prebattle pep talks like "You're not here to die for your country; you're here to make those so-and-sos die for theirs." The Wolfhounds' proud combat record showed that they believed him, and they had eagerly adopted their commander's no-nonsense brand of soldiering. I was more than ready to do the same.

The 2d Battalion's XO pointed the way up the road to where the rifle companies were deployed. The first unit I came to was Company G, where I reported in to First Sergeant Edwin Rager. "I can always use another sergeant," this giant of a topkick roared, then and there assigning me to 3d Platoon. Finally, with the assurance that I'd be picked up on the morning report (so I wouldn't be considered AWOL or MIA), I joined my new family.

At first it was not the happiest of unions. I should have realized it wouldn't be easy. It's always a bitch to join a unit (particularly one as tight as the Wolfhounds) as an individual replacement, and for some reason it's even worse when you're an NCO or an officer. You don't know anyone, and no one trusts you until you've proved yourself in battle. You get all the lousy details and only the worst battlefield horror stories; you're just "the new guy," you're just "fresh meat." And to add insult to injury, though I'd been a squad leader and acting platoon sergeant in Italy and a section leader in the 25th Recon, now in the 3d of G, I found myself an *assistant* squad leader. I was damned unhappy with the demotion—I probably had more noncom experience than any of the squad leaders in the platoon—but the fact was that in their eyes I was untried, and all protests to the contrary fell on deaf ears.

I didn't help my cause any that evening, soon after my arrival, when just at dusk I got caught in a rice paddy right smack in the middle of a blistering Chink mortar attack. I started to run, but slipped and fell in the paddy. When I finally got back to my foxhole, I discovered that my water-repellent outer trousers were covered with human shit, which the Koreans used for fertilizer. Unsurprisingly, the guy sharing my hole was as unhappy about this as I was. I took the trousers off and made do for the night with the two pairs of long johns and two pairs of OD trousers I had on underneath. (Lots of layers were the key to staying warm, I'd learned. Bulky stuff like pile jackets were too heavy and constricted movement; light clothes were more comfortable and much better for trapping body heat.) Then I sacked out until it was my turn to go on guard, leaving my foxhole partner to contend with the lingering aroma of my "accident."

Guard was a grueling ritual, mainly because everyone was always so tired. Each squad had its own sector, normally four foxholes, each about four yards apart (the spacing dependent, as were all things in combat, on the enemy, the terrain, and the weather). Two guys shared a hole and took turns throughout the night searching into the darkness. You'd look until you got tired, then glance at your buddy sacked out at the bottom of the hole. Then you'd look a little longer while you thought, *Should I wake him now? Has he had enough sleep?* Few guys had watches—to own a watch in an infantry squad during that first Korean winter was a luxury beyond imagination—so you spelled each other based on the honor system, and you only asked for relief when it was impossible to keep your eyes open any longer. Then your buddy would ask for a sitrep (SITRPT, or situation report) and that was it; you'd be asleep almost before you'd zipped up your feather-down fart sack.

"What's happening?" I asked, when my foxhole partner woke me for my turn.

"Not a thing," he replied, and was out like a light.

Still inside my sack, I sat in the darkness on the edge of the hole, got my eyeballs unglued, and tried to remember where I was. I was fantasizing about smoking a cigarette, drinking a hot cup of coffee, eating a charcoal-black rare steak (bite by delicious bite), and getting a squad of my own when, to my amazement, I saw a man lying prone to my immediate left rear. I woke up my buddy. "There's a goddamned Chink almost on top of us!"

We whispered through our options. We could toss a hand grenade, blast him with a rifle, or crawl out and get him with a knife. We decided on the third alternative, because the guy was right in the middle of our squad position, and rifle fire or a grenade could easily start a firefight among our own guys. The Chink wasn't moving and his back was to us. My buddy covered me while I crawled out of the foxhole with my trusty M-1, a ten-inch-long razor-sharp bayonet attached.

In a crouched position, I silently slipped up behind the enemy soldier. When I got within sticking distance, I drew back my rifle and thrust it with full force. Branches crackled and it was over: I'd bayoneted my own frozen-stiff trousers, which I'd earlier hung over a bush behind our foxhole to dry. The next morning, I had to put the shitty things back on again (now with a hole in the ass as well), and for some reason the "fresh meat" was the only one in the squad who didn't think it was very funny.

The war seemed lost; at best it was hopelessly confused. I'd thought wars, at least America's wars, had happy endings, like capturing Berlin and Tokyo. All we were doing was yo-yoing back and forth across the Korean peninsula. Defeat, then victory, then defeat and defeat. With G Company, too, we were retreating: shuffling along, heading south, colder—sometimes the temperatures were twenty degrees below zero—and more tired than we'd ever been in our lives. One day a snap thaw had us wading through mud on both sides of a mire that had once been a road. Jeeps and trucks sloshed through it, too, each vehicle trying in vain to miss the rut of the vehicle in front so as not to become bogged down. One jeep stalled and would not restart just as our column was passing by. The driver and lieutenant passenger unassed the thing; the lieutenant called for help to push it over to the side. But before we could slosh through the quagmire and give him a hand, he whipped out his pistol and aimed it at one of the tires. I figured his daddy must have been an old horse soldier and this guy was going to follow the Cav tradition of shooting his disabled mount, and sure enough: *Pow. Pow. Pow. Pow.* But the last shot missed the tire. It glanced off the rim and boomeranged back to strike the lieutenant right between the eyes. We pushed the jeep and the warm, still body off the road and then returned to our column. Soon the temperature dropped, the road turned to ice, and we just kept heading south.

It hadn't meant anything, the lieutenant's death. For openers, what he'd done was dumb. But more than that, we'd become immune. Fighting a war on the ground is like working in a slaughterhouse. At first the blood, the gore, gets to you. But after a while you don't see it, you don't smell it, you don't feel it. *So what's another dead body?* It's almost as if you don't care. In this case, we just leaned forward, kept walking, and tried to ignore the song in our heads, the one the troops called "The Bug-Out Blues."

So this is the life of the groundpounder, I'd often think. The risks were higher in the Recon Company, but life in George was far more harsh. At least in the recon we frequently rode on the backs of our tanks and thus kept warm; in the infantry it was just a plodding grind, one foot after the other, until the column stopped and we'd flop down, sound asleep before our heads touched the ground. In the recon, we were seldom hungry because we stashed rations on the tanks; in the infantry, growling bellies were our constant companions. In the infantry, many men lost their will to live. Frequently guys would just quit, drop out of the moving column, and plunk down on the side of the road—sometimes with the Chinese within sight. You'd say, "Come on, buddy, get up. Let's go! You're going to be captured!" And he'd say, "I don't care. I can't go another step." A day felt like a week, and the more tired an infantryman became, the more he wanted to lighten his load. First to go would be the souvenirs (the captured goodies like SKS rifles), and then his extra ammo. Next would be bulky gear—field coats, pile jackets, and down sleeping bags—even though he knew he'd freeze that night. In the infantry, I found, you live for right now. You don't give a damn about tomorrow, because you don't even know if there'll be one.

Now and then, if we were really lucky, we'd stop in a village and commandeer an abandoned house for ten or twenty winks. A Korean home had adobe mud floors under which lay an oven, the purpose of which was to provide central heating for the entire house. Of course, American soldiers had no idea how these things worked and the first time around we built the biggest fire we could and went to sleep shivering and bitching that the gooks didn't know how to do anything right. It turned out, though, that the previous occupants of our temporary abode had the last laugh. Throughout the night the floors got hotter and hotter, until some of the guys' jackets spontaneously combusted and the ammo we'd laid on the floor blew up. Snow never looked so good.

On most nights, though, to stave off the cold we employed old soldiers' tricks from the bleak, frozen days of Valley Forge. One was to stuff hay in a poncho and wrap it tightly around two guys to keep in body heat. Another was to fill your steel pot with hot coals and embrace it all night long (a practice that continued despite a number of tired soldiers who died this way from asphyxiation). Another was to put a slug through your foot. I'd thought about that one—most of us did—but it always seemed too risky: you might blow your foot off, or you might be caught and court-martialed. But one bitterly cold night, when I would have done anything to get out of that place, I came up with the perfect solution.

If I emptied most of the powder out of a grenade, I could toss it into my foxhole and blame it on a sneaky Chinaman. Better yet, if I chipped a trench on the side of the foxhole with my bayonet, I could contain the damage to my leg. All I'd have to do would be lay my body in the trench, stick my leg in the hole, toss in the grenade and *Bang!*—a million-dollar wound. It was a wonderful idea—somehow a lot better than the one I often saw during a firefight, when a guy would stay in his hole and wave his arms or kick his legs like a chorus dancer, hoping to catch a slug and the first boat back to the States—and I spent all night digging away, working on the trench, and thinking how warm I'd be back in Santa Monica, the war vet who got it in the leg. I chipped and chipped away at the frozen ground, completely forgetting about the cold, the time, the fact that I needed some sleep, or that my buddy (who was sleeping behind the hole) may have had enough. Finally it was ready. I hoisted myself into the trench, prepared the grenade, and dangled my leg in the hole. And I was just about to pull that pin when I saw the most beautiful sight, a sight that every infantryman in Korea dreamed of seeing. It was the sun, slowly rising. It meant the terrible night was over. It meant I could light my fire and be warm again. So I forgot my little trench (and for a long time afterward wondered if I really would have pulled that pin), and for a moment forgot the other thing the sun meant: the beginning of yet another long day, another step south, the never-ending, bitter taste of defeat in all our mouths.

And then, as if overnight, everything changed. It turned out that despite the fact that I never saw a general on the battlefield, apparently one Lieutenant General Matthew Ridgway had been all over the Eighth Army front, assessing the situation and making his plans. "I rode in an open jeep," he would later write in his memoirs, "and would permit no jeep with the top up to operate in the combat zone. Riding in a closed vehicle in a battle area puts a man in the wrong frame of mind. It gives him an erroneous sense of warmth, of safety. His mental attitude is that of an ostrich poking his head in the sand. Also, I held to the old-fashioned idea that it helped the spirits of the men to see the Old Man up there, in the snow and sleet and the mud, sharing the same cold, miserable existence they had to endure. As a consequence, I damn near froze . . ."[1] Nevertheless, Ridgway persevered, with no quarter given: he banned the word "retreat" from the English language, at least insofar as correspondents could describe our miserable trek to the south; "I'm more interested in your plans for attack," he told a staff officer when the latter offered up those for another withdrawal.[2] He recognized even before we did that the Chinese offensive was running out of steam, and sought to take advantage of it with deep patrols to the north to find out exactly how stretched the enemy was. Operation Wolfhound was the first of these, and the Fire Brigade, under the command of Colonel Michaelis (one of General Ridgway's WW II Airborne protégés), was on the attack once more.

Two platoons of G Company and elements of the 89th Tank Battalion made up one of the task forces. Named for and commanded by our company commander, Jack Michaely, Task Force Michaely was given the mission of taking Suwon, and on the sixteenth of January it did just that. The enemy was totally unprepared for the daring daylight assault. George was outside of artillery range, and Captain Michaely, an old Horse Cav man, approached Suwon in the only way possible—frontally, down a road never probed for mines, and fast. My platoon, the 3d, was not involved in the blitzkrieg operation at all, but when the other guys came back (having killed 150 enemy without a casualty of their own), in high spirits and with stories of Captain Michaely sauntering across the streets of Suwon while enemy machine-gun slugs thudded all around him, our morale went sky-high—we were ready to take on the world.

Meanwhile, I got my squad and immediately set about instilling it with my TRUST standards and beliefs about the way things should be done. I got out a notebook and wrote down each man's name, rank, and serial number, his blood type, weapon number, next of kin, and whatever training and combat experience he had had. I started demanding that rifles be cleaned and that soldiers shape up; if I saw a soldier walking around without his weapon, the next thing he knew he'd be on the deck crawling to it, while I stood by kicking him and telling him with each kick that he was being hit with a slug. Brutal stuff—I'd learned it in basic training when Lieutenant Kramer at the Fort Knox rifle range kicked my arm until I'd positioned it correctly under my weapon—but that's how a guy learns. Besides, better my foot and a mythical slug than an enemy slug and good-bye friendly foot, arm, or life.

My guys thought I was crazy, and a prick to boot. They still didn't believe I'd paid my battlefield dues. Little did they know that *they* were doing the paying, in spades, for making me get that Sergeant Combat feeling all over again. But then came 6 February, part of another reconnaissance-in-force mission (code-named Operation Thunderbolt, which turned into a full-scale attack), and I never had a complaint again. In fact the reaction was the direct opposite. No longer was I the hard-ass sergeant who arrived out of the blue with strange ideas of discipline and training. Now I was just "Hack"; Hack, the Great Fighter, who'd gotten shot in the head courageously saving lives and inflicting punishment on the enemy. It really was a great relief, knowing I would not have to prove myself to anyone anymore—but what I didn't know at the time was that the name I made for myself on 6 February 1951, was one I'd have to live up to for the next twenty years.

It seemed ironic that the thing that saved my life on that day was the very thing I hated most in Korea—the cold. The blood kept pumping, but it froze almost as soon as it came out of my head. After the doc patched me up with a Carlisle bandage (I felt like the little drummer boy in a Fourth of July parade), I radioed Captain Michaely and gave him a sitrep. I'd already appointed another NCO to skipper the platoon; Michaely told me to head for the road behind which Gilchrist's platoon was fighting. He would send a litter jeep there to pick me up. The platoon doc, always worried about his flock, wanted to tag along; I told him I'd make it, policed up one of our dead's M-1s, and headed off.

I kept low and used the rice-paddy walls and irrigation ditches for cover. I probably wouldn't have felt it if I'd gotten hit again anyway, because during my run back down the drainage ditch I'd fallen through the ice and been soaked from the waist down. The water and zero-degree weather had turned my lower torso into a block of ice—my head was spinning and my balls were frozen, and I wasn't sure which worried me more.

Then I came upon PFC Charles, the guy I'd earlier tasked to take the two North Korean POWs we'd captured that morning to the Old Man for interrogation. Charles was sitting in a drainage ditch by the road, eating a can of C rations. At his feet were the prisoners stretched out in the ditch—dead, each from a single bullet in the back of the head. I was outraged. "Why'd you kill them?"

"They tried to escape," he said simply, but I didn't believe him. "Besides," he continued, "I wasn't going to risk my ass to get two gooks out of here." There wasn't much I could do; I told him to report back to the platoon. Gilchrist told me later that Charles had received word only days before that his brother had been KIA over in the 2d Division. "Not too good a choice of an escort, Hack," he'd remark, drawing on his pipe.

I continued on. Small-arms and machine-gun fire was skipping down the road. I gave it all a big miss and kept to my little ditch. I headed south until I met Lieutenant Colonel Gordon Murch, our old pro battalion CO, who was controlling the battle from his tactical CP behind a roadside knoll a few hundred yards from the front. There I was placed on a litter in a medical jeep, and as we bumped down the road all I could think was *Hallelujah, I've got it made. I'm leaving this goddamned place.*

Or so I thought, because just then the jeep's radio crackled on: "First Platoon, George Company . . . got a serious wound . . . real bad . . . Get there fast. He'll be on the side of the road." I couldn't believe it. *Let me out! I'll wait here,* I thought, but I was too weak, too tired, and too cold to get the words out. The jeep spun around and headed back up that fire-swept road, past Colonel Murch, right into the jaws of the whole goddamned Communist Army. We stopped. The medics calmly sauntered out to pick up the other casualty. They took all the time in the world, or so it seemed, while the enemy used the large Red Cross markings on the jeep for target practice. The jeep's canvas sides were being ventilated, the slugs passing above and below my litter; I felt totally helpless, and swore that whoever the wounded guy was, I'd hate him for life (which, from the way things were going, was not going to be long).

It turned out he was a buddy through the "Hawaiian mafia" connection, a handsome six-footer named Ray Mendez. I almost kept to my word, though, when I found out his critical wound was a slug in the thigh. When he'd been hit he'd rolled up in a ball; blood had squirted out of his leg all over the front of his jacket, and someone had concluded he'd taken it in the gut. Oblivious to the fight raging on all sides of our thin-skinned ambulance jeep, Mendez became chirpier and chirpier as we headed out of the battle area. He sang the praises of his million-dollar wound and spun dreams about his imminent return to the Islands—"Me one big war hero, brah," he said.

The regimental collecting station was jammed with casualties. The surgeon who bent over my litter was covered in blood, like a butcher. "We're going to bypass Division Clearing and send you right to MASH at Suwon," he said. "You're on your way home."

The next stop was quick. The MASH was near the runway at Suwon; the doc there wrote on my wound tag "Emergency—Air evac," which somehow scared me, and before I knew it I was strapped down on the deck of a C-47.

We took off, just at dark. *Why don't they close the goddamn door?* I thought—it *had* to have been open, because I'd never been colder. I was shaking like a jackhammer, and I couldn't feel my hands or feet. A flight nurse stayed right with me (another ominous sign); she piled on blanket after blanket, with no effect. Just as I was reaching the point where I didn't know if I could take it anymore, we landed in Pusan, and it was another world. Paradise, in fact. A heated ambulance was waiting, and as they loaded me in I felt like that old boll weevil who lived in a red-hot fire—"mighty warm, but nice," I'd found a home. I fell asleep and didn't wake again until I was being winched aboard the hospital ship USS *Haven* in Pusan harbor.

I opened my eyes and everything was white, clean, and oh-so-warm. Medics were starched; the nurses all looked like Doris Day. I was stripped, placed in crisp white sheets with soft blue blankets—I was safe, and suddenly starving. A medic came to the immediate rescue with a delicious hot meal; I wolfed it down just in time for the next wonder of wonders: a beautiful young nurse in a tight little white outfit who came to clean me up. *Why didn't I join the Navy?* I thought.

Except for my bath in the Korean tub, I hadn't washed in more than two months. I was caked with dried blood, Korean mud, and God only knew what else, and each time the nurse scraped off one filthy layer, she'd have to change the sheets and start again. It took four sheet changes, with no help from me, because as a "head wound," I wasn't allowed to move at all. Next, the poor girl had to shave off my ratty beard. Bad hygiene and ingrown hairs had covered my face with boil-like pimples; it was too terrible to be funny, watching the nurse bobbing and weaving all over the place to avoid the flying debris every time that razor hit one of the antipersonnel mines buried in my cheeks.

The next few days were a haze. Sleep, really hard sleep; people standing over me, having whispered consultations. Blood, IV, X ray after X ray; doctors probing, asking questions—"How many fingers do you see?" I slowly regained my strength. Somebody commandeered my Waltham watch; I never saw it again. The sleep was good; I caught up on months of it lost. But then I started getting restless.

The ward, though spotlessly clean and staffed with talented, dedicated pros, was an extremely depressing place. We were all head wounds, most either terminal or vegetable cases. It was amazing that many—young boys, all of them—were still sucking in air. One guy had tubes running out of everywhere—he'd caught a slug between the eyes.

I wanted out. I'd had my little vacation. I told the docs, "I'm ready to return to my platoon. There's nothing wrong with me." The doctors probably thought that the bullet had done some pretty serious damage to my brain—nobody wanted to go back to the front. They didn't realize that the guys in the 3d Platoon were my brothers, my family, and I loved them. I'd only been with them three weeks, it was true, but in combat that's a lifetime, and I didn't want to leave them out there alone, if by being there I could help keep them alive, keep them out of a head-wound ward. "I want to go back," I kept telling them. "Sure," they'd say, giving one another those *he's-a-little-screwy* looks, and soon they sent me to Osaka General Hospital in Japan.

The regiment had been based in Osaka before Korea; the city was the Wolfhounds' lair, so we were looked after wonderfully, not only by the medical staff but by the distaff side of the regiment as well. The wives visited us often, brought little presents, helped us write letters home, and gently reintroduced us to the civilized world. A wife would find out through the grapevine that a guy from her husband's company was hospitalized and she would rush to his bedside: "How is my husband, Sergeant Rager?" she might ask.

"Mean as ever," you would say.

But sometimes the replies were not so glib, especially if a few days earlier you had seen the husband cut in two. Looking into the anxious faces of warrior wives, I thought that only a foolish woman would allow her man to earn his living as a moving target.

After a lot more tests, the docs concluded that I was okay. There was no brain damage; the wound had actually been superficial: the bullet had passed under the skin on the left side of my head, grazed along the top of my skull, and then punctured through the skin again in the back. All it had left me with were two buzzing ears, a neat V branded on the back of my head where the slug had come out, and a hankering to get out of the hospital and on with the promised convalescence leave.

A G Company guy told me he had seen Mendez up in the Leg Ward. The bullet had done a job on him; he was still a bed patient. "Your little scratch almost cost me my life," I joked with him. "If I'd been the doc I would have left you there with a Band-Aid."

Mendez laughed as only a Hawaiian can laugh. "It Hawaiian mafia, brah, got me out. They fake whole thing. Now I go home. *Me pau*, man . . ." ("I'm finished") he said, with more belly laughs.

The "Hawaiian mafia" was a term we had that referred to the large number of Hawaiians among the Wolfhound ranks. The 27th had spent years on Oahu before World War II; even though the regiment had not been back to the Islands for almost a decade, the Wolfhound history was such that Hawaiians coming through the replacement pipeline fought, lied, and cheated to get into the outfit. Consequently, most of the companies had tons of islanders. Individually and as a group they were the most stalwart and loving of friends, and they stuck together like glue. They were also the wildest, bravest, and most undisciplined fighters on the block. They had an almost obsessive drive to prove themselves on the battlefield, a drive I always thought came from their older brothers who'd made up the fierce 442d Regimental Combat Team during WW II. Of course, the 442d—the most highly decorated regiment in that war—was a hard act to follow, and part of the charm of this generation was that they never stopped trying ("Go for broke," the 442d motto, was the favorite expression among them), with act after act of sheer guts.

Mendez and I caught up on where George was, what lumps the company had taken, and all other bits of information we could garner from new arrivals. It turned out that on 6 February we had taken on a reinforced North Korean regiment and really torn its ass: 170 enemy bodies were found on position, with additional killed and wounded estimated at 500 men. Before being ordered to withdraw by battalion CO Colonel Murch, we'd captured five antitank weapons, two 120-mm mortars, and nine machine guns. We'd knocked out three artillery pieces, too, and come within two hundred yards of overrunning the enemy unit's regimental CP. (The next day 2d Battalion had continued the attack, but the North Koreans had met their match with gallant George, and bugged out to prevent an encore performance.) Third Platoon, despite the mauling we'd taken in the first moments of battle, had hung on tenaciously; we only now found out that we'd been operating in an area intended for an entire *company*—Fox, which had gotten hung up with a lot of enemy behind us, and whom George's tank-infantry task force had "hauled ass and bypassed."

We heard that Captain Michaely had been shot in the ass but kept on fighting; that Lieutenant Land had three thousand dollars of poker winnings in his pocket when he died (but that the guys had left it on him, even though they knew it'd be knocked off at Grave Registration), and that 1st Platoon was putting *me* in for a medal—for saving their ass *after* I was hit! Well, that was news to me. I hadn't done anything of the sort—or if I did, I didn't (nor would I ever) remember it. Still, word of this and the rest of the stuff that happened on 6 February started flashing around Osaka General (though all of it exaggerated to hell and back), and suddenly I found I was Big Man in the Hospital.

An ardent admirer came in the shape of an Army nurse. Her shape, to be exact, was that of a tackle for the Rams, and she would look at me adoringly as she gave me my shots. I was getting penicillin every four hours, in the ass; to this nurse's credit she was so magic with that dreaded needle that I seldom felt a thing. But I was into cheerleaders, not tackles, and the unhappy day came when she started suggesting that we take leave together. At first I tried the soft line: "Love to . . . but sergeants can't socialize with officers." This tack got me nowhere. If anything, it increased her passion for a little hard scrimmage at some idyllic Japanese hideaway. Finally I had no other recourse but to lay it on the line. "There are only two things in life that interest me," I blurted out. "One is sex and the other is adventure, and you don't offer either." I was too young to know about the "woman scorned" bit, but until I escaped a week later, she managed to find needles with square points, which she drilled into my aching cheeks with a vengeance.

On the first day of leave I met a lovely Japanese girl. She was probably a pro—some were, some weren't—but it didn't matter; at the end of your leave you always gave your little girl-san whatever money you had left anyway. She'd made you forget the war for a while, and that was worth something. So maybe she wasn't a pro. In any event, she was gentle and kind and fun, and we had a glorious, roaring two-week party together. And that was all you wanted on leave, convalescence or other. To live as high as you could, which meant good food, good women, lots of booze, and staying blasted all the time; to spend all your money and have a lot of fun, and try not to count the days before you had to go back.

The Han had been crossed and Seoul retaken; George Company was once again north of the city when I returned to my unit in mid-March. The company was tired; it had seen continuous hard combat since I'd been evacuated. But it had done a great job throughout, and was even in for a Presidential Unit Citation for the action on 6 February.

I took over my old squad. Things hadn't changed that much. Every day was still a grind, with one steep hill following the next. But there *was* one big difference: now it was the enemy who were on the run.

The yo-yo was headed back up the peninsula. Our spirits were higher than ever before—like Montgomery at El Alamein, who'd given the Allied forces their first victory in three years of war (*and* heralded the turning point of WW II), Ridgway had completely turned his defeated Army around. It was undoubtedly the most significant leadership achievement in modern military history. We were miraculously well equipped with winter gear and weapons; the supply system was belching out all kinds of good things. Tac air and outgoing artillery were plentiful; no matter how hard the enemy fought, they couldn't hold us back. We had two BARs per squad* and two

* The Browning automatic rifle was the best infantry weapon in Korea. Rugged and reliable, it seldom jammed, and a good gunner could mow the grass with its blistering and sustained rate of fire.

light machine guns (LMGs) in the platoon. We had cold-weather shoepacks, too, and hot chow at least once a day. All things considered, we couldn't have asked for much more, and it really wasn't until 30 March, when Company G was tasked to seize and hold a high, craggy hill designated Objective Logan, that the good times seemed to come to a screeching halt.

Korea was a bitch of a place to fight, because you weren't just fighting Chinamen and North Koreans. You also fought the hills themselves. Most were steep and razor-backed; many were solid rock, which meant an attacking force had to contend not only with enemy fire raining down from above, but also with rock fragments—as bad news as the flying steel. Objective Logan was one rocky hill. It resembled the top of the Rock of Gibraltar, and was so steep that only one platoon could attack on the company front at a time. After the lead platoon secured a ridgeline about five hundred yards from the objective and established a base of fire, 3d Platoon, originally tasked as the reserve element, passed through and became the assault force.

We moved along a ridge, concealed by low-lying clouds. But as the sky opened up, so did the enemy, with 75-mm pack howitzers, 60-mm and 82-mm mortars, and wall-to-wall automatic-weapons fire. We had casualties from the first shot, including our new medic, a black sergeant named Brown, who took a slug just below the heart while pulling a wounded kid to safety. We were pinned down, and would have remained so forever but for Phil Gilchrist, who'd recently taken over as 3d Platoon leader. Gilchrist told us to move out and we moved out, with him at the point, up Objective Logan with weapons blazing.

On top of the hill, the Chinese were well dug in and fighting a tenacious and determined defense. They were throwing the world at us, and for every inch of ground we gained, they extracted a terrible price. It was tough slugging, not unlike the fighting in Italy in 1944–45—the same sort of determined enemy; the same rough, difficult terrain. The Chinks flung grenades at us in barrages of three and four by ringing the pins around their fingers and throwing a handful at a time; we could see their hands rising over the crest of the hill, bedecked with grenades, which, an instant later, were hurtling toward us. The grenades, bullets, shrapnel, and flying rock fragments took their toll: by the time we reached the top of the hill, only seven effective fighters remained in the platoon. Everyone else was badly wounded or killed.

We etched out a little fingerhold by stacking up stones around shell craters. It was still broad daylight; we'd crested the hill and now looked down on the reverse slope to see the Chinese leaders below getting their men together for a counterattack. U.S. artillery and mortar fire were adjusted through the company radio net—the stuff was popping in so close it was amazing we had no friendly fire casualties. I'd recently taken over the weapons squad; now I placed our one remaining light machine gun in a 155-mm artillery crater, and for a while Thacker and Wells's blistering, effective fire kept the enemy at bay. But it was still hot. Very hot. The Chinese concentrated all their fire on our little redoubt. Mortars, artillery, and small arms thundered around us; one round landed so close that it knocked over our LMG and filled the hole with fragments. Amazingly, none of us was hit. A six-inch-long, jagged shard of shrapnel landed an inch from my knee. So close and yet so far from a million-dollar wound, without thinking I picked it up to show to Thacker and Wells, meanwhile burning the hell out of my hand on the red-hot steel.

We stayed low in our crater—even looking over the brim was a guarantee to be blown away—and for a while had to go blind, returning fire by holding our rifles over our heads and pointing downhill. We were so low on grenades that Lieutenant Gilchrist ordered that we get his permission to throw one. I was down to my last when gut feeling told me it was time to unlimber it, right in front of our position. I motioned for Gilchrist to come over. Indicating that we were not alone, I requested permission to pull the pin on the frag. He gave it.

I was lying on my back with my head pointed toward the attackers. When I pulled the pin, I spent a lazy second or so setting the grenade on the crater's edge (which didn't make Gilchrist, still lying beside me, too happy). Then I gave it a little flick with my fingers. It slowly tumbled down and exploded. *Bwam.* The hole shook, debris rained down, and then the air was filled with gently floating feathers. A down-jacketed Chinaman had gotten what he was going to give us—except gut feeling had told me to get there first.

We were quickly running out of ammo. Thacker had no more than a belt and a half for the machine gun, and our rifles were down to a couple of M-1 clips. Strict fire discipline became the rule; we couldn't afford to waste one round. We policed up a case of Chinese potato-masher grenades. They were probably World War I German Army vintage and about as effective as cherry bombs, but they made a lot of noise and at least they were something. Funny how a few hours before we'd been a rifle platoon loaded for bear, and now we were on our ass, hurling firecrackers and not making a dent.

As we broke up the last belt of LMG ammo and distributed it for the M-1s and BARs, Gilchrist told us a squad from Sergeant Reeves's 2d Platoon had volunteered to join us on the hill. What a great sight it was, moments later, to see their lead element coming up behind us. "Hello, brah," said their point man, Aguda, as his buddies ran past, tossing us bandoliers of M-1 ammo, grenades, and several boxes of machine-gun ammunition. "Big fight here, huh?"

James Aguda was one of my friends from the Hawaiian mafia. He'd just returned to his platoon a few days before, after having been wounded during a previous operation. When I'd first seen him after he'd gotten back, I'd noticed he was not wearing shoepacks. "Get rid of those leather boots," I'd told him. "You Hawaiian Buddha-heads have enough trouble with the cold. No sense asking for frostbite." I'd given him a pretty hard time—intentionally, because I was trying to find out how much his wound had affected him. Sometimes a man would come back from the hospital and say, "Yeah, Sarge, I'm cool . . . only a scratch," and the next thing you knew he'd crack up. But Aguda had taken everything I dished out, and finally I'd said, "Okay, fine . . . but you better get yourself some shoepacks."

Aguda had just shrugged and said, "I'm not going to be around here long enough to need them."

I'd dismissed the comment; such fatalistic statements were par for the course, especially before a big fight. I hadn't thought any more about it, nor did I now, on the hill. All I thought was that help had arrived. More ammo, more rifles, the staying power we needed to hold our objective. Now we just needed a little time. Aguda, casually sauntering past with his BAR, gave us that.

The crazy bastard stood up. He didn't go prone like the rest of us. He just walked to the forward slope and started mowing down the attacking Chinese ranks like John Wayne in *The Sands of Iwo Jima*. His BAR was singing as he fired magazine after magazine. And the whole time he was screaming to the Chinese, "Come on, you motherfuckers, come and get me." I yelled, "Get down! For Christ's sake, Aguda, get down!" But he just kept firing and reloading, firing and reloading—the perfect killing machine. Slugs were snapping all around him. I knew he was going to be killed. Then I could see he was getting it. *I could see it.* In the leg, in the arm, then two more in the legs. But he just kept shooting and screaming, and I kept yelling for him to get down. Finally he took one in the chest. It spun him around and he dropped. KIA.

Aguda's action, and similar actions from the other brave volunteers of 2d Platoon, turned the tide of the fight. They bought us time at perhaps the most critical phase of the battle—time in which the men of 1st and 4th platoons could get into position and start putting down the effective fire that broke the back of the Chinese counterattack. But the strange thing about Aguda was that he really had known he was going to be killed. It wasn't just his shoepack comment; after the battle, a poem he'd written was found among his personal possessions, predicting he would die in battle on a cold, windswept hill. I guess he knew his number was about to come up, and he just decided to go out fighting.

The Chinese had broken off their attack, and we had time to consolidate our defenses and evacuate our casualties. An ad hoc platoon aid station had been set up in a rocky outcrop near the crest of the hill; at one point in the battle it had been crammed with forty-two casualties, all of whom were cared for by an amazing infantryman who, armed with knowledge gleaned from a YMCA first-aid course, had taken Sergeant Brown's aid bag at gunpoint when the severely wounded medic insisted he could still do his job. We couldn't dig—the hill was solid rock—so we modified Chink bunkers, stacked rocks in front of our fighting positions, and hunkered down as best we could. The position was still hot, with plenty of incoming mortar and small-arms fire. Our platoon, which was now less than a squad, drew most of it; Thacker's machine gun had been the focal point of the complete battle so far, and we still occupied the high ground in the company center.

I was looking for a better machine-gun position when the enemy launched another attack. I hopped into the nearest hole, a large Chinese foxhole that had probably been a platoon CP. Now its sole occupant was one dead Chinaman, curled up in the bottom. I lay there with him, and whenever there was a lull in the firing, I'd pop up, fire eight rounds, and go back down to reload and wait until I could jump up again. It was kind of like playing human jack-in-the-box, and during one of these routines I caught a slug. *Oh, shit,* I thought, *not again, not in the head.* My helmet, which I had on backwards, was ripped off my head and I was propelled to the bottom of the hole.

If someone took a baseball bat and swung it at you—at your arm, your leg, or your head—with all his might, that's what getting hit with a bullet feels like. *Bam!* and then you don't feel anything for about twenty or thirty minutes because of the trauma caused by the speed of the projectile. Only after about half an hour does it really begin to hurt, so when I got it this time, all I knew was it felt just as it had on 6 February.

My head was spinning. I slowly reached up and touched my forehead, and then looked at my hand—no blood. I found my steel pot. It looked as if it had been neatly parted with an ax. The bullet had struck the helmet between the bottom lip of the steel and the liner, but because the back of a steel pot is reasonably oblique, the bullet had skipped along between the liner and the steel before coming out the top. If I hadn't been wearing the thing backwards (a habit I'd picked up from my dear friend in the weapons squad, machine gunner Jerry Boyd), I would have been as dead as the Chink who was sharing my hole.

The incident took the fire out of me for a bit. Ears ringing and in a daze, I was stuck in the hole and didn't know how long I'd be there. I decided to get to know my Chinese companion a little better. I looked through his pockets and found a wallet full of Chinese money and some pictures of his family. The pictures stung me inside—this dead Chink had been a real person. I didn't want him in my hole anymore. I rolled his body up the side with my feet. I got him to the top and was about to tip him out when a Chinese machine gun hosed him down and blew off his head. This scared the hell out of me, and I dropped him. Now I was sharing my hole with a headless Chinaman whom I liked less with every passing second. It took a dozen tries before I finally rolled him out.

Dusk brought a lull to the fighting, but it brought nothing else—no food, no water, no resupply of ammo. The word was that the Korean *chogi** party, our human resupply train, had gotten lost. We were so thirsty, all we wanted was water. We'd been in constant hot contact for hours, using up a lot of adrenaline, generating a lot of fear—and fear dries you out. One of the guys found a knocked-out Chinese water-cooled heavy machine gun. We drained the stagnant, filthy water into a steel pot and filtered it through a piece of dirty cloth; it was still oily when we drank it, but to us it tasted beautiful, like a nice cold beer on a stinking hot day.

When you're fighting, you're scared. And it's such an all pervasive sort of fear that you can't even pinpoint what the feeling is. It's a gnawing, a churning in the gut. You become so afraid that it's as if you're not afraid at all. And that's what bravery is. It's not *fearlessness*; it's the ability to get off your ass and charge even when your mouth is dry, your gut is tight, and your brain is screaming *Stay down!* But even the bravest of men have a breaking point, and on Objective Logan, a couple of good men reached theirs. One was one of our best NCOs. He'd been a great fighter and a fearless leader. At the Pusan Perimeter in the bleak, early days of the war, he'd taken a newly issued 3.5 bazooka and destroyed three T-34 tanks single-handedly. So he was not a coward—nor, I discovered, were most men who lost their nerve on the battlefield.

Over time I concluded that a man is like a bottle. On the battlefield, fear is what fills him up and fuels him to perform. But some bottles are smaller than others. When a guy becomes unglued during a firefight, it's just that his bottle has filled up and overflowed; it's time for him to get away and let the fear drain out. But even when it does, there is a catch: from that moment on, the man is like a spent cartridge, and no amount of gunpowder will ever make him a real fighter again.

* *Chogi* was our nickname for the Korean laborers who worked for the Eighth Army. In Korean, *chogi* means "over there" (as in "put it over there").

*   *   *

As darkness fell, the Chinks started attacking again, with great enthusiasm. "Hold at all costs" was passed from Company. Ominous words—"all costs" meant die on position. We stacked up more rocks and got ready. I just hoped the Chink CO hadn't told his guys to *take* the hill at all costs. A major Chinese breakthrough occurred on the right; we could hear their bugles and see their flares in the valley to our rear. New orders: "Conduct a night withdrawal. First and Second platoons start pulling back now. Third Platoon hold. You fight the rear guard." To the few men left in our platoon, that sounded even worse than to hold at all costs. But the shake of the dice is never fair in combat, and in retrospect the order was sound. Third Platoon held the high ground and was marginally combat effective; we could delay, and if destroyed, our skipper would still end up with two strong rifle platoons (less 1st Platoon's weapons squad, which was tragically destroyed by an enemy mortar round just moments after it arrived on the hill).

The company's main body slowly pulled back, and by the time the order came for us to withdraw, we were engulfed in Chinamen. I was the last guy down from the few left in my squad; I walked backwards, slowly, down our well-reconned escape route, shooting Chinks as they crested the hill. When I reached the safety of the saddle, I shagged ass and caught up with the rear of my platoon. I arrived just in time to see a badly wounded Sergeant Connie Moore about to be tipped out of a makeshift poncho litter and over a gorge by the two new men who were packing him down the hill. I jabbed one of them in the ass with my bayonet. "We'll take him back, won't we, guys?" I asked, leveling my M-1. "Sure, Sergeant" was the kids' startled reply. I stuck with them in case they needed more cold-steel encouragement, but they didn't. I never mentioned the incident to either of them again and both turned out later to be great fighters. They'd just been scared, and ill prepared for their baptism of blood.

Last of all off the hill was Lieutenant Gilchrist, who made his way along the ridge with friendly artillery—his only security—crashing in just fifty yards away. His uniform was caked with blood, his own and that of a boy who'd taken a direct mortar hit and disintegrated to (in Gilchrist's words) "a purplish mush" before dying in the Lieutenant's arms. Now, as he reached the area of the ridge where the fight had begun so many hours before, he heard a voice. "Is that you, Lieutenant?"

It was the medic, Sergeant Brown, who'd lain on the ridge all day with a hole in his chest, for the sole purpose of checking the bandages of every casualty the YMCA first-aid-class rifleman had treated on the hill. The medic was new, he was a black man in a white unit, he was grievously wounded, yet he was there. He didn't have to be; common sense would have dictated *Get out while the going's good!* but he'd stayed. And if that didn't epitomize the spirit, the loyalty, and the guts of 3d Platoon and the rest of George as well on this terrible day, then nothing ever could.

We were all dead on our feet by the time we passed through the dug-in 1st and 2d platoons and set up. Soon First Sergeant Rager arrived with the lost carrying party. We gobbled down yesterday's breakfast (cold pancakes and even colder black coffee). It was delicious. Then the First Sergeant handed me a stack of mail for 3d Platoon. *Mail call in the pitch-black night,* I thought, and most of the guys already evacuated or dead. I tossed the packet down next to my rock-pile wall and was asleep before I'd stretched out on my stone bed. For once, the mail could wait.

When a unit got a bloody nose as we did in this fight, it was seldom broken up. Normally it was sent to the rear, where it received replacements and was refitted before going back to the front. Unfortunately, the 3d of George was not so lucky; there was too much going on and we regrouped on the hoof. With First Sergeant Rager rotating home, and the 3d's great platoon sergeant, Maurice Flemings, being bumped up to topkick, there was some shake-up, but Walt Schroeder, one of our squad leaders (who'd knocked out two enemy machine guns on Logan), slipped smoothly into the role of platoon sergeant, and I became his assistant.

The Wolfhound Regiment had been in constant combat for nine months now. The 3d Platoon, whose dead and wounded on Objective Logan alone numbered thirty-two out of thirty-seven, had probably turned over two dozen times since July. It was like musical chairs with stinging bullets playing the tune: a man would get hit, he'd be replaced; the replacement would get hit, and he'd be replaced. Sometimes you didn't even get to know a guy's name before he was gone. About half the wounded would rejoin the platoon within weeks; we got a lot of experienced men back this way, some who'd been wounded two or three times.

A large number of the replacements during this period were pros—recalled WW II vets who had seen a lot of combat. We welcomed them with open arms; by now many of us had seen our fair share of combat, too, but the guys from the big war were older and wiser, and there was plenty to be learned from them. Of course, as happy as we were to have them was about as unhappy as they were to be there. They felt they had gotten a raw deal. They'd fought their war. They just hadn't read the fine print that got them in the inactive reserve. One day they'd been university students, or hustling away at their postwar careers; the next day they'd found themselves on a slow boat to Korea, with no transition training, and little chance to get in physical shape for the big game. Their first few weeks in-country were pure hell. The vets were very bitter, they took shit from no one, and pity on the leader who didn't know what he was doing. But these angry men were still damn good soldiers; however they felt inside, they did their jobs. Their previous battle experience and leadership talents did wonders to improve the Army's combat efficiency during a grim period when it was a pretty battered and inept fighting force; now they provided much-needed guidance to us all and along with the hospital returnees helped keep our green guys alive.

It only took a couple of days for a new replacement to become a seasoned veteran. Before that, in fast-moving, heavy combat like we were in, he was a liability—cannon fodder—the first to get hit. We always tried to match up new kids with the best old-timers. The old guys looked after them for the first few days and taught them the tricks of the trade—even the little things, like the importance of a spoon, which to an infantryman is probably second only to that of a rifle, with the only things running close being a toothbrush and a dry change of socks. These—and lots of ammo—were the real essentials in a doughfoot's kit, a fact that was one of those things you just had to learn. The second pair of socks is the quintessence of a foot soldier's mobility; bad feet can't walk, and if you can't walk, you can't fight. You don't just clean your teeth with your toothbrush; sometimes you clean your rifle with it, too. You don't just eat with your spoon; you can use it to scratch out a hole, open a beer, and, in between, wear it like a badge of honor poking out of your pocket, or snugged neat in your canteen cover. Uses for that damn big wonderful spoon were just a few of the things the new kids were spoon-fed; all they had to do was be willing to listen and learn, and with a little luck they'd make it through. But then there were kids like O'Toole.

He joined us one evening just before dark, the chalk number used to control replacements debarking from the boat still printed on his helmet. "You'll stay with me tonight," I told him. "Keep a sharp eye to the front while I finish up our hole." He sat down in his new, very green fatigues—fat and sloppy, out of shape.

"What's this, Sergeant?" he asked.

I looked up. "Chink antitank grenade. Leave it alone. I'll tell you about them later."

Bam.

Luckily I was bent down in the hole, digging. O'Toole had just blown the shit out of himself. Good-bye, O'Toole; next replacement, please.

We kept attacking north. Resistance was light. With twenty replacements joining us during this time, we used every spare moment to train. We hammered away on the basics: clean weapons, shoot low, fire and maneuver, cover and concealment. The first U.S. troops to come to Korea from occupation duty in Japan had been soft and badly trained, and each generation of replacements seemed worse. Those of us who'd been there awhile quickly became training madmen, and we had full authority to train as we saw fit without interference, even from Company. When the situation allowed, we'd attack a hill even if the enemy was long gone, teaching simple battle drill: how to hit the ground, roll, and fire; how to flip a grenade into a Chinese position without its rolling back on you; how to close with the enemy and destroy him without taking excessive lumps. Defensive procedures were easier to teach because we went through them for real every night.

One evening, though, we ran into a bit of a snag. Third Platoon, on the left flank, was supposed to tie in with a unit from the 1st Cav Division, but the Cav guys were nowhere to be seen. It was almost dark when Captain Michaely told us to find them; the platoon dug in and fishhooked a rifle squad with a light machine gun on the open flank, while I took one guy and wandered down into the dark, silent valley to have a look for our lost Cav friends. We never found them, but we did find hundreds of Chinese, and got out of there in a hurry. I called Captain Michaely and told him what we'd seen.

By now it was pitch-dark. Hot chow was ready at the company CP; half our men stayed in their defensive positions and the other half went down to eat. It was standard procedure; they'd bring back food in their mess kits for the security force. About a half hour later Jerry Boyd, who was manning the machine gun at the fishhook, called me. "I got some movement over here," he whispered. Jerry was a black guy who'd gone AWOL from a trucking company and joined our all-white unit. He was one of only a dozen or so black troopers in the entire regiment; I had been his squad leader or assistant platoon sergeant for four months now, and loved him like a brother. He was a good man, and a good soldier.

I crawled to his position. "Look there," he said. "There's Chinks down there." I looked into the blackness and didn't see a thing. "There," he insisted, "right in front. . . . Look! They moved again!"

I carefully scanned the area, back and forth—nothing. "Are you sure, Jerry?"

"Yeah, man . . . look, there! They're moving again!"

"Okay," I decided, remembering the swarming Chinese I'd seen earlier in the valley, "I'll flip a couple of grenades and see what happens."

The beauty of grenades is that they don't give away your position; the enemy doesn't know what direction they're coming from. I tossed two. *Bam. Bam.* Then silence. I looked hard. Jerry whispered, "Look over by those trees. There's a squad—standing out in the open!" Sure enough, I could see them, too, and they were moving right toward us. We each threw two more frags. The sound-power telephone (which ran between the platoons and the company CP) rang. It was Captain Michaely.

"What's happening up there?"

"Enemy squad, sir. It's under control. But I think we should go to one hundred percent, and get our people back from chow soonest."

"Okay, Sergeant, keep me posted."

Captain Jack Michaely was one fine soldier. In World War II, after his Horse Cavalry unit had evolved to Mechanized (later Armored) Cav, he'd been an officer in the regiment that screened the front of Patton's army. It was dangerous work, but he'd made it through, and now, alive and well at twenty-eight, he was "The Rock" of George Company, the one who stood firm when the world was crashing in around our ears. In Korea, Michaely had been George Company's CO for seven months, longer than any company commander had been with any rifle unit in the 25th Division. He'd gotten us through a lot and we trusted him, then and always, to get us through a lot more.

Michaely was cool as ice. He exhibited little emotion; the worse things were on the battlefield, the calmer his voice sounded on the radio. Later he said that as cool as he was on the outside, inwardly he'd churn: "I learned in WW II," he said, "that the slightest bit of excitement in a leader is transmitted to the men. You might be afraid, but the fear gets magnified in the troops. Somebody has to keep his cool. If you're a decent leader, you don't dare lose it—for your *own* good. You've got to keep your unit up there doing its job."

Which he did, brilliantly, and this evening was no exception. Time passed. The guys returned from chow and I stayed with Jerry in his hole. Jerry got more and more edgy as we watched for the enemy through the darkness, and so did I. "There they are again! They're coming at us!" he suddenly cried, and started blasting away with his machine gun. I immediately started flipping grenades and firing my M-1; the foxholes around us joined right in. The phone rang: Michaely.

"Why are you people firing that machine gun?"

"There are a lot of Chinese now, sir. And they're moving toward us."

"How many?" he snapped.

"At least a platoon, sir."

"All right, Sergeant. But I'll tell you something. There'd better be a pile of dead Chinks out there in the morning. You don't fire a machine gun unless there's a strong attack."

"Yes, sir. I know."

A machine gun is the firepower of a rifle platoon; it was the first thing the enemy tried to knock out. Thus, to fire it except as a last resort was giving its position away on a silver platter. A supreme no-no. So after things quieted down I decided I'd better crawl out and have a look. The truth was, I was more afraid of the Captain than of the whole damn Chinese Army.

I couldn't find a trace of the enemy in the grove of trees where we'd seen them. No tracks, no blood, no smells. But the barks of the trees, which had been partially blown off by our grenades, were flapping in the breeze—white silhouettes, which, to tired, tired eyes, seemed to move. I was in big trouble.

I went back and chewed Jerry's ass. I told him that come first light his sorry ass was going to become a rifleman—the point man in bold Fred "Chris" Crispino's squad. Then I tried to sleep, but couldn't. I sat inside my fart sack, leaning my back against a little knoll, worrying about Captain Michaely's early-morning visit. Around 0400, I saw about twenty *real* Chinks creeping up the hill behind our fishhook, trying to outflank us. It was pure luck that I was awake and looking in that direction. I slowly unzipped my bag, an inch at a time so as not to make any noise. I pulled out my rifle and rolled a couple of frags down the hill. When the grenades exploded, I took the Chinks under fire. The CP group woke up and joined in about the same time the platoon to our right was hit as well (the Chinese game plan must have been to probe from both sides at once and try to determine our tactical disposition). We fought them off without too much trouble.

I fell asleep, and woke just before dawn to see Jerry Boyd dragging a dead Chinaman toward his gun. "What the hell are you doing, Jerry?"

"Wait and see, boss. Wait and see."

He kept dragging bodies until he'd stacked fifteen dead Chinks in front of his gun. It was a stroke of pure genius. At first light, by his word, Captain Michaely walked into our position.

"Morning, Captain."

"Had a probe, did you, Hackworth?"

"Yes, sir. Two. They also tried to come up behind us."

"Uh, huh," he replied as he walked to the machine-gun position, where fifteen dead Chinamen—and a smiling Jerry Boyd—were waiting. "Good job, son," said Captain Michaely, looking over the dead. He walked back to me. "It was work for rifles and grenades. Not the most important weapon in your platoon. Smarten your gunner up. Good morning, Sergeant."

In early April, still getting in shape after Logan, 3d Platoon was strung out in single file as the reserve element behind the rest of G (who were assaulting yet another objective). We were passing through Chinese fighting positions that the lead elements had already cleared when a Chink soldier, weaponless, leaped out of a bunker right in the center of the platoon and took off running like a scared rabbit. Every weapon fired, from ranges of fifty to two hundred yards, and no one hit him. Lucky Chinaman. Thirty bad riflemen (many new replacements). Soldiers were not trained to hit moving targets. Marksmanship in the U.S. Army was taught on a known-distance (KD) range—fixed target, big bull's-eye, plenty of time. It didn't make a lot of sense.

A little later, Fox Company's assault platoon on our right was stopped dead in its tracks by one lone Chinaman holed up in a pile of rocks. We could see him tossing grenades, firing, and ducking from rock to rock, single-handedly pinning down the entire platoon. I took up a prone position. Schroeder marked my shots with a pair of binoculars, and three shots later, I hit home; from five hundred yards, the brave defender didn't know what hit him. One Chink down, and a new nickname for me, which stuck among some friends for life: The Rifleman. As for myself, I just thanked Steve Prazenka, the greatest shot I knew.

Fighting was not always confined to the enemy—if nothing else did, MacArthur's 11 April snap relief from command showed that. All of us who'd admired the General as a god had lost some faith in the man by now (four months after Christmas and we were still here), but it was a hell of a shock—one of America's most legendary soldiers being fired by the President in the middle of a war he'd been the first to turn around. Still, he'd been outspoken and he'd gone too far—first to the Yalu (or so it seemed), then in publicly disagreeing with the Commander in Chief. It was insubordination to the highest degree, and we figured MacArthur should have known better. Our own Eighth Army commanding general (CG), Matt Ridgway, immediately replaced him (with Lieutenant General James Van Fleet taking over Eighth Army command); we were saddened to see Ridgway go, but proud (and greatly relieved) to know that the new Supreme Commander of all U.N. forces in Korea would still be around, with his finger on the pulse of the war. Happily, Van Fleet was cut from the same bolt of cloth as Ridgway. He'd led the assault regiment onto Utah Beach at Normandy, and was the first U.S. general to fight Communists in Greece in 1948. Like Ridgway, he was a good fighter and a soldier's soldier, so the Eighth Army remained in good hands.

Down at company level, mixing it up with fellow friendlies was far more common than fights between five stars and Presidents. Sergeant Reeves, the 2d Platoon sergeant, was a Texan who was in for the Distinguished Service Cross (DSC) for his part in the battle up on Logan. (Among his many derring-dos on that grim day, at one stage he'd been crawling forward on his belly, and as he parted the grass in front of him he'd run right into an enemy soldier who was doing the same thing; the platoon sergeant had grabbed the Chink's weapon and killed him with it, and then killed the Chinaman's comrades who were sneaking up behind their leader.) Reeves was a bold, aggressive, good soldier, but for some reason he rubbed me the wrong way. One evening, the company was in battalion reserve and a squad from 3d Platoon had drawn outpost duty. The chow line had formed and it was a rifle company long; I took the outpost detail to the front so they could eat first and be on their way. The next thing I knew, Reeves came along and put one of his squads in front of my people. "Look, Sergeant," I said, "my men are going on outpost duty. That's why they're first."

"So are mine" was his reply. "That's why *they're* first. And nobody is going to get in front of them."

I said, "Oh, yeah? Well, your people are not eating before mine."

Words led to fists, and was I ever outgunned. With most of G Company looking on—175 soldiers with ringside seats—Reeves cleaned my clock. I don't think I even got a hit in. I hadn't been whipped so badly since Sergeant Oscar Reyes beat me in the TRUST lightweight championship, and Reyes went on to be European lightweight champ and a world contender in his class. It turned out that Reeves was no slouch either. He was a former division heavyweight champion himself, and he tore my ass simply because I'd failed to follow an age-old military axiom: Know your enemy. Needless to say, his guys ate first.

A few days later the battalion moved behind the 24th Regiment with the mission of passing through and seizing a bleak, craggy hill designated Objective Jake Able. The only approach to the thing was almost vertical, with little concealment and cover; it was a formidable piece of real estate, so steep that even a pastoral walk up the thing looked enough to kill an ordinary man (let alone the fact that there were people up there already, whose sole mission was to shoot us long before we reached the top). All in all, to me it looked like a suicide trip—we'd be easy pickings from the second we crossed the LD—and even though George Company was the reserve unit for the operation, there was little doubt we'd be committed. I was so worried about it that the night before the attack I couldn't sleep.

It was very rare for me not to be able to sleep on the battlefield—normally I could sleep through anything. One night not long before this fight, my platoon got clobbered with dozens of rounds of incoming. The guys, deep in their holes, thought I'd gone to ground, too, but when first light came, they found me stretched out like a log behind my foxhole, covered with dirt and rocks thrown up from the incoming shells. The ground around me looked like the face of the moon—shell craters everywhere. "Christ, guys, what happened?" I'd yawned.

Not so the night before Jake Able. I tossed and turned, and again and again in my mind's eye saw 3d Platoon painting the slopes of Jake Able red with its own blood. Finally I gave up and went to the company CP to see the topkick. In terms of my education, First Sergeant Maurice Flemings was to me and footslogging infantry what Prazenka had been to me and recon—a real mentor. Flemings had fought from Sicily to Germany in WW II, and when the Korean War broke out he'd been one of a number of battle-hardened senior NCOs who were cleaned out of Fort Benning's Infantry School and sent over to provide some muscle to an otherwise pretty sorry-assed Eighth Army. All in all, he was just a fine old pro to whom I often turned for battleground advice.

Flemings was wide-awake, too, worrying the operation. I told him what I'd been thinking and how anxious I was; we walked to a point where we could observe the ominous hill and he chalk-talked me through the attack. Then I went back to the platoon assembly area, feeling better but not much. I was still afraid for my unit, and had the clearest premonition that Jake Able was going to be my last attack. I even wrote a letter to my brother, Roy, one of those "I-don't-think-I'm-going-to-make-it-back" numbers that I gave Carroll, the platoon radio telephone operator (RTO), who was awake on security. He said, "I'll give it back when we get to the top, Sarge." I talked to him about the attack, even though confessing my concerns violated all my leadership training as far back as TRUST (*Leaders do not cry to their men. They are resolute islands in the center of all the insanity*). But Carroll was older than I; he was a smart college-graduate draftee replacement, and I felt calmer having talked it through.

As it turned out, for G Company Jake Able ended up being more like a training exercise. Easy and Fox bore the brunt of the Chinese defense of their hill, both companies losing almost all their officers (wounded and dead) and many men. (Their wounded streamed past us to the rear in an endless, bloody line. It was a scene of unimaginable impact for us as we moved forward into the same fray that was gutting their ranks.) The Chinese, reinforced in preparation (we later found out) for a major offensive, had cut down trees and bushes to deny any semblance of a covered and concealed avenue of approach; Easy and Fox fought coura-geously for every inch. Over in E Company, one platoon was pinned down early in the piece by a Chink firing an automatic weapon from a fighting bunker. Every time the guys fired on him, the Chinaman would bob down, then pop up again and fire on Easy's men. The company commander, a reputedly fine shot named Dell Evans, got into the act, and after three tries the enemy position was silenced. When Evans later went out to check the bunker, he found a pile of three Chinks behind a Bren gun, each with a single hole in his forehead.

By the time George was committed on Jake Able's west flank, our sister companies, in concert with the 21st AAA Battalion (which called itself the Wolfhounds' Fangs) and our direct-support artillery unit, the 8th Field (the Wolfhounds' Bark), had broken the enemy's back. The ridgetop was an erupting volcano of U.S. artillery and quad .50-caliber fire, as well as tac air's napalm, white phosphorous (Willie Peter), and delay bombs. Round after round of Willie Peter pounded in only fifty yards in front of George's advance—tactics right out of World War I that denied the enemy visibility and allowed us to close in. We could almost have caught the shells as they exploded before us in red-hot white plumes. But then I heard one falling short. I heard the shrill whistle, and I knew my name was on that round.

I was with the point—two guys just a few yards ahead, then me, then the rest of the platoon well spread out on the ridgeline. The round exploded in an airburst. The force of it knocked the three of us down. I rolled and looked up to see burning white phosphorous streaming down—kind of majestic, deathly snow fingers. I thought. *You were right, Hackworth. You're dead. And the thing that killed you isn't even Chinese, but made in the U.S.A.* I started to roll, and then, for an instant, I was back at home, at Ocean Park Pier. Al Hewitt had gotten us jobs at the amusement park, working on the Whip, and one morning, before anyone was there, we'd decided to see how fast the thing could go. Al manned the controls and I sat in one of the cars; when he got it to full speed and beyond, he released my car. But his timing was off—the car slammed into the iron trestle and I was flung onto one of the ramps. When I looked up, a ton of steel (in the form of the car I'd been sitting in just moments before) was screaming down on top of me. I rolled and kept rolling out of harm's way. The Whip car, and now the Willie Peter, didn't touch me. I was alive and unscathed. Both point guys had multiple burns, but they were more scared than hurt. I emptied my canteen in a patch of dirt, made some mud (just like the good book said), and heaped it onto their wounds. Both returned in a couple of weeks.

The men of George were almost at the top of Jake Able before we ran into any serious enemy. And even there, the Chinese were so shaken up from the "record-breaking" artillery and mortar fire (as the 27th's S-3 journal for April described it), the tac air, and E's and F's assaults that they fought badly, and finally didn't fight at all. But they'd certainly made a dent, particularly when they got Spotlight Sims. This fine lieutenant's luck ran out on Jake Able, which was a damn shame; maybe he didn't know that in combat you only get so many passes before you crap out.

Derwood "Spotlight" Sims was F Company's commander. He was a brilliant leader; his troops loved him because he approached the battlefield like a matador, parading around during firefights with a walking stick and acting as if he were invulnerable to bullets and all the other shit that came in. The story on Jake Able was that as F Company made its way up the hill, the lead platoon got pinned down by a Chink machine gun and its platoon leader was killed. Hearing this, Sims went to the point. His men shouted, "Stay down, Lieutenant! There's a machine gun here!" But Spotlight said, "Screw the machine gun," walked right into the thick of things, and got himself shot in half—not-so-living proof of the old adage: "There are old warriors and there are bold warriors, but there are no old, bold warriors."*

We secured Jake Able, consolidated our positions, and were preparing to dig in when I got into another pissing contest with Sergeant Reeves. We could not agree on our Company-assigned platoon boundary; I held it was one place, and he reckoned I was wrong. "Look, Sarge, we tie in here."

"No, Sergeant, you're wrong. It's here." He was vying for a shorter line, and so was I; a shorter line meant less area to defend. I thought, *Christ, here we go again. It's going to be another fight on top of this damn hill, and this cocky bastard is going to clean my clock all over again.* Just as we were getting hot and heavy about it, out of the corner of my eye I saw movement in the Chinese bunker we were arguing in front of. There was a Chinaman in there, big as life, holding a weapon. I shoved Reeves aside and flipped a grenade into the position, killing the Chink and sending a small shard of shrapnel from the grenade flying into Reeves's hand. For a long moment we just looked at each other—he was stunned—and then we both doubled up with laughter. I told him I was sorry he got hit, but couldn't resist commenting on what a lousy job his guys had done clearing their positions. For once, he didn't fight back. We quickly agreed on the boundary, but I don't remember who got the shorter line.

Then Carroll came up and handed me the letter I'd given him the night before. Jake Able was secure, and I was still here. He smiled and walked away without a word.

Carroll was with me a few nights later when I picked out an abandoned Chink fighting position for the platoon CP. I told him to get commo with Company HQ, and for the rest of the CP group to make the place livable

* Given the fog of battle, there ended up being a number of stories about how Sims died. Most likely, in fact, it was a grenade, but legends live on beyond death, and if the Spotlight had to go out, it had to be with a flair.

while Schroeder and I got the squads set up. (In the middle of the fight for Jake Able, Lieutenant Gilchrist had been sent over to take command of Easy, whose CO had been evacuated. Walt Schroeder replaced him as our 3d Platoon leader, and I became platoon sergeant. It's called "fall out, one.") After our defense was squared away I headed back to the bunker, and not a moment too soon. With the darkness had come Chink 82-mm mortar fire, which pounded throughout the company sector. A round exploded too close for comfort just as I found the CP. "Shit, will you listen to that incoming!" I said as I ran inside. The guys were sitting there in the dim light, but no one answered me. *Here we go,* I thought, *another big funny game.* I sat down. "Look, cut the crap, you guys." No reply. "Carroll, did you get commo with Company?" Still nothing. "Talk to me, you bastards." Still not a word.

A combat soldier's sense of humor can be pretty bizarre. My favorite trick was to sit by the fire, wearing my scrounged tanker jacket all zipped up. I'd be there bullshitting with my buddies, and at the perfect moment I'd unzip the jacket really fast. The movement of the zipper—up or down—sounds exactly like an incoming artillery round in the final seconds of its trajectory. *Zzzppt!* and everyone would hit the ground while I'd have a big laugh. Now I figured my CP group was just paying me back for the times I'd scared the living daylights out of them.

"You know, you guys are something else." I took out my Zippo lighter and flicked it on, right under the nearest guy's nose, and almost jumped out of my boots. I was staring eyeball-to-eyeball into the face of a Chinaman. I looked at the others—two more Chinks sitting and staring at me, looking perfectly healthy but all three stone-cold dead. I was definitely in the wrong hotel. I forgot about the incoming and shagged ass out of there in a big hurry. The next morning we concluded that napalm must have sealed the aperture of this bunker and burned up all the oxygen inside—including what was in these guys' lungs—while they'd just sat there, feeling safe.

After Jake Able came Jake Baker, Jake Charlie, and Jake Dog, each just another objective, another "critical" hill to take "at all costs." The Eighth Army offensive, which had been roaring along since 25 January, was running out of gas. I'm not sure the generals knew this, but we at the cutting edge damn well did. The Chinese were getting stronger. We were facing good-looking, well-equipped Chinese troops who had plenty of ammo and lots of fighting spirit. The feeling among the 3d Platoon's old-timers was that we'd be hard-pressed to continue the attack much farther north. The situation was beginning to feel eerily like November 1950 all over again.

We hauled ass across the billiard-table-flat terrain of the Chorwan Valley to reach our new positions along a railroad line. Enemy ground resistance was light, but Chinese artillery, mortar, and self-propelled (SP) fire was fierce. With little cover and no concealment, most of us were actually wishing we were back on the steep, much-bitched-about hills. At least there we could disappear in a fold in the ground or behind a tree.

We reached our objective by midday, and with barely a word of guidance, the boys in the platoon began digging like moles. Fortunately the railroad embankment ran as straight as an arrow in an east-west line, and the high mound gave us the most perfect defensive position I had ever seen. There was no letup in the incoming. It rained down on the line, but soon our holes were deep and we took no casualties. A platoon of 89th Battalion tanks lumbered up behind us, but they drew so much fire that Schroeder had me send them away; they'd creep back after dark and set up in hull defilade on the south side of the railroad track.

Captain Michaely trooped the line. He said the complete Eighth Army front was under heavy attack and that several major units on our flanks were in trouble. He said that Battalion expected us to get hit that night as well, and that our positions were not strong enough. He wanted deeper holes, overhead cover, more ammo on position. A little later a small observation helicopter buzzed the front. Shortly thereafter word came that the eye in the sky had been "Lightning 6," the CG of the 25th Division, and apparently he was not happy with our positions either. So we kept on digging, uprooted railroad ties to provide overhead cover for our crew-served weapons, and steeled ourselves for what portended to be one hell of a night.

By dusk we were set. We had flares and booby traps in front of us and plenty of ammo and grenades on position. Our recon patrols went out at dark (just as the 89th Battalion's tanks slipped into place as planned), but moved only a few hundred yards when they ran into a serious bunch of Chinamen, and came zooming home.

At 0230 hours, 23 April, our positions were blistered by savage mortar and artillery fire. In the darkness we could hear the unnerving, unmistakable sound of enemy tanks moving toward us, and the whistle-bang of our own tanks' 76-mm main-gun fire. Next came bugles and flares, and then waves of Chinese infantry, who struck simultaneously across the battalion front. For two and a half hours, the Wolfhounds' 2d Batt held like a stone wall in our well-prepared positions, against an estimated enemy regiment.

Then, suddenly, like a curtain coming down in a theater, exactly at 0500 hours the battlefield became quiet. In the early light of dawn we could see the ground to our front littered with enemy dead and knocked-out tanks. Regiment later estimated that the battalion had inflicted more than seven hundred casualties on our Chinese attackers that night; in George Company we counted forty-two enemy dead within hand-grenade distance of our holes alone. George's losses were amazingly light for the total—just two KIA and four WIA.

It was one of the few times in my battle experience that everything went according to plan. We could not have asked for a more ideal battle position to make our stand, or for better support. The brass had figured the enemy's move to a T; all the ass chewings about digging deep and getting tough had been well founded, and thanks to the vigilance of our leaders, not only had we chopped up a force three times our size, but we stood ready to do it again. But word soon came down from Captain Michaely that there would be no second show on this bloody ground. The units on our flanks had collapsed, and we had to get moving south quick or be cut off. At 1030 hours we carefully leapfrogged down the valley. Just as we were thinking we were home free, a U.S. Air Force B-26 bomber came swooping over us, all twelve forward-firing .50-caliber machine guns blazing. The pilot did a couple of enthusiastic strafing runs down the valley before someone gave him the word he was firing on his own people; we unscrewed ourselves from the ground and flipped him the bird in unison while he flew off into the early-morning light.

We continued fighting a delaying action south through the Chorwan Valley until we received the welcome word that we were going into reserve. Instantly high spirits charged bone-tired feet. The only news that could have been better would be word that the war was over. All of us looked forward to a few days off, to sleep, take hot showers, sing, and drink booze. In reserve we'd pay a hundred dollars for a bottle of shit whiskey, ten bucks for a can of beer, and whatever the going price was for that great 190-proof alcohol (the docs got it through their black-market medical outlets), which, even mixed with pineapple juice, was so powerful that it made the insides of our canteen cups look like they'd been chromed. Then we'd sit around our fires and get drunk, and then we'd talk about the war.

Reserve gave us a chance not just to unwind, but also to examine a fight. It would be like putting a jigsaw puzzle together, with each guy fitting in his piece: "I was here and there was a Chink machine gun there," one man might say, and then another voice would add, "Yeah, and I saw Mitchell blow it away with a grenade just as he got drilled." Finally we'd get the general story, and by dividing it in half—to account for all the fantasy and exaggeration—we'd pretty well have a factual account. The problem was that in the middle of a firefight you only see what's going on in front of you, and maybe what's happening directly to your right and left. You can't get the big picture, so you never really know what happened. But you want to—you *need* to—to account for friends dead and wounded, to find out what you did wrong so it doesn't happen again, and to give credit where credit is due, because in reserve, we'd also talk about the Gilchrists, the Deboers, and the Agudas.

Reserve was where the heroes were recognized and legends were born and nurtured. It was also the time when award recommendations would be submitted. Normally, Company would call and ask for recommendations. We'd scratch them out in a crude fashion on C-ration boxes, cardboard from ammo cartons, or whatever writing material we could scrounge. "Hey, brother, how do you spell 'machine gun'?" we'd ask one another—there were few Hemingways at platoon level. We were just a bunch of dumbshits trying to articulate a comrade's courage, as in the case of Aguda.

All the old 3d Platoon guys wanted him to get the Blue Max—the Medal of Honor. This was most unusual, given that he was in another platoon, but we wrote it up as best we could: "We recommend PFC James Aguda for the Medal of Honor. James Aguda was a brave soldier. He shot a lot of gooks and saved our ass up on Logan. Aguda was a good man. He deserves the big one." This recommendation went back to the rear, to a very literate captain (sitting in a nice warm tent at Regimental Awards and Decorations) who determined who got what by reading our statements. With Aguda's he probably said, "So what? 'He shot a lot of gooks'—*well, that's what we're here for!* He was a 'brave soldier'—*well, we're all brave soldiers!*" So James Aguda got the Silver Star posthumously, and not the Medal of Honor he deserved. A Silver Star is a damned high decoration, but it's not the Blue Max, it's not even a Distinguished Service Cross. Aguda's bravery, which to our minds saved our platoon, perhaps our whole company, went unrecognized only because we didn't know how to say it.

Infantrymen were fighters, not writers. In one way, we prided ourselves on it; we didn't have time for such "pussy" stuff. But the fact was that infantrymen in Korea came, as a rule, from the bottom rung of the social and economic ladder. The squads were mainly made up of poor whites, blacks, and yellows—a dispensable rainbow—uneducated, with nothing to keep us a step ahead of the point of a bayonet. And if a doughfoot got killed, his parents generally didn't have the education to write and ask why. They'd silently, stoically wear their loss like a sad badge of honor. In Korea, a heroic, dead comrade-in-arms; at home, a gold star in a cracked window in a little house on the wrong side of the tracks.

Reserve was not as long as we'd expected; in fact, it was only a few hours. At 0245 the following morning we were roused with the news that elements of the "Deuce-Four," one of our sister regiments, had been overrun by Chinese. It was a real emergency, and the Wolfhounds' 1st and 2d battalions were tasked with restoring the 24th's positions.

H (How) Company jeeps shuttled us toward the scene, the infantrymen literally stuffed into the heavy-weapons unit's vehicles, a squad to each jeep, more squads standing upright in the attached trailers, or hanging on all sides around How's own equipment. Finally we reached the base of a mountain ridge; the 3d of George was in the lead as we started climbing a hill far steeper than Logan—it was steeper than any hill I'd encountered in Korea, and covered with boulders. The winter had passed now; frostbite casualties had given way to those of heat exhaustion, and our out-of-shape replacements were now falling out in droves. I spent as much time pushing, dragging, and cajoling the new guys up the hill as I did cursing the Deuce-Four for bugging out for the eighteen millionth time.

At this stage of the war, the 25th Div was extremely handicapped in that it had only two effective regiments—the 27th Wolfhounds and the 35th Cacti. The division's third regiment, the 24th, was an all-black outfit, and as a fighting force it was sorrier than any unit I'd ever seen. It had not always been that way; in fact, the Deuce-Four had been responsible for the first significant American ground victory of the war, at Yechon, in July of 1950. But the regiment had been badly bloodied since then, and with the attendant loss of many of its fine black NCOs (too many of whom were replaced by white NCOs who were unable or unwilling to bond with the troops—and vice versa), it seemed the 24th had gone to hell in a hand-basket. Individually, many of its members were great—the Deuce-Four certainly had its share of Medals of Honor, DSCs, and Silver Stars—but as a fighting organization, its leadership was too thin and its combat scars too many. ("You don't know what low morale is until you get into an organization like the Deuce-Four," said Lieutenant John Arvidson, a white platoon leader recently in the unit. "Everybody thought he was going to die. Nobody thought he'd get out alive. And that type of feeling is contagious.") So to its sister regiments the Deuce-Four was simply an undependable liability, and whatever the rivalry between the 27th and the 35th,* both joined forces in often bitter resentment over the 24th's battlefield conduct. "When the Chinese yell 'banzai,' the Deuce-Four says 'good-bye' and heads south" was how we described our mutual sister unit, as month after month we carried its load. This situation led to much bad blood between units, though as it happened many 24th guys agreed with the white regiments' assessment. After this mission, one of our people, passing back through a Deuce-Four outpost, heard a black soldier throwing shit on the Wolfhounds

* "What makes a cactus grow?" a guy from the 27th would shout; "Wolfhounds' piss!" the rest of us would scream in unison, in a standard routine. "Try wiping your ass on a cactus," the 35th guys would respond, "and you'll really hear a Wolfhound yell!"

only to hear another 24th man say, "Man, don't you bad-mouth the Wolf-hounds—they done reassed *too many* hills this Deuce-Four unassed."

One by one, our herd of disenchanted mountain goats finally reached the top of the hill. The seven of us who got there first had a chance to rest; the enemy was nowhere in sight. Soon we saw another unit, Fox Company, coming down toward us from an adjacent, slightly higher hill. We lazily watched them come, and it wasn't until they were about three hundred yards away that we realized it wasn't Fox Company at all, but three or four hundred Chinamen, many wearing abandoned Deuce-Four steel pots, who, with bloodcurdling screams, started steamrolling down the hill in a mass, like an avalanche. We were in shock, and with only two BARs and five rifles to take them on, we were also in very serious trouble.

I heard Lieutenant Bell, George Company's artillery forward observer (FO), before I saw him. How he'd gotten to the top of our hill with that bulky arty radio I'll never know, but he was there, calmly calling for fire. "Fire mission . . . battery one round . . . rifle company in the open. Fire for effect."

The whole salvo fell short. It hit behind us, and sounded as though it landed right on the finger the rest of the company was climbing. It wouldn't make the trek any easier. Bell, standing there without a helmet, his long hair blowing in the breeze, didn't blink; instead, he made one of the boldest adjustments I'd seen in a long while. "Add four hundred, left two hundred, battalion six rounds," I heard him say through his huge handlebar mustache. "Fire for effect."

One hundred and eight rounds of 105-mm high-explosive (HE) shells flew through the air. They landed right smack in the center of the wave of Chinese attackers; their ranks simply disappeared from earth as bits and pieces of arms, legs, heads, and bodies flew skyward. *Iron on target*, I thought. *Thank God for Lieutenant Bell and the 8th Field.*

Allan Bell was the best FO I ever saw, and fifteen years would pass before the next great one came along. He wasn't even a field artilleryman; by training he was an antiaircraft officer who'd been caught up in the merger of AA and field artillery just before the Korean War. Bell was as cool as they come. Once the executive officer of his battalion actually told the lieutenant he worried him because while the other FOs called in all excited when they had six enemy out in the open, Bell could call in a steamroller enemy attack and sound as though he was bored. As it happened, Bell was a self-confessed disciple of Captain Michaely (which accounted for his cool); they comple-mented each other in a way absolutely essential in a commander/FO relationship. He was also a thinker (which is enough to send a lot of guys around the bend on the battlefield; thinking too much can be a liability, particularly if you've got a vivid imagination), and he used it to his advantage when, upon volunteering to go on line as an FO, he was told his life expectancy would be only twenty-one days. Why is it twenty-one days? he'd asked himself, assuming that if he could figure it out, he could beat the odds. His conclusions were simple battlefield common sense that apparently too many FOs never lived long enough to learn. The first was "he who hesitates pretty quickly gets blasted away." The other was that the minute you get to a lay-up point you have to look around for an extra bit of good cover in case things don't go according to plan, because, in Bell's words, "Once the unexpected occurs it's too late to start looking around to see where you're going to go." For almost nine months on line, George's FO used his latter guideline every day of the week; his former axiom had been particularly effective up on Objective Logan, when Bell's request for a fire mission was denied after the battalion liaison officer pointed out that the coordinates Bell called in were only three hundred yards from our forward elements, and a division regulation stated that you couldn't fire within six hundred yards of friendly troops. "I know how far it is from our forward elements," Bell had rejoined, "because I *am* our forward elements. There's no point in firing six hundred yards out because the enemy's not out there, they're here. Now if you'd like to come down here and be the FO, go ahead. If not, I'd appreciate it if you would just relay my fire mission," which the now-sheepish battalion liaison captain did.

So Bell had saved our asses again—momentarily, at least—with the help of the 8th Field, a unit so good that Chinese POWs often swore we'd been firing automatic artillery. Now on the hill, the last stragglers stumbled in (with word that no one had been hit by the opening short rounds) and took up positions around us.

George Company dug in and hunkered down for a battle that raged all afternoon. With the help of Fox Company, we stopped a three-battalion Chinese counterattack force dead in its tracks, but it was hard, hard fighting all the way. Then, just before dark, somebody somewhere must have decided the best course of action would be to blast holy shit out of the enemy force with every bit of firepower we had. And for the only time in my life, I thought my bottle was going to overflow.

P-51s and Navy Corsairs strafed and bombed from the air; artillery, half-tracks, and tanks boomed from the valley floor, and it felt as if all this friendly fire was going directly over 3d Platoon. We were being showered with spent shards of U.S. shellfire and hot brass from the fighter-aircraft machine guns. Rounds were bursting so close that every one of them seemed to have our names on it. We couldn't dig in on our solid crag, so we squeezed into cracks and crevices, and I wanted to stand up and scream *"For God's sake, shut it off!"* The noise was incredible—whining, whistling, zinging sounds as plummeting bits of steel ricocheted against the boulders all around us. The longer it went on without my being hit the worse it became; every near-miss brought the odds down, and I was more sure than I'd ever been that soon some tank gunner would screw up and I'd be one dead hombre, with a 76-mm round right through my ass. *Well, get it over with, goddamnit!*

The inferno blazed forever, or so it seemed, until blessed darkness came and all was quiet. Well, not all. Although the U.S. war machine had dampened it, it had not put out the enemy's fire, but our M-1s and automatic weapons sounded like popguns after the thundering hell of the last couple of hours.

The fight continued, and in the dark we could see and hear Easy and Fox engaged as well. The Chinese kept coming, and so did the word from Company: "Hold at all costs . . . hold at all costs." But the problem was that the word was not coming from Captain Michaely (who'd gone on R&R that very morning), but from a new CO whom I'll call Lieutenant Peterson. The fact was that all of us had been shaking since the first short rounds were delivered more than twelve hours before. Add to that the fire storm we'd just survived, and Peterson's inability to hide his anxiety had us scared stiff. We were stuck on this boulder of a hill while the enemy pushed south, and by the time we got permission to withdraw "as best you can," it was midnight and we were cut off well within enemy territory.

We had some trouble getting out—not just enemy pressure, but a couple of the replacements. One kid, who'd complained the whole way *up* the hill, and whom I'd convinced to come along by firing a shot right behind his heels (a little trick I learned watching Western movies), now decided he couldn't go one step farther down. "Do you know there's Chinese back there?" I asked him. "That when we leave they're going to come here and eat you up?"

"I can't move, Sergeant."

"Well, that's fine," I said. "You just sit there and relax." With that, I left him and a few minutes later he got off his ass and followed me down. It was nice to know you didn't even have to finish high school to understand reverse psychology.

When the word came to withdraw we'd been told to pull out one platoon at a time, with 3d Platoon last off the hill. I'd tasked Sposito, a reliable corporal in our platoon, to follow 4th Platoon down and then come back to guide us out. This he'd done, but now, as the 3d reached a particular junction on the ridge, Sposito had forgotten whether the 4th had gone right or left. It was pitch-black; we couldn't see a trail nor could we feel a track on the sheer rock path. With fifty-fifty odds we took a guess—it was the wrong one—and ended up on the valley floor with jabbering Chinks to our east and southwest. Not a little unnerving, and only made worse by the bugles the enemy blew incessantly (as part of their communications system, which had the fringe benefit of driving the U.S. troops nuts) and their eerie flares, which were popping to our front, flanks, and rear. Schroeder and I got the men into a perimeter around a dry creekbed; then squad leader Chris Crispino and I went out looking for some English-speaking comrades. When we finally found H Company's 81-mm mortar platoon merrily firing away, we crept back to the creekbed to lead our guys out.

I could not believe my eyes when we arrived at the perimeter. With Crispino out with me, and Schroeder holed up on the other side of the position, a few of Chris's new replacement troopers were openly smoking cigarettes, as if they were at a downtown bus stop, not in the middle of enemy territory. Crispino and I exploded; that madness on the hill was nothing compared to what the smokers experienced with our flying feet and fists as we hissed under our breath the rules about smoking on the line. The cigarettes went out in a big hurry; luckily neither they nor the asskicking compromised our location, and we slipped on silently to the H Company positions, and then on to rejoin George. The next day, as the regiment continued south with the entire Eighth Army front (exchanging ground with the Chinese attackers for huge mounds of their dead), Chris continued punishing the smokers in his squad with as much dirty work as he could find, and he could be pretty imaginative. Crispino's military career had started in Italy at the age of six, when he became, and remained until he and his parents wised up and fled to the U.S., a member of Mussolini's Black Shirts. Meanwhile, the kids tried to defend themselves by complaining that in basic training no one had told them they couldn't smoke in the field. *Shit*, I thought to myself, *what else didn't they learn?*

Any hope of reserve was lost when orders came down that we were to set up in a delaying position on the east side of the Chorwan Valley, and execute delaying actions across yet another mountain range. The Chinese were attacking on a broad front; it was November all over again, only this time it was called the Chinese Spring Offensive, and we were confronting even more Chinamen than we had last time. "Spring is here, wish we weren't," cracked the jokers. And if there was any comfort in knowing that at least we were not fighting in sub-zero temperatures this time around, the feeling was more than offset by the fact that the warming weather held torments of its own. As the ground thawed out and the spring rains came, the battlefield became a sea of thick, oozing mud. It built up on the bottom of our boots and made them as heavy as lead. Movement was not just putting one boot in front of the next; it was slipping and sliding and damn hard work. The mud fouled our weapons and equipment. It stuck to our shovels, making the daily foxhole-digging ritual a nightmare. Then the rains filled the foxholes, and the futility of it all flooded our hearts. The roads became quagmires. The rivers and the creeks were swollen and hard to ford. The two things that we had going for us over the Chinese were mobility and firepower, but they were advantages greatly reduced in the conditions we now faced. Even so, there was no panic, as there had been in those hard winter days. Ridgway had left his mark on the Eighth Army, and mud and rain, big numbers and all, we were set for Joe Chink.

We arrived on position at midday. G Company was deployed with two rifle platoons in the valley and my platoon, the 3d, on a little piece of high ground to their left. The battlefield was quiet, less the occasional rumble of a firefight to our front. But as darkness came, the outpost line (consisting of the 5th Ranger Company, the 25th Recon Company, and B Company, 89th Tank) started passing through us with word that the Chinks—"millions of them"—were right on their ass. This rear-guard force had been in heavy contact all day, and they'd had a hard time breaking contact. "They'll be here soon," they warned of the Chinese. "Good luck."

Schroeder and I made it a policy that almost to a man each rifleman in the platoon carried two extra (250-round) boxes of .30-caliber machine-gun ammo in addition to his basic load. When the men sat down, the ammo sat down; when they walked, the ammo walked. We all hated the extra weight, but it meant the ammo was always there when we needed it for our LMGs, and when things got really bad, we could break it out for our M-1s and BARs. Now, in light of the latest word from the outpost line, we had a good look at our ammunition level and then sent our scroungers out for more. And as the rear-guard force rolled through, they tossed us stacks of hand flares, grenades, and even more machine-gun ammo, so by 1700 hours the platoon was loaded for bear and well dug in, with good fields of fire for our two light machine guns and our one captured Chinese Bren gun.

Schroeder sent a two-man outpost out with instructions not to get engaged, but bug back when they heard the enemy coming. There was a big gap between 3d Platoon and Fox Company to the west, but a platoon from the 5th Ranger Company was now on the move. They would fill in the gap, making the main battle line complete.

We picked out three great positions for the section of tanks we were getting. They'd be able to put flanking fire right down Company G's front, and cover in front of G Company, 35th Regiment, whom George was tied into on the right (two Georges in a row—not the best configuration in the world). The tanks would also be able to cover the north-south road that ran smack into George's position and was a good high-speed enemy-tank approach, plus they'd be able to pummel the hell out of anyone coming directly at 3d Platoon. We were going to be tougher than the Siegfried Line.

I heard tank motors and decided to guide them into position myself. "Follow me. You're spending the night with the 3d Platoon of George."

"Okay, Lieutenant. Let's get cracking," shouted the tank commander, competing with the roar of his Sherman.

The voice was as familiar as an old coat, and since he'd just promoted me to lieutenant, I decided to hop up and have an eyeball talk with the owner. I should well have recognized the voice: Master Sergeant Francis, Company C, 89th Tank Battalion, had been my platoon sergeant in the recon unit in Italy. He didn't immediately recognize me in the fading light, but he looked the same: tall, craggy, and handsome in a Gary Cooper kind of way. We had a good laugh when he realized he was working for his former gunner-private. "It's because I trained you so good, Dave," he said in his soft Kentucky drawl.

Hard as we tried, we could not get the tanks up the muddy hill leading to 3d Platoon's positions. After an hour, Francis decided to pull back and laager for the night behind us. Mud had led to Napoleon's defeat at Waterloo; now, 136 years later, it had just played a significant role on a small piece of Van Fleet's tumultuous western front, and specifically in the fate of George Company. But as I watched the M4s with their mighty 76-mm guns disappear down the road, I was not to know that yet.

Schroeder told Lieutenant Peterson about the tanks. The CO assigned the company's 57-mm recoilless rifle section to replace the armor, and reported that the Ranger platoon would be in position within the hour. With that, I went back to the platoon CP to enjoy the sheer luxury of my new air mattress. I'd just gotten it that morning. Maybe it was Van Fleet's or someone else's way of saying "I'm sorry" for cheating us out of reserve. All in all our supply tail was indeed wagging—a lot of creature-comfort goodies were coming our way these days. In general I liked to think it was a grateful thanks from the stateside war machine, which was running along again at full bore (even if no one seemed to know that by the time a trooper dug a hole big enough to fit his 5'7" x 2' air mattress and then inflated the thing by mouth he'd probably be too bushed to fight the enemy).

At 2015 hours, just as I was beginning to think the rear-guard force had either overreacted or had been pulling our legs about all the Chinese, several green flares popped about five hundred yards in front of our positions. The outpost was back in a flash, with reports of countless enemy out there.

It remained deathly quiet. Peterson was informed of the situation, and we requested max harassment and interdictory (H&I) defensive artillery fire and flares. *Bam, bam, bam*—the 8th Field Artillery barked obligingly, and simultaneously our front lit up and shook with the impact of outgoing rounds. Then, under the cold, eerie light of slowly descending parachute flares and the WW II antiaircraft searchlights we'd asked for (the beams of which, bouncing off the clouds, lit up the battlefield), we saw the enemy. They were marching in column. Neat formations as far as the eye could see, each at least a company in strength, marching down the north-south road, one after another. They were not firing. They weren't even in battle formation. It was more like a pass in review. Schroeder called in an artillery fire mission with his report to Peterson, and told the recoilless rifles, who had a good supply of canister shot, to start blasting. The 8th Field plus all available artillery pounded rounds in front of us and turned the valley into an inferno of high-explosive geysers. FO Lieutenant Bell said later he'd had all the American artillery going in the 25th Division's sector—fifteen battalions, the second-largest barrage of the Korean War (the first being when the division recrossed the Han)—yet all this fire did not seem to put a dent in the Chinese mass attack. The enemy just continued to march like mechanical robots, one foot in front of the other.

More Chinese signal flares lit up the cloudy, starless sky. Bugles, whistles, and high-pitched Chinese screams were interspersed with the dull thud of high explosives thumping down in ugly red-black fireballs all along our front, and the steady tap of our machine guns, BARs, and rifles. The Ranger platoon was right behind us now, on its way to fill the gap between us and Fox Company. But it got caught. It couldn't get in position between us and the steadily advancing Chinese, who walked right over their dead and, from the high ground, played taps on their bugles to signal "objective taken." We shifted a light machine gun to cover the open flank. The Rangers withdrew and the Chinese kept coming. Where they were going, I didn't know, but wherever it was, they'd been tasked to get there *at all costs*.

Third Platoon had three Chinese columns marching toward us, on separate axes. Ironically, each was headed directly into the field of fire of one of our automatic weapons. We cut their ranks to pieces; enemy dead were strewn all along the platoon front. Our LMGs were red-hot, firing longer and longer bursts of grazing fire from point-blank range. I thought the machine guns would melt before we ran out of ammo, and that, I felt sure, would happen before the columns ran out of Chinks. But it was impossible to enforce any fire control as long as they kept coming.

But then they stopped. Suddenly the Chinese broke off their attack on our well-armed position, leaving only their dead to litter our front in scattered mounds of broken, twisted bodies. Like a rich man down to his last million, I guessed even these bastards finally realized that some things cost too much.

Not so in the valley below, where the main battle raged on. The Chinese left us alone. We were still putting down fire, but we became more like spectators, watching a ball game from the fifty-yard line. From our high perch I could see the tracers from our machine guns pouring rounds upon rounds onto the enemy; I could see the Chinese controlling their formations with flares. It was really quite spectacular, in a nightmarish kind of way: in the dark, the artillery, recoilless rifles, and machine guns firing; the Chinks' whistles and their screaming; the silhouettes of both friend and foe moving through the half-light of flares and searchlights and exploding shells; the huge mounds—four to five feet high—of enemy dead mounting in front of 2d and 1st platoons' positions.

I checked the squads. We had three U.S. wounded and one dead KATUSA (Korean Augmentation Troops, U.S. Army). Our light-machine-gun crew had vanished from the left flank and no one could account for it. We redistributed ammo and reconfigured our defense into a tight perimeter ringing the top of our perch. And then we heard the most incredible sound.

As if someone had blown a whistle to stop the game, suddenly there was no shooting in the valley at all. For a split second, there was no firing, no artillery, no flares. Then, in their place was a hum—a drone—as the Chinese yelled in terrible, bloodcurdling unison and steamrolled their way through our 1st and 2d platoons, like a great wave washing over the battlefield. They smashed the position in half, creating a gap of five or six hundred yards. The floodgate was open and the enemy was pouring through. From the high ground we could see them rushing behind us, flattening everything in their path. They washed down the valley guiding on the north-south road. George's mortars were firing; we could see white sparks as the rounds left the tubes. Then the flood hit them and the little sparks were submerged. No more mortar section.

The 5th Ranger Company (less the platoon originally tasked to fill in the gap on the main line) had set up a blocking position on the valley floor behind George Company. Their plan was to let George pass through them and then meet the Chinese attackers head-on. But George did not come back as an organized force, platoon leapfrogging through platoon. According to Ranger witnesses the men came back as a "panic-stricken mob," and hot on their heels were the Chinks. The Rangers could not tell the friendly from the enemy. They held their fire as George Company people ran through their position screaming, "Don't shoot. Don't shoot. George Company," but the enemy was mixed among George's people and some got behind the Rangers. It was bedlam. Captain John Scagnelli, the Rangers' fine CO, had no choice but to pull back and try to regain control of his unit, which had unavoidably been split up and intermingled with George guys and Chinese. Through it all we could hear Master Sergeant Francis' tanks' main guns thundering like bass drums from the direction of the battalion CP, and I sent up a silent prayer for a good man.

Before long, we were at least a mile behind the penetration. We could hear Chink bugles and whistles deep to the south, far beyond where the battalion CP, the Rangers, and other isolated units were somehow hanging on. The Chinese were still all around our little knob, but they ignored us as if we were not there. U.S. artillery was blistering George's vacated positions in the valley, and now we were starting to catch a few rounds of this friendly (but no less lethal) fire. The arty had long since cut our sound-power line—a problem at any time, but disastrous now because our SCR-300 radio (which had been acting up all night) was dead. Schroeder, grumbling that "the damn thing only seems to work when you don't need it," had me try to call Peterson. "George 6, this is George 3-5, over." Nothing. "George 6, this is George 3-5, do you read me? Over." Nothing.

I was about to give up when I heard my radio break squelch and the faint whisper, "George 3-5, this is George 6 Able."

I had connected with Peterson's RTO. "Let me speak to the Six," I said, referring to the commanding officer. The RTO whispered back, in a tearful voice choked with fear, "He's gone. I'm lost. There're Chinks all around. I'm alone."

There was no way I could help him. "Keep moving south, and keep cool. Destroy your radio. Good luck. . . . Out."

By midnight our area was reasonably quiet. The Chinese were pouring down the road past where our 1st and 2d platoons had been dug in. Their medics were picking up the dead and wounded. It was pretty obvious they thought our hill had been taken. We were cut off.

I had learned four things about being cut off: keep a cool head, maintain tight discipline and an even tighter perimeter, and don't let the troops panic. Walt Schroeder had won a Silver Star in September in a situation like we were in—only then the whole battalion had been cut off, and Schroeder had saved George from certain annihilation when he pretty well single-handedly intercepted and destroyed a North Korean force moving directly toward the company perimeter. In the great scheme of things, 3d Platoon was cool; over the winter months we'd all become pros at being cut off. Danny Abella said, "Call Eddie at Battalion. He'll give us the skinny."

Eddie Abella, Danny's brother, had been in G Company. Now he was the official 2d Battalion Operations sergeant and the unofficial don of the Hawaiian mafia. Danny was still a squad leader in our platoon, and on calmer nights, the Abella brothers always checked in with each other. If trouble was brewing, Eddie was on the horn to let us know; if one shot was fired anywhere near the vicinity of the 3d Platoon of G, Eddie called up to see if Danny and the rest of us were okay. It was great to have a private line into Battalion Operations and Intelligence—there was nothing like being informed.

Eddie reported that the Chinese main attack had bypassed the battalion CP and raced southward. He said the CP had been hit by a couple of half-assed probes, but that a Ranger officer named Joe Ulatoski had put together a scratch force of cooks, clerks, and George and Ranger company stragglers who drove off the enemy with the unexpected help of Sergeant Francis' tank section (which had roared into the CP perimeter seemingly out of nowhere). I thought to myself that if *we'd* had those tanks, none of this would have happened at all. The only guidance Eddie could give me was "Hang on, and get the guys out the best way you can." He said that F Company, on the high ground to our left, was quiet, and gave me their radio frequencies. "Look after Danny," he said, "and good luck."

Our withdrawal route to the south was a sea of Chinamen. We had to link up with Fox, but after all the trouble that Ranger platoon had run into, we couldn't chance going directly up the ridge to their position. So Schroeder and I talked about it, and decided to go north, parallel to the Chinese axis of advance, and then double back along the high ground leading to F Company's front. We had all the guys throw their steel pots away—the Chinese didn't wear helmets—and went down the hill into enemy lines, hoping we looked like Chinese medics toting out wounded. We hadn't gone fifty yards when the radio crackled with the most welcome voice we'd heard all night. It was Captain Michaely, back from R&R. In a whisper, Schroeder explained the mess we were in and the course of action we'd chosen. Michaely agreed, and on we went.

We snaked across the valley floor, dodging medics and stragglers, U.S. artillery, and the Chinese columns still moving south. Once on the ridge directly in front of F Company, we contacted the CO, Lieutenant Norman LaFlamme. In the middle of outlining our situation, the SCR-300 radio went dead again, and we spent agonizing minutes reestablishing commo. Finally Schroeder was able to get through, this time on F Company's internal net.

"This is George 3," he whispered.

"George 3, this is Fox 1" came the reply. I recognized the voice: it belonged to one Lieutenant Barney K. Neil. *Oh, shit,* I thought. He and I had met before, and it hadn't been pleasant.

About a month earlier I'd been sitting with some of the guys by a fire on a very cold day, when this bundled-up figure walked up and asked for directions to the G Company CP. "Just keep walking, buddy," I'd told him. "Straight ahead. You'll find it."

"Do you realize you're addressing a lieutenant in the United States Army?" he'd boomed, followed quickly by "Why aren't you standing at attention, soldier?"

Then I'd seen the brass bar of this young, parade-ground-perfect second lieutenant. My guys just watched, waiting to see how I'd handle it. No way was I going to stand up. I said, "Look, Lieutenant, I'm doing the same damn thing you're doing in this war—*without* bars—so don't pull that rank bullshit on me, okay?" It wasn't exactly true—Schroeder was the platoon leader in our outfit, not me—but I didn't care. The guy made me mad. And anyway, officer platoon leaders came and went so fast that unless they were really something they didn't even make a dent in a unit in the first place. Only the NCOs did that.

Neil tried to get bad, but my guys and I went back to staring at our fire. Finally he melted behind his little bar and disappeared with "We'll see what your company commander thinks of this, Sergeant."

His Oklahoma accent had been indelibly etched in my brain. Now, as Schroeder continued to talk to him, I kind of wondered whether I'd be better off staying out in the dark with the Chinese. Schroeder asked him to throw two illuminating hand flares in succession (we couldn't be sure with just one, which could just as easily be a spooked trooper popping a flare) so we could get a fix on his position with a compass. When we started to move, our big worry was no longer the Chinese; it was that we'd get ironed out by our own artillery (which was still blistering through the valley), or a friendly-but-nervous trigger finger. There are few more dangerous movements than entering a friendly front line when a fight is going on, but Neil assured us that Fox Company's H&I was shut off and the whole unit knew we were on our way. "Fox Company. This is George," Schroeder yelled, taking no chances, when we were a couple hundred yards out. "We're coming in!"

"Hold up," Neil called. "I'm sending a guide. Got booby traps and flares out there."

We were received with open arms. We split the guys up, one in each of 1st Platoon's holes; the Lieutenant didn't recognize me, but he was so friendly that I decided to confess I was the insubordinate sergeant he'd met that cold morning in March. It turned out Neil was not at all the garrison-soldier martinet I'd thought he was. He'd just been reacting to our generally surly fireside attitude. So we sat up the rest of the night bullshitting, and Barney K. Neil and I began a friendship that would last for the rest of his life, until he was killed as a battalion commander in another war, nineteen years later.

At first light, 3d Battalion's K (King) Company arrived. Theirs was not a happy lot. The whole 3d Batt had been on the move as the regimental fire brigade for more than a week already, and they were flat worn-out. Most recently, after George and the Rangers got brushed aside, the 3d Batt had taken the Chinese attackers head-on in their blocking position deep in the valley behind our battalion CP, and stopped them cold. Then K Company was attached to 2d Batt and sent on a sixteen-mile hike in the dark back over the rugged terrain the enemy had steamrolled through, with the mission of sliding behind F Company, and then fighting through and sealing the initial penetration by occupying G Company's holes. It was all standard procedure, but to the guys in King, there had to be an easier way to fight a war.

So K slid down through F, just before first light. The company commander was not in a good mood. He didn't want to go down in the valley. It was *very* bad down there—a lot of Chinese, a lot of artillery (both Chink and American) blasting the hell out of everything on the valley floor. He asked Barney K. for a sitrep. Barney said, "Talk to Hackworth, he's from G Company." I thought, *No, no! Don't let him know I'm from G Company! Don't tell him!*

Too late. King's CO said to me, "You'll lead the way."

"Like hell we will. You've got the job of closing the hole—it's not our job."

"Yeah, but you're the bastards who bugged out."

"We didn't bug out, we were overrun. And no way are we going to be your point into that valley. No fucking way." I quickly added, "Lieutenant," realizing that this little bantam was bone-tired, pissed off, and would not take much more from me. He looked as if he was just angry enough to blow me away.

Still, I felt guilty. My company had caused this mess. Maybe we did bug. Maybe we were just a bunch of "yellow-bellied bastards," as the King Company lieutenant went on to say. And now, with his bad-mouthing my unit, it became a point of honor. I told him we'd go down with him. "You take the Second and First platoons' holes—Third Platoon will occupy its own."

Down we went. King successfully sealed the penetration, and the Chinese were caught in a net. As the dawn was breaking, from our old positions I could see the complete battlefield. The Chinese were like chickens in a slaughterhouse yard, running in circles with their heads cut off while P-51s darted down from overcast skies, bombing and strafing anything that moved, and artillery kept pounding in.

"The Rangers have been given the mission of sweeping and clearing the valley," the CO of King informed us. "Your platoon is attached to them. I'm squatting in G Company's holes. Good luck." In that at least two-thirds of George had been scattered to the winds, and for all practical purposes we were no longer an effective combat force, it was logical to follow King's CO's orders. We joined what was left of the Rangers, under Captain Scagnelli's command.

John Scagnelli was a soldier's soldier. In his WW II paratrooper's uniform he looked the quintessential devil in baggy pants;* tough, squat, with the smashed face of a boxer, he was one bad, pugnacious hombre. His 5th Airborne Rangers were among the finest fighting men in the U.S. Army—strictly professional. "You'll sweep on the right of the valley. Tie in on line with my First Platoon," snapped The Scag. I was proud to be part of his operation. Its precision reminded me of the old 351st in Trieste.

We formed a skirmish line (soldiers lined up abreast, ten yards apart) that stretched across the valley floor—a moving wall of weapons on the hunt for human beings. Soon we came across the body of a Ranger lieutenant; it was a gruesome sight. Fred Lang was a huge guy, an ex-Oklahoma A&M football star, who, I later found out, was a classmate of Barney K. Neil's. The lieutenant had been hit in the legs earlier on, and the story (as I gathered from the Rangers' shorthand discussions over his body) was that Lang, who was far too heavy to carry, had told his men to prop him up by a trail with a bunch of ammo and grenades and get the hell out of there. Lang had done a Custer's last stand, blowing away Chinamen until they blew away him. But apparently that wasn't enough for the Chinks. Then they'd gotten him with their bayonets.

The Chinese bayonet on the Soviet SKS rifle was only about eight inches long. It was not so much a bayonet as a large and lethal three-pronged leather punch. It didn't make a clean cut; it made more like a rip, and the dead Ranger officer was just ripped to pieces. With jagged punctures all over his body, he was just a mound of shredded, bloody flesh; it seemed to us that every Chinese trooper had administered his own coup de grace as he filed past the lieutenant's body. This pissed the Rangers off. It got to all of us. The word went out: no prisoners. The Rangers were like NYPD cops when one of their own was shot down—vengeance, swift and without mercy.

What followed that day, walking through the valley, was not a sweep but a bloodbath. Chinks were coming at us and we just mowed them down.

---

* "American parachutists—devils in baggy pants—are less than 100 meters from my outpost line. I can't sleep at night; they pop up from nowhere and we never know when or how they strike next. Seems like the black-hearted devils are everywhere. . . ." (Extract from the diary of a German officer who opposed the 504th Parachute Infantry of the 82d Airborne Division on the Anzio beachhead in 1943.)[3]

Many played possum, lying motionless on the ground, pretending they were dead; when this was discovered, every single "corpse" got a slug in the head—if blood pumped out you knew you'd gotten a live one. It'd be fair to say that we were all a little in shock by the time the "mop-up" was over. Regiment would later estimate that 722 casualties were inflicted on the enemy that morning, but all we knew at the time was the valley floor was blood-red and littered with dead Chinese.

And then there was nothing more to do. We headed south, the platoon passing through the 3d Batt positions where they'd stopped the Chinks the night before. "Hey, boys, here comes G Company, the cowards," someone shouted.

"Yeah, 'G' for Guys Who Bugged."

"You rotten sons of bitches."

We all hung our heads and walked as fast as we could, trying to ignore the jeers. "Bug out" was an officially forbidden phrase in the Wolfhounds; its use, even in a whisper, tended to cause panic on the battlefield. Now that the whole thing was over, though, it was open season on old George, and it was humiliating. We were a proud company, not the kind that bugged. Still, 3d Platoon had had a machine-gun team disappear in the middle of the battle and no one had seen it since. In the heat of a firefight, a platoon leader can't be everywhere. Neither can a platoon sergeant. Somehow, as the battle warmed up, neither Schroeder nor I got over to the left-flank light machine gun, and by the time I did, it was gone—Jerry Boyd and friends, vanished. Maybe they'd bugged. Maybe they'd been killed. Maybe it was our fault.

We walked down the muddy road, passing by the gun positions of the 8th Field. And who should be there with them but Jerry Boyd—a totally intact Jerry Boyd—with the rest of the guys from our missing gun crew, sitting around with the 8th Field as if they belonged there. We kept walking. Jerry came running up. "How're ya' doing, boss?"

He wasn't wearing a steel pot, just his pile cap, earmuffs askew. He looked like Pluto the Dog. I wouldn't look at him. "What are you doing over there with the Eighth Field?"

He said, strutting along now with his jive accent, "I'm a motherfuckin' gunner now, man! Au-to-matic ar-till-er-eee. Bam, bam, bam, bam, bam—that's me!"

Looking straight ahead I said, "Jerry Boyd, what happened last night?"

"You told us to move out, so I moved out. I'm not going to be staying around when somebody's saying to move out and the Chinese are coming at me like some roller-skating snowmen."

"I never said 'move out.' I don't want to talk to you, Jerry Boyd. I don't want to know you. You've lost me for life." Now this was to Jerry, my *brother*, my foxhole buddy, the guy I shared my toothbrush and all my secrets with.

Jerry kept swearing that he was telling the truth. Then more of the missing guys came up, and they said it happened, too. Finally we were able to piece the story together. When the Ranger platoon—which happened to be the Rangers' 3d Platoon—got hit going into position between us and Fox Company, a Ranger had yelled to his people, "Third Platoon, let's go," and Jerry Boyd and crew had automatically saddled up and gone with them. (And there I'd been, worrying because two George companies were tied in together on the other side.) Then, when the Rangers got into more trouble down on the valley floor, my guys split for safer ground, and walked until they found the 8th Field.

"So I'm not the bad guy you thought I was," said Jerry. "I know what your mind was thinking. You were thinking when those Chinamen yelled '*banzai*,' old Jerry said 'good-bye.' Now you got the truth. Think I should get a medal, Hack. For saving my boys."

"Let me tell you something, Jerry Boyd. I've got your medal. Hanging. The last time I saw you, you were holding a machine gun. My machine gun. You do not have a machine gun right now. And I don't want to see your face until I see you holding a machine gun again, just like the one you had on that hill. Until I see you with an M1918A6 Browning machine gun, caliber thirty, brand-new, I don't know you. Got it?"

"Sure thing, boss!" Jerry said, and he bopped away, shining his giant smile, to find a new MG.

We kept heading south, leapfrogging through other units. At 1600, when the column halted and the battalion dug in, George Company was tasked as battalion reserve and reorganized behind the new front in an abandoned village. In a cluster of Korean mud-walled huts we found many tired, familiar faces—G Company brothers from the other platoons who'd straggled in a few at a time—and huge mounds of new gear. The company had almost nothing except its rifles and what we had on our backs. Everything else had been abandoned in the battle—our asses in exchange for our equipment. *Not much of a deal*, I thought, even as we took what we wanted from big piles of brand-new cartridge belts, weapons, steel pots, sleeping bags, pile jackets, and anything else we could need.

Everyone was still bad-mouthing us. No one had a good word for George.

"Watch out . . . there's Bug-out George!"

"When they said 'push on,' George heard 'Pusan,' and they've been heading south ever since."

But G Company had not run. As we gathered our unit together and started swapping stories around our ubiquitous campfires, it became clear that 1st and 2d platoons couldn't have fought more valiantly. The Chinese had just poured through. Regiment reported that two reinforced battalions had blasted through the positions; to those on the ground, two reinforced regiments—perhaps even a division—was closer to a true figure. One little Hawaiian guy, who was a machine gunner in the 2d Platoon, told me he'd been firing long bursts of machine-gun fire—twenty or thirty slugs a hit—into the advancing Chinese ranks. The Chinks didn't even try to knock out the gun. They just kept coming, until in the end the machine gun got so hot it wouldn't fire. The Hawaiian whipped out his .45-caliber pistol and started blasting away with that. Eight dead Chinks later, he found himself sharing his hole with an empty pistol and a live Chinaman. He beat that guy to death with the butt of the pistol, and it was only then that he decided he'd better get his ass out of there.

There really wasn't anything more he, or any of the guys in those two platoons, could have done. The Chinese had literally steamrolled right through. Meanwhile, Lieutenant Peterson (who showed up in the village to a few choice words from Schroeder) said he'd withdrawn the company under pressure, and swore he'd tried to get the word to 3d Platoon that the rest of the unit was hightailing the scene. When he couldn't raise us on the radio, he said he'd sent up a runner; it was pretty damn apparent the kid never got there, and we went on blaming Peterson even though Lieutenant Bell took full responsibility for the decision to withdraw in the first place, *and* for leaving 3d Platoon behind. From his FO perch on the northeastern slope of our little hill he'd watched the whole battle, knew the company could never survive the massive onslaught, and felt the rest of the unit would be zeroed out if they stayed until we got the word. Bell's decision had been the right one, but it was not easy to convince any of us in 3d Platoon.

The bottom line, though, was that the whole thing had happened without "The Rock" at the helm. Had Captain Michaely been there from the beginning, maybe we, as a company, could have held. I know damn well we would have executed an orderly withdrawal. Continuity of command is extraordinarily important on the battlefield. On a night like 26–27 April 1951, it was essential, and it wasn't there. Besides, Lieutenant Peterson just wasn't cut out to be a company commander. He was too nervous, and we felt his every quiver. His heart was in the right place, and he wasn't lacking individual guts: the story went that he'd been an NCO with a reserve commission working in a finance office in Japan; he'd felt guilty he wasn't in Korea, and put in for active duty so he could go over. In his first fight, in November, he'd gone out with a platoon as an observer, and when the platoon leader was hit, he'd taken over as platoon leader; when the rest of the platoon leaders *and* the company commander were hit, he'd found himself as the company commander. Then *he'd* gotten hit and was evacuated back to Japan. A Silver Star winner, he'd come back from the hospital and joined G Company as executive officer in a way that reminded me of my first encounter with Barney K. Neil. Schroeder told me that just before the Han River crossing (I was still in the hospital) he'd picked out a great hut for the NCOs, only to have Peterson come by and make all the sergeants move out—the hut was for the officers, he said. Later that day some booze found its way into the company through an R&R returnee, and Schroeder and another sergeant named Baxter got so drunk they decided to burn the hut down. Captain Michaely raked both men over the still red-hot coals for that one, but all the NCOs thought it was the best laugh south of the Yalu.

The reason Peterson was given command of George was simply that he was the ranking lieutenant at the time Michaely went on R&R. When the Captain returned the night the Chinese broke through (having danced at the Osaka Officers' Club with Spotlight Sims's wife, all the while having to pretend that Sims was alive and well because the wife hadn't received news of his death on Jake Able through official channels), he'd immediately been assigned as battalion Operations officer. That's why we'd heard him on the battalion net during the fight, and also why we'd ended up having to go it alone—things were so screwed up in the battalion chain of command that Michaely had ended up running the whole 2d Batt show. Without him the whole unit, not just George Company, might well have been destroyed.* When all was said and done, unquestionably the battle had been a hell of a mess from beginning to end, but when all the stories were told, we knew George had done the best it could, and as a company, we started holding our heads up again.

The guys continued straggling in, and after a good night's sleep and a packet of new replacements to fill our ranks, we headed south again as part of the regiment's rear-guard action. As April drew to a close, the Wolfhounds' official S-3 summary for the month reported the result of the Chinese Spring Offensive and this period of the most intense fighting I would ever experience: "Offensively, the [27th] Regimental Combat Team (RCT) . . . advanced for a period of forty-five days from the Han River; defensively the RCT withdrew approximately the same distance in six days."

---

* Our brilliant commander, Colonel Murch, had left 2d Battalion in early March. From the first this departure created some upheaval: neither his first replacement (who was relieved of command early in his tenure) nor the new CO, whom I'll call Colonel Cork, could come anywhere close to Murch's brand of leadership or tactical skill. Most of the battalion leaders felt that Murch's ability and example were responsible for the uniformly fine performance of the 2d Batt from the outset of Wolfhound involvement in the war; that we'd continued on in fine form since was a credit to the foundation he laid during his eight turbulent months of command.

On our way back, we passed an element of the 25th Recon Company set up in a delaying position along the side of the road. They were from my old platoon, the one I'd gone AWOL from a hundred years before. There were a number of guys from my scout section there as well, and when we saw one another it was like a family reunion. The guys walked along with our column for a while, and soon my old platoon sergeant (whom I'd always gotten along well with) heard I was there and joined us. He told me that the platoon leader lieutenant who'd provoked my going AWOL had been killed; he'd fought bravely, died heroically, and won the DSC in the process. I was truly sorry to hear he'd been killed, but glad to know he'd shaped up and become a proper leader before he cashed in his chips.

"And what about you, Hackworth? I hear you're quite a hero yourself," the sergeant said. "And you keep coming back for more?" He shook his head. "You're a glutton for punishment, young sergeant." I laughed and told him that maybe I was. But then he continued, "You know what I think, Hackworth? I think somewhere along the line you got stuck by the glory bayonet."

The glory bayonet. I'd never heard that expression before. At first I thought the sergeant was just using it to describe my gung-ho attitude to soldiering. But after we'd parted company and I continued walking down the road, I couldn't stop thinking about what he had said.

What made me a fighter—a warrior—was a combination of TRUST training and family tradition. My grandmother had told me, from as early as I could remember, the glorious battle record of the Hackworths from the moment they landed in the Virginia colony in the early 1600s. Two had been high-ranking officers at the Battle of Point Pleasant in 1774, she said, and one, Augustine, had been Andrew Jackson's deputy in the War of Independence in 1776. It wouldn't be for many years that I'd discover my high-ranking ancestors had actually been privates, and realize that Andrew Jackson was nine years old when the colonies revolted against the Brits, but it didn't matter. Gram's faulty memory helped give shape to a feeling that maybe I was born with: I was going to be a soldier.*

Gram's brother, Uncle Roy, had served as a buck sergeant in WW I. He'd won a Silver Star ("That and a nickel will get you a cup of coffee, boy," he'd say, whenever I asked if I could see it) and lived in Arizona in an old soldiers' home due to mustard-gas wounds he'd suffered in the trenches. He died

---

* Gram didn't get it completely wrong. My great-great-great-grandfather, John Hackworth, and his four brothers did all fight in the Revolutionary War. John Hackworth's father, George, was given land by King George for fighting Frenchmen and Indians in the mid-1750s. My great-great-grandfather, also named John, was a captain in the 56th Kentucky Regiment in the early 1800s and his son, Jeremiah, wearing blue, fought his cousins in gray during the Civil War. The strong soldiering tradition continued right up to World War II, when my brother, and then I, too, took up the call.

when I was nine, but I'd never forget sitting with him behind Jerry's Liquor Store in Ocean Park whenever he came to visit, listening to the bleak, inglorious war stories I'd beg him to tell, which he'd always punctuate with a slug from the bottle of cheap wine he carried in a brown paper bag. One time I'd gone racing into the newly installed indoor john of our house, not knowing he was in there taking a bath. I'd never seen Uncle Roy in anything but his clothes, and what I saw in the bathtub was a body that was kind of half a body. It was as if there were no muscles in one of his shoulders—just a discolored mustard-gas-burned bone that stuck straight out. An exposed ligament seemed to be the only thing preventing his arm from falling right off; it was without a doubt the most horrific thing I'd ever seen. But as horrific as it was, for me, at the age of six, it was equally compelling—the horror of the battlefield and the quiet dignity of a soldier all rolled into one—and the image would stick with me for life.

So Gram and Uncle Roy did their bit, and the movies, too—*The Dawn Patrol, The Fighting 69th, Sergeant York, All Quiet on the Western Front*—were my inspirations. And after 7 December 1941, I'd gone to sleep every night not counting sheep, but instead shooting imaginary Japs out of imaginary trees with an imaginary gun, inflicting imaginary—but very heavy and extremely *justified*—damage on a very real enemy who had committed the outrage of Pearl Harbor. All the groundwork for my future had been laid, long before TRUST, long before I had a war of my own, here in Korea. Given that, how could I have been stuck by a glory bayonet?

The enemy now, the North Koreans and the Chinese, had not committed the same offense as the Japanese in WW II. But I'd learned that they represented something even more sinister, the Communists, who were hell-bent on taking over the world. They had to be destroyed, and that was my job; the only glory in that was the feeling of being part of the force that was going to protect all the free world held near and dear. The more Reds you killed, I guessed, the more well thought of you were; maybe that was what the recon sergeant was talking about. But there was certainly nothing glorious about being tired and dirty all the time, and watching your friends get blown away.

And yet, right there lay the key to why I was so gung ho, and why I'd never quit. Sure, I was fighting for America, for all that was "right" and "true," for the flag, the national anthem, and Mom's Apple Pie. But all that came second to the fact that the reason I fought was for my friends. My platoon. And as I walked on, I concluded that that was why most other soldiers fought, too. The incredible bonding that occurred through shared danger; the implicit trust in the phrase "cover me"—these were the things that kept me going, kept me fighting here in Korea, and why I'd come back for more, for as long as my bottle held out. And though I did like the "glory" inherent in my steadily growing reputation as a good warrior, the most important thing was that I knew with other troopers' respect came their *trust*: they knew that I wouldn't let them down. And to the best of my ability, I never would. *So much for the glory bayonet*, I thought, and picked up the pace to catch up with my platoon.

5 BY THE DIRECTION OF THE PRESIDENT

Hack lived every day as if he were on top of a big, big wave. He was very excited about his military career, and wanted to prove his worth as a leader. The only problem he ever caused me—and it wasn't really a problem—was that any time I issued an operation order, Hack always wanted his platoon to lead the attack. Some discretion had to be given to the fact that he was not only volunteering his own life and safety, but the lives and safety of forty-two other soldiers in his command, but Hack's demonstrated example rubbed off on the members of his platoon—soon they all wanted to fight and be like him. It was a delightful experience having such an effective fighting "machine."

Lieutenant Colonel Dell Evans, USA, Ret.
Company Commander, E/27th Infantry
Korea, 1951

VAN Fleet's Line Lincoln, five miles north of Seoul, was where the Chinese offensive finally ran out of punch. It was a defensive position right out of World War I, with deep trenches, bunkers, and heavy field fortifications protected by minefields and barbed wire. The Chinese attackers (whose logistics tail was well overextended) couldn't make a dent in it. With the enemy on their knees, the hard-fighting Eighth Army was preparing yet another offensive, but as of 3 May 1951, the only American defense to be let down was mine.

"They want your ass down at Division, Hack," First Sergeant Flemings remarked as he walked into the 3d Platoon CP. "Looks like you're going to be commissioned whether you like it or not."

"Top, you know I don't want to be a lieutenant," I replied.

"Tell that to the boys at Division."

It was not a new conversation; in fact it was one I'd had as far back as TRUST, with Captain Eggleston, when he'd recommended me for Officer Candidate School. Luckily (or unluckily, depending on how you looked at the war), Korea had broken out before my OCS orders came through, and I'd been spared the ordeal. With Sergeant Flemings here in George, we'd been going over the same turf for the last two months. The only difference was that our discussion, which had been more or less hypothetical, was now a full-blown reality.

Soon after I'd returned from the hospital in March, Phil Gilchrist had recommended me for a battlefield commission. He had taken the case to Captain Michaely, who'd approved the promotion, then on to Colonel Cork, who only recently had taken command of the 2d Battalion. The criterion for a battlefield commission was simply to be a proven combat leader. Education, family connections, even officer potential played little part. It was an honor won only on the battlefield, its recipients the spirited frontline fighters who got the job done, and could inspire their fellow troopers to do the same.* In ten months of Korean combat, only eight men in the 27th Infantry Regiment had been commissioned in the field. Most of them were dead; the price paid for being a "mustang" (as the Marine Corps called their battlefield commissions), for never being reluctant to stand up and charge when the chips were down, was often one's own life. In truth, I felt honored to be considered worthy of inclusion among this distinguished group of warriors, but there was one problem—I didn't want to be an officer. Being an officer didn't jibe with my childhood expectations of Army life, or with the reality of my seventh-grade education (in TRUST, I'd had so little self-confidence that the only thing I was sure of in terms of my ability to handle OCS was that I'd flunk out the first day). Now, having been a noncom for more than two years, I'd concluded that I was an NCO through and through, and there seemed little reason for jumping into the officer ranks.

"I don't want to be like all those ninety-day wonders, Sergeant Flemings," I pleaded with the topkick, referring to OCS graduates. "They don't show me anything. I want to be a platoon sergeant like I am now, and just run my platoon. Then one day maybe be a master sergeant. I'll be happy as shit when I've got three stripes up and three stripes down. I don't want to be a lieutenant."

Flemings nodded. "And what if you don't make master sergeant? Look, Hack, if you don't take the commission, one day some second balloon

---

* As a board of officers reported to the commanding general of the European Theater at the end of World War II: ". . . on the battlefield, if a platoon sergeant, whose platoon commander has just been killed, can successfully lead fifty scared, confused men who depend on him for everything, and who must be made to accomplish what they think is impossible, it is of no consequence if the AGCT [Army General Classification Test] score of that man is less than 100 and he never attended high school. . . ." ("A Brief History of Battlefield Commissions in the Armed Forces," the National Order of Battlefield Commissions.)

[second lieutenant] might come in and take over your platoon. He also might get a lot of your people killed. Then how would you feel? You've got to take the promotion and look after your troops."

The First Sergeant had a point. And besides, he'd been there and done it all while I'd just been dreaming about it; he was a *From Here to Eternity* NCO, and straight as a die. Flemings knew the score, and I knew he was right. This time, when it counted, he'd worn me down. "Okay, Top," I said. "You got a deal, if I can keep my platoon."

The paperwork was done at Division Rear, 150 miles to the south, near Taegu. The Adjutant General, Lieutenant Colonel Master, put me in a tent where casuals slept; I stretched my fart sack out on the dirt floor and marveled at the luxury of my plush quarters—electric lights, no less. I went to be processed, which meant closing out my old records and opening up new officer's ones, and the next day, "by the direction of the President," the AG swore me in. He pinned a second lieutenant's bar on my right lapel, and then asked me where my crossed-rifle infantry insignia was. I didn't have one; as it turned out, neither did he. So he pinned another brass bar on my left lapel (which is how they're worn in the U.S. Navy) and said, "Well, that's it, Lieutenant. Congratulations. Report to Division Forward soonest."

"How do I get there?" I asked him.

"*You* figure it out, Lieutenant."

I hadn't told the guys I was sharing the tent with that I was there to be commissioned, so when I went back to collect my trusty M-1 and my gear, they all thought it was quite amusing that I was now an officer, and a naval officer at that. I was pretty embarrassed by the whole thing, especially because I didn't feel any different at all. I'd sort of thought something would happen—I didn't know what—but something, and nothing did. I was still Sergeant Hackworth, with bars. Two, to be exact. I went to the road and put out my thumb.

A truck picked me up, and for the first time in my life, someone called me "sir." The driver said, "Where are you going, sir?" I told him north, and that I'd been a sergeant up until a few minutes ago, so don't call me "sir." "Yes, sir," he replied, and we roared down the road.

At Division Forward, I met another Wolfhound who'd just been commissioned—Lieutenant Ushida, from C Company, 1st Batt. Ushida was an old guy of at least twenty-seven, who'd served with the famed 442d Regimental Combat Team in World War II, fighting his way through Italy, Normandy, and across Europe. I'd always admired the 442d (it was just a great fighting team, and, with 314 percent casualties, had won more Purple Hearts than any other regiment, as well as more than eighteen thousand individual awards and seven Distinguished Unit Citations), so I guess it was only natural that I admired Ushida, too. We spent the day together; I pumped him for war stories and in the course of it all really became close to him.

That night, after the division briefing, there was a little ceremony. Ushida and I stood up, and Brigadier General J. Sladin Bradley, who'd recently taken over the 25th Division from General William Kean, pinned on our bars. Bradley was a fine fighting general himself, and now he gave us a quiet speech, making no bones about his belief that we, as battlefield commissions—as "mustangs"—were among a rare breed of fighting men. With that, I said good-bye to Lieutenant Ushida, with the hope that someday we'd tie in on the line or something. But it was not to be, and when I heard he was killed in combat soon after we were commissioned—a fate this good man shared with the majority of the 27th's battlefield commissions, most of whom did not survive the war—it knocked me for one very serious loop.

I reported in to 2d Battalion HQ, for what was to be my first eyeball-to-eyeball with our new battalion commander, Lieutenant Colonel Cork. I'd heard little good about him in the month or so he'd been with the unit; from the scuttlebutt, it seemed that 2d Batt would have gone to hell in a high-speed hand basket had it not been for our S-3* (battalion Operations officer), Captain Michaely, who more or less ran the battalion, not just in late April during the Chinese Spring Offensive, but every day of the week. On first impression, Cork was not my kind of soldier. He was drunk, or well on his way, when I reported in at midday. He slurred out that I was going to Easy Company; I protested, telling him I was from George, and that the First Sergeant had said I'd return to my unit. "Well, George Company's First Sergeant doesn't run this battalion, does he?" Cork asked.

The First Sergeant is far more capable of running this battalion than you'll ever be, you drunk, silly-looking son of a bitch, I thought to myself, but kept my mouth shut. "You're assigned to Easy Company. Dismissed," mumbled Cork, and then something more about not getting myself killed.

It was the middle of the night by the time I found Easy Company's trains. There I met First Sergeant Cox, a good man who'd been with the Wolfhounds as far back as Japan. He was a real pro, a fine soldier who helped me one hell of a lot until I got the hang of this platoon-leader business. I was a little afraid of it, despite the fact that I'd been doing the job,

---

* Staff officer positions are numerically designated: -1, Personnel; -2, Intelligence; -3, Operations; -4, Logistics. The command level on which the staff officer works is designated alphabetically: the prefix "S" refers to Special Staff on the battalion, regiment, or brigade levels; "G" refers to General Staff on the division, corps, or Army levels; and "J" refers to Joint Staff (combined services of Army, Navy, and Air Force).

in one way or another, on and off since Italy. Now Cox said the battalion was on line; E Company was up forward, and since I was eager to get cracking, why didn't I take up the resupply trains? It was a reasonable suggestion, and off we went into the pitch-black night. No one really knew where we were going, least of all me; we didn't know exactly where the front was, and before long we didn't even know where *we* were. *Shit*, I thought, *if Cox had known what a rotten ground navigator I was, he'd never have given me this job.* But he had, and on we went—me, a few troopers, and fifteen Korean laborers loaded down with more than twice their weight in ammo, water, and other supplies.

The Korean laborers were the third tier of Korean nationals involved in the war under the auspices of the Eighth Army; the Republic of Korea (ROK) Army and the Korean Augmentation Troops, U.S. Army (KATUSAs) were the other two. The ROKs had disintegrated in the first moments of battle, almost eleven months ago when the North Koreans invaded the South. Since then they'd re-formed, gotten into fighting shape, and now fought side by side with units of the United Nations forces. The KATUSAs' origins were the beginnings of the war itself, when Syngman Rhee, president of South Korea, declared a state of emergency and initiated a draft. About 100,000 young men were rounded up, both to train and to be kept out of North Korean hands; when the time came to farm them out to ROK units, it became apparent that a huge surplus of replacement troops existed. Someone then had the idea to integrate these soldiers into the U.S. units (which had arrived in-country with only two understrength battalions per regiment), and before long the "augmentation" occurred. Unfortunately, most of these KATUSAs were not worth shit as fighters; for them, bugging out was the rule, not the exception. But it really wasn't their fault. They had no understanding of the English language, and U.S. infantry guys on the ground knew no Korean. As Captain Michaely explained the KATUSA problem best: "How could they have full faith in somebody they couldn't even talk to?" Still, the KATUSAs came, and stayed until they bugged or were wounded or killed; they generally worked in pairs, with the survivors normally ending up as ammo bearers for their units.

Communication was just one of the problems between Korean and U.S. troops. Ethnic customs and religious beliefs were often miles apart in the two cultures, and little or no effort was made to bridge the gap. One crisis that occurred among the laborers in our battalion began when, for morale purposes, it was decided "Lion White" (the code name for 2d Batt/27th) needed a new battalion sign. Design ideas went back and forth, and the one finally chosen and executed included a human skull, which was perched on top of the sign itself. By the next day all the Korean *chogi* bearers had disappeared. Captain Michaely went out to find them; the laborers were well down the road to the south by the time he caught up. When he asked why they'd left, they replied it was because of the sign with the skull. They said they just couldn't work for people who had so little regard for human beings as to do something like that. Michaely had to promise he'd have the skull removed, and that it (and its body) would receive a decent burial, before they said they'd come back. All of us may have become jaded enough to think the sign was a real masterpiece, but to the poor Koreans our attitude was simply barbaric.

But the *chogi* bearers did come back, and the fifteen with me now just smiled and strained and trudged along as we stumbled around in no-man's-land, looking for Easy Company. We heard movement; I hid the noisy carrying party in a draw and went off with one of the guys to have a look-see. M-1s at the ready, within moments we made contact with an element of Easy Company on their way back from a patrol. The chance encounter scared the hell out of them *and* us, but at least they were able to point the way to the company's positions.

It was about 0400 when I finally got to the mud house that served as the company CP. I sat down, then stretched out on the porch outside, and the next thing I knew, gallant Phil Gilchrist was waking me up. Now he was running Easy, and as it turned out, he was the one responsible for my not returning to George. He'd been called by Cork a few days before, regarding the commission he'd recommended me for months ago: "If you think so much of Hackworth you can have him," the battalion CO had said, and the next day I'd gotten the word to report to Division. Having Gilchrist as my CO certainly relieved some of my disappointment over being yanked out of George; ironically, this ideal situation lasted a grand total of four days: on the tenth of May, Lieutenant Dell Evans (who'd commanded Easy until he got hit on Jake Able) returned to resume his command.

Gilchrist assigned me to 3d Platoon. I was lucky; my platoon sergeant was a damn good NCO, a DSC winner named Crawford, and the squad leaders, Marvin Hardburger, Stephen Stranzle, John "Whitey" Snyder, and Bobby Stokes, were all pros, too. It wasn't too common to have a top company skipper *and* five crackerjack NCOs; *Not a bad start,* I thought, except that during the first couple of days these bad hombres of Easy tried to run me—or at least scare me—out of town.

I didn't tell them I'd come from George, and neither did Gilchrist. I'd scrounged a new set of fatigues at Division, and with my shiny second lieutenant's bar I looked like a brand-new replacement officer, fresh off the boat. So I played out the new-guy role, and the war stories of the Thirsty Third—"bloodthirsty, that is," they said—came hot and heavy: Desiderio and Easy up north in November when "The Man got the big one the hard way"; Millett and Easy and the February bayonet attack.[*] There were countless war stories, from the "Bowling Alley" at Taegu to the Yalu and back, all concerning the trials, tribulations, and heroics of Easy. It was small wonder that any other units were needed in Korea at all, judging from Easy's own accounts of their derring-do. But I enjoyed the little game. It gave me time to take the measure of my new outfit, and I was pleased with what I found. They were a spirited, proud company, and besides, most of their stories—to some degree anyway—were true.

A day or so later we moved into a blocking position and tied in with G Company. As soon as I got my platoon busy digging, I paid a visit to mighty George, which I'd left five days before. It was like a homecoming, with bear hugs, slaps on the back, hoots and hollering and exaggerated salutes. "Come see me after you get your shit squared away," I told them, "we're just down the line." And they did—the whole platoon dropped in at my CP, so happy that one of theirs had made it, one of theirs was a lieutenant. None of them called me "sir," just Hack, and a very put-on "Hack" at that. Now it was the 3d of E who had to listen to overblown war stories—all about their "green" second balloon, no less: "Man, he got us in some deep shit there . . ." the George guys were saying. "Hell, he's the baddest guy in the valley! You guys in old Easy Company might just have to get off your asses now that you got Hack here." The George boys' visit sent my stock up 100 percent with the new platoon. They stopped looking at me under invisible microscopes, and it was total acceptance all around. *Now*, I thought, *we can get on with the business at hand.*

" 'Two up and one back. Feed 'em hots and keep 'em in clean socks.' That's about all you've got to know to make it in the infantry," drawled Platoon Sergeant Crawford as we moved up a few days later, with George and Fox on line and Easy in battalion reserve. We were married up with a platoon each of tanks and quad-50 half-tracks; our job was to be a counterattack task force in case the Chinks broke through the front line. Every day we rehearsed various counterattack plans. During these maneuvers I had the opportunity to have a good look at 3d Platoon, and there was no question that I'd inherited a strong, solid outfit that knew what it was doing. The platoon was full of characters, too, like PFC "Red" Smalling, a

[*] On 7 February, the day after I got hit, Lewis Millett, then CO of Easy, led his men in a bayonet charge that Army historian S. L. A. Marshall deemed the most effective bayonet attack in the history of the U.S. Army. With all the attendant publicity (and Marshall's gifted hand writing the commendation), Millett ended up getting the Medal of Honor. But a number of George's guys who'd witnessed the assault thought that as actions go it was remarkably oversold. On the other hand, G Company always resented Easy's glamour-puss reputation; George quietly prided itself on being steady and solid instead.

freckle-faced kid and brilliant combat soldier from Arkansas, who'd walk up and down the line at night making sure the guys on guard were all awake. If one wasn't, Smalling would hold his .45 against the side of the transgressor's head and fire off a round. And as if that wasn't enough to wake the kid up and teach him a lesson, the next day Red would follow him to chow and beat the shit out of him, with the First Sergeant making sure the fight wasn't broken up until Red had done a good job. This particular routine was explained to me by weapons squad leader Bobby Stokes, who also introduced me to the machine-gun duo of John Lipka and Richard Sovereign, two gunners who knew their weapons as well as a guy knows every curve of the body of his first great love. They practiced night and day, and had down pat a "shave and a haircut, two bits" duet, which they'd play on the machine guns during enemy attacks so Bobby would know their positions hadn't been overrun. It was a brilliant idea, and it worked.

There were also some great characters among the officer corps in our havenlike reserve. The character of characters was one Lieutenant Milo David Rowell, a West Pointer, class of 1950, and commander of the track platoon co-locating with us. Milo was from a wealthy California family and was the heir apparent to the family fortune. We were all less than impressed—we basically considered Milo an outsider (he wasn't infantry for openers, and all of Easy's officers thought he was a pampered prude)—and though we'd never say so to his face, we managed to let him know how we felt by ganging up on him when the officers got together to play hearts. The way we did it was by making sure Milo got the queen of spades and every single heart—except one. We'd set it up in such a way that he thought he was going to "shoot the moon"; he'd get all excited, and then he'd lose, with twenty-five big points. All of us took almost sadistic pleasure in this, because then Milo would throw tantrums: we inferior infantry morons were ganging up on him. Not fair. Not cricket. One night after he got his usual shaft, he blew up. He threw down his cards, jumped up from the makeshift table, and yelled, "You guys are a bunch of cheaters! I'm never playing with you again!" He stormed away, never to return—I think we'd been playing for a penny a point.

The funny thing about this was that we'd really been living the good life during our reserve duty. The work wasn't hard, there was plenty of time for laying back in the warm spring sun, we lived in "liberated" Korean huts, and we were eating the Army's gourmet food line—beautiful, hot A rations. Milo was so pissed off that he moved his platoon out of our cozy village and laagered them in an open field. He wouldn't even let his guys continue to eat with us. So they slept under ponchos and ate C rations while their offended leader fumed; we couldn't help but laugh, despite our feeling sorry for the poor folks in Milo's command.

Soon our combined team, designated Task Force Evans (after Dell Evans, our company commander), was ordered to pass through the front and probe a series of small Chink-occupied hills in preparation for a U.N. limited offensive, which was jumping off the next day. We breezed out, riding the backs of tanks; when we got close to the hills, the infantry dismounted and deployed in a line of skirmishers. "Mines! Mines!" came a sudden, urgent cry. We froze. A quick recon revealed my platoon was in the middle of an American AP minefield full of Bouncing Betty types—for infantry the worst in the inventory. We carefully reorganized at a respectful distance behind the tanks, and while the Chinese watched us from the hills, well outside effective rifle range, the tanks proceeded to lead us through the field, blasting lanes with their tracks. Meanwhile, the enemy started lobbing a few mortar rounds, but never got close; one advantage the Americans always had over the Communists in Korea—and thank God, because they'd have eaten us alive—was that the Reds could never quickly and effectively adjust their indirect fires (mortar and artillery), nor, with their bad commo, easily coordinate fire support.

Once out of the minefield, we started maneuvering up the ridgeline. The tanks and tracks supported our attack with overhead fire from the valley floor. It was standard procedure, attacking a hill under an umbrella of fire—except that after a while, we were getting rained on: the tracks' quad-50s were chewing up the ground with long bursts, right into my people. I screamed on the radio, "Shut it off, shut it off! You're firing right on top of us!" but the slugs kept coming. I grabbed the air panel my RTO dragged behind his radio and started waving holy hell out of it—this long, brightly colored panel would show a blind man our forward edge. The quad-50 fire lifted. Miraculously, we had no casualties. *First U.S. mines, now U.S. fire. Who needs an enemy?* I thought. Then I remembered who commanded the tracks, and though I *did* know he hadn't done it purposely, for a fleeting moment I wondered if that "friendly" fire hadn't just been Milo Rowell's trump card.

From the map (and from the valley floor, too), the ridge had looked as if it ran to the top of the objective assigned to me by CO Dell Evans. But about four hundred yards from the top of the hill, we found that it was a military crest; to continue the attack, we'd have to move across a long, pool-table-like shelf, and then come back up. There was no cover, no concealment, no avenue of approach. It would have been a Pickett's Charge—no more healthy for infantrymen in Korea, 1951, than it was at Gettysburg, 1863. I held up the guys and called Dell with the lowdown. He switched the main attack to 2d Platoon (commanded by a former NYPD cop and recalled WW II vet, First Lieutenant Jim Lynch), which was coming up another finger. Our job would now be to support their assault by rifle and machine-gun fire. We'd been "pinched out" of the assault, and for the 3d of Easy, it was a lucky, lucky case of being in the wrong place at the right time.

Second Platoon did not have an easy road. The Chinks were solidly dug in and were not about to be shoved off their hill (the first part of the mission, to determine the enemy's disposition, was accomplished the minute we locked horns). The second part of the mission, to inflict maximum casualties on the enemy, was also accomplished, all guns and weapons blazing within the company, and supported by tank, quad-50, artillery, and Corsair-delivered bombs and napalm. Still, the assault force took casualties. One trooper was blown down the hill and rolled into the pool table in front of my platoon. He lay in the open, right under the Chinks' guns. Brave Corporal Victor Kozares from my platoon, acting on his own, quickly stripped his gear and took off like a shot. He grabbed the guy as though he were a bag of potatoes and charged back through a hail of enemy fire to the safety of our hill's reverse slope. Our doc patched the kid up, and he lived.

Kozares was later awarded the Silver Star for his act of unselfish gallantry. Still, his feat could have backfired: he could have been hit, and then *two* disabled troopers would have lain exposed on the open, fire-swept crest until *another* brave soldier rushed to the rescue and got hit himself. I'd seen and heard about it a million times. A leader has a difficult time preventing such waste. The problem is simply that if enemy fire can cut down one man, the same fire can cut down a hundred. In a hot firefight, a rifle platoon can take ten casualties before you can cry "Medic"; and if you multiply by ten the one rifleman who falls out to look after his buddy, suddenly you've lost the guts of the platoon's firepower. So a leader has to be hard-nosed. He must remember his *mission* comes first, and only then the welfare of his men. If a guy stubbed his toe three feet from a cobra, you wouldn't let his buddy sit down, take off the guy's boot, and assess the damage, especially when a tiger is lurking just behind the snake; a leader cannot give the enemy the initiative by allowing his unit to become ineffective as a result of care for the wounded becoming first priority. *"Keep your weapon downrange and don't play medic"* was my standing operating procedure (SOP), and I tried my damnedest to enforce it. Any other course carried not only the risk of failure to accomplish the mission but also the loss of a hell of a lot more men than necessary.

*   *   *

The sun was going down. We were supposed to be home before dark, and having accomplished his mission, Dell Evans sent word to break off. Third Platoon provided covering fire while the 2d and 1st broke contact, but the Chink fire was still so hot that 2d Platoon's dead could not be gotten out without a still greater cost in lives. Dell wisely decided to continue our withdrawal as planned; we'd pick up our KIA in the morning.

Early the next day, a Turk unit attached to the 25th Division secured the hill as part of the offensive, and I drew the task of recovering our dead. When we got up there, the Turks had completed mopping up and were now lazing around and smoking in the sun. Great fighters, the Turks—mean, loud, and awesome-looking—damn near impossible to like, but the kind of soldiers you were generally glad to have on your flank. Interestingly, the Turks felt the same way about the Wolfhounds. According to FO Allan Bell (who worked with them for a while), the 27th was the only unit the Turks even admitted existed.

I found the Turk commander, and he took me to our dead—four bodies stacked up, neatly wrapped in ponchos. Then he said, "You Americans no can take hill. Turks take hill! We *walk* up! Chinese say, 'Ah, Turks come . . . we run away! We afraid of Turks!' Everybody afraid of Turks!"

Now, as individual soldiers, the Turks *were* great, but the reason the Chinks were even on that hill was that the Turks had lost it to them a few days before. Furthermore, our mission had not been to take the hill in the first place, and on top of that, the only reason the Chinese defenders were easy pickings when the Turks took off in the attack was that Easy had blown the shit out of that hill—we'd reduced the position to a pile of rubble—the day before. But tell that to the Turks. Tell that to this puffed-up dude with the huge mustache. It really wasn't worth the effort, so I just took the broken-Englished shit he laid on my unit and hauled ass and bypassed (as it were) the fight to which my protests eventually would have led.

The second phase of the Chinese Spring Offensive was petering out; now it was the U.N. forces' turn to attack north. Happily, the Wolfhounds' 2d Batt was given a break from the fighting; we went into corps reserve at Uijongbu. There, a tent became the Officers' Club, and a few nights later Colonel Cork summoned an officers' beer call—my first of such social outings since I'd been commissioned.

In heart and soul I was still an NCO (after only two weeks wearing a bar not much more could be expected), so I guess it was only natural for me to be uncomfortable, socially speaking, around officers. For the main, we came from different worlds. I didn't know a dessert spoon from a soup spoon, and because I didn't have an education, I doubt I even knew the difference between a noun and a verb. When one of my first Officer Efficiency Reports (OER, or ER) stated that I was "quiet and unassuming," the rater had been dead right, but only because I was too afraid to open my mouth. So at Cork's party, besides having a few beers and bullshitting with Dell Evans and Phil Gilchrist (who was now Michaely's assistant in the battalion S-3 shop), I kept quiet and watched.

The whole thing wasn't my scene. Parties never were. My conclusion at this one was that officers' parties were the same as NCOs', except that I'd rather be raising hell with the noncoms than playing out this "officer and gentleman" game. I was about to slip out and return to my platoon when the new battalion XO called out, "Hackworth, get the Colonel a beer."

"The Colonel can get his own beer," I replied.

It was an immediate reaction, like ducking when someone shouts, "Fire in the hole." I didn't think I'd said it in a loud voice, but it seemed as though everybody in the tent had heard. And now they were waiting for the other shoe to drop, in the most deafening silence I'd ever known. Then quick-thinking Dell Evans pulled my ass out of a big crack. He stood up and said, "No, no, Major. Not Hackworth. It's Lieutenant Johnson, from H Company. He's the junior lieutenant. He was commissioned a week after Hackworth. Johnson, get the Colonel a beer." And Johnson, who'd been an NCO for a long time (but unlike me, knew how to move and groove in these circles), jumped up with a big smile on his ruddy Irish face and got the Colonel his beer. Dell took me aside. "Hack, it's Colonel Cork's policy that the junior officer act as Mr. Vice. It's an old officer custom. Goes back to the British Army."

"I thought we kicked their ass in 1778," I retorted. "I ain't getting no beer for no man, Dell," I said, because that's where I was coming from—always had and always would.

Dell put his arm around me. "Come on . . . I'll walk you back to your platoon. I'm going to have to teach you some social graces, Hack," he said in his rich Arkansas twang, "or start keeping you in a cage."

Lieutenant Dell Evans was one officer I really liked. He was a small, slight guy, a paratrooper, and a very brave and distinguished soldier. He'd already won a Silver Star, and was in for the DSC for an action in February when he'd been the only man of a seven-man volunteer patrol to reach an objective still in enemy hands. Firing his carbine on full automatic, he'd stormed the hill under some serious automatic-weapons fire and a skyful of grenades, until he'd reached an occupied Chink hole. Only then did he find he was out of ammo, so he jumped into the hole, swinging his carbine like a baseball bat. The two defenders naturally fought back, and after the carbine stock shattered, Dell grabbed the enemies' own potato-masher grenades and beat the two Chinese unconscious with them. About that time he saw twenty-five or thirty enemy soldiers coming up the hill toward him. "Right away," he told me later, "I decided if I were going to survive I'd better learn how to use their grenades." He did, and after he threw about three, the Chinese reinforcements bugged out. Dell gave the two Chinks in his hole one more bash with a potato masher, set a grenade between them, pulled the cord, and hauled ass out of the hole. People who watched the incident said he flew out, like a bird.

The net result of Dell's single-handed action was the breakup of a serious counterattack that threatened both the men of his patrol and all of Easy Company. When it was over he was so shook up over what *might* have happened that he began to stutter, and couldn't stop for three days. (A funny sidebar to the story was that this incident occurred just ten days after Easy Company's bayonet charge, and despite Dell's gallantry, there was much talk about why he hadn't used his bayonet to finish off the defenders. Old soldier Colonel Murch, who was still the battalion CO at the time, even brought the subject up in a note he sent Dell along with a bottle of bourbon and a new M-2 carbine. The note was attached to the bayonet and it read, "This carbine and attached bayonet is a token of my appreciation for your today's tremendous act of valor. However, you are reminded that the next time you are expected to use the bayonet or you will be expected to sign a statement of charges for the misuse of government property.") In a word, Dell was just a stud of the first order. Besides that, he was a brilliant gambler—much better than I was—and through shared combat and a lot of money won and lost, he'd become not only my idea of a fine combat officer, but also a most respected teacher and friend.

One day, soon after the Officers' Club affair, Dell had a visitor to our reserve camp at Uijongbu—an ROTC buddy from college days by the name of Lieutenant Lloyd Leslie "Scooter" Burke. Scooter Burke did not look like a big war hero. He was of small build, with metal-rimmed glasses; he was Clark Kent, not Superman. But by May 1951, he was well on his way to becoming a legend in his own time. He'd already won a Bronze Star, Silver Star, and, in November of '50, the DSC for almost single-handedly stopping a large Chinese force from destroying his 1st Cav unit. By the time he'd leave Korea in November 1951, he would earn three Purple Hearts and the Medal of Honor, too, the latter as Company XO, just about to rotate home, when he heard his battalion was in deep shit on the line, and led about thirty-five men left in his company in a final attack, catching live Chink grenades and tossing them back on the enemy, killing or capturing about a hundred Chinese, and generally playing Audie Murphy on his way to successfully securing the battalion objective.

Scooter was a great warrior indeed, but he was also a great guy. He loved poker, and played the game with the same daring as he led his troops. But probably the most memorable game that occurred during his visit was one he, Dell, and I missed. Fortunately. I don't know where those two were, but I'd taken my men on some night training, and about midnight, when we were hiking back to the battalion assembly area, we heard Bedcheck Charlie making his nightly rounds. Putt, putt, putt—his little biplane (said to be WW I vintage) sounded like a one-stroke lawn mower. The battalion area was far behind the light line, so it was lit up like a circus (a perfect target for the Chinese Red Baron). Down below, the battalion doc and some staff officers were in the middle of a poker game. From our position on the high ground, we saw Charlie start dropping 120-mm mortar shells all over the area, one after the other. Even as the mortar "bombs" exploded all around them, the poker players refused to bug. They held fast, and while 3d Platoon remained riveted to our ringside seats, Bedcheck Charlie blew up the game.

The next night Dell, Scooter, Captain Eugene Snedeker (CO of H Company), a couple of other guys, and I decided to reliberate recently liberated Seoul. We jumped into Dell's jeep and drove down the road; the first stop in our quest for excitement was the Fifth Air Force Officers' Club. The place was dim and garish inside, but plush compared to where we'd come from. We were wearing our Sunday-best field gear, and it got us a lot of heavy looks from the Wild Blue Yonder gang in their Class A's. They acted as if we were savages invading their territory, and it pissed us off—these fly-boys had the world by the ass while we lived like rats in the field, yet they resented us being in their club. *Screw 'em*, we thought, and sat down anyway.

The chips on our shoulders grew larger by the drink. We became more antagonistic, more obnoxious, more profane. There were a number of complaints about our conduct, and the more complaints, the grosser and badder we got. Before long, the Club Officer, a big fat major, came over: "You people are not authorized. You're in the wrong uniform, and your conduct is unbecoming to officers." Scooter, who was the baddest of us all, grabbed him. He put a .45 against the major's belly and looked at Dell.

"Say the word and I'll blow him away."

Dell gently convinced him that greasing this guy would ruin our party, so Scooter just pushed the petrified pilot away, and we left. We jumped into our jeep and headed home, taking potshots at passing streetlamps just to entertain ourselves. An MP jeep gave chase (we were driving in a blackout zone with our headlights on): "Turn those lights off!" we heard. Paratrooper Gene Snedeker whipped out his .45 and shot a hole through the instrument panel of our jeep. Somehow that kind of sobered us up, and we started concentrating on avoiding the MPs until we successfully cruised into the reserve area and crashed into our beds.

Soon Scooter went back to the Cav, reputation intact; the next little Uijongbu escapade Dell and I were involved in did little to enhance ours. Five South Korean policemen had, for some unknown reason, beaten up "Big Stoop," Easy Company's number-one *chogi* boy. They'd really done a number on the kid, hanging him upside down from a tree and beating him with their rifle butts. Dell was outraged, and rightfully so. I was among the five volunteers who, in accordance with Dell's wishes, "put the cops in the same condition as Big Stoop, or worse." This second incident ended up in a CID inquiry, and while the five vigilantes got off scot-free, the thing cost Dell dearly. Every time his name came up for a battlefield promotion, it would be crossed out—the Lieutenant had shown poor judgment, and should have known better. Dell resigned himself to his fate, looking at the events as "a lesson for me in the use of power and how it can be abused"; I personally believed in the "eye for an eye" justice we'd dished out to those cops who'd abused *their* power, but was sorry it had cost Dell his tracks. He was only twenty-two years old, but he damn well deserved them.

By the end of May, U.N. forces in the east were really giving the enemy a run for their money, and now the 25th Division was ready to put the squeeze on the Chinese from the other side. The Wolfhound and Cacti regiments were to lead this assault from the west, jumping through the Deuce-Four to attack into the Kumhwa Valley. The day before the operation, 31 May, our unit was trucked from Uijongbu down a dry creekbed which was to serve as our main road. Easy Company's assembly area was a ridge running down behind the front line, with the company CP located at the bottom.

It was payday, traditionally the peacetime Army's day off, that wonderful, lazy day once a month when you put aside soldiering for the roll of the dice and the snap of the cards. We were still in reserve (which was as close to peacetime as anything in a war zone), so we whiled away the hours pretending we were in Las Vegas. I'd learned to play poker in Trieste, the same place I learned the basics of just about everything. I don't know whether I'd read it in a book or seen it in a film, but at some stage early in life I'd concluded that great warriors were usually great poker players (it made sense, too, because in many ways the skills required in poker are the same ones you need on the battlefield: boldness, a cool head, and the ability to bluff), so it was only natural for me to feel compelled to be the best poker player on the block.

In Italy, on payday (or "the day the eagle shits") we got paid early in the morning by the officers, who'd then go away for the day. The company area would then become our own gambling casino, the recreation room a makeshift Las Vegas devoted to blackjack, craps, and poker. NCOs and enlisted personnel could play, but usually by midnight only four or five NCOs would be left, the novices having long before been tapped out. After a couple of days (or nights, really) more, most all of the company's money would be consolidated further, between a couple of guys. These two would play the big winners from the other companies, the money being consolidated even more, until finally the big winners of the three battalions—each of whom might have ten thousand dollars to play with—would meet at the Regimental NCO Club for the final play-offs. The next day, it wasn't unusual for news to filter down that some guy had won up to fifty thousand dollars the night before.

In that poker is very much a science, you can read as much as you like about it, but you really can't be good at it without playing a hell of a lot. I'd started as soon as I got to Italy, and it took all four years I was there to really get it down. At first I'd been limited by finances: every month I was sending $37.50 home to my grandmother (in the form of a $50 savings bond), and I couldn't play much poker with the twelve and a half bucks left over from my pay. Like most guys, I sold my cigarettes on the black market, which brought in a couple of hundred more—it was sufficient to get started with, at least. At first I'd last about an hour at the table, then two or three. But whenever I got tapped out, I didn't leave. Instead, I'd go to the sharpest guy I saw there, sit down behind him and watch. There were some great players—Sergeant Neil, who was in charge of the mess hall, and Sergeants English, McAlweny, and Randall Johnson—who knew, simply from my hanging around, that they were teaching me; sometimes one of them might even show me his hand, and I could see how he played, what he played, and *when*—and I would just take the best I could from him. As time passed, I began to stay in the games longer and longer, until, by the time I left Trieste in 1950, I was always in the finals and frequently a big winner.

My luck hadn't left me in Korea (except when Dell Evans was around), and now, waiting to jump off into the Kumhwa, I was on a bona fide winning streak. We played all day, and one by one, all my opponents fell by the wayside. At nightfall we continued by the light of our campfire, but by then I'd pretty well cleaned out the gamblers, so we decided it was time to quit. I must have won at least two grand; I didn't bother counting it, just stuffed the loot into my fatigue jacket, feeling a bit disappointed that I had nowhere to blow it.

Throughout the day we'd taken light incoming, but nothing close and nothing big. Our platoon CP was in a draw, and since we hadn't taken any incoming in our area, we hadn't bothered digging in. I'd made the platoon dig for sure, but not the CP, and now that it was dark, it seemed pretty pointless to get carried away scratching out a hole, since we were jumping off first thing in the morning. The rest of my CP group—the doc, RTO Lee Livesay, assistant platoon sergeant Whitey Snyder, and platoon sergeant Charlie Greer—agreed, so we snapped together our ponchos and made a big lean-to, which we hunkered down under solely to keep out the drizzling rain.

Soon after we'd settled in, the Chinese artillery got serious, blasting all over E Company's position. Then our guns got into the act, and the next thing we knew, a big artillery duel was raging between the good guys and the bad guys. The only problem was that our lean-to was right in the middle, getting the overs and shorts from both. For some reason, it didn't bother me. The guys were saying, "Shit, we should dig," and I kept telling them not to worry about it, that we had a great position here in this draw. "Natural protection," I said.

But then I heard the son of a bitch coming. I could hear the incoming whistle, loud and clear in the dark. And it started coming in louder and louder. We flopped onto our bellies and hugged the ground. Greer was next to me; he flung his arm across my back as the incoming round kept screaming. It was going to land right on top of us, I knew it—and it did, right at the edge of the goddamned poncho, with an earsplitting roar.

"Everybody here? *Anybody* here?" I asked when the dust settled and the ringing stopped.

The doc, Lee, and Whitey all said they were okay, and then Greer said, "I'm hit."

Greer had just returned from a wound he'd gotten up north. A .50-cal slug had torn through the muscle and tissue of one of his arms, just missing the bone. He had an incredible scar from it, and now the poor guy told me he'd gotten it again, this time in the other arm.

The rest of the CP group, in the meantime, were beginning to sit up, checking out all the places where mud, debris, and equipment had slammed against them when the round exploded, to see if they'd been wounded. Amazingly, Greer was the only one. I was still prone, waiting for Greer to move his injured arm. When he finally tried, I felt blood, and a lot of pain. "Wait a minute," I said. "I think I'm hit, too." At first we couldn't work out the connection. Then we discovered that Greer's arm was nailed to my back.

A shard of shrapnel, about eight inches long and half an inch thick, had pierced his arm in exactly the same way the bullet had. It had missed the bone, gone the whole way through the muscle and tissue, then out the other side and into my back. If Greer hadn't been such a big guy, if he hadn't had such huge arms, and if he hadn't thrown one of them across me, I would have been dead. But as it was I was alive and kicking, with a good wound and a kit full of money; as we pried Greer's arm off my back, all I could think was *Japan, here I come.* With great delight, I flipped on my radio and called Dell. "I'm hit, Greer's hit, and Whitey's taking over."

"How bad are you guys hit?"

"I think it's pretty bad. In the back for me. Greer got it in the arm. We're going down to the aid station now. I'll see you on the way out."

Greer and I started down the draw, hindered by thorny bushes and scrub trees growing on the ridge, as well as by the artillery that was still popping all around us. We got to Dell's CP. He was concerned about our wounds, and about losing a platoon leader and platoon sergeant just before jump-off. I took his mind off it—first of all, I reminded him, Whitey had been a WW II combat platoon sergeant and he could handle the platoon better than Greer and I put together, and second, I was going to Japan and I was loaded with dough, "So you're not going to get a goddamned cent of it!" (The thing was, if I hadn't gotten hit, the next big game would have been the play-offs down at Company, and Dell would most likely have cleaned me out.) I really rubbed it in, but my poker-playing nemesis wasn't even ruffled. He knew there'd be a next time. Just before we left the CP I gave Dell my treasured German Mauser machine pistol. It was a Chink officer's pistol—a real prize—and I didn't want it to be knocked off by some rear-echelon doc, as my Waltham watch had been after 6 February. "Look after this, will you?" I asked him; for some reason, it really mattered.

The battalion aid station was overflowing with wounded. *Screw this*, I thought; *we'll wait in line forever.* A litter jeep was parked outside; we piled in and the jeep slowly rocked its way down the creekbed road. Much heavier Chink artillery was coming in now, fast and furious. Fires blazed in the darkness—American artillery pieces that had taken direct hits. It was a bad scene: rounds were smacking all around the jeep, and there we were, well outside the battalion area, traveling about three miles an hour with the headlights off. I told the driver to flip on his lights and make tracks. No can do, he said, we were beyond the light line. I said, "Fuck the light line. We're talking about our asses!"

He flipped on the lights and we buzzed down the creekbed at a fast clip, leaving all that incoming behind. A few miles down the road, an MP stopped the jeep. "GET THOSE LIGHTS OFF!"

"Battalion surgeon!" I called out. He shot his flashlight at my bar, which I'd pinned onto my steel pot. "Got some critically wounded here, got to get them out!"

"Yes, sir!" he said with a smart salute. We tore off.

The regimental aid facilities had taken a direct hit; there were wounded everywhere. Some of the medics were in worse shape than their patients. They were brave men, the docs, patching people, ignoring their own wounds. An aid man came along. "Where're you hit?"

"The back," I said.

"Does it hurt when you breathe?"

As a matter of fact, it didn't. But I was glad he asked the question; it was the million-dollar question, which—if I answered correctly—would be my magic ticket to Japan. "Yeah, doc," I replied. "A lot."

A surgeon came up next, had a look, and asked if it hurt when I breathed. I felt really guilty bullshitting this guy, because he looked a lot worse off than I did—he'd gotten it in the back, too. But I kept thinking of the bright lights of Japan, and all this dough I had burning a hole in my pocket. "Oh, shit, doc, yes. Yes! Like daggers, every time I breathe."

Both Greer and I were evacuated to Division Clearing. The medics suspected that my left lung was collapsed, and a splinter of shrapnel was still in my back. By this time it was morning, and I was a litter case marked "Critical." I still hadn't been x-rayed, but again came the million-dollar question: did it hurt when I breathed. My response, which was getting better all the time—"It's killing me! Doc, do you think I'm going to make it?"—got me back to MASH, and from there onto a hospital train back to Pusan.

Litters were stacked three-high on both sides of the crowded ambulance train. The wounded composed a fair slice of the United Nations forces fighting in Korea: Turks, English, French, Greeks, Aussies, and Yanks. Most were noncritical—leg, arm, and back wounds that didn't require intensive care—which was all for the best, because our nurse was a bulldog. No compassion and strictly business. She thumped a needle in my ass and lectured me about staying put, lest the shrapnel splinter lacerate my collapsed lung further. I moaned and groaned and nodded, all the while keeping my eye on the hot crap game that was roaring in the aisle at the foot of my litter. "You must keep on your left side!" she barked. *I want into that game*, I thought.

The minute the Iron Florence Nightingale went on to the next car, I was in, knee-deep. I still had two grand of 3d Platoon's loot, and with that kind of backing, I could almost buy my luck. And I was hot—red-hot. On one occasion I made seven straight passes. The bucks were rolling in, in U.S. Military Payment Certificates (MPCs), lire, drachmas, pounds, and francs; my left hand could barely wrap itself around the wad of United Nations funny money I was collecting, as my right hand went on making pass after pass. Just as I lost the dice and faded into the crowd, Florence marched back into our car. I slipped back into my litter and was following orders by the

time Her Sternness came by. Trying to ignore the resentful glares of my
fellow gamblers (who'd lost the chance to win back their money), I
concentrated on sorting and counting my loot—now close to four grand—
and daydreaming about Japan.

The train pulled into the station at Taijon. Delayed for four hours, we
were told. Walking wounded could visit a nearby Red Cross Club, but litter
patients had to stay on board. *Shit.* But then dear Florence was replaced by
a laid-back medical corpsman who, not knowing about my "lung condition," told me he'd look the other way "if you want to stretch your legs,
Lieutenant."

The Army sergeant who ran the train depot was wearing the Wolfhound
crest. I hadn't known him; he'd been badly hit, placed on limited duty, and
was now a railroad man. "Come over to my place," he offered. "Got a bottle
of Daniel's there." The guy's "place" turned out to be a railway car that he'd
converted into a plush—at least by an infantryman's standards—mobile
apartment. One corner was stacked with loot. "I take what I need from the
supply trains and a little extra for swapping," he said. "Sure beats climbing
hills and getting shot at."

I readily agreed, especially as I looked over the fine body of his little
Korean mama-san. The railroad man caught my hungry stare. "She's yours,
old buddy." He told her he was "going out to check my trains—take care of
my friend here," and he left. The girl and I cracked open another bottle of
whiskey and hopped into the sack; she wasn't much to look at, but I didn't
spend a lot of time looking.

There's a thing about combat soldiers and sex. On one hand, it's the most
important activity in the world. On the other, it means nothing at all. Sure,
sometimes it was a love thing, but most times it was just a good, hard screw.
You were always horny and never discriminating; you weren't looking for
love, you were looking for pussy. *Pussy.* One word. And no matter who it
was or how it was, that's what it came down to in that all-male,
ultramasculine world of the Army. You'd come back from leave and the first
question your buddies would ask was, "Did you get some pussy?"

"Yeah, it was great," you'd reply, even if you'd struck out. "Best pussy I've
had in a long time."

"*I want some pussy*" rolled off a soldier's tongue as easily as "I want a
drink." Getting as much pussy as you could was part of the role: proving
yourself in the cot was as important as proving yourself on the battlefield.
Tribal behavior, I guess—the great warrior, the great conqueror of all lands
and all broads—or some deep psychological thing: knowing you might get
killed and wanting to plant the old seed before you went. Or maybe it started
in Hollywood. Who knows? Who cares? All I know is we talked about it a

hell of a lot more than we got it—but when we got it, it was pretty damn good.

"Train's leaving in twenty minutes, old buddy," said the railroad man when he returned to find an exhausted, drunk, but well-screwed trooper. He walked me to the train; I thanked him for his hospitality. "We Wolfhounds gotta stick together," he said. "Hope you get to Japan. Take care, ya' hear?" I'd known the guy less than a few hours, yet he treated me like a brother—the Wolfhounds were a very special fraternity. We said good-bye. I got back on the train, slipped into my litter, and dutifully laid down on my left side to take the pressure off my poor overworked lung.

The 3d Station Hospital stuck out like a sore thumb in the Pusan shantytown that surrounded it. What a terrible place for my journey to end. The doc who examined my wound said, "Good news, son. No lung damage whatsoever. You'll be back with your unit in no time." It hit me like a death sentence. No lung damage meant no Japan. No Land of the Rising Sun. No place decent to spend my money. It really was a hell of a blow, and the only compensation was my new officer status, which had me living like a king in semiprivate luxury.

It was an eye-opener, this difference between the officer and soldier worlds—like a first-class hotel to a Salvation Army flophouse. In the enlisted wards, the rows upon rows of crushed bodies were "requirements" with numbers; just to provide basic maintenance, their nurses had to run around like needle-prodding machines. In the officers' wards, a guy's every need was catered to. He was special, and the nurses had time to be human. It was like two different planets. The highlight of my stay, though, was the afternoon I shared my bed with Jennifer Jones, the movie star, who was on a USO tour. Sad to say, I was asleep at the time. She sat on my bed, talked to the other guys, and left before I woke up. What a razzing I took from my roommates.

Pusan was the asshole of the universe: a drab, dirty war town where the sun didn't shine. The train ticket was open; it was an unstated hospital policy that a returnee could lose himself in the city for a few days. I couldn't stand the place, so I took the next train north, thinking I might hop off and visit my railroad buddy and his girlfriend in Taijon. Before I left I bought a case of Southern Comfort from a PX sergeant for fifty dollars a bottle. The stuff sold legally for three bucks, but I didn't care. What else was I going to spend my loot on? At least I could get the boys drunk, and besides, they really bought it with their own dough. (Gambling money was "easy come, easy go" anyway; it didn't have the same value as the stuff you'd sweated for.)

On the train I got drunk with a young 187th Airborne squad leader. He had Shirley Temple dimples, which he'd gotten catching a slug. "Went in one cheek and right out the other," he said. "I was hollering at my squad. Didn't even know I was hit till I tasted the blood." We toasted his Rakkasan paratroopers,* and then we toasted the Wolfhounds; we even toasted the Chinese, and got so drunk that I slept right through Taijon.

"But goddamn, Hack, it's good to see you. And especially good to sip a little Comfort," Dell Evans said when I got back to Easy. He was still the skipper, but his days were numbered; it seemed that his promotion papers to captain had been removed from channels as a result of the Uijongbu "Big Stoop" affair (which meant the first guy with tracks to walk into the battalion would probably be sent to Easy to take over the reins). It was a damn shame.

I got back my Mauser and we caught up on events. Dell told me the division had been on the attack since the day after I got hit; Easy had spearheaded the breakthrough and led the way ever since. Now they were in the fourteenth day of humping over hill and dale in the Kumhwa Valley. They'd overrun enough guns and matériel to equip two Chinese divisions, as well as a field hospital; Easy was moving so fast that the new battalion CO (Colonel Cork had been relieved) ordered Dell to stop so that his flank units could catch up. "To hell with slowing up!" Dell had responded. "Let them catch us. We're on the enemy's heels—we have to pursue the advantage now!" Finally the CO agreed, as long as Dell sent patrols back during the night to keep contact with the flank units—a two-mile ordeal for the men assigned this duty.

Dell himself was in for another Silver Star. On about the fifth day of the action, he'd discovered a large enemy force to Easy's rear. At the time, the company's assault elements had been in the middle of some serious hand-to-hand combat, but Dell had successfully disengaged them, gotten his reserve platoon into good blocking positions and heavy artillery fire onto the Chinese, and brought the enemy to their knees. "The boys did good, Hack," Dell said, smiling. But that had been the high point of the whole two weeks; generally it had been far less than fun. At one stage Easy outran its supply tail, and some of the men had been on the verge of mutiny after three full days without so much as a C-ration meal. And to top the whole thing off, somehow word had gotten around that Easy was lost somewhere in the valley, so when the guys had reached the hill above their tie-in point with the 89th Tank, the tank battalion thought they were enemy and opened fire on them. "Now that'll ruin your whole day for you!" Dell laughed. Luckily no one got hurt.

I dropped a bottle of booze in to the topkick, and gave him six more to

* The men of the 187th Airborne were the Rakkasans just as the men of the 27th Infantry were Wolfhounds. *Rakkasan* is Japanese for parachute.

safeguard until 3d Platoon went into reserve. Bearing gifts of the remaining three, I rejoined my unit. Japan or no Japan, it was good to be back. All the old guys gathered at my platoon CP, leaving the replacements to guard the front; we drank down the Comfort all at one sitting, and told tales of war and railroad stations until darkness broke up our little reunion.

We continued attacking north through the Kumhwa Valley. It was bitching terrain—straight up and straight down, with no roads and few trails in our sector. It took nine hours to pack wounded to Battalion, and about the same time to bring up ammo and supplies; it was no fun, with the only redeeming feature being that the Chinese were struggling even more than we were. Enemy resistance was virtually nonexistent. Had someone given us the word we could have marched right on to the Yalu. As it happened, we did get the word, but the message was entirely different from the one we'd expected to hear.

In late June, after one year's hard fighting, the U.S. Eighth Army started digging in deep on some high ground north of the 38th parallel, which we'd recently restored. We built sandbagged bunkers and installed barbed-wire barriers, with plenty of mines and booby traps. The Chinks were nowhere in sight—if ever there was a time to keep moving this was it—but the word was *stop*. There were rumors of peace talks, though, which was good news for everyone; we all shared the hope that we would soon see a cease-fire. All things considered, it was probably for the best that our youthful naïveté prevented us from recognizing the enemy's real intention: to fuel the peace flame only to gain time to rebuild its gutted forces. Still, once the heavy field fortification work was over, we started enjoying the sitzkrieg life until someone remembered that, peace talks or no peace talks, there was still a war going on, and the regiment started vigorously patrolling deep into no-man's-land.

One of 3d Platoon's first missions was to conduct a combat patrol a few miles in front of our position—an air observer had seen Chinese in a bombed-out village. I stripped the platoon down to three lean squads and moved out before dawn. By first light we were set up on a small hill a few hundred yards from the reported sightings. We took the enemy by surprise, killing fifteen and capturing four with no friendly casualties. There was no question in my mind now that the Chinese were on their last legs. Our opponents in the village were sick and hungry, with little will to fight, and seemed more like rear-echelon troops. I sent the POWs back with a squad while the rest of us poked around the valley. We found two more Chinamen who looked as if they'd been abandoned by their unit. Both were more dead than alive, too weak even to brush away the flies. We pretended we didn't find them.

The squad with the POWs was still an hour from friendly lines when we caught up with it—the men had been slowed down by the wounded prisoners. We had instructions to get home before dark; "Get back as soon as you can," I told them, as the rest of us passed through and hotfooted it back so we could be in our defensive positions by nightfall.

Several hours later the squad joined us. I called Company on the field phone. "Where's the Old Man?" I asked when an unfamiliar voice answered the call.

"Lieutenant Evans is checking the line."

"Okay, listen. The POWs are here. I'm sending them to your CP."

"Don't bother, Lieutenant," replied the voice through the wire. "They've got no intelligence value. Battalion has seven already from their outfit. Just shoot them."

"No way."

"What do you mean, no way?"

"Just what I said. No fucking way."

"All right, Lieutenant, how do you propose we get them to Battalion, then?"

This joker was looking at the POWs not as a human problem but as a logistics one: four weak and wounded POWs, a nine-hour walk at night over rough terrain to Battalion HQ—we'd lose at least four rifles as escorts. But it wasn't that simple to me. It wasn't even the issue. These were innocent soldiers, unarmed prisoners—and always in my head was the strong belief, *But for the grace of God, there go I.*

"Look," I said, "I'm not doing anything till I talk to Lieutenant Evans. He'll figure out something. Meantime I'll get the prisoners dug in."

As I hung up the field phone I saw one of my guys hanging around the CP door. I didn't know how long he'd been there; he was kind of a weird guy anyway—never said much and *always* seemed to be brooding over the problems of the world. The funny thing was, when you put this kid in a battle he was a tiger—a brilliant, brave combat stud—but the minute it got quiet, he'd revert to being resident weirdo. Anyway, he was a good man and I knew I could count on him to organize the POWs; I gave him the job and he shuffled out without a change of expression.

A short while later, I headed out of the CP to check 3d Platoon's positions. I saw Soldier Weirdo overseeing the prisoners; he had them digging in for the night, each with his own little foxhole. I went on down the line, and then, out of the blue, I heard gunfire back behind my CP. I ran over to find Soldier Weirdo holding a still-smoking pistol. He'd emptied the magazine into the POWs after he'd made each one dig his own grave. "They tried to make a break," he explained.

We never spoke again. The kid had lost me forever, and within a week, I got him transferred out. And I was pissed off at whoever that bastard was at the company CP (he was probably laughing now). I knew why he'd said those guys should be shot, but it didn't make it right. It was not the way to play the game. It was an atrocity. But he and Soldier Weirdo alone would carry the burden of those deaths for the rest of their lives—I didn't blow the whistle. No one blew the whistle. All of us had seen too many atrocities, and what is war anyway but one big, raging atrocity? It was something every doughfoot—regardless of which side he was on—knew to the bottom of his soul. Both sides had killers and sadists (Like PFC Charles in George Company, who shot the two POWs on 6 February. It wasn't until a month or so after that that I realized he was crazy. We'd been walking down a road when we passed an old South Korean man with a long, flowing beard; Charles had pulled out his Zippo lighter, grabbed the old man, and set fire to his beard.), but each side had battlefield pragmatists, too. One of the guys in the platoon summed up the most recent incident, in his friend Soldier Weirdo's defense, with, "The fuckers would have kicked off before they got to Battalion anyway. The kid just shortened their misery."

Soon after this event, Dell Evans became the battalion Intelligence officer, replaced in the company by a mouse named Captain Pierson. Within a week Pierson, who wasn't even an infantryman (he was Artillery), had virtually destroyed the morale of Company E. It seemed impossible, but it was true. *Shave your face, blouse your trousers, wear your helmet and all your equipment,* he ordered. Unshaved and stripped down, Easy had spent the previous year achieving one of the finest fighting records of any company in the U.S. Army. It had been awarded several individual Presidential Unit Citations, and had been skippered by Medal of Honor winners Reginald Desiderio (awarded posthumously) and Lewis Millett, as well as DSC winner Phil Gilchrist (for Objective Logan) and Dell Evans. An outfit is only as good as its commander—Desiderio, Millett, Gilchrist, and Evans had made Easy the proud, effective unit that it was. And now this little mouse was tearing us apart.

Morale and fighting spirit plummeted. "Hope the bastard doesn't get in front of me during an attack—I might slip and blow his head off" was the old-timers' attitude toward the new Easy 6. Fortunately for them *and* Captain Pierson, the much-rumored rotation program (which eventually would make Korea a one-year tour) had started in April, and everyone was too busy adding up his points and keeping abreast of the changing policy to grease the new Old Man.

After forty-five straight days on the line, we were relieved. "Hooray! It's back to beers, broads, and the good life," shouted ace machine gunner

Sovereign as we loaded trucks and headed south. But the trucks didn't take us to the rear. Little did we know we were being shifted from the quiet western sector of the Kumhwa Valley to the red-hot eastern side.

The enemy held the high ground; from the towering slopes of "Papasan," Hill 1062, the Chinese had commanding views of the entire valley. And as well as having such brilliant observation, the enemy also had plenty of indirect mortar and artillery support—the Wolfhounds had jumped out of the frying pan and into the fire. The hardest hit by this reality were the high-point rotation guys, who had figured they'd never see the front line again. There were no celebrations that day in the Land of the Morning Calm.

That evening we conducted a night relief without incident, but when the fog lifted in the morning we found ourselves looking straight into enemy guns on the higher ground across the valley. Fortunately, 3d Platoon drew the open right flank, which was the farthest away from both the Chinese *and* Captain Pierson's CP.

The first two days we followed the schedule of the relieved unit so the Chinese wouldn't get wind of the switch until we were set. We stayed in our holes and dug even deeper. Just at dusk on the second day, the Chinks clobbered the company front with a stiff barrage of mortar fire. This was followed by a PA announcement from the Chinese trenches: "Welcome, Wolfhounds. We kill all of you." So much for military security and our clandestine relief. This message was repeated over and over, until a crazy little Hawaiian in my platoon, Takashi Maki, jumped out of his hole, stood in the open, and screamed back, "Fuck you, Chinamen. Fuck you! Come and get us, you lousy sons of bitches!" Chink psychological warfare couldn't faze a Hawaiian, especially the likes of Maki, who attacked up hills shouting "Yea, Wolfhounds!"

I did love those Hawaiians, and after eight months of being knee-deep in little Buddha-heads, I'd kind of become one. I spoke pidgin ("Ey, man, me go down company CP and get order, okay, brah?"), scooped poi with my fingers, and, with them, waited with great anticipation for the next "care" package of abalone and other Island goodies. When Dell had found out how much I respected the Hawaiians, he'd gone out of his way to assign as many as he could to 3d Platoon, and when the fighting was heavy, we all got along fine. But when the war became static and boring, and with the arrival of the Pierson types, the Island boys were a wild bunch to control. I was constantly in hot water because of their shenanigans.

Now Pierson called on the sound-power from his CP, demanding the name and platoon of the soldier who had yelled back at the Chinese. He didn't get it. We hadn't heard a thing.

Down at Battalion, Intelligence Officer Dell Evans needed a prisoner—a POW could tell him who we faced on Hill 1062 and what their intentions were. It was only natural for him to call on his old comrades for help: "Hack, you should conduct this raid. If you volunteer, I'll fix it so the operation comes directly under Battalion control. You can plan it yourself, however you want, and I'll get your platoon off the line for a few days to get ready." Bored with just sitting there day after day on the receiving end of Chinese incoming, and with the assurance that 3d Platoon would get a break and Pierson would not be involved, I said yes. We were moved off the line and were given three days to plan, rehearse, and execute the raid.

We set up at E Company's supply trains. It was the first time 3d Platoon had been off the line in more than two months, and immediately one of our scroungers went out to get some steaks. While the other guys cleaned up and rested, Dell, a few key leaders, and I planned the operation in detail. What we devised was simple, bold, and maximized shock and surprise.

I decided on a lightning tank-infantry daylight strike that would put us into the Chinese positions before they knew what hit them; shock action and speed would be the key to the Chinks' front door, similar to the way Captain Michaely had zoomed through Suwon in January. We'd go with a stripped-down platoon—only rifles, BARs, and fighters—the heavier stuff and the timid could stay home. The surprise would come from our daring (no one in his right mind would ever attack a Chinese main battle position of at least a couple of regiments with one platoon in broad daylight) and our timing (we'd jump off at 1700, which was unheard of—the Americans had been attacking at dawn since Washington was the Main Man). The timing element was something I'd learned from Prazenka; whenever we'd patrolled the Trieste borders and outposts, we'd vary our times and routes to keep the Jugs off guard. "You can't be like some bus pulling into a station the same time every day," he'd said.

Surprise through stealth was impossible—we'd be crossing a wide-open field of no-man's-land—but I figured we could still catch the Chinese asleep, hit them while they were dazed, and run before they woke up. We laid on a fire plan that included every artillery tube in the corps area that could strike Hill 1062 and its adjoining hills. A maximum mix of smoke, Willie Peter, and high explosives would be used to blind and shock the defenders—it would slam down on the enemy in a wall of smoking steel from the moment we jumped off until we got home.

The first night behind the lines we ate steaks, sang around a big bonfire, and got knee-knocking drunk on the six remaining bottles of Southern Comfort, augmented by a gallon or two of scrounged medical alcohol. The next day, with heads slightly the worse for wear, we conducted rehearsals with the tank and track platoon that composed our little task force, on terrain similar to our objective.

That night, while the platoon finished up the medical alcohol in a half-hearted attempt to recapture the fun of the night before, I took two NCOs for a recon. We started at the LD and carefully probed with trench knives, clearing out a dozen cake-sized U.S. antitank mines as we marked a path for our track vehicles with small pieces of white engineer tape. A bomb-damaged bridge spanned the north-south main road; I looked at it carefully but concluded it probably wouldn't take the weight of a Sherman, so we probed a big looping path around the bridge through a fordable creek, then across an open rice paddy and back to the road.

The map showed the road forming a lazy S, and the contours indicated a slight slope at the top end. This was the ridge where we planned to dismount and commence our assault into the rear of the Chinese positions, so I wanted to have a look at it. We carefully slipped along the side of the road, our movements masked by darkness and the whoosh and impact of U.S. artillery H&I fire.

U.S. flares were popping in the valley to our west. We had coordinated our patrol and asked that no flares be used in the 2d Battalion's area during our recon, but in battle at least 10 percent never get the word. Tonight it was a welcome snafu. One came in close and we hit the ground, only to see in its surreal light a Chinese sentry on the road about twenty-five yards away. We couldn't chance getting around him, and knocking him off would risk blowing tomorrow's raid. *Live and let live*, I thought as I signaled to withdraw.

August eighth dawned, an overcast, rainy day. It was a perfect day for the mission; the Chinks would be like us, all hunkered down in their positions, trying to stay dry. We made final preparations for the attack: test-firing and cleaning weapons, last-minute briefings, and organizing a forward aid station just behind the LD. We married up with the tanks and tracks, and at 1700 hours we shot down the road like an express train, to the deafening roar of massed artillery fire. The tanks, with the stripped-down 3d Platoon riding piggyback, quickly and easily rolled through the lanes we'd cut in the minefield, and swung behind the enemy positions. The operation was going exactly to plan. Hill 1062 and all key enemy terrain around our objective were simultaneously being blistered with HE, Willie Peter, and smoke. The enemy was blind and surprise was ours. We dismounted the tanks and rushed to the base of the hill. And stopped. I could not believe what my eyes were telling my head.

The gradual slope we'd expected from the map was absolutely vertical. *The best-laid plans of mice and men . . . and one goddamned Chinese sentry,* I thought. "You can read all kinds of books you want and you can make all kinds of plans you want," Steve Prazenka had said, "but when you get out in the field those books and those plans might not meet the eye of the situation you find there. So you just have to roll with it." *Right, Steve. Let's roll . . .* I thought as I slung my M-1 across my back and started climbing hand over hand, straight up. My guys followed. No orders were given; the men in the 3d Platoon were a magnificent team—they'd stayed loose, flexible, and, above all, cool. Meanwhile, the tanks had pulled back off the road and joined the tracks in the cleared lane through the open rice paddy east of the road; together they were laying down welcome, murderous overhead support fire.

When I got to the top I jumped into a trench, almost on top of two enemy soldiers. I shot them both, then started blasting stunned Chinamen on my left and right. Meanwhile my guys poured into the trench. We fanned out through the intricate, mazelike trench system, knocking the Chinese defenders off as we went. When we crested the ridge we looked down onto the enemy's main battle positions. They were manned only by a light security force, but behind the main positions, in a deep draw, was what looked like a complete rifle company. They'd been eating; now they scurried for cover while our point-blank plunging fire took a heavy toll.

Our artillery was still slamming in. We were now in complete control of the ridge and had captured three prisoners—it was time to withdraw. We quickly slid back the way we had come while the tanks returned to the base of the hill to pick us up. I sent the wounded down first with two squads and the prisoners, and stayed with a couple men to hold the Chink positions until the WIA were loaded and our task force ready to split. Artillery, quad-50, and tank fire kept the stunned Chinese at bay when we, too, finally slid down the hill.

After I'd given the order to withdraw, one of the tracks had panicked, left the cleared lane in the rice paddy, and hit a mine. Now the disabled vehicle was sitting right across the lane itself, blocking our only escape through the minefield. Meanwhile, the Chinese were getting themselves together. They started putting down a lot of fire—small arms, mortar, artillery, and SP. As yet they didn't have our range, but even with their lousy commo, it wouldn't take long. There was only one alternative. I shouted to the tank platoon leader, "Let's try one tank over that bridge, and if the son of a bitch holds, we'll go out that way."

The thirty-six-ton Sherman gingerly rolled across the semicollapsed bridge. The bridge sagged, swayed, but held. I radioed the crew of the damaged track to abandon their vehicle, load on other tracks, and follow the lead Sherman's trail to get the hell out of there. Once my own tank had crossed the bridge, I ordered the tank platoon leader to fire a couple of armor-piercing rounds into the disabled track. No way was I going to have those four .50-calibers dismounted by the enemy and remounted on the hill facing my platoon. The rounds split the thin-skinned vehicle in half, and it burst into flames.

We made it back—sixteen wounded and nobody badly hurt, no friendly dead, and three prisoners. Not a bad show. I got off my tank and was making sure our wounded were being looked after when a lieutenant colonel raced up, bellowing like a bull. "Who's in charge here?"

"I am, sir. Second Lieutenant Hackworth."

"And who gave the order for destroying my track?"

"I did, sir."

"Well, I'm going to have you pay for it! That's a hundred and twenty thousand dollars! You do not have the authority to destroy my vehicles!"

Lieutenant Colonel Henry, CO of the 21st AA Battalion, raged on, chewing my ass for not going into the minefield with a tank and winching his damn track out. I tried to explain that it was so hot out there that no infantry soldier would have lived, that we'd barely gotten his crew out alive. He did not want to hear. Finally I got pissed off. *Very* pissed off. I told him that no way was I going to risk one infantryman for a rotten piece of twisted steel, that my people's lives were more important than his goddamned clapped-out track, and that if I had to make the same decision again I would do it "in spades."

Colonel Henry was livid. *"You will pay for this!"* he screamed.

A jeep screeched up, and out of it jumped my regimental commander, Colonel George B. Sloan; the divisional commander, Major General Ira P. Swift; and the corps commander, Major General John "Iron Mike" O'Daniel, all three great combat leaders of World War II. General O'Daniel boomed out, "Where is the platoon leader?"

Oh, shit, I really must be in trouble now, I thought. "Sir, Second Lieutenant Hackworth," I reported.

"Second Lieutenant, you are a First Lieutenant as of now. And," O'Daniel said, thumping a Silver Star on my chest, "I'm also recommending you for the Distinguished Service Cross. I watched the complete attack from the regimental OP and it was outstanding. Outstanding! It was one of the finest demonstrations of professionalism and leadership I have seen in combat. Your platoon operated as a perfect military force. I want you to tell me which soldiers you want me to decorate."

"All of them, sir!" I said, and right then and there, every man of my platoon who went on that raid was given a Bronze or Silver Star by this fine fighting corps commander.

Sometime during my chat with General O'Daniel, the outraged Colonel Henry crawled away, and I heard nothing else about his precious track. More and more I was seeing officers like him, ones whose priorities were, to my mind anyway, 180 degrees out. This guy happened to be insanely obsessed with his machine. Others, like Captain Pierson and the guys who replaced Colonel Murch as 2d Battalion CO, seemed unskilled in their trade and didn't understand—or even try to understand—what made combat men tick.

By the time of this raid, I'd had a gut full of all of them. And I'd really enjoyed the opportunity to organize and execute my own plans for this mission; it had been great not to have to bow to the demands of men who didn't know what they were talking about to begin with. So when, soon after the 8 August mission, Colonel Sloan offered me a volunteer unit—a completely independent command, a unit that I could handpick, organize, and train as I saw fit—it was difficult to refuse.

I told the guys in my platoon. "We're going with you!" they said, and a fair number of them did. I talked to Schroeder and Crispino, who were both still over in G Company. "Roger on that, Hack . . . I'm on my way," Chris said, but good, steady old Schroeder, who'd been with the 3d of G since long before the war (and by now was the only original member left), decided to stick with George. Chris brought a bunch of my old platoon with him, though, and along with the Easy guys, they provided a cadre of men whom I knew and trusted, who knew me and my style of leadership, and who, in their individual ways, would give shape to the unit we soon would create: the 27th Wolfhound Raiders.

6 THE ONLY GAME IN TOWN

It's not a simple matter to get a company of infantry and say, "You guys are going out on a patrol tonight to capture some Chinese prisoners"; the average military unit doesn't have the unique skills necessary for the conduct of successful night operations against an entrenched enemy. We decided we needed a specialized unit, for the specific purpose of conducting patrols against enemy positions all along the regimental front, with the specific mission of taking prisoners as a means of gathering intelligence and information. The question of who would command this unit, which we called the Wolfhound Raiders, of course, received a lot of attention, and I recall being surprised that the name of this young lieutenant percolated right up and everybody said, "Yeah, that guy is something else," and it was Hackworth.

Colonel George B. Sloan, USA, Ret.
Regimental CO, 27th Infantry
Korea, 1951

RAIDER volunteers came from every outfit in the regiment, about four hundred in all. Colonel Sloan had not set a strength limit, but four hundred we did not need—our requirement was more like forty.

Other than the guys from G and E, the volunteers were a mixed bag: super gung-ho types who did not like trench warfare, eight balls a cunning topkick was trying to unload, bored troops just looking for adventure. We had little time to cull through the herd of would-be warriors—we were on a short fuse to get ready, with our first raid scheduled within a month—so I relied on a few of the former E and G NCOs (who knew what we were looking for) to conduct the initial interviews. They quickly sent the jerks and thrill seekers marching; the best and bravest they sent to me. Crispino, whom I'd made Raider platoon sergeant, sat in on my sessions with these "first cut" candidates, and between the two of us it was usually easy to assess a man's mettle. For the times when it wasn't, Chris had devised a brilliant screening technique that instantly separated the men from the boys.

He'd taken the powder out of a frag grenade and fired the primer cap separately. Then he'd reassembled the thing, and now, as I interviewed potential Raiders, Chris would sit there playing with this dummy grenade. Near the end of the session, if I still wasn't sure about a man, I'd give Chris a wink and he'd "accidentally" drop the grenade. The safety pin would fall out and we'd jump back—horror and shock on our faces—meanwhile studying the guy's response to this "live" grenade spinning around on the floor. If the volunteer froze, we knew we didn't want him. If he threw himself on the grenade, we thought he was nuts (or at least suicidal) and we didn't want him either. But if he grabbed the thing and threw it out of the tent, or if he cut a trail out of the place himself, we knew he had good sense—he was a cool hombre, and real Raider material.

We were faced with the same dilemma a high-school football coach faces each fall, when every freshman expects to make the varsity squad. Probably three hundred volunteers were weeded out with our shotgun approach—a lot of good men, too. Some, the persistent, kept coming back and finally made it as we needed replacements. After Chris's and my cut, we still had far too many people, but at least it was a manageable number, and I knew that, as with parachute or Ranger training, more than half of these men would fall by the wayside over the next few weeks.

Training started the minute an individual was accepted. The first week was all basic individual stuff—how to scoot and shoot. My foundation was solid: Crispino, Costello, and Wells from George and McLain, Smalling, Ropele, Lipka, Sovereign, Bill Hearn, and Jimmy Mayamura from Easy were all seasoned combat warriors. The Raider NCOs taught most of the classes—all hands-on, no classroom shit—and every hour of every twenty-hour training day became a test in which someone was eliminated. The weak fell out, the strong made it, and by the end of the week we were down to sixty guys.

The second week was squad training. "Your squad," I'd say to an NCO, "train it." The men practiced ambush and counterambush techniques until they could do them in their sleep. The volunteers progressed from the basics to the more specific skills needed when operating behind enemy lines: how to cut throats, use a garrote, and toss a razor-sharp hand ax with pinpoint accuracy. Attitude, motivation, discipline, intelligence and common sense, physical fitness, and the ability to think under pressure were harshly measured: more men fell out, and we were down to fifty.

The final week we trained as a unit, repeating, repeating, repeating until everything was second nature. Well-planned raids on U.S. and South Korean installations served as the final exam. I figured if novices could infiltrate friendly positions protected by armed and shaky clerks who'd shoot to kill, then operating behind enemy lines would be a piece of cake. When one Raider "patrol" managed to uproot and abscond with a thirty-foot flagpole from a South Korean Corps HQ while guards goose-stepped all around the joint, I knew we were ready. We'd bottomed out at forty-seven lean, mean, and damn proud Raiders—the graduation exercise was a ten-mile run with full gear.

Colonel Sloan had given us a blank check. His word alone was the magic key to all the fat supply depots, and what could not be obtained legally we bartered, scrounged, or stole. The training had already paid off: stealth, and plenty of it, made the Raiders the best band of thieves ever assembled in the U.S. Army. We knocked off tents, trucks, jeeps, beds, and even a complete operational field kitchen; we had enough rations and other goodies in our larder to keep a regiment going for a few days, including a bunch of epicurean rations from the General's kitchen, which we scrounged while making off with two stoves. Nothing was safe and nothing was sacred; we sharpened our skills while improving our life-style. Life at our camp was good, and promised to get even better—and our Raider flag (a skull and crossed bones) flew high.

The Raiders' initial organization was four eleven-man squads, all identical in organization and equipment. Later, based on lessons learned and mission change, we would add a scout squad and beef up the assault force with a couple of LMGs. I decided that every guy could carry the weapon of his choice, as long as it was automatic. The M-3 submachine "grease" gun was easy to get and, despite its weight and the weight of its ammo, was a favorite, but better still (if you could get one) was the snazzy, more reliable Thompson, which was in short supply.

The Thompson had been phased out of the U.S. Army after WW II. Chiang's Nationalist Chinese Army had had them for a while (before the Red Chinese kicked Chiang's ass in 1949 and took them away); now we were getting them back from dead Reds in Korea. Musical Thompsons. And since both sides were dug in and the war was no longer one of movement, the game continued, with combat soldiers swapping the weapons for firewater with noncombat types who wanted to play out the role of a tommy-gun-toting warrior. MPs confiscated the Thompsons from the rear-echelon commandos as unauthorized weapons, and because automatic weapons could not be sent back to the States as war souvenirs, piles of them were ending up on the floors of Ordnance depots. To the Raider way of thinking, this was a real waste, and Chris took it upon himself to make a deal with an Ordnance sergeant in Seoul: one jeep for his Thompsons. The 25th Signal Company graciously provided the jeep (when the driver failed to chain-lock the vehicle and pull the distributor), and the next morning *two* Raider jeeps bumped down the main road to Seoul to make the swap. The ex–Signal-Company jeep's paint job wasn't totally dry, but with its new Raider markings, it had no problem clearing the checkpoints where MPs were always on alert for hot vehicles.

Our little convoy consisted of Chris and me and Bobby and Johnny, two Korean kids whose last names we never knew. Bobby was about twelve, an orphan, his parents having been killed in the winter of 1950. He'd adopted me and the 3d of Easy when we were at Uijongbu; now he was the Raider mascot and had come along today to find out what was left of his family outside Kimpo. Johnny was a sixteen-year-old Korean *chogi* bearer who'd been with us in George. He'd followed Chris to the Raiders and was, in his own words, Chris's "number-one fix-it man." Chris was virtually the Buddha incarnate to young Johnny, and the boy tagged along everywhere, including raids, wearing a constant, lopsided grin.

The weapon swap went well, netting us eighteen Thompsons and several hundred magazines. Bobby's family turned out to be two very lovely sisters, about seventeen or eighteen years old, who wanted to be Raiderettes. Chris and I figured they'd be great in the kitchen and even better with other housekeeping functions, so we quickly scrounged fatigues and headgear for our new recruits. I remembered the time in Trieste when the I&R had relieved a unit on the Jug border. We'd gotten there before the guys in the outfit had awakened, and we'd been amazed because, zipped up in their fart sacks, all the men looked as big as Paul Bunyan. As the camp came to life, we'd discovered (and had been even more amazed) the reason the soldiers appeared so gigantic: as each sack was unzipped, out crawled not just a trooper but a Yugoslav girl who'd kept him warm all night. The platoon sergeant of the outfit explained that the girls were just part of the "hill property" and now they were ours. Prazenka had said, "You can't break up a good thing, can you?" and let them stay, for a few days at least. Like the Jug girls, Bobby's sisters couldn't speak English, but they giggled and jabbered with their brother as they pushed long, black hair inside helmet liners and slipped lovely bodies into baggy green fatigues. Glancing at the girls hunched down in the back of our jeep (they looked like two green Korean soldiers on the way to the front), I inwardly thanked Prazenka for setting such a considerate precedent on that hill in Italy. In every way now, the Raiders were ready to go.

*   *   *

Our first mission, kind of a crawl-before-you-walk thing, was chosen by our immediate boss on Colonel Sloan's staff, Major Willard Stambaugh, the regimental Intelligence officer. Chink snipers were coming down from the hills before dawn and setting up in the flat ground facing B Company of the 27th. By first light they'd be in position and masterfully concealed; they used smokeless, flashless ammunition, making them impossible to spot. The men of B Company were afraid to stick their heads up, and rightfully so. Our job was to eliminate the snipers, and try to snag a prisoner.

The role we were about to perform was one previously fulfilled by Ranger companies across the front, whose very raison d'être was this sort of mission. But as of 1 August, all Ranger outfits in Korea had been inactivated. One of the Pentagon-stated reasons for this move was that if there's only one guy in a regular unit squad who wants to fight, he's needed there to influence the other men; this same guy, went the logic, was the one who would join a Ranger unit, thus leaving the squad "bare of inspiration."[1] It sounded reasonable from Washington, but it seemed like a big mistake for the war as it was. If nothing else, Colonel Sloan's urgency in getting his ad hoc Raider unit up and running within a month of the Rangers' shutdown attested to that.

Our shakedown cruise began at dusk on 28 August. We assembled behind B Company, where I had a chance to talk to Lieutenant Jerome "Jim" Sudut, whose platoon we'd go through at dark. Good man, Sudut—World War II vet, twenty-six years old, a battlefield commission—really a stud of a guy. Sudut's platoon was dug in along a raised railroad line that ran east–west along the Kumhwa Valley. Fortunately, the position's rear slopes provided good cover from the sniper fire, and relative ease of movement as long as you kept your tail down and moved fast. Unfortunately, there was no patrol path going out. Earlier another U.S. unit had seeded the area knee-deep in antipersonnel mines without keeping a record of where they were buried. Their short-term protection meant only long-term agony for subsequent units, who had to find uncharted mines the hard way. It was a problem that had confronted infantry since the introduction of mines, and now it was ours.

When it was dark Sudut guided us to the edge of his wire and wished us good luck. "I'll have you know, Hackworth, I volunteered for your job," he said. It had turned cold; I hadn't brought my field jacket and Sudut took off his, insisting that I wear it. "There'll be coffee waiting for you in the morning," he added. I gratefully slipped on the jacket and eased out into the darkness.

Crispino and I swapped turns at the lead. It was good to work with him again. I hadn't realized how much I'd missed him since I'd gone to Easy three months before. Chris had come to George in March, when the 8th Rangers (which is where I'd first met him) broke up. He was about five years older than I, but we had a great affinity. Destined to win two DSCs, two Silver Stars, and five Purple Hearts over two tours of Korea ("I don't fuck around with the small change," he'd say, years later, when asked why he'd never won a Bronze Star, too), Chris was a first-class fighter and, from our experience in the 3d of G, one of the finest point men I'd ever seen. He was also the unit's lead singer around those inspiring "Closer Walk with Thee" campfires. He was a really talented musician who could play anything— beer bottles, spoons, whatever was available, but mostly it was his guitar. Chris also liked to gamble, fight, screw, and generally raise hell, which suited me right down to the ground. He was a great guy to have for a friend, but not the sort you'd take home to Mother—or to an Officers' Club, for that matter.

A few days before this first raid we'd gone back to Kimpo for supplies. We had a little time to kill, so we thought we'd get a drink and some decent food while we waited. But Chris, an NCO, couldn't get into the Officers' Club; the only way around it was to give him a phony commission. I took an extra insignia out of my pocket and pinned it on him. "Just do what I do, Chris," I said. "They'll never know." That got us into the club. We had a few drinks at the bar and then sat down to eat.

Now, when a waitress asks, "Would you like mushrooms on your steak?" the average guy might say, "Yeah, that sounds great." But not Chris. He was working overtime to be a proper officer. His response was: "Mushrooms [rolling his eyes to the ceiling] . . . ah, yes . . . mushrooms. Yes, I do believe mushrooms would be just fine. Thank you so very much, miss . . . and would you mind terribly bringing us another bottle of that most delightful red?" I could not believe my ears (nor could the Korean waitress, who probably spoke ten words of English), and I couldn't wait to get him out of that club so I could bust his ass back to sergeant.

Well, neither of us is a proper officer now, I thought, creeping along through the dark. After almost a year of combat each and a big chunk of it together, here we were still leading patrols, still playing point man, still probing through minefields. We had little choice about the minefields. Few Raiders as yet were trained for this kind of work (let alone when it was black as a coal digger's ass), and it was not a job to delegate to green guys. Even combat engineers got spooked by the task, and that was *after* training, and in daylight conditions.

The first mine disarmed was a Bouncing Betty on a trip wire, but there were others to contend with, too—pressure types, which were the worst, those mean little bastards with small pins barely sticking out of the ground. We crawled on hands and knees, clearing the area to our direct front, and then carefully sweeping one hand in a long, slow arc. If a wire was found it would be followed to the mine; the mine would be disarmed and set aside. If no wire was found, then we'd probe with trench knives. Anything solid would be dug up; sometimes we'd sweat out a rock and sometimes it was the real thing. After "all clear," we would crawl another yard and repeat the process. I didn't need Sudut's jacket now. I was soaking wet.

The day before, I'd conducted my first aerial recon. We'd overflown the patrol route just once, and the path I'd seen coming off one particular hill confirmed Sudut's suspicions that the snipers were operating from a bald knob to the west of Hill 1062. To a groundpounder, seeing the battlefield from the air had added a tremendous new perspective, but the whole time up there I couldn't help thinking there must be better ways of spending an afternoon than flying over enemy lines in a canvas-and-aluminum shell with a lawn-mower motor. I didn't like it. At least on the ground I could always find a hole. Up there I felt altogether too vulnerable.

But there must be better ways of spending a night, too, I thought, when we finally finished clearing the minefield. It had taken three hours to cut through that uncharted maze of death. We'd cleared ten mines and my gut ached as if I'd done a thousand sit-ups. It wasn't work to keep you young.

We high-stepped through tall grass—a silent, single file of ghostly night marauders, now a mile behind Chinese lines—toward the ambush site, a spot where the path I'd seen from the air intersected a well-used north-south trail. As we set up our killing zone we found horseshit, no more than twenty-four hours old. When the Chinese first came into the war, they'd used horses in Genghis Khan-like, sword-swinging cavalry attacks. Since then, many of their horses had gone wild (in George Company we'd captured a few riderless beasts ourselves, but with nothing for them to eat on the bare winter's ground, after a few days we'd let them go); the ones the Chinese had managed to hold on to (or had infiltrated throughout the year) were for the sole purpose of resupply. So the horseshit on the trail was a good sign: most likely, we were going to have visitors.

We waited—forty-seven men, including rear and flank security—lying prone in a killing zone about one hundred yards long. Our weapons were set on full automatic with safeties off; grenade pins were straightened, too. All the Raiders were connected to one another by way of a thin wire running from hand to hand. Three quick pulls on the wire meant ENEMY, then one pull for each joker entering the gauntlet. I was in the center of the ambush. I'd trigger it with a blast from my submachine gun only when the fish were well into the net, with Don Neary, my RTO, simultaneously firing a hand flare. Our SOP then called for each Raider to fire one mag, toss two grenades, and pour in another mag.

After three hours of waiting, the only blood drawn was our own: the ambush site was in mosquito country—*big* mosquito country. None of us used repellent (Chinks could smell it as easily as after-shave, soap, tobacco, and toothpaste); we couldn't slap at them (noises traveled loud and far at night). So we waited and reluctantly contributed our blood. I was well protected. Jim Sudut was a giant of a man, and his jacket was like a tent. I could almost crawl up into it. A lot of the guys who, like me, hadn't thought they'd need their field jackets were not so lucky, but just as they'd set up the ambush, now they were maintaining it like pros, despite the thousands of little stinging bites on hands, faces, and necks. We made no contact. The mosquitoes finally won by a TKO—we had to get home by daybreak.

We saddled up and took a different route back to avoid the possibility of a Chink ambush along the path we had taken out. We had about four hundred yards to go when the sun started to peek its nose out of the eastern sky. Chris was leading and I told him to pick up the pace. Suddenly he stopped dead in his tracks. He slowly turned and whispered in my ear, "I smell gooks."

I took a long sniff. "Chris, you're hallucinating. There are no gooks here."

He insisted, "No, I smell them. They're around here somewhere."

The sun was really starting to make its move now. I had the monkey on my back—we had to return to our lines in a hurry or we'd get the shit chopped out of us in the middle of no-man's-land. No one had told *me* the Raiders' maiden voyage was code-named "Titanic." "Let's get the hell out of here," I whispered.

Good soldier Crispino started off again with me breathing fire down his neck. He took one more step. "Look, Hack, they're here. I smell 'em . . . no shit."

"Chris, get behind me, I'll take the point."

I had taken no more than five steps when I heard a metallic click. I knew the sound: a bolt going back on a weapon. A fraction of a second later little red flames licked out of the darkness from a distance of five feet—slugs leaving a Chinese burp gun. I felt the slugs smashing into my stomach even before I heard the report. I hosed down the flames with a long burst of .45-caliber slugs, simultaneously jumping to the right and hitting the deck. The Raiders took up their antiambush positions automatically, as I tossed two grenades while spraying another mag. After one more grenade I charged the ambush, blasting away. Steve Prazenka, look out—you taught me well. Moments later, six dead Chinamen were stretched out in the tall grass. But

Chris was also down, and very still, about five feet away. It was light enough now that I could see his head was covered with blood.

I felt sick as I slowly turned him over. Chris looked up at me with vacant eyes. Then, slowly, a sly, mischievous grin crossed his face. "See, Hack, I told you I smelled 'em," he said.

And the enemy did smell. "Having a nose" for trouble on the battlefield, for contact, was not just an instinctive thing. Particularly at night: smells seemed to carry as far as sound in the darkness. The Chinese had a smell of rice and garlic, a putrid, unmistakable odor that started the adrenaline flowing with the first whiff. Curiously, the intelligence value of the enemy's smell seemed apparent only to the troops on the ground; the rear-echelon commandos took little stock in it, as evidenced by a story Phil Gilchrist told me some time later.

After Phil won his DSC, he'd been moved to Division as the assistant Operations officer. He was in the division tactical operations center (TOC) when I once reported—through Regiment—that my Raider patrol was close to the enemy because we could smell them. According to Gilchrist, the boys at Division thought this was funny and asked one another, "Just how many can he smell?" Phil (who was the only one there who had smelled the enemy on a night patrol) kept his mouth shut, having learned long before, in his own words, that "the last thing a combat officer can do is intrude upon the ruminations of the nonfighting elite of the Army." Was it any wonder, then, that the average U.S. fighting man in Korea was sent into the field smelling like the corner drugstore? Of course, I wouldn't let the Raiders go that way; we went as natural as Tarzan in the jungle. It didn't bother me if our aroma wouldn't have set well with the folks back home; I was concerned about the Chinese. After all, *their* enemy smelled, too.

When I realized Chris wasn't dead and there was no chance of him dying, I had another look at the dead Chinks. They looked like an FO team, but a number of them were armed with SKSs. They had not set up yet, but it looked as though they were just going into position when we surprised them by coming up from behind. Their mission had probably been to put a little heat on the main line with some well-directed H&I fire and selective sniping. *Well, not this time,* I thought. It was broad daylight by the time we scooped up their radio, weapons, and papers and made tracks to the cut in B Company's wire. When we arrived, Sergeant Costello, another G Company stud who'd also served in the 8th Rangers, loaded the Raiders on our waiting trucks and took them home. Sudut took Chris and me to his CP so the doc could go to work.

I felt no pain. *Hell, I should be dying with multiple slugs in the gut,* I thought, but except for my hands, which were covered with small wounds and swelling to the size of mini baseball gloves, there was no blood gushing from anywhere. Doc Brakeman said, "Lie down here, Lieutenant, and let me have a look."

I glanced over at Chris. He was kneeling a few feet away, drinking the steaming hot coffee Jim had promised (and which I wasn't allowed to have with my gut wound). He was a casting director's dream, old Crispino—the wounded warrior, blood still dripping down the side of his face. "No, no, doc, don't worry about me. Take care of Crispino. Take care of the enlisted swine."

The doc went over to Crispino. Chris said, "Oh, no, doc! I'm just a lowly enlisted man. Take care of the officer. The officer is far more important. We EM can always be replaced." We continued playing the game, ricocheting poor, confused Doc Brakeman back and forth. The doc didn't really know us yet and couldn't understand our warped sense of humor. Finally he gave up trying, and took care of Chris.

It turned out his wounds were not serious—they just bled like hell. One slug had clipped his earlobe and the other had grazed his skull like a razor slash. By the looks of things, the Chinese gunner must have panicked. He hadn't held his weapon down, and the recoil had lifted the fire from my gut to Chris's head to the stars. But we were just damn lucky the Chinaman wasn't a pro. He could have cut both of us in half and done some serious damage to the Raider column, too.

Then it was my turn. But when the doc laid me down and cut open the side of my jacket, he found no wound. He unbuttoned the jacket and pulled back the other clothes. There was no blood, no nothing. I had small cuts and lots of steel splinters all over my face, neck, chest, and the backs of my hands, but no bullet holes. But I'd been hit in the gut—I *knew* it—unless *I* was the one who'd been hallucinating.

It was time to call it a night. We said good-bye to Sudut and his gang, and gave them a couple of SKS rifles for their hospitality. Between my blood and Doc Brakeman's knife, the jacket Sudut had loaned me was pretty well done for; I promised to send him a new one with something fluid in the pocket. But I never saw him again. He was killed two weeks later leading a platoon attack against a firmly entrenched enemy position. When his body was found, there were half a dozen or so enemy dead scattered all around him in the trench. The lieutenant had run out of ammo but not out of fight: the last of the enemy defenders had been killed with Sudut's trench knife.*

The doc at the regimental aid station patched us up properly. Chris would

---

* Sudut was awarded the Medal of Honor, posthumously, for this action.

be down for a few weeks, but my wounds were superficial, nothing that couldn't be fixed with a few shots of penicillin, Tennessee whiskey, and some deft strokes with a scalpel to get the steel out. An easy Purple Heart, but I still couldn't understand it.

My next stop was Regimental S-2. Major Stambaugh had set up his Intelligence shop in a large, sandbagged general-purpose (GP) tent surrounded by concertina wire in the Regimental Headquarters complex. I placed my weapon on the table out front, following SOP: magazine out, bolt back, weapon on safety (too many well-armed clerks had blasted each other with "unloaded" firearms inside tents), and went inside. With Stambaugh, I covered everything that happened after we crossed the LD: the minefield, the terrain, the vegetation, the horseshit, the smells, the noises, the contact. At the end, in passing, I told the Major how certain I was about getting hit in the gut. He jokingly suggested that I'd "gone Asiatic," whatever that meant, and I left, picking up my weapon on the way out. But when I flipped the grease gun over to close the bolt and insert the magazine, there, staring up at me, was a jagged hole the size of a fifty-cent piece. So I wasn't crazy; I *had* been hit, and the steel splinters were bits and pieces from my all-metal M-3. I couldn't resist running back into Major Stambaugh's tent so he could have a look at it. He told me to go home and get some sleep.

Dell Evans heard I'd been hit, and he came to visit the Raider camp later that morning, to check on friends and get the full scoop. He disassembled my damaged weapon, and upon examination we saw that three slugs had ripped through the trigger housing assembly. The slugs had gone through the oil thong case, then through the bolt retracting mechanism, and smashed into, but not penetrated, the other wall—the wall that was up against my gut. My weapon was an M-3 A1, modified with a recess in the bolt to draw it back; the retracting mechanism had been made redundant by this modification, and shouldn't even have been there. So it was almost as though some thoughtful Ordnance man had left it in, somehow knowing that it would be perfect to slow down three 9-mm Communist slugs, and thus save my life.

Chris managed to get out of the hospital early. I think he was worried that I, of all people, would take advantage of living alone in our tent with the two lovely Raiderettes (who'd gotten tired of the full-time Army life, but who still visited on occasion). The thought had not crossed my mind, because Costello had moved in with me as acting platoon sergeant while Chris was away.

Costello was actually on his way home, through normal rotation. Because his days were numbered, I wanted to be sure he experienced the best of the Raider life, and on one particularly hot day between the early raids, I was dismayed to find him stretched out on his rack, sleeping. I woke him up. "Costello, let's go for a swim."

"Fuck that," he mumbled. "I want to sleep." He was wearing only a pair of GI shorts, and his cock was hanging out his fly and down between his legs. I couldn't resist. I grabbed my little patrol pistol, a 9-mm Beretta, off the top of a nearby field desk and pointed it at his cock.

"Costello, I'll blow your cock off if you don't get out of that sack and come with me."

Costello knew I'd pulled the clip and emptied the thing upon returning from the previous raid, so he told me to get fucked. I took careful aim and squeezed. *BANG*. The son of a bitch was loaded. The slug missed Costello's dick by an inch and blew a hole in his air mattress. I don't know who was more shocked as we both watched his bed slowly deflate—but he did go swimming. I doubt I've ever seen anyone happier to rotate home. Jack Speed—my favorite Tennessee wheeler-dealer and, at twenty-three, the oldest Raider besides Chris—took Costello's place, and watched me like a hawk.

By the time Chris got back, the Raiders had completed six successful missions with no casualties, save on the first one. The tasks had been varied and chosen by Major Stambaugh according to Intelligence needs; all required stealth and skill, but not every one required the full Raider force. We only took as many men as needed to do the job, be it taking a prisoner for interrogation, getting enemy uniforms for line crossers, raiding an outpost—whatever the S-2 assigned to us—and from each raid we learned more and got better. The missions gradually became more difficult, taking us farther and farther behind enemy lines, or into territory so hot it might take five hours to crawl a hundred yards. Advanced training was dictated by mission requirements, and anyone with experience shared in the teaching (like Costello and Crispino, who'd both been Ranger-trained at Benning, and McLain—who, in some hard Pacific fighting, had taken shrapnel from a Jap round right in the face—and his fellow Texan, "Tex" Garvin, who were both WW II ex-Marines). My own "snooping and pooping" I&R experience was invaluable, too, and we'd all sit around and discuss techniques, the old pros adding much to the ever-growing repertoire of Raider tricks.

With Chris's return came a mission to destroy four caves burrowed into the side of a hill deep behind enemy lines—what aerial photos and the Intelligence "experts" suspected to be a supply depot. Artillery had already tried to close the place down, with zero effect; tac air couldn't get in there at all, because the Chinese had too many automatic weapons on Hill 1062, which fired on the aircraft. Our mission was simply to blow the caves and return. It sounded easy, but it wasn't—few of them were. We had to slip through the main Chinese defensive line, make it through real bandit country before we even got to the caves, then blow them up and get out as if nothing had happened—all in exactly ten hours. It was not much time.

During an aerial recon (the uneasiness I'd felt during the first one had passed, and now I requested them whenever possible), I found the simplest way to make the raid. Many trails and secondary roads crisscrossed the area around the objective, and a large creek ran almost to the caves. We'd wade up the center of that creek; it would cover any noise and simplify navigation. I would take only two squads into the objective area: Mayamura's scouts to get us there, and David Forte's demolitions people. We took lethal packages of plastic explosives (C-4) and, in addition, each Raider carried two thermite grenades. I figured if we didn't blow them up, we'd burn them out.

We registered artillery concentrations along our route, and for two nights before the raid, the gunners hammered away. We'd use them during the raid, too. The noise would help cover our movement, and the flying steel might encourage the enemy to stay in their holes. Another benefit was that the guns would be warm and gunners ready in case we needed their magic punch to get our asses out of a crack.

At 1600 hours, Raid Day, everyone was standing tall. The Raiders' standard uniform was fatigues or coveralls, and black knit caps and sneakers. Black was the order of the day as much as possible—our faces and hands, too, smeared liberally with the end of a burned cork. Loose clothes, dog tags, and anything that made noise were tied down with OD tape or held tight with rubber strips cut from inner tubes. Chris conducted the inspection, which by now was SOP: each Raider had to run in place, hit the ground, and roll without making one sound before he could board the truck.

We slipped through friendly lines at dark, and by 2000 hours we were behind the main enemy line. We moved fast, with Mayamura and two of his scouts far to our front. About a hundred yards from our objective we halted and formed a tight defensive perimeter. Jimmie insisted that he go alone for a look at the caves.

There was no point in debating the issue; Jimmie Mayamura was like a cat at night—totally unafraid. We'd been together for four months in Easy, and by now I was well used to his little midnight walks through enemy lines. I loved Jimmie. We all did. He was a no-bullshit gunfighter, a samurai warrior who preferred operating by himself. But he was also a quiet, unassuming first-generation Japanese-American, and he had this strange thing about rank. Jimmie was a PFC when he joined the Raiders, and every time I tried to promote him he wouldn't accept it. He was ready and willing to do any job (as it was, his role as squad leader called for the rank of E-6), but he just didn't want to be an NCO. It didn't matter to me, but somehow I really felt that after he went home (which was in only a couple of months) and got out of the Army, the time would come when he'd regret his attitude about not wanting rank. So without telling him, I decided to promote him anyway, one stripe at a time, and little did he know, but PFC Jimmie Mayamura was already a staff sergeant.

An hour after he had gone, Jimmie returned with the word that there was nothing in the caves, that they hadn't been used in a long time. There was also no sign of Chinese, but the main track was well used (with horseshit all over it), and north of the caves there was a rough wooden bridge that spanned the creek we had come up. Jimmie suggested we blow the bridge. It seemed like a good idea (we had enough demo to blow up the Golden Gate anyway, and it was crazy taking the stuff back), and besides, it was good training. Jimmie provided security while Forte wired the bridge to explode when we were sixty minutes down the track; we hustled out of there, and an hour later the bridge blew with a thundering roar.

Whether or not we made contact with the enemy, it was near impossible to relax, much less sleep after a raid. It took a long time for the adrenaline to stop pumping; you couldn't just flop down and switch off. Most of us would go for a good swim in the river that flowed right by our little camp; we'd play on the beach and in the water, just to let off some steam, and slowly, slowly unwind. Afterwards, we'd pick the raid apart—lessons learned, screwups, and who should get his walking papers—over a mighty breakfast of steak and eggs washed down with beer. Then we might play some softball, and only around noon would we crap out and sleep for ten or twelve hours. By midnight, most guys were up again and a party would be rocking the Raider camp, complete with open kitchen, 190-proof on the rocks, and, weather permitting, midnight swims. It wasn't bad duty. We raided one night and had the next three off. It sure beat the hell out of hiding in the bottom of a hole on the front and having HE dumped on you twenty-four hours a day.

One evening, for some reason I wasn't in the mood for the usual "first night after the raid" roaring party, and hit the sack early. The rest of the guys got drunker and drunker and, deciding I was a party pooper, marched into my tent to tell me so. I was asleep; I woke up to find myself weaving in midair in the pitch-black night as six Raiders held my cot over their heads and congo-lined through the darkness. I told them to leave me alone, but the more I protested, the more convinced the troops were that I had to come to the party. Then one guy got the idea to toss me, cot and all, into the river. This course of action was hotly disputed (there seemed to be two knee-knocking-drunk schools of thought on the issue: "Leave the Old Man alone"

versus "Drown the bastard"); meanwhile I just swayed in the air, listening to
all this and contemplating my fate. I was about to do a parachute landing fall
(PLF) off the thing when the conflict accelerated with the introduction of
firepower: one of the troopers pulled out a pistol and started shooting into
the sky. *Scratch the PLF*, I thought, lying as flat and thin as I could in my
little cot, looking at the stars and wondering if I would soon be among them.

The water was cold. But everyone jumped in to salvage my bed, my
blankets, and me. And the boys had their wish—I warmed up by the fire and
joined in the fun, as the Raiders continued to party on through the night.
War stories flew, and we were just a bunch of kids having a big old time.

At dawn on our second day off, we'd suit up and head down the road for
an eight-to-ten-mile run. Our singing, counting, and shouting woke up the
regimental rear-echelon commandos, and sweated out all the poison we'd
inflicted on ourselves the night before. The run would be followed by two
days' and one night's hard training, and then another raid. By the beginning
of October our tactical proficiency became so sharp that I cut out all training
except for replacements and rehearsals. To me, there was no sense fixing
something that's already fixed, and there's nothing worse than an anxious,
overtrained unit. Besides, it gave us more time to improve our life-style.
Since the Raiders were formed, logistical units in our vicinity had begun
chaining everything down. It was, of course, to no avail—we had bolt
cutters—but no one ever came to our camp to look for things. Maybe they
assumed that the Raiders, the darlings of the regiment, were above all that.
How very wrong they were.

One night the Raiders set up an ambush on a track in front of the 1st
Battalion, about a mile and a half behind enemy lines. My guys set up on
a small, four-foot-high ledge that paralleled and overlooked the track, on the
other side of which was an orchard enclosed by a long, rectangular rock
wall. It was a perfect ambush site, and with Jimmie covering our rear with
his element (on a small knob to the south overlooking the track), anyone
coming down the track or through the orchard would have nowhere to run.

As soon as we were in position, we saw a Chinese squad carefully picking
its way through the orchard. A larger force was following this point element,
and another enemy squad, much closer to us, was moving in single file
down the track as flank security for them all. The Chinese were careful, and
well spread out.

We let the complete group enter the orchard. Just before their point
cleared the southern rock wall, thirty automatic Raider weapons began to
blast as our ambush force poured magazine after magazine of lethal fire
throughout the orchard area. Chris called in artillery and we had some

harvest; the Chinks had no cover other than behind the small trees, and we splintered them with grenades.

Suddenly, we started taking machine-gun fire from behind the northern rock wall. It peppered along the ridge but snapped far over our heads. At the same time, Jimmie radioed: "Got an enemy force, size unknown, moving between us and your rear. What's happening over there?" I gave him the details of the ambush and directed him to take the force under fire—we were about to be outflanked. I told him we were going to head down the track and into his position as soon as we could shut down the machine-gun fire; Chris adjusted the artillery, and when it was on target we moved. We joined Jimmie's perimeter and waited. The force he'd engaged took off to the northwest (which was fortunate, because Raider enthusiasm and all automatic weapons had just about gobbled up our basic load of ammo). We took no casualties, but I made a mental note: in future, Raider SOP would be, per man, an additional two boxes of .45-caliber slugs, taped to prevent them from falling apart and carried in the jacket pockets. We'd never know when we'd need the ammo, and in the meantime it would provide an excellent armored plate over each lung.

Chris scattered artillery along the enemy's probable routes of withdrawal. We kept it crashing down around us, a warm (if somewhat noisy) security blanket, while Jimmie went to have a look at our own withdrawal route to make sure it wasn't blocked. Meanwhile Chris, Speed, a few other guys, and I snuck back to the ambush site to see if anything of interest could be scrounged from the enemy dead. Not even Superman could have escaped the amount of fire we'd poured into the ambush area, and we figured we'd net a couple of Thompsons, if nothing else.

The battlefield was dead quiet except for the friendly incoming. Only a couple of hours had passed since we'd sprung the ambush, but now, to look at the orchard, it might have been days. There was not one dead Chinaman to be seen. Not one. There were plenty of pools of blood, a lot of spent brass, but no fallen warriors. *Shit,* I thought to myself, *maybe it didn't happen.* The Chinese had responded that quickly to the task of pulling out their dead, wounded, and weapons. Our final report: one bloodstained, well-pruned orchard. No corpus delicti. The Chinese were pretty slick.

A new outfit set up across the river from the Raider camp. I did not like such close neighbors. That's why I'd selected such an isolated position in the first place, far away from any other unit so the guys could let their hair down without complaints from sleepless rear-echelon folk in the wee hours of the morning. From the start, I'd also decided we'd have no hangers-on in the camp—no fat logistics tail to cut down on our fighting strength. Raider personnel performed such secondary jobs as cooking, driving, and administration (like Jack Sprinkler, the Raiders' clerk, who got the job because he was the only one who would admit he could type), but every swinging Richard in the outfit was a warrior first. Now, suddenly our lean, mean crew was being crowded out, and I wanted to know by whom. Chris made a quick recon and reported back that the intruder unit was the regimental bakery. The regimental bakery officer, he went on to say, was none other than Lieutenant Barney K. Neil, who'd saved our platoon's ass back in April when G Company was overrun.

What the hell is Barney K. doing as the regimental bakery officer? I wondered. I didn't believe it; I refused to, until an hour later when Barney himself arrived at the Raider camp. And was he down. Just one look at him told me how badly he was hurting, but it wasn't until we sat down with a bottle of hooch that I found out why.

Simply put, he'd cracked on the battlefield, in the same attack that killed Jerome Sudut. But no story is that simple, and the one that Barney K. related told me plenty. Only days before the operation, the stated purpose of which was to straighten up the lines around Hill 1062 (Papasan—that huge thorn in the United Nations forces' side, destined never to be removed), the newest battalion CO apparently decided that Barney K. was too familiar with his platoon. The night before the attack, the CO transferred him to George (which was spearheading the operation in the morning) as a replacement platoon leader.

At the best of times taking over a unit isn't easy. Before a big attack, it can be a horror story. No one knows you, no one trusts you, and it'd be fair to say the reverse is true as well. The one thing Barney K. had going for him was Master Sergeant Moore, one of the few black soldiers to serve in G Company besides Jerry Boyd. Moore had come to George as an AWOL volunteer from some rear-echelon quartermaster outfit, and had worked his way up from rifleman to platoon sergeant in an all-white outfit—a remarkable feat in a unit heavy with Johnny Rebs. Moore was a damned good man, but it was no consolation to Barney K., who, until that moment, had been the longest-serving platoon leader in the battalion. In Korean combat so far, the average platoon leader lasted no longer than a month. Barney K. must have had nine lives. In ten months straight of heavy, heavy combat with Fox, he'd never once been hit, though he'd seen his platoon turn over, through bullets, at least five times. It was almost as if he was now being punished for living so long. The new battalion commander had used his eyes but not his head: he'd seen overfamiliarity, but had not taken time to *think*, to realize that Barney K.'s easygoing attitude with his guys came from the platoon's and its leader's mutual understanding, respect, and trust.

With one order, the CO had destroyed it all, and my friend was heartbroken.

At first light the following morning, just as they were about to jump off, Barney K.'s new unit started getting the shit blasted out of it with Chink mortar fire. A 120-mm round landed nearby, a little too close for comfort, but Barney K. wasn't touched. Scared, yes, and ears ringing, but otherwise— physically—intact. But he couldn't take it. He told Sergeant Moore to take command and walked down off the hill.

Shoot him, court-martial him, or give him a medal—no one seemed to know what to do. Probably the powers that be thought he'd gotten a bad deal (which he had, like a jockey whose horse had been pulled out from under him and another thrust in its place just moments before a big race), so they gave him the job of bakery officer.

Barney K. stayed at the Raider camp more than he did at his place of business. All the Raiders loved this infinitely lovable Oklahoman. They knew what he'd been through, and that he was a good man. So they jollied him out of his depression and gave him back his dignity. Meanwhile I got the straight skinny on the Army I could expect to find stateside: Barney K. told me all about protocol in the officers' world. I tried to put him back on his horse, too; again and again I invited him along on our raids. But while again and again he promised to be there, on the night itself he never was. Barney K.'s bottle had filled, and only time would empty it.

The regiment was changing; the old warriors were fading out and new leaders straight from the stateside Army took informality and comradeship as signs of a loose, sloppy, undisciplined outfit. The irony of it all was that while General Van Fleet was telling the world that the reason for his Eighth Army's limited, large-scale attacks was that "a sit-down Army is subject to collapse at the first sign of an enemy effort," and that he "couldn't allow [his] forces to become soft and dormant . . . and slip into a condition that eventually would cause horrible casualties," his new COs seemed to be hurrying the negative process along by punching huge holes in morale.[2] One captain, for example, introduced himself as the new CO of proud George Company by telling that unit that if he saw one man from the company run (probably referring to the bullshit "bugout" tales of the past April), he'd shoot him in the back.

Fortunately, we Raiders had a patron saint in Colonel Sloan—nobody, but nobody, messed with us. We had no visits from higher headquarters, no staff inspections, no checks to see if we were following regulations right to the letter. We'd get a mission order that said "Do it" and we trained and planned as we saw fit. We wrote the book for the sorts of things we were doing, instead of blindly following field manuals that didn't always apply.

Sloan trusted me, so I had total freedom to get the job done. I trusted my NCOs to help me do it. My guys trusted me to stand up and fight if someone tried to screw us over, and I trusted Sloan not to use us as a kamikaze force.

And it worked. The Raiders were the cockiest, most gung-ho sons of bitches on the block. The men approached each raid with superhuman confidence, knowing just as well that it could be their final journey. Last-minute wills would be drawn up (*"If you get killed, I want your jump boots." "Oh, yeah? If you get killed, I want your knife and watch."*), but the wills weren't signed or even sealed with a handshake, and since no one was getting killed, it was a big, fun game. Sure, you'd have gotten those boots if the guy who was wearing them bought the farm. But trust was what made the guy with the boots risk his life on the battlefield when you said, "I'll cover you"—he knew you'd keep him alive because you wanted him alive far more than you wanted his goddamn boots. Trust meant you'd risk your life for your buddies, because you knew they would do the same for you, and they'd never leave you dead or dying on any hill, for any reason.

"Trust" was a magic word with the Wolfhounds, but it was falling out of use a little more as each new boatload of senior stateside officers unloaded. Something was happening to the combat army of the past year, but I couldn't put my finger on it. The new people knew all the cosmetic stuff: how to shine your shoes until they gleamed, how to stand ramrod straight and click your heels at appropriate moments. I'd learned all that peacetime discipline in Trieste—good stuff, at times, but it just didn't go well on the battlefield. The *yes, sir, no, sir* bootlicking business had gotten into our Army through the influence of the British, the French, and the Germans, way back in the von Steuben days of 1776. We'd modeled our system after theirs, and the incoming commanders knew the routine cold. They'd learned everything, except that combat is no place for martinets. The Raiders were a damned disciplined unit, no less so because no one called me "sir." I treated the guys as I wanted to be treated—fair, square, and honest; we operated on mutual respect. They knew I loved them, and they knew I'd never ask a man to do anything that I had not done on the battlefield, or wouldn't do again. So we called one another by our nicknames; there was rarely any pulling rank; and even when guys had a little too much sauce, there was no breakdown of Raider authority, or submerged hang-ups ticking away like bombs, waiting to explode when sufficient booze had been slurped up. Except, I think, the night when Chief decided to kill me.

All Indians in an Army unit seemed to be called Chief. In Italy, in the 752d, it had been Chief Robert Ventura, from Texas. This "Chief" had been my Indian Al Hewitt. Ventura was an old man of at least twenty-three when I was sixteen; he'd fought through Europe and the Pacific during the war, and I was in awe of him. With or without firewater he was a powerful guy. He could lift a Sherman tank's heavy engine compartment door single-handedly, or shoot all the bottles off a wall in a village bar (like in some Western movie) and not get caught only because the barkeep was afraid to even look at him. With his friend Polk, from Georgia, Ventura taught me old-soldier tricks, among them two vital uses for gasoline: one, to kill crabs (you take a shower with it), and two, to wash tank engines (you pour a fifty-five-gallon drum into the engine compartment while the tank is revving up). They taught me the first of these outdoors in the dead of winter; I'd never forget watching Polk hold a five-gallon drum of 80-octane gasoline over Ventura's head, while the Chief stood under it, rubbing and scrubbing the crabs away in the subfreezing temperatures. It would have killed an ordinary man. The engine-cleaning shortcut was not nearly as memorable, except in its potential: one stray spark would have blown the tank, its basic load of HE ammo,* and all of us to kingdom come. But Polk and Chief weren't afraid of that or anything (and besides, that's how they'd done it the whole way from Africa to Germany), and if I was going to emulate them, I couldn't be afraid either. So I wasn't.

In the Raiders our Chief was Chief Denny from Arizona. Denny was a great, powerful stud of a guy. He was a super soldier, an original Raider who'd come from 3d Batt; he was also the silent type, who never seemed to say a word about anything. One night, we were all sitting around in a GP medium tent having yet another after-the-raid party when out of nowhere Chief decided he was going to kill me, and the only reason I could think of for him wanting to kill me was that I was an officer. All I knew for certain was that I was sitting on the ground in the center of the tent, drinking and bullshitting and leaning against the tent pole with a canteen cup of Raider booze in my hand, when suddenly I looked up to see Chief swinging a pick mattock down on my head.

Luckily, the 190-proof had not zeroed me out completely. I rolled to one side, and the pick plunged into the ground exactly where I'd been sitting. It took half a dozen Raiders to wrestle the Chief onto a nearby cot; they tied him down with commo wire and left him alone until the next morning. When we cut him loose, he didn't remember anything about the night before. I certainly wasn't going to mention it, and even though we did lock up all the picks (to be on the safe side), nothing like it ever happened again.

Every weekend I sent a few Raiders back to Seoul for a little unofficial R&R. Besides the readily available pussy there (which kept the guys happy

---

* Seventy-one rounds of 76-mm shells and thousands of rounds of .30 and .50 caliber.

and out of trouble), Seoul was a scrounger's paradise. On one such journey the boys brought back a full generator and lighting set in exchange for a few captured weapons; on another, one Raider returned with a large refrigerator, which he told me fell into his truck as he was driving past a Seoul Officers' Club in the early hours of the morning. But even with the essential items that kept finding their way into our camp, I was always bellyaching that we didn't have enough vehicles. We had three jeeps (one authorized and two hot), but more times than not they were out with some joyriding Raiders, and never there when I needed one. The final straw came when I had to report to Regiment—a ten-minute jeep ride—and had to drive a two-and-a-half-ton GMC truck (of which we had two—one authorized and one hot—but that was not the point). *What*, I asked myself, *is the leader of the Raiders driving a truck for? Would Lieutenant Patton drive a truck? Would Lieutenant Rommel?* I was very pissed off. I tore Chris's ass: "Three fucking jeeps and I've got to take a truck. I want one jeep here at all times! My own personal jeep that no one—but no one—will even look at. Do you understand?" I immediately regretted blowing up at him, but of course would not apologize. None too popular that night, I went to bed early to do some hardcore sulking.

I woke up about midnight to the blinding headlights of a jeep, which was sitting in the middle of Chris's and my tent. On the hood and all over the damn thing were very mellow Raiders who'd rolled up the side of the tent and pushed the vehicle through. Chris stood nearby; I knew he was still pissed over the ass chewing I'd given him, because he smartly saluted and said with the utmost correctness, "Here is your own fucking personal quarter-ton, Lieutenant." He stormed out of the tent, the other Raiders in tow. It was all quite humbling. I had to get up, reverse the jeep out of the tent, roll down the side, and wait for Chris to come home to thank him. So much for pulling rank.

In the morning, all was forgotten as the Raiders' shared mission became to make this jeep our own. Chris had stolen it early the night before from the 35th Regiment's Medical Company; all 35th markings (bumper numbers and Cacti insignias) had to be painted over and our markings and Wolfhound heads painted on instead. Each military vehicle had a War Department number on it as well, and we assigned the same number (RAIDERS 1) to all four of ours, so if a jeep was stopped we'd just produce the trip ticket and no one would be the wiser. The only problem was we could never park them all in one place at the same time.

In the Raider camp it wasn't too much of a problem, though, because we allowed few visitors. Besides Barney K. Neil, the only people who saw the inside were Raider volunteers, buddies from the trenches (like Phil Gilchrist, whom I'd invite to watch the Raiders train—I was so proud of my boys), or poker players. Poker was still big on my list; our games were frequent, with good-sized pots and big-league pro players brought in for the challenge. I won a lot, so I always had a big bundle to donate to Dell Evans whenever he came to collect. The consensus of Raider opinion was that Dell must have been a Mississippi gambler in another life—I could never beat him. Once I had him for a few hundred bucks, but given that he'd taken thousands from me over the last year, it just wasn't enough. So I persuaded him to shoot craps. Dell wasn't too interested ("Just two guys shooting craps, Hack?"), but he took me on. A short time later I was completely wiped out, and, according to Dell, still mumbling to myself when he pulled away in his jeep.

But my brand-new RAIDERS 1 was compensation enough for any other losses. The only other person who was allowed to touch it was Bobby, who loved it as much as I did. The two of us were like little kids with a new toy; Bobby washed it, polished it, and kept it shiny for his combat "dad," and in return, whenever I went for a drive I took him along. One afternoon we decided to pay Dell a visit at the 2d Battalion Forward CP. We picked him up and spun down the main supply route (MSR) through the 2d Batt positions and on toward the U.S. main line.

The battlefield was deadly quiet, as if the war had been shut off. It was a lovely sunny day, perfect for Dell to see and feel my new set of wheels, and he was suitably impressed. Then out of nowhere roared a P-51 fighter. It was in trouble; smoke was pouring out its rear, making a trail across the sky as the plane headed right into enemy lines. We gave chase as the fighter powered to gain altitude. Right in the middle of no-man's-land the pilot bailed out. "Let's get him!" Dell shouted, and we zoomed down the road. Within moments we passed a big sign that read "You are now leaving the Wolfhounds' Lair. Northbound traffic should be able to speak Chinese," or something like that, but we could see the chute opening and the pilot coming down, and we were so caught up in the excitement of this adventure that we figured we could scoop him up and make it back to our lines before the Chinese were any the wiser.

The first round smacked in front of the jeep—a Chink SP gun was firing straight up the road. I slammed on the brakes. We unassed the thing, and by the time the next round hit (behind the jeep), Dell, Bobby, and I were lying in a ditch on the side of the road in the middle of no-man's-land. Dell gave Bobby his steel pot; the kid looked incredibly silly as he sat there beaming out from under it. The helmet had enough room for two little Bobby-sized heads.

We had to get that jeep turned around before the Chink gunner got its range, but the road was very narrow, so it wasn't a matter of a quick U-turn. I ran to the jeep, and in the short lull between incoming rounds, went forward, then backed up, and then went forward again before jumping out of the vehicle and hitting the ground as the Chinese gun blasted away. Forward, back, forward. Over. Forward, back, forward. Short. He was having as much trouble getting our range as I was getting the jeep to head south. Finally Dell and Bobby piled in and we got out of there. I don't know what happened to the pilot—the word was the 35th got him out—but I do know my hot little jeep did very well on a very hot road, and one little orphan boy had not had so much fun in a long time. I can't say the same, though, for me and Dell.

Night attack. We fell out, checked gear, loaded trucks, and moved—the Raiders were about to take their first hill. Ironically, it was the same ridge I'd raided with Easy on 8 August, which had brought me to the Raiders to begin with. The big attack, which had killed Sudut and knocked the fight out of Barney K. Neil, had pushed the main line forward as it tidied up the lines, and now the 8 August ridge was the U.S. front. It was strange riding down that road in perfect safety, seeing again the familiar landmarks—the bombed-out bridge that had saved our asses, now rebuilt; the S-turn in the road, where once stood a lone Chinese sentry illuminated by a flare; the hill itself, jutting up from the ground. The front line was still far to our front.

Since September the raiding business had gotten very serious. It was no longer easy to slip through the front lines and disappear behind enemy positions. The Chinese had wised up to Raider activity, and were countering with raiders of their own, and with damn good ambushing and observation teams. Meanwhile, regular units were slowly atrophying—as Van Fleet had predicted—in long, windy trenches that snaked from one side of the Korean peninsula to the other. Barriers, booby traps, and alert listening posts (LPs) now filled the little holes that in the past we'd virtually meandered through. The enemy hugged the Allied positions with their own siegelike trenches (they had to in order to avoid U.S. superior firepower); in some places the lines were within hand-grenade range. The war had become a contest between a modern industrial state and a regime of fast-digging primitives who had little but numbers on their side. Limited major attacks by both sides "to keep the pressure on" seemed to be the politics of the peace table at Panmunjom far more so than practice for the troops: special units like the Raiders were springing up all over the front to take up the slack and carry on the day-to-day fighting.

So while Truman sent the word to keep casualties at a minimum and the

Chairman of the Joint Chiefs of Staff, Omar Bradley, visited the Korean front, and while the Pentagon recommended the use of nuclear weapons if a large Chinese attack threatened our forces with military disaster and the USAF conducted simulated tactical nuclear strikes on North Korean targets,[3] the Eighth Army's I Corps' 25th Division's 27th Infantry Regiment's 3d Battalion's K Company's position had become untenable in the daytime, and the Raiders were on the road again.

But then came the sneer.

"There go those big, badassed, motherfucking Raiders."

Chris slammed on the brakes, whipped the jeep into reverse, and came to a screeching halt next to the loudmouthed trooper. It was chow time for members of the 3d Batt on the side of the road. The Raiders were going to work and we weren't in the mood for eating shit, especially the shit of someone from the battalion whose asses we'd come to save. The Chinese had dug a virtual siege line only a couple of hundred yards from K Company. Their manned spider holes made it impossible for anyone in King to stick his head up during the day without drawing a sniper shot between the horns. Our mission was to get rid of the whole shebang.

I grabbed my trench knife out of my boot and held it next to the wisecracker's throat. "All right, joker! If you're so big and bad you can come with us." Under great protest the guy was pulled into the back of my jeep. I smiled; we'd just see who was big and who was bad.

Jimmie and crew slipped through King's wire at first dark. It was more like an ominous twilight, really—the full moon was so bright I would have canceled the raid except for the fog. McLain went with them. He'd be trying out our newest acquisition, an infrared night device, to knock off the Chink OP. The scope was mounted on a carbine, and McLain assured me (with the confidence only an ex–Marine Corps Expert Marksman can) that it was accurate to at least forty yards. We needed it; artillery would cover the noise of the shots, and we'd be hard-pressed to get past the OP otherwise on a bright night like this.

Next, I pushed our captive out of the trenches and told him he was going to lead the way. The guy became totally unglued. He cried, he begged, but I wasn't having any of it. I thumped him with my weapon and shoved him up toward the enemy hill. More Raiders slipped through the wire.

By this time Jimmie and Mac were far ahead, all set up. I was getting nowhere with the kidnapped, sniveling wiseass, and he was so damned noisy I could see he was about to become more of a liability than the lesson was worth. I handed him over to Neary, with the instruction to let the bastard go after the elements had reached their probable line of deployment. Still,

I figured the kid had learned his lesson. It would be a long time before the old green-eyed monster got the best of him again. *Might even make him president of the Raider fan club*, I thought.

Three rounds of artillery smashed into the top of the hill; I didn't hear the carbine fire even though I was only fifty yards away. Sure enough, Mac had neutralized the two-man OP with two clean shots between the eyes. We'd hold on to that infrared device.

The hill was steep and void of all vegetation. We inched our way forward, slithering along like snakes, carefully shifting loose rocks out of our path. One careless move, one tumbling rock down this artillery-battered hill could mean serious trouble; it would alert the defenders to forty very exposed and vulnerable Raiders right in their killing zone.

When we got to the first Chinese trench, no one was in sight. Our artillery had driven the defenders underground. I covered "Red" Smalling, my old friend from 3d/Easy, as he poked his head into a bunker. At the same time, two Chinks came down the trench. Smalling gave both a short burst from his stripped-down BAR, and the battle was in full swing. But the Chinks had been had—Raiders were all over their positions—and the fight was almost over by the time the enemy at the top of the hill began their usual barrage of potato-masher grenades.

While we were mopping up, Smalling got into a jack-in-the-box duel with one die-hard, burp-gun-toting Chinaman. They went at it for a while—one popping up, firing, and going down, and then the other—until finally, both of them popped up at the same time. Smalling cut the guy in half, but the Chinaman's last burst stitched Red right up his left side with half a dozen slugs. "Hack," he said (with Arkansan understatement), "ah'm hit." His left leg was virtually shattered, but he was still mobile, so I told him to go down the hill and Doc Brakeman would patch him up. "What about my weapon?" he asked. SOP in Easy was if you were hit you passed your automatic rifle on to some able-bodied guy (you don't want to lose that kind of firepower on a hill). But we Raiders had plenty, and besides, we were almost through up there. I told him to keep it.

The cleanup continued. We had a few casualties, mostly from grenades being thrown by a couple of hardcore jokers in a bunker on the reverse slope of the hill. Johnny "S'koshi"* Watkins, a young kid of about seventeen who was the size of a jockey with the heart of a lion, got a chunk of his ass blown away, and dear old Ropele had the tip of his generous Roman nose sliced off by a shard of grenade steel. I was especially sorry about Ropele's wound. He owed me about five hundred bucks from jawbone poker, and it was a Raider

---

* *Sukoshi* is Japanese for little.

rule that if you got hit you were cleared of local gambling debts. I always hated to see good money bleeding off a hill.

Suddenly Smalling reappeared. "I thought you'd gotten the hell out of here, Red."

"Yeah, Hack," he drawled in his lazy kind of way, "but I bumped into some gooks on the way out. I thought you should know." He went on to tell me that after Brakeman patched him up, he'd been heading back toward King Company's position when he'd run into six Chinese setting up a machine gun to our rear, along our withdrawal route. He'd killed them all, but then, despite the fact his left side was almost paralyzed, had felt he should come back to tell me. What a good man. After I sent Chris to deal with the threat (his force knocked off another dozen enemy and left a squad behind to secure our withdrawal route), I turned my attention back to the reverse-slope bunker where those potato mashers were coming from.

We couldn't use artillery because we were too close. Our own grenades, thrown blind, seemed to be having little effect. The only answer was one of Forte's bunker busters.* We'd just have to keep the enemy down and stop the incoming grenades long enough for the charge man to toss the thing in. McLain, that tall, brave *Semper Fi* Texan, volunteered for the job. Just before he walked up the hill, he hung his patrol cap over the end of his weapon and thrust it far out in front of him. The cap dangled down like a Lone Star flag. Mac turned to me. "Right out of *The Sands of Iwo Jima*, huh, Hack? Sit down, John Wayne!" Grenades—ours and theirs—popped all around him as McLain made his way up the hill. He set his weapon down, armed the charge, and spun it around his head like a lasso. *Yahoo*. He flung it over the top. Good-bye, bunker. Good-bye Chinamen with your piss-weak grenades.

An infantry platoon from King replaced us before dawn. It had been another good Raider show—mission accomplished, four friendly wounded and no dead. Statistics say that for every three Purple Hearts there's one dead. God was keeping his eye on us crazy young fools.

Colonel Sloan had promised us a unit R&R after the tenth raid. Morale was high as we returned from yet another night assault on yet another small hill in front of the 3d Batt. We'd had no friendly casualties (for the dozen or so Chinese we'd killed) and in a few days we'd be in Japan. We carefully wove our way along King Company's patrol path, which cut through a triple strand of barbed wire and mines. No more than thirty yards from the fighting positions, an LMG let go a long, long burst—it must have been

---

* A satchel charge, composed of C-4 explosive and a short-fuse detonation cord.

thirty rounds. I could see the tracers coming in one long, fiery flood; they skipped over my head by what seemed to be inches. I screamed, "Raiders, Raiders! Shut off that fire!" No one was hurt except the gunner—Chris jumped into his bunker and stomped him to a pulp. The gunner's platoon leader, NCOs, and fellow soldiers watched, silently condoning our on-the-spot Raider punishment. The guy had been asleep at his post. He must have awakened and panicked when he saw our dark figures coming at him. Fortunately, his firing was as accurate and reliable as his vigilance. The bastard could have killed a dozen good men.

Getting ready for R&R was almost as complex an operation as any raid. All we could leave in the camp was authorized stuff, which meant packing, storing, and hiding just about everything we had. The last thing we needed was some inspector to find anything irregular about our special unit. We'd grown accustomed to the luxuries of life, and the stakes were too high to leave the place anything but perfect. The biggest problem was our vehicles, most of which we ended up hiding in a deep draw behind the camp. My new jeep went off to Ordnance for engine repair, and when everything was squared away, Barney K. Neil organized a few of his bakers to stay at the Raider camp for security. Barney K. himself came with us.

Rest and Recreation or Rape and Run—it all depended on what manual you wanted to believe. But the Rest was nonexistent and the Rape was paid for in advance, so to a guy fresh from the front, R&R was simply 120 precious hours, all of which would be accounted for and none of which would be wasted. Lovely little girl-sans floated between guys; every five days they honeymooned with a new husband. The stars of the group were passed through units like a good weapon, many of them as proud of "their" outfit as regulars. "Me Wolfhound girl-san . . . never happen me stay with Cacti. You want Cacti girl-san, go see Rosie."

If we could have just frozen time. Countdown Korea began the minute you touched down in Japan, even before the first sweet, cold sip of fresh milk you'd had for a year passed your lips in the R&R center in Osaka or Tokyo. The hardest thing during those wonderful five days was to stop the clock running in your head. *Deep-six the clock*, you'd tell yourself, *in a sea of booze*, and drink some more to drown each tick, which brought you that much closer to the front.

Eat, drink, and be merry—finally the world of death and horror is far away. Danger, that constant cruel companion who haunts you every day, is suddenly cut loose and left behind. The best clubs, the best steaks, the best girls are yours forever, until a car backfires, and you're hurtled back to the whole mad thing while frantically searching for cover in the middle of the Ginza strip.

I steered clear of the other Raiders in Tokyo. Basically, I didn't want to cramp their style, like a chaperone at a high-school dance whose mission in life is to take names and kick half-bared asses out of darkened hallways and janitors' closets. I joined forces instead with Barney K. (I didn't want the Raiders to cramp *my* style either), and though Barney stayed true to his stateside bride, Belle, the two of us still managed to take the city by storm.

Five days and a three-hour plane ride later, it was back to the front for most of us, and one mean shock. There were no smiling faces, no eagerness to pick up those Thompsons and go on a raid. Of course, this was probably for the best, given that it took almost a week before all the guys got back—about half of the Raiders who'd gone to Tokyo had ended up in jail. One group had smuggled in a Chinese submachine gun; on a drunken spree they'd shot out neon lights all over the Tokyo nightclub district. Another squad had infiltrated a nearby U.S. Navy club; they'd tried to drink all the rum, torpedo the ladies, and sink all the swabbies. All in all, the Raiders hitting Japan as a unit had led to a pretty rough five days for the old Land of the Rising Sun, leaving the natives only to shake their heads and rue the day they decided to bomb Pearl Harbor.

Colonel Sloan was not amused by the conduct of his elite creation. The Raiders had gotten into more trouble in five days than the whole regiment had in six months of R&R. We had sinned, but sinned good. No one suggested deactivating the force (in fact, Sloan's XO, Lieutenant Colonel Smith, a man so caring we called him "Mother," did wonders to prevent Sloan getting the full skinny on the Raiders' R&R escapades), but the good Colonel did lock my heels together. He told me there would be no more unit R&Rs, and it was highly doubtful there would even be individual Raider R&Rs for some time down the track. "Your boys are all volunteers, and they're taking on extremely dangerous assignments. I don't expect them to be Boy Scouts. On the other hand, I cannot overlook gross violations of discipline," he said, suggesting I return order to the ranks *muy pronto.*

Jack Speed, spokesman for the transgressors, explained their shit behavior the best: "You know, Hack . . . you get over there and they give you a goddamn steak and a glass of milk and all that, and you finally realize what life is all about. I don't know . . . we just went goofy." I understood, but it wasn't going to wash with Sloan. So I took the boys on long runs especially close to the Wolfhound CP, all the while barking, "All right, you bastards, you think you're so bad," and the Colonel and staff could hear the Raiders chant their mournful repentance.

It took a different kind of leader to understand and handle the sort of animals I had on my hands. I was well suited for the job, mostly because I helped make them animals, and probably because I was one of the biggest animals of them all. So for me as their leader, the worst part of the R&R business was not the embarrassment with Sloan, but the fact that the only difference between my boys and me was that I didn't get caught.

It was just a case of a unit with *spirit*. Uncontrolled, maybe, but still spirit, which is the essence of success in battle. Spirit makes all things possible. Spirit is what made the Raiders. And if, from the outside, it looked as if we had too much, that was something only I had to deal with. My boys didn't give a damn about rules and regulations, but neither did I. What was the point? Every day we lived with such danger, we kind of figured the next would be our last anyway. And if it wasn't, and we had to pay the price with higher command, what could they do? Put us back in the Raiders and send us behind enemy lines?

The Japan raid might well have been forgotten but for two incidents. First, two weeks after our return a couple dozen cases of clap appeared among the Raider ranks. The regimental surgeon congratulated me for having my unit equal the regimental VD record for the past month. Second, the jeep we hid in Ordnance was found by its owner. It seemed that a wise old motor sergeant from the Cacti Medical Company had recognized his missing chariot in my RAIDERS 1. He must have remembered some little dent or other odd scars or modifications; he'd pulled out his jackknife, and a few careful scrapes across two coats of paint revealed the Cacti insignias.

"Sir, that jeep is not a Wolfhound jeep," I explained to regimental XO "Mother" Smith. Unsmiling but sympathetic, Smith assured me he was well aware of this. But how, he wondered, did it come to have 27th Raider insignias? I couldn't exactly say, "Well, sir, the jeep was found on post, and some gumshoe artist was fiddling around and suddenly our numbers were on the vehicle, and what the hell, it belonged to that rotten 35th Regiment," but I did. Colonel Smith was not amused. The 35th wanted a head. Someone had to be court-martialed. But he said we could probably do a deal—hold the court-martial, satisfy the 35th's CO, lose the paperwork, and the matter would be forgotten.

The Raider mafia met before the sun set. "Why don't we tell the truth?" suggested Chris. "S'koshi got the jeep."

"What do you mean, I got the jeep? Crispino, you're a lying son of a bitch," little Johnny Watkins cried, as he grabbed his weapon and slammed a magazine into it. Chris belted him in the mouth. The blow sent S'koshi flying, but no one intervened; after all, Watkins had been about to blow Chris away.

"Shit, S'koshi, I'm just pulling your leg," Chris told him, as he helped the boy to his feet. "We wouldn't make you take the rap. Okay, look," he

My grandparents, John Hackworth and Ida Stedman ("Gram"), circa 1890, Cripple Creek, Colorado. It was the frontier values of these two that molded and guided me from my earliest memory.

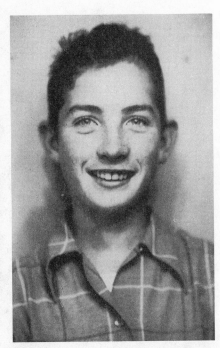

With my brother, Roy

Trieste, Italy, 1947. My platoon in the 752d Tank Battalion at Banne Barracks. Second and fifth from the left are, respectively, my dear friend Jimmy Sparks and Sergeant Ernest Medina, who almost got Sparks and me thrown into the stockade for life. First and fourth from the right are, respectively, "Chief" Robert Ventura and Sergeant Wilbur Polk, who taught me many an Old Soldier trick. The guy in the middle holding the mops is PFC Hackworth on barracks orderly duty.

The 15th Tank Company (formerly the 752d Tank Battalion) on parade in downtown Trieste, 1947. Tank 7 (foreground) is being driven by me.

Sergeant Steve Prazenka, my reconnaissance mentor and one of the greatest soldiers I ever knew, polished up for parade. Trieste, 1949.

"The more sweat on the training field, the less blood on the battlefield." I learned this in Italy, 1946–50, in the demanding charge of many World War II NCOs and officers who had learned it themselves the hard way.

Trieste United States Troops (TRUST) 351st Regimental Headquarters Company precedes the regiment in review, June 1950. Captain Kenneth Eggleston, my commander and inspiration, leads the way, and newly promoted Staff Sergeant Hackworth is just a step behind, proudly carrying the company guidon.

Korea, April 1951. 3d Platoon of George Company, 27th "Wolfhound" Regiment, crapped out on the side of the road. Good buddy and platoon leader Walt Schroeder is standing; platoon sergeant Hackworth (foreground) takes a load off his feet with the rest of the troops.

Veteran warrior Captain Jack Michaely. As skipper of G Company/27th Wolfhounds, in the first year of the Korean War Michaely was the longest-serving rifle company commander in the 25th Division.

"Thru these portals pass . . . the best damn soldiers in the world." The Wolfhounds, Korea, October 1951.

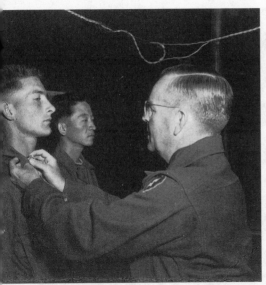

The battlefield commissioning of Sergeants Hackworth and Ushida. Brigadier General J. Sladin Bradley pinning on my gold bar at 25th Division Headquarters, 5 May, 1951.

Great fighter and great friend, Federico "Chris" Crispino. Korea, September 1951.

At my 3d Platoon, Easy Company, CP, planning the 8 August (1951) raid. Note the looted clock in the foreground, which gonged every hour on the hour, keeping time for both friend and foe on the next ridge.

Hell-raiser and brother, Raider Jack Speed toting the much-sought-after Thompson submachine gun. Korea, October 1951.

A break from the Raiders. R&R with Barney K. Neil (center) in Osaka, Japan, September 1951.

Receiving a Silver Star medal from General Bradley for the action on 6 February 1951. That action established the "legend" and reputation that I would have to live up to for the rest of my Army days.

The only photo left of the Wolfhound Raiders, taken by Easy buddy Bob Stokes on a visit to the Raider camp. Front rank from left: Salazar, Evans, Mayamura, Lipka, Sovereign, McLain. That's Platoon Sergeant Crispino in the middle distance, and I'm in front, walking to greet Bob. Korea, October 1951.

1st Lieutenant Hackworth receiving an award from Wolfhound regimental commander Colonel George B. Sloan. Korea, 1951.

March 1952. On leave in Los Angeles after my first Korean tour, with my brother Roy.

Korea, December 1952. This photo was taken from the east side of "the Gap" and shows Fighter Company, 223d Infantry's trenchline snaking up the ridge to our western boundary on the top of the hill.

Manhattan Beach, California, 1956. Fighter Company's Uno Rentmeister (left), my childhood idol Al Hewitt, and I.

Germany, 1962. There were a number of damn good Old Soldier NCOs in D Company, 1/18th Infantry, but none came better than 1st Sergeant J. J. Sweeney (front and center). On the right is XO Captain "Big Ed" Szvetecz, and on the far left, my lifelong friend Tim Grattan. Tim, Ed, and Dave Adderley (standing next to Grattan) were all top collegiate football players, and together formed the nucleus of D Company's winning team.

August 1961. The Cold War heats up. Khrushchev builds the Berlin Wall, and Kennedy tasks the 1/18th Infantry "Vanguards" to reinforce the American garrison in West Berlin as a show of force.

Colonel Glover S. Johns, a soldier's soldier, leads his 1/18th Battlegroup triumphantly into Berlin.

A reflective Colonel Johns, after the Vanguards' harrowing trek to Berlin. This is the photo which was compared in *Life* magazine to Rembrandt's *The Man in the Golden Helmet.*

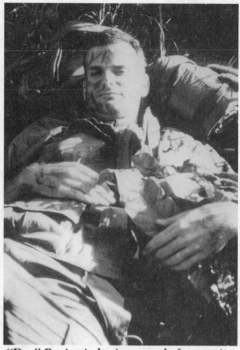

With the 1st Brigade, 101st Airborne Division, Republic of Vietnam, February 1966. Lieutenant General John A. Heintges, Deputy Commander, MACV, gives me a pep talk at My Canh, in the rice paddy where a day before the 1/327 Tigers ran into an NVA buzzsaw. The enemy was deployed along the hedgerow to our rear.

"Doc" Benjamin having a rest before an air mobile assault. Raphiel was the bravest of the brave.

June 1966. 1/101st Brigade Commander General Willard Pearson and I look on as PFC James Deardorff, a C Company, 1/327 trooper, receives a cold drink from a Viet beauty upon our triumphant return from the Dak To battlefield. This was the proudest day of my Army career.

"Doc" Raphiel Benjamin took this snap of me, Johnny Howard and Don Chapman the day after the My Canh fight.

"Up front" (at Battalion Rear) with Army historian S.L.A. "Slam" Marshall, after the Battle of Dak To, June 1966. Note the spoon—one of the infantryman's basic tools—sticking out of my fatigue jacket pocket.

The Pentagon, October 1966. Army Chief of Staff Harold K. Johnson presents me with a number of awards.

The Pentagon, 1967. As a member of the Department of the Army's "stable of studs," a Speakers Bureau whose job was to "sell" the Vietnam war to the American people.

The 1/327 Airborne Infantry Battalion marches proudly into the Screaming Eagles' base camp, after their victory at Dak To, June 1966.

Vietnam, 1968. Brigade Commander Hank "the Gunfighter" Emerson confers with battalion CO Don Schroeder in the Mekong Delta with the 9th Division.

With the 4/39 "Hardcore" Battalion, 9th Div., in the Mekong Delta, RVN, 1969. A very informal awards presentation. Captain Takahashi is the recipient.

Briefing the brass. Mekong Delta, Vietnam, 1969.

Pleiku, RVN, August 1969. Receiving a medal from Army Vice Chief of Staff General Bruce Palmer.

Getting the straight skinny from Intelligence officer Ralph Palmieri in front of the mess hall. Note the pull-up bar by the mess-hall door. If a man couldn't do ten on the way in, he didn't eat. Team 50 Compound, 44th Special Tactical Zone, February 1971.

A memorial service for the men of D Company, 4/39 Infantry, who died when their position was overrun. Fire Support Base Danger, March 1969.

The spoils of war. Some of the booty netted from the Hardcore's destruction of the VC 261A Battalion. FSB Danger, March 1969.

General Lu Lan, II Corps Commander, says goodbye to me as I leave the US advisory detachment at Pleiku for the Vietnamese Airborne Division. Colonel Binh, my G-3 counterpart, is on the right. December 1969.

With the Vietnamese Airborne Division. Looking over a captured NVA arms depot at Cam Pak, Cambodia, June 1970.

There's no point in trying to win an argument with Ben Willis, but I always gave it a damn good try. Cambodia, June 1970.

My promotion to bird colonel. The dark patches on my uniform are the result of the old Army tradition of "wetting down" the new insignia with beer. Congratulating me is ARVN IV Corps CG, Lieutenant General Truong. Cao Lanh, RVN, March 1971.

Ben Willis (center) provides wise counsel during the filming of "Issues and Answers." Standing by is ABC Television's Howard Tuckner, who conducted the interview. Cao Lanh, Vietnam, April 1971.

Brisbane, Australia, 1983. On the peace trail. At left is Mike Higgins, producer and presenter of "The Living Will Envy the Dead," a documentary that began the process of waking up the Australian people to the dangers of nuclear weapons.

said, turning to the rest of us, all business. "We'll tell the truth. *I* got the jeep. I found it."

Another voice chimed in. "Yeah, it was abandoned over near the shower unit. It wasn't locked or anything. And it was getting dark. Thought a Korean would steal it."

"Yeah, so we brought it home for the night. Next morning one of the guys was just screwing around and painted on our markings."

"Right," said Chris, "and by the time I woke up, the new Raider jeep was on its way to Seoul for a scrounging trip. And when it came back . . . well, it was three days later, and nobody had been asking about no jeep. And then we'll tell 'em it belonged to the 35th anyway, and they're just a bunch of no-good sons of bitches, so we kept it. I'll take the blame."

Chris was court-martialed by one of the regimental staff officers the next afternoon. He was found guilty, admonished, and fined part of a month's pay. The two of us drove back from Regiment, pleased that the heat was off and "justice" had been done. We knew the guys had been worried. We hadn't told them about our back-room talks and that the court was fixed (some things had to remain sacred), but as long as they were still in the dark, we decided to play out just one more scene in the drama.

We arrived back at camp, our faces grim. Chris went into our tent and began to pack his gear. "How did it go?" the guys yelled in unison. "What's he doing?" asked Johnny Watkins. I told them that Chris was getting his no-good ass right out of the outfit, that in order to save himself from jail he had squealed on us and all of our unauthorized activities—the Raiderettes, the other stolen vehicles, the rations, everything. A couple of the guys got so pissed off they grabbed their Thompson submachine guns and started for our tent, as if to finish off the job S'koshi had tried to start the night before. I hadn't expected that. Our script called for a happy ending, not Chris's brains splattered all over the camp.

I took the weapons away. "Look, let me handle this." Mercifully, on cue, Chris came out of the tent. As per script, we went to an open field about three hundred yards from where the Raiders were sitting. There, I proceeded to stomp the hell out of my friend. Then Chris started to stomp the hell out of me—a kick in the face, a fierce blow to the head, a thundering flip on the back. But it was all stuntman stuff, like buddies faking it on the back lot: every boot and every blow was stopped before it sank home. Finally we both got bored. It was time to wind the thing up. The finale came when Chris, the villain, kneed me. I rolled into a ball, and he started to finish me off with vicious kicks to the face. But like the true, clean-cut, all-American boy I was, I pulled myself up on his tattered uniform, coldcocked him, and walked away, victorious.

"That'll take care of that squealing son of a bitch," I said, slapping my hands together, as the rest of the Raiders looked on in horror. "Let's have a beer." When Chris got up, dusted himself off, and joined the party, everyone had a good laugh, but it'd be fair to say the two of us had a hard time making the Raiders believe much of anything after that.

A few more good raids made Regiment forget all our transgressions, and by late October there was not one hill or valley throughout the regimental sector that the Raiders had not ventured across. It was indeed difficult to find an objective where we had not been before. Battlefield circumstances and Chinamen in depth had phased out our original Raider role; our mission assignments now came from Operations. We had become the de facto regimental assault force.

I was always on guard against higher headquarters playing games with my unit. I well remembered how the 8th Rangers had been misused and virtually destroyed in November, and most of the other specially trained Airborne Ranger companies in Korea met the same fate. Historically, special units have always been thrown into the breach to stem the tide. Everyone knows that ten spirited fighters are far better than a herd of a thousand listless drag asses. But many commanders on the Korean battlefield were beginning to behave like desperate gamblers, ignoring the reality that it was far easier for the planners to draw a circle on a map and claim it as a critical objective than it was for mortal men to seize it. So, with morale in the trenches already lower than whaleshit, COs across the front were calling for well-trained, well-motivated cannon fodder—Ranger/Raider specialists—to do the jobs their own dough-foots would, or could, not do themselves.

It took great command wisdom not to ruin a fine thoroughbred by having it pull the plow when the mule was down. Colonel Sloan exercised this wisdom, and the Regimental S-3, Major Robert Glaser, backed him up to the best of his ability. Glaser was a seasoned combat man with two wars under his belt. Until his recent promotion, he'd commanded a 3d Batt rifle company, so he knew well how to keep his planners in tight rein, and make certain the grease-pencil warriors did not promote schemes that would put the Raiders in serious jeopardy. Still, our missions were no longer based on stealth and skill but rather on shock and firepower. It didn't help that little by little, through battle casualties and normal rotation, we were losing some of the original Raiders. Fortunately, the replacements adopted our what-the-hell attitude, and we accepted each mission as we had all to date— fatalistically. Even when it meant retaking a position in broad daylight.

For three days we'd sat in foxholes behind the 1st Batt, to whom we were temporarily attached. Indications had been that the Chinese would attack in force right down the center of the regiment. The Raider role was to block an enemy penetration. If the guys ever thought they were prima donnas, this duty quickly dispelled the idea: our position should have been held by a two-hundred-man rifle company. We had less than a fourth of that number and were armed with only assault weapons, great for close-in stuff but not red-hot in the defense. We did not have mortars, entrenching gear, or even steel pots. We were David waiting for Goliath, minus the slingshot.

The Chinese threw a fair amount of artillery and mortar fire around but did not launch the expected attack. It was when they overran an outpost in front of A Company that 1st Batt decided to send "their" Raiders to get it back in daylight. Why not? I guessed the rationale was that we were attached to them for the moment, so why get any of their own killed when someone else will go for free?

The OP was located on a little knob about six hundred yards from the main line. We moved up before dawn. I would have preferred making a night attack, but Lieutenant George Creamer of A Company had said that at night there was no way to crawl through the barbed wire and mines that previous U.S. defenders had laid on the slopes. We clobbered the hill with artillery and kept it pouring while we worked our way to the top in single file, disarming mines along the OP patrol path. The position did not have any tactical value to the enemy; the attack had either been a feint or a psychological exercise—a demonstration by kamikaze troops that the Chinks were the baddest guys in the valley. In any event, the Chinese raiders had flown the coop by the time we reached the top. I called the main line to tell them the goddamned position had been retaken courtesy of the Raiders and they could come out and relieve us any time they wanted. Now it was just a case of tidying up before they arrived.

We stacked up the U.S. dead (it looked as if they'd been asleep at the switch; the Chinese must have slipped through their defenses and knocked them off all at once) and started cleaning up the position. Down below, a few of my guys began opening a wider path through the minefield for the relieving force; I went down to have a look. I moseyed around the position a bit, and when the boys yelled, "All clear," I started back to the top, only then noticing that one of my boots had trip wire wrapped all around it—normal debris from defused mines. I gave my leg a mighty kick to get rid of the stuff. My troops hit the ground—instantly. Before I could figure out why, a Bouncing Betty exploded about four feet away from me, sending scores of ball bearings into the air. When the dust settled I was still standing up, untouched. "What the hell are you guys doing down there?" I asked, as the boys slowly got up and looked at me in amazement. The fact was, my hearing had deteriorated a lot after I got hit in the head on 6 February. The only difference between the mine clearers and me was that I hadn't heard the "click" when the firing mechanism went. "Thought you fuckers had cleared this area," I barked, and hotfooted it back to the top of the knob—so I could go into shock in private.

It would just become part of the legend: *Let me tell you about our Old Man . . . our CO doesn't give a damn about anything. You know how he clears a path through minefields? He just walks out and stomps and kicks. He blows the shit out of mines and isn't even touched!* Or the time when Chris was chopping wood in front of our tent, standing there in his shorts, legs apart. His pistol lay on top of his rack; I picked up the weapon and squinted through the sights right between Chris's legs. What a tempting shot. I took careful aim at the log he was splitting no more than six feet away, and squeezed the trigger, figuring the pistol wasn't loaded. *BANG!* The slug went between Crispino's legs, missed the log, and cut the ax handle in two as Chris followed through on a downward chop. It scared the shit out of both of us, but I pretended I'd hit my target: "Bull's-eye."

I never squeezed rounds off an "unloaded" weapon again; it was a lesson I should have learned years before, when I overheard old Sergeant Walker in Italy counseling a young kid who'd playfully pointed his weapon at him. ("Don't ever point a weapon at someone unless you intend to kill him," said Walker, who'd seen combat in Africa, Sicily, and Italy. "I know, because some damned fool killed me that way. But when I got up to the Pearly Gates, Saint Peter said, 'You're too young and too handsome to be here now. I want you to go back and *teach* all those careless young fools who point their weapons at their friends.' ") Even so, the legend only grew with stories like that: *And yeah*, says another one of my guys in the rear, *not only is the son of a bitch scared of nothing, but he can shoot an ax handle off an ax between a guy's legs!*

I knew the minefield incident was built on bad hearing, and the ax-handle shot was just sheer stupidity canceled out by good luck. But that's the stuff a legend has to keep to himself. Soldiers need legends. It's a way to deal with the madness of war. Like the legend of Rodger Young, a quiet, shy man who won the Medal of Honor in the Solomon Islands in WW II for leading a daring attack against strongly defended Jap positions. He'd died in the attempt, courageously ignoring his buddies' calls to stay down, and was immortalized in a number-one hit song among the boys in olive drab: "For the everlasting glory of the infantry/Shines the name/Shines the name/of Rodger Young." Only after the war was it revealed that Rodger Young was almost totally deaf. He'd faked his hearing test to get into the fighting, and his bravery on the day he died was most likely a result of not hearing the warning shouts of his friends. But it didn't matter by then. Rodger Young was a legend, and his very name got many soldiers through the night.

"Living legends" serve a similar purpose. If the troops can go into battle secretly knowing that among them lurks a Scooter Burke—a Superman in Clark Kent's ODs—they'll fight better, they'll fight harder, and they'll somehow believe that immortality is theirs, too. But this presents a problem for a leader "legend," because you reach a point where you can't let your men know you make mistakes. You just can't, even when it means you become trapped somewhere between who you really are and what they want you to be.

All I ever wanted was to be a good soldier, and I was. But to myself, I was certainly not a hero. Inside I was an embarrassingly uneducated, insecure kid of twenty with a terrible temper and lots of luck (both traits more than likely inherited from my Irish mother). Fury accounted for most of the heroic acts chalked up to my name. Going after that sniper on 6 February, where the whole legend began, was more than anything the work of a hungry Irishman temporarily off his nut. Still, on the outside I played the role, and even encouraged the hero business. After all, showmanship is vital to being a good troop commander. The only problem was that my audience kept demanding encore after encore. Many, many times in a firefight— when the slugs were really snapping—I'd find myself snugged up close to a solid dirt wall or behind a tree enjoying perfect cover, and just as I'd begin thinking how comfortable I was, I'd start feeling the eyes of my command boring in, saying, *We're in a real tough spot here, baby. Just what trick are you going to pull out of the old hat to save our sweet asses?* And I always pulled out something, with one more wild or brazen stunt, confirming to my troops (and maybe to myself, too) that I was the bravest dude on the block.

Before Napoleon promoted a general to field marshal, he would ask one question: "Are you lucky?" And only if the answer was yes, would Napoleon pass on the baton. I was lucky. That little bit of magic followed me as closely throughout my career as the smell of battle. And it followed the Raiders, too, in the fall of 1951, through dozens of raids (behind enemy lines and within our own), irrefutable cases of insubordinate and wild behavior, and enough 190-proof to keep a hospital going for a year. Yes, the Raiders—my own little army, composed solely of field marshals—were lucky. And we were going to live forever.

7 HILL 400

What made a guy right for the Raiders? You had to be someone who just didn't give a shit. It isn't a big deal to die, you know—"Live with honor, die with dignity," that was the Raiders' slogan. See, Hackworth had pride in people. And for a twenty-year-old man to be able to make a person want to fight and die and be happy about it—shit, we were *happy* to die for our country. That's the kind of spirit we had in the Raiders.

Master Sergeant Jack Speed, USA
Squad Leader/Platoon Sergeant
27th Raider Platoon, Korea, 1951

We few, we happy few, we band of brothers;
For he to-day that sheds his blood with me
Shall be my brother; be he ne'er so vile,
This day shall gentle his condition;
And gentlemen in England now abed
Shall think themselves accursed they were not here,
And hold their manhoods cheap whiles any speaks
That fought with us upon Saint Crispin's day.

William Shakespeare
Henry V, Act IV, iii

I never wanted to die, but I never feared death either. I guess I always knew that the price of admission to life was one owed death; my father and mother both paid it before I was a year old, and Uncle Roy just eight years later, his a lingering death from the mustard gas and other wounds he sustained in WW I. With me, I figured when it came it would be with the roll of the dice. It was really a matter of luck and probability: the more missions, the more point duty, the more hot engagements, the higher the probability of getting zeroed out. And if you had to go, sure, you wanted to do it heroically, but real heroism, I believed, was just returning to the front—when you knew the score and how the game was played, and when you knew what it was like to have hot steel ripping through your body, and your wounds healed in a ward full of kids your age who might never walk, see, and think the same again.

On the occasions (and there were a good few) when death and I stood eyeball-to-eyeball, when I knew I'd used up my odds and in the next few moments I would be dead, I was always perfectly calm. There was no fighting, no raging to hang on. I was always perfectly at peace, and almost invariably I'd think to myself, *So this is the way it is; what an uninspiring way to go.* In its way, it was a good feeling, because then I'd settle back and rock into whatever was going, just as cool as ice. Men had been dying in battle for ages—what else was new? "Live fast, die young, and have a good-looking corpse" was how I and the rest of the Raiders saw it (along with John Derek, who said it first in the 1949 movie *Knock on Any Door*); the only thing to do was not worry about it at all, and have the best damn time you could while you were around. Of course, being a leader helped. You were always too busy bringing in air and artillery, moving your people and shepherding your herd, to take time to focus in on yourself, on where *you* might be in a moment's time.

On the battlefield you become very superstitious. You're always looking for something that's going to protect you from being killed. It might be a photo of the girl next door. It might be a rabbit's foot, or a blanket (yes, a security blanket), which you huddled under in the night. Phil Gilchrist's was a white T-shirt with a blue band around the collar. He never went into battle without it. My Chink Waltham watch might have become a lucky charm for me, if it hadn't been knocked off in the hospital after 6 February. But as it was, I didn't need it or any other. Because I had an inside thing with God.

I prayed all the time. But early on, I'd made a pact with myself: it was never *Dear God, please look after me*; it was always *Dear God, please look after my men and make sure that no one gets killed.* I suppose if I could have been objective about it, I would have realized that to lose men was just the breaks of the game. But I had built my little house of hope and God dwelled therein: since I'd returned from the hospital after the 6 February wound, which meant all of March until now, 1 November, we'd been in some really heavy combat, taken stacks of WIA, but among my men we'd never taken any dead. The Man and I were tight.

"We've got a tough job for you. It will be the hardest one your outfit's had," Colonel Sloan explained to me quietly. "How many men have you got and how soon will you be able to jump off?"

Colonel Sloan's "tough job" was a Raider assault on Hill 400, what the

Infantry School would have called *key terrain*. It was a rocky, volcano-shaped hill that sat astride the left boundary of the Wolfhound Regiment, dominating the battlefield like a Spanish hilltop fortress. The enemy had occupied it for a long time. According to Intelligence there were no more than fifty Chinamen up there, but the enemy had burrowed deep into the hill's rocky slopes, and despite all tactics used or vast firepower employed, the Wolfhounds could not secure that piece of ground.

We were assured it was not a kamikaze attack. Instead, Sloan said that it was critical, and an operation perfectly tailored for our fleet-footed band of hill runners. Though I might have mentioned that this perfectly tailored operation had only been designed for the Raiders after two or three different units of infantry had assaulted the hill (taking extreme casualties in the process), I accepted the mission without comment. But my gut started to churn; 400 was that Jake Able feeling all over again.

We'd jump off in three days. On the morning of the first day, key Raider leaders and I conducted a visual reconnaissance of Hill 400 from Item Company's forward outpost position on Hill 275. The OP was set on a gray knob a mile from the front, with our objective about one-half mile farther north along the ridgeline. "Shit," said Speed. "This one won't be so goddamn tough." I wasn't sure I agreed. For one thing, there were the ubiquitous mines and booby traps to be disarmed before we even got near. For another, our objective was a formidable piece of real estate, with steep sides and a rear anchored securely by the Chinese main battle positions on Hill 419 to the north. And the third thing was there was only one avenue of approach: it would be hi-diddle-diddle, right up the middle.

Item Company's grim-faced soldiers didn't help the foreboding feeling. They had a fugitive, hunted look about them. They all kept their heads down, moved fast, and didn't smile much. Everything about their hill reminded me of Uncle Roy's 1918 stories about Château-Thierry and the Marne: the dugouts, the muddy slopes, the shell-ravaged trenches where brooding men just waited to be overcome by rolling yellow clouds of mustard gas, or to be ordered to hurl themselves into machine-gun fire.

Tooling around in RAIDERS 1 had already shown me the sharp contrast between the life-styles of the frontline troops and those located behind Battalion Forward: bleak, endless trenches versus all the comforts (under canvas) of a stateside billet. The Raiders were unusual—as a rule the Army kept infantry "have-nots" far from the rear-echelon "haves"—and though none of us felt guilty about the good life we led behind the lines, I often wondered what fighters like these guys up in Item thought when rotation came and they saw all they'd been missing.

That night Jimmie, Chris, and I left Item's outpost for a closer look at the Chinese defensive positions on Hill 400. We'd been all around that fortress on previous operations and never had been able to find a weak point; now we were up there on it for almost six hours. Item Company guys who'd previously attacked the hill warned of accurate 82-mm and 120-mm mortar fire and a damn tight defensive system. We disarmed a few mines (but nothing to get too excited about), found three outposts on the hill's southern nose, and behind that a trench bunker system. But that was all. We still couldn't find Hill 400's Achilles' heel.

We returned to our camp and worked out the plans. On request, the artillery people had been punching the shit out of 400 with heavy eight-inch delay stuff since we'd gotten the warning order (causing big sections of the enemy's breastworks to crumble in), but on the night itself there would be no artillery preparation or illumination. Our initial attack would be by stealth: we'd knock off the OPs, move to our deployment position, and, after forming a line of skirmishers, hit the trenchworks. Only when the shooting started would supporting fires be brought in to clobber the Chinese reverse slopes, reinforcement routes, and likely mortar and artillery positions.

Sloan approved the plan. He also told me he'd have a regimental forward aid station set up behind Item's outpost, a comforting thought, but one that did little to assuage my concern about the operation. Then, reminding me that I was long overdue to go home, he added, "I don't want any heroics up there, Dave." *No heroics*, I thought. *Right—like telling Johnny Reb not to click his heels together when "Dixie" was played.* Besides, just going up that hill was worth a double Blue Max—for all of us.

We briefed the troops. Every man knew exactly where he was to go and what he was to do when he got there. I guess Chris and I were snapping out orders and carrying on like real badass Regulars—in the hospital, a thousand years later, Sprinkler told me that's how the guys had known we were in for some deep shit. So while Forte made satchel charges and Scaglion played fireman with his scrounged portable flamethrower, the rest of the Raiders rehearsed the operation and readied their gear. The boys looked good. I was pleased.

We moved up behind Item under the cover of darkness the night before the raid. I didn't want to tip our hand, but I wanted my guys on the hill in the morning so they could get a good look at 400 during daylight, then be rested and set to go at first dark. They had their look and then, spread out among Item's reverse slope bunkers, caught some shut-eye. A number of the guys wrote letters—some in earnest, some in jest, the latter group wrinkling them up and rubbing them in the dirt, so that if they got zapped, whoever was on the receiving end would know that life in the trenches was tough and war was hell. After a last look at foreboding 400, I sacked out for the rest of the day. Unlike Jake Able, I slept like a bear.

The sun dropped out of the sky like an incoming round. Suddenly it was pitch-black—the perfect night to attack—no moon and a thick blanket of fog that settled over the battlefield. Jimmie moved first; his scout section was through the wire and gone without a sound. Jack Speed's squad was next, followed by me and Don Neary with his radio. Next were Bill Smith's and Tex Garvin's people. All was going just like rehearsals. For once everyone seemed to have gotten the word. No one fired at us from Item; no flares were sent up to make us sitting ducks in no-man's-land.

The inevitable first hitch occurred just as I'd cleared Item's wire. Word was passed up that a Raider in Smith's squad was refusing to go a step farther. I had Neary halt the infiltrating column, and I went back to find this guy hunkered down in the patrol path like a mule. Until now, he'd been a good man—he had at least a dozen raids under his belt—but now he wouldn't budge. He said he'd had it; he couldn't go on. I told him that his timing was off—he should have turned in his quit slip before we left home—and that his ass was going up that hill. Sobbing, he told me to get screwed. I hit him on both sides of his face with my pistol and said that there wasn't a Raider out there who wanted to go, but they'd all made the commitment when they'd gone through the wire. The boy wouldn't be moved. I pulled my trench knife out of my boot and laid it against his throat. "I'd just as soon cut your throat as fuck with you," I said. "You either go on this raid or die. If I kill you I'll report that you bought the farm in a big burst of glory. Make up your mind." After a few seconds, between muffled sobs, he said he'd go.

The crews of the three enemy OPs must have forgotten the old soldiers' creed: *Stay alert and stay alive*; Jimmie and his gang knocked them off with ease. We moved up to the deployment line, then crept forward, one slow, quiet step after another: toe down, then heel; crush, not snap—taking more care than in a minefield.

All the Raiders around me were now in, or entering, the trench. A short way down, Tex Garvin made the first kill. He'd just finished putting his men into their attack positions and was standing just above the trench when an enemy soldier came strolling by. Garvin reached down, splattered the Chinaman's head with the butt of his weapon, and rolled him into an empty bunker. Meanwhile, I checked with Speed to see how his guys were doing—everything was okay. Neary and I started creeping down the enemy trench line to where Speed's and Smith's squads were tying in. Then I saw a Chink not more than four feet away. I froze. The guy was standing in the trench, looking downhill with only his head sticking out, a difficult target for a knife or a garrote, and I didn't want to shoot him until we were really ready to go. But I couldn't see how I could get at him, or past him, silently. Neary covered me. I slipped my pistol out of its holster, laid my Thompson down, and started bellying along the top of the trench line. Definite heart-in-mouth stuff. I was about a foot away from him when I came to the interesting realization that Chinese sentries were no different from a lot of Americans I knew. He was fast asleep.

He never knew what happened. I grabbed him with one arm, covered his mouth, snapped his head back, and cut his throat. Neary, who was at least six feet four and built like a fullback, moved up behind me and pulled the sentry out of the trench as if he were a feather pillow. He dragged him down the hill and stuffed him into a shell crater.

Everyone was in place, and Forte's satchel charges were ready and waiting at sleeping bunker doors. "Let's get this show on the road" was the word from Jack Speed. Jimmie Mayamura appeared in front of me. He whispered, "Hack, I think we're going to have to change the plan." He reported that there were some additional, heavily fortified positions between the trench we were in and the top of the hill. We hadn't found them on our reconnaissance (it would have been too risky to have gone beyond the trench; we could have blown the operation). Now Jimmie, roaming around as if he were on a Sunday picnic, had stumbled across them. They were unoccupied, but another scout, Bobby Evans, had gone into one large bunker and estimated at least ten men in there. He'd set a trip-wire grenade booby trap to nail them when they came out.

Before I could reassess my battle plan, Hill 400 exploded. Evans dispatched four Chinamen who were moving down a connecting trench into the one we occupied. His BAR had barely started singing when every weapon on the line started hammering away. Forte ignited his satchel charges and an earth-shattering roar shook the trench line as bunkers blew across the position. The remaining Chinks in the immediate area didn't have a chance. If they were not trapped underground, then Raider grenades blew them sky-high. Farther up the hill, the enemy were wide-awake now and frantically firing in every direction. They hit nothing. We'd cracked their main line and not a casualty reported so far. I was beginning to count on my Jake Able premonition. This time, like the other, it was a false alarm: this hill was going to be a piece of cake.

I told the boys to use regular daylight assault procedures; we'd fire and maneuver and blast our way up. Cordite hung heavily in the air as Chris formed a reserve of Forte's and Mayamura's people and took over our positions with the mission of guarding our ass. The prearranged artillery fire blistered the top of the ridge as Scaglion kicked off our attack with two fiery blasts of his flamethrower. The Raiders started slugging, but then the world fell in.

The Chinks always relied heavily on potato-masher grenades. Already we'd policed up what looked like enough to give each enemy soldier on 400 his own monogrammed case. But even when they threw them at us in bunches (as they had on Objective Logan, ringing the pins of each around their fingers or on little sticks), potato mashers didn't pack much punch in the open. They were virtually harmless firecrackers we'd learned to dance around and (more or less) ignore. The problem on Hill 400, though, was that the defenders weren't just throwing potato mashers. They were also hurling frags. We hadn't counted on that, and the sky was black with them.

Many rolled down the hill and exploded out of range behind us (proving one of Captain Michaely's pet theories over in George: it was actually safer up front doing the fighting than hiding behind where you became a sitting duck for grenades and incoming), but many found a Raider target. Smith's guys had a hard time; they took a number of casualties and couldn't gain an inch of ground until Speed's fighters thundered forward in a wild attack. These men overwhelmed one of the unexpected positions, and now Speed's complete force was in there, mopping up. The price filtered back to me: we'd taken three dead and more than twenty wounded. *It's just a nightmare,* the words bubbled up in my brain.

Almost to a man, the wounded Raiders refused to leave the hill. Doc Brakeman was performing miracles in his ever-growing "field hospital" in a shell hole behind the trench below us; the kids determinedly returned to the fighting the minute they got patched up. Some, like Jimmie (who'd already gotten shot in the ass and the arm), didn't even bother with the patching— everyone knew we were a lean outfit and that every gun counted. It was that family bonding again: no one was going to let his brothers down, especially in a fight like this. Even at the cost of his life.

I called for Chris and Forte to bring up their people. We needed everybody on line. Fuck a lot of rear security—if you're losing the fight, a strong rear won't do you any good. We were running low on ammo and grenades so we took all we could from enemy dead. I told the leaders to let me know when they were rearmed, reorganized, and set to go. We had to *banzai* the shit out of the hilltop in a hurry. It was the only way we'd take it, and if we didn't jump off soon we'd be nickeled and dimed to death by what seemed like ever-increasing scores of frags bouncing down from above.

Green tracers from a machine gun raked our position. It was set up in a rocky outcrop near the top of the hill, firing right down Speed's throat. No way could he get his people through that. The way it stood now, they couldn't even return fire. The gun had to go.

Brave Raiders Smith and Salazar, on the left, took on the deadly challenge. There was little cover and no concealed approaches to the gun, just a fold in the ground in the center of Smith's front, which the machine gun could not depress low enough to cover. Raider weapons laid down good covering fire as the two volunteers crawled up the hill. I liked these men. Especially Smith, an Alabamian who I initially hadn't been sure was Raider material, because he'd gotten his stripes the National Guard "weekend warrior" way. The funny thing was that Smith didn't think he deserved those stripes either. He was embarrassed about them, and always seemed to go out of his way to prove himself, even when it was no longer necessary. Maybe it still riled him a bit when we called him "NG" (due to his National Guard origins); still, by now he did know it was just a loving nickname for a brave and trusted comrade-in-arms.

Now, under our fire, he and Salazar snaked through the dead space toward the gun. About twenty yards from their objective, Salazar blasted with his weapon and Smith rushed forward, screaming as he unleashed two large Chinese antitank grenades. Both hit home, exploding on impact. The machine gun and crew were blown to a million pieces. The two Raiders turned and started back toward us. Then a Chinaman jumped up on the outcrop and fired a long, long burst. Both men fell, their momentum sending them tumbling into our position. Smith died in my arms. I cried as I held him; *It's just a nightmare,* I thought. And then I swore we'd take that fucking hill.

Speed had jumped off as soon as the machine gun blew. Garvin, picking up the reins from Smith, attacked on the left. Item Company put 60-mm mortar fire all over the top of the hill; we came up right under it. Speed's people hit the top like a bulldozer, closely followed by Garvin's squad. The die-hard Chinks were making a determined last stand as Raiders fanned out; savage close-in fighting and hand-to-hand combat were the bloody order of the day.

"Shift the mortar fire to the back of the hill!" I yelled to Neary.

"Grenade!" shouted Raider Mendoza, who was kneeling about three feet away from me. We went for cover. Mendoza and Neary hit the ground. I spun, but tripped and rolled down the slope. I stopped rolling about the same time as the grenade. The same place as the grenade. It was under me when it exploded—the blast propelled me into the air like a rocket. Moments later a 160-pound rag doll fell to the ground with a heavy thud.

I could not get any air. I was choking and gasping. Horrible sucking sounds were coming out of my chest. *Fire,* I thought, my chest and left side were on fire. I groaned and tried to breathe. I figured my lungs had burst. Then I stopped moaning. It took too much energy. "Hackworth's done for . . ." the words floated down. "The Old Man's dead." *No, Speed, no. I'm not dead.*

I moaned again, louder, but Jack was gone. *Fuck you, Jack Speed, I'm not dead, and I ain't gonna die, not on this goddamn hill.*

I dragged myself to my feet and headed for the doc. He checked me out and got me breathing while I sent word to Chris to take command and get a prisoner. My left arm was broken and hanging from my shoulder by ripped flesh and torn muscle; scores of shrapnel wounds covered my burned chest. But I would live, and for the second time, a submachine gun had saved my life. A submachine gun, and good TRUST training. When I'd rolled down that hill, I'd tucked my Thompson into my gut as I'd been trained, and rolled with it under me; the weapon, not I, had taken the full impact of the explosion.

Johnny Watkins drifted in. A grenade had blown the shit out of him. He said things were heating up, that Chris had been hit in the leg and Speed had assumed command. I could hear the increased fire above, and after a shot of morphine and a little Brakeman bedside manner (he wrapped my arm in a heavy Carlisle bandage and made a sling out of an empty M-1 bandolier), I headed back to the fight. It was almost dawn.

The Chinese had been counterattacking since I'd been hit. Only now was the assault beginning to falter. Raiders, all wounded, had been pushed back; they lay near the crest of the hill and cut the enemy down as they came over the top. I picked up a little M-2 carbine. It was nothing like my Thompson (now a black and twisted mess), but I could fire it like a pistol with my one good hand, and I joined in the fray.

It was getting light enough to see now. To my right lay Chief Denny and ex-Easy trooper Hearn. Both had been hit: Denny in both arms, and Hearn down from a head wound. Hearn couldn't see and Denny couldn't shoot, so the Oklahoma cowboy and the Arizona Indian brave had formed a posse of one: Denny gave directions while Hearn fired the weapon. *Red man, white man, kill 'em yellow man.* Tex Garvin was over to the left, both legs badly blasted by shot. He couldn't move, but he put down effective fire as calmly and deliberately as if he were at the KD range at Camp Pendleton, striking for a USMC Expert's Badge.

Neary crawled over to me with a message from Colonel Sloan: *Put Crispino in command and get yourself down to Item.* "You never got that message, Neary," I snapped.

"But, Hack, he was serious."

"Shut off the radio."

All colonels are serious. But there was nothing Sloan or anyone could have done for us right now. We needed to know what the hell was happening. It seemed as if we'd already wiped out the whole Chinese Army and the bastards were still coming. I asked Neary if the guys had gotten a prisoner yet. He replied in the negative and slipped into the cordite dawn, while I backed off from the top of the hill to take a moment to examine the situation. All but a handful of Raiders had been hit. Most, twice and more. More than twenty-five wounded and, at last count, five dead, including the boy who'd tried to quit at the LD. *Had he known something I hadn't?* Most of our leaders were down. Speed had taken a shot in the belly and was shooting with one hand, holding his guts in with the other. We were totally dependent on captured weapons. Our ammo supply was gone. We'd reached a fish-or-cut-bait situation.

There is seldom a Mexican standoff in battle; you either win or lose. And in many fights, a commander reaches a point where he thinks he's lost. He sees only his losses, and knows only his *own* situation, not the enemy's. The carnage surrounding him erodes his confidence. Wellington at Waterloo thought he'd lost; so did Easy Company under Desiderio, in the fight on the hill up north. Grant summed up the feeling best, at Fort Donelson during the Civil War: "Either side was ready to give way if the other showed a bold front." Well, we'd certainly shown a bold front, but so had the men from China.

Neary appeared again, this time carrying an unconscious little Chinaman. I found out later that after I'd told him we needed a prisoner, he'd taken it as a personal assignment. He'd charged up the hill and stormed the top unarmed. Once in the enemy position, he'd smashed this Chink on the head with his fist and hotfooted it back to me. Unfortunately, the POW died before we got the skinny—he'd kept trying to pull one of the grenades off Neary's belt on the way back, and Neary had stomped him, obviously a little too hard. So we got another prisoner, but then, just when we needed him most, our interpreter, Kim Upsu, decided to bug out. Speed saw him running down the hill. He stopped him. "I go, I go," said Kim, and edged away. Jack didn't know what to do. He was good and ready to waste him; instead, he leveled his weapon and shot off Kim's hand. This persuasive little tactic worked, and as we bandaged him up, Kim decided he liked our company after all.

The word from the POW was just what we wanted to hear: our artillery had clobbered the enemy reinforcing unit (Intelligence had been off by about three hundred men in terms of enemy strength on Hill 400; the Chinks were reinforcing through a tunnel-trench network on the reverse slope, which ran through to Hill 419 behind), and no one on the hill had any fight left in him. I told Jimmie and the others to round up every gun that could walk, limp, or crawl. We were going to storm the top.

Twenty bloodied and battered Raiders soon crested the hill. Its surface was covered with enemy dead. The Chinese defenders who hadn't been killed on position had chanced running the gauntlet of artillery shot (which continued to blast the back of the hill); judging from the carnage on the reverse slope, few had made it. But an intact Bren-gun crew was still raising hell among our tired band. There were more casualties, until Jimmie and Evans went on the attack. They killed the crew, but paid the price.

Jimmie lay like a broken reed next to the gun. He'd taken a shot in the face that ripped through his right eye and lower jaw. Evans lay nearby, staring at Jimmy with wide, lifeless eyes and a satisfied look on his heavily-mustached face. It was the look of a winner. He'd probably just said to Jimmie, "Well, we got the son of a bitch," before a burst of enemy fire, most likely the last of the fight, hit him full in the chest and ripped the life out of him.

Neary switched on his radio to report the capture of Hill 400. Relief was en route, he was told, dispatched by a worried Colonel Sloan when we went off the air. *"Oh, say can you see,"* I thought, as in the dull light of morning we collected our scattered and broken fighters from the blood-soaked, *American*-held hill. The inexhaustible Brakeman was kneeling over Jimmie, pumping life into him with a container of albumin. Some piece of cake: we had seven KIA, twenty-nine WIA, and one Raider, Salazar, missing. The only two Raiders who were not hit were Lipka and Sovereign, the two gunners. Their machine guns had been out of range of the frags that had depleted our ranks. It was a strange turnabout—normally the gunners ride in the death seat.

We turned the hill over to the relieving Wolfhound unit and continued looking for Salazar. We wouldn't leave the hill without him, and any man who could walk joined in the search. He'd been patched up after he and Smith had knocked out the machine gun, but no one had seen him since he'd returned to the fight. A faint moan was heard in a draw on the steep left-hand side of 400. It was Salazar, more dead than alive; he'd been blown off the hill by a grenade, and somehow, with twenty-nine slugs or shrapnel wounds in his body, that tough Texan hombre was still sucking in air. The doc got some blood into him, and we started down the hill.

We carried all our dead and the wounded who could not make it under their own steam. Speed and I brought Jimmie's broken body down in a poncho while Brakeman kept the albumin going. Regimental medics took over, and carried the litter cases down by stretcher. There had been no free rides on that terrible hill—Chris's boy, Johnny, bled, too, as he accompanied Chris through the low-lying fog. Chink 82-mm and 120-mm mortar fire continued to smash in around us, but it was ignored by all. After what we'd been through, it didn't mean a thing.

Colonel Sloan had walked alone to meet us on Hill 400's forward slopes. He, too, ignored the incoming as he went from Raider to Raider, helping, comforting, praising. Tears streamed from his eyes in that early-morning light as he helped us down. He led us to the aid station, and there I saw seven figures, all lined up, each covered with a poncho. *It's just a nightmare*, I thought, but I didn't believe myself at all. I went to each body, and pulled the sheet back off the face. One by one I cradled those men and rocked them in my arms, crying and mumbling and damning God because he had let me down.

Now that the curtain had fallen, the shock of it all came on. Suddenly I felt empty. Every part of me ached. My mouth was dry as a beachful of sand. Sloan helped me to my feet. He was a fine, caring man and a great commander. A medic came up, looked at my wounds, and hit me with another Syrette of morphine. It dulled the pain but not enough; he told me to lie down in a litter so I could be evacuated. But I was not about to go anywhere. The welfare of my men was not a responsibility that could be delegated. Until everyone had been cared for, I'd stay right there.

I walked into the small tent that had been set up to act as a temporary surgery. Jimmie was on the table. He was bad—ashen white, almost no blood pressure, and little sign of breathing. He was about to check out. The medical officer could not get blood into him. He kept saying that Jimmie had lost too much, that all his veins were deflated. But Doc Brakeman had gotten a needle into Jimmie's arm up there on top of the hill, in the dark, and *he* was being shot at. I couldn't understand why this surgeon was jabbing everywhere but where it counted. Then I realized he was drunk, or that he'd been on a big binge the night before. He smelled like a barroom rag and his hands were shaking as he frantically stabbed that needle into Jimmie's arm. I pulled my pistol out and put it against his head. "Man, if you don't get that thing in the next time, you're one dead doctor." The needle went in next round, and the grim death mask Jimmie wore slowly began to fade.

Steady, brave Doc Brakeman gently led me outside the tent. He said everyone was fine and he wanted me to rest on a stretcher. Combat medics are mountains of courage and wisdom; Brakeman stood out as the ultimate among these fine men.

I lay down. The shot was taking effect—I was so sleepy. There were faces: Colonel Sloan, Major Stambaugh, Dell Evans from 2d Batt, and then Phil Gilchrist, who'd come the whole way down from Division Forward to lend a hand to his old George and Easy buddies. Then I was being lifted, and swung in the air. And then a motor and hard bumps, like knives, sending sharp pains throughout my body. And God hadn't yet explained why he'd forgotten us.

I woke up thinking I was in the Raider camp. Eyes closed, familiar voices were all around. Laughing. Bullshitting. Talking about 400, talking about the fight. *The fight.* I opened my eyes. I was in a long tent ward at a MASH. The bed next to mine was occupied by Chris, and then as far as I could see were Raiders, carrying on as though they were at a Boy Scout jamboree. I turned to Chris. "What is the status of the unit, Master Sergeant Crispino?"

"Raiders! Listen up!" Chris shouted down the row of beds, and the roll call began: Beasey, Denny, Evans, Hearn—the wounded and the dead, all present and accounted for.

Jimmie and Jack fell into the heading of "accounted for." Neither was in our wing; they were down in intensive care. Chris cornered a medic and asked him for a status report on our friends. "They're in a bad way," the medic said flippantly upon his return, "I wouldn't take any bets on their making it."

Chris lashed out. "You better watch your mouth and get some respect, motherfucker, or I'll get out of this bed and kick your ass all over this tent." Chris was always so diplomatic. But if he hadn't said it, one of us would have. It was not because of the news the medic brought; something like it had been in the cards for months. But they were cards *we'd* dealt. Yes, we'd lived on the edge of death. Yes, we'd made the choice to gamble recklessly with our young lives, the only thing that could not be replaced. But who was this rear-echelon callous bastard to see our fate, and the fate of all his charges, as potential stakes in his own floating crap game?

"Where are they?" Chris snapped. A contrite and more than a little worried medic gave him the layout of the MASH.

We found Speed first. He was as white as his sheet and filled with tubes. His belly was swollen and painted a bright, ugly orange color. His spleen had been removed. He'd lost a massive amount of blood and there was a good chance of infection. But Jack was a gambler—he dug the challenge of long odds—and I knew he was going to make it. He was talking now, and in my mind's eye he was already sitting on the edge of my bed in the morning with a bottle of Jack Daniel's. "Now, *son,*" he'd be saying in that slow Tennessee drawl, "*take a slug of this, 'cuz ah'm 'bout to taeell you the goddamnedest story 'bout a leetle heel called 400.*"

Except for his mouth and one eye, Jimmie's face and head were completely covered in bandages. So was the rest of his body. In addition to any other wounds, it seemed that a grenade must have exploded on top of him and filled him with shrapnel. He lapsed in and out of consciousness; he twisted and tried to turn, and muttered in Japanese. Chris and I tried to talk to him, but he was far away. We talked to him anyway, and somehow our voices brought him back for a moment. "The Chinks . . ." he said. "Evans, get down." Then he came off 400 and moved back in time. "I got pineapple, man." Poor, crushed Jimmie was back with Easy, where the practice was to carry your C-ration cans inside your fatigue jacket over your belly. Fruit was a C-ration prize. It could slow or stop a slug with the best of them, and tasted far better than most.

"Jimmie . . ." I said. Then I stopped. What do you say to your friend when he's dying? I loved him. I wanted him to make it. I wanted him to fight harder. Maybe if we could bring him around he'd zero in and concentrate on staying alive. "Jimmie," I said, "you're a sergeant . . . a sergeant first class!"

His good eye fluttered and slowly opened. He seemed to focus in on me for a second. "Aw, shit, man . . . why'd you do that?" Then he slipped back into his deep, dark coma. A gentle nurse chased us back to our beds, assuring us that Jimmie looked far worse off than he really was. She said he was getting stronger, and that, in fact, it was Jack who was not out of the woods.

Over the next few days, one, two, and three at a time, medics wheeled us into surgery. "If you don't make it, I'll have your watch" . . . "If you don't make it, I'll be on top of your woman before you hit the slab"—the same, great Raider spirit followed Chris and me as we went down that long hall together. The injected pre-op cocktail had stung, but it took away most of the pain, and some of the fright.

An arm that was somehow familiar was strapped to a board under the watchful eyes of masked people in green clothes. A glaring spotlight beamed overhead. It seemed even brighter with the second needle, as if someone had brought the sun inside. A gloved hand holding a forceps skillfully probed around the ripped flesh of the restrained arm. The instrument went in empty and came out holding shards of steel. Like pulling a rabbit out of a hat, I thought. A scalpel went in next and carved a doughnut around the jagged hole. Debridement, it's called, I found out later. The chunk of meat was extracted. The gloved hand balanced it deftly on the end of the scalpel. With a flip of the wrist, the meat sailed through the air into a bucket of blood and other discarded chunks of damaged government property. They should empty that thing, I thought, as blood slopped out of the brimming pail and slowly dripped down the white surgery wall.

A voice behind a green mask said there were no complications and to leave it open to drain. "Lieutenant Hackworth," the same voice said, "do you want the shrapnel as a souvenir?" I climbed back through the looking glass. The arm was my arm. The bucket held my blood. And Jimmie's, and Jack's, and all that flowed down 400. And now this man with gloved hands was asking me if I wanted a souvenir. As if I were a tourist, as if in my old age I'd want something—need something—to remind me of that terrible hill, this stinking tent hospital, all the wounded and all the dead. I tried to tell the skillful hand what he could do with his fucking souvenir, and for that matter the whole fucking war, when another gloved hand administered another needle and I drifted away. They cleaned up my chest. But I didn't watch.

I awoke next on a hospital train. I'd come this way in the summertime and now it was cold—my semiannual vacation south. *Hey, mister conductor,* I thought, *let me off at Taijon. My friend lives there by the railroad track . . .* and then I fell back into a heavy, drugged sleep. We were unloaded at the Pusan train station. I asked the medic to put my litter next to that of Raider Charles Beasey, who'd lost his right hand on 400. Beasey was from a farming family in Indiana; he'd been destined to take over the business and now he was worrying how he'd manage. He was down, really down. I'd kind of been looking forward to the old officers' ward, but it didn't seem like a good time to leave him alone.

As the medics sorted through the sea of litters on the platform, I disappeared my medical tag. A sergeant assigned Beasey to the Swedish Hospital. Then he knelt by my litter. "Where's your tag?"

"Don't know," I said. "Just woke up." He said he'd make me a new one; I told him I was Sergeant Hackworth and gave him my old enlisted serial number. "Can I go with my friend?"

"Sure," he replied, and Beasey and I rode off in an ambulance, side by side.

I fell off again and awoke with an Ingrid Bergman look-alike in hospital white standing over me. "Who stole the tea?" she asked, or at least that's what it sounded like.* *I just got here,* I thought, *haven't been here long enough to steal anything.* She wanted to know my name and where my medical card was. I told her I was a Wolfhound Raider, which for some reason she thought was quite funny, and then I went through my sergeant, U.S. Army, EM serial-number routine while a grateful Beasey in the next bed bit his lip to keep from laughing. I thought of my brother Roy, in L.A., who was now on a first-name basis with Western Union. This would be the fourth telegram: THE SECRETARY OF THE ARMY HAS ASKED ME TO EXPRESS HIS DEEP REGRET THAT YOUR BROTHER SGT HACKWORTH DAVID H WAS SERIOUSLY WOUNDED IN

---

* In Swedish, *"Huru mår ni?"* ("How are you?").

ACTION . . . and I hoped he wouldn't read it carefully—last round I'd been a lieutenant. I knew Roy would handle the wound part, but I wasn't sure about the bust. On the other hand, having a brother who's a sergeant was probably better than one who was an inmate at San Quentin, which as kids is where I'm sure he thought I'd end up.

Beasey was still down. I tried to cheer him up with stories about my father, who had lost most of his right hand in a mining accident in Colorado, but from everything I'd heard, he'd managed quite well. Besides, I said, the VA would give him a special tractor each year and plow his South 40 on request. He'd find a blue VA check on the first of every month, and really, I told him, he had it made—a grateful America would never forget him.

The patter didn't help much. Beasey's "good fortune" would only hit home when he started to look at the other wounds on our ward: down a few beds, the kid with no legs and only a little stump for an arm; across from him, a guy whose guts were sitting outside his stomach; next to him, a Chinese soldier who'd lost both forearms. The Chinese boy had been brought in by two tall, chrome-plated MPs. They'd dropped his litter a foot from the floor—I guess they thought we'd be pleased. But we'd booed, cursed, and hissed them out of the room. Had there been a gun around, someone would have shot them. There was no "enemy" on our ward. Hospital clothes had no patches or flags. Away from the battlefield, there was instead an unspoken bond, camaraderie based not on a uniform but in a barely hatched notion we shared: that one and all we were just battered pawns in a larger game that had nothing to do with us at all.

But after lights-out, the game went on. Boys in their sleep fought battles over and over again. Our moans, often tortured screams, punctuated each others' dreams—a horrific, endless war movie, playing on through the night.

I spent my twenty-first birthday in the Swedish Hospital, one week to the day after Hill 400. My birthday present was a rash—*the worst rash*, I thought, *ever experienced in the history of mankind*. I scratched myself to pieces; the rash got worse. Few of the doctors and nurses spoke English, so even if I'd known, I couldn't have explained what was wrong. They thought it was from the antibiotics, so they changed them; that didn't help, so when I started to scratch until I bled, they tied my hands and feet to the bed. Modern medicine. I wiggled and squirmed night and day, until finally an American doctor stopped by for his weekly visit. "Man, I'm dying," I told him. "I'm going crazy!"

"You should be," he said. "That's the worst case of lice I've ever seen." *Hill 400*, I thought; *it'll never go away*. I must have picked them up crawling through enemy positions—Mao Tse-tung's revenge. The nurses trundled me off into the shower, and then they bathed a sheet in calamine or some such lotion and wrapped me up in it. *Joy*.

The civilian doctor in charge at the hospital had told me my arm and chest were healing well. On the fourth day there (fortunately before the lice reared their itchy little heads), the drain was pulled and I was stitched up with wire. After my short glimpse of heaven in a pink sheet, the American doctor returned to tell me they'd take the stitches out in the morning. But then he dropped the bomb. He said he wasn't sure I'd ever be able to straighten my arm again. I'd lost too much bicep muscle, and so much flesh.

Now it was my turn to worry. Much as I joked with Beasey, there was nothing too glorious about being a twenty-one-year-old cripple. When the doctor was two beds down, I flopped out of mine, went to the floor, and did a push-up. It hurt like hell, but I straightened my arm until the elbow locked. The doctor and his assistants came running up, thinking I'd fallen out of bed. I told them I hadn't fallen, I'd rolled, and that if I was going to have a stiff arm for the rest of my life, no way was it going to be hanging there like a crab claw. A dozen or so stitches had ripped out, but I didn't care—my goddamn arm was parade-ground straight.

A young boy across from us had been shot in the dick. The docs had sewed it up as best they could, but its owner said it had an odd twist to it. He talked about it all the time, really worried that it wouldn't work. There was only one way to test the damage, though, so the ward's old-timers organized a ladder for our second-floor window—Destination Whorehouse, just down the road. A pussy patrol climbed through almost as soon as the lights went off, to give young Twisted Dick an operational checkout. When (hours later) they returned, all concerned hit the sack, and some bragged awhile to the nonmobile. Soon the ward was quiet. I couldn't sleep—lying in bed day after day, napping all the time, makes normal sleep almost impossible—and after a while I heard muffled sobs. They were coming from the bed of Twisted Dick. *What a shame*. I thought. *What a shame*.

Beasey was shipped to Japan and from there he'd go stateside. My own wound was still raw and leaking fluid; the word was I'd be discharged in a few weeks. I was getting regular mail from the Raider camp and had an idea what was happening: light wounds were drifting back . . . the unit had been re-formed . . . Lieutenant John Arvidson, a gung-ho Californian who'd participated in the 1948 Mideast war, had been assigned as new skipper, and he'd filled the Raiders up. But he did not seem to have an eye for quality or was being rushed by the higher-ups; the outfit seemed full of guys we'd rejected. It didn't matter now that Chris was back, and that the lieutenant and RTO Neary had gotten shot up helping out a George Company operation on 400 (that jinxed hill, which, totally beyond my belief, had been abandoned soon after the Raiders took it). Now there was talk that we might be disbanded. Raids had been canceled, Chris was going to see Colonel Sloan, and when was I coming home?

I was bored without Beasey and had no reason to stay in this hospital. I figured Doc Brakeman could look after my arm, and besides, it was somehow discovered that I was an officer impersonating an NCO and all along had been the ringleader of much of the havoc on the ward. They told me that if I didn't shape myself up they'd ship me right out to an officers' ward. But I didn't want to go to another ward, officers' or not. I wanted to go back to the Raiders. So I got myself some gear and said good-bye to my wardmates and lovely Nurse Bergman. I caught a midnight train back to Seoul and hitchhiked up to our camp.

A truck driver let me off on the MSR. I ran down the little side road; it was cold, but I was too excited to notice. The Raider camp was covered in snow. Our flag was gone, skull and crossed bones replaced by the Stars and Stripes, which flapped majestically in the wind. Newly whitewashed rocks in perfect formation around the camp made our renegade outfit look like the 25th Quartermaster Company, but I didn't care—smoking stovepipes said someone was home, and so was I. I ran past the Raider gate and burst through the tent flaps of the mess.

The guys around the stove jumped up, and in an instant the old Raiders were all over me like a *welcome* rash. One and all they tried their best to break my back with giant bear hugs. Our yelling and carrying-on brought everyone else to the tent, and it was more of the same. The new guys in the outfit stood on the outside looking in—*So this is Hackworth*, their expressions seemed to say. God, it was good to be back.

Chris limped in. "What the hell took you so long?" he said, but his hug was that of a long-lost brother. "Good to see you, man. Good to see you." Then we caught up. Each Raider was accounted for, including Jimmie and Jack. They'd made it—Chris had checked with the nurse before he left MASH; both were strong and would soon be shipped to Japan.

We unlimbered some well-stashed hooch and the reunion got serious, just like the old days. The new guys drifted out, as unwelcome as an ex-husband at his former wife's wedding reception—this homecoming party was exclusive to the brotherhood of 400. We refought the battle, and as the story unraveled, we knew it had been one mean, bloody fight, but what the hell, we'd won, we'd kicked their stinking asses. And as the booze flowed, our glorious achievements and heroic acts became even more so. No one got sentimental or teary, but no one pulled out the Raider photo either, the one we'd had taken with all of us in all our gear, which by SOP after previous raids we'd laughingly update by crossing out the faces of our lucky comrades evacuated because of wounds. And no one talked about the dead. There was no way we could understand why they had died and we had lived, so we just pretended they had not gone. It was the only way. The pain would otherwise have been too great, the loss too traumatic. So they were as alive to us as they'd been in the battle, and any moment now they, too, would come bursting through that tent flap and join in the fun.

Next came the ritual parade of scars. Everyone bared their wounds—favorites, of course, were the ones that could be seen on the beach. When I was a kid I'd had *Death Before Dishonor* tattooed on my arm; the shrapnel that had ripped right through it on 400 made me candidate for "Mr. American Legion." But the booby prize went to one poor hero who had a long, wicked, red-stitched welt across one cheek of his ass; it wasn't at all good beach material to prove he'd been gored by a fierce Chinese bull.

"But what's with the white rocks?" I asked. "And where is the Raider flag, and Bobby and the girls?"

"There's been a lot of housecleaning . . . think someone figured we'd fight better if we were strictly GI," replied a drunken Raider. It didn't sound promising to me. I shot Chris a glance. He nodded. We'd have to take a long jeep ride. . . .

Colonel Sloan hadn't thought he'd see me back. When I told him he couldn't get rid of me that easily, he said I was wrong—he was sending me home. He thought I should go to the Infantry School and get some formal military education, that I'd used up all my chances on the battlefield. I reminded him I had not seen combat compared to those guys who had fought through Africa and Europe or during that long island-hopping campaign in the Pacific, but the Colonel (who'd fought in both theaters) would not be moved. "What about the Raiders?" I asked. Sloan wasn't sure. He hadn't been able to find the right man for a Raider leader. He needed a fighter, and apparently they were becoming a rare breed. I suggested he commission Crispino, who knew the score better than anyone. Sloan said he'd think about it, and in the meantime, I was to shape the Raiders up. They'd go on operations with Chris as the skipper while I, banished from the front line, conducted training and played liaison officer between them and Sloan. *Yes, sir.*

As I was leaving, I was stopped by the Regimental Adjutant. Colonel Sloan, he said, had directed that every deserving Raider be decorated for the operation on 400. The Adjutant had tried to get it moving while I was in the hospital, but the few remaining NCOs wouldn't help; it was as though there was some conspiracy not to put in for any decorations.

Good men, my Raiders. Back in August, when we'd formed the unit, the NCOs and I had decided not to play the medals game. It was honor enough, we thought, just to be a Raider. About decorations Napoleon had said, "Some people call them baubles; well, it is by such baubles that one leads men," but in our judgment the RAIDER tab the guys wore over their 25th Division patch was just as good, maybe even better. And besides, we did not want the Raiders to become a watering hole for glory hunters. Hill 400 wasn't the first time I'd been asked to get recommendations together; always in the past I'd say, "We're working on them,"and let it go until the fast turnover of combat clerks through rotation made the boys at the top lose track. Now I told the Adjutant about our policy. He said it wouldn't wash, but that he'd provide specialists from his Awards Section to facilitate the paperwork.

It was time to rebuild the Raiders. I sent most of the new replacements packing, and started recruiting all over again. But few people wanted to join up these days. It wasn't like last August, when we had a line a mile long waiting outside the Raider camp. Still, we managed to scratch together a unit, and immediately started to train. But none of the old guys really had their hearts in it anymore, and neither did I.

The Awards team came down. They stayed with us, interviewed the guys, and then typed up all the necessary supporting papers. It was a snap. All we had to do was tell a few war stories and sign our names. Bill Smith was put in for the Medal of Honor, and Jimmie, Chris, and Jack Speed went in for the DSC. All the rest were for Silver Stars. Then, at Division, a few of these recommendations were knocked down to the next lower awards. To me, that was wrong, like James Aguda's Medal of Honor being knocked back to a Silver Star was wrong. It was only much later that I realized my own idealistic policy regarding decorations for the Raiders had been wrong, too. For myself, especially after Aguda, decorations had lost most of their meaning. But for the others, my prejudice meant that so many deserving fighters would grow old with nothing to show for their extraordinary gallantry with the Raiders—or just one tin medal for the last hurrah.

They should have had one for every damn time they suited up.

There were a few more raids with Chris as leader, but everyone was jittery. Sometimes the words were spoken, sometimes they were not, but no one wanted another 400.

A week before Christmas, Jimmie's sister wrote to ask for the circumstances of his death. *His death.* I refused to believe it. None of us would. We got knee-knocking drunk and argued about it until midnight, at which point Chris and I and two other guys decided to go to the horse's mouth. We drove by open jeep in a bitching snowstorm (a sobering experience itself) to get to the MASH where we'd last seen him. We woke up the doc. He remembered our mass unit visit but could not recall Jimmie. He pulled all the records, and starting from 4 November he worked forward through the papers. When he hit the eighth, I could tell by his face before he spoke that our brother was gone. Strong, soon-on-the-way-to-Japan Jimmie Mayamura had died on the operating table. They'd gone in to take a sliver of shrapnel out of his brain; when it was pulled, his clock had stopped running.

The news about Jimmie was the death knell for the Raiders. It would have been, even if Sloan had commissioned Crispino, but even that was impossible because some thorough clerk had not disappeared the paperwork from Chris's court-martial over the hot jeep, and a guy couldn't be commissioned if he'd had trouble with the law. And although, years later, Colonel Sloan would say of his decision to disband the Raiders, "Even though they were volunteers, and they'd volunteered for this specific sort of thing, I didn't think it was reasonable for these people to carry the combat load for the whole regiment," among ourselves we knew there was still another reason. The Raiders were burned out. We were all used up.

We turned in our gear and folded up our tents to the strains of Chris's favorite campfire tune, *That Old Gang of Mine.* It was the saddest duty I had ever performed. Colonel Sloan organized good jobs for those not eligible for rotation (not on the battlefield, though; putting a Raider in the trenches would be like locking up a panther in the East Podunk Zoo). We exchanged permanent addresses and swore we'd keep in touch, maybe even have a reunion every ten years or so. Chris still had another year and a half on his hitch; he didn't know where he was to be assigned back in the States, so he gave me his mother's address in Connecticut. We made a pact: if either of us was crazy enough to come back to Korea, we'd grab the other and take him along.

Just as I was about to leave for the division's Replacement Depot (repo-depot) to start outprocessing, I was again hospitalized and evacuated to Pusan. My arm was wildly infected; another operation revealed that the souvenir-touting doc had left a large chunk of steel in there. This time they cut in from the other side and cleaned it out properly. *Too bad the boys won't get to see this,* I thought, because along with the old scar, it was a humdinger.

*   *   *

By the time I got out of the hospital, the Wolfhounds had been shifted from the front lines to the small island of Koje, off the southern tip of Korea. I couldn't imagine why the best regiment in Korea had been pulled off the line and sent back to this place. Rumors were flying in every direction: the Wolfhounds were returning to the States to lead some parade down Pennsylvania Avenue; the regiment was to be trained in amphibious operations for another invasion of North Korea. I got the real story before we tied up at the docks. It seemed that Koje had become a huge stockade for enemy POWs. Of late the little mothers had been rioting, embarrassing Uncle Sam and disrupting the peace talks. The Wolfhounds were there to bring order. Not one to miss a good firefight, even Jack Speed was back for the battle in Compound 62, a bloody affair that saw one Wolfhound killed by friendly fire at the height of the madness. But all these happenings didn't matter much to me. The Wolfhounds had changed so much that besides the surviving Raiders scattered throughout the regiment, I hardly knew any of the people. Friends from '50 and '51 were long gone. I'd be there only long enough to have my points tallied up and get processed to go home.

I checked in and was assigned a cot in the regimental transient officers' tent. That night I sacked out and had a wild nightmare. The Chinks were yelling and screaming in a mass attack—we were surrounded. I forced myself awake inside that dark, unfamiliar tent, scared shitless, with cold sweat dripping down. But the dream wouldn't go away; the screaming continued. I pulled up a corner of the tent and peered into the early-morning half-light. There were thousands of Chinese out there, on the road right next to my tent, all in formation, running, singing, and counting cadence like sheep. But I was safe—Wolfhounds with fixed bayonets were shepherding them along. Strangely, the POWs were wearing brand-new U.S. Army officers' gear—pinks and greens (the current, classy officers' dress uniform) as well as Ike jackets, OD trousers, and WW II officers' greens—but on the back of each was neatly stenciled POW. Apparently the U.S. Army Quartermaster had found these surplus uniforms unsuitable, either through obsolescence or slight wear and tear; most of the Wolfhounds were picking the eyes out of the best stuff and sending it home. *If you can't beat 'em, join 'em,* I thought, as I headed over to the POW supply center later in the morning to get a complete (and free) issue of new officers' gear myself.

Jack Sprinkler had gotten the top ex-Raider job. He roamed around the island with ease as a driver/secretary for the regimental Red Cross man, Charles Delmonico. We got together my first day there and had a few drinks from Mr. D.'s bountiful Red Cross grog larder. As the drinking went on I commented on the island beauties I'd been noticing. Jack informed me solemnly that pussy was off-limits. *What else is new?* I thought. *Pussy is always off-limits.* But as Jack went on, the Army's policy against fraternization suddenly became most appealing. It turned out that before it became a POW camp, the island of Koje had been a leper colony.

Kind of makes you lose your interest. We decided on the next best thing. Jack put the word out and all former Raiders on the island got together the afternoon before I was to leave. We had to meet at the NCO Club, so I plucked off my insignia; the Army's fraternization rules dealt not only with the opposite sex but also between officers and enlisted. In other words, it was okay for an EM to die in your arms but most unbecoming for you to drink with one in his club.

It was the first time we'd partied together outside the Raider camp. We pushed tables together and covered their tops end to end with the only thing going, whiskey and Coke. So many faces were missing, but we still had a merry time—fueled by the booze, the war stories, and our love and respect for each other—until some sergeant from one of the battalions recognized my face. "Hey! You're a lieutenant. Hackworth . . . from the Raiders. What are you doing in our club?"

The sergeant started to heavy me, but then my boys stood up, and by the end of the brawl about the only thing left of the NCO Club was the concrete floor and roof. The Raiders may have been low on numbers, and it was certainly not our most professional fight, but there was no doubt at all that we'd won.

The following morning, hung over and with a bashed-up face, I packed my bags. The boys saw me off at the coastal steamer that would take me to Pusan, then Sasebo, Japan, and then home. And as I looked at all the black eyes and split lips around me, I knew the NCO Club incident was the only fitting end for the Raiders. We'd been born in battle, and that's how we finished up, too.

8 THEY DON'T HAVE COBWEBS IN KOREA

We must get down to the essentials, make clear the real difficulties and expunge the bunk, complications and ponderosities; we must concentrate on registering in men's minds certain vital considerations instead of a mass of less important details.

General George Catlett Marshall
Assistant Commandant
Fort Benning, Georgia, 1927–32

THE style of leadership I developed with the Raiders would stay with me for the rest of my Army career. I had more balls than brains; I was a reckless buccaneer on one hand, a nimble high-wire artist on the other, always teetering on the thin edge of regulations. Many times I'd be right on the verge of falling. Sometimes I'd even take a plunge. But there was always someone—an Eggleston, a Gilchrist, an Evans, a Sloan—to help me regain my balance, or hold the net.

And I would need him, whoever he was. Even my short stay at Sasebo did not bode well for me as a stateside officer. Monkey see, monkey do—with the help of a big book on "The Army Officer" and a few Wolfhound buddies billeted in my Bachelor Officers' Quarters (BOQ), I began my conversion from combat warrior to garrison lieutenant. It was not going to be easy: I suddenly found myself in a most competitive, utterly foreign Army world, where the object was not to win battles against an enemy but to shine among your peers (even as every one of you conformed to the same rigid code of behavior). Most of my contemporaries were very smart and system-savvy; they knew just what to say, just how to say it, and whom to say it to. I didn't, so I had little choice but to use the same tactics I had since I'd been commissioned: *Watch, listen, and learn, but for chrissake, keep your mouth shut*. It was the only way I'd survive.

The only person in Sasebo who did not make me painfully aware of my lack of education was a girl named Katie, who worked for the Red Cross. Katie, from Iowa, was the nicest girl I'd ever met. She had dark hair and flashing blue eyes, and we fell madly in love. We became so involved, in fact, that Katie went to a senior Army friend to see if I could be assigned to the Sasebo base. DA had assigned me to Fort Benning for the Infantry Company Officers' Course, but I was so lovesick I was ready to give it all up and inventory sheets for the rest of my life just to walk in Katie's shadow. But it was not to be. The Army, my stern, unyielding father, said "No way." Katie and I were heartbroken; our tragedy left Romeo and Juliet's for dead.

The night before I shipped out we went to a local officers' club for a last, special evening. The club was a huge place—multitiered, with dining tables on each level, all overlooking a dance floor, bar, and more tables on the ground floor. Both in uniform (because that was the rule) and wearing brave smiles, Katie and I sat by the railing on the second tier and made plans for our future over a candlelit dinner and a couple of bottles of wine. The perfect evening might well have gone on forever, but we were interrupted by some Navy John Paul Jones, who'd known Katie before. She asked him nicely to leave. He did, but soon started sending his buddies over, one by one, to ask her to dance. The nonstop harassment started taking its toll (my blood was boiling), but Katie reminded me that discretion was the better part of valor, and we decided we'd just leave. Unfortunately, John Paul Jones decided to block our way. So I asked him to move. He told me to get fucked. I *told* him to move, and before he had a chance to say, "I have not yet begun to fight," I fired a torpedo that sank his wise ass to the bottom of the dance floor. He took the railing with him, and a clubwide fight ensued, with the Navy crowd below starting to charge the stairs, only to be ambushed by Army guys at the bar, led by *Nec Aspera Terrent* (No Fear on Earth) Wolfhounds, who'd watched the whole thing build up.

I grabbed Katie and the wine and we retreated to better defensive ground—the third floor. The gladiators below (who'd already forgotten who started the fight) were duking it out most enthusiastically, so we hung around, drinking wine and enjoying the show until the wail of MP sirens told us it was time to bug. Katie led me down the back steps to her chauffeur-driven Red Cross sedan; with me hiding on the floor under a blanket, and Katie's little feet plunked down on my back, we drove out just as the police threw a cordon around the club to prevent any participants from leaving. It had been a fine evening after all, and we spent the rest of the night giggling about sinking Navy in the brig.

The next morning, Katie came down to the pier and waited on the dock while tugboats pushed our long, gray transport ship into the channel. As the ship pulled away, we waved and shouted last-minute "I love you"s—me, pushing my way back toward the stern of the crowded ship, calling at the top of my lungs; she, walking down the dock to the end of the pier, tears streaming down her cheeks. I stood on the fantail as we sailed away, until Katie got so small that all I could see was the waving of her long red scarf. I never saw her again.

And then we were home. The Golden Gate Bridge rose out of the fog. It brought back memories—I'd come this way before. The first time had been in early 1946, when I returned from my tour with the merchant marine. I'd been fourteen when I joined that outfit, disgusted that World War II had ended without my assistance, and on the run from juvenile authorities. The judge had given me one last chance: after I'd run away from one foster home in Lancaster, California (it had been more like a slave-labor camp for children), he'd sent me to another home in Palmdale, where a gentle lady named Mrs. Ordway waited for her husband to come home from the war. I'd liked that place and I'd liked Mrs. Ordway, and I might have stayed there forever but for my terrible temper and one of the other kids, a bully named Milton, who rode me one step too far. I knew it'd be the end of the road when Mrs. Ordway found out I'd cleaned his clock—I'd be on to Whittier, Preston, and San Quentin, in that order—so I ran away from Palmdale, too, and started hitching my way back to Los Angeles. What I'd do when I got there I didn't know (I figured I'd probably try to join the Marine Corps or the Army again), but at least I was on the road.

I'd been waiting at a gas station for another ride when a Dodge station wagon pulled up, a 1942 model in mint condition. It was a most incredible sight in 1945; the Dodge was probably one of the last cars off the line before they stopped making them in '42 as part of the war effort. While the attendant was busy filling it up, I'd moseyed over to the driver and tapped him on the shoulder. "Hey, mister, are you going to L.A.?" I asked. The guy turned, and my heart skipped a beat—he was a cop in plain clothes.

"Yes, I am, boy. Hop in."

It had been too late to run away, and in the desert of Southern California, there weren't too many places to run anyway. So I got into the car, looking around for radios and whatever else cops keep in their vehicles. I didn't see anything, but I still expected the guy to put me under arrest any second; the scariest part was that I was convinced he knew me and was just biding his time. I knew him—I'd recognized his face.

We'd headed toward L.A. When we stopped for lunch it became pretty apparent I didn't have ten cents in my pocket, so he bought me a sandwich and a Coke. We started to talk (he really was a nice guy), and suddenly I realized that he wasn't a cop, but the guy who always played the cop—or the priest—in the movies. Straight from one of my favorite war films, *The Fighting 69th*, it was Pat O'Brien—and one of the great thrills of my life.

I'd told him I was going to visit my grandmother in Ocean Park, but not much more (I couldn't see Pat O'Brien wanting to be a real-life accessory to my "escape"), and when we hit L.A. he insisted on driving me home. I hadn't counted on that. The fact was, I couldn't go home, because Gram would haul me right back to the judge if I stepped in her door. He started asking me about my address when we got to Santa Monica; I suggested he drop me off right there.

"You said you lived in Ocean Park," he said. "How are you going to get home?"

I told him I'd take the bus.

"Thought you didn't have any money."

"I'll walk."

He stopped the car, and put his hand on my shoulder.

"How old are you?"

"Fourteen, sir."

"Let me tell you something, kid. I know you're on the lam. You don't have any money, and every time a police car's gone by all day, you've as good as slid under the seat." I started to explain, but he stopped me. He reached into his wallet and pulled out a bill, and as I sat there thinking Pat O'Brien was going to give me a dollar and the bus only cost a nickel, he handed me a twenty.

"Keep it, kid, you'll need it," he said.

I'd gone right over to Al Hewitt's, but his mother knew I was hot so she wouldn't let me stay. With my newly acquired twenty bucks I'd checked into a boardinghouse for a week, which left me four dollars and seven days to decide my future. It had been Al's idea to join the merchant marine. He told me our schoolmate Kenny Carpenter had just come back from somewhere out in the Pacific, that he was a big war hero, had lots of money, and all the girls in town were throwing themselves at him. I liked the sound of that, and if Kenny's reception on the home front weren't compelling enough reason, about the same time, my brother Roy, who was seventeen, joined the Navy, and my cousins, John and Donald Hackworth, came home war heroes from the South Pacific.

So the merchant marine it would be, except for the problem of my age. Al had been all right; he was a couple of years older. But I needed to be sixteen and even then (because I was still a minor), the permission of my father. It had been a tall order for a kid—to age two years overnight and resurrect a father who'd been dead for thirteen. Still, where there's a will, there's a way: we just went down to the beach and found a suitably aged wino to whom we gave a dollar (with the promise of another) to come with us to a notary public, call himself my father, and give permission for his son, born 11 November 1928, to join the merchant marine. Within a few hours one wino had a windfall, and Al and I were at San Pedro, joining the Seamen's Union and being assigned berths on a ship that was leaving at noon the following day. I stowed my gear and stayed on board while Al went home to say good-bye to his parents.

The next morning, no sign of Al. At twelve o'clock, just as we were pulling away, I saw him running down the dock.

"We're gonna leave without you, Al! Hurry!" I called from the deck.

"Can't go!" he yelled back.

"Why not?"

"Mother won't let me!"

So long, Al.

The name of the merchant ship was the SS *Marine Lynx*; its role, to shuttle personnel and supplies between Guam, Saipan, Eniwetok, and Tinian. My job had been that of an apprentice seaman, eight-hour days spent shifting ballast, and chipping, priming, and painting anything on board that didn't move. I had no area of responsibility—the ship didn't depend on me in any way—so I had plenty of time to look around, and by the time we got to the islands I pretty well understood how things worked. (Like, if I took care of the cook with an extra can of paint when he needed one, he'd take care of me with huge sandwiches and other goodies, as requested, day or night—a perfect arrangement, given a kid of fourteen's bottomless pit for a stomach.) I'd also figured out that because the *Marine Lynx* was such a huge ship (C-4 Class), it wouldn't be tough for a guy to disappear himself for a day or two at a time, so whenever we were in port at Guam, I'd go AWOL at first light.

I'd wrap my clothes in a plastic bag and throw them into the ocean. Then I'd dive in, swim the mile or so to shore, get dressed, and find myself a Marine outfit to tag along with on patrol. I'd stay with them the rest of the day, crawling through knocked-out Japanese tanks and bunkers, and picking up rusting weapons and other souvenirs in the jungle. On more than one occasion, I'd found myself hugging the ground, too—it was late 1945, and the Japanese left on Guam were the ones who, fanatically refusing to accept that the war was over, were determined to fight it out on their own.

When the patrols came in at night, I'd catch a Landing Craft Infantry (LCI) back to my ship (no one ever checked up; you needed permission to go ashore, but not to come back on board), but the best nights were the couple when I missed the LCI. I had little choice then but to follow the Marines back to their village and spend the night with them, too, listening to war stories and watching them get drunk. Some of the Marine guys kind of adopted me, as had members of the Army regiment that was billeted in

Ocean Park when I was a kid. It was really a dream come true. Although I'd been an eager Army mascot at home (complete with a little uniform, WW I campaign hat with blue braid, and starving to learn anything the GIs would teach me), secretly I'd always wanted to be a Marine. One reason was Gram had always said my birthday was 10 November, Marine Day; the other was because there were lots of Marines in Santa Monica during the war, and they'd had the snazziest uniforms and the shiniest shoes of all the services. And I knew shoes, because I'd made a small fortune shining them for the Army guys up the road.

All in all the merchant-marine tour had been just a great, great adventure, which ended only when I cut my foot badly on some coral during one of my forays. The wound became infected, and I was sent home by hospital ship in March 1946.

To my great surprise, the welcome our vessel received in San Francisco (seven months after the war had ended) was probably as enthusiastic as on V-J Day itself. Banners and signs dotted the shoreline, thanking us and proclaiming "Job well done." Boats with bands jammed the harbor, and spilling across the horizon were what seemed like millions of beautiful, waving girls. It was a great warriors' homecoming, and amidst all the excitement I was transferred to the Marine Hospital, where I spent three weeks recovering from my "wound." And if anyone asked how I got it (and didn't ask too quickly), I'd tell them a little story about *those Japs on Guam* . . .

But it was not 1946 anymore. It was 1952, and though the Golden Gate appeared on cue, then and there the similarity ended. Before we'd even docked I knew that no one would be asking me this time how I got wounded, or even how went the war. The shoreline was empty, save for a few curious onlookers. The harbor was ours alone, other than the pilot boat with its grim-faced officials who came on board to facilitate our unloading. There were no bands, no banners, no signs, no girls. There was nothing, really, at all.

My arrival in Santa Monica was a bit more auspicious. My friend Erwin ("Erkie") Cheldin's father (who'd been really good to my grandmother and me during a lot of lean times) organized a parade through the streets of my hometown, and a lot of people came out to cheer for their bad boy who'd made good.

I always loved parades—military ones especially. We'd had them all the time in Trieste, from a simple "pass in review" almost every night at retreat to a humdinger once or twice a month for some visiting VIP. It wasn't just the ceremony I loved, or the shivers that went up my spine every time the martial music began to play; it was being part of the parade itself. I was so proud to be a cog in that finely tuned machine. I loved the discipline: the relentless repetition—basic drills reinforced again and again—that conditioned a soldier to react to orders not only on the parade field but on the battlefield as well. When we'd practiced, two guys would hold a string along a whole rank of men to make sure we were perfectly lined up. We'd stand at attention until someone dropped; then we'd ignore him and stand there, unflinching, even longer. When we'd marched, every heel hit the ground at the exact same time; all arms swung in perfect unison, no man's white-gloved hand moving an inch farther back or forth than any other trooper's in the column. The precision was most incredible. "Right shoulder . . . ARMS! Right turn . . . MARCH!" would come the order, and twelve hundred men in Class A uniforms and perfect synchrony would pass in review, one company after another, each fluidly and simultaneously executing mass turns and staring straight ahead as if it were the most natural thing in the world. In the I&R I'd usually been guidon bearer for Captain Eggleston's Regimental HQ Company, so for me there was always the added thrill of high-stepping it with The Man in the front of the unit.

But it was a lot easier, I decided, being custodian of the company guidon in a TRUST parade than being the complete focus of a parade in your own hometown. I didn't mind the fact that there was no military precision among the flag wavers lining the streets. It's just that I had nothing to do, except smile and wave and be pretty embarrassed about the whole thing.

Gram beamed. I'm sure the only parades old Ida Stedman Hackworth ever thought she'd share with me were those forced marches she'd taken me on between our house and Juvenile Hall; the path had been well beaten, through misdemeanors accrued between the ages of seven and fourteen. "What have I done," she'd moan, "to deserve such a terrible child?"

Roy was there, my somber, studious older brother. I used to tell people the reason we were so different was that our mother's maiden name was Kenefick, which translated from Gaelic as both "great warrior" and "great scholar." On the playground I'd duke it out with anyone who gave Roy a hard time, but in our own games, it had been every man for himself. Once we were playing war with dirt clods and BB guns in an empty lot down the street from our house. I'd deployed my troops throughout the battle area, and posted myself so that no one could outflank us by slipping around the front of Jerry's Liquor Store (which was against the rules anyway). I'd sat there biding my time, and admiring the brand-new Daisy single-shot BB gun I'd wanted all my life (and had just gotten for Christmas), when who should suddenly appear around the off-limits area but my brother, one of the aggressor soldiers. "Halt!" I'd called. "Put up your hands. You can't go any farther. You're a prisoner of war and I'm taking you in." Roy wouldn't surrender, so I shot him. At the parade, now ten years later, I noticed he still carried the scar, uncomfortably close to his eye. My BB gun, which had been unceremoniously broken over my back by Uncle Frank, Gram's other brother, was probably still under the house where Frank had thrown it, warning me never, EVER, to go down there to get it. (Frank had been dead for almost five years now; I'd gotten the news in Italy, the very morning the Jugs tried to take Trieste. Though I'd long gotten over the tears, time had done nothing for the fears: Uncle Frank could rest easy in his grave, because the BB gun would stay right where it was.)

The parade passed by all the old haunts. The area around Jerry's Liquor Store was now built-up; in my childhood, it had stood vulnerably between two vacant lots and had been too much to resist: my gang—Harry Brown, Sidney Dworkin, R. Lee Carrigan, Richard Johnson, and I—used to knock it off at least twice a month. We'd used an old abandoned touring bus in a junkyard as our HQ, and every raid was planned, written out, rehearsed, and executed with strict military precision. Pint-sized commandos: *Okay, Sidney, you're the lookout. Richard, go by this window with a rock. When you throw it in, I want you, R. Lee—you'll be across the street—you start bashing on the lid of that garbage can. That'll cover the noise. Harry, you jump in the window and throw the loot out. We'll grab it and get the heck out of there. . . .* One of the first raids had been a total mess. An old-fashioned window came down like a guillotine and speared Richard's hand with jagged glass. We'd barely dragged him under a nearby car when the cops came. I could still see them there in my mind's eye, holding pistols and searching around with flashlights blazing while we lay under the car, scared shitless, trying to stop the torrent of blood from Richard's hand. After that, though, we'd conducted a string of successful break-ins. We'd read about ourselves as the mysterious Santa Monica boy burglars and have big laughs; we were very proud of ourselves. Our undoing had been knocking off the hardware store. We'd gotten away with a couple of hundred jackknives, one of which was unknowingly sold to a cop's son, and the next thing we knew, we were in Santa Monica's brand-spanking-new jail. It was one of the scariest moments of my life. We were all put into separate cells; everyone was crying and looking at me because I was the leader. I told them not to say anything—the only evidence the police had were a couple of knives. Sidney Dworkin was the first to crack. He told them about our bus and all our loot. Then they found the bus, and I was the fall guy.

As the parade swung by Robert's Market, I thought how different it all might have been had Bob Ross not gone off to war. His family owned Robert's Market when I'd started working there at the age of eight. First I'd just hung around and helped Bob close up at the end of the day. Eventually he started to pay me, out of his own pocket. First a quarter a day, then a quarter an hour, and I worked for him whenever I could. Bob was like a real father—he was the one person who took a genuine interest in me as a kid—but then the Japs bombed Pearl Harbor, and he went into the Air Corps to be a fighter pilot.

So there'd gone my father figure. Still, Bob had written me pretty often. He told me about flight school and the Army Air Corps life. I used to tell people the reason I didn't have a father around (a point of great embarrassment to me) was that he was a Marine fighting on Guadalcanal. All the kids at school believed me, so it worked out well and I felt a little important, and in my head it kind of made up for losing Bob to the war effort. But without his strong man's influence around, I'd gone on my merry, delinquent way. I was already at Mrs. Ordway's when, in 1944, Bob Ross was killed in action. Maybe it was the news of that that made me upset enough to stomp that bully and run away, I don't know. But Bob Ross's death was yet another big signal for David Hackworth to go marching off to war.

So I'd marched off to war, and now I'd returned to what I'd always dreamed of—a hero's welcome, a hometown parade. And for a moment it was just all the pomp, and none of the pain, of being a soldier boy.

Jimmie Mayamura's family lived in a tiny apartment in the Japanese section of Los Angeles. His sister opened the door to the very neat third-floor walk-up and led me into the pale-green living room where Jimmie's parents were waiting. Above the mantelpiece were hung two small crossed American flags. Below them was a basic-training photo of Jimmie—young, innocent, grinning. Below the photo, Jimmie's medals from Easy (it could take up to a year for his Raider award to be approved, if it was): Silver Stars, Bronze Stars, and Purple Hearts, all hung up in a neat line. On the mantel itself rested the American flag that had draped his coffin, neatly folded in a tight triangle, as per regulations. It was a little shrine to a fallen son.

Jimmie's parents spoke no English. His sister translated for us, and somehow it all came out in the present tense: "He is such a fine boy" . . . "Such an honorable son" . . . "He loves you all like you are part of his family." They told me how they'd waited on the station platform for the train to arrive, and how proud they were when Jimmie came out. *Shit! He's not dead!* I thought. And no matter how hard I tried to flash back to the hospital, and to that cold night when we went back to talk to the doc, I couldn't shake the feeling that any second now Jimmie would be tearing through that front door with a huge grin on his face, that he'd sit down and join us for tea.

Then his sister started talking about "when they put him in the ground . . ." and in a rush I was brought back to my senses. Tears streamed down my cheeks, my eyes burned and my heart broke. After all this time, reality had finally struck home. Jimmie was dead. His father said, "Do not be sad. Rejoice he dies defending this great country of ours. We are proud our son dies in this country's name." I told them what a wonderful boy Jimmie was, and how we all loved him. Then I gave them the last picture I had of him, which was my (unmarked) copy of the Raider group photograph, with all the guys in all their gear. As we said good-bye, the father took my hand and held it for a long time. Then he bowed and wished me a happy life.

I called Bill Smith's family from a phone booth in Mobile, Alabama, on my way through to Fort Benning. Bill's father's English was easy to understand, and his message short and sweet: "I don't want to see you, you murdering son of a bitch. You killed my son for the sake of a bunch of yellow-assed gooks. Don't come around here unless you want trouble."

I was dumbstruck. Was this how most Americans viewed the war? In my mind's eye I saw the Mayamuras: shy, humble Japanese who had come to America and had not yet taken for granted our wonderful land of opportunity and freedom; who had not become callous when, just ten years before, their new country had locked their people up as security risks simply because they were of Japanese descent; who were not bitter now, though their new homeland had taken their only son. And then to hear Smith's father—a real live, probably seventh-generation nephew of Uncle Sam— who'd for so long taken the American way for granted that he'd forgotten (if he'd even known) that there was a price of admission sometimes. But why young Bill Smith had had to pay—with his life—for his family's ticket was something I, at twenty-one, could not begin to explain, just as I could not explain Korea itself, to a heartbroken father through a telephone wire.

The U.S. Army Infantry School at Fort Benning was like a circus in the spring of 1952. *And in the main ring,* I thought as I drove through the MP checkpoint at the front gate and on to Post Headquarters to sign in. On one side of the road, men from the parachute school were descending from 250-foot towers; on the other, students were running, shouting, and sweating down the road in tight formations of forty. Though not immediately within sight, I knew that somewhere on the huge, ever-expanding base men were getting training in Ranger, Pathfinder, and other specialty skills, and that somewhere else the Officer Candidate School was pumping out platoon leaders at a furious rate. There was a great sense of urgency at this Mecca of all things infantry—and I had a sense of relief. At least there was one place in America that fully understood we were engaged in a war. As for the rest of the country I'd just driven through, it seemed strictly business as usual, and very unfamiliar to me.

Since 1945 I'd been stateside for a total of—maybe—three months. My memories were of the war years, the lean years when no one was unaffected by events transpiring across the seas. My four-year stint in dark, war-torn occupation Italy had me miss out on the postwar boom at home; now, seeing only the results, I saw a country without a cause. There was a war going on, yet there was no hardship on the home front. There was no rationing, no "making do." Employment was high, prices were low. Production lines were going full tilt, not just in the war effort, but to keep up with Everyman's desire for a second car in his garage. Happy days were certainly here again; it was as if Korea, that distant battlefield, did not exist at all, or that Killed, Missing, or Wounded in Action were words reserved for someone else's son. To date, more than 105,000 Someone Else's Sons.

I was the first student of the 121st Student Officers' Course to report in; my orders had been fouled up somewhere along the line and classes didn't start for a week. I spent the first couple of days bumming around the post while future, unfamiliar classmates trickled in. On the third day I was walking out of the barracks when I saw, lugging a duffel bag up the steps, my hero, my mentor, and my friend—one Second Lieutenant Steve Prazenka. I don't think anything in the world could have made me happier at that moment.

"Combat!" he bellowed, dropping his gear and wrapping me in a huge Czechoslovakian bear hug.

Gasping, I told him that "Combat" was now a first lieutenant, and though I made it a rule not to speak to second balloons, since he'd been instrumental in my development I would make an exception. With Slavic straightforwardness, he told me where to go, and that rank among lieutenants was like virtue among whores. (Of course, he was right.)

We spent the rest of the week reminiscing. I'd stayed in touch with Captain Eggleston and the I&R guys throughout my time in Korea (in fact, I'd used TRUST as my permanent address, like Boys Town). When I'd been commissioned, an article had appeared about it in the TRUST paper, and apparently Steve, before he got his direct commission, had borne the brunt of my "success."

"They harassed the shit out of me, Hack! 'Just wait till you get back to the States. . . . You're gonna see Hackworth and he's gonna be a goddamn lieutenant and you'll only be a master sergeant!' they said. So what happens? I come back and who's the first goddamn guy I see? Hackworth. *First Lieutenant Hackworth!*" Steve laughed. "But I'm proud of you, Combat, I really am." More welcome words I could never have hoped to hear.

Meanwhile, the class filled up, 243 students in all. There were a few West

Point and university ROTC Distinguished Military Graduates (Class of '51), but the majority of the students were battlefield promotions from Korea or direct commissions from Europe and stateside. The direct commissions were all infantry platoon sergeants with an average of about ten years' service; like Prazenka, most were World War II vets and many had at least a year's Korean combat under their belts as well. We were one of the first classes back from the present "Police Action"—a formidable bunch, with one Medal of Honor, six DSCs, and limps, scars, and Purple Hearts attendant to the hundred Silver Stars (at least) among us.

The class formed into platoons, and student leaders were selected based on rank to handle routine administrative details, like getting us to class on time. But there were discipline problems from the start. Our CO was an Air Force major who did not know much about much. Just off the battlefield, the wild groundpounder pros gave him a hard time, and eagerly awaited his next mistake so they could start in on him all over again. It was a tough job for an airplane driver, and all the harder for him, because making him the butt of our jokes was about the only pleasure we got in our earliest days at Benning School for Boys. The place, for us newly returned Korean vets, was an insult and a joke.

The Company Grade Course should have been something on the order of an obedience school for feral animals. Our class already had enough talent and combat knowledge to cadre a division and within six weeks make it the strongest, fightin'est unit in the U.S. Army. What we needed was instruction on being an officer in a peacetime role—things like protocol, administration, report writing, and which fork to use. We didn't get it. Instead, we were treated to sixteen hours' instruction on the M-1, sixteen hours on the BAR, twenty-four hours on the LMG, and so on—all taught by fresh-faced Lieutenant Combats whom the class's collective fruit salad* would have had shitting for a year. It was ridiculous, like sitting Ernest Hemingway down and teaching him the alphabet. So it was little wonder the old pros who had packed these weapons across Europe, the Pacific, and Korea became resentful, then openly hostile; no wonder we all started looking toward the other side of the fence. The grass over there probably wasn't much greener, but it sure was a hell of a lot more fun.

A trooper passing through Benning never had to worry about being alone. There was no shortage of women in Columbus, Georgia, the parasite city living off the booming Army post. But if he didn't watch his ass, even the most hardcore bachelor could leave the Infantry School with not just a gold

* Awards and decoration ribbons.

bar, but a gold ring: since George Catlett Marshall had taken a Columbus resident as a bride many years before, it seemed that the major cottage industry here was the entrapment of freshly appointed young officers by the fair city's southern belles. Geographical bachelors, the ones who took off their wedding bands and stashed them upon signing in on post (then carefully tanning the telltale white flesh on their ring fingers until even the most expert scrutiny would not reveal a home fire burning somewhere else), would have had it made, except that the husband hunters were pros at ferreting out the truth. The ladies knew well how the system worked, and the place was so incestuous that there was always a friend or cousin who knew someone, or could get the information themselves.

But there were also plenty of fast available types who couldn't have cared less about your marital status. There were the ones who'd ring the BOQ at the start of a new class, introduce themselves, and let you know (sight unseen) they were willing to be your girl until graduation. If you clicked on the phone, this type would pick you up within minutes (for inspection or a quick roll in the back of her car); if it didn't work out, there was always another on the phone the following day. The temporary girl of your dreams could also be found in the dilapidated honky-tonks on the Strip just beyond the main gate. Generally, these were the war brides—from Germany, Japan, and Italy—who, upon arriving in the United States, had dropped their husbands to continue their camp-following ways. A GI overseas in the post–World War II days seldom met a nice girl. Most were whores and bar girls who knew how to manipulate lonely and often not street-wise kids. So he'd fall in love, they'd get married, and the blushing bride got her coveted passport back to the Land of the Round Doorknob.

Not so brazen or daring as the others, but right near post, was yet another class of woman. This was the lonely Army wife, whose husband was on an unaccompanied tour. These were temporary widows looking for company; if the magic was there, you had an odds-on first-night score, and guaranteed good meals and high times for the rest of your Benning experience, with no strings attached.

The fact of the matter was, if you were looking for pussy you couldn't miss, because even if you couldn't find what you wanted in Columbus, all you had to do was put on your steel pot and drive across the Chattahoochee River to Phenix City, Alabama. This modern-day Sodom made Columbus look like a proper Bible-bashing town. The press called it Sin City; a movie made in the fifties about attempts to clean it up helped Governor Patterson make his name. Anything went there—gambling dens, red-light districts, crooked cops, murder, and intrigue—you name it, Phenix City had it. A visit there was excellent precombat training for Korea. And for us returning guys, it served as the perfect way station between the battlefield and what civilians were telling us was the real world.

So we took full advantage of it, and for the first few weeks of class, every morning at least one or two dozen students were missing. Of those who did show, about half turned out in dress uniforms, the other half in fatigues. Some were still in khaki and reeking of booze from the night before; it was conduct unbecoming an officer, en masse. Our USAF class leader, backed up by the permanent party CO, took strong and forceful action: enough horrible examples were made of guys kicked out of the course for disciplinary reasons that finally we settled down—the mustangs broken and saddled and dutifully trotting off to class. But then it was the old story of leading a horse to water . . .

Instructor: "What is the muzzle velocity of the M-1 rifle?" Most of the old pros would be asleep.

Eager Beaver (waving his hand frantically, jumping up from his chair): "Two thousand eight hundred and five feet per second!" Those of us awake and writing letters would make a neat stroke in our notebooks. We called them "Spring Butts," those eager beavers whose impressive memories had them enthusiastically bouncing out of their chairs and up the road to being first in the class.

Instructor: "What is the weight of a model 1922 BAR?"

Eager Beaver (springing to his feet): "Nineteen point two pounds!"

Now the guys reading *From Here to Eternity* or *Esquire* behind their training literature would look up with interest, as the letter writers made another stroke in their notebooks.

Instructor: "What is the chamber pressure of the M-1 rifle?"

Eager Beaver: "Fifty thousand pounds per square inch!"

With a sigh, Eager Beaver's latest effort would be added to the tally. In 1927, as the Infantry School's Assistant Commandant in charge of the academic department, George Catlett Marshall had tasked himself with ridding Benning of the "bunk, complications and ponderosities." It was hard to believe, but it seemed that all that great general's work had been lost in just twenty-five years.

By the time Eager Beaver answered his fourth question, a great sense of anticipation would fill the room. *Will he do it? Can he?* We'd sit on the edges of our seats; guys would jab sleeping students sitting close by, to rouse them from their slumber before the big moment. It was time for question number five.

Instructor: "What is the cyclic rate of fire for the M-2 carbine?"

Eager Beaver: "Seven hundred fifty to seven hundred fifty-five rounds per minute!"

"BINGO!" we would all shout in unison.

Sleeping, writing letters, reading, and keeping score on Spring Butts alleviated the boredom and killed a little time. But every week the class got smaller. Suddenly another friend would be missing, expelled for flunking too many exams, or for disciplinary reasons like trouble with the law, whores, or not getting to class at all. The "failures" slipped away, rarely to be seen again on post. A failure at Benning essentially meant the end of your career; what's more, it was mighty embarrassing suddenly to be found wanting in the very thing you've done brilliantly for a decade or so. I kept passing, not because I studied, or even cared, but because of TRUST. We were walking encyclopedias then. A good PFC in that command probably had more military knowledge than a captain in a stateside unit. So for me, Benning was more like a refresher course in "You're in the Army Now."

In Trieste there'd been a position in the 2nd Battalion known as Colonel's Orderly. It was just an honorary thing; the trooper who got it was the one who displayed the best military bearing and knowledge during the inspection of the guard. "Who is the President of the United States?" the inspecting officer would demand.

"The President of the United States is Harry S. Truman, sir!"

"Who is the Secretary of the Army?"

"The Secretary of the Army is Kenneth Johnson, sir!" Right down the chain of command you had to have it to the letter.

"What is the weight of your weapon?"

"Sir, the weight of my weapon is nine point five pounds."

"What is the First General Order?"

"Sir, the First General Order is to take charge of this post and all government property in view!"

Colonel's Orderly was a plum position, though it only lasted for the day, during which you sat in the office of Colonel "Two Guns" Lyons (so named for the pair of pearl-handled revolvers he always wore), answered his phone, went around with him on inspections, and generally picked up anything you were willing to learn. Even better than the day itself was the pass you'd get for the next three; I never liked guard much, but I loved that three-day pass, so standing tall and looking good, I made a point of making Colonel's Orderly sixteen times in a row.

Funny how priorities change. PFC Combat Hackworth would have been the Benning School for Boys' Spring Butt of them all.

*   *   *

The classes droned on. Our instructor in first aid was a young Medical Service Corps (MSC) lieutenant, full of enthusiasm and seemingly sympathetic to our deep-seated resentment. "All right," he began. "All of you may have noticed that instructors flag probable test questions. Some make it obvious by raising their voices and repeating the information. Some say, 'Listen up, you might see this again.' In my case, what I'm going to do when it's something important is stamp my foot three times." (*Stamp stamp stamp*, he demonstrated.) "So whenever I stamp, you'll know you're going to see it again." He then continued: "Cobwebs have a coagulative property." *Stamp stamp stamp.* "So a good way to stop bleeding, if you're in a difficult situation on the battlefield and a medic's not around, is to get a big handful of cobwebs and place them over the wound." *Stamp stamp stamp.* This young MSC lieutenant really was concerned about how to keep wounded men alive on the battlefield, even though he'd never seen a wounded soldier—or the battlefield—himself. And the cobweb cure was a sensational bit of information; we all wrote it down for the test. The only problem was I had never, in almost fifteen months of combat, seen a cobweb on the battlefield in Korea. I hadn't even seen a spider.

The school solutions we were being taught simply didn't work. They had absolutely no legitimate basis given the realities of the present conflict. We'd started from square one with basics and tactics; now we were moving on through squad, platoon, company, and battalion-sized operations. Some of the company and battalion stuff was related to Korea 1950–51, but most of the instruction was World War II revisited, with weapons, tactics, and mind-sets right out of 1945. As the course went on, the instructors sought to introduce the subtler aspects of infantry in combat, too, but they were subtleties for the wrong war at the wrong time and with, *most definitely*, the wrong students.

One afternoon, a shiny staff car pulled into our training area. A lieutenant aide-de-camp jumped out and he was looking for me. "General Meloy wants to see you," he intoned. I didn't know what to think. I'd only met the General (who was Benning's Assistant Commandant) once, a few days before at an awards ceremony. I was suddenly scared (the feeling was even worse than having to go to Juvenile Court to face the judge when I was a little kid; at least then I'd known what I'd done wrong), and I immediately began ticking over my latest transgressions in my head.

Brigadier General Guy S. Meloy II was a slender old combat soldier who'd recently commanded an infantry regiment in Korea. The word among classmates who'd served in his command was that he was both a brave warrior and a good man. When I walked into his office I immediately felt at home with him, and his friendly smile dispelled any fears I'd had of getting my ass chewed. But the General did come right to the point. He told me he'd been looking over my records and, based mainly upon my combat performance in Korea, he'd concluded that I had the qualifications to attend West Point. I was speechless. To me, it was like Jesse Owens telling a one-legged sprinter he could join the Olympic team. Maybe Meloy didn't know the only reason I had a high-school diploma at all was a lot of luck on the General Equivalency Diploma (GED) test I'd taken in Italy; on the other hand, maybe he did, because he outlined a plan that entailed my attending West Point Prep School first, where I'd be tutored in math and other areas where I was academically deficient. (He didn't know, I'm sure, that that meant *every* area.) I needed time to think it over; he said I could take all the time I wanted, and then turned the conversation to the Officers' Course. Never one to miss an opportunity like that, I told him exactly how so many of my friends and I viewed it. General Meloy seemed well aware of the curriculum's shortcomings from the point of view of the returning Korea vets, and said he was working toward making it more relevant. Unfortunately, he went on, there was a lot of red tape to wade through, which didn't make for quick changes. *Hell,* I thought, *if I were wearing that star, I'd kick ass and take names and have this place turned upside down in a week.* I didn't know then how the Army's educational system had been poured in concrete, and that only a bunch of satchel charges under the desks of a lot of higher HQ bureaucrats would even stand a chance of shaking it up.

None of my friends thought I should go to West Point. And it wasn't just the mustangs; it was even the guys who wore the big ring themselves. *Particularly* those guys, many of whom were still smarting over the cheating scandal that had rocked West Point in 1951. Ninety students had been expelled in the incident, tarnishing the reputation of both the Academy and its students. The investigation had not been completed by the time the '51 class graduated, and though (as it turned out) none of that class was implicated, its members now at Benning felt the Academy had done them a great injustice by not clearing their names before they were commissioned. As for my own attendance, both West Pointers and mustangs alike said that if I made it (a long shot at best), five years from now I might be able to explain the dark secrets of calculus, but I'd also be a second lieutenant again, and in terms of the skills needed to perform as a proficient combat leader on the battlefield, I'd have gained nothing at all.

Their arguments were sound; I took them a step further by thinking that if I'd not been offered this opportunity, I'd never have given West Point a minute's thought. I had no desire to take refuge in well-protected ivory towers; I was not particularly interested in becoming a well-groomed gentleman officer at (what I perceived to be) the expense of being a capable combat leader. But my brain kept coming back to my favorite U.S. Army soldier of them all, Jim Gavin. Gavin had joined the Army underage, as I had; he'd served in the ranks in Panama, learning his trade hands-on, as I did in Italy; then he'd entered West Point, as I might, through the prep school. Now he was a three-star general, CG, VII Corps, Germany, and most insiders believed he would one day be Chief of Staff.

Gavin had been one of my great heroes since I was a little kid. During the first years of WW II he'd commanded a battalion and then a regiment of paratroopers, all fresh from the Army's first jump school (which he'd helped establish at Benning in 1941). And in 1944, even after he became CG, 82d Airborne Division—the youngest major general in the U.S. Army and one of the youngest in its history—thirty-seven-year-old "Slim Jim" still packed an M-1 and lived on the front line with his men. Gavin was the kind of soldier I'd always wanted to be, and he went to West Point. So despite all the reasons I could think of for not going, in the end Slim Jim's example left me with little choice: I submitted my application to a very pleased General Meloy. Hello, Duty, Honor, Country.

That settled, I had to get my seven-year-old fraudulent enlistment papers and date of birth straightened out. What with all the cheating and cribbing trouble at West Point of late, I didn't think it would be too good if I entered on a lie. Eugene Ernst, a classmate, was an AG officer doing a two-year Regular Army (RA) detail in infantry. He'd just graduated from the University of Pennsylvania, knew how the system worked, and said he'd fix it. He wrote a letter to DA simply stating that a review of my records indicated that my date of birth was incorrect; we enclosed a copy of my birth certificate, and a few weeks later DA responded with a letter stating that my records had been corrected, and thanking me for bringing this oversight to their attention.

The course plodded on, the attendant bitching and moaning from all of us becoming almost as boring as the instruction itself. Our Air Force company commander had shaped up well. He'd gained our respect (for a man in blue, he'd turned out to be a pretty good groundpounder), so we couldn't even have fun at his expense anymore. We kept ourselves amused in much the same way as the temporarily widowed Army wives (sometimes *with* the temporarily widowed Army wives) who spent their days watching soap operas, the latest rage. Far more interesting, though, were the soap operas among my spirited and daring classmates, scenarios that were well beyond fledgling television programmers' wildest dreams. One of the best was the story of the lieutenant, a Korean battlefield commission, who got caught in the rack with the wife of one of the U.S. Army's top pistol marksmen. Sergeant Deadeye had returned earlier than expected from an out-of-state tour with the marksmanship detachment; for the rest of the course the lieutenant had to use every bit of evasion training Benning could impart to escape old Deadeye's systematic terrorization (which began when the cuckolded husband sank eight rounds into the back of the guy's brand-new fire-engine-red Kaiser as the poor lieutenant attempted to make a quick getaway from the scene of the crime).

As for me, I shared many nights of war stories over dinner and drinks with other Wolfhounds stationed at Benning, among them Dell Evans, who was on the leadership committee with Lew Millett (for a career NCO or officer, an assignment at Benning, preferably as an instructor, was an essential station of the cross), and dear old Barney K. Neil, who was a tactical officer at OCS. But I hardly recognized my romping, stomping wartime buddies. In the peacetime setting they were proper fathers and husbands. Little children scampered around; efficient Army wives served drinks and smiled benignly as they passed around hors d'oeuvres. The evenings I spent with these old friends were among the best I had at Benning, but all the domestic stuff left me cold. I couldn't quite believe that these animals I had known on the front line were now being led around by a short leash; I didn't understand how they could do it. The thing was, if you were going to be a good soldier, you had to give in to the Army's demands for all your time, devotion, and energy. But the Army wife and family seemed to demand the same. For myself, at twenty-one, I took comfort in the old, old saying: If the Army had wanted you to have a wife, you'd have been issued one.

The nicest surprise at Benning was a wonderful reunion with Jimmy Sparks, my dearest friend from the Trieste days, now a sergeant first class. Jimmy was in the school troop's tank unit; he'd heard I was at Benning, and I came home from training one afternoon to find him waiting for me at the barracks. He was the same old Jimmy I'd left two years before—the same wire-rimmed glasses hiding shortsighted eyes, the same build, tall and strong, like an Indiana oak tree in the state from which he hailed. We'd been wild teenagers, Sparks and I. We'd both enlisted at fifteen; we'd gone through basic together (though we hadn't met until we were on the troopship to Italy), and had been friends from the very first day. We'd raced tanks down hills, chased big-time operators (BTOs) who tried to screw us in our small-time forays into the black market, fought in the TRUST 15th Tank Company smokers, and together gave up soldiering for about four months to be jocks on the regimental boxing team. We'd drunk ourselves blind and screwed ourselves silly, and spent as much time imagining what we'd do when we were NCOs as we did discussing the finer points of our little Italian girlfriends, Dolores and Lauradonna.

Jimmy was married now to a girl named Barbara (who was as small as he was tall), and in honor of our reunion, she gave him leave to go out on the town with me. We had a wonderful time, though totally unlike an evening with Dell and Barney K. Instead of war stories there were reminiscences of a youth so recent and yet long past. Jimmy said he was proud to see I'd become such a good soldier, but that he was a little surprised. Since I'd spent a lot of time in the early days in Trieste puffing my chest out and talking about Muscle Beach, California, he'd kind of thought I'd end up as a beach bum. I told him I was surprised we both hadn't ended up dead, particularly after our adventure on leave in Lido, when we'd tried to stop a fight between three Italian guys and a TRUST tank sergeant named Medina. During the brawl one of the Italians had knocked Jimmy down and tried to gouge his eyes out; I'd then hit the guy with a body block, with little noticeable effect. Only when a shot rang out did the eye gouger go limp: Medina had intervened with his Beretta.

That might have been the end of it except that the sergeant, who was a fiery, hot-blooded Mexican, turned to the other guys who'd been hassling him and at very close range shot each of them in the heart, dead. Medina was out of his head. Then he opened fire on the crowd that had gathered around throughout the drama, and kept shooting until he'd emptied the pistol. I couldn't believe it. "Let's move," I said. Jimmy and I decided to split up and meet at the Wagner, our Venice hotel. I ran down to the ferry, but at 0300 it had stopped running hours before. It was a long swim to Venice, but a good Santa Monica beach bum on the run couldn't be afraid of that, so I jumped in and swam across.

There was no sign of Sparks when I got back to the hotel. I washed my gear while I waited for him, put on fresh khakis, and when he still hadn't shown, I made tracks for the cabaret. Jimmy wasn't there either, but the Venezia Giulia police were prowling around all over the place. One little Italian officer noticed I was wearing the same tanker insignia as Medina. Did I know him? Had I talked to him? No, I hadn't even been to Lido that night. They chained me up and dragged me down to the police station, where I found Jimmy. He'd run into Medina during the great escape, and they'd both been hauled in together. At least a dozen other GIs had been brought in as well; it seemed to me the whole thing had gotten out of hand. So I got smart with the officer and he slapped me. Then, when two of his men grabbed me from behind, I kicked the officer in the balls. Unfortunately, he recovered and belted me in the mouth while his goons held my arms. At this point, Jimmy and I (and the rest of the totally innocent troopers) were thrown into a cell, where we were interrogated for almost a week.

Medina was found not guilty of premeditated murder. He got the maximum sentence under Italian law, though—twenty-four years—for the killings, but because it was a holy year, the Pope immediately took eight of them off. Meanwhile, the regiment chipped in to the "Medina Fund" every month, to give money to the families of the dead. This knocked another eight years off the sentence, and in the end, the sergeant would pull only about six. When it was established that Jimmy and I were just witnesses, we got off scot-free—or so I thought when we laughed about it in Columbus, Georgia, four years after the fact. It wouldn't be for another seven that I'd be sorry I'd ever met Ernest Medina.

During the course of the evening, I noticed a tall, stunning Columbus blonde—beautiful enough to be Miss Georgia—staring at me with bedroom eyes from across the room. I started feeling mighty warm, and no sooner had old Jimmy gone home to little Barbara than I found myself with the blonde in the back of a Cadillac El Dorado in Chad's parking lot. *Don't know what to say, officer . . . it's called spontaneous combustion or something.*

Miss Georgia was something else. Mrs. Georgia, to be exact—two times over. Her first husband had been killed in 1944; now she was married to one of his West Point classmates (the Army, and particularly the Academy, is a very closed society—it takes care of its own). Her present husband, a major, was now off fighting Communists in Korea, so Mrs. G. was a lovely, lonely lady who wanted someone to fill the void: a live-in mate for the duration.

I liked her, but I didn't like the role. At first it was great—home-cooked meals, drinks by the pool, solitude, and warm magnolia nights on her lovely property in the country. But it didn't take long before I felt like my old buddies in their ticky-tacky government-issued wood-framed cottages, who envied me and my freedom. Mrs. G. was a good woman, but I was getting kind of bored. I missed kicking around with my friends. And even worse, I felt like a real shit, screwing this nice lady while her husband was over there fighting. I'd been assigned to Camp Roberts after my course ended; soon Mrs. G. started talking about moving to Paso Robles with me—she said she'd just wait for her husband there.

I stopped feeling bored. Now scared seemed more appropriate. First I tried to avoid her, but that was impossible. She had a copy of the class's weekly training schedule, which listed what, where, and when for my every move throughout the day. (I'd even find her waiting with the dutiful Army brides at the company area when buses brought us back from distant classes.) Next I tried hiding from her. I stopped answering the phone messages she left with the CQ. I'd never been one who liked to give the bad news to ladies; the way I finally escaped was by telling her I'd busted the course and had to leave immediately for Camp Roberts. A friend scratched my name off the CQ's roster and annotated it "Returned to unit," and I stashed my yellow convertible in a nearby pine forest (next to a bright-red Kaiser with eight slugs through its ass), having unwittingly joined at least one of my classmates as a desperate fugitive who knew he'd done nothing particularly wrong, except make a lonely Army wife's nights a little shorter.

The hide-and-seek with Mrs. Georgia was probably the final straw. I hadn't liked anything about my stateside tour. The training was not only bad, it was depressing. I was uncomfortable in the peacetime role, a sow's ear that didn't especially want to be transformed into a silk purse. And I was afraid to go to West Point. I was never one to joust at windmills; I never took on a job I knew I couldn't win, and I wouldn't win in those hallowed halls.

I probably had a postcombat hangover too. Nothing here felt *real*. I read the papers every day; across the ocean, in Korea, was where it was happening. The peace talks had come to naught, the war was going hot and heavy; our units under Eighth Army CG Van Fleet seemed to be on the move and I wanted to be there, too.

My friends, especially the WW II vets, tried like older brothers to talk me out of volunteering for a second tour. *Do as I say, not as I've done,* I thought. I wrote Crispino to tell him to meet me at the Wolfhounds. I submitted my paperwork to AG; the young clerk who processed my application said I'd have to attend a Korea precombat orientation course. I didn't even argue. There seemed little point in telling this pink-cheeked kid I'd been down the road before.

The four-month Company Grade Course was drawing to a close; out of a class of 243 there were 180 students left, none any the wiser about our profession. I graduated 108th. Not brilliant, just crammed to the gills with TRUST knowledge gained in a period of history just peaceable enough to have time for that "mass of less important details." Those of us who made it could separate ourselves from the failures only by good memories, and an ability (or willingness) to regurgitate on command for an exam. None of us had learned to think. It was not part of the required curriculum.

The instructor in our last class was a rugged infantry lieutenant colonel, of weathered face, boxer's build, and starched, neat khaki uniform. He wore a polished blue helmet liner with a white instructor's band. He wore combat medals, too, from two wars—he'd done well. He was the kind of stud warriors immediately respect. His subject was "The Rifle Company in the Defense in Korea," and he gave us an amazing example of a company that had held a hill against incredible odds. The Chinese had thrown thousands of men against it, but the company held like a rock. The unit was cut off from its battalion, isolated deep in enemy territory; battered and bruised, it held on, and when ammo and food ran out, the troopers lived off the land

and used captured weapons. They built a barrier wall of tree branches, like the men at Valley Forge; the Chinamen came and the Chinamen went and the valiant unit did not give an inch, until finally a U.S. tank force broke through and extricated it.

It really was an extraordinary example, and the colonel left no doubt that only the rare skill, strong leadership, and tremendous courage of the company commander had made it all possible. "I am proud to tell you," he went on, "that this unit was from my battalion. Its skipper, who has been recommended for the Medal of Honor, is one of your classmates."

We all looked around, applauding, wondering who among us had so ably worn Superman's cape.

"Lieutenant Doug Anderson," said the colonel, "will you please stand up?"

There was a long pause. Then our Air Force class leader stood up at rigid attention. "Sir," he shouted, "Lieutenant Anderson was dismissed from this class three weeks ago . . . for academic deficiency."

And that just about said it all.

9 DON'T LOOK BACK

When First Lieutenant Hackworth reported to me at the north rim of the Punch Bowl late one October afternoon in 1952, I remember returning his casual (but soldierly) salute with the immediate thought of *What a wonderful, cheerful grin.* Later I would call him the "happy warrior"—he was that. We spent one or two days and nights together; for me it was a stimulating, interesting, professional time, and from this brief episode I came to think of Hack as one of the infantry officers who epitomized the best in combat leadership. His background was rough and his education incomplete, but to my mind he brought the skills, attitude, and courage to the American battle effort that West Point tried to indoctrinate in her graduates. Thirty-three more years of experience have not changed my view.

> Colonel Joseph B. Love, USA, Ret.
> Company Commander, G/5th Infantry
> Regimental Combat Team
> Korea, 1952

We called him Hack—he was one of the boys. We did respect his rank, though, and everybody respected *him*, because he'd been around and he was good, and he kept us alive.

> Uno Rentmeister
> Squad Leader, F/223d Infantry
> Korea, 1952–53

WHEN I left Korea in early '52, the Eighth Army had been dug in for six months. As a Raider, I'd been spared life in the trenches, so despite the glimpses I'd had of this reality during Raider operations, in my mind's eye I still saw the lean, mean mobile Army of the first year of the war—racing up and down the peninsula, hardly ever spending two nights in the same place; getting our asses kicked and reeling in defeat, or kicking ass and driving the enemy back in resounding victory. From the moment I made my decision to return to the front, I'd really looked forward to getting back to that sort of fighting. As a result, I was almost totally unprepared for what I found when I got there: my second tour would prove to be a different war.

Upon arrival in Pusan, I was sent marching not to my beloved Wolfhounds but to the (former) 40th California National Guard Division. It was a heartbreak of the first order. The 40th had been mobilized in January '51, but, sent to Japan to train, it didn't get to Korea for another year. Its members had not seen any combat other than patrol actions and a few company-sized operations, and all of these had only reinforced the unit's reputation as a sorry, undisciplined, ineffective fighting force. Its nickname—the California "Crybaby" Division—spoke for itself; I just couldn't see myself growing old and telling my children that during the war I'd been a member of such a candy-assed organization. If the truth be known, I didn't intend to stay there even one day.

The CO at the division's Replacement Company accepted every insult I could dish out about his unit. He calmly explained the Guard was being phased out and the new CG had asked that every available stud (Airborne/ Ranger warrior types) be assigned to the 40th to give it some muscle. But I didn't want to hear about it. As far as I was concerned, I'd made a contract to return to the Wolfhounds when I volunteered, and I'd been betrayed.

I railed my way up the chain of command until the AG received instructions to take me to the Chief of Staff's office at the Division Forward command post. To my great surprise, I was impressed with what I saw when we got there. The Division CP was shades of Trieste: everyone and everything dressed right and stood tall. The place actually had an Airborne feel: the sparkling-clean jeeps were painted that blue-black Airborne color; the perfectly pressed and polished Division Security Platoon wore black-lacquered steel pots. It was strictly military and looked more like an 82d Airborne unit than the 40th Crybaby boys. The AG got the first nice words out of me since we'd met. He took the opportunity to tell me the Airborne "feel" was no coincidence, that the CG, Major General Joseph P. Cleland, had come from the 82d, and had brought a number of his Airborne people with him. And, the AG added, it was his impression that General Van Fleet had asked for Cleland by name to convert the 40th to a regular division.

This should have been enough for me, but it wasn't. I could be very stubborn when I wanted to, and to my mind if God himself had been CG of this unit, I still would have refused to wear the 40th patch. I told Colonel Dillinder, the paratrooper Chief of Staff, just this, and demanded that I be sent to the Lightning Division. No sooner were these words out of my mouth than a small, neat figure with snow-white hair and mustache appeared before me. "Glad you're here, Lieutenant Hackworth. Come inside, would you? I want to have a few words with you."

I followed him into his office. He guided me to a chair. "Now, why is it you don't want to belong to my outfit?" he asked. The voice was cool and quiet, the complexion smooth and rosy against the shock of white hair—kind of like Santa Claus. There was a magic twinkle in his eyes, brighter even than the two stars on each of his lapels. Major General Joe Cleland, the man who was to become my unsolicited patron, drew up a chair beside me.

He listened intently as I told him I was a 27th man, a Wolfhound, and that I'd come back to Korea to fight, not to play nursemaid to a bunch of NG third-string weekend warriors. Cleland smiled. He knew the Wolfhounds and he knew what I was talking about. "But you have to remember," he told me, "there are no bad outfits. Only bad officers." He said he was now getting his pick of the best, and that the 40th would be exactly what he and his collection of warrior-leaders made of it. I could go back to the Wolfhounds, he continued (those merry eyes dancing), but only if I wanted to be in the *second*-best unit in Korea.

Cleland was persuasive. Confident, but not manipulative. I knew in my gut he was very much a soldier, and a soldier's soldier at that. So he'd won me hands down even before he said that if I stayed he could do more for me than any other CG in the country: "I'm going to give you a rifle company, Lieutenant, and see you get a damn good chance to fight it." It was the biggest surprise of my twenty-one years.

I spent the night at Division CP. At dawn I awoke to the sounds of running and the count of calisthenics; I looked out of the tent to see a superbly fit General Cleland double-timing down the road with members of his staff. Probably half of this bunch were still Guard types—fat, out of shape, wheezing with every step—but Joe Cleland, fifty years old if a day, led the pack, shaping up the 40th Division from the top, by personal example.

The drive from Division to the 223d Regimental HQ gave me the opportunity to see exactly how far blitzkrieg had moved to sitzkrieg in this war. Everything seemed to be poured in concrete. Arty was dug in to stay. At Regiment itself there were volleyball courts, snack bars, EM and officers' clubs, and officers' messes but a maître d' away from the Ritz. It was not just the permanency that struck me, but the attendant luxury. All the goodies were there: nightly movies, well-stocked PXs, starched fatigues, even an outdoor amphitheater with a stage and row beyond row of green sandbag seats. And all this was within earshot of artillery crashing down on the poor bastards in the trenches. "Gibraltar—the rock—home of the 223d," said the sign. *Complacency under canvas*, it might have read. I was shocked, and actually frightened by this living, breathing example of an Army in the defense. Had it been this bad during the Raider days? Had I misread the newspapers back at Benning, or read more into them because I so badly wanted to come back? The Army I saw now obviously had no intention of attacking, and without that, it had no hope of winning.

The HQ was an "Airborne all the way" mini replica of the 40th Division CP, but from the moment I entered the CP area I felt that none of it was quite real. The adjutant, Major Doak, greeted me as if I were his replacement rather than a pimply-faced lieutenant. "The Colonel is waiting to meet you at his quarters," he gushed.

I had a chance to have a good look at my new regimental CO while he glanced over my service record. Colonel Louis Truman was smooth. Exceptionally handsome. Immaculately dressed in tailored fatigues and infantry blue scarf. Manicured from the top of his head to his buffed and clipped fingernails, he had the theatrical presence of Douglas Fairbanks, or maybe that other Douglas—MacArthur. When we'd met moments before, he hadn't walked up to greet me—he'd glided. He hadn't talked—he'd purred. "Yes, Lieutenant . . . the Old Man rang me . . . gave you the highest recommendation. He wants you to have a rifle company." He was still purring as he made small talk over my record: "A lot of combat . . . four Purple Hearts . . . excellent background. . . ." Then came the hook: "You've known the General before?"

I should have said he was my father and I his bastard son. Cleland must have given me one hell of an introduction. Now this good politician before me—it was all becoming clear—wanted to know how deep the connection was. How it might affect him I couldn't imagine. The story about Truman was that he was the President's nephew, and a guy couldn't get much more clout than that.

The Colonel then briefed me on the regiment. It was in reserve and, like the rest of the division, phasing out the Guard and assimilating new replacements. The unit had the numbers but not the experience; it was suffering from an acute shortage of tried-and-true NCOs and qualified junior officers. At company level, most COs had less than two years' service; platoon leaders, less than one. That's why Cleland was trying like hell to get seasoned people, and why, explained Truman, "We're so glad to have you aboard."

So glad to have you aboard. I looked around for the gangplank so I could

jump ship. About this time Major Arthur Hyman, the regimental Operations officer (fresh out of the 82d, too) glided in. Maybe he took lessons from
Truman. "Colonel," he said, "hate to bother you but this is hot."

That's how they talked. Cliché after cliché, with a kind of manufactured
urgency. Soon Hyman glided out again, the plans for the next morning's
"hot" training exercise burning holes through his hands. Enter Adjutant
Doak, who had a hurried whisper with the Colonel before exiting stage
right. Truman turned back to me with sympathetic, doleful eyes. "Lieutenant, there is no rifle-company command position available in the
regiment. But what we can do is assign you to the First Battalion as CO of
D Company." *Heavy weapons*, I thought. *Great. The minute I walk out of
this room I'm going back to Division and get on my pony for the Wolfhounds.*
But Truman read my thoughts. "You understand, Lieutenant, this is just a
stopgap position. You will get the first rifle company that opens up in the
regiment. In the meantime, I think the experience will be good for you. I
notice you've only had rifle-company experience. This will round out your
career, so to speak." *So to speak.* *

Lieutenant Colonel John C. Young, down at 1st Batt, was a poor
imitation of Colonel Truman. He wore the same tailored fatigues, the same
infantry scarf, but everything was a bit wrinkled and nothing seemed to fit
quite right. Young explained that the battalion was training hard, and would
go on line in about five weeks. As he gave me a rundown on Company D's
strengths and shortcomings, I was struck with the strongest feeling that this
CO didn't know what he was talking about. Like a professor of mechanical
engineering who knows the language but has never seen a motor or had
grease on his hands—that's how this guy was with the jargon of infantry.

Or so it appeared to me. I gave myself a good talking-to as I left his office.
After all, Young was a light colonel of infantry; he was probably very
qualified to run this outfit. Maybe I was just used to rough cobs skippering
battalions. Young was just different, as Truman was so different from Sloan.
And maybe it was my own anxiety about taking over a company. I'd never
expected such an opportunity; I hadn't thought I had enough experience.
Now it was obvious, at least in a comparative sense, that I did, but what a
place to do it in. All-green guys in an all-green regiment. No famous
heritage like the Wolfhounds' to build esprit upon, when esprit was probably
the only win/lose factor left in this war. My new charges—whatever unit I
ended up with—would probably be most un-Raider-like. They'd have read
the papers. Surely they'd know the peace talks were ongoing (even at a snail's

---

* As it happened, Truman was right: the heavy weapons experience was good for me. Through it I
learned the importance of the infantry's organic supporting arms, knowledge which would prove
invaluable to me in my subsequent higher level infantry commands.

pace), and all would be waiting for the breakthrough, none wanting to be the last casualty in a no-win war. It was a hell of a big leadership problem: how would I motivate these guys, fire them up for the big game, when all they'd want to do would be hide in their bunkers and hope they'd make it until it was time to go home? As it turned out, I had far fewer problems with my men than I did with Colonel Young: I lasted in his command just over a month.

Our first confrontation was over what Young considered my "unorthodox" supply procedures. Ammunition was rationed for training, but when my supply sergeant found a ROK supply depot that would swap us ammo for C rations, the Raider in me (logically) told him to go for it. Sure it was irregular—as a matter of fact, it was totally illegal (the ROKs would no doubt sell the Cs on the black market)—but I didn't care. My job was to knock these troops (only about 50 percent were NG now, but that was plenty to keep the outfit bopping along more like a fraternity than a military unit) into shape with heavy-duty, hands-on training. And if I could do just one thing, it would be to make damn sure that when I went on to Truman's promised rifle company, these guys in the rear would be proficient enough not to clobber us with inaccurate, but no less lethal, fire. Young locked my heels together for not going by the book. "You have to go through the regular supply channels, Lieutenant!"

"You can't fire requisitions, Colonel," I replied.

Our second confrontation was about my "unorthodox" troop-leading procedures. Having taken just one look at the sorry condition of D Company, I'd implemented a dawn-to-midnight training schedule. The boys didn't know what had hit them, but whatever it was, they were none too pleased. I also established an open-door policy, a period every day when troops could see me without going through the chain of command. My first visitor was a young NG sergeant. "Why don't you just cut out all this training shit?" he demanded. "Most of us are going home and then out of the blue you come in like a madman and give us all this extra work. We don't like it, and we're not buying it."

I told him he didn't have to buy it, that I was giving it away free of charge. I reminded him he was in a Regular Army unit now, and if he didn't like that, I'd extend his sweet ass in Korea for six months by tossing him into the slammer for insubordination. The kid didn't care. He charged right back, telling me he was going to see some NG major up at Division. "I'll tell him what you've been doing here and he'll fire you."

I could not believe my ears. And why, I asked, would he fire me?

"He works for my father. He's a supervisor in Dad's company in California."

I told him I didn't give a damn what his father did for a living, he had nothing to do with this outfit, nor did I take orders from majors who were not in my chain of command. And furthermore, I wound up, if the California National Guard sergeant opened his mouth one more time, I'd fill it up with my good old California Regular Army fist.

The trooper got the message and the word got out to his NG buddies. Day by day some rotated home; the new replacements and those who remained started to snap into shape and play by the rules. But in the meantime, word got back to Young that I'd "threatened" this kid. It was a small thing that he made a big drama. He did not stop for a moment to see that the unit was coming together, that maybe these guys *could* be made ready in the few weeks remaining until they went on line.

I gave up on the CO completely. It was just too frustrating. Fortunately Colonel Young had a brilliant S-3 by the name of Captain Joe McDonough, who, the more I watched, I could see actually ran the battalion on the quiet. McDonough (who would go on to make two stars) was a West Pointer, a jumper from the 82d. *What is it with this battalion?* I'd asked myself when I first walked into his S-3 tent and saw a sign over his desk in Latin. When he'd translated it for me ("Don't let the bastards wear you down," it said), I'd breathed a sigh of relief; it was the first down-to-earth thing I'd heard since I'd left General Cleland. I felt even better when Captain Mac confirmed my initial feelings about Young. It turned out the battalion CO was a Finance officer who'd branch-transferred to Infantry. So he was just a brilliant guy with stars in his eyes; he had little hands-on experience to back himself up. Worse, though, was that he was not alone in his inexperience. At this point in time, Joe McDonough was the only officer in the battalion who'd commanded a rifle company in combat.

Still, the unit was shaping up, not just in terms of proficiency, but in terms of spirit. And this was due to the ever-present Joe Cleland. He came to be known as the Great White Father, whom you might find running along with your company in the wee hours of the morning or suddenly standing behind you, listening in as you worked through a tactical problem. His style and techniques mirrored Ridgway's ten years earlier, when the latter ramrodded the 82d into Airborne perfection. No one ever knew when Cleland would appear, so everyone was always on the stick. His energy seeped through the whole division. Within weeks the organization became worthy of the bright-yellow sunburst on the 40th's blue shoulder patch: no longer the California Crybabies, through Cleland's personal example we were well on our way to becoming—in deed as well as name—the Fireball Division.

Finally 1st Batt was tasked to relieve another unit on the line. I was pretty confident that my D Company charges wouldn't do too much damage on the battlefield except where it counted, and the rifle-company commanders and I went forward a few days early to plan and recon the relief.

As the heavy-weapons CO, I was responsible for the battalion fire plan. When I first got this job I'd scrounged a copy of the heavy-weapons field manual and begun reading up, almost wishing I'd paid more attention at Benning when we'd discussed the functioning of a heavy-weapons company. But I hadn't given it any thought at the time. I saw myself as a frontline infantryman; heavy weapons had seemed like rear-echelon shit. To my mind, they still were. But if I had to be a rear-echelon commando, I was determined to be the *best* rear-echelon commando, and had studied long and hard, at night and on the job, to this end. Now, on the line, my task was first to establish interlocking bands of grazing fire across the battalion front; then, to cover dead spots with indirect fire starting with D Company's mortars; and finally, to deploy the principally antitank recoilless rifles to cover tank and infantry approaches.

I walked along the front selecting my sites and alerting the rifle-company COs so they could plan to shift their own weapons as necessary (heavy weapons had priority of sites, in that the interlocking bands of fire had to tie in with the battalions on either side, as part of a Red-proof line that stretched the whole way across Korea). All went well until one of the company COs refused to shift a BAR to make way for a heavy-machine-gun section. We got into an argument, which heated up (à la Sergeant Reeves back in G Company) to the point where we were ready to duke it out. Reason came to my aid at the last moment: the CO had a chip on his shoulder the size of a mortar tube (he was a short guy with a runt complex) and I decided to let the battalion commander intervene.

After I finished my deployment plan, I left the line and headed back to Colonel Young. I told him the story and requested he talk to the CO. Young rubbed his hands together like the worried old bookkeeper he was and said, "It's Charlie's area . . . he knows what's best."

"Colonel, we're talking about an integrated fire plan. Right out of FM 7-15." I took the field manual out of my jacket and thumped it on his desk.

"It's quite pointless to argue, Lieutenant."

"Look. I will read from the book," I replied, and read the thing, chapter and verse. I slammed the field manual down again. "So it has no goddamned bearing on whose area it's in. Heavy weapons has priority of sites."

"Lieutenant, I suggest you not use profanity in my presence."

That was the absolute limit. I blew up. "Colonel, you can take this battalion and stuff it right up your ass. After forty days in this limp-dick outfit

I'm convinced you could not run a good Boy Scout troop." With that I saluted, whirled around, and stormed out.

It all had to do with a deep moral feeling on my part. The book was the book. You could play with it—make it better based on your own experience—but on basic tactical matters it held proven principles for success that had evolved from a lot of wars over a lot of years. I should have realized Colonel Finance wouldn't know this. He probably didn't know an M-1 from an adding machine. On the other hand, maybe I had realized it and I'd just been looking for a final shoot-out. But I think what pissed me off even more was that the guy did not have the guts to stand tall during a fight between two subordinates.

I decided I was right—morally right and Army right—but that Truman would not know this. The last thing I needed now was to blow my top at the regimental CO, too. (I was already worried about what I'd said to Young; not that it wasn't true, but it was just not the way one addressed his CO.) I went straight to General Cleland and told him what happened. He agreed with me on the tactical end of things; as for my tact, he was less impressed. In fact, he chewed my ass royally. With much fire in his voice he said I needed to learn patience, respect for my superiors, and, most important, control over my temper. I agreed down the line, but told him it was hard. I'd learned in 1950 that war was a serious game. People died in it. But guys like Young didn't seem to know this, and it seemed that the Youngs were in charge wherever I looked. "Sometimes, Hackworth," the General replied, "it's better to be like the Three Monkeys—'see no evil, hear no evil, speak no evil.' The Army is changing. You must do the best you can, even while you're changing with it."

Before I left he called Truman. A rifle company had miraculously opened up in 2d Batt; Cleland assured me that the old Airborne CO, Bill Locke, was my kind of soldier. "You'll be on line in a couple of days, son," he concluded as he walked me to the door. "Good luck, take care of yourself . . . and watch that temper."

I returned to Company D, packed my gear, and split with no regrets. To my great relief, there were no repercussions from my blowup at Colonel Young, or so I thought. His last laugh came long after he'd been killed in Korea on the reverse slope of A Company's sector. He'd taken the opportunity to render an Officer Efficiency Report on me—a form I'd never paid much mind to in Easy or the Raiders—for my short tenure in his command: the words "impetuous" and "immature" on that ER (an accurate assessment, I had to admit) were to sting my ass in a big way for almost a decade to come.

I arrived at the 2d Batt CP, and for the first time really knew I'd soon be back on the line. Everyone was moving briskly, packing up and getting ready to go. A rush of adrenaline ran through me. Long dormant, that familiar buzz, which resonates in your gut all the time you're in combat, awoke with a start. I liked the feeling. I also liked this place. Precise, neat, military. Young's battalion had looked good, too, but there it seemed the precision was all for show. A "just in case" exactness, as if to prevent God, or at least General Cleland, from suddenly swooping down and catching the outfit short. Here, the exactness was organic. It thrived on itself. No one seemed to be looking over his shoulder for higher command's approval.

Dick Weden, the battalion Adjutant, told me the Colonel was up front on a recon. I filled the time processing in, and being briefed on battalion SOPs and the operational readiness of Fox Company, my new command. At one point the battalion XO, Major Charles Brown, took me aside to tell me Colonel Locke was one mean hombre, the worst-tempered, toughest guy he'd ever worked for. Brown would know—he was a hard old warrior himself, wounded three times in WW II—and I began to wonder if maybe I should have stayed with Colonel Young.

A bit later Weden said the Old Man was back and would meet me in the battalion mess. I went in. No colonel. A small, thin captain wearing Medical Service Corps insignia and a Korean Military Assistance Group (KMAG) patch walked in; as the mess was about to close, I decided not to wait any longer, and ate with him. We made the usual small talk, and then he started asking me what I thought of the 40th Division, what I'd heard about 2d Batt—really strange questions that started my sixth sense screaming. Why would an overage-in-grade MSC KMAG captain give a damn about this division or this battalion? Maybe he and the Colonel were pals; hell, the guy was so old, maybe his only friend in the world was the Colonel. So I answered his questions, but in a very guarded kind of way. About this time Weden came in. "Oh," he said, "I'm glad you found each other. Have you been introduced to the Colonel, Lieutenant Hackworth?"

Not only was this Colonel Locke mean, he was very, very sneaky. My new CO dismissed his trick with a shrug, saying he'd forgotten about his recon disguise. *Like hell*, I thought. The minute his disguise was dropped, he got down to business with the most colorful vocabulary I'd ever heard. The scuttlebutt was that Locke had been a mule skinner in the old Horse Cav; all that was certain was he did swear like one. Poor old George Washington must have been rolling in his grave—in July 1776, he'd issued an order to the Continental Army that swearing, that "unmeaning and abominable custom," was forever banned. The order still stood in 1952. General Washington of all people should have known that one must never issue an order that cannot be enforced.

Colonel Locke was Old Army through and through. The word was he'd risen to topkick before the war, then was battlefield commissioned while with Merrill's Marauders in Burma. Since 1945 he'd served with the 82d, as battalion CO and regimental XO. The man was mean as a snake and looked like one, too—a rattler about to strike. He was thin, almost bald, with a long face and thin, tight lips he mashed together like Humphrey Bogart. He chewed tobacco, had a stain from it on his cheek, and his teeth were ground down like an old horse's. He also minced no words. He said the battalion was locked, cocked, and ready to go; we would go forward in the morning, coordinate with the outfit we were to relieve, stay twenty-four hours to get the lay of things, and return to our unit. From Locke's point of view, the terms of my own employment were simple: if I fucked up, I was out. Then, having made himself so succinctly and painfully clear, he rose to leave. His last unsmiling words: "Welcome to the Second Battalion."

Weden was pleased I'd gotten along so well with the Colonel, though it was news to me. Now I understood the flawless condition of his unit: he ran it on pure fear. His men had no time to worry about surprise visits from Cleland. They had enough on their plates just watching out for their mule-skinner CO.

Fox Company had talent. Untried, but it was there. The platoon leaders were West Pointer ('51) Joe Rice, ROTC grad Joe Stokes, and Boyd Guttery, an AG man doing his infantry stint. None had more than twelve months' troop experience to bring to his platoon, yet instinctively I knew each was a good man. Eager and bright, in a few months (with lots of work) they'd be studs on the battlefield. As their fledgling company commander, though, my biggest concern was who was going to hold their hands through the worst of it. Normally green lieutenants leaned on their old sergeants until the realities of combat caught up with their West Point, OCS, or ROTC book learning. The problem in Fox (and across the front) was that the U.S. Army had totally run out of NCOs.

I had to put two corporals, Thelbert Allison and OCS dropout Homer Smith, in platoon sergeant positions. These jobs were normally held by master sergeants, but even my topkick, Gregory, was only a staff sergeant whose complete infantry experience had been as a company clerk somewhere along the line. My saving grace in the unit was actually a PFC named Herschel Hudson, whom I assigned to round out the rifle platoon sergeant team. "The Hud" was a WW II platoon sergeant who'd reenlisted for Korea. All in all, I had a good team (though it looked as if officer and NCO would be leaning on each other for the next little while); my own job was already shaping up to be not just commander but chief instructor.

I got the company together to give them my "I am your new CO" talk and set in motion a training program for the period I was on recon. In this respect, I did not feel daunted by the number of men (two hundred) I was now responsible for. The two-day, forty-hour crash course would concentrate on the same basics (battle drill, night defense procedures, field fortifications, and night relief) I'd taught and reinforced in my George squads of eleven and the Easy and Raider platoons of forty to fifty. I set up a relief rehearsal for the night I returned; with that, my recon party cut off our 40th Div patches, taped over the unit markings on our vehicles, and slipped up to the line.

The first thing that struck me was that if a unit is a reflection of its commander, then First Lieutenant Joe Love, skipper of George Company, 5th Regimental Combat Team (the unit Fox would be relieving), was one of the best I'd seen in Korea. Love was a tall, handsome, southern charmer; West Point, Class of '50, and a total pro. In a no-win war where defeat and counting days until DEROS (Date Eligible Return from Overseas) had grabbed hold of the boys in the trenches in rolling tides as poisonous as mustard gas, Love ran a high-spirited, enthusiastic outfit. He did credit to the 5th RCT, one of the hard-fighting sister regiments of the Wolfhounds (in the Hawaiian days); from range cards to hill weapons to fire plans, George Company was ready.

The same, unfortunately, could not be said for the position. It wasn't Joe's fault. The worst of the place had been thrown up more than a year before when Siegfrieditis set in, and George Company hadn't been there long enough to make major fixes. The place was a maze and in bad repair. Bunkers were falling apart all over the hill, their sandbags bursting from age and shell hits, the supporting log beams sagging from initially bad design and worse construction.

The fighting positions were badly laid out; they'd been thrown up on top of the barren hill like little forts. Most had terrible fields of fire: not only could the weapons not reach down to get grazing fire, but one good enemy SP or MG across the valley could slam rounds right into the bunkers' firing ports and close them down. It was a wonder they were still there, especially when you looked at the junkyard in front of the position. The wire barrier had been as badly laid out as the fighting line, and as sadly neglected. Along its helter-skelter barbed-wire apron were bits and pieces of rat-gnawed enemy dead in bloody khaki; the whole thing was just a broken-down hodgepodge of stakes, concertina wire, and mines, thrown up or buried by one generation of defenders after another. I'd seen it all before, with the Raiders, but somehow it was different now when I realized I'd have to live there (and of course, there was no doubt the frontline dilapidation had continued most enthusiastically in the months I'd been away). As usual, there were no barrier maps. "Where are the mines?" was the logical question; "*Out there*" (with a broad sweep of the arm) was the standard reply. I couldn't understand it. The positions had been there one year. They'd been occupied by elements of four different divisions, and it seemed as though not a damn thing had been done to improve them. They were death traps, nothing more or less.

Who's kidding whom? I wondered, as I headed back to Fox the next morning. The fighters knew the truth, but maybe the generals really believed the story they fed the politicians, that the Eighth Army defense was an impregnable line in depth. But "depth" meant good defensive positions behind the main line that were, or could be, occupied by soldiers in a snap. Our "depth" was snack bars, volleyball courts, and the regimental Greek theater. Those perfect green sandbag seats belonged on the line. It was criminal.

The only depth we had was out front: two fortified half-squad OPs (one astride each major avenue of approach, and both death traps I'd already decided to change), LPs, and patrols. But they were not depth. Their function was security: to delay the enemy and provide early warning, and to deceive the enemy as to where the defense was. Yet the latter was hardly possible given the big forts we had sitting astride the trench line like Humpty-Dumpty on a wall. *Well*, I thought, *Humpty-Dumpty's going to have his great fall if we don't get it together in a big hurry*.

That night Fox did a slow walk-through rehearsal of the night relief. Patience had never been one of my strong points, and I saw it slipping now: the rehearsal was by no means a disaster, but it was painfully clear that my boys could barely go through the motions. God only knew what they'd done in training, but they were not ready for the big game. I realized then it was going to be a question of just getting them on the hill. The front line was no place to train, but there was no alternative. I had fledgling architects when what we needed were gnarled old carpenters; I just prayed we'd have time to forge a fighting team before the enemy blew our house down.

After the rehearsal I met with the leaders and issued my order. Simplicity was the word. We would follow the book: company assembly point to platoon assembly points to squad release points, to filling in the line next to Joe Love's fine soldiers. As each Fox platoon leader took over, Joe's relieved force would reverse the procedure and finally they would slip off the hill. The troops were so green I wondered whether we should lock and load; I finally decided that the weapons would be loaded, but with no rounds in the chambers, and there'd be no firing without an officer's approval.

We got the troops into the sack early and let them sleep in the next morning. There wouldn't be much rest in the next forty-eight hours and they'd need all the energy they could muster. I snuck my mess truck forward by day infiltration; this wasn't allowed—a security risk, went the reasoning— but the way my selectively insubordinate mind saw it was, first, I knew how good hot food would taste to the boys in the assembly area before the swap, and second, who ever heard of a mess truck leading a relief anyway?

After the company had placed luminescent tape on the backs of their helmets, tightened their gear to make it noiseproof, and blackened their faces à la Raiders, I gave them a little pep talk. Fox Company was dead, I told them. From this moment forward we were Fighter. We would answer the phone with "Fighter Company." We would call ourselves by the new name and use it loud and proud enough that no other unit in our vicinity could be mistaken about what we really were.

I saw a lot of smiles. The troops got a charge out of it, at least the ones who could understand me. It was during the rehearsal that I'd realized many of them didn't speak English. Puerto Ricans and Koreans were sprinkled liberally throughout the unit; between them and the Guamanians, I'd lost track of who the all-American troops really were. It was a problem. The policy of requiring units to be integrated down to the squad was as unworkable now as it had been when first implemented in late '51. In a firefight there's no margin for misinterpretation, no time to gesture and stumble through pidgin English instructions to get the word across. Yet, with up to four languages spoken among any group of ten soldiers, we had mini Towers of Babel every hundred yards across the U.S. front.

But at least the men of F Company had one thing in common: they were all Fighters now. And with heads held a little higher, we saddled up and started on our way.

It was Halloween night and quiet, less the routine hammering of H&I fire. Along with my advance party, Joe Love had his guides at all critical points of the relief route. It was still his ball game; I slipped through a sandbagged tunnel near the edge of the road and waited in his CP. The large bunker was split in two with a log interior wall. Half was the company switchboard and commo center; the other half was the CP itself, with a couple of painfully uncomfortable sacks of interwoven commo wire for the CO and topkick. It was a good setup. The only thing I'd change would be the beds.

I had a chance to watch Joe in action. He was calm, cool, and professional. His 3d Platoon leader was one Master Sergeant Bob Fowler, whom I'd known in the Wolfhounds and who could only be described as Huckleberry Finn in fatigues—sandy hair, freckles, a mischievous smile. I asked Joe if Fowler could stay with us a few days; Joe went along with it when he realized we were old pals. This led to an agreement in which, in addition, Love would leave a good NCO with each platoon, plus someone from his FO party to gently introduce my green unit to the place. Neither of us told our next higher-ups—they'd have said no—just as we didn't tell them I was keeping G Company's machine guns (I wanted the firepower on the hill, zeroed in and ready to go), leaving mine at the bottom of the hill for Joe's boys to pick up on the way down. I promised Joe he'd get no "dogs" among Fighter's equipment; the bottom line here was *trust*, and in that regard, the two of us were from the same school: in Joe's words, years later, "We trusted—the scheme worked."

And so did the relief. At dawn I finally had the numbers and assumed command; Joe wished me good luck and moved out with his CP group. A few days later his transition team was gone, too. *What a good man*, I thought as Sergeant Bob Fowler slipped off the hill. Little did I know that sixteen years later his fine soldiering and leadership would lead to his death. Just before he was to be promoted to sergeant major in a battalion of the 1/5th Cav, he'd be killed walking point (as a company first sergeant) in a bad battle in another no-win war, which, like Korea, would gut the Army of its very fiber, its NCOs.

The 40th Division was deployed on the east coast, near a large valley called the Punch Bowl. The right flank of the division was on the Punch Bowl's northern rim, linking up with other units to form a human wall stretching from coast to coast. Fighter Company's defensive sector started on a high hill where we tied in with Easy. We had the top. A ridgeline sweeping up from the valley floor on this eastern edge of our position was a company-sized enemy avenue of approach, right into my 3d Platoon.

The sector ran downhill into a draw, then up another hill to our west about a hundred yards, where we tied in with George Company. The draw led into the valley, widening as it went, and by the time it hit the valley floor, it was wide enough to take almost two enemy battalions abreast. Called the Gap, it was a most dangerous regimental avenue of approach, and it didn't take much to see (and it was recognized the whole way from Army to Corps to Division, Regiment, Battalion, and especially to me) that Fighter held the critical ground. To overrun the Punch Bowl the enemy would have to strike through my position; if they secured the high knob (my left flank), it would be smooth sailing, walking or rolling (the draw was also a good tank avenue of approach) from there right through the Gap to the flatlands behind. It was not a great place for a green regiment.

My tasks were many, and competed in priority. Holding the hill and keeping the boys alive were the key governing factors. Patrols had to go out and the men had to be trained, but keeping them alive also meant an immediate rebuild of the breastworks and the solving of a serious field sanitation problem. Rats fed off the enemy dead on the wire (as well as on any food they found on position), and infested every bunker. Some were as long as an arm. I worried about hemorrhagic fever, a killer disease, the first sign of which was the whites of the eyes going red with blood, like someone had given them a good poke. I remembered Uncle Roy telling me about the big influenza epidemic that roared through Europe in 1918. More people died at the end of WW I from the flu than were knocked off by shot. But as far as I was concerned in the Somme-like Korean trenches of 1952, one was no worse than the other; be it a slug or a bug that got him, I'd still be losing a valuable soldier.

The bunkers were death traps, not just because of their high profiles, but because they were too heavily built, easily twenty thousand sandbags to many of them. The men piled the sandbags on like the Crusaders had piled on armor. But the sandbags weakened the heavy wooden timbers, and just like the Crusaders (who became so heavily protected they couldn't even stand up to face the enemy), soldiers across the front were being crushed to death or mangled when a direct hit or heavy rain caused their sandbagged bunkers to collapse on top of them.

Joe Rice did justice to his West Point military engineering degree by designing a sleek, low-profile fighting bunker. We figured each platoon could manage one rebuild per night, the troops filling sandbags in chow bunkers on the reverse slope (unobserved by the enemy) by day, so come nightfall the bunker building would be a simple assembly job, with all materials prestocked. At the same time, the OP in front of 3d Platoon would be relocated and rebuilt, while the one at the Gap would be abandoned and booby-trapped (I decided to replace this one with a two-man "roving" OP whose members could provide early warning and hightail it home).

I ordered rat poison by the ton and no "care package" food on the hill. I abolished the practice of throwing empty C-ration cans (a rodent delicacy) in front of the trench, and had the enemy dead burned off the wire with napalm. The wire itself would be upgraded when the weather changed; we'd have a slightly better chance of working through the uncharted AP mines without blowing ourselves up when the ground was frozen hard. And whenever all this was completed, we'd rebuild the reverse slope bunkers.

I woke up on 4 November 1952, thinking that a year had passed since that terrible night on Hill 400. *What had it been for?* I wondered. The month of November '52 saw the heaviest fighting of the past year, with U.S. casualties up to a thousand a week. The peace talks dragged on and on,

while troopers on the ground still sat on death row, waiting for a reprieve
that never came. More firepower—air and arty—had now officially been
used in Korea than in all of WW II. Fighter was catching hundreds of
incoming rounds a day, mostly 82-mm and 120-mm mortars, and 45-mm
and 75-mm pack howitzers. The thing that always got to me was that while,
pound for pound, we had the enemy incredibly outgunned (they had none
of the good stuff we had—no tactical barbed wire or minefields or tac air),
it didn't stop them from nickel and diming us, literally around the clock.
Their artillery was burrowed, corkscrew fashion, into the hillside, sometimes
on tracks. The guns would be pulled up along the track to their firing
positions, poop out a few rounds, and then be slid back. Like the Chinese,
the North Koreans needed a lot of preplanning to concentrate heavy fire in
support of a specific operation, and lousy commo made them inflexible
once the show got on the road. Still, we'd been on line less than a week and
had taken a couple of WIA every day, mostly from direct artillery hits that
ripped into the bunkers. Joe Rice had an 82-mm round slam through three
layers of sandbags and split the fourteen-inch logs in the roof right over his
head as he lay dozing in his bunker one afternoon. Luckily, it didn't go off
("A lot of dirt but no problem," he said); about 20 percent of all incoming
(much of it old Soviet ammo) were duds. But tell that to your heart as you
sat listening to the whine, the whistle, and the crunch—about one round's
worth every three minutes across the company front.

Fortunately, U.S. artillery was responsive, accurate, and plentiful during
this period. The emphasis on it, pretty well a whole new ball game
compared to my last tour, was (I figured) based on Napoleon's concept of
depending on firepower when the infantry is weak. God knows we were
piss-weak, so the arty, historically the doughfoot's best friend, was ours, too,
in this old-style trench war.

By the eighth day on line, I was exhausted. I hadn't clocked too many
hours of sleep since we arrived (little did I know it would be that way the
whole time we were in this sector, which came to be known simply as the
Gap); there was always something to fix or rebuild, always someone to train.
It amazed me how much there was to do. At platoon level, I'd somehow
come to assume that on a day-to-day level we were the ones doing the work,
while the company commander just sat back and took it easy until the
operation warning order came. How very wrong I'd been. The respect I'd
had for Michaely, Gilchrist, and Evans only grew as I came to appreciate
the heavy responsibility and the great demands of a job they'd performed so
well. Still, the work in Fighter was worth the effort—our position and our
people were looking better and better. We were becoming a company in
spirit and proficiency as well as in fact. The patrols were already meeting

with some success; in the first week, men of Fighter killed half a dozen North Koreans with no casualties of our own. Our first enemy probe, which occurred near where the 3d Platoon OP was being rebuilt, was also nipped in the bud, despite the fact that the North Koreans were at their finest at probes, with specially trained sappers for whom patience *was* a strong point. The sappers would crawl along on their bellies, snipping their way (with cloth between their cutters' teeth, which muffled the metallic "click") through minefields laced with booby traps, flares, and barbed-wire entanglements and be in your position without your hearing one sound. But Joe Stokes, platoon leader of the 3d, had wisely placed an outguard on a knob a hundred yards from the OP to provide the work detail with security, and a squad of North Koreans walked right into them. It was total surprise all round, but the final result was no friendly casualties and three more enemy KIA. Little kills like these did wonders for morale, and even more important, they dispelled the rumors that the North Koreans were ten-foot-tall monsters roving through the valley like slanty-eyed Frankensteins.

I spent many daylight hours out in my observation post (OP), studying the battlefield. Joe Love had rebuilt this critical facility. It was a first-class command center that allowed a good view of the entire company front plus a clear view of No Name Hill (the grim enemy-held fortress dominating our immediate battle area). This was my battle station. In it I worked out Fighter's "flashfires" (complete defensive barrages of mixed artillery, mortars, and flares, prearranged and code-named) with my artillery FO; from it I would initially control my unit during an enemy attack.

At night I worried my fledgling patrols through their paces as if they were my sons out with the family car for the first time. I'd gone on a few patrols myself, to help the boys through their opening-night jitters, but as the company CO I really had no business being out there in no-man's-land, and with great reluctance I now remained in the trenches and lent moral support. The self-exile had certain advantages, though. If nothing big was happening (like a patrol getting lost, which in the early days happened with painful regularity), I'd walk the front line from end to end a couple of times. I'd check each position, talk to the troops until I got to know their names and could recognize their voices in the dark, and give quiet, impromptu classes on everything from weapons maintenance to leadership to how to stop homesickness ("Hey, sir, when's the mail coming?" kids would ask again and again).

I'd take a hike out to the 3d Platoon outpost, which was under construction. I'd have a look at the rebuilding and then just sit there, thinking, *If I were the enemy CO, how would I attack this position?* I did the same thing down at the Gap. Then I would wargame all the options. *How would I maneuver? Where would I set up my supporting weapons? What would be my main attack? When I penetrated, how would I roll up the flanks?* Out of all this pondering, night after night, came our defensive organization and local counterattack plans.

Every time I walked the line I'd find troopers asleep. Sleeping on the front was a court-martial offense—one snoozer weakens the whole defense. But I didn't believe in court-martials. There's more than one way to keep people awake, and I preferred the Old Army NCO way. Company procedure required anyone coming up the trench to be softly challenged: "Halt, who goes there?" No challenge generally meant the trooper was asleep, or at least not doing his job. I'd sneak up and toss the guy on the trench or bunker floor; he'd wake up with my trench knife against his throat. "If I were a North Korean you'd be one dead son of a bitch." Then I'd bring in the chain of command so every responsible leader got into the act; I'd call in the kid's squad and platoon leaders and, on the spot, have them explain why he was sleeping. But I knew why. A lot of troopers could sleep all day long and still nod off on the line. It was their escape. Many were so damn scared they'd fall asleep just to make it all go away. But sleepers placed the rest of my soldiers at unnecessary risk, so alertness became top priority. NCOs and officers started patrolling their sectors like cops on a beat. This cut the number of sleeping incidences way down, but there were still too many offenders. Finally I came up with the ultimate punishment: habitual sleepers would man the outposts. Nobody would dare screw off there.

It's only fair to say that from time to time I fell victim to the sandman, too. One night during the first week, I'd done my walk through the position and returned to my CP running on empty, afraid to even grab a catnap in case something happened and I'd be too foggy to deal with it. I sat down on my ammo-box-and-air-mattress bed. I couldn't lie down; lying down meant instant sleep. *Should have kept Joe Love's commo-wire contraption,* I thought as I lit another cigarette. That "bed" virtually guaranteed sleepless nights. I'd chain-smoked from the minute I came inside the CP, and between the smoke and the heat from our little squad stove, my bloodshot eyes were beginning to sag. I got up and poured my millionth cup of black coffee (which had been reheated for about the two millionth time since dinner); I sat down again, thinking that my breath would kill an elephant, and closed my eyes.

I awoke with a fright. The sun was just rising. "Adkins!" My commo-cum-operations sergeant appeared at the doorway. "What's happening with the patrol?"

He gave me a puzzled look. "Sir, you brought it in an hour ago."

Adkins had thought I'd been resting my eyes. The whole time I'd been sitting there he'd been bopping in and out saying stuff like "The patrol is at Checkpoint Red. Shall I move it according to plan to Checkpoint Blue?" Apparently, each time I'd pondered the question and then issued clear instructions. But I had no recall; sound asleep, I'd just moved the patrol all over no-man's-land and home again. *Not cool.* From that moment onward, I made Adkins have me on my feet every time I gave such instructions. *In the meantime,* I thought with great misgivings, *all's well that ends well . . .* and wondered if I should assign myself to OP duty, too.

Total U.S. casualites for the Korean Police Action as of 10 November 1952, were KIA, 21,471; WIA, 89,263; MIA, 10,793; and POW, 1,868. A lot of numbers, a lot of good men; Gold Stars, Purple Hearts, and brokenhearted families. A couple of the most recent WIAs were mine: we got an extra ration of incoming the day they did their tallying, and the night of the tenth, 3d Platoon was caught in a twenty-minute torrential downpour of accurate MG fire from No Name, mixed with the usual mortar and artillery fire. It started inexplicably and stopped just as quickly; we tended to our wounded and all was quiet.

The eleventh, my birthday, was a day like every other, only a bit colder. At dusk my patrol men were chomping at the bit, waiting for the shot of first dark to send them dashing off to the valley floor. This is how the war went. During the day both great armies lived underground, hoping not to get knocked off by the unrelenting bursts of artillery and mortar fire coming from across the way. At night the war moved into the valley, where small, lightly equipped patrols hunted each other down in no-man's-land.

The key to the ambush patrols was to beat the Reds down to the choice ambush positions. Most sites, like the Pines (a favorite, just north of the Gap, where the boys were going tonight), were no bigger than a city parking lot, with only limited places to set up. The patrol would then set up a killing zone with all-round security in the hope, ideally, of taking a prisoner before dawn's first light. Excepting the work of U.S. Raider-type units, to date the enemy had been far craftier and usually more successful at this sort of operation than the average American doughfoot. Basically this was because among the other "good" things the North Koreans were lacking was rotation, an insidious system that caused U.S troopers to pay more attention to counting days than fighting Reds, and to make not even the slightest attempt to get to know the lay of the land, a crucial element in staying ahead in this war. The North Koreans, on the other hand, knew every fold and wrinkle of the battlefield as well as a game warden knows his reserve; they'd been there since the beginning and they'd be there for the duration, unless they went out feet first. This fact alone gave them a decided advantage: the motivation for taking the job seriously.

Dark came, and out went the patrol; I'd stay in my CP, ready to pour in the supporting fires, until the men reached their lay-up position. I thought about Colonel Locke, who'd paid his daily visit that morning. That was the only bitch I had about the great, relatively safe road network that ran behind our position. As a result of it we got "hots" for breakfast and dinner (no complaints there), but we also got many—too many—sightseers. Every visiting fireman seemed to come to Fighter (mainly because we were so accessible), completely destroying any chance of sleep during the day. The road ran but a few steps from our CP, and out of the jeeps they'd hop—fat politicians in new, green fatigues, and high muck-a-mucks complete with entourage, from Regiment, Division, Corps, and Army—directly into a well-constructed bunker. They'd take a quick look at the enemy positions from my OP, pile back into their vehicles, and get to the rear just in time, I assumed, for Happy Hour. Locke's visits, however, were somewhat different. He usually walked the trenches before coming to the CP, casting his Old Army eyes over everyone and everything. Hearts throughout the company would freeze with fear. It took till the next morning to thaw them out, and by then he was on his way up the line again. He was an odd guy, Locke. His attention to discipline and exacting detail no doubt saved a lot of lives. But I didn't agree (nor would I ever) that fear was the only way to get results.

This morning, for some reason, the troops had been spared. The Colonel had come directly to the CP and flopped down on my rack. How he was able to do this without wrinkling his starched, immaculate uniform I'd never know. We'd talked about the company, the battalion, and the other world "out there"; I'd been amazed at how cynical he was. Then, as usual, we'd taken a walk down the long tunnel that led to my OP. About halfway, there was a small step down and, as usual, I'd said, "Now watch your step, Colonel." He'd missed the step (which was also as usual), thumped his head on a supporting beam, and cut loose with the foulest tirade imaginable, in my direction: "Yougoddamnmotherfuckingrottensonofabitchbastardofapis-santlieutenant! Why don't you fix that fucking step?" That had been just the start, and, as usual, Locke's assessment of Fighter's Old Man was broadcast for miles, to both friend and foe alike. I'd just "yes, sirred" and "no, sirred" until the barrage slowed down, only then reminding him (as usual) about the two-ton rock that lived under the step, and that to modify the tunnel fell into the category of building the Hoover Dam. Thinking about it now, I had to laugh. Locke had skinned his head this morning. Pretty soon his skull would be as worn down as his teeth.

The patrol reported in from the first checkpoint. Negative. Nothing in the Pines—at least not yet—and no enemy in sight. Then, just as I was about to leave the CP, a huge wall of enemy fire crashed over the company sector from end to end. I ran to my OP. It looked like the Fourth of July out there, with artillery, mortar, and direct-fire MGs blazing in the meanest barrage I'd ever seen. I called for all flashfires to lock our position in. If we were getting hit, the enemy attack force would be out in the open now; we could smash them with our counterwall of fire.

The platoons had flipped on their radios. All reported heavy incoming but no ground attack, though 3d Platoon leader Joe Stokes had lost contact with his outpost. He said he'd send some people out to check on it as soon as the worst of the present barrage ceased. In the meantime our patrol at the Pines had seen no enemy movement. I told these men to sit tight and try to avoid making contact. I only wanted one ball game at a time.

Stokes reported contact—infantry force, size unknown, on his reverse slope. They weren't in his trench line; he'd had no penetration and didn't know where they'd come from. The other platoons still had no contact when I called Locke with a sitrep; he said E Company had been penetrated, which at least answered the question of where the North Koreans were coming from, but it had been a damn gutsy maneuver on the enemy's part. They had to have come up right through their supporting fires.

I had our FO lift the defensive fire everywhere along the company front except 3d Platoon, and I took off for Stokes's position. In their first real fight, my boys, God bless 'em, were cool, alert, and professional. Squad and platoon leaders moved back and forth checking their positions; troops challenged me right down the line.

We passed through 2d Platoon and entered 3d Platoon's trenches. It was a whole different scene at the top of the hill. Total panic. The boys had bunched up, leaving large areas of the trench abandoned. Mortar and artillery fire was still raining down; MG slugs were stitching the top layer of sandbags. The Humpty-Dumpty bunkers that hadn't yet been rebuilt were taking fire right through the apertures; the guys inside were pinned down and couldn't return fire. I suddenly realized that was what the barrage the previous night had been all about. The North Koreans had been zeroing. Clever bastards.

I ran over to the E Company tie-in point. The penetration had come at Easy's first fighting bunker; enemy tracks in the wet ground ran right over the top of it. My guys got themselves together and sealed the penetration. We could hear a good firefight raging on the reverse slope near Stokes's CP—no one had a clue as to how many bad guys were down there, but at least now they had no way out.

I went inside the E Company bunker, only to find a certified frontline recreation center. A poncho was over the aperture. Candles were burning.

Magazines and playing cards were strewn all over the place, and in the middle of it all were the bodies of two Americans who'd died having fun on the firing line.

Stokes appeared, steady and very much in control in his first big firefight. He was a good man, Joe Stokes. I'd liked him from day one. He'd graduated from Oklahoma A&M in agriculture the year after Barney K. Neil; his father had destroyed his dreams of turning their panhandle plot into a prosperous farm by finding oil all over the joint. Stokes had actually been disappointed. Now he reported in, with his dry sense of humor, that gooks were still alive and well on the reverse slope, but being contained and "whittled down to size," with a dozen enemy dead already. He said there were no friendly KIA but at least ten wounded, and he'd still had no word from the OP.

I told him to clean up the reverse slope; I'd go down to the OP myself as soon as the incoming lightened up. Stokes moved out while I directed the Weapons Platoon leader to get tank, recoilless rifle, and .50-cal fire onto No Name to shut off the goddamned MG fire still ripping right into the position, and I organized a squad of Stokes's people under PFC Lindeman (a great former 1st Cav combat man we'd picked up as a replacement) to check on the OP. I finally had a chance to touch base with my CP; the patrol still had no contact. I told Adkins to return these men to the main line and have Joe Rice meet them at the patrol gate in front of 1st Platoon. No doubt the boys below would be a little trigger-happy with so much action just up the ridge, but if Rice was out there, he'd make damn certain that weapons remained locked and the patrol not be chopped up by jittery friendlies.

In the middle of all this, Lindeman appeared with a struggling KATUSA and dropped him at my feet. "This yellow little bastard was on the OP. He saw the gooks coming and bugged out."

The KATUSA was crying. "Everyone under poncho. Every night one guard . . . same . . . me. I see enemy come. I run away."

The rage built up so fast I didn't know what I was doing. Stuck in the trench wall was an M-1 cleaning rod—all metal. Without thinking, I grabbed it and lashed out at the Korean. I picked him up and threw him over the trench—he'd lead us through the bullets to the OP—and whipped him with that cleaning rod until he got his cowardly, weaponless ass moving.

It was another page in the continuing, unfortunate saga of the KATUSAs. Through attrition, their numbers had dwindled as the war dragged on, and they'd become less and less effective as their untrained ranks continued to be integrated into American units (leading, naturally, to more and more resentment among their U.S. counterparts). It wasn't until a short time after this fight, when I put all the Koreans in one unit under a great little Korean liaison-sergeant-turned-line-NCO named Chung *and got results*, that I finally understood how much of the damn problem was the Yanks themselves. Most American leaders had given up trying to communicate with the KATUSAs, except through sign language (more often than not obscene) and name-calling. The war had made all the U.N. troops cannon fodder, but the KATUSAs were treated like *subhuman* cannon fodder. The Americans came and went every nine months; it was the KATUSAs who stayed on these slopes for the duration. And as time passed, we, the Americans, were the ones who, through the continued introduction of green EM and in most cases even greener officers, were becoming increasingly less proficient in our trade. It should have been little wonder that the South Korean soldiers were cool, cunning, and more adept at keeping their heads down than joining in the fray; no wonder, in a jam, that they'd save their own asses and not their U.S. "buddies."

But I was too mad to think about that now. We arrived at the outpost to find two men dead, bayoneted and their throats slit. The third man, Haley, was missing, and the enemy long gone. The OP had been taken by stealth and surprise; there were no spent cartridges to be seen, just long gray ashes from cigarettes that hadn't died as quickly as their smokers. A poncho lay crumpled at the bottom of the hole—a picture worth a thousand words. Haley and the two KIA had been sleepers. I'd ordered Stokes to make them permanent OP until they got their shit together; they must have thought school was out when they covered the foxhole with that poncho and lit up.

I spent the rest of the night with Lindeman and his squad, searching for the missing man in no-man's-land. We went all the way down to the valley floor (which was still being pulverized by U.S. artillery fire), but Haley was nowhere to be seen. Fresh tracks gave us the first clue as to the size of the raiding enemy force: two, maybe three, platoons. Then it was getting light so we gave up the search, and with heavy hearts moved back to the OP to pick up the dead and take them to our lines.

By the time I got back to 3d Platoon, the enemy dead had been searched and neatly stacked, like sacks of potatoes. The North Koreans had put on a good show, even if they'd lost two dozen men. They'd knocked off the OP and taken a prisoner; they'd sneaked up the hill and slipped right through the weakest and most critical point in a defensive position—the tie-in point between two separate units—and swept undetected over the reverse slope. Only now did I find it was just the North Koreans' bad luck that ten of Stokes's men were leaving a sleeping bunker to relieve some buddies on line at the same time the enemy appeared on the scene, that I'd come up and closed the penetration behind them, and that the beautifully detailed map of our position (both fighting and rear), which undoubtedly had been made with inside information (probably one of the Korean laborers was a spy) and which we found on one of the dead, was a direct replica not of our position but of Joe Love's when we'd relieved him two weeks before.

The major lessons learned concerned sleepers, smokers, and sloppy procedures. Henceforth (following the lead of Red Smalling in the Easy Company days), sleepers would have the shit beat out of them by their leaders. Cigarettes, which could be seen for miles, were as good as an engraved invitation to the enemy to "come and get me," so from that moment forward, smoking was prohibited from sunset to sunrise anywhere on the hill. The rule applied to chain-smoking me, too, and there were to be no exceptions, even within the deepest, safest bunkers on the reverse slope. Transgressors would meet the same fate as the sleepers.

It had been sloppy not to inspect the Easy Company tie-in position every time we checked our line. If I'd been the 3d Platoon leader, I was sure I would have done so—at least I thought I would—but as company commander, I *definitely* should have, so this was as much my fault as Stokes's. Henceforth, though, it would be the rule. We also placed tactical barbed wire, complete with mines and flares, along our reverse-slope boundary with E Company. This caused quite a row between me and the Easy CO, but I wouldn't bend. I was rarely burned more than once.

During the attack, the guys of 3d Platoon had bunched up, five and six guys in bunkers designed for two. It was a natural herd instinct I'd seen a million times, but it might have been prevented had a local counterattack force been appointed the moment we got on the hill and the guys trained accordingly. It should have been SOP; instead, more sloppiness on both Stokes's and my parts (and worse for me, because I should have known better).

After the wounded had been evacuated, I went back to my CP to record the action: the mistakes, the casualties, the lessons learned. My little book would be a valuable teaching aid; I'd go over it with the troops, and when we got into reserve we'd go over it again, again, and again. But I did not write down my own mistakes. I didn't have to. For all the work we'd done, for how on top of things I'd been feeling, that such a thing should happen *and why*—I was sick, guilty, and ashamed. My own lesson learned was indelibly etched in my brain: the image of two dead soldiers whom I'd known were irresponsible yet whom I'd tasked with the safety of my unit. I'd violated security and sent them to their deaths. Haley, the third man, was the only soldier ever captured from my command; he was released some months later as part of Operation Little Switch. But the tragic, unnecessary losses—a direct result of the worst command decision I would ever make—were crosses I would bear for the rest of my life. *Happy birthday, Hack. How's it feel to be twenty-two?*

Other documents found on the KIA with the map (he'd most likely been the CO of the raiding party) caused higher headquarters to believe a major North Korean attack was imminent. Nothing came of it, but it was good psychological warfare compliments of the enemy (sometimes these sorts of documents had exact dates and times which kept us on our toes, and higher-ups milling around the position. In the meantime, we rebuilt and reorganized, starting with the pisstubes the 11 November North Korean raiders had grenaded out, in what was probably the only humorous moment of the whole affair. We used metal 105 ammo canisters both for stovepipes and urinals. The pisstubes were dug into gravel pits with lime all around them, and were interspersed with the stovepipes of the sleeping and warming bunkers throughout the platoons' reverse-slope positions. The North Koreans must have been drilled that a tube sticking out of the ground meant a stove, which in turn meant a bunker, which meant throw a grenade down there and blow it all up. Stokes had seen one gook send down a grenade only to have it blow up at his feet, killing him instantly and showering him with Yankee piss. Guess the North Koreans didn't know Indian folklore: American braves always said the white man pissed too close to his own tepee.

We absorbed new replacements, many of whom were combat-ready for a change. I had a lock on good people through Boyd Guttery, who'd left as one of Fighter's platoon leaders to be the regimental Personnel officer. He was a good man I'd fought to keep when he was ordered back; though I'd lost that battle, I'd won the war, because Boyd sent us the best: former Trieste studs (like SFC Sewell and PFC Maguire) as well as Airborne/Ranger types, Korean returnees like Lindeman, and, my favorites of them all, good old country boys from the hills of Kentucky, Tennessee, and Virginia, who, unlike all the city boys, had grown up with a weapon in their hands and took to combat like Alvin York. Danny Forrester, from Tennessee, was one of these. He was absolutely fearless, and with him, ex-187th man Bob Gruber, and Uno Rentmeister (an ex-82d man who reminded me of Jimmie Mayamura—he could walk through unpacked snow without leaving a trace), I had the basis for the best of Fighter's recon patrol teams.

Uno Rentmeister was probably the deadliest weapon Fighter had against the North Koreans, basically because unlike the National Guardsmen and draftees in the company, *he believed.* Uno had grown up in Estonia. As a child he'd seen what the Russians did to his homeland and that of the neighboring Finns, and at twenty, he hated all Communists and what they represented. "I felt a little bit different than a lot of the guys," Uno would say, years later. "I volunteered to go to Korea and fight the Communists, and most of the draftees were thinking about going home. But that's why I'm here and so many of them are buried." Uno was a small guy, completely at home in the dark, snowy woods; he knew how to dress lightly, and was able to train his fellow patrolmen in this and other subtleties of the dangerous recon work (for example, not to open candy-bar wrappers on patrol, as one uninitiated volunteer did one night, the paper crackling like thunder in the silent valley). The two biggest problems Uno ever had were the night I sent him back to the rear to get a good night's sleep (he found a few guys sleeping in a tent full of litters, commandeered a vacant one for himself, and in the morning awoke when two guys from Grave Registration started carrying his bed away; he'd unwittingly spent the night in the Regimental Morgue), and the Puerto Ricans in his squad, who disobeyed his orders on the pretext that they couldn't understand Uno's second-language English. But in the case of the Puerto Ricans, that was just one of the excuses in one of the squads. Nobody had an easy time with these particular islanders.

The Puerto Rican contingent of the company, like the KATUSAs, had proved virtually ineffective as individuals fighting alongside their mainland counterparts. They got spooked at night, and caused the same major disciplinary problems within Fighter as they had when I'd first encountered them on the ship coming over for this tour. Then, they'd had big chips on their shoulders because their Puerto Rican regiment (the 65th Inf) had been broken up. So much for the Army's quest for integration. The voyage from Puerto Rico had been marked by complete anarchy; the Puerto Rican NCOs had no authority, and every day saw another punch-out or some kind of problem, with the troublemakers (who, in fact, were running the whole damn ship) traveling in gangs, isolating a few whites and doing a job on them.

I'd been assigned as mess officer for the San Francisco–Pusan leg of the trip. I knew nothing about the job, but you didn't have to be too smart to see that serving chow to twenty-five hundred men under gang rule was impossible. As the Puerto Ricans steadfastly refused to comply with the ship's meal-shift schedule, with the troop CO's blessing I let the word go forth: "You will eat by compartment"—as the ship was divided for control purposes—"or you will not eat at all," and backed up the ultimatum with a bit of muscle in the form of a dozen tall paratroopers armed with hickory batons. The first day saw numerous skirmishes, but the brig had been readied for immediate occupancy and the hooligans were off to the slammer before they knew what hit them. It didn't take long to get back on schedule. The only problem was that the ringleaders were still at large. Then I found out they were scrounging like crazy from the ship store and the crew mess; like squirrels getting ready for a long winter, they were storing rations for the trip so they wouldn't have to play by my rules. I got the store closed and the mess secured, and by the end of the second day on board, the Battle of the Midsection seemed won.

Until the third day. Luckily, we'd been tipped off by an old Puerto Rican NCO. My paratroopers were in perfect riot-control formation when two dozen bad guys launched a bold attack right down the steps leading to the mess. Order was quickly restored, and the well-thumped leaders of the gang spent the rest of the trip in the brig nursing their wounds.

In Fighter Company, it was pretty obvious that all the energy these Puerto Ricans used up fighting the gringos would be better spent fighting the enemy across the valley. But they needed a leader to bolster their confidence and give them some self-esteem. A Puerto Rican sergeant named Rivera, who joined us through the replacement system, was the one. He'd made a combat jump with the 187th Airborne RCT on a previous tour—white, black, Puerto Rican or green, that was no small thing—and under his leadership the new Puerto Rican Platoon (which wasn't nearly platoon-sized, but it sounded good) became a great fighting force almost overnight, just as the Koreans became under Sergeant Chung. Sometimes all the motivation a guy needs is a little respect, and a damn good leader who shares common ground.

Even before the big influx of replacements, the leaders I'd inherited had begun to show their true, capable colors. Gregory, my top, was damn smart and growing into his position every day. Fighter's platoon sergeants, Hudson, Allison, and Smith, were magic on patrol and doing fine with their acting-master-sergeant roles, too. Though I had no power to promote—acting or otherwise—above corporal (in the Raiders, I'd organized promotions for Jimmie Mayamura and other deserving guys through Colonel Sloan), I got the stripes and had the guys sew them on as if they were the real thing. Authorized, permanent stripes did come down from Regiment each month, so over their time in Fighter, the guys would, one by one, start getting paid in accordance with what they were wearing on their sleeves. But in the meantime, my acting-promotion scheme worked wonders: within days, each man and his respective unit were functioning like they'd been at it for months. We were not the best yet, but we were getting there—the sterner the challenge, said Toynbee, the finer the response—and it impressed the visitors, too, to see all these "senior" NCOs in one little company.

But we were still a bit green in the great scheme of things, so I was elated when Colonel Locke rang to say he was sending me his sergeant major. I couldn't believe my luck. I remembered the guy—he was a young parachute master sergeant, a walking recruitment poster. "Great!" I said. "I'll make him my first sergeant."

"No," replied Locke. "I want him busted. He's no goddamned good. I'm sending him to you because you're the hardest guy I've got. I want him to be a private within a month. Bust him for inefficiency."

A few hours later a short, blond-haired, blue-eyed, all-American stud by the name of John Westmoreland walked into my CP. I explained to him that the Colonel wanted his stripes, and asked why he was on Locke's shit list. "Well, sir," Westmoreland began (with a wonderful Tennessee twang), "you know the Colonel has a mighty wild temper. . ." and went on to tell me it had all started the day before when Locke's field telephone at Battalion CP wouldn't work. The Colonel had flown into a rage and thrown down the phone. It broke. He'd snapped at Westy to get him another one, and though Westy was not the commo sergeant, far be it from him to disobey an order during a tantrum. The second phone hadn't worked either, and, according to Westy, Locke had gotten so mad he'd taken a swing at his sergeant major. But Westmoreland, who'd been middleweight champ of the 82d Airborne Division, had just stepped back and cleaned Locke's clock—in the middle of the command bunker with the rest of the CP group sitting at ringside.

I now understood why Locke wanted him reduced. I also knew I'd do everything in my power to make sure it didn't happen. The Colonel had had the right idea to send Westy to the line, but he'd picked the wrong CO to bust his ass. The challenge was just too great to resist. Westmoreland had no infantry experience. He'd been trained as a medic and worked his way up to sergeant major of a medical battalion at Fort Bragg before being transferred to our infantry unit. But he was very sharp, and I could tell he was a good man, so the first thing I did (with his consent) was make him an assistant squad leader. This was three big steps down for a master sergeant, but the guy was willing; I told him I'd work with him and instruct his platoon leader and sergeant to do the same. The fact was, I'd been down the same road myself. In both the Recon and George companies, someone had always seen potential and taken me under his wing, but I'd had to prove myself on the ground before I got any real responsibility. I'd continued the tradition in the Raiders: NG Bill Smith got a lot of attention from the rest of us and he'd proved himself a fine young leader. Like Smith, Westy had all the makings; he just needed the techniques. So every night when I walked the line I made a point of seeing him in his squad sector. I'd fight him through hypothetical attacks, deploying mythical men and machine guns until he got a feel for the game. Most of it was common sense anyway.

Westy was just one more act to juggle, in many ways the easiest, because he was alert and eager to learn. Maybe it was because he'd been a medic; he had an intuitive understanding of the tides of battle and a heightened sensitivity to the needs of his fellow troopers. And that was far more than could be said for many men, both on the line and at the regimental country club.

During this period we found ourselves inundated with inspectors. The only good reason I could find for this was that higher headquarters had nothing else to do. The stagnant Korean War presented many problems for the Army, not least of which was a whole bunch of rear-echelon staff officers working in headquarters that were designed to move, but with nowhere to move *to*. So these officers were made inspectors and then sent traipsing off to the trenches to look at the way we lived. And for morale purposes, I guess, they were supposed to "help" us. Not only did they inspect our food, our bunkers, and our weapons; they inspected our teeth, too. Yes, dentists would visit the frontline positions and wake troopers (who'd been up all night pulling guard or on patrol) to examine their teeth. That kind of help we didn't need. Morale could have been lifted far better if they'd just stayed away and let us sleep.

Another "innovation" in this trench war was the Korean Certificate of Loss (KCL). We were told that Congress, concerned about Army waste, had adopted the KCL as a watchdog mechanism. Anything that was lost, in the trenches or in combat, with a value of fifty dollars or more had to be accounted for by a certificate signed by the company, battalion, and regimental COs. Not only did this mean an enormous amount of paperwork at the company level (the last thing we needed as we attempted to fight a war), but it also made liars out of us all. In Fighter we blamed, for example, the problems of a six-man patrol for the loss of more gear than would be carried by a platoon, including the otherwise unexplainable disappearance of two kitchen fire units. Even the regimental COs knew this; from time to time our KCLs were sent back with a note to find "a better story" to cover a loss unacceptable under the KCL rules. How this was supposed to jibe with an officer's integrity I didn't know. From Congress to the boys in the trenches, the war had become a useless drain not just of resources but of credibility, and why the higher-ups didn't just end the thing was beyond everyone's comprehension.

The first snow came on 17 November. Unlike the previous Korea winters, we were well equipped: warm as toast with cold-weather gear (including experimental pocket warmers) and lightweight, bulkless eight-pound armor vests that a .38 slug wouldn't penetrate. The latter reduced casualties and kept chests, backs, and guts warm; it was SOP to wear them on the hill twenty-four hours a day. The cold weather was, in a way, a blessing; it made the ground like concrete and really reduced old bunker collapses. It also solved a lot of our sanitation problems: the decaying flesh along the wire froze up, and without the usual revolting stench, the rats found it a less appetizing target. We still had rats, of course, but were slowly winning the battle through our rat-poison campaign. For my own CP, though, I had a simpler, more straightforward solution. Lying in my sack, I'd watch the huge bastards scampering along the logs over my head. I'd lead on their tails (which would dangle over the side of the logs) and, with a little Kentucky windage, blow them away with my .38. The scheme worked well on two counts: I greased a lot of rodents, and few people entered my side of the bunker unannounced.

With the cold as well came more incoming and more enemy probes. It seemed as if the North Koreans were making one last effort before the real winter set in; only then would they go to ground and more or less hibernate for the season. But the boys—who were getting better ever day on the line—weathered it all, including some savage hand-to-hand combat against probes that made it through the barbed wire.

One morning Locke rang: "What's the situation with Westmoreland?" *Thirty days to the minute, the son of a bitch,* I thought. "Working on it, sir . . . working on it," I told him. "Things have been a little rough up here." The Colonel accepted this, and I bought a little more time for the inefficient ex-sergeant major who, with no outside influence from me, had already been promoted to squad leader. The other item on Locke's agenda was the barbed wire: higher headquarters wanted it cleaned up. So did I, I assured him, but hadn't figured out a way to do it without getting people killed, and I'd been delaying making a decision until the frost. The Colonel decided the time had come, and said he was sending up his Ammunition and Pioneer Platoon to get started.

The Pioneers arrived, none too pleased about this duty. The next thing I heard was that their platoon leader was refusing to go out with his troops. I coaxed him out myself, at rifle point, and assigned one of my guys to keep him there. Meanwhile, the Pioneers' platoon sergeant, a hot-blooded Italian stud, was snarling that it was the stupidest job he'd ever seen. And he was right. First Sergeant Gregory had calculated that Fighter was the eleventh company to occupy this position; the wire defenses were eleven generations worth of mines, booby traps, and as many Rube Goldberg–like explosive devices as ingenious American teenagers could devise. It was a bad, bad place, which would have been better left alone. The Pioneer sergeant went down to Battalion to protest, warning that someone would be killed. He was told to press on; the mission prevailed. Back on the line, he was so pissed off he began stomping through the field, screaming, "If they want mines, I'll find their motherfucking mines." One of Fighter's fine squad leaders, Sergeant Simmons, a black stud and damn good man who was providing the Pioneers with a security detail, had a hell of a time reasoning the guy out of blowing himself up. Good, calm Simmons got the senseless operation going again. Ironically, he also stopped it once and for all, when he tripped a U.S. hand-grenade booby trap while helping an entangled Pioneer. Simmons' face was not touched, but the blast took off the back of his head, splattering his brains around for yards. "Forget the mine clearing" came the word from 2d Batt, and the Italian Pioneer sergeant shook a clenched fist in the direction of the battalion CP, shouting, "Fuck you, fuck you all!"

Losing men to friendlies was always a bitter pill to swallow. But when it happened through sheer carelessness, it was enough to make you ready to kill. Some time after the minefield incident, Sergeant Louis Bravo, a great, brave parachute sergeant, found his Fighter patrol stuck out in no-man's-land, the two outposts having heard enemy activity along both withdrawal routes in our sector. In the end I told him to bypass Fighter entirely; after he finished the patrol he should come up through G Company instead.

I rang the CO of George, explained the situation, and asked him to alert his people that my guys would be coming through about 0500. He assured me he would. When 0500 came, as did Bravo's patrol, one of the George OPs opened fire on them. Two men were killed as Bravo screamed, "Hold your fire! Hold your fire!"

As soon as I heard, I called George 6. "Your OP is firing at my people! Didn't you notify them?"

"Why, yes, I did," he said (which was a lie, as we later found out from the George OP sergeant). "Perhaps they panicked and thought they were under fire."

"Well, shut it off!" I screamed. "We just took two dead!"

"Pity," George 6 replied in a cool, even voice. "Pity, pity, pity."

By now I'd organized a group of good shooters to act as a sniper unit. They were excused from night duty and spent their daylight hours surveying the enemy trenches with damn good scopes mounted on .50-cal MGs and rifles. To give my CP group a chance to be part of the action, I'd placed one of the sniper positions on top of our CP bunker under camouflage-painted burlap. Now, at first light the morning of the Bravo patrol, I felt like going up there, turning the rifle around, and blasting George 6's head right off his shoulders. I didn't, of course, but I should have. As it turned out, it might have saved another man's life.

✳   ✳   ✳

In late November, the Assistant Division Commander, Brigadier General Gordon B. Rogers, visited the company. I took him through the little tunnel out to my OP to have a look at No Name. Then we went back to the CP and drank coffee until there was a letup in the somewhat heavier-than-usual afternoon shower of incoming. As soon as the steel rain stopped, he ran out to the road, got into his jeep, and drove away. A few weeks later, the daily dispatch included a General Order (GO) awarding this very general a Silver Star. Since the date was the same as the day he'd visited Fighter, I read the GO with interest. Apparently, Rogers had "with great courage and utter disregard for his own personal safety, exposed himself to sustained enemy artillery and mortar fire over open terrain while personally inspecting front-line positions." *Well,* I thought to myself. Maybe he'd put something in his coffee I didn't know about.

I kept reading the GO, trying to figure out exactly what he'd done (on the assumption that this was not a load of shit, but that perhaps he'd visited another unit that day in which he didn't spend the whole time hunkering down in a safe CP) to deserve the third-highest combat decoration the U.S. Army awards. So far he hadn't done one thing under any worse conditions than my platoon leaders and NCOs—or for that matter every swinging dick in the company—didn't do twenty-four hours a day, every day of the week. Then I found it: "The presence of a General Officer in an area that was being continually shelled was an inspiration to all troops." Now I understood. Stripes and bars just don't dazzle like stars; it wasn't what you did, but what you wore on your shoulders when you did it.

My revelation was not quite accurate, as it turned out, for about the same time, word came quietly down that all battalion commanders were to get a Silver Star for something, too. Joe Rice was asked to sign a statement that Colonel Locke had come into his platoon CP under "heavy and deadly fire"; a quiet but serious fuss transpired when Joe refused. But somehow all the awards went through, with each battalion CO showing great "courage and personal disregard for his own safety," each exposing himself "to sustained enemy artillery and mortar fire over open terrain while inspecting all of his units." This was no mean feat for the 3d Batt CO who, the widespread rumor was, had actually been on a boat coming over to Korea on the date he performed so gallantly in action.

For field-grade officers and above, it seemed as if the awards system had become little more than a giveaway program, Silver Star "kisses" handed out by higher HQ to recognize these guys' spending five minutes on the front and getting a speck of dirt on their neatly starched fatigues. *Stars and Stripes* announced all awards, deserved and other. Once, I pinned up the weekly list in my CP when Silver Stars went to a bunch of senior visitors to Fighter who, with complete disregard for their own personal dignity, ran through our trenches during a short (and not even close) mortar barrage, right past one of my patrols that had just returned from a balls-to-the-wall firefight in no-man's-land, for which none of the men received even a "thank you" from higher HQ, much less a valor award. I concluded then and there that a valor decoration awarded to anyone above the rank of captain, unless accompanied by a Purple Heart, was an unearned one, and that the men who took them had a hell of a lot to answer for, not only to their troops but to themselves when they looked in the mirror.

Even putting aside the Silver Star business, as time passed I'd begun to lose a lot of respect for Colonel Locke. There'd been a postscript of sorts to the mine-clearing exercise, over in George Company. Roy Herte, a West Point platoon leader and fine, fine stud whom I'd have been thrilled to have in my unit, was tasked to take a patrol through an area in no-man's-land full of uncharted mines. He asked Locke a number of times to reconsider the mission until the area had been cleared, but the Colonel was adamant. The result of the action was three men blown away by mines. Directly afterward, Locke asked Herte to make out a report stating that the Support Engineer detachment had told him the area was cleared of mines. When Herte refused, Locke said the lieutenant would be court-martialed for "dereliction of duty," having knowingly taken his troops into a wall-to-wall minefield.

Guys who worked with Locke at Battalion said he'd often work himself into such a rage that he actually looked as if he were foaming at the mouth. One of the best stories I heard was of the time Locke chewed out his staff, repeating again and again that they were "boys, little boys." During the tirade the phone rang, and the S-2 answered it, "Boys Town, Father Flanagan speaking." The others in the CP thought Locke would hit him. When I heard he'd just stormed out of the room, I figured judgment had prevailed, in light (maybe) of his disastrous duke-out with John Westmoreland.

And of course, the Colonel was still after Westy. "Working on it, sir . . . working on it," I said in the most recent of his many calls, not having the heart to tell him that Westy, again with no outside influence from me, was now a platoon sergeant, and running his unit brilliantly.

One night soon after, Westy led an ambush patrol to the Pines, where a North Korean patrol walked right into their trap. Westy's force blew them to bits—about ten enemy KIA and a lot of wounded—and hightailed it home without a single friendly casualty. The next day Colonel Truman came up from Regiment to congratulate the patrolmen and give out some medals. He was impressed with the whole group, but most of all with Westmoreland. He liked the sergeant's attitude and appearance, and was knocked out with the perfect condition of his platoon, despite the fact that many of the boys had just gotten back from a twelve-hour, very hairy operation. He immediately suggested I recommend Westmoreland for a battlefield commission.

I refused, inwardly damning Colonel Locke, whose heat I could feel already. "Sir," I explained to Truman, "it's regimental policy that once an NCO is commissioned he's transferred out of his unit. Sergeant Westmoreland came here as a medic. He knew nothing about infantry, and we didn't train this fine platoon sergeant ourselves just to lose him to another outfit."

"What if I let him stay?" mused Truman. *Hallelujah.* Unwittingly he'd executed an ambush as perfect as Westy's.

"Then go ahead and commission him."

Colonel Locke, as it happened, was on R&R when the paperwork came through a few weeks later. Westy went back to Division to have General Cleland pin on his bar. When Locke returned to find a Lieutenant Westmoreland in his midst he went absolutely crazy. He ground his teeth down another inch, and screamed and swore until I was sure a stroke was imminent. When he came up for air I addressed him as apologetically and sympathetically as I could. "I tried to stop it, sir, but what should I have said? That the sergeant had a fistfight with the Colonel and shouldn't be commissioned because he knocked you on your ass?"

I might have just been a dumbshit pea-brain of a pissant lieutenant, but Colonel Locke had to agree I'd chosen the proper course of action.

The weeks went by, the patrols went out, training continued, and casualties decreased. Lieutenant William Price, an OCS graduate, joined us and I found myself set with good stud platoon leaders and platoon sergeants, and squad leaders who were coming along well. It was much easier to build a unit while defending (there was nowhere near the number of leader casualties as you'd get on the attack); as a result, more time was available to concentrate on working with the troops. Even sleepers were learning their lesson; Platoon Sergeant "Knock 'em out" Hudson's enthusiastic and ever-bruised fists attested to that. The Hud was a big guy, but small-boned; I always found it hard to match up his little paws with the damage they did to the screw-offs. Sleepers looked as if they'd done a round with Joe Louis by the time he got through with them.

The Hud was "not all there" according to some of the guys who knew him well. He boasted that he'd killed his wife (something we were never able to substantiate). It wouldn't have surprised me though; he seemed capable of anything, because nothing seemed to faze him. When a Fighter sniper took one right between the horns in one of Hudson's positions, I went down to the .50-cal bunker where it happened to see what should be done. As Hudson and I looked out the aperture, a slug ripped through the opening, missing our heads by mere inches. I went to ground faster than I think I'd ever done in my life. Hudson, on the other hand, continued staring out the aperture. "Saw that flash, sir," he drawled. Another slug ripped in. Hudson didn't blink.

"Get the fuck down, Hudson!"

"Yes, sir, Lieutenant, I got him pinpointed. I'm gonna get me that sorry son of a bitch. Come on up and have a look."

"No way."

Hudson shrugged. He carefully sighted the .50 cal. "I've got him in my sights, sir." The gun fired. Hudson turned around. "Got him, sir. You can get up now." I felt pretty sheepish (*At least you're alive*, I consoled myself); as for The Hud, well, maybe he was a little crazy, but I preferred to think he just had nerves of steel.

Then Homer Smith got into a jam on patrol, but he performed brilliantly and the next time Colonel Truman trooped the line he wanted Smitty commissioned, too. He got no complaints from me. Truman really was an enigma to me. He came up to the line, frequently recognized deserving people with awards, and on these occasions seemed to be a great leader. But other times he'd glide through the motions with his great stage presence and prove he just didn't know which end was up. Back in D Company during a formal battalion inspection (just before we went on line), I'd escorted him through my company area. We'd been up most of the night getting ready; the men looked great as did our crew-served weapons, which were set up on canvas tarpaulins in front of the troops. All went smoothly through the MG and recoilless-rifle platoons, and then we arrived at the mortar platoon. The Colonel stopped in front of one of the squads whose 81-mm mortar was not set up (every weapon so far had been assembled on a bipod or tripod; in this case the bipod was in Ordnance for repair, so the tube was laying flat on the canvas).

"Soldier," Truman addressed the squad leader, "where is the ah . . ." He stopped. "Uh, where is the ah . . ." He was desperately searching for the magic word "bipod." Colonel Young, standing to his left, did not know the word. Nor, it seemed, did anyone else in Truman's entourage, judging from their quickly paling faces and anxious, darting eyes. Finally the Colonel came to his own rescue: "Uh . . . uh . . . soldier, where is the ah . . . holder-upper?" It was horrible. The squad members, who had been standing at rigid attention throughout Truman's struggle, could no longer contain themselves. They burst out laughing while I just looked down at my feet. Luckily, Truman flashed out of there in a big hurry.

Once, on the line, he stopped a Fighter Company jeep driver right in the middle of the impact area on the road to chew his ass for speeding. *Who,* I asked myself, *wouldn't speed in an impact area?* The term itself referred to the relentless incoming that clobbered that part of the enemy-observed road day after day. And who with a brain in his head would *stop* there? Adkinson, the driver, returned to the CP, telling me a colonel had stopped him and taken his driver's license. I told him to forget about it, that I'd put someone to work to organize a new one for him. A few minutes later the field phone rang; it was Colonel Truman calling to tell me what had transpired on the road. He said he wanted the man in a rifle platoon by sunset, and was completely unmoved by the fact that the soldier had been hit three times in a rifle platoon, which was why I'd made him a driver in the first place. It pissed me off—it always did—how guys in the rear used "the line" as the ultimate threat to make people heel (and as if Adkinson, driving that jeep and simultaneously dodging mortar and sniper rounds, wasn't "on the line" enough). I got off the phone. "Just don't let him catch you again," I told a very relieved young troop from Kentucky as I asked him what name he wanted on his new driver's license. As for Truman, I'd just have to make sure he was never the wiser.

I eventually came to conclude that Truman wanted very much to be a good soldier. The problem was he'd just been away from troops too long. Once he commanded Roy Herte to take out a daylight patrol to capture some wounded enemy soldiers reportedly in front of George's lines. Herte told him it was altogether too dangerous, that the route the patrol would have to take would make it both visible to the enemy and vulnerable to their small-arms fire. Truman was not impressed, insisting that the mission go on. As only a day had passed since he'd been threatened with Colonel Locke's court-martial, Herte figured he had little to lose, and took command of the patrol. The group was less than a thousand yards from George's position when its RTO and point man were each shot in the chest. Artillery support shut down most of the subsequent small-arms fire that Roy had predicted; the patrol was still receiving incoming mortar fire when Lieutenant Dave Jennings (then the CO of G) led a relief patrol out to lend a hand. Fourteen hours later, Jennings was dead, blown in half by a mortar round that missed Herte by barely a foot; all WIA had been evacuated and Roy was out in no-man's-land again, determined to recover Jennings' body before the enemy got to it. He did, and upon his return to the company was told to report to Regimental HQ to receive a Silver Star. "To this day," Herte said years later, "I contend that the award was made not so much for any heroism on my part but to placate the consciences of those who made the inept decision to send the patrol out in the first place." He was probably right, though there was, and is, no doubt in my mind that Roy Herte deserved the Silver Star and more for his almost single-handed salvaging action that horrible day, acting—of mortal necessity—above and beyond the orders of men who'd long since forgotten, if they'd even known, the deadly realities at the cutting edge.

Whenever I could get permission from Battalion, I'd have a turkey shoot. At Benning they'd called it the Mad Minute—a demonstration designed to show students the Army's available combat power. On position, it served much the same purpose (it gave the troops confidence in our punch), but it also allowed us to test all weapons in a major shoot-out. On signal, after coordinating with units on our right and left so they wouldn't think the world was falling in, we'd fire every available weapon at the enemy's position: rifles, BARs, MGs, and recoilless rifles as well as supporting artillery and whatever else was around, like tanks, mortars, and quad-50s. I set out in advance the number of rounds each weapon would fire, so the whole thing was controlled, but for those few deafening minutes it was the wildest fireworks display you could ever hope to see, with red tracers arching gracefully through majestic Willie Peter, and HE shells thundering down. You name it, we had it, and the troops loved it. The turkey shoot also helped rotate ammo, thus ensuring good, fresh stuff when we needed it; on top of that, it must have had a pretty devastating psychological effect on the North Koreans across the valley (not to mention the damage it did to any enemy caught roaming around in no-man's-land).

As confidence grew among the troops, so did improvisation. In the daylight hours, where any movement in the trenches brought mortar fire right onto your head, or a dalliance near an aperture of a fighting bunker was an odds-on bet you'd get one between the horns, the troops (besides Uno Rentmeister, who went on "rat patrols" with his carbine) stayed underground sleeping, writing letters, and inventing more savage ways of sticking it to the enemy. An old standard by now was the placing of fifty-five-gallon drums of napalm (each with a white phosphorous grenade set in the top as a fuse) in front of each platoon. In an enemy attack, a long wire running back to our lines would be pulled, and the whole jellied mess would go up in a fiery roar, lighting the battlefield like day and denying the enemy even a moment to hotfoot it out of there. Another was the old napalm-inside-the-suitcase trick: empty .50-cal ammo boxes filled with napalm, fitted out with a fuse and wrapped with barbed wire. This device could be thrown over the trench wall; the explosion ignited the napalm and scattered metal and barbed-wire fragments right, left, and center of the attacker. Unfortunately there was a lot of wastage with this one (troopers had a tendency to throw it at any and every noise), but at least we always roasted a couple of rats, and they were the enemy, too.

Higher headquarters kept insisting we were about to get clobbered. They wanted more patrols out, a screen to lie in wait and provide early warning. I fought them. It was true that patrols had the best vantage point of the front, and that it was mighty difficult for the enemy to move large formations without being picked up by them. But the temperatures were fast approaching zero at night, and the minute the boys got into position, their sweat-filled, heavy rubber "Mickey Mouse" boots (newly issued, and so named for the striking resemblance they bore to those worn by Walt Disney's famous rodent) froze from the inside out. I'd seen too many frostbite casualties in the 27th to go through that drill again, and proposed short, roving patrols instead—in and out, but no laying up. Of course, because few at the top had ever been on patrol, much less in these bitching conditions (the nightly vigils in the valley were more often than not controlled by Corps, and the starched set up the chain of command didn't seem to have the guts to challenge them), the order to stay out and ambush stood. Fortunately, it wasn't hard to fool the powers that be, since we never had nighttime visitors. Each night I sent a small recon party down to the valley to have a good look around ("no laying up" was the rule) while back at home we phonied radio traffic with the "patrol leader" in his platoon CP. The only reason we bothered to dummy up the traffic at all was Westy had told me Locke and staff monitored our internal radios. *If only they had something more important to do,* I thought, all too often. Once Locke commented about the excessive number of frostbite casualties Easy and George were experiencing, while we in Fighter had none. His casual interest was the only time I thought our scheme would be found out; happily, when I told him the boys of Fighter changed their socks when they got in position and kept their fingers and toes moving, he dropped the subject and never brought it up again.

It was a lie; in terms of the Officers' Code of Conduct a lie as bad as any other lie, including the blatantly approved lies then running amok through the Officer Corps prompted by those Korean Certificates of Loss. But the fact was, I was slowly beginning to see myself developing my own Code of Conduct; rather a Code of Conscience, the rules of which were based on the needs and welfare of my men versus regulations, or the desires of my higher-ups. The switch was unconscious (it had probably come with the Raiders, if not before); the long-term ramifications were enormous (something I couldn't have known in 1952). But the little book of What Really Matters, what's *really* important, had begun to write itself in my head, and it was something I'd trust in the rest of my life.

*   *   *

The morning of 18 December was cold and snow-covered. I'd stood the company down to 10 percent (we stayed at 10 percent during the day, 50 percent at night, and only when it hotted up did we "stand to" in the old British naval tradition, with 100 percent of the force locked and cocked behind their weapons and in their fighting positions), and because there wasn't anything urgent to attend to, I went out to my OP to have a look at the battlefield before catching some shut-eye.

The OP was equipped with a battery commander's (BC) scope, a highly magnified binocular periscope with which at a thousand yards you could tell if a soldier had shaved that day. It was hard to put the thing to the test in the trenches though: our North Korean counterparts were masters of camouflage and deception, and during the day you could look into the enemy positions no more than six hundred to eight hundred yards distant and not see a thing. Aerial photos for our area of operation showed their line to be entrenched in great depth—on the average, fourteen miles—with the mazelike, stacked positions having no tactical integrity, at least from a Western point of view. We'd heard that some of the Communists' underground chambers could shelter whole battalions; I believed it—they were great diggers—but to look across the valley you'd never know.

As I'd expected when I peered through the scope, all was quiet. But when I turned my attention to the Pines, I saw white-on-white movement against the snow. I could barely believe my eyes. Bold as life, like animated snowmen, half a dozen North Koreans in over-white camouflage gear were rolling up commo wire abandoned by U.S. patrols. At 1130 hours! Guess they thought *It's daytime . . . Yanks sleep . . . no one will see*, and to the naked eye, it would have been true. Without the scope, there would have been no way to discern them against the landscape.

I called Joe Rice, a great patroller at any time but one who personally preferred daylight work. He immediately moved out with a five-man patrol. He packed his own radio so we had great commo; it meant I could watch Joe's movements and provide direction at the same time I kept my eye on the snowmen.

In the meantime I rang up newly commissioned Second Lieutenant Smith to get cracking with a backup element, and gave my FO a warning order to be prepared to blow No Name sky-high. I brought the company to stand to, told the platoon leaders the situation, and ordered a good old-fashioned turkey shoot as accompaniment to Joe's action in the valley (firing on order, keeping the stuff high and only at the enemy trenches). I didn't tell Battalion what was going on until the very last moment. I wouldn't have told them at all except they'd have gotten the word when the arty people requested fire, and I knew it'd be better for me if I broke the news. (It was just that I knew the minute I did, I'd have the entire chain of command, from Corps on down, on the horn, telling me how to run my company.)

From my OP I watched Joe positioning his people. I saw the carefree North Koreans working through the Pines and disappearing into some old bunkers. I told Joe exactly where they were. It was like watching a silent movie—an amazing thing to watch an entire action from beginning to end in such detail and in such safety. Joe moved like a stalking tiger, his men providing security from concealed positions. A North Korean stuck his head out of a bunker. Joe shot him. The guy fell back, and Joe threw a grenade. I told him another North Korean was crawling out the left side of the bunker. He moved over and shot that guy, too. The North Korean rolled down the hill as Sergeant Allison opened fire on him.

In the meantime, the North Koreans in the trenches on No Name woke up. A machine gun opened fire. One of our patrol men fell. I pulled the chain and the turkey shoot began, like an erupting volcano. One enemy soldier got so excited that he jumped on top of the trench line, waving his arms wildly till he took a direct hit and was splattered across the hillside. I figured he was the company CO (who must have been even more shocked by what he saw in the valley than I'd been; imagine watching one of your patrols being scooped up in front of your own main line of resistance [MLR] in broad daylight).

It was a magic morning. With only one casualty of our own, we'd netted two POWs and two enemy KIA, not to mention those killed during the company turkey shoot. Through my BC scope I watched Smitty's nine-man support group move swiftly forward to evacuate the POWs and our WIA. I told Joe's people to shift the enemy dead to a small clearing. That night we laid an ambush, using the dead as bait. An enemy patrol fell right into the trap: their comrades had frozen fast to the ground, and while a couple of white figures worked to break them loose, our ambush went into action and killed the whole enemy crew. All in all, it was not a bad day's work for Fighter.

Within a few hours of Joe's return, our position was inundated with visitors: Battalion, Regiment, Division, Corps, and Army. Had President Truman bopped in, too, I doubt I would have been surprised. But it was my own fault, really. I'd unplugged my phone as soon as the patrol got home safely, when I was besieged by everyone for a firsthand report. Our prisoners were the first to be captured in ages, and when the POWs spilled the beans that they'd been tasked with getting intelligence for a regimental-sized attack (the North Korean recon patrol had moved into the Pines that morning to get a head start but had been undone by their patrol leader who couldn't resist picking up the rich man's wire), higher headquarters got so excited they could barely contain themselves. We got stacks of replacements and top priority on everything. Another element was brought in east of the Gap; G Company shifted over and took part of our line to give Rice's platoon (who would take the brunt of an enemy attack) a tighter, stronger position.

All this was very nice, except that the whole thing had been completely blown out of proportion. What we'd had was a local fight. Beyond Regiment, no one should have given it more than a second thought, and in a normal shooting, scooting war, no one would have. They'd have been too busy worrying about the big picture: how bad they were making the enemy hurt across the *entire* front; the hows, whats, and wheres that were necessary to break the enemy—positive, *winning* thinking—to make them reach the point of giving up. But at this point there was no big picture, save the peace talks, and no thoughts of winning at all (or so it seemed). As a result, bored, frustrated higher-level commanders and their staffs had nothing to do but mess with the troops the whole way down to squad level. In this, the third year of the war, whether or not to hold a pimple of a hill had become an issue for Eighth Army, the Pentagon, and sometimes the President. The only problem was that while these guys hemmed and hawed over whether to withdraw or reinforce (and the political ramifications of each option), down at the cutting edge American soldiers died.

It would come to be known as centralization. It gave middle management (Battalion and Regiment) an easy way out: they simply passed the buck up the chain of command ("What do you think?" "I don't know, what do you think?" "Maybe we should call higher headquarters." "Yes, that's what I think, too.") with no risk of failure to themselves. I generally unplugged my phone, or reported only what I absolutely had to until the action was over or we really needed a hand. The big problem was artillery. Higher HQ could track your situation by that traffic. I always said I was going to get my own cannons, then no one would know a damn thing until I was ready to tell them.

During this period, a regimental CO came to call. He told me he was planning (contingency planning, that is) a regimental attack to take some high ground directly to our front, in an effort to "tidy up the lines." He wanted me to have a look at the problem; we couldn't get a good view of the objective from my OP, so we drove up to 1st Batt, where the picture was clearer. "If you were a regimental commander," this colonel asked, "and you were given the mission to take that objective, how would you go about it?"

Why he was asking a first lieutenant whose military schooling was the seventeen-week Infantry Company Officers' Course at Benning I didn't know, but based on what I knew from my Wolfhound experience (and the countless hours I'd spent with Master Sergeant Flemings), I outlined a general plan: I'd jump off here, take that knob there, run some tanks and tracks down the valley while I had HE and Willie Peter artillery going on the top, maybe a couple of air strikes here, some quad-50s there, then launch another battalion this way...etc., etc. The colonel soberly took it all in. Afterward, I forgot about it. About a week later I was called in by the battalion S-3 to be shown an operations plan (OPLAN). Word for word, tactic for tactic, it was exactly what I'd outlined to the colonel. I was amazed. It was like the Pope accepting and expounding an altar boy's interpretation of the Bible. The plan was never executed, but looking at it (like the phony Silver Stars for high-ranking guys who hadn't earned them, and the accepted lying on KCLs) was a real bolt from the blue.

But General Cleland made up for all the pretenders, in spades. He'd visited the company every couple of weeks since we'd come on line, usually just a quick stop as part of his larger look at the regimental front. I'd liked him more every time I'd seen him, and he'd adopted a fatherly kind of attitude toward me. Now, just before Christmas (on the eve of the suspected enemy attack), he came up and spent half a day, wishing the troops Merry Christmas and checking the positions. The General was the finest senior troop leader I'd known to date. He certainly knew his trade: he could slide behind a machine gun and know in an instant if its field of fire was right; he accepted incoming like Hudson, as a matter of course and without even a blink. Before he left the position, we shared a pre-Christmas C-ration lunch in my CP. He asked me about my background and if I'd considered West Point; I told him about General Meloy and my minimal education. Cleland nodded, but did not comment.

Christmas came and went. The big enemy attack came to naught (the North Koreans probably called it off on the assumption that the POWs we took had compromised it), and word flashed through the division that Cleland, the Great White Father, had walked a soldier's post in a bitter snowstorm on Christmas night, after sending the Catholic trooper off to Mass in the General's jeep. My only present was a letter from home with a clip from *Time* magazine. It said that one newspaper, intent on gauging its readership's interest in the Korean War, ran the same story ("Reds blasted from vital knob") three days in a row. Apparently there was not one call, from either readers or reporters from competing papers. Yet, the editor was quoted as saying, "If the paper omits a comic strip or football score . . . the office switchboard begins working frantically."[1] I wondered if the friend who sent the article was trying to tell me something.

With the New Year came the final good-bye to Colonel Locke. The meanest mother in the valley was going home. His visits had grown less frequent as he became a short-timer. On one of the last he'd been sitting on my sack, chewing tobacco and musing that he had only twenty-eight "goddamn days" to go. Without thinking, I'd replied, "Oh, no, sir, you only have twenty-seven," and he'd been surprised. How did I know? he asked. I was used to having to think quickly with Locke around: "In your battalion, sir, it's an officer's duty to know every important detail." I couldn't tell him we 2d Batt officers were counting down his DEROS almost as eagerly as he.

Locke's last day in the battalion was related to me by Dick Weden, now HQ Company CO. Dick usually lived at Battalion Forward, but he went to the rear CP to make sure the Colonel got off all right. He told me Locke had gone into the mess about 0530 (old soldiers don't know how to sleep in), and when the mess sergeant served him his eggs, Locke had looked at them, put his hand under the plate, and slammed the eggs over onto the table. "You goddamn people will never know how I like my eggs!" he'd snarled. With that, he put on his hat, picked up his gear (one tiny AWOL bag, when most senior officers had two or three footlockers), got into his jeep, and drove away—without looking back even once.

At the end of February, we were relieved and sent back to Eighth Army reserve to train. Once again we switched with the 5th RCT. The relief went without a hitch, but Joe Love, now a captain, was nowhere to be seen. He'd gone back to the States, chosen by General Van Fleet to lead an Eighth Army honor guard at the head of Eisenhower's first inaugural parade. Joe was a good man; he well deserved the recognition.

As we slipped off the hill I saw my company together for the first time in four months. It was one of the great shocks of my life—suddenly I thought I'd been commanding a company from the King's First African Regiment. There'd been no natural light in the underground bunkers; while Adkins had devised a great lighting system for the CP (a truck battery hooked up to a sealed-beam headlight), the troops had had to come up with a field expedient. Some had candles, but for most it was mosquito repellent with a cloth wick. The latter sent off pounds of black soot, and with water rarer than good wine, no one ever thought to wash the grime off his face and hands. So it just sat there, getting darker and thicker, until now, standing before me on that cold, cold morning, wearing Mickey Mouse boots, long, green field coats, and pile caps tied under their chins, were almost two hundred black-faced hill people with straggly, long hair, haunted eyes, and bedrolls under their arms.

*   *   *

Six weeks later we were back on the line, this time east of the Gap. *Oh, for the days*, I'd sometimes think about our last position. It hadn't been good, but this place was horrific. We relieved a South Korean unit that must have known as little about field sanitation as it did about fighting. The position on Hill 930 was basically a foul-smelling, open-air latrine; our predecessors had crapped wherever the urge came. The stench only got worse as the snow melted, revealing North Korean bodies hung on the protective wire in various states of decay. When our CP line went out and wireman Hansen left the trench to fix it, in the dark he found a Chinese tennis shoe near the wire. It was a great souvenir and he brought it back to show us. "Look what I found!" he shouted as he burst into the CP, only then noticing in the CP's dim light the greenish-black Communist foot that was still inside the shoe. He turned green, too, and immediately puked his guts out.

The sun never seemed to shine here. Cordite and smoke-generator fog kept the place gray and stinking. Nothing was growing; it had all been pounded away, making the hill like an elevated sandpit. Yet the incoming was still as regular as breathing, the noise so deafening, the barrage so intense sometimes that you were sure no one would survive. *It's always the one you can't hear that gets you*, you'd think, crawling inside your flak jacket while trying to figure the odds of one of those 120-mm Soviet mortar shells bearing your name. Amazingly, we took few casualties. The troops just screwed themselves deeper and deeper into the ground.

I was proud of Fighter Company. The six weeks in reserve had been excellent as far as training was concerned; it had also been a fine "getting to know you" period between the boys and me. The thing was, I'd only been with them two days before we went to the Gap, so there'd been no time to forge a relationship with them, as a unit, until we left the line.

I'd sent an advance party complete with mess truck back to the reserve area early, to square things away for the troops' arrival. It was snowing hard when the men detrucked, but no one seemed to mind. They stood around or sat in the snow, wolfing down their first meal in months without an ear cocked for incoming.

When I arrived, Dick Weden (who'd become a great friend and whom I'd requested and got as my XO) had bounced up to my jeep to usher me into the officers' mess tent he'd scrounged up, complete with tables, chairs, tablecloths, silverware, plates, and a red-hot stove. *But this ain't right!* I'd thought. The boys had just walked two miles through a snowstorm to the open trucks, where they'd shivered for six hours in brutally cold winds the whole way back to the reserve area. They'd passed through the light line, beyond which their rear-echelon counterparts (squeaky clean and ever so warm) bitched in their heated tents and their heated mess because the guys on the line got forty-five bucks more than they did (combat pay) and four points versus their three for each month they were there. Now Fighter's men were eating the same old chow in the snow, right in the shadow of the only restaurant in town. I told Weden to strike the tent. We'd eat outside, in the snow, and *after* the troops. That's how it was done in the Army I came from.

So the little officers' tent was struck, a move that had a dramatic effect on the soldiers. For the four months I'd been their CO, all they'd known about me was that I was a warrior. Now they saw another, more caring, side.

The thing was, you had to look after your soldiers. It was true that a CO's first priority was the mission, but a conflicting requirement was the welfare of the men. It was true that the whole purpose of the military establishment was to get a doughfoot eyeball-to-eyeball with the enemy, and it was equally true that the troops were the ones who paid the price, in blood, for an objective secured. These facts made—and make—an infantry CO a hanging judge. He has incredible power over the lives and deaths not only of a faceless enemy but of his men. Sometimes this power causes a leader to become hardened: he stops seeing his troops as human beings. They become faceless assets to him; he becomes afraid to get close or to feel, instead constructing a concrete barrier in his head to keep out the guilt and the pain of lives lost at his behest. In the process he forgets that though he may give the orders, it is the soldier who makes them happen—or doesn't. He forgets that if you want 100 percent from a trooper, you have to give him 200 percent as a commander. You have to keep your boys well fed and well clothed whenever possible, and well trained *always*. You have to show respect for them, and you have to remember that every trooper is a priceless asset, not some easily replaced, numbered part to be abused or wasted. An American leader cannot just take his place in a Prussian kind of caste system, with its huge gaps between officers, NCOs, and enlisted men, and expect his men to die for him in battle. It is as unrealistic (given America's long history of citizen soldiers) as it is wrong; the troops might respond for a while, but not for always—especially in an unpopular war.

Of course, I didn't like eating in the snow any more than the men, so on top of the things-to-do-in-reserve list had gone the mission of building ourselves a proper mess. Everyone pitched in with the building and selective scrounging; within three or four days the thing was finished and we'd gone on to the serious phase of what the reserve was all about: training.

I'd worked out a training plan based on what I considered my unit's deficiencies, and gone over it with Major Jack Hemingway (who'd replaced Locke as battalion CO). The two could not have been more different. Locke had been a foul-mouthed, ass-chewing, hard-driving son of a bitch.

Hemingway was an antiswearing, nondrinking, very serious meeting man. Most of the battalion officers had adopted Locke's habit of swearing every other word, so Hemingway's first order of business had been to clean up our mouths.

The new commander had approved my training program, as long as I incorporated the official regimental training schedule as well. Regiment had lots of inspectors running around here, too; I got around their snooping by having my training area about ten minutes from Fighter Company's sign, with an EE8 telephone connecting the two. That way I was able to do what I wanted, and if the training inspectors came around, my company guide at the sign would ring up and I'd have ten minutes to get back to the regimental schedule.

The boys were out of shape from four months underground, so we started with the basics, taking it slowly: physical training (PT), short runs, and individual refresher stuff, including the "lessons learned" that I'd recorded in my little notebook. "You all remember Private X and how he blew himself away? The reason he killed himself was he didn't know how to correctly probe for an antipersonnel mine. This is how you do it." We used a hands-on approach; we didn't talk about probing for mines, we probed for them, using dummy mines.

We took long hikes, working up from five to twenty-five miles; afterwards I always checked the troops' feet (if I ran a trucking company I'd look after the tires) and ordered all leaders to do the same, and to make sure their units had plenty of clean socks and changed them regularly.

Fighter Company was excellently trained in defensive matters by the time we hit reserve, not just from "being there" in the trench war, but through our leaders and NCOs' constant drills on staying alert and staying alive. But in war, the purpose is to strike your enemy, not to sit back and wait for him to strike you. You defend only long enough to reach out, attack, and clobber your opponent. And you have to be prepared to do it confidently, at a moment's notice. Any soldier who lived through that first year of the Korean War knew this. Unfortunately, young leaders who tried out their wings since we'd dug in did not, which was why, I supposed, the Army had cooked up reserves like this one, which was for training in the offense. (This is notwithstanding the fact that no big attacks were in the cards at this stage of the war. Colonel Sloan, who'd gone from the Wolfhounds to Eighth Army as Chief of Plans, repeatedly made plans for full-scale attacks at Eighth Army CG Van Fleet's request, only to have them all turned down back in Washington. It seemed the basic criterion for *any* offensive operation, including those on the smallest of hills, was, in fact, a defensive one, to wit: "Is this piece of real estate a threat to our position?")

Fighter's unit training had begun with the smallest and most important element—the squad. Eleven men would go on the attack with live ammunition, repeating the drill again and again, one squad at a time, until they were truly proficient. I made them train at night, too; one of the major shortcomings of Army training was its stupid dawn-to-dusk philosophy of fighting, despite the known fact that our enemy, who had almost zero air power, was forced to operate at night.

Once the squads had their act together, we'd moved on to the Platoon in the Attack. When that became second nature, the training culminated in a Company in the Attack program, in which the whole unit jumped off with live fire—just like a full-steam-ahead Wolfhound assault (except that no one was shooting back)—and attacked a series of hills in the training area. It was fun, exciting, and a great learning experience for me—the first time I'd commanded a company-sized attack versus being one of the cogs that made the thing happen. But I just pretended I was old Jack Michaely back in the gallant George Company days, and it all seemed to turn out right.

This final phase of the training had given Fighter a great sense of cohesiveness and confidence. It gave the men a chance to see for themselves what the maneuvering of infantry was all about: the employment of every possible bit of firepower brought down on an objective to pin the enemy down, and then the fire being lifted and shifted at the last moment, so the guys could come up from under it to close with the enemy and destroy them with rifles and bayonets. The men could see the mortars dropping in, watching their interplay with the recoilless rifles, then understand how the machine guns—and finally they themselves—fit into this great concerto. All support fire was free fire; in real offensive combat, mortar rounds would pop right in front of the men and machine-gun fire zing just inches over their heads, so the guys had to learn how to trust themselves and their buddies, to know the gunners weren't going to hit them with poorly aimed fire. Safety was stressed, but not at the expense of overall, *realistic* training value.

The whole thing was very successful. General Cleland came down to watch and decided that all the rifle battalions in the regiment would conduct a Company in the Attack problem, with Fighter as the demonstration unit for each. At thirty to forty thousand dollars' worth of ammo a shot, this was no small demonstration, and we got to do it three or four times.

On the side, I'd conducted some classes on the basics myself. One evening toward the end of the reserve period I had all the machine gunners in my CP, teaching them MG night procedures I wanted followed. Then, in the darkness, came the unwelcome growl of the EE8. Lights off, I groped around and finally found the phone. The voice at the other end said, "Hackworth? This is Colonel Herrick." (Colonel Curtis Herrick had recently replaced Colonel Herman Kaesser who'd replaced Colonel Truman as regimental CO. Three in one year—bingo.) "I'm calling to tell you you've been promoted to captain. Just got your orders. I'd like to see you tomorrow."

"Thanks, Dick," I said, thinking it was Dick Weden (who did stuff like this). "But you don't sound a bit like Colonel Herrick and I know I'm not promoted. Besides that, you're interrupting my class, so I'll talk to you later." I hung up.

Within minutes the phone rang again. This time I recognized the voice: it was the regimental XO. "Listen, Hackworth, you were just talking to the Colonel and he was quite surprised with what you had to say."

"You mean I'm really promoted?"

The next day I went to see the Colonel. He had a little laugh about my unbecoming conduct the night before, but it didn't stop him from pinning on those tracks. When I left, I went right back to training, but I wasn't able to hike that day—I high-stepped it, about ten feet off the ground.

And so did the boys of Fighter, which was probably the nicest part of all.

Confidence and morale soared for all of us in reserve. The bunker nerves, the little tics brought on by incoming, disappeared, replaced by the cocky swagger of well-trained, well-motivated, confident studs. My only fear was what returning to sitzkrieg (after six weeks of training "blitz") would do to their spirit, but it proved to be an unnecessary concern. The guys were all old hands now as we went through the whole cleanup and rebuilding procedure we'd followed at the Gap. It went a lot quicker this time, and we saved a number of bunkers on the verge of collapse due to the early spring weather.

Hill 930 was a steep, winding, thousand-yard climb from the nearest road. A sandbagged station at the base held prepackaged supplies; SOP was "both hands full," and a trooper's minimum load on the way up was two five-gallon cans of water (one hundred pounds' worth) or a case of Cs, ammo, or radio batteries. This made for a bitch of a climb; it took a good hour considering the load you'd carry and your frequent dives into foxholes dug in along the way. (We lived right in the shadow of No Name and another high, enemy-held peak the troops called Stalin Hill, both of which looked right down our reverse slope. Smoke generators belched out clouds of heavy white fog to deny enemy observation of particularly hot spots on this slope, which the North Koreans enthusiastically blew the hell out of; the ruse worked beautifully except that the clothes, hair, and tongues of the hill people ended up coated with an oily, horrible-tasting film. We used large camouflage nets, too, to deny the enemy observation of the position, but these were frequently blasted, and it was a big, dangerous maintenance task to get them up again.)

The relentless incoming notwithstanding, the position was easier to defend than the one we'd left six weeks before. It consisted of three long ridgelines, each a steep, narrow company-sized avenue of approach, with damn good wire and mine work (other than the sanitation conditions, the South Koreans we'd relieved had actually kept the position in fine shape) that channeled the enemy right into our defensive fires. The outpost line was excellent—well dug, good wire, with a formidable squad-sized bunker on the military crest of each ridge, with a deep, connecting trench back to the main line. A couple of hundred yards below we had nighttime floating LPs, which would find the enemy and bop back to the nearest outpost, which, in turn, would call for help. Then we'd get artillery going— thousands of rounds' worth—and flares to light up the sky, while the OP took the attackers under fire and scooted back to the line. By then the rest of the company would be at 100 percent and ready to do battle, be it with grenades, bullets, or bayonets.

There were no trees left on the hill, yet looking into the nighttime darkness beyond which lay the enemy, it almost seemed like an impenetrable jungle out there. In silhouette you'd see metal stakes jutting up at weird angles, wrapped in barbed wire and haphazardly rooted in the earth; around these were big rolls of concertina wire. In a way it *was* a jungle—an awesome jungle of death—but by no means impenetrable. The North Koreans still had their gutty little sappers—damn good soldiers, all of them—who'd crawl up to the line and silently clip through, or blow a hole in the wire with bangalore torpedoes. Their infantry would be right behind, to rush through the custom-made gap.

Our OP/LP system nipped most of the not-infrequent enemy attacks right in the bud. Alert soldiers meant no Pearl Harbors, and our artillery defensive concentrations hammered down on the aggressors before they could breach the wire. One night we got more than fifty enemy KIA without one trooper's weapon being fired: the enemy walked right into a killing zone and got smashed. The new Eighth Army CG (an arty man from way back when), Maxwell D. Taylor, must have been crowing. I know we were.

The Americans really had the best—and best-supplied—artillery in the world. Historically it, and the eager outpouring of our assembly lines, had won every war since the North's heavy industrial base brought the South to its knees in the Civil War. Tactical skill, the abilities of generals—both came second to our capability to outequip and outshoot our opponents. I often remembered Italy in 1946, when I was detailed to guard German prisoners of war. One of the prisoners was a damn tough lieutenant captured at Salerno. He spoke English, so I whiled away my duty hours giving him a hard time. Once I asked him why, if he and all his Kraut friends were such brilliant soldiers and such supermen, was fifteen-year-old me the one holding the weapon and he was a prisoner of war. He answered me with a story. "I was an 88-mm antitank battery commander," he said. "We were on a hill, and the Americans kept sending tanks down the road below. Every time they sent a tank we knocked it out. They kept sending tanks, and we kept knocking them out, until we finally ran out of ammunition. The reason I'm here," he finished his story, "is that the Americans didn't run out of tanks."

Now the Air Force was doing a job on North Korea: seven hundred tons of bombs and thousands of gallons of napalm sometimes dropped on the capital, Pyongyang, in a day. It was a strategy of sorts: bomb them back to the Stone Age to keep them at the bargaining table at Panmunjom. The only thing that didn't track was my memory of things I'd read about Nazi Germany. We bombed them to kingdom come, too, but a month before the surrender, their wartime production levels were at an all-time high. Still, this doubt was easy to put aside when you were stuck in the trenches and the enemy was on the move: the more arty, the more air, the better.

One attack that did get through Fighter's barrier defenses was localized to 2d Platoon. When I saw that the rest of the company wasn't under attack, my RTO and I went racing down the trench to lend a little moral support. A mortar round came crashing in on top of the sandbag-lined trench right between us. Fortunately, it didn't knock me down. In fact, it kind of inspired me to pick up the pace on the downhill stretch. The RTO was packing a PR10 and I had the handset; the radio cord between us went taut—he wasn't keeping up. After a few feet of this I turned around to tell him to stop dragging his ass, only to find it was about all he could do, and that was only because I was there pulling him along by the radio cord. The RTO no longer had a head. He must have walked right into that mortar round. Three feet ahead of him, I'd been untouched. It was the luck of the draw—and my first thought was I needed another RTO.

One of the things about combat that remains unexplainable to those who've never experienced it is the apparent callousness in the face of death. I'd learned the first year in Korea that in war a soldier or a leader is about as indispensable as the hole left by a finger in a glass of water. Every good leader is missed—as an individual—and there are never enough real leaders, but there is always someone to pick up the chips and do the job. A few days after my RTO was killed, I had to brief four NCOs who were to lead a complicated patrol. We met at first light, the only time we could get away with it without being blown away by enemy sniper or mortar fire, and lay down in an open 75-mm recoilless-rifle position. The sun was just rising as we poked our heads up, eyeballed the fog-enshrouded objective and rally points, and discussed the plan. When I was finished issuing my order, I ducked and weaved my way back to my CP bunker, leaving the two patrol leaders and their FOs to tie down final details between themselves. Just as I was about to enter the bunker I heard a WHOOSH and an earth-shattering thump. Ugly, black 120-mm mortar smoke rose from the position I'd just left. I ran back to find one leader dead, one guy with gaping chest wounds, and the other two minus legs—all from one round, out of the blue, right on target. I couldn't do anything for the chest wound (not a cobweb in sight), but I thrust my hands into the legless men's stumps to stop the wild rush of blood pumping out of their femoral arteries. I held on until the medics took over; before long, litter bearers had the KIA and wounded leaders on their way down the torturous windy trail, and I was left with the problem of who the hell I'd get to lead the raid. Of course, replacements were found, and the patrol crossed the LD on time.

The fact is, generally there's no "time-out" for mourning on the battlefield. But it's really no different than the father of ten who comes home to find his house on fire with all his kids sleeping inside. He doesn't stop and cry over the first child he finds dead. To do so would be to sign a death warrant for the other nine. A CO is often in the same situation. To do anything but continue on would be complete dereliction of duty, and, in the larger picture, could possibly lead to even worse carnage among his troops. So you do what you have to do, and only later, when things settle down, do you allow yourself to grieve.

Lieutenant Colonel Herbert Mansfield (who'd replaced Major Hemingway who'd replaced Colonel Locke as battalion CO) came up to see us every week or so. I liked him. He was an old friend of Cleland's, well educated, a WW II Airborne vet who regularly held forth on international and big-picture events. He took a keen interest in my development, offering almost fatherly advice about military ways; all in all, he was a good man who always wore his .45 along his spine under his web belt (a trick I loved and immediately adopted for my own). Mansfield was always cheerful when he trooped the position. At first I'd been worried, because just days before we went back on line he and I had gotten into a flap over parade-ground antics (I'd thought the troops' time could be better spent, and told Mansfield so in downright rude terms). It was not very wise, but at twenty-two I never got high marks for tact; I always charged in and ended up with my size-eleven boot right in my mouth or ass. In this particular case I'd inwardly excused myself somewhat, because I was still excited over another big surprise I'd received in reserve, in some ways even bigger to me than being promoted.

I'd been about to take the company on a tactical field march when I saw a Wolfhound jeep coming down the battalion street. It had no business being there; the Wolfhounds were about 150 miles away, on the west coast. The jeep had come to a screeching halt in front of Fighter, and out jumped this little guy with a walrus mustache. He started running toward me, and by the time I realized who it was, the one and only Fred Crispino had thrown his arms around me in a big bear hug.

Chris had been over in the Wolfhounds waiting for me all that time, as First Sergeant in dear old George. He figured I'd never made it, and I'd plumb forgotten our rendezvous because of the rush of getting Fighter's edge honed sharp. He'd only found out where I was when he noticed my name in an article about Fighter Company in *Stars and Stripes*, at which point he'd gotten permission to make tracks for the Eastern Front.

We had a wonderful reunion, like the good old Raider days. Chris stayed in the BOQ and we drank, sang, gambled, and told war stories the whole time he was there. It was great seeing this dear friend whom I respected so much. I tried to talk him into coming over to the Fireball, but he wouldn't; we were best buddies, but Chris was a Wolfhound first. We decided that the war was shit, and nothing in Korea was worth fighting for (if for no other reason than South Korean president Syngman Rhee; in a drunken rave, we realized that an Oriental with a name like that should have been suspect from the beginning). Still, the war must go on, we'd said with a final hug. Then he got back into his jeep for the journey west, and I lost my temper with Colonel Mansfield.

Happily, we'd patched it up by the time we went up the hill. Mansfield had ordered us to paint our faces with C-ration instant coffee. He really was a smart old fox who realized the yellowish-skinned disguise might buy our U.S. unit a bit of time after our relief of the South Koreans. Now that we were up there, his visits were uniformly welcome. Besides the Colonel, though, guests were few and far between to this position. Even without the incoming, the steep climb to reach us was generally enough to keep them away. Still, Mansfield would occasionally call to say he was going to bring up some VIP or another—senators, congressmen, generals. To them, coming to our position would mean they'd "been there." To me, it meant my troops were going to be harassed, since they would have to be preparing for an inspection when they could be getting some sleep. So we developed a very effective technique to keep unwanted guests away.

Whenever I heard a VIP was scheduled, I'd have the attached 75-mm recoilless-rifle section poop out a few rounds. *Boom, boom, boom*—very loud, with the attendant puffs of black recoil smoke, which looked exactly like incoming. Within moments the phone would ring. "What's happening up there?" Battalion would ask.

"Just an extra dose of incoming," I'd say. "Nothing to worry about." It wasn't exactly a lie; we averaged from four hundred to eight hundred rounds of incoming a day across the company front anyway, and by now the enemy had usually thrown a little something extra our way in response to the recoilless rifles.

"I see," would be the reply. "Maybe it's not such a good idea to come up there. Maybe we'll take Congressman Smith over to Easy instead."

This game ended when word came down that ammo was to be rationed. Every round, including M-1 slugs, would be accounted for. The rationing was off if you got hit, but in the meantime it was lean time, with the austerity program greatly restricting even H&I, as the most severe rationing was of mortar and 155-mm ammo.

The "whys" for the rationing were first explained as long-term strikes in the U.S. This had a devastating effect on the troops' morale. It was hard enough to live like cavemen and risk death every second in a meat-grinder war to "keep Asia free"; for the soldiers to be short-changed because of stateside greed and industrial strife was more than a little hard to accept. Then word filtered down that wrapped around the strikes were miles of Pentagon red tape. New procedures set up to improve the system had actually stopped it dead in its tracks. An ammo order now had to go through forty-two different departments before even one round was issued.

To the guy on the line, this snafu was just another stitch unraveling from the seam of the American effort. And how it was all happening with Eisenhower in the White House was hard to believe. Most of us were so happy to have him there. We knew "Ike" would stop this carnage, even if he had to drop the goddamn A-bomb to do it. But it was hard to square this great General-President with the bullshit that Eighth Army continued to put out, to wit, that we were the best-supplied Army in the world. They continued to chant that the enemy was being stretched to the breaking point logistically, while down at the cutting edge we knew the truth. Every day we saw and felt the Communists hitting us with twice what we could answer back with. Fortunately, the rationing did not last that long, but a minute would have been too long.

Meanwhile, life went on on Hill 930, and an interesting thing started to happen in Fighter Company. The boys doing all the fighting were doing it very well. They seldom got rattled, they handled incoming and probes in steady stride, like pros, and day by day were getting even better. Yet at the same time, the quality of the chow was getting worse and worse. We had only one hot meal a day, and every night it was colder and more awful than the one we got the night before. An army travels on its belly, or so said Napoleon; food, mail, and thirty-six points were about the only damn things the troops had to look forward to, and the crap they were eating limited the horizons a bit too much. I began a little investigation, only to find that the mess sergeant and cooks were completely burned out. Cajoling and threatening them didn't work, and when I realized nothing short of lining them up against a wall would, the only course of action was to fire everybody. I made rifle squad leader Sergeant Bravo mess sergeant, and he went to the troops: "Any of you guys cook in civilian life?" He got about two hundred volunteers (it seemed that every hill person had been a French chef in some fancy restaurant, or so he said). Bravo took the most promising off the line, and almost immediately they started putting out truly incredible meals. Unlike the old crew, my gung-ho, newly ex-infantry cooks knew well how important food was to the guys on line; suddenly we were eating French and Italian, and Bravo's hailing from New Orleans guaranteed some wild Cajun delights. How the new cooks scrounged all the good things they did was something I was probably happier not knowing, but there was no doubt in my mind that Napoleon would have decorated Bravo's raiders on the basis of the first bite, every night of the week.

The mess experiment worked so well I decided to do it on the supply end, too. My supply sergeant was a nice guy, but his heart wasn't in it. He just didn't appreciate that extra pair of socks or that extra can of rations. So I replaced him with Sergeant Toohey, another fine rifle squad leader, who instantly became a master scrounger. There was nothing that boy couldn't get. "Here you are, sir," he'd say, flashing a great grin as he plunked his newest acquisition down before me. Sometimes I wondered if I should ask him for North Korean General Kim Il Sung's head on a platter. It might have brought the war to a speedy end.

After the food was squared away, Bravo got the idea of giving the troops a midnight snack of soup and coffee. Brinkley, one of the new ex-infantry cooks, thought this was a great idea and volunteered for the job. He organized a hill kitchen in a vacant bunker near the company CP, and soon every night we had hot soup (from those delicious dehydrated soup packets) and fresh, strong coffee just when we needed it most.

Then, in accordance with the Great American Dream, evolution occurred. Before I knew it, Brinkley had a big production bakery going on top of the hill. He carefully lined the hub of his booming enterprise with ammo containers to make it rat proof, and outfitted it with stoves and all kinds of kitchen paraphernalia. At midnight the warm aroma of cinnamon rolls and coffee cakes, hot soup and coffee wafted through the position. Runners from each platoon shuttled mouth-watering treats from the bakery to their buddies. No doubt it pissed off the North Koreans, who didn't get a share; now and then they'd send a mortar round in Brinkley's direction, and our resident baker was probably the only cook in Eighth Army to get wounded four times. But the wounds were always superficial, none of the cakes seemed to fall, and the bakery was always open for business the next night.

About this time I heard a story that the George CO who'd gotten Bravo's patrol shot up had shot and killed a young Oklahoma A&M DSC-winning lieutenant. I was sick. I didn't know the lieutenant, but still felt a heavy weight of responsibility for the incident, because I'd had a confrontation with George 6 in reserve, which almost mirrored the events that led to the young lieutenant's death.

I'd been sitting at a long table in the BOQ, with Smitty, Westy, Price, and a new, great young officer from Boston named Richard Alexander, when suddenly George 6 came storming through the door, followed by his redheaded XO.

"What's up, Captain?" I asked him. He looked really weird—eyes all bulged out, melted snow dripping off his flushed red face—but just about the same time I realized he was drunk, he pulled a .45-caliber pistol out of his parka and pointed it at me. "I'm going to kill you, Hackworth," he said.

I didn't know what was going on. I would have thought it was some kind of drunken gag, except that he then advanced toward me, pointing that cannon at my head very earnestly. I shot a glance at Westy. *Do something.*

"Hold on, hold on. What's the flap here, Captain?" I asked.

"You took my machine gun, and I'm going to kill you."

"What machine gun?"

I was at the center of the table. Westy was on the corner a little farther down, rear and flank, so to speak, of the drunken CO as he moved closer and stuck the pistol under my nose. As George 6 began a disjointed tirade about the recent relief and hill property and some machine gun he said we'd taken that screwed up G's switch with her relieving company, out of the corner of my eye I saw Westy slowly moving his hand toward the strap of a steel pot hanging nearby. In an instant Westy had hurled that pot at the side of George 6's head, and I was on my feet, smashing at the Captain's wrist. He dropped the weapon, and I hit him from the ground up. The punch drove him into the corner of the GP tent; I rushed over to his spread-eagled, bullying ass and stomped him with my Mickey Mouse boots. I stomped him with the fear of the last minutes. I stomped him with longtime hate accrued since he'd shot up Sergeant Bravo's patrol and killed two of my men. The cleats and metal shoelace hooks on my boots did a job on his face; I stomped him until he was almost dead. Then a couple of us picked him up and threw him out into the snow. We roughed up his XO a little, too, and booted him out the door.

The next day Hemingway mentioned that George 6 looked as if he'd run into a freight train. "Yes, sir," I'd said, "I heard he fell in the snow." Hemingway glanced at my raw fist. "Yes, Hackworth, I heard that, too."

Now, in light of the news about the lieutenant killed by George 6's hand, I realized I should have told Hemingway what happened. I should have pressed charges on that drunken madman. I don't know why I didn't. Perhaps because I'd reported the "Pity, pity, pity" incident to Locke at that time, and nothing had been done about it. Besides, I'd seen tons of examples of what too much booze and combat-raw nerves did to people— from my first day in Italy, in fact, at the end of the war. Usually a little "eye for an eye" justice straightened these guys out, and I figured it would work on George 6, too. But it hadn't, obviously, and the circumstances of the lieutenant's death were too close for comfort. The story went that George 6 had pulled his .45 on the kid (who was a regimental liaison officer) and threatened to kill him if he didn't get out of his sight. The lieutenant was reported to have said, "You don't understand, sir. The regimental com- mander has asked me to come and discuss this matter with you, and I'm here on his authority," to which George 6 replied, "I told you to get out, and I told you I was going to shoot you if you didn't and—" BAM. George 6 blew the lieutenant's brains out. I never heard if the Captain was put away over the incident, but it was too late anyway, and it was something I would regret for the rest of my life.

When General Cleland established a King for a Day program and selected me as the first "king," I didn't want to go. I'd been with Fighter almost nine months now, and I'd never left my unit before; some protective, superstitious instinct kept me there, as if something terrible might happen and I wouldn't be around to help. But I got leaned on by Colonel Mansfield, and when he assured me the whole thing would be only twenty-four hours, I hotfooted it down the hill, all the way back to the land of electricity and running water.

The purpose of Cleland's program was to find out problems at the fighting level firsthand, and at the same time honor the rifle company skippers who carried the true burden of the war. As such, it was VIP treatment from the moment I arrived at Division until the moment I left. I took my first shower in three months, put on clean new fatigues, and dined (with the few awkward manners I had) in the generals' mess, a room full of white tablecloths, crystal glasses, and gourmet food served on sparkly china by orderlies in starched white jackets. Tough way to fight a war. But I couldn't begrudge Cleland; he was every bit a soldier despite the luxury that came with his job.

I sat with the General during his morning and evening briefings, and spent much of the rest of the day checking in with G-3 Operations to find out what was happening in Fighter's sector. That night Cleland and I had a long talk about my future. He was worried; he told me the Army was going through one of its most significant changes in a hundred years and there could well be no room in it for me. For the first time ever, America was going to have a standing Army—this Cold War was here to stay—a new army where being a top fighter and troop leader would not be enough. The war would soon be over; there would be cutbacks, and the first to go would be officers without education. I had to go to college, he told me, or West Point; he felt I had great potential to rise to senior rank if I got that little bit of sheepskin to show I was a thinker as well as a warrior. And he said he would help me in any way he could.

Cleland was from the Army of Soldiers. He seemed saddened by what he was telling me, by all the changes he saw coming. And for myself, after two years in the officer world I still thought like a sergeant—meaning, I just assumed I'd go from one unit to the next throughout my career, training troops and making them better. Now suddenly the emphasis was on making *me* better—in the classroom, of all places—and I didn't know what to think.

I lay awake most of the night on the wonderful fat mattress of my three-quarter bed at Division. I hadn't given much thought to my future. I still had a while before my three-year officer commitment was up and had hoped to see it out with Fighter. Mansfield was pushing me to go home (I had my thirty-six points), but I didn't want to; the war would soon be entering its fourth year, and as much as I hated it, I couldn't see myself walking away.

A slow bitterness welled up inside me, I'd served my country—well, I hoped. *Goddamnit,* I thought, *what's so damn important about a college education or West Point?* I only wanted to be a company commander, and after almost seven years at company level, one thing I was sure of was you didn't need to be some mental wizard to kick ass, take names, and run a good outfit. All you had to do was know your job and be fair and square. In reserve I'd been asked a million times, "What class are you?" (meaning what class of West Point); I'd never known how to respond till somebody said, "Tell them you're Korea, Class of '50." Well, that I was, and damn proud of it, too. I'd helped kick Red asses with every bit of energy I had that first horrible year of the war. I'd raided through their positions during the second year when the war turned static, and then come back to sit in the goddamn

trenches for another year still. I'd watched green forces, commanded by a lot
of self-serving amateurs—field-grade officers and generals who got medals
they didn't deserve, colonels who used twenty-two-year-olds' experience to
develop plans they couldn't or wouldn't work out themselves—be nickeled
and dimed to death in a stupid, pointless war that no one at home seemed
to care about. I'd trained my units like crazy to make sure my boys did not
suffer the same fate, and succeeded so well that from my first four-month
line period with Fighter, where we'd taken an average of one casualty a day,
in the second period we had just two KIA and fifteen wounded, even as both
incoming and enemy attacks were four or five times as intense. The ratio
should have been about twenty dead and four hundred WIA. I was proud of
that, too, but obviously it didn't mean a thing to anyone but me, my troops,
their parents, and Joe Cleland. The Army, *my* parent, and my one real
teacher, was now ready to boot me out for being street-wise and school-
dumb. It was all too painful to be real, and somehow very hard to
understand.

I didn't make a decision about my future that night. I turned my thoughts
to Fighter, which I was anxious to get back to in the morning. My unit made
sense to me, at least, and finally I fell asleep, just a tired Old Man who'd
been King for a Day.

If I had to leave my company and go home (and Mansfield kept insisting
I did), I didn't want to leave Fighter with anyone but the best. It became a
running argument between the Colonel and me. He kept suggesting people
and I kept telling him they were wimps. I wanted Lieutenant Alexander,
who'd proved himself to be not only a stud, but the kind of guy who'd lead
Fighter with the same spirit I had.

The thing was, when you're with a unit for a long time, it becomes a
raging love affair. Fighter and I belonged together, and the hand-and-glove
factor could be seen in the faces and manner of all the troops. They weren't
exactly carbon copies of their Old Man, but they'd developed a certain style,
I guess it could be called, from me. It was only natural; since I was a little
kid I'd always latched on to someone I respected, an Al Hewitt or a Steve
Prazenka, and knocked off anything I liked about him to make my own. It
was the same in the Army (my adopting Colonel Mansfield's pistol-packing
procedure, for example). If a trooper likes his CO and the CO wears his hat
at a bit of an angle, the trooper starts wearing his hat like that, too. If the CO
acts cocky, confident, and sure of himself, so do the boys. It's kind of like
tailor-making your own coat. You steal the best-designed sleeves, pockets,
buttons, and lapels you see, and one by one put them on, until you've got

the perfect coat, which, just by wearing it, you grow into until it fits, and becomes uniquely yours.

I wanted Alex to replace me because we were cut from the same bolt of cloth. What I liked about him was he was a brave, no-nonsense man who was never exactly insubordinate, but close. Nothing was worth taking seriously, according to Alexander; as a result, he was a calm, cool platoon leader who looked after his troops (and they loved him for it), at the same time leaving lots of room for showmanship. I'd never forget the night an enemy force got itself behind Alex's patrol and I couldn't raise him on the radio to tell him. About the time I knew he'd be saddling up to come home, I got artillery and flares peppering in all over his planned return route (which was where the North Koreans were laid up). It was kind of dangerous, but I figured Alex would come up on the radio to tell us to shut it off and I could tell him about the enemy and an alternate return route. He didn't. In desperation, just when I knew he had only enough time to make it back to our lines before light, I stood on top of a frontline bunker and yelled at the top of my lungs into the dead-quiet valley below.

"Alex! This is Hack! Come back through the First Platoon. Don't go as planned. Come back through First Platoon!"

A moment later, a voice bellowed up from the dark valley floor. "Okay, Hack!" he replied. "First Platoon!"

"*Let me tell you about my platoon leader,*" Alex's legend might have begun. "*He's not afraid of anything. He stands right in the middle of no-man's-land and yells right up the enemy's nose.*" He told me when he got back safe and sound that his radio had gone out; he'd assumed with all the friendly fire and all the light that something wasn't right, and had already decided to come back a different route. No sweat.

So I wanted Alexander. Mansfield refused. He didn't like Alex; he told me he was a "wiseass." Which was true, but all my guys were wiseasses. Cocky wiseasses, in fact, because that's what I wanted them to be. You've got to be pretty confident to spend your days as a moving target. The next thing I knew, Mansfield decided to send one of his staff captains to take over Fighter. I hit the roof. I'd known the guy in Trieste. He was worthless as a troop commander, and I didn't want him having anything to do with my unit. Mansfield and I got into a very big argument, and as usual when I lost my temper, I said a lot of things I shouldn't have said. In the end, I lost anyway. The staff captain came up to take command of the company, and I went down to Battalion staff until I got my orders to go home.

Less than a week later I stood outside the battalion CP with Colonel Mansfield, watching my old company being savaged. The hilltop home of

Fighter's CP and Brinkley's bakery had become an inferno. Staring up in the dark, it looked to us as though they'd been overrun, but there was no way to find out: Fighter was silent, with no one up there manning the radio or switchboard. I was getting more anxious by the second; the Colonel was worried, too, so when I suggested I go up and find out what was going on, he gave me the green light and I was off, radio operator in tow. We ran straight up the hill, through Easy's trenches. It was a quick trip, mainly because hardly anyone bothered to challenge us. When I hit Fighter the first thing I heard was "Halt!" Just one of the guys doing as he'd been taught.

"Hackworth!" I yelled and kept running.

"Halt!"

"Hackworth!"

"Halt!"

"Hackworth!"

"Shit, sir, it's great to hear you," I heard again and again as I moved through the trench. All I wanted to know was what the hell was happening. No one had any idea. All they knew was they got hit bad, no artillery went out, no one could raise the CP on the phone, and it looked as if the penetration had been right up the center of the company sector. I bumped into Alex, who'd taken command by default. He'd sealed the penetration and was now cleaning up the gooks on the reverse slope. When everything was under control, I ran down to the company CP.

Inside, all was quiet. The commo sergeant was dead, blown up by a grenade. The inner door, between the commo shack and the CO bunker, was closed. I kicked it open. There, sitting on the little chair that used to be mine, was the new captain, head down between his legs, crying. I walked up to him and belted him in the mouth.

I got on the horn to Battalion. I told Mansfield the situation, and that I'd assumed command from this babbling son of a bitch. And I told him he damn well better give Fighter to Alex, whose platoon had just saved the whole unit moments before. *Now* he agreed.

I went out to the OP in front of 2d Platoon. It was just getting light, and in about fifteen minutes it would be a very uncool place to be. But I wanted to have a last look. I wanted to figure out for myself how it had happened, how—after all the months of combat, all the knowledge, the love, the hard, hard work all of us had put into it—I had come to receive as my farewell present the vision of my company being overrun.

Fighter's men were cleaning up the battlefield, evacuating our dead and wounded. An occasional enemy mortar round came crunching in. The sights and sounds of death were all around me, yet I was not there; I was, somehow, removed. As if I were watching, from a great distance, a surreal dumb show not intended for an audience.

For almost three years I'd seen, heard, and smelled death among my friends and among my men. But as I hovered over Fighter in my mind's eye, I knew that never before had I felt death so strongly as I did now. It was a dull horror that spread from my gut to my heart, to my limbs and to my head. And I knew that the fate of Fighter was no longer in my hands, any more than George or Easy or the Raiders would ever be again.

It was time to go home.

10 BLACK SHOES

They called it the Brown Shoe Army, and then it was the Black
Shoe Army. It's funny how the little things changed everything
somehow. What made it different? I don't know what the hell it
was. You're still the same guy, still the same son of a bitch you
ever were, still good or still bad—but that changing of the shoes
really put something in the air.

Captain Steve Prazenka, USA, Ret.
Intelligence and Reconnaissance Platoon Sergeant
Trieste United States Troops (TRUST), 1947–50

"WHERE'D you get all those medals, 'Captain'?" The voice, close
behind me, dripped with sarcasm. "You buy 'em in the PX?"

I turned around, only to be confronted by two MPs with big grins and
hard eyes. They looked strangely out of place in the St. Francis Hotel bar.
"Looks to me like you're impersonating an officer, boy," said the other one,
putting his hand on my elbow and easing me to my feet. "I think we should
step outside."

He'd gotten my number all right. As far as I was concerned, I'd been
impersonating an officer since the second I was commissioned. But I didn't
like the way he said it, and I didn't like that arrogant son of a bitch touching
me.

I'd just gotten home. Assigned to Fort Mason for processing, I'd spent the
last couple of days wandering around San Francisco—the other end of the
earth, it seemed, from the trenches of Korea—trying to figure out what I was
going to do with my life. It was the toughest decision I'd ever faced, and I
only had three days to make up my mind. The only two options, according
to the Personnel officer at Mason, were to sign up for another three years as
a Reserve officer or to get out of the Army. It shouldn't have been so
hard—General Cleland had pretty well convinced me to get out and go to
school—but I'd rotated home with Roy Herte, that G/223d, West Point stud

of a platoon leader (whose father was a colonel) and he'd spent the whole damn boat ride persuading me to stay in.

Now, as the MPs led me out of the bar, all I knew for certain was that a purple rage was washing over me. I was embarrassed. The other patrons, who hadn't even glanced in my direction when I'd arrived (let alone come over to slap me on the back or say "job well done") were now gawking, and I could see on their faces their collective disdain for "just another Army guy in trouble."

So much for the glory of being a soldier, I thought, as the MPs hassled me, now in the hotel lobby, for identification I didn't have. I finally convinced them to call Fort Mason, and as one of them marched off to the phone booth, the other stayed and kept an eye on me. In the meantime I thought about the Army, to keep myself from punching out my smart-assed captor.

There was no question but that it was my life, or at least it *had* been, for seven years now. I'd been a private, I'd been a noncom; I'd jumped into Korea eyes wide open and suddenly I was an officer—a little leap that had cost me, on paper anyway, three more years' service. I'd gone back to Korea not just because I couldn't handle the idea of stateside duty, but because of the Sergeant Combat complex that had fueled me since Trieste: I'd been determined to get as much combat experience as possible, so that no one could ever put me down again for not being the most qualified at my job. It seemed to me that was a career choice in itself.

But now the war was almost over, and combat "qualifications" would have nothing to do with anything. Reserve officers would be getting the ax en masse, according to General Cleland, and even if I signed up, there was no guarantee that I wouldn't be chopped within months. It seemed so unfair (particularly since I still had almost a year to go on my three-year "wartime" officer's contract), but I guessed it had always been that way: the Reserve men were called in to do the (platoon- and company-level) dirty work while so many Regulars hid under (staff duty) rocks; when the shooting was over, the Regulars pranced out into the sunlight and ruthlessly ground the fighters into the dirt.

I saw the MP who'd called Fort Mason striding across the hotel foyer, a sheepish look on his face. Guess someone had told him I was, indeed, boy-Captain Hackworth, and that the medals were well earned and all mine.

"Sorry about that, Captain," he said.

"Gee, Captain," the other jumped in, "no hard feelings, huh?"

For a moment I just looked at the two polished MP pricks sniveling in front of me. For some reason, they said it all—whatever "it" was—and in that instant I made up my mind. "Just get fucked," I said. "I'm getting out of your Army anyway."

I was off active service for two years, the two longest of my life. I'd never know whether I made the right decision in quitting over the MPs; one thing I was sure of, though, was that I regretted it from the moment I left Fort Mason. Civilian life was boring. It just wasn't my bag. From the outset I missed the adventure, the kinship, and the sense of belonging that came with being in the Army. I probably missed the structured, disciplined life, too—I couldn't find a *purpose* in the world outside the military—and the same unknown variable that had compelled me from childhood to join up now had me counting the days until my self-imposed exile was over.

General Cleland had been assigned the top soldier job in the Army, as CG, XVIII Airborne Corps. We corresponded frequently; he urged me not only to hit the books but to remain active in the Reserves so I wouldn't lose touch. Accordingly, I joined—or, more precisely, rejoined—the 40th Division, which was transferred back to California and National Guard ineptitude when the Korean War ended six weeks after I came home. It didn't take long for me to realize why the 40th had been so screwed up when it first deployed to Korea. There was nothing military about this NG organization except that we wore uniforms when we met once a week to drink coffee and shoot the breeze. Each summer we had a two-week training period at Camp Roberts, but by the time we'd unpacked and got set to play war, it was just about time to go home. Without General Cleland to fuel the flame, the light of the Fireball had flickered and died. For myself, I started out as an enthusiastic troop CO in the Division Recon Squadron, but when I found I was one of the few guys on the block who even gave a damn, I decided not to make waves. Instead I rocked along with the rest of the weekend warriors and refused to feel guilty over the absolute waste of taxpayer dollars.

I was at loose ends. It was a postcombat hangover for which no "hair of the dog" cure existed, made all the worse by newspaper and magazine coverage of the unsatisfying conclusion of the war. The *Time* magazine wrap-up, for example, which contained an excerpt from a wartime interview with General Van Fleet, damn near killed me:

"Reporter: 'General, what is our goal?'

"Van Fleet: 'I don't know. The answer must come from higher authority.'

"Reporter: 'How may we know, General, when and if we achieve victory?'

"Van Fleet: 'I don't know, except that somebody higher up will have to tell us.' "[1]

What, I asked myself, *is a war without a goal?* What was victory, if not something you could taste and breathe and feel? Instead, there'd just been three years of fighting—for nothing. Twenty-two billion dollars spent, and no decisive victory; more than 33,600 American lives lost, 103,000 men wounded in action, 13,000 men captured or MIA.[2] And that was not to mention the ROK civilian-military casualties of almost 844,000, and the 3.7 million left homeless in South Korea alone.[3] It was such a horrible waste, and Secretary of State John Foster Dulles' war's end proclamation, that "for the first time in history an international organization has stood against an aggressor" did little to justify it, at least in my eyes.[4] We hadn't lost, but we hadn't won; even worse, we—meaning not the guys on the ground, but the U.N. governments led by the United States—hadn't even *tried*, at least after the first year. It was something I didn't think I'd ever understand.

I settled in Santa Monica, dutifully enrolled in Santa Monica City College, and began to educate myself. It meant nothing to me; I just managed to scrape by. I felt bitter, hurt, betrayed; most of my energy was spent drinking, fighting, and chasing pussy, till finally I reached the point where I gave up the first for about a year to stop the second (but that's where I drew the line).

When my grandmother, who'd still lived right down the road in Ocean Park, died in 1954, I was surprised at how deeply it affected me. She'd been a bigoted, opinionated old lady; so many of the 1860s values she'd stamped into my impressionable child's mind had been proved inaccurate in the years since I'd left home that I thought I'd dismissed little pieces of Gram herself, as each of her "truths" bit the dust. But I hadn't. She was as much a part of me as I was of her, and at twenty-three I realized that that was never going to change.

Gram was a brave frontier lady whose family had traveled overland from Virginia to Kentucky to the rich mining country of Colorado, with the dream of carving out a new life. Many times she'd told me about that life—how she'd hidden in her prairie house as Indians on the warpath stalked around outside; how her father, John Stedman, would load up his rifle and shoot the red men to protect his kids. In her nineteenth-century way, Gram had had the same lust for adventure as the men of the Hackworth clan she married into, and though it was Uncle Roy who spun tales of "the war to end all wars," it was Gram who drummed into me the litany of Hackworth military feats throughout America's history. Inaccurate as most of her accounts proved to be, the constant commercial for duty, honor, and country instilled in me a fierce patriotism, which guided me every day of my life. Thanks to her, I grew up believing that my family made this country—with an ax in one hand, a rifle in the other—chopping down

Indians, trees, or anything else that stood in the way of progress, of manifest destiny, and what was "rightfully" ours.

After the funeral, two of Gram's children raided her little house in Ocean Park. Years before (prior to his disappearing down a Cripple Creek mine shaft never to be seen again), John Hackworth, Gram's husband, had been a successful gold miner and mining superintendent; now their kids, who still lived in Colorado, were convinced my grandmother had a stash of gold stock certificates concealed under her bed. Having suffered the indignity of receiving relief packages on our doorstep all through my Depression childhood—powdered milk, instant margarine, and all kinds of other stuff (including clothes and cardboard shoes for me that you could tell at a hundred paces had been issued by the state)—I could have told them that if Gram had anything, it was the money I'd sent her every month since I joined the merchant marine. But they didn't ask, and when I walked into the house they were literally ripping it apart. My aunt Freda was wearing a gold watch I'd bought for Gram in Italy; I tore it off her arm and told everyone to get the hell out, that I'd just come back from killing a lot of people and I was perfectly prepared to kill them, too. In his way, big, tough David Hackworth was still the same little kid who'd clung to Gram's legs as she stood by the door holding a suitcase and threatening to leave if I didn't shape up. (The trick had worked for a few years, until the time the suitcase popped open and I found out it was empty.) Now, as then, having lost my Army family, I was a brand-new orphan, with nothing to fall back on.

One thing I was, though, was a survivor. I transferred to Woodbury College after a year at SMCC, majored in salesmanship, and became a part-time insurance man for Prudential. Both Jack Speed and Uno Rentmeister came out to visit for a while (and to get to know some of my female clients); while they wined and dined, I just kept on selling, and in three months I'd sold enough insurance to qualify for the 1955 Million Dollar Round Table. I had to admit there was great satisfaction in finding out I wouldn't be a complete bust in civilian life—but I was still counting those days, because I had no intention of being a civilian even one minute longer than necessary. (Besides, I was finding out that civilian life could be damn dangerous. According to Jack Speed, some of my beloved Raiders had pulled off a final, *stateside* raid, long after the unit broke up, with the help of a submachine gun one of them had managed to smuggle back from the battlefield. Apparently, when these three Raiders were not appropriately welcomed in San Francisco, they decided to announce their return by raiding a downtown bank in broad daylight. The submachine gun prevented heroics on the part of the bank's staff, but the guys got caught a short time later and were now serving twenty to thirty years in a California federal penitentiary.)

In mid '55 I wrote General Cleland to tell him I'd almost finished those magic two years of college, and had submitted my application for active duty. I told him I'd requested assignment to the 82d Airborne at Fort Bragg; within days, a paratrooper friend of Cleland's at the Department of the Army's Office of Personnel Operations (OPO) called and tried to persuade me not to go there. He said the Airborne was finished; Army aviation and "choppers" were the new wave, and he could get me in on the ground floor at the Aviation School at Fort Rucker. *And that's about where I'll stay, too,* I thought, having just completed fifteen hours of fixed-wing lessons, only to find myself an unsure, uncoordinated, and dangerous pilot. No, I told the OPO colonel, if I was going to be in the Army, and if I could have a choice, I wanted to be in a paratroop outfit; it was a Jim Gavin–inspired dream that all the progress in the world would not keep me from fulfilling. With misgivings, the colonel agreed with my rationale and said he'd do what he could.

It was a different Army I returned to in December 1955. Manpower was out; missile power, in. The darling of the armed forces was the Air Force, with the Eisenhower Administration determined to hinge the nation's defense on strategic intermediate and long-range nuclear weapons, such as USAF's developing five-thousand-mile-range intercontinental ballistic missiles (ICBMs). Military strength, which at the height of the Korean War had numbered 3.6 million, had already been reduced to 2.9, with deeper cuts in manpower expected across all services. Eisenhower's "New Look" had already reduced the Army's force by a third, bringing its total to little more than one million men.

Although the McCarthy era had ended ignominiously, the Red Scare was alive and kicking; the Russians were coming, said the military experts, with their own A-bombs and H-bombs, to blow our cities off the map. As such, Air Defense (AD) was the password of the decade, with the 35 percent increased military budget mostly dedicated to the improvement of our continental air defense, and to radar facilities in the Arctic. The Army's share of the new funding was devoted, in great measure, to the development and deployment of a twenty-to-thirty-mile-range AD antiaircraft missile system known as the Nike-Ajax.

The AD facts of life notwithstanding, it was a rude shock when I found myself assigned not to the 82d Airborne as requested, but to the 77th Antiaircraft Artillery (AAA) Battalion in Manhattan Beach, California. I was sure it was a mistake; I didn't know a damn thing about AD. I called Cleland's friend in OPO; the essence of his reply was beggars can't be choosers. Apparently he'd had a hell of a time recalling me, even with the Cleland influence and my combat record. He'd gone so far as to try bringing me in through the expanding chopper program against my wishes, but the results of my entrance physical were so poor (hearing loss and left arm still not 100 percent) that he couldn't even manage that. The OPO colonel assured me it wouldn't be more than a year or so before he got me back to infantry; in the meantime, he suggested I use this period as an opportunity to continue my education. It seemed that while I was struggling to get through two years of college, word was coming down from the top that only a master's degree made one a certified thinker in the New Army.

I reported for temporary duty (TDY) to Fort Bliss, Texas, to be retrained in Air Defense. Bliss was home to the Antiaircraft and Guided Missile School and, like Benning during the war years, was expanding at an incredible pace. Against a backdrop of blue skies and cacti, adobe buildings left over from the Horse Cav's Indian-fighting days served as monuments to simpler times; all around them, in various stages of construction, were new classrooms, offices, barracks, and ultramodern training facilities.

Besides polo, which in Old Army tradition was played every Sunday, Bliss ran like most civilian organizations: strictly nine to five, five days a week. It was my first encounter with the gentleman's Army, a world all its own. Each day began when I woke up in my well-appointed private suite, put on my Class A's, and left my laundry by the door for the maid to pick up. After breakfast at the first-rate mess, I'd head off to class for a nine-o'clock start. The day's instruction was punctuated by lunch and a couple of coffee breaks, and exactly at five it was over to the plush Officers' Club for a few drinks. As much as to wind down, this last stop was necessary to avoid the evening rush hour: hundreds of soldiers going home after their long day staring at the sky, waiting for the Soviet air armada to strike.

There was an in-crowd, clubbish feel at Bliss, which was emulated throughout the whole Air Defense arm. And it didn't matter that the Army had come to realize a guy could get pretty lazy sitting by his gun waiting for an enemy who never came, and had begun infusing super gung-ho infantry and field-artillery people into the program. The guys in charge—at Brigade, Region, and Army Air Defense Command (ARADCOM)—were still mainly WW II Air Defense men, who'd spent their lives in step with the Air Corps and that organization's minimum military ways. It didn't make for changes, and again and again I was struck not only by the overall sloppiness, but by the utter lack of urgency among permanent party personnel. It was an Air Force attitude: unshakable confidence that "we're here to stay."

And they were, despite the fact that AAA would be phasing out all its active-duty gun units by the end of 1956 and replacing them with missiles. The new Nike-Ajax units, to most, were more of the same, even if somewhat more complex: once their training was completed, these AD guys would go right back to staring at the sky. The only difference would be they'd be part of a new club: the Nike battalion "package," which included all key people from the CO to the lowest radar technician.

For someone like me, with absolutely no background in AAA, Bliss was more often than not a nightmare. The Antiaircraft Battery Officers' Course was so hard that I would have given up my infantry colonel's standard of living and dug a foxhole every night if it would have helped unlock the mysteries of E/I = R (electricity over current = resistance), horizontal slant ranges, or superheterodynes. Still, in direct contrast to what I'd known at Benning, the quality of instruction at Bliss was of the highest caliber. The dawning missile age had no precedent in history. The Army could no longer depend on its pink-cheeked virgin lieutenants to parrot after-action reports of WW II, or even Korea, to teach us how to fight tomorrow's wars. Granted, many of our instructors at Bliss were young lieutenants; some were even draftee PFCs. Most had no combat experience either, but they did have Ph.D.s from MIT or similar institutions. These whiz kids knew their stuff, and taught it in a no-nonsense, professional way; their ability was enough to make dumbshits like me want to cry—I was worried sick about flunking out and blowing my Army career just when it was starting.

I made good friends with a couple guys who were in much the same boat. Tom Trainer, a WW II battlefield commission (now a fire chief in Chicago), and Bob Streena, a private eye in Palo Alto, were both members of NG units that had been converted from Infantry to AAA and recalled in response to the Red Scare. The three of us lent each other moral support, and spent many an evening drowning our sorrows across the border in Juárez, Mexico. For more concrete assistance in passing the damn course, I turned to two Marine Corps officers, Lieutenant Casey and Captain Everett, both longtime AD men stationed at Thousand Palms, California. We'd met through a shared passion for physical fitness. I was a fanatic about running and push-ups at this time, and because that was pretty unusual among our classmates, I guess it impressed the two gung-ho Marines, who made no bones about their feeling that the Army was a pretty Mickey Mouse organization. Marines being Marines, they no doubt didn't believe me when I told them Fort Bliss was not *really* the Army, but I was desperate enough for their assistance not to stand in the door over it.

In the end, I graduated thirty-two out of thirty-six in the course, but just as the guy who comes in last in medical school is still called "Doctor," I was still, record- and MOS-wise, considered a fully qualified Antiaircraft Battery Officer. I took comfort in knowing that as a commander, I wouldn't have to remember the details I'd held in my brain long enough to pass the tests; I'd just have to make sure I got some smart guys on my team to do that kind of thinking for me.

Battery C of the 77th AAA was smack-dab in the middle of Manhattan Beach, California. So much for the great adventures I'd dreamed of upon recall to active duty. My new Army home was half a block from my favorite beach, across the street from Pancho's (one of my favorite haunts over the last two years), and ten minutes from where I was born. The post didn't have a BOQ; the departing battery XO, a University of San Francisco basketball star named Jim Ruane, was checking out of the service and I took over his bachelor pad on the beach. All in all, it seemed as if the only notable difference in my life-style was going to be wearing my soldier suit every day instead of just weekends, and, thanks to Jim, a whole new list of Southern California beauties to look up in my off-hours.

C Battery was one of four identical firing batteries in the 77th. It was composed of four 90-mm AAA guns and two radar (acquisition and tracking) sections. Soldiers manned the guns, but in fact, the system pretty well ran itself. The acquisition radar was designed to pick up a target (as far out as a hundred miles), and transfer it to the tracking radar once it got into range. The tracking radar would then send out an identification, friend or foe (IFF) signal; if no response was received, the aircraft would be considered hostile, and we (the human element) would prepare to fire. The gun crews' tasks were simply to set the 90-mm shells with an automatic fuse setter and load the guns; the tracking radar locked onto the target and did the rest. It all sounded good, but over the next nine months we came close to blowing friendly aircraft out of the sky on a number of occasions. There was much room for error in the system, if only because of the incredible amount of ordinary air traffic in and out of L.A. Luckily, jet fighters dispatched by the Antiaircraft Operations Center (AAOC) to intercept, identify and/or shoot down the presumed hostile always saved the day, finding that the IFF equipment on board was malfunctioning, or that the target was a friendly civilian aircraft that had simply lost its way.

I inherited C Battery from Lieutenant David Cramer, who stayed on as my XO. Cramer was a good officer, with about eight years' service and a lot of experience in Airborne field artillery. He'd run a damn good AD outfit, a fact that, in its way, made both of our new jobs harder. No one likes to see someone come in and mess with his "perfect" unit (especially if that someone was as undiplomatic as I), and when I decided to shake the natural

AD sit-on-your-ass mentality out of C Battery with hard training, tough inspections, and an immediate halt to those nine-to-five days, ex-CO Cramer had no choice but to back me up.

Initially (and naturally) my men hated me. Most were draftees, a number were Regular lazy-assed AD NCOs. All of them reminded me of the National Guardsmen in Company D/223d, and I pushed them just as hard as I had the heavy-weapons company boys, from the moment they stood reveille at 0600. The only people who hated me more were the Army wives (who'd gotten pretty comfortable with their husbands' sixteen-hours-at-home, nonsoldiering soldiers' lives), the local community (which had to bear our singing and counting as we ran down the beach every morning), and my battalion CO, Lieutenant Colonel George L. Theisen, a weak, unsure, ex-lawyer commander who knew precious little about soldiering and nothing at all about leadership. Swayed by the bellyaching of some of those shrewd career NCOs who'd figured AD was a good way to mark time until I'd come in and upset their Sunny California vacation, Theisen was constantly after me to cut out the training. Air defenders, said he, did not have to be paratroopers. My stock answer was that the 6th ARADCOM CG, Major General E. G. McGaw, had put out a training memo calling for an hour's PT every morning, and I was "just following orders, sir." In truth, I knew the sort of training I was putting these men through was unnecessary; in AD the odds of their needing the stamina or the infantrylike skills I insisted upon were slim to none. But at the same time, these were *line soldiers*. There was no excuse for their not being kept physically tough and ready to go, regardless of the cushy jobs they had going at the moment. My concern was not without precedent; during the Battle of the Bulge, in December of '44, the U.S. command flat ran out of infantrymen, and because there was no Nazi air threat, AD people were sent to fight in infantry units. The same happened in Korea. Who was to say it could not happen again? So just like the proverbial new broom, I kept up the training, and the boys learned pretty quickly that the good old days were over and a new man was sweeping the floor.

Of course, when a new CO is a hard-ass, his men look first for the chink in his armor. As a result, a leader sometimes finds himself in a situation of having to hide his more human side. One morning in the early days, for example, I had a bitch of a time running on the beach—terrible stomach pains, so bad it took every bit of willpower I possessed to keep going. But I couldn't fall out—not ever, let alone with the eyes of one hundred unwilling air defenders boring in on me. Somehow I made it back to the battery; the doc there took one look, called for an ambulance, and before I even had a chance to protest (in the words of good Sergeant Prazenka) that only the lame, the lazy, and the screw-offs go on sick call, I was on an operating table at Fort MacArthur, having my near-bursting appendix removed. I'd never know what kind of celebrations arose out of my untimely leave from C Battery, but I'm sure *that* was all for the best. It was the first time I'd hit sick call in almost ten years of service.

When I'd first arrived at the battery, the WW II–vintage prefab facilities on post were falling apart as quickly as they'd been thrown up in the face of the "imminent" Red attack. The barracks were open squad rooms with no privacy. It wasn't all that easy to distinguish between the mess and the latrine. Unquestionably, something had to be done, and it was number one on my list the second I got out of the hospital.

"Sir, work orders went in . . . Fort MacArthur just doesn't have any money," explained Master Sergeant Allison, my supply sergeant. Allison was a fine old soldier—he probably had thirty years' service by then, starting out long ago as a "buffalo" soldier with the illustrious black Cavalry Regiment—and I loved the guy. He drank his share of booze every day (gulping it right down, a water glass at a time) and still ran the straightest supply room I'd ever seen.

"Well, Sergeant, work orders won't get this place fixed up. What do you think we should do?"

Not since the thirties, when the Army was so broke that General George C. Marshall at Benning had had to mow his own lawn, had units had such a hard time making ends meet. The problem was that for the first time in a long, long time, the man in the White House knew what was happening at Fort Huachuca or Camp Breckinridge; when the budgets hit Ike's desk, he could take one look and know that the money being requested for a radar testing station would actually be used to build a golf course or a snazzy Officers' Club. Eisenhower had definite ideas as to what was needed and what was not, and with a confident stroke of a pen, he axed anything that didn't fit in with his overall military austerity program. In the meantime, the troops lived in hovels and scrounged shoelaces to hold their morale up. The President was a far cry from the Ike I'd met during an inspection of my recon company nearly ten years before in Cormons, Italy. Then, as Supreme Commander of all Allied Forces, he'd asked me whether I was being fed well. I'd said no, and he'd been surprised; he'd immediately called over the Mediterranean Theater commander.

"General Lee," he'd said to the three-star relation of Civil War fighter Robert E. Lee, "there's a boy here who's not getting enough to eat."

"No, sir," I'd interrupted, "I'm getting enough. It's just that it's always the same thing. I've been in this battalion for three months, and all we've had for breakfast, lunch, and dinner is dehydrated scrambled eggs and Spam."

"Is that true?" Ike asked General Lee.

"We've had a big surplus of Spam, General, and we've been trying to use it up . . . well, let me check on that a little further, Ike."

Before I knew it there'd been a hushed conference of Ike's general staff, right in front of me; finally Ike had turned to me again and flashed his famous grin. "Don't worry about it, son. We'll fix this up right away." And he did, because, surplus or no surplus, we never had Spam again.

In 1956, a lot of units were just wearing the poverty-line conditions being imposed by the New Ike, but just like that little kid in Italy who'd gotten fed up with Spam, I wasn't going to, and I didn't expect C Battery to do so either. So Master Sergeant Allison started to wheel and deal for building material. The hardest thing to come by was timber. SFC Normal Crot, an ex-Marine and damn good soldier himself, solved this problem when he let on he knew of a big stack of pine two-by-fours just screaming to be liberated from a civilian construction site down the road. For the next month, we made frequent midnight hits on the site and a number of others in the area. It wasn't exactly lawful activity, but it was good combat training for the men of my new command—who proudly started calling themselves "Hack-worth's Rangers."

In the meantime, gun sergeant Charles Landry, who'd been a concrete man in civilian life, arranged to get us the excess a local concrete guy was dumping at the end of each day. The merchant got a tax break and we got concrete walks and driveways as well as permanent, maintenance-free revetments to replace the eroding sandbags around the guns. When we got enough wood, we rebuilt the barracks to provide individual rooms. We renovated the latrine, too, and by the time PFC Richard Plumer got through tiling it with seconds from a local factory, it was (in all our opinions) the Mona Lisa of shit houses. Finally we rebuilt and redecorated the mess to look like a fancy seafood restaurant (complete with fishnets draped all over the place), and the battery was something the men could be comfortable in and proud of. The building program had given them a break from the monotonous waiting game they'd become locked into, and combined with the training, which improved both individual and team proficiency, now the guys' drag-ass defensive attitude was being replaced with a keen offensive spirit.

Anything C Battery could be the best at, it was—Best Supply, Best Motor Pool, Best Mess (the latter under the watchful eye of mess sergeant SFC George Clark, a graduate of Tuskegee Institute with a B.S. in food administration, who could create gourmet feasts out of any Army-issue rations). We won the 47th Brigade Championship in softball and basketball, cornered the market on Brigade Soldier of the Month selection, and in the 47th's annual inspection, out of thirty batteries ours was number one.

The irony of it all was that despite our successes, I personally remained number one in both battalion CO Theisen's and the Manhattan Beach community's bad books. The concept of small posts being located in residential areas was somewhat new to the Army; it was one, I was convinced, the Manhattan Beach homeowners were none too pleased with. Though a lot of organizations came onto our renovated post for tours and went home suitably impressed, the next day I'd still get a phone call from some Soroptimist or another complaining that our morning run or battery alert siren was annoying the sea gulls. When I'd politely explain to the caller that it was "just tough shit," she'd ring the Colonel. Colonel Theisen, meanwhile, didn't even talk to me anymore. Instead he sent reports and warning messages through his S-3 or XO, or through old Milo Rowell, the hearts-losing, millionaire AAA officer who'd co-located with me and Easy once upon a time in my Wolfhound days in Korea. Milo, now a captain, was assigned as the 77th's battalion Adjutant (S-1); he crashed at my place until he found one of his own, and kept me abreast of what the Colonel was thinking. The word was never good: I demanded too much, I pushed too hard, I was insensitive to the representatives of the Sea Gulls Right to Nest Foundation, he was considering relieving me. The litany went on and on, and I was sick, because I wanted the Colonel to like me, and I wanted him to appreciate my unit. After all, it wasn't as though C Battery was some sad-sack organization. We were damn good, and I truly believed the reason for it was the deeply ingrained TRUST standards—of proficiency, dedication, and esprit—I'd brought to the outfit. But if I'd learned soldiering in a Trieste time warp, if TRUST was a throwback whose standards had long since died, then it was "just tough shit, Colonel Theisen," and so be it—I couldn't have changed my ways even if I'd tried. But I didn't try, because I knew my ways were right.

Until a weapon disappeared. Not just any weapon, but an M-2 automatic carbine. I'd been doing my monthly inventory of the armory and noticed that the bright, conscientious Mormon armorer had listed six weapons on guard, and I knew we had only five posts. When I mentioned it to the kid he broke down and spilled all: it turned out the carbine hadn't just recently gone south. It had been missing for three full months, its absence undetected through ninety daily Duty Officer checks and two of my own monthly serial-number inspections. It was little wonder the armorer was afraid to tell anyone (a missing carbine was FBI material), and now I couldn't either. To report it would make C (the Best) Battery a laughing-stock, and give Colonel Theisen a damn good reason to relieve me. I told the armorer to keep it all under his hat for a few more days while I figured out what to do.

Supply Sergeant Allison had a deal going with the guy who picked up the battery's garbage. It brought the trashman a bit more money, gave Allison leverage in his swapping activities, and served as preventive ass-covering for me. A battery CO was responsible for all the property in his concern. As one of the last things he did before leaving a unit, he and the new CO would take a complete inventory, and whatever was missing—blankets, sheets, forks, webbing, jeeps—would have to be paid for by the departing man. The bill could run to thousands of dollars, so a savvy, reliable supply sergeant made a point of knowing what he had, what was missing, and an SOP for replacing things in time for his CO's change-of-command stocktaking day. The little stuff that disappeared in a unit was usually the work of unthinking troopers who just chucked things into rubbish bins; as a result, by the end of any given week, the trashman's truck was always full of GI gear, so much, in fact, that the vehicle was more like a disorganized traveling supply depot than anything else. So the deal we had was simple: since the trashman got paid per cubic foot of stuff he collected, Allison would sign for more trash than the guy took out of the battery, and in return, the trashman would give Allison all the GI gear he found, no questions asked.

So I invited the trashman for coffee. He was a Damon Runyon kind of guy—shrewd, shifty, and very sharp—and when I mentioned I was looking for an M-2 carbine, he just shrugged and said he didn't come by too many of them in his truck. But, he added casually, he had one of his own, a rusty old M-1 model he'd brought back from WW II. Did I want it? *Did I ever*.

The weapon was in sorry shape, but with the help of Mess Sergeant Clark, Allison reblued the serial-numbered receiver in the mess-hall oven and replaced all the other parts. By the time they'd finished, we had what to the naked eye was a brand-new M-1 carbine. The M-1 became a brand-new M-2 (the later model had a selector switch that enabled it to fire fully automatic) when old Allison drilled, glued, and blued a dummy switch onto the vintage carbine. He also made a new "old" page in his property book to square the different serial numbers (no easy chore in itself, as it required probably ten different typewriters and pens, as well as a master forger's touch to age the paper), and finally only one step remained: to turn the weapon in to Ordnance, get credit for the turn-in, and remove the number from the books once and for all.

I'd stayed out of the whole operation; the minute Clark and Allison, those two fine Old Army men, got into the act, I took the carbine off my worry list completely. So when Allison dropped by my office the day before payday, at first I didn't understand the mysterious poker face he was wearing.

"Would the Captain have fifty dollars?" he asked.

"What for, Sergeant?"

"Well, Captain, I'm aiming to finish off the little project George and I've been working on."

The light went on. "You got it, Allison," I said. "What've you got in mind?"

"I'm thinking I'll just mosey on down to Ordnance. I got a buddy over there who'd be mighty happy celebrating my win at the races, sir."

Allison's plan was simple, and absolutely brilliant. Traditionally, the day before the eagle shit was one when most old regular sergeants were broke and *very* thirsty. The supply sergeant knew his Ordnance pal was no exception, so with my fifty bucks, he took his friend out on the town that night. Late in the evening, when the Ordnance man was sufficiently mellow (knee-knocking drunk, in fact), Allison mentioned he wanted to do a weapons turn-in in the morning—first thing, he said, so he didn't have to waste a minute of his day off. No problem, slurred his friend.

Still feeling no pain from the night before, the next morning Allison took the weapon over to Ordnance. By then the "M-2" had been further modified to include a bent, "no longer serviceable" barrel. Within moments the twisted rifle was on the junk heap and a receipt had been written out; my career was saved and Allison and his hung-over buddy were off to wet their furry tongues again.

For a long time I worried where that carbine would surface—whether I'd open up the paper one morning to find a bank full of people had been gunned down on full automatic—because despite all else, I took my job in sleepy Manhattan Beach very seriously. After almost ten years in the Army, it was my first stateside command: the first time I'd actually been tasked with the defense of the nation (Italy and Korea were both so far from home that the connection between their defense and America seemed thinner than the slack in a hair trigger). In truth, I was not as caught up as the Administration and the general populace seemed to be in the fear that the Soviets were coming any second, but there was no doubt in my military mind that the Communists were the enemy, and my job entailed being on alert and always ready—to fight them on the beaches, in the streets, anytime and anyplace, and beat them at all costs. Sometimes, though, it was very hard to stay enthusiastic—in my neighborhood at least.

David Cramer had been transferred out of the battalion by now; he'd joined the Army's first nuclear-equipped division, the low-yield Honest John–packing 101st Airborne. My new XO was a fine young black lieutenant named Herb Williams, and one Saturday afternoon the two of us stopped for lunch on our way back from a meeting at Fort MacArthur. Both in uniform, we sat down in a busy San Pedro restaurant. A half hour later, without so much as a glass of water being brought to our table, the headwaiter came over to tell me we might as well leave: they didn't serve "coloreds" there. I was ready to tear the place down. Herb himself was the one who stopped me, insisting it was no big deal, he was used to it. But at twenty-five years of age I was as surprised as I'd been when I was eight and carving Halloween pumpkins after school with my friend R. Lee Carrigan, and Gram had dashed out of the house and told me to "get that nigger off our front porch." At the time I didn't even know the meaning of the word; later I chalked it up to the fact that Gram was just an old southern lady with Civil War values. But it was 1956 now, not 1865; it was California, not the Deep South; and there was no excuse—except, maybe, that there were still two Americas, and to many people only one was worth defending. I guessed America's white civilian population, most of whom had waltzed through the Korean War painlessly by turning directly to page two of the newspaper, had also managed to bypass the words of Kipling (which spoke most loudly for the black soldiers who served as cannon fodder in all America's wars to keep the country free): *"Tommy ain't a bloomin' fool—you bet that Tommy sees!"*

C Battery continued to move from success to success. I'd weeded out most of the troublesome old air defenders; in the main the team ran itself now (from then on, my goal in any of my commands) with senior NCOs who weren't locked into the "that's the way we've always done it" mode, and younger NCOs and smart draftee troopers whose minds and eyes were open. When we had the annual firing battery tests at Camp Irwin, I basically went along for the ride; Herb Williams, Tony Escover (Radar), Warrant Officer Yoshio Morikawa (Maintenance), and my great old top, Master Sergeant Lee, ran the whole drill. We'd come a long way; the boys worked in perfect harmony with one another and their weapons systems, as, one by one, C Battery shot robot-controlled "Soviet intruder" drones out of the sky, and we came home named the best firing battery in the brigade. It was not insignificant that Colonel Theisen did not write or call to say "good job"; his leadership skills wouldn't have coaxed the most eager lemming into the sea.

With all the good in my unit, C Battery still had its share of losers. One of these was Private Russell, whom I caught one night trying to slip through the barbed-wire fence surrounding the battery. I was Duty Officer that evening and had just returned from my tennis-shoe-clad silent sneak-up on all the guards when I saw him in the motor pool with a blanket under his arm. "Where are you going, young soldier?" I asked.

"I'm going to the beach with my girl. We're going to watch the stars."

"Are you now?" I replied. "I don't think you have a pass. Do you have a pass, Russell?"

"No."

"Right. And what's that I see under your arm? Looks like that blanket is government property. Government property cannot be taken off post, can it, Russell?"

"No."

"Okay. So why don't you just march your sweet ass back to your barracks before you find yourself in more trouble?"

"You don't like me," he said.

The kid was absolutely right. I didn't like him at all, but it was only because I didn't like screwups. "You've got the potential to be a damn good soldier, Russell, if you'd just get off your ass and get that big chip off your shoulder."

"You think I have a chip on my shoulder?" he retorted. "Well, why don't you try and knock it off?"

"Might be just what you need."

"Take off that jacket."

He wanted us to be equals. Never one to let rank get in the way of a good lesson, I took off my jacket and fatigue cap and laid them on the hood of a parked jeep. I let Russell have the first swing; I blocked it and let fly four punches that sent the private reeling to the ground. "Now pick yourself up and go to bed," I told him. It was too dark to see the damage as he staggered to his feet and shagged ass to his billet. *A little NCO justice never hurt anyone*, I thought as I watched him go. More than once I'd had my clock cleaned by Jesse O. Giddens, my platoon sergeant in the tank company in Italy; as far as I was concerned, getting the smart-ass knocked out of you was part of growing up. So I didn't give the incident another thought as I cleaned my bleeding knuckles and hit the sack.

The next morning when we moved out for our daily run, Russell was not with his platoon. Suddenly the little incident of the night before took on awesome dimensions. NCO justice was one thing, but I was a captain and the kid's CO. In my mind's eye I saw the private standing with a bashed-up face in front of Colonel Theisen's desk, while the good Colonel rubbed his hands together with evil glee, and plotted the most horrible way to relieve me. I worried throughout the run.

As it turned out, the whole time I was sweating, Russell was just pulling his normal, rostered KP. From my first day with the unit, I'd organized George Clark to have a big stainless-steel pot of orange juice ready for the boys when they returned from their run. This morning when we got back, who should be ladling out the juice but my midnight foe, Private Russell—sporting two black eyes, a split lip, and a slightly battered nose. "Good morning, Russell," I said. "What happened to you?"

"Fell down, sir. Last night, in the motor pool."

"You okay?"

"Just fine, sir."

And that was it. Word never got to the Colonel, and Russell and I never spoke of it again.

The job of Duty Officer was rostered, and a week or so later when I was pulling it again, a young soldier with a strange, old man's face told me (with draftee directness) that I should learn to be more tolerant. I told him I'd think about it and dashed back to the Orderly Room to look up the word in the dictionary. Upon consideration, the boy was right, so the following week I practiced tolerance. But I wasn't very good at it, so I decided to give it up. Even so, it had been a good week, because during this broad-minded phase I decided to try to straighten out another wiseass draftee soldier, Gary Weinstein, from New York City.

Weinstein, who had a master's or a Ph.D. from some hotshot eastern university, hated the Army. His dress and manner bordered on insubordination from the moment he woke up until the moment he went to bed. His attitude was not uncommon among the draftee EM of the fifties; during its boom years, AD got all the brains the Army could commandeer, and guys like Weinstein often worked overtime to logically and articulately incite riot among their less-educated peers. In Weinstein's case I decided to use his quick tongue and brilliant mind to my advantage. DA was always sending down "we of the white hats" anti-Communist propaganda and other guidance to be served up to the troops; even though Weinstein was an eight-ball private in the radar section, I made him Troop Information NCO, responsible for getting the word out through weekly Troop Info lectures. It was the perfect job for him. He jazzed up the talks a bit, the other troopers loved listening to him, and almost before I knew it this sad-sack EM became the sharpest soldier, not just of C Battery, but of the entire 47th Brigade, winning the highest honor of Brigade Soldier of the Year. Weinstein was so proud of that one (and so was I) that he gave me an autographed photo of brigade CG Willis Perry presenting him with the award.

I'd been wearing my soldier suit again for almost nine months now. It had taken about three to get the battery into shape; since then I'd been bored and increasingly restless. I submitted numerous applications to go to the newly forming Special Forces, but was again and again rejected on the grounds that the unit did not require AD officers at this time. My protests—that I was not an AD officer—fell on deaf ears.

The establishment of Special Forces seemed to be the New Look's only concession to an Army growing increasingly automatic. Talk within the military (and without) was of push-button warfare, a concept that would make ground forces more or less redundant. I found the whole idea difficult to believe, much less accept (to begin with, an army with no reliance on the soldier could hardly call itself an army), and though I was as enthusiastic as the next guy for the "bigger bang for the buck" weapons systems under development in 1956, it seemed to me that, except in the event of all-out war with the Soviet Union, the new gear would be as appropriate as using a sledgehammer to swat at flies.

When I'd first arrived in Italy in 1946, I couldn't understand why the one-man guard box at our camp at Cormons was exceptionally thick-walled, solid concrete. But I'd gotten the picture pretty damn quick when one day I found myself sharing the thing with Jimmy Sparks, both of us shaking in our boots as sniper fire (which moments before had caught us in the open) zinged and thudded against the sides of the box. Only a couple of hundred yards from our tank gate, a hidden, Communist Yugoslav partisan was making his presence known. But no one could ever get at him; every time we tried, the Jug and his weapon would simply disappear.

It had been my first introduction to guerrilla warfare, and as time passed in Italy during those initial Cold War years, again and again I saw examples of insurgent war on the cheap. When they could get the explosives, the Jugs would mine the road; the first KIAs I ever saw were an American captain and his driver, both killed when their jeep hit a mine. (Strangely, at the time what had struck me even more than the dead men was the blanket of twenty-dollar MPCs that covered the ground all around them—the captain had been an 88th Division pay officer.) When the Jugs couldn't get the big stuff, they just tied piano wire across the road between two trees, at about jeep-windshield level. Then they'd go away, leaving the Americans to lop their own heads off when they came barreling through the invisible wire, windshields down, at forty or fifty miles per hour. Once, on patrol, someone on the lead vehicle had seen strands of piano wire stretched across the ground; immediately, the entire column stopped, and while we spent the next hour probing for mines, in my mind's eye I saw a little Jug laughing in the woods at how he, single-handedly, had held up a whole Yankee armored recon company.

Nuclear weapons, with Eisenhower's threat of massive retaliation if the Kremlin made a move, had not stopped war; they had only changed its face. Though Hiroshima and Nagasaki had marked the end of WW II–style unconditional victories (and the advent of Korea-style no-win conflicts), in the ten years since V-J Day there'd been dozens of decisive wars, not the least of which was the Chinese revolution under Mao, where from a tiny band of insurgents came the overthrow of a government set in granite. Guerrilla war, not push-button war, was the wave of the future—it could only flourish under the protection of the Bomb—and it was my kind of war, because it was the kind that a man, not a missile, had to fight to win.

I spent those restless months in the 77th studying everything I could on the subject of guerrilla warfare: the Colonies' Indian-style tactics in response to the French and then the British prior to and during America's Revolutionary War; the Filipino tactics after the Spanish-American conflict (which had young Lieutenant Douglas MacArthur inches from buying the farm when a Filipino guerrilla sniper shot his hat right off his head); the Soviet, French, American, and Yugoslav guerrilla activity during WW II; the British struggle in Malaya; and, most recently, the humiliating French defeat in Indochina. And I watched with particular interest the ongoing activities of a young Cuban stud named Castro, who was beginning to nickel and dime that tyrant Batista to death. *More power to him*, I thought.

In the meantime, life at C Battery went on uneventfully, until the morning one of my soldiers fell out on the beach with a collapsed lung. As the Colonel's phone ran hot with beachfront property owners complaining that their breakfasts had been disturbed yet again by that maniac (me), I put in my application to be relieved from active duty. Colonel Theisen now had his reason to can me, and through Milo Rowell, word came down in a big hurry that that was just what he intended to do. The rumor was I was to be transferred to Battalion Staff as S-2; to my mind, selling insurance was preferable to being the Intelligence officer in a AD battalion in Manhattan Beach, California, especially when the reassignment was, in fact, punishment for just doing my job.

Training had always been the bane of all the armed services. After WW II it went soft, well attested to by the horrific casualties in the early days of Korea. The American people were shocked: how could the government have allowed their sons to go off to war so ill-prepared? Those of us who'd been trained well and fought through those bleak days wondered the same thing; those who survived to become training madmen in Korea carried the same passion into their subsequent commands. There, we were thwarted before we'd hardly begun: with neither the means nor the blessings of the powers that be, apparently there was no room for training madmen in this peacetime Army.

Ike's budget cuts were the first obstacle toward maintaining a combat-ready Army ground force. Gasoline, live ammo, and adequate training facilities all cost money; Ike's austerity kick gave us barely enough dough to conduct morning PT. Then there was the draft, which brought into the Army not just uneducated kids from the wrong side of the tracks, but university graduates with minds of their own. Many were pampered punks for whom a drill sergeant had two choices: either spoon-feed them into acquiescence or ramrod them into submission. Most (good) sergeants chose the firm-but-fair latter course. The Army was never meant to be a democratic organization; on the battlefield there's no time to say "please" or to take a vote on who's going to knock out a machine gun. The fact is, a soldier's response must be automatic, and based in a philosophy about killing that simply cannot be taught in a classroom. "Kill or be killed" hands-on training, in the control of a seasoned, hard-assed NCO, can often mean the difference between life and death for a boy on the battlefield. Take the case of Willie Lump Lump, whose tragic story—well known among my men—went something like this:

After WW II, a boy named Willie Lump Lump enlisted in the Army. He went to Fort Benning to take his infantry training, sixteen weeks of sweat and tears and lots of punishment, to turn him into a hardened soldier. Along about the seventh week of training, a sergeant stood up in front of his class and said, "Gentlemen, I'm Sergeant Slasher, and today I'm going to introduce you to the bayonet. On guard!" With that, the sergeant went into the correct stance for holding the bayonet. "On the battlefield," he continued, "you will meet the enemy, and there will be times when you will need this bayonet to defeat the enemy. To KILL the enemy! Over the next weeks you'll be receiving a twenty-hour block of instruction on the bayonet, and I will be your principal instructor."

Willie Lump Lump went back to the barracks, deeply upset. *Man, that was so brutal out there today,* he thought. *The war is over. We're living in peace and tranquility, and still the Army is teaching us how to use these horrible weapons!* "Dear Mom," he wrote home. "Today the sergeant told me he's going to teach me how to use the bayonet to kill enemy soldiers on the battlefield."

Willie's mother was shocked. She got right on the phone: "Hello, Congressman DoGood? This is Mrs. Lump Lump. I want to tell you what's happening down at Fort Benning, Georgia. Here it is, 1949, and they're teaching my baby to kill with a bayonet. It's uncivilized! It's barbaric!"

The congressman immediately got on the horn. "Hello, General Playitright at the Pentagon? This is Congressman DoGood. I understand the Army is still giving bayonet training."

"Yes, we are."

"Do you think it's a good idea? I don't think it's a very good thing at all. It's even . . . somewhat uncivilized. I mean, really, how many times does a soldier need his bayonet?"

"Not very often, sir, it's true. Actually, I was just reviewing the Army Training Program myself, and I was thinking that the bayonet is a pretty obsolete weapon. I agree with you. I'll put out instructions that it's going to stop."

The next day, seven hundred miles away: "Gentlemen, I am Sergeant Slasher. This is your second class on bayonet training—" The sergeant was interrupted by a lieutenant walking purposefully toward him across the training field. "Stand easy, men."

"It's out," the lieutenant whispered.

"What!" said the sergeant.

"It's out," the lieutenant whispered again.

The sergeant nodded, his mouth wide open in disbelief. He returned to his class.

"Gentlemen, we'll have to break here. It looks as if bayonet training has been discontinued in the Army."

A year later, PFC Lump Lump, the model soldier, deployed to Korea with the 1st Battalion, 15th Regiment, 3d Infantry Division. He was standing on a frozen hill and the Chinese were coming at him—wave after wave after wave. Willie stood like a rock. Resolutely, he shot the enemy down. Suddenly he realized he was out of ammunition. He looked at his belt—not a round left. He saw a Chinaman rushing toward him. He remembered the first class on bayonet training. He reached down and pulled his bayonet out of his scabbard. Shaking and fumbling, he tried to fit it on the end of his weapon, but by that time the Chinese soldier was standing over him, with a bayonet of his own.

The Secretary of the Army signed his thousandth letter for the day: "Dear Mrs. Lump Lump: It is with deep regret that I must inform you that your son, PFC Willie Lump Lump, was killed in action 27 November 1950."

Heartbroken, Mrs. Lump Lump wrote to some friends of young Willie's in the company. "How?" she asked. "Why???" "Willie wasn't trained," they wrote back. "He didn't know how to use his bayonet." Now Mrs. Lump Lump was not only heartbroken, but outraged. She didn't even bother to call Congressman DoGood. She barged right into his office.

"Why?" she cried and screamed. "Why wasn't my son trained for war?"

The mythical Willie Lump Lump was my training aid. I used him in every unit I commanded, to explain two things to the troops: first, that the training they were about to receive was in their best interests, and second, that the civilian population didn't know diddley-squat about the realities of war. Because as much as any other factor, civilian interference was what was leading the post-Korea Army training program down the tubes.

A few months before my trooper fell out on the beach, there'd been an incident at the Parris Island Marine Corps training center. A drill sergeant named McKeon had gotten his seventy-four man platoon of recruits out of bed for a night march, in order, he said, to teach them discipline. The end result was six dead boots, swept down a fast-running creek on the island.

McKeon was court-martialed, and the entire military training system went on trial by the press. Heads rolled on Parris Island, as bleeding-heart civilians got on their soapboxes and called for an end, essentially, to any training that carried with it even the slightest risk of danger.

The military overreacted. When Parris Island's CG was transferred out of his command, a chill went down the spines of all the new-style, self-serving commanders I'd met in (and since) my second tour in Korea, who put their careers above their missions and their men. *But for the grace of God . . .* they thought, and gratefully accepted the new training safety regulations sent down from the top. It was a long, long way from Blue Devil Day in Gorizia, Italy, the one day each month when all units in the 88th Blue Devil Division were put through their paces. At one of these I'd been going through the bayonet training drill and managed to vertical butt-stroke my squad leader (who was dancing in front of me, daring me to get him) right in the chops with my M-1 rifle. My regimental commander, Colonel Ball, who'd strolled by just as the sergeant fell to the ground in a shower of blood and teeth, hadn't even flinched. "Good work, soldier," he'd said, speaking from the experience of three years of the toughest combat of WW II, in Africa, Sicily, and Italy. "Good training."

The only way to prepare men for combat is to train them in conditions as close to the real thing as possible. A CO has to be prepared to take his lumps in training. Soldiers cannot be trained in a classroom, then be thrown onto a battlefield and be expected to cope. In Fighter Company, I'd taken my share of wounded in our Company in the Attack demonstrations—guys hit by shrapnel from a shell landing a little too close in—but I'd been willing to take that risk, because I wanted those people to know what it was like to have a mortar round slam down in front of them and hear machine-gun slugs snap over their heads. The average 2 percent training casualties we had, to my mind, were a small premium for an insurance policy that could cover a whole unit when the real shooting started.

The McKeon case was just a terrible tragedy. The sergeant was charged with six counts of involuntary manslaughter, oppression of recruits, and drinking on duty. With the help of powerful testimony from the greatest Marine of them all, Lieutenant General Lewis B. "Chesty" Puller, McKeon was eventually acquitted of the manslaughter and oppression of recruits charges,* but the verdict did not calm the fluttering hearts of Colonel Theisen and his ilk, and peacetime Army training continued its downhill spiral, the horrible consequence of which would not be seen for another decade. (As just one company commander in the next war would say, "We got kids in combat who believed that people were just shooting blanks at them. They really believed they couldn't die out there.")

The 47th Brigade XO, Colonel William Shanahan, persuaded me not to quit the Army over Colonel Theisen. He told me a new unit, the 108th Arty Group, had recently been formed to control the four Nike-Ajax Missile Battalions being deployed around Los Angeles; if I wanted a new job, he said, he could organize me to be Group Logistics Officer. I jumped at the offer before it was halfway out of the Colonel's mouth.

My primary mission in the new assignment was to coordinate all missile-site construction with the Army's Los Angeles–based District Engineers. I also handled special logistic work, mostly written studies on everything from relocation of established facilities to reports on moisture content in missile storage areas (and what corrective action might be taken). Based at Fort MacArthur, I was most fortunate to have as a boss Major Edward McKinnon, an old soldier and a damn good man. Major Mac was a joy to work for; he played the role of teacher in the early days of my first staff job, patiently rewriting my papers (with me by his side) until I got the hang of it. Senior Clerk Master Sergeant James Cook saved my ass on more than one occasion, too, as he helped me negotiate the maze of jargon that characterized all Army correspondence. As well, because the job required considerable traveling, I was authorized both an Army sedan and a driver/logistics clerk of my choice.

The first time I saw Private Tom Martin he was mowing the lawn in front of Group HQ. Without a doubt, he was the sloppiest American soldier I'd ever seen in my Army career. His fatigue cap was kind of hanging off the back of his head. His fatigue uniform was so wrinkled that there was no doubt in my military mind that he slept in it. His boots weren't shined, his trousers weren't bloused, his hair badly needed a cut, and big clumps of stubble darkened his extraordinarily poorly shaved face. The term "sad sack" took on new meaning for me.

I went over to him to deliver a little on-the-spot correction. To my great surprise, he obligingly got himself together, and as we talked I realized this sad sack was one very smart guy. A new replacement trained in high speed

* McKeon *was* found guilty of negligent homicide and drinking. He received a harsh sentence, most of which was commuted by the Secretary of the Navy a few months after the trial.

telegraph, Martin was still awaiting assignment; when he said he could drive, type, and had thirteen years of Jesuit schooling, that was all I needed to know. I went to Captain Johnson, the Group HQ Battery commander, to organize the private as my clerk/assistant.

Johnson thought I was crazy. "Have you seen him? He's a disgrace to the uniform!" The Captain went on to tell me that Tom was a smart-ass college draftee whom nobody wanted, and whom, he felt sure, he'd end up kicking out of the Army. I insisted, saying that I thought the boy had a lot of potential, and I'd really like the challenge of shaping him up. Finally, with great reluctance, Johnson assigned Tom to Group S-4.

Tom got to work on time the first day, but that was about all that could be said in his favor. He hadn't shined his shoes—he'd painted them. His brass was positively green. His khaki uniform looked even worse than his baggy fatigues, and he was wearing white socks. I knew in an instant that the guy wasn't going to change, and that the hardest part of my job would be just keeping him out of Captain Johnson's sight.

So I became Tom's protector, and at the same time, he became mine. I taught him how to shine his brass, badgered him to keep his uniform neat and tidy, and made sure he and Johnson's paths never crossed. In return, he wrote the staff studies. Each evening we'd come back from our little sojourns in the field and talk through the problem; I'd provide the guidance from a military standpoint, and Tom would take my views and work them into a knockout of a paper. From the first one we submitted, the kudos kept on coming.

With Tom at the wheel of our Army sedan, the two of us drove around Los Angeles virtually every day doing our logistics thing. It was good duty; we usually finished the work by noon, and because my secondary, self-assigned mission was to keep Tom as far from HQ and Captain Johnson as possible, I felt totally justified in taking the afternoons off and not bringing him home until dark. The job was great for Tom, too; after all those years in the seminary (he'd quit just a couple weeks before he was to take the priestly plunge), now he was like a kid playing hooky from school. He was brilliant at playing the horses—the Jesuits had sharpened his keen, mathematical mind to a razor's edge—and we spent as much time at Hollywood Park as we did at our job. In the line of duty we'd often go out for lunch, too, and took great pleasure in destroying the complacency of Southern California suburbia. One afternoon, for example, we were sitting at an outdoor restaurant near Hollywood. The waiter was hovering anxiously nearby (probably because we were in uniform and carrying rolled-up blueprints and building plans), so in a low voice, just loud enough for his benefit, I said, "You know, Tom, I really think that real estate across the street would be perfect for a missile site." The "real estate" in question was like Saks Fifth Avenue.

Tom immediately picked up his cue. "I've just been thinking the same thing, sir. And we could put the acquisition radar on that little hill over there . . . it wouldn't be too tough to move Griffith Observatory, would it, sir?"

"No sweat," I replied, "this is military priority! We're talking about the defense of the nation!"

The waiter's eyes bulged out of his head; Tom and I often wondered how far or how fast the land prices in that neighborhood came tumbling down after the whisper got going that the military was about to condemn it all and take it over.

Another day, we'd just picked up some stuff downtown at the L.A. District Engineers and decided to go to the Hilton for lunch. As we walked into the lobby, Tom suddenly stopped and dramatically unrolled a blueprint he was carrying. Now *I* was the one to pick up the cue. I looked from the blueprint to the hotel lobby. "Yes, I think this will be fine. We'll just cordon off this area here . . . shut down all the elevators, except this one here. Of course, we'll need security on top."

Meanwhile, Tom had whipped out his pad and was taking notes. The assistant manager came bustling up.

"May I help you gentlemen?"

He'd caught me off guard. I put on my most official voice. "Haven't you been informed?"

"No, sir, I haven't."

"Well, I don't have the security clearance to tell you myself, but you will be informed. The Chief of Staff of the Army should be ringing any minute to tell you who'll be coming." (I tried to make the mysterious VIP sound like God.) The assistant manager hurried off; just before he got out of earshot I turned back to Tom: "We'll have to remove all that glass, too, in case someone decides to bomb the joint." With that, we went into the dining room, and within a few minutes, the hotel manager came up to the table.

"I understand you've been looking over the hotel. May I ask for what reason?"

By this time, both Tom and I realized we'd been guilty of overacting. We'd surreptitiously taken off our name tags the second we sat down, to prevent our little joke from blowing up in our faces; still, we were in too deep now not to play the drama out. I told the manager how sorry I was for the slipup in communications, that I was not authorized to tell him why we were there, but the minute we got back to headquarters we'd advise the General, who would, of course, call him. The manager was really thrown as he walked away from the table; I felt kind of bad, but there wasn't anything I could do. Finally we finished our meal and went to pay the bill. "Oh, no, sir!" the cashier said, whisking away the check. "The manager said it's on the house—compliments of the Hilton." And who said there's no such thing as a free lunch?

On one of the rare days I was working at my desk, a good-looking E-4 walked into the office. At first I didn't recognize him; all I saw was a snazzy starched uniform, perfectly polished brass and shoes, a rigid attention, and a brilliantly executed salute. Then I noticed the 77th's Battalion crests on his epaulets. It was ex-Private Russell, whom I'd decked in the 77th's motor pool. He was at Fort Mac Separation Center being discharged; he come in to say good-bye, and to thank me for kicking his ass. "I deserved it," he said, "and I kind of figured if you were willing to risk your career to make a soldier out of me, maybe I should give it a try. But you know something, Captain?" he continued. "I could have nailed you. My uncle is Senator Richard Russell, and if he'd heard about that fight . . ."

And with that, the nephew of the chairman of the all-powerful Senate Armed Services Committee tossed me another great salute and marched out in style. And as everyone in the office commented on the fine-looking trooper and asked who he was, I quietly quaked in my boots and told them he was "just one of my boys . . . a fine Georgia boy."

Russell's visit really moved me. But for a while afterward, I wondered whether I'd have let him get on a first-name basis with my fists if I'd known who he was. Chances were, the answer was yes, for two reasons: first, because you always go with what you know (and I knew the kid needed a little knuckle drill), and second, because as a rule I lived and worked by gut feeling. In my gut I knew Russell was a good man, just as gut feeling told me Tom Martin was a good man. If you went out on a limb for guys like that, they'd come through for you, too—as Tom did, one Saturday morning a couple of weeks later, when I overslept after a big poker game with some Woodbury College buddies. A big briefing had been planned for brigade CG Perry and his staff, and at H minus ten, I (the briefer) was still in bed. I jumped up, shaved in ten seconds flat, and raced down to Fort Mac at a hundred miles an hour. I got there with about a minute to spare, only to find the charts already set up and Tom Martin standing by—shined, starched, and spruced up like a perfect TRUST trooper—prepared, if necessary, to give the briefing himself. As it turned out, the General was delayed so I had a chance to wash the blood off my face, but the point was, I'd never seen old sad-sack Tom voluntarily get himself together before, but when I needed him most he was there, looking like Soldier of the Month.

My roommate during this period was General Perry's aide, Bill Cowart. Bill was a stud of an officer—a lawyer from Florida who'd commanded a missile battery in the 933d before moving up to Brigade. We'd become friends when I was in the 77th; when I moved up to Fort Mac we got an apartment together. As two of the few single officers around, our nights were as busy as our days; it was an exciting time, and whoever scored first would hang a "Do Not Disturb" sign (in the form of a necktie) on the front doorknob, so the other knew to find himself another place to sleep for the night. Living with the General's aide had lots of benefits, not the least of which was getting the hot skinny on virtually anything, often before it happened. Bill had been instrumental in getting Shanahan to persuade me to stay in the service; now he told me he'd heard, because of the good work I was doing, I could well be scooped up and promoted to Brigade as a staff officer in S-3. I got Major McKinnon to block that move; thanks to Tom I was thinking and writing more clearly and logically every day, but I was afraid I'd sink without him around to put those words on the page.

Then, good Major Mac fell victim to the Reductions in Force (RIF) program, just one of thousands upon thousands of casualties in Ike's continuing savage attack on the Army's ground strength. The RIF program was another great tragedy of the New Look: it weakened the fiber of the Army by destroying not only its might but its morale. No Reserve officer on active duty with less than eighteen years' active service *to the day* was safe: scores of men at Fort Mac, well into their seventeenth year, left work on Friday and on Monday reported to their units only to find they'd been canned. The chop always came without warning, or even apparent thought—a bad ER from a decade ago, no college degree, a letter of reprimand, or the tiniest recorded indiscretion carried more weight than Purple Hearts or valor awards won in the service of the country. Still, a man wasn't forced to quit if he were RIFed. But if he wanted to stay in, he had to take whatever sharp, equally arbitrary demotion the Army selected. Most who stayed were (understandably) bitter. In the 77th, I'd had a first sergeant who had been a lieutenant colonel, and he simply could not adjust. Finally I'd eased him out to a plush job at Fort Mac, and replaced him with proud, longtime NCO Master Sergeant Lee.

The most pathetic case of all was that of Fort Mac's deputy post commander. This bird colonel, with enough valor decorations and Purple Hearts from two wars as an infantry commander to run from his belly button to his epaulet, was RIFed. He'd had about seventeen and a half years' active service and another decade in the Guard. When I heard about it I didn't give it much thought (except that it seemed funny they'd RIF a full colonel) until I walked through the PX and saw him—now a staff sergeant—stocking goodies on the shelves. I said hello, and couldn't stop myself from referring to him as "sir"; he could barely look me in the eyes. He had the saddest expression I'd ever seen on a man's face. It was as if his self-esteem and dignity had been stomped to dust on the PX floor. *What a load of crap*, I thought as I walked away, *about the Army taking care of its own.*

As bad as RIF was for the guys getting axed, some of its worst casualties were in outstanding young officers like Bill Cowart. The Army was no longer a safe harbor. Job security was a thing of the past, and many, many good men, who might otherwise have made a career of the military, saw the writing on the wall and got out. And it wasn't just the young Regular officers shagging ass for the door. A lot were enlisted and draftee studs with high IQs who'd been trained, at enormous expense to the government, to operate and maintain the new high-tech military equipment. Instead of settling for an uncertain career in the Army, these men eagerly snapped up the bait of civilian defense contractors, who offered ten times the Army salary for the same skills and frequently the same jobs. The losses were probably even more serious in the NCO corps, where thousands of WW II and Korea vets, tough old squad leaders and platoon sergeants with five to fifteen years' service, were tossed out of the Army during the RIF simply for not meeting the Army's arbitrary IQ scores. How much money was actually saved through the RIF program would be hard to estimate, but if you stopped to consider the quality lost and the damage done to the Army as an institution, it probably wasn't much. For myself, I considered every day I remained a captain another day under Damocles' sword, especially after the ER Colonel Theisen rendered on me when I left C Battery. If that wasn't RIF material, I didn't know what was. It was so hot, in fact, that it burst into flames the minute it hit the office of Brigade Personnel. Luckily I had a friend there who contained the damage, but he couldn't do anything to save that poor, charred ER. So it never found its way into my DA records, and I was safe, at least for a while.

It was more likely General Cleland's influence than anything else that kept me from being RIFed. The only preventive measure I took (besides alerting the volunteer "fireman" at Brigade) was to enroll in night school to finish my Associate of Arts degree. With Tom around to help write my term papers, it was pretty much a breeze, and the extra-long days were well worth the effort if they'd keep me from being chucked out of the Army. Before I had a chance to become too sure of myself, though, a kick came in the form of Army Chief of Staff General Maxwell D. Taylor. At a meeting of the L.A. Association of the U.S. Army, the General spoke passionately about the necessity for higher education among the officer corps; I'd already heard the drill about getting a master's, but now Taylor added his desire that all of us achieve fluency in not one but two other languages. And I had enough trouble with English.

The New Look had brought with it not only a new kind of weaponry, but a new kind of warrior as well. Actually, the new breed was kind of a warrior-diplomat; as bloodless ballistics seemed to be phasing out the role of fighters on future battlegrounds,*the emphasis increased on the diplomatic side of soldiering. The competition was fierce: you either learned to dance and prance and speak Chinese, or you sat back and waited for your RIF notice in the mail. Now it was not *what* you said or did that counted, but *how*, and old soldiers, for whom diplomacy and tact were harder to master than jumping out of a plane or *banzai*ing a hill, were left shaking their heads, like puzzled commuters staring at the schedule and wondering how they got on the wrong bus.

The scenery was just so *different*. The most familiar, the most steeped in history, the most inspiring landmarks were, one by one, being razed to the ground. First to go were the distinctly-Army brown shoes. In the name of cost efficiency, the New Look policy was that black shoes would be worn by all services. Next on the hit list was the square-frame belt buckle. I found this one kind of strange—unlike the new "standard-to-all-services" brass buckle, the old one could not only hold up your trousers but also open a beer faster than a conventional bottle opener. It was hard to believe that Old Army Ike would sanction our giving up such a versatile item for a junky thirty-nine-cent single-function variety, but he did, again in the name of cost efficiency. Funnily, the belt buckles often separated the old warriors from the new diplomats: one glance around a room to see who was wearing what (because a lot of us refused to comply) was generally enough to pinpoint which Army a guy was coming from. It might not have seemed like much; in the end what difference did black shoes or brass buckles really make? But the fact was, it made a lot of difference. An institution was an institution, and for the old guys who balked at the New Look, it wasn't a simple story of resisting change. Instead, it was an attempt to stave the flow of blood, which was pumping hideously out of an increasingly ashen Army's veins.

But then, suddenly, it was too late, even for a tourniquet: Chief of Staff Taylor disbanded all the Old Army regiments, with all their history and tradition, to make way for New Look "battlegroups," each composed of five rifle companies. This battalionless, five-sided system, designed for the nuclear battlefield, was fittingly called the Pentomic Army, and was

* In fiscal 1954, the missile program accounted for $500 million of the defense budget while conventional hardware got $3.7 billion; by fiscal 1959, we'd see a 180-degree swing: missiles getting $3.4 billion and conventional equipment $600 million.[5]

virtually the first such major reorganization of forces since Valley Forge. It had its own jazzy vocabulary—an outpost line was now a combat outpost line (COPL), the front line was now the forward edge of the battle area (FEBA)—but the new lingo was more a public-relations exercise than anything else: after all, a killing ground by any other name is still a killing ground. Within five years the Pentomic concept would prove completely unworkable and the Army would furtively reorganize once again, but the damage done in the meantime was —in a word—irreparable.

One more of the last vestiges of the Old Army disappeared when we traded in our familiar OD uniforms for new forest-green ones. Modeled before Congress by none other than Captain Joe Love, that fine soldier I'd met in Korea when we relieved his unit at the Gap, the new gear was a close copy of the German Wehrmacht uniform of WW II, from the Prussian-style billed service cap to the heels of the coal-black shoes.

The German look didn't bother me much; no question but the Germans were brilliant in all things military (even if they didn't win many wars), and in the years following WW II all kinds of German designs went on permanent loan to the U.S. Army. The M-60 machine gun bore a striking resemblance, in function, to the German MG 34; our self-propelled anti-tank weapon (SPAT) was much like the famed Kraut 88-mm except that ours, like the new belt buckle, was on the cheap, tinny side (and was down with maintenance problems most of the time). The missile program was in the hands of former Nazi scientists who'd surrendered to the Americans at war's end, led by Wernher von Braun, developer of the "space-age" ballistic V-2. Somebody up there was definitely fascinated with the German war machine; it seemed to me we copied virtually everything the Germans had to offer except their leadership and discipline techniques. We would have done well to examine this aspect of German might, too, as in fact, it accounted for much of their military strength. Instead, the Army dealt a thoughtless blow to the very *foundation* of leadership by instituting yet another New Look policy: name tags, to be sewed onto all fatigues, and personalized badges (the name in white, on black plastic, like the ones Tom and I'd deep-sixed at the Hilton), to be pinned on all dress uniforms.

The philosophy behind those name tags was as transparent as cellophane, and about as flimsy. To me, their advent was a sure sign that U.S. Army leadership was on a downhill slide. Napoleon was said to have been able to recall fifty thousand of his soldiers by name; in the New Army, a CO didn't even have to learn five. Yet *know your men* was a crucial principle of leadership, and that meant not just their names, but where they were from, what they thought, what made them tick. Name tags were all very well for the new-style officer who stayed in a peacetime command only long enough to jockey his way into a better, career-furthering slot: why bother memorizing names, went his thinking, he'd never use again? But for the trooper, personalized uniforms were just another gimmicky example of an increasingly impersonal, almost corporate Army—one difficult to love, let alone have the allegiance to that would serve him and the country well in the event of war.

In July I replaced Tom's nemesis, Captain Johnson, as the 108th Arty Group's HQ Battery CO. It was good-bye staff work, hello, command—and I was thrilled. HQ Battery was responsible for the administration of the Brigade-Group Air Section, motor pool, acquisition radars, and the AAOC itself; I was the only officer in a command of more than four hundred men, which necessitated two things pronto: one, a good first sergeant; the other, a couple of sharp assistants to help with the stacks of paperwork that came with the job.

I was dumbfounded when I couldn't find one decent master sergeant to be topkick. None of them wanted it. Most were longtime AD men who'd found their niche in jobs such as Gym or Reenlistment NCO; they were happy as hell with their short hours and minimal responsibility. Finally I gave up the search and appointed an enthusiastic SFC named McRae; as I'd done with Hudson, Allison, and Smith in the 223d, I let McRae wear the stripes, and the guy turned out just fine.

I picked the eyes out of the new replacements to get my own staff together: Richard Caughey from Notre Dame, Ron Gerrard from San Diego State, and Ph.D. Joe Perez from NYU were the core of my brain trust, all of whom troubleshot for the battery and the boys, and (since Harbor College was ongoing) occasionally gave polish to my rough-as-a-cob term papers. Gerrard became a particularly good friend; he shared the same mania I had for running, and early on we got into the habit of doing six to ten miles every morning.

When the 77th was inactivated, I grabbed Gary Weinstein to be HQ Battery's Troop Information NCO, and my dear friend "Cordon Bleu" George Clark to take charge of the mess. George was also the battery barber, a weird combination of talents I chose to ignore, especially when I started hearing he had a habit of dropping hot cigar ashes onto the heads of his barbershop customers, then brushing the clients' hair off his uniform while dishing out chow. Tom Martin came over to the outfit, too, and continued a practice he'd initiated in the S-4 shop—breaking the bank of a local bookie, with the help of superb contacts he'd developed in the racing world as well as his own horse-race enthusiasts' cartel. Tom's prerace selection committee meetings were always held in my office; I often had an inner chuckle thinking how Captain Johnson would have reacted to the knowledge that every week his most hated sad sack was holding court at his very own old desk.

The men I inherited with the unit were exceptional. I got to meet them all right away, through my policy of paying every soldier myself. One poor troop was getting only nine dollars a month; when I asked him why, he said he was on Statement of Charges: he'd been a driver in D Battery, 77th, when a truck he'd parked rolled down a hill and caused four grand's worth of damage to it and other vehicles in the motor pool. The soldier was found responsible; now it looked as if he'd be paying off the bill for the rest of his life through his meager Army salary. The whole thing didn't seem too fair to me. I immediately put my brain trust to work to find a loophole. They did, and not only did the guy never have to fork out another cent, but we also managed to get back all the dough he'd paid in to date. Meanwhile, my stock went up 1,000 percent with the rest of the men of HQ Battery; this one act let them know that I was on their side.

When I saw how the unit operated (everyone had a fixed job, generally shift work and not too much bitching and moaning going on), I concluded these guys didn't need a shake-up as the boys in the 77th had. Instead, I decided on an informal command style: no formations, no police call, no inspections. I was studying sociology at school, so I looked at it all as an experiment of sorts. I simply put out the word that I expected the guys to keep themselves and the barracks looking good, that each man was to police up our area of the post as he went through the day (meaning, pick up cigarette butts, candy wrappers, etc.), attend mandatory training, and get to work on time. The experiment proved to be a great success—from day one there were few problems—which is probably why I was compelled to do some ass chewing (a rare opportunity these days) the morning, early in my tenure, that I walked out of an HQ Group building while Jerry Lewis was shooting a scene for his movie *The Sad Sack*.

When I stopped to watch, I noticed a couple of troopers (not mine) at the edge of the crowd. Both were leaning on their M-1 rifles as if the things were goddamned canes—hands over the barrels, the ultimate of no-nos in my book. "Get your hands off the muzzles of those weapons," I snapped, as I moseyed up behind them. Then I walked on, and went back to watching the filming. A few minutes later I glanced over, only to find that the two troopers had not moved their hands one inch. Such blatant insubordination was mind-boggling to me. I rushed over and chewed their asses into hamburger, only winding up the tirade when it became clear they weren't even listening.

"What company are you from?" I demanded.

"Paramount," one replied.

"So fuck you, Jack," said the other.

There wasn't much more I could say. I snuck away, only then noting the long hair each kid wore, which alone should have told me they were movie extras.

Captain Johnson had left me with one unresolved problem: an RA corporal by the name of Jack Gallagher, who, at the time I took over the battery, was residing in L.A. County Jail on the charge of drunk driving. Under Army regulations, a soldier in a civilian jail was one well on his way to being booted out of the service; in Johnson's opinion, Gallagher's demise as a serving member of the U.S. Army could not come one day too soon. "A big boozer and an even bigger troublemaker," he explained, and recommended I let the corporal rot in the slammer until Army justice took its course.

As soon as I got my new command squared away, I paid a visit to the wayward noncom. My first impression was that Jack Gallagher was a real soldier. Tall, thin, a few years older than I, Jack had fought with the 1st Ranger Battalion in WW II. That fact alone told me virtually everything I needed to know; since most Rangers were cut from the same bolt of cloth, it was only natural that in a peacetime setting any of them would have trouble toeing the Army line.

Gallagher, who'd gone on to serve with distinction in Korea, reminded me of my Wolfhound friend George Creamer, another fine soldier who was stationed at Fort Mac. George's job was recruitment, and to look at him was to look at a walking Army recruitment poster—paratrooper/Ranger, Korea battlefield commission, a high-stepping, highly decorated, good-looking, hard-fighting stud. But he was always in trouble. Every time he went into a bar, he'd get into a fight. George also had a glass jaw, which was unfortunate for someone with a penchant for duking it out, and most of the time I knew him at Fort Mac it was broken. Sometimes I'd find him sitting at the bar of the Officers' Club, hungry as hell, bitching and moaning through his wired-up jaw that all he could eat was soup; a few martinis later, he'd be trying to push crackers through his teeth. The guy was an animal. And he didn't give a damn that he didn't fit into the stateside scene. He'd just shrug and say through his wireworks that what the peacetime Army needed was a deep freeze to put the fighters in. "Just leave 'em there," he'd say, "till you've got a war. Then thaw 'em out and let them go win it." And he was right. George spoke for all the warriors who couldn't make it in the peacetime Army. Most were just too abrasive and outspoken; too often, they said exactly what they thought, and lived by the only law that counted to them: the one forged on the battlefield, where what was true and what was false—what was real and what was not—was as clear as a burst of Willie Peter in a midnight's starless sky.

And that's the kind of guy Corporal Gallagher was. He wanted to stay in the Army, but regulations or no regulations, he simply could not handle anything that didn't jibe with his own code of honor and justice. He made no excuses for his brushes with authority; he just explained them away. "You know the movie *From Here to Eternity?*" he asked me. "I went to see it, and got so excited I went right down to re-up, thinking I'd be getting back into the Old Army. But you know what I found? Pink curtains, black shoes, and no bugler." It didn't take much for me to see that Jack Gallagher was my kind of soldier, and when I found out he shared an 11 November birthday with me and George Patton, there wasn't a doubt in my mind.

I went to the judge who'd heard his case and worked out a deal to halve the sentence. Then I went back to the battery and organized the paperwork to give Jack "leave" for the duration of his time in the hoosegow. Within two weeks he was back at Fort Mac, performing just like the hard-assed, good man I knew he'd be—and he kept his promise never to drink and drive again.

Alcoholism was a common problem, especially among long-term Regulars. Booze was cheap and easy to get, and with all the social activities of the peacetime Army—"happy hours," officer and NCO parties—it was virtually an accepted thing. In the military, drinking fell into the same category as pussy: the more you could put away, the more macho you were among your buddies. The only problem was that the line between being a stud and an alcoholic was a fine one, and once crossed was really hard to reverse. We'd had a brilliant clerk in S-4 who bought scores of half-pint bottles of vodka every payday. Then he'd hide them throughout the Administration Building—in air-conditioning vents, in the water cabinets of toilets, in file drawers. He even had one hanging from a string inside a water-filled fire extinguisher. He'd be sloshed to the gills till his pay ran out; then he'd start in on this secret cache. Unfortunately, unlike old Supply Sergeant Allison in the 77th, this senior Specialist was totally ineffective when he was drinking. Major Mac, being the good man that he was, hadn't wanted to bust him (the guy was close to retirement), so he assigned me the additional duty of "vodka patrol": the only way we knew to get this guy dried out was for me to ferret out all his little bottles before he had a chance to get to them.

Major Mac himself was replaced by an alkie, a mean little man who did nothing all day but drink and stare out the window. One morning I'd walked by his office and he was drinking out of a Brasso can. I'd seen guys, if they were really hard up, drinking after-shave lotion, but Brasso? A few days later (when he was out) I snuck a whiff of the can: it was good old Kentucky bourbon, incognito. I guessed the guy's logic was that sipping hooch out of a Brasso can was better than buying a decent flask, an act that to him might have been just too close to admitting he had a problem.

In HQ Battery my favorite drinkers were James O. Johnson and Motor-Pool Sergeant "McNasty" McKown. Johnson had also been with me in the 77th; now, according to Jack Gallagher, he was never without a bottle of cheap wine and a Bermuda onion in his lunch bag. When he was broke he'd hock his wife's toaster (and anything else that wasn't nailed down), and if those proceeds didn't last till the next payday, he'd just sidle up to me with a big smile and say, "Does the Captain want his bee-yootiful Chevy convertible polished? Sure does look like it could use a good shine." Twenty dollars and one sparkling-clean car later, Johnson's smile was even broader, and it was watch out, Miss Sweet Lucy.

Master Sergeant McKown ran the best damn motor pool I'd ever seen. We had about three hundred vehicles; he kept them up, running, and looking good, and the Brigade-Group Best Motor Pool award was in HQ Battery's hands more often than in any other unit. The only problem was come payday Mac himself was up and running—and non compos mentis— until his dough ran out. After a couple of months' observation I decided his problem was not booze, but money, so every payday I gave him a couple of back-to-back three-day passes. He'd drink himself blind, spend all his cash, and when he was broke he'd come back, dry out, and run that motor pool like no one else could.

The living was easy that first summertime with HQ Battery (all told, I spent twenty months there) until the last days of August 1957, when the realities of the Cold War chilled the Southern California night air. In quick succession the Soviets announced the first successful launching of an ICBM (the U.S. Contender, the Air Force's Atlas, had yet to take to the skies), and then, only weeks later, the first-ever space satellite was orbiting the earth in the form of Russia's Sputnik. We had indeed been caught with our New Look pants down.

A-bomb rattling had been going on for more than a decade. The four years the U.S. had had as the world's only atomic power had been the best for brandishing the nuclear sword; as early as 1946, when I was a little kid in Italy, word once filtered down to the troops that Truman was going to drop a "superbomb" on Yugoslavia over an incident involving an American plane shot down while overflying Communist Jug airspace. And even after the Russians developed their own A-bomb in 1949, and their H-bomb in 1953 (nine months after the U.S.), we'd still been able to use the Bomb to great effect, or so it seemed, to coerce the Communist Chinese to the

Panmunjom bargaining table in Korea, to dampen Mao's enthusiasm for the islands of Quemoy and Matsu in 1954 (and would, again, in 1958), and generally to keep the Kremlin itself at bay with warnings of "massive retaliation" with high-yield nuclear weapons already developed in America (like the 60-megaton bomb, "the meanest and dirtiest in the arsenal . . . a vengeance weapon against Russia's cities if the Kremlin ever struck at U.S. cities first," announced by Livermore Laboratory just a month before the Soviets' triumphant ICBM launch).[6] At the time it sounded ominous enough, but the Reds had been playing their atomic cards close to their chests. The realities of "push-button" warfare were now brought home through the Russian breakthrough in the means of delivering the weapons, and our threatening claims appeared about as credible as the work of the House Un-American Activities Committee. To make matters worse, only three days after Sputnik a Pentagon study revealed publicly that the Nike-Ajax short-range (antiaircraft, antimissile) missile, despite the billions of dollars spent on the crash program, was ineffective, with a jet-aircraft and rocket kill rate of between 30 and 50 percent.[7] Heretofore the public had been told the system was close to 100 percent effective.

There was a lot of hysteria. Los Angeles Air Defense went on full alert, and HQ Battery was faced with the requirement of organizing a special supply scheme for the acquisition radars. We had to be fully operational twenty-four hours a day—not one system could be down lest the Kremlin decide to go for broke—and the routine requisitions setup was simply not designed for emergency resupply. We called our new section Bluestreak, and in the capable hands of now-Staff Sergeant Jack Gallagher, not once in the rest of my time with the unit were we caught short on spare parts or equipment. Bluestreak got the highest priority, complete with jet airplanes and special couriers. It reached the point that a replacement part was there before anyone, save Jack, even knew we needed it. As HQ Battery CO, I was supposed to sign all the requisition forms, but it quickly proved to be an impossible requirement: they sometimes ran to a couple of hundred a day, and with elements of the battery spread over hundreds of coastal miles, often I'd be an hour's drive from HQ when a request had to go. I got around the problem by changing my signature to one of big block letters that could be forged by Gallagher and First Sergeant McRae (I'd learned as a young lieutenant that if you can't trust your NCOs you're dead), and I never worried about it again.

As a soldier, the thing that got to me most during the early post-Sputnik days was that I knew Los Angeles could not be defended by AD. Those very expensive, super-duper radar systems that could spot enemy aircraft three hundred miles away could not detect a target over the ocean three hundred *feet* away in war games with the Navy. The planes got through simply by flying on the deck (below the radar's effective range) or through heavy ground clutter, and succeeded in bombing the shit out of the California coastline (theoretically) every time. It seemed so obvious that money was being spent on the wrong things or, at least, on things that were not worth the money being spent, but those of us at the user level were like wrinkled old carpenters who knew the futility of arguing with whiz-kid architects: "I have a degree," the architect would say, "I've studied these matters for five years. Just keep your mouth shut and drive in the nails." *Yes, sir*, we'd think, and five years later stand aside and watch as the multibillion dollar Air Defense house came tumbling down.

As a rule, the judgment of those on the ground was respected less and less in the post-Korea years. Centralization of command, which had characterized the trench war of '52–'53, was alive and growing stronger every day. And it wasn't just know-nothing commanders making the decisions (which would have been bad enough); now it was a combination of computers and peacetime procedures that ignored the human variables: initiative, potential, and personal growth of an individual soldier. In the 77th, I'd applied to go to an advanced Nike missile course, only to have my request denied on the basis of my "impulsive and immature" nature. These attributes had been ascribed to me in Colonel Young's ER back in the 223d; the computer that used the ER to weed me out of the course couldn't stop to think that I might have grown somehow in the *five years* since I'd told the Colonel he couldn't run a Boy Scout troop. Apparently, no human being thought to do so either.

"Time in grade" was another such nonthinking, computerized measure of worth. The concept (that a man, from the lowliest private to a lieutenant general, could not be promoted until he'd spent a certain number of months or years at his present rank) had been around for a while, but never before had it been so rigidly enforced. What it meant, down the chain of command where it counted, was that a company commander could no longer award an eager, clean-sleeved trooper even the tiniest morale booster of his first stripe. I had two great privates in the battery who'd volunteered to paint the barracks at night, during their off-duty hours. They did such a great job that I promoted them both to PFC. Within days the computers at Personnel spat out that it was no go—the kids had four months to play private. I ignored the guidance, paid the boys the salary difference out of my own pocket, and let them keep their well-earned stripes.

When my top, McRae, officially made master sergeant (E-7, by Army shorthand), it was about the same time the NCO computerized "super-grades" of E-8 (first sergeant) and E-9 (sergeant major) came out. With the attendant rise in an E-8's pay and prestige, suddenly every fat-assed master sergeant in town came clamoring to the door begging to be my topkick. When I told them to get stuffed—after all, where were they when the job was just eighteen hours a day, six days a week?—a number of them went over my head to the Group CO, Colonel Charles A. Jenkins, to cry that not only was I hurting their chances for promotion, but McRae didn't even have the *time in grade* to sit in the E-8 chair. Luckily, Jenkins was a real soldier, a well-decorated, former field artilleryman who didn't give a hoot about time in grade (or a supergrade slot gone a-wasting). He'd brought me to HQ Battery in the first place; now he backed me all the way, and McRae stayed right where he was. That is, besides the day I had him along with eight or nine other NCOs—and me—pull KP for the troops' Thanksgiving dinner. The night was a great morale booster for everyone (in particular for the old NCOs, who got a kick out of peeling potatoes again); booze flowed fast around the mess hall, and only later did Jack Gallagher remind me that the next day about half the outfit had to go on KP just to clean up after us.

In May 1958 eight Nike-Ajax missiles exploded at a site near the sleepy New Jersey city of Middletown, killing six soldiers and four civilians. It was an accident that, according to public information officers (PIOs), "couldn't happen," and thus another big PR blow for the Army. Twenty-three major industrial areas in cities across the country were "protected" by Nikes, and the same citizens who had cried for increased security in the wake of Sputnik now screamed for blood. The irony of it all was that the Army was just beginning a quiet phaseout of the five-year-old Nike-Ajax for the faster, longer-range, nuclear-capable Nike-Hercules. Now, on top of the change-over, the PIOs had to contend with homeowners who suddenly looked upon the Hercs as little Hiroshimas just waiting to happen in their backyards.

We felt the heat of Middletown three thousand miles away, but for me an even more scorching wind had blown in January, when Lieutenant General Jim Gavin retired from the Army. The Army's Chief of Research and Development—my hero, and the man who was destined to go "all the way"—quit over what he perceived as an Army, and an overall U.S. military strategy, fast going wrong. For me, it was a hard pill to swallow. In my heart I felt he was right, just as General Matt Ridgway had been right with his damning assessment of the New Look, delivered after he'd turned the reins of Army Chief of Staff over to Taylor. But I told myself there was probably another, hidden reason for Gavin's retirement; I just couldn't understand how "Slim Jim" could just turn his back, especially at a time the Army needed him most.

The New Army said to get a degree, so I was getting a degree. I finished my Associate of Arts at Harbor College (it went to my head a little, too: I offered to take part of a GED test for Gallagher; he accepted and I flunked it for him), and enrolled in California State at Long Beach to get that aptly named B.S. This mission was complicated when the Group XO and my direct boss, Major Robert Stanek, was transferred to AAOC and was replaced by one Lieutenant Colonel Charles Jackson. Stanek had been a great guy to work for; he gave me a free hand but was always there to provide inspiration and encouragement. He'd been particularly pleased that I was going to school; in the ER he rendered on me just before he left, he called my "personal off-duty educational program . . . impressive." Unfortunately, about the time he left and Jackson arrived, I found myself in a situation where I had to take a class during the on-duty day. The new XO told me loud and clear that this was unacceptable, but I needed the course (which was offered only once a year), so I had little choice but to employ a little *delay and deceive*. The tactics were simple. Step one was my personally organizing to see the Engineers about the same time I had to be at school. Then, as soon as I was out the door, McRae would call over there and tell them something had come up, the Captain wouldn't be coming by, and to pass all calls for him to Signal. Then he'd call Signal and tee up the receptionist there, saying I'd gone on to Quartermaster and to pass all calls for me there. And so went the drill, all over Fort Mac. So if the Colonel was looking for me—as he frequently was—he'd end up spending the whole morning chasing me down around the post, by which point I'd be back from school, ready to impress him with how much had been accomplished so early in the day.

Around this time I discovered a subtle change in myself. I'd never be a yes-man, but I was as aware as any of my peers were of the rules for getting ahead in the peacetime Army. Sometimes I just couldn't comply; when, for example, I'd been deemed antisocial by the officers' wives in the 77th because I wouldn't go to their functions (I found out through a good friend, who was one of those wives, that I was the number-one target for gossip at many afternoon bridge clubs), I'd refused to do anything about it. I'd given officer parties probably three good tries and all I knew was: one, the chain of command "pecking order" among Army wives was as strict as among their husbands, and two, it seemed that every Army wife brought a lovely niece or a sweet younger sister along with her, who was "just perfect" for single-officer me. The bitch of it was that the wives generally had enormous influence over their husbands; career-wise I was crazy not to play the game. But I couldn't, any more than I could play golf or tennis, or sit around the Officers' Club shooting unadulterated horseshit with my superiors in the quest for a good ER. The only way I would get ahead, I figured, was by being the absolute best at my job, or at least appearing so. With nine-to-fiver Colonel Jackson, I climbed the ladder by arriving to work early, consulting the "things to do today" list he kept on top of his desk, and then doing as much as was humanly possible before he even came in. So if he ever called and said, "I want the latrine painted green," I could say, "Just done, sir," and he'd think I was a mind reader. There was another advantage to this system: if I had a look at the list and there were things on it I didn't want to do, I'd just steal the list itself (my guerrilla-warfare study was already paying off) and have a couple days' reprieve while the frantic Colonel tried to reconstruct his "things to do."

It was a hard time for all career, or potential career, officers. Mistakes or petty indiscretions could blow up in your face before you even knew you'd committed them. When Colonel Jenkins (or his clerk) left his "Classified" document safe open one night and I discovered it while on Duty Officer, I knew that to follow SOP—calling the brigade XO, writing it in the Duty Officer report, and alerting the Counterintelligence Corps (CIC)—would have meant a lot of rain on one fine soldier's parade. Instead, I just called the Colonel and he came over. Nothing had been disturbed in the safe, so he locked it, and I told him I hadn't seen a thing. With the Army inchingly infusing AD with combat-experienced field artillerymen to replace the deadwood, no way would I be responsible for destroying one of the best men to happen to the 108th Arty Group for what ended up being a harmless oversight.

In this New Army, no one could afford to tell the truth, make an error, or admit to ignorance. The only major guidance I gave my men before the annual 6th Region Inspector General (IG) inspection was that if the inspecting officer asked them a question they didn't know the answer to ("Corporal, what is the weight of your weapon?"), the boys should say, in a soldierly manner, the first thing that came to mind ("Sir, the weight of my weapon is thirty million tons!"). Anything was better than "I don't know," and besides, chances were the inspector wouldn't be listening, or, if he were, he wouldn't know the right answer himself. Still, when we won Best Battery in the Region with this minimal direction and little hassle to the troops or to me, even I had to admit it was not just because we really did run along like a well-oiled machine. There was also a certain amount of "M-1 penciling" going on.

The M-1 pencil was like any other pencil, except that its sole use was to beat the system. It got its name from the hole a sharpened pencil made—exactly the same size as an M-1 bullet—if you poked the end through a cloth target. In execution it meant that on the known-distance rifle range, even Little Stevie Wonder could get a perfect score, simply by organizing his buddy in the pit to poke the old pencil right through the bull's-eye and mark it accordingly. M-1 penciling had long ago left the KD range and become synonymous—Army-wide—with cheating in all the little ways. Commanders condoned its use by looking the other way (just as they'd looked the other way in the trenches when we'd produced absolutely ridiculous Korean Certificate of Loss statements), and wrong as it was, they had little choice. Maybe the KCLs started it, I didn't know, but the post-Korea Army had an unquenchable thirst for perfection which parched the throats of even the most dedicated leaders, and the M-1 pencil was the only water to be found. A CO simply couldn't fail. His troopers' shooting ability, their parade-ground skills, even their attendance at Troop Information classes over the past year all had to be 100 percent, or at least look 100 percent, if a commander was to survive on the peacetime battlefield. Everyone knew it, and as we got better and better at stretching the truth, we came to believe that some lies were even "okay." We never failed, and in the quest for "zero defects," we made sure our subordinates never failed. Our sham of perfection set an unspoken precedent for bigger lies and far more serious half-truths; little did we know that just a few years down the road, each and every one of them would ricochet back on the Army as an institution, with the repercussions of it all enough to shake America to its core.

George Creamer of the glass jaw was about to check out of the service. Having put all his stock in the Army for the last twelve years, it seemed to me a hell of an investment to throw away, but George had bigger plans: he intended to go to Cuba to help Castro. One by one he was recruiting an incredible team of adventurers and buccaneer types; he'd bought a yacht for the journey, and each time I saw him, there was yet another guy living on board. The boat itself, tied up at the Fort Mac wharves, was kind of like a pirate ship. Like so many other California yachts, it was reputed to have been owned by Errol Flynn; more certain, however, was that it had belonged to the California Sea Scouts. In any event, day by day it was settling deeper in the water as George scrounged weapons, ammo, rope, rations, and who knows what else for his big trip to Cuba. If I took my guys to the rifle range, George was usually waiting in my Orderly Room when I got back. "Hey, Hack," he'd say, "what's new?" Then he'd just happen to notice I had a couple of cases of ammo left over. "Sure could use them," he'd purr, "and it'd be a hell of a lot easier for your guys than having to lug it all back down to Ordnance." So I'd give him my surplus as, apparently, everyone else did on base, until it reached the point where I wondered if his loaded-down galleon would ever make it out of the harbor.

George tried to persuade me to go with him. It was very tempting. In 1958 I looked at Castro as Cuba's Patrick Henry, rightfully fighting to free his country from Batista's evil regime. The only problem was that the timing was wrong, on three counts. First, Colonel Jenkins had just been transferred out of the 47th Brigade; his successor, a well-decorated, good old West Point soldier named Raymond L. Shoemaker, Jr., had given me permission to relocate HQ Battery, and we were right in the middle of the move. George accepted this excuse, to a point; he was not particularly impressed with my second reason—that I'd just applied, at the urging of Colonel Jenkins and Brigade CG Perry, for appointment to the Regular Army. I tried to explain that despite everything I didn't like about the new Black Shoe Army, the fact still remained that the Army was my home and I loved the soldier's life. Besides, I said, I'd already had two years out, and spent the whole time counting the days till I could come back. "All this New Look crap will pass," I told him, remembering Roy Herte on the boat coming home from Korea telling me the same thing: if we just waited it out, we'd be Old Army again. George just grunted through his wired jaw, and I knew it was no time to tell him the third reason I didn't think I'd be setting sail for the Cuban revolution—that being a girl named Patty Leonard.

Even though the Army had yet to issue me a wife (so personally I was in no hurry to find one), more and more I felt the pressure to get married. To start with, there were the gossiping nags in the distaff, who were finally beginning to get to me. Then there was the fact that I was almost twenty-eight years old; most of my friends—military and civilian—were already hitched and working overtime making babies. Al Hewitt, my childhood hero, who, by sheer coincidence, lived right near Fort Mac, had already taken the plunge with a nice girl named Anna. Bill Cowart, my bachelor brother roommate, was getting pretty serious with another girl around town. So there I was, single, getting old, and beginning to worry about people thinking I wasn't into girls. I guess I felt it was becoming a now-or-never situation.

Patty, who was studying to be a nurse, looked amazingly like Elizabeth Taylor. In terms of Army-wife selection, she was a perfect choice: nursing, I figured, was akin to the military in terms of discipline (and it pretty well assured me she'd be a good mother), and with her looks and manners I knew she'd be an asset in the peacetime social scene. We'd actually dated almost two years before, when I was with the 77th in Manhattan Beach; then the romance was cut short when her father caught us necking one afternoon in Patty's bedroom. The door had been open (and one foot on the floor the whole time), but all that carried little weight in the mind of Al Leonard, protective Irish father, who threw me out with the warning not to return until

I developed a sense of "propriety and decorum." Now, many months later, I still didn't know what those words meant, but Al was posted somewhere overseas (he was a brilliant engineer; he designed the hydraulics for the *Nautilus*, the first nuclear-powered submarine), so Patty and I got together and stopped worrying about that one foot on the floor.

"Don't start a fire if you can't put it out," Uncle Roy had told me when I was nine and he caught me playing "doctor" with little Geraldine Carey behind the liquor store. I guess I hadn't heard him right, because eighteen years later I suddenly found myself with a wife who had to give up her nursing career before it even started. We'd planned to keep the marriage a secret until Patty finished her training (like West Point cadets, nursing students couldn't be married), but when she got pregnant and then, as her last practicum, she was assigned communicable diseases, it was a question of reporting herself in or risking the health of our kid. We chose the former course; ironically, she lost the baby anyway.

So now I was married. But from day one it was bigamy, pure and simple, and the Army was my first and favored love. I was a soldier twenty-four hours a day. I liked to stay with my troops; I liked spending my off-hours reading up on my trade. Women, even good women, had always run second (and they always would), so poor Patty, whom I loved as best I knew how, never had a fair chance. She was a good wife, a great cook (Mess Sergeant Clark taught her how to make a mean Thanksgiving turkey), and she turned out to be a fine mother, too. But all I could think to myself, day after day, was *This is not for me*. It hadn't helped matters much when I'd told George Creamer I couldn't go with him to Cuba because I was getting married; a few days later, Patty and I'd bumped into him at the Fort Mac Officers' Club, and he'd come up to the table to meet her. "So you're the bitch!" he'd said. "You're the bitch who's going to housebreak old Hack!" The next thing I knew, Patty was crying, and I didn't know what to do. I mean, George was a Wolfhound. A war buddy. A friend. So I couldn't knock him on his ass, or even tell him to shut up. It was something Patty never understood and, rightfully, held against me for years. But what could I say? The simple fact was I was married to the Army—and the new Mrs. Hackworth deserved better.

So George went off to Cuba to help old Fidel overthrow the government. Patty stayed home and talked Catholicism with Tom Martin and the Group chaplain (every damn time I walked into the house they tried to convert me, with Father Paul invoking my mother's Irish-Catholic name: "If she'd lived, me boy, you'd be a Catholic, too."). As for myself—having decided not to tell the good chaplain my grandmother had hated Catholics, that it had, in fact, been the bane of Loretta Kenefick's life and even now Gram was rolling in her grave over my marriage to Patty—I escaped to Fort Bliss for a one-week working holiday.

The Atomic Weapons and Guided Missile Course was designed for senior officers. I got to go only because the 47th Brigade's top brass had already attended and there was a space in the Brigade allocation that had to be filled. It was a lucky break: it was a gentleman's course with no exams to struggle through, so I could just sit back and take in this introduction to the "more bang for the buck/more rubble for the ruble" basic weapons in the Cold War arsenal. I found the whole thing most interesting, and when I left Fort Bliss a week later, I came away with the firm belief that as a tactical weapon the A-bomb was just another highly effective weapon in my kit bag, to help me get the job done.

Back at HQ Battery, we completed the lock, stock, and barrel move into "The Hole" (as it was known in Fort Mac-ese). Our new home was actually a tunnel complex on the order of Corregidor; it had been built many years before, prior to WW I, when military and public hysteria over prowling enemy fleets had caused Fort Mac to commandeer and annex a large hill, nicknamed "Topside," for a coast artillery stronghold. The underground maze of firing positions, offices, and barracks had fallen into disuse with the threat, renewed in WW II, long past—or transferred now, to the skies; I'd been eyeing it since I'd arrived a year before (I never liked being too close to the flagpole, and HQ Battery was set up back-to-back with Group HQ). Now that we were finally settled in just up the road (and under the ground), I felt the exercise had been well worth the wait. Group HQ had nothing to bitch about either. Part of my deal with "the Shoe," as we affectionately called the new Group CO, was that we'd rehabilitate two of our old Topside buildings for Group's use. This project, too, was finished, and everyone, according to Colonel Shoemaker's clerk, Bill Rean, seemed to be living happily ever after. Rean was a good friend of Tom Martin's, and through him, I always had an inside line to what the Colonel was thinking. Fortunately, unlike the news brought by Milo on Colonel Theisen's behalf, the word from the Shoe was always good, and the biggest problem I had in my latter days at HQ was when Gallagher called from Las Vegas to say that he, Acquisition Radar Master Sergeant "Big Steve" Stevenson, and another of my boys, Burkhardt, were stranded, having lost all their dough gambling. I had to send the battery's laundry money to get them home, and while I chewed Big Steve and Burkhardt's asses for being irresponsible—they were both married—Jack fell asleep in his chair. "I'll get to you later," I warned his comatose figure.

In February 1959 I got orders to attend the surface-to-surface Corporal Missile Course at Fort Sill, Oklahoma, TDY en route to a missile assignment in Germany. Talk about big bangs: I was being yanked out of school one semester short of my B.S. in sociology. Still, an even bigger concern in leaving HQ Battery was what I was going to do with Tom Martin. Captain Johnson was long gone, but I could see there were plenty of officers and NCOs just waiting for me to split so they could get the boy. And he really was asking for it. In his eighteen months in the Army, he'd learned well how the system worked, and just how far he could push it. He was downright insubordinate most of the time in every aspect of soldiering; the only thing standing between him, the slammer, or an irate NCO's dukes was me. So I had to get him an Army job as far from the Army as possible if I hoped to keep him out of the stockade until his Expiration Time of Service (ETS) in six months' time.

Through another good Irish Catholic, Major Quinn at Special Services, I arranged for Tom to finish out his Army career as the lifeguard at the officers' swimming pool. It was the ideal assignment for an almost-priest who'd yet to be fully awakened to the pleasures of womanhood (thirteen years in a seminary ain't no place to produce Valentinos, but when I introduced him to Patty's sister, even I was dumbfounded by his transformation into Melvin Fumbler), and Tom took the job gladly. Little did I know at the time that I'd be creating a monster. Some months later, when I came back to Fort Mac on leave, Melvin Fumbler was now Joe Cool, smiling and flashing his big blue eyes at the generals' and colonels' daughters around the pool, tossing lines like "Right, honey . . . maybe tomorrow. Just hang around . . . we'll see."

Fort Sill, another old Cav post, had none of the gentleman's Army feel about it that Bliss did. Sill had been the home of Field Artillery for a long time; besides the Corporal Missile Course, there seemed to be little acknowledgment of the nation's rapidly changing strategic defense posture, or—to my relief—the Army's New Look. The men on this post were still in the business of soldiering. The Corporal Missile Course itself was about a thousand times harder than the antiaircraft one I'd taken at Bliss. There were only ten of us in the class; all, save me, were majors and lieutenant colonels (most of whom had master's degrees in electronics), and as they breezed right through, I sweated over every detail. The bitch was that all the instruction was classified SECRET. I couldn't take anything home, so night after night I'd go back behind the high-fenced, well-lighted security perimeter and read in the classroom until the instructors (who had to be there to answer questions) finally just fed me the vital test information and sent me home.

The Corporal missile was sort of an updated Nazi V-2. It could pack a

100-kiloton nuclear warhead, but with a range of only one hundred miles, it was actually on its way out, soon to be replaced by the longer-range, more powerful Sergeant. Even so, the basic theories we were taught—the Doppler effect, liquid fuel systems, firing procedures, and so on—would be applicable for some years to come, and in addition to the technical stuff, we learned the basics of deploying nuclear devices in the field. There was a psychological aspect taught in the course as well. "Nuke the Pukes" was an expression I heard for the first time at Sill, and as we war-gamed tactical exercises in which atomic weapons were employed, and calculated the damage a 100-kiloton A-bomb (five times the firepower dropped on Hiroshima) could inflict upon an enemy, the phrase sat as a righteous watchword in the backs of all our heads.

I never finished the course. In April my Secret security clearance was revoked ("the character and trustworthiness of subject individual does not meet the criteria as set forth in AR604-5") and I was summoned to a "show cause" board to determine if I'd purposely misled the Army about my background.

I was knocked on my ass. The whole thing revolved around my "criminal record," which the Regular Army Board had dug up while considering my RA application. Now they wanted to know why I'd answered "no" to the question on the application: "Have you ever been detained, held or arrested," under either civil or military codes, when, in fact, I had. All things being equal, it was a fairly reasonable query on their part, but the stuff they were about to hang me for was the night in Lido with Jimmy Sparks (when Ernest Medina shot those three Italians), and my gang's hardware-store jackknife heist when I was twelve. I couldn't believe an almost bankrupt Army would spend valuable time and money terrorizing a little kid who'd long since grown up. What pissed me off even more was that the Personnel sergeant in Trieste had told me, *and* Army regulations themselves stated, that juvenile offenses were not recordable. On top of that, Medina— who'd actually killed the guys in Lido—was already out of jail, and eleven years after the incident here I was taking his rap all over again.

I immediately asked for and received legal counsel in the form of a wonderful Will Rogers–type lawyer named Captain Harry Pitchford. I had no assigned duties while he prepared the case, so I spent the month in the post library, reading Nietzsche and feeling like shit. It was a horrible, soul-searching time; though I came to understand a bit more about Hitler, not for one moment did I grasp why it seemed that all the Army wanted was to get me out, when all I wanted to do was stay in. Still, I was in good hands with Captain Pitchford. He'd been a Washington newsman before WW II, during which time he'd been a big poker-playing buddy of President

Truman's. He loved telling Senator Truman stories, and again and again assured me that if all else failed he'd go to "Harry" to straighten this thing out.

Fortunately it didn't look as if that would be necessary. The investigating officer, Major Harold Dean, was a distinguished combat man who was on my side from the start. On his advice Pitchford got supportive letters from Colonel Jenkins and Generals Cleland, Truman, McGaw, Perry, and Honeycutt (Perry's wonderful Field Artillery old-soldier replacement). He even got one from my old Wolfhound regimental CO, General Michaelis. The letters improved my morale considerably, but better still was the quick trip I took to nearby Fort Hood to see Dell Evans, who'd been stationed there as a company commander (now he was a battalion training officer) in the 37th Armor. Elvis Presley was one of his soldiers and, according to Dell, a damn good one. We had a fine visit, but by the time I'd told all my secondhand stories about the President and he'd told all his firsthand ones about the King, we had just enough time to glorify the Wolfhounds before the all-too-short weekend was over. Then it was back to Sill for me, to await the sword to come crashing down on my career. In the end I was found "not at fault"; before I had a chance to celebrate, though, I was summoned a second time for other screwups in my record, among them my 1928 date of birth on a form I'd filled out in 1950. I called Eugene Ernst, my friend from Benning, to prove I'd taken the necessary steps to rectify that error, and finally, on the ninth of June, I got my security clearance back, and I was free. When they had the balls to ask if I wanted to reapply for RA, I said, "Thanks, but no thanks"—I was rarely one to make the same mistake twice.

With that, Patty and I packed our gear and left Fort Sill. And after a quick stop at Fort Mac to watch Tom Martin (the lady-killer) in action, it was off to Germany, where I would officially become part of the Nuke the Pukes world, as CO of my first atomic missile unit.

11 THIS AIN'T THE ARMY, MR. JONES

I remember him as a gentleman, perhaps a bit naive in his
expectations of people. . . . He was an idealist, not prone to
make allowances for human foibles.

Colonel Richard E. Dryer, USA, Ret.
Chaplain
Nürnberg Post, Germany, 1958–62

"How is it, sir, that the personnel system can take a doughfoot,
spend thousands of dollars making him a missileman, and then assign him
to be a horse holder for generals?"

The Deputy Chief of Staff, Personnel (DCSPER) of the Army, Lieutenant
General James F. Collins, seemed a little taken aback by my question, but
no more so than I'd been a month before in Heidelberg, when I'd been
assigned not to a Corporal missile battalion but to Southern Area Command
(SACOM), at the U.S. Army Hotel in Nürnberg. *Is this peacetime Army
SOP,* I'd asked myself, *to put guys in jobs they were totally untrained or
unsuited for?* It seemed as if it happened to me every time I got a Permanent
Change of Station (PCS). So, just as I had when I'd been assigned to the
40th Division in Korea, and then to Manhattan Beach's Air Defense, I
screamed bloody murder. And, just as had happened on the previous
occasions, it hadn't made a bit of a difference. Despite shortages of
missile-trained officers (or so we'd been told at Sill) and of combat arms
captains in the European Theater, I'd arrived at a time when a more
immediate, urgent requirement had to be met: a young combat officer "with
plenty of fruit salad" to run the new Visitors' Bureau for VIPs passing
through the Nürnberg area.

"Don't bitch" was the word. The Personnel guy had tried to show me the
bright side. "You don't have your bachelor's degree," he'd said. "This is a
great chance to finish it off, get another language, and start cracking on your
master's. Besides," he'd added, "you'll make some good contacts with the
top brass. Can't hurt your career, you know."

I knew, which was why I'd buttonholed the DCSPER in the elevator of the hotel the minute the doors closed. By the time they opened at his floor, General Collins had promised to lay the groundwork with Heidelberg to get me back to infantry. Now at least there'd be something to look forward to as I spent my days playing hotel executive (I was also designated assistant hotel manager) cum dog robber for transient senior brass.

All things being equal, I had to admit it was a pretty easy assignment. The Visitors' Bureau job basically entailed my playing Johnny-on-the-spot—coordinating transportation, providing info, and generally looking after the occasional NATO and other VIP guests. But things are never equal, and the good in the job was far outweighed by having to live in, and work under the command of, the Nürnberg Post.

There was nothing onward and upward about Nürnberg Post. It was a drab, lifeless eight-to-five organization whose senior officers were, for the main, an odd collection of has-beens and never-weres. While it was little wonder that the post was staffed with officers who were not headed for bigger and better things (its basic mission was not exactly a warrior's dream: to baby-sit the American community in Nürnberg, providing housing, schools, and dependent evacuation if required), most of these guys acted as if they'd retired a few years before and were only marking time till their final parade. Coffee calls were the most pressing engagement every day, the sense of urgency accompanying them only matched by the morning ritual of reading the *Stars and Stripes* at one's desk. The Post CO, Homer Chandler, looked kind of like Errol Flynn (albeit a *fading* Errol Flynn), but it seemed to be all he had going for him. As a West Point colonel he must have screwed up pretty badly to have ended up at this shabby Fort Nowhere. The same, I assumed, could have been said for his adjutant, Lieutenant Colonel Smith.

Patty and I lived in the American colony near the post. She was pregnant, which at least gave *her* something to think about in our sturdy but styleless government-issued apartment when I disappeared early each morning, through the looking glass, into the opulence of the hotel.

The U.S. Army Hotel had been built in the early 1930s by the Nazi Party as an annex to the next-door Grand Hotel. It was a huge place (then called the Grand Hotel Guesthouse), with a couple of hundred beautiful, high-ceilinged rooms, and ornate VIP suites complete with those grand old European baths. In the cellar was what I was convinced was the biggest kitchen the world had ever seen. The cooking pots alone were the size of mini cement trucks, and they worked about the same way: pour in five or ten sacks of potatoes, crank up the pot, and feed a thousand people mashed spuds. The mammoth scullery was connected by a mini underground railroad to the Nürnberg stadium. All the cooking for Hitler's big rallies had been done at the hotel and then choo-chooed over to feed the Fuehrer and his tens of thousands of misguided followers. Neither kitchen nor railroad was used anymore, but everything was in military mothballs—perfect condition—meticulously maintained by the all-German civilian staff (though why, I'd never know, because I wasn't game to ask).

Hitler had used the Grand Hotel Guesthouse exclusively for the Nazi Party Organization Days, a fourteen-day conference held each summer. At the end of WW II, the U.S. Army had confiscated the building as a spoil of war. Now it was open to any U.S. forces in Europe, and catered primarily to transient personnel and guys on leave. The hotel was run on a nonprofit basis; rates were cheap (you could sleep, eat, and drink like a king for just a few bucks a night), but like most U.S. Army facilities in Europe, slot machines on the premises (which provided everyday entertainment for guests and permanent party personnel) made a small fortune. They were always in use. Day after day, from morning to night, I'd see the addicts— mainly women—hanging on the handles of the slots, disappearing thirty-cent highballs as fast as they did their quarters. Some of the biggest one-armed–bandit junkies were the wives of officers assigned to the Nürnberg Post. Their desperate, lonely love affairs with the slots spoke as vividly as the swollen, failure faces of their husbands did for the dead-end street of a Nürnberg assignment.

In my role as assistant hotel officer, I worked with Hotel Custodian Glenn Faulks, a fine, strapping paratrooper captain who'd been with the 101st at Bastogne, and had only recently left the new Pentomic/Atomic "Screaming Eagles." He was another round peg in a square hole. How he'd ended up ramrodding a hotel was no less of a mystery to him than it was to me. Still, the two of us found the jobs themselves not too terrible (if we remained detached); over time I learned a great deal about the inner workings of the establishment, and the ongoing Peyton Place among the staff.

Most of the hotel employees had been with the place since the war's end, if not before. They knew one another well, and joyfully traded their own and other staff's and guests' secrets to anyone who would listen. One of the favorites was the story of Eva, the pop-eyed hotel switchboard operator, who was rumored to be having a long-term affair with a U.S. infantry division commander (who happened also to be president of some heavy-duty religious organization). One evening I walked by the switchboard, only to find the goddamn thing lit up like a pinball machine and Eva nowhere in sight. I asked the night clerk where she was. "Dat Eva!" he roared, with a lecherous look in his eye. "She ist upstairs, mit der General. Eva ist der General's little playmate!" Yuk, yuk, yuk, he laughed, his huge belly shaking all over his desk. But he wasn't wrong. Every time this general called—he summoned her up to his suite like an order of bratwurst and sauerkraut—Eva disappeared. Then, when she'd finally return to her post, she'd look down at the rest of the staff from the dizzying heights of the two stars she'd just ridden bareback (according to the all-knowing, all-seeing desk clerk, anyway) and remain completely insufferable for the rest of the general's visit. Unfortunately for the overloaded switchboard, his visits were frequent.

The hotel employees were comrades-in-arms in a bureaucratic war with Tom Marucca, the new civilian hotel manager. Tom, far more than Glenn or I, took care of the hotel's day-to-day functions. He was a roly-poly American in his mid-forties who'd held similar jobs throughout Europe for the last fifteen years or so. Conscientious, hardworking, and always smiling, Tom reminded me of a superefficient Italian headwaiter. His huge brown eyes saw everything that happened in "his" hotel (which meant he saw plenty), and the staff, in their crisp, immaculate, identical uniforms, stared wholesale daggers at him every time he cast a glance in any of their AOs. Be it in one of the bars or coffee shops, the à la carte restaurant (for which a manageable kitchen did exist), the corridors, the rooms, or the big, plush lobby, there was someone who resented Tom Marucca. One reason was probably his three-generations-removed origins; after two World Wars, there was no love lost between the Germans and any of those "treacherous" Italians (particularly the Mussolini-shaped ones). On top of that, Tom represented and implemented change, something the German staff had lost the knack for. So if there was any way they could bring him down, there was little doubt that they would.

I'd been strolling around the hotel for about two months when I was summoned to an interview with Colonel Theodore Mataxis, CO of the 8th Div's 505th Parachute Battlegroup. DCSPER General Collins had been true to his word, and when Mataxis gave me the thumbs-up, it was only a matter of time before I'd have an infantry (Airborne!) troop assignment again. I was ecstatic. Unfortunately, it was a short-lived euphoria, because at about the same time, Tom Marucca came to me (Glenn was on leave, so I was in charge) to report that brass from Nürnberg Post and the surrounding area were doing some heavy freeloading from the hotel. He said big parties of these guys and their friends—sometimes twenty or thirty people—had more than once come to the dining room, had complete banquets, and left without paying the bill. No dockets were even written out, he said, just slips of paper that subsequently disappeared. The logical course of action was to report it immediately, but the problem was, *to whom,* because Tom suspected the irregularities reached the highest levels of Nürnberg Post. But the situation couldn't go on, so I had little choice but to take the matter to Colonel Chandler.

The CO immediately set his post Criminal Investigation Division (CID) to work to uncover the facts. In the meantime, I got with my own private "intelligence agent," an American girl who sang at the hotel every night (and thus could fill me in on what happened when I'd gone home from work). She provided information that backed up Tom's comments; it looked as if Mr. Marucca had unwittingly opened a huge can of worms. As it turned out, the results of the investigation reflected just that: numerous irregularities were indeed found at the hotel. But the prime mover behind them all, according to the report, was none other than Tom Marucca.

I was knocked out. Somehow I hadn't expected this sort of whitewash. Suddenly Tom, one of the straightest guys I knew (in a business full of temptation), was being accused of abusing the system in every way possible: booze and food management, the slot machines, using the hotel facilities for personal forays into illicit sex, etc., etc., etc. His ongoing feud with the staff didn't help. Most of those guys supported the investigation's findings with great enthusiasm. Then, when I went to bat on Tom's behalf, I was accused of being his partner in crime.

A great slander campaign ensued. Among other things, I was accused of having an affair with the singer at the hotel (which pissed me off no end, in that for the first time in my whole life I was actually being straight-arrow), and Patty was more upset by the day. In the middle of it all I was summoned to SACOM: "We understand you know what's happening at the hotel, and would like all evidence you can provide. A staff car has been sent for you."

Down I went to Munich, to the commanding general, Paul Gavan. I said my piece: that Marucca, the singer, and a few key German staff members all corroborated the fact that senior officers, several generals from a nearby division included, were taking advantage above and beyond the call of freeloading. Gavan listened intently, and in the end assured me he would start an investigation immediately, so the real "guilty parties" would be identified and prosecuted. *Great*, I thought. But there was still one area of concern. Although I'd been summoned to Gavan (I found out later the girl singer had tipped SACOM off with an anonymous letter), from the points of view of Nürnberg Post's Chandler and Smith, I had violated the chain of command, and I'd questioned their findings with the General. I couldn't afford another bad ER, and the one those two would render would be a doozy. I voiced my concerns to General Gavan. "Don't worry," he said. "I'll personally rate you for this period."

In the Army, as everywhere, there are all kinds of ways of not telling the truth. You can avoid it, omit it, color, fabricate, or forget it. Which one, if any, General Gavan used I'd never know, but one thing was certain: whatever SACOM's findings (if indeed an investigation was even carried out), Gavan took no action. The whistle was never blown, and though the free lunches came to a screeching halt, the brass got away with their game. However, there were casualties, among them Patty and I, who'd become personae non gratae at Nürnberg Post, with the majority of post personnel siding with Colonel Chandler and the original results of his kangaroo court.

It was a very lonely period. Our friends could have been counted on one hand: Mike Krumpac, an Armed Forces Network (AFN) radio announcer whose place of business was a suite on the top floor of the Grand; Joel Prives, a Boston-born Army dentist (stationed in Nürnberg), and his wife, Roberta; Ron Gerrard, my running buddy from Fort Mac, whom I'd gotten to Nürnberg through an old 108th supply sergeant (now the assignment NCO in Heidelberg); and Harold Borger, an American businessman who lived next door at the plush Grand Hotel and frequently visited the annex.

Harold was a white-haired forty, a well-educated, well-dressed, highly successful import-export man from New York. What he saw in Patty and me neither of us knew—we guessed he didn't have too many friends, either— but over time he'd become part of our family. He came to dinner frequently and talked Big Apple with Patty (who was a native New Yorker herself) and Castro with me. I was still very enthusiastic about old Fidel, and read as much as I could get my hands on about his victory in Cuba. Harold shared my views that the young revolutionary was a great, great patriot, and we spent a lot of time debating how the United States would ultimately come to perceive him. Harold traveled a lot, too, and was trying his damnedest to encourage trade between Eastern and Western countries. He believed, and I totally agreed, that if both sides had heavy financial commitments and trade relations with each other, they would inevitably reduce the war talk and lessen the likelihood of blowing each other up. In a job where the heaviest thinking I had to do was give directions to Nürnberg visitors, my talks with Harold were a breath of fresh air.

Our first child, Laura, was born on the twenty-second of October 1959. She was the only bright spot in the fast-approaching holiday season; for us, Thanksgiving around the post was very bleak, and Christmas promised to be even worse. My annual physical found me "not fit for a combat assignment." Though I'd had a series of shots to break down the scar tissue in my left arm (tissue that over the last years had gradually grown up around the nerves and numbed my arm all the way down to my hand), my hearing had not improved at all. So my 8th Div orders were canceled, and for the time being at least, I remained an unhappy prisoner of Nürnberg Post.

One evening just before Christmas, Ron Gerrard dropped by our house. "Man, are they screwing you!" he said. Ron's job at the post was (ironically) Officer Efficiency Report clerk, and in that role he'd managed to smuggle out a copy of my ER, prepared not by General Gavan (as I'd been promised), but by Colonels Chandler and Smith (as I had feared). And it was *bad*. I exploded. General Gavan had given me his word on three counts: one, he'd promised to conduct a fair investigation; two, he'd sworn he would punish whoever was at fault; and three, he'd assured me I wouldn't get zeroed out on an ER. Point for point, his word had proved no good—and he was a general officer!

I was disillusioned as I'd never been before. My only consolation was that this guy didn't spell his name like *the* General Gavin; old Slim Jim would have struck the sleazy command of Nürnberg Post like lightning. I wanted to quit the Army then and there. I didn't want to be part of an organization where flimflam was the order of the day at every level of command. Patty and I talked it over, but quickly realized we were between a rock and a hard place: with only fourteen years' service and a three-year overseas commitment barely begun, I would have had to foot the bill to get us and all our belongings back to the States. We just couldn't afford it, particularly when we had a brand-new kid to think about as well.

So instead of quitting, I stormed back to Munich and General Gavan. I slammed the ER down on his desk and asked him what had happened. He explained that there'd been an oversight; he'd cancel the report and rate me personally. At that point I was so angry I almost didn't care—whatever he'd write in his ER would be less than honest anyway (he'd seen me twice in his life and didn't know me from Adam). I told him all I wanted was out of that hotel and out of Nürnberg Post, pronto. On this, at least, the General came through. He organized my immediate transfer to a staff division of the United States Army, Europe (USAREUR) Command Headquarters. He disappeared the condemning ER, too, and though he didn't rate me himself, his chief of staff did, in glowing terms. Strangely, I never saw the report again; for reasons I'd never know, it disappeared from my permanent file.

The Palace of Justice sat along the main road just outside Nürnberg. Now home of HQ USAREUR's Special Activities Division (SAD), this majestic building was better known as the site for the postwar War Crimes Tribunal. The courtroom where Hess, Goering, and a score of other Nazis were tried for crimes against humanity was sealed up and preserved as a historic monument; the few times I went in there I stood in awe. It was as if the place was haunted; in the stillness I could feel the presence of the guilty, and of those courageous souls who testified against them in the hope that such crimes would never happen again.

After a couple of months as HQ detachment commandant, my job at the Palace of Justice was that of SAD's administration branch chief. I was assigned a sergeant major, a good man in his late thirties by the name of Slattery, as well as a secretary, clerks for every occasion, a message center, and a big, plush office of my own. It was basically fat-cat city, and as I sipped coffee out of Rosenthal china cups (served deskside twice daily by two stout, efficient German women behind a coffee cart), I'd contrast the torment at the hotel with this easy living, and truly marvel at my good luck.

Next door to me was a bigger, plusher office that belonged to The Boss's secretary. Adjoining hers through an inner door was the biggest, plushest office of them all, that of The Boss himself—the Chief of Special Activities Division, whom I'll call Colonel C. William Willard. "The All-Seeing," as we called him, was among the most consummate staff men I'd ever seen. He was a paper pusher supreme, able to consume and pass judgment on thick studies in a blink of an eye, before zooming them back through appropriate channels to go sailing out all around Europe. The man was also rumored to be as erratic as a V-1 Nazi rocket; I'd been told to tread carefully with him the moment I arrived. At first I couldn't understand why. I reported to him each day and we got along beautifully. He told me he respected a "real" warrior, because he was a warrior, too. "The big war, you know," he'd say.

My first inkling that The All-Seeing didn't have both oars in the water was when he carefully explained to me his "stud book" procedure. When I got to work at seven each morning, my first stop was always the message center to get all communiqués from higher HQ. The Colonel's routine was that if there were promotion orders among these notes, specifically from colonel to general or generals going up to a higher grade, the next thing I had to do was go to Willard's office and see if the lucky guy(s) were in Willard's "stud book" (which was actually the *United States Military Academy Register of Graduates*, and contained brief biographies of all alumni). If he/they were, I had to place a marker by the name(s), and the entire book neatly in the center of the Colonel's desk. Then for the rest of the hour, until Willard arrived at eight, I'd wander around the building telling the staff to brace themselves. This last bit was not part of the Colonel's SOP; it was a wrinkle I added over time, based on the old adage that to be *forewarned is forearmed*.

The problem was that The All-Seeing, a West Pointer himself, was never among those selected for promotion. Why this was so, no one knew, least of all (apparently) Willard himself, who would fly into maniacal rages the minute his bespectacled eyes darted across the first name I'd dutifully marked for him. The first day was always the worst; for the staff it was like being locked in a cage with a crazed lion. (On one occasion, when a fellow classmate got a star, I thought the Colonel would have a stroke. Not only did he rant and rave, stomp his feet, bulge his eyes, and turn a royal purple, he also got on the horn to other West Point classmates to bemoan an Army that would award a star to "the moron of the class.") After that came an unlimited number of days' sulking from our chief. In the end, he'd always shake his head sadly, tell me there were more generals from his class than any other, and life would go back to normal with a very likable, considerate chief at the helm—until the next promotion orders came out.

Or until some unsuspecting officer left a toilet seat up in the men's room. One poor captain, a quiet, former combat infantryman, committed this heinous crime one morning, not knowing that The All-Seeing was in the next stall. Willard stood him at attention in the hallway outside the bathroom door and chewed his ass for all the building to hear: "You know my policy! All toilet seats will be down when not in use. You have violated a direct order! I should relieve you. You are an incompetent, unthinking . . ." on and on and on. And the captain (who'd just relieved *himself*) could do nothing but stand there and wear it.

Colonel Willard really must have screwed himself somewhere along the line. Most of his contemporaries were at least brigadier generals, and many already held the key spots in the Army. Still, Willard, who *had* graduated in the top 10 percent of his West Point class, had not given up hope. Until his appointment, the position of SAD chief had always been a two-star billet, and The All-Seeing reasoned that the logic behind his assignment here was as a testing/proving ground for "bigger things." As a result, under the Colonel's reign every project and paper was urgent (regardless of its relative importance), to be delivered to USAREUR HQ absolutely perfect and by special courier. With these superefficient ways, the Colonel knew that one day USAREUR commander General Bruce Clarke would recognize his brilliance, and "battlefield commission" the frontline paper warrior into the star-studded big leagues.

Somehow I managed to escape Willard's wrath, and all in all I found my new job great fun. Tom Martin had trained me well; I was surviving pretty effortlessly as a staff officer on my own, with a little help from Sergeant Major Slattery (who was a smart and thorough admin NCO), and the host of civilian and military administrative specialists running around the palace. My work consisted basically of digesting the huge staff studies into a couple of paragraphs for the Colonel to sign off or give his inimitable guidance on;

but through the job I inadvertently found myself in another role as well, that of the staff's barometer for Willard's moods.

"What's his disposition? Do you think I should see him now or wait?" Grown men—light and full colonels with proud combat records—would cringe and shake at the prospect of catching The All-Seeing on a bad day. And they had every reason to fear him. The competition for promotion was so stiff that anything less than "the best" was unacceptable, and an ER in the hands of a mad son of a bitch could zero a guy out before the ink had dried on the page.

I started going to school again, three or four nights a week, through a degree program offered by the University of Maryland. Since the Army had begun putting such a heavy emphasis on college educations, a number of American universities had jumped on the bandwagon and designed courses like the one I was taking, specifically for Army personnel overseas. Their standards were all greatly reduced, and most were like diploma mills. U of M seemed to be one of these; a bachelor's could be obtained simply by going to class and breathing. The Army apparently didn't care what school you went to, or even what degree you ended up with. It was the degree itself—just the degree—that counted.

I always figured this emphasis in quantity versus quality came from the fact that our service branch had gotten the short end of the stick throughout Ike's time in office. Interservice rivalry was intense on all levels; since the other services got all the money and the weapons (and we only got the cuts), it seemed as if the Army was determined to have the corner, at least, on smart guys. Personally, I didn't care; of more real use to me were the various courses I took through Fort Bragg's Department of Non-Resident Instruction to complete the Special Forces guerrilla training I'd started in the 108th. One of these, an updated demolitions course, discussed the employment of atomic demolition munitions (ADM), and though it came as no surprise to me that atomic weaponry was being considered as a replacement for the good old antitank land mine on future battlefields, what *was* surprising was the explosive force being envisioned—ADMs with punches of 25 kilotons to 20 megatons each. *Step aside, Grand Canyon*, I thought—but at least it would make the Russians think twice.

Schooling aside, it was an easy life. Exactly five days to the work week, with many a weekend spent skiing at Garmisch or Berchtesgaden, where the Army managed more plush, former Nazi hotels. With rates of three bucks a night at some of Europe's top ski resorts, it was hard to bitch.

On one cold winter's day I took Patty to Dachau. The horror of Hitler's vision was alive and well in this grim death camp: the barracks, the ovens, the electrified barbed-wire fences, remained intact. A mound here held the bones of ten thousand Jews; the one over there, twelve thousand more. The place was a monument to the darkest side of man, and yet—despite the smoke and ash that rained down on their homes from camp incinerators, despite the sickly smell of burning flesh and hair, which surely carried with the slightest breeze as far, probably, as Munich—the villagers claimed they hadn't known. I couldn't square it, anymore than I could square the fact that not one of the laughing, backslapping, congenial comrades I met (in their beer-belly-filled lederhosen and their jolly Bavarian green caps) had fought the Americans in the West. All assured me they'd been on the Eastern Front, fighting "the real enemy," the Russians. It was a story I heard in the cities, too. In fifteen years the Germans had come a long way in their rewrite of history. *But at least there's Dachau*, I thought to myself, *to remind them of the truth.*

Harold Borger had been traveling a lot lately; when he finally touched down for a while I invited him to the Palace for a visit. I gave him the full tour: the courtroom, the grounds, the marble halls, the grandiose offices filled with heavy antique furniture confiscated from the Nazis. As we walked by the steel door leading to SAD's classified-document vault (for which I was custodian), he stopped and asked what it was. When I told him he nodded, both solemnly and knowingly. He'd been a major in the Air Corps during WW II and had held a similar job. "Many a career has been ruined by a lost document," he warned. After lunch in the Palace's swanky dining room, Harold said good-bye with the promise of dropping by to see Patty and Laura soon. "Oh, by the way," he concluded, "do you think you could get hold of an extra fatigue cap? My nephew in New York keeps asking me for one."

"I'll see what I can do, Harold," I said, and soon forgot all about it.

Harold asked me about the fatigue cap the next time we met. When I told him I'd forgotten, he seemed unconcerned but wondered if, when I *did* fulfill his request, I could get him a field jacket as well. "The kid'll love it," he said.

Well. I liked Harold Borger. A lot. And he'd been nothing but a good friend to Patty and me. But it suddenly occurred to me that all might not be as it appeared. As far back as Trieste I'd been taught that people in espionage did their recruiting by methods quite similar to those Harold seemed to be employing. They start with something easy, like, "Can you get me a fatigue cap?" The next might be, "Can you get me a field jacket?" It wasn't such a big deal to scrounge a cap or a coat, but it *was* against regulations. So some poor schmuck breaks the regs once or twice, and before he knows it, the requests from the "friend" become a bit harder, with more serious regulations involved. A guy breaks a couple of these and he's hooked. He can't get out.

But Harold's a great guy, I kept insisting to myself, even as my instincts went on screaming. He *had* told me he'd been to Russia a few times and went to East Germany regularly on business. He was as enthusiastic about Castro as I was, but I started to wonder if, actually, he thought Castro was my Achilles' heel, and a way he could bring me into the espionage world. And with me as custodian for thousands of papers ranging from Confidential to Top Secret (including all the war plans for the European Theater), I would be a good catch.

In short, I began to think Harold Borger was a spy. I went to the Counterintelligence Corps, told them about his request, and asked that they check him out. What was his background? Had he been in the military or was that part of the game? The guys at CIC thought I was a nut. It took everything in my power to persuade them to look into the matter any further. When they did, they found that he *had* been in the Air Corps in WW II, but with a somewhat spotted record, and that he had longtime leanings to the Left.

In the still-lingering McCarthy era, everyone at CIC now concluded I was being set up as spy apparent. They immediately asked me to become Harold's "handler" while they went about identifying his contacts. It was a lousy job. I didn't want to be a counterspy any more than I'd wanted to be a hotelier. I didn't like being treacherous—what if Harold was clean?—and I didn't like the way the spy role quickly became all-encompassing. For every request Harold made, the agents made another; I couldn't tell Willard, yet almost every other day I was taking these long lunch hours with my friend. From all outward appearances, I was just screwing off. But duty first: every time Harold asked for something, I passed it on to Army Intelligence and they provided the item. Harold got his fatigue cap, his field jacket, the Army's new protective gas mask (he told me he'd been a chemical officer, too, and wanted to see the latest equipment), nonclassified books on atomic warfare, and anything else his masters desired.

As Harold Borger fell deeper and deeper into his own trap, the main thing I noticed was that our Intelligence guys were the fumblers of all time. They often followed us to restaurants or on our walks through the lovely inner city of old Nürnberg. I'd look behind me and there they'd be, like walking, talking Sears and Roebuck catalogs, dressed in the latest PX flash gear. They might as well have been wearing neon. I'd concluded that my friend was indeed a spy, but an amateur; if he hadn't been so inept he would have caught on to the game from day one.

"We've got to see his passport," said the CIC.

"How?" I asked.

"Invite him for dinner."

Right. The following night, Harold came to the apartment. CIC had set the trap earlier in the day: they'd jimmied the heating system, and now the place was getting hotter by the minute. Naturally, I couldn't fix it, and always proper Harold began to sweat. Soon the perspiration was streaming down his face and neck; he still hadn't taken off his jacket, and I began to think he would melt. Finally I *insisted* he take it off; he handed it over gladly, and while Patty (whose mission along with fellow guests Joel and Roberta Prives was to keep Harold occupied) gulped water in the kitchen to quench her fear-parched throat, all the while chatting bravely with the Priveses and our unsuspecting spy, I sat in the spare room rummaging through Harold's things like an apprentice spook. What a life.

In June I was promoted to major in the U.S. Army Reserve. It was a great relief; it meant that Colonel Young's ER back in the 223d and all the trouble at the hotel had not effectively destroyed my career. I did not get to wear the insignia, however. Though this was a "permanent" paper promotion (whatever that meant, but fitting somehow, for the peacetime paper war), not until the active-duty promotion board met would the little gold leaves be mine to wear.

In the meantime, SAD was about to move, to co-locate with USAREUR HQ in Heidelberg. Colonel Willard approached the move as though he were invading Normandy; our Operations Order (OPORD) was about as detailed (three desks to be displaced here, a file-cabinet assault there) and as thick. It was my responsibility to make it happen, but the job was complicated not only by Willard's mania, but by my wife and my friend the spy.

Patty was pregnant again, but having a hell of a hard time keeping the kid. She was placed in the Nürnberg hospital, where she'd remain for the rest of her term; I had to leave Laura in the care of our Nürnberg Post neighbors, Jewish Chaplain Richard Dryer and his wife, Arlene. As for Harold Borger, when I told the CIC guys I was leaving, the first thing they suggested was I invite Harold to live with us—at the Army's expense—in Heidelberg. For me, that was the end of the line. The whole affair had put an incredible strain on our lives already, and I was just sick of it. I told them there was nothing in my MOS that said I had to be a spy handler and I wasn't going to do it another day. The CIC guys hit the roof. "But you're involved in this!" they said.

"Like hell I am. I found a spy. I told you about him. Now he's your spy. He ain't mine."

The latter-day Neanderthals leaned on me very heavily. Finally I'd had enough. "Okay. This is what I'm going to do. I'm going to see Harold Borger, I'm going to tell him you're on to him, I'm going to tell him I'm a dirty rat of an agent myself and that I was the one who turned him in in the first place. Then he'll run away, the game will be over, and you won't need me anymore. Do you want me to do it that way or will you just let me go?"

"Oh," they said, "under the circumstances we'll just say you're not very cooperative."

"You're damn right. And you can put it in capital letters: HE'S NOT VERY COOPERATIVE."

Finally I was given leave to continue with my own life. My last big scene in this spy drama was to introduce my DJ friend, Mike Krumpac, to Harold. Somehow the CIC had managed to con him into taking my place as handler, although by now Harold had a couple of other "friends" to confide in, too. (Little did I know that even Chaplain Dick Dryer was involved. Borger's basic modus operandi was to seek out Jewish soldiers and tell them he was a spy for Israel. No one ever believed him, but the Jewish guy in Nürnberg who became another handler henceforth always met him at the Jewish Chapel. Borger's ultimate capture was actually timed to the end of one of Chaplain Dryer's services.)

SAD moved to Heidelberg without a hitch. About the same time, the division reorganized internally as well, and although I still dealt directly with Colonel Willard, my immediate boss was Lieutenant Colonel Clayton Quig (pronounced Queeg). An infantryman whose last post had been as an instructor at Benning, Quig was a truly dedicated officer, and a wonderful man. He was also a longtime student of the military, and one day he told me a story. Years before, he said, a bright, forward-thinking German general divided his officers into four classes: the clever, the stupid, the industrious, and the lazy. The general believed that every officer possessed two of these qualities. The clever and lazy, for example, were suited for command (they'd figure out the easiest way to do a task); the clever and industrious were suited for high-level staff. The lazy and stupid, he maintained, were an unfortunate by-product of any system and could be slotted in somewhere; but the stupid and industrious were just too dangerous, and the general's standing order was to have them removed from the military completely, the moment they were identified.

In Colonel Quig's opinion, the stupid and industrious were now running the Army, which was why the organization was in such bad shape. No one had the smarts to see a problem, he felt; everyone was too busy running after the bus driver to get his "ticket punched." It was the first time I'd heard the expression, which over the next years would become the catchword of all Army officers. *So it has a name,* I thought: ticket punching—the syndrome that had me chasing down that elusive degree; struggling, at the behest of Maxwell D. Taylor and his Chief of Staff successor Lemnitzer, to learn more German than *"Wo ist das schlafzimmer?"* ("Where is the bedroom?"); and generally covering my ass in every way possible. I was yet to know (and later wondered whether Colonel Quig had, as early as 1960) that ticket punching was like an infectious disease for which no cure existed; that, over time, it would become to the Army like the Plague, crippling its effectiveness and its strength at a time when both were needed most of all.

The flawless move to Heidelberg had me high on Colonel Willard's list. I was Boy Wonder, and even the Colonel's secretary—an abrasive, inconsiderate pain in the neck who'd worked with generals for so many years that she thought she was one—had to at least affect being civil to me. One evening as I was closing up for the day, I realized I had a staff meeting at USAREUR the following morning at the same time Colonel Willard expected a huge, not-yet-assembled staff study on his desk. I went to Sergeant Major Slattery and The All-Seeing's secretary to make sure the report would be there on time and looking good. I wasn't too concerned; the major point I made to them actually regarded the binding of the document.

Colonel Willard had an aversion to a certain kind of paper clip. If he saw those big, bulky silver ones that stuck out at the top, he went berserk. He'd explained to me in the earliest days that only the flat-edged ones (which folded down over the pages, giving the paper completely clean lines) were acceptable. So I told the Sergeant Major and Mrs. I-Would-Have-Been-a-General-if-I-Didn't-Have-Tits to be absolutely sure that the correct paper clip went on the finished work.

It didn't get there. The next morning, in the middle of my meeting, Sergeant Major Slattery rang up. "Get back here soonest. The Colonel is out of his mind. He's been screaming and cursing you since the minute he walked in."

With heart in mouth, I drove back to our HQ. "What happened, Sergeant Major?"

"I don't know. He's been raging for an hour."

"Did you get the paper to him?"

"Yes, sir."

I knocked on Willard's door. "Captain Hackworth, reporting as directed, sir!" I announced, as properly military as I could be.

"You have failed me! You have let me down! You are incompetent!" Willard cried. He picked up the assembled staff study from his desk. "Look!"

I looked. The paper was bound with the forbidden paper clip. "Sir, there's been a mistake. I briefed people not to use that clip—"

"It's YOUR fault! You're the officer in charge! You're responsible!"

"Sir, I wasn't here this morning. I left instructions. That's the best I could do."

"Well, it's not good enough, Captain. You're responsible for lives!"

Lives? I thought. *What lives am I responsible for?* The man was truly crazy. And the more he raged, the more embarrassed I became. My face was burning, probably as much as the many ears cocked and listening on the other side of those paper-thin walls in our new building. Finally it became too much. "Colonel Willard, I've heard enough. I won't accept your speaking to me in this manner. I'd gladly take responsibility if it was something of significance, but what we're talking about here is a case of clinical insanity!"

I turned around without saluting and started for the door. Willard ran from behind his desk and threw his arms around me. "Hackworth," he said, "you have to understand. I'm just under such pressure!" *Pressure?* We were a goddamned staff division. All we did was generate paperwork that went to someone else who generated more paperwork. I turned on my heels and walked out.

For the next month, Willard wouldn't even talk to me—a little awkward, given that I was his administrative officer. I got all directives through Colonel Quig (they should have switched names, those two; besides the little silver balls, Willard was Herman Wouk's Captain Queeg to the T), Sergeant Major Slattery, and Willard's secretary. Finally Quig released me from my increasingly tortuous job by organizing a special section called Review and Analysis and making me its chief. I knew nothing about the job; it was a big Harvard Management School scene through which, in chart form, the division's expenditures and performance in all areas could be monitored. I was assisted by some finance books I sent for from Fort Benjamin Harrison and by my one-man brain trust, an E-4, Tom Martin–like financial whiz-kid named Cybocal. Operating from a small, specially built office in the bowels of the building, we put on dog and pony shows with multicolored charts and graphs every quarter, and everyone seemed happy with yet another neat, new, quantitative measure to feed into the computers.

By now it was October 1960. I traveled back to Nürnberg every weekend to see Patty and Laura, and began to prepare for my annual physical in November. After nine years without any improvement, I realized that my "artillery ears" (as they were known by military tradition) were never going to get any better. The only way I'd ever get a combat assignment was to learn to beat the hearing-evaluation machine at the hospital. If Medal of Honor winner Rodger Young could do it, so could I. I studied up on how the thing worked, and found I could dramatically "improve" my hearing simply by counting beeps and pushing the button early. Just when I'd pretty well perfected the sham, I was knocked on my ass yet again: I was called to another "show cause" board for irregularities in my Personal History Statement that had been discovered while my reinstated security clearance was being updated. It appeared that the Intelligence paper pushers had misplaced the whole Fort Sill investigation file. I couldn't believe it. And besides, what did a fellow have to do to prove he was a loyal American? If I'd wanted to be a spy I could have joined Harold Borger's team. Fortunately, my file was found again some three months later, and that was the end of it.

The winter came and went. Leslie Allison was born a month after Laura's first birthday, and the family was finally reunited in our little apartment in Heidelberg. And was I ever married. The full weight of it didn't strike me until the day after Leslie's birth, when I met Dell Evans (who'd been assigned to an Armored Cav Regiment near Nürnberg) and his family at the Frankfurt airport. I couldn't help but remember the first time I'd met Dell outside of Korea, at his little house at Benning eight years before. Then, I (the freewheeling bachelor) hadn't understood how he could handle the adventureless, married, family life; now, as I took the whole Evans crew to our home for their first night in-country, it suddenly occurred to me that I *still* couldn't understand it, but that I'd damned well better figure it out, because with a wife and two kids, I sure was there, too.

On the other hand, maybe an adventure was not as far off as I thought. I passed my annual physical—including the hearing test—with flying colors, and, with Colonel Quig greasing the skids, immediately transferred out of missiles and back to the infantry. Quig, who was a great friend of Colonel Mataxis, also set in motion my request to go to an infantry unit, and suggested that I apply for Regular Army. No way, I told him; the last time I'd taken that suggestion I'd almost been shot at dawn. Besides, I didn't care if I were RA or career Reservist; in fact, in some ways being a career Reservist was better. The DCSPER managers more or less regarded us Reserve types as Christmas help, so with no tickets to punch we were virtually assured of having repeated troop duty assignments. As well, it seemed that my infantry friends who'd gone RA had had to branch-transfer to Armor in the process; the Army had switched off (to some degree, at least) push-button war, and was now grooming its Regular Army studs like Dell Evans and Phil Gilchrist for command of tank units, to be employed in a conventional ground war against Russia in Europe. I'd done my tank duty, and I knew it was not for me; all I wanted was just what I got: the chance to wear those crossed rifles again. Now I just needed a crackerjack unit to wear them in.

On 20 January 1961, forty-three-year-old John F. Kennedy was inaugurated as the thirty-fifth President of the United States. We were in Berchtesgaden skiing that day, and I rushed back to the hotel to hear his inaugural address. It was like being a kid again, crowding around the radio with Gram, Uncle Frank, Roy, and our sister Mary (who'd come to live with us after a few years of being shunted around among our relatives in Colorado) to listen to FDR during the grim war years. *"Let the word go forth,"* the new President said, *"from this time and place, to friend and foe alike, that the torch has been passed to a new generation of Americans. . . . Let every nation know, whether it wishes us well or ill, that we shall pay any price, bear any burden, meet any hardship, support any friend, oppose any foe to assure the survival and the success of liberty.*

"This much we pledge—and more."

President Kennedy filled us all with such hope. His words gave the nation a sense of purpose, and I was never prouder of being an American, or of wearing the uniform, than I was at that time. And I was not alone—servicemen all over Europe were standing with heads held just that much higher. Germans greeted us on the streets and saluted; it was as if Kennedy were their new leader, too. JFK brought about a relationship between nationals and "occupiers" unlike I'd seen since Italy in 1946. We'd been viewed as saviors then; it was only with the passage of time that our familiar faces began to breed contempt among the citizens of that land. How long the Kennedy magic would last, none of us could guess, but for the moment he was the shot in the arm America, the U.S. military, and the free world desperately needed.

The last months of the Eisenhower Administration had been pretty bleak. On 1 May 1960, Gary Powers had been shot down over Soviet airspace in his high-flying, spying U-2. Although such reconnaissance flights had been going on for four years (or so Defense Secretary Thomas Gates admitted some months later), this one, just weeks before the East-West summit in Paris, dampened any hopes for progress in relations between the two major powers.[1] The whole affair was made all the worse by America's first denying any knowledge of a spy mission, then coming up with excuses for Powers' straying into the Soviet sphere, and finally having to admit the truth when Powers began to tell all. It had been horribly mortifying for the Administration to be caught red-handed, and even worse was the absolute glee with which Khrushchev announced his catch. Finally, in Paris, the West's worst fears had been confirmed when Khrushchev walked out of the summit conference in fury. The Cold War was heating up.

On the home front, the ongoing fight between Ike and the three services had raged on, while interservice rivalry reached a fevered pitch of its own. Maxwell D. Taylor's *The Uncertain Trumpet* had been published, beseeching the Administration to abandon "massive retaliation" as a strategy and replace it with one of "flexible response." Eisenhower, still determined to balance the budget (for fiscal year 1961) in the twilight days of his presidency, made *everyone* mad by deciding to hold defense spending exactly where it was. In the meantime, in order to halt the flow of gold going out of the country, Ike decided to cut American spending overseas by ordering dependents of servicemen based abroad to come home. The order was almost inconceivable from the guy who used to wear five stars; in terms of Eisenhower's track record, though, it was just another morale buster for a hell of a lot of soldiers.

And then there'd been the emergence of a "military-industrial complex," which Ike pinpointed in his farewell address three days before Kennedy's inauguration: "In the councils of government, we must guard against the acquisition of unwarranted influence, sought or unsought, by the military-industrial complex. The potential for the disastrous rise of misplaced power exists and will persist," Eisenhower had warned, and in the last years of his Administration, claims had come fast and furious that abuses were already occurring. Ex-military officials were being snapped up as chairmen, executives, and/or key employees of the defense contractors as fast as they retired,* and it was claimed that many used the old-buddy net to get their new bosses a piece of the action. On the ground, none of us really cared much; of greater interest was what Kennedy, the new President, would do to dismantle Ike's New Look. One of the first things he did (almost the minute he took office) was rescind the "all dependents home" decree; most of us just waited with bated breath for what would come next.

What *did* come next was one of the biggest bloopers of all time. It was committed by the new Secretary of Defense, whiz-kid Robert McNamara, who told newsmen there was no "missile gap" between America and the Soviet Union. Given that this "gap" was an essential plank in Kennedy's election campaign, both the press and the Republicans had a field day until the position was clarified through typically political semantics: a missile gap did indeed exist, but, according to the newly battle-tried Secretary of Defense, there was no "destruction gap," at least at the moment. To assure

---

* In 1959, 721 retired military men of the rank of colonel or above (or navy captain and above) were employed by the top eighty-eight defense industries in the United States.[2]

that this latter gap did not become a reality, JFK raised Ike's FY '61 defense budget by $2 billion, one half of it devoted to missiles, launchers, and blast-resistant underground silos for our Atlas and Titan ICBMs.[3] At the same time, to the relief of the few die-hard remnants of the Old Army, renewed emphasis was placed on conventional war capabilities, with an initial five-thousand-man increase in the Army's ground forces (and three thousand more Marines), and nonnuclear weapons to cope with "brushfire" wars for which nuclear retaliation would be somewhat of an overreaction.[4]

I thought it was quite funny how similar ex-militaryman Ike and ex-Ford Motor Company President McNamara were in terms of "stroke of the pen" defense-spending decisions, yet with such different results. With one slash, for example, McNamara had Kennedy ax a nuclear-powered airplane program on which the Eisenhower Administration had lavished a billion dollars.[5] At forty-four, McNamara was a far cry from Ike's first Secretary of Defense, Charles Wilson (of whom a Chief of Staff once said, "He was the most uninformed man, and the most determined to remain so, that has ever been Secretary"[6]); McNamara wanted to know everything, and if the generals had anything to bitch about at all it was that McNamara wanted his information "yesterday"—not next week or next month—and was less concerned about each service's pet projects than he was about developing a worthwhile, cost-effective defense program. So with McNamara's no-nonsense, corporate approach to America's defense, and JFK's apparent vision, it seemed in those earliest days that maybe the Army and the nation were about to get back on track. But then came a debacle of the first order, one the fledgling Kennedy Administration inherited from Ike.

Time was showing that my idol Castro, the nationalist patriot, had never been much of a democrat. Though the Eisenhower Administration's fear of a Soviet satellite in our backyard had yet to come to pass, Castro's communistic leanings were growing more apparent by the day. From the start, the U.S. position hadn't helped the situation much. As if to show Castro "who's boss," the U.S. moved to deny Cuba access to American sugar markets. In turn, Castro sought (and received) economic assistance from the Soviet Union. Meanwhile, a not-insignificant proportion of middle-class Cubans were less than happy with the new regime, and by the time Kennedy was elected, the overeager CIA believed that, given the means, Castro could be overthrown. *The people are ready*, they told the President. *They'll rise up and meet us on the beach. We can liberate them!* What followed was the Bay of Pigs. The faultiness of the intelligence for this operation could not be overstated: the U.S.-based Cuban exiles who stormed the beach were not met by cheering crowds but by a well-armed Cuban Army. This disastrous attempt at a countercoup resulted in 87 wounded among the invasion force,

250 dead, and long columns of POWs, most of whom were returned in an extortionlike exchange for farming equipment and medical supplies. It caused the new Administration extreme embarrassment, and sent Castro scooting firmly into the Soviet camp. I don't know which disappointed me more, Kennedy's bad judgment or Castro's losing his white hat once and for all. Now old Fidel was just the enemy. Now he was just a goddamn Red.

The beautiful Heidelberg spring gave way to summer. Patty and I took the kids on picnics and bike rides through the vineyards and the manicured Black Forest, by the castles and the Neckar River. I really enjoyed being a husband and father at times like these, but with no childhood role model for either, it was pretty much a touch-and-go situation—I could only handle each in small doses. Like most American servicemen and families overseas, we didn't socialize with the "Rads" (short for "comrades," our name for the German people), and everyone seemed to like it better that way. We lived in the "Mark Twain" American military village; we listened to American radio, saw American films, drank American booze at the American officers' clubs, and shopped at the American PX for American goodies. All in all, a tour in Germany was not that much different from a tour at Fort Benning, except that things were cheaper overseas and the Germans were so damned efficient.

Our only close German contact was the housekeeper I'd employed while Patty was in the hospital. She was a skinny old lady who looked more like an ostrich than a human being; she had a mind of her own, and from the moment Patty got home it was all-out war. The final battleground was the kitchen floor, which Frau Gobbler was cleaning with the sponge ordinarily used to wash dishes. It had happened before and Patty, with her sterile, surgical nursing background, couldn't bear it. She hit the roof, and the housekeeping arrangement was terminated on the spot. Some time later I was summoned to a German magistrate court to explain why Frau Gobbler was released without notice. When I related the sponge incident, the courtroom audience broke up laughing; I squirmed with embarrassment in my neat green uniform, and quietly paid the fine for firing the old birdlike troublemaker.

Finally, finally my infantry orders came through: I was to report to the 8th Div, 1st Battlegroup, 18th Infantry, near Mannheim. It was a nice twist of fate: the unit was a direct descendant of the U.S. 18th, which my great-grandfather Jeremiah and his oldest son, George Washington Hackworth, belonged to when they fought their Hackworth cousin, Billy (who was with Bedford Forrest's 4th Tennessee Cav, CSA), during the Civil War. Though I was authorized a few weeks' leave between assignments, I raced over the second I said good-bye to Colonel Quig, because I was absolutely panicked that the clerks at Personnel would change their minds, or call for another hearing test.

I'd been away from infantry, and from the Army I'd grown up in, for far too long. Walking through the gates of Coleman Barracks was stepping into the welcome past—the Old Army had not died after all. The 18th was military perfection. Men stepped smartly across meticulously kept grounds. Starched uniforms, blue infantry scarves, dazzlingly shined brass and boots, snappy salutes, and cheerful "Good afternoon, sir!"'s marked my journey to the HQ where I'd sign in. The spirit of this fine unit was already infecting me. The hot, stifling, windless day, the ragweed pollen that blew in from adjacent fields, covering the camp and immediately activating my hay fever (which would continue to plague me throughout my time with the 18th), the run-down, boring camp itself—none of it mattered, as inwardly I was transported to an island oasis untouched by turbulent seas.

And it was all thanks to one man, the battlegroup CO, who would forever after be my model, mentor, and friend. Colonel Glover S. Johns was the finest senior infantry commander I'd ever seen, or would ever see again. We shared a mutual, abiding respect almost from the moment we met: he was my kind of soldier and I was his. He was a warrior—Patton's aide before WW II, then during the war he'd hit the beaches of Normandy as part of the 29th Division, and fought from those bloody shores all across Europe until victory was achieved. As a battalion CO, he'd headed the task force that captured the critical French town of St. Lô. Chronicled in his own hard-hitting book, *The Clay Pigeons of St. Lo*, the WW II feats of Johns's men (and Johns himself) were well known to me long before I had the good luck to serve under him.

In Korea he'd served as XO, then regimental commander in my own 40th Division. His reputation there was awesome. One story that made its way through the division was that a wild new XO had come to the 224th, gotten down on his belly in the mud to check the unit's machine-gun fields of fire, and promptly moved two-thirds of the MG bunkers that had sat there for two years. I'd immediately thought of my own Fighter Company renovations and wished to hell that this savvy character had been assigned to the 223d. Later, when he took over as CO of the 224th and the unit moved to a new sector, he'd outposted a spur about two hundred yards in front of one of his companies so the North Koreans couldn't do it first. "I didn't intend to wake up some morning and find a couple hundred gooks looking down my throat," he said. But this move was considered "seizing ground" and against the no-win rules of the war, and soon the X Corps CG, I. D. White, flew down to Johns's position to discuss the matter with him. After examining the situation, General White (of whom Johns was a favored son from their Fort Riley days) told him he could keep the spur, but was never to "advance" again—even his outpost line—without express permission from Corps.

The 40th Division combat patch I wore on my right shoulder made conversation easy when Colonel Johns greeted me at his office door. He talked with a soft, Texas drawl, similar to that of the Vice President, Lyndon Johnson. As he ushered me inside, I noticed that his blue eyes sparkled, like those of a wise and truly tested man who'd long since realized that humor could be found in just about anything. He had seen his share of horror. His cheeks were rosy and the dueling scar (or so went the story, from his prewar, postgraduate training at the Munich Technische Hochschule) that crossed one of them in no way detracted from his rugged yet gentle Old-Soldier face. Maybe the scar even enhanced it, I don't know, but it sure gave it more character, and provided a good yarn to boot.* In any event, Colonel Glover S. Johns was a forty-nine-year-old stud.

He wanted me to be his assistant S-3. I wanted a rifle company. He said I'd already had far more than my share of command experience as far as the career-balancing Pentagon paper shufflers were concerned. I said I'd been out of infantry since 1953 and the only way to get caught up on the ins and outs of the changing Pentomic setup would be to learn it down with the troops. Besides, I knew I'd soon be promoted to major and this would be my last shot at command at the company level. After that, with virtually no command billets for majors, I'd go to Staff, and with promotions so slow, unless there was a war somewhere I could expect to retire in five years at that rank, without commanding another trooper at all.

Johns gave me a long look. Then, with laughing eyes, he said, "Well, son, I can only give you the best I've got," and went on to tell me about Company D, which, under the command of Captain Donald Hanson, had just passed its company Army Training Test (ATT) with max scores, and was well reputed as the finest unit in the battlegroup. *Oh, boy,* I thought—it's a bitch to take over the best. If you take the worst, anything you do is considered great. But with the best, even the most spectacular accomplishments are treated as everyday occurrences, if they're treated at all. On top of that, it's damned hard to make a mark on a unit already full of hotshots. Johns knew all this, of course (or, as he would have put it, "natch," for "naturally"); it was as though he'd thrown down a gauntlet, and it was my choice whether or not to accept the challenge. But, "natch," he knew I would.

Before I left the office, Johns told me one last 40th Division war story,

---

* In fact, Johns received that scar in an automobile accident in Taipei. He was drunk at the time, and barely missed receiving a general court-martial upon his recovery.

about his first night with the Fireball. "I was in a battalion HQ on the line," he said. "At about 0300, the whole staff went nuts. I thought maybe I'd rouse myself a little to see what was happening. Turns out they'd just had word a patrol was fired on. Someone said, 'God! We better get this to Corps immediately!' while the rest of them were running around like headless chickens.

"Now, Captain," Johns continued in his slow drawl, "I would have reduced any company commander of mine to a bloody pulp if he'd called me at 0300—had I been asleep, which I usually was not—to say one of his patrols had run into a problem. All I'd want to know was who caused it and what they did about it, and I wouldn't want to know that until I could get it in detail after the patrol got back. Unless, of course," he added, "they'd run into something serious in the way of an enemy move.

"But, you see," he said, becoming a teacher, as if I were one of the fortunate cadets who had studied at Virginia Military Institute (VMI) while he was commandant there (his most recent assignment before the 18th), "the Army took a hell of a beating in Korea, and the greatest part was *after* the heavy fighting was over. First there was the 'no-win war' spirit. Then there were the political limitations imposed on us during the peace negotiations. And the Army meekly submitted, raising higher and ever higher the point of responsibility for the smallest action. I was a regimental commander, and if *I* couldn't send out even one patrol without Corps approval of the plan—submitted forty-eight hours in advance—what did that make all you company and battalion COs? Messenger boys. You had no authority. You had no room to run. No room to fail.

"I believe a young officer should have room to fail, Captain Hackworth."

And as Colonel Johns showed me to the door ("Now get on out of here . . ." he said), I knew I was home.

12 THE VANGUARDS

When Hack came to take command, we were on a field problem. He tagged along for a week or ten days, just observing and saying nothing. Finally, at the change-of-command ceremony (which was in the field), he said something to the effect of "Gee, this sure is a good company, and I'm proud to take command of it. But you ain't seen nothing yet—just wait till I'm done with you."

My thoughts at the time, and those of my peers, were, "He's not going to be able to teach us anything. He's just a muscle-bound, egotistical SOB who'll probably end up ruining a very good rifle company we're proud to be in."

Boy, were we wrong.

First Sergeant Jack Frye, USA, Ret.
Fire Team Leader/Squad Leader
Company D, 1/18th Infantry, Germany, 1960–62

"Let's get something straight from the start, Captain."

"What's that, Top?"

"You're the skipper. You command this outfit. But I run it. Don't you forget—I run it."

So counseled my first sergeant, Master Sergeant James J. Sweeney, as if by way of introduction. I could have hugged him. Sweeney's record spoke for itself: four combat jumps with Jim Gavin's 505th Parachute Regiment in the 82d Airborne, attendantly fighting with distinction across Europe, and then in Korea six years later. Now this leathery old soldier of twenty-some years' experience (who still carried all his worldly goods in two duffel bags) stood straight as a West Point plebe before me, his deep-set eyes challenging and confident as he told me the lay of the land in D Company, 1/18 Inf. And I couldn't have agreed with him more.

I'd found myself with a commander's dream: a great, enthusiastic unit ramrodded by the best NCO corps I'd seen since Trieste. The NCOs were real professionals—*From Here to Eternity* types, most with WW II and

Korean combat experience—who knew what they were doing, did it well, and made my job a breeze. In garrison I seldom had to give an order. If I looked at my watch and said, "Top, it's time to fall the company out," the First Sergeant's response would be, "They're out in the company street, sir, like four rows of corn." If I said, "Sweeney, are we set for the alert?" his reply would be, "Yes, sir. The troops are leaning forward in their foxholes."

It was about this time I finally concluded that the Army—if it hadn't had the ongoing requirement of producing senior officers—wouldn't need good lieutenants, or even good captains at the company level, as long as it had good sergeants. I'd probably sensed this all along, but it had taken me sixteen full years to *know* it as a military "truth." In a company, one of the main things that was needed was continuity. Officers were moved from job to job so frequently (I'd seen it time and again in Korea) that they could provide little of that; a wizened old sergeant could. Among the other essentials, besides raw leadership, were hands-on knowledge and good common sense; in these regards, an experienced senior sergeant was usually far better qualified to lead than the average company-grade officer. No doubt I was a bit biased, but I found that by giving my noncoms the free rein I'd had as far back as Trieste under Captain Eggleston, they pulled like hell for me. And with Sweeney and his NCOs anticipating every drill, D Company ran like a well-greased machine.

Most of the 1/18th's NCOs had been with the unit for at least six years—three at Fort Riley, Kansas, before the 1st Division became Pentomic and its battlegroups were gyroscoped to Germany for a three-year tour. Bottom-line professionalism was probably the only thing that had kept these fine, dedicated men from outright rebellion during the big switch: when in Germany they found that in the interests of saving money, the 1st Division's maneuver units were to be reassigned to the 8th Div, while their own 1st Div colors stayed at Fort Riley (controlling the 8th Div units that had gyroscoped home).

It was the nonthinking Pentagon movers in one of their more infamous hours. The proud regiments of the 1st Division—the 16th "Rangers," the 18th "Vanguards," and the 26th "Blue Spaders"—had been 1st Div regiments since 1917, when the division was formed; the unit had a glorious battle record, as well as the distinction of being the first to fight in both World Wars. The 8th, on the other hand, first saw combat in WW II, was inactivated after the war, and was reactivated five years later as a training division. In fairness, the 8th had fought well during the war, but that was not the point: the Big Red One patch allowed no one to forget that unit's place as America's premier division. To expect a longtime 1st Div man to exchange it for another was tantamount to asking him to join the WACs.

Talk about morale busters. As it was, most of the old NCOs were just marking time until their overseas tour was up and they could go back to Fort Riley and their beloved Big Red One.

Still, while they were there, the NCOs gave the 8th Div their all, and they were of particular assistance to me in my first weeks with D Company. The outfit I'd inherited was good, but not (or so said then weapons platoon leader Lieutenant Brian "Tim" Grattan some months later) as good as its members thought. Right away I saw little areas here and there where I could make it even better, and set about making changes with great enthusiasm. Most, as was becoming my style, regarded training.

When I first arrived in the 1/18th, I was surprised to find that many mornings at reveille the troops had to recite, like robots (in unison at the top of their lungs), a little number called the "Code of Conduct for Members of the Armed Forces of the United States":

> I am an American fighting man. I serve in the forces which guard my country and our way of life. I am prepared to give my life in their defense.
>
> I will never surrender of my own free will. If in command I will never surrender my men while they still have the means to resist.
>
> If I am captured I will continue to resist by all means available. I will make every effort to escape and aid others to escape. I will accept neither parole nor special favors from the enemy.
>
> If I become a prisoner of war, I will keep faith with my fellow prisoners. I will give no information or take part in any action which might be harmful to my comrades. If I am senior, I will take command. If not, I will obey the lawful orders of those appointed over me and will back them up in every way.
>
> When questioned, should I become a prisoner of war, I am bound to give only name, rank, service number, and date of birth. I will evade answering further questions to the utmost of my ability. I will make no oral or written statements disloyal to my country and its allies or harmful to their cause.
>
> I will never forget that I am an American fighting man, responsible for my actions, and dedicated to the principles which made my country free. I will trust in my God and in the United States of America.

The Code had been developed by an all-knowing Pentagon study group in response to the appalling manner in which American POWs conducted themselves during the Korean War (becoming turncoats, denouncing America, playing footsie with the Reds, etc.; in all, 43 percent of men captured collaborated with the enemy in some way).[1] The purpose of the thing was to steel the will of soldiers in future wars, but it was closing the proverbial barn door after the horse had bolted. If we'd had hardened, well-trained, and well-led soldiers in Korea, we wouldn't have had all those POWs to begin with. The U.S. Marine Corps had very few; outfits like the tough Ethiopians had none. To me, the "Code of Conduct" was a silly and degrading exercise. And it was potentially dangerous, too, in that as an Army-wide preventive wartime cure-all, it could easily lead to even worse complacency in the peacetime training program. Now six years old, the Code was a quick fix that addressed the symptoms, not the disease.

But not in D Company, or, for that matter, in the whole 1/18th Infantry Battlegroup. For the first time since I'd said good-bye to the Great White Father, General Cleland, I was in an organization whose commander (Johns) and deputy (Colonel George Couch, another great Brown Shoe Army soldier and a WW II Big Red One man) concurred totally with my unwavering belief that "the more sweat on the training field, the less blood on the battlefield."

Every morning in D Company began with a long, hard run ("Hi de di de, God Almighty/Who the hell are we?/Rim ram, God damn/We're the infantry!"), the length depending on how much time I had up my sleeve and how mean I felt. The platoon sergeants, platoon leaders, and I ran backwards, counting, chewing ass, encouraging, and using up twice as much energy as the troops; with all the usual bitching that accompanied the runs, the boys got stronger and, as important, *felt* stronger. I took them on long marches in full gear, and reintroduced my Korea policy of having every soldier's feet examined immediately afterward by his squad leader, platoon leader, and me. All this nuclear battlefield shit notwithstanding, I still maintained that an infantry trooper's feet were the mobility of the nation; the kids knew I cared when I squatted down over their sweaty feet to make sure they were okay, and in the process I was able to instill my troop-leading style into the young studs who would be commanding during the next war.

As well as my great NCOs, I'd been blessed in the officer department, too. Lieutenants Al Ferraro, Dave Adderley, Joe Woodridge (whose admiral father had been one of the planners for the Bay of Pigs), and Tim Grattan were all Distinguished Military Graduates (DMGs) fresh out of university ROTC or the Military Academy. Adderley, Grattan, Ferraro, and my XO, Ed Szvetecz, had been football stars in their college days (Szvetecz was All-American, and captain of the West Point team); all five men were in fine shape, as well as being well-motivated, sharp young Regular officers. We'd had a somewhat rocky start (they all thought I was crazy), but after these boys were introduced to Willie Lump Lump, and I had them and their units sit down in front of a movie projector and watch the WW II Italian campaign documentary *The Battle of San Pietro*, they began to understand what I was all about, and why I was training them so hard. I'd shown the film in every unit I'd commanded to date. It was a brilliant picture that showed on-the-ground, real-life infantry in combat. I loved it for a lot of reasons, the main one being it dispelled all myths of war as a cops-and-robbers game; I always felt they should have given salty old John Huston the Blue Max just for making it.

I gave as many classes personally as I could, not only for the benefit of the troops, but for myself. I found that the teacher learns as much as, if not more than, his students, and it also kept my own skills sharpened to a fine edge. It's easy to lose touch with the basics, and you become less inclined to get them back once you've moved up the ladder; I'd seen too many high-ranking officers who'd stopped trying, having decided, I guessed, that they were "above all that."

Colonel Johns was not among this group, though. Johns was a "basics" man and a total soldier. He taught—and insisted that his company commanders teach—things like terrain appreciation, the knowledge of which was a basic tool of a soldier's trade: to be able to look at a piece of ground and appreciate the slightest differences in the contour; to notice how the ground unfolds and be able to think *There's cover over there*—cover, the one essential, providing protection from direct enemy fire; to recognize a stream line, a gully, or a treed area as an avenue of approach through which a unit could move unseen; to understand and identify the best ground from which to launch or repel an attack. Shoot, scoot, and communicate—the "three R's" of infantry were where Johns began and worked his way up. The morning battle drill began with fire and maneuver, one man firing while his buddy moved, a fire team moving while its counterpart fired. Colonel Johns likened it to a fighter's "bobbing, weaving, and jabbing"—we kept the mythical enemy pinned down while we jabbed our way to close on his position. The Colonel was right there with us to set the example, and we did it—just as we had with Prazenka in the I&R—until we got it right. We'd end up black-and-blue (running, hitting the ground, and rolling into firing position with full field equipment on is not without pain), but no one bitched because Johns again and again reinforced the simple equation: the quicker you get to the ground and get your weapon into position, the sooner you'll be delivering effective fire on the enemy and the longer you'll stay alive.

Still, this truism was just one part of the overall, strive-to-better-your-best philosophy that characterized the 1/18th under Colonel Johns and Deputy CO Couch. In Couch's words: "It was our policy to encourage excellence among the soldiers, particularly in bayonet training, unarmed combat, shooting, and total physical fitness. This is what really makes a soldier; if he masters these subjects, he'll fight." From my experience in Korea, I could not have agreed more.

D Company trained hard, staying in the field at least four days a week. We never set up tents or any other administrative comforts; instead, we'd form a defensive perimeter or pretend we were on line, tied into another unit. Everything was tactical: steel pots on, faces and uniforms camouflaged, no one bunched up, rifles at the ready. Even chow call was done tactically: the mess truck covered with a camouflage net, guys well spaced out as they filed through, their weapons at no time more than an arm's distance away. I stressed the basics all along. I'd have one platoon aggress against another and then reverse them, until they were masters of both defense and attack procedures. I wanted each unit trained so well that a PFC could take a platoon and run it. "If I drop dead, one of you guys better be able to take my place—and do a damn good job of it," Prazenka used to say; now, stressing that it happened *regularly* on the battlefield, during training exercises I'd tell a platoon leader he was dead and to put one of his PFCs in charge. The first time I did this troopers panicked, claiming they didn't know what to do. "You've just had twelve hours' instruction on the Platoon in the Attack," I told them. "You've got the knowledge. Just get cracking and do it. When we get in a real fight you'll be a leader. So learn it now." And they did, with confidence soaring all the way. Even without live fire, all tactical training was conducted as close to actual battlefield conditions as I could make it. When attacking or defending, I insisted that leaders go through the drill of adjusting artillery and calling in air strikes, even though neither was available on the training field. I made the leaders pretend they were talking to the Air Force forward air control or artillery people. They felt damned foolish, but were more afraid of my thunder than the embarrassment they felt playing make-believe. Eventually the calling for fires became an instilled habit, which was the object—just another tool in the kit bag to be pulled out by second nature as needed on the battlefield.

The Army's prototype T-44 rifle was now in production and, renamed the M-14, had been issued in small numbers to the battlegroup. The M-14 was a good solid rifle, with semi- and fully automatic capabilities, which made it the perfect replacement (as it was intended) for the M-1, M-3, carbine, and the BAR. It was only a matter of time before all of us were issued them; in the meantime I borrowed every M-14 I could get, scrounged ammo (the weapon used NATO's standardized 7.62 cartridge as did the M-60 MG, which would ultimately make the logistics of resupply a hell of a lot simpler), and trained the whole company in order to guarantee my boys' instant proficiency with the weapon when the changeover day came.

We still fired on KD ranges; my constant bitch was that we needed combat ranges where the targets popped up at varying distances and behind rocks and trees—after all, that's how it was on the battlefield. Johns couldn't do anything about the KD range, but in his own way showed marksmanship for what it ought to be. This full colonel would stroll along the range for a while giving encouragement and instruction, then stop by a soldier: "You got a quarter, son?" he'd ask.

"Yes, sir."

"Give me your rifle there." The trooper would hand over his weapon. After taking a good hard look at it, Johns would turn to the kid. "Now you just throw that quarter up in the air. High as you like."

The trooper would toss up the coin, and before he had a chance to blink, Johns would put a bullet—sometimes two—right through the middle of it. He'd hand back the kid's rifle as the quarter ricocheted to the ground, and continue down the firing line until he got the urge to display his prowess once again.

The "Johns Quarter," as it was called, was a sought-after prize. More than that, though, was the pleasure of watching him "produce" one. The troops loved it. Johns was a showman in the truest sense of the word (and he was also the first to admit it)—for him it was a basic principle of leadership.

Every Friday night we had a beer call, a somewhat formal exercise that all battlegroup officers attended. Promptly at 1800 the battlegroup band, an ad hoc little team composed of eager battlegroup medics and litter bearers (whose renditions probably had J. P. Sousa rolling in his grave), would begin to play and we'd start drinking from huge German beer steins, each personalized with the officer's name and embossed with the 1/18th Infantry insignia. During the evening, Colonel Johns would give a little speech recapping the past week's events; then he'd present the Fugawi Award, a wooden plaque with an infantry blue background on which was painted a caricature of an Indian (big nose, busted feathers, broken arrows, tomahawk, and so forth). The legend that accompanied this prize was that there once was an Indian tribe that was always lost. At the Battle of Little Big Horn, Sitting Bull had tasked this tribe to go down a ravine and come up behind Custer's Easy Company, but they went down the wrong ravine and, as usual, got lost. The chief of the tribe, realizing his error, went up to the top of the hill and called out mournfully, "Where the fuck are we?" Resonating throughout the hills, his call sounded like "Fugawi," and Sitting Bull said, "From now on they will be known as the Fugawis." In the 1/18th, the Fugawi Award went to the company or individual staff officer responsible for the biggest snafu or screwup of the week. Johns would give a kind of humbling but often hilarious recapitulation of how it had gone; in this neat way, lessons were learned and admonishments given, but no one was hurt because it was all good fun.

And *fun* was a necessary component in an otherwise painfully boring peacetime scene, particularly for "combat" units like ours. The 8th Division acted as Seventh Army reserve. We were way back from where the main fighting lines would be, and because there were Airborne battlegroups in the division as well, we Vanguards would be the last to be employed. A year before, the 1/18th had received the highest combat-readiness rating in Seventh Army; as a result, our role had become (theoretically) that of a general fire brigade, with all kinds of contingency plans and NATO responsibilities. As well, only a stone's throw from Heidelberg, USAREUR, and that great general Bruce Clarke, we had more than our share of visiting firemen, which meant honor guards, parades, and jumping through flaming hoops on command. These created a lot of pressure, but on a nuts-and-bolts level, life in the 1/18th consisted mainly of training, practice alerts, and waiting for the East-West balloon to go up for real. Or, if you were into that kind of thing, paperwork.

The paperwork was enormous. With directives coming from DA, USAREUR, Seventh Army, V Corps, Division, and Battlegroup (all of which requiring answers, reports, and further implementing instructions), if a company commander chose, he could easily spend his time fighting this bureaucratic war and never see his troops at all. Swollen HQs, like the one I'd recently left, had nothing else to do; as they scribbled away *their* boredom, they did not consider the impact of their work down at the maneuver level. Personally, I refused to get wrapped around the axle in red tape from higher HQ, or in normal company administrative detail; I left it all to "Big Ed" Szvetecz, who was brilliant at this sort of thing, and stayed in the field instead, working to create some excitement and adventure for my troops while getting them prepared to fight a real war.

Knowing how important food was to them, I often broke regulations and snuck my mess truck forward so a piping-hot breakfast would be waiting when we got to the field. I had a great mess sergeant who converted the truck into a mobile diner; it reached the point where he cooked on the move and the boys could file through and pick up steaming coffee and huge sandwiches of scrambled eggs and bacon on toast (it sure beat cold Cs), which they ate on the way to the LD. Often I'd call the mess sergeant in the middle of the last day of an exercise and tell him I wanted to surprise the troops for their job well done. I'd give him our ETA, and he'd be at the front gate to meet us, bearing a hamburger and a big bottle of German beer for every guy. No one had to pay (we always did this toward the end of the month when everyone was broke); money came from our highly irregular, totally unauthorized slush fund.

Monitored by Szvetecz, we generated capital for the fund by renting out our mobile mess (as a snack bar) to other companies when they were in the field. We also had an unauthorized company bar where the guys could go during off-duty hours in their fatigues, for drinks, pretzels, and sandwiches. What was so good about all this (besides the obvious morale lift) was that it gave us the means to improve our overall life and times, throw an occasional party, and send guys off in style. No one had to go around asking people to chip in a buck to buy some guy a going-away present; instead, through slush-fund proceeds, I had little Company D "being there" trophies made. It was just a small thing, this memento of our service together, but it did wonders for team spirit.

Every few months the 1/18th went up to Baumholder, a former German training area north of Mannheim (and home to the 8th Div live firing ranges and maneuver areas), for a couple of weeks of field exercises. Baumholder was a dreary, desolate place that seemed to have a corner on rain, mud, and ragweed. Tim Grattan was my partner in misery there during hay-fever season, both our allergies further aggravated by the dust kicked up on maneuvers. Neither of us could open our eyes in the morning; it sometimes took half an hour to soak the dried pus off before we could even muster a blink.

But the battlegroup maneuvers were great. The old NCOs knew every fold in the ground by memory; they were like Indian scouts. They seldom used maps, and referred to objectives as "the hill where Captain Holland got lost" or other event-tied coordinates. Colonel Johns (natch) was magic in the field. General Grant of the Civil War was reputed to have had a somewhat simple captain whom he vetted all his orders through, figuring that if this guy understood, everyone would. Johns employed a "Grant's Captain" (as it had become known) of his own, and as a result his operations orders were always clear and to the point. He also left the door wide open for questions if, for whatever reason, a subordinate wasn't sure of his task: "Find out what the goddamned mission is," Johns would counsel, "before you go slapping off the walls." It was a most welcome invitation. The average company commander, especially in the new "gotta be perfect" Army, was one afraid to admit he wasn't sure. He might (perhaps) ask one of his peers for clarification or advice, but heaven forbid he should go to the source and be branded a little slow on the draw or just plain dumb on his next ER. Johns didn't give a damn about ERs; in fact, he was repulsed by what he saw them doing to the Army. In the field he just wanted results, and knew the only way to get them was to make sure his people knew what they were doing, and got it right the first time around.

One night on maneuvers the battlegroup Operations officer, newly promoted Major Sapenter, kept bugging me for my flag location. It was pitch-black and pouring rain, and I didn't know where the hell we were, except that we were still not settled in. "When we're set up, I'll give you the coordinates," I told him. The constant harassment on the field phone continued. "According to battlegroup SOP," Sapp boomed through the wires, "I should have had your report thirty minutes ago. You are violating battlegroup SOP, Captain."

I really did hate staff officers, even good ones like old Sapp, whom I'd known since Korea. I grabbed the phone out of the hands of Robbie Robinson, my wonderful RTO. "Look, Major," I snapped, "if it'll make you happy you just take the battlegroup SOP and shove it up your ass, 'cause I'm not giving you a report on anything until I'm goddamn well ready!"

Next thing I knew, the phone sounded again, and through it came a slow Texas drawl. "Hack," the Colonel began, "Sapp here just told me about this little problem you've got. I think you might be being a bit hard on him. What do you think? How about just stretching a poncho over your head, flipping on a flashlight, and giving us those coordinates so we can send 'em on to Division?"

"Colonel Johns, if you have a look at *Clay Pigeons of St. Lo* you'll see that the young battalion commander tells his regimental S-3 exactly what I've just told *your* S-3.* Seems to me that's following the *real* battlegroup SOP."

Johns laughed. "It's mighty hard to argue with that, son. You've got your SOPs right. Get back to us when you can."

When we came in from the field, Johns and I laughed about it again. Even though he cautioned me to think twice before blowing my top, he added that from his experience he'd concluded that in combat a CO will put up with just about any insubordination as long as the subordinate wins the fight. It made sense to me, but it wasn't for a few years yet that I'd know exactly what he meant.

If Colonel Johns was an old soldier's soldier, our battlegroup chaplain, Father Francis Xavier O'Connor, was an old soldier's padre. This huge ex-football player Irishman drove around the battlegroup to give absolution

---

* "The Major [Johns] was very tired and his temper was definitely showing signs of wear. He launched his attack without preliminaries, 'Warfield, I'm Major Johns. Just how the hell did you expect my company commanders and my S-3 to make you an overlay in the middle of this black night when there's Krauts all over the place and no more shelter for light than the palm of my hand? . . . In the future before you go asking for impossible things you better make it your business to find out what the situation is.' "

and say Mass in an unauthorized jeep (borrowed from the Cav) with a machine gun mounted on the back. He could also drink and curse with the best of us. Still, only once did I witness even a temporary slip from grace, and that was one night at the Baumholder Officers' Club. Father O'Connor played the piano, and regularly led the battlegroup officers in rowdy sing-alongs. "I Just Want to Play Piano in a Whorehouse" was one of the tops on his and that other Irish lad Tim Grattan's personal hit parade. At Baumholder we were right in the middle of one such off-color little tune when the Assistant Division Commander bustled in, chewed every one of our asses (including the Chaplain's), and banned us from the club for singing unbecoming an officer. "There are ladies in the club!" he raged. We moved out, our heads hung low, but not before giving winks to the "ladies," who had, in fact, been humming (if not singing) along as well.

But how did the other ladies, the wives, fare throughout the days on end when their husbands were in the field? As well as possible, but all things considered, theirs was a pretty empty lot. Too, dreams of romantic reunions upon our return were regularly shattered; "so close yet so far away" well described life for the Company D officers' wives in Mannheim while we were "home" at Coleman Barracks. And the wives collectively (unfairly, I thought) hated me for it. Sure, it was my fault the car pool to work left at 0500, and it probably was my fault that we didn't knock off until around seven in the evening. But could I be blamed for the fact that by the time we'd finished drinking a few beers and shooting the breeze it was ten at night before "Hi, honey, what's for dinner?" rang out through most D Company apartments in Benjamin Franklin Village?

We men just never stopped. Each evening we'd discuss the day's events. Then we'd talk about what we were going to do the next day *and* the next week. Sunday, the one full day off, was spent sleeping and gearing up to start all over again. I might have started the ball rolling, but now it was total gung-ho dedication on all our parts to make D Company the best rifle company in the world. Having such a tight group of officers did wonders for the morale of the whole outfit, but it took a hell of a toll on the home front. None of us consciously decided to lock the girls out, but there was a certain perverse pleasure in speaking in the silent shorthand we'd developed over many a beer (dozens of signals, like the hand over the mouth, palm up, meant "Say no more, you've said enough"; a forefinger pulling down at the bottom eyelid meant "I, indeed, know better"; a forefinger on the nose meant "Surely this guy is bullshitting") while our wives, oblivious, chatted away by our sides.

So they shouldn't have married military men. It's a terrible life that never gets better. The job has top priority; the wife and family get what's left. The wife has to be a perfect woman to match up with and help advance her ambitious, "perfect" husband. She has to put up with loneliness. She has to be prepared to move at a moment's notice and at the same time have the old quarters (which were always too small for active little kids, and by no means childproof) unscratched, unscuffed, and so clean that even the most tyrannical housing inspector with the keenest eyes and whitest gloves in the world could not level a statement of charges, hold up the move, and put the word out that she (and by extension, her husband) was a slob. And should she manage to get away with max scores for housekeeping, all it meant was starting the same thing all over again in another billet identical to the last. The villages looked like serial German-made Holiday Inns. Quarters were close—eight families per single four-storied stairwell—and on rainy days there'd be scores of toddlers racing up and down the steps. It was a wonder none of the mothers jumped off their roofs.

Worst off were the newlyweds. Lieutenants brought home $220 a month, and with all spare change going to buy cribs and strollers for a kid (almost invariably) conceived on the honeymoon, by the end of the month, husband and wife were eating Corn Flakes and powdered milk. And if by chance they weren't, or were driving a Chevy (wagewise, a captain's car) and not a VW, the gossip would begin: everyone knew what everyone else made, and if a family lived beyond its means, well, *someone must have a rich daddy*.

But the wives made do, scurrying back and forth between apartments, borrowing sugar, playing bridge, and solving one another's problems. Many got involved doing charity work; others hit the bottle or played around (with word somehow always getting back to the cuckolded husband). I personally was my normal, rotten self, having neither time nor patience to understand my family's needs. When Patty knocked out two of her teeth in a bicycling mishap, she rang me at work; my response was "What the hell do you expect me to do? For Christ's sake, go to the dentist. And don't ever call me at work again!"

XO Ed Szvetecz' wife, Pam, was not really like the others. She was an ex-airline stewardess, and a liberated woman long before it was fashionable. Every Wednesday afternoon Ed had to go home and wax their apartment floors (or so went the word). We all gave him a hard time about it: what was a West Point, Airborne/Ranger, All-American football player, U.S. Army stud doing waxing the floor while his wife stood nearby with her arms folded across her chest (or so we imagined)? Unfortunately, I had to give up my personal razzing. Ed was my neighbor at Benjamin Franklin Village, and our wives became good friends. Pam "corrupted" Patty into believing that she didn't have to shine my shoes or my brass (a job I'd assigned her at the outset of our marriage), and that I could damn well do it myself. One evening I arrived home only to have the riot act read out, and Patty steadfastly refused to do this wifely chore ever again. How much nicer it would have been had she followed Colonel Johns's suggestion, offered up to the wives at one of their regular luncheons: "When your man comes home from the field you should be at the door to meet him . . . martinis in one hand, your panties in the other." (Unfortunately, it was a suggestion ably countered by Tim Grattan's wife, Darlene, who said, "Colonel Johns forgot one thing—by the time you guys get home, you're too sloshed to even know the difference.")

Among the top EM in the unit was my driver/RTO, William "Robbie" Robinson. Robbie was bold and fast behind the wheel of our brand-new state-of-the-art M151 jeep (which was actually a death trap, with individual wheel suspension and a tendency to flip over). I called him "Stirling" when he was driving, after race-car driver Stirling Moss, and spent most of my time on the road hanging on tight and sucking up the seat. In the field, though, in his guise at RTO, Robbie was diligent, careful, and almost spongelike in the way he soaked up the skills necessary to command and fight a unit. In this respect he reminded me a lot of Don Neary, my RTO in the Raiders, who as a corporal was actually given command after Hill 400 when all the leaders were evacuated, until Lieutenant Arvidson was found to take my place. No one had bitched, not even the more senior noncoms left in the unit; everyone knew that Neary, because he'd been with me all the time, had the best know-how to keep the unit going strong.

The relationship between commander and RTO is a unique one. In the field or in combat, a CO goes nowhere without his radio; as a result, he and his RTO are together twenty-four hours a day. It's a very tight relationship; over time, an RTO knows his CO as a woman knows her man. This puts the RTO in a uniquely powerful position. He lives with the troops, and because he's usually the first guy to determine what you're all about (i.e., if you care for your people or if you're a phony), he can, with a few words, make or break you in his buddies' eyes. At the same time, because the RTO is "in" with "The Man," he often becomes the sounding board for the rest of the EMs' bitches, who figure he can get through where they can't. I always tried to develop my relationship with my RTO on the order of: *Look, man, if something bad's happening, I want to know. If the troops are unhappy, you've got to tell me. I don't want names, I don't want you to be a squealer, but things ain't going to improve if I don't know what's wrong.*

RTO Robinson was just terrific—eager to learn and fun to be with, even when conditions themselves were far from pleasant. One bitterly cold night on maneuvers, the battlegroup was fighting a withdrawal exercise through mountainous terrain. D Company was located on the COPL; our mission was to delay, deceive, disorganize, and deny the mythical enemy's attack, with my units to fall back on my order and not before. At present, everything was going smoothly, so Robbie and I were just sitting under a poncho on the hood of our jeep, the motor running to keep us warm. I was exhausted—during maneuvers you often went days without sleep (it was usually worse than combat)—and now I found myself nodding off again and again. Finally I told Robbie I had to catch a few winks. "Wake me if anything happens," I said.

Some time later he shook me out of a sound sleep. "Come on, Captain, we're moving!"

"What do you mean we're moving? I haven't ordered the COPL in."

"Sir, I did it an hour ago."

"You what!"

"Sir, I—"

"Do you realize it takes a corps commander—a *general*—Robbie, to call in the COPL?" (How it worked was, if I felt the unit was under serious pressure—like about to be overrun—I'd call the battlegroup commander, give him a sitrep, and recommend the COPL's withdrawal. He in turn would call the division CO, then that guy would call the corps CG, who'd decide from the "big picture" whether it was time to pull in his protective screen.)

"I know, sir. We were under a lot of pressure on the left flank. I notified S-3. I've seen you do it a hundred times, and you were so tired I thought I'd go on and organize it for you. Now, let's go!"

No one's indispensable, I thought as we drove off in the jeep, though, in the final analysis, Robbie had only been the replacement "messenger boy," as Johns had put it to me on my first day with the 1/18th. In the old days, a company commander had full authority to bring in his outposts. Now, in the modern, post-Korea centralized Army, the fate of my two hundred-odd men rested in the hands of a lieutenant general a hundred miles away. But who would know better—the company CO on the ground, who sees the enemy charging up the hill and knows it's time to haul ass or have his unit smashed and cut off, or a corps CG who is so far up the chain of command he lives in a constant state of vertigo? Now and then, while waiting for permission to give an order to my troops, I contemplated whether I should try to radio my aunt Freda in Colorado: she was no more removed from the situation we were encountering than the corps CG was, really, and besides, it might bring some excitement to her life.

"A systematic robbing of authority and prestige," Colonel Johns was later to write to me, describing the lot of company commanders and NCOs during this period, indeed, since the end of the Second World War. Reports emanating from the postwar Doolittle Commission, calling (in part) for mammoth reforms in the selection and training of officers, and in the relationships between officers and enlisted men, were largely ignored. With the introduction of computers in the fifties, the "caste system" Doolittle pinpointed became even more deeply etched in stone, even among the NCOs, with the race for coveted supergrade (E-8 and E-9) promotions becoming a ticket-punching exercise in itself. Then there was the Uniform Code of Military Justice (UCMJ), adopted in 1951, which robbed a company commander of the authority to administer punishment on his own, and certainly tied the fists of an Old Army NCO: since the UCMJ's inception, the use and abuse of the court-martial had become widespread.

Personally I sat on few court-martials. I had more important things to do with my time, like training my troops, and little by little (usually over a couple of beers) let the word go forth throughout the battlegroup that I thought any man up for a court-martial was guilty, and that any evidence produced on his behalf in an upcoming trial would not change my predetermined conclusion. This "attitude" generally led to my being challenged, so I didn't have to sit on the court-martial board at all. But few could completely escape the web of frustrated overreaction; even Colonel Johns found himself tangled in it when one of the company commanders court-martialed a staff sergeant for being thirty minutes late for reveille (hence AWOL). This was the kind of thing that, in Trieste, would be dealt with by the guy's platoon sergeant, who'd say: "Do you want to work for me or the Captain?" and nine times out of ten the transgressor would opt for NCO justice. That might mean a whole bunch of nights making little rocks out of big rocks with an eighteen-pound sledgehammer, but it also meant no bad marks on the guy's record. In this case, it was the sergeant's second offense, and the court-martial verdict that came down was "bust him." Colonel Johns, who had made a rule about second offenses, had no choice but to uphold the finding. The E-5, as a result of the bust, could not keep his wife and children on in Germany. Johns told me later it was the hardest thing he ever did in his life, and felt it never would have happened had authority not been wrenched so completely from the hands of officers at the company level.

The particular irony of all this was found on the potential battlefield. While company COs could not take a piss without consulting higher HQ for the time, place, and manner in which to do it, in the field they were responsible for a staggeringly large defensive area. Our "war positions" in the event of a Soviet attack into West Germany were top secret, so secret that the maps were classified and locked away. We conducted recons without them, in civilian clothes under the guise of picnickers. (It was ridiculous, really—four or five white-walled American men in a field, having a picnic with binoculars and absolute military correctness, then strolling as "aimlessly" as possible, given our ingrained military sense of urgency, through farms and villages selecting fields of fire and defensive fallback positions.) When Tim Grattan showed me the battlegroup's war position at the Fulda Gap, I couldn't believe my eyes: my company front was three miles long— in Korean or World War II terms, regimental-sized, meaning nine times bigger than any company front I'd ever held. The rationale behind it was, obviously, nuclear; in the Pentomic master plan, the enemy would be driven into "killing zones," such as the Fulda Gap, at which point they would be creamed with tactical atomic weapons. Tactically it was, in a word, crazy, for European terrain and for anything less than a decision to begin total war.

The Army had backed itself into a "damned if you do, damned if you don't" corner, with those on the ground the ones who'd pay the price regardless of the chosen course of action. If tac nukes were employed and general war followed, the risk was there for massive destruction of foe and friend alike, throughout all of Europe (if not on a global scale). If the U.S. powers that be decided not to use tactical atomic weapons at all, our Pentomic configuration, confronted by a conventional full-strength Soviet ground force, would only lead to the wholesale slaughter of friendly troops along the frighteningly thin battle line. The strategy was so weak it should have been disposed of hot off the drawing boards, along with the stupid and industrious staff officer/managers who'd cooked it up.

Everyone at the top—and it filtered down damn quick to the junior-officer level—was too busy *doing* to do any thinking, any real appraising or reevaluating. On one of our secret recons we bumped into four young West German officers. They were not examining future war positions. They were not even on duty. What they were were four totally professional soldiers on leave spending their time going over the ground of previous battles. Studying. Being reflective. Theirs was a serious interest in the business of soldiering, and one seen all too infrequently in the U.S. Army of the day. This was especially so in infantry, where being labeled "introspective" or "studious" was close to the kiss of death, those words having become almost synonymous with "distracted," "lazy," or "antisocial." Instead, we had "Hell, will you look at that Lieutenant Wonderboy? Isn't he moving! Boy, isn't he aggressive! What a can-do guy!" with the admirers themselves moving and grooving at breakneck speed, unable to stop long enough to notice that Lieutenant Wonderboy was actually like a dog chasing its own tail, and never getting anywhere at all.

The Pentomic structure lent itself particularly well to fostering a can-do, don't-think officer mentality (though the 1/18th, under Colonel Johns, was an exception to the rule). The battlegroup concept ignored basic, known principles of command and control, and dug a huge chasm between the battlegroup CO and his individual company commanders. In the old organization, three rifle companies, which made up the battalion, were commanded by a lieutenant colonel. Three battalions, which made up the old regiment, were commanded by a bird (full) colonel. With the Pentomic concept's destruction of the regiment and the fattening up of the battalion, as it were, to become a five rifle-company battlegroup, a decision was reached to make the new battlegroup unit a full colonel's billet. The immediate result of this was a frantic scramble among thousands of infantry birds for about eighty battlegroup command slots (an essential step on the stairway to those stars), and an enormous gap, in both age and experience, between battlegroup and company COs. The longer-term result was that not only infantry majors but now lieutenant colonels, too, went without a command assignment. And though it was ideal for them in terms of time to run after their tails chasing degrees, DA staff assignments, and other essential punches on the old ticket, it meant that in the event of war within the decade, the Army would find itself with a generation of middle-level commanders who had little, if any, command experience beyond the company level.

If this alone were not cause to make a student of the military a bit uncomfortable, there was the problem of span of control. Generally speaking, the known, effective span of control for a CO is five subordinate maneuver elements. In the old organization this worked just fine; a battalion CO would have three rifle companies, a weapons company, and maybe a tank unit as well. But in the battlegroup, a CO reached his optimum number with his rifle companies alone. Beyond these, he was responsible for the employment of the (newly configured) battlegroup Combat Support Company, which included mortar, recon, AT, and radar platoons, and, in the field, additional attachments such as an engineer company, a couple of tank companies, and an artillery battalion. So, on the Pentomic battlefield, a CO could easily find himself with at least nine maneuver elements, well beyond the effective span of control for most colonels of the day. Of course, some COs—the ones who were calm, proficient at their trade, and well versed in the ebb and flow of battle—could handle that number and more. But they were the exceptions, not the rule, and I completely shared Colonel

Johns's wish that the battlegroup concept die a quick and quiet death. The system had been devised by Chief of Staff Maxwell D. Taylor and many of his 101st Airborne protégés; like others who held top spots in the Army, a lot of these men had made their names in a few months' combat in WW II and, through quick wartime promotions, found themselves as battalion commanders at the age of twenty-three. They'd barely had time to experience life at the levels of platoon and company, and now they were the decision makers, making authoritative, grandiose policies that, on the ground, meant life or death to the small units they were essentially ignorant of.

Nevertheless, we dutifully looked over the war positions assigned to us, kept silent the thought that attempting to defend them against a Russian attack would be about as futile as trying to put out a forest fire with gasoline,* and once or twice a month had our enthusiasm and readiness put to the test through practice alerts.

The alert would come at three or four in the morning. While the troopers and on-base NCOs jumped out of their sacks, a couple of off-post personnel would be informed. By roster, each of these men would call two more people, who'd call two more, and so on, until everyone had gotten the word to get his ass to his unit. By that point the on-post NCOs would be readying the troops, and trucks would have arrived to provide lift for our rations, petrol, water, and ammo (all of which far outstripped the capacity of our organic vehicles). All equipment was kept in a state of readiness for these alerts; you never knew, with all the contingencies we had going, if it would be the real thing. Within two hours we'd be at our war assembly areas, and while higher HQ inspectors clocked us in (a screwed-up practice alert could mean the end of a CO's career) and ran around checking to see that we were all there and had left nothing behind in our rear area, I'd make sure my boys got maximum training value out of the exercise by having them set up defensively, get camouflage on, and make out range cards.

Company D was almost always "fustest with the mostest" at the assembly area, but I could take little credit for our consistently fine performance. My top-notch NCOs ran the show; all I did was walk around during the outloading, making my presence known. "An organization does well only those things the Boss checks," Bruce Clarke always said; the first time I'd heard the adage was when the General had it printed on thousands of 7" x 5" index cards to distribute around the USAREUR command. I'd gotten mine in Nürnberg and loved it so much I'd had it framed, with the thought of hanging it in every office I had for the rest of my career. It was a simple and straightforward command philosophy I'd adopted for my own,

---

* According to Colonel Couch, the 1/18th's "share" of the enemy in a Soviet attack would have been three and a half *divisions*.

and no one could say they weren't warned when out of the blue I'd arrive for a quick look-see, and tear asses if things weren't up to par. (Like the night out in the field when I caught 100 percent of one of my platoons sound asleep—no security on the line, no one even on the radio in the platoon CP when I stomped in there. I roughly shook the platoon leader awake and started chewing his ass royally. He scrambled out of his sleeping bag, and suddenly I forgot why I was so mad at him. I was struck dumb. This lieutenant, in the field, in a fart sack, was wearing silk pajamas. Suffice to say, it was an ass chewing never to be forgotten.)

One of the most gung ho of all the 1/18th's Regular officers was Lieutenant Tom Johnson of C Company. He was a fine stud, and so enthusiastic that we called him Ranger Tom. One afternoon during a daylight training problem, Ranger Tom saw a uniformed Soviet officer in the distance observing Tom's platoon through field glasses. Johnson immediately went to ground and, with the finesse of my best Raiders, snuck up behind the guy, tackled him, and took him into custody. Only then did he find out that the Comrade was authorized, belonging to a military observer group based in Potsdam (which allowed the Soviets and the Americans to inspect and monitor each others' training and troop deployment). All of us had a good laugh over the incident, but with Khrushchev crowing about Russia's superiority in both nuclear *and* conventional war making, it was little wonder that guys on the ground got a little jumpy. And for myself, I'd learned the hard way that it was pretty tough to trust anyone: after all these months, I'd received word that I would soon have to appear as a witness against Harold Borger, who'd been arrested while buying secret documents at the Nürnberg railroad station.

It was a strange period of conflicting signals, not only between East and West but within the U.S. Army as well. "Know Your Communist Enemy" dominated the Troop Information Program, yet Major General Edwin A. Walker was admonished and relieved of his 24th Infantry Division command just down the road at Ulm, West Germany, for preaching impassioned anti-Red doctrine to his troops.[2] Being the well-indoctrinated, anti-Communist storm troopers that I and most of my friends were, we felt he'd been given a raw deal. After all, the Cold War was basically a war of words, and Walker had just gone in with all dictionaries blazing. Some months later it came out that the two star was a John Bircher from way back and, according to Secretary of Defense McNamara, had quite likely violated both civilian and military law by trying to sway his troops toward ultra–right-wing voting in the 1960 congressional election. Acknowledging Walker's "sincerity of purpose in attempting to fight Communism," McNamara's testimony regarding censorship seemed to assert that there was a time and place for everything, but with the Soviets and Americans like two evenly matched prizefighters dancing and prancing around the ring deciding whether or not to take the first swing, now was not the time or place. Nor would it ever be (except through the vote) for Walker, or any other man wearing the uniform. "The military establishment," said McNamara, "is an instrument—not a shaper—of national policy."[3]

I continued to work a few nights a week toward that elusive bachelor's degree. It was not an easy task, since most of my time was spent in the field, and whatever was left generally went to temporary duty as an umpire out with other battlegroups. I got a hell of a lot out of these umpiring assignments (I never knew what new trick or technique I'd pick up to slip into my own kit bag), but they were a long way from satisfying the diploma-mongers of the New Army. Once again, Colonel Johns came to the rescue. If I were on maneuvers, he'd send me his helicopter, and Jerry Hileman, the battlegroup aviation officer and a good friend, would fly me to Mannheim and guard my steel pot while I went to class. Two hours later I'd dash out with the next week's assignment in hand and fly back to the field. Had I known that a "world event" was in the making that would effectively cancel any hope of finishing the degree (in Germany, at least), no doubt I wouldn't have gone to the trouble. But my own ticket needed that punch; without that "smart guy" foundation, my career was just a house of cards.

In mid-August 1961, all of the 1/18th's company commanders were assigned as umpires for Operation Wind Drift, an Army/Air Force joint Airborne exercise, one of the largest of its kind held in Europe since WW II. Two 8th Division battlegroups, the Airborne 504th and 505th, were marshaled in France; those umpires who didn't jump in with them were to meet our units at their initial drop zone (DZ) in northern Germany.

Whoever had chosen this DZ should have been put against a wall and dispatched with extreme prejudice. It looked as though it might have been an artillery range at some point (or maybe a convenient practice range for the old German antiaircraft artillery school, to which the field was adjacent), but whatever its original purpose, it was the last place in the world a person in anything less than a Crusader's armor would want to drop. There were knocked-out tanks, trucks, and other obstacles all over the area. All had been carefully padded with mattresses, but you only had to jump out of an airplane once to know that no mattress is going to save you if you come down and land smack up against the turret of a tank.

The terrible conditions on the ground were matched only by the lousy weather, and the drop was delayed most of the day. My great buddy Dick Coker, a fine young captain who was CO of B Company, joined me in the long wait at a local *Gasthaus*; it was late afternoon before we heard the buzz of approaching aircraft, indicating the drop was inbound. We hauled ass out to the DZ just in time to see one of the first guys come down: a West Point lieutenant who did everything right except that he smashed right into a tree and broke both his legs.

Soon Dick and I joined our respective assigned companies. The maneuver continued for a few hours, when suddenly a large Army helicopter flew over the scene. "Attention, attention," we heard booming down from the PA system on the hovering craft. "All personnel from the 1/18th Infantry report to this chopper."

In the bird we were told the battlegroup was moving out for some big emergency, but what it was no one knew. Colonel Couch, who'd also come up for Operation Wind Drift as its chief umpire, was equally in the dark. Of all the contingencies we'd been prepared to meet, none particularly stood out; we finally concluded that de Gaulle must have run into serious trouble in Algeria (this was just about the time the French Foreign Legion revolted) and we were going there. It was all very exciting. For weeks and months I'd been telling my company we had to be prepared, and now it was happening: we were going to war.

My biggest concern was how D Company, left to its own devices, had done in this real-life alert. Just weeks before, we'd gotten a new topkick—an E-8 issued by DA. He was Infantry Branch, but had been holed up in some higher HQ for so long he didn't have any idea about what was what at the rifle-company level. He was short and fat, and his uniform fit him like a duffel bag; he didn't look anything like a soldier, and though his name was Ball, his extreme fumbling from day one quickly earned him the name of "Fingers" among the troops. I'd fought and screamed to get rid of him, but to no avail. Even with Johns backing me all the way, DA wouldn't budge. My only recourse had been to make Sweeney my unauthorized "Field First" (I had to; the rest of my fine NCOs were in shock with this new jasper in charge) and, as much as possible, leave Fingers Ball in the office with the company clerk. He was the first computer-issued, ticket-punching top I'd ever had to deal with; it was agony just to hold my temper day after day.

Logistic problems kept us at one of Operation Wind Drift's CPs until 0200 hours, at which point we and our jeeps boarded "Dumbo" choppers and headed south. As we passed over the autobahn I saw a huge military convoy—close to five hundred vehicles—winding its way north up the road. We arrived at Mannheim to be met by a calm and smiling Colonel Johns just as the last trucks were moving out from Coleman Barracks. "Hi, boys, where've you been?" he said, grinning. "Looks as though we're reinforcing Berlin, so I want you to go on home, get yourselves a change of clothes, say good-bye to your wives, and try to catch up with your companies. Hack, you're leading; Coker, you're next in the column."

So we're going into Berlin, I thought, as I hurriedly packed my gear, hardly (if at all) noticing Patty's anxious eyes. I guessed it had probably been inevitable; the divided city had been a thorn in East-West relations since the moment it was created at the end of WW II, and in recent years Khrushchev's favorite taunt, it seemed, toward the United States.

It would be the third major confrontation over Berlin. The first, in 1948, arose when three of the four powers that occupied Germany (the U.S., French, and British) decided to unify their zones and rebuild "West" Germany within these borders. Berlin, similarly divided deep in the heart of Soviet-occupied Deutschland, naturally went the same way, much as the British and Americans had merged their forces in occupied Trieste when I was a kid. Thus provoked (from his point of view), Stalin began to close down all ground access to Berlin until there was none, effectively holding the citizens of the "free" part of the city hostage. The brilliant response on the Allies' part was simply to supply West Berlin by air, and for almost a year that was exactly what they did. Beaten so beautifully at his own game, Stalin finally gave up and reopened the road/rail access routes.

In 1958 the whole show began again, with new Premier Khrushchev threatening another blockade if the West didn't pull its troops out of Berlin. To Eisenhower, in Paris, and to Kennedy, in Vienna, Khrushchev made known his intentions to sign a separate peace treaty with East Germany, giving that "host" government control over the fate of Berlin. In 1959 Eisenhower stated firmly that the U.S. would go to war over the divided city should access to it be denied for whatever reason.

In both clashes, the U.S. had listed the nuclear response as a proposed solution to the problem. In the first, the Americans were still the sole possessors of atomic weapons, and though this did not stop Stalin from imposing the blockade, it seemed to keep him from any further hostile activities when the blockade proved ineffective. In the second case, during Ike's Administration, the risk of war over Berlin was once again nuclear, but this time it was for the simple reason that Eisenhower had gutted the armed forces of the ability to wage conventional war.

The past months of the new Kennedy Administration had been plagued with the problem of Berlin. And, after the Bay of Pigs debacle in Cuba, and talks in Vienna with Khrushchev that were no more productive than Ike's last round in Paris (Khrushchev minced no words: "We'll bury you," he'd said), the President couldn't afford to screw around. He needed to act decisively on this powder-keg issue—and soon—both to regain face and get the message to Russia that he meant business. The first step had been taken in July, when Kennedy boosted military manpower ceilings by 100,000, increased the draft call, and raised the defense budget about $3 billion to cover these and other preventive measures should Khrushchev decide to fight over Berlin.[4] Our reinforcement seemed to be step two, but the question was *why?*

Coker picked me up in front of my apartment; we raced out of Mannheim and tore up the autobahn. Finally we caught up with the tail end of the steadily moving fifteen-hundred-man convoy. It was a formidable bunch: the entire battlegroup plus artillery, engineers, and signal. All normal attachments were present less tanks, moving smartly up the autobahn in tactical formation, twenty meters apart.

We didn't reach the midpoint of the column until late in the day. There, the convoy had stopped, or so it appeared, dead in its tracks. The 8th Division CG, Major General Doleman, was there with his chopper; he and S-3 Sapenter joined Colonel Couch (who was with us) to discuss the problem. Apparently the military gas tankers that were supposed to refuel us on the move had failed to arrive, and the task force was now, vehicle by vehicle, topping off at a lone European Exchange Service (EES) gas station on the other side of the road. It was a snafu of the first order; road guards had had to stop all southbound traffic while the entire convoy exited the autobahn, filled up their tanks, and looped back across the center grass strip to continue the northbound trek. We found out later that tankers *had* been on the move, but some unthinking logistician from division's G-4 shop had sent them not from Bremerhaven (a logical choice, in that they would have met the head of the column with time to spare), but from south of Mannheim, and *after* the convoy had moved out. How anyone could have expected those huge mothers to catch up with, much less double, the moving column to give us the juice was beyond nearly everyone's comprehension.

Meanwhile, Coker and I were getting anxious. We wanted to join our companies. Dark was falling; the bottleneck at the EES station involved other units—companies D and B were long past it. So we persuaded General Doleman to let us borrow his chopper, and flew off in the failing light.

The guys greeted me at Brunswick Airfield (where the task force would bivouac that night) with welcome smiles and even more welcome C rations. Szvetecz, who'd been acting CO in my absence, filled me in on how things had gone since the alert; the company leaders, officer and NCO, had done well, and handled the emergency like pros. I finally found out what had prompted our mission. After years of threats, Khrushchev had finally decided to act on *his* greatest problem with Berlin.

Since the end of WW II, East German residents had been pouring from the Red Zone in flood proportions. The last decade alone averaged well over 200,000 per year, with the majority choosing the easy way out—Berlin, where freedom was just a few unguarded paces beyond the Brandenburg Gate.[5] Such an obvious show of voting with one's feet was a huge, continuing embarrassment for the Kremlin and the puppet government of East Germany—so much for the utopia of the Communist system. So Khrushchev had decided to stop it once and for all. And while Kennedy and Company planned for contingencies like another blockade of access roads into Berlin, Khrushchev and his gang pulled the plug from the other side: overnight, the legally divided city became physically divided as well, with barbed-wire and roadblocks strung along the entire 193-mile East-West Berlin border. Guarded twenty-four hours a day by East German and Soviet soldiers, this interim barrier was the beginning of the Berlin Wall, and early the next morning, we'd slowly make our way through the access corridor on East German soil to see it for ourselves.

At the airfield that night, the battlegroup was, to the man, professional. Few commanders or anyone else got much sleep, not only because of the amount that had to be done in the way of briefings and organization, but through sheer excitement. We were sorely understrength—the division staff had arbitrarily decided that anyone with less than thirty days left on his tour was excused from the mission—but that didn't concern me as much as the rumor that we would not be going into Berlin with our trusty old M-1s. Instead, went the word, at this eleventh hour all the men were going to be issued brand-new M-14s. The logic of this was beyond me. It was as if someone were already planning the postmortem of a failed, suicidal mission: *no one can say they weren't armed with the latest and greatest.* Maybe the powers that be remembered Custer, who declined the offer that his 7th Cav be equipped with the new Gatling gun to take on the Indians at Little Big Horn (confident that the red men wouldn't stand and fight), and wanted to be sure we had all the firepower we'd ever need. The only problem was that much of the battlegroup had never fired the M-14. Some probably hadn't even seen one. My guys, who at least knew how to handle and fire the weapon, wouldn't be at any real advantage, because factory-fresh M-14s had no zero. And behind a weapon with no zero is a trooper—even an experienced trooper—with no confidence. It didn't seem the smartest way to go into a potential World War III situation, and I was not the only one who breathed a sigh of relief when the Helmstedt changeover did not come to pass.

Johns had put the word out that when we jumped off the next morning, every man in the battlegroup would be clean-shaven and perfectly polished from helmet to boots. "I want you not only to be the best soldiers," he said, "but also look the damned best." Johns's particular measuring stick of soldierly appearance (and even more important, a barometer of unit discipline) was the steel pot's chin strap fastened precisely over the point of a man's chin; at 0400 Sunday morning, when he took a final look at his battlegroup, the good Colonel saw fifteen hundred walking recruitment posters in his very own image.

Johns was in the lead vehicle when we approached the first Soviet checkpoint. The crossing was without incident, and we began the hundred-odd-mile journey through Red territory. The day before, Colonel Couch had seen a Russian general and a few officers hurrying along the autobahn in a sedan toward Berlin, as if trying to find out what we were all about; now, in every tree line, on every hill and every bridge, there was a Soviet or East German unit, tracking us with the main guns of their tanks. All told, 110,000 East German soldiers and twenty Soviet divisions surrrounded Berlin that morning.[6] Suffice to say, it was a very scary ride. We were the Vanguards, not just in name but in fact—and sitting ducks if even one round was fired. *Johns's last stand?* I thought, remembering the Colonel's remark early that morning, "We'll end up like Custer if those goddamn Ruskies take us on, but we'll take a goodly number of the sons of bitches with us when we go." I worried about my marginal soldiers. What if they panicked and opened fire themselves? Tim Grattan called and asked if he should set up mortars if we got hit. "No, just fight as infantry," I said as nonchalantly as I could, knowing full well it'd be over as soon as it began. Infantry in trucks was no match for wall-to-wall Soviet tanks.

The tension was almost unbearable. Waiting, waiting, waiting—for an explosion, a shot, a *something* that would start the shooting match. Then I heard a roar coming directly toward us from the road up ahead. At first I thought it was a tank. The closer it got I realized it was a twin-engined jet bomber, flying about sixty feet off the ground. As it got closer I saw its bomb-bay doors were open. *He's too low to bomb us,* I thought. *He'll blow himself out of the sky.* But then, *My God, he's going to strafe the column!* How no one panicked in the face of this thing—each of our vehicles had an air guard with an M-60 or .50-cal MG—could only be attributed to the great training of the 1/18th (or just plain old fatalism acquired of necessity, like Dick Coker's first thought when he saw the Soviet bomber: *Well, they're going to take us out right here.*). But whatever the reason, not one shot was fired, and as the plane swooped over the convoy we could see it was just a Soviet recon aircraft taking photographs. Bastards. Fine pictures could have been taken from a thousand times the altitude, but the Reds just couldn't resist one truly provocative act.

But then we reached West Berlin, and the enemy stepped aside. Swords remained snugged in scabbards; there was no blood, but the castle was under siege no longer. We, the Vanguards—fifteen hundred white knights in trucks and jeeps—had saved the day. The people were overjoyed. As far as the eye could see were smiling, tearful faces, estimated later at 300,000 strong. Colonel Johns's jeep was immediately swarmed with Berliners throwing flowers and kisses. Their cheers were deafening. I had to strain to hear the Colonel's voice on the radio: "Hack, we're going to have a little march through the city now. You're leading. Now I want you to stand up on your seat and hold on to that windshield. Wave and smile all you like. Pretend you're Caesar going into Rome, ya' hear?"

"Yes, sir!"

With that, Johns pulled up at a reviewing stand where stood Vice President Johnson along with West Berlin mayor Willy Brandt and the high-ranking muck-a-mucks of the Berlin Command, Major General Albert Watson II (U.S. Commandant) and Brigadier General Frederick Hartel (CG). When Johnson (who had flown in for the occasion) had arrived earlier that morning, he'd received the same hero's welcome as we were getting now, and excited the crowd (in the best cowboy-and-Indian tradition) by hitching up his trousers as he got out of his car, "a Texas symbol of determination," *Stars and Stripes* reported.[7]

Meanwhile I stood up in my jeep as directed and led the parade through the cheering crowds. "*So jung!*" I heard again and again. I guessed they thought I was the "so young" Colonel, since I was in the lead vehicle, and I knew I had to be on my best behavior. It wasn't easy. The entire convoy was, in Tim Grattan's words, "up to its armpits in flowers" thrown by the crowd, but we were also being bombarded with Ping-Pong balls and wads of paper. Why, I didn't know, till finally I caught one of the balls: printed neatly on it was "*Mein Name Ist Polly*" (or "*Heidi*" or "*Gertrude*"), and a telephone number. Well. It's no mean feat to remain a composed and dignified liberating hero and collect flying Ping-Pong balls at the same time, but I gave it my best try.

By the time we got to Andrews Barracks, Colonel Johns and the VIPs had already arrived. We unloaded, stashed Ping-Pong balls in pockets, and stood tall in formation. After the Vice President gave his welcoming address, Colonel Johns was asked to speak. Undoubtedly everyone expected a corny Old-Soldier talk (not knowing Johns spoke five languages); when he opened his mouth and poured out a beautiful speech in fluent German, jaws dropped open across the podium. Talk about showmanship. *That cool hombre*, I thought. *He's probably been writing the thing since we left Helmstedt!*

We'd arrived intact and, besides the petrol fiasco, without a single hitch. Over the 435-mile trek, not one of our 491 vehicles had broken down (to the credit of the battlegroup motor officer, Captain Weaver, an Army aviator doing his ground-duty hitch), and not one soldier had screwed up (to the credit of Colonel Johns). Now everyone just needed a little sleep. We weren't the only ones, though; later I heard that four thousand miles away, cadets at VMI, having heard their old commandant was leading the Berlin task force, had posted maps and tracked our route full-time for the last two days. A week later a photograph taken of Colonel Johns at this tired time was published as a full page in *Life* magazine. In it, he looked exhausted and pensive (though still every inch a soldier). Some weeks later a *Life* reader wrote in to remark that the Colonel bore an uncanny resemblance to the subject of a Rembrandt painting called *The Man with the Golden Helmet*. We all thought this was kind of spooky, because, having scrounged around to find a copy of the Rembrandt ourselves, it was absolutely true.

Johns designated D Company as the battlegroup's reaction force. As such we moved over to Tempelhof Air Force Base (TAFB), the whole way across town from the rest of the battlegroup (which suited me just fine), and about sixteen hundred yards from the Friedrichstrasse border crossing. Also known as Checkpoint Charlie, this heavily guarded crossing was the only access left between the two Berlins. Augmented by a platoon of M-48 tanks and nine armored personnel carriers (APCs), we were to be on a five-minute alert (sleeping in full gear with boots on; ammo and load-bearing equipment stacked, guarded, and ready) until tensions eased in this showdown.

TAFB had fine facilities. We were given a huge, unused hangar, perfect for barracks, mess, and offices, with plenty of room left over for a complete indoor training ground. But before we all had a chance to move in, the base commander, an Air Force colonel, arrived to welcome us to his command and tell me he'd arranged for the D Company officers to stay at the USAF hotel (the Columbia House) nearby. As well, a new, chauffeur-driven Mercedes-Benz was mine simply for the asking. I loved that, not just from the personal standpoint, but for the international irony: there we'd be, joyriding in one of Western capitalism's finest works of art, right in the heart of a failing Communist state.

The following day, while the company rested, we officers took a general orientation jeep drive around West Berlin. We were begrudgingly escorted by members of the 6th Infantry (two battlegroups of which, the 2d and 3d, were permanent units in Berlin), who were incredibly jealous about the welcome we'd received the day before. Still, it was their job, and one of the first places they took us to was the Wall.

We got out of the jeep. The barrier was still a maze of barbed wire, but already concrete blocks were being laid for the permanent structure. A few West Berliners jeered and hissed at the robotlike Communist workers and their guards; they were, naturally, ignored. The whole situation pissed me off. I started walking toward the barricade, playing the role of some badassed hombre; why I'd chosen this moment to be a showman I'd never know, for on the other side stood a very wary East German soldier holding an AK47 submachine gun. More accurately, this mean-mouthed Vopo was *training* an AK47 on my precious body. It had been a long time since a weapon was pointed at me in earnest. It got my attention.

In my mind I flashed to Trieste, to that day I heard a Jug patrol moving through the valley on the Yugoslavian side of the whitewashed border. I'd squatted on the ground and duck-walked my way down the hill toward the thin white line, sweeping the valley floor with my binoculars. At first I'd seen nothing of interest; then I saw nothing at all, as a man stepped out of the woods directly in front of me and blocked my view. I put down the field glasses. The Jug soldier was a couple of feet away, just across the line. The only thing grimmer than his expression was the sight of the barrel of his submachine gun, pointed right at me. I was unarmed; in my early Sergeant Combat "find 'em, fix 'em" enthusiasm, I'd unconsciously inched much too far from my weapon. I slowly got to my feet, heart and mind racing through very limited options; it was *High Noon*, Cold War style. I kind of gave the guy a smile, and slowly reached into my pocket. I pulled out two cigarettes, lit them, and offered one to the Jug. He didn't refuse it, but he didn't let his weapon drop either. We smoked in silence for a very long minute. Then, with a nod, I turned my back to him. Heart in mouth, I walked over to my abandoned rifle, picked it and my helmet up, and kept on walking up the hill.

Looking back, though, that had been easy: I'd been alone. Now, with a readied AK47 burning a hole in my chest, and the eyes of my guys burning a hole in my back, I couldn't exactly offer this Vopo a cigarette. So (albeit scared stiff) I kept walking. *Poker bluff*, I thought. *I've got jackshit in my hand, but I'll raise him the pot.* Finally I got to the evolving Wall. And with one glaring eye on the Vopo, I kicked the concrete part as hard as I could.

It was a stupid, frivolous act. If the guy had shot me—an American soldier—we might have had WW III on our hands. As it was, I think the East German was as surprised as I was that I'd done it, so I just gave him what I hoped was another hard glare, turned around, and walked back to my jeep. And as the guys slapped my shoulder and congratulated me on my balls, I just held my breath until we'd driven away and the Wall was out of sight.

Things in Berlin settled pretty quickly. I reorganized the company into two rifle platoons and one weapons platoon to counter the manpower shortage (about two weeks later we'd get a slew of replacements to bring us back to full strength); we were stood down from our full-time alert after a week, with the duty rotated around to other units. There were a number of confrontations at Checkpoint Charlie, usually with Soviet and American tanks rolling right up to the gates, playing "chicken." All such incidents caused general alerts, but fizzled before a shoot-out (quite fortunately, really, given that if we'd gotten into a real firefight in Berlin, "our longevity," to quote Tim Grattan, "would have been about five minutes."). The Vopos sometimes used mirrors to reflect sunlight into our cameras and binoculars, a weird "weapon" that was right out of the Bible, where shields were used to blind the enemy. They also used water cannons, but not necessarily with water: one 1/18th patrol got hit with a load of "night soil," aka human shit. Colonel Couch's retaliative suggestion for that was to zap them with adamsite grenades, which produced a host of unpleasant though temporary effects, including severe nausea. The countereffort worked and the East German "night soil" assaults ceased once and for all.

Meanwhile, letters of commendation praising our move to Berlin were pouring in from President Kennedy on down. The Berliners, calling us liberators and saviors, showered any man wearing the 8th Div patch and the 1/18th green-and-white fourragère with all the love and affection in their hearts. The 6th Infantry got surlier and surlier over all the attention we were receiving; inevitably this led to some tremendous fights in clubs and bars around town. The 6th guys would grab one of our men by his "fireman's rope" (the fourragère) for leverage, take a swing, and it was on. Colonel Johns counseled the battlegroup to use restraint, personally shared the nightly duty (with Colonel Couch and other field-grade officers) of roaming around the trouble spots and making his presence known, and even talked to the 6th's COs to put an end to it. When nothing helped, he gave permission for "his boys" to let fly. Unbeknownst to the friendly enemy, a couple of guys in the 1/18th were karate black belts, and before Berlin, "unarmed combat" had been part of the training schedule. So when our boys let loose, they were like a buzz saw running amok through the 6th Inf's ranks. Soon after, the two permanent party battlegroup COs got with Colonel Johns to find a better solution, and much of the violence stopped.

Happily, Company D played little part in all this mayhem. The worst of it sprang from the fact that the 1/18th was co-locating with the other battlegroups and stealing all their girls. Over at Tempelhof our only competition were the fly-boys, and because the little fräuleins who milled around the base were equally enamored with them, there was hardly any friction at all.

In truth, there shouldn't have been any to begin with—the ratio of girls to guys in Berlin was seven to one. It was a soldier's paradise. I knew we were on to something when I saw the ugliest guy in my company—a short, dumpy albino kind of guy with scars and boils all over his face—strolling through Tempelhof like Valentino, with a Prussian beauty on each arm. Guys like Ed Szvetecz and Tim Grattan were as straight as the arrow on their 8th Div patches, but the rest of D Company's officers were bachelors and they took full advantage of it. The players and strayers among the married officers in the 1/18th came to Tempelhof for their dalliances, far from the eyes of Johns and the rest of the staff; as for myself, Berlin was simply a belated conclusion to the journey I'd set out on with Al Hewitt fifteen years before. *This is the Army of occupation in Germany, Al. You've got to join up!* I'd say to myself from time to time, wishing my dear old friend were with me to help cash in on all the Ping-Pong balls.

It didn't take long for word to get back to the wives in Mannheim that the married "liberators" were taking too many liberties of their own. Johns intervened on behalf of the ladies, organizing R&Rs for them with their husbands in Berlin (the unstated rule being that the Tempelhof Officers' Club was off-limits), or letting each of us go home for a few days. One of the married NCOs in my unit got his chance to go home the morning after his Berlin girlfriend planted a wicked hickey on his neck. When he came to me for advice, the only thing I could think to do was call in the medic for some emergency surgery. The doc took a scalpel to the angry red blotch, made a first-class wound out of the thing ("Ripped it on barbed wire," the guy could say bravely), and bandaged it up. Apparently the ruse worked, because the guy came back still married. And that was no mean feat, in that the divorce rate within the battlegroup skyrocketed during our stay in Berlin (as did marriages between troopers and West Berlin girls).

One of the most successful American ladies' men in Berlin was a brilliant, young Army aviator captain named Dale Le Clerc. Twenty-four years old, short, solid, and built like a bull, Le Clerc would have been among the top three on my list of "Animals I Have Known." I met him through Jerry Hileman, who'd been one of his flight-school classmates, and we became good buddies despite the fact that—even by my standards—Dale was an absolute wild man. He'd stand in the Officers' Club sipping a martini; when he was through, he'd eat the glass—just nonchalantly stand there and crunch it down to sand. It was a good trick that must have taken some time to master; in the interests of showmanship, I tried it once, only to cut all hell out of my lips and tongue. (But since all my boys were there, I had to keep on chewing, and pretend it was perfectly natural for me to be slugging down the booze with blood gushing out of my mouth.)

Dale Le Clerc's unparalleled success with the fräuleins was most likely the result of his imagination and his extraordinary charm. He'd fly his chopper over the Berlin lakeside beaches, for example, throwing out leaflets that read, "The handsome young man flying this helicopter is Captain Dale Le Clerc. If you would like to meet him in person, ring him at . . ." with, of course, his phone number and the best time to call. These things would flutter, en masse, onto the tanned bellies of the West Berlin sunbathers, and the results were mind-boggling. Once I went back to his apartment with him, only to find a line of girls waiting patiently at his door, all of them ready to live the day as if it would be their last (the prevailing philosophy among most West Berliners at this time). Dale didn't know a single one but, with both good judgment and generosity, allowed a few to introduce themselves to me. Sadly, he had to abandon that particular airborne promotion scheme when one of his leaflets landed on the lap of one of the Chief of Staff's (Berlin Command) dependents. She took it home to her daddy, who failed to see the humor of it.

As part of the Berlin Aviation Detachment (whose basic purpose was to fly VIPs along the Berlin Wall), Le Clerc was permanent party at Tempelhof and responsible for all the helicopters there. One afternoon he did a favor for an elderly Berlin-based civilian photographer, letting the guy take a bird's-eye look at the Wall. Berlin reporters were not authorized on U.S. Army aircraft, but by any stroke of good luck Dale should have gotten away with it. He didn't. As the chopper tooled around in the air, it was fired upon, a single projectile crashing through the bubble of the aircraft. Had the flight been authorized, this incident could have been yet another serious East-West flash point; since it wasn't, the warrant officer pilot reported nothing and hightailed it back to Tempelhof immediately. Upon Dale's investigation, the damage had come not from a bullet but a bolt, which some East German must have sent up with a slingshot. Dale got a new bubble for the chopper, swore everyone to secrecy, and that was the end of it.

A week later, the unauthorized flight became an international incident. The warrant officer let the proverbial cat out of the bag, and Who-did-what-to-whom? and Why-the-hell-was-that-chopper-up-there-in-the-first-place? were just the preliminary queries in an investigation that involved everyone from Dale's CO up to the highest levels in Europe, if not to the President himself. It didn't do wonders for Le Clerc's career; he received an Article 15 (nonjudicial punishment) and, to my great disappointment, was removed from the Berlin Command.

The bolt incident was only one of a number of potential flash points in the early days of life in the physically divided city. Another was TV personality Jack Parr's visit. In this episode, eighty U.S. soldiers in full battle gear plus seven U.S. jeeps armed with machine guns and recoilless rifles came rushing, unprovoked, up to Checkpoint Charlie. As cameras rolled, they were joined by seven officers, and while the Vopos looked on anxiously from the other side, Parr began his razzle-dazzle report "on the ground with the troops." The public information officer of the Berlin Command was relieved by Theater CG Clarke in the wake of this cops-and-robbers affair (which the info officer had organized, and which the Pentagon later called "a disgraceful episode"), and the battlegroup CO who provided the troopers was admonished.[8]

All of us played hard in Berlin, but the 1/18th worked damn hard, too. The unit-wide issue of M-14s took place only days after we arrived (we turned in our M-1s simultaneously, so despite the Helmstedt reprieve, we still found ourselves with unzeroed weapons in what was considered a combat zone). We got priority on the lighted KD ranges and zeroed them at night. I hadn't zeroed a weapon at night since Camp Drake in Tokyo the night before I shipped to Korea for the first time. Then it had been cold, and I remembered how awkward it was to zero my M-1 wearing the gloves I'd been issued. Of course, now it was late summer in Berlin, with warm, balmy nights, so there wasn't really much to the exercise except a nice bit of nostalgia.

After the M-14 changeover, serious training began, and for all our fire-and-maneuver field troops and most of the officers as well, it was a whole new ball game. Riot Control—fixed bayonets, skirmish lines, bullhorns, tear gas, and feet stomping on cue—was pretty boring, particularly since the only potential riots in West Berlin were between the U.S. units stationed there. But Combat in Cities, the next block of instruction, was great. The Berlin Command had built a complete mock city for this training. I'd learned much of the stuff as a private in Italy—fighting door-to-door, using grappling hooks to climb up buildings, employing snipers and grenades in a city environment—but I quickly learned that the view of the one being employed is dramatically different than that of the one doing the employing, so as a company commander I got a hell of a lot out of the instruction. The 6th Infantry were experts in both city fighting and riot control; despite their "Palace Guard" flabbiness, they proved able teachers. Still, to prevent their becoming too cocky, a while later we "fought" them in a tactical field exercise in Berlin's Gruenwald Forest and whipped their asses—in the process, rekindling their outrage at our very presence in "their" city.

There were few good training areas around the air base for field exercises, but we made do. In direct contrast to the Manhattan Beach community, the Berliners—who were right into anything military—loved watching us train. And we put on a pretty impressive show, with Szvetecz singing a mean version of "When the Saints Go Marching In" during our runs, and the company chiming in on each line at full voice, without missing a step. PT was designed as much for fun as to work up a good sweat; sometimes I'd challenge the guys to beat me in push-ups and we'd do hundreds, until none but the studs were left. It was the same with the runs. On one occasion I gave the order to "go for broke," and while most of the group fell out at ten or twelve miles, the studs kept moving. In the end the only ones left were Adderly, Grattan, and Szvetecz (the jocks), me, and that hardcore mother of them all, Sergeant Sweeney.

We continued night training in a limited way. One of the first exercises was a company night attack across the runways at Tempelhof. Consideration for all elements of the maneuver was taken into account, or so we thought, until simultaneously with a red star cluster shooting into the sky (signaling the commencement of the attack) and my two hundred men dashing across the airstrip firing blanks, a commercial jet came roaring into Tempelhof on its final approach. The pilot thought the airport was under attack, and he pulled out all stops and zoomed off to abort the landing. Naturally, a lot of people (not least of them the pilot) were a bit upset about infantry playing cops and robbers on the on-line runway, and the next morning Tim Grattan, who was the training officer, was summoned before the TAFB command. "I was scared to death," he reported when he returned, "but when I saw the infantry CIB on this Air Force guy's chest, I knew we weren't going to be too far up shit creek." He was right. We had our wrists slapped, and thereafter coordinated our night maneuvers a little better with the air-base authorities. Failing that, I'd send "Big Ed" Szvetecz over, after the fact, to smooth things out again. ("Thank God it only lasted three months," Ed would later say. "I used to think it was your way of keeping my weight down. I lost a few pounds off my backside every time I made a call.")

The comparative freedom D Company had in Berlin resulted from time to time in little lapses in discipline, even among the more solid young soldiers in my command. One of these guys was an E-4 I'll call Jack Frye, who was reported AWOL early one morning. It was a pretty straight-forward case; the rumor was he'd fallen in love and was shacked up in the British sector of the city. The easiest course of action was simply to wait, and when he returned, court-martial him, but I didn't want to do that. As a kid I'd come in late off a pass a few times; the only difference between Frye and me was I never got caught. The boy—he was only nineteen—was not a screwup. In fact, he was a damn good soldier with a lot of potential, and my gut feeling told me not to use him as a horrible example. So instead, I authorized a three-day pass, had someone forge Frye's signature on the sign-out roster, and asked his own platoon to go out looking for him that evening. Of course, if he'd been found floating facedown in the river overnight and was now lying in a morgue somewhere, it'd be kind of difficult to explain how he managed to sign himself out, but I kind of felt the odds were on our side.

When Frye strolled in later that day, he was brought to my office. "This won't go on your record, Frye," I told him. "I could bust you, but I've decided to turn you over to Sergeant Sweeney instead. He'll determine what your punishment will be. But let me tell you something, young soldier. I just laid it on the line for you. You owe me one. You've got the potential, so don't screw it up." The boy agreed to smarten up his act, and I never had any trouble with him again. He was always a bit of a wise guy, but that was probably another reason why I liked him.

Soon after this incident (and the funny thing about it was, little did I know when I saved Jack Frye's ass that a decade later he'd save mine), I decided to make acting sergeants out of a number of my E-4s until we got some E-5 allocations in the battlegroup. (Another of Chief of Staff Taylor's Black Shoe innovations had been to abolish the rank of corporal and replace it with the "specialist" system—a stupid, stupid move, in that corporal historically was, and should have remained, the first rung on the NCO leadership ladder.) There were about eight guys due for promotion. I gave it to all of them save Frye; he was fully qualified, but I wasn't going to reward a guy who'd just been late off a pass. At the weekly inspection, just hours after the promotions were announced, Frye stood at a stone-faced attention. "Frye," I said as I inspected his weapon, "I was thinking about promoting you to acting sergeant, too. But I really think you're too young."

"Well, if I understand it correctly, sir," the E-4 rejoined immediately, "you were a sergeant when you were sixteen."

He was off by a couple of years, but he got to me (I guess I was a softer touch than I'd thought). As soon as the inspection was over I had the First Sergeant cut Frye a promotion order, too.

I always tried to give guys the benefit of the doubt. Generally I worked on the baseball principle "Three strikes, you're out," but now and then my hair-trigger temper got the better of me. What followed then was like a period of temporary insanity (though the rage itself was justified), and at times like these I could do absolutely anything. On the battlefield this fury was a gift; at other times, a definite liability. When, for example, during a general alert, our (attached) truckmaster staggered in late (which was very serious in itself) and drunk (which was inexcusable), if the whole company hadn't been assembled there, I probably would have pistol-whipped him to a bloody pulp. Only some unconscious survival mechanism stopped me; instead, I stood the truck sergeant at attention in the middle of our hangar, whipped out my loaded .45, and thumped it on his chest while I chewed his sorry ass to shreds. Grattan told me later the guy wanted to press for a court-martial, until Sweeney and a number of other noncoms counseled him that it would be a pretty dumb thing to do. The guy was lucky to have people like that around. My own counselor was Tim Grattan himself, who, when I was about to go half (or fully) crazed over a trooper or a policy, would just shake his head, and with a grin declare, "Sir, I think you're pissing in the wind."

And it was so much better to leave the "dirty work" to Sweeney anyway. Not that I couldn't have done it as well, but to my Old Army brain it was more appropriate for an NCO to shape people up. When a guy missed reveille one morning simply because he'd drunk too much the night before, Sweeney tasked Frye and another sergeant to get him out of the sack and bring him to the mess hall. "Being the good First Sergeant," Frye explained later, "Sweeney wanted the trooper to eat before he disciplined him any, so he put the guy in line. The kid took a tray, put scrambled eggs right on it instead of on a plate, and dumped a cup of coffee over the eggs. Then he went over to sit down at a table. Needless to say, this made the First Sergeant awfully mad. So J. J.* braced him, facing against the wall, and told the kid to stand there and eat. The kid said something smart to him, and J. J. told him to turn around. He did. So now the guy was standing there holding the tray, and J. J. just hauled off and hit the tray from the bottom, right up into the kid's face. Scrambled eggs and everything went flying all over the place, and all the German KPs went running for cover. Then the First Sergeant had me and the other sergeant take the kid outside, where we took turns running him until about two or three hours later, when he literally dropped to the ground and we had to haul him back over to the barracks."

The net result of Sweeney's NCO discipline was not a demand for a court-martial by an aggrieved screw-up. Instead, the kid did a 180-degree turnaround; like Private Russell in the 77th, he became a damn good soldier. And since that was what being in the Army was all about, the moral

---

*Sweeney's nickname when the troops spoke about him, but *never* to his face.

of the story is that experienced, hard-assed NCOs like Sweeney are not, by design, brutal, unfeeling individuals. They do not break soldiers for the hell of it; they know what a trooper will need when the time comes, and if they break him at all, it's only to rebuild him again with a stronger, life-prolonging foundation, to support him when the bullets begin to fly.

Of course, the NCOs policed themselves, too. "Well, how's it going, Top?" I might ask Sweeney.

"Looking good, sir."

"Any problems?"

"No problems at all, sir."

"I thought I smelled something with Sergeant Misfit yesterday."

"He's been corrected, sir. Everything's under control."

Generally speaking, this worked just fine, but now and then there'd be a guy who'd manage to defy correction. One of these was a buck sergeant I'll call Keen. This small, heavily built guy was a marginal squad leader, a troublemaker of the first order, and had a reputation for abusing troops. How bad he was I didn't know until the afternoon I was walking through the company area and saw him beating holy hell out of a refrigerator-sized cardboard box. I thought he'd gone crazy.

"What's up, Sergeant?" I asked.

"I'm giving a soldier discipline, sir."

I asked him to open the box. He did, only to reveal a soldier cowering inside as though he was waiting for the next blow. This was not discipline; it was victimization, and kind of a revelation for me. I hadn't seen anything quite so sadistic since Charles burned that South Korean papa-san's beard off in G Company many years before. I made a pledge to myself then and there—my complete trust in the noncoms to take care of their own notwithstanding—to keep a sharper, personal eye on the goings-on of any reputedly unsteady NCOs.

The only thing in life you can be sure of is you can't be sure of anything. When the *Army Times* published the promotions list and my name was not on it (for the whole world to see), not only was I humiliated, but I was completely and totally crushed. At first I thought there'd been a mistake. I read the thing again and again. Everyone tagged for promotion to major was listed, and my name just wasn't there. I couldn't understand it. I'd been promoted to the permanent grade of major only months before in the Reserve, and had had nothing but glowing ERs since. And to be passed over . . .

I was heartbroken. Fortunately, I was in Munich when I found out, having been summoned to appear at Harold Borger's grand jury. Within twenty-four hours I'd be back with my unit, struggling to keep a brave face, but with Patty, who'd joined me for the court appearance, at least I got over the initial shock.

We went to the court and sat outside while I waited to be called to testify. Patty was sympathetic, supportive, and truly wonderful throughout, but my misery over the pass over was only compounded during the wait—all the deception I'd been through with Harold came back with a rush. At least it would be the last time we'd have to be each other's two-faced friend; I was sorry he'd been so stupid, and that I'd been the one who recognized it.

Finally they called me in. Harold, as impeccable as ever, was sitting in the dock. "Hello, David. How are you?" he asked. "It's lovely to see you." I nodded, but couldn't look at him. "And how are Patty and the girls?"

"They're fine, Harold. Just fine."

"Well, give them all a big hug for me, will you?"

"Sure."

With that I took the stand and testified against my friend the spy. Six months later Borger would be the first American ever to face the West German Supreme Court for espionage. Then, he'd testify that his motives were pure, that he'd spied for East Germany solely to "further the cause of Israel," believing there was a revival of anti-Semitism and militarism in West Germany, and that he'd "meant no harm to the United States or West Germany" themselves.[9] There was no evidence at all to back up his claims; he was found guilty and was sentenced to two and a half years. Where he went after that I'd never know—I never saw him again.

I left Patty, who had proved once again (just as she had at Fort Sill during the show-cause investigation) to be the epitome of the solid, steadfast Army wife, and headed back to Berlin, just a passed-over captain. Worried that my troops would find out their "stud" CO was a failure, that they'd see my disappointment and my heavy, heavy feet of clay, I worked overtime being cheerful while, in fact, I went on a bender that lasted for days. I told no one save Dick Coker, who stood by during many a drunken night to provide whatever support he could; I found out only later that a number of my men knew the truth from the first day, but mercifully kept it to themselves.

Meanwhile, Colonel Johns started pulling strings to find out what had happened. First he called an old buddy, Colonel Beverly "Rock" Read, who was working with the Chief of Assignments for infantry officers. From Read came the news that I'd not been passed over (which was a relief; two pass overs and you're out of the service) but, under a new system, was deemed "fully qualified but not selected." The reason: Colonel Young's *nine-year-old* ER (rendered after forty days' observation of me when I was twenty-one), which stated I was "impetuous and immature."

Colonel Johns was furious. Always looking after "his boys," he fired every cannon he could get his hands on. While Colonel Read took the case before his boss, Brigader General Reuben Tucker (a much-renowned WW II regimental commander with the 82d Airborne), Johns turned to USAREUR CG Bruce Clarke. General Clarke started pulling strings of his own, and when Tucker approved Colonel Read's recommendation that my record go before a special board of study, it promised to be a pretty smooth road. In the meantime I stopped bleeding, shook off the enormous blow to my pride, and finally got my ass wholeheartedly back to work.

When Maxwell D. Taylor, JFK's personally selected Military Representative of the President, decided to visit Berlin, Colonel Johns designated Company D as the airport honor guard. Under the new style of Army leadership, this sort of thing would have been a nightmare; under Johns's Old Army command style, it was a dream. No staff officers came prowling around for pre-inspections. Johns himself gave me the mission ("Put on a show for him, will you? Right by the book. And if you need anything, just holler."), and I didn't see him until about ten minutes before Taylor arrived four days later.

"How're you doing, Hack?" he said.

"Just fine, sir. Would you like to inspect the honor guard?"

He glanced toward the eighty-stud force I'd culled from the company. "No, they look good to me." Then he paused. "On the other hand . . . I'll tell you what. Why don't I just put the boys through their paces?"

"Right, sir."

He strolled over to the honor guard. "Atten-hut!" he bellowed like a drill sergeant. "Present arms!" The men quickly complied. "Order arms!" Johns grinned. "Stand easy, boys. Well, that's fine," he said with his gentle drawl. "Throw me your rifle there, son. I mean THROW IT!" The kid he was addressing hurled his M-14 at the Colonel. "Now, gentlemen," Johns continued, catching the weapon easily, "it's been a long time since I did this kind of thing, but when you're doing the drill, put a little extra SNAP into it!" With that, he whipped that weapon around as if it were a two-pound cane, each movement with complete precision, as though he'd been doing it every day of his life. "See what I mean?" he asked offhandedly as he tossed the rifle back to the trooper. All the boys were working hard not to smile. Johns had that effect on them. He was so obviously in love with his profession and his troops that just seeing him in action was an inspiration. And it seemed as if everyone admired him. A lot of times troopers would come to my office and ask to see him. *Oh, shit,* I'd think. *What now?* "Can I help you, Sergeant?" I'd say.

"No, sir, I want to see the Colonel."

"It can be arranged, but I don't think it would hurt for you to tell me what's on your mind."

"Yes, sir. My wife had a baby last night—little boy. I want to tell the Colonel we're naming him Glover Johns." This happened all the time, particularly among the black guys in the outfit. Johns was just a stud and a charmer who knew soldiers and soldiering even better than his namesakes' names, and it was that very thing, his total confidence as a leader of men, that gave us the room to breathe, to fail and to grow. A screwed-up honor guard for Maxwell D. would have done little to advance Johns's career, but the Colonel trusted me enough to know I wouldn't blow it. And, of course, I busted my ass (the honor-guard stint went off without a hitch) to make sure he was right. Trust, that magic word, was not dead after all, at least while commanders like Johns were around.

We left Berlin before Christmas, replaced by a 24th Division battle-group out of southern Germany. There was no fanfare, just a cold, cold morning to remember the Cold War city by as we retraced the route we'd taken some three and a half months before. The Soviets had dubbed the reinforced U.S. presence in Berlin "military hysteria"; we'd ignored them and stayed on, as would the 24th, to remind them of our military strength and commitment to Berlin, while life in the West's side of the divided city pretty well went back to business as usual. The building of the Wall had provoked one of the chilliest moments of the Cold War, but considering everything, it was just a political game. After all, our presence didn't stop the Wall going up even one minute. And had there been a serious confrontation, our forces wouldn't have stood a chance, a fact just as obvious to the White House as to the Kremlin.

The thing about the Wall was that despite Khrushchev's big offensive threats in the years preceding his decisive act in Berlin, the Wall itself (as any soldier should know) was a defensive concern. It wasn't defensive in a strategic, war-making sense; it had not been built to prevent the West invading Soviet-controlled soil. Berlin had been like an hourglass, the people of East Germany flowing to the Western sector relentlessly, like grains of sand. And no matter how much the Soviets narrowed the aperture, the people kept on coming. Every day we were there, East Germans tried to escape, and the Vopos—besides the scores who made the break themselves—tried to stop them. At least two were brutally slain swimming the fifty yards between East and West across the Teltow Canal, shot in the back by East German soldiers. Double strands of barbed wire along the canal bank had closed that escape route, but it didn't matter; the determined still found a way, and always would. The Berlin Wall was simply an exceptionally effective monument to the failure of the Communist "people's" system. Khrushchev had solved his problem, but at a very high price.

At the checkpoint coming out of Berlin, my unit was inspected by a Soviet captain. The Russians were mad people and truck counters; we'd gone through the same drill (governed by provisions in the Potsdam Agreement) on the way in—detrucking, lining up in files, and waiting for the okay to keep moving. Though I'd thought these inbound checks had been without incident, when we reached Berlin I'd heard one quite amazing story involving a member of one of my squads. The rule was that though the Reds could make us unload and reload any time they wanted, and though they could inspect the contents of our vehicles at will, they were not allowed to touch the vehicles themselves in any way. Apparently a Russian third lieutenant, too short to adequately inspect one of the trucks, had stood up on the tongue of the attached trailer to get a better view. One of our spec fours, an old WW II guy who'd been a master sergeant but never seemed to be able to hold his rank (thanks to the three-day binges he went on every time the eagle shit), and who was sitting in the truck by the tailgate, had hauled off and butt-stroked the Soviet in the face with his M-1. The third lieutenant landed, bloody and dazed, at the feet of his boss, a colonel; everyone in the truck had figured that this was it—hello, World War III. Instead, the Russian colonel had jerked the boy to his feet and dragged him away behind a building, where he chewed the lieutenant's ass to borscht, at the top of his voice. What had interested me most about this episode was that despite the overall tension, despite the Soviet bomber's too-close-for-comfort provocative overflight, and the Vopo and Soviet guns tracking us the whole way up the East German corridor, that Russian colonel—the guy on the ground—had been in no hurry to start a big confrontation. Still, as I saluted the Red officer now, on our way out, I just hoped our spec four would not give an encore performance. "Sir," I said, "my unit is ready for inspection."

The captain returned my salute. He was a small guy with high cheekbones, almond-shaped eyes, and thin, determined lips pursed tightly together. As we walked toward the company, I noticed he could not take his eyes off my pile cap. He was wearing one, too, of similar type, but the fur was almost blue; I thought maybe it was the paratrooper wings or captain tracks pinned to mine that had grabbed his attention. So I took the cap off and offered it to him. He put it on and gave his to me. He finished his counting, each of us wearing the other's hat, and told us we could go. Then he looked at me, and for the briefest instant, he smiled. And in that moment there was no Cold War. We were simply the day-to-day custodians of someone else's suspicions and fears; we were just two soldiers, trapped into hating each other by the roles our countries had ordered us to play.

We traded hats again, and the 1/18th started the long trip home. It was uneventful, all things considered, except when one platoon of Captain Rosenstein's E Company somehow got off the autobahn and took a scenic drive through East Germany. Colonel Couch, who was traveling with Rosie's unit, decided to halt the column, and while the boys took advantage of this unscheduled "comfort stop," a Soviet lieutenant colonel tasked to monitor the withdrawal pulled up on the scene. "He laughed," related Couch, "got on his radio and told the Russian Command we'd stopped 'to wet.' " XO Charlie Rogers offered the guy an Irish coffee, which, according to Couch, "he really put away"; when Couch asked him about the missing platoon, the light colonel cheerfully said they'd taken the wrong turn and were going in the other direction. Even before Rogers poured a second shot of coffee, the Russian officer had agreed to take Rosenstein with him, and together they'd bring the missing element back to the main column. The stragglers, unharmed and intact, were ultimately rounded up on the road to Dresden (it was no big mystery who'd get the Fugawi Award that week) and put back on track; the Russian had been good to his word. And considering him, the Soviet colonel who'd chewed out his third lieutenant, and the Soviet captain who'd worn my hat, it kind of made you wonder what all the hating was about.

When a green West Point or ROTC lieutenant joined D Company, I always had Sergeant Sweeney or another of my Old Army NCOs sit in on my first conversation with him. "Glad to have you with us," I'd say. "Looks as if you have a fine record from the Academy. But let me tell you something—now, I don't want to upset you or anything—but you don't know shit about soldiering. You see old Sweeney* here?" I'd gesture to the sergeant sitting across the room. "When I was a little kid, Sweeney was a platoon sergeant in Sicily. Dropped with the 82d. Is that correct, Sweeney?"

"Yes, sir."

"And he fought that platoon from Sicily to Normandy and all the way to the Elbe, where he met up with the Russians. Isn't that right, Sweeney?"

"Yes, sir."

"And when *you* were a little kid, Lieutenant, Sweeney was commanding a platoon in Korea. Matter of fact, he's been an infantry platoon sergeant for . . . how long, old man?"

* Sweeney's name is used here as an example only, as this great NCO was Field First now, operating on a company, not a platoon, level.

"Twenty-two years, sir."

"Twenty-two years. Now, when you're a full colonel, Lieutenant, and you're sitting in the Pentagon with your feet up on a desk, getting fat, and *your* kids are little—or maybe even grown-up and going to college—old Sweeney will still be running a platoon somewhere. Don't you think so, Sweeney?"

"More than likely, sir. Can't think of anything else I'd like to do."

"So, Lieutenant, I think it's fair to say he knows more about infantry than you will ever know. So what's going to happen here is Sweeney's going to be your teacher. He will command the platoon and you will follow his instructions. You are not commanding shit. Don't give orders and confuse things. Just do what he says. When he's ready to let you command the platoon, he'll let you know. Do you understand?"

By now the new lieutenant's face would be ashen white. "Yes, sir," he'd say, his perfect military bearing marred only by a meek and trembling voice.

"Okay, Sweeney, take him away."

The kids were always shocked. But it always worked, and was a technique I used with Sweeney, or a guy just like him, in every command I ever had until the NCO corps was bled dry. Becoming a competent infantryman is no overnight transformation. The toughest job in the U.S. Army is that of a rifle platoon leader. This is the guy who is at the cutting edge of the whole war. Yet historically the platoon has been led by the most inexperienced (and thus the most incompetent) guy in the chain of command. Even if a guy comes in with talent, it still takes five or ten years of really hard work to get the knowledge and develop the skills to the point of second nature (General Patton is reported to have said that an officer needed ten years of troop experience before he started to earn his pay, and some never did). In the case of the new lieutenants in my company, the old, seasoned NCOs always treated the greenhorns with the respect due their rank ("Look, sir, this is how you do this . . .") as they taught them all they knew, but at the same time, and as important as the teaching, the lieutenants developed an abiding respect for the role of NCOs in a unit, and for the NCOs themselves. It was something they just weren't taught at the Academy or through the ROTC program.

On the other hand, there were a lot of things not taught to the enlisted guys about the officer world—things that might have been kind of helpful to know—and one thing that long bothered me after my commissioning in 1951 was the zero preparation I'd had to make an easy adjustment from EM to officer rank. In D Company, a number of soldiers wanted to go to OCS. Since I was the one who made the recommendations, I figured the best thing to do was give these eager beavers a shot at command, and while I took the opportunity to assess their potential, they could get an idea of what being an officer was all about.

In the Regular Army at this time, a squad leader generally had twelve or so years in the service. For my program, I organized a provisional squad that one OCS hopeful at a time would run. We'd feed the guy the basics, and then we'd observe his leadership style in action. If we thought he had what it took, he'd next become the company's training NCO. In this role he dealt directly with me, the rest of the company officers, and the senior noncoms. This gave us the chance to find out what made the guy tick, and because I was right on top of training (there wasn't one detail I didn't want to know), it was pretty easy to determine how efficient and capable he was. The program was not authorized, but it worked quite well; and to my great pride, a number of men who'd been through it went on to Benning and became honor graduates in their OCS classes.

Sergeant Hartman was one of these OCS hopefuls. From all the facts on my desk, this heavily-built but fit former Marine seemed a shoo-in for the Benning assignment. But something about him always made me uneasy. To start with, I didn't like him. To me, he was an apple-polisher and an asskisser, and he approached soldiering like a kid playing war on the back lot. He'd done a competent job in the squad leadership phase of our program, though, and in fairness I'd had to bring him in as my training NCO some months before.

By the time we left Berlin, I'd had it with him. More than once I'd caught him in lies meant to cover numerous training screwups I'd already noted; more than once I'd come back to my office to find him sitting behind my desk, wearing an officer's camouflage scarf and smoking a big long cigar (with his skinhead haircut, he looked like a piss-weak Mussolini). "Who the fuck do you think you are, Hartman?" I'd say. "John Wayne?" Hartman had proved himself superambitious—in itself, no crime—but with a power obsession that spelled nothing but trouble. I felt he was the kind of guy who once he got in charge of troops would initially abuse them, and ultimately get them killed.

So the day finally came when I told him he wasn't officer material. "You can stay on as a sergeant or transfer out," I said, "but you're not going to OCS from my company." Hartman didn't take it very well. In fact, about two weeks later he went AWOL, and a few days after that, his uniform was found neatly folded on the bank of the Rhine River with a letter to Colonel Johns. Its message was pretty straightforward, something like: "Dear Colonel Johns, I've committed suicide here in the river because Captain Hackworth is an unfair, no-good prick who wouldn't let me go to OCS."

Now, had Johns been anyone else but Johns, I probably would have been in serious trouble. As it was, he called me in, and when he realized I wasn't actually responsible for the guy's death, it pretty well ended the matter. But Hartman's body was never recovered, and I kind of blamed myself for his death. I did a lot of soul-searching: *Was I just too hard?* Maybe my personal feelings unfairly overrode a proper assessment of this guy's worth. On the other hand, if he'd jump into the river over not being appointed to OCS, God only knew how he'd have coped with the stress of being a leader in combat. Still, it bothered me for about a year, until the day I came across an Army Intelligence memo that reported a deserter—my old buddy Sergeant Hartman—had been apprehended in America. The story was he'd never jumped into the river; instead, he'd caught a merchant ship home from Bremerhaven. Then, apparently, his mother got so sick of having him around her house that she reported him to the MPs, and they, in turn, threw him into the slammer, where he belonged.

Colonels Johns and Couch had a thing about company mascots, and after Berlin we all jumped on their spirit-building bandwagon. Coker's B Company got theirs first—a bulldog they aptly named Big Bad Johns. John Ward's Charlie "Cougar" Company brought home a huge old alley cat that could fight like its namesake (in keeping with Ward's favorite expression, "sustained superior performance"), and D Company had to think quick. I asked my guys what the deadliest creature on earth was. When they reported back it was the cobra, I asked what could kill a cobra. The answer was the mongoose, and before long "Mongoose Delta" Company had a stuffed mongoose living in the Orderly Room, its teeth sunk deep in the neck of a full-sized stuffed cobra. It was a real class act. Unfortunately, I barely had a chance to get used to seeing it there, because in early January 1962, Colonel Johns transferred me out of D Company to take over the battlegroup's Combat Support Company.

I hadn't expected another company command—it would be my eighth in the last ten years—and as exciting as the prospect was, I was somewhat ambivalent about it. I hated leaving my unit, just as I'd hated letting go of the Raiders and Fighter Company in Korea, and C Battery, 77th Arty in California. When you work hard and see improvements, when you get to know your troops and watch them grow, you can't remain unattached. Your outfit is not just "the best" outfit; it's the *only* outfit, and it becomes hard to imagine your life outside or beyond it. On the other hand, there's not much better in the world than a challenge, and Combat Support would certainly be that. Since I didn't have much choice in the matter anyway, I chose to look at the bright side, and after turning command of Mongoose Delta over to (recently promoted) Captain Ed Szvetecz, I moved across the company street to start sweeping out my new home.

The unit was in good shape when I arrived, with damn capable officers and NCOs. All they needed was a little tightening up: each platoon* had organic vehicles, and the troops had grown accustomed to driving everywhere; they had to be reminded they were infantry foot soldiers first and combat supporters second. But it was easy. Essentially all I did was walk in, explain my SOPs (most important being the emphasis on basics), and let the guys get on with the work.

I brought Robbie "Stirling" Robinson, my RTO/driver, over to Combat Support with me, and over time managed to grab more studs from D Company to round out the team. I inherited some fine young men with the unit, too, most notably Lieutenant John "Jack" Peppers, the SPAT platoon leader, who reminded me of Eisenhower (the soldier, not the President) somehow, and whom I made the mortar platoon leader soon after my arrival when I realized the captain in charge there was less than adequate for the job. It was a decision I was never to be disappointed with.

All too soon, Colonel Johns received orders back to Berlin as Chief of Intelligence. Most of us had known the magic couldn't last forever, but it didn't change the fact that we were incredibly sad to see him go. On 15 January 1962, the battlegroup fell out smartly for its final review before our favorite soldier. The weather was bitterly cold, but no one noticed. We were all too busy standing tall and greedily soaking in the Colonel's farewell address.

Johns was a leader who taught by example, so most of the points he made weren't exactly new to us. But to hear in a single speech this great man's basic philosophy of soldiering was like being let in on the secret ingredients of some magical formula. To wit:

- Strive to do small things well.
- Be a doer and a self-starter—aggressiveness and initiative are two most admired qualities in a leader—but you must also put your feet up and *think*.
- Strive for self-improvement through constant self-evaluation.
- Never be satisfied. Ask of any project, *How can it be done better?*
- Don't overinspect or oversupervise. Allow your leaders to make mistakes in training, so they can profit from the errors and not make them in combat.
- Keep the troops informed; telling them "what, how, and why" builds their confidence.

---

* Combat Support Company was composed of antitank, radar, recon, and maintenance platoons as well as a 4.2-mortar platoon, which, commanded by a captain, was virtually a company within a company.

- The harder the training, the more troops will brag.
- Enthusiasm, fairness, and moral and physical courage—four of the most important aspects of leadership.
- Showmanship—a vital technique of leadership.
- The ability to speak and write well—two essential tools of leadership.
- There is a salient difference between profanity and obscenity; while a leader employs profanity (tempered with discretion), he never uses obscenities.
- Have consideration for others.
- Yelling detracts from your dignity; take men aside to counsel them.
- Understand and use judgment; know when to stop fighting for something you believe is right. Discuss and argue your point of view until a decision is made, and then support the decision wholeheartedly.
- Stay ahead of your boss.

When Johns had finished, Colonel Couch gave the order to pass in review, and company by company we marched by with just that little extra precision, our shoes, uniforms, and brass earlier attended to to provide just that little extra sparkle. As was the custom, the company commanders peeled off after their units passed the reviewing stand, and congregated nearby for a final good-bye.

Our moment with the Colonel was delayed by the 8th Division CG, Andrew Goodpaster, who had replaced General Doleman in October. The minute the last company passed in review, Goodpaster grabbed Johns off the stand and began to chew his ass over something to do with the police of the post. Johns had watched the parade with tears in his eyes; the tears remained as he stood at attention while this prancer (who obviously hadn't heard a word of Johns's speech) berated him in front of us, totally oblivious to what this day meant to the Colonel. Perhaps more couldn't have been expected from this engineer/presidential aide to Ike now "managing" an infantry division, but we were appalled. Later Johns would write to me that Goodpaster's behavior that day was "so incredibly thoughtless" that it made him wonder at the man's ability "in anything that requires subtle thinking." On the other hand, Johns continued, "maybe that's the only thinking he can do, as he damn sure couldn't lead a squad of real soldiers to the PX for a cup of coffee."

Johns's biggest problem, in his own words, was his "uncanny ability to alienate my immediate superiors." In WW II, he'd told his regimental CO he was a "stupid son of a bitch" when Johns's unit was having the shit kicked out of it and the CO refused to support him with tanks or artillery. To add insult to injury, then-Major Johns next violated the chain of command and

personally called the Div Arty commander to organize the firepower he
needed. In Korea, his attempts to reverse the dangerous apathy that had
accompanied the slide into trench warfare put him in constant hot water:
"My OER for that war was hardly a world-beater either." In Berlin, his
stealing the glory from General Doleman and the 8th Div staff didn't go
down too well at all: "In effect all we got was a kick in the ass for being good,
as witness that after-action report that had not one kind word for what we
did—only grave criticism for the tie-up at the gas point. . . . When I
pointed out that an after-action report, the way I understood it, was
supposed to enumerate all that was done right, and all that was done wrong,
and the lessons to be learned as a result, I got a *very* snotty letter from
Goodpaster calling me contumacious. I didn't even know what the word
meant, but have about decided that it should be my middle name most of
the time when dealing with dumb shitheads in the rear."

Colonel Couch later told me what the farewell-ceremony confrontation
between Johns and Goodpaster was all about. The problem had actually
begun when we first got back from Berlin. In our absence, half our buildings
at Coleman Barracks had been given away to a reserve tank battalion, which
had been brought over from the U.S. to reinforce the division during the
Wall affair. This was clearly unacceptable, and Johns, as senior CO and
installation coordinator, had moved everyone around until we got back our
fair share of the post. Colonel Gershenow, CO of Heidelberg Post (of which
Coleman Barracks was a satellite), who'd commandeered our buildings to
begin with, was not impressed. Next, when Johns and Couch, who before
Berlin had daily provided one of the 1/18th's rifle companies for the police
of the entire post, decided "the devil with that" and insisted that all units
within the *Kaserne* take their turn at police detail, the colonel responsible for
housekeeping had gone bitching and moaning to Goodpaster. The result
was the obscene farewell ass chewing by the reviewing stand.

Still, despite what had seemed an immediate obscenity to all of us waiting
to say good-bye to the Colonel, it was nothing compared to the venomous,
petty faint praise Goodpaster and his ADC, Brigadier General William
Rosson, offered in Colonel Johns's Permanent Change of Station efficiency
report. Though the Colonel was "well groomed," "well grounded," "vigorous," and "self-confident," with an "exemplary military appearance" and
"an unusual ability to inspire his officers and men and to obtain maximum
response from his unit" ("well demonstrated," remarked Goodpaster in one
of the understatements of the year, "when his battlegroup was sent into
Berlin with no prior notice"), Johns also "remained aloof from operational
detail and close personal supervision" . . . "on occasion applied himself less
diligently to his role as installation coordinator than desirable," and "with

some neglect of important details and ancillary or supporting activities."

"Internecine warfare," Colonel Couch would later say of Colonel Johns's relationship with certain powerful men up at Division. "I think they were a little jealous of his capabilities. They didn't like his personality. They couldn't come up to him as a leader and a soldier, and I think it galled them."

Or, in Colonel Johns's words: "I drove hard and raised hell when I didn't get what I wanted. I made waves. I bitched about supply procedures. I fought for my men if I thought them unjustly accused by a higher HQ. I fought problems too hard, from a love of *my* men (as opposed to someone else's men, or my own boss's interests), because I had identified too closely with them due to my WW II experiences. I think I saw too many men killed, and bled too deeply inside, with the result that I was overprotective."

Overprotective he may well have been, but Colonel Johns translated his love for his men into the one thing that would save them when he was not there to wield the sword himself—good, realistic training, esprit de corps, and high morale (or unabashed cockiness, some might say) within the units in his command.

And while guys like Andrew Goodpaster and William Rosson made their way up the glory ladder, gaining four stars and the attendant influence, while Lyndon Johnson inherited the Presidency and then won it, too (it's been said that a longtime family feud, perhaps even a class war, between the Johns and Johnson families in Texas was the only thing that prevented Johns getting his first star on the spot in Berlin), Glover Johns of the non-world-beating ERs was destined to retire right where he was, as a colonel. "I hung on," he later wrote me, "even though I knew I had no chance for promotion as early as while we were in Berlin. I did so because I found it hard to believe, and because I just plain liked what I was doing."

And, Glover Johns, in case you didn't know, you made us like it, too.

I'll call Colonel Johns's DA-issued replacement Gus O. Newbreed. Watch out, Fingers Ball. Newbreed did not look like a soldier. Short and dumpy, with blue eyes, red-blond hair, heavy jowls, and a rumpled uniform, he always reminded me of a potato sack. He did not act like a soldier either. He was a staff officer, had no infantry combat experience, and was simply not qualified to command a battlegroup of combat troops. He carried pockets full of candy and handed it out to troopers as he talked to them in the field ("the field" being any troop position he could reach by jeep and not have to walk); instead of endearing the guys to him, this practice only earned him the derisive nickname "Candy Bar 6." While Johns could run a unit in the field with his eyes closed, Newbreed stumbled, bumbled, and screwed up everything he tried, with eyes wide open. As CO of Combat Support Company, I worked with him directly on maneuvers (Combat Support platoons operated separately in the field as dictated by the tactical situation); Newbreed would ask things like "Where's the I&R platoon?" which the Army had disappeared five years before, or "Where's the SCR-300 radio?" which went out not long after Korea.

And it wasn't as if it was tough to stay up on the profession if a guy wanted to. There were professional magazines and journals, correspondence courses galore, but I guessed this guy, bottom line, didn't care. His standard response to voice disappointment and disapproval was "Oh, balls!" in a tone of voice bordering on the effeminate, and when pushed, he had temper tantrums that rivaled Colonel Willard's.

People started scrambling to get out of the battlegroup. Those who remained talked mutiny, and feared going into combat with this guy in charge ("Don't worry," said one, "he wouldn't last a day, and you can bet your sweet ass it ain't gonna be enemy who gets him."). He was just such an embarrassment. The young officers were disillusioned; guys from other battlegroups jeered loud and long at the clubs—the formidable 1/18th was losing its grip.

Thank God for Colonel Couch, we'd think, who stayed on as Deputy Battlegroup CO under Newbreed. Couch didn't look much like a Prussian soldier either, and certainly not when compared to Johns, who was a casting director's dream for the perfect military man. Couch was of medium build and Grant-looking; he wore glasses, and always seemed to have a huge cigar hanging out of his mouth. But he knew his trade inside and out, and if he ever felt rusty with the basics, he took personal remedial action. He and his driver used to carry practice grenades in their jeep; on the way to the training areas they'd stop, pick out targets, go prone (or kneel behind trees, rocks, or other cover), and throw these dummy grenades. This was pretty exceptional behavior, but perfectly logical to Couch, who explained, "I'd been sitting on my tail for about five years in a staff job. Pitching grenades requires practice; I needed to get back in the groove." And, he added, "It was really a rather closely guarded secret, but old Glover and I would practice with the pistol quite a bit, too."

Couch had played tough guy to Johns's benevolent father role. The first six months I spent with the 1/18th I'd been scared to death of him, until I came to understand his subtle sense of humor, and to realize that he, too, had a heart of gold. One time in D Company, on a brutally cold, snowy day, I'd started moving my boys out for a few days' training in the field when Colonel Couch came driving by in his jeep. "Where are you going, Captain?" he'd asked.

"Training, sir!"

"In the snow?"

"Yes, sir. It's on the training schedule. And besides, sir," I'd added, being a smart-ass, "it does snow in combat."

"Good point. But I want to tell you something, Hack. To learn, you don't have to suffer."

That particular concept had never crossed my mind. I'd always had a Spartan kind of attitude toward soldiering (on a personal level, anyway, given that one of the first things I tried to do in a new unit was make the garrison life-style for everyone as comfortable as possible). When I joined the 1/18th, I'd gone back to shaving with cold water and sleeping on the ground on maneuvers, figuring that I might as well get used to it in case we ended up in a battlefield situation.

"What are you going to be teaching out there?" Couch asked.

"Rifle Platoon in the Attack and weapons platoon crew drill, sir."

"Fine. Now you just take these boys back to their barracks. Chalk-talk it with them. They'll love you for it, but don't tell them *I* said that. Just take them to the front gate, stop the company, call all the lieutenants together and say, 'Gentlemen, do you think it's too cold to train?' They'll all say yes. Then you say, 'Well, I think so, too,' and take them back. Everybody will think you're a wonderful leader, and you'll get a lot more value out of the thing than you would freezing all your nuts off out in the boonies."

"Right, sir."

Couch had proved right, on all counts. It was a great lesson learned for me, and a morale boost for my near-frozen chosen. How fortunate we would have been had the deputy succeeded Colonel Johns as battlegroup commander. This was a fairly normal procedure, but Couch himself had bent more than a few noses out of joint, and so was not considered for the job by higher HQ. (The reason stated was that the job called for a full colonel and Lieutenant Colonel Couch had six months time in grade left before promotion.) Now, the bitch of it all was that although Couch was still there to hold the unit together in terms of tactical proficiency, he could not counter the morale bust of the new CO.

But we'd take what we could get. In only a few months the 1/18th would be taking its annual battlegroup Army Training Test, in which we'd be judged for combat readiness. The ATTs, through which careers could be made or broken, were the most important tests in the peacetime Army. The 1/18th had missed the 1961 exercise because of Berlin; in 1960, under Colonels Johns and Couch, the 1/18th had proved itself the best battlegroup in Seventh Army. At the best of times that would be a hard act to follow: add to that Newbreed, and the fact that we were still pretty rusty from our Berlin stint as parade ground/garrison warriors, and Colonel Couch's intensive tactical training was the only hope we had.

Even as the battlegroup made preparations for its August test, smaller-scale ATTs were also going on at the company level. Couch designated me chief evaluator for these ATTs; it was a challenging, interesting, and fun job until B Company's turn came around. Since Dick Coker had been reassigned to Division, Bravo Company had been commanded by a captain I'll call Hale. Hale was loud, affected, and incompetent; his troops had his number (and hated him for it). My own first serious encounter with him had been during the platoon ATTs, for which he was officer-in-charge and I was an observer. When an aggressor detail hit the platoon of an old Hawaiian ex-Wolfhound master sergeant named Solomon, Hale had rushed up to demand Solomon fire his machine guns. "Make some noise," he'd said. To begin with, Solomon already had the problem under control. Also, the platoon sergeant (who'd had far more combat than Hale would ever care to see) knew the role of the machine gun was not to make noise, that it was considered the last weapon a platoon in the defense should employ. Solomon had turned to me. "I don't want to teach my men bad habits, sir," he'd explained, and because I totally agreed, I backed him up all the way. Understandably, I was not overly impressed with Captain Hale, nor he with me.

B Company was one of the first units to take its ATT. The test, which lasted about five days, was an unquestionable fiasco. Bravo's commander could do nothing right. If the unit was not lost, it was attacking the wrong objective. If the guys were not attacking the wrong objective, they were withdrawing and leaving half the unit behind, because Hale hadn't given them the word. Their final mission in the test was to attack and secure a small hill on the Baumholder training grounds. The CO roared to the foot of the objective with his company riding in APCs. The troops deployed at the base of the hill (about seven hundred yards from the top) and then, in the best Pickett-at-Gettysburg tradition, they started marching in a skirmish line, straight up. I was on top of the objective with a handful of the aggressor detail. We watched the suicidal maneuver below us in amazement; had just we few soldiers been enemy defenders in actual combat, we would have wiped out Hale's entire command.

It was true that I didn't like B Company's CO, just as I'd not liked that oddball Hartman. Yet to flunk him on the ATT would completely end his career, and it was not the kind of a decision to be made lightly. But the company was sick. According to all my subordinate platoon umpires, it had failed every test. In combat, that would equal a lot of dead men. Looked at that way, the unanimous decision among all the umpires and myself, to flunk the company, was more or less made for us.

And did the shit hit the fan. Besides being loud, affected, and incompetent, Hale was also black. When he was relieved, he immediately submitted a reclamation that held that I was racially prejudiced, and had so influenced all the other umpires. This pissed me off no end, because among all the things that I was—and I was able to name a lot of them these days—one thing I was not was racially prejudiced.

When, now and then, one of the black guys in the 1/18th would beg the regs and grow a little goatee just below his bottom lip (but above the chin so it couldn't be classified as a beard), my SOP was to go to the soldier, give his beardlet a tug, and warn him that if it wasn't gone before the sun went down, his ass was going to be grass, with me playing lawn mower. Black or white, I wasn't going to stand for that crap, and no one ever accused me of anything more than doing my job. These guys may not have liked me—I didn't care—but it was a hell of a lot fairer than following the widespread cover-your-ass (CYA) procedure of nailing the white kids and leaving the black guys alone.

I would have failed Hale if he were white. I would have failed him if he were green. I just had no tolerance for "leaders" who'd get kids killed on the battlefield. Soon after the ATT incident, for example, when I heard from one source too many that a (white) weapons platoon leader in one of the companies was grossly incompetent, I sent Peppers over to have a look. The class he observed was on 81-mm mortar fire direction. What he found was that the lieutenant in question was not using the required sharpened pencil to plot his points; instead, he was teaching his men to use grease pencils. It was like teaching surgeons to perform open-heart surgery with baseball gloves on. When translated into a combat situation, these big, grease-penciled dots on a plotting board could throw the mortar fire off by hundreds of yards, meaning it could easily land not where required, but smack-dab in the middle of friendly troops maneuvering underneath. I'd had my share of friendly fire back in Korea, and no way was I going to set this supremely stupid individual free to kill or maim our own boys in the field. After numerous other reports of gross deficiencies on this lieutenant's part, I raised hell until he was relieved.

A board upheld our decision to fail Hale's company. Soon after, he left the battlegroup, and a couple of years later he left the Army completely. Colonel Newbreed had been in a state of panic throughout the investigation and had refused to back me up on our initial findings; it really was more than a little tiring to serve under this categorical wimp and his new XO,

LTC Charles Sniffin, who was married to a senior general's daughter and had been away from troops even longer than old Gus. Luckily "the Sniff," as we all came to call him (I found out later that he'd nicknamed me, too—"Sackworth"—after the Hale and mortar lieutenant affairs), was in a staff role, and we were spared his dubious command talents for a long while.

Robbie Robinson was about to go home, so I needed a new RTO/driver. I figured that since I'd be spending a lot of time with the new guy I'd get someone really smart, who could fill me in on all the books I hadn't read (which were most, besides military stuff), and if he were really articulate, maybe that would rub off on me, too. So I went to Personnel and asked for a man with a degree in English literature.

My reward was a Harvard graduate. I was stoked, and for a couple of weeks we drove down the highway and through the field, this new guy giving me instant courses in things literary while Stirling (having broken the Ivy Leaguer in on the killer jeep, the radios, and our SOPs) hung out in the back seat waiting to go home. One day on maneuvers we went up to the top of a hill so I could transmit a couple of radio messages. On the way back down it became quite evident that my new driver was losing control of the vehicle. The old M38 jeep could negotiate cross-country driving; the latest and greatest M151 could not. The jeep went into a slide, the driver turned his wheels, and as night follows day, the thing flipped over.

Robbie and I were lucky—we were thrown out. When I'd recovered from that, I looked up on the hillside to see the new driver trapped underneath the overturned vehicle. Gas was pouring out of the jeep, and the big command radios were throwing sparks; it looked as if we were about to see a pretty spectacular bonfire. Robbie and I ran up the hill. The driver's legs were pinned under the jeep. I picked up the back end of the thing and, with Robbie, slid the guy out. (Pretty staggering what a human being can do under stress, when the adrenaline starts pumping. I tried to lift the back end of that jeep again when the emergency was over and couldn't budge it an inch.)

I looked at the boy and knew he was gone. He wore that ashen death look I'd seen too many times. I started up all the old battlefield stuff—"You're doing great, kid. You're going to make it."—while I watched him check out of the net. Then he started praying. I thought it was Hebrew, but I didn't know; the main thing was he knew I was bullshitting him and he was going to die. At the same moment I heard an Army helicopter flying overhead—maybe God *was* listening. Miraculously, I got the pilot on the radio without even knowing his frequency; when I popped a smoke, he came down and whisked the kid off to the hospital. The long and short of it was the boy didn't die. His pubic bone had been broken in the accident and had become like two razor blades cutting his insides apart; he had massive internal injuries and ended up pretty badly crippled for a few years, but ultimately got on his feet again. Still, the bottom line of the incident was that *it shouldn't have happened*. All this boy's pain was due to a newfangled, Army-issued piece of junk, which had everything and could do anything except get you from point A to point B in safety.

I called it "wonder gear," all the Army's experiments that made it past the prototype phase and into the hands of human guinea-pig troopers. Much, in general terms, was useless; some, incredibly dangerous. In Combat Support I had the opportunity to see a hell of a lot of both. The SPAT, for instance, was a 90-mm antitank gun sitting on a full-track chassis. The concept was great—it was modeled after the German 88-mm, which darted in and out of the action and wreaked havoc all over European battlefields in WW II. But the American version had a gun too heavy for its base, spare parts unavailable through the normal requisition system (the weapon had actually become obsolete during its short life, and was being phased out for the SS-10 and SS-11 antitank missiles), and a weak track system that almost invariably had us towing the things back from maneuvers as if they were beached whales.

Another bit of wonder gear, the brand-new M-113 APC, was a totally unnecessary vehicle, and a first-class disaster waiting to happen. To begin with, infantry didn't (and don't) need armored personnel carriers; in fact, the last thing an Army should want is foot soldiers dependent on vehicles. The tried-and-true method for carrying infantry squads into battle was to have them ride piggyback on the backs of tanks; if the spearhead of my company had been in APCs on 6 February 1951, every single one of us would have been dead. If an APC hit a mine, you'd lose a squad; as it was, by default, you invariably lost one or more effective members of an eleven-man squad just to the driving and maintenance of the vehicle. And then there was the M-113's basic design, which was so miserable that you'd almost believe all America's enemies had joined together to have it built: the thing looked like a huge shoe box—on the battlefield, an irresistible, high-profile target. But the *worst* thing about the new APC (which we, and the Army, didn't know in 1962, but would soon find out at great cost in lives) was that the M-113 was also a crematorium on tracks. The M-113 APC was made of a highly flammable magnesium alloy. In the next war, based on the vehicle's fiery track record from its earliest sparks of battle, drivers would reach the point where they'd refuse to get inside it. Instead, they'd sit on the (heavily sandbagged) top, and control the thing with wires they'd attached to the steering column and gears below.

Still, among the many wonder weapons available at this time, the greatest of them all was the atomic cannon, the Davy Crockett. As early as 1956 this subkiloton, frontline tactical nuclear weapon was in production, but only now was it being issued at the troop level. Combat Support Company, 1/18th Infantry, was to be the first unit in the European Theater tested for operational readiness in its use.

Gus O. called me on the phone; our careers hinged, or so he said, on getting a Davy Crockett platoon together that would pass a technical proficiency inspection (TPI) in about three months' time. This was very serious stuff. I had my pick of any men in the battlegroup for platoon leader and other personnel. The first thing I did was grab Tim Grattan out of D Company and make him CO. We got top priority for replacements; Tim picked about fifteen top-stud troops for his command from the new guys, or through stealing the best from other companies. (According to Newbreed, the only "off-limits" man in the entire battlegroup was the Colonel's own driver.) We were issued a fine old combat paratrooper NCO named Boltz, who'd been trained at Benning on the Davy Crockett and would be our resident expert on the system; Tim and he organized firing teams and began to train day and night.

They used dummy warheads, large watermelon-shaped projectiles that fit onto a rocket launcher (mounted on a jeep or tripod). "It was designed to throw the thing out there far enough to use the warhead without hurting us," Tim would say later, "but I don't think the system ever could have worked correctly." It didn't seem likely, for a number of reasons—just one being the SOP for permission to fire. It went like this: The section leader who first saw Soviet tanks roaring over the West German hills would ask Tim for permission to fire. Tim would then call and ask me. I would ask Newbreed. Newbreed would call Goodpaster at Division, who would then call the Corps CG, who'd call the Seventh Army CG, who'd call the NATO CG, who'd call the Pentagon, who'd call the President, who'd make his decision and send it back down the chain of command. By the time the unit got the green light (some two and a half hours later) and coordinated with nearby units to make sure their guys knew not to look at the fireball, the Soviet tanks originally sighted by the gunner would be in Paris. On the other hand, as Field Marshal Montgomery had said regarding atomic weaponry, that he'd fire first and ask questions later, it was kind of hard to envision a nervous corporal, while watching Soviet tanks barrel into his position, waiting patiently for permission to nuke them.

"The key thing about the Davy Crockett," said Tim, "is that the weapons system itself was designed by a bunch of intellectual pinheads who'd never seen a battlefield. And if they thought that young troops on the battlefield could throw one of these nuke devices out about three thousand meters and not have the effects of the nuclear blast on themselves or their own unit, they were crazy."

Nonetheless, the training went on, the TPI took place, and Tim and Boltz passed it with flying colors. Tim was the only man in the theater ever to fire a live Davy Crockett HE training round. The only problem left then was where the unit would get live atomic warheads if it needed them. Even Tim *as platoon leader* did not know where they were kept, or an SOP for procuring them in an emergency. Curiously, I found out many years later from a man who helped develop the Davy Crockett, who was *not* "an intellectual pinhead" and had, in fact, spent many years on battlefields (which to me made the weapon's uselessness even more unfathomable), that live warheads could have been procured within about two hours. It was good if not somewhat belated news. The Russians would still have gotten to Paris, but maybe we would have been able to stop them before they started to mix vodka with Dom Pérignon.*

About this time, word came down that General Yakabofski, Chief of the Soviet Army in East Germany, had accepted an invitation to inspect our battlegroup. Project Yankee, as it was called, would prove to be the greatest show on earth. While four and a half years before, Chief of Staff Maxwell D. Taylor had spoken about the difficulty of obtaining New Look funds for the day-to-day needs of conventional ground forces (and cited as an example a suggestion he'd heard regarding motor transport replacement: ". . . the only way to be sure of getting such a program is to have our research and development people produce a truck with an atomic warhead"[11]), now we of the 1/18th had a better, surefire approach: invite a Russian general for lunch.

Even with Kennedy's injection of funds, the Army was still ridiculously poor. We'd become used to knocking off the Coleman Barracks ordnance parks and motor pool in nighttime raids, simply to keep ourselves operational. (Everyone else did it, too; another problem with the SPAT was that ours had been nocturnally cannibalized by the 504th and 505th battlegroups.) But now, nothing was too good for us. It had been decided Yakabofski would inspect Combat Support Company because we had all the battlegroup's goodies; I took full advantage of our good luck to bitch about the equipment problems and shortcomings I had previously been resigned to, and the weeks preceding the general's visit were like Christmas. Carryover equipment from WW II was replaced with ultranew stuff. If the

---

* Quickly realizing the system's limitations, the Defense Department stopped all Davy Crockett production within two years of its deployment. Within four years the Davy Crockett was withdrawn from Germany entirely.[10]

seat of a jeep was slightly worn, we were given a new seat. On the basis of the tiniest scuffs or scratches, entire vehicles were repainted or replaced. It was wonderful.

But the greatest show was also the greatest sham. All the barracks were painted—but only the sides visible to the Russian on his flight path in. A patch of dirt near the HQ, which was used for a parking lot, was also painted—green, to look like lush grass from the air. Combat Support was immediately issued dozens of six-foot-tall Russian-speaking CIC agents to replace our less regal-appearing troopers. We trained them in "their" jobs so that when the general made his inspection, he could speak directly to the U.S. troops and conclude that every one of us in this average old battlegroup was a multilingual stud. Charismatic Tim Grattan, who really was head and shoulders above the very best of the battlegroup's fine young officers (as well as being quite high on Newbreed's list since the Davy Crockett test), was appointed escort officer. General Yakabofski was so impressed with him that when the flawless tour was over he offered Tim the job of CO in a Soviet rifle company if the American lieutenant would come over to the other side. Of course, Colonel Newbreed just puffed with pride.

Like Tim, I'd managed to stay on the right side of old Gus. I tried as hard as I could to be respectful, and only faltered when he started acting crazy or interfering with my command. When former senator William Knowland from California was due to pay a visit to the battlegroup, Newbreed called me to say the senator would be inspecting my company. Gus's order couldn't have come at a more inopportune time. I had a big remodeling program going in the unit and it wasn't quite completed. The mess hall, admin, and arms rooms looked great, but the supply room was a complete shambles. "What about this one?" asked the guys who were working there.

"Lock it up," I said.

On the morning of Knowland's visit, Gus rolled in for a preinspection at 0800. Knowland wasn't to arrive until 1100, which gave Newbreed three hours to provide close, personal supervision and not to be aloof to operational detail. In other words, to nitpick, drive us crazy, and do all the things Colonel Johns wouldn't have conceived to do for an honor guard for a four-star general, much less for some bored ex-senator's blink-of-an-eye, walk-through inspection.

"What's that?" he demanded outside the supply room.

"That's the supply room, sir."

"Yes, but what's that?" he persisted, pointing to the padlocked door.

I could feel the pangs of insubordination coming on. "That's a lock, Colonel. It means the door is locked."

"Don't get smart, Hackworth. Open it up!"

"No, sir. My supply room is in the process of being renovated. It's closed."

"I want you to open that door!"

"Yes, sir."

I let the Colonel in. He looked it over—shelves were down, tools and other building material strewn around, and sawdust all over the floor. "I want it ready by the time he comes," Newbreed ordered.

"Sir, it won't be ready."

"It will!"

Gus bumbled out on his short legs. "Sergeant," I said to the guy in charge, "shut that door and lock it."

Eleven o'clock rolled around and so did Knowland. "How are you, Senator? Welcome to Combat Support Company. This is the arms room. This is the orderly room. Here's the mess hall and the day room for the troops. That's the supply room—if you don't mind I won't take you in there. We're in the middle of renovating it."

"I understand completely, Captain," said Knowland. "You're from California, aren't you?"

When Knowland finally drove away, Newbreed scurried up, his face red as a beet. "You didn't follow orders! You didn't take him into the supply room!"

"No, sir. I did not. I told him we were renovating it and he accepted that. If he hadn't, I would have let him go in, just as you did."

"You're relieved, Captain!" Newbreed screamed.

"Very well, sir."

By this stage in Newbreed's tenure, I was just about the only officer in the battlegroup who hadn't been relieved. Some men had gotten the boot two or three times. The HQ Company CO, Captain Harrelson, seemed to get it every other day. Once, I heard, it was because someone had stolen some cookies from the Colonel's trailer. Next to "Oh, balls," "You're relieved!" seemed to be Gus's very favorite expression. Invariably what happened next was Newbreed would find himself without a commo officer or a driver or a company commander, and move quickly to reinstate him. In this instance he sent Colonel Couch over to see me.

"Hack, the Colonel's having regrets about relieving you. He wants you to come back."

"No, sir. No one talks to me like that." (The last thing I wanted to do was leave my company, but I also wasn't going to play Gus's game.)

"The ATT's coming up, Hack."

The ATT. If we flunked, unit pride in the 1/18th would be destroyed for the next twenty years—the worst follows a unit, more strongly even than the best—and even more painful than leaving my company was the thought that this obscenity of a commander would degrade the name of the Vanguards. So I relented, went back to work, and vowed to let the Colonel relieve me whenever he wanted. *Besides,* I told myself, *my time in Germany is almost over.*

After the ATT I'd be going on to a new assignment. For some time now I'd been looking seriously at my options, and they seemed limited to two. One was a staff assignment, most likely in the United States. The other, which I preferred, would take me to a tiny country in Southeast Asia.

Throughout my Germany years, it had become increasingly clear that among the world's "little wars," one with no end in sight was that of Vietnam. There had been little peace in that country since the French defeat at Dien Bien Phu. The U.S. had sunk $1.9 billion in South Vietnam since its birth in 1954 (which helped President Ngo Dinh Diem rebuild the war-torn country), but the $80 million spent per year specifically to strengthen South Vietnam's military capabilities had done nothing to slow down Viet Cong (VC) guerrilla activity all over the countryside.[12]

The Cold War dimension of the struggle in Vietnam was stated (in general terms) by Khrushchev in Moscow, four days before Kennedy's inauguration: "There will be liberation wars as long as imperialism exists, as long as colonialism exists. . . . Communists support such wars fully and without reservation and march in the van of the people fighting for liberation," and by the President, after the nightmare of the Kennedy-Khrushchev Vienna talks, when he reportedly told James Reston, then Washington bureau chief of the *New York Times*: "Now we have a problem in trying to make our power credible, and Vietnam looks like the place."[13] A month later, in July 1961, the Americans pledged to increase their advisory "training mission" from 685 men to almost a thousand,[14] and now, less than a year later, there were more than three thousand American soldiers serving as "trainers" for the Army of the Republic of Vietnam (ARVN), with "the number," according to a 26 February 1962 *Newsweek* magazine piece, to "shortly double."

I wanted to go. Whether or not the conflict would grow into a full-blown war I didn't know or care; for me it was just a great opportunity to sharpen my skills. I talked Tim Grattan and Jack Peppers into volunteering with me, and soon they received orders to Vietnam, with language and adviser school at Fort Bragg en route. I, on the other hand, was rejected. "Too much combat experience," the guys at Personnel said. This knocked me on my ass. How could a potential adviser to a disintegrating army have *too much* combat experience? Even if I'd given the matter a lot of thought, which I hadn't, it never would have occurred to me that the Army wasn't sending its more combat-savvy personnel to get ARVN (pronounced "arvin") on the road to victory. Tim and Jack represented the best of the young officers of the day, but their only experience was ROTC, standard basic officer training, and their stint with the 1/18th Inf. How could young lieutenants be of value as advisers to the Vietnamese, a people who had been fighting nonstop for the last twenty years? How could sending highly motivated but inexperienced people to train indigenous troops result in anything more than what was reportedly already there—an inept, inefficient South Vietnamese army? It was early days yet, but it seemed as if the primary purpose of our being there had already been compromised; only now did it occur to me that in 1962 Vietnam was not just "the only war we've got" for me as a combat infantryman who didn't particularly want to go to a stateside staff assignment, but for the entire U.S. military establishment.

In July I was finally promoted to major. It was eight months overdue, but I was on top of the promotions list and absolutely overjoyed. I didn't even mind the rumor that had sprung up over my initial nonselection: according to Ed Szvetecz, the scuttlebutt was that I'd been passed over for failure to salute a superior officer I didn't respect. Patty and I threw a big party at the Benjamin Franklin Village Officers' Club. We'd planned to have the bar open for three hours but ended up letting it run till the club closed. Phil Gilchrist even came over for the celebrations (he was now a senior major commanding an armor battalion at Kaiserslautern) and it was just a great night. The cost was well over a year's pay difference between a captain and a major, but what the hell—I was a major. Still, it took a long time to get past nine years of captaincy. For weeks after, I still answered the phone as "Captain Hackworth." Finally Grattan made a sign, and every time I picked up the phone, he held it up. "You're a major," it read, "you dumb son of a bitch." I finally got the word.

The ATT was now fast approaching. Preparations were going well until Colonel Couch was seriously injured in a night field training exercise (FTX)—another M151 jeep turned over. Couch was tossed out and the retinas of both his eyes were detached. He was flown to Frankfurt in critical condition, and as soon as possible he'd be transferred back to the States for whatever was necessary to save his sight. It was a tragic accident for both the man and the battlegroup. Without Colonel Couch around to cover Gus's ass during the test, the 1/18th was going to be in big trouble.

Then, out of the blue, Newbreed called me to his office. "I'm making you my deputy," he said. I was dumbfounded. Colonel Couch had to be replaced, but there were five majors in the battlegroup who outranked me, plus Sniffin, who, as a light colonel, by all New Army criteria should have gotten this senior lieutenant colonel billet hands down. Still, *a commander will put up with any amount of insubordination as long as the junior officer gets results,* Johns had said, and I guessed it was true.

I wanted to see Colonel Couch before he was evacuated. His nurse met me at the door of his private room to tell me I could stay only ten minutes. She took the cake I'd brought (which Pam Szvetecz had made and asked me to deliver) and I went in to see the Colonel. Couch's eyes were heavily bandaged, but his great sense of humor was still in fine form. We had a nice visit, and toward the end the nurse came back to tell him about the cake. Couch suggested we have a piece, which we did, and then I said my good-byes and left. On the way down the hospital corridor, I realized I hadn't told Couch that I was only the bearer of the cake, that Pam Szvetecz was its maker. For a moment I thought about running back and telling the nurse, so she could pass the word along. *But no.* I thought. *Screw it. He'll think you did it, and you'll get the credit for being a good guy.*

Well. Take the credit and lay the blame—the motto of the superambitious. I was becoming just like those I despised, and as I drove back to Mannheim I didn't like myself very much at all. But to my great, long-lasting shame, I never rectified the situation either.

Finally it was August, and up to Baumholder for the week-long ATT. According to a friend who was one of the ATT controllers at Division, apparently there were grave doubts as to both Newbreed's ability to command the unit, and whether a fair evaluation of the battlegroup could even be made with Gus at the helm. All of us shared the same doubts; nevertheless, rehearsals were over and, sink or swim, it was opening night. As Deputy CO, my role basically was to run an alternate battlegroup CP (in case the main CP took a nuclear hit, went the reasoning), and be prepared to take over or lead a separate task force if required. I made Tim Grattan my S-2/S-3, took a couple of jeeps and communicators, and fitted out an APC as a mobile command post. I wanted to travel light, like Rommel, whose command style I'd admired forever.

The show got under way. Early in the piece, a German hunter in lederhosen wandered into the main CP area, complaining about "maneuver damage." He was immediately apprehended; civilians were not allowed anywhere in the CP grounds. But the hunter refused to leave, demanding to see the commander. Finally he was taken to the CP. When Colonel Newbreed, who'd been worrying the "battle," turned to talk to him, the guy said in English, "I'm not a hunter. I'm an enemy agent and I've been given the mission to assassinate you." With that, it was KABOOM, as the hunter "terminated" Gus with a blank from his shotgun. The umpire stepped in and told Newbreed he was dead for the next two days. Outraged, Gus rose up red-faced from the dead and relieved on the spot HQ CO Captain Harrelson (who was responsible for security of the CP area), for the millionth time.

I took command. A few pathfinders were picked up on an open field to our rear. I concluded we were in for an enemy helicopter assault or parachute drop, and had the engineer company simulate the seeding of all probable landing and drop zones with AP mines. With a rifle company (tanks attached) placed in the tree line, and the engineers instructed to fight as infantry as required, the aggressors fell right into our trap. I found out later that the airmobile assault was the largest helicopter airlift of troops ever attempted in Europe. All I knew at the time was that we absolutely destroyed them, in the process capturing a couple of hundred POWs and winning that part of the battle.

We attacked across a river, and all in all were doing quite well by the time Gus was deemed alive and allowed to resume command. "Doubts concerning Newbreed intensified," my controller buddy later told me, when promptly "he got lost and placed his tac CP in front of friendly lines." But that was not all. He set up his command post in a draw, effectively blocking all radio commo with the maneuver elements. The exercise started to fall apart. Nothing was coordinated. No one knew what was going on (except that at this rate we were going to lose the battle and, far more serious, fail the test). In the meantime we'd been surrounded by aggressor elements. The controllers took matters into their own hands. They decreed that the battlegroup CP had taken a direct artillery hit and had been wiped out. With Newbreed thus "killed" again, I was back in command.

Tim and I moved our tac CP up to the highest hill we could find. The battlegroup was surrounded, cut off, and about to be gobbled up—shades of Korea, 1950–51—and though there'd be no dead or POWs to rot in enemy camps, the honor of the Vanguards made the stakes seem just as high. We established good commo with all fighting units, and then maneuvered them into a tight perimeter defense. From then on it was easy. As Tim described it, "We were just drawing circles and arrows on maps, and talking to people on the radio. We were not using all the correct codes, but it was like fighting a real battle—and it worked."

For me, the whole thing was just plain exciting. I fought the battlegroup as I'd fight a rifle company; the only difference as I saw it was that I had more and bigger toys to play with. Radio reports kept coming in with new situations and the latest intelligence; I kind of felt like a doctor in the middle of a big operation. The doc's primary mission might be a straightforward appendectomy, but he's still always on his toes, getting sitreps from the nurses on the patient's blood pressure, heart rate, and whatever else is going.

The doctor has his SOPs, but he also has contingencies; in an instant he has to filter all the info his assistants give him, and be able to alter his procedure as necessary, on the spot. On the ground during the ATT, my decisions based on the latest info seemed to come completely naturally. It came as no small surprise, but I'd never felt more confident in my life.

In the middle of it all, I received a panicked call from Colonel Sniffin. A life-and-death reality had gotten mixed up with the mythical war. He said one of his ammo trucks had tipped over in a muddy field. The driver's arm was pinned underneath; the truck was on fire and in serious danger of blowing its load sky-high. "What do we do?" asked the senior lieutenant colonel who, as XO, was in charge of all supply trains. After ascertaining that there were no vehicles capable of winching the truck off or pushing it out of the way, and realizing the kid was going to burn to death or be blown to smithereens, I told Sniffin to get an ax and chop the boy's arm off. He'd lose a limb, but not his life.

I went back to fighting the battlegroup. Last time around, Colonels Johns and Couch had turned the 1/18th ATT upside down by "going through the aggressors like the well-known fecal material through a tin horn," as Johns put it to me later, which resulted in a whole new schedule and artificial delays to keep the thing going. Now, Tim and I worked our asses off to do the same thing. We attacked when we were supposed to defend and threw the whole scenario out the window. We used Larry MacDonald's recon platoon as if it were a tank company and blasted holy hell out of the attacking forces. These recon guys found a hole in the aggressor line and spearheaded the breakout. A couple of rifle companies augmented with tanks gained the high ground to cover the rest of the battlegroup's night retrograde river crossing; when these last defending units successfully withdrew across the river, we'd all but won the little war.

Tim and I both worked around the clock for two days. When there was no doubt we'd pass the test, the Test Chief, Brigadier General Clarence E. Beck, had me "killed" so I could get some sleep and put Newbreed back as the battlegroup CO—"Fortunate," in one of my platoon leaders' words, "that there was one left to command." Beck termed the shambles Gus made of the exercise "neither pretty nor pleasant," but as for myself, it had been exhilarating, good fun. As well, the good word came that the boy trapped under the ammo truck had kept his limb *and* his life. A jeep full of evaluators had arrived on the scene in the nick of time, extricated the trooper, and got him off to the hospital. For a long time, though, I wondered why I'd been the recipient of Colonel Sniffin's frantic call. Shouldn't he have been competent enough to handle the emergency himself? The question remained with me for many years, particularly as

Sniffin continued to climb the stairway to the stars, and didn't stop until he hit major general.

Leaving the 1/18th wasn't hard. Under Colonels Johns and Couch, we'd been warriors (in our heads at least, and as much as peacetime allowed) twenty-four hours a day. We'd paraded proudly in battle uniform (complete with shrimp-net camouflage gear on our steel pots), while everyone else wore dress; we'd looked different, and we'd *felt* different. But without those two Old Soldiers, the special, spirited unit I'd joined was like any other route-step outfit of fifteen hundred men dressed in green. Still, it kind of hurt to go without so much as a "thank you" from old Candy Bar 6 or the Sniff, or a special ER for having pulled their nuts out of the fire at the ATT (Gus was spared even a routine ER because I'd not been in the deputy CO slot for the minimum sixty days). But there was nothing to be done about it, nor, ultimately, did it matter. Newbreed's breed of soldier would always do their damnedest to bring warriors to heel. If they could not engender respect, then they'd work on fear. If they could not engender fear, then they'd simply fix your career by means of an Army truism for which there was no recourse: the painful reality that "the boss"—whether or not he's qualified, or even knows what he's talking about—"is always right."

I spent the last days at Combat Support Company writing ERs for my own boys. Having been burned pretty badly myself, I went out of my way for the likes of Grattan and Peppers, both of whom, even as young lieutenants, I felt would one day be outstanding generals (which, indeed, Peppers went on to become). Writing ERs was an art form in itself; no longer was "a fine, conscientious, good man" the ticket to a successful career. Instead, "the finest, most conscientious, best man ever to wear the uniform—a God-given waterwalker" was the shot. Everyone had to be rated as if he were a future Chief of Staff, and though such inflation made the whole system meaningless, any attempt to evaluate even the best young officer objectively and realistically was, in effect, about the same as cutting his throat. It would result only in an early pass over or nonselection for him down the track.

I popped into Heidelberg one afternoon to say good-bye to Cybocal, my old partner in the Review and Analysis section. I figured I'd find him just where I'd left him two years before, in our little basement office far from the eyes of The All-Seeing. He was there all right, but he was not alone. Our little two-man team, conceived by Colonel Quig essentially to keep me out of trouble, had exploded into a full-blown staff—a lieutenant colonel, a major, a captain, about nine whiz-kid troopers, and four or five civilians— doing the exact same thing Cybocal and I had managed quite well alone. It was like some living, growing organism that once started didn't know how to stop, resulting not in greater efficiency but in an absolute waste of money and manpower.

It would be good to go home. We had a choice whether to fly or ship over; I chose the "slow boat" to unwind and work Germany out of my system. For me, it had been a period of the highest highs and the lowest lows: JFK's golden Camelot after Ike's barren reign; the boredom of the peacetime Army giving way to the wonderful adventure in Berlin; the brilliance of the 1/18th under Colonel Johns, trampled in the dust by his successor, Colonel Newbreed; being "not selected" for major and finding that Johns and, by extension, Rock Read, Reuben Tucker, and Bruce Clarke believed in me enough to come to my aid; turning thirty, then thirty-one, and recognizing a little better who I was, what I wanted, and what made me tick.

I had a gift for selecting good men, for putting them in the right jobs, and for recognizing the magic buttons to push in order to get the max out of them. I was impatient and intolerant with the lazy, the incompetent, and those lacking common sense. I came down hard when things were not done as quickly as I wanted and the way *I* wanted them done—unless, of course, someone else's way was better, faster, and wiser. Even in my increasingly ticket-punching programmed mind, I could not suck up to phonies. I was caustic and openly insubordinate to superiors I did not like. General Tucker once told Rock Read that I had a flair for shooting myself in the foot with superior officers and that it might do me in one day. He was probably right, but I'd worry about that when the time came. Meanwhile, any man, regardless of rank, who had the potential to stupidly endanger the lives of my troops was my enemy for life; another of my qualities, for better or worse, was a long, long memory.

I was an NCO in officer's gear. I loved to talk to the troops. More than that, I loved to listen to them. In everything but training I listened to their bitches and tried to make their lives a little better. When it came to training I kept it up until the bitching turned to boasts, as Colonel Johns had identified in his farewell speech. I had a great memory for my troopers' names and used that talent to let the boys know they were not just faces in a crowd. I wanted to be liked—it was an ongoing-since-childhood search for approval—but I didn't mind being hated. I took great pride in both the mark I made on a unit—when I left it was always spirited, well trained, mission oriented, and infinitely cocky—and, perversely, in the lower scores on my ERs, which were always in the areas of tact, tolerance, and discretion.

I found myself more and more grateful for having entered the Army through the TRUST gate, and being taken under the wings of Steve Prazenka and other Old Army soldiers, even as my TRUST trooper priorities were giving way to those of a combat-oriented warrior (I even surprised myself the morning I chewed out one of my squad leaders because he'd spent his time shining his boots to mirrors but, as a result, was not prepared for a class he had to teach: "Get your priorities straight," I'd snapped), and for being battlefield and not West Point or ROTC commissioned. Although I'd mostly gotten over my basic disdain for school-trained officers (which was born of my own insecurity anyway), I really believed that I approached the battlefield in a freer, simpler, more flexible way because I'd learned it on the ground, where the unexpected was the norm and all the school solutions in the world were not adequate preparation.

Added to the hands-on experience was all the military reading I'd done since I was a kid. I'd lived in my uncle Roy's WW I picture books, and had since read anything and everything I could get on battles and wars throughout the ages. And because it was all independent of formal education, I had to draw my own conclusions, which, remolded and reshaped based on what was happening at the moment, had already proved a great foundation for decisions I would make myself on the battlefield.

My next assignment was the 101st Airborne Division at Fort Campbell, Kentucky. I'd wanted Vietnam, but I couldn't bitch; my lifelong dream was finally coming true: a paratroop assignment with one of the best divisions of them all. I'd resigned myself to the fact that, as a major, I would not command troops; I was well grounded in staff work now, and confident to boot. *As long as I just remember to put my feet up occasionally and think,* as Colonel Johns had urged all his boys.

But little did I know, as the ship neared New York, that for the Army, the days of introspection were over.

PART II

13 SCREAMING EAGLES

When I arrived at Fort Campbell in January 1965, the cluster of
World War II barracks shrouded in a cloud of coal smoke didn't
at all resemble my mental image of the home of the 101st
Airborne Division, the Army's premier fighting force. But I didn't
have a lot of time to think about it. The 101st was definitely the
"big leagues." To make your mark in such a unit a second
lieutenant had to hit the ground running, and those of us from
the Class of '64 did just that. We worked hard and we played hard
and we were damn proud to be members of the best team in
the U.S. Army. That Screaming Eagle patch meant a hell of
a lot.

> Brigadier General John D. Howard
> Platoon leader, 101st Airborne Division
> Republic of Vietnam, 1965–66

THE 101st Airborne Division was rated as one of the U.S. Army's
top units. Like its sister division, the 82d, it had captured the American
imagination from its earliest days, with jumps at Normandy and Holland. Its
role in the Ardennes offensive of World War II produced a rich supply of
battlefield lore, immortal words such as McAuliffe's reply of "Nuts" to
German demands for surrender, and an unknown paratrooper's "They've
got us surrounded, the poor bastards," in response to the division's plight. *
Though inactivated after the war, in the late fifties the "Screaming Eagles"
dusted off their parachutes to meet another "rendezvous with destiny": with
the backing of then Army Chief of Staff Maxwell D. Taylor, who'd
commanded the unit from Normandy to the war's end, the 101st became
the Army's first nuclear-equipped division.

In October 1962, "the spirit of Bastogne" was alive and well at Fort
Campbell, Kentucky. The paratroopers of the 101st Airborne were lean and

---

* The fact that the 4th Armored Division also lays claim to the latter comment in no way detracts from
the morale-boosting value it has had for generations of 101st troopers.

mean and infinitely proud. Their parachute wings and scrupulously polished brass shone brightly in the sun as, all over the huge, spotless post, they moved purposefully in cut-down, starched fatigues and mahogany Corcoran jump boots. "Airborne, sir!" they shouted to passing officers as they executed snappy salutes; "All the way," the officers barked in reply. For me, walking around Fort Campbell for the first time was like a dream come true. Having "refound" TRUST perfection in the Vanguards, I could hardly believe that now, back-to-back, I'd found it again.

The 101st was ready to go anywhere, anytime, and at a moment's notice. It took a lot of hustle to be prepared to jump a hundred different ways, but there was never any panic, it seemed. In an emergency anywhere on the globe, the division could have its first combat element in the air thirty minutes from the initial alert, with a reinforced battlegroup on the way within two hours, and the rest of the division following within thirty-six. (By comparison, it might take thirty-five to sixty *days* to move a heavy-in-equipment "leg" infantry [non-Airborne] or armor division.) This ability to deal quickly with the unexpected was a distinction shared only with the 82d during this 1962–65 time frame. In terms of equipment, we were the only two light divisions in the Army.

I hadn't been in the 101st for two weeks when I got my first taste of the motivation, discipline, and pure professionalism of the crack troops and leaders of the Screaming Eagles. The occasion was Soviet leader Khrushchev's getting caught in his mighty gamble to deploy intermediate-range ballistic missiles (IRBMs) in Cuba, just ninety miles off the coast of Florida. In response, the U.S. Joint Chiefs of Staff recommended massive air attacks on the missile sites and all air-defense installations in Cuba. An invasion, too, was planned, in which the 101st and 82d Airborne divisions (as part of XVIII Airborne Corps) would jump into Cuba and form an airhead while the Navy conducted amphibious operations to subsequently link up with the paratroopers on Cuban soil. It would be like Normandy all over again, and the adrenaline was pumping. At Fort Campbell, plans were drawn, loads were rigged, and the troopers, eager to jump off on a great adventure, were brought to a razor's edge of readiness.

Like so many soldiers who grew up in the Cold War (certainly those of us who joined after WW II), I took it for granted, and I think most American citizens did, too, that one day the Soviet Union and the United States would square off and go at it. In the meantime we all lived with the situation as one might live with malaria, never knowing when and how severe the next bout would be, but never really believing it was something we would not ultimately survive, not ultimately *win*. But then came the Cuban missile crisis. It shook all of us, both military *and* civilian, out of our complacency, at least momentarily. For the very first time, the war of ideology between East and West was not being fought by proxy in China, Greece, Korea, or Southeast Asia, but by the superpowers themselves. And neither Kennedy nor Khrushchev looked as if he intended to back away.

I called Patty, who was visiting her mother in Los Angeles, and told her to take the kids and get a cabin in the mountains to ride out the unknown. The specter of war seemed ever closer when, in the midst of the crisis, Castro shot down an American U-2 and another U-2 intruded Soviet air space near Siberia. Kennedy had called off all overt and covert military operations during the emergency, so neither aircraft should have been up there in the first place. Afterwards he would say of this breakdown in communication that "ten percent never get the word," but in such a matter of global life or death, the figure seemed chillingly high.

At the eleventh hour, Khrushchev accepted Kennedy's firm "suggestion" that he dismantle and remove his missile sites from Cuba *muy pronto*. Neither U.S. air strikes nor an invasion proved necessary; the Kennedy Administration's naval blockade coupled with the obvious fact of the United States's overwhelming military superiority in a conflict just off its shores was enough to turn the immediate situation around. (Which was all for the best for the 82d and the 101st, because had we jumped in, our casualties would have been horrendous. Aerial intelligence photographs taken after the operation was put on the back burner revealed that the Cubans had cut the sugarcane on all our planned drop zones at an angle and about knee-high, to skewer any paratrooper who landed on it, and the DZs were covered by Cuban antiaircraft guns.) The confrontation in Cuba, undoubtedly the most dangerous thirteen days civilization has ever known, did, in a way, provide a brief pause in the Cold War, with Khrushchev admitting during the crisis that "one is afraid to say good night to one's family," and the affair being the impetus to establish a "hot line" between Washington and Moscow. But the only real lesson the two powers came away with in this brinksmanship duel was that each needed bigger, faster, and longer-range weapons, and in the end, all the Cuban missile crisis led to was a new round in the nuclear arms race from which there'd be no turning back.

I'd actually been on my way to Fort Benning when the Cuban situation erupted, to attend the Infantry Career Course, a vital station on the career cross designed to be like an advanced degree in infantry. I went as scheduled, as did the rest of the 101st, 82d, and Army aviation personnel in my class, though all of us remained on alert throughout the crisis to rejoin our units in a flash should the planned Cuban invasion become a reality.

Benning had changed significantly since I'd last been there ten years before. With the military now permanent big business, the Infantry School was certainly getting its share of McNamara's greatly expanded defense budget. Like Fort Sill and Fort Bliss during the missile boom, new buildings, classrooms, training facilities, and quarters at Benning reflected heavy expenditure. Columbus, too, had a new face; it was now a prosperous, modern southern town. Happily, all you had to do was peel back the makeup, though, to find the same honky-tonks of the forties and fifties that we old-timers had known and loved.

The Career Course adopted an academic approach to training infantry officers. As such, when our class was the first to get the welcome word that the Pentomic Army division was out, we were also the first to receive instruction in the new structure, known as Reorganization Objectives Army Division (ROAD), set to replace it the following year.

Basically the ROAD reorganization redressed the imbalance, inherent in the Pentomic scheme, between an Army division's nuclear and conventional capabilities. In keeping with the philosophy of Maxwell D. Taylor, by then serving as Chairman of the Joint Chiefs of Staff, ROAD moved the military's "massive retaliation" thinking of the mid to late fifties toward one of "flexible response." Under the ROAD concept the battlegroup was disbanded and the battalion was reintroduced; unfortunately, that one step forward was followed by two steps back, with ROAD sounding the final death knell for the proud regiments, which were to be replaced with characterless "brigades" numbered one, two, and three. While the regiments had actually been disbanded in the Pentomic structure, the battlegroups that replaced them had carried along the names, the history, the lifeblood, and the spirit of their colorful ancestral units—the troops of the 1st Battlegroup, 18th Infantry, for example, felt themselves as much the Vanguards as did their older brothers in the 18th Infantry Regiment. But when ROAD came into being, all real regimental affiliation was lost. The new brigades were nothing more than basic control headquarters under the division umbrella, to which any number of the division's battalions and support units would be attached as required by the mission. The concept was called tailoring. ROAD was designed like an accordion, one that could be expanded or contracted at will to deal with the widest possible range of military scenarios.

There was no doubt that ROAD was a far more workable organization than the Pentomic structure. Its battalion orientation meant fewer jobs for full colonels and more for light colonels, lessening the gap, agewise, between company commanders and their immediate bosses, and afforded a more reasonable span of control. Still, I always felt the Army division had fought three good wars with the regimental configuration, and though I was as relieved as anyone to see the Pentomic Army axed, ROAD seemed to be just more change for the sake of change, and the work of staff men who didn't understand the vital role tradition played in causing fighting men to risk their lives. Ironically, in practice ROAD ended up where the whole reorganization had begun. As a rule, the same three maneuver battalions were attached to the same brigade all the time, so in fact we were back to the old regiments again, only without the attached heraldry, historical élan, battle honors, and the "I'm a Wolfhound!" pride and built-in esprit that made soldiers do the impossible. As time passed, individual battalions sometimes picked up the names of their regimental forebears, like the 1/27 "Wolfhound" battalion or the 1/7 "Gary Owens." But unless these battalions had unusually strong commanders who really pushed the history and the pride of the regiment that had come before, the names were names and nothing more.

The many hours the Career Course allotted to introducing us to ROAD were nothing compared to those assigned to counterinsurgency and related subjects. Counterinsurgency was *the* thing in the early sixties. It was endorsed enthusiastically by Kennedy and his brain trust, and with Vietnam on everybody's lips, in the Career Course we studied guerrilla campaigns from as far back as biblical times. But in what I thought was a strange twist, unlike the right instruction for the wrong war I'd received at the Infantry School fresh off the battlefield in Korea, Benning in '62 was teaching for the right war but using the wrong instruction. Little emphasis was placed on the late-forties to early-fifties French experience in Indochina, the most likely arena for America's first foray into guerrilla war since our campaigns in the Philippines at the turn of the century. Instead, the emphasis was on the recent British experience in Malaya, which related more closely to the U.S. Indian campaigns of the 1860s to 1890s. The guerrilla techniques taught to our class were of Napoleonic vintage, and, according to the dozen or so of my classmates who'd just returned from U.S. Special Forces assignments in Southeast Asia, would be of little use in the Highlands and paddies of Vietnam in the 1960s. The outspoken Green Berets, among them Mike Phelan, Chuck Darnell, John Firth, Bill Angel, and one of the great all-time legends of Special Forces, Larry Thorne, also warned that the counterinsurgency training we were receiving wasn't counterinsurgency at all, but conventional tactics with increased mobility provided by helicopters, or "choppers." (As it was explained by one helicopter-enamored commander, with choppers "we can bring in fresh troops, hit fast, and in thirty seconds we can clean them out.")[1] "We need *new* tactics," the Special Forces pros pleaded, "for a protracted guerrilla war."

But the pleas fell predominantly on deaf ears, in large part because whatever the character of the war at hand, Benning's mentality was first and foremost one of stopping the Soviets on the plains of Europe. Put simply, Benning was just not *interested* in counterinsurgency. So however many hours the Career Course devoted to the subject because the Kennedy Administration demanded it, from the Infantry School point of view, it was just a *requirement*, to be given a good load of lip service but little more. And that was what it got, regardless of what the soldiers and officers truly needed or what the war to come required. On the other hand, even if Benning had wanted to change the curriculum or course content, its hands were tied. The fact was that the Infantry School couldn't update or change anything without a doctrine change from higher up. My big bitch during the course was the river-crossing training. I knew about river crossing. In Germany, the 8th Div had made its members total pros in this critical maneuver. We'd practiced it in the attack and in the withdrawal, in both conventional and nuclear scenarios, and on a regular basis. Most of the ex-8th Div guys in the Career Course agreed that Benning's methods would have been just right for a Napoleonic plan to invade the British Isles. But when I went to Colonel Swearinger, the deputy committee chief (and a good man who'd been the 1/18th's deputy commander before Colonel Couch), to try to get some reality brought into this training, he said there wasn't a damn thing he could do. He suggested I write an article on the subject for the Benning-published *Infantry* magazine. That was the best way he knew to get the establishment's attention, he said, and possibly start the ball rolling for meaningful change in the curriculum. I started writing that very night.

There was also a lot of talk about the atomic battlefield at the Career Course. About 10 percent of our training had us sitting in the classroom and theoretically blowing away Soviet tank regiments and divisions on a European battlefield, then estimating the damage with little plastic wheels that calculated the number of deaths by blast, radiation, and fire. Neat, clinical, and academic, we could spin the wheel and with a theoretical press of a button eliminate more enemy than Grant did in a campaign. To an infantry soldier of the time, tactical atomic weapons—nuclear-tipped Honest John, Corporal, Sergeant, and Davy Crockett missiles, as well as eight-inch atomic cannons—were just a logical progression from the bow and arrow. But with Cuba still hanging in the balance, I found the classes about them more than a little sobering.

By the time the Career Course was over, Cuba was off the boil. I said good-bye to old friends and new, took a short leave to finish my river-crossing article (it was never published—my writing skills, I'm sure, left much to be desired), and moved Patty and the girls to Fort Campbell. There'd been no academic highlights to my 1962 stint at Benning except that I did graduate just shy of the top 5 percent of the class, having accepted Benning's emphasis on memorization and pat school solutions to fluid problems, and giving in to the required "garbage in, garbage out" approach to our exams. It was only in retrospect I recognized that what I had considered a six-month nonevent was actually the end of an era for me, and the person I saw it out with was Steve Prazenka. Just as I'd run into him at the Infantry School in 1952, a decade later he was there again—now married, now a captain, now a company commander, his career being "managed" by an Army that felt everyone should be general officer material even when—as in Steve's case—the guy didn't want to be a general in the first place, but just wanted to lead his troops and make his company the best in the world. As always, it was great to see him, to thank him for kicking my ass when I was a kid and teaching me my trade, both of which were fundamental to the warrior I became. Then General Cleland had come along, to build my confidence and give me incentive in those frustrating limbo years, and then there'd been Colonel Johns, who provided the anchor. Johns taught me the skills to be an officer (*and* a gentleman, when absolutely necessary) but never to lose sight of my primary responsibility, my troops; it was Prazenka who'd set me on the right course years before, but it was the man Johns had guided whom I would have to be now, whom I would more and more become over the next years. Somehow it was significant—though I didn't realize it at the time—that I never saw Steve Prazenka or Colonel Johns again throughout my life. Each had done his job, and when I said my final good-bye to Steve, I was really on my own.

When I first reported in to the 101st, I tried like hell to get assigned to a battlegroup, but no jobs were available. The word was I *might* be able to get an S-3 or XO job in a battalion when ROAD was introduced in '64. Meanwhile, upon my return from Fort Benning I was assigned to the 101st's logistics shop as G-4 Operations officer. If I had to be a staff officer, I could have done a lot worse. G-4 Operations was a real *team*, and a damned efficient one at that, thanks in large part to Captain John Anderson, my sharp assistant, and Master Sergeant Haultman, our twenty-year paratrooper Operations sergeant. My immediate superior, Major Robert E. Saksa, and his boss, G-4 Lieutenant Colonel James D. Abts, were brilliant staff officers, with reputations as fine commanders as well; they knew how to delegate authority, and always got the best out of their subordinates.

In general terms, the job itself entailed writing plans for the logistics side of any Division operation or contingency mission. The most difficult part of it was the stamina you needed simply to stay on top of everything. Each operation the 101st was involved in (be it a major maneuver anywhere from

Alaska to Iran,* or a battlegroup or division-size exercise in America's South that might cover more ground than Grant or Lee did in the entire Civil War) required ground recons, coordination, and detailed organization. That work, coupled with the division's ongoing contingency planning (to invade, assist, attack, defend, or reinforce countries from Algeria to Zambia), meant for us in the G-4 shop that there were simply not enough hours in the day.

I was responsible for the logistic side of all Division outloading. As such, though I'd never been a detail man, I soon found myself memorizing weights and cubes, calculating maximum loads to be carried by the C-124 and the C-130 aircraft according to how far the plane had to fly and whether the operation was tactical (i.e., jumping in) or strategic (landing at a friendly field and unloading). I became a pro at filling those aircraft to the limit with a mix of passengers, vehicles, and preconfigured pallets of water, ammo, fuel, and medical supplies for every possible contingency. Another one of my early tasks was to rewrite the division's outloading SOP from the first page, which meant from the moment the whistle blew and the first combat element of the Division Ready Force (the half-hour Immediate Ready Force) swung into action until the division's ash and trash had been safely landed at the final destination. When completed, the document was the size of the New York City Yellow Pages. For me that mission provided a particularly great learning experience, for I had the chance to work closely with our Assistant Division Commander, Brigadier General Patrick Cassidy, a twenty-year Airborne vet and probably the Army's expert on Airborne operations at this time. Cassidy was to Airborne what Prazenka was to recon—a total pro.

One morning General Cassidy called me in and tossed me an all-metal rifle that looked about as lethal as a child's toy. "Take this out and see what you think of it, Hack," he said. To date, the AR-15, as the rifle was known, had been used as an Air Force survival weapon, but it seemed that DA was considering arming Airborne units with it, too: with every pound counting in Airborne in terms of mobility and resupply, the recently issued M-14 was just too big, and it and its ammo too heavy, to make it an ideal paratroop weapon. The AR-15, on the other hand, was small and light, with lightweight ammo—at first glance, exactly what was needed.

I took the weapon out and pumped thousands of rounds through it in every conceivable situation an infantryman might find himself—in sand, mud, cold, rain, and dense foliage as close to "jungle" as I could get at Fort Campbell. I took it apart, put it together, fired it dirty, fired it clean. And whatever the situation, the AR-15 did one thing with consistency: it jammed.

---

* The 101st's primary orientation was the Middle East, so much of the training was in desert warfare, affording the units of the division more than occasional travel to exotic lands.

Far more than it fired. The weapon had serious teething problems. But, in my estimation, even if it went back to the drawing board and the Research and Development whiz kids ironed out some of its more glaring faults, the AR-15 would never be worth a pinch of salt as an infantry weapon. It just wasn't rugged enough. It wasn't GI-proof. The thing required almost surgical cleanliness (damn hard to achieve on a battlefield) and exacting maintenance that the average Airborne infantryman wasn't going to perform in a combat situation. The AR-15 *looked* good, but to me, sending a trooper into combat with it would be sending him on a suicide mission.

I made my report to General Cassidy and to his boss, the wonderful 101st CG, Major General Harry Critz. After going over all my findings, the two men agreed with my conclusions, and the official Division position was that the AR-15 was simply not an infantry/Airborne weapon. All of us felt that Material Command would get similar reports from the 82d, as well as from any groundpounder unit that got a sneak preview of this latest wonder gear; it was therefore an incredible surprise to find, two years later, that the rifle the 101st was issued to carry into battle in Vietnam was the shit-piece AR-15 down to the last detail, except that the new version had a stock and was called the M-16.

Each year XVIII Airborne Corps held a huge maneuver called Operation SWIFT STRIKE. SWIFT STRIKE III, held in 1963, had a maneuver area that encompassed almost all of Dixie, and the primary purpose of the exercise was to ascertain whether Army or Air Force aviation was more conducive to the movement of large bodies of troops in a battlefield setting, to the use of unimproved runways, and to aerial resupply overall. The outcome of the exercise was of enormous importance to the Army: ever since the Air Corps, originally a branch of the Army Signal Corps, broke away and became a separate service (the Air Force) in the late forties, the Army had been trying to get an air arm back. To this end, in the early sixties it was already gearing up a fleet of its own helicopters, and to assure maximum independence from the Air Force in the fixed-wing department, during SWIFT STRIKE III the Army would pit its twin-engine CV-2, a Canadian aircraft also known as the Caribou, against the USAF's C-123 and the mighty C-130 Hercules. Interservice rivalry was, in fact, the bottom line of this competition. There was no small truth in the joke that our Army, Navy, and Air Force hated one another as much as, if not more than, they hated the Soviets.

Airborne had evolved enormously since its birth more than twenty years before. The basic tactics hadn't changed, but whereas in the Airborne operations of WW II, arriving *with* one's unit, and even remotely close to the designated drop zone, was the exception not the rule, by the early sixties, Airborne was a truly sophisticated system, complete with electronic homing devices that led planes right to the drop zone, and different methods of jumping that got more men and matériel out of the planes and onto the ground faster, and in reasonable proximity to one another. Even so, Airborne carried with it its own peculiar risks, and SWIFT STRIKE III highlighted quite a few.

G-4 Operations was responsible for all troop movement and resupply from the outset of the exercise. As such, I jumped in with the Division tac CP on the second drop. Just as I recovered and assembled with the small tac CP group, I saw General Critz's jeep plummeting through the sky. Its cargo chute had "Roman candled" (i.e., the silk had rolled and twisted around itself), and there wasn't a hope in hell that it would open. So all we could do was look on helplessly as the quarter-ton smashed to pieces on the DZ. The vehicle had been carrying General Critz's command radios and most of our bare-bones tac CP gear. The dilemma wasn't nearly the pickle Ridgway found himself in at Normandy (when he landed, he was *completely alone* for hours before finding his CP group), but the mishap showed well how in Airborne a little thing like the CG's jeep clobbering to the ground could potentially change the course of a battle. In this instance, the division signal officer quickly commandeered some radios, and Critz was back in control before the troops had even begun to push the flattened jeep off the DZ.

Other than a strong enemy presence on the drop zone or bad ground winds, there is nothing more dangerous in an Airborne operation than a cluttered DZ. By the time of the next drop, General Critz's jeep was gone, but a number of our (so aptly named) Mules were still sitting right in the middle of the drop zone—already stacked with containers of machine guns, 81-mm mortars, recoilless rifles, and ammo that had just been dropped as well—refusing to start. The Mule was another of the modern Army's wonder-gear vehicles. It was a wagonlike flatbed on wheels, about five feet long and capable of carrying a thousand pounds; its mission in life was first to move dropped equipment and supplies off a DZ quickly, and then to serve as a utility vehicle. Like the AR-15, in theory the Mule was ideal for Airborne. In practical terms it was a pain in the neck, because you never knew whether or not it was going to cooperate. At SWIFT STRIKE III, obviously most of the Mules were balking, and we had the monkey on our backs to clear the DZ to make way for heavier loads, such as jeeps, 105 howitzers, and light bulldozers, which were next in line to be dropped.*

---

* The first priority in an Airborne operation was to get fighters in to secure a drop zone. Next came more fighters, then light weapons and artillery to support the ground troops. The whole sequence was like a slowly expanding inkblot, with small bulldozers then dropped and used to build an assault airfield out of the initial DZ; when that was accomplished, planes could begin to land with more soldiers, supplies, etc.

Every spare trooper ran out to help clear the DZ. Among the volunteers was an old man, ramrod straight in civilian gear, busting a nut with the rest of us as we hurriedly pushed Mules out of the way. Only later was I told he was retired Major General Thomas Sherborne, who'd commanded the 101st when it went Pentomic and who, until the Mule problem, had been at the SWIFT STRIKE III DZ merely to observe the drop. I also heard that the Mule had been one of Sherborne's favorite innovations when he'd had the division. It must have broken this old paratrooper's heart to see that the vehicle lived up to its name only too well.

Night fell and our tac CP group was still without shelter. But the maneuver had to go on, and to maintain light discipline a poncho was stretched out under which all of us—the CG, Chief of Staff, G-2, G-3, and me—crawled, our legs sticking out like the spokes of a wheel as we studied our maps by flashlight. But as the General gave his guidance, the flashlight began to dim. I pulled a candle out of my pack and lit it. As wax dripped all over my hands and the map while Critz issued his orders, I suddenly thought how on that very same ground, a hundred years before, Grant had probably huddled under a poncho with his aides and a candle, planning battles against Lee in the Civil War. I felt I was living out a real historic irony: here we were, a hundred years later, as members of the best, most effective, most modern division in the U.S. Army, and things hadn't really changed much at all.

As SWIFT STRIKE III progressed, of necessity I roamed the battlefield to ramrod the aerial resupply. Aircraft were thundering down on farmers' fields, dropping off troops and supplies or picking them up and flying them to distant AOs. Both Army and USAF fly-boys were busting their asses to "git thar fustest with the mostest" 1960s style, and I soon found that the guys on the ground were playing the game the exact same way. At one stage, I watched several 101st rifle companies making their way toward a small hill that controlled a road and a wide valley below. The battlegroup commander accompanying this force spotted an "enemy" element moving toward the same objective, and suddenly the exercise became a contest of who could get there first. Before my eyes I saw the 101st's units storming the top of that hill; there was no tactical formation, just a mob of four hundred paratroopers, waving their weapons, running like hell and screaming. They reached the top of the objective before the "enemy," and were rewarded by an umpire who ruled that as the 101st "had the combat power" on the hill, they'd won. I was amazed. No one—the umpire, the battlegroup commander, the company leaders, or the troopers themselves—seemed to realize that their shortcut to success would never have worked on a hot battlefield. "Men will do in battle what they have been in the habit of doing in training," General

Bruce Clarke, one of the U.S. Army's greatest training generals, had written in his then recently published *Guidelines for the Leader and the Commander*: in this case, both leaders and their men had been patted on the back for doing it wrong, and I wondered how many were going to die when King of the Mountain was played for real.

By the time SWIFT STRIKE III was over, aerial-resupply and troop-movement procedures had been hatched that would form the basis of all such procedures in future Airborne/airmobile operations. Unfortunately the Army lost its battle for an air arm: the final result of the test was that while the Army would control the small, tactical choppers (to be used for small-unit troop movement and command and control), USAF would take over the Caribous, as well as all other choppers save the Chinook, which the Army got to move its artillery.

The Kennedy Administration was committed to integrating the South. Units of the 101st had already been used at Little Rock, and we remained the primary enforcer now. When Governor George Wallace of Alabama proclaimed "Segregation now . . . segregation forever!" Task Force Cassidy, under the direct control of the President, was sent to Birmingham to prove he was dead wrong. From our Task Force headquarters at Fort McClellan, we began contingency planning in neighboring Mississippi and Georgia. The hatred of the time was incredible, and with blood spilling as passionately as it had during the Civil War, fears were high that all of Dixieland would soon be engulfed. One recon in Mississippi had me cruising in a Hertz rental car with two FBI agents, General Cassidy, and Major Joe Wilson (Task Force G-3). We played the average tourists as we drove around picking out landing zones, radio and TV stations, and staging, assembly, and enclosure areas (the latter to wire in anyone who was arrested), but just like the reconnaissance "picnics" we'd taken in Germany, we didn't fool the rednecks for a minute. Our skinhead paratrooper haircuts and the FBI guys' short top, back, and sides (not to mention their identical black plastic sunglasses) made us about as inconspicuous as a band of black guys at a Ku Klux Klan rally.

I was the Task Force G-4, responsible for keeping the troops fed, the vehicles maintained, and all other logistic considerations. Part of the job was to submit a daily logistics report to the Pentagon's Tactical Operations Center (TOC), and one evening I made my usual call.

"TOC, this is Task Force Cassidy. I've got the equipment status report for you."

"Okay, give it to me," replied a young, brash voice that I disliked immediately.

I made the report. When I finished, the guy said *very* cuttingly, "Yesterday you had four hundred vehicles. Today you have three hundred ninety-nine. You're missing a vehicle. Where is it?"

Smart-ass whiz kid, I thought. "I wouldn't have a clue. It's no big thing—we're still one hundred percent operational. Probably a truck is down with a broken axle. Vehicles get sick, you know, just like people."

"Don't get smart with me, soldier."

"Look," I said, "I don't have time for this. Do you want the report or don't you?"

"Do you realize who you're talking to?" the guy roared through the line.

"Yes, I'm talking to a wiseass who's overimpressed with his own importance and who's got nothing better to do than mess with the troops."

"Let me speak to your commanding general!"

I suddenly realized I'd probably gone too far. "Well, who are you?" I asked.

"I am Robert F. Kennedy. I'm the Attorney General. I'm *commanding* your organization. I'm *responsible* for handling civil disturbance, and if I want to know every last detail, soldier, you'll provide it. Now get me your boss right now!"

Talk about centralization. I put the phone down and went to see General Cassidy, whom by now I knew quite well, and vice versa. "General, you won't believe what I've done."

"I'll believe it, Hack," he said, "just tell me."

"See, I thought he was some clerk at the Pentagon TOC giving us a hard time—but I just told the Attorney General of the United States that he was a wiseass."

Cassidy moaned, "Of all people, Hackworth! Of all people!" and headed for the phone in the Task Force TOC. It was just lucky for me that both men were Irish. Cassidy managed to convince Kennedy that it was the Irish in *me* that had started all the trouble, and the Attorney General accepted Cassidy's apology on my behalf. With that, the good general hung up the phone and left the TOC, shaking his head. "Of all people, Hackworth. Of all people."

General Cassidy was not quite so sympathetic the next time I got a little carried away in Alabama. On that occasion the problem had actually begun at Fort Campbell, when it occurred to me that Master Sergeant Haultman, my Operations sergeant, was retiring in a few weeks. Haultman had been a fine teacher for me in my early G-4 days; besides that, he was a friend and a great soldier, and I wanted him to have something special to remember the Army by. But he didn't want a parade. He didn't want anything, he said. Then, a few days short of his retirement, he changed his mind. Now what he wanted, he told me, was to go up with me in a helicopter full of parachutes, and for the two of us to keeping jumping out of that chopper until all those chutes were gone.

"It's done," I said.

Having learned early in the Army that the system virtually ran on IOUs, I was fortunate to have a few of my own out at that time, to include both a helicopter pilot and a parachute maintenance officer. So the day before Haultman was to retire, as per his wish, I had a big stack of parachutes and our own personal chopper standing by. We flew around the Alabama countryside until we found a good drop zone in some farmer's field. With that, we put on our first chutes and jumped out. On the ground, we rolled up the chutes, threw them in a stack, got picked up by the chopper, and, as the bird gained jump altitude, slipped into the next chutes so we could do it all over again. I don't know how many jumps we made, but I do know we were bone-weary by the time we'd finished (the body wasn't made for so many opening shocks in a row), but if an old paratrooper wanted to go out that way, who had the right to deny him?

Few would disagree that paratroopers were an unusual breed of men. Some might say they were a little nuts. ("Why would anyone jump out of an airplane?" went the rhetorical old saying. "The thing is flying along perfectly well, and there's a guy up front who can put it down on the ground for you. So why jump out of it?") But despite this "leg" sentiment, few could honestly argue that the paratroopers weren't the elite of the Army, or that paratroop units were not filled with a cross section of the best studs around. "Slim Jim" Gavin was right when he said that if you want to find out if a guy will fight in battle, find out if he'll jump out of an airplane (if he will, you'll know he's a fighter); the average paratrooper was motivated, aggressive and proud, tough-fibered, hard-living, sometimes reckless and even wild.

Airborne was unique. There was the adrenaline rush of the jump itself—the butterflies in your stomach beforehand, the cold wind lashing your face as you stood in the door waiting for the green light, the merciless prop blast as you took the plunge, and then the falling, falling, confident your chute would open but never sure until (thank God) the violent jerk that told you it had. Then you simply sailed, feeling pretty invincible, with your main concern a rendezvous with the DZ and not with trees or poles or other hard, immovable objects on the ground. And then you landed, and when it was over, everyone was smiling, laughing, happy. Airborne provided a unique sense of oneness among its ranks. From the lowliest private to a two-star general, the shared danger of jumping out of a plane—onto a hot or cold DZ—had a leveling effect. When the Mules failed on the drop zone during SWIFT STRIKE III, for example, rank had no bearing as everyone pitched in to push them off. No one wanted to see even a single unnecessary casualty.

The bonding effect of shared danger meant, too, that no one was unaffected when another man's exhilaration turned to terror, as in the story of the aircraft that ran into engine problems after it had dropped all its troopers, leaving the two static jumpmasters to decide whether to bail out over the DZ or limp back with the plane to its base in Ohio and go through the hassles of getting home. The jumpmasters chose to bail out with the aircraft's emergency chutes, and on the way down one of them had a malfunction. When the man's body was recovered, it revealed that he'd clawed the whole way through his field jacket, his fatigue jacket, his T-shirt, *and* his own stomach, frantically searching for the D handle on the reserve chute. It was an ingrained thing—main chute malfunctions, pull the D ring on your reserve over your belly. The problem was that the two jumpmasters had used Air Force chutes, which had no reserves. *But for the grace of God there go I*, thought paratroopers all over the land.

The other unique thing about the Airborne was its NCOs. Even the short, stocky ones looked lean and mean. Their faces were leathery, their bearing ramrod straight, and on jumps, most—particularly the jump-masters—wore a cold and beady-eyed look that took years to master. I'd met the quintessential Airborne NCO at Campbell on a jump just before Task Force Cassidy. We'd been standing up in the aircraft, hooked up and ready to go, but on the approach to the DZ the wind velocity increased and the drop was aborted. We tried again, but the wind was even worse. The turbulence was knocking guys all over the aircraft. We had to throw our arms over the anchor cable just to keep upright. Next came the puking, all over the troop compartment. Meanwhile this jumpmaster just stood there, staring at us with those beady eyes, seemingly immune to it all. I was fascinated, especially when his granite face started to turn pale green. Then olive drab. Then jade. Then, suddenly, like a snake striking out, the jumpmaster pulled the front of his jacket open and threw up inside it. And without even a blink he was back to staring at us with his old Airborne sergeant eyes. To me, that said it all.

The Airborne NCO was just one tough hombre. Airborne was his life: he usually went from one Airborne assignment to the next, be it from Fort Campbell (101st) to Fort Bragg (82d) to Germany (8th Div) to Okinawa (173d) and back to Campbell or Bragg again. The attachment to Airborne was certainly not for love of money—jump pay was a big fifty-five dollars a month, and at least twice that amount was spent monthly on tailoring and laundry costs alone. (Every day in the Airborne began in a freshly washed and starched pair of cut-down fatigues, and both officer and NCO "broke starch"—put on a fresh pair—once or even twice throughout the day.) This was not to mention the nonissue (but mandatory) Corcoran jump boots, the cost of sewing patches, stripes, and insignia onto all those uniforms, and the Silver Fund, Community Chest, Red Cross, Old Soldiers Home, etc., etc. handouts everybody and his brother wanted come payday. (With unit competitiveness spilling into the area of "greatest contributions," too, the NCOs were invariably set back in this area themselves, in the effort to set the example for their troops.) No, the job was one of love alone for these old-time gunfighters, a dying breed; in the end, any price was insignificant for the honor of being Airborne.

By the time Haultman and I got back to Fort McClellan it was getting dark. The mess was empty, and as the two of us sat there eating and bullshitting, a trooper from G-4 rushed up to me, looking mighty worried. "General Cassidy wants to see you ASAP," he said.

"What's the deal?"

"I don't know, but whatever you did must be real bad—he is one *pissed-off* guy!"

Haultman came with me over to Cassidy's office and waited outside while I went in alone. "Hackworth," the General began, "I got a call this afternoon from Lieutenant General Truman, Commanding General of Third Army. He asked me if I had any paratroopers out jumping in a field in Alabama. I checked with my Operations and determined that there weren't any, so I said no. Afterwards, to be on the safe side, I checked with the aviation officer to see if there were any aircraft out today. It turned out that one helicopter *had* been checked out—to you. Now, would you like to enlighten me on what you've been doing today?"

"No problem, sir. I've been out jumping."

"You've been out jumping," Cassidy repeated. Calmly, like before the storm. "Without authority from me, without authority from Third Army"—now the General was red-faced and beginning to thunder—"*who*, Hackworth, YOU KNOW has to give permission for any parachute jump. You didn't de-energize the power in the area. You didn't have a medical jeep on the drop zone to take care of jump casualties. You didn't have a drop-zone safety officer. You didn't have shit!" he roared. "Goddamnit, Hackworth, you've violated every regulation in the book! Meanwhile, I told General Truman it couldn't have been anyone from my outfit. Now I have to go back and tell him I don't even know what's happening in my own command! Hell, Hackworth," General Cassidy wound up his totally justified tirade, "I should sack your dumb ass."

I had never seen General Cassidy's temper so aroused. I didn't say a word, for fear of setting him off afresh. It didn't help. "Well, why'd you do it?" he blew up again. "Just explain to me *why*. I'm going to have to tell the General *something*."

I said, "Sir, Master Sergeant Haultman wanted to go out this way. He retires tomorrow and he wanted to make a few jumps rather than have a parade."

"Haultman, huh?" said Cassidy. "So old Haultman's retiring, is he? Now, *that's* a good man. Did you know we served together in World War II?"

"Yes, sir. He's in your outer office waiting to say good-bye. Look, General, I know I really screwed up this time. No question about it. I should have followed regulations. I just didn't think we'd get caught. But wouldn't you have done the same thing for an old paratrooper?"

"Okay, Hack," Cassidy admitted, "I would have done what you did, but a goddamn lot slicker. I wouldn't have found my ass in here at the end of the day. Now how do you suggest I get out of it with Truman?"

"Lieutenant General Louis Truman, sir?"

"That's the one."

"Easy, sir," I said. "You call him up and say you found out the problem. When he says, 'What?' you say, 'It was Hackworth.' He'll say, 'Dave Hackworth?' You say, 'Yeah, he was a company commander in your regiment in the Fortieth Division.' And he'll understand. And you tell him about Haultman, and tell him you're going to burn my ass—but not severely to ruin my record, because I don't think he'd want my career ruined." (As a rule, if you served well with someone in combat, the bond established went on forever, and many an indiscretion could be overlooked.)

So Cassidy rang Truman and said, "Sir, it was Dave Hackworth . . ." and that was the end of it. Of course, had Cassidy not been Cassidy, a real soldier from the old school, my career could well have ended that day. But since he was and all was well that ended well, and Haultman retired just the way he wanted to, when I thought about the incident afterwards, all I knew was I wouldn't think twice about doing it all over again.

Task Force Cassidy continued without interruption, reaching its zenith when 101st troopers plunked George Wallace out of the front door of the University of Alabama and a black student named Vivian Malone walked inside. With that, we went back to Fort Campbell. But there the pace didn't slacken for even a minute. We were kept hopping, not just with the day-to-day workings of the G-4 shop, but also with some tremendous upheaval in the division: there was a continuous turnover as more and more people got orders to the advisory effort in Vietnam. I still wanted to go, but for reasons I'd never know, the assignment was not forthcoming. G-4 Colonel Abts, meanwhile, tried to take my mind off the situation by pushing me to attend Austin Peay College in Clarksville, Tennessee, through an Army-sponsored "bootstrap" degree-completion program.

In a world where a second or third language and a master's degree were among the tickets to success, my bachelor's degree (or lack thereof) was becoming of crucial importance to my future. Without it there was little chance I'd be selected for Regular Army, and unless Vietnam broke open into an all-out war, no RA meant automatic retirement as a Reserve major in 1968, at the tender age of thirty-seven. The idea of giving up the Army—my life—in my prime was pretty hard to swallow, but after my University of Maryland degree fell through the cracks in Germany when the Berlin Wall went up, I'd lost heart for ever getting one. In G-4 Operations there was no time for going to class, much less for studying, so despite Colonel Abts's insistence that I try again, I'd resigned myself to the fact that it couldn't be done. But Abts would not be swayed. He called a friend of his at OPO's Infantry Branch, and before long returned with the word that both DA and the 101st's Chief of Staff, Colonel John T. Berry, had cleared the way for me to take time off from Army life to join the academic world. I halfheartedly submitted my paperwork and waited for the necessary rubber stamp that would finally lead to my degree.

Then, in early November, Ngo Dinh Diem, who had governed South Vietnam since its creation in 1954, first as premier and then as president, was assassinated. Over the years the once respected Diem had grown further and further away from the needs of his people even as he insisted that he knew what was best for them. Despite the millions of dollars the United States provided in both economic and military aid, Diem, the head of a Catholic regime in a predominantly Buddhist culture, had paid only lip service to U.S.–suggested reforms that might have eliminated the base cause of the ongoing war of liberation in his country. Assassinated with the president was his brother, Ngo Dinh Nhu, a power-hungry mandarin who, with his wife, the much-hated Madame Nhu, had actually run the country in recent years as the weak, ineffective Diem retreated into personal isolation in the face of the escalating crisis in Vietnam. While history would suggest that the United States had instigated, or at least condoned, the coup that lead to the Ngo brothers' deaths, whatever the circumstances, the joy that greeted the news in many quarters of South Vietnam signaled that one way or another perhaps it had been meant to be.

Twenty-one days later came the death of another head of state, but this one shocked the world. I was sitting in a dentist's chair at Fort Campbell; twelve thousand shots of Novocain couldn't have numbed me more than the news, flashed on the radio, that John F. Kennedy was dead. At first I thought it was some Orson Welles hoax. To me JFK was an invincible comrade-in-arms. I felt we had shared combat somehow, in Berlin and then again during the Cuban missile crisis; both times the U.S. had emerged victorious, and it was Kennedy who'd given me those proud moments of my life. So when I found out it was true, that he was dead, the pain was as deep as that of losing a close friend on the battlefield. Meanwhile, U.S. military units around the world went on full alert should the Soviets take America's grief as a sign of vulnerability and launch some kind of preemptive strike. They didn't, of course, and though Communist sympathizer Lee Harvey Oswald was captured and charged with Kennedy's assassination, his live-on-prime-time death at the hands of Jack Ruby meant the facts of the case, as in the death of Diem, would never be fully known. In any case, November 1963 marked the end of an era in both Vietnam and America. The violent deaths of their leaders set both countries careening toward each other like runaway trains, before hardly anyone—certainly not the American people, or even Lyndon Johnson, the new President, himself—even knew they'd jumped the tracks.

When Colonel Abts received his own orders for an advisory assignment in Vietnam, I assumed it was all over for my bootstrap degree. The thing was that while the 101st's Chief of Staff had approved my going to school, he would not give the G-4 shop a replacement major (none were available) during my absence. Colonel Abts had accepted this, but I doubted his successor would. To expect a new boss to go shorthanded in our extremely busy staff section for almost a year was really too much to hope for. So in early December, when Lieutenant Colonel John Neff, the new G-4, called me in to say I was off to Austin Peay, I was knocked out. A replacement still had not been found for me, but Neff, an urbane, thoughtful West Point officer, seemed unconcerned: somehow everyone would manage, he said, and it was important for me to get the degree. I was amazed. In a more often than not self-serving Army world, Neff, who had every right to cancel my orders, was thinking of me.

Despite its belly-to-belly proximity to Fort Campbell, at Austin Peay College a sense of urgency was looked upon as some kind of dreaded Yankee disease. It was a *big* switch. Almost twice the age of many of my classmates and a thousand times more serious, I needed some time to settle in to the peaceful and relaxed style of this sleepy southern school. Once I tuned out the 101st's hectic goings-on, though, I began to enjoy my TDY civilian life. I loved the people, maybe because the Hackworth family roots were anchored deep in the hills of Virginia, Kentucky, and Tennessee; I enjoyed the academic side, too, and drove myself hard, majoring in history, with minors in sociology and journalism (based on interest and what seemed to be most applicable to being an Army officer). Patty, the girls, and I still lived on post at Campbell, but if my temporary break from the pressures of G-4 work had lifted the family's expectations for a more complete home life, they were soon dashed: I drove off to school in the morning, and when I came home I locked myself in my study and hit the books until bedtime. I knew this was my last chance if I was going to "make it" in the Army.

Historically, the only thing Austin Peay had going for it was that Woodrow Wilson's father had taught there when the place was Southwestern Presbyterian University. When that school relocated to Memphis, Austin Peay, the governor of Tennessee and a Clarksville boy himself, had headed the push to bring another college to the town, and my soon-to-be alma mater was the result. Academically, Austin Peay had more in its favor— many fine professors, for one thing, among them Dr. Wentworth Morris, who in particular opened a lot of doors in my head (including some I probably would have preferred to remain shut). Until a few months passed and I started to loosen up and listen to other people's points of view, no doubt Morris considered me his resident Nazi storm-trooper student. I was as hard-line as anyone could be, and in that Morris and many of the other academics at Austin Peay were vehemently against America's creeping involvement in Vietnam, I often had to bite my tongue and force myself not to jump up and defend what we were doing. To me, although I disagreed with the advisory effort as it was being carried out, i.e., using it simply as a combat training ground for our inexperienced young officers (or so it appeared from my point of view as one who desperately wanted to go and was again and again refused), I truly believed we were right to help the South Vietnamese. It was as good a place as any to take a stand against the Communists, who were behind the Viet Cong (I was an avowed and enthusiastic proponent of the "better to fight them in Southeast Asia than on the beaches of Santa Monica" philosophy), and besides, wasn't that what America was all about, to help the poor and downtrodden, to help preserve freedom for those who couldn't do it alone?

Over time, one of the things I liked most about being in school full-time was the chance to talk with civilians about the world "out there," and find out what the civilians "out there" thought about. One of the strangest things I heard was over a Monday-morning cup of coffee with a friend who was a light colonel's wife and a Radcliffe graduate getting her M.A. at Austin Peay. I'd just finished telling her a story about a jump I'd recently made, in which a quarter-ton jeep was parked right in the middle of the DZ where I was about to land. The only thing that saved me from crashing into it was the lieutenant DZ safety officer who'd parked it there in the first place—as luck would have it I flew close enough to the guy on my way down to grab him and use him as a mattress. As I explained to this woman, there was no great satisfaction in creaming the safety officer into the side of his jeep, but at least he learned a little lesson about parking vehicles on a drop zone. "You Scorpios are all the same," she responded. "You always go for the jugular."

The comment seemed like the biggest load of crap I'd ever heard. That was not to say my friend was wrong about *me*; it was just that I was not about to accept her amateur astrological analysis of my character. In the Vanguards I'd been fond of saying over a glass of beer that men fell into three categories: lovers, fighters, and killers, and I'd always prided myself on being a killer. The categories had nothing to do with the battlefield, or, for that matter, with loving, fighting, or killing; instead, they were my ways of describing how a guy looked at life. And while the categories were very distinct, they weren't mutually exclusive: you could start out as a lover and work your way up to a killer and still not lose any of the apparently more positive aspects of the less "lethal" categories. A killer was really just a lover and a fighter who would use any method to get what he wanted, and was willing to risk it all in the attempt. A killer had to win. Killers *did* go for the jugular; they *were* the ones who lashed out, in my friend's terms, with a "Scorpio sting." And although I dismissed what she said when she said it, I never forgot what that Radcliffe lady said, and when, over time, I discovered that four of the great generals of WW II—Patton, Montgomery, de Gaulle, and Rommel—were all Scorpios, I came to add to my Why I Am a Warrior list this accident of my birth.

On the second and fourth of August 1964, North Vietnamese patrol boats attacked two U.S. destroyers in the Gulf of Tonkin, thirty miles off the coast of North Vietnam. I was outraged. So was Professor Morris. The 4 August episode prompted President Johnson to order U.S. air attacks on mainland North Vietnamese military installations (the first use of overt American force in the conflict), and while all I hoped was he'd flatten the whole goddamned Communist country, Professor Morris said the whole thing was an election-year sham. He compared the Tonkin Gulf incidents to Hitler's chicanery just prior to invading Poland, and said that LBJ's "we seek no wider war" proclamation was bullshit of the first order, and that the exercise had been orchestrated to give the President the popular support of the American people. A Harris poll conducted soon after the U.S. Tonkin Gulf reprisal proved Morris right on at least one count (the nation's approval rating of LBJ's handling of the Vietnam War soared from a pre-Tonkin 42 percent to 72 percent), and while history has proved him right on the other counts, too, at the time I felt as if I were sitting face-to-face with Benedict Arnold.[2] Couldn't Morris see that the North Vietnamese, not the United States, had been the aggressor at Tonkin (thought I), and such acts had to be dealt with? But the professor just raged on, much in the spirit of Oregon senator Wayne Morse, who was simultaneously raging in the Senate that "we are going to be bogged down in Southeast Asia for years to come if we follow this course of action, and we are going to kill thousands of American boys until finally . . . the American people are going to say what the French people finally said: 'We've had enough!' " Coming as I did from the viewpoint of a soldier in the world's best army, I quietly disagreed with Morris' *and* Morse's assessments, but as I was just a few weeks shy of finals and then graduation, I just bit my tongue again and kept silent.

But there would be no finals for me at Austin Peay. Graduation, yes (with a B.S. I could not have been prouder of), but finals, no, when Dr. Bowman, the college's dean, assented to DA's request that my exams be waived so I could attend the Army's Command and General Staff College (C&GS) at Fort Leavenworth, Kansas. All of this came as a big surprise to me. I'd never even put C&GS on my wish list: that particular school was a big, big chop point in the Army, in that only 50 percent of the officers eligible to attend got the nod. Selection meant light colonel, no sweat, and I was thrilled. And as if that *and* not having to take finals weren't enough, I found out that after my tour at Leavenworth, I'd been reassigned to the 101st, giving me my third troop-duty assignment in a row. Somebody was *definitely* looking after me.

C&GS was a gentleman's course, 99.9 percent in the classroom, and only five or six hours a day. There was a fair amount of homework involved, but fresh out of college, I was used to studying and I found the whole thing a snap. The instruction duplicated much of what I'd learned at the Career Course at Benning. It seemed to me students would have been better served had Benning concentrated on tactics and troop-leading procedures taught in the field, and Command and General Staff College dropped the "Command" out of its name to concentrate on staff procedures (which were taught damn well there) and related paper-shuffling techniques. I never believed you could teach command anyway. Sure you could sit a guy down and teach him the *principles* of it, but command itself came from experience, from on-the-job training under solid vets and from doing it yourself.

The mismatch of warrior and clerk instruction could well have been at the root of the initial misunderstanding between my class's Airborne students and the C&GS school commandant, Major General Harry J. Lemley, Jr. Soon after we arrived, an edict came down from the Commandant's office stating that no student could wear jump boots, berets, or Airborne overseas caps to class. The Airborne guys were most pissed off. It was an outrageous policy emanating from clerks at the top who didn't know what made any gung-ho soldier tick. Still, we grudgingly followed the order until our Alabama Airborne classmate Lee Mize stood in the door.

Lee Mize, a 3d Div Medal of Honor winner from the Korean War, now on TDY at Leavenworth from the Special Warfare Center at Fort Bragg, was a friend from my Germany days. He'd served in Ted Mataxis' 505th Battlegroup, and I'd met him when the Vanguards invited the officers of the 8th Div rifle team (of which Lee was a member) to one of our Friday-night beer calls. Unit rivalry between hosts and guests had run at a fevered pitch throughout that rowdy evening, and before it was over, Colonel Johns's personalized beer stein had disappeared. Happily the thievery occurred early enough for significant retaliation: I knocked off all the 505th guys' fatigue caps, which were hanging on a hat rack outside the club, and took them home with me. The next day I'd received a frantic prereveille call from short and feisty Lee Mize. His master-blaster "blood wings" were on his hat and he desperately wanted them back.* I told him the wings were being held hostage, the ransom being Colonel Johns's beer stein; Mize readily agreed, and the swap was soon made.

But that incident was the only time I ever saw fine fighter Lee Mize not 100 percent on top of things. At Leavenworth, as far as he was concerned, the situation was simple: no way was he going to let anyone see *him* without his beret or jump boots on. "Maht as well go on back to Bragg," he said. "Ah'm a paratrooper first, not some chickenshit leg schoolboy." Since it wouldn't have looked too good for the commandant of C&GS to have a Blue Max winner quit his school, Lemley quickly backed down, and soon we paratrooper students went back to dressing "Airborne all the way."

The three big areas of conversation outside C&GS classrooms were the 1964 elections, the expanding Vietnam commitment, and ticket punching. Ticket punching was by now a concept set in concrete. Everyone from brand-new West Point second lieutenants on up talked about the punches they had, or had to get (at Campbell I'd often been amazed by the stuff coming out of the West Point–educated junior officers' mouths; most of them worried and war-gamed their punches as if their entire Academy experience had been programming in how to get stars some twenty years down the track, never mind becoming a competent leader of men today). Now there were actually ticket-punching formulas, discussed openly at C&GS. A master's degree punch, for example, plus a DA staff punch plus a battalion command punch equaled assignment to War College; a War College punch equaled a star. A combat punch was considered essential,

---

* Blood wings were the first set of parachute wings a paratrooper received upon qualification at the levels of novice, senior, and master rating. Master blood wings were attained on the occasion of a trooper's sixty-fifth jump.

and everyone wanted to get his as a counterinsurgency adviser in Vietnam. Not a whole lot of Regulars wanted command of U.S. troops if there was any way to avoid it. Troop duty was where you got burned. There were too many booby traps, too many things to go wrong. In the "one strike, you're out" zero-defect Army of the early sixties, the prevailing attitude was that it was much safer to be in a staff-swollen HQ, where a mistake could be shunted off to bureaucratic never-never land and no one was responsible. Meanwhile, dumbshit that I was, *all* I wanted was to be with troops. And I couldn't wait to get back to Fort Campbell, where I was ready to beg, borrow, or steal to get down with the soldiers again.

The presidential election was fast approaching. Most of my classmates were Goldwater fans; *None Dare Call It Treason*, a book that accused the Democrats of being soft on Communism, was making the rounds throughout the class, and the general feeling was that Goldwater, an avowed hawk, would take care of Communist North Vietnam one way or another, even proposing nukes to get the job done. Goldwater promised to get us into a war and Johnson promised peace; little did anyone know that a vote for LBJ would get the country everything Goldwater had promised. It would be my first real lesson in politics.

Vietnam was quickly closing in on U.S. forces, both in the war-torn country itself and at home. Well over one hundred American lives had been lost there so far. The U.S. was spending $1.5 million every day, with the only significant result being the Viet Cong growing bolder. In November, three months after the Tonkin Gulf incidents, the VC attacked the U.S. airfield at Bien Hoa, killing four American soldiers and destroying an entire B-57 squadron—ten million dollars' worth of airplanes. Maxwell D. Taylor, who as President Kennedy's special representative had visited Vietnam in 1961 and concluded that he saw no military means of defeating the VC in the near future, in 1964 (now as U.S. ambassador to South Vietnam) was pushing for escalation: his 1961 belief that a coordinated military and political program under American guidance could settle Vietnam's problems in a matter of a few years had been dashed since Diem's death, during which time U.S. support had been received only by an increasingly unstable, coup-plagued country whose leaders agreed on nothing and paid scant attention to American wishes anyway. The ray of hope in the first quarter of 1963, when U.S. intelligence estimated Communist defections to South Vietnam had doubled,[3] by late '64 was dim, with Taylor home from Vietnam with the observation that "the ability of the Viet Cong continuously to rebuild their units and to make good their losses is one of the mysteries of this guerrilla war."[4] Meanwhile, the South Vietnamese Army was growing weaker by the day, as untrained units were more and more being thrown into the breach. Division adviser Lieutenant Colonel John Paul Vann (who, a dozen years before, had welcomed me to the 8th Ranger Company in Korea) warned in 1963 that "unless the Viets start fighting better themselves," chances were the Americans would find themselves even more involved in the struggle for Southeast Asia;[5] the Viets *weren't* fighting any better in late 1964, and the many head-shaking Vietnamese officers, many of whom understood and spoke English only marginally, whom I saw scurrying down C&GS corridors as guests of the U.S. Army, did little to give the lie to Vann's belief.

All in all C&GS was an uninspiring period. But it was a vital punch on my ticket and augured well for my future, so I wasn't going to complain. And I had to admit I was damn proud to be there the day I was called to General Lemley's office to find Joe Cleland, the Great White Father himself, waiting to see me. The eleven years since we'd last met had been kind to him. His rosy cheeks, snow-white hair, and lean, mean paratrooper's shape were all intact. So was his command style: he was just passing through Leavenworth, heard I was there, and wanted to see how I was coming along. I was happy to tell him I'd recently been selected for Regular Army, particularly since without him I probably would have still been selling insurance. General Cleland was thrilled, and especially so when I told him I'd accepted only on the condition that I be commissioned Infantry. Few others would have understood as Cleland did why if I couldn't belong to the Queen of Battle I wouldn't want to belong at all.

By the time I returned to Fort Campbell, ROAD had been introduced to the division, and Colonel Berry, the straight-shooting Chief of Staff (another good, solid soldier who should have gotten a couple of stars and ended up with none), assigned me to the newly designated 1st Brigade, 101st Airborne (1/101). I wasn't with troops yet, but at least I was getting close. The brigade CO was Colonel James S. Timothy. A West Point DSC winner from his WW II European combat days, he had all the right punches (company and battalion command duty, a master's, War College, DA and Joint Staff duty) and was well on his way to his first star. Thoughtful, cool, considerate, and polished, "Gentleman Jim," as he was known (though we called him "Tim" behind his back), was a fine, articulate, and knowledgeable man. The best way to describe him was as James Mason in fatigues, and his only real failing was an insistence on wearing his contact lenses when we jumped (one of which he'd invariably lose when he hit the ground, resulting in a mad search of the DZ).

Colonel Timothy made me his brigade Operations officer. Brigade Headquarters was located in the old 327th Battlegroup HQ, and since most of the brigade HQ staff were from the 327th, I was fortunate to have inherited a well-oiled S-3 team whose years of experience in working together had boiled the whole drill down to SOPs. My sergeant major, for example, Grady Jones, besides having a recent tour as an adviser in Vietnam under his belt, knew more about the paper side of the S-3 job than I'd ever known existed. He and his solid and dedicated right-hand man, Master Sergeant Billy Sullivan, could run things with their eyes closed. My principal assistants, Captains Henrik "Hank" Lunde (Operations and Plans), Phil Stynes (Chemical), Richard Meyer (Communications), and Second Lieutenant Joel Stevenson (Training), were equally adept, and my immediate superior, Brigade XO Lieutenant Colonel Joseph Rogers, gave us a free hand to get the job done. Rogers, whose favorite expression was "It's nice to have studs to hold back by the belt instead of guys who need to be booted in the ass," was a joy to work for, and the only pain he ever caused me was when we jumped together on maneuvers. He was a master jumper, but even I hurt when he hit the ground—rather than doing a PLF, he kind of thumped down on his side, like a bag of potatoes falling off the back of a truck.

S-3 was a seven-day-a-week job, the weekdays a minimum of twelve to sixteen hours each. Though I was working in a different capacity, the requirements at Brigade were the same as they'd been on the division level: desert training exercises, Division Ready Force (which tied up one battalion minimum every third week), and myriads of other drills that had the unit hopping all over the world. The overcommitment was wild. Fortunately, civil-disturbance commitments had slacked off, but the parades, inspections, and normal ash and trash of peacetime soldiering, not to mention the mandatory participation in the individual pet projects of DA, Continental Army Command (CONARC), Third Army, XVIII Airborne Corps, and Division, *plus* parachute operations and contingency missions (for which, when we were alerted, everything else was just dropped), left barely enough time to sleep, much less to concentrate on the basic essentials of soldiering. This was no exaggeration. At about this time, Lieutenant Colonel Henry "Hank" E. Emerson, the G-3 of our similarly overcommitted sister division, the 82d, did a study which concluded that to actually fulfill all the training requirements laid on us by all levels of command would necessitate, in real terms, 450 training days *per year*. So, like the guy who spends more than he makes, each day we got further and further behind.

Among the worst drains on individual and small-unit training time were General Paul D. Adams' Strategic Army Command (STRAC) requirements and Command Material Maintenance Inspections (CMMI). In the case of the former, the most positive thing to come out of it was the addition of a new adjective—"STRAC"—to Army jargon. A STRAC trooper or a STRAC unit was one of military perfection. STRAC requirements, on the other hand (or Stupid Troopers Running Around in Circles, as the men themselves translated the acronym, although Scatter, the Russians Are Coming was also heard), were just more of the same tests to see how fast we could load up and move out. The Command Material Maintenance Inspection, on the other hand, was a perfect example, in action, of the zero-defect syndrome of the sixties Army. Designed as "spot checks" to make sure all equipment was in working order, the CMMI program was, in the words of Hank Emerson, "a specter that the lazy guys in the logistics business used as a crutch to keep all the equipment properly prepared, [leading] to people just parking their vehicles in the motor pool and not using them for fear of being gigged for some minor malfunction." Emerson, who would become one of the great captains of the Vietnam War, also had strong words about the large-scale unit exercises that cut deeply into individual training. His pet hate was the SWIFT STRIKE maneuvers: "a total waste of soldiers' time after the initial jump—and the thing was a two-week exercise." Emerson believed the emphasis on large-scale maneuvers was due to the fact that the men in charge were the ones who got to be lieutenant colonels overnight in WW II and never had much experience at the platoon and company levels. I agreed. The purpose of the big maneuvers, which was principally to test staff and communications procedures, could have been met through command-post exercises that required little more than a few guys with radios, and almost none of the taxpayers' money. But the men in charge, who'd been big-unit movers from the early days of their careers, still saw themselves as big-unit movers now, and these exercises gave them their only chance to play with all their toys and boys. What they didn't recognize, however, *because* they'd never spent much time at platoon or company level, was that their big units were made up of small units and individual soldiers whose training needs had to be met, not just for the soldiers' own survival (which big-unit movers did not concern themselves with anyway) but for the ultimate success of the big-unit maneuvers. This lack of recognition on the part of senior leaders did not bode at all well for the future.

"The only time any emphasis was placed on squad and platoon training was when we were expecting visitors," said Platoon Sergeant Robert A. Press of the 1/327 Battalion, who'd served in the 40th Div in Korea at the same time I did. "Everything else seemed to have priority. Every day it seemed we were in the middle of, or preparing for, some sort of maintenance inspection—motor stables, maintenance of weapons, A-bag inspections to determine if everyone had a shaving brush—never used—and three sets of underwear. In all my years [with the 101st] as a platoon sergeant, I can only remember running my outfit through live-fire exercises four or five times. Add on once a year on the range, and that was about it for the live firing. But nothing seemed to interfere with the big operations, barracks locked up and all of us going out to sit in some defensive position for a day or so at a time." Sergeant Press was one who'd know: the nucleus of the brigade's NCOs came from the old 327th paratroop battlegroup, and Press had been with the unit almost since its reactivation in 1956. Others, like First Sergeant Leo B. Smith and Master Sergeant John Humphries, had been together for more than a decade; this group had fought in Korea as part of 3d Battalion, 187th Regimental Combat Team, which was redesignated the 327th in '56.

Pound for pound, there was no doubt that the 1st Brigade's NCOs were the best I'd ever seen. Most were like Sweeney, dedicated professionals without an ounce of bullshit, who started with the troops at 0500 reveille and worked long, uncomplaining days. The brigade's (and the division's) young officers were also the best of the best. Most were Regular Army and dozens were the sons of generals;* most of the platoon leaders were West Pointers or ROTC Distinguished Military Graduates who had augmented their basic training with Benning's Airborne and Ranger courses. If you added to this collection of stud officers and NCOs the tough, resourceful, highly motivated troops they led, a vast percentage of whom were black or Hispanic, you had the makings of one hell of a fighting team. But what concerned me when I got to Brigade was that having "the makings" was not necessarily the same as having the goods.

Because the brigade had such STRAC personnel, and because we accomplished well the myriads of "big picture" tasks and requirements assigned to us, the overall impression we gave was that we were combat-ready. Unproved but also unchallenged, this belief filtered all the way up the chain of command: we were like the best-looking, best-equipped track team in town, so studly and intimidating that even the coach didn't bother to fire the start gun to see if we could run. I knew how little time was devoted to individual and small-unit training. My cursory view from Division and SWIFT STRIKE III the year before had told me the individual battlegroups (now battalions) were not nearly as sharply trained as they should have been. The fact that the 1st Brigade S-3 training officer was only a second lieutenant—and this was true of every brigade in the division at this time—said everything to me in terms of the division's overall complacent

---

* The 101st produced more generals than any other WW II division, and almost twenty years later, it was still the gateway to the galaxy of stars. Every brigade commander during the time I was there got at least one star, and every CG went to three or four.

attitude toward *the* vital component in preparing a combat-ready force. So now that I was at brigade level, I thought it was essential that we find out what our unit's strengths and limitations really were, so we could build from there. To this end, Colonel Timothy approved a tough, realistic Operational Readiness Test (ORT) for each of the brigade's three battalions.

The ORTs were similar to the ATTs we'd had in Germany, only not quite as long or as demanding. After all three battalions had been tested (the "Above the Rest" 1/327, commanded by Lieutenant Colonel James Wilson; the "Second to None" 2/327, skippered by Lieutenant Colonel Edward Collins; and the 2/502 "Strike Force," led by Lieutenant Colonel Wilfrid Smith), one thing was clear: had any of our war scenarios been the real thing, we would have had a lot of dead paratroopers on our hands. From Company HQ and up, all units functioned well. They produced clear, timely OPORDs and the staffs performed brilliantly. Below Company HQ, though, i.e., at the fighting level, the units performed very badly in two of the three battalions.

It wasn't that the troopers weren't gung ho. They wanted to be good, and they *thought* they were good. But for the main, the fact was they just didn't have what it took. The depth of the problem was one of the more unexpected shocks of my life. These soldiers of the illustrious Screaming Eagles—who could jump out of airplanes, who could strut on a parade field as chrome-platedly perfect as TRUST troopers, who had the bearing, the spirit, and the physical fitness of prizefighters—wouldn't have lasted a minute in the ring, because they were almost ignorant when it came to the basics. All the Johns stuff—fire and maneuver, hit the deck and roll—the stuff that keeps you alive, had little meaning for them. It was a great relief to find that at least one of the battalions, the 1/327, was in damn good shape, and besides reflecting well on its commander, Jim Wilson, the 1/327's fine ORT result spoke eloquently for the (unusual) continuity of strong command that battalion had recently seen. Wilson, himself a Wolfhound Korea battlefield commission, had inherited the unit from Colonel Herbert E. Wolff, a WW II draftee who'd won a Silver Star as a PFC, was battlefield commissioned during the Luzon campaign in the Philippines, and came up through the ranks (ultimately to retire as a major general), and Wolff had taken it from Colonel William A. Kuhn, who'd coined the "Above the Rest" unit motto and had been a tough training commander from as far back as his WW II 327 days.

In any event, after the ORT I was totally convinced that if the 1st Brigade was committed to anything more than a parade, we'd be shot down in flames. It'd be Kasserine Pass, or Korea, June–September 1950, all over again. I was equally convinced that the deteriorating situation in Vietnam would soon require U.S. troops. (The South Vietnamese were not holding their own at all; three days after I joined the brigade, Christmas Eve, 1964, the VC smuggled a hundred-pound bomb into a six-story building in downtown Saigon that just happened to be the largest U.S. Bachelor Officers' Quarters there, killing two Americans and one Australian, wounding eighty-five more Americans and Vietnamese, and demolishing the entire BOQ itself.) There was little question that the harder the VC pushed, the more likely the Johnson Administration would be to commit troops. And with longtime paratrooper Lieutenant General William Childs Westmoreland now in charge as recently appointed Commander, U.S. Military Assistance Command, Vietnam (COMUSMACV), there was equally little question that the troops would be Airborne, and very likely the 101st itself, which Westy had commanded from 1958–60.

So we had to get cracking if we were going to be up for the big game. "The More Sweat on the Training Field, the Less Blood on the Battlefield" read the shingle that hung on the wall behind my S-3 desk; from the moment I put it there I made the 1/101's combat readiness my personal mission. First came my "Training Policy" paper, written with the total support of Colonel Timothy. "Results of our battalions' ORTs," I wrote in the opening statement, not exactly endearing me to the battalion commanders to whom it was addressed, "have shown that our battalions are 'combat-ready' insofar as the commanders, staff, and senior NCOs are concerned. The people who are not 'combat-ready' are the ones who must do the fighting. . . . All leaders in this brigade have failed in their responsibilities to train the individual soldier. . . ."

Of course, Colonel Timothy (who appreciated good small-unit training, having had two full years of it with the 79th Infantry Division prior to its landing at Normandy) couldn't go to his general and say, "I just tested my three battalions, and they're not combat-ready." In the zero-defect stakes, it would have been suicide for his own career. So instead, with Timothy's backing, bit by bit, block of instruction by block, I took over the training of 1st Brigade myself, to make it more realistic and more worthwhile, to instill in the men the *right* way of doing things, as well as the killer instinct: the will to win.

We slowly worked toward giving the unit a jungle rather than a desert orientation. We changed the umpire system, too, from a "combat power" orientation to a tactical-ability one. No longer was the winner the one who got the most troops, weapons, and firepower on an objective the fastest, but the one who proved skillful in the basics, i.e., proper tactical procedures, en route to getting there. I found one West Point–trained platoon leader, for example, attacking a dug-in "enemy" across a pool-table-flat field. I chewed his ass, only then realizing he really didn't know any better. He'd had a lot of book learning thrown at him, but little hands-on training to experience how to do it the right way. His NCOs were as good as the brigade had, but they did what the lieutenant told them, and didn't argue. So I made the guy do it again. I made him call for simulated supporting fires this time (to ingrain a habit that would save his and his unit's asses a million times on the battlefield), made his troops use fire and maneuver and concealed avenues of approach. Then I made him do it again. And again. He learned, but it shouldn't have been my job to teach him: why hadn't his company commander shown him the right way? Or his battalion commander? The problem was that these guys were so busy juggling commitments they didn't have time. Some probably didn't know the basics themselves, but it was the preoccupation with potential failure—coming up short on a CMMI, blowing it on an ORT, not getting out on time in a Division Ready Force alert—that put blinders on many an officer to the needs of his subordinates. The rigidity of the system brought out the worst in the ambitious, aggressive Airborne personality of the early sixties, leading all too many officers to forget that their primary responsibility was to their troops, and not to the ground-laying of long careers. And the problem was exacerbated by the widespread belief that assignment to the 101st was reserved for the Army's studs. Because of this, fine but inexperienced platoon leaders were loath to even ask the right questions, much less to fail. One excellent example was one Second Lieutenant Pat Graves, who joined 1st Brigade after a stint with the 1/506: "I didn't get any guidance," he said. "I guess I was supposed to be the epitome of the Army officer, a second lieutenant, because I graduated from West Point. But quite frankly, I didn't know what the hell I was doing."

Among the real hotshot Airborne types in the 1st Brigade was one Captain Frederick Garside Terry, Jr. Terry was from a long line of military men, a descendant of both the Sharps and the Bennets, and, by marriage, Ulysses S. Grant. His father had been killed on Saipan in 1944, and his grandfather John Bennington Bennet just two weeks earlier in Burma. Young Terry himself was a West Point (Class of '60) star lacrosse player fresh from a couple of Special Forces tours in Laos and Vietnam, followed by "chopper school" and now the 101st. He really was a stud of a soldier, but from the moment I laid eyes on him I decided he was an overconfident, eager-beaver ticket puncher, nothing more, nothing less. Sure he had the credentials, but to me he was just another guy who knew a little about a lot and not much about anything. Fresh from flight school when he took over the 1st Brigade's aviation section (which worked directly for me), I didn't trust him at all, so I continued to depend on the lieutenant who'd been aviation officer until

Terry's arrival, who'd gotten us through all sorts of difficulties and was both a fine pilot and a solid aviation commander.

One day around lunchtime, I received a call from Division: "Your aviation section will have a Corps ORT in two hours." The whistle had blown the minute I picked up the phone—in exactly two hours every aircraft in the section, all supplies, all records and so forth had to be configured and ready to fly off into the afternoon sun. I called Captain Terry's quarters, only to be told he was out playing golf.

I *hated* military men who played golf. Not unlike I hated guys who made a point of socializing with their superiors at the Officers' Club. (I'd actually resigned from the Officers' Club at Fort Campbell, and had to report to General Critz and explain why). To me, it just had nothing to do with being a soldier. So this was just one more mark against young Terry. I immediately called the aviator lieutenant, gave him the job of organizing the ORT, and alerted Colonel Timothy, who would have paid the highest price of anyone should the test not go smoothly. As it turned out, the ORT went fine, the aviation section passed with flying colors, and that was the end of it until about half an hour later, when this six-foot-tall captain came storming into my office, fresh from the golf course, in a rage.

"Major Hackworth," Terry said, "I don't like the way you handled the ORT."

"That's the way the ball bounces, Terry," I replied. "I wanted to be sure we passed the test, and you were out playing golf. With the CG, I presume. What did you want me to do, send one of my men out to chauffeur you and your little golf cart back to where you should have been for openers? If you weren't so busy playing the social circuit, Terry, you might have had your sweet ass where it belonged, and that is in the brigade aviation section!"

"If that's how you feel, Major—"

"That's how I feel, Captain."

"Then all I can say is I'm sorry I'm only a captain."

It wasn't exactly a subtle challenge. I stood up. "Okay, have a swing."

Terry didn't need a second invitation. He took his swing and we went at it. He was one pissed-off hombre, and by the time we finished, the only thing more bruised and battered than the two of us was my cubicle of an office, which had not been exactly the best place to duke it out. So we just sat on the floor, both of us bleeding and panting, until Terry asked, "Are you going to report me?"

"No," I said. "I didn't like you. I thought you were a ticket puncher and a phony, and I didn't go out of my way to find you for the inspection. You came to me and you were pissed off. You were right, so it's over. We understand each other." And we did. That fight was actually the beginning of a close friendship between Fred Terry and me. Only then did it occur to me that I'd probably just been jealous of this guy for being such a complete stud (with everything and heritage, too), and over time I realized he was only doing what was necessary to advance his career. And I realized, too, that I'd had no right to be so quick to judge in the first place. I coveted those C&GS, bachelor's degree, RA, and General Staff punches on my ticket as much as the next guy—and in the name of my career, I'd already found myself war-gaming how and when I'd be able to get a master's degree, too.

In January 1965, U.S. estimates counted 40,000 full-time Viet Cong guerrillas in South Vietnam, and up to 100,000 if the "part-time" VC (who doubled as "civilian" farmers) were added to the tally.[6] Against this enemy, despite more than 30,000 U.S. advisory and support people in-country to assist, the poorly trained South Vietnamese were losing a battalion a week. Time was not on our Southeast Asian friends' side. The Americans, too, were taking their share of lumps. In February, during Tet (the Vietnamese New Year), the Viet Cong attacked Camp Holloway, a U.S. helicopter base in II Corps at Pleiku. The casualties were 7 American KIA and 109 wounded, six choppers destroyed, and seventeen other aircraft severely damaged. The Johnson Administration retaliated with a forty-nine aircraft air raid on the North Vietnamese town of Dong Hoi, where South Vietnamese Communist cadres were known to be trained and housed. The following week, twenty-one Americans were killed when Viet Cong guerrillas destroyed the U.S. adviser barracks at Qui Nhon. The tit for tat continued when, in response, 160 planes took off for a bombing raid into North Vietnam. In March, as the U.S. launched Operation Rolling Thunder (a series of USAF and Vietnamese Air Force [VNAF] air raids against North Vietnam), President Johnson sent thirty-five hundred U.S. Marines to Vietnam with the sole mission of protecting our air base at Da Nang. Three weeks later, the VC bombed the U.S. Embassy in Saigon (killing two and injuring more than two hundred Americans and South Vietnamese), and within two days LBJ made the Marines available for "combat support" for the first time. Regardless of what anybody said, we were in the war now, boots and all.

I received orders to go to Vietnam as an adviser to the Vietnamese Airborne Brigade about the same time Patty gave birth to our son, David Joel. Patty wanted to stay in the Campbell area while I was away. My Raider buddy Jack Speed owned a home in the country just outside Memphis, and when he said the house right next door was for sale, we bought it immediately. I had to stay at Campbell to work throughout the week, but thanks to Fred Terry, who clocked his required "cross-country training" by shuttling me back and forth to Memphis every weekend in his chopper, I was also able to get the new house squared away and ready for family occupancy.

The 1st Brigade, meanwhile, was about to embark on a big training exercise at Natchez Trace State Park, in western Tennessee. Its genesis had occurred in long talks Hank Lunde, my brilliant S-3 Operations officer, and I had had about counterinsurgency, and about the probable inability of the 101st to fight a war of that nature given that the division's entire frame of reference was conventional war. Drawing on Lunde's own considerable (four years) Special Forces experience and the latest Vietnam-tested SF doctrine for insurgency operations, the object of the Natchez Trace exercise was to teach the troopers of the 1/101 to respond offensively to the insurgent, using the traditional principles of war as our guide but the methods of the guerrilla.

Lunde was project officer for the exercise, which used Vietnam-experienced Special Forces personnel from Fort Bragg as part of the guerrilla/aggressor forces, and which required our men not only to beat the "enemy" but also to win the support of the "locals" in four mock villages. It was a damn good field problem that would have given the soldiers a fair idea of what was soon in store for them; unfortunately, before the exercise had barely begun it was canceled, when the ongoing problems of the Dominican Republic (since the assassination of dictator Trujillo four years before) exploded, and American interests there were no longer assured.

LBJ called in the Marines. Meanwhile, the 82d (whose orientation was Latin America) was alerted, with the 101st designated the follow-up unit. Fortunately, the 82d and the Marines provided enough of a show of force to bring the tiny island country under control, and the 101st "Dom Rep" alert was over as quickly as it had come on. But then, without even a day to catch our breath, the word we'd long expected to hear finally came down: the 101st was being alerted for deployment to Vietnam. Colonel Timothy's 1st Brigade had been chosen as the spearhead; *Ready or not*, I thought, *here we come.*

14 TIM'S TRAVELING TROUBLE

I lie in my tent
  Thanking God for free rent
While outside the rain pours
  And inside my buddy snores
Muddy floors and a wet cot
  But still thanking God a lot.
Got hot chow every day
  Rain or shine, come what may,
Got a dog 'bout two weeks old
  Eats C-rations hot or cold.
Special Forces all around
  Keeping safe this hallowed ground
1st Cav in the air
  Landing, fighting here and there.
Ain't got much but could be worse
  Just ask the men in the *101st*.

"Ode to the Infantryman in RVN" by an anonymous
Signal Corpsman in Nha Trang, Republic of Vietnam.
(From the *Vietnam Reporter*, October 1965)

THE arrival of the Screaming Eagles' 1st Brigade in July 1965 brought the total number of American personnel in Vietnam to seventy-nine thousand. Though the first few weeks after the troops' long boat journey were scheduled for everyone to regain land legs, adjust to the heat, and square away gear, within three days of the brigade's welcome at Cam Ranh Bay by General Westmoreland and Ambassador Maxwell D. Taylor, our units were conducting squad- and platoon-size local patrols throughout our area of operation. We were aided by Vietnamese guides, assigned one per platoon; they only knew a dozen English words, but they were invaluable as instant teachers in Vietnamese customs, and greatly facilitated our dealings with the locals.

At night, on position along the perimeter, skittish green troopers saw a VC behind every bush. Exploding grenades, tracers, and the *bang-thump* of M-79s kept everyone awake and on edge as many of the soldiers created a mini war among themselves. What I had felt was insufficient stateside training had been compounded by Army-wide safety regulations that prevented our soldiers from learning about living in an armed environment. It didn't help that the Army at this time was predominantly made up of city boys who not only had not grown up with a rifle in their hands, but had no idea about coping with the bush either. After a few nights' worth of Custer's Last Stand, Colonel Timothy issued an order that no weapon would be loaded. This stopped a lot of the panic, but shadows and jungle noises were still fought with great enthusiasm. Two medics in our support battalion, for example, became the brigade's first Purple Hearts when their unit took on another of ours in a wild firefight. In another early case of friendly fire casualties, one of our troopers on patrol tripped while carrying a loaded— against orders—M-79 with the safety off. His fingers hit the trigger and *bang-thump*, he wounded a dozen troopers on another patrol a couple of hundred yards away. As Ridgway said at Bastogne of the newly committed 17th Airborne Division, "I can never get over the stupidity of our green troops."

The two short months since the 1st Brigade was alerted for deployment to Vietnam had been nonstop for everyone. Word of the move had spread through Fort Campbell like wildfire: I for one had been given the "Top Secret" news at 1000 hours, and when I went home for lunch at noon (with no intention of telling my wife), the first thing Patty said was, "So the First Brigade's going to Vietnam?" Turned out Brigade XO Rogers had told his wife, and she passed it on to Patty in a flash. So much for security.

My advisory orders had been canceled, and Colonel Timothy and I headed to Vietnam immediately for a short recon to see what we were in for. When we returned, while the troops began concentrated training on fighting in a jungle environment, we assembled all the guys in the brigade who'd had previous duty in Vietnam to get their input for the move. Logistics was a particularly serious concern, so S-4 Herb Dexter, a 7th Div Korea battlefield commission with three Special Forces tours to Vietnam under his belt, was an absolutely invaluable source of information. So was S-2 Joe Hicks, already a two-war veteran—with the Marines in WW II and the 24th Div in Korea—who'd had two SF tours in Vietnam as well. (Hicks was a damn good man who, on top of everything else, had survived sixty-nine days cut off and alone behind enemy lines during the Korean War.)

We'd then centralized the planning—operational, logistic, and personnel—to the S-3 shop. I was the coordinator. We'd gotten max support from DA, including a direct hot line to them, which allowed us to bypass the multiple layers of headquarters in between. Amazingly, the only serious flap we had in the planning stage was when DA insisted we deploy with winter gear and dress blues, a ludicrous requirement for Vietnam's tropical climate. They also insisted we take all our organic Table of Organization and Equipment (TOE), even after we'd pointed out that many items, such as recoilless rifles and Mules, were of little value on a counterguerrilla battlefield. The feeling I got was that DA didn't think we'd be there too long and wanted us to retain our tactical integrity in every way. Through our hot line I tried my damnedest to at least spike the winter- and dress-gear requirement, but it was not until Colonel Timothy took the matter to our CG, Major General Beverly Powell, that DA modified its position. Winter stuff became officially "out," but we did have to take our dress greens and summer uniforms, though none of us could figure out when we'd possibly be expected to wear them.

Lunde got the mission of writing the OPORD. He and Grady Jones, who'd only returned from a Vietnam advisory stint ten months before (but good man that he was, he volunteered to go back with the brigade), produced an absolute masterpiece, which, in part, utilized commercial air and rail transport to get the brigade to the west coast of the United States and onto its slow boat to Southeast Asia. The plan—a document a foot thick—required few adjustments and later would be used as a model for such operations at the Infantry School. When it was finished and its planners recovered from their celebratory binge, the final coordination of the move had been left to Assistant S-3 Captain Terry McClain, and Lunde and Jones had gone back to Vietnam with me as part of the brigade's advance party.

The party had been composed of a stud lieutenant from each infantry battalion and attached unit as well as a small Brigade S-2/S-3 staff and a few other key people. Our mission, to prepare for the rest of the unit's arrival, had proved nearly impossible for a long time: the MACV staff orchestrating our deployment was, in Grady Jones's words, like "the young boy who got his first girl in the bushes: 'Now I got it, don't know what to do with it.' " We'd initially left Lunde as our liaison in Saigon at General Westmoreland's request. It proved a particularly frustrating job for him, in that the destination of the brigade was being changed almost every day, and Lunde was caught between keeping up with the confused MACV planners and keeping me at bay. I had lots of questions and, through no fault of his own, he couldn't get the answers. (MACV was violently shifting from a slow-paced advisory concern to a full-blown war headquarters, and our problems were just part of the overall rough transition. The command was not structured to become an instant field army. How much easier it would have been had DA sent over such an HQ, and kept MACV free for its advisory duty and the overall coordination of the war effort.)

Finally, just days before the brigade arrived in-country, MACV decided where our unit would deploy—Cam Ranh Bay, where the Screaming Eagles would secure large-scale construction activities eventually to result in a first-class harbor, air base, and other huge logistic facilities along the bay's nineteen-mile peninsula. And it was at this time, when Hank Lunde, Grady Jones, and I went to recon the huge area for the first time and to work out how to defend it, that the war really began for me in Vietnam.

We'd borrowed a jeep from the Special Forces team who were so kindly hosting us at their camp at nearby Dong Ba Thien, and we tooled down the road toward Cam Ranh Bay. The Green Beret Intelligence sergeant had said Dong Ba Thien was a "safe area," so we took our time. The weather was absolutely beautiful, and there was much to be admired in the peaceful, lush green countryside. But as we drove along admiring it, the sultry afternoon air was punctured—*ba dit dit dit*—as a hidden automatic weapon suddenly sent a dozen slugs over our heads. We unassed the jeep in a big hurry and went prone. All was quiet. We searched the area, but there was nothing to see. No sniper, no weapon, no tracks. It was almost as if we'd imagined it. Except that we hadn't, and from this old trick (no different, really, than the Yugoslav sniper who had terrorized Jimmy Sparks and me in our guard box at Cormons almost twenty years before), I'd learned the first of many valuable lessons in the new war: there were no safe areas in Vietnam.

Gradually the brigade settled down. The soldiers got used to the jungle and its noises, and their shadow-shooting campaign died a slow but natural death. Quickly on its heels, however, came boredom. The men wanted to mix it up with "Victor Charlie," the Viet Cong. "Those were such dull days," one of the brigade staff would later say, "I wondered if the war would ever start." I knew what he meant, even though we both knew the war was ongoing, and all around us. There were just no front lines. The war was a sniper on the "safe" road near Dong Ba Thien, a child with a grenade, the old woman or young girl who sold Coca-Cola (a ubiquitous feature of the South Vietnamese landscape) on the side of the road who just happened to be simultaneously scoping out your positions, and who spent her off-hours planting booby traps and manure-tipped bamboo "punji" stakes along the patrol paths you'd be using that night, or putting crushed glass in that Coke you'd be drinking. All the Vietnamese, friend and enemy alike, spoke the same language, a difficult tonal tongue that few Americans spoke or understood. Enemy troops and noncombatants often wore the same style clothes, with results often tragic and sometimes almost slapstick, like the time, two weeks in-country, when the brigade began conducting operations near the city of Nha Trang and one patrol netted a dozen armed VC, black pajamas and all. Only afterwards did we find they were actually part of the friendly Popular Forces (PF), local militia that no one had informed us were operating there, and vice versa. In fact, despite Province intelligence claims that the high ground overlooking Nha Trang held *"beaucoup"* VC, we saw very few during the five major operations the 1st Brigade conducted in its first month in Vietnam. Instead, our guerrilla enemy was like an audience at a play in which we, the counterguerrillas, were the unwitting actors: the VC sat in their darkened redoubts and watched and learned, while we played out our roles, warts and all, on a well-lit stage.

When the 1st Brigade, 101st Airborne Division left Cam Ranh Bay in the last week of August, it would prove to be only the first of many moves. Our mission, in Colonel Timothy's words, was to serve as "a reserve reaction force capable of airmobile or parachute assault anywhere in the theater." We were to General Westmoreland what the Wolfhounds had been to Generals Walker and Ridgway in Korea fifteen years before. Only the name had changed: Colonel Michaelis' "Fire Brigade" was now, in honor of our commander, Colonel James S. Timothy, "Tim's Traveling Trouble."

Over the next six months the brigade would travel hundreds of miles by air, water, and road to hot spots in South Vietnam. We went from the Central Highlands jungles of An Khe to the rice paddies of Qui Nhon, from the dusty, Arizona-like landscape around Phan Rang to the rubber country of Lai Khe and Ben Cat. In An Khe we secured the deployment of the twenty-thousand-man-strong 1st Air Cavalry Division and their 420-odd choppers; in Qui Nhon we did the same for the Korean Capital Division, but that was the end of any similarity between the two missions—the move from An Khe to Qui Nhon could have been a million miles, so different were the two terrains and how Charlie fought. In the Highlands there were vast jungles complete with tigers and monkeys and an enemy who, until our arrival, was systematically strangling the countryside, totally disrupting the economy by mining and cutting deep, impassable trenches in the roads, thereby preventing the rural community from getting its products to market on the coast. At Qui Nhon, on the South China Sea, vast expanses of rice paddies (whose harvest we were tasked to protect) offered little cover and concealment to us but somehow plenty to our cunning opponent, who whittled away at our ranks with snipers and booby traps and the overwhelming support of the people.* Lai Khe–Ben Cat was different yet again, with vicious mines and booby traps planted deep within virtually impenetrable double- and triple-canopied rubber-tree jungle. And though only one "big" battle was fought throughout this six-month period, of necessity the men of the 1/101 day by day became more flexible, more competent, and combat savvy.

An Khe was probably the hardest for everyone. Though the brigade successfully opened up and secured Route 19 for the 1st Air Cav's deployment, it was not a fear-free walk in the sun. The road, which linked Qui Nhon on the coast with An Khe and Pleiku in the Central Highlands, was the one on which Mobile Group 100 (*Groupement Mobile 100*, or GM 100), France's finest, had been annihilated eleven years before at the end of the Indochina war. The burned-out hulls of French vehicles, still dotting both sides of the road, provided a sobering image for even the most gung-ho "let's go get 'em!" guys in the brigade. There was no small amount of bitching as to why the studs of the 1/101 had to hold the Air Cav's hand with vigorous, deep patrolling operations around their base-camp area while they shuttled their gear from Qui Nhon to An Khe and got set up (after all, the 1/101 troops griped, no one had patrolled and secured the base area at Cam Ranh Bay when the 1st Brigade arrived). In truth, though, the brigade's bitching was less real resentment of the Air Cav than a manifestation of their own frustration on those long, deep patrols. For the main, the VC avoided contact. They just sat in the audience and studied the Yankees' patterns and procedures. For our troops this generally meant endless hours of waiting for something to happen, and then usually little to nothing did, except perhaps a deadly rendezvous with a punji stake, a booby trap, or a sniper. And yet, if something big *did* happen, the troops were as often as not paralyzed, unable to act—not out of fear, but because of the MACV rules of engagement, specifically the one that precluded a U.S. soldier firing his weapon if not fired upon. Just one incident, in the 1/327, found a 2d Platoon, B Company patrol observing five or six VC sitting in the bush, their weapons propped up against a log. When Dennis Parker, the fire-team leader who discovered them, informed his squad leader of the find, he was reminded of the strict rules of engagement. Parker had to inch around, get the enemies' attention, and make them go for their weapons before he could take them under fire. The net result of the skirmish was two dead VC, but as Parker wrote after the fight, "I would like to make it clear why it is hard

* It didn't help that the Americans had inherited the taint of European colonialism from the French. Like our predecessors, we were called "long noses" by the Vietnamese (or "monkey men," in recognition of our substantial body hair, which was virtually unknown to the Vietnamese), and because the French had worn the same type U.S. gear now we did, it was not unheard of for Viets to actually mistake us for them, thinking they had returned to reimpose French rule.

for the American fighting men in Vietnam today. After fighting sharpened bamboo stakes, man traps, passing through several ambush sites *and* seeing men with rifles, we still couldn't shoot first."[1]

A few nights later one of our ambush patrols had a much easier time when they took on an enemy force that had walked right into their killing zone. The platoon leader reported the contact to his battalion, which reported it to Brigade; as S-3 I relayed it to Task Force Alpha Headquarters at Nha Trang,* which reported it to Westmoreland's MACV Headquarters in Saigon. Before long the brigade S-3 phone was running hot with questions from higher HQ: how many enemy? what kinds of weapons? what direction were they moving? etc., etc. The platoon leader couldn't see anything in the pitch-black night, so he tentatively reported some ten or twelve enemy dead, with details to follow when day broke and he could have a look for himself. This went down fine with Battalion and Brigade but not with higher HQ. MACV continued to bug Task Force Alpha, and they had no recourse but to pass on the requests to Brigade. It was shades of Korea 1952–53 all over again, only worse. To me it was truly incomprehensible that some four-star general would be getting all lathered up about a platoon ambush so cleanly executed that the enemy did not return one round of fire. The barrage of questions continued until finally I'd had enough. From then on, every time I answered the S-3 phone I made sure I had my battery-operated electric razor in my hand. "Okay," I'd say, "here's the latest on that contact. Are you ready to copy?"

"Yes, sir. Ready to copy."

"Okay, here it is. An ambush patrol made contact at 0330 hours when—" *bzzzzzzz.* I'd hold the razor up to the phone. "Did you get all that?"

"Not a word. There's static on the line. Can you say again?"

"Sure can. An ambush patrol made contact at—" *bzzzzzzz-zzzzzzz.*

The razor effectively kept us out of commo with higher HQ the rest of the night. Day broke, and the ambush team went out to search the killing zone. There were indeed ten dead, a significant "body count," as the soon-to-be-infamous measurement of success in Vietnam was known and stressed from above from the minute we arrived. The only problem was they were all unarmed men, women, children, and old people. It turned out the ambush had been sprung on an unarmed family of Montagnards, a nomadic people much like the American Indians, who lived and roamed throughout the Highlands jungles of Vietnam and didn't give much

* In that the 1st Brigade was an independent unit (i.e., it had no division headquarters in Vietnam), Task Force Alpha was our immediate higher HQ. The Task Forces, soon to be renamed Field Forces, were each the equivalent of a U.S. corps. The Field Force label arose in order to prevent confusion with the South Vietnamese corps command structure. Task Force Alpha, commanded by Major General Stanley "Swede" Larsen, would soon be renamed I Field Force, Vietnam, or IFFV.

thought to curfews, or the rule that all movement after sundown was to be considered enemy.

The Montagnard incident, like the rules of engagement and the frustration of not being able to lock horns with a major VC unit, did little for morale while the brigade was at An Khe. So when a contact on Route 19 yielded one enemy dead carrying documents identifying him as a member of the 95th Battalion, 2d VC Regiment, it was a day worth celebrating. At Brigade, Major Joe Hicks's S-2 shop had been working overtime to locate the 95th, which we'd known all along was operating somewhere around An Khe. Now that one of them had been killed along Route 19, we doubled our efforts to get a fix: there'd be no Mobile Group 100–style ambush sprung on the Screaming Eagles' 1st Brigade.

The 95th was a force to be reckoned with, the fight the troopers needed to get over their boredom and frustration, to have their shot at the VC and feel as though they were really in a war. As intelligence came in and began to form a pattern, the brigade continued to beat the bush. A Hawaiian cook in the '02 brought us our first substantial clue: a People's Army, Vietnam* (PAVN) troop he'd captured while scrounging for souvenirs during a patrol he'd joined for the fun of it. The POW was a talkative guy who assured us his comrades were in the vicinity. S-2 Joe Hicks had him flown over the area to see if we could get an exact fix on where. Unfortunately, the POW was scared stiff on his first airplane ride, and couldn't recognize his own belly button at one hundred miles per hour, much less the battlefield on the ground below. Fortunately, just about the same time a USAF Forward Air Control (FAC) aircraft took fire from a .50-cal machine gun in the vicinity of what we believed through radio intercept was our opponent's battalion command post. After that we thought we had all the pieces of the puzzle, and moved quickly to prevent the 95th from moving first. Little did we know that our haste could not have led to more waste.

Operation Gibraltar, the 1/101's first major confrontation with Charlie, kicked off as scheduled early on the morning of 18 September. Two A1E Skyraider airplanes prepared the single landing zone (LZ) with bombs, and the 2/502, under the command of Wilfrid Smith, conducted an airmobile assault into a clearing in the village of An Ninh. Insufficient troop-lift helicopters meant the '02 had to go in piecemeal, three platoons at a time. Insufficient planning time meant no one at brigade or battalion level had had a chance to scrutinize the aerial photographs we'd received late in the evening the night before, which would have clearly shown that An Ninh

---

* Soon to be known as the North Vietnamese Army (NVA).

was not the wisest place to conduct an airmobile assault: the area around the LZ there was nothing less than an armed camp. "Many comrades said they wished the Americans jumped down from helicopters right in this area so they could deal them a long-remembered blow," claimed the author of a VC after-action report on Gibraltar captured months later. ". . . Their landing from helicopters in this area will be a golden opportunity for our unit to achieve merit because we do not have to move, nor minutely investigate, or to spend sleepless nights and exert any effort. Their landing here means certain death for them."

The anonymous scribe was not far wrong. The '02 landed dead in the middle of the 95th Battalion's training base. Their LZ was the very same dry rice paddy the VC troops used to train for defense against airmobile assaults. Though the first lift came in more or less unopposed, when the second lift arrived fifteen minutes later, the LZ was an inferno. Two helicopters were downed right there on the LZ. Wilford Roe, CO of B Company, was hit while still inside his chopper and was evacuated immediately. The seven U.S. Marine choppers provided to augment elements of Lieutenant Colonel Cody's combat-seasoned 52d Aviation Battalion refused to land at all, and instead just turned around and took the troopers they were carrying back to the loading zone.

A third lift, onto an alternate LZ eight hundred meters away, met with equally heavy ground fire. Alpha Company's CO, Captain Gerald Landry, was hit as soon as he landed (and was also immediately evacuated), and in total, the third lift managed to discharge only thirty-six men in two isolated units, totally cut off from each other and the elements of the other two lifts. Meanwhile, C Company's Captain Rawls, who'd come in on the first lift, was killed by machine-gun fire while rallying his troops to attack,* and Colonel Smith, who was pinned down behind a paddy wall, found himself with no company commanders and fragments of companies fighting independently all over the battle area against a well-entrenched, well-equipped enemy who had rehearsed just such a contingency dozens of times. The VC had gotten their wish.

Smith himself had come in on the second lift. "What's your situation?" Colonel Timothy asked some minutes later, from the Command and Control (C&C) chopper in which he, Joe Hicks, and I were hovering above the battlefield, as soon as the ground commander established contact with us from the hot LZ.

"We've got a hundred and thirteen dead!" Smith cried.

Timothy looked at me, incredulous. "He's panicking," I said. "There's no

---

* When Rawls's body was recovered, his arm was outstretched, his hand pointing directly toward the machine gun that cut him down.

way he could take that many casualties in five minutes." And even if he could have, it would have been impossible for him to make any sort of accurate assessment in the time he had been on the ground. Under fire like that everything becomes exaggerated; my biggest fear in the C&C was that the colonel was going to lose complete control of himself as well as the battle. But as one of the '02 officers opined later, "Colonel Smith was never *in* control to lose it," and I believed it was true. From the moment the first elements of the '02 hit the ground at An Ninh, it seemed that anything that could possibly go wrong with the operation went wrong, and with a vengeance.

The landing zone Smith had chosen was outside the range of our artillery. The task force the arty was moving with was being held up on the wrong side of a mountain range, due to roads bogged by heavy rain or cut by the Viet Cong. Smith had knowingly taken this risk of being beyond the artillery fan: "I don't need artillery," he'd declared in response to Lieutenant Colonel William Braun's concern that Braun's 2/320 Airborne Artillery would not be able to support Smith's assault, "I've got my tac air." The only problem was, come the morning of the operation, Smith did *not* have his tac air. After the first two A1E Skyraiders prepped the LZ and flew away, there was no tac air at An Ninh for a full hour and a half after the '02 landed there. Back at Qui Nhon it had been discovered that the fuel for the A1Es had somehow been contaminated, and the planes were grounded. Until MACV scrambled jets out of Bien Hoa to pick up the tac-air slack, the '02, less helicopter gunships, was on its own.

Meanwhile, up in our C&C bird, we received word that not one of the twenty-six troop-carrying choppers designated for this mission was still operational. All had taken multiple hits and could not fly. One of the faint-hearted suggested we tell the '02 to E&E—escape and evade— forgetting completely that this situation was, in fact, tailor-made for Airborne. The Airborne's very purpose was to drop behind enemy lines. Its men were *trained* to be surrounded and to fight in isolated pockets of resistance. So I called Grady Jones, who'd been traveling with the waylaid task force in a jeep outfitted with all our maps and S-2/S-3 gear; he parked on the side of the road, popped a smoke, and soon Timothy, Hicks, and I joined him on the ground to decide what to do next.

Colonel Timothy organized another task force composed of elements of the 2/327, the remnants of the two '02 companies that never made it to the battlefield, and elements of the 23d ARVN Ranger Battalion. Captain Duane Messer, the Rangers' fine senior adviser, was authorized to send only two of his companies, but when he heard what a mess we were in he brought the whole battalion anyway and said he'd worry about the legalities later.

We had to tap the 1st Air Cav for lift; with every troop-carrying chopper attached to us down, theirs were the only immediate air assets in the vicinity. But when Bob Miller, the brigade S-3 Air, called over to the Air Cav to request some helicopters, the Cav's Chief of Staff said, "No way."

"What do you mean, 'no way'?" I yelled through the radio when Miller reported back to me.

"That's what I said," he replied. "I told him we had a battalion getting the shit kicked out of it to protect the 1st Cav's ass and it'd be a nice idea if they'd give us a little support. He said they didn't have flak jackets and flying without them would violate all their SOPs." (Later I heard the Cav's real bitch was that our action would cheat them out of a few of the thirty precious combat-free days they'd been promised in-country to get themselves set up at An Khe.)

Word traveled fast that we were getting zapped. Before long Lieutenant General John L. Throckmorton, Westmoreland's deputy, flew up from Saigon to find out who was responsible for this disaster and what the hell we planned to do about it. By then we were locked and cocked except for the Air Cav's assets; Timothy explained the situation to the General, Throckmorton made a few calls, and the next thing we knew the "Flying Horsemen" 1st Air Cav came galloping to the rescue.

Sort of. For reasons unknown, the Cav dropped the second task force (Task Force Collins, named for the 2/327's CO) at an LZ not two kilometers from An Ninh, as Colonel Timothy had chosen, but *five*. This destroyed any hope of their linking up with and taking the heat off the '02 at all that day. Two daring Air Cav pilots did get much-needed ammo resupply and an 81-mm mortar into the battle zone, though, and were able to evacuate five wounded before they had to break off because of heavy enemy fire. ("The choppers weren't even landing," said one participant after the fight. "We were just throwing bodies in.")

On the ground the battle was fought by the NCOs, who'd become the commanders by default as the officers were, one by one, killed or seriously wounded and Colonel Smith remained pinned down behind his paddy wall. But the biggest sting of the fight was word that Herb Dexter, who'd only recently transferred from Brigade S-4 to the '02 as S-3, was also killed. In this, his fourth tour in Vietnam, he, too, had become a platoon leader in the effort to turn the battle around. He was hit five times as he led a small band of courageous paratroopers up a heavily fortified, enemy-held hill that dominated the landing zone. "Don't pull back. Don't pull back," he said as he died, and his men heeded him, taking the objective a short time later in hand-to-hand combat, with one brave trooper even storming an enemy mortar and ripping its sights off with his bare hands. The guys probably best off were the thirty-six who'd come in on the third lift. Though under constant attack, cut off from one another (in groups of eight and twenty-eight men) until noon, and then cut off together from the main body of the battalion the rest of the day, throughout the battle these men were in the good hands of platoon sergeants Robert Jack and Robert Wightman, two old soldiers with years of combat between them. Wightman had actually found himself in, and fought himself out of, a virtually identical cutoff situation a dozen years before in Korea.*

The '02 troops performed magnificently throughout the battle, but never more so than in the early, crucial hours, in the absence of air support, artillery, *and* the commanders all had assumed would be there to lead them. They survived their baptism of fire with sheer guts. At one stage late in the day, a recon man named Freeman even took five prisoners with his disassembled M-16. (The weapon had jammed and he was cleaning it when he saw a VC patrol approaching him. He jumped up and pointed the barrel assembly at them; they threw up their hands and he marched them into his unit's nighttime perimeter.) Fortunately for all concerned, by midafternoon tac air was in abundance, close to all that was available in-country. Bob Miller had so many planes stacked up he had to provide alternate targets throughout the battlefield just to unload the ordnance. The first day's forty-seven air strikes punished Charlie royally, suppressed a lot of his fire, and let our troops come up for air, but close-in requests within one hundred meters of friendly positions during the belly-to-belly fighting accounted for two B Company deaths and a number of injuries throughout the day. By nightfall the Air Cav had lifted the 2/320 Artillery into range of An Ninh. At our request, they also set up one of their own batteries nearby to support Task Force Collins (which was beyond the 2/320's fan), and mistakenly proceeded to blast the shit out of Collins' CP. It wasn't the Cav's fault. In the hurry and the heat of the battle, no one had thought to make sure they used the same artillery deflection as the 2/320. Obviously they did not, and it was just luck that among the eleven friendly casualties that resulted from the accident no one was killed.

That night, flareships circled overhead, keeping the area lit up like day. By morning the VC had gone to ground, and though Operation Gibraltar continued for two more days, with the 2/502 being extracted and Task Force Collins mopping up the area, the worst was over. The net result of the

---

* According to retired Lieutenant General Henry "Hank" Emerson, Bob Wightman was one of the greatest combat leaders the Army was fortunate enough to have among its ranks. He was one of the greatest combat leaders Emerson had ever seen, and though the sergeant was well beyond the age limit, Emerson fought the bureaucracy to have him battlefield commissioned. In the end, though, it was Wightman who refused the commission, telling Emerson he'd rather be a good NCO than a lousy officer any day.

fighting was friendly casualties of thirteen KIA and forty WIA (twelve of which were from friendly fire), for an enemy body count reported to be 257 KIA, most the victims of our tac air. Only twenty-one enemy weapons were recovered, but twelve prisoners were taken, a number of whom were unquestionably hardcore NVA regulars, "fillers" infiltrated down to join VC Main Force units and buck up their southern counterparts. So much for North Vietnam's chant, "No NVA troops south of the seventeenth parallel."

General Westmoreland, along with some twenty reporters, was at Brigade Headquarters at An Khe when the '02 was extracted. Colonel Smith was immediately flown there to meet him, to give his report and quash early press accounts that the '02 had been badly mauled at An Ninh. The following day he was flown to Saigon to do it again for the press there. Though Smith had been pinned down throughout the first bloody day, and destroyed most of his documents in anticipation of being overrun, he would receive a Silver Star for gallantry in action during the operation. His battalion was awarded a well-deserved Presidential Unit Citation, though less for their tactical brilliance than for their guts and absolute refusal to give in.

How lucky the unit actually was, in the earliest moments of the battle, to survive what ended up being the buzz saw of a well-trained, well-armed Main Force VC unit, would not be known until the 1st Air Cav captured that VC after-action report on Gibraltar some six months later. According to that document, the VC knew we were coming as soon as we started planning. The minute we'd informed the "friendly" Viets in the district that we were going into the area, the word was passed along to the VC. The 95th also had a pretty good idea where we would be landing, and for two days before the battle, they trained on position there. But since nothing ever goes exactly according to plan, as prepared as the VC at An Ninh had been to receive us, when the '02 made its initial airmobile assault, Charlie ended up being as surprised as we were. While huge pots of still-boiling rice, ammo, and other gear found by our troops in hastily abandoned enemy campsites told the tale on the ground, the VC after-action report filled in a noteworthy blank: as the initial A1E air strikes and the first '02 lift went in, all the VC leaders, from squad level on up, were at their battalion CP, chalk-talking a sand-table exercise of the expected battle. The air strikes cut the phone wires between the battalion commander and his companies, and throughout the subsequent fighting the VC troops fought as isolated bands with no guidance from the main boss. And at the outset of the battle, until the squad, platoon, and company leaders got back to their units from the battalion CP, the VC troops fought with no guidance at all. Just one irony of this could be seen in a story related after the battle by '02 recon man John Reed, in which, soon after they landed as part of the first lift, a number of '02 recon guys saw a dozen Viet Cong in black pajamas tearing across the river just beyond a tree line north of the LZ. The recon group opened fire, only to be stopped by their sergeant because the enemy did not appear to be armed. It was General Westmoreland's strict rules of engagement again, and these VC got away. But they were never identified, and the question would always remain: what if they'd been among the unit's platoon and company commanders? And if they were, how different would the battle have been had our recon guys killed them and the enemy lost all its key leaders, as the '02 lost theirs?

Operation Gibraltar, the first major battle waged by the U.S. Army in Vietnam, was hailed by General Westmoreland as a great victory for U.S. troops. To me, Gibraltar was many things, chief among them a learning experience—about the necessity of artillery, the allowance of sufficient lead time before an operation, the worth of Airborne training (even if Airborne operations themselves were obsolete against a sophisticated enemy with tac air and tactical nuclear weapons), instilling as it did the "they've got us surrounded, the poor bastards" fighting spirit that served the '02 troopers on the ground at An Ninh in fine stead. But one thing Gibraltar most definitely *was not* was a great victory. Later, one '02 officer participant diplomatically called it "a blundering success"; another was a little more blunt when he said, "The VC saved the day by walking away," which, not at all to downplay the spirit and performance of the '02 soldiers or the professionalism of its NCOs, was indeed the case. Still, the "great victory" at Gibraltar sounded the start gun for many more big battles and many more "great victories" for American units in Westmoreland and DePuy's "search and destroy" war of attrition;* and while the 1st Brigade had learned plenty to arm it for the next confrontation with Charlie, so, of course, had the VC.

Because of the tremendous losses in helicopters during Gibraltar, extracting troops from An Ninh, a function of the brigade S-3 shop, was a slow, complicated, piecemeal process. Still, Bob Miller, the S-3 Air and a truly exceptional officer (he was also a VMI boy from Colonel Johns's days as commandant, and loved the old man as much as I did), had things under control. The redeployment was going smoothly when Major Charles W. "Bill" Dyke, S-3 of the 2/327, burst through the tent flaps of our S-3 tent, demanding assets to get his battalion out of the battle area.

Bill Dyke was a hard-charging, superconscientious officer. So conscientious, in fact, that to me he always looked on the verge of going tilt. He reminded me of an overbred hunting dog, so finely tuned that all it could

* Brigadier General William E. DePuy, Westmoreland's J-3 at the time, was and is widely considered the primary architect of the U.S. strategy of the Vietnam War.

do was shake. As far as I was concerned, Dyke's was not the kind of personality we needed around at the moment. Most of the brigade S-2/S-3 staff hadn't slept in three days and tempers were reasonably short. In my case, I was holding on by a hair trigger. Nonetheless, Dyke came charging in, demanding priority on air. My primary concern was getting the 2/502 back on (pre-Gibraltar) station; Miller went on organizing just that, with Dyke breathing hot and heavy down his neck. Finally I said, "Okay, Dyke, we're ready to outload your fucking battalion."

"Don't call my battalion a fucking battalion!" Dyke screamed in reply, and before I knew it, he came charging at me like a red-faced, raging bull. Automatically, I put up my dukes and the second he was in range I hit him. Not once, but three or four times, and knocked him on his ass right then and there. After he got his bearings, Dyke slowly got up from the deck and grabbed my hand. "Hack," he said, shaking it wildly, "you're a better man than I." *What a weird guy*, I thought to myself as he madly pumped away on my hand. *This is one weird guy.*

By the time the 1st Brigade left An Khe for Qui Nhon, the men were well on their way to becoming seasoned vets. Gibraltar had bloodied us and taught us to respect our foe. Overall confidence had steadily risen, both through the countless patrols and company- and battalion-size operations, and from observing the predominantly nonparatrooper 1st Air Cav guys going through *their* opening-night jitters. How quickly our men had forgotten their own. Comments like "What were ya'all shootin' at last night, Leg?" (which had been heard from the moment the Air Cav arrived), now, on the eve of our departure, had given way to "Hey, Leg, what're you gonna do when we're not here to protect your ass?"

About the same time that we moved out of An Khe, Colonel Timothy made good the promise he'd made me as far back as Fort Campbell, about letting me go down to a battalion. I was thrilled. Brigade staff was no place for a warrior. Though I enjoyed working for Colonel Timothy very much, from the way things were shaping up, the war in Vietnam was one fought almost solely at platoon, company, and battalion levels, and a staff officer at brigade, division, and above was nothing more than a manager's assistant, a small cog in a huge paper-shuffling machine, whose function was little more than matching assets against requirements and writing reports. I probably would have been happy with any job just to get off the brigade staff, so when Timothy told me I was going to the 1/327 "Above the Rest" battalion as executive officer, it was like a dream come true. The 1/327 was head and shoulders above the other two battalions. It was a close-knit, spirited crew, a unit that well reflected its long history of strong leadership.

And since the new CO, Joe Rogers, had already been my immediate superior (as Brigade XO) for almost a year, it was yet another break for me: there was no time or energy lost having to establish or prove myself with my new boss.

. A battalion XO actually wore two hats. One was that of battalion chief of staff, and the other, that of deputy commander of the battalion. As chief of staff, an XO's main responsibilities were to ramrod the battalion staff and run the administrative and logistics side of the unit. As deputy commander (a hat that had to be worn most carefully), if the XO made sure he adhered to the "good guy" or "bad guy" role his CO tasked him to play—and the differentiation of roles between the pair was essential—he could find himself an integral part of a damn good command team. For example, since Colonel Rogers was an unassuming, relaxed intellectual and I was a hard-driving son of a bitch, we fell very naturally into our respective roles in the running of the 1/327. Like Colonel Couch to Colonel Johns in the Vanguards, I snapped the whip and Rogers applied the salve, and though generally the commander played the bad guy, our arrangement suited me right down to the ground. On top of anything else, it gave me leave to kick ass and take names, and to hammer in the basics from the first day I walked into the battalion. Fire and maneuver, weapons clean and within arm's reach, wearing steel pots and proper camouflage—all these were things the troops of the 1/327 knew, but they'd gotten lazy about them during two months on the battlefield, and laziness could kill.

For the troops, the forty days the brigade spent in the Qui Nhon area were characterized by snipers and booby traps, mines and monsoons, and one rice paddy after another. The paddies all looked alike, and as such made navigation hell. On one occasion, a company landed on two separate rice-paddy LZs, only to find both were wrong. Booby traps were responsible for many, many casualties in the 1/327 during this period. The enemy had an incredible array of the things, which they attached to the doorways of vacant houses and shrines, on gates, and especially along the tops of paddy walls. There were hand-grenade booby traps with one or multiple trip wires secured to trees and rocks. There were more grenades, pins removed, held tight by a bag of rice, a rock, or a potential souvenir (a VC flag, for example), that were activated simply by picking up the item under which the primed grenade lay. Some of the best VC booby traps were made in the U.S.A.: Air Force "dud" cluster bomblets, modified with a pressure device and buried just below ground level to blow when a trooper stepped on them, or 81-mm and 60-mm dud mortar rounds, buried "nose up" and similarly pressure detonated. The VC used anything careless American soldiers left behind (C-ration cans, for example, formed the basis of many lethal enemy devices); deadlier still were the items the VC gave *back* from time to time, like U.S. grenades they policed up on the battlefield. A less-than-savvy American trooper might pick up one of these seemingly abandoned grenades and add it to his kit; during a fight days or weeks later he might use it and find himself dead the second he pulled the pin: the VC who'd found it first had replaced it on the battlefield only after removing the delay.

This sort of thing really played with the troopers' minds. It was hell never knowing if you were going to have a foot after your next step. It also gave rise to enormous frustration and anger among them. They seldom saw Charlie at Qui Nhon (though he was actually much more plentiful there than he'd been at An Khe), yet every day Charlie was bleeding them. They'd go into villages almost completely bereft of males, and after the women and old men had explained that all their husbands and sons were in the Army or dead and "No, no VC here," our soldiers would move on a few hundred meters only to have one of their number killed or wounded by a sniper holed up in the village they'd just left. The vast majority (up to 80 percent) of the heavily populated countryside were supportive of or influenced by the VC; add to this that the enemy at Qui Nhon was a far more cunning and evasive opponent than he'd been at An Khe, and his strategy of hit, bite, and run was all too effective.

The coastal monsoons made things even more grim. With the onset of the rainy season, the flat, open rice paddies, already sniper-, booby-trap-, and punji-stake infested, became like rivers. At one stage the brigade CP was actually washed away when it was set up on ground a speck too low. While Fred Johnson's C Company used captured sampans to improve their mobility through the flooded paddies (Johnson was an invaluable asset to the 1/327; as the only officer in the battalion who'd been to Vietnam before, he was our continuity link to the war), most of the troops just sloshed through the chest-deep water with weapons held over their heads, simultaneously trying to fight an unseen enemy who could see them for miles. Immersion foot, a condition where continuously wet feet blistered and then became a mass of painful ulcers, quickly became a serious problem among the men, the only remedy for which was to pull the sufferer out of the field and make him wear flip-flops (a.k.a. Ho Chi Minh sandals) until his feet dried out. It was hard to disagree with the sentiments expressed in a captured VC document from this period, that "U.S. troops walk in the open and look like bewildered ducks"; the only consolation for us was that whoever wrote the thing (he went on to say that in action we ran slowly and looked funny) had obviously never seen Harry the Horse.

Lieutenant Harry "The Horse" Godwin, a platoon leader in A (Abu) Company, began his legend at Qui Nhon. After deploying his best sharpshooters, this six-feet-three-inch ex-Marine and top college athlete (Henderson State, producer of studs—Dell Evans and Scooter Burke to name just two) would get on top of rice-paddy walls and run. The purpose of the exercise was to get a concealed VC sniper to take a shot at him. Then, as the long-legged basketball star kept on running, his sharpshooters would nail the sniper. The scheme worked very well, but as cat-and-mouse games go, it was altogether too dangerous, and I quietly told George Shevlin, the Abus' capable skipper, to put a good harness on "The Horse" and rein him in. Even so, I couldn't help but admire old Harry and wish his legend well; he was a top combat leader and a soldier revered by his men.

I was not involved in many combat activities while my new battalion was at Qui Nhon, but I *was* involved in a few battles, most notably with the 1st Brigade staff, which I managed to alienate within about two minutes of leaving there and joining the 1/327. The problem began when I realized that on the user level the battalion was playing guinea pig for the Research and Development (R&D) people back in the States, not unlike the German Army scheme almost thirty years before, when the Spanish Civil War became the Nazis' R&D field laboratory. Every time I turned around, our unit was being given some new piece of equipment to test on the battlefield. Then we at Battalion had to send the untried wonder gear down to a company commander, who'd give it to an appropriate user; the user would try it out and report his results back to his skipper, who'd make a verbal report that would be formalized at Battalion S-3 and sent on to Brigade.

The first to suffer for this game was the user/tester, who, concurrent with his efforts to adjust to and fight the war, was being made to fumble around with equipment he'd never seen before and had no confidence in. On the ground at company level, people were already terribly overworked, and the net result of this sort of "testing" was snap judgments on costly and often critical equipment, not to mention enough related paperwork to drown the whole war effort.

As battalion XO, I did not agree that our job in life was to be an extension of DA's R&D, or to answer mail from higher HQ just because they sent it. "You will *not* answer that. We will *not* make that report," I'd tell my people when what I considered unreasonable requirements were sent down, "we are here to fight a war. Our primary purpose is to kick Charlie's ass, not to write reports." I was particularly annoyed with the brigade S-3, Mark Hansen, with whom I'd swapped jobs. Though it was only natural for him to send little "projects" down to his old unit, I really felt he laid altogether too many requirements on us. On top of that, since he knew all the good people in my battalion from his XO days, it seemed as though every other damn day he and Jim Wilson (who was now the brigade XO) were stealing the best and taking them to work in their already overstaffed brigade HQ.

One afternoon a stinging Reply by Indorsement (RBI) letter came down from Brigade: "Why haven't you given us an evaluation report on the feasibility and desirability of the 'Over and Under'?" The RBI landed on the desk of the battalion Operations officer, Major Don Hilbert. "Look," he said, "they're yelling for this report. What's the priority?"

I grabbed the RBI. "Don't worry about it, Don. I'll do it." I was furious. Where the hell did they think they were, Fort Benning? "If I attempted to answer the mass of futile correspondence that surrounds me, I should be debarred from all serious business of campaigning," Wellington once wrote; as I jammed a piece of paper into a typewriter, I wondered what exactly Wellington did with the stuff he didn't answer, and, more importantly, how he'd gotten away with it. "TO:" I pounded on the keys, "THE OCTOPUS." I banged the carriage return so hard I thought it would break off. "SUBJECT": I continued, "THE PERFORMANCE OF THE OVER AND UNDER," and proceeded to report that this Rube Goldberg wonder weapon (which was an M-16 with an M-79 fixed underneath) was an ineffective, undesirable piece of shit. I ripped the rough draft out of the typewriter and gave it to the clerk to final type, forgetting completely that I'd addressed the thing to "The Octopus" instead of "Commanding Officer, 1st Airborne Brigade," to whom it would go. So the kid typed it up as it was, I only read through the text of the message, and off it went.

Thank God the commanding officer was Colonel Timothy. Over the last year we'd developed a wonderful relationship. He was an infinitely patient man who, as a caring father would with his wayward son, took great pains to try to smooth out my character. (A dinner we shared in Hawaii, for example, on our way back from the Vietnam recon in May, became Colonel Timothy's opportunity to work on my manners. We both ordered chicken, and while the Colonel properly cut his into bite-size pieces, I picked mine up and started hoeing it down with gusto. Tim was able to ignore this, but I guess when I started licking my fingers it got to be too much for him. "Dave," he said gently, "gentlemen do not eat chicken with their fingers.")

In Vietnam, since he'd sent me down to the 1/327, Colonel Timothy always backed me up and wore, on my behalf, the bitching of his brigade staff about me. The Octopus memo, however, was one step too far: "You have no idea how close I was to relieving you," Tim snapped when I saw him soon after. "There you were, calling *me*, your commanding officer, an octopus!"

"Well, you *are* an octopus," I replied, feeling a little bad (after all, Timothy had his own octopus to contend with—the lion's share of his time was spent briefing VIPs like the Secretary of Defense and visiting senators, congressmen, and firemen), "or at least your headquarters is. They're always coming down here with their long tentacles and wrapping them around us and strangling us with red tape so we can't get on with our job. Then they whip in again and steal all our best people. The minute we get a man trained and looking good, somebody decides he's wanted at your headquarters!"

"That is not the issue, Dave."

"It *is* the issue, sir!"

As with all my run-ins with Colonel Timothy, this one soon passed, and he even thumped his people for raiding our good men. There wasn't much he could do about the R&D testing requirements, however, and the battalion continued to play guinea pigs for many new toys, few of which were practical, GI-proof, and applicable to what we were doing in this war.

And that was my *real* bitch with the Buck Rogers wonder-junk laboratory team we were an unwilling part of. The rotten M-16, for example, which we'd brought over with us, was still a real sore point with me, and quickly became one for the warriors whose lives depended on its working. Many troopers picked up Soviet AK47s off the battlefield, lugged heavier M-14s or Thompson submachine guns—anything to avoid the M-16, which still wasn't GI-proof and still jammed more than it fired. And even when it was working, the M-16 wasn't worth a tinker's damn in the bush: though its projectile was incredibly lethal when it struck a human target, it was easily deflected by vines, bamboo, and other undergrowth. What good, I kept asking, was a weapon that couldn't hack the jungle, when we were fighting a jungle war? And since a competent soldier is, first and foremost, a confident soldier, how the hell were these kids expected to perform well carrying a weapon they couldn't trust? The same questions applied to the M-72 light antitank weapon (LAW), which had an electrical firing mechanism that completely shorted out if any moisture developed inside it. In the hot, humid conditions of Vietnam, half the time a guy would be better off throwing that weapon at the enemy than trying to fire it. Ditto the PRC-25 radio handset, which was so fragile it virtually fell apart when you blew on it, and was so susceptible to moisture that it had to be wrapped in plastic to keep it dry.

The R&D people didn't always get it wrong. The PRC-25 radio, for example, less its handset, was first-class and totally reliable. And the R&D guys did produce the M-79 grenade launcher, the finest infantry weapon fielded since the BAR. Colonel George Couch helped develop this compact, lightweight, reliable miracle, which ensured that infantry would never again have to find itself pinned down fifty meters from an entrenched machine-gun position, too far away to toss a grenade, too close for artillery, and nearly impossible to reach and knock out without severe casualties. With the M-79, one well-placed HE round could do the trick. The M-79 also fired shotgun shells, which made it an excellent area-fire weapon, well loved by point men and at night; unlike the M-16, with the shotgun shell the M-79 could penetrate the bush, which led to many resourceful troopers carrying both weapons at all times (the M-79 to tear a hole through the jungle, the M-16 to fight in the resultant "clearing"). Conceptually, this made the "Over and Under" M-16/M-79 combo a winner, too. But like everything else, the weapon—half of which (the M-16) had enough problems of its own to be worked out—was being sent down to troops before anyone had even begun to address its teething problems or basic bugs. In 1965, the Over and Under was a malfunctioning suicide weapon in the hands of a young soldier. But that didn't stop us from getting them to test, more and more and more.

As Over and Unders, LAWs, and all the other too-often useless and/or dangerous wonder gear poured in from the States to be tested on the ground, basic, *essential* things seldom found their way to the troops. A perfect example was the hand-grenade pouch. Ever since Matt Ridgway wore an uncovered frag grenade on his harness in Korea as a showmanship trick, it seemed we'd not had a secure way to carry grenades. Despite conditions on the ground in Vietnam that pleaded for such an item, such as "self"-inflicted casualties arising from grenade pins catching on jungle vines and being pulled out while unsuspecting troopers walked along, the R&D and logistics people did not take time to have a look and see for themselves. The soldiers, of course, made do; the canteen cover, which we'd used in Korea to carry extra frags, became the grenade pouch in Vietnam, too.

But the soldiers doing the fighting shouldn't have had to "make do," for grenade pouches or anything else. And it was this truth that made the priority given to R&D the most incomprehensible, especially in the first few months we were in Vietnam. We had LAWs and M-16s out the ass (which would have been a godsend if we could have counted on them to work), but in every other way, the logistic support we received during this period was criminally inadequate. General Westmoreland had made a bold decision to send combat troops to Vietnam with no logistics tail to speak of. And it was true that at the time we arrived, the roads between all provinces and most districts in the Highlands had been cut, and the war effort there (and throughout South Vietnam) was on the edge of collapsing to the Viet Cong. But this fact meant little to the troopers of the 1st Brigade, 101st, who were on canned C rations for three solid months. There were now 125,000 Americans in Vietnam with the number ever growing, but there were few cleaning rods or gun patches and little preservative oil for the line soldiers' weapons. About the only thing the logistics people made sure there was an ample supply of was beer for the troops to drink. While I was still at Brigade, Grady Jones had finally given up his in-country search for tires for our S-3 jeep. He wrote to his wife in America and she sent him two by mail. He got them. Our stateside fatigues were too hot for tropical operations. The troopers' first-rate Corcoran leather jump boots had begun to fall apart within two weeks of traipsing around in the jungle (the leather cracked from the dampness and the soles fell off), and with no resupply, the result was many soldiers going into battle in scrounged sneakers, or with their boots held together with commo wire and tape. Early in the piece, when General Westmoreland came up to give the 1/101 troopers a pep talk, even he was shocked by the condition of their boots. The next day he sent up dozens of pairs of proper jungle boots from Saigon,* taken, I was told, right off the feet of the rear-echelon commandos at MACV, who had an abundance of *everything* while we lived like Washington's forces at a humid Valley Forge. When, as newly appointed XO, I walked into the 1/327 for the first time, I was appalled by the lack of just about the works. Fortunately for me and the battalion (though I didn't know it at the time), the battalion S-4, whom I'll call Captain Tom Hancock, and whom I summoned to tell I wanted this situation changed *muy pronto*, was one of the greatest scrounger/wheeler-dealers in the U.S. Army, and all he'd been waiting for was a green light.

I'd met Tom Hancock at Fort Campbell when I was a tag-on on one of his platoon's jumps. Back then he'd been a cheerful, gung-ho second lieutenant (ROTC Distinguished Military Graduate) who ran one damn fine platoon. After the jump I'd written his name down in my "People to Watch and Grab Later" book. Even so, it was just good luck that I'd ended up with him in the 1/327, and even better that, in the words of one of his peers, Hancock "made an art form out of stealing."

"Hancock," I'd say, "I don't care how you do it or where you get it, but we need it now. Don't tell me your troubles, just get it done." Hancock was not the only one who got caught up in the scrounging spirit I instilled in the battalion's leaders (a carryover from Fort Mac and my D Company, Vanguard days), but he was by far the best: one of his first acquisitions at Qui Nhon was a real coup—an ice machine for the troops, set up right on the beach. (Ice was cold gold in South Vietnam's blistering summer heat, and from the moment we arrived at Cam Ranh Bay, our greedy South Viet allies had taken full advantage of our need for it, raising the price in the first week from about one dollar to a hundred dollars a block.) While it would later be

---

* Quick-drying and comfortable, these new jungle boots were another positive R&D development, as were the new, lightweight, quick-drying jungle fatigues and jungle blankets, if only the supply system could have gotten them to the men who needed them.

said of Hancock that stealing was "a narcotic to him—he just stole and then stole that much more," I liked to think of my master scrounger as Robin Hood in fatigues, scrounging, at my direction, for the troops of our destitute battalion.

The thing was, we all could have accepted the lean times if they had applied to everyone. But they didn't. MACV, USAF, and Army service and support units lived Fat City while we struggled to get the basics. And then they had the balls to look down on our people when we "dared" to ask for a few crumbs, or to go to their snazzy clubs in dress that did not meet their standards. As a result, as far as I was concerned, survival was the only law of the land: our combat units just took what they needed to ensure the troops' welfare was looked after. When I told Hancock, for example, that I wanted the battalion to have a decent hot meal when the companies returned from the next Qui Nhon operation ("I want steak, chicken, potatoes—not stuff out of a can, for Christ's sake. They've been on C rations forever . . ."), Hancock, who'd once been a general's aide, put on his aide-de-camp insignia, commandeered a small boat, and motored out to a ship in the Qui Nhon harbor. He told the captain he represented "the General" and that he needed some steaks, etc., for a VIP show for some Vietnamese. Whether the ship's captain was more impressed with Hancock or with the souvenir gifts of captured weapons the S-4 presented was hard to judge, but he gave Hancock everything he wanted, times three.

When the troops next got back from the paddies, the wonderful smell of grilled steaks and barbecued chicken was wafting through the camp to greet them. Hancock had scrounged an extra load of beer, too, and before long one slightly mellow, very happy battalion was moving through the chow line, courtesy of Tom Hancock. Unfortunately, one of the cooks had received a "Dear John" letter that morning, and elected the middle of the party as the moment to blow his brains out. He lay down on the ground, stuck an M-16 in his mouth, and let loose on full automatic. Though I wasn't there at the time, word had it that his hungry fellow troopers, deprived of decent food for so long, didn't miss a lick.

Like the rest of the battalion scroungers, Hancock understood I'd cover for him if he got caught red-handed. Unlike the understanding I had with the other battalion scroungers, however, I found myself covering for Hancock in all kinds of ways, for all kinds of activities, including the time he walked into a Qui Nhon bar, told a few legs there that they'd better leave, and when they didn't, he shot an M-79 through the bar window. (At the time, I was just thankful he wasn't drunk; when he was drunk he was much worse.) Hancock's enthusiasm for the ladies got him into even more trouble. We called him "Peeping Tom" when he was on the prowl (which was most of

the time), and since he didn't seem to be able to do anything halfway, he fell
in love fast, and very, very frequently. His only failing was a somewhat
indiscriminate bent. Had I known about this before the war, I would have
loaded up on shares in companies that manufactured penicillin. All in all,
I quickly realized Peeping Tom Hancock was going to be a handful, but
maybe because he reminded me a lot of myself when I was a hell-raising kid,
I put up with the bad to get the best out of the good, and the two of us got
along fine.

By the time the brigade left Qui Nhon, it had been on continuous
missions for one hundred days. Our next stop was Phan Rang, home of the
1/101's new, permanent base camp, for a much deserved rest. The Qui
Nhon mission (code-named Sayonara) had been very successful. Not only
had we held the Korean Capital Division's hand until they set up and got
through the same opening-night heebie-jeebies we and the 1st Air Cav had
had, but we'd allowed the local people to harvest their rice in peace,
unmolested by the Viet Cong. As well, the brigade had captured hundreds
of tons of the stuff from VC caches while pushing the enemy back into the
hinterland. The casualties at Qui Nhon had been mostly the result of VC
snipers, mines, and booby traps, with friendly fire accounting for the
remainder. In the Above the Rest battalion, we'd taken a total of fifteen KIA
and fifty-one WIA, the most tragic losses being in the recon platoon, where
five were killed and four wounded when the platoon leader erroneously
adjusted U.S. mortar fire right onto his own position. Gastroenteritis and
malaria had also taken their tolls at Qui Nhon. Some slackers saw these
illnesses as a way out of the war, and, not unlike the Korea days, went out
of their way to drink rice-paddy and well water without halazone tablets, or
did not take their antimalaria pills and then went around inviting mosquitoes
with their sleeves rolled up and shirts unbuttoned when the sun went down.
The malaria situation got so bad (and was made all the worse by a lethal new
strain that targeted black troopers as its main victims) that we finally issued
an order that squad leaders had to administer the huge, antimalaria "horse
pills" to each trooper personally, and record the event in a notebook.

Phan Rang gave the troopers a chance to relax and have a few beers while
the battalion organization went through a major reshuffle. All but one
company commander was replaced, and a new, fourth maneuver element
was established. The company command shake-up was not by choice. It was
instead based on the Army's Vietnam policy that a company CO's command
tour was to be three months long. The philosophy behind this policy, which
ended up being a policy of command musical chairs, was to spread
command experience around, with the long-term view of having an Army
full of experienced combat commanders. In practice, however, the policy

only *prevented* a man from becoming a good commander and leader: just as he began to get the hang of the role, to get to know his troops and understand how to employ them, he was yanked off the line. Meanwhile, the troops had no continuity, and if a wimp replaced a stud CO (and good or bad, the best or the worst, unless a guy was relieved he stayed with his unit three months), morale and fighting confidence could plummet overnight. It was a terrible way to run a combat unit, but it was the rule, so at Phan Rang there wasn't much we could do except make the changes and hope the new guys had what it took.

A more welcome adjustment to the battalion at this time was the establishment of an all-volunteer, Raider-like unit called the Tiger Force. The Tigers' personnel assets came from our recon and antitank platoons, which at Qui Nhon I'd recommended to Colonel Rogers that we inactivate. Rogers agreed that we had little requirement for antitank weapons, and the units' vehicles made them roadbound anyway. The Tiger Force troopers, in their distinctive Special Forces "tiger suits" (fatigues permanently camouflaged with black and brown stripes and scrounged from the Green Berets by Hancock), gave the battalion a long-range reconnaissance and ambush element that would operate independently, as well as the flexibility of a handy fourth maneuver element.

The need for—and value of—a fresh concept like the Tigers was intensified in the battalion by virtue of recent goings-on in the 2/502. Wilford Smith was gone; now Lieutenant Colonel Henry Everett "Hank" Emerson was in charge, breathing fire into the '02 and implementing a kit bag of bold ideas. There's nothing like unit competition to shake off the cobwebs, and in the 1/327 we knew that unless we got off our asses, the Above the Rest would soon be Below the Best. Lieutenant Jim Gardner, most recently the recon platoon leader, became the first Tiger CO. He was a hardworking, redheaded, Dyersburg, Tennessee-born Irishman, a natural leader whose gentle demeanor belied the cocky, profane Tigers he helped create. Gardner was a no-bullshit kind of guy. The story went that he'd been kicked out of West Point after turning himself in for violating the Academy's strict honor code. Undeterred, he'd gone to OCS, and been commissioned a few months before his West Point peers. He had loads of common sense (rare among young lieutenants) and truly loved his soldiers; unfortunately the latter attribute would have him blaming himself the rest of his life for the five recon platoon deaths at Qui Nhon, when he'd mistakenly put mortar fire onto his own position. In any event, Gardner was my kind of man. He had no trouble getting volunteers for the new outfit either, and soon he'd organized and begun to train his very mean two-platoon Tiger Force.

As soon as things were squared away, Captain Raphiel Benjamin, our new battalion surgeon, checked me into the hospital at Nha Trang. I'd picked up a severe case of gastroenteritis at Qui Nhon, probably from drinking Viet "33" beer (rumored to be made, in part, from formaldehyde); I'd been sick for a couple of weeks, and even the unquestionably brilliant new doc hadn't been able to bring it under control. As events proved, the docs in the hospital couldn't either, despite an entire week under their care, but while they poked and prodded and scratched their heads trying to figure out what had gotten to me, I watched my near-empty officers' ward fill to capacity, with casualties all from the 1st Air Cav and all from a single battle—the battle of the Ia Drang Valley.

The first casualties in were from Lieutenant Colonel Harold "Hal" G. Moore's 1/7 (Gary Owen) Battalion. The stories they told of their baptism of fire began as echoes of Gibraltar: inadequate lift and piecemeal commitment, landing virtually at the enemy's front door, and being incredibly outnumbered. The first day found Moore's understrength (little more than 50 percent) unit surrounded and caught in a vice of two-plus NVA battalions. The second day was more of the same, except that the two, possibly three, North Vietnamese battalions assaulting the weary 1/7 were entirely fresh troops. The enemy made their main attack into Moore's C Company, inflicting heavy casualties and rendering that brave band of men ineffective as a fighting force. But the survivors hung tough and held their ground. Savage hand-to-hand combat was the order of the day as the enemy closed as tight as they could to avoid the Air Cav's superior firepower; close-in employment of artillery and tac air severely punished the NVA troops but took its toll in friendly casualties, too, the worst case being when a canister of USAF napalm was mistakenly dropped just twenty meters from Moore's CP, scorching many and burning to death one of the troopers dug in there.

Despite these dire stories I heard in my hospital bed, Moore's Ia Drang fight did not smell like a disaster, or a "blundering success" like Gibraltar. While Moore would later describe his battalion's fight as "a fight-to-live situation," which was not unlike what the '02 had experienced, a critical difference between the two battles was that the commander of the 1/7 was completely in control from the moment his fight began. At An Ninh, Colonel Smith was denied this control by going in with the second lift of troops. Moore, on the other hand, had been on the first lift, in the lead chopper; he'd made sure he had a chance to eyeball the LZ and the terrain surrounding it before the fight broke.

Hal Moore was a comer in the Army. By the grade of lieutenant colonel, an officer's reputation was generally made or broken, and if the guy's a comer, at that point he starts being described as "one star" or "three stars," that is, what rank he'll achieve before being retired arbitrarily in keeping with the Army's senseless age rules. At the time of the Ia Drang fight, Hal Moore was already being described as an "all the way" man, meaning four stars and probably Chief of Staff one day. That reputation was only enhanced by his performance at Ia Drang, where he fought his battalion brilliantly against incredible odds, taking severe casualties but inflicting even worse ones on the enemy, including a spectacular coup de grace just before his battalion was relieved and extracted from the ground they'd fought over for forty-odd hours. Using the "sixth sense" he'd developed over years and years of troop-leading experience and plenty of combat, just as dawn was breaking Moore ordered a controlled Mad Minute with every available weapon in the battalion blazing. The net result was the annihilation of an NVA company, cut down in their attack positions just moments before they were set to launch an assault on Moore's unit.

As the week passed, Ia Drang casualties continued pouring into the hospital at Nha Trang. But the mood of these, my latest ward mates, was as grave as Moore's men's had been elated. They were members of Lieutenant Colonel Robert McDade's 2/7 Cav Battalion, which had relieved Moore's forces and that very same morning walked right into an estimated five-hundred-man NVA ambush. The word I was getting from the wounded Air Cav officers was "disaster"—annihilation, almost to the man, of 2/7 units as big as company size. Despite this, however, and despite the fact that American KIA would number more than two hundred by the time the battle ended little more than a week later, both at the height of the fighting and when it was over, COMUSMACV General William Westmoreland confidently stated that the battle of Ia Drang was "an unprecedented victory" for American units in the war.

"Victory" is one of those words—as hard to define as "light," "moderate," and "heavy," three more of those words that MACV had chosen as the official words to describe friendly combat casualties to the press corps and the folks back home. These words would have pleased Humpty-Dumpty, sitting on his wall in the world inside Alice's looking glass: "When *I* use a word," he'd said, "it means just what I choose it to mean—neither more nor less." Victory had been used to describe the 1/101's near-disaster at An Ninh; now it was being used again to describe Ia Drang, where, despite the incredible NVA losses (official U.S. totals, unconfirmed by eyewitnesses, were well over a thousand enemy KIA), nowhere near did the Americans come to beating the oft-stated equation Ho Chi Minh had taunted the French with during the Indochina war: "You will kill ten of our men and we will kill one of yours, and in the end it will be you who tire of it." Ia Drang put another word, "ambush," into the Humpty-Dumpty dictionary, too. The destruction of McDade's battalion didn't fit in very well with the otherwise "victorious" fight, so despite all evidence to the contrary—platoon leaders were telling me how the hidden enemy had been everywhere, even dug into the tops of the six-foot-tall anthills a few feet off the ambushed trail—the 1st Air Cav's Assistant Division Commander, Brigadier General Richard Knowles, told reporters McDade's battalion had *not* been ambushed, that they'd probably surprised the NVA unit that subsequently destroyed them.

In terms of scale, in terms of the nature and number of the enemy, and in the way the NVA initially stood and fought instead of running away, the battle of the Ia Drang Valley was unprecedented in America's involvement in Vietnam. Also, Ia Drang (and in fact the entire Central Highlands Pleime campaign, which had begun five weeks earlier and of which Ia Drang was a part) heralded a major change in the face of modern warfare. The first real test of America's airmobile might proved, in combat, the wide-ranging capabilities and worth of the helicopter for the movement of troops and artillery, the evacuation of casualties through medevac choppers, and resupply. The fact that the Air Cav covered enormous distances throughout the battle in comparatively insignificant amounts of time certainly changed the complexion of warfare as any of us knew it, but especially for the North Vietnamese, whose previous enemy, the French, had (as a rule) hacked their way one foot after the other through the Highlands at a maximum speed of five hundred meters per hour.

The big question of Ia Drang was why the NVA stood its ground in the face of our awesome firepower, and allowed such diabolical casualties among its ranks. Indeed, a significant part of the high-level American ecstasy after Ia Drang was its "proof" of the suitability of a war of attrition (the style of war General Westmoreland was waging) in Vietnam. But while Westy opined that the reason the NVA stood was to protect a new supply and staging base in the mountains above Ia Drang, it was John Paul Vann (who by now had quit the Army as a lieutenant colonel and had returned to Vietnam as an Agency for International Development (AID) civilian adviser and recognized expert on the situation there) who correctly suggested that the NVA's purpose at Ia Drang—and hang the expense in lives—was to figure out how to beat the Americans' incredible firepower and amazing mobility. And they accomplished their mission. Sure, they were knocked on their asses and took a long time to recover, and they had to cut back on their fledgling "Stage Three" set-piece battles and return to "Stage Two" guerrilla hit-and-run operations. But from the fight they also learned to "hug the belt" of their enemy, to come in as close as they could in order to neutralize the killing power of our artillery and air support. At Ia Drang, the North

Vietnamese *learned how to fight us*. And looked at in this way, even if the battle was an unprecedented victory for the Americans in our war of attrition, it was an equally unprecedented victory for our enemy in their protracted guerrilla war.

The brigade was conducting local security missions around our Phan Rang base camp by the time I returned to my battalion. The Above the Rest training program we'd established, which incorporated lessons learned so far, was also in full swing, but other than that nothing was happening, and life at our base-camp "home" would have been boring beyond words if all the free time hadn't given me the opportunity to get to know the young officers in the 1/327, and find out what they were made of. Cards being just about the only nightlife Phan Rang had to offer, this "getting to know you" generally took place around a poker table; I cleaned out most of the guys on a regular basis, but as testimony to their mettle, they always came back for more. Lieutenant George Perry from Abu Company, for example, was one of the worst card players I'd ever met. It finally reached the point where I'd tell him to stay home and get a good night's sleep, that I'd be happy to prorate his losses against his track record and bill him in the morning. Whatever I said, though, Perry was always at the table that night.

Sparkling entertainment at the officer card parties was provided by battalion assistant S-3 John Dalton Howard, a.k.a. "Gentleman John," a West Point lieutenant who'd struck me as being outstanding the first minute I laid eyes on him. Johnny was a very serious young soldier with a John Denver wholesome look about him. Underneath, he was also a great practical joker and one of the funniest guys I'd ever met. He viewed playing poker with me somewhat as Hank Lunde did ("That dumb I'm not," my former assistant S-3, now making his mark as the top company commander in Emerson's stable of '02 studs, would say when asked to participate); Johnny came to every game, but when asked to play he'd usually sit back, beer in hand, and say, "No, my job here is to enhance the conversation." And enhance it he did, with jokes and complete recitals of Rudyard Kipling and other military poems. When he wasn't playing Gentleman John, though, Johnny was a tiger. The main reason he was up at Battalion was that I'd pulled him out of his platoon in Abu Company when he started doing Harry the Horse–like stunts. I knew in my gut if I didn't he'd get wasted.

Also at the poker table in Phan Rang, though I hated to admit it, I finally met my match. Captain Benjamin L. Willis, a volunteer replacement from MACV, was the best poker player I'd met since Dell Evans in Korea. My longtime belief that great warriors were (or should be) great poker players was certainly borne out by Ben; his incredible common sense and street fighter's cunning belied his West Point education. Even he said most Academy graduates were too smart to be infantrymen, and he freely admitted he'd graduated at the bottom of his class. I had enormous respect for Willis' judgment and ability—in my view he was probably one of the best American guerrilla fighters in the Republic of Vietnam—and if I personally taught him anything in the three tours we would ultimately serve together, in the early days of our friendship he taught me even more.

From time to time, on nights when poker got old and/or a fair amount of boozing had gone down, we'd conduct a raid on downtown Phan Rang, specifically on Madame Nhu's House of Pleasure. It hadn't taken long to find out who shared my view of combat soldiers and sex (those of "rampant libido," as Johnny Howard so succinctly would observe); on the nights themselves I'd send word down to the company CPs that "Major Hackworth requests your presence at Madame Nhu's," and when all interested officers were assembled (normally a wild, drunken mob), we'd pile into jeeps and head into town. Usually the subsequent events were pretty straightforward, although one notable exception was the night everyone wanted a second round and no one had enough money to pay for it. The Vietnamese madam happily accepted a transistor radio as compensation for her girls' double rations rendered (the radio belonged to one of the lieutenants, though God only knew why he'd brought it along); from that point we had it made in the shade until the MPs started banging on the whorehouse door, presumably because of all the Airborne jeeps outside. My guys were all on the second floor. As the situation hotted up, we scrambled to make our getaway, and I found myself scaling down the side of the building with another battalion officer, employing tactics neither of us had used since our rappeling training days back at Fort Campbell. Fortunately, the whole group got out intact and we soon roared off into the night, beyond the clutches of the law.

We were like a college varsity football team, and I was the coach and captain. I didn't think twice about drinking and gambling and letting off steam with the men off-hours. I always thought the Army's rule against fraternizing with subordinates was wrong anyway. If you can tell them to die you should be able to get blasted with them—as long as they knew that come the morning it was all duty, and they got no break from partying with the boss.

Of course, they got no break from *not* partying with the boss either. When a contingent of the young officers went to the opening of the base camp's Brigade Officers' Club, didn't invite me along, and got themselves into a huge drunken fight, *I* was the one who got my ass chewed by Colonel Rogers, who correctly believed I was responsible for infusing the fighters with such wild spirit. I wouldn't have minded this if I'd been invited, but as it was, the following morning I assembled all the transgressors. "You're a bunch of bums," I said. "That was a brand-new club you destroyed. Are you crazy? I'm telling you now, and I'm only going to say it once: this drinking to excess has got to stop! Do you understand?" Judging from their collective hung-over moans as they shuffled slowly out of the room, my young friends got the message. That evening I paid my own visit to the Brigade Officers' Club. Hancock came along with me, and we seriously tied one on; when we came staggering home, we decided we ought to drop by the battalion's TOC and give the duty officer, who that night happened to be Gentleman John Howard, a hard time. As luck would have it, all was quiet and Johnny was asleep when we arrived. We woke him up by grabbing his hands and feet, and before he could even protest, we'd carried him out of the TOC, tied him to the hood of my jeep, and proceeded to drive him all around the base camp. Johnny had been one of the guys who'd withstood my morning tirade on the abuse of alcohol; when we finally untied him from the jeep, he just looked at me, deadpan, and said, "So much for a new perspective on moderation, sir."

To be able to successfully slip between the roles of buddy and boss was a skill I'd learned from Steve Prazenka and the other TRUST NCOs. The 1/327 officers accepted the ground rules; as Tiger Lieutenant Dennis Foley later explained it, I had an ability to violate one rule of leadership, and that was: overfamiliarity breeds contempt. "You could be 'overly familiar' with Hack," he said, "but it was always on *his terms*. Because when he pulled the reins back, it was as if you never even knew he had a first name. We could go out with him and raise all kinds of hell till dawn, but the next day—God forbid we mentioned that we went, or failed to perform adequately, or looked as if we were hung over or needed some sleep. We soldiered and it was not discussed." And it was with this understanding that a foundation of love and respect was established all around, which would add mightily to the battalion's strength not long down the track.

I'd liked Dennis Foley from the minute I met him. He was a tall, skinny, bespectacled kid, an Army brat who'd gone to OCS after a couple of years' enlisted service. When I gave him command of one of the Tiger platoons, I'd also given him my "Sergeant Sweeney" talk. Foley was as ashen-faced as most lieutenants were when confronted with the fact that they didn't know shit about leading troops, but according to Phil Beldon, the old pro NCO who actually ran the unit while Foley learned, the new lieutenant was shaping up fine. One thing Foley was a bit slower off the mark with, though, was the art of scrounging, a fact that became painfully clear to me the day I received the humiliating news that he and his boss, Tiger CO Jim Gardner, had been caught in the act.

Apparently the two had decided they were going to scrounge a refrigerator for the HQ company mess (a fine and generous idea) from the USAF base just down the road in Phan Rang. Their fatal error had been to trust the Air Force lieutenant they met at the USAF Officers' Club, who, in a moment of drunken camaraderie, told them the easiest way to get a refrigerator was use his name at the base's supply dump. The fly-boy was correct, but just as Gardner and Foley finished loading up the refrigerator, no questions asked, and started driving away, back at the bar the supply lieutenant got scared and reported everything to the Air Police. Within minutes my Tigers (who were probably drunker than the Air Force lieutenant) were ambushed by the base security guards, and when confronted with the fact that they had a stolen refrigerator in the back of their truck, they confidently maintained that it must have fallen in. The first I heard of the matter was the late-night call I got from an irate USAF colonel. When he finished chewing my ass (which took a fair while), I told him I'd take care of it, and two very drunk Tiger lieutenants sobered up quickly when told by the colonel to report to me ASAP ("Can't we just go to Leavenworth?" young Foley reportedly asked). I *was* mad as hell, but the two lieutenants needn't have worried. I didn't want a pound of flesh. I just couldn't believe that these two guys—these two *Tigers*—had screwed up so badly. It wouldn't have happened in the Raiders. "Just don't let it happen again," I roared as the two men stood miserably at attention before me. "If you can't do it without getting caught, then don't do it at all!"

General Westmoreland visited the brigade at Thanksgiving. Hands on hips, his square jaw jutting out, he stood on a box and inspired the troops with cheers that we were beating the VC into near-submission. Before he left, the brigade was issued, per man, two little cards to carry around in the jungle and study like the Bible. One was MACV's "Nine Rule" card, which spelled out MACV policy for winning the hearts and minds of the people, and the other, the "Standing Orders, Rogers' Rangers," written in 1759 (see Appendix). The latter item was a decided plus. Even Maxwell D. Taylor had said the VC was "an enemy as shrewd, well-trained, and with the guile of the American Indian during his best days,"[2] and Major Robert Rogers' two-hundred-year-old guidelines were as applicable in Vietnam as they'd been in the American colonies during the French, Indian, and Revolutionary wars. Unfortunately, the card creators at MACV HQ in Saigon soon went into the same overdrive as the Research and Development people in Washington. Before the Vietnam War was over, American combat soldiers would virtually need a truck to carry all their prompt cards: a troop-leading card, a Code of Conduct card, a patrol leader's card, a mines-and-booby-trap card, a five-paragraph field-order card, a card-for-every-occasion card—you name it, the troops had it.

The holiday was rounded out with a traditional Thanksgiving feast, complete with all the trimmings. It tasted great despite what old paratrooper First Sergeant Leo B. Smith told me, that at least one of the turkeys was twenty-five years old (a surplus bird frozen since the Second World War). Still, I couldn't help but marvel at how screwed up MACV's priorities continued to be. After four months in Vietnam and a home-style, nothing-is-too-good-for-the-troops Thanksgiving dinner, we were still short on the essentials: jungle boots, jungle fatigues, gun patches, oil, and cleaning rods. After four months in Vietnam, no one had recognized that the 1/101 was not being used in a normal Airborne role,* and we were still ridiculously ill equipped in terms of vehicles, weapons, and equipment to function as the regular infantry unit we'd become. So as delicious as that turkey dinner was, there was no question that the troopers would have been a lot more thankful on Thanksgiving, 1965, if MACV had given us chicken sandwiches instead, and spent their time, energy, and money addressing our critical operational shortages.

Thanksgiving had barely passed when the 7th ARVN Regiment was decimated in a battle with Main Force VC units at the Michelin rubber plantation near Ben Cat, just forty-five kilometers northwest of Saigon. The VC had had the run of the rich rubber country around Ben Cat and nearby Lai Khe for twenty years. The area had been the birthplace of the Viet Minh's insurgent effort against the French, and though our predecessors had fought many a bloody battle there, in the end it was always the guerrillas who prevailed. Curiously, the French-owned Michelin plantation had operated continuously in this VC stronghold since the fall of Dien Bien Phu, its only acknowledgment of the ongoing war being signs all over the place demanding that combatants not damage the trees. October 1965 put an end to the operations, however, and to this typical French complacency, when the VC infiltrated the plantation, demanded taxes from the owners, and made a lasting impression on all the workers by executing their South Vietnamese foreman right in front of them. Michelin closed down, and the 7th ARVN was sent in to guard the real estate. Upon their routing (a disaster only compounded when American aircraft dropped HE bombs right in the middle of a 350-man relief unit of ARVN Rangers), General Westmoreland ordered a massive retaliatory operation to secure the plantation and get the VC. His choice of allied units for the job (elements of the U.S. 1st Div, the

---

* Traditionally, paratroopers were lightly equipped, "in and out" troops who, after an operation, immediately went back to Army Reserve to train, refit, and await another jump mission. As such, traditionally the Airborne didn't need a lot of vehicles or a long logistic tail.

173d, the 1st Battalion, Royal Australian Regiment [1/RAR], and a two-battalion task force from the 101st) was, to me, unstated testimony that he and DePuy had concluded the ARVN didn't have a hope in hell of winning this war and it would soon become—if it was not, basically, already—an all-American show.

The initial role of Tim's Traveling Trouble in this operation was to take over the defense of Bien Hoa Airfield from the 173d and 1/RAR—the Aussies were under the operational control (OPCON) of the 173d as its third maneuver element—while those two units conducted operations. It wasn't bad duty, though the troopers were restless and aching for a fight; with the exception of Saigon, Bien Hoa (halfway between Saigon and Lai Khe–Ben Cat) was as close to the Land of the Big PX as one could probably get in South Vietnam in 1965: lavish, air-conditioned clubs with floor shows, open-air barbecues, slot machines, long, slick bars with drinks no more than two bits a shot, top-quality food, and even Broadway entertainment, most recently *Hello, Dolly!* starring Mary Martin. (*Pinch me,* I thought when we first arrived, *for a minute there I thought I was supposed to be in a war zone.*)

The last time I'd been to Bien Hoa was in June, during the advance-party days. While the other members of our party were farmed out to the individual units already deployed, to observe, learn, and be prepared to pass this knowledge on to their own units when they arrived, I'd taken the opportunity to visit almost all the U.S. outfits in the field to get an overall view of what was happening. The walkabout had proved invaluable, if only to find there was little point in placing any of our party with the U.S. Marines (who were operating in the north, up in I Corps) or with the 173d at Bien Hoa, because they would only learn bad habits. It was not that the Marines or the 173d were short on good soldiers or strong leaders. But they were sloppy on the basics of staying alive in an armed environment, and their gung-ho, "assault 'em on the beachhead" (or drop zone) tactics could not have been more wrong for a guerrilla war. I'd quickly discovered that besides the U.S. Special Forces A Teams, who ran (and manned, along with the Montagnard soldiers they'd trained), the Civilian Irregular Defense Group (CIDG) frontier border camps, it was the Australians, under the command of one Lieutenant Colonel Brumfield, who seemed to be the most knowledgeable in terms of how to fight a guerrilla in a jungle environment. So I'd begun encouraging the infantry members of the advance party to mosey on over to 1/RAR to have a look.

The Australians' expertise was not exactly surprising. It was based on experience gained not just in their Australia-based training program (which concentrated solely on jungle warfare at a ten-thousand-acre tropical rain forest training ground), but also on the jungle battlegrounds of New Guinea and Borneo during WW II, as well as during the postwar Malayan conflict, a war of insurgency the Aussies shared with the Brits for a dozen years. Historically, the Australians were a well-respected foe, a fact expressed best by Field Marshal Erwin Rommel a quarter of a century before, when he said during the fighting in Africa, "Those damn Australians." A single admonition found in a captured VC diary proved the Aussies had already made a similar impression in the present conflict: "When you're engaging the Australians," it warned, "watch your flanks with special care."

Major John Essex-Clark was the 1/RAR's S-3. He was a giant of a man and a stud of a soldier; one of the last battlefield commissions in the British Army, he'd spent thirteen years fighting guerrillas in Rhodesia and the Belgian Congo, and two years on long-range patrols on special operations in Malaya. We'd met during the advance-party days, and even in that short time he'd taught me plenty about guerrilla fighting. Now that the 1st Brigade was at Bien Hoa, we had a chance to become reacquainted, and not a few beers were sloshed down at the Bien Hoa USAF Officers' Club as we picked up where we'd left off. Essex-Clark was no more impressed these days than he'd been when we first met by the large-unit (company- and battalion-size) tactics of his gung-ho American counterparts in the 173d. The Aussies used squads to make a contact, and brought in reinforcing elements to do the killing; they planned in the belief that a platoon on the battlefield could do anything, "including get out." While the 1/101 was starting to develop small-unit tactics with the Tigers and Hank Emerson's Recondos, what would prove to be the biggest stumbling block to the widespread adoption of such tactics among the Americans was senior commanders' unwillingness to break down their organizations into such seemingly devourable chunks.*

In any event, I still maintained that the Australians understood the war better than our guys ever would, so at Bien Hoa I pitched Essex-Clark a cross-training proposal I'd been thinking about since we first met: that of sending Above the Rest platoon leaders over to the pros at 1/RAR to gain jungle-fighting knowledge that they could bring back and infuse throughout their units. Essex-Clark agreed to the idea, and we decided on a post-Christmas start for the program to give me time to clear it with Colonel Timothy.

When the brigade was relieved of its airfield security mission, we moved

---

* And this was despite the not uncommon attitude expressed to John Essex-Clark by one American brigadier general in these early days of the war, to wit: "We've got to take casualties. If we don't, the Vietnamese won't believe we're serious about this."

overland along Route 13 to Lai Khe and the Michelin plantation. It was an expensive journey: before our first day was out, the 1/327 had taken three KIA and ten WIA when VC command-detonated mines destroyed two of our jeeps and a troop-carrying two-and-a-half-ton truck.

The 1st Brigade's Operation Checkerboard commenced on 12 December with a massive airmobile assault. After all the months of scratching around for whatever lift we could get, we in the 1/101 could not believe the number of helicopter assets assembled for the task. The first lift alone was composed of forty UH1D troop carrying choppers (also known as "Hueys" or "slicks"), able to carry two complete rifle companies into the battle area simultaneously.

Airmobile assaults were both exciting and frightening. Each one was a gut-churning event not dissimilar to the moment before you unassed an airplane with a parachute on your back. The chill down your spine and the tightening in your stomach started the moment you loaded into the chopper. You sat down on your steel pot—few trusted the Huey's thin underbelly to keep them in full possession of their most vital organs—and soon you were bolting skyward, as if ascending in a high-speed elevator. The slicks moved in a line, like giant locusts; approaching the LZ, they swung into a big orbit, staying out of the way of the tac air preparing the ground below—you could see the napalm and cluster bomblets crunching down and the big geysers created by heavier bombs. Then the tac-air aircraft pulled away with a flourish, and artillery rained down as the slicks were joined midair by gunships, which would, when the artillery was lifted, hose down the tree lines with machine guns, rockets, and fast-firing M-79 guns while the slicks sat down and discharged their troops. Only when they'd landed did the slicks' door gunners open up, while troopers (eight per bird, four per door) hit the ground running with hearts in mouths, bent double to avoid the whirling *thump, thump, thump* of the chopper blades, through the noise and confusion, to secure the tree line for subsequent lifts to go in without covering fire. It was a concerto of awesome firepower coordinated with split-second timing, an intricate ballet of man and machine. Everybody had to have his act together—troopers, crews, artillery, and Air Force supporters—because on top of everything else, it all happened at more than a hundred miles an hour.

I was on the ground with the troops during Checkerboard, sent (with no need for a second invitation) by Colonel Rogers to see how the companies were doing since the Phan Rang game of company-command musical chairs. No major contacts with the VC occurred during the operation. While the Lai Khe–Ben Cat area proved to be a major logistic base for the Viet Cong, complete with a hospital complex, training facilities, and large-unit base camps and mess halls, judging from the lack of booby traps among these installations and the freshly prepared, still-warm food we found in cooking pots, the VC units who lived there had decided to run away rather than take us on. Still, they'd left calling cards throughout the rubber plantation and double-canopied jungle, making the battlefield particularly grim. Like Qui Nhon, wherever a trooper walked there seemed to be a mine or an explosive booby trap. We had a number of casualties, and countless near-misses. Other primitive but highly effective devices we encountered included tiger traps with their razor-sharp bamboo spears at the bottom, but much worse were the huge logs the enemy had rigged up and hidden in trees. The unlucky infantryman who sprang the concealed trip wire of one of these would find two hundred pounds of teak, usually studded with spikes, catapulting down on him at fifty miles per hour. The jungle held the routine unpleasantries of red ants and leeches as well, but more dangerous to the soldiers was their own behavior within the bush. Just one example was the several friendly casualties that occurred when a grenade was tossed, hit the trees, and bounced back on the troops. It was a common accident; the men still had not come to terms with jungle fighting. The Screaming Eagles' long orientation for desert warfare was one of our worst enemies: the overall lack of training for this terrain had troopers sounding and acting like a herd of elephants crashing through the forest.

Nowhere was this more clear to me than when Operation Checkerboard drew to a close and I accompanied Lieutenant Pat Graves's B Company platoon on the way out of the jungle. It was an experience that made me well respect the enormous difficulties the groundpounder in Vietnam faced: machetes wielded against the dense, uncompromising bush that rose into double and triple canopy (making the day like night), point men changed again and again as the exhausting job of hacking through it overtook them. Then, suddenly, the dark, dank, impenetrable jungle opened up. But it did not reveal daylight; instead, the presence, five feet in front of us, of another unit. Fortunately, they were 2/502 guys, doing the exact same thing we were. Due to Graves's unerring navigation, we'd hacked our way right into our linkup point with the '02. But what was most amazing was that neither group had heard or seen the other until that very moment, both so busily and loudly hacking away. It was just good luck all around that neither was VC.

But where *were* the VC? While Checkerboard proved successful in terms of disrupting the enemy's logistic system—VC tunnels were blown up, half-built VC villages were burned down, enormous quantities of rice, ammunition, and items such as VC black pajamas were uncovered and destroyed—the major purpose of the five-day mission, to find and destroy the VC unit that had mauled the 7th ARVN Regiment, was not met. In the biggest U.S. operation to date, with probably fifteen thousand troops beating the bushes, we failed to even find the enemy (that is, in large formations or numbers), much less destroy him. But where had he gone? He had to go somewhere. No doubt to his sanctuaries in Cambodia, or somewhere within the densely forested War Zone D, adjacent to the Cambodian border, or War Zone C, which led virtually to the gates of Saigon, or perhaps even under our very feet, in his vast tunnel complexes. So early in the war, the failure of Operation Checkerboard to find the enemy was ample illustration of the limitation of the Americans' large-scale, incredibly expensive multibattalion operations. They were simply no match for a cunning foe who lived by Mao's conviction, "Give me a path wide enough to move a mule and I will move an army."

Christmas came and went, and on 27 December Lieutenants Harry "The Horse" Godwin, Pat Graves, and John Dorland (another fine West Point stud) went over to 1/RAR in Bien Hoa, as John Essex-Clark and I had agreed. The three lieutenants commanded platoons in each of the 1/327's rifle companies; the plan was that they'd stay with the Aussies for a month, bring back to their companies their lessons learned, and if the program proved worthwhile, they would be followed by three more of our lieutenants. I hadn't exactly "cleared" this cross-training idea with Colonel Timothy. When I'd brought the subject up, he'd said he'd have to check with the people in Saigon, and within days word had come back that the concept was a "no go," the reason given that sending American troops, *particularly* troops from the 101st, America's finest, to the Aussies would be like admitting we didn't know what the hell we were doing. Since I thought the issue was a little more critical than MACV's potentially bruised pride, I'd then assessed the likelihood of being found out if I ignored the guidance and sent the lieutenants anyway. When I concluded the odds weighed heavily in my favor, I'd gone ahead. It was selective insubordination that I truly believed would benefit the whole battalion.

Although the 1st Brigade, 101st Airborne Division would continue to play fire brigade the rest of its first year in Vietnam, the days of Tim's Traveling Trouble were coming to an end. In early January, Colonel Timothy led the 2/327 and the 2/502 on his last operation with the brigade before moving on to Pleiku to become the II Corps senior adviser. The operation took the two battalions to the city of Tuy Hoa (one hundred miles to the north) and its rice paddies by the sea. In years past, 80 percent of the rice harvest there had been gobbled up by the Viet Cong; the mission of the brigade was, as it had been at Qui Nhon, to protect the farmers and their crop even as they found Charlie and kicked his ass. The 1/327 was left behind to secure the brigade's base camp, and to conduct operations in VC-controlled villages southwest of Phan Rang.

For us at Phan Rang, the month of January was pretty uneventful. The high point of all was when a Tiger Force medic, who also happened to be an American Indian, somehow missed an airmobile assault and, in the fine tradition of his forefathers, traveled overland alone through VC territory until he'd tracked down his unit in the middle of the jungle. Though the supply situation was improving all the time (by Christmas we'd been set up with most essentials through regular supply channels), the Above the Rest had well augmented its share through its enthusiastic scrounging effort, which was ongoing in the first month of 1966. But how far Hancock and friends had gone to upgrade our standard of living I don't think even I comprehended until Colonel Timothy's successor, Brigadier General Willard Pearson (whom few of us knew anything about except that he'd most recently been an assistant division commander in the 101st at Campbell) joined me in a chopper to have an orientation look at the base camp from the air a week or so before he took over the brigade.

We flew over the 2/327's area, and below us we saw a few dozen tents. Then we flew over the '02 Strike Force, which also had a few dozen tents. When we got over my battalion, which, thanks to Hancock and his merry men, had a GP tent for virtually every eleven-man squad, from the air it looked as if we had a million tents. "Where'd you get all those tents?" General Pearson asked. It was a logical question.

"We scrounged them, sir," I replied, praying that this unknown quantity of a commander-to-be was not going to be a strict book man. And General Pearson didn't say another word. My guess, as I looked down at my unit area with a mixture of heartfelt pride and great relief, was that the new commander didn't want to know. And it was true, he didn't. Pearson had no time for the small stuff: he had already moved on, pondering how his new command might get the VC even better.

15 THE YEAR OF THE HORSE

If you were encountering problems that he didn't think were problems, he'd call you on the radio and really chew your ass. He called me one afternoon and he wanted something done and I said, "Hey, we've already been at this for a couple of days and we're falling on our ass. We're tired." He said, "I don't give a damn what your problems are. You guys get moving." So I grumbled a bit and he said, "Look—if you don't think you can do it, put your second-in-command in charge."

Well, we went ahead and did it—as it turned out we were able to do just what he wanted us to do. He was the kind of guy who understood the necessity to drive people beyond what their normal capability might be. He made us all understand that combat is a battle of wills as much as it is a battle of physically doing in the enemy, and you've really got to be a stronger-willed fighter than he is if you eventually want to beat him. And he was able to impart that to his commanders very well. But sometimes he could be damn ruthless about doing it.

> Brigadier General John C. Herrling
> B Company Commander
> 1/327 Battalion, 101st Airborne Infantry
> Republic of Vietnam, 1966

On the twenty-first of January, the Vietnamese New Year—Tet—ushered in the Year of the Horse. Knowing nothing about the Chinese zodiac, I didn't know at the time that I'd actually been born under the sign of the Horse thirty-five years before; I didn't know either that the Year of the Horse, 1966, was going to be *my* year, the year I established myself once and for all in the big leagues. It happened just as I would have wanted it to—on the ground, in battle, with damn good troops; and by sheer coincidence, it all began on 7 February, fifteen years and one day after Sergeant Combat made *his* name on a frigid morning in Korea.

The 2/502 and 2/327 were heavily committed up at Tuy Hoa. Hank

Emerson's '02 was operating in a brigade-size AO; "the Gunfighter," as the Strike Force commander had been dubbed, had fights going all over the battlefield. He'd already committed his reserve when the morning of 7 February brought that one fight too many: elements of Emerson's C Company, commanded by Captain Robert Murphy, were pinned down and in danger of being flanked and destroyed by an NVA force of unknown size. The 1/327 had been called up from Phan Rang a couple of days before for just such a contingency; now new brigade commander Pearson said he wanted me to take a task force to relieve and reinforce Murphy. "You have the Tigers and Bravo Company," he said. "Now go get 'em."

I assembled a light CP group, which included the assistant battalion S-3, Don Chapman, our 2/320th Artillery LNO, Don Korman, myself, and all relevant RTOs, and hopped into a waiting chopper. We made contact with Murphy (who was mighty cheerful for a guy whose company was up against a force with what he estimated were at least a dozen machine guns), and after having a good look at the battle area, we selected LZs, coordinated fire support, and returned to Tuy Hoa, where I briefed Bravo's CO, Al Hiser, and Tiger commander Jim Gardner on the plan.

Murphy's company was stuck in the northwest corner of the bombed-out ruins of a village called My Canh 2. My idea was to have the Tigers come up on the surrounded unit's flank, while B Company swung around to the south and set up a blocking position deep behind the enemy. After tac air and artillery preparation, the Tigers would hit the enemy and roll up their flank; I figured at that point the enemy would break contact and run, only to get caught in the trap I'd set behind them with Bravo Company.

The Tigers led the way out and I went with them. We landed at an LZ quite close to the battle area. The men spread out and moved like old pros through waist-high grass. I, on the other hand, was walking on air. I felt like a bit player at M-G-M might feel, after years and years and years of hard work, seeing his name above the title of the movie, or in lights on a theater marquee. Ever since I'd arrived in Vietnam—now some eight months ago—I'd lived for the prospect of another combat command. Hell, I'd been dreaming of another combat command since 1953. And then to get one as a major, *and* with the Tigers (whom I'd secretly considered "my boys" since the creation of the elite force), was the greatest break I could have asked for.

We guided on the sound of Murphy's firefight. C Company's commander was also putting max tac air and artillery on the enemy surrounding him, but it wasn't doing much good—the enemy soldiers were belly-to-belly with Murphy's men, and to close them down effectively would have resulted in a hell of a lot of friendly casualties as well. We moved forward continuously, killing as we went about ten enemy stragglers who'd been dumb enough to take potshots at the Tigers. These men were dyed-in-the-wool NVA troops complete with khaki uniforms and armed with AK47s—upon examination, members of the elite 95th NVA Regiment, the unit known to be operating in this area, whose activities during the Indochina war had given the bloody Street Without Joy its name. They were probably the most formidable enemy fighters in South Vietnam. "Do I get the CIB now?" Don Chapman, who was hiking along behind me, asked only half-jokingly each time an enemy shot rang out. "No, Chapman, not yet," I'd reply, having a quiet chuckle, remembering what that blue badge meant to me when I went through my much-longed-for baptism of fire.

We reached a small knob by a river, across which we could see Murphy's people lying on the ground around the foundations of blown-away houses. I wasn't satisfied with the update Murphy now gave me by radio, so I took advantage of a bamboo bridge that crossed the river very close to our little knob and went over to the village to see what was happening myself. Unfortunately, a wide-open field about fifty meters long lay between the far side of the bridge and Murphy's position, so when Darryl Nunnelly, my longtime RTO (who had to accompany me lugging his bulky PRC-25 radio) and I dashed across the bridge, we became shooting-gallery ducks for some very professional marksmen armed with automatic weapons.

After crawling around the battle area a little bit, talking to Murphy, and eyeballing the situation as he saw it on his side of the river, Darryl and I ran back across the field and the bridge, unscathed despite the enemy machine guns, which fired as enthusiastically at our backs as they had at our chests, arms, legs, and heads on the way over. My original plan still held. After telling Gardner what I knew about the location of enemy positions in a hedgerow to our front, I ordered the Tigers to strike the enemy's flank and roll it up, in order to unpin Murphy and send the NVA scurrying into Bravo's waiting ambush. It was a neat, clean "hammer and anvil," right out of Fort Benning. With that I gathered Korman, Chapman, Nunnelly, and the rest of the CP group, and with the Tigers behind us providing effective covering fire, we hightailed across the bridge. Korman, who was the best artilleryman I'd seen since Allan Bell in Korea, neutralized the fire-swept open field on the far side with smoke and HE arty shot, and though the run was a little hairy, the shortcut saved us valuable time.

"Do I get the CIB now?" Chapman panted when the CP group arrived intact at Murphy's position.

"No, Chapman, not yet," I said, and directed my guys to dig in fast and deep: automatic weapons were stitching all over the area. We set up in the rubble of a bombed-out building, and while Korman put together his artillery fire plan and Darryl and the other RTOs started digging a foxhole large enough to hold the entire CP group (a trick I'd learned from Colonel Johns's *Clay Pigeons of St. Lo*), I took Chapman with me on a little mosey around the battle area. We crawled through the rubble of a couple of buildings, then crawled on through a ditch along a paddy dike. Suddenly an NVA soldier popped up in front of us, out of a hole he'd burrowed into the side of the dike. He was a little above us as the three of us started shooting, but we hit him first and all his slugs went high, right over our heads. "Do I get the CIB now?" Chapman asked dryly.

"You got it, man." I laughed.

The first thing I saw when we got back to our command post was Darryl setting up his 292 (two-niner-two) antenna, a heavy, unwieldy son of a bitch to carry around but worth every pound and more in terms of the best possible commo. Then I saw Korman talking on the radio. Then I saw the Tigers on the attack—and I couldn't believe my eyes. Gardner and his people were walking across the open field between the bridge and Murphy's position. They'd forded the river (many of them were soaked to the neck), and now they were marching straight across that field in a perfect skirmish line, like Pickett's division at Gettysburg. I was stunned. I'd given Gardner a mission-type order. I didn't tell him how to do it. He was one of the best and most experienced lieutenants in the battalion, so I'd just assumed he would take the well-concealed approach to My Canh—quite obvious from the knob where he'd begun—along a dry streambed on his flank. Now it was too late for him to turn around, and there was no way to stop him; all the '02 guys in the village could do was start putting as much suppressive fire as they could on the face of the hedgerow to Gardner's front, to keep the enemy down. Incredibly, the Tigers were taking no casualties as they advanced toward My Canh. In fact, it seemed as though they weren't even being fired on. But then, about twenty meters from our position, with one step they walked into a wall of lead.

Our opponent was indeed a force to be reckoned with. The discipline of this element of the 95th NVA, so skillfully dug in and camouflaged along their hedgerow wall, was iron-tight. Not one shot had been fired prematurely, and when they did open up, they mowed my Tigers down from end to end across that open field. Those who survived immediately charged the tree line through the fire (an act that took courage beyond words), and from that moment on, for both Tigers and members of C2/502, it was bloody hand-to-hand with the enemy all the way.

I watched from my tac CP forty yards away. It was like a 3-D movie—a collage of khaki, green, and scarlet red—and wholly outside my experience. This wasn't guerrilla warfare as I had studied it. Not even the French had encountered this enemy tactic of hugging the belt, as it would become known, rendering any U.S. air or arty support useless. I'd read Hal Moore's Ia Drang after-action report, but I'd never seen with my eyes our Viet enemy voluntarily intermingle with American troops. I'd never seen him stand and fight. It quickly became clear that he wasn't going to fall into the trap I'd set for him with Bravo Company, so I called Hiser and told him to punch through the enemy's rear.

The dug-in NVA had numerous heavily reinforced machine-gun positions at My Canh, but one in particular, about a hundred meters from our CP, was causing problems. That machine gun had one of my elements stopped. As I talked to the tac-air forward air controller about closing it down, an Australian voice came through the radio: "I've got a Canberra light bomber here with two-hundred-fifty-pound delays on board. Can you use them?"

"Are you real accurate?" I asked.

"I reckon," the Aussie pilot said.

I told him the situation and where the bunker was, popping a smoke for reference. When he did a dry run to have a look at the bunker himself, his twin-engine bomber flew in so low I almost could have reached up from my hole and touched it.

"I see it," the pilot's voice came through the radio as he pulled his plane up. "This'll be a live run, so tell your chaps to get their heads down."

I watched the first bomb being released. It came in on an angle, and as it zoomed over our hole it looked as if it was no more than a few feet away. On delay, it sank into the ground not far from the targeted bunker and exploded with an earthshaking *bwoom*. After examining the damage, I asked the pilot if he could shift the next run three meters to the right.

One by one, all the Canberra's bombs were dropped onto this single target. The pilot's accuracy was incredible; he was able to carry out every adjustment I made precisely, no matter how small. We never did get a direct hit on the bunker, but close enough that even the most hardcore NVA inside would have been battle-rattled into submission, if not unconsciousness.

"How was that, mate?" the pilot asked when the last of his ordnance was expended.

"Great, man, you saved our ass. Thanks a lot."

"Good hunting and good luck," he said, and flew away.

"Okay, let's see if we can clean up that position now," I said to my held-up element. The men started toward the position, but—*rat-tat-tat-tat*—the minute they stuck their heads up, they felt the fury of the exact same machine gun from the exact same bunker.

It was a bolt from the sky. We were all being told—even the President was being told—that our combat power, unleashed on the enemy, would either blast him back to the Stone Age or make him give up. We were being told that our air power would, ultimately, be the magic panacea to cure Vietnam of all its Communist ills. But if we on the ground were using it as precisely (and as excessively, some might say) as I'd just done on one tiny position and it wasn't doing the job, then what the hell good was all the saturation bombing in North Vietnam? Air power was great if you caught the enemy out in the open. But if he was fighting from well-dug-in positions as these cats were at My Canh, and if the fortified positions were manned by hardcore mothers who didn't give up even after their eardrums had burst from the concussion of our bombs and blood was pouring out of their noses and their ears, then the exercise was almost counterproductive. All it did was make the enemy hate us even more, and become that much more determined. So it was a mighty lesson learned in that split-second machine-gun burst from a primitive mud-and-log and well-shook-up bunker at My Canh: whatever the answer to this war was I certainly didn't know, but one thing I could confidently say was that bombing alone would never be it.

By now the afternoon sun was waning. I was damned anxious; we had no semblance of a perimeter, and with no luck in knocking out the most lethal of the NVA positions, with dark on its way I was really worried about medevac and resupply. Throughout the day, through trial and error, we'd discovered a way to bring helicopters in without subjecting them to direct enemy fire. What concerned me now was that dark would prevent the critical accuracy required on the pilots' parts in maneuvers like "Go back one klick [kilometer] and get on the deck, come in on the deck at 182 degrees, and when you see a smoke in front of your nose, flare back and land right on top of it." (And the final warning: "Don't go beyond that smoke, or you're gonna find two antiaircraft machine guns firing right down your throat.") I was also terribly worried about getting the men set up for the night. While B Company had run into some heavy fighting and broken off their attack, the Tigers and Murphy's men were still in the thick of it, with the Tigers being held up in a trench by four machine guns. As daylight grew shorter, so did my patience with my boys. "Goddamn it, Jim," I yelled at Gardner on the radio, "get those positions cleaned out right now. No more fucking around, do you understand? It's getting dark. Knock out those guns, and I mean now!"

I was not in a position to see what happened next, but as the story was related to me by Dennis Foley, Gardner's XO, Jim made my words his personal mission. He took as many grenades as he could carry in his shirt and started running up the trench by himself. Slugs were snapping all around him as he ran to the first machine-gun bunker; he threw himself against it below the hole, pulled the pin on one of his grenades, and threw it in. As the grenade went off and the machine gun in the bunker went limp, Gardner moved on to the next position. He repeated the drill, only this time someone inside the bunker threw the grenade out of the hole, in front of him. Jim was hit as it went off, but he just took another grenade, threw it into the hole, and permanently closed down the gun inside. To the astonishment of his men, he pushed on to the third bunker, an antiaircraft position that contained a machine gun mounted on a tripod. The Tiger CO destroyed that gun, too, with another grenade, and then burned an X across the aperture of the bunker with his rifle to make sure there was no one left alive inside. But this moment proved his downfall: simultaneously, an enemy machine gun in yet another position took him under fire, and hit him four times across the chest. Jim reportedly turned around and said, "It's the best I can do," and then he dropped, KIA.

The Medal of Honor Jim Gardner would receive posthumously for his heroic stand, like the belief (expressed to me by a couple of his men) that he'd made his charge to absolve himself for the deaths of his recon troops by that short mortar round three months before, was little consolation. For all our partying as equals, and for all his scrounging escapades where my seniority meant nothing except that I'd keep him out of trouble, Gardner and all the other young officers who were my friends never forgot that I was their commander, that when I said "Jump" I might mean to the moon and I'd expect it done with no questions asked. They performed because they trusted and respected me, and they knew I wouldn't ask them to do what I wouldn't do or hadn't done myself. But when someone dies for you, as Jim Gardner died for me (a fact I repressed for many years), it's the worst of all crosses a combat leader has to bear.

Gardner's courageous bunker-busting did not unpin the Tigers, and I needed them to break contact and link up with Murphy's people. It was the only way we could set up a defensive perimeter before dark. I moved as close to them as I could (which still left us separated by a fairly open space in the village), and got Dennis Foley on the horn. "You're in charge," I said. "I want you to collect your guys and get out of there. I'm right across from you. We'll lay down covering fire and a lot of arty. When it comes in, haul ass over here to my position."

The brave Tigers dodged and weaved their way across that open space under heavy fire, and arrived, miraculously, 100 percent intact. When Dennis joined us, Darryl and I were lying behind a blown-down coconut tree, on the other side of which a whole bunch of pigs were frantically running around. While we remained sheltered from the steel cyclone going on just over our heads, from time to time we'd hear a loud squeal as one of the pigs got caught in the cross fire. One pig had the good sense to hide on our side, but then, when we suddenly got an intense amount of small-arms fire, the pig stuck its head up and got blown away. Insufficient training. Meanwhile Foley took a slug through his helmet; it came out the front, not touching him but knocking one of the arms off his glasses. It was the second time he'd been hit like that since the battle began. The first had been during the Tigers' initial attack, when he'd taken a slug in the back that actually went right through his jacket and equipment, missing his body entirely. The boy had luck.

I'd been talking down choppers all afternoon with great success. One of the most recent lifts had carried a magazine reporter who jumped out of the bird in a yellow short-sleeved shirt and baseball cap and dashed over to our fallen coconut tree. "Hi!" he chirped. "Where's all the action?"

I pointed straight up and went back to fighting the battle. A short time later I noticed the reporter was poking his head over the log, taking a few photographs and coming back down. "Hey, Mr. Reporter," I said, "that's not a very cool thing to do. Stick your camera up and take pictures, but not your head, or it'll be good-bye, Clark Kent." Not five minutes later I looked over again, only to see one very dead reporter—he'd taken a slug between the eyes.

I'd just finished telling a couple of Tigers to stack the reporter's body with the rest of our dead when the voice of an unknown chopper pilot came up on the radio. "Savvy Volley 5," he said (addressing me by my call sign), "this is Outlaw 5-3. Inbound. Resupply and PAX [passengers]. Mark LZ. Over."

"Outlaw 5-3, this is Savvy Volley 5. Look, it's really hot down here, so I'm going to tell you how to get in."

I started giving the pilot my detailed instructions, but almost immediately he interrupted me. "Savvy Volley 5, just tell me where you want me. Don't tell me how to do it, okay? I think I'm a little more qualified than you in this job."

"Look, buddy," I snapped, "this is a bad, bad LZ here. Come in a certain way or you'll be blown out of the sky."

"I say again: if you want these supplies, just mark your LZ."

"Roger on that," I said, and popped a smoke.

It was like watching a movie in slow motion. First the ship was coming in. Then the ship was being stitched, as greenish-blue NVA tracers burst out of the dusk-darkened hedgerow on both flanks. Then the ship was losing control. It was quietly beautiful and, in a way, exceptionally funny to see it spin out and crash on the deck. I sent an element over to retrieve the supplies and the freshly wounded. No one was badly hurt, though Doug Holtz, who was kicking out the supplies as the battalion's support platoon leader, got an easy Purple Heart when a bullet zinged across his ass. Holtz was another lucky guy: this was his fourth Purple Heart and he'd never received more than a scratch. The worst casualty in the incident was the chopper itself: $300,000 worth of lift destroyed with a couple of nine-cent bullets and the help of a smart-ass pilot who knew it all.

As night fell we buttoned up. I had Bravo Company set up a perimeter on the outskirts of the village, and the Tigers and C2/502 set up the best perimeter they could in the village itself. We brought in mortars and dug in deep, concentrating our efforts on blocking the enemy's withdrawal routes, mostly with artillery. Enemy dead were strewn all over the area; while I was sick in my heart over the Tiger casualties, at least we, not the enemy, held the village of My Canh.

Then Al Hiser called me with his casualty figures. Nineteen KIA, he said. A score of wounded. I felt as if I'd been slugged in the gut with a sledgehammer. "What?" I asked—I didn't believe him. He repeated the figures, and tears sprang to my eyes. All told, the battle had claimed the lives of twenty-six of my men and wounded twenty-eight. It was a terrible price, in no way justified by the sixty-six NVA bodies and twenty-odd Chinese-made crew-served and individual weapons we found the next morning, or the fact that we were the proud possessors of this demolished village, which we'd soon pull out of anyway.

The casualty figures sickened me even more as the story of Bravo's fight unfolded. Hiser had launched his attack just as the Tigers had—across a wide-open field. His 2d Platoon had been mowed down. The whole thing was just a shining example of bad, bad training. At the Infantry School they taught "always use a concealed avenue of approach," but these were just words, taught mainly in a classroom, when on the training field, troops learned that all they had to do was *get there first* (and damn how they did it) to be declared King of the Mountain by an umpire who knew no better himself. I'd seen it with my own eyes at Campbell, and now the chickens had come home to roost. At fault, too, perhaps, were the habits Gardner and Hiser had brought to My Canh: Gardner's formed in the open rice paddies of Qui Nhon (where our opponent had been skillful, but in the final analysis he'd still been a local guerrilla), and Hiser's from the superaggressive 173d. In their eagerness to cross swords with the NVA, perhaps neither man had realized how tough the big leagues could be.[*]

---

[*] Tiger XO Dennis Foley shed additional light on his unit's tragic maneuver. Apparently the choice not to take the concealed avenue of approach along the dry streambed had been made after a quick recon revealed that thick, six-foot grass—excellent concealment—was growing out from the riverbank for some distance. Gardner had acted on the assumption that this grass would provide a concealed avenue of approach all the way to his destination on the enemy's flank at My Canh.

As for my own mistakes at My Canh, as yet I wasn't sure, and it would take a lot of thought and another good battle before I would be. For now, all I knew was our losses were far too heavy to claim "victory" (although that was how the newspeople and higher headquarters would describe the battle, with the price in U.S. lives only "moderate"). The fact was we'd been sucked in and eaten alive. We had attacked machine guns as the British and the French had in WW I, and I was heartsick at the result.

Task Force Hackworth was disbanded when Colonel Rogers and the battalion staff flew into My Canh the next afternoon. (After a first-light artillery and tac-air strike, the remnants of Bravo Company had entered My Canh unopposed that morning, the NVA having run away throughout the night to fight another day.) I couldn't have been happier to see Doc Raphiel Benjamin, the battalion surgeon, hop out of that chopper. He was the one person I knew I could talk to about the tragic events of the day before.

Raphiel was my friend. The good doctor had volunteered for the 1/101 to get out of a boring job with the 70th Engineer Battalion, and we'd hit it off from the first day he joined the 1/327. We'd started out sharing meals (Raphiel would take his, all the medics', Darryl's, and my C rations plus whatever else he could scrounge and cook up big delicious stews); before long I'd started sacking out on one of the stretchers in his aid station, and at night when there were blackout conditions and we couldn't read, we'd just bullshit across the tent until we fell asleep.

Tall and thin enough to stand between raindrops, Raphiel hailed from Baton Rouge, Louisiana. At twenty-seven, he'd been drafted into the Army right out of medical school, leaving behind his wife, Karen, and two small sons. He was a brilliant doc, brave and caring and well loved by the troops; he was an unflappable kind of guy, who, as a civilian, found that the hardest part of the soldier's life was having to live like an animal for months on end. From the Korea days I didn't even think twice about living like an animal, or how uncomfortable or unpleasant it might be for the troops, who'd never had to do it before. Raphiel, who'd sing his little blues song about drinking muddy water and sleeping in a hollow log, did a lot for my awareness that way, opening my eyes to things I'd stopped noticing, and he became one of the great teachers of my life, about things I'd never noticed at all.

And now he would be my sounding board for the disheartening events that had taken place at My Canh the day before. But that night, just as we started talking, a firefight broke out on the east side of the perimeter, complete with flares, grenades, and blazing rifles. We ran over there. "Hold your fire," I shouted over the din. "Hold that fire!" The leaders along the perimeter heard me and took up the call. Before long the weapons were silent. "All right, what's happening here?"

"There was a lot of firing at our outpost, sir," Johnny Adams, the 4.2-mortar platoon leader, reported. "Then there was firing into our perimeter, so we fired back."

I called out to the two men on the outpost, but there was no reply. Raphiel and I headed into the night.

We snaked our way out of the perimeter until we came upon the OP. It had been overrun, and a still-lit cigarette glowing in the darkness beside two very still bodies explained how. For me, it was 11 November 1952 all over again.

The two men were still alive, if only barely. After spraying the area and flipping a couple of grenades, I took one of the guys by the legs while Raphiel tried to grab the same one under his arms to take him back to our position. But the doc's hand kept slipping away—one of the guy's arms had been blown off at the shoulder. Raphiel got hold of him somehow, and we rushed back to the perimeter, yelling our names to prevent being knocked off by our own people. We put the first guy into Doc Benjamin's tiny hex-tent foxhole/surgery and the good doctor went right to work. But it proved to be a losing battle. Just as one of the medics got back from the OP with the second casualty, Raphiel shook his head. "No," he said, "I've lost this motherfucker. Pass me the other one." We put the second body down, but it was too late. He was already dead. "Shit," said Raphiel. "Shit, shit, shit."

My eyes stung. Raphiel, unlike myself, was not prone to using profanity. He probably wouldn't have called a dead patient a "motherfucker" back home in Louisiana.* But back home in Louisiana he wouldn't have been living like an animal either, or trying to save lives by flashlight in a muddy hole in the dark of night.

Johnny Howard took an M-79 and, alone, started out into the darkness to see if he could find anything. He fired at some movement but couldn't see the result; though we didn't find a body in the morning, some bloodied gear on the ground nearby was evidence at least that Johnny had hit home. Meanwhile, I let the word go forth that at first light every leader was to take his men out to that OP to have a firsthand look at that cigarette and the blood of those two dead men in that foxhole. Furthermore, I said that anyone who smoked between seven in the evening and seven in the morning—on the line, in the base camp, even on R&R in Hong Kong—might as well get his ass out of the battalion, because if I caught him he'd spend the rest of his tour with a split lip and two black eyes, courtesy of my fists.

* On the other hand, in the Airborne, the term "motherfucker," unless spoken harshly, was among the highest terms of endearment.

Operations in the Tuy Hoa area continued. Task Force Hackworth was reestablished for one independent mission when Colonel Rogers wanted a little extra experience on the team, and with Abu Company, a platoon of Tigers, and a little CP group, I eagerly moved out into the unknown.

We infiltrated into our AO by stealth, moving out of the battalion's temporary fire base on foot and at night. Choppers would have gotten us there a hell of a lot faster, but they made enough noise to virtually guarantee there'd be nothing to get when we got there: any enemy within five miles would say, "Yanks come, we run away," and be gone before we even set down.

The operation was five days in length. At the outset I made a rule that for the duration there'd be no resupply aircraft buzzing around dropping in hot food or ice cream or beer, and no commo with higher HQ either, except a daily report via Darryl's radio and two-niner-two antenna. The kids weren't shook by the new ground rules at all. They sneaked through the forest like a silent pack of Daniel Boones, all of them so much into the spirit of things that even the wounded didn't bitch; they just hobbled along on their sprained ankles, knowing the pain could be lived with and there was something more important going on. ("Look, man," I'd explained, "we're here sneaking up on the enemy and we're not giving our position away. Sure you've got a little scratch. You don't see any helicopters evacuating the NVA out, do you? What do they do? They stick with their outfit and walk and heal up. They're hardcore. But *you're* hardcore, too.") Why the troops took so easily to the on-the-job-training (OJT) guerrilla game was probably partly because it was different, partly because it was fun, and partly because they knew we really were right on the NVA's tail. Signs were everywhere—recent camps, recently used trails, broken branches. Meanwhile, for the first time since I'd arrived in Vietnam, I was having my own opportunity to *feel* the deceptively quiet battlefield, and the enemy's presence therein. I became convinced, for example, that when a U.S. unit was in the bush in an enemy AO, it was always followed by an enemy recon element, maybe just two or three men, whose whole purpose was to watch, work out the mission, look for weaknesses, and then report back to their parent outfit. So one morning I had my CP group fill an empty case of C rations with dirt (for weight), restrap it with its original wire (to make it look unopened), and then bury it with a live frag grenade underneath. We moved out, and not twenty minutes after we'd left that night position, *BAM*. I sent an element back and they found the booby trap had killed two VC. This technique became standard practice. Until now, with good reason the enemy had considered the wasteful Americans a principal supplier of ammo and raw materials for his own booby traps and mines. Having our units police up, bury, and booby-trap everything the Viet Cong would otherwise have scrounged gave the enemy a much-deserved taste of his own medicine and our troopers a hell of a lot of satisfaction. Another technique that evolved from this was to have an ambush element stay back in our vacated night positions. Fifty percent of the time they drew blood.

As my task force crept on, I could feel we were on the edge of a great fight. The adrenaline was pumping; with each more careful step I knew we were getting closer. Then, after so many of my troops had braved their minor wounds without even a whimper (or at least one I heard), my own operations sergeant got sick. Sick-sick, like he was going to die, according to the doc, who was the senior aid man and a top medic.

Thanks to Raphiel Benjamin, I thought I knew quite a bit about diagnostics and field medicine. I felt particularly savvy about hepatitis and gonorrhea; these, along with malaria, were the most common complaints voiced by the scores of battalion members who wandered through the doc's tent in the middle of the night while I tried to sleep on the other stretcher. For suspected hepatitis cases, Raphiel always stuck his hand under the trooper's rib cage to see if his liver was hard. For gonorrhea he'd just say, "Reel it out and let me have a look," and then if things looked drippy he'd tell the guy to come back in the morning for a shot of penicillin. It seemed pretty straightforward, and I was sure a little of Doc Benjamin had to have rubbed off on me by now, so I got the operations sergeant to lie on the ground and, having ruled out clap from the outset, put my hand under his rib cage as I'd seen Raphiel do a million times. Though I had nothing to compare it with, the patient's liver felt pretty hard, and since he was moaning, I concluded he had hepatitis. It broke my heart to blow our cover and call in a medevac (our prey would undoubtedly fly the coop the minute the chopper blades whirred), but I wasn't going to let the guy die out there. While some of the men started cutting out an LZ, I took a piece of cardboard from a C-ration box and wrote a note to Raphiel. "To Doc Benjamin, Battalion Surgeon. I'm referring this patient to you because, in my opinion, he suffers from acute hepatitis. Please have a look at him. I will be interested to know what your conclusion is. Sincerely, David Hackworth, Forward Doctor." I gave the tag to the sick sergeant and he was flown out.

Sure enough, our elusive enemy disappeared entirely, and we came back to the fire base the next day empty-handed. That disappointment, however, was nothing compared to the news I got when I went to Raphiel to check on my patient. "About that diagnosis," he said. "He had pneumonia. Good try."

Deciding from that moment to give up medicine and concentrate on soldiering, I used the Tuy Hoa mission to think through our tactics, and to try to find a way to fight the enemy without paying such a heavy price in casualties. For me, it was just a question of synthesizing all the ideas and input I'd received from my reading (notably *Street Without Joy*, by the French on-the-ground scholar of the Indochina war, Bernard Fall), my mentors (especially the Special Forces guys I'd met at the Career Course), and my own growing experience. Colonel Rogers was open to suggestions, and we began to experiment in the battalion. It became virtually SOP to infiltrate company-size units into the bush during the night, for example. These units would form small company perimeters and radiate patrols out from there, to comb the bush for unsuspecting enemy troops. We began practicing what the Australians preached, and what Hank Emerson, the bold, forward-thinking Gunfighter, had been doing successfully in the '02 since Lai Khe: finding the enemy not with unwieldy company-size formations, but with small patrols fanning out in all directions of the battlefield (with backup elements available to reinforce—"pile on," as Emerson would say—if a contact was made), taking the risk and wearing the consequences of seven-man patrols possibly being gobbled up in the search. It was at night that the value of these decentralized, company-controlled operations became most clear. At the end of each day, these small teams became individual ambush patrols spread out all over the battle area. Besides regularly drawing blood, the nighttime patrols continuously allowed us to interdict the enemy's ingress-egress routes—in essence, to take the battlefield away from our foe. Again and again they proved what the Raiders had proved in Korea, that small units with capable leaders can make a significant, even vital contribution. Still, at first it was not easy to sell our young leaders on the new techniques, or even on the adoption of the "scouts well forward" Australian way of moving through the bush, which reduced the risk of an entire unit getting wrapped around the axle. Right after My Canh everyone was running scared, and while naturally they settled down, never again did I sense the "let's go get the bad guys" enthusiasm I had seen before that bloody fight. As Operation Gibraltar had for the 2/502, 7 February woke everyone up in the 1/327 to the reality of war. Slowly the men began to understand a little more about their enemy and to respond in kind. Slowly they began to develop patience, that VC strong point, that characteristic that gave the enemy the inner resources to collect, flatten and tack together empty beer cans, one onto the next and the next, like shingles, until he'd made a metal roof.

"I think you better get back here soonest," Ben Willis said, calling me from the battalion's temporary base camp at Tuy Hoa. "Something's come up."

He couldn't have sounded any more cryptic, and it was so unlike Ben that I took him at his word. Fortunately, things were quiet out in the field and I could easily get away, so I grabbed Darryl and as soon as we could we hitched a chopper ride back to Tuy Hoa.

Ben met us at the airstrip. "You'll never guess who's here," he said. "Miss Vinh."

"Who's Miss Vinh?"

"She said she knows you from Nha Trang. Heard you were here and flew up by civilian aircraft." (In one of the more bizarre aspects of the war, Air Vietnam, a commercial airline, operated virtually unimpeded throughout the fighting, taking off and landing on the same strips as our fighter aircraft, with few destinations off limits, whatever was happening on the ground.)

We walked into the airline terminal and there she was, looking absolutely beautiful with her long, black hair, in her sexy *au dai*. I knew Miss Vinh. She was the sister of the equally beautiful Vietnamese nurse I'd met when I was in the hospital at Nha Trang, who'd taken it upon herself to look after me after I got out of the hospital but before I returned to my battalion. The nurse worked during the day, so it had been left to Miss Vinh to provide half of the tender loving care I received in the quiet little house she shared with her sister in the city. Though we had had no contact—no letters, no nothing—in the three months since I'd left, she'd heard the 101st was in Tuy Hoa, and with the innocent faith that so many of the Vietnamese had, she figured if the 101st was there, I'd be there, too, and we'd be able to get together.

It had been a long, long time since I'd seen a woman. At least it felt that way. I couldn't even think. "Where are we going to stay, Ben? I can't take her back to the battalion area. What about the city?"

"You don't want to go there, man," Willis said. "It's all VC!"

But in the end there wasn't any choice. VC or no VC, Tuy Hoa was the only place around. So we did a quick recon, found a hotel with an empty top floor, and while Willis and the girl organized the accommodation end of things, ever-resourceful Darryl started outfitting the room with commo equipment. Young, married, moral, poor Darryl—all the stuff he had to put up with from me. Still, after he finished setting up my PRC-25 radio and organizing a couple of extra batteries for it (so I could stay in constant contact with the battalion in the field and with Willis' rear CP), and Ben provided a box of hand grenades and plenty of ammo for my M-16 and M-79 (at the same time promising to pull me out of a jam if necessary), the two of them left me and Miss Vinh in peace. And for a couple of days of bliss overlooking the South China Sea, I gave instructions to the battalion staff as necessary through the radio, and Ben covered for me when Colonel Rogers asked where I was. It was not a bad way to fight a war.

No sooner had I said good-bye to Miss Vinh and made arrangements to go back to the field than General Pearson came looking for me. "Do you have people down with the Aussies?" he asked, right out, in such a way that it was kind of hard to evade, avoid, or change the subject.

"Mmm," I said.

I did have people down with the Aussies—our third group, in fact. Graves, Dorland, and Godwin, the first group, had come back with a much better handle on the war (or so I felt), so I'd continued the program, was damn happy with it, and until Pearson confronted me, no one had been the wiser. Now, since I had to confess anyway, I asked General Pearson how he'd found out. It seemed that it was all due to Pat Graves, who, in his usual self-effacing and matter-of-fact way, had neglected to tell me that while with the Aussies he'd had occasion to take over the platoon he'd been observing when the Australian platoon leader was hit. Apparently he'd performed most heroically, the result of which being the Australians sending a commendation for him to MACV, which had reportedly landed on the desk of none other than General Westmoreland, the man who'd vetoed the plan to send men to 1/RAR in the first place.

Pat Graves really was the best and the brightest. He was the ultimate West Point officer, a six-feet-tall, straight-as-a-die romantic from Alabama, who believed passionately in America and his fellow man. Firm in the conviction that we were embarked upon a noble cause, Pat had volunteered from the 1/506 Battalion at Campbell to join the 1st Brigade when word came we'd be going to Vietnam. Compassionate and dedicated, in the field he'd proved to be one of the best platoon leaders the 1/327 had. Throughout his first tour Pat kept a diary of his experiences, and he also wrote a piece called "Observations of a Platoon Leader," with the hope that he could give the young officers who followed in his footsteps in Vietnam a head start, with pointers Pat would have liked to have known before he arrived. The piece was used at the Screaming Eagles' replacement camp at Bien Hoa as well as by West Point's tactical department and the Infantry School; later Pat would expand it into a three-part series, which would be published in *Infantry* magazine and then Army-wide, as a DA pamphlet. This was a real coup for a young lieutenant, and in the career stakes really put Pat "above the rest."

Even so, this fine platoon leader now had me in hot water. General Pearson really locked my heels together for disobeying Westy's original directive to Colonel Timothy, and I had no choice but to suspend the 1/327's "Aussie connection" for the rest of my tour. But while the whole thing then blew over, to me an irony remained: I was told Westy had deep-sixed the cross-training idea because it wouldn't have looked good from a public-relations angle to have the Australians nursing the Screaming

Eagles along. But from a public-relations angle, what could have been more perfect than to have a 101 guy picking up the chips for the beleaguered Aussies?

The people of Tuy Hoa successfully completed their rice harvest, and the 1/101 turned its attention to the jungles and mountains in the surrounding area. The next ten days or so were singularly uneventful, until the morning of 4 March, when I saw an old Viet gentleman walking toward the 1/327's battalion perimeter. Australian John Essex-Clark always said that the Americans put too much stock in electronic intelligence gathering rather than feeling the pulse on the ground, so I told our S-2, Lieutenant Jerry Nakashima, to go talk to the guy and see if he knew anything.

The old man told Jerry he'd just seen "men from the North" wearing khaki and carrying "long stovepipes" moving toward the village of Thanh Phu. The only reasonable interpretation of this was that a North Vietnamese unit carrying large mortars was setting up in a village to our southwest, but the question then was whether the old Viet was for real or a setup—a VC supporter, or perhaps just an innocent old man whose family was being held hostage by the NVA—to lead us into a trap. In either case, this kind of "volunteered" information was a typical enemy ploy, and in assessing it, the only thing I had going for me was my instinct and the quaint way the Viet described what he'd seen to make me feel he was telling the truth.

I gave Colonel Rogers the intelligence and the circumstances in which we got it. He swung A and B companies, which were just returning home from another operation, toward Thanh Phu on separate axes, and by the time we'd organized our tac CPs (the Colonel decided to tag along with the Abus while I went with B Company), Bravo had already made contact just outside the village hamlet of My Phu.

The subsequent fighting in and around My Phu was vicious. What seemed at first to be light fire from a squad-size enemy element within a short time became heavy automatic-weapons fire from an enemy force of two to three companies. For a moment it seemed we'd been lured in: the enemy was fighting from well-dug and fortified positions just as they had at My Canh. But all was not as it appeared. When I landed in the middle of B Company's fight, one of the first things I saw was an NVA company running around like headless chickens. We'd caught them on the move, a fact confirmed later in the day by a POW (who added that the NVA unit's intention had been to set up mortar positions to blast our fire base while hitting us with a three-company ground attack). The old Viet man had been right.

B Company was fully engaged, kicking ass but also taking casualties. Even though they'd been surprised, the NVA's SOP when on the move, to always have pre-dug defensive positions for just such a contingency, diminished our initial advantage. One of Bravo's medics took a slug in the back of his head. Raphiel, who was on the ground treating the wounded the whole time, didn't think he'd make it but felt it was worth a try, and together we dragged the medic along the ground in a poncho to a safer spot. ("Safer" in this fight was relative: across the battle area you couldn't lift your head without drawing fire.) I called for a medevac and instantly a chopper was on the scene, its pilot asking for landing instructions. "Look, it's really hot down here," I told him. "You're going to have to volunteer for this one 'cause you may not make it out."

"Just tell me how to do it," he replied.

I told him what I thought the best route would be, and the pilot followed my instructions to the letter. As the chopper landed, Raphiel and I rushed the wounded medic to the open door. The chopper crew chief grabbed him and pulled him inside. Slugs were buzzing and snapping around the chopper like flies in a slaughterhouse as I turned to thank the pilot. Only then did I find this was no ordinary airplane driver, but Major Dave George, a dear old 8th Div friend of mine and rival from the Fort Benning Career Course days.

We shook hands and started catching up on old times over the din of his helicopter, completely forgetting we were on the battlefield. It was probably the only reason neither of us got hit. "You've won me for life, stud," I told him as he prepared to carry the wounded away; it was the first of many medevac runs that good man and his brave crew would make to My Phu.

Enemy dead were strewn all over the hamlet. Hiser and the men of Bravo had learned well at My Canh: at My Phu they did not assault fixed positions. Instead, they hunkered down and let firepower dig the enemy out. Still, in the wake of their casualties and in the fog of battle, I wasn't sure who had the upper hand. All that changed when I saw one young black trooper firing like fury down a wide ditch with an M-79. I raced over there to see that he'd killed some thirty NVA soldiers single-handedly. Such carnage on so small a section of the battlefield was a picture that said everything to me— suddenly I *knew* we had a solid victory on our hands.

Meanwhile A Company had taken seven casualties in an attempt to come to our assistance and encircle the enemy forces. Over the radio Colonel Rogers (who had gone airborne in his C&C to have a look at the whole fight) told me he thought we should break off. "No, sir," I said. "We've got to capitalize on this. We've got the enemy on the ropes. We're winning this one."

"I agree with Hack," said General Pearson, who was monitoring our net from his bird above the battlefield. The two commanders then decided that because I was on the ground I should take command of the engaged troops. It was another lucky break, but it was almost nipped in the bud when, a short time later, Raphiel, Darryl, and I were leaning against the blown-out wall of a house and an enemy machine gun opened up right at us. How the gunner managed to stitch the wall *between* Darryl and me, and move on to stitch *between* me and Raphiel, and not hit any of us was a miracle or a fluke beyond belief, but that was exactly what happened. Of course, we immediately shagged ass out of there—it wasn't a very cool place to be.

The battle began to settle down to a slow, methodical, inch-by-inch finding of the enemy's dug-in positions and one by one destroying them. Just as dark was coming on, Abu's company commander, Hal Eaton, staggered into our position. It was very strange. He came out of nowhere, and he had to have walked from A Company straight through the NVA positions to get there. But we quickly found out how he'd done it: he was in shock, having taken grenade fragments in his throat.

Only then did I get the full story on Abu's casualties. They were staggering. Not one officer of the three rifle platoons remained. All had been killed or wounded, with the greatest shock of all being word that Harry "The Horse" Godwin was dead.

At dark, the Abu weapons platoon (which was fighting as a rifle platoon, and had been held as such in battalion reserve throughout the day) infiltrated the battle area and linked up with the remnants of its company. While Bob Press, Abu's First Sergeant (who'd actually hit a mine the previous day but had chosen to stay with his unit when it was redirected toward Thanh Phu), took command of the company, I radioed Harry the Horse's platoon. I spoke with Staff Sergeant Travis Martin, the only NCO left, and asked him if he thought he could run Harry's platoon for the night. "You bet, sir," the squad leader replied, "I've been training for a situation like this for ten years."

I directed A Company to get themselves squared away along the enemy's escape route to the south. Bravo, meanwhile, consolidated its positions along the escape route to the west. As both companies evacuated their casualties I knew we desperately needed more men on the ground; with C Company off on a brigade mission, all I had as reserves were the Tigers, who'd spent the fight so far securing our fire base (a stupid damn job for them anyway). I decided to bring them in.

"What about my security?" the artillery battery CO screamed through the radio when I gave him the word. "I need the infantry to secure me!"

"Well, you're not going to have them tonight," I replied. "Look at your

TOE statement, young captain. It says you are capable of defending yourself. So let's see you do it."

Denying the artillery its security was far less a concern to me than eliminating my reserve. But I was convinced we were soundly trouncing the enemy. What I wanted now was to get as many escape routes blocked as we could, then blow the hell out of the center of the NVA positions and catch the enemy troops with infantry ambushes as they scurried for safety. More and more, through my own experience and as it meshed with what I'd read of the French experience, as well as the views of the old Indochina hands and what Emerson was doing in the '02, I was concluding that this was the way to fight the NVA and the VC. The ammo was free—only the taxpayer paid for that—and it made a lot more sense than trying to close with our hardcore opponent as we had at My Canh and suffer excessive casualties.

The Tigers were inserted at 2100 hours, in the brigade's first nighttime airmobile assault. They moved into their multiple ambush positions without casualties, despite being under fire from the moment they stepped out of the choppers at their one-bird LZ. Of the score of NVA stragglers killed throughout the night, the Tigers were responsible for about a dozen. Unfortunately (though predictably) many NVA escaped, too, through our far-too-open net, and bugged back to the hills.

Come the early dawn, Darryl Nunnelly and I left B Company, where we'd spent the night, and moved out to the Abus' position. With us, as well, was the redoubtable Tom Hancock, who would replace the wounded Hal Eaton as A Company's commander.

To appreciate how the tragic events of 4 March affected the men of Abu Company, it is necessary to understand the Abu spirit and the Abu history. The Abus had actually evolved from another unit, the Ibus, a.k.a Item Company, 187th RCT. As the story went, in 1952 the companies of the 187th decided that rather than use standard military phonetics (i.e., Alpha, Bravo, Charlie) to identify themselves, they would give themselves names. Animals seemed to be the order of the day (L Company became Lion, M Company became Mighty Moose, and so on), but poor Item found the only animal that began with an *I* was a wading bird called an ibis, which just wouldn't do. It was Item Company's commander, Captain Robert Channon, who came up with the mythical Ibu (in fact, an acronym for *I is the Best Unit*). All that was needed then was to decide what this never-before-seen creature looked like. Remarkably, the task was accomplished in a very short time: the Ibu had a gorilla's body, a lion's head, a moose's horns, and an alligator's tail, and wore (for all eternity) a parachute and jump boots, and clutched a pistol in its right hand and a knife (dripping blood) in its left.

The Ibu proliferated quickly, finding its way onto guidons, company signs, swagger sticks (an ivory Ibu on one end, an ivory jump boot on the other), and the legs of many an Ibu NCO, in the form of a tattoo that stretched virtually from ankle to knee. When, in 1956, the 101st was reactivated and the 3d Battalion, 187th RCT (of which Ibu was a part) was incorporated into the Pentomic 1/327 Battlegroup, instead of gracefully bowing out, the Ibu, fierce figure of yesteryear, just changed its name: Abu, to accommodate its new company designation (A Company, 1/327).[1]

For old-timers and newcomers alike, the legend of the Ibu/Abu was the glue that cemented the men of A Company together. At Fort Campbell, a good number of Abu's NCOs had been with the company since its early Ibu days; even with rotation and normal attrition in Vietnam, on 4 March many original Abus, like First Sergeant Bob Press (who'd started out as a squad leader in 1956), remained. Unlike Bravo Company, which had had its baptism of fire in February, the fine, cocky troopers of Abu had not seen a major battle in Vietnam before My Phu. Their losses, thirteen KIA and almost forty WIA, knocked the remaining members for one serious loop. The shock was only compounded by the death of indestructible Harry the Horse—if Harry died, the company's collective thought seemed to be, how could any of the poor mortals among them survive? The unit's morale had not just been damaged, it had been destroyed, or so it appeared when we arrived at their position (a rice paddy in the center of which were Abu's dead, neatly stacked row on row, and covered with ponchos) on the outskirts of My Phu.

I was quietly briefed on the events of the previous day. On Hal Eaton's order, Abu's 3d Platoon had assaulted across a dry rice paddy and taken eleven WIA in less than fifty yards, with six more lost when they'd attempted to advance over a dike on My Phu's perimeter. Harry Godwin's 2d Platoon had attacked across another open paddy, this one seventy-five-yards long with absolutely no cover or concealment; the strength of the platoon had gone from thirty-five to eight men before they were halfway across, with the weapons squad suffering 100 percent casualties. Among the KIA were Harry the Horse (who'd led the attack) and his RTO, Reuben "Sweet Daddy Grace" Garnett. The story went that Harry fell first, and when Sweet Daddy automatically went to his aid, he was dropped by the same gun that had killed his friend. Sweet Daddy was holding Harry's hand when he died; so far from home, the bond of love and friendship these two men shared in life and death transcended the separate worlds they'd known in America—Harry Godwin was a dyed-in-the-wool southerner, and Reuben Garnett a black man born and raised in the ghettos of Philadelphia.

The Abu survivors sat dazed and defeated, hunkered down behind rice-paddy walls. I knew I had to get them back on their horses immediately or they'd never ride again. "So you guys have taken your lumps," I began, and proceeded to remind them of who they were ("The Abus, the best!"), and what Abu, the 1/327, and the U.S. Army paratrooper was all about. Then I tore their collective ass for violating the basics, which had led to all their problems in the first place. First Sergeant Press later told me the whole speech had been good news, especially to the older NCOs, who'd been trying to get their platoons to act and react tactically as they'd been trained, rather than taking on all the bad habits sanctioned by the most recent company commander, who'd brought *his* gung-ho, ultra-aggressive bad habits from his last unit, the Airborne-all-the-way 173d.

I must have begun my speech squatted down near the troopers and then stood up and started walking around, because suddenly a sergeant called out, "Get down, sir! There's a machine gun in that house" (referring to a substantial stone structure in the village behind us).

"Fuck a lot of machine guns," I replied, and marched over to the paddy wall beyond which stood the house. I turned to the men. "Who's going with me?" I asked, and hopped over the wall. I started moving toward the house, using paddy walls as a concealed and covered approach. I was damn scared—I didn't want to go like Jim Gardner—but since I'd gone through the village with Darryl and Hancock on my way to Abu's position and hadn't seen a single live enemy, I figured the odds had to be on my side. Besides, the exercise was worth it if only to set an example, and make the Abus grab hold of their bootstraps and pull themselves up. Some, mostly NCOs, were already doing so—about a dozen had followed me over that first paddy wall.

When I got to the side of the house, I threw a grenade through the window, then jumped up and hosed down the dead crew inside. Then I formed a skirmish line of the troopers who'd joined me for a sweep through the village. I was end man, moving along a paddy wall. We hadn't gone very far when I saw sudden movement on my right. Out of a spider hole popped an NVA soldier holding a rifle in one hand, a grenade in the other. The guy was about to throw the grenade in front of the skirmish line. I could see there was no way I'd be able to spin my rifle around fast enough to stop him, so I just dropped my weapon and tackled the guy. I threw his grenade away and dragged him out of his hole. He was wounded, probably in the previous day's fight, and I turned him over to Press with instructions to get a chopper to evacuate him to Brigade HQ, and make damn sure no one killed him in the meantime. The Abu boys weren't butchers, but after what they'd been through, the passion for revenge would naturally be high.

Hancock and I personally counted 118 dead NVA troops on the ground at My Phu before I left him to his new command. He was a good choice as skipper, as competent an officer as he was a scrounger, and the ideal guy to charge up the Abus, having been A Company's XO both at Fort Campbell and in the early Vietnam days. Unfortunately for all concerned, however, Hancock was not so lucky on the battlefield. Less than twenty-four hours after he took command of the Abus he was evacuated to the States, his hand badly wounded in the mortar attack on our fire base that the 95th NVA, our opponents at My Phu (as they'd been at My Canh), went ahead with, just as one of the POWs had outlined, despite the beating we'd given them the day before. So Hancock was gone. Captain Wayne Dill, a replacement from the 82d, and a brave, solid soldier who was not afraid to tell the boss what he thought, became the Abus' new Old Man.

No sooner had I left the Abus than I received a radio message to return to Brigade immediately. I got in a chopper and headed for Tuy Hoa, where I was met by General Pearson in his clean, starched fatigues. I, on the other hand, was filthy from head to toe, with a two-day scruffy beard to boot.

"General Westmoreland would like you to brief him on yesterday's battle," Pearson said.

"Shouldn't I change clothes or shave, sir?"

"No, you're just perfect. You look just great!"

Pearson escorted me to the briefing tent, and I told Westy about the fight. I did feel we'd acquitted ourselves well, though the casualties we'd suffered were still far, far too high for the result. Though we'd caught the enemy on the move, he'd been able to take advantage of his already-established, dug-in positions, and by not specifically restraining Abu, Colonel Rogers and I had allowed them to attack right into the buzz saw, with typical Airborne aggressiveness.

But naturally I did not tell any of this to General Westmoreland. He got just the highlights. When I'd finished, he said, "You have done a good job, and you're to be congratulated. It sounds as if you've pretty well mauled a VC battalion. Now they're groggy and you've got to keep after them, which I presume is your plan."[2]

"Yes, sir," I replied.

The briefing over, I headed for the door, only to be stopped by a final congratulations from the theater commander. "Well done, Major," he said, and then added, "Now you've just got to pursue, pursue, *pursue!*"

"Yes, sir," I said.

Pursue? I thought, as I walked out of the tent. Did he really mean he wanted us to charge into the woods and get our asses torn apart by the enemy's inevitable delaying screen of snipers and booby traps? In WW II there were numerous cases of one sniper stopping a rifle battalion for hours, killing and wounding dozens of soldiers in the process. Did Westy really want us to make that investment in lives here in Vietnam for so little return?

Surely not. This was not the same kind of war as WW II. This was not a war of terrain objectives (a fact I'd come to appreciate the hard way at My Canh), each one worth the price in lives if in taking it you moved closer to your final objective, your Berlin, your Tokyo or Pyongyang. Vietnam was a war where more often than not our elusive enemy just went to ground or ran away while we swept through and "cleared" a village, only to return, rebuild, and reoccupy it again the minute we'd moved on. My Phu was a classic example. Twenty-one of our men were dead in a battle for a piece of real estate that elements of the battalion, even A Company itself, had searched a number of times in the weeks previous to the 4 March fight. And unlike WW II, where, in just one example, ten thousand U.S. Marines were stacked up on the beaches of Saipan in four hours because we *needed* that island to construct an air base to bomb Japan to end the war, in Vietnam, at My Phu, twenty-one of our men were dead in a battle for a piece of real estate that had no strategic or tactical value, and that would be abandoned by our "pursuing" forces as soon as the dust settled.

I left My Phu feeling as I had after My Canh: there must be a better, less expensive way to fight these sons of bitches. The whole Tuy Hoa experience led to a big jump in my tactical thinking. I recognized my error at My Canh: I'd fought the battle by automatic reflex based on my previous combat experience, and with everything happening so fast, it hadn't occurred to me that my second-nature reactions might be wrong. I'd fought the battle as I would have done in Korea. Hal Moore had fought Ia Drang like Korea, too, but in his case it had been a Korea-style battle—the NVA attacked the Cav in waves, not unlike the Chinese had attacked us in the winter of '50 and the spring of '51. In my case I'd had a mission to relieve a besieged unit. I'd deployed my men with one element blocking in case the enemy broke and ran (which is what he was supposed to do); the other's job, to roll up the enemy's flank, was a sound employment of forces for a set-piece battle. Except that My Canh had not been a set-piece battle. The enemy's disposition had not been well defined. He'd had no flanks per se, and his discrete, unorthodox (in terms of the U.S. style of fighting), brilliantly concealed and fortified positions had not exactly been conducive to being rolled up. My brain had automatically told me that to relieve Murphy's unit I'd have to take the village where the men were besieged. I'd fought for a terrain objective, which the student of guerrilla warfare in me *knew* was not the way to fight this war, but which the Korea-seasoned warrior in me did not have time, or take time, to remember.

Drawing on the My Canh experience and the subsequent weeks' fighting that culminated in My Phu, as the Tuy Hoa mission drew to a close I began to advocate more and more small-size patrols for the battalion, and more and more night operations to steal the darkness from the enemy, who up until now had moved freely through it. Though Emerson would be the first to conduct a full-scale, battalion-size nighttime airmobile assault, never again would I let the night hamper *me* as it had at My Canh—again a result of my Korea experience, which demanded with the coming of darkness that a unit consolidate, dig in, and get set to be hit.

I realized, too, that the presence of a large enemy element should not be the green light for a full-scale assault by our men. After all, what had caused the carnage at Tuy Hoa were the heroic "Airborne" charges. Tuy Hoa proved to me once and for all that paratroopers were innately unfit for guerrilla warfare, even Phase II (battalion- and regiment-size) guerrilla warfare. So were Marines, of whom Harry the Horse had been one before he joined the 101st. Both types of warriors were trained for shock action—to violently close with the enemy and destroy him, and then go back to a rear area to marshal, refit, train, and wait for the next mission. Both were eager, motivated, and aggressive, all admirable characteristics in a conventional war, but on a guerrilla battlefield they became *too* eager, *too* motivated, *too* aggressive. Both Airborne and Marines were determined, but they had no patience; they were always long on guts but sometimes short on brains. After Tuy Hoa I also realized that, my attitude toward decentralized command and mission-type orders notwithstanding, there were times when the issuance of more exacting instructions to my paratroop units was absolutely essential to get the job done right, with the minimum of casualties.

But the main thing I learned at Tuy Hoa was that there was simply no point in taking an objective you had no intention of holding, no point in using men when firepower could do the job. Tuy Hoa's battlefields may have looked like the hedgerows of Normandy, but if (as was the case) the taking of such objectives one by one wasn't ultimately going to *lead* you anyplace, and if (as was also the case) you were going to abandon each objective after you'd taken it, only to take it again and abandon it again, *again and again and again,* as the French did before us and as we were doing now—well, it wasn't worth the life of even a single soldier.

I'd learned.

Just after My Phu, Colonel Rogers finished his six-month command tour with the 1/327. In and out like clockwork—battalion commanders had six months, company commanders had three—just long enough to figure out what they didn't know. Rogers' replacement, Lieutenant Colonel Walter Meinzen, had been away from troops for a long time. Fortunately, I was to stay on as the 1/327's XO to provide continuity in the battalion.

Not long after this change of command, word came from Nha Trang that

Gentleman John Howard, who was hospitalized there with malaria, was to be evacuated to the States. This came as a hell of a blow, to me because I loved the guy, and to the battalion because he was just such a damn fine officer. Though I'd once put him on ice in the S-3 shop to keep him alive, after Jim Gardner was killed I'd sent him to the Tigers—he'd wanted more action and the unit had needed him.

Since I had a few logistic things to take care of in Nha Trang anyway, Raphiel and I decided to use the trip as a little R&R and visit Johnny in the hospital. Apparently our young friend was one sick hombre, but in Raphiel's expert opinion he looked "pretty good" when we arrived, so we persuaded Dr. Barton "Black Bart" Pakull, a friend of Raphiel's and one of the hospital doctors, to let us take Johnny out for a temporary holiday, just to sit in the sun at the beach and enjoy himself. Black Bart wasn't exactly convinced when we promised that his patient wouldn't drink or eat the wrong foods, and that we'd have him back in his hospital bed by 1800 hours, but because Raphiel was a doctor and a damn good one at that, he gave us the nod.

We really did mean to keep our word. It was just that we kind of got sidetracked when we hit the first of the Nha Trang clubs. By 1800 we were drunk enough to forget to take Johnny back to the hospital, and instead stumbled over to Le Frigate, an open-air restaurant that Johnny promptly (and at the top of his lungs) renamed Rick's American Café. We drank and ate the richest food on the menu, and despite the fact that Johnny grew greener by the second, good trooper that he was he still got up on a table in the middle of the club and began his Rudyard Kipling recitation. A few less-than-romantic souls kept interrupting him until we threatened to clunk their heads together; Johnny soldiered on, orating eloquently as he swayed from sickness and booze, until he got knocked in the head by a whirling ceiling fan and fell off the table.

I think that's when we decided to take him back. Black Bart was in a rage when we dragged his patient back to his hospital bed. Besides the fact that we hadn't kept our end of the bargain, we'd unknowingly triggered such a relapse in Johnny's condition that for the next couple of days the docs thought he was going to die. He didn't, thank God, but then they contemplated court-martialing him for abusing his government-leased body. Fortunately, that didn't come to pass either, and he was soon sent home where he fully recovered. Johnny would return to Vietnam to distinguish himself at the 1972 Battle of An Loc, and subsequently go on to become a boy general.

A few days later, my other Tiger platoon leader, Dennis Foley, got a Nha Trang R&R of his own, thanks to the battalion's policy that a wounded trooper, wherever he was, had to be paid on payday just like his buddies, and he had to be paid by one of his own officers. This SOP was good not just for the soldier's morale but also for the officer's: an unwritten rule was that after the hospital visit, the rest of the day—and the night—was his. Foley planned to take full advantage of it. He'd gone to Nha Trang almost directly from the field, unshaved and unwashed in his distinctive Tiger Force fatigues. After he'd paid the troops, he planned to clean himself up and head over to Marie Kim's, a favorite Screaming Eagles watering hole for falling in love.

As he headed up the street from the hospital, an OD Army sedan with two stars on the bumper standard pulled up beside him. General Larsen, the IFFV commander, opened the door and stuck his head out. "What are you doing in town, Lieutenant?"

"I came to pay the troops," Dennis replied.

"Got a place to stay tonight?" the General asked.

"Not yet, sir."

"Well, hop in."

Dennis didn't have much choice. He got into the sedan and they drove off. Larsen, who loved the 101st, had recognized Foley's Tiger fatigues and took the chance encounter to get a firsthand report on how we were doing. The two men chatted in the car, and before long they'd arrived at Larsen's quarters, a stately old French villa. A valet showed Foley to his bedroom for the night and pointed out the bathroom. The valet brought him a drink and Dennis took a shower, but by the time he got back to the bedroom, all his clothes were gone. In their place was a set of General Larsen's fatigues, complete with stars embroidered on the jacket. "Put these on," said the valet. "We're washing yours."

Again Dennis didn't have much choice, and before long the second lieutenant in the major general's gear was having cocktails with the genuine item in the dining room of this villa. Drinks led to dinner, dinner led to coffee, coffee led to adjournment into another room for cognac and cigars, and war stories flowed throughout. It was an extraordinary event, but for Dennis, the experience was double-edged: few lieutenants would ever dream they'd spend a pleasant evening at home with their commanding general, but on the other side of things, Dennis *had* been dreaming—of getting laid—ever since he'd left Tuy Hoa, and the General just wouldn't let him go. Larsen was like a lonely prisoner in his own headquarters. He was a corps commander who had no corps to fight; a major general without a Berlin or Tokyo to capture; a superb field soldier, battle-tested in almost four tough years of Pacific fighting in WW II and another year's combat in Korea, stuck in the ultimate nothing-to-do job.

The long Nha Trang day turned into night, and Dennis knew he'd lost if not his chance then at least his options at Marie Kim's. He finally excused himself by saying he had to get some sleep—he had an early plane to catch. "I'll have my driver take you over to the airport," Larsen volunteered, and any hope Dennis had had of grabbing a morning quickie evaporated in an instant.

Foley went back to his bedroom to find his Tiger uniform newly washed, pressed, and starched, and his boots polished. Just as he began undressing for the night, one of Larsen's aides appeared at the door of the room. "The General has retired for the evening," he said. "He asked me to pass on to you that if there's any place you need to go, or anything you want to do before you retire, please feel free to do so. You'll find a driver and a car outside, and one of us will be here to let you in whenever you return." Swede Larsen may have been a hell of a general, but he was also a soldier's soldier.

The 1st Brigade received a well-earned Valorous Unit Citation for the Tuy Hoa operations, and the 1/327 got a separate one for My Phu. VUCs weren't easy to come by, so both brigade and battalion were damn proud. For my guys in the 1/327, though, the experience at Tuy Hoa had meant a lot more. The soldiers had begun to get hard there, not just physically, but upstairs, where it really counted. After eight months in Vietnam, they'd dealt death and seen death in numbers none could have imagined. They'd endured leeches and jungle rot, constant, heavy rains and clammy clothes that chilled them in their sleep, and the "wait-a-minute" bushes that could hold a trooper as tenaciously as a strand of barbed wire. Many fought malaria and hepatitis; all fought fear, not just of the enemy, but of the snakes, the tigers of the Central Highlands that reportedly pounced on troopers, the monkeys that dropped out of trees at night like stealthy Viet Cong (at least one of these was hacked to death by a trooper with a machete in the dark), and of course the night itself. But through it all they'd learned, and little by little exchanged bravado for real confidence. Everyone did, if they stayed long enough—even the pilots like Outlaw 5-3, who'd insisted on having his chopper blasted out of the sky at My Canh. I met him again four months later, at a big party we threw in celebration of the battalion's brilliantly fought, end-of-tour graduation exercise, the battle of Dak To. When Outlaw 5-3 heard one of my guys call me Savvy Volley 5, he came over to introduce himself and tell me that as a result of our last encounter he'd left his know-it-all, God's-gift-to-aviation days behind. That same evening a lot of other pilots came up and introduced themselves as White Eagle 4 or Splendid Horse 2 or whatever their call signs were, and mentioned the operations where we'd served together. It wasn't too often that guys on the ground met the men who supported them and vice versa—we were all generally just voices on the radio—so there was an immediate camaraderie among us. And there was a lot of mutual respect, too. We looked in awe at the pilots for some of the amazing risks they took in our support, particularly to evacuate wounded soldiers on the ground; the pilots treated us infantry guys as if we were Wyatt Earp gunfighters in the old Tombstone bar, the ones who dished it out and had to take it the hard way. In a high-tech world, the pilots somehow made their helicopters a romantic symbol of a bygone era; they rode those choppers as they would have done their horses in the old Cav or cowboy days, coming in guns ablazing, swooping down over the battlefield "to save the day" with their tremendous mobility and firepower. Unfortunately, the feeling of power most chopper drivers felt could work both for the infantry and against us: overenthusiastic pilots sometimes got a little carried away, firing first and only then ascertaining whether the target was friend or foe. This developed in the infantry a definite ambivalence toward the fliers and their gallant steeds, but like a lot of relationships, love-hate or other, if it were all weighed up, we wouldn't have dreamed of letting them go.

While the Screaming Eagle fire brigade moved to the coastal town of Phan Thiet to prepare to do battle in what intelligence reports indicated was a large Viet Cong stronghold somewhere along the nearby Vietnamese II and III Corps boundary, I prepared to go on R&R. "Raphiel," I said to Doc Benjamin, who was going as well, "organize us a kit—a pill for every possible contingency. If we get malaria, we've got to cure it for five days. Hepatitis—cure it for five days. The runs, VD, *anything!* I don't want to miss one stroke on this R&R!"

We arrived in Hong Kong, and each of us got a suite at the Hilton. In mine, I filled the tub with hot water and bubble bath, rang room service and ordered champagne, hors d'oeuvres, and a tailor. Neither Raphiel nor I had any civilian gear; in Hong Kong everything was beautifully (and instantly) made to order and cheap as hell, so we spent our first wad of dough on clothes, in duplicate, triplicate, or by the dozen. Then Raphiel wanted to go out and buy some stuff for his wife, and I decided that whatever he got for Karen I'd get for Patty. We bought mink stoles and diamond rings (it didn't hurt that the night before we left Vietnam I'd gotten into a poker game at the Nha Trang Officers' Club, and in the course of the evening won almost a five-figure bundle of free money to round out my Hong Kong kit bag), beaded sweaters and beaded purses, and finished off the spree by buying ourselves each a gold Rolex watch, at that time a mere couple of months' pay. We probably spent six grand each the very first day, but what the hell—we were there, we were having fun, and we were *alive.* What else mattered?

Upon returning to the brigade base camp at Phan Rang, I was informed I was to report to Brigade Forward at Phan Thiet soonest. Lieutenant Colonel Melvin Garten, CO of the 2/327, had been badly wounded when a VC mine blew his jeep to hell and back. He'd taken a bad hit in the leg and shrapnel in the head; it was a terrible waste of a WW II DSC winner, bearer of a "perfect attendance" (three-war) CIB, and all-round brilliant soldier. A hell of a combat commander, Garten had breathed fire into the previously sluggish "Second to None" 2/327, renaming it the "No Slack" battalion and *cutting* no slack until the unit shaped up. It was just beginning to come into its own as a great, spirited outfit when Garten was hit, so his loss was felt the whole way down the chain of command. Fortunately, Lieutenant Colonel Joe Wasco, the brigade XO and another fine, longtime Airborne man, had been sent up to the 2/327 to take Garten's place and keep up his good work. The reason I had to report to Phan Thiet soonest was that I was to replace Colonel Wasco.

The brigade XO was the third most senior person in the brigade, right behind General Pearson and his deputy, Colonel Ted Mataxis. The position generally went to a senior lieutenant colonel (of which there were a number in the 101st), and I was only a major. General Pearson's decision immediately put me in a very difficult position. Just as in the Vanguards, where Colonel Newbreed had catapulted me over his senior majors and Colonel Sniffin to become his deputy for the ATT, now I was in charge of a staff where almost everyone outranked me. Army officers being a breed keenly aware of such things as date of rank and the attendant pecking order, there was a lot of resentment among the staff. This was only compounded by the fact that their new boss was the one they'd sniped at and bitched about continually during the "octopus" days, the one who refused to play their paper-pushing game at the battalion level. Still, to me the irony of it all was wonderful, and even I was surprised at how diplomatic I was in my initial Letter of Instruction to these no-good pricks who were suddenly showering me with love and affection: "Some of you, I know from experience, do everything you can to help the units. Some of us have the attitude that the units are here to make our job easier. Our responsibility is to do everything possible to help the battalions, and the individual companies. No one on the staff will say no to a subordinate unit. Only the General will say no." The friction eased pretty quickly, or maybe I just stopped noticing it. General Pearson was a damned efficient paper man, and from day one I was too busy burning the midnight oil to stay ahead of the Old Man to get involved in staff politics.

Pearson was a high-intellect kind of guy, more a staff man than a commander. He drove his people hard, a result perhaps of his own iron self-discipline. He'd taken a memory course and henceforth never forgot a thing. He could fall asleep in an instant and wake up fully rested ten minutes later. He was a no-nonsense man who hurried his briefers along with a "Next point?" that cracked like an M-1 rifle. He was ruthless in a quiet way, but a strong supporter of those who served him well. Though he lacked the Johns type of showmanship that electrified the troops, Pearson was a knowledgeable and fair man, and the perfect general for the war in Vietnam, which was a battalion—not a brigade—commander's war. (An exception to this was when a brigade commander was a romping, stomping warrior type with a real feel for on-the-ground battle. Then the war could be a brigade CO's war. But Pearson generally stood back from the action. He ran his unit more like a division than a brigade, but in the 1/101st this suited his romping, stomping warrior-type battalion subordinates just fine.)

The way it really shook out was that '02 commander Hank Emerson was the tactical brains of the brigade, and I was his assistant. We were both innovators who bounced ideas off each other (the quality of these ideas was often propelled by the competitive spirit we shared, a clean and comfortable competition based on abiding mutual respect); we'd sell them to Pearson, and if an idea really worked, the General would implement it across the board in the brigade. Somehow this created a great rapport among us—Hank and I, the sometimes crude, always maverick warriors; Pearson, a man with the dedication and spirit of a modern-day Cromwell, as straight as they come yet able to look the other way when necessary, as he had when he'd seen the millions of tents in the 1/327's battalion area, or when he'd found out about my unauthorized Australian connection. When it came to Hank, Pearson knew that having Emerson on his team was like having a Cadillac (albeit an extremely tall, gangly, hook-nosed Cadillac) in the garage; Hank Emerson was one of the most unlikely-looking warriors one could ever imagine, but he was a winner, a brave, inspiring leader whom Pearson knew better than to play musical chairs with. By the time the 2/502 left Phan Thiet, the Gunfighter had been with the outfit for eight months. With his own gushing enthusiasm he'd built a great, spirited unit from the ashes of Gibraltar the previous September; now, as the brigade moved on to the bamboo labyrinth of Nhon Co to begin operations, the '02 and its leaders stood poised for their finest hour with the 1st Brigade, when Hank's boldness and combat savvy, coupled with his troops' total professionalism, would turn a potential massacre into the very model of how to fight this war.

But there was still one thing to be learned from Phan Thiet. The Phan Thiet operation ended not much differently than it had begun: nothing happened. At least in the first week one funny encounter had a Tiger or

Recondo long-range reconnaissance patrol bursting into a VC training camp in the middle of a class, the subject of which was "Beware of American Long-Range Patrols."[3] But in the second week, after combing the area side by side with troops of ARVN, the Regional Forces and Popular Forces (RF/PF), and other friendly Viet elements (probably five thousand men in all) with only light and minor contact, the only thing the 1st Brigade discovered was that the intelligence had been wrong. The VC did not have a huge redoubt on the II and III Corps boundary in that area after all. So the fire brigade picked up again, and as XO I was responsible for kicking the brigade out.

Our security perimeter got smaller and smaller as one battalion and then another took off in C-130 Hercules aircraft. As the support elements left, the area shrank even more, and just because it couldn't have been done any other way didn't make it any less precarious for the men left on the ground, or any more comforting. Finally only a few vehicles and some twenty-five or thirty people, the team involved with coordinating and executing the move, were left on the ground. ARVN was in the area for security, but since I'd learned early never to depend on them,* I was damn anxious to get us all out of there. Finally our aircraft arrived. Equipment was stacked on, jeeps driven in and tied down, all of us got on board, and soon the plane turned around and took off.

Just as we cleared the airfield, there was a terrible explosion in the back of the plane. We'd taken multiple hits, with at least one slug cutting a fuel line, sending JP4 aviation gas spewing around the cabin. The crew chief shut off the valves that controlled that line and opened another to direct the fuel around it; we were rerouted to Nha Trang, the nearest airfield that could be foamed, and soon landed safely. But to me, there was a significant message in the incident. For fourteen days, at a cost of probably thirty million dollars, five thousand men beat the bush looking for Charlie, and they didn't find him. And yet, on the very last day, at the end of our very own airstrip, one VC with an automatic weapon brazenly peppered our very last aircraft full of slugs on its way out. "Good-bye Yanks," each one seemed

---

* A lesson learned during our first major operation together, as a matter of fact, when the brigade opened up Route 19 for the 1st Air Cav. At the time, since we were operating in the 22d ARVN Division's AO, Colonel Timothy had told me to coordinate the brigade's passage through the area with the Viets, and to get the 22d to secure the three bridges between Qui Nhon city and the base of the critical An Khe Pass. Those bridges were essential for the safe movement out of Qui Nhon of two Screaming Eagle battalions' worth of ground attack forces. I was so impressed with the 22d ARVN CG's "No sweat, Major," Airborne-all-the-way attitude when I conveyed Colonel Timothy's request to him that come the morning of the operation I was absolutely shocked to find not a single ARVN trooper in sight. We'd had little choice but to send our ground forces on, and just pray the bridges hadn't been blown or mined. Luckily the operation went on without a hitch, but the experience taught me a very valuable, if harsh, lesson: never to give a Vietnamese unit a role that was critical to any operation, and never to trust a Viet again. And on both counts I never did, over the entire four years I spent in Vietnam.

to say. "See you again real soon." It was as if, whatever *we* thought, we were really playing the game by their rules.

I was at the Brigade Forward CP, merrily shuffling papers when the 1/327 and 2/502 began operations at Nhon Co (on the II and III Corps boundaries, like Phan Thiet, but well inland, along the Cambodian border). Again the battalions were faced with terrain they'd never experienced before: from the air the triple-canopied jungle obscured the maze of solid bamboo below, so thick in places that with every man hacking through it, progress was still no greater than thirty meters an hour. Two divisions could simply disappear in a few kilometers of that kind of bush.

For the troops, plagued by long, black wood leeches whose bites led to infection on top of infection, little to no sunlight for days on end, and the beginning of the monsoons in this region of Vietnam, the first week of the operation was a strenuous, exhausting fight with the jungle and nothing else. Hank Emerson got even more ornery than his men as day after day brought no contact for the '02. On a hunch he decided to slip his unit south, across the boundary into III Corps, and take advantage of an airstrip at Bu Gia Mop, an abandoned Special Forces camp.

When Emerson's L-19 was fired upon in an early-morning reconnaissance of the airstrip, he knew his hunch was going to pay off. A short time later, Hank Lunde's Alpha Company made contact and captured a malaria-ridden, panic-stricken soldier from the 141st NVA Regiment. Lunde gave the prisoner water and got him covered with a blanket. Then Emerson landed, and before he hit the guy with a long barrage of questions, he gave him some cigarettes and a much-needed meal. The POW's reaction to this kindness was simply to break down. Hank's interpreter explained that the NVA had been told he'd be beaten, tortured, and then shot if captured by the Americans. As this was obviously not the case, the grateful prisoner eagerly provided Emerson with the straight skinny on the disposition of his unit: a four-company ambush was waiting some forty minutes away, and six more companies were behind them, at a further forty-minute walk.

From the moment Hank Emerson treated that prisoner right, he could do no wrong. Lunde had already discovered a well-used track; now, little by little Emerson's scattered units tightened up as Lunde moved forward to converge on the enemy position. Emerson maneuvered his people brilliantly. His bold, small-unit "checkerboard" tactics, which he'd developed at the War College in 1964 specifically for Vietnam while everyone else was still wallowing in the British experience in Malaya, gave way to an almost conventional configuration in another turn of the evolutionary wheel on how to fight these guys. For what Hank wanted to do he needed combat power, so conventional was about the only way to go.

The final confrontation with the four-company ambush did not take place until the following day. Emerson told Lunde, his senior ground commander (who'd proved to be as fine a combat leader as he was a staff and peacetime man—a rare combination), to plan the ground operation, and it worked like a charm. Lunde's men, along with Captain George A. Hamilton's A Troop, 17th Cav, and Captain Ronnie Brown's composite task force of Cavalry, Recondo, and "Apache" Montagnard troops, silently encircled the waiting NVA ambush. Using massive air and artillery support, they proceeded to bushwhack the enemy bushwhackers in good old Yankee fashion. When it was over, of the 450 NVA troops who'd been lying in wait, only 50 remained alive and more or less intact.

As for the six-company ambush the first prisoner had mentioned, Emerson chased these guys to the Cambodian border. There he could only look on helplessly as what was left of the 141st NVA slipped safely across into the "neutral" ground, where trucks could be seen waiting to ferry our enemy to the safety of his Cambodian sanctuaries.

The successful operation at Bu Gia Mop was a newsworthy item, jumped on by the press and higher HQ. Directly after his crowning success, Lunde and his people received the dubious honor of clearing an LZ in the shattered jungle for Dan Rather and his television crew (an eight-hour job, but it was that kind of a war). Swede Larsen came up to the border to see the battlefield and talk to Hank Emerson about the fight. It was one of the last things he'd do before going back to America to brief the Pentagon press on what was happening in IFFV. During that briefing, besides declaring that the 101st was the best fighting unit in Vietnam, Larsen would relate the fact, well known at the highest levels in Vietnam and proved beyond doubt at the bayonet level at Bu Gia Mop, that the North Vietnamese were operating out of Cambodia. This information would be big news in the U.S.A., which by day's end would be vehemently denied by the Secretary of State and the Secretary of Defense. The press would then go back to General Larsen, whose innocent, honest heels had been hurriedly locked together in the interim, and he would say, "I stand corrected," from the corner he'd been backed into for reasons he didn't know. This incident well characterized one of the biggest problems in the war, which only got worse as the conflict went on. Out there, every day, American men were playing for the ultimate stakes. Yet back home, it seemed as if the politicians and bureaucrats who sent them there were playing by a different set of rules, if not a completely different game. There *were* NVA in Cambodia—so far, four to six regiments' worth—who were already killing American soldiers in South Vietnam. If they remained unstopped, they would kill many, many more. To the guys like myself on the ground, it was as simple as that. So none of us could figure out why things were not that simple.

When Walt Meinzen was evacuated the night before the 1st Brigade's next big mission, I had already been in Vietnam for thirteen months. On top of that, I was scheduled to rotate home in just four weeks, so I was incredibly surprised to find, the morning of the operation, that I was to take Meinzen's place as commander of the 1/327. "You were down there seven months and you know it better than anyone," General Pearson explained when he called me to his command tent at the Central Highlands Special Forces camp at Dak To. "We're going to have some tough opposition this time, so get read into the plan. Any questions, come back to me."

It took everything in my power to keep from dancing out of the tent. "Darryl, we got a battalion!" I sang to my patient RTO/driver waiting by our jeep. It was not just my fondest wish come true, but at that time in my career, the highest accolade I could receive.

"I'll get our gear together immediately, sir," Darryl replied with a huge grin, knowing full well that after I'd taken him with me from Brigade to Battalion and back to Brigade, I would surely want him by my side now, when I confronted the challenge I'd been waiting and preparing for since I was a rifleman in Italy so many years before.

I arrived at the battalion and it was old home week. All the old-timers rushed up with a chorus of "Great to have you back"; it was as if I'd been away at Brigade a year rather than a month. I had a look at the battle plan. The 1/327's mission was to relieve a nearby Special Forces camp at Tou Morong, atop a high mountain reportedly surrounded by a large NVA force and under the constant harassment of mortar fire. A year before, the June monsoons had set the stage for the enemy to successfully overrun eight such outposts (including our present base at Dak To) near the Laos–Cambodia–South Vietnam border; with the monsoon season of '66 about to start any day, the powers that be felt it better to relieve and abandon Tou Morong rather than take the risk of a replay of the events of the previous year, which had caused incredible panic that South Vietnam would be cut in half by marauding Communists.

No two commanders see a tactical problem the same way. As I examined Meinzen's attack plan, I knew I'd alter it after the airmobile assault phase, which in just two hours would put us in at LZs behind the Tou Morong objective. My reasoning was simply that I didn't think the NVA gave two hoots in hell about destroying the Special Forces camp at Tou Morong. What they wanted was to destroy the relieving force. I was sure we were being enticed into a very conventional (by guerrilla standards) Viet Cong insurgent trap, that of luring the counterinsurgent force into a situation by making it believe that one of its camps was threatened, and that a quick victory could be achieved in the process of saving the day. The fact that two NVA "ralliers" had just given themselves up at Dak To (and reported that the SF camp would soon be hit) only added to my conviction that Tou Morong was a trap.

Meinzen's plan called for two rifle companies to attack parallel with the two roads that led to the camp (one from the north, one from the east), with the third company remaining at the LZ with our command post and mortar platoon. I felt sure this was exactly what the enemy expected, and they would be waiting along the two roads in ambush. So I decided after the airmobile phase we'd go cross-country instead, despite the hellish navigation and difficult terrain. We'd take our time—Tou Morong had been "under siege" since the middle of May (it was now 3 June) and another day or so wouldn't hurt them.

I had only one instruction to give to the battalion before we jumped off. Since the Joe Rogers days ended, the light, Wolfhound-style "bum's roll" he and I had insisted the Above the Rest troops carry (just the basics: one set of fatigues and dry socks, a poncho, jungle blanket, and C rations all tied up with commo wire and thrown over the shoulder, able to be flipped off easily when a firefight developed) had gradually been added to and added to until the men were going into battle like mules again. (As Johnny Howard used to say, "Give a trooper a rucksack and he'll fill it.") But the big loads were disastrous in these Highlands of steep mountains, tall trees, and thick undergrowth, catching on everything and sapping vital strength long before contact was even made. So the single order was a simple one: *Lighten up!* The only question I had about the operation was how I was supposed to go into battle with a call sign like "Bald Eagle" (especially with Emerson going in as the glamorous Gunfighter). I told Pearson I wanted to be *Bold* Eagle, not Bald, and he quickly had his commo officer change it with a matter-of-fact, "Yes, Hack, that fits you better."

The Tigers had secured our LZ on D-1 (the day before I joined the battalion), and now our airmobile assault was made unopposed. We made our way overland with a scout section moving Aussie-style, well in front of the main force of each company. With our big fists locked together, the enemy realized he wasn't going to get his pound of flesh for free, and in the two days it took to get to our objective, we had less than a handful of contacts.

We reached the Tou Morong camp and prepared for the movement of its 150 inhabitants down the hill to Dak To. The North Vietnamese had broken off their mortar attacks on the outpost, no doubt damn disappointed we hadn't stumbled into their trap. Still, their plans had not been completely foiled: according to Don Korman, who'd heard about it over the artillery net, while we were traveling cross-country the day before, the 1/42 ARVN Regiment had made *their* approach to Tou Morong along one of the roads, been ambushed just as we would have been, and taken four dead and nineteen wounded.

Hank Emerson and General Pearson and his staff flew into Tou Morong for a "what to do next" conference: should we continue to look around here or give up and move elsewhere? Between the ARVN ambush and my gut feeling, I knew that regardless of his present silence our foe was still in the area. But before I joined the powwow, I wandered over to one of the inhabitants of Tou Morong, a Montagnard corporal, who confirmed it. I pulled out a map. "Where are the NVA?" I asked him.

"Down there," he replied, indicating a valley below the outpost.

"Are there many NVA there?"

"Many, many. Maybe a regiment. Maybe more."

"Do you know that for a fact?"

"Oh, yes," the Montagnard said, "I patrol there, but I never go there now. None of my men will go there."

"Thanks a lot," I told him, and joined General Pearson and his staff, the latter of whom were firmly of the opinion that the 24th NVA Regiment, our reported opponent, had vacated the battlefield and therefore so should we. Of course, Pearson's staff didn't know what the Montagnard corporal had told me, but as I listened to their argument, it quickly became clear that through some very serious breakdown in communication they also didn't know about the previous day's ambush of the ARVN unit on the road to Tou Morong. As such, their arguments for leaving were totally logical, even if they were totally wrong. Meanwhile I was smelling an incredible firefight (that in the unit competition stakes would put the 1/327 well in front of Emerson's '02), so when Pearson asked for my opinion, without going into details I said I thought I might stick around Tou Morong for a while and have a look in the valley.

"It's all yours," the General said.

I deployed my units in a recon screen, little fingers to wind carefully down the valley, each platoon no more than an hour's reinforcement time from another. Ben Willis' Abus* made three sharp contacts with an estimated reinforced platoon of NVA; tragically, during the fight a friendly artillery barrage landed right in the center of one of Ben's platoons, killing five

---

* Willis had taken over the Abus some six weeks before, when Wayne Dill came down with malaria. Since his recovery, Dill had commanded C Company.

troopers and wounding five more. Everything stopped while we sorted out the debacle and evacuated the casualties. It wasn't exactly the greatest way to start the operation.

As darkness fell I had everyone hold up and dig in, planning to continue the hunt come first light. All was quiet until 0200 hours. Then Captain Don Whalen's B Battery, 2/320 Arty, which was in direct support of us (and under the 1/327's operational control), came under attack from an estimated battalion-size enemy force. Heavy mortar fire preceded the assault; then, with bugles blowing, the NVA came at the position in waves, as the Chinese had in Korea, and as the Viet Minh had against France's elite Mobile Group 100 on this very same Central Highlands ground a dozen years before. The gunners quickly found they were virtually on their own: only one platoon of A Company, 2/502, which was OPCON the 1/327 under the command of XO Karl Beach and had been tasked with securing Whalen's battery, actually got into position to help them. (The '02 company had been too spread out from the first; as such, some of the company's number got pinned, with the outpost squad closest to the enemy's ingress route nearly being trampled by racing hordes of enemy soldiers intent only on Whalen's position.) Meanwhile, with a "Smokey the Bear" flareship hovering over the battlefield, dropping flares and lighting the ground like day, Whalen's artillerymen fought like lions for their lives and their positions, even reclaiming overrun guns and firing them point-blank into their attackers' ranks.

Dawn was fast approaching. I called Sterling Fairchild,* whose Tigers were near the action, and ordered him to set up an ambush on the trail I was sure the enemy would use to withdraw before first light. The Tiger CO started to bitch over the very busy battalion command net that he didn't want to do it. He was close to rotation and didn't want to get knocked off. I had more things on my mind than Fairchild's DEROS. "Just do it," I snapped. Next, I got Ben Willis' Abus moving toward Whalen's battery (while supporting the defending gunners with 81-mm mortar fire), and B and C companies poised for a first-light airmobile assault deep behind the enemy's escape route. Between these units and the A2/502, I had five strong forces to chop up the NVA withdrawal and pick off their stragglers. I was confident because I felt I'd been down the road before. The situation was not that much different than what the Wolfhounds had experienced in April of

---

* West Pointer Sterling Fairchild (as I will call him) had gone to the Tigers at the same time Johnny Howard did. I did not consider him a warrior in the least, but he was an exceptionally bright staff man who thereafter had played the role of Tiger administrator/S-3 while Howard's and Dennis Foley's platoons rotated in the field and fought the war. Dennis Foley had been wounded at Phan Thiet, and with Jim Gardner dead and Johnny Howard evacuated, Fairchild was now in charge of the unit's maneuver elements.

'51, at the outset of the Chinese Spring Offensive. Then, the Chinese had penetrated G Company and had us all on the run, but by the morning the penetration had been sealed and the Chinese could not withdraw. They were caught in a sack not unlike what I was trying to draw now, and we had destroyed them in detail.

I don't know how or when I got word that Fairchild had disobeyed my order. All I know was that the ambush was not set, no sack was drawn, and come the dawn many an enemy soldier slipped away down that very trail. Fortunately the plan was not totally blown despite what I considered Fairchild's act of cowardice. Between my other elements and our tremendous supporting fire (including "Puff the Magic Dragon," an aircraft whose mounted Gatling guns spat 450 rounds per second, enough to cover the area of a football field in three seconds, a slug hitting every square foot along the way), a first-light sweep of the area revealed eighty-six enemy dead from the 24th NVA Regiment. Our own casualties for the night were four American KIA and ten wounded.

Still, I was furious, and after moving B and C companies out by chopper to sweep down from Whalen's position toward the valley of the Montagnard corporal's "many, many" NVA, I brought the Tigers in and relieved Fairchild on the spot. I didn't give a damn if he was a short-timer. Almost everyone was, and some were well past their rotation dates. The Vietnam one-year rotation policy was already panning out as it had in Korea: when people got short, they just wanted to go back to the base camp and hide under a rock. They were deadweight in an outfit; they didn't do their share, and their lousy attitude was infectious. And in Fairchild's case, while it was bad enough that he, a Regular officer (*and commander of the Tiger Force!*), bitched out loud on the battalion command net, the fact that he clearly disobeyed an order that might have changed the course of the battle soon to follow was inexcusable. So I relieved him, and brought in another young captain whom I'll call Neville Bumstead to take his place. I wanted to get the Tigers out into the field again right away, just in case any of them had soaked up their erstwhile commander's cold feet. (To me, the most striking irony in Fairchild's behavior was that this officer had not only graduated from West Point, but he'd graduated at the top of his class in *leadership.* Classmates said, and I had seen for myself before this incident, that the guy couldn't make a decision; the system, or at least the criteria, at West Point had to have been seriously flawed to single out and honor a man seemingly so inappropriate to exemplify this basic and essential quality.)

In the middle of all this, a reporter came up to me, introduced himself as Ward Just from the *Washington Post,* and said he wanted to go along on one of our patrols. I gave him to Bumstead and the Tigers and hoped he'd keep his head down. Fortunately the initiative was all ours as the Above the Rest companies, each broken into platoon-size formations (giving me nine maneuver units plus the Tigers), combed the dense Highlands bush killing stragglers, two here and four there.

It was the beginning of six days of continual contact for the battalion, trying days, but ones in which the men, after a year of growing and learning on the battlefield, remained strong, resolute, and courageous. Besides an enemy who hugged our belts to neutralize our incredible firepower, the men fought lung-busting hills and virtually impassable jungles—terrain as bad, if not worse, than the worst in Korea, more like the Huertgen Forest along Germany's Siegfried Line.

Though I'd long believed the CIDG effort to stop NVA movement across the Laos and Cambodian borders was pretty futile, it took me years to truly appreciate how insane it was for infantrymen to fight in the Highlands. Yet my troopers knew, with every step they took, and weren't exactly shy about saying so. At one stage, when my tac CP and I were tagging along with one of the rifle platoons, the column halted for some reason and I took a hike up to talk to some of the troopers stretched out along the jungle track. Even though the troops knew I was "The Man" (I wasn't wearing brass, but with an "antenna platoon" of at least five PRC-25 radios with me, it was kind of obvious), they pretended they didn't and started telling me about the stupidity of it all, how infantry couldn't fight through this terrain, that their weapons couldn't even penetrate the bush, and that the guy in charge (me) must be some dumb son of a bitch. I loved every second of their rave and joined right in; as I scooted back to my tac CP, I thought those kids were the ones who should be the goddamn generals.

Because, really, what *was* the point of fighting in the Highlands? If the NVA wanted to cut the country in half, so what? All they'd have had would be a lot of thick jungle, a few Montagnards, and one hell of a lot of malaria. The Highlands had no real strategic value. The key to the war was the people. Protect the people, make their lives better, win *them*, and you'd have won the war.

But in early June 1966, such thoughts had not occurred to me, and the Central Highlands Dak To fight continued. On the second full day of combat, 7 June, Bumstead's Tigers wandered right into the middle of an enemy base camp. By midafternoon they were under a tremendous amount of fire, and the new skipper was beginning to crack under the strain. Charlie Company, under the command of Wayne Dill, moved to reinforce and got into a wild fight of its own; Willis, who'd been in a tough fight since his Abus jumped off the day before, also went to the rescue while we kept the Tigers alive with 155 and 105 artillery fire blasting with pinpoint precision around their position. Meanwhile, word came that the Tigers had taken terrible casualties, among them the reporter, Ward Just. A wounded civilian was a drama I didn't need at this moment, and the only thing worse was the news that Dill's unit, having extricated itself from one fight, had again locked horns with the enemy just one hundred meters from the Tigers. As night fell, Willis' Abus formed a perimeter around the Tigers *and* the beleaguered members of Charlie Company, giving all within a chance to breathe while continuing to slug it out with the enemy themselves.

From the Tigers came word that eight of the wounded were critical: without medevac they wouldn't last until morning. But medevac seemed like an impossible dream. No way could a chopper land at the Tiger position, heavily wooded and ringed as it was by determined, well-entrenched enemy troops, and in the dark yet. Still, an all-volunteer chopper crew dared to try it. They used a USAF HH44 "Husky" rather than a slick or other medevac aircraft. The bird hovered over the Tigers and, one by one, the brave crew winched the eight critically wounded on board, as the enemy fired enthusiastically at them from below. All eight cases made it off the battlefield alive, but later, when Ed Abood, my XO, brought me the casualty list from the brigade collecting station, the flawless operation suddenly displayed a worrisome hitch. The civilian reporter's name was not among those reported to be evacuated from the Tigers. Civilians had priority in this kind of situation, so I was pretty concerned; when I called Bumstead he explained that Just had refused evacuation because there were men far more seriously wounded who deserved priority. It was an exceptional gesture on the reporter's part, and one that won me for life. Through it Ward Just joined the brotherhood and became my friend—and little did I know that *my* life would never be the same again.

When the balance of the Tigers had been sprung and had come home the next morning, they totaled just sixteen effectives, nine of whom were wounded, and a single NCO, Pelham Bryant, who fortunately for the Tigers was one of the best ever to come along. We filled up the unit with new volunteers, but whatever plans I may have had for them or my companies went on hold in the afternoon, when Hank Emerson called me and said his C Company was in a big jam and about to be overrun. Battered Willis and the Abus, who had already been in constant, tough contact with the stubborn NVA for more than two full days, were in the best position to go to the rescue; I turned them around and on they went. For better control of the operation I made Ben OPCON Emerson, but mother hen that I was, I set one of my radios on the 2/502 battalion frequency to make sure he was okay.

What happened next, on 9 June 1966, was one of the great tragedies of the entire two-week battle. The 1/327 had so far borne the brunt of the fighting at Dak To, and we would continue to do so for ten more hard-slugging days. But the newspapers did not report that Ben Willis and the Abus got into the fight of their lives that day, taking twenty-six wounded and six dead on the way to rescue the C2/502, or that one of Ben's platoon leaders, Lieutenant Ken Collins, had his eye blown out during the battle, but continued directing his platoon, holding his eyeball in his hand, or that, when the whole thing was over, Ben's men, wounded and all, refused to be lifted out, determined as they were to go out under their own steam. Instead, the headlines blared that West Point football hero Captain William S. Carpenter, Jr., onetime All-American "lonesome end," now commander of C2/502, dropped napalm on his own troops.

The reason for this drastic course of action, so the story went, was that Carpenter was surrounded, had taken heavy, heavy losses, and believed his unit was on the verge of being overrun, with the enemy already swarming among his people. When the incident was over, while it turned out that his unit had suffered some six KIA and twenty-five seriously wounded, enemy dead on C Company's hill were as scarce as hen's teeth.

The publicity that ensued was not Carpenter's fault, nor were the John Wayneesque embellishments of the story each time it was reported. Still, in terms of unit pride and unit rivalry between the '02 and the 327 (units that, at Bastogne twenty-some years before, had stood back-to-back, taken the best the enemy could dish out, and stopped them cold), the effect of the affair was devastating. And when it was all over, ironically, about the only one among the men of the 1/327 who had a good word to say about the tragic incident was Ben Willis, whose Abus had taken the brunt of it in the effort to relieve Carpenter's company. "I can't in my heart blame Carpenter for anything he did," he said. "Unless you're there, on the ground, in that damn jungle, under that triple canopy, nose to nose with the other guy, you don't know. And if you don't know, you shouldn't pass judgment." Ben was right, of course. But for me as the battalion commander of one damn heroic battalion, it didn't make the heavy Abu casualties, or all the Carpenter headlines, any easier to swallow.

The next day the refitted Tigers were on their way out again to join Dill's Charlie Company in the attempt to relieve Willis, who was still engaged. Dill found himself in continual contact throughout the day, however, and Willis was left on his own to conduct a nighttime withdrawal from his position. By that time Pearson had told me a B-52 "arc light" strike was on the way; I left Charlie Company (which remained in contact much of the next day) and the Tigers in the area until the very last moment, fixing the NVA in place with dummy radio traffic so the enemy wouldn't realize we were pulling out in preparation for it. The arc-light strike dropped silently from thirty thousand feet, cracking like a thousand thunderbolts on impact, leaving the ground pockmarked with deep craters, like the dark side of the moon. Both the 2/502 and the 1/327 went in right afterward with little resistance. It was estimated the million-dollar strike was responsible for some two hundred enemy casualties.

Like most of the men in the battalion, I went from the sixth to the twelfth of June with no sleep. I was a walking zombie by the time we pulled back for the B-52 strike; as soon as Willis got out and we got him refitted, I hit the sack for twelve straight hours, and I doubt if I ever slept better in my life. Fortunately the first couple of post-arc-light days were quiet, giving everyone a chance to catch up on much-needed rest. Only then did the monsoons come. Luck alone had brought them late, but their absence had been decisive. The NVA's plan had been to lure a major U.S. unit into this area of Vietnam at a time when the terrain and weather favored them. If the NVA had had their way, the monsoonal rains, mists, and low cloud cover would have rendered our air power impotent, and only two forces, theirs and our infantry, would have squared off against each other at Dak To. In that scenario, they thought, the Americans would have been chewed up, just as we'd been in the past. But while the good weather did foil the NVA plan, I felt sure they would have had a harder time with the 1st Brigade than they'd expected even if the weather had gone their way. We'd learned quite a bit over the last year, and air power notwithstanding, for the main, this time around we had refused to attack the enemy's buzz saw. The only time we really played into their hand was during the relief of Carpenter, and had that not all happened so quickly, I might have recognized that the '02 company, like Tou Morong, was just the lure, and that it was the relief element—the Abus—that was really the juicy morsel the NVA were after.

It would have been good had Operation Hawthorne, the name given to the relief of the Tou Morong outpost and the subsequent events, ended after the B-52 strike. As it was, the search-and-destroy missions in the area continued, and on the seventeenth of June, the weary Abus, low in NCOs and platoon leaders, high in new replacements and guys just days from rotation, made contact with a small NVA force. There was no point in taking a lot of casualties. Willis played it safe and called for fire support. But the 1st Air Cav gunships that came to his aid made a terrible error: instead of shooting up the enemy, they shot up the Abus, wounding twenty-one (including Willis and the rest of the officers, most of the NCOs, and, worst of all, every single medic) and killing XO George Perry, our not-so-good-at-poker but very good buddy, with a tiny piece of shrapnel through the heart. It was a tragedy only compounded by the fact that Perry, two weeks over his DEROS, hadn't even had to be there. He'd just wanted to help Ben and his beloved Abus, and the plan had been for him to take the first resupply chopper out, get his gear, and go home the next day. It was a damn shame.

Word of the fiasco quickly got to my tac CP. I immediately grabbed Darryl and called Raphiel at his aid station at Dak To. The doc in turn grabbed Milton Turner, the medical platoon leader, and a medic named Nichols, and together with a couple of engineers with chain saws, they made their way by chopper to the battle area.

There was no landing zone near A Company's position (hence the chain saws to cut one out), just steep hills and thick forest no different from most of the Highlands. In my C&C I told the pilot to get as low as he could. We churned through the underbrush, the chopper blades cracking like gunfire against the bamboo and treetops as we cut a hole inching us toward the jungle floor. About fifteen feet above what might have been the LZ, Darryl and I jumped out, and radioed Raphiel that that would be the only way in for him and his people, too.

The doc was none too enthusiastic about the idea of jumping in. But when he got to the site, the longer his chopper hovered with him sitting inside it (so he told me later), the more he started thinking he'd be a lot safer on the ground than up in the air, because in his mind's eye he could vividly see an enemy trooper taking aim at him at that very moment. After a very long few seconds, it just became too much for him, and he jumped out of the bird, picked up his aid bags, and headed into the bush. Turner and Nichols were delayed in joining Raphiel in patching up Ben and his troops when the engineers jumped out of their chopper and each promptly broke an ankle, but soon things started getting squared away. Luckily, Willis wasn't hurt too badly and could stay with the company. When there was nothing more to be done, Raphiel and Turner hopped onto the last medevac chopper out without even a good-bye, leaving young Nichols, Darryl, and me out there without ponchos, without anything to protect us from the torrential rains that followed that night. Having assumed the good doctor would want to suffer right along with me, I was a little aggravated that Raphiel hadn't stuck around, but I couldn't really blame him. After all, he'd been there when we needed him, to care for the wounded and set an example for the medics in his charge, and he hadn't even had to do that. No one forced Raphiel Benjamin, the battalion surgeon, to tag along on operations, or to jump, figuratively *or* literally, into the fray, though that was exactly what he did throughout some of the worst of the 1/327's fighting at Tuy Hoa and Dak To. The adventure part had died quickly for this civilian doctor whom I considered among the bravest of the brave, but still he was always there, because he knew we needed him. And in just the same way, the gutsy forty-man medical platoon Raphiel oversaw knew we needed them. Consequently they flinched at nothing, and as a unit completely turned over three times in one year.

I didn't know what it was about medics. I used to think they joined the Medical Corps because they had a double load of courage, but maybe it was just the title itself that transformed them into the most valiant band of men I ever knew. Medics didn't wait for a miracle to pull the wounded to a safe shelter—they *were* the miracle that pulled, slid, dragged, and packed shattered bodies out of danger. And they performed miracles: stopping bleeding, stopping shock, relieving pain with morphine, and getting IVs going to pump life into broken fighters. Many packed M-16s along with their forty-pound medical kits, but their job was to save lives, not take them, and they risked their own, again and again, answering calls that took them right into the line of fire—machine gun, mortar, sniper, mines—without hesitation. Their most powerful medicine was their encouragement ("You got it made . . . just a scratch . . . you'll see that girl again"), a never-ending patter to keep minds occupied while deft hands administered aid or tried to sort out a stomach or a chest ripped open by shot. Grievously wounded soldiers were further assisted by the brave pilots who performed medevac missions, but it was the medics who made the difference on the ground, until the choppers could get in. Selfless and serving beyond good sense, countless medics died in the line of duty to save not just their buddies but the life of every man who fell on the battlefield. From two wars, it is these men, the medics—the "docs"—who hold the most special place of respect and trust in *my* infantryman's heart, and I'm sure there are a couple of million other men in the United States alone who feel the exact same way.

On the eighteenth of June, a resupply aircraft arrived at Willis' position with the bum's roll (complete with poncho) I'd neglected to take along with me in my haste to get to the Abus the day before. The first thing I did was brush my teeth—in the jungles of the Central Highlands it was about the only thing you could do to remember you were a civilized human being. You couldn't wash up there (during the monsoons you were always wet anyway), you couldn't shave (the slightest nick, like the inevitable cuts, rashes, or jungle sores, turned septic). The damp, dark jungle was not particular: *everything* rotted there—your boots, your clothes, your skin. So much for my insistence on an extra pair of dry socks. I learned not to wear them at all at Dak To, or undershorts either. Since you couldn't keep them dry anyway, the only purpose they served was to rub you raw and start the rot. It was a hell of a way to have to fight.

We spent the day beating around in the woods, but no contact was made. The enemy force had pretty well vacated the area; after the severe beating we'd given them, we figured they'd slipped back into Cambodia to regroup. With that, word finally came we'd be heading back to the brigade's Dak To base, where it had all begun some seventeen days before. General Pearson popped into my forward CP to tell me about the move: "Hack, I've given Emerson the aircraft. They're going to pick him up first, and then come back and get you."

I quietly imploded. The 1/327 had done the bulk of the fighting; the 2/502 ended up getting all the press *and* all the glory as a result of the Carpenter incident, and now, to top if off, Emerson's people were getting the aircraft and going home before mine.

"Never mind, sir," I told the General. "I don't want any choppers. I'll walk my battalion out of here."

"What do you mean?" asked Pearson.

"We'll just sweep back," I said. "I got over a hundred replacements in the last two weeks. Almost all the platoon leaders and NCOs are new. It'll give them a good shakeout, and we'll screen the battle area right back to the Dak To airfield."

The ten-mile walk took a night and a morning, and it *was* a good training exercise, not just for the new men but for the guys who'd been there all along, if only to shake out their hangover from the big fight. We made no contact, but almost lost a man when a viper crawled into his fartsack and bit him. A night medevac saved his life and the rest of the journey was without incident. Just shy of Dak To proper, I sent a radio message to battalion S-1 Glynn Mallory to bring out the battalion colors and company guidons. I assembled the company commanders, and told them we were going to march home walking tall, and show the '02 and the rest of the brigade who the *real* soldiers were in this outfit. Soon my well-proven battalion had lined up at proper intervals in a column on each side of the road, and we began to hike home.

I was leading, followed by the colors, my command group, and the Tiger commander, and then the rest of the battalion, each company led by their individual commanders and company guidons. And as we got closer to the base camp, the little "entrance" Glynn Mallory and I had set up just started to build. It was as if someone had said, "Hey, there's a parade!" and everyone wanted to get into the act. All the support people rushed to the side of the road to cheer us on—even an ad hoc band that started playing "Stars and Stripes Forever"—and with every cheer my boys stood taller and their stride grew that much jauntier. As we passed the 2/502 assembly area, about twenty feet from the road stood Hank Emerson, by his CP. He was fresh out of the shower, and he was shaving. He looked toward the road for a moment, his mouth agape, and then he just shook his head. "Hackworth, you son of a bitch!" he called with a smile.

"Above the Rest, sir," I shouted and gave him a snappy salute. It was a rare thrill to outgun the Gunfighter.

In a totally uncoordinated effort, people were coming from everywhere to look at the warriors. General Pearson had even fallen out with his staff in front of the brigade HQ to salute the battalion as we marched by, and just before I peeled off to join them, a group of aviators did an impromptu five-airplane flyover of the columns in our honor. I, too, saluted my fine companies as they strutted past, filthy and unshaven, jungle boots rubbed white with wear, still with camouflage in their helmets, some bandaged up and limping like little drummer boys. It was, then and forever, the proudest moment of my life. We'd taken 27 dead and 129 wounded, but we'd killed 276 NVA for the price. The men had fought bravely and well against terrific odds and in bitching conditions—they'd been in Vietnam for a year and *they'd learned*.

16 BOX SEAT

No lesson seems to be so deeply inculcated by the experience of
life, as that you should never trust in experts.

Lord Salisbury

BY the time I finished my first tour of Vietnam, the Infantry
School at Fort Benning was again in full swing, mass-producing infantry
officers to replace the combat and rotation losses of units fighting in the war.
I wanted to go there as an instructor when my tour with the 101st ended. To
date, the Infantry School had not had the benefit of combat people fresh off
the battlefield with U.S. units to pass on "lessons learned," and I couldn't
think of a place my experience or talents would be better used.

Instead, newly promoted to lieutenant colonel, I was assigned to the
Office of Personnel Operations (OPO) at the Pentagon. On paper, this was
a very important career assignment (DA duty was a *key* punch on the old
ticket). In reality, it was a two-year jail sentence in an office deep within the
bowels of the Pentagon, with little more to do than sign papers for the
twenty-five civilians I apparently managed, but who kept me and my
deputy, Major William Kesterson, blissfully ignorant of what was really
going on. No eager soldiers on limited tours were going to disturb *their*
well-oiled bureaucracy.

Throughout the six-week leave I took between Vietnam and the beginning
of the Pentagon assignment, no amount of pleading on my part was enough
to sway the career managers that it would be much better for me *and* the
Army to send me to Fort Benning. Consequently, I sold my house in
Tennessee, bought a new one in Burke, Virginia, and in the course of things
got to know Patty and the kids again. As hard as life is for the Army wife, for
the children it is that much harder. Dad's seldom there, and when he is (for
any length of time), it generally means the family's about to move
again—new house, new school, new friends. Laura and Leslie, not yet
seven and six years old, were on their fourth such move. At fourteen
months, Joel was too young to understand that part of the Army life, but it

was just as well. Having suddenly lost his year-long position as lord of the castle, he had enough on his plate trying to figure out who the hell this strange man was who called himself his father and wouldn't let him sleep in Patty's bed. Also, kids—my kids, anyway—got away with murder with their mother in charge. Undoubtedly it was quite a shock to their little systems when I came back with a whole new set of rules and banished anything less than *ordered* chaos from my home. I don't think it was easy for any of us at first, but the worst part was that just when we were beginning to function really well as a family again, I was on a plane back to Vietnam.

By then I'd been at the Pentagon for two stir-crazy months. But just before Thanksgiving the sun began to shine in my windowless, subterranean office when, without warning, Brigadier General S. L. A. Marshall came to visit. I was stunned. "Slam" Marshall, as he was known, was a legend of sorts in the Army. He'd walked and talked with the greats (Ike, Ridgway, Patton, Bradley), and he was the author of such widely read books as *Night Drop* and *Men Against Fire* from his WW II days, and *The River and the Gauntlet* and *Pork Chop Hill* from Korea. He was a historian cum military analyst, considered by some to be *the* American expert on soldiers in combat; to be sure, he was fascinated by the ultimate game of war. He had already been to Vietnam, where his study of the 1/101's Highlands fighting provided the stuff for his soon-to-be-published *Battles in the Monsoon.* I'd met him during that trip, when he was interviewing the participants of our Dak To fight (a fight that would win the brigade a Presidential Unit Citation), and in the months since, we'd had occasional contact, always when the General was chasing down some detail to go in his book. But I had not seen him, nor was there any reason why I should have, which made his sudden visit, in civilian gear, to my Pentagon cranny all the more mysterious.

General Marshall came right to the point. "Hack, I've been talking to Johnny Johnson,* and we both feel the Army has dropped the ball in Vietnam. We aren't learning from our experience there. The lessons learned are not being recorded and passed on, and we're taking unnecessary casualties because of it. Now, I told Johnny I'd go back and set up a system that will use my postcombat interrogation techniques, but I'd like you to come with me. I'm too old to be trudging around battlefields on my own. Besides, we click well together, and it'll get you out of the Pentagon." (In our previous correspondence I'd made no secret of my hatred for the aptly named "Five-sided Puzzle Palace.")

I was flabbergasted. For weeks and weeks I'd badgered and harassed

---

* General Harold K. Johnson, the Army Chief of Staff, the mere mention of whose name brought Kesterson and me to attention.

OPO's Infantry Branch for a change of assignment. I'd been told to "keep quiet or chance ruining a promising career," and I'd finally taken another step forward in the ticket-punching parade by accepting that guidance in the interests of the "bigger things" my counselor said I was "earmarked for." But then in walks S. L. A. Marshall—a man whose World War II books I'd read and reread since childhood, a man whom I was admittedly in awe of—and offers me not just an out from my horrible job, but the opportunity of a lifetime. It was almost unbelievable.

"When do we leave, sir?" I asked.

General Marshall told me the Chief of Staff would want to see me before we headed off in just over a week's time. Even so, when I was called to Johnson's office, I felt not unlike a parish priest might feel upon being told to report to the Pope in Rome. I viewed the meeting as a rare opportunity to have the Chief's ear, so I prepared a list of points to squeeze into my audience with him, all regarding what I felt was needed to improve our combat efficiency in Vietnam. Much to my disappointment, when I arrived at his office I was told exactly five minutes had been scheduled for our meeting. "Take no more," said the General's aide, Colonel William Caldwell, "the Old Man has a very busy afternoon. You'll be in and out."

I'd met General Johnson once before, about a month earlier at an awards ceremony. Then, as now, when I was called in to see him, I was struck first by the size and splendor of his office, and by the windows (wonderful windows we in the dark depths of the Pentagon could only dream of) that looked out over the swollen Pentagon parking lot and beyond, to the Potomac. The Chief greeted me in his formal, no-nonsense way. At the age of fifty-four, Harold K. Johnson was the youngest Chief of Staff since Douglas MacArthur—no mean feat for a man who spent three years of World War II in Japanese prisoner-of-war camps after the fall of Bataan. Tall, straight, and handsome, Johnson *looked* like a Chief of Staff. He was a sincere, kind, and genuinely good man, who, word had it, was also devoutly religious, with a deep dislike for such soldierly pursuits as hard liquor, fast women, or foul barracks talk. I knew to be on my best behavior. "Sit down, Colonel," he said to me now, "I want to brief you on your mission with General Marshall."

It took him about three minutes, the gist being that with a view toward improving the collection of basic data on U.S.-fought battles in Vietnam for a future, official Army history of the war, Slam would teach the after-action reporting techniques he'd pioneered during WW II to selected U.S. Army officers in all divisions and separate brigades in the theater. Because General Marshall would be visiting Vietnam as a private citizen, Johnson went on to explain, my job throughout the tour, rather than simply assisting him, would be that of representative of DA's Chief of Military History. Privately, I didn't understand the General Marshall-as-private-citizen twist, but I barely had a chance to contemplate it when General Johnson, after a considered pause, said, "Take care with Slam, Colonel. He is the Army's powerful friend, but he can be a treacherous enemy." I masked my surprise. As far as the conversation *I* was following went, that comment came straight out of left field.

With two minutes left out of my five, it was small-talk time. The General had met my family at the awards ceremony; now he asked how they were, and how my work was going. "Everything's fine, General," I replied, painfully conscious of the clock running out. "But, sir, if you have a minute there's something bothering me that I'd like to discuss with you."

"Let's hear it," he said.

"We've had U.S. Army units in Vietnam for eighteen months," I blurted out. "Almost one-third of the Army is committed to that war. But at Fort Benning there is only a handful of field-grade officers with Vietnam experience, and half of these were advisers. They weren't with U.S. units. We're just not putting our best and most recently experienced combat officers into the school system, which is where I believe they belong. We're sending them everywhere else to get their tickets punched, as if their careers took priority over the war. Vietnam is the toughest war we've ever fought, and we're going at it as though we're fighting World War II all over again."

"Now just a minute, Colonel Hackworth," the General bristled. "In terms of enemy and terrain, the fighting in Vietnam is no different for infantry than when we fought in the Philippines after Pearl Harbor."

"Sir," I said, "that statement is about as far from the truth about the nature of the war in Vietnam as I have ever heard!"

I couldn't believe the words had come out of my mouth. I could feel my face getting hot as General Johnson, red-faced with anger, stared at me from behind his desk. After a moment he leaned back in his chair and took a deep breath. He picked up his phone and called his aide. "Cancel all my appointments for the rest of the afternoon," he said. Then he turned to me, his face grim and his voice icily stern. "I will give you the rest of the day to justify that remark, Colonel Hackworth."

Johnson walked briskly over to a large worktable across from his desk and pulled out some Vietnam battle maps. "Every general who has fought in Vietnam has briefed me at this desk and with these maps," he said.

I'd gotten his attention, so I decided to go for broke. "Sir, maybe that's the nub of the problem. Maybe those generals do not know how different the war is either. In my experience over there—and I have to admit, I was only with one brigade, but we were all over Vietnam and I talked to a lot of people—the only people who really know how to fight this thing are the Australians and the Viet Cong."

General Johnson and I talked at the worktable for about an hour and a half. We refought the 1/101's battles at Tuy Hoa and Dak To, discussed enemy tricks and tactics, and how, until we'd learned, the brigade fell for the enemy's lures and got itself chewed up again and again. When I'd made my case, the General put his arm around me and walked me to the door of his office. "Son," he said, "I'm going to think about all you've told me. I'm sure you've made some valid points. But if you're right, I must say it is most discouraging. I only hope this tour with Slam proves you wrong." Johnson patted my back. "I'll have a look at what's happening at Fort Benning, too," he said. "Meanwhile, Colonel . . . good luck."

I felt as though I'd won him, I really did. And it felt great.

At the end of the day, I met General Marshall for a drink. I told him about my meeting with the Chief of Staff, and how knocked out I was that Johnson would compare Vietnam to Bataan or island combat. Marshall said, "I agree with Johnny. Infantry combat is infantry combat." I could have fallen off my chair. *Does he really believe that?* I wondered, but I had no time to ask him, because just then we were joined at our table by one of Slam's old friends, General Moshe Dayan. When you traveled with Slam, I was beginning to discover, it was first-class all the way.

The former Chief of Staff of the Israeli Army had recently returned from Vietnam, where he'd looked at damn near everything. He'd accompanied platoon- and company-size U.S. units deep into the Highlands jungles (something I never heard of any American general doing in Vietnam at any time throughout the U.S involvement); he'd observed larger actions, too, and come away incredulous over the American style of war. He thought our companies too eager to rush to battle at any price. He was amazed at our use of firepower, citing one case where the Americans fired more than twenty thousand rounds of artillery in a single action. Yes, Dayan admitted, the action did result in some two hundred enemy dead, but at a price of more than all the artillery used during the Sinai campaign! Dayan's personal study had shown him that the enemy almost invariably had the initiative on the battlefield, and he quoted Mao's rules of warfare verbatim,* suggesting that until these simple guidelines were acknowledged by our leaders, the enemy would continue to have the upper hand.

Dayan confirmed many of my own thoughts (or, more accurately,

---

* "When the enemy advances, we retreat. When he escapes, we harass. When he retreats, we pursue. When he is tired, we attack. When he burns, we put out the fire. When he loots, we attack. When he pursues, we hide. When he retreats, we return."

instincts) on the war, which was a great relief, given that they were thoughts I'd expressed that very afternoon to the Chief of Staff of our Army. General Marshall, meanwhile, countered all the Israeli's arguments with "We'll wear them down. No one can take the kind of punishment we're dishing out and win. Look at the Germans and the Japs. . . ." Finally, having now heard Vietnam compared to World War II twice in one day (by no less than the Army's boss and by one of America's top military analysts), I decided it was best to excuse myself and go home to wish Patty and the kids a happy Thanksgiving and a merry Christmas—*I won't be home for the next four months, ya' see.* . . . The poor Army family.

Both United States Army, Vietnam (USARV) and MACV's Saigon headquarters were incredibly plush, and worlds away from the city that throbbed just beyond their respective gates. Outside were taxicabs and bicycles, and beautiful girls with long, black hair and lovely *au dais* that flew like kites in the steamy breeze. Inside were charts and graphs and aides and assistants bustling busily through air-conditioned rooms. The staffs of both HQs, officer and enlisted, wore jungle fatigues complete with the new, canvas-black embossed insignia recently developed to be sniperproof in the bush. They wore the cleated canvas boots of the warriors, too, but unlike the real warriors, whose battle scars were mirrored in those boots rubbed white by rocks and undergrowth, these rear-echelon commandos (or rear-echelon motherfuckers [REMFs], as they were known in the parlance of Vietnam) were peacetime Army perfection. The only thing mirrored in their gleaming, polished boots were the overhead lights in their busy offices. I would have been amused by the whole scene if it weren't for the knowledge that the guys here in these pristine headquarters received the same "combat pay" as the soldiers who really did the job, living in the mud and risking their lives every day.

The MACV briefing General Marshall and I received before we went into the field was suspiciously rosy in its assessment of how went the war, but it matched well the view Slam had professed to Dayan and me in Washington. As such the General was positively jubilant as we proceeded on to Saigon's Tan Son Nhut airport. There, a VIP two-engine aircraft bearing a one-star red standard was waiting for us, its pilot, copilot, and crew chief all lined up in front of the plane waiting to salute and shake the hand of Slam Marshall. This was a far cry from what I was used to. The way most guys got around Vietnam was by hitchhiking a ride, often after waiting at heliports and airports for hours, or even days. But with Slam, it was red-carpet treatment all the way—doors held open, people bowing and scraping wherever he went, and not a moment's delay.

Given his reputation and all the respect accorded to him, one who had never seen Slam might easily imagine that he was an imposing presence, like a MacArthur or a Gavin. He was not. On the contrary, Slam Marshall was a small, very plump man in his mid-sixties, whom one would be immediately forgiven for mistaking for an animated sack of potatoes rather than a flag officer. He was no doubt the most unmilitary-looking general since the Civil War. His uniform, which he always wore in the field, was permanently wrinkled World War II khakis or fatigues. His shirt pockets, which were always unbuttoned, were home to numerous felt-tipped pens, all sticking out. His fatigue cap had embossed on it, front and center, a general's star twice, perhaps three times larger than, the regulation size. Marshall actually looked more like a caricature of a general than the real McCoy, but because he wore his ridiculous costume with complete self-confidence, while a trooper or an officer might look at him in utter amazement, he'd never, *ever* allow himself to laugh.

When everyone at Tan Son Nhut had finished kissing Slam's ring, we got into the VIP twin engine and took off on the first leg of what Slam would describe, ten years later in his autobiography,* as my "journey into disillusion." He would not be wrong. But all the sad and sorry revelations I would make were still well down the track that day at Tan Son Nhut, and for the first few weeks of my tour with Slam I was perpetually high, with the mission, the man, *and* the extraordinary opportunity being with him allowed me, as an outsider, to play in the inner circle of the general-officer world.

Our first stop was the 1st Air Cav Division's base camp at An Khe, where we were greeted effusively by its CG, Major General John "Jack" Norton. Norton was an old friend of Marshall's, the two having met in 1944 when Slam was doing his postoperation study of the Normandy invasion.† As the two men reminisced, I stood back and marveled at the metamorphosis of the 1st Air Cav's Highlands home. It bore almost no resemblance to the place the 1/101st had secured for the Flying Horsemen in mid-1965. What had then been a village of perhaps twenty-five hundred mostly mountain people had sprung up into a ticky-tacky cardboard instant city with more than eighteen thousand Viet and Montagnard camp followers. The jungle was gone. The Cav had chopped it away to build a barricade—eighteen kilometers in circumference—inside which was the base camp, a fine airfield, and the towering How Kow mountain, which sat in the middle like a silent giant. Choppers and fixed-wing aircraft filled the sky overhead. Many more could be seen dotting the long runway, or in sandbagged

---

* Published two years after his death, in 1979.
† Then a whiz-kid major, Jack Norton had been G-3, 82d Airborne, for that operation.

revetments on either side. The 1st Air Cav truly was a going concern, and if ever one were looking for a "we're winning" reading on the wartime barometer, An Khe was certainly it.

General Marshall and I went to work immediately, setting up the first of four "schools" to teach his postcombat interviewing technique. Essentially a copy of the system police use for reconstructing a crime, Marshall's method entailed bringing together the participants of whatever action was to be reviewed, and, with a trained interviewer guiding the discussion, reconstructing that action as a group. (For Slam's schools, the actions we examined were recommended to us by a unit's Operations people or commander, and we conducted the interviews at the An Khe base camp or by visiting the participant units near their own positions.) While each man, whatever his rank, was allowed to speak freely about what had happened on the ground, the reason the interviews were conducted in groups rather than with individuals was to minimize the bullshit factor. The men kept one another on track, so not only could a fuller picture be developed with everyone's input, but a truer one, with a minimum of exaggeration. It was a very good system. And though the fighters eagerly did most of the talking, the interviewer was a crucial element, because a good one could capitalize on the tiniest scraps of information to get to the crux of a story. Yet the interviewing drill itself could be as simple as a trooper saying, "Small-arms fire was tearing into us. I saw four men go down and then I saw Whitey running up on my left holding a grenade," and then the interviewer breaking in to say to Whitey (who would also be among the participants gathered for the occasion), "Okay, Whitey, what happened then?"

The object of the endeavor for Slam and me was not to draw conclusions about the fights we examined in the schools. (Though it would quickly prove unavoidable—like the disturbing observation that, a year after Ia Drang, the Air Cav was still looking for big battles, still war-gaming huge, totally unimaginative hammer-and-anvil operations à la Benning, though the enemy had long before reverted to *economy of force* tactics that made the Cav's WW II approach like swatting flies with a sledgehammer.) Instead, our job was simply to train our students, all officers from the Army's Military History Detachments already in place in Vietnam, in a method of after-action scrutiny that could be easily set up and maintained in their own units. *They* were the ones to draw conclusions from their own battles while collecting their historical data, and make any fallout "lessons learned" available to their commands to prevent the same mistakes being repeated in future engagements.

A tireless worker, General Marshall conducted all the interviews in the first school while the officer-students observed the technique. Slam really was a master at it, with a natural feel for battle and a great understanding of squad and platoon tactics, his specialty. He also had a most incredible memory, bordering on total recall. On one occasion he stunned everyone in the room when he turned to a burly, old-soldier platoon sergeant in his mid-thirties and insisted he knew him, though the sergeant was positive they'd never met. "It's in my book *Night Drop*," said Slam. "I met you at Normandy, right after the 82d jumped in at Ste. Mère Église. You were in the 2d Battalion, 325th Glider Regiment."

"No, sir," said the sergeant. "That wasn't me, but I'll be damned if you're not talking about my older brother. He was in the 2/325 Glider, just like you say."

We stayed at An Khe for two weeks, working solidly by day and enjoying the expansive hospitality of General Norton by night. The Cav CG was most supportive of Slam's effort here in Vietnam, and made sure our every need and comfort was looked after, both in the field and in the Cav's Hilton-like VIP quarters where we were put up. We ate in the generals' mess, a room with three long tables forming a horseshoe, the head of which was reserved for the generals and VIP guests like Slam. The staff and less important guests (like me) sat opposite one another at the two legs perpendicular to the generals' table, and throughout each evening's three-course, five-star-quality gourmet meal (presented on fine china embossed with the Cav insignia and served by black waiters in starched white jackets—probably line infantrymen who'd found a home in the rear), we politely eavesdropped on what the VIPs were saying. There was little, usually no, talk of war during these formal dinners. In fact, you'd never even know a war was going on unless the generator sputtered, coughed, and went out, plunging the room into darkness. Fortunately, an efficient generator operator (probably another line soldier who'd found the good life in the rear) would promptly switch on the backup unit, and the lights would go on all over the mess hall. Usually this was just in time for after-dinner cigars, liqueurs, coffee, and conversation, at which time the guests normally told some well-worn anecdotes.

Slam was a marvelous storyteller, and as "senior" guest, most evenings of our stay with the Cav he held the mess-hall floor. One night, however, found him sharing the spotlight with author John Steinbeck, who was in Vietnam to visit his son, a radio announcer for Armed Forces Network in Saigon, and to take home all the "good news" on the war effort. In his last years of life, Steinbeck was in pretty shocking physical condition, particularly compared to Marshall, his contemporary; the two distinguished guests had equally healthy egos, though, and there soon proved to be insufficient room at the head table to contain them both. At the happy hour before dinner, the two old men had spent their time sniffing at each other like bulldogs.

Throughout the meal, normally cheerful, twinkly-eyed Slam had been stony-faced as his Nobel Prize–winning rival showed him the respect he might show a copyboy for an insignificant weekly rag. When the dinner was finished, the two men spent the rest of the evening fighting for the floor to deliver their respective tales of "the time I talked to" kings or presidents, and by the time the whole thing was over, I'm sure I wasn't the only one to gratefully tumble into bed, absolutely exhausted.

After reconstructing two of the 1st Air Cav's actions for the students of the first school, we said good-bye to Jack Norton and his luxurious An Khe home and flew off to the equally sumptuous 1st Division base camp at Di An. The base-camp mentality in Vietnam was an outgrowth of the static days of the Korean War. Back then the Vietnam-era generals had been majors and lieutenant colonels on the outside looking enviously in; no doubt many of them had thought, *When I'm a general I'll have that, too,* and now that they were, they were going to, even if the base camps had even less place in this war than they had in the last. In Vietnam, a frontless war, the security requirement alone at these base camps was massive. At the 1st Air Cav, an entire brigade—fully one-third of the division—was engaged solely in protecting the unit's An Khe home. Similarly, by the time I'd left the 1/101st in June, one-third of its combat power was tied up guarding Phan Rang. In the 1/101st this was particularly significant, in that when we'd originally gone to Phan Rang, the position was almost Charlie-free. But the longer we stayed, the more interest the enemy took in the place. By the time I left, they were regularly blowing up vehicles, lobbing an occasional mortar shell, and doing selective sniping. So almost by design, the base camp invited enemy activity, and then depleted the fighting strength of a unit in the effort to counter it. Frontline troop strength was continually drained, too, by the number of men needed to stay behind simply to service the base camps as they grew bigger and more plush. And in that the camps created an extra layer of diversion in which a trooper, fresh out of the hospital or back from R&R, could lose himself before returning to his unit, it wasn't long before these massive installations were really as much the enemy as the enemy himself.

But you'd be hard-pressed trying to convince the high-living generals of that, or even Slam, who took to such splendor as if it were his God-given right. As for myself, no doubt I was initially seduced by the good life at An Khe, and even at first in Di An, where I was assigned to share the air-conditioned bungalow (complete with a bar in the corner of the living room and a full-time Viet maid who kept shoes polished, clothes washed and pressed, and beds made with perfectly starched white sheets) of one of the Big Red One's assistant division commanders, Bernard Rogers. But my enthusiasm disappeared pretty quickly when I saw the terrible complacency such living engendered. ADC Rogers, for example, emerged from his room each morning wearing pajamas and a dressing gown. Worse, even though the information we gained during Slam's schools exposed critical deficiencies in the U.S. effort from the level of the individual soldier the whole way up the chain of command, most of the generals at their evening happy hours seemed blissfully unconcerned, if not totally unaware, that any such problems existed.

Operation Attleboro was a prime case in point. With more than twenty thousand Americans involved at the height of the fighting, and more air and artillery used than on D-Day of the Normandy invasion, as of December 1966, Attleboro was the biggest operation of the war so far. And according to Colonel Stoutner, G-3, II Field Force (who practically begged Slam to study it as part of his second school), it was nothing less than a classic, brilliant victory over the Viet Cong. But something smelled very funny to Slam and me about the perfectly planned, stunningly fought, triumphantly concluded battle—our briefers' contention that the Viet Cong no longer controlled their time-hallowed refuge of War Zone D, for one thing. And indeed, when Slam and I took Stoutner's suggestion and turned our undivided attention to Attleboro, what we found was an operation that was rotten through and through.

Attleboro was initiated in the middle of September by the 196th Brigade, the first U.S. brigade of its kind to fight in Vietnam. Less than a year before, the unit had been a band of two thousand raw recruits. After six months of training, from "This is a rifle. . ." to the Brigade in the Attack, this instant unit had been declared combat-ready, and prepared to deploy to the Dominican Republic to replace the 82d Airborne element that had been there since the beginning of the unrest. But at the last moment the 196th was rerouted to Vietnam. The new destination would prove a hell of a place for them to have to wet their feet, because all declarations to the contrary notwithstanding, the 196th was *not* combat-ready.

The unit had not been trained correctly from the outset. The initial NCO cadre was mostly artillery or armor, and even the brigade's operational report for the period ending 31 October remarked that "the serious shortage of infantry personnel made the training mission extremely difficult to execute." As Steve Prazenka always said, "Learn it right and you'll do it right the rest of your life. Learn it wrong and you'll spend the rest of your life trying to get it right"—if the 196th's training mission was difficult to execute, it shouldn't have been hard for the powers that be to imagine how a combat mission would go. To make matters worse, Colonel Frances S. Conaty, the 196th's initial commander (and a Medal of Honor winner with a reputation as a good infantry soldier), was relieved when the unit arrived in Vietnam, and was replaced by one Brigadier General Edward H. deSaussure, Jr., an artillery-man who had never before commanded or served in an infantry unit. So the stage was set for a very messy baptism of fire for the first instant brigade.

From the commencement of Operation Attleboro, for almost seven weeks the 196th had a leisurely walk in the sun. They made few contacts with the enemy but accomplished a lot in their wide-ranging mission by uncovering and destroying many VC supply depots and logistic installations. It wasn't until 3 November that the brigade's good life came to an end, when it became apparent the enemy was going to strike back. In good World War II fashion, General deSaussure requested and got the 25th Division's 1/27th Wolfhound Battalion to act as the anvil while two of the 196th's organic battalions played hammers to drive the VC into a killing zone. At least that was the plan. On the ground, all intentions quickly went by the boards when C Company, 1/27th landed on a cold LZ and proceeded north right into a VC ambush that got them from the front, both sides, *and* the rear. Within two and a half hours the company had taken fourteen WIA and ten KIA, the latter figure including the company commander, the first sergeant, one of the platoon leaders, and one of the platoon sergeants. Until the 1/27's battalion commander, Major Guy S. "Sandy" Meloy III, came and took control, the senior officer on the ground was a brand-new second lieutenant on his first operation.

A1/27 was brought in to reinforce its battered sister company, and was ordered to "roll up the VCs' flank." DeSaussure, meanwhile, ordered three companies from two of his battalions to go to the rescue. All were made OPCON of the 1/27th, giving CO Meloy control of five companies by the end of the first day's battle.

By the end of the second day, a wounded Sandy Meloy was simulta-neously commanding *eleven* rifle companies from four different battalions. In lethal action that found A1/27 hanging on in the face of numerous frontal attacks (after being ambushed just as C1/27 had been the day before), deSaussure had begun to commit unit after unit piecemeal, without rhyme or reason. Somehow all these units ended up under Meloy's operational control, and it was just fortunate that Meloy, the son of General Guy S. Meloy II (who fourteen years before had taken such an interest in me at Fort Benning), was an able commander with a hell of a lot of troop-duty experience under his belt. He fought his ad hoc mini division beautifully for thirty straight hours, until Major General DePuy (late of MACV, now CG, 1st Division) arrived to relieve Meloy's forces and take over the battle from the totally unqualified deSaussure.

It was at this point, according to all the official reports, that the battle turned in favor of the Americans: DePuy apparently decided to turn the entire region into a parking lot. Practicing what he preached as the author of the big U.S. search-and-destroy operations, he employed huge "Rome Plow" bulldozers that plowed, ripped, and sheared through the jungle, leaving bare swaths a thousand feet wide in which VC movement could be easily spotted from the air. In some areas he had engineers use ditchdigging machines to slash into the Viet Cong's ingenious network of underground tunnels and bunkers (most of which, time would prove, remained untouched, unshaken, indeed *undetected* throughout the U.S. involvement) that ran through both War Zones C and D like a poor man's subway system. DePuy believed in maximum firepower, too, and by the time Attleboro was over, a total of twelve tons of tac air, thirty-five thousand artillery rounds, and eleven B-52 strikes had rained down on the enemy.

DePuy was actively and aggressively seeking what he called the enemy's "threshold of pain," the point beyond which he believed the enemy could not sustain the punishment we were inflicting. It was his solution to end the war. Therefore, not unlike Sherman when he marched across Georgia, wherever DePuy went he left destruction in his wake. In the Iron Triangle, for example, more than six thousand peasants were moved to refugee camps and their abandoned villages were burned and bulldozed to the ground so their land could be declared a free-fire zone (with anyone caught within it considered VC, fair game for all choppers and spotter planes that hunted there). Defoliants like Agent Orange were sprayed frequently throughout the 1st Div's AO of War Zones C and D, and the ground had been bombarded so frequently by B-52 strikes that it looked from the air as if it had been pressed in a waffle iron.

DePuy would have had no complaints from me for what appeared to be his Napoleonic "the weaker the infantry, the heavier the employment of cannons" philosophy. There was no question that using firepower was better than wasting lives. But the problem was that a lot of lives were being wasted, too. Each day as Slam and I collected our information on Attleboro, visiting unit after unit that had somehow been involved, I got more and more depressed to find the same problems occurring, the same lethal mistakes being made again and again—and they were the exact mistakes we'd made in the 1/101st as far back as a year before. The Viet Cong, those dumb country hicks (or so we perceived them), were still fleecing us city slickers every day. Irrespective of Attleboro's official report of victory, the fact was that the operation (which claimed 155 U.S. lives and another 741 WIA) was just another case of dancing to the enemy's tune, a tune written years before during the Indochina war. The tactics the NVA and Main Force VC employed at Attleboro were right out of *Street Without Joy*. The standard bitch of the French ("I just *know* the little bastards are somewhere around here—but go and find them in that mess")[1] was the same complaint Slam and I heard again and again from the Yankee "long noses" a dozen years later, as their accounts of the fight revealed that the VC initiated or controlled almost every action. (During Attleboro, they sucked U.S. units into well-prepared killing zones—almost a replay of the lure we fell for at My Canh—and then ate the Americans up at eyeball-to-eyeball range. All our men could do was try their damnedest to extricate their dead and wounded and themselves, and get some distance so they could hammer the enemy with our unbeatable firepower.) And yet, when I asked the company and battalion commanders who'd participated in Attleboro whether they'd read Bernard Fall's basic primer on the war, few could answer in the affirmative.

During our reconstruction of Attleboro, Slam and I found that other U.S. units were being devastated without meeting the enemy at all. In the 199th Infantry Brigade, for example, one company had taken sixty casualties over a three-month period, forty of which had been from booby traps (generally constructed of American "debris" and generously emplaced by the VC throughout War Zones C and D). I did a quick calculation of how many of the remaining twenty had been friendly fire WIAs, and when it was all shaken out the enemy might as well have stayed home. "To subdue the enemy without fighting," said Sun Tzu, "is the acme of skill."

This is not to say that these U.S. units were not making any kills. At Attleboro alone the enemy KIA by body count was reported to be 1,106.* The operations Slam and I studied *were* hurting the enemy, but it was not at a price the opposition could not sustain. According to one of the basic principles of guerrilla warfare, if the G is not losing he is winning, and if the G's opponent is not winning he is losing. As long as the VC and NVA could sustain their losses, they were not losing the war, whatever "defeats" their foe ascribed to them. And there was no reason to believe they would not be able to continue to sustain their losses, even in the face of Westy and DePuy's search-and-destroy tactics and the rich man's war the Americans were waging. If the VC and NVA "lost" at Attleboro, it was a conscious decision to run away to fight another day. No doubt they would go to ground and lick their wounds, but just as had been the case in the Indochina war, going to ground was just the first step in rebuilding, in strengthening their ranks and their will to prepare to meet us again on the very same ground as

---

* The number of individual weapons captured during the fighting at Attleboro was only 141, however, which made that body count highly suspicious: while a 4:1 body count/weapons captured ratio was fairly reasonable, 12:1 was extremely unlikely.

before. So even if Operation Attleboro was a victory for us in the WW II
sense (i.e., we held the ground at the end of the battle), in terms of the
material losses in both choppers and ammo used, in the number of U.S.
dead and wounded, *and* the fact that the enemy would (and did) move right
back into the area the minute our units pulled out, Attleboro was a Pyrrhic
victory at best.

But no one wanted to know. While all the generals Slam and I met
seemed wholly behind our endeavor, none showed any real interest in the
findings the schools uncovered. The same base-camp complacency that did
not see the need for self-examination in the first place had led to what
appeared to be a total absence of curiosity (even when the hard work was
done for them) about what was happening around them. I would have liked
to tell these generals what we were learning on those many occasions when,
to my utter amazement, one or another sought my advice on some future
plan, but since Slam never broached the severity of the problems when he
was turned to for guidance, I certainly didn't think it was my place. I should
have gone right ahead, though. By the time we'd finished the second school,
I realized that in the power game I was way ahead, and could probably have
said anything I damn well pleased.

Traveling with Slam, I was accorded respect well beyond that due my
rank of light colonel. I was not a general and I didn't belong, but the real
generals seemed to forget that or put it aside. For the purposes of the trip at
least, I was one of them. It didn't hurt that I was representing the Office of
the Chief of Military History on the express recommendation of the Army
Chief of Staff; everybody assumed I was tight with General Johnson, and
again and again I found flag officers who wouldn't even have acknowledged
my presence at other times slapping my back and acting out the role of big
buddies. I was knocked out that the guys who wore stars still had to play the
political game, and even more so that they thought I had the power to give
any one of them a little career jump. And it was General DePuy, of all
people, who was the most striking example of those who sought to take
advantage of my "close" relationship with the Chief.

William Eugene DePuy was considered by insiders to be the prime
architect of America's war in Vietnam, and a principal in the development
of the U.S. "frontier" strategy there. He was an extraordinarily brilliant
man, or so went the word, who had made his name as a staff officer, having
had little command experience at all and none on the company level. After
he took over the Big Red One, DePuy quickly became infamous throughout
Vietnam for on-the-spot relief, firing some thirty battalion commanders,
most within days of their arrival. While this was actually more the work of
DePuy's no-bullshit ADC for tactics, James Hollingsworth (a gravelly-

voiced, colorful character who cursed a blue streak, had five Purple Hearts from Africa, Sicily, and Europe during World War II, and was undoubtedly the real power and spirit behind the 1st Div), * what was interesting was how, when DePuy finally settled on the battalion commanders he wanted, their average height was at least six feet. It was a Frederick the Great thing, I was sure. DePuy himself was very short, and ferretlike in both look and manner, and whenever I saw him conferring with his towering subordinates I couldn't help but think of old Frederick and his runt complex. Still, DePuy would go on to have an unparalleled impact on the Army. Under his continued patronage, in subsequent years his handpicked Praetorian Guard would slip into the Army's top jobs. DePuy himself would never go "all the way" to Chief of Staff or Supreme Commander, NATO, but his incredible influence as a power broker in the top tiers of the Army would have much to do with who did (and who did not). Later still, he would expand his base and take on his most ignoble role, that of undeclared head of the crusade to rewrite the history of U.S. involvement in Vietnam, of which he was so much a part.

But that was all in the future. In 1966, DePuy was already a powerful, powerful guy, so I was totally unprepared for the ingratiating smile he flashed me when Slam and I arrived at Di An, or the way he took me aside as soon as he could for a private word. Though I'd met with him quite regularly the previous year when, as J-3 of MACV, he'd visited me in my S-3 role with the 1/101, one thing I never would have expected would be to be greeted by DePuy like a long-lost brother. (DePuy was even more fawning and deferential to Marshall, but since most of the generals we met treated Slam not unlike a king, in that respect his behavior was unremarkable.) "Hack," he said, "I'd like you to do me a favor if you get a chance when you talk to the Chief. Just tell him I'm a good man. And tell him—sure, I curse and carry on a bit, but it's all an act. It's what the troops in the Big Red One expect. So if you could just tell him I'm a good man. . . ."

Slam and I spent Christmas with the 1st Division. On the twenty-sixth, Bob Hope gave his traveling show for a huge Big Red One crowd. It seemed like madness to assemble such a large target for VC mortars and rockets, but the antagonists had declared a cease-fire and the show went on despite intelligence reports that the Viet Cong would strike during the Christmas truce. I didn't go. Besides the fact that it was mind-boggling to me that

* Jim Hollingsworth went on to become one of the most effective high-level advisers of the Vietnam War. At An Loc in 1972, he virtually took command of ARVN's III Corps, and used B-52s like tac air to stop the major NVA offensive dead in its tracks.

DePuy would take such a mammoth risk with the lives of his men, I'd made a practice of missing Bob Hope shows since Korea, because I didn't like his slick brand of humor and I'd just preferred to stay with my unit and avoid all the confusion. Slam, on the other hand, was a Bob Hope fan, and a distinguished guest at the performance. He was still chuckling when I met him after his return, and repeated what he considered the classic Hope joke: "The U.S. bombing raids on North Vietnam are the best slum-clearing program Uncle Ho ever had."

The following day, still during the cease-fire, a VC unit ambushed a 1st Division platoon whose patrol also violated the truce. The ambush took place less than two klicks from the now vacant Bob Hope venue; with the VC armed with both a machine gun and a mortar, a day earlier they would have made some impact on that show. The Americans took seven KIA and several WIA in yet another classic "no one's learning" scenario: a young, OCS-trained lieutenant had allowed his platoon to cross a wide-open rice paddy. The first I heard of the incident was when DePuy came dashing into the generals' mess as excited as a second lieutenant going to his first guard mount. He told Slam to saddle up—they were off to battle. As DePuy dashed out again with Slam in hot pursuit, I marveled at this incredible example of oversupervision: *a division commander rushing to the scene of one of his platoons' open-and-shut screwups?* Where were the platoon's company and battalion commanders? Where was the brigade commander? From the information Slam's schools were routinely revealing, most likely they would be on the scene as well, overhead in choppers, all of them issuing orders and playing what became known as the Great Squad Leader in the Sky, creating absolute chaos in an already confused situation. Such was not the way to win a war, but the longer the war went on, the worse this situation got, as many senior officers saw their units' fights and patrols only in terms of the glory it could bring them, or in terms of the medals and ribbons they could win (awards so common that they only became conspicuous by their absence in a guy's fruit salad) without leaving the beyond-rifle-range comfort of twelve hundred to fifteen hundred feet.* In the case of DePuy's and Slam's dash toward the sound of guns, by the time they arrived on the scene the guns were silent; there was little to do but evacuate the dead and wounded and come home, which they did.

For New Year's Eve, I took Slam with me to a party at the New York Bar on Tu Do Street in Saigon. The place was owned and operated by my dear

---

* The worst case I heard while with Slam of the Great Squad Leader syndrome was one of a platoon leader who, pushed for time by *his* Great Squad Leader in the Sky, ordered his men to use a well-traveled trail through the jungle. The unit fell victim to a single command-detonated claymore mine set up along the trail; the result was eight wounded and seven killed, the latter figure including the lieutenant, who, according to survivors, had always made a point of traveling through the bush and never using trails.

friend John Westmoreland, who, since his battlefield commission in my Fighter Company in Korea, had risen through the ranks to make light colonel (I was so proud). After a couple of early-sixties tours of Vietnam, he'd recently quit the Army, joined the State Department detachment as a civilian, and come back to the war zone, where he'd made a life for himself. He'd met and married a Vietnamese woman named Jackie who had a penchant for having children and making money; they had one kid already, as well as two or three very successful bars on Tu Do Street. My personal favorite was the New York, with its mirrored walls, laminex tables (each separated from the next by a curtain), and big American tape decks that blared out down-home country-and-western and popular Beatles tunes. Troops went there on pass to fall in love with any one of Westy's resident tea ladies, those fragile Oriental dolls who melted hearts with their lies ("I see you one time, I love you too much . . ."); the boys fresh out of the bush didn't care, as long as they could pretend it was true.

Westy had a cozy corner organized for us when we arrived at the bar, and a strikingly beautiful good-time girl for Slam. I'd been more than a little apprehensive about taking him along (anyone with a discerning eye would say that the New York, like most of the bars on Tu Do Street, was actually pretty sleazy), but it proved to be a wasted worry—Slam loved the place. The hardest part of the evening was actually in getting from the front door to the table. Very rarely did one see a general on Tu Do Street, so when Marshall walked in wearing his distinctive rumpled khakis and huge general's star, it caused a tremendous stir (to his great delight).

The rest of the evening was drunkenly wonderful. Slam displayed an incredibly earthy side which meshed perfectly with Westmoreland's, and when the New Year came and went and Westy suggested we go back to his house to continue the party, Slam was all for it. So everyone paired off, made our way to John's villa, and drank our way through the dawn. At some stage in the wee hours Slam and his tea lady disappeared, and I had a good chuckle thinking the old fox had gotten (or was getting) his ashes hauled by the Viet bar girl. She was probably the first Vietnamese civilian he'd even *talked* to. Sadly, all was not as it appeared. In the morning, before I stumbled out of his house, Westy told me the girl had reported in on her night with Slam. "General have many things in head but nothing in dick," she'd said. "He go to sleep right away. But Number One general! Big man!"

Months before, still in Washington and thinking I was stuck in the Pentagon for life, I'd written an article titled "No Magic Formula" to pass on some of the knowledge I'd gained fighting with the 1/101st in Vietnam. With my deputy Bill Kesterson's magic edit and polish, we'd forged it into a great piece, and I'd sent it to "Gentleman Jim" Timothy, my old CO, now a general and Assistant Commandant at Fort Benning. Tim had said it would be published in *Infantry* magazine early in the new year, so when Slam and I arrived at the 173d Airborne Brigade's base camp at Bien Hoa, I was surprised to see a stack of mimeographed advance copies of the article on the desk of the 173d's CG, Brigadier General John Deane. Even more surprising, I found that Deane had attached a glowing cover letter to each copy addressing my qualifications to write same.* Apparently the piece was mandatory reading within the 173d.

It would be a tremendous understatement to say I was very proud of that. But as pride goes before a fall, it was soon evident that few of the brigade's soldiers at Bien Hoa had done their homework. The 173d, now the oldest serving U.S. Army maneuver unit fighting in Vietnam, was battle-scarred but not battle-wise. Commanders seemed preoccupied with the big picture. They didn't notice how the small things, the things that made a unit effective and prevented unnecessary casualties, were slipping, and slipping badly. Guys were using soap, toothpaste, and shaving cream before operations. They were smoking and wearing mosquito repellent on patrol. I even saw one guy returning from patrol bopping along to the strains of Jimi Hendrix pouring out of a portable radio the kid had bought at the PX and carried with him into the field. Few NCOs and company-grade officers were doing anything about the slow disintegration. Old NCOs were already getting scarce, and the young captains weren't with their companies long enough to make a dent. More than a few of the men Slam and I talked to didn't even know their company commanders' names. It was a bad situation, and one made all the more worrisome by the fact that the 173d had some of the *better* officers, NCOs, and enlisted men we'd seen among the units we'd examined to date. If an elite Airborne outfit like this one was falling apart, what more could possibly be expected from the average, unglamorous, footslogging infantry unit?

Visiting the 173d was not an uplifting way to begin the New Year. Fortunately the next stop was my old home, the 1st Brigade, 101st Airborne Division at Phan Rang, and there my spirits were lifted instantly. Unlike any other Regular unit I observed during my tour with Slam, the Screaming Eagles were routinely employing tactics that actually fit the war. General Pearson, still in charge after almost a year, called them "semiguerrilla" tactics—stealth, deception, and surprise, units infiltrating the battlefield at night and without the use of choppers or accompanying artillery H&I. Basically they were evolvements on what Hank Emerson had developed a year earlier, and *they worked*.

---

* As Chief of Staff of IFFV under Swede Larsen, John Deane had been my endorser on the special ER rendered for my short tenure as the 1/327's battalion commander.

The 1/327 was being commanded by Lieutenant Colonel Joseph E. Collins (son of retired four-star J. Lawton Collins), and the unit looked great, particularly the Tigers, who netted five dead VC and five weapons in a classic ambush the day Slam and I arrived. "Gunfighter" Emerson's old outfit, the 2/502, was now in the infinitely capable hands of "The Gunslinger," Lieutenant Colonel Frank Dietrich, a paratrooper since World War II who'd come up through the ranks.* At one stage during Geronimo I, the thirty-seven day 1/101 operation we started to examine for Slam's third school, Dietrich maneuvered his entire battalion into one square mile of thick jungle to box in an estimated 100 NVA soldiers who'd fired on a Recondo patrol. It was a measure of the fine discipline among the 2/502 troopers that *not a single friendly fire casualty* resulted from this very tight, very dangerous situation. As the operation continued, over three days of fighting the '02 killed forty-one enemy and took thirty-six prisoners on the way to rendering the 5th Battalion, 95th NVA Regiment ineffective as a fighting unit.

Dietrich's was the biggest engagement of the Geronimo campaign, but there were other equally impressive ones, like the dawn ambush in which a very patient, reinforced squad of fifteen men killed nineteen NVA, took one prisoner and eighteen weapons for no casualties of their own. The significance of Geronimo I lay in its close to 10:1 (enemy to friendly) kill ratio, the very high weapons-to-body-count ratio (143 weapons, individual and crew-served, to 149 enemy dead), and the fact that many of the seventy-six prisoners taken had voluntarily surrendered in the face of the American brigade's superior tactics—economy of force tactics that gave the enemy a taste of their own medicine. I was elated. There was no question that the continuity of General Pearson's command over the past year and his openness to good ideas were essential ingredients in the brigade's success, but I also knew that if the 1/101's procedures, starting with its basic philosophy of "Know Your Enemy," became a standard among U.S. units, we could have the same success all over the Vietnam battlefield. We would be able to beat this foe. We'd be able to fight the same protracted war of attrition the enemy was willing to fight, without paying the heavy, heavy price in American lives. The Screaming Eagles were proving again and again that alert, well-trained soldiers could out-G the G.

I shared my enthusiasm with Slam, but he was more distracted than impressed. "Their load's too heavy, Hack," he said, and proceeded to give me his well-developed World War II argument about the soldier's load (he'd

---

* Dietrich was also a featured hero (as "F. Dietrich Berkely") in Ross Carter's one-of-a-kind book of war stories and war truths, *Those Devils in Baggy Pants*.

written a book about it) and how too much weight will exhaust a trooper long before the first shot is fired. What he said was absolutely correct, but the point he missed was this was *not* World War II, where there was a "front" and a main supply route right behind, from where goodies could be brought up as required, or that resupply Vietnam-style (by chopper) would compromise the paratroop guerrillas' very modus operandi. Neither would Slam acknowledge that while the troopers' loads were heavy when they went into an AO, centralized caches in the bush kept the men light when it came time to fight. And when I suggested that for the first time since we'd arrived in Vietnam we were seeing a Regular American unit doing it right, Slam said irritably, "Let's face it, Hack, there's no juice here."

"No juice" was Slam's way of saying there was no stuff at the 1/101st for a book. No Vietnam War *Night Drop* or *The River and the Gauntlet* or *Pork Chop Hill*. Immediately I could feel my face burning. I'd known for some time Marshall wasn't concerned about the schools we were running for the Military History Detachments, but I hadn't realized he, the military operations analyst (as he sometimes called himself), had no higher purpose at all in his analysis of military operations.

When we first planned the trip, Slam had talked about visiting every one of the ten divisions and separate brigades in Vietnam (which we eventually did). I'd suggested we streamline the effort by conducting not four schools, but one, at An Khe, and bringing all the student officers there. The interviewing technique was the same wherever it was taught and regardless of the action being scrutinized, and I'd figured there would be plenty of material to work with even if we just reviewed the 1st Cav's operations since July. Besides, it didn't make sense to go hopping and rushing all over the country when the students could come to us. But Slam had put his foot down. "We must visit every unit," he said. "I want to cover all the major U.S. Army campaigns since I left in June." Logistically speaking, this was a moderate pain in the neck, because it meant we had to take all the student officers with us when we went from unit to unit. But even that would have been okay, except it soon became clear that Slam, whose job it was to teach these men being flown all over South Vietnam at the Army's expense, couldn't have been less interested in them or whether they learned the technique at all. Not just in the first one, but in all four schools, the Military History Detachment officers sat on the sidelines and watched while the General conducted the actual interviews. Slam never placed them in charge or asked them any questions—in truth, he simply ignored them. Meanwhile, every evening Slam counted the longhand pages of notes he'd taken that day as most people would count money. He'd glance through the pages, noting all the soldiers' names, which he'd taken down during the interviews perhaps even more assiduously than the action—"Every name is worth ten books at the cash register," he'd declare.

So even before the "no juice" comment, I'd recognized that Slam's priorities on this trip were not the same as the Chief's or mine or the officers of the Military History Detachments who traveled with us. But I was still not prepared for his reaction when, about a quarter of the way through our examination of Geronimo I, Jack Norton called from An Khe to say a hell of a fight had just finished around an Air Cav fire support base (FSB) designated LZ Bird, and Slam ought to come up and have a look. "Wind it up," Slam directed me, fire in his eyes for the first time since we hit the 1/101st. Already he was seeing in his mind's eye another *Pork Chop Hill* (commercially his most successful book), only this time he'd call it *LZ Bird* and keep the TV rights. He'd given them away for *Pork Chop Hill* and often talked about how, as a result, he felt sick every time the film of his Korea story played on the tube and he didn't get a red cent. "I'll never let *that* happen again," he'd vow each time he wound up his lament on the subject.

So we folded our tent at the Screaming Eagles' nest, and headed back to the 1st Air Cav, where Slam got all he needed for his book. He also made sure the Cav CO on the ground at LZ Bird, a captain who'd led his men courageously in the very heavy hand-to-hand battle, was put in for the Medal of Honor. Unfortunately, this generosity of spirit on Slam's part was, I knew by now, as calculated as it was real. Besides the boost to book sales he envisioned should the real-life lead figure therein win the Big One, the award would be another notch on his own belt. Because Marshall had a thing about making heroes. One of his favorite pastimes was dropping names, generally in the context of his having "made" the subject (who was usually some illustrious three- or four-star general, past or present), and a favorite Korea tale was the one in which, through his clever prose and big-league contacts, he got the Medal of Honor for Lew Millett and his bayonet charge. By the time of the LZ Bird episode, I'd grown used to his chatter, so I silently wished the captain presently the recipient of Slam's attention well in the Blue Max stakes, and tried to let the rest of the affair wash over me.

But it was hard to watch an idol moving closer and closer to the edge of the pedestal I'd placed him on. Despite his glowing reputation, I was beginning to see that Slam was less a military analyst than a military ambulance chaser, more a voyeur than a warrior, the Louella Parsons of the U.S. Army. Because although it was the 1/101's hard-learned, well-proven economy of force tactics that held the key to winning the war—wearing the enemy down on our terms for a change, without paying the price—Slam responded only to heroes and heroics, men fighting against impossible odds and, as necessary for the drama, dying. This wasn't to say he was a bloodthirsty man, it's just that that was how he saw war. But that wasn't something I understood at the time.

We never did return to the brilliant Operation Geronimo I or the "juiceless" 1/101st. Instead, we went up to Pleiku and the mostly draftee 4th Division, an outfit relatively new to the war. As we had with all units to date, we told the division's G-3 we wanted to review what he considered one of the more significant actions his unit had been involved in. Without hesitation he chose Paul Revere IV, an operation conducted along the Cambodian border the previous November, and suggested we meet in one hour's time for a full briefing. I was amazed. It usually took at least a day to organize such things. Promptly an hour later, however, the briefing officer and his entourage appeared before us with a set of full-color charts and graphs and the slickest presentation I'd seen throughout my time with Slam.

It was a fine diversion, especially considering that the content was nothing new—Paul Revere IV, we were told, was a classic encounter. *Ho hum, here we go again*, I thought as we heard how early intelligence had picked up a large NVA element, which the 4th Division and some OPCON units promptly and skillfully deployed around; how the U.S. forces proceeded to push their foe into a trap in which the enemy was savagely punished and all but destroyed, with the tattered remnants limping across the border into Cambodia while the Americans marched home in glorious victory. Slam and I exchanged more than one dubious glance as the briefing went on. We'd heard it all before, in unit after unit—though the numbers always changed, the victories remained decisive. When it was all over, I couldn't help but ask the briefing officer how he'd gotten the remarkably comprehensive presentation together so quickly. "This briefing is the same one we gave to General Westmoreland, General Wheeler,* and Defense Secretary McNamara a few days ago, sir," he replied crisply, as briefing officers tend to do.

We began our interviews with the 4th Div participants. Then I went to the POW camp and interviewed all the prisoners taken during the battle. This examination of the POWs, coupled with the horror stories of 4th Div troops, whose squads or platoons were chewed up and spat out by their NVA opponents, revealed that there was almost *no correlation* between the official Army report on Paul Revere IV and what actually happened on the ground. I was astonished. There was no question that our boys had

---

* Earle G. "Buzz" Wheeler, Chairman of the Joint Chiefs of Staff.

performed heroically. And no question that the enemy had been punished—the official figure was more than a thousand KIA—by the Americans' incredible firepower. And our boys *did* hold the terrain at the end of the battle (even if it was an empty chunk of steaming jungle), so if the operation were measured against our World War II experience, it was indeed a victory. But if Paul Revere IV was viewed as it had to be, from the perspective of the war of insurgency that it was, then we did *not* win and we were *not* brilliant. In fact, we were stupid, lethally so, and Charles won the day. The enemy initiated the action, using tried-and-true Highlands methods, i.e., threatening a CIDG border camp and using NVA decoys to entice U.S. forces into an airmobile operation. The enemy sucked the American units into well-dug-in killing zones along the Cambodian border, killing more than 140 and wounding more than 560 of our men on terrain that favored them completely (once they'd accomplished their mission, they could scoot right across the border to regroup). As General Vo Nguyen Giap, North Vietnam's Minister of Defense, later wrote of the operation in his September 1967 statement on the war, "In the high plateau area the LAF [Liberation Armed Forces] lured the U.S. troops into coming to Plei Djerang* and annihilated them in bloody battles along the banks of the Sa Thay River"; while neither Slam nor I would have used the word "annihilate" to describe U.S. losses, after reconstructing the battle, our assessment of Paul Revere IV did in fact track much more closely with Giap's than with the sanitized U.S. report of the events.[2]

That the official and true stories of Paul Revere IV were so distinctly different was bad enough (though really, it was just a question of degree in relation to the only slightly less glowing and slightly more true reports we'd seen previously in unit after unit). But what was worse was that for the first time I realized that probably no one at the very top had any idea that the official reports were wrong. Slam knew, and he agreed with me that there was a regular and heavy-handed use of the M-1 pencil in the effort to put our debacles in their best light. But if the M-1 pencil was being applied starting at the company level, with embellishments added all the way up the chain of command, whatever underpinnings of truth remained by the time these reports got to division and corps were probably accidental. So from there, these reports—reports like Paul Revere IV, full of relatively honest but totally false optimism—made it all the way back to Washington unchallenged. And then they became the basis of critical decisions made on the war.

It was the study of Operation Paul Revere IV that most profoundly shook

---

* The CIDG camp pivotal to the action of Paul Revere IV.

what Slam would later call my "almost childlike faith" in the honesty of the after-action reporting system. But it was Slam himself who sent me hurtling down the road toward disillusion at this time, because he saw as clearly as I did what was going on, and didn't raise a finger or utter a word to try to change it. It wasn't as if he didn't have the power or the influence to do so. Slam had made himself virtually a one-man media effort to keep the American public informed on how the war was going. Besides his soon-to-be released book, he had a syndicated newspaper column and regular TV and radio shows (all of which he continued to write and/or tape while we were in Vietnam), and he had the ear of every CG in the country, including COMUSMACV Westmoreland. Only after Paul Revere IV did I reflect on a conversation Slam and I had had a short time before, after I'd witnessed (from a respectful distance) what appeared to be an animated, friendly talk between Marshall and General Westmoreland. Slam had returned to my side and promptly informed me that "Westy's a dumbshit" who didn't know what he was doing. At the time I was flabbergasted by the comment, but now I wondered what the hell else Slam expected, if the information Westy got was rah-rah bullshit such as we'd heard about Paul Revere IV.

I felt Slam had a responsibility to tell Westmoreland and the rest of the establishment the truth about what was happening to the war effort. But instead he continued to play the distinguished guest at every unit, and ruffled no feathers. I didn't get it. If Marshall had the balls to tell me that Westy was a dumbshit who didn't know what *he* was doing, why didn't Slam have the courage to take a real stand on the mess we were making of the war, instead of falling back on the "we have firepower on our side/the NVA can't sustain those losses/we'll wear 'em down" argument?

As our trip drew to a close, my observations gained throughout began to line up to form a very bleak picture. It wasn't just that we were losing the war. Instinctively I'd known that was the case for a long time. But what I couldn't have guessed was how much faster we were losing than I had imagined. To me, General Westmoreland was like the poker player who hadn't won a pot all night—in the desperate hope of changing his fortunes, he kept bumping the ante and forcing everyone to play faster. But it seemed he was throwing good money after bad. From the beginning of the escalation, as fast as we dispatched new units, the NVA matched them, the enemy, too, upping the ante, confident that we could be tapped out. Westy authorized huge search-and-destroy operations, but whatever return they brought was temporary at best. The enemy just went to ground and waited until the coast was clear to return and rebuild. In every action Slam and I examined, save the 1/101's Geronimo I and the activities of Colonel John

Hayes's Special Forces "Delta Force"* (the last unit we visited, which, pound for pound and weighed against its cost, was the most effective fighting force in Vietnam), U.S. forces had come out badly bloodied. Our casualty figures for 1966 equaled those for the Battle of the Bulge more than twenty years before. And though it was true that it took troops in Vietnam twelve months to chalk up such figures while it took less than two at the Bulge, at least with the Bulge one could say the bitter fighting there virtually ended WW II in Europe. But what greater good had our 1966 casualties in Vietnam achieved? An end to the war was nowhere in sight.

The emphasis on body count, a system already as obsolete as the CIDG border camps, was also taking its toll on the war effort by making everyone a bounty hunter and a liar. This yardstick of enemy dead had proved very effective during the British counterinsurgency experiences in Palestine and Malaya (indeed, according to John Essex-Clark, it was the only real measure of success in Malaya, where a platoon could patrol for a year and not see a single guerrilla). But in Vietnam, as the war escalated on both sides and Main Force and regular VC and NVA units expanded the conflict out of the guerrilla realm of banditos chasing and being chased through the bush, body count completely outlived its usefulness as a reliable measure of anything. Yet, with the passage of time, the reliance on it among the top brass of the military, the Defense Department bureaucrats, and the politicians would only increase. The more bodies we counted, went the thinking, the better we were doing. In fact, my experience with Slam revealed that the pressure for a high and instant body count interrupted the flow of battle, tied up communications, and created unnecessary casualties among troopers tasked with the job of doing the counting during a fight. Body count was also well on its way to destroying whatever was left of the moral code of soldiers and officers in the zero-defect Army. Leaders did not challenge suspect figures reported by subordinate units (who themselves knew the importance of a significant count) and too often actively inflated their scores to please their ER raters or just to get higher HQ off their backs. Sometimes a body count was completely made up to mask a screwed-up mission. In just one

* Project Delta (Delta Force) was infinitely successful with its tactics, doctrine, and a basic philosophy completely at odds with the Army's Regular units. The same success was not to be found in the other, more traditional half of the 5th Special Forces operations—the SF/CIDG border camps like Tou Morong and Dak To. The border-camp program still looked good on MACV's "big picture" operations map, but in fact had long outlived its usefulness as a means to interdict replacement troops and equipment streaming down from the North. At this point in the war the camps were ineffective, enemy-battered defensive concerns that served as little more than bait for the NVA and VC to lure reinforcing or relieving units into large-scale ambushes. While one would have thought something would be done to change the mission, configuration, or tactics of the border camps to have them again contribute positively to the war effort, no alterations to that end were made, and the border camps seemed set to remain what they'd been too long already—just a very expensive drain on manpower and matériel.

instance, a battalion commander asked one of his company COs over the radio to tell him his college football jersey number to have *something* to report for a botched operation ("Eighty-six," said the company commander; "Eighty-six!" exclaimed the battalion commander. "Great body count!"). Body count was much in the tradition of the Korean Certificate of Loss, in that it assuaged sectors of the public and the government that might otherwise have grown indignant over the waste the war was responsible for. But body count was infinitely more dangerous, because, like Paul Revere IV and other such essentially bogus after-action reports, the inflated counts made it all the way up the chain of command, where they became the proof-positive statistic that we were winning.*

The colonels and generals Slam and I met on our trip were, in the main, very much entrenched in the can-do (at all costs) bureaucracy that fostered inflated body counts and the like. As such, they seemed truly blind to the crucial shortcomings in the war effort. It was a bad situation only exacerbated by the obscene luxury available to many at base camps like the 1st Air Cav's and the 1st Division's. Vietnam was as complicated a conflict as the U.S. had ever known, yet the longer many of these generals stayed, the less they understood the war or even tried to, so caught up were they with the finer things in life available in a war zone. I found it interesting that these guys, many of whom had learned little in their last combat commands in the sitzkrieg days of the Korean War, still managed to take the worst lessons Korea offered and make them the standard for Vietnam. (Of course, as a European-style war superimposed on an Asian mainland, the Korean conflict was an extremely poor training ground for a new kind of warfare, even if the generals had taken the time to try to learn from it, which the vast majority did not. It is also worth noting that in Korea, while the warriors commanded the first year's bitter fighting, the Army's legion of clerks, dancers, and prancers only volunteered their services to the effort after the war settled down, when it was much harder to screw up or get hurt and there was plenty of time for empire building.)

Our rifle units, which were turning over every ninety days, were ragtag and shamefully inefficient. Young draftees were running squads. Company commanders were kids with an average of three years' commissioned service, an experience level shockingly low to do battle with an enemy who'd been fighting all his life. Old NCOs were few and far between, the NCO corps well on the road to being totally gutted through death and injury, or because the old noncoms simply saw the writing on the wall—many, many good NCOs were quitting after a single tour rather than

---

* Hank Emerson has suggested that rather than a body count, a weapons count should have been employed in Vietnam, as such a statistic would be very difficult to fudge on the battlefield.

find themselves being sent back again and again for another Korea, another war there seemed no intention of winning. Without the NCOs, there was no muscle within the units, and with the constant rotation of company and battalion commanders (i.e., the moment they stopped looking green), there was no institutional memory either, to prevent repeated mistakes and to make things happen. The companies themselves were paper-thin. Almost all of the one hundred we came across in our travels were operating at around 50 percent of their authorized strength—at about 115 men, that was barely more than two platoons. So where were the rest? R&R, or sick, or lost in the logistics-and-support maze emanating from the base camps.* It made no sense to me. In the peacetime Army, if a CO fell out with only 50 percent of his men for an ATT or an ORT, or even for everyday training, he'd be relieved. In the peacetime Army a CO had to account for the whereabouts of every single trooper in his command. Yet here in Vietnam, in combat, I never heard one senior officer complain, much less worry, about this problem. It was hard to believe they didn't notice; after all, it was not unlike driving a car on two tires. Nor did anyone seem to notice the pungent smell of marijuana that now permeated many a base camp. It was sold everywhere, for a nickel a joint or in a pack of twenty disguised as a sealed box of Marlboros. With three-quarters of the soldiers in Vietnam now draftees, Regular Army booze was taking a backseat to the weed, and though I didn't see it this tour, it was more than obvious that it was just a matter of time before marijuana made its way from the rear areas to the fighting line. MACV denied there was a problem and stuck their heads in the sand; in 1968, when heroin found its way into those Buddha grass "Marlboro" joints (eventually turning some 20 to 30 percent of the U.S. military in Vietnam into junkies before you could say "Far out, man"), it would be too late to turn the tide.

"Hack, all armies are inefficient," Slam counseled whenever I tried to share with him the litany of formidable woes our tour had uncovered for me. "Why, at best they operate at twenty percent. Right now the VC are limping along at six percent, so no matter how screwed up Westy's army is, it's twice as well off, if not more, than the enemy. Concentrate on tactics, Hack. That's your forte. I don't give these Communists more than a year. Surprised they've held on this long."

Slam's regularly offered prognosis on the war almost invariably led to an argument between us on the subject of firepower versus the will of the

---

* At any rate, only a fraction of our Army in the theater was out beating the bush. The "tooth to tail" ratio of fighters to supporters was thought to be as low as 1:10, with a preponderance of the supporters working at the huge administration setups at Long Binh, Nha Trang, and in the Saigon area as typists, truck drivers, and the like.

people and guerrilla versus conventional war. At first I thought I'd win such a debate hands down. Slam knew next to nothing of the history of the Vietnam conflict, having never read Bernard Fall or General Giap, or even Jules Roy's recently translated *The Battle of Dien Bien Phu*. But even when I could prove that the operations he and I had examined were chillingly similar to those of the French—change the name from Paul Revere IV to Operation Lorraine, replace "helicopter cav squadrons" with "mobile groups" and "All the way, sir," with "*Bien, mon commandant*" and one couldn't tell the difference except that the Americans were losing on an infinitely larger scale—Slam's routine and obstinate response was that war was war and I didn't understand it.

Okay, I said to myself in early discussions on the subject. Unlike Slam I had not participated in or written about two World Wars and two land wars in Asia (which was one of Marshall's most compelling and frequently voiced claims to credibility). And Slam was right, there was no question that the pounding our forces were administering was, day by day, sapping the enemy's strength. But one thing I knew was soldiers, and while I, too, could see the enemy getting physically weaker, I also saw his will growing stronger. Throughout the trip, on those days Slam holed up in his VIP quarters to bang out his newspaper column (Dateline: "Somewhere in the Central Highlands") or flew to Saigon to do his television and radio tapings, I tried to go to the POW compounds and talk to some of the prisoners. I always told them I was just a historian trying to understand how both sides waged the war, and when they realized I didn't care what unit they were from and I wasn't there to get any secrets, from commanders to the lowest ranks they became openly friendly and helpful.

I learned plenty, and by the time the tour with Slam was over I had a damn good idea of what our North Vietnamese and VC enemy did and how he thought, both on the battlefield and off. I came away convinced that though our opponent wasn't invincible, his ability to endure was. He had the will, he had the numbers, the Eastern bloc kept him moderately well supplied, to date he controlled the hearts and minds of the people, and he knew he had time on his side. It had taken him a thousand years to kick out the Chinese, and less than one hundred to get rid of the French. What did it matter how long for the Americans, who actually made things easier by repeating the mistakes of the French? When I asked how long they were prepared to fight, almost every prisoner, from the uneducated, simple farm boys to the better-versed officers, said ten to fifteen to twenty years. They were going to win, they said, and they were prepared to stay in South Vietnam as long as necessary to do so. "Are you?" one asked.

I told Slam all this, and point for point invariably won every debate we had, or would have won had Slam not always launched into his "war is war" discussion ender. Strangely enough, I had a gnawing feeling he actually agreed with me much of the time, that he was as aware as I that we were sinking deeper and deeper into a quagmire. But he refused to add up the facts, or at the very least wouldn't let the facts get in the way of his prejudgment of the situation. Meanwhile, body bags were filling with American youths at a rate of two hundred to four hundred a week, and through it all there were the infantry troopers, who clung to the belief that somehow in all this madness someone, somewhere, had to know what he was doing.

After Project Delta, we packed our bags for Saigon for the last time. Slam insisted we stay at the Oriental Hotel, a sleazy flophouse in the fish-stall area of the city where no Westerner in his right mind stayed. The place was located in a narrow alleyway not even wide enough for a jeep. Our cramped, stifling room (awash with Saigon's big-city sewer smell, the result of longtime uncollected garbage left to ripen in an unrelenting sun) was on street level, and Viets were always crowding around the window, peering in at Slam's fatigue cap, which he had the habit of "posing" in plain view when not in use. I'd shudder every time someone pointed at the huge star and joined in the chorus of *"Dai-Tuong! Dai-Tuong!"* ("General! General!"). Half the onlookers were VC, and a general (even a private-citizen-pretend-general like Slam) would be a great prize. I took to throwing a towel over that fatigue cap, wearing civilian gear, and spending every spare moment with John Westmoreland at his house or at the New York Bar. The few nights I had to stay at the Oriental, I slept with one eye open and pistol at the ready. Meanwhile, the Tet of '67 celebrations had begun, ushering out the Year of the Horse and ushering in the Year of the Goat. A year later it would come as little surprise to me how easily the Viet Cong's Tet Offensive got under way. As Slam and I walked through the city one afternoon, dodging huge, uncontrollable crowds and frequently screaming at each other to be heard over the din of wall-to-wall exploding firecrackers, we even talked about how simple it would be for the VC to use the noise and confusion of Tet to launch a great attack. "They're bound to use this cover sometime," Slam remarked. I agreed and hoped it wouldn't be that evening as I asked permission to spend another night at Westy's.

It was just madness to stay in the back streets of Saigon, especially at that time. By regulation, as a civilian Slam couldn't stay in MACV quarters, but there were two lovely, secure hotels to choose from in the city, the Caravelle and the Continental Palace. Though Slam would later write that we stayed at the "native" Oriental because "we liked the people," the real reason was a bit less convivial: Slam was incredibly cheap when the Army was not picking up the tab, and besides, the high-priced Caravelle and Continental were off limits because (as Slam would say derisively) "that's where the press stays."[3]

Slam hated the press, of which he did not feel a part despite the fact that he made most of his money the same way "they" did. With few exceptions, he thought they were freeloaders on the system, spending their time in Vietnam doing virtually everything *but* covering battles in the field. It galled him that the slant of many of the young journalists' work appeared "antiwar" (leading him to brand such men as David Halberstam and Neil Sheehan "Commies," and truly believe they were), or dealt with the politics rather than the strictly military aspects of the conflict. He simply could not see that each was inextricably intertwined with the other, any more than he saw any incongruity between his public disparagement of so many of his fellow media men and women as cowards and cynics and his own privileged position as guru to the generals. I could no more have imagined, for example, Slam Marshall on the ground in a firefight as any number of the other journalists were on a regular basis than I could any of those other journalists standing in a generals' mess saying (as Slam would, and often did, in an offhand, cheerful way), "I always think better with a bourbon at hand," and a horse handler immediately being dispatched to fill his glass and charge his battery.[4]

The night after our obligatory exit briefing with the USARV staff, Slam and I stayed at the Oriental Hotel and roared through some bourbon ourselves. The briefing had gone well for Slam but not so well for me. My view, that we desperately, *immediately*, needed to find a new strategy for the war because we were losing and losing fast, was not well received. Fortunately, Slam was there to lift the spirits of the entire top-brass audience with his opposing "we got 'em on the ropes" assessment; this view was accepted unquestioningly for the reason (I could only guess) that most of these guys didn't have a clue as to what the war was all about in the first place, so were more than happy to shuffle their staff papers, endorse exaggerated after-action reports, and accept good General Marshall's assessment that it was going just fine. Mercifully, I was not invited to Slam's exit dinner with General Westmoreland. The following evening, however, as the bourbon took hold, I took the mellow opportunity to try to tell Slam for the millionth time that the summing-up he invariably gave to the top brass bore no relation to the facts we'd gleaned over the last few months and he knew it.

But Slam was unconcerned and flying high. As the evening continued and the bottle emptied, he just became more and more expansive, talking about the success of our trip as if we'd just made a major contribution toward winning the war. "A million words, Hack!" he exclaimed, patting the stack of notebooks at his side (which he never let out of his sight), in which were recorded all the after-action interviews from all the schools. "And every one of them is gold. I've got eight solid books here," he continued. "How's *that* for an insurance policy for Cate and the kids?" Cate was Slam's wife and, he often said, the power behind him. She was much younger than her husband, and Slam was always very concerned about providing for her beyond the grave. "I'll write them in advance," he said now, "and she can publish them one at a time when I'm gone."

Personally, at that point my thoughts were of the thousands of young infantrymen who would be gone long before Slam if somebody didn't pick up the overall game in the ground war. I'd kept my own notebook during the trip, in which I'd kept an ongoing list of my observations of our Army's repeated tactical failings as well as the details of my discussions with over one hundred POWs. I felt there was a book there, too—a handy-dandy little guide of do's and don'ts on how to fight the bad guys—that could be a significant contribution to the fighting men. But Slam didn't want to do it. His eyes flashed dollar signs only when he talked of his own eight potential *Pork Chop Hills.* And considering that the Army had thousands of manuals and dozens of schools, it really was crazy that a book such as I was proposing was needed. But in my view it was urgent, and I badgered Slam nonstop until he changed his mind. I started to write the minute he gave me his halfhearted okay. But pretty quickly he, too, got into the spirit of it, and before we left Vietnam, the first draft of the *Vietnam Primer* was done.

The night before we headed home, the General and I went to the Rex Hotel for dinner. We sat under the stars at the rooftop bistro, perfectly situated to drink, eat, and watch the war. Artillery was popping in what was left of the jungles around Saigon. Operation Cedar Falls, which had replaced Attleboro as the largest operation of the war so far, was just winding up its Sisyphean mission of destroying the Iron Triangle and all other VC redoubts in the area. (The Iron Triangle would prove no more "no more" after Cedar Falls than it had been when Butch Williamson proclaimed it so more than a year before; what had "once consisted of fifty square kilometers of the unknown," he'd said back then, "has now been destroyed . . . one more enemy bulwark [psychological and physical] has been completely marked off the situation map.")[5]

As I watched Puff the Magic Dragon lighting the sky with flares and whining over distant contact areas, I thought of the "Saigon cowboy" Pat Graves met here once on leave from his 1/327 platoon. Saigon cowboys were a breed of rear-echelon soldiers so called for their latest and greatest, dressed-to-the-hilt warrior look that they took no closer to the combat zone than absolutely necessary. One of these guys sat down with Graves and fellow platoon leader Chuck Olyphant and after a time reverently drew their attention to the brightness of the flares in the Saigon night sky. The Above the Rest boys looked at each other and then at him in disbelief—the "flares" under observation were in fact neon lights on the building across the street.

Just then the Joint U.S. Public Affairs Office (JUSPAO) lieutenant commander who'd been assigned as Slam's Saigon contact approached our table. With him was a VIP he wanted the General to meet. It was Bernard Fall, the greatest writer on the Indochina war, and through his books, one of my greatest teachers. A native of France, Fall had lived the history of his country's Indochina conflict, a history many Americans, including Slam Marshall, chose to ignore. Unlike Slam, who flew from CP to CP in his own personal chopper, ate off china plates, and gathered his information and gained his "expertise" second- and thirdhand at secured base camps after the firing was over, ever since 1953 Fall had strapped on his pack, carried his rations, and tagged along with combat soldiers on both sides of the conflict to understand the war. He had also spoken with many top leaders on both sides, including Giap and Ho. Himself a guerrilla with the French underground at the age of sixteen, Fall knew insurgent and counterinsurgent warfare inside out, yet his views that the Americans were going about the problem much as the French had—which was to say "all wrong"—were wholly unwelcome to the Johnson Administration and, it would seem, to the top Pentagon brass as well.

Fall believed that, like the French, we could not win the war. Oh, we could win it *militarily*, he said when he'd sat down at Slam's and my table for an exchange of ideas, and we *would* win it that way—like Slam, Fall was convinced that our enormous firepower and stunning mobility, two things the French didn't have, would prove decisive.* But, he continued, a military victory was somewhat irrelevant, because Vietnam was first and foremost a political war, which the Americans, just like the French, did not understand. The Americans would never win the war politically, so they would never win the war.

Marshall's position was his usual "war is war" and we were winning this one. "I don't know anything about the politics," he said, all he knew was Vietnam was a just war; in the short term, we would save the Vietnamese from the Communists, and in so doing would, in the long term, stop worldwide Communist aggression.

---

* According to Fall, less bomb power was brought to bear in the fifty-six-day battle of Dien Bien Phu than in any single day during the present U.S. involvement. One U.S. mission, he said, employed more aircraft than the French had possessed in all of Indochina throughout their entire involvement there.[6]

In the course of the evening, Fall gave Slam a quiet education on the Vietnamese—their culture, their history, their unflagging determination since before the Common Era to rid their country of outside invaders. Bombing the enemy back to the Stone Age, he said, was not the answer to the problem the Communists represented. Social reform was: offer the Vietnamese a better life and watch them come over to our side.

Late in the night Slam went back to the Oriental to sack out. I'd said very little throughout the evening, but now Fall and I talked for another hour or so. He told me he was going up to I Corps next, to join the U.S. Marines who were operating on the Street Without Joy.

"Can I tell you something?" I said. "I've been an infantryman most of my life, and one thing I know is you can only go tagging along with squads for so long before you get killed. It's like rolling the dice, Bernard," I continued, and was stunned to hear myself almost pleading, "you can make so many passes, but eventually you've got to crap out. You'll buy the farm if you keep on going out on patrols. You're going to have to find another way to look at the war."

"You tell me how one can understand the war without dealing with the people," Fall challenged me, "without seeing how they are fighting. Without seeing the results."

He was right, of course. There was no other way.

Two weeks later, Bernard Fall was walking along the street he'd made famous, the Street Without Joy, with a U.S. Marine Corps patrol. He was talking into his tape recorder, reporting the war. ". . . shadows are lengthening and we've reached one of our phase lines after the firefight," he was saying, "and it smells bad—meaning it's a little suspicious. . . . Could be an amb. . ." Fall's monologue was interrupted by an exploding booby trap, and in that instant he was dead.[7]

Bernard Fall's death at the age of forty was undoubtedly one of the great tragedies of the tragic war in Vietnam. Although persona non grata among the military and top Washington political men who were actually running the war (those, that is, who turned to Slam Marshall for the good news), at the time of his death Fall had a large and growing following. Through his books he was awakening people all across America, not only members of the intellectual community but many a perceptive soul in the military and the Defense and State departments as well. Perhaps, had he lived, he could have made a significant impression on the Nixon Administration. *If only he could have convinced Marshall*, I thought many times. Slam had the audience. Slam had Westy's and the President's ears. It didn't matter that he would have been out of his depth talking strategy. I'd come to realize Slam was out of his depth on most subjects, but he was a great Sammy Glick of all things military and everyone still listened to him. But Slam was not convinced. He couldn't be—the war itself was his insurance policy for Cate and his kids. To tell the President, the military, and the American people that it had to stop would have been biting the hand that fed him, and it was not something Slam was about to do.

So our boys went on fighting, Slam went on writing, and one by one the predictions of Bernard Fall—based not on some superhuman prescience, but on being there, studying, and caring—became realities. And when the observations he made and desperately tried to convey from 1953 onward became impossible for the American powers that be to ignore (and much later, when the war was long over), it was Fall's widow, Dorothy, who would time and again receive the shamefaced apologies of men who'd refused to listen.

Slam paid his hotel bill in green—American dollars—and got a good rate. This practice was forbidden by MACV currency regulations, but anyone who'd been in Vietnam long (or for that matter, in almost any inflation-ridden country) did it. "I learned this trick in Spain when I was covering the civil war," Slam said unabashedly of his exchange as he pocketed his wallet and we headed for Tan Son Nhut airport and home.

We stopped in Hawaii, where we were debriefed by the U.S. Army, Pacific (USARPAC) staff. After the USARV briefing, I'd narrowed my wide-ranging concerns to three suggestions for improving our combat efficiency in the war; though I doubted I could make an impact, I shared them with these USARPAC people now: that a unit-replacement rotation policy be instituted, rather than the current individual one; that the one-year rotation policy apply to combat troops only, while the clerks and officers of the rank of major and above would have a two-year tour (and only receive combat pay if they earned it); and, most important, that a training school specifically for battalion commanders be formed pronto, to get these critical leaders read into the nature of the war and the proven U.S. and enemy tactics. Unfortunately, as had been the case at USARV, my views were shrugged off as alarmist by these guys who were even more out of touch with the war than the boys in Saigon, and Slam did nothing to change their minds.

For me, the weather improved considerably when we got back to Washington. General Johnson not only approved our idea for the *Vietnam Primer* and extended my TDY with Slam for another month so we could finish writing it, but he also took a very personal interest in the project: "The liaison on this book is between you and me, Hackworth, so come up anytime." The two of us went over the manuscript together word for word in the next weeks, and although the final product bore the disclaimer that Slam's and my opinions did not necessarily reflect official DA positions, I really felt Harold K. Johnson *did* agree on almost every point therein. The only areas he really objected to in the original draft were our harsh discussions of the M-16 and of body count. In both cases Johnson felt we got carried away, that the M-16 was an emotional issue with me (which it was, and the results of our interviews in Vietnam had only reinforced my hatred of the weapon) and that body count was too sensitive an issue in itself to be the subject of my literary wrath. He personally rewrote part of the M-16 section, and though he kind of took the teeth out of the body-count discussion, he didn't change the intent.

But most importantly, the Chief of Staff pushed the *Vietnam Primer* from the word go. The book was basically a "lessons learned," covering the areas of our own and the enemy's security, communications, movement, weapons, intelligence, and training, as well as a substantial chapter devoted to enemy ruses, decoys, and ambushes. Johnson himself wrote the foreword, and the book's publication became a top priority. When I took it to the Adjutant General with a simple "General Johnson asked me to come by and get this printed right away," almost before I knew it there were a million copies being distributed all around the world. Meanwhile, Slam insisted the *Primer*, which was also produced in Thai, Viet, and Korean, be classified "For Official Use Only," which prompted another mini battle between us. "If we classify it, then soldiers won't be able to carry it into battle," I said.

"Don't worry, Hack, it'll get around."

"But what's there to classify in there? There is nothing secret in the whole damn thing. It's enemy tactics. Don't you think the enemy knows what their tactics are?"

"Hack," Slam replied patiently, "the reason I want it classified is so it will not be in the public domain. That way later on you and I can rewrite it and publish it commercially." For Slam, it was just another way to make a buck.

Slam Marshall would remain an enigma to me throughout our relationship and for many years beyond. He was a mean, power-rapt little man who threw his weight around shamelessly—how often I saw him in Vietnam offhandedly promising hungry, enraptured colonels and generals alike a mention "in the daily dispatch" (Slam's syndicated column) or in his next conversation with "Johnny" or "Westy"—but who also had the capacity to be sincere and generous and kind. He'd once told me the secret of his success was his philosophy of "do one thing well." ("Long ago, I decided to specialize in the infantry squad and platoon in battle," he said, "so while most of the other fellows were spreading themselves too thin grappling with the big picture, I became the Army's expert. . . .") Yet he had long since abandoned that tack and instead had actually come to believe he knew almost everything about everything. And incredibly, he was able to convince a lot of people who counted that he really did. (On the other hand, there were those like Captain Eggleston, my TRUST company commander, now a lieutenant colonel, whose one and only encounter with Marshall, at a lecture at Fort Benning, had immediately conjured up for him one of his father's old sayings, "If you could buy him for what he's worth and sell him for what he thinks he's worth, you could retire.")

Marshall could be a braggart of the first order ("I could write on toilet paper with a crayon and sell it" was a routine boast), but his favorite claim to fame was at first the most puzzling to me, and years later, the most significant in terms of unraveling the hustler and the phony that he was, and how he was nonetheless able to make such a mark on the U.S. Army. Slam regularly brought up the fact that the Army had made him a general despite his never having attended even one military school, and that he was the only general in the Army to have this distinction. He neglected to say (and never would have, had I not followed it up out of sheer curiosity) that he'd gotten his star *not* in the Regular Army, but in the Reserve. Meanwhile, with no reason not to believe him, I accepted Slam's stories of World War I, his experiences as an infantryman in all the major campaigns, his battlefield commission to become the youngest second lieutenant in the U.S. Army during the war, the romantic tale he spun of Armistice Day, when he saw in the end of the war sharing his canteen with his brigade commander in the trenches. With no reason not to believe him, I accepted Slam's tales of World War II, too, his participation in the fighting in the Pacific as well as his service in Europe, which had him in the front line of the Normandy invasion. It would be many, many years, years in which Slam repeated the stories endlessly, in which his reputation was only further bolstered as one or the other appeared in everything from *Current Biography* (1953) to the obituaries upon his death in 1977, and in his autobiography published two years later, before I would discover that it was all a lie.

Slam had been an enlisted man with the 315th Engineers (90th Inf Div) during WW I, and spent his time not fighting as an infantryman but repairing French roads until just before the war's end. He had *not* been battlefield commissioned, and he wasn't anywhere near the trenches on 11 November 1918, being instead at the Army's France-based Officer Candidate School (then called the Infantry Candidate School). The self-proclaimed youngest lieutenant in World War I, who in fact never served as an officer in a TOE outfit—Reserve or Regular—in any capacity, ever, was not commissioned until April 1919, long after the last angry shots were fired. According to his service record, Slam saw no infantry combat in WW

II either (though he was awarded the CIB for the Marshall Islands campaign while serving on the DA staff), and far from being on the ground from the earliest hours of the 6 June 1944 Normandy invasion, Slam didn't even arrive in the European Theater until July, and then it was as a staff officer/historian reconstructing the operation. And while Slam would speak with pride of being the only American soldier to serve in all four of America's great wars in the twentieth century, it was a claim more than a little deceptive: his Korean War experience covered exactly three months (December '50–February '51), when he was recalled from the Reserves to active duty as a historian/"Operations Analyst" for the Eighth Army (a stint for his country that produced *The River and the Gauntlet* for himself), and his "service" in Vietnam was undertaken as a six-year retired Reserve general and a forty-year experienced journalist (Slam's job when he wasn't wearing khaki) looking for a story on the Army's tab.

A historian as careless with his own history as Slam Marshall was could hardly be a careful historian, and Marshall proved the rule. Veterans of many of the actions he "documented" in his books have complained bitterly over the years of his inaccuracy or blatant bias. For the lay audience, however, his "gift" was that what he lacked in accuracy in his books with regard to names of people, places, and units (not to mention events) he made up for by the immediacy he brought to the stories. He always wrote as if he were on the scene—jumping out of the plane, storming the beach, assaulting the hill. It was a conscious effort on his part to give the audience the impression he was there. Sometimes he wrote that he actually *was* there, conferring with and giving advice to the generals, or virtually sharing a foxhole with the troops. He didn't seem to care that what he wrote was totally inaccurate and easily disproved. He seemed to have relied (and successfully so) on the notion that no one would ever dare to correct him, to say, "No, General Marshall, you weren't there during the mortar attack," or "No, General, the enemy was not surrounding us."

The thing was that Slam wanted with all his heart to be a real general. But in fact, he was more like the Howard Cosell of combat: he'd never commanded troops either on active duty or in the Reserve, but he wanted to command great *armies*. He wanted to be like the other Marshall, George Catlett, for whom he took great delight in being mistaken (and frequently was, which no doubt accounted for more than a little of the blind respect accorded him, in that he never bothered to correct an awestruck fan), and his books reflected this. "...Having wintered with our line forces and Green Berets in the forward areas...," he would manfully encapsulate our tour together in his autobiography, and perhaps not even consider the dishonesty of the statement.[8] The truth was, in the air-conditioned, five-star-dining, one-day-laundry luxury we lived in (or in the oh-so-secure base camps to the farthest rear of the forward areas where we did many interviews and not once, *not once*, came under fire), the only serious danger we faced was a hangover from one too many martinis in the generals' mess. But with Slam, the voyeur warrior, the truth never got in the way of a good story.

Slam Marshall was very good to me. Until the day came four years later when he had to choose between the Army (his meal ticket) and me as a soldier and a friend, he went out of his way to be a help to my career. As a civilian, he couldn't give me an ER for our tour together, but he wrote a glowing letter to go into my record about the excellence of our relationship and my contribution to the mission. He was still concerned, however, about the four-month "hole" in my record, so far as my efficiency reports were concerned, and suggested to General Johnson that *he* rate me for the lost period. Light colonels do not get rated by the Chief of Staff of the Army, but I did, a highly complimentary report (though like everyone else, Johnson cut me on tact) that secured the future of my Army career and virtually guaranteed me a star. When Marshall did stuff like that I always felt a twinge of conscience that bordered on extreme guilt—there I was, dismissing him as a phony when he was being his most magnanimous. I felt a similar ambivalence when I considered the incredible opportunities being Slam's favored son afforded me, things like sitting down for a drink with Moshe Dayan or Bernard Fall, or such ticket-punching necessities as making myself known among the general-officer ranks, for which Slam expected nothing in return.

With it all, though, the truth was that Slam was a fallen and irrevocably smashed idol in my eyes. He knew I'd grown away from him throughout our time together, but it was not something to discuss: I cherished my career too much to risk getting on his bad side, and I was opportunistic enough to see the value of staying on the good side. But there must have been many like me, whose silence in the face of Slam's power only added to it and gave credence to his dubious expertise, who allowed him to have an absurd amount of influence, which fed his ego and lined his purse, and for years and years did an incalculable, horrific disservice to the Army (the thing he professed to love above all), not to mention to the nation and to the men who fought and died in Vietnam. When General Johnson had warned me, "Take care with Slam. . . . He is the Army's powerful friend, but he can be a treacherous enemy," I had not understood what he meant. But when I finally did, I understood, too, that the Chief of Staff had gotten it backwards. The reality was that Slam Marshall was the Army's powerful *enemy*, because he was its most treacherous friend. And if he were alive today, perhaps even more than the Vietnam-era generals who determinedly maintain we won the war we lost in their hands, Slam Marshall would have plenty to answer for.

Soon I was back to work at the Pentagon and Slam was home in Birmingham, Michigan, writing *LZ Bird, Ambush, West to Cambodia*, and *The Fields of Bamboo*, the four books that ultimately came out of our trip. None proved to be the next *Pork Chop Hill* Slam had been hoping for to cash in on the film rights; for that matter, none was even particularly well received by the critics or the public. The General did stop by my new Pentagon office (General Johnson had gotten me released from my old job in the bowels of the building and into a new one where I could actually be of some use, in the Directorate of Individual Training) to tell me he'd organized half the *LZ Bird* royalties to come to me. I didn't understand his motive, and so refused the offer; Slam knew how I felt when we'd returned to the 1st Cav to study the Bird operation, and that I hadn't done one thing toward the writing of that book.

The program we went to Vietnam to teach was high priority until no one was looking anymore. Slam himself didn't give it a second thought; I wrote an article on the technique that appeared in *Army* magazine a few months after we got back, but when I returned to Vietnam twenty-three months later, I didn't see the system being used at all at the bayonet level. For me, the value of the whole experience was digested in the *Vietnam Primer*. While the book did center around what we had seen, in it as well were a lot of *hunches* I'd developed throughout the journey on how to fight more successfully in Vietnam, perhaps even to win (at least militarily), by beating the little bastards at their own game. And while it would be a long wait until I had the opportunity to try those hunches out, at least—despite what Slam so obstinately had to say—it wasn't as if the war was going away.

17 CORPORATE HEADQUARTERS

> I expected the military crowd to be different. I was looking for the square-shouldered majors and colonels with a bright "can do!" attitude about their job of defending the United States of America. While I saw a few people like that . . . I was shocked to realize that many of [the] military men [in the building] were just bureaucrats in uniform. I later learned that a dedicated military man dreads assignment to the Pentagon. But, I also learned, the bureaucratic military men made their best career advancements there.[1]
>
> Dina Rasor, Director
> Project on Military Procurement

PENTAGON duty was not for the nervous or the fainthearted. The pressure was enormous. You had to look good and perform well under working conditions that would make an industrial psychologist reel back in horror. The Directorate of Individual Training (DIT), where I worked, was especially taxing. With more than 400,000 people in Vietnam at that time and the numbers set to expand another 100,000 (even as rotation and casualties were constantly removing personnel from the theater), the stateside training base was struggling to keep up. Current training facilities were in a constant state of expansion. New courses were being developed to meet the heavy training demands of the battlefield, and their geneses were almost all on, or in the immediate vicinity of, my desk.

My office, a claustrophobic hole no larger than 20 × 20 windowless feet,* housed fifteen people, three clattering typewriters, and some dozen or two constantly ringing telephones. A typical day there found your "In" box spilling over with a foot or two of papers when you arrived at work in the quiet of the morning, but you hardly had a chance to read even the first sentence of the first one, much less try to write anything, before your

---

* The Pentagon was laid out as five concentric circles labeled (from the inside out) "A" to "E." As such, only the "E" ring, which contained such offices as those of the Joint Chiefs of Staff and their staffs, had windows that looked out on the "real world."

phone(s) started ringing. Before long you found yourself juggling four phone calls in four time zones from four agencies with four problems. Add to that the fact that your office mates were simultaneously juggling *their* phone calls, their voices raised in the struggle to be heard above the din of which you were all very much a part, and you suddenly had one very uptight organization. Warriors with even two wars under their belts were not seasoned vets to this sort of combat. If Sherman said *war* is hell, it was only because the Pentagon hadn't been built yet.

My first job at DIT was that of Chief of the Individual Training Branch. After a few months I moved over to DIT's Schools and Education Division (SED-DIT) as Chief of the Schools Branch, where I was responsible on the policy level for the operation and functioning of all U.S. Army service schools in the United States. In the second job I also served as one of the five "action officers" in my branch, with my specific areas of concern being the Infantry, Airborne, Jungle, Counterinsurgency, Military Police, and Ranger schools. With training my longtime passion, if I had to be in the Pentagon it was probably the best job I could have had: provided that a way could be found to blast through the concrete that locked obsolete Army doctrine in place, for the first time in my career I was actually in a position to do something about it.

Among the first things I learned at DIT was that U.S. Army doctrine was not created by the generals. Major and lieutenant colonel "action officers" like myself, spread throughout DA's General Staff (another vital punch on the old ticket), could and did start the ball rolling in all areas of policy change. Whoever sat in a particular action officer's chair was considered the "expert" in his field. He did the hard legwork, and wrote "recommendations" that often rivaled the thickness of a Sunday *New York Times*. All the three-star generals had to do was make the decisions, which were usually based on one-page summaries attached to the action officers' recommendations. But I quickly learned that changes in policy were in no way expedited by this procedure. In fact, this system was just the tip of the bureaucratic iceberg. The "expert" action officer who initiated a recommendation had to coordinate it with other "expert" action officers and their bosses in other directorates affected by it throughout the Pentagon. Be it in intelligence, operations, logistics, doctrine, or whatever, each agency had to give the project or study a "chop," or concurrence, before it could go to the Assistant Chiefs of Staff or the Chief himself for the final judgment. Just one problem with this was that almost everyone along the line felt compelled to put his two cents in, even when he had nothing to offer. Virtually everyone rewrote your work. Usually it wasn't even a question of content, it was a question of style. And when you were on a short fuse to get the thing upstairs, as was generally the case, it could really start to get to you.

There were many major and lieutenant colonel clerks who thrived in this atmosphere, where the means were ends in themselves and only trivia was all-important. But putting a warrior in the Pentagon was kind of like telling a street fighter to put down his dukes and take up hairdressing. And a Pentagon assignment was a strange reward for a leader fresh off the battlefield—one day a commander of a thousand men, the next day a lackey in a crowded bureaucracy, working in little better than sweatshop conditions. I'd hated the place when I was there after my tour with the 1/101, and I hated it when I came back after my trip with Slam. And among the only people who hated it more was my SED-DIT boss (and old 1/101 rival), Hank Emerson, who'd arranged my transfer to his Schools Division in the first place. Both of us knew we had to put in our time, but it didn't stop us from actively looking for a way to escape with honor. Emerson had been trying to get out from his first day, but was consistently blocked by the DIT director and our boss, Major General Melvin Zais, who told him he had enough awards and decorations and now needed some "sophistication" if he hoped to advance further in the Army. For myself, even as I plotted how I'd get a master's degree to kill two birds with one stone (one more vital punch on the ticket *and* an out from corporate headquarters), I knew I had a lot to be thankful for. Hank Emerson was a warrior and a war buddy, and we were like-minded in many ways, not least of which being our mutual drive to be totally professional in our trade. So I could bitch and scream and carry on (which at the Pentagon was easy to want to do), and even if Hank didn't agree 100 percent, at least he understood how I felt. Imagine how it would have been had I found myself working for a Pentagon hero who loved being there.

At the time I switched over to SED-DIT in mid-1967, the Army schools system was in total disarray. Although the war was in fact going very badly, the basic optimism about it that permeated the Pentagon at this time made fundamental changes in training policy close to impossible to achieve. Even if there had not been the layer after layer of virtually immovable bureaucratic rock to blast through, from DA to CONARC to the individual service schools at Benning, Bragg, Knox, Sill, and Bliss, to name just a few, there was a basic problem of philosophy at the highest levels. Two years into the jungle-oriented war in Vietnam, all our schools were still geared up for "two up, one back, hi diddle diddle, right down the middle" confrontations on European battlefields. The Infantry School was still teaching to "close with the enemy," which was the worst thing you could do in Vietnam. Meanwhile, our guerrilla, nonconventional enemy was making hay while the sun shone on our conventional, yesterday's war approach to the conflict. Though everyone agreed that something had to be done, the general feeling was that Vietnam was a hiccup: we could not scuttle our basic mission, i.e., preparation for war in Europe or Korea, for an aberration soon to pass. (This attitude persisted despite the fact that as the Vietnam War continued, our forces in Korea and Europe were reduced to third- and fourth-string status, with second lieutenants commanding companies and PFCs running squads as the more seasoned, combat-ready personnel were "drawn down" from Seventh and Eighth Army resources to fill urgently needed battlefield requirements in Vietnam. This situation alone should have proved to those in charge that the Russians had no intention of making war on Europe at that time, if they didn't attack when we were so obviously vulnerable.)

But whatever the philosophy that ruled the schools system and dictated the general direction of the instruction, with almost half a million U.S. troops rotating through Vietnam, the fact remained that the war machine had to be fed. And in that the schools system was responsible for preparing the bodies, an overriding philosophy developed within the system that could be summed up in one word: output. High attrition rates in the schools became totally unacceptable. In the effort to produce, produce, produce, little thought was given to the product itself. How many graduated rather than how well or appropriately trained they were became the vital statistic— more fodder for the cannon and never mind that the gun was pointed in the wrong direction. In January of 1967, when Dennis Foley, my 101st Tiger Force leader and himself a 1964 OCS graduate, returned to Benning as a captain and an instructor (the first officer assigned to the Company Operations Department with Vietnam U.S. troop experience), he found that the normal two or three OCS classes a year had blossomed into dozens of classes run concurrently.* He also found that the almost 50 percent attrition rate that attended classes in the peacetime years had dropped to, at max, 5 percent. The running joke at Benning, he told me, was "the standards of OCS haven't been lowered—it's just that the students aren't required to meet them anymore." Colonel Floyd "Gib" Gibson, my counterpart over at CONARC, was actually sent to the Infantry School to investigate whenever a class showed an excessive attrition rate. And when Gib, a warrior from the old school, suggested that one of the purposes of OCS was to weed out undesirables (rather than "recycling" them to follow-on classes until they passed or the instructor gave up), he was told by his superior he "harbored a negative attitude." (Of course, Gib had a knack for rubbing clerks the wrong way. Three years previously, he had volun-

---

* Between FY 1966 and 1967, OCS officer production at six branch schools (Benning, Belvoir, Sill, McClellan, Gordon, and Knox) jumped from 3,881 to 18,334 men and WACs.[2]

teered to serve as a Province Senior Adviser in Vietnam, and with four years' experience learning about the Oriental mind as a MAAG adviser to the Nationalist Chinese Army, he was a perfect choice. But the war had begun in earnest for the U.S. by the time Gib got to Vietnam, and his advisory abilities notwithstanding, as a veteran of two wars—with the command of two platoons, nine companies, and a battalion under his belt—Gib was an equally fine choice for a combat assignment. He got neither. Instead he was banished to a desk job in the J-3 shop of the Rural Reconstruction Division at MACV's Saigon headquarters. Gib couldn't believe it, and began a somewhat vociferous campaign to get a job where he could actually be of use to the war effort. But all *that* earned him was a haughtily plunged knife in the back by a clerk-rater in his next ER: "Lieutenant Colonel Gibson has strong emotional feelings and frequently expressed his opinion that a soldier's duty is to fight. This attitude limits his value to the service, his desire for self-improvement, and adversely affects his subordinates.")

The schools system was also plagued by a severe shortfall of instructors. More and more were being authorized by DA to each school to cope with the ever-expanding requirement for new courses and additional classes, but fewer and fewer were actually being assigned. The numbers simply were not available. It was the blind leading the blind all over again. Just as I'd found fresh back from Korea in early 1952, many of the instructors were pink-cheeked lieutenants who'd never heard a shot fired in anger, who, in fact, had only just finished their *own* training, but had been considered studs enough by *their* instructors to be given places on the faculty. In this atmosphere, it was little wonder that hands-on training out in the boonies with pros teaching their tricks was replaced with handy-dandy training films and dull classroom lectures.

No one, myself included, stopped to say "Enough!" It was much simpler to juggle class sizes or add an extra Vietnam-oriented lesson to an existing curriculum. The gung-ho, can-do, zero-defect Army spirit did not understand the word "impossible," and in our branch we were run so ragged just setting up the mechanisms to make particular training available (every detail having to be cleared by half the Pentagon along the way) that there was rarely time to consider what we were even doing. How truly inefficient our system was only became clear to me when the requirement arose for me to liaise with the Navy to establish a particular block of training. The proposed course was for replacement commanders and staff officers bound for the Riverine Force, a U.S. Army brigade tasked with conducting amphibious operations from U.S. Navy ships in the Mekong Delta. Only God and General Westmoreland knew why this Delta mission hadn't been assigned to the Marines (who were qualified for that sort of thing as a matter of course), but mine was not to reason why, and I called my counterpart in the Navy Department about how to get the program established. He gave me a contact at Mare Island, an extremely accommodating lieutenant commander.

"What do you want?" he asked. I told him. "What's your input?" he continued, and I told him that, too, about twenty-five people every two months. "When do you want to start the first class?" he asked, and when I told him the following month, he said, "Fine, just have your people report to me."

"What about funding?" I asked.

"Forget it," he replied. "You're talking such small numbers we can absorb it, no sweat."

I was knocked out, and told him so. This lieutenant commander—the equivalent of an Army major—had full authority to set up a program that in the Army would have taken the approval of the Chief of Staff. The Navy was still damning the torpedoes and moving full speed ahead while the Army was floundering on the shoals of centralization. I'd seen it in Vietnam with Slam, and now even more clearly at the Pentagon. The closer a man got to the top, the more control he wanted over the smallest detail. He couldn't let his underlings be completely in charge of anything; if they screwed up, he might pay the price with a bad ER or a pass over at the promotions board. Yet at the same time, he needed those underlings, because without them he'd have no empire to command. And empire building was a human tendency the Army exhibited with great enthusiasm. It guaranteed swollen headquarters under swollen headquarters from the Pentagon on down, all of them justifying their existence through the amount of paperwork they generated, even if most of it duplicated the work being done at the next higher level and nothing came of it in the end. If the truth were to be known, it was a wonder anything got accomplished at all. With twenty-seven thousand people working in the Pentagon alone, I always felt that if someone stood at the front doors and told every fourth person, whoever he was and whatever his function, not to show up for work the next day and each complied, the running of the place wouldn't even miss a beat.

Except, that is, if they tossed out Hank Emerson and the very rare men like him. Hank rammed good ideas through the bureaucracy faster than even the most sincere and accomplished ticket puncher could say, "Yes, but . . ." And even when he failed with one thing, he made sure we had a contingency plan to get as close to what we wanted as possible through the back door. We devised a Platoon Leaders Course, for example, when one of our studies revealed that only eleven out of every one hundred platoon leaders who went to Vietnam had ever stood in front of a line platoon. Over a six-month period, the participants in this all hands-on program (designated the "company") would have rotated among themselves leadership of the "squads" and "platoons" that made up their ranks, while a seasoned Vietnam-experienced lieutenant colonel infantryman like Frank Dietrich acted as company CO. Though we lost the battle to get that course off the ground, we were able to expand the eight-week Ranger training program—the hardest, most realistic, *only* course in the U.S. Army that prepared young leaders for the war we were now waging—to take more personnel. Under Hank Emerson SED-DIT also got a much-needed orientation and refresher training program going for battalion and brigade commanders en route to Vietnam for the first time, and another essential little course entitled simply "The Enemy." But perhaps most significant among SED-DIT's achievements under Emerson was the creation and implementation of the Infantry Non-Commissioned Officer Course (INCOC).

By the autumn of 1967, two and a half years into the war, the line NCO shortage I'd noted with Slam had become critical. It was Korea, 1952, all over again, only worse: in 1952 at least the war was defensive, and a good company commander plus just one decent NCO were enough to spoon-feed and forge a team. It was a whole different story in the ever-changing, small-unit jungle fighting of Vietnam, 1967–68, where, with only a couple of years' service, the average rifle-company commander couldn't pour piss out of a boot much less mold a draftee unit into a cohesive whole. The need for tough NCOs had never been greater, and the absence in force of these old pros on the battlefield in Vietnam was, at least among warriors, great cause for alarm.

Hank and I brainstormed the problem, first looking at the mix of men who formed the pool of second lieutenants who fought in Vietnam. We concluded that OCS officers statistically made better platoon leaders than ROTC or West Point graduates because they had more hands-on training. (In the long term, the latter probably had more potential because of education and motivation in the areas of staff work and future generalship, but for the moment we didn't need staff officers or generals; we needed studs who could whip Charlie's ass and keep kids alive on the battlefield.) From there we concluded that there must be a large pool of capable soldiers coming through the system who would have made good officers except that they missed OCS entry by a few points on the school's IQ requirement. We designed the NCO Candidate Course to grab guys with leadership potential out of this pool and get them trained up as squad and platoon sergeants.

We modeled the program on OCS, and in order to get it going as quickly as possible, we used much of OCS's support plant (instructors, curriculum, etc.). The first candidates were almost all volunteers. They'd all completed their Basic Combat Training (BCT) and Advanced Individual Training (AIT) where their leadership potential had been evaluated; the NCO Candidate Course afforded them another twelve weeks of training, about one-third of it at night, plus nine more weeks of OJT in line units or at various training centers around the United States before they began their year's tour in Vietnam.

The program looked brilliant on paper, and from the feedback we received, it appeared to work well in practice. The graduates weren't Sweeneys or Presses or Gallaghers, but they were a lot better than a PFC in a firefight who inherits a squad by default, and they provided considerable relief on the ground in Vietnam. DIT Chief Zais hung the heavy-duty name of Skill Development Base on the course and forbade us to call its graduates "instant NCOs"; little did he know there were worse such monikers—within the Army the instant noncoms quickly and forever became known as "shake and bakes." And, like all things Army, almost immediately the program was expanded from infantry to armor to artillery and the rest of the service branches.

The NCO Candidate Course, which really was Hank's and my baby, was an essential innovation at that time in the U.S. Army's war in Vietnam. Still, to me it came second in importance to what I considered the *most* significant thing I did at the Pentagon, which was a study of U.S. friendly fire casualties in the war. If my tour with Slam told me anything, it was that the U.S. Army was its own worst enemy in Vietnam. Hank Emerson agreed (on the basis of his 1/101 experience alone), and about two minutes after I got to SED-DIT he tasked my branch to prepare a study outlining the problem and recommending solutions. At our request, the Adjutant General provided us with all casualty cards (which were the actual tags written in the field by the medics) for a one-year period. While we pored over them, I also solicited the views of respected warriors paying their Pentagon dues, like Hal Moore, the hero of Ia Drang, who was working in the Office of the Secretary of Defense.

During the study, I was surprised to discover that a new system had been established to count KIAs. Now, if you died after you'd been loaded onto a chopper, you were not KIA, you were DOW, or Died of Wounds. It was a cynical but clever ploy that reduced (and thus made more palatable) the percentage of KIAs served up daily by the Army to the American public. But if the Army thought it was fooling the people, it had no idea how badly it was fooling itself. As our study shook out, the fact became inescapable that a staggering *15 to 20 percent* of all U.S. casualties in Vietnam were caused by friendly fire.

The paper we wrote, which explored both the problem and the radical changes in training, equipment, and doctrine essential to rectify it, proved difficult for some powers that be to swallow. As Lieutenant General James K. Woolnough, the DCSPER, wrote to DIT Chief Zais of our study: "A most thorough, provocative and dangerous (Public-Relations-wise) document. If we are really as bad as this infers all of Westy's and other commanders' comments on how well trained our troops are are rendered false! I believe in the enthusiasm of the authors . . . they have unintentionally painted a much too damning picture—therefore perhaps you should have all copies classified." Zais gladly followed the suggestion, and the true but terrible word didn't get out. Fortunately, General Woolnough did not let the subject drop there, which he easily could have done. He felt most of our points were valid and required immediate attention, and in record time (from a Pentagon point of view) our recommendations were doled out among the appropriate action agencies. Some changes were implemented immediately and some took a little longer; our recommendation that the Colt .45 pistol be eliminated and replaced (having caused, since WW I, more friendly casualties than enemy) probably took the longest, at some eighteen years.

But the main problem of friendly fire casualties—unrealistic, oversupervised training—was never solved, and of the some 58,000 Americans who died in Vietnam, on the basis of our calculations, between 8,700 and 11,600 of them shouldn't have. It was the saga of Willie Lump Lump repeated again and again, only by now congressional interference and fear of congressional investigation had weakened the quality of Army training across the board. The irony of this was never greater to me than when the countless "Congressionals" bounced down to DIT and my desk during my short tenure as Chief of Individual Training—inquiries by congressmen on behalf of the Mr. and Mrs. Lump Lumps who'd complained that their sons were killed in Vietnam as a result of inadequate training. Our job then was to call the training facility the soldier had attended, make sure he had received the relevant training, then rush a letter to that effect back to the congressman via the Office of Legislative Liaison. It was not our job to determine whether the "relevant" training had indeed been relevant, hands-on, or worthwhile, and after a short time, when we'd answered every possible question at least ten times, my marvelous secretary, Eloise Whitfield, organized the responses by paragraph and slipped the pages into a book of clear acetate folders. Then, as each inquiry came in, I could call the school, get the training records checked, circle the appropriate paragraphs on our acetate-covered master letter, and have the Congressional on its way in fifteen minutes. From where I sat in the Pentagon, there was nothing else to be done.

*   *   *

AWOLs were a large and growing problem throughout the Army at the height of the Vietnam War. Although I wasn't directly responsible for these reluctant souls, there was no doubt that if they had been trained properly in the first place the problem would not have exploded as it had. Or so said Lieutenant Colonel Harold "Ace" Elliott, the Corrections action officer in the Office of the Provost Marshal, and he was right.

Ace Elliott was an unlikely cop. That is to say, he never struck me as a cop, even from our earliest meeting when he called me at SED-DIT about the AWOL problem. Nor should he have, really—Ace was an early Airborne infantryman who'd come up through the ranks in World War II and Korea. He'd learned his trade from the likes of Jim Gavin, for whom he had been an RTO, and he'd only left the infantry for the military police when complications from a severe leg wound he'd received as a 187th paratrooper in Korea had him on the verge of being put out to pasture. Like his assessment of the AWOL situation, Ace's solution to the problem was as much, if not more, an infantryman's than an MP's: establish a correctional facility specifically for the AWOLs, where they could get the concentrated training they had obviously not received to date. Well remembering how bums had become chargers after a stint in the "correctional facility" of the TRUST stockade, I was enthusiastic about the plan, and in the first of a number of actions we worked on together, Ace and I got his brainchild off the ground at Fort Riley, Kansas. And with Ace handpicking the trainers, the program was a great success.

The MP with the infantryman's eyes was soon promoted to Chief of Operations for the Provost Marshal General, and we had occasion to work together again during the fierce antiwar and race riots in Detroit, Chicago, New York, and scores of other cities around the country. The widespread outbreak of violence prompted Harold K. Johnson to order Ace to form a team to go to every police department in the U.S.A. to train civilian officers in civil disturbance/riot control operations. Thirty-seven police departments later, Ace returned to the Pentagon to tell the Chief this one-on-one scheme wouldn't be finished until the turn of the century. Once again he got in touch with me, and with a little help from SED-DIT, Ace was soon able to realize his concept of a single school at a central location (Fort Gordon) to which members of the civilian law-enforcement agencies would come for the training program. That we were using the military to train civilian authorities to put down disorder (the origin of much of which was the military's role in Vietnam to begin with) among the civilian population was an irony lost on me at the time. Though I knew we were fighting the most unpopular war in our country's history, it wasn't mine or any of our jobs to find out what all the people's hollering was about. It was simpler to set up the mechanism to keep them in line, or put them in cages until they calmed down or came around.

As tied as I was to my Pentagon job, I still got out among the civilian population a lot during those turbulent days, not just in Washington (where people expressed their feelings about the war outside the White House gates with the chant of "Hey, hey, LBJ, how many have you killed today?"), but all over the country. Slam Marshall's *Battles in the Monsoon* had been published, and because Slam had written glowingly about me and my battalion during the Dak To fight (despite, incredibly, identifying us as the *2d* Battalion, 327 rather than the 1st), I became kind of an instant celebrity. Before long I was called upon to join the Chief of Information's (CINFO) Distinguished Speakers team, a stable of well-decorated studs who, on request, had to speak/sell the war to whomever CINFO targeted. At first I did preaching-to-the-choir VFW and American Legion functions, Rotary and Lions clubs, and universities in the Washington, D.C., area. Later I was appointed the Department of Defense (DoD) representative to a presidential briefing team whose job was to sell the war through a lecture tour of major U.S. universities, countering in the process, it was hoped, the effects of the anti-Vietnam movement on the campuses.

The other speakers on the presidential team were from the Agency for International Development (AID) and the State Department. Our presentation was a slick dog and pony show designed to convince our listeners that America's purpose in Vietnam was pure, and that our effort there would bring peace and democracy to that war-savaged land. Most of our audiences were already supporters, but we generally ran into some organized student protest at each assembly, too. There was always a lot of heckling, but after a while my cospeakers and I each developed perfect put-downs that set the majority of our audiences cheering while the protestors were hustled out or meekly disappeared within the crowd. All in all, the tour was tremendously successful, and the only problem for me was the more I did the rounds with it, the more I knew what we were saying was bullshit.

My AID and State Department counterparts didn't believe what we were saying either, but it didn't seem to bother them as much. My problem was that by this time I was completely obsessed with the war—how we got into it and the mess we were making of it—and having given up trying to deceive myself, I couldn't stand the fact that I was deceiving the American people. Always before I'd studied the war from a military angle. For the CINFO job I'd had to read other things—the terms of the French cease-fire, for example. And for the first time I discovered that *we*, not the North Vietnamese, had violated the terms of that agreement; that *we* had refused to allow the planned plebiscite in 1956 to decide whether Vietnam would remain divided or be reunited, because the result—a reunited country with Ho Chi Minh at the helm—was as unacceptable as it was easy to foresee. In years to come, this and other ironies would be common knowledge. But back then, to me, they were a whole new set of truths, and they gave my view of the war a schizophrenic quality. *Maybe we shouldn't be there at all*, said one voice in my head. *But we are there and we're not leaving, so let's get with it*, said the other—and that was the voice I listened to, because that was the military angle again, the one I felt I could possibly do something about.

I found myself searching wildly for a magic solution. The Army was my life, and I could not accept that this institution—my mother, my father, my only real sustaining love—could blow it so badly. In the stacks of the Pentagon library I found dozens of after-action reports covering the French experience in Indochina, 1946–54. The French had well documented every operation; translated into English, their frustrations, failures, and lessons learned were exactly the same as those that U.S. troops were experiencing in '67–'68. Yet a lot of people really must have believed the American four-star general who suggested that since the French hadn't won a war since Napoleon, nothing could be learned from them—judging from the unmarked "due date" form in the front of each book, not one of these French after-action reports had ever been checked out. Neither had *Modern Warfare*, the insurgency treatise of one of my renegade mentors, French colonel Roger Trinquier, available in English since 1964. "The fight against the guerrilla must be organized methodically and conducted with unremitting patience and resolution," wrote Trinquier. "Except for the rare exception *it will never achieve spectacular results so dear to laurel-seeking military leaders* [his italics]. It is only by means of a sum total of perfectly coordinated, complex measures that the struggle will, slowly but surely, push the guerrilla to the wall."[3] And yet there we were, getting wrapped around the axle with big-unit missions just like the French before us, arrogantly looking for the decisive battle and the attendant glory, while the unread Trinquier gathered dust in the Pentagon library.

I had to do something about all this, to educate my apathetic colleagues and do my part to turn the tide of the war. I began to write articles, shooting for one to be published every month in one of the military magazines. Given the amount of time I was on the road speaking, there was never any more light at the end of my In box than Westy had at the end of his tunnel in Vietnam, so I took to writing in my car on the way to work. With traffic flowing at about five to ten miles per hour and a CW Morse code key clamp to hold my clipboard on my knee, it was quite possible to write a good solid paragraph in the eleven-mile stop-and-start trip between my house in Burke, Virginia, and the Pentagon. As soon as I got to work I'd give it to my secretary to type when she had a chance (it paid to be tight with your secretary at the Pentagon; if you liked each other she'd always expedite your work, put your periods and commas in the right places, and watch out for your flanks), and between the two of us we'd rewrite/retype it three to six times at odd moments throughout the day until it was perfect. That night I'd take it home, add it to my finished stack, and start the next paragraph the following bumper-to-bumper morning. The final products, which appeared in such magazines as *Army*, *Army Digest*, *Military Review*, and *Infantry*, generally sought to redress what I considered some of the worst of our Vietnam failures, and/or to provide how-tos from my own experience and study.

I was greatly encouraged to write by Ward Just, the *Washington Post* journalist who'd gotten hit with the Tigers at Dak To. Now recovered from his wounds and living in Washington, D.C., where he was assigned to cover the Department of Defense, Ward was to have an inestimable impact on my thinking during this period. Two years before, Doc Raphiel Benjamin had asked questions that opened my military mind and sprinkled seeds in my brain. Now Ward cultivated these budding thoughts. He had just completed a book, *To What End*, a collection of pieces born of his Vietnam experience. He asked me to review it, and the manuscript brought home to me that not only was the war effort madness, but we were probably fighting on the wrong side. Ward was no preacher, but his feelings toward the war, in black and white on the pages of his book, were a major step in my enlightenment. As I looked at the political side of the war—a war much more of America's own making than I'd ever thought before—I realized for myself that the goal of the conflict should not be the defeat of the enemy. Beside the fact that such a result was militarily impossible on our present course, it was clear that an American victory would not address the fundamental problems that had fueled the conflict all along and sent so much of the population down the Communist road. Instead, what the goal had to be was the rebuilding of the nation *by itself, from within*, and along democratic principles. But how could this possibly happen? The people hated us; it was only the kids who shouted "GI Numbah One, Ho Chi Minh Numbah Ten," in the same breath as their rapid-fire "You got gum? You got candy? You got C ration?" In cities and villages alike, we moved families from their ancestral homes with the same disregard for their culture and religion as we'd shown the red man in America, and made them prisoners in "strategic hamlets" about as free as concentration camps. Meanwhile we ruined their crops with our chemicals and their economy with our Yankee dollars, supported a chain of corrupt governments and a corrupt Viet military machine, and won hearts and minds by destroying villages to save them. It had taken me this long, but I finally concluded, as Bernard Fall and a number of the more sensitive journalists in Vietnam already had, that unless some extraordinary miracle happened, the war was irrevocably lost.

But in the Pentagon there was nothing I could do about it anyway. I gave up my quest for a magic solution, though I did continue to write articles for military publications. I continued my studies of guerrilla warfare also, and began to clip every news item I found in the *Washington Post* and *New York Times* on guerrilla incidents and activities in Latin America. "That's where it's going next," I told Ward during one of our many meetings, "because the bastards think they can win it all now." When he asked me where I'd be in ten or fifteen years, I said I'd be COMUSMACL—Commander, U.S. Military Assistance Command, Latin America—but I wasn't going to screw things up as Westmoreland had in Vietnam. I was going to follow Slam Marshall's advice and become *the* expert on Latin America in the U.S. Army—on the history, language, culture, values, religion, you name it—and in how to fight a cheap and efficient counterinsurgent war down there when Castro, with Soviet assistance, started playing his cards against the gringos.[4]

Meanwhile life at the Pentagon went on, and I was tasked to brief the Chief of Staff, the Army staff, and the Army commanders on all the goings-on at DIT at the quarterly Army Commanders Review. The middle-range anxiety I'd gotten used to feeling while working at the Pentagon soared to apoplectic proportions at the thought of addressing some forty-four stars in one room. I started rehearsing a full week before. Over the weekend I took almost-three-year-old Joel with me to the Pentagon briefing room where the real thing would occur, sat him on the very chair General Johnson would sit in during the briefing, and recited my report to him until he was so bored it would have been inhumane not to take him home. The morning of the briefing I bolted out of bed before the alarm, showered, shaved, and dressed to perfection. Just as I was about to head out the door, Patty turned over in the bed. "Where are you going?" she asked.

"Work," I whispered.

"At midnight?"

I carefully got undressed and got back into bed. But sleep wouldn't come, so I just laid there at attention, rehearsing the briefing over and over until the alarm went off some five hours later. The Pentagon was one uptight place.

My briefing for the Army Commanders Review went well. When I finished I took my place in the back row with the other Indian-level briefers to await the discussion of Ranger training, which I'd made sure was placed on the agenda for the meeting. During the period Hank and I had been studying the feasibility of expanding the Ranger program. I'd noticed that despite the mere nineteen hundred Ranger spaces available per year at that time, per class there was a continual shortfall in enrollment. This was a big concern. Besides being the most valuable training available, Ranger School was very expensive to operate, and I had to ensure it was filled for each and every class. So I'd set up a program to monitor input very closely, and alerted the Army staff to the problem. By getting the subject placed on the agenda for the Army Commanders Review (the whole purpose of which was to discuss the most important issues facing the Army at the time), a lot of pressure was brought to bear to get people thinking Ranger. Meanwhile, I discovered that a major cause of the shortfall was that while DA paid for a soldier's Ranger training, the Army to which the soldier belonged (First Army, Second Army, etc.) had to pick up the tab for his round-trip transport to Benning plus twenty weeks' per diem. So it seemed that the Army commanders, in the effort to save money, were giving the first chop to the only course in the Army that produced qualified battlefield leaders.

The subject finally came up at the quarterly review, and one of the Armies reported a 300 percent increase in Ranger training input. The Chief of Staff was delighted. "Yes, sir, we've really been pushing it," the reporting Army CG said proudly.

The Chief looked back toward me. "Hackworth, are you pleased with the progress we're making on Ranger training?"

"Well, sir," I replied, "the three hundred percent figure just mentioned is based on the fact that for the past six months this particular Army has had zero input into the Ranger program when it should have been sending twenty-two people each time. This last quarter it sent three, which is indeed a three hundred percent increase. But it's still shortfalling nineteen people."

A flustered three-star sent me an "I'll get you later" look, but those were the breaks. *Figures don't lie but liars figure*—I'd learned early in the piece the unofficial motto of the Five-sided Puzzle Palace.

Throughout this period at the hub of Army decision making, I also tried to rectify some of my pet hates, among them the M-16 and the command musical-chairs rotation policy. An old paratrooper friend from Campbell was the action officer for the M-16 in the Office of the Assistant Chief of Staff for Force Development (ACSFOR). I went to see him and tried to persuade him to stand in the door over the weapon. Even though the system had endorsed it, he agreed with me that it was far too delicate for infantry, probably on any battlefield, much less in a jungle/rice paddy setting like Vietnam. But like most of us ticket-punching drones in the Pentagon, this action officer was very career-minded, and despite his being *the* person in the U.S. Army who could have made the difference, he couldn't bring himself to buck the system. As I was leaving the office, another guy even piped up, "Don't fight it—just buy Colt Industries." And so the saga of the M-16 went on. Time would prove that one of the major problems with the M-16 in the war years was its ammo, bought on the cheap by an Army cutting costs at the expense of its men's lives (and later, when the ammo situation was straightened out and the mammoth teething problems were addressed, the weapon did get better). But in the final analysis, that situation—as obscene as it was—was still secondary to the fact that the weapon was a worthless piece of junk that never should have gotten down to the troops to begin with.

Initially I had better luck on the command musical-chairs question. Over time I'd become friendly with one Dr. Martin Bailey, who was working in Assistant Secretary of Defense Alain Enthoven's systems analysis office. Bailey was one of those Ph.D. whiz kids who were trying to make sense, quantitatively, of all the data coming out of Vietnam. Army guys generally didn't go out of their way to talk to these brainy types; in truth, most of us were scared shitless of McNamara and his entire crew, and demonstrated it by ridiculing everything to do with them or their beloved systems analysis. But Dr. Bailey was very approachable on those occasions I had cause to work with DoD personnel, and we actually seemed to agree about the stupidity of it all. When I felt confident I could express my views to him without having them boomerang back on me, I broached the subject of the command musical-chairs program. Speaking as a soldier, I told him that constantly rotating company, battalion, and brigade commanders through Vietnam was not leading to an Army with great depth in experienced battlefield leadership (as OPO was crowing), but instead to the loss of more blood and more lives, the presence of more dilettantes/ticket punchers in vital command roles, and a criminal lack of continuity on the ground (as John Paul Vann would later express the latter point, the U.S. was not in Vietnam ten years, but one year ten times). Bailey agreed that it did not seem the best way to win a war, so I suggested he send a letter to the Army, through McNamara's office, simply asking why our brigade, battalion, and company commanders changed so frequently, and why they couldn't stay in place longer.

Dr. Bailey wrote the letter. It bounced from McNamara's office down through the Army staff to General Zais at DIT. Zais gave it to Hank

Emerson to answer, and Hank, who didn't know I had anything to do with it, gave it to me. "Hack, I want you to take care of this."

I couldn't believe my luck. "Yes, sir," I replied. "Any guidance?"

"Shoot it down," Hank said.

I couldn't believe my ears. "Shoot it down? You know as well as I do that's the crux of the whole damn problem over there."

"I know, I know. And I'm sorry. But that's the guidance from Zais and DCSPER and the Chief."

"No, sir," I said. "I won't do it. I can't." In my incredible naïveté, I'd just assumed Bailey's question would catch the Army with its pants down, and it would have to confess that it had been so eagerly punching tickets that men were being sent into battle improperly led. Then (according to my scenario) the Army would immediately take action to rectify the problem, and many more young men would live happily ever after.

I realized I didn't know the system as well as I thought I did.

In the end, Hank got Major John Rogers, the Budget Branch chief, to do the paper. I watched him working on the thing, secretly praying he'd get stuck and have to give up. But he didn't. The conclusion finally arrived at was something like: "Having culled through our World War II and Korea battle records, it has been determined that in the Italian Campaign a battalion commander lasted thirty-two days, in the South Pacific a battalion commander lasted sixty-four days, and in Korea a battalion commander lasted sixty-eight days. So in Vietnam, our battalion commanders are getting three to six times more experience than they did in World War II and Korea. And by the way, we won those two wars. So, Mr. Civilian, up there in your ivory tower, go back to sleep. This matter doesn't concern you. The Army knows what's best."

My next attempt at causing change was a book Ward helped me tee up with Stackpole Press, *The Platoon Leader's Combat Guide*. I was already correcting the galley proofs when the publishers called to say they wanted me to change the entire thrust of the book, to make it less Vietnam-oriented and more "institutional." Located in Harrisburg, Pennsylvania, Stackpole must have picked up the optimistic drumbeat from Carlisle Barracks and the Army War College just a stone's throw across the river; they felt the war would soon be over and wanted my book to be "less perishable." I told them the Vietnam War had some way to go yet (almost six more years of U.S. military involvement, as time would prove), and that I'd contracted to write a book designed to keep our platoons alive there and to sharpen their combat skills. It quickly became clear we were two immovable objects, and it was no big surprise when the project "fell through the cracks," as one might say (and usually did, those days) in

Pentagonese. Fortunately I got a lot of the information out anyway, in articles based on the finished chapters, and I didn't have to give back the seven-thousand-dollar advance, which had been a windfall to Patty and me. (Majors and lieutenant colonels on Pentagon duty could starve in Washington, D.C. The cost of living was so high and the salaries so low that to own your own home was an incredible luxury, and whatever little money you had left over tightened in direct proportion to every inch each of your children grew.)

By no means was I the only one trying to effect change in the Army at this time. Another was one of my great heroes and one of the greatest trainers the U.S. Army has ever seen, General Bruce Clarke. Throughout his career, Bruce Clarke had been a leader of men. With more than forty-three years in uniform, not once did he serve in the Pentagon; he'd gone from command to command in peacetime and war, commanding in combat a squad in WW I, a corps in Korea, and being the unsung hero of the Battle of the Bulge when his 7th Armored Division Combat Command held St. Vith against the German counteroffensive in December '44. In 1967, when I saw him, white-haired and in civilian gear, walking by my office in the C ring of the Pentagon, he'd been retired five years. I jumped up and went into the corridor to say hello (although I knew he wouldn't remember me from our only previous meeting eight years before, in Germany, when he'd interviewed me to be his junior aide-de-camp). As it turned out, the General was knocked out that I recognized *him*, and our talk of the old days, Seventh Army, Berlin, and Colonel Johns as we walked down the hall was the beginning of a fine relationship. From time to time he'd write me letters asking for information, or send me studies and ask for my views; I soon realized Clarke, too, saw the Army he loved slipping, and was single-minded in his postretirement effort to get it back on track. I often thought about him as it became increasingly clear to me that the track had been destroyed, and as I wrestled with my own future, because during those Pentagon days my career, too, had come into question. Should I stay in and try to repair the Army from within, biding my time until I got to the top and could flush the whole thing out? Or resign while I was still young and could do something else? General Zais once told me if he didn't get a division command in Vietnam (his next vital punch) he'd get out early, become a vice president for General Electric or some other big company, and not look back: "Because even if you stay in," he said, "what have you got when you leave the service after a really long career? A handful of ashes." Zais, a highly decorated, movie-star handsome, charismatic, longtime paratrooper and comer in the Army, was always a good one for one-liners and the occasional turn of a phrase. But that one, "A *handful of ashes*," was almost too good, saying it all too well for the Bruce Clarkes of the Army, who, as impassioned and as vital as they'd been when they were known on sight by perhaps hundreds of thousands of troops, just a few years later could walk unrecognized and truly powerless down Pentagon halls.

While I remained undecided about my career, Tim Grattan, my 1/18th Vanguard buddy and the finest young infantry officer I'd ever known, called me to say he was hanging up his suit. He was well on his way, but his basic nature of calling a spade a shovel, he said, was going to run him afoul of the system sooner or later, so why not get out while he had the ideas and energy to start afresh? I was sick. It wasn't that Tim was not in good company— Regular Army captains, young majors, and NCOs with up to fourteen years' service were resigning in droves these days. It was just that I couldn't think of one good rebuttal for his grounds for quitting, much less give him a decent reason to change his mind.

I walked into our little SED-DIT office one day to find Hank Emerson listening intently to a wild-looking, very strange man he introduced to me as a "cave expert." The guy was giving Hank a whole routine about how, through his knowledge of caves, he was sure he could pinpoint the Viet Cong's underground cave-and-tunnel complexes throughout Vietnam, and he wanted to go over and give it a try. Most Army comers wouldn't have given this sort of fellow the time of day, but Hank, who was one of our Army's few lateral thinkers, was always open to the unusual, and besides, what the guy was saying made sense: if the location of the tunnels and caves were known, they could be systematically destroyed. So after checking him out through a Washington speleologists' organization and finding out he was for real, Hank bought the idea and in his characteristic way blasted through all layers of red tape virtually overnight to convince the Chief of Staff that this guy should go to Vietnam immediately. A cable was sent to the Hawaiian headquarters of Admiral U. S. G. Sharp, Commander in Chief, Pacific (CINCPAC), strongly recommending that our newfound speleologist be given the green light for his study. (As the strategic headquarters for the war in Vietnam, CINCPAC had to approve all such things, though why, five thousand miles from the war zone, CINCPAC was the strategic headquarters for the war in the first place was a totally unanswerable mystery, particularly given how completely out of touch the command was with what was happening in Vietnam.) Predictably, the answer on the cave expert was no. And it was yet another good idea trampled in the dust by just another big, far-removed headquarters that needed something to do, another solid layer of World

War II–thinking, close-minded, unimaginative bureaucracy throwing around its weight.*

Things seemed a hell of a lot less bleak the morning I got hold of a copy of the captain-to-major promotions list. All of my guys from the 1/327—Peeping Tom Hancock, Ben Willis, Wayne Dill, Don Chapman, Glynn Mallory—had made it "below the zone" to major. I was prouder than a new father, and since promotions lists were supposed to be about as closely held as the most secret of war plans, I waited at least five minutes before calling each man to give him the word. I waited another five minutes to call Ronnie Brown, one of Emerson's 2/502 studs who'd also made the 5 percent list—it took me that long to believe what my eyes were telling my head, that his name was even there.

It wasn't that Ronnie Brown wasn't a good soldier. In fact, he was a great one—a natural fighter, and a dedicated leader and trainer. But he was also way up there with Dale Le Clerc as one of the Animals I Have Known. He even looked like an animal, rivaling the Abu with his tough, squat (maybe five feet four) gorilla body and a face the dead ringer of a bulldog. Ronnie graduated from West Point, but how he'd gotten through was one of the unsolved mysteries of the twentieth century. He had a tendency to laugh uproariously in the face of any authority higher than his own, and he probably set a record for walking off demerits at the Point for insubordination bordering on the suicidal. (Just one example of his problem with authority in those formative college days was the speech he felt compelled to give as captain of the 150-pound West Point football team to the entire Corps of Cadets and officers the night before the all-important Navy game. "I don't give a damn about West Point," he said. "And I don't give a shit about the black, gray, and gold. And screw all the men who came before—we're going to go out there and kick Navy's ass for *me*, Ronnie Brown!")

In the end Ronnie defied all odds and graduated with his class. At Fort Campbell, where he was first assigned, he defied all odds by not being court-martialed. First, he ring-led a drunken "hose-down party" in the BOQ: one of his gang had a girlfriend down for the weekend, and when the two took an early-evening siesta, Ronnie and Co. stuck a fire hose under their friend's door and flooded the place. Then they took a fire ax and chopped through the door. All this would have been bad enough, but then

---

* The irony was, of course, that the tunnels and caves in South Vietnam were the Viet Cong's secret weapon. Regardless of what after-action reports for Operation Attleboro, Cedar Falls, and Junction City had to say, while sections of the tunnel complexes were destroyed by the Americans, for the most part they survived our bulldozers and B-52 runs and the rest of the technology the U.S. war machine brought to bear on them throughout the war. Both the Tet Offensive of '68, which more or less signaled the end of the U.S. war effort in Vietnam, and the final attack on Saigon on 30 April 1975, which finally ended the war, were launched from the VC's labyrinth of tunnels and caves that stretched over an area of some 100,000 acres.

the gang did the same to the rest of the rooms on the hall. The only thing that saved Ronnie from a cell at Leavenworth that time was the fact he wasn't alone; so many guys ended up being involved that in the end they all got off with an official reprimand. Ronnie didn't fare quite as well when he lost about five thousand dollars of his company's payroll while standing in the middle of a bank. Not only did he have to pay back every cent (the Army withheld his pay for about two years), but he also received an Article 15, which in the Army of the day was a basic guarantee he'd be a candidate for "premature retirement." And that was *before* the ugly fight he got into with members of the 501st Signal Battalion in the Officers' Club. Finally he was sent down to the Recondo School (whose instructors all had a tendency to be uncontrollable animals) as deputy commandant. In his element, he acquitted himself well there, as he did again in Vietnam with the 2/502, and when he returned to Fort Belvoir, Virginia, where he won the honor of Best Instructor. Even so, in the warrior-diplomat, zero-defect Army world of the mid-sixties, it would not have been unfair to say Ronnie Brown was *not* field-grade officer material.

Yet, there he was, on the 5 percent promotions list. So I called him on the phone. "You've got to be kidding me," he said when I gave him the news. "Are you sure you've got the right guy?" I read him his service number. "You've got to be kidding me," he repeated. "With *my* record? Man, Hack, if the Army's that fucked up, I'm quitting." And that was it. He quit.

Counterproductive as it turned out to be, Ronnie Brown's place on the promotions list proved that at least some of the less-refined battlefield animals—the real warriors—were getting through the system. It *was* unusual; as General Zais explained, old blood-and-guts leadership was neither needed nor desired by an Army that now placed management and executive skills well above those essential to inspire men or turn around an army on the ropes, even in the middle of war. In 1967–68, Grant, Teddy Roosevelt, Patton, Gavin, Ridgway, and Van Fleet wouldn't have stood a chance. Zais, on the other hand, went out of his way to fill his directorate with combat studs, so I always thought he bemoaned the direction the Army had taken as much as I did. But then came the day I tried to get a young major who'd worked for me in the 101st, now over at Fort Belvoir and very unhappy, to come to DIT as a replacement for Bill Kesterson, who was leaving for less squalid pastures. I took Zais the major's personnel file for consideration, and later that day he called me in. "This guy," he declared, "he's not our kind of man."

"Why's that, sir?" I asked.

"First of all, he doesn't have any medals."

"What's that got to do with it? You have my assurance he's a good man."

"And he doesn't have any gray in his hair."

"He's got a master's degree in nuclear physics."

"He's a young, skinny-looking guy, Hack. He's not a stud. I want studs, with a little gray and a blaze of medals."

"Sir," I replied, "I can't believe these words are coming out of your mouth. Since when do you have to be a hero to shuffle papers?"

"My staff is a reflection of me. When the Chief of Staff or the DCSPER looks at DIT, I want him to see studs. *All* studs. I have a fine stable now, and I'm not bringing in any limp dicks. This man is not acceptable."

The boss is always right even when he's wrong, and the major didn't get the job. Meanwhile I was left surprised and disappointed. The good of the Army was no more at the root of Zais's partiality to warriors than it was of the clerks' desire to zero the warriors out. It was all just part of the big scramble to get ahead, and ironic to me that just as junior officers would grab onto the coattails of up-and-coming superiors, the up-and-coming superiors were always on the lookout for what they perceived to be up-and-coming juniors to propel them ever starward from below. (The big problem with these relationships was that for the junior of the pair, if too strongly identified with his patron, the end could come without warning and finish a promising career. One colonel I knew, a combat-savvy DSC winner well on his way to a star or maybe even two or three, actually put in his retirement papers the day after "his" general had a stroke and medically retired. "No chance for me now," he explained with a shrug. And despite his having a hell of a lot left to offer, it was true.)

Politically speaking, the Army was broken down into a number of unofficial "clubs" (Airborne, Tanker, POW, Aviator, etc.), and the object for the career-minded was to maneuver himself to be a favored son of one (or preferably more) of the older members in the club to which he belonged. (Military Academy graduates also had a safety-net organization in the form of the unofficial but very real West Point Protection Association, or WPPA, whose members took care of their own.) Then, if a guy was lucky, he'd find himself in the right club at the right stage of his career. For example, it didn't matter that Airborne was inappropriate for the counterinsurgency war in Vietnam, or that Westmoreland, as an Airborne *artilleryman*, was even less appropriate as an overall commander. The fact was that with Westmoreland in command in Vietnam the Airborne club ran the show, and a hotshot Airborne officer had much greater command and career opportunities than he might in another branch. When Westy came back to Washington to become Chief of Staff, the tankers got in the driver's seat in

Vietnam, as Westy's COMUSMACV replacement, General Creighton Abrams, gradually surrounded himself with cardholders of the Tanker club, of which he was a charter member.

Why the Army in its infinite wisdom chose an Airborne cannoncocker (with his entire frame of reference being that of protecting his artillery, Westmoreland was directly responsible for the unwieldy fire support bases in Vietnam that destroyed U.S. mobility and initiative on the battlefield) and then a tanker for the top job in what was nothing if not an infantryman's war was something for future historians to decide. But at least Abrams, whose formidable reputation as a ruthless badass was only matched by his undisputed combat savvy, actively sought the opinions of officers who'd served there. After it was announced that he was to become Westy's MACV deputy and likely successor, Vice-Chief of Staff Abrams started calling us into his office. My one-hour interview with him consisted of exactly one question: "If you were COMUSMACV, what changes would you make?" Then the Vice-Chief said nothing for what was for me a very uncomfortable hour. His clear blue eyes seemed to penetrate, like an X ray, right through to my brain as he nodded occasionally and emitted gruff little grunts while I talked and he took notes, all the while chewing on a huge cigar. What he was thinking was anyone's guess, but when time passed and he took his place as COMUSMACV, it was obvious Abrams had taken to heart suggestions that I and others like myself had made. "If you can't eat it, wear it, or shoot it, don't bring it" was his solution to the blowout luxury that had occurred under his predecessor; in terms of tactics, he started replacing the wasteful search-and-destroy missions with extensive economy-of-force operations such as long-range reconnaissance patrols (LRRPs), and phasing out the CIDG border camps. On the other hand, these changes also coincided with the end of the Tet Offensive and the Khe Sanh siege, two milestones of the war that could not help but affect the way it was being waged.

Contrary to official U.S. reports, as of late 1967 the NVA was having great success in the Central Highlands and border areas. A month-long enemy siege at Con Thien, a Marine outpost near the DMZ, never developed into a full-scale enemy attack, but a thousand Marines were wounded or killed by continuous NVA artillery shelling on their position. Twenty-two thousand tons of American bombs were dropped by ever-faithful B-52s throughout the siege, until the Communists finally slipped away and Westmoreland pronounced Con Thien "a crushing defeat" for the NVA, invoking its likeness to the 1954 siege at Dien Bien Phu, only "in reverse," because we had prevailed.[5] But as with most things he said about the war, Westy spoke too soon.

About a month later the battle of Dak To was refought, with elements (ten-thousand-men strong, by the end of it) of the 4th Div, the 1st Air Cav Div, and the 173d Airborne Brigade taking a tragic pounding. A friend who'd fought with me at Dak To in 1966 was there this time, too, now as a member of the 173d. He said the fight was a "bloodbath," with his brigade alone taking 833 casualties, 191 of them KIA. Once again the NVA had lured U.S. forces into the most rugged terrain in Vietnam using one of the oldest tricks in the guerrilla handbook—an NVA "defector"—and even the (173d's) CG, Brigadier General Leo H. Schweitzer, admitted that "the enemy . . . chose the time and place in which decisive engagements would be fought," that "only when and where the tactical situation, terrain, battlefield, preparation and relative strengths of opposing forces favored enemy action were significant contacts initiated."[6] Eighteen months after Pearson's fight there, no one had learned. Twenty American troops were killed when a U.S. fighter aircraft put a bomb right on top of a friendly company. Twenty more died when enemy artillery scored a direct hit on the Americans' ammo dumps at Dak To. Two C-130 aircraft were lost and forty choppers were hit or destroyed. And even if the Americans' 1,644 enemy KIA reported by body count at Dak To was an accurate figure to the last man, was it worth the 2,096 air strikes (almost one and a half air strikes per enemy dead), and the expenditure of 151,000 rounds of artillery (92 rounds per enemy dead) it took to get them? Or the 344 U.S. troopers who lost their lives, or the 1,441 American WIA?

General Westmoreland, meanwhile, was back in the United States during Dak To with America's ambassador to Vietnam, Ellsworth Bunker. LBJ had requested their return to beat the "we are winning" drum, no doubt in some part because of Secretary of Defense McNamara's public and growing disenchantment with the war. Westy did his commander in chief proud during the brief tour, using even the ongoing, hugely expensive (in U.S. lives and matériel) Dak To battle to signal "the beginning of a great defeat for the enemy,"[7] and proclaiming in an address before the National Press Club that "I am absolutely certain that whereas in 1965 the enemy was winning, today he is certainly losing."[8] Perhaps his most amazing cheer was the one that we were now really winning our battle of attrition, that we had "raised enemy losses beyond his input capability," and that the enemy's "guerrilla force is declining at a steady rate."[9] I was not the only one who found this extremely hard to believe, but even though the events of the next two months would prove that Westmoreland's "best foot forward" in the U.S. ended up right in his mouth in Vietnam, it would not be for nearly a score of years that the country would know that the enemy-strength figures had actually been manipulated to back up Westy's claims, and that the COMUSMACV had handed out the M-1 pencils himself.[10]

But having juggled the figures, Westy must have come to believe them, and when he returned to Vietnam he enthusiastically embraced the siege on Khe Sanh as the Dien Bien Phu (in reverse) of the war (with the events at Con Thien barely filed away), from which would spring his ever-longed-for set-piece battle that would turn the tide of the war decisively in the Americans' favor. It was only Mao who said "there is no such thing as a decisive battle" in guerrilla warfare.

Over a period of months in late 1967 and early 1968, some forty thousand NVA troops surrounded Khe Sanh, an isolated Marine base supplied strictly by air and located near the Laos border. In turn, Westy expanded Khe Sanh to six thousand Marines, in preparation for what he was sure was the inevitable NVA attack. It never came. Instead, for more than two months, day and night, day in and day out, while World War II–minded generals warned of the horrors of abandoning the camp (the "Western anchor of our defensive line," said one, that, if surrendered, would allow the enemy to "turn our flank and two or three provinces would be in serious jeopardy"), the Marines sat on the receiving end of the same horrific incoming we hill people had endured in Korea in 1952–53.[11] Throughout the siege the NVA got theirs, too—from B-52s alone some seventy-five thousand tons, and in casualty figures fifteen to twenty times those of the Marines' five hundred KIA. But as Ward Just had titled his book, *to what end* was the whole damn thing?

General Giap knew, even if Westy did not. Eleven days after the Khe Sanh siege began, seventy thousand Communist troops launched a surprise attack on more than a hundred cities, towns, and bases throughout South Vietnam almost simultaneously. The attack commenced under the cover of the Tet celebrations, just as Slam and I had discussed a year before, but even I was surprised by the size, violence, and initial success it achieved. The Tet Offensive of 1968 gave the lie to almost everything stated publicly by General Westmoreland and his staff, such as the VC were on their knees, both in strength and morale, and would never be able to mount a sustained attack, or that "pacification" was working: almost every city considered to be a "secure" area in South Vietnam was attacked during Tet of '68. If Westy and Co. maintained the merest vestige of credibility with the American people after the U.S. Embassy in Saigon was attacked and penetrated by nineteen Viet Cong at the outset of the offensive (for all the world to watch on the six-o'clock news), it was lost less than a week into the fighting, when the first official body count was announced: the absurdly precise figure of 14,997 enemy KIA (to 367 American dead).[12] A week after that, the figure had been rounded off to (an incredible) 31,000 enemy KIA, but even this trouncing had its price—U.S casualties were also the highest of the war:

920 KIA and 4,560 WIA.[13] The American mission's credibility with the South Vietnamese people also plummeted during Tet of '68, and new battalions of Viet Cong were created every day as the percentage of civilians mistakenly added to the official enemy body count grew and grew. In the city of Can Tho, in the Mekong Delta, the opening rounds of the fighting saw half of the civilian casualties caused by the Viet Cong and half by the Americans. But as the Americans geared up their war machine in counter-attack, close to all the civilian casualties were from U.S. activity.[14]

Westy, meanwhile, like LBJ, was so obsessed with what was happening at Khe Sanh that he determinedly believed the Tet Offensive was simply a feint to draw U.S. troops away from his potential Dien Bien Phu in reverse. That he might have the scenario backwards, i.e., that Khe Sanh was a feint to draw American troops away from the cities on the eve of the Tet attacks, was not considered. Only General Fred Weyand, the IIFFV commander, was prepared for the huge offensive that caught U.S. military intelligence with its Pearl Harbor pants down: he took the advice of his civilian adviser, John Paul Vann, who'd been the first to notice the enemy was massing and suggested strongly that Weyand's units stay closer to home rather than go out on search-and-destroy missions. (Not insignificantly, Weyand, a thinking man who was determined to understand the war in depth, had chosen Vann as his senior adviser over Westmoreland's protests that Vann was "a troublemaker.")[15]

The Americans did achieve a tactical victory in the Tet Offensive. Ho and Giap had unwittingly been cursed with the same kind of bad intelligence that led to Kennedy's Bay of Pigs: much to their surprise the people of South Vietnam were *not* ready, and did not rally around the revolution. But while our firepower proved decisive on the ground and on the day, the strategic and psychological victory the Communists achieved during Tet—among the South Vietnamese people, the American public, *and* the American fighting men—was incalculable.

The siege at Khe Sanh was ongoing throughout the Tet Offensive, and back at the Pentagon it was the main event. Unable to do anything about what was happening there or anywhere in Vietnam, I was angry, frustrated, and ashamed for the Army and the country. I had a friend working in the Office of the Joint Chiefs of Staff and I went to see him frequently in his E-ring office to get the latest skinny on the siege. When I heard the Joint Chiefs were considering using tactical nuclear weapons at Khe Sanh, *I* exploded. As Chairman of the Joint Chiefs, J. Lawton Collins in May of 1954 had recommended the use of atomic weapons at Dien Bien Phu. In Korea in 1950 and again in 1953 we'd talked about using them, too. Every time we'd gotten into a crack since 1945, everybody had started yelling, "We *gotta use nukes!"* Talk about upping the ante. So for Khe Sanh (which couldn't have fallen anyway, because our conventional firepower alone was too great*), the recommendation to use the Bomb as a way to get us out of the terrible, stupid, and totally avoidable trap we'd gotten ourselves into because few people had read the French report on Dien Bien Phu pissed me off so much that without even thinking I blurted out, "I'd take my son to Canada before I'd let him fight in this goddamn war!"

I astonished myself. Not for the sentiment, but for the conviction. And as for the words, I regretted them the minute they were out of my mouth. In true ticket-punching fashion I immediately launched into damage control. "My God, I can't believe I said that! Jesus, Jerry," I implored Major Jerry Scott, an old 101st paratrooper friend who also worked in DIT and was witness to my blasphemy, "you didn't hear me say that! Please, please, don't tell anyone I said that!"

Nuclear weapons were, of course, not used in Khe Sanh. And after Tet, when the ruse was no longer needed, the enemy ran away to fight another day. The thirty thousand American troops Westmoreland had tied up in reserve in preparation for the attack went on to other jobs, and Khe Sanh itself, by now rat-ridden and shell-shattered, its significance as the "Western anchor of our defense line" now forgotten, was abandoned by the Marines with no enemy response at all.

It was the end of LBJ and the end of Westmoreland, even if the latter did go "all the way" to Army Chief of Staff three weeks after Khe Sanh was quietly abandoned by General Abrams. Westy left behind in Vietnam 533,000 U.S. troops and enough high-hype charts and graphs and formulas and systems to do everything but resolve the conflict. With almost twenty-five thousand American lives lost in his four years as COMUSMACV and nothing to show for it save TV images of enemy troops swarming through every major city in South Vietnam, Westmoreland returned to the United States to an angry national will. Shortly thereafter, sixteen officers were selected from throughout the U.S. Army to express their views in writing to the new Chief on problems facing the Army then and in the immediate future. I was one of those sixteen officers, and in the resulting "Compendium of Comments" I let go with both barrels, writing:

> The U.S. Army has badly botched the war. I have concluded, after exhaustive study, that we have lost. Here are the main tenets of my study:

---

* As it was, fundamentally, in all of the Americans' major engagements in Vietnam, making it totally impossible for U.S units to "lose" any battle at brigade or division level in a conventional, WW II sense. Vietnam was the first of America's wars where a division commander *never* had to fear losing his unit.

1.　We have not required the government of SVN (GVN) to establish reforms. It remains a corrupt, inefficient, graft-ridden collection of divided opportunists who have little interest in the people of their country. As a result of these factors, the people have no interest in the GVN and are either actively supporting the VC or completely indifferent to the programs of the GVN. Without the active assistance of the people, an insurgent force cannot be defeated.

2.　Failure to develop overall objectives and a plan of strategy to support these aims which would bring the war to a successful conclusion.

3.　Failure to develop small unit tactics which would support an overall campaign plan.

4.　Failure of our Army to understand the nature of guerrilla warfare. As a consequence of this almost criminal shortcoming, we have been reacting to the enemy since mid-1966. It boils down to the hard fact that we don't have the initiative and are strictly on the defense—the enemy plays the tune and we dance. . . .

We have sent a large force which is top-heavy with supporters and thin on fighters to Vietnam. This force is organized conventionally and thinks conventionally. Its objective has been to fight big multi-battalion battles where generals can display their "generalship." The net result of this is we have had our "clock cleaned" in almost every major fight.* The VC hide when confronted with a large force and fight only on their terms (when victory—either tactically or psychologically—can be assured).

5.　The tactical know-how that senior officers (LTC and above) have displayed in Vietnam is deplorable. This condition has resulted in a failure to understand how to fight the guerrilla. The root cause for this debacle is, that for the past decade our Army has been concerned with developing high-level corporate managers and, in the main, our officer corps has been scurrying busily about collecting tickets—C&GS, War College, DA and JCS [Joint Chiefs of Staff] staff assignments and command experience sufficient only to get by. Consequently, we have few soldiers who understand what it is all about at the point of the bayonet level. And that, as you well know, is where wars are won. We do have a great number of well-ticketed Harvard graduates who are very swift in the area of management, but know little about the "nuts and bolts" of their profession.

6.　To win in Vietnam we need a Wingate, Giap, Rommel, Jackson, McNair-type soldier. But I doubt if our present system will produce such an

---

* Lieutenant Colonel Robert C. Schweitzer, another contributor to the report who went on to three stars and the job of head of counterinsurgency on the Joint Staff, provided a different view of America's performance in Vietnam, and one that would prove to have a lot more "takers" than my own. "Whether or not Vietnam is regarded as a defeat will depend on the face that is put on it . . ." Schweitzer declared. ". . . there will be plenty of those who will put the face of defeat on U.S. efforts. Silence on the part of the Army et al. will both corroborate and add numbers to the voices of defeat; the Army must lead the way in conducting a 'Psyops [Psychological Operations] campaign' to the end that American Arms accomplished their mission in Vietnam."

individual. They are too: *abrasive*, opinionated, undiplomatic, nonconform-
ist, and effective.

* * *

The capable combat leader has traits which are inconsistent with today's
criteria for high-level positions. As a result, the men who know how to win in
battle, with rare exception, just don't get ahead. Instead the second stringers
who talk a good game in the shower room and are adroit at fixing the blame
on others, succeed.

The system desperately needs an enema. Better yet, it requires a violent
purge. . . . This purge will have to be initiated from outside the Army because
the "system" is poured in concrete and it will take 10 to 20 years to weed out
the "ticket punchers" and to reorient the policy makers.

* * *

The system doesn't lend itself to fresh ideas. A new idea means waves.
Waves mean causing people to be flushed out of their comfortable ruts. I have
recommended numerous projects which could have led to a better trained
Army, but most of my recommendations have not been acted upon even
though all hands agree that they were damned good. So I found myself
refusing to initiate anything and thus the process of vegetation started setting
in.

To succeed in today's Army one must be quick on his feet and dazzle all
with shifty footwork. To be a winner you cannot rock the boat and you must
be willing to change your positions to accommodate the views of your
"superiors." I found my head starting to nod in agreement though I knew
down deep inside that I was in complete disagreement! My growing Pavlovian
tendencies scared me to my roots!

Aside from word that the new Chief was "not happy" with what I had to
say, I received no feedback on my contribution to his study. Still, there was
always something happening to reinforce the views I'd expressed therein.
Just one was the DoD briefing I attended in which Dr. Herman Kahn
pontificated about the consequences of the Tet Offensive. Kahn, one of the
gurus of American nuclear policy, felt he was an expert on Vietnam
because, as he explained, he had visited the country every year since the
early fifties. In fact this made him just another tourist, but the Defense guys
and military men nonetheless gushed over everything he said. The military
men were particularly enthusiastic, perhaps because, having been so
conditioned by their own can-doism not to *think*, they were mesmerized by
people who used their brains for a living. In the old days I may have been,
too, but being with Slam had taught me well. Kahn, a huge-bellied
intellectual, looked like a sloppy bohemian rabbi even as he acted as smooth
and glib as Billy Graham. He didn't strike me as being into learning,
though: he was into power, the way Slam was into power, power that you

could almost feel when you were with men who knew they'd arrived. I'd felt it with Slam, and I felt it whenever I traveled with a three- or four-star to visit one of my branch schools. As tagalong notetaker and horse handler I was always kind of in the back of the bus, but being close to that power was still some rush—from private planes onto waiting choppers, flags snapping, bands playing, and precise schedules of honor guards, inspections, and receptions. It wasn't hard to see why someone would want to be a general.

Or an intellectual. Kahn, his power masquerading as knowledge, was of the opinion that Tet was the beginning of the end for the Communists, that even if the war raged on into the eighties, it would be bandito stuff that would ultimately fade away. He went on to propose that the U.S. build a network of "freeway canals" in the Mekong Delta to further economic development in that rich rice region, but his proposition on how to secure the scheme (high-speed patrol boats) was about as realistic and sensible as the multimillion-dollar electronic fence McNamara wanted to build across the DMZ. ("Do something—anything—to win the war," McNamara and LBJ had tasked Lieutenant General Alfred Starbird, director of the Defense Communications Agency and Planning Group in mid-'66, and an electronic Maginot Line was the fundamentally flawed result of this straw-grasping exercise. A barrier field of sensors could be only as effective as the men on the ground who protected and defended it; an electronic fence would have required troops just to keep it safe from enemy hands, and even then the NVA could have just gone around it, using their well-traveled Laotian infiltration routes.) Kahn seemed to be one of the few who persisted, after Tet, with a confident, rosy view of the war effort. Why no one, myself included, challenged his blind-eyed opinions, his qualifications to express same, or his harebrained ideas, I'd never know.

Research and Development was full of civilian would-be Kahn types who made a living dreaming up Buck Rogers wonder gear (for which no scenario existed to justify its use) or Buck Rogers scenarios (to give themselves something to design wonder gear for). R&D was so remote from the user level that it was almost as if the soldier in the field was considered a pesky, somewhat irrelevant nuisance who, as much as possible, must not be allowed to interfere with the Grand Plan. "It doesn't take a year-long study to determine the 40-mm grenade launcher attached to the M-16 as an unsuccessful gimmick," wrote Lieutenant Colonel Robert Sunell in the same sixteen-officer study of problems facing the Army that I participated in, "yet we all went through the agony of installing it. I often wonder who is dictating what to whom. The Army to industry or reverse order." In the same study Major Fredric Brown, a tanker like Sunell, wrote of mine detectors in the world of R&D with the same passion I had for a simple grenade pouch: "We seem overly taken with exotic gadgets . . . while my reaction is certainly emotional, it seems to me if we can go to the moon we can develop a lightweight, effective density mine detector." Brown also wrote of the oversophistication of equipment in terms that would become familiar in the years that followed, as the American people got less and less bang while U.S. defense contractors got more and more bucks. "I have a feeling that everybody has written down everything that he believes [a piece of equipment] should be able to do, then all requirements are totaled. The result is a very expensive, highly complex, long lead-time weapons system which the average soldier has great difficulty in mastering."

The military-industrial complex was alive and kicking and growing stronger by the day. Industry *was* dictating to the Army, but more than ever that "industry" was composed of ex-military men who one would have thought would know better, or at least care more about the service they had left behind. As of March 1969, 2,072 officers of the rank of colonel or navy captain and above were working for the ninety-five top military contractors, a number that had nearly trebled in the ten years since Senator Paul Douglas' study identified 721 retired military officers working in the top eighty-eight defense industries.[16]

In May '68, Slam Marshall rang me to ask if I'd go back with him to Vietnam—Westy wanted him to have another look at the war. I impulsively said yes, but as we talked I realized the purpose of the trip was actually to whitewash the effects of the Tet Offensive through Slam's considerable media power. One of the reasons I'd jumped at the invitation in the first place was that I'd had it with running around the U.S. selling the war on those speaking tours, and I'd be damned if I was going to go back to Vietnam only to continue the charade. So I told him I'd have to think about it, and then that I'd changed my mind. Slam was shocked. He wouldn't take no for an answer, and I finally had to arrange with my new boss, Colonel Kenneth Buell, to take a short leave just to get away from the constantly ringing phone. I went to Tim Grattan's in Seattle, but even there Slam or his wife, Cate, called every day, urgently looking for me. Darlene or Tim would always say I was "out fishing," until the Marshalls finally got the message. I didn't know whether I'd screwed myself by not giving in to Slam's desire, but I did know I was damn relieved when the phone fell silent.

I did not mourn the lost opportunity to go back to Vietnam, because I knew it was just a matter of time until I went anyway. The previous December, Major General Julian Ewell, an old 101 man from Bastogne (one of the many Slam said he "made" with his book *Night Drop*), had been assigned command of the 9th Division by his fellow "All the Way" Airborne

club member William Childs Westmoreland. Ewell had asked Hank
Emerson to be one of his three brigade commanders, and in turn Emerson
had suggested to Ewell that I be brought on as one of Hank's battalion COs.
Ewell had agreed, and naturally so had I.

But I'd needed General Zais's approval as well, as I was nowhere near the
end of my DIT tour, and Zais had invested enough time in me to give him
every reason not to let me go. Both Ewell and Emerson came along when
I went to plead my case. Thankfully, General Zais was completely
understanding. Putting the interests of the troops above those of the
bureaucracy of which he was a part (a rare instance at the Pentagon, I
thought), he told me on the spot, in front of Ewell and Emerson, that I
could go.

I was fully appreciative of the sacrifice Zais was willing to make on my
behalf. I was walking on air, and even the response of my career branch to
the news ("You don't want to go back. You've commanded your battalion
there. If you go back and get into a donnybrook you'll ruin your chances for
a star. What you need is Joint Staff duty.") couldn't dampen my excitement
about going back to the cutting edge. The career managers, those number-
one string pullers when it came to directing your life, had no appreciation
of the individual as they worked out the same equation again and again to
prepare everyone to be a future Chief of Staff. Their pat response to my own
news was the final straw for me; I said to myself, *Screw their advice*, and paid
no attention to them ever again.

Months passed. Ewell went over to Vietnam, Hank went over, and then
so did Slam Marshall. Then, when I was just beginning to think about
putting my house on the market (*Guess what, Patty, I'm going back to
Vietnam, so I'll see you around . . .*), General Zais called me to his office.
"Hack, goddamn, would you believe this! Westy just called—he's giving me
the 101st!" *The* prize in the Army was to command the 101st Airborne
Division, and there Zais had been, worrying whether he'd get a division at
all. "So now we've got to get the team together," he continued. "You're
going to be my G-3." It was probably the most important lieutenant
colonel's spot in a division.

"I'm not going to be your G-3, General Zais. I've got a battalion in the
9th, remember? You told General Ewell in this very office you'd let me go."

"Fuck Ewell!" Zais exploded. "He's got his fair share of studs. I'm going
to get some studs, too."

"You gave him your word, sir!"

"I've changed my mind. The situation's different now. Ewell's got the
best guys there are. He's practically cleaned out the whole Army!" (Which
he had.)

I came to a rigid attention. "Fine, sir," I said.

"You don't have to stand at attention, Hack," Zais burbled. "Come on, let's start lining up the team!"

"I'm not going, sir," I said.

"Why not?"

"Because I'm quitting, General Zais. If there's no trust in the Army, if you can't trust a general to keep his word after he's given it to you, and after he's given it to another general—as you did, General Zais, to General Ewell right here in this office—then I'm checking out of the net. It's all over."

"Oh, Hack, forget it," Zais said.

"No way, sir," I replied, and meant it from the bottom of my heart.

I put in the paperwork. I had more than twenty years in and, after all, had it not been for Vietnam I'd intended to get out in '68 anyway. But I didn't want to get out. After months and months of ruminating on the issue, at the eleventh hour I knew it was true—I was fed up with the system and the war but I still loved the Army. And besides, I didn't know what the hell I'd *do* in civilian life. I'd quit on impulse. I had no training. I had no prospects. It was 1953 all over again, and for the first time in a long time I was damn scared.

And then Slam called. Just back from Vietnam he'd heard through the grapevine that I was getting out, and he wanted to know what I was going to do. The million-dollar question. "I don't know," I said.

"Well, come work for me," he offered. "I'm getting old and tired of all this war and traveling. You can write. You know my style and technique, and you'd be the ideal person in the Army to replace me."

It was an incredible offer. And I was touched or saddened or *something*: my ambivalence was almost painful about this man who cared for me as he might a son and would have been truly proud to have me carry on his work. And Marshall was right, working for him would be the perfect job for me, and once established in my own right I wouldn't have to wear the same mantle I saw Slam wearing all too comfortably now, that of the Army's top apologist. But then again, too much water had gone under the bridge with Slam and me. We stood so far on opposite sides of the fence that I knew it would not take long before we found no common ground at all. So I had to tell him no. And I never saw or spoke with him again.

Just days before I was to be discharged, Swede Larsen, at this point CG of Sixth Army, called me from his headquarters in San Francisco. He'd heard I was quitting and urged me to change my mind. "You're a good soldier and we need good soldiers," he said.

"The die's been cast, sir."

"You've still got the suit on, haven't you?" he asked. "What would you want to do if you stayed in?"

"General Larsen, all I want to do is to command a battalion."

"All right," the General replied. "Then why don't you come out here? I'll give you a battalion at Fort Lewis."

"You can do that?"

"I can do it."

Larsen's offer was a reprieve. I still intended to get out, but at least at Fort Lewis I had Tim Grattan nearby, with whom I could plan my civilian life. The boys at OPO smirked and sneered; compared to DA or a combat assignment, a training battalion at Fort Lewis wasn't exactly upmarket. (There were no TOE infantry battalions at Fort Lewis. Instead they were all training battalions, composed of troops going through Basic Combat Training or Advanced Individual Training en route to Vietnam.) "You won't be doing your career any good," they said. "It's a retrograde step." Little did they know that I was having the last laugh, because I didn't care.

I read in the *Army Times* that First Sergeant Sylvester Wilson had been killed in Vietnam. A million years before, when we were both kids, Wilson had been my TRUST I&R scout, my navigator who always kept me going in the right direction. I hadn't seen him in all the years since, but his death was that of a brother, and the pain of loss cut deep. Then, on the Fourth of July, Fred Terry, on his third tour of Vietnam, died in a midair chopper crash during a 1st Div combat operation. Tears streamed down my face in my Pentagon office as an unknown officer's voice formally asked me over the phone if, at the request of Fred's widow, Carol, I would deliver the eulogy at his funeral. I couldn't. Fred and I had met in battle in my S-3 office at Fort Campbell, the result of which had been a true and lasting friendship. He, like my friend Sylvester Wilson, had died a senseless death in a senseless war and I knew I'd never find words to describe any of it at all.

On my last day at DIT Major General William Henderson, the Australian military attaché whom I'd met through his interest in the *Vietnam Primer*, invited me to a farewell lunch. The last time we'd gotten together was in April at his home on the west bank of the Potomac, where we'd sipped cocktails and watched Washington burn as the death of Martin Luther King set off riots unlike the city had ever known. It had felt strange to be with a non-American, much less a British subject, watching our capital in flames. The last time Washington had burned had been by a British torch in the War of 1812. Try to explain it all.

Anyway, Henderson wanted to have lunch, and just before I went to meet him, I stopped in to see Colonel Buell. After a boss like Hank Emerson, Buell had been pretty much a nonevent. But we'd always gotten along fine, had never had any big shoot-outs in the seven months I worked for him, and now when he showed me the ER he'd rendered on me (which was customary) and congratulated me on my "well-earned" max scores, the atmosphere was nothing but congenial. I told him the only thing I had on my agenda that afternoon was to be backup briefer for General Pearson at his 1530 briefing for the Chief of Staff (it was just my good luck that Pearson had replaced Zais when the latter went off to the 101st), that I had a lunch appointment now and if he had no objections I'd be off. He didn't, and I went.

I met General Henderson at the Australian Embassy. We each had a stiff scotch in his office, and then went to lunch at a place called the Black Beret. We ate and drank some more (in the drinking department Henderson was a typical Aussie, and I had to make a point of not even trying to keep up with him if I intended to get back to work standing upright) and time slipped by. As the hour approached for me to leave it became harder and harder to break off. I explained to General Henderson that I had to get back for the briefing, but he wouldn't hear of it. "No worries," he said. "I'll just call Westy and tell him you're with me."

That may have been the Australian way of doing things, but I rather doubted it would go over too well with the Chief of Staff. "No, sir," I said. "Thanks, but no, don't do that. I've got to be there. I really need to get a taxi."

I finally broke away, but the little bit of extra effort cost me time I couldn't afford. I jumped into a cab, zipped back to the Pentagon, ran up the steps and into my office to get the briefing paper I'd need if called upon by Pearson to elaborate for the Chief. But the paper was gone. Someone said Jerry Milam had taken it. Pearson had come in looking for me, and when I wasn't there, Jerry, my Artillery and Air Defense action officer and de facto principal assistant (due to his overall brilliance and essential Tom Martin qualities), had said he'd stand in at the briefing. At least I knew Pearson was in good hands.

I went next door to Colonel Buell's office, to find him in a quiet rage. "I guess I screwed up, sir," I said.

"I guess you have. I guess you have," Buell responded without looking at me.

"I'll just shoot up to the Chief's office and see if there's any flak."

"No, you won't, Colonel. Major Milam has taken care of your duties since you weren't here to acquit them."

"Yes, sir. I'm very sorry. I should have gotten away earlier. I didn't, and I'm fully responsible."

"Indeed you are."

I did feel bad about what had happened. I'd let Pearson down. But there was nothing I could do about it now. As I left Buell's office, his secretary stopped me. "Buell changed your report," she whispered.

"Why?" I asked.

"Something to do with your not being on the mark with this briefing."

I turned around and went back into Buell's office. "Colonel Buell," I said, "I'm glad we were able to get this situation squared away, and I really am sorry if I caused you any concern on my last day here. But I did want to thank you again for giving me that great report, and I was just wondering if I could have another look at it."

Buell got all flushed. "Well . . . uh. . ." he said.

"Well, I have seen it, you know. You showed it to me yourself this morning."

Very reluctantly Buell handed over the efficiency report. In a glance my blood began to boil. In the revised edition, he'd cut me on judgment. "Wait a minute, sir . . ." I said as innocently as I could sound with boiling blood. "There seems to be a mistake here. This '1' has been changed to a '2.' "

"Well, you did screw up."

"Oh, I see. I worked for you for two hundred and nine full days, and for one mistake I made today you decide to give me a '2' in judgment? Well, if you're going to do that, why don't you just change the whole goddamn thing, Colonel Buell? You have attacked me on my most vulnerable point. What I'm all about, and what any good Army officer is all about, is judgment. And if I don't have good judgment I shouldn't be wearing this suit."

"I think you're overreacting, Colonel."

"Well, I don't give a damn what you think."

At that point a buzzer sounded on Buell's desk. It was General Pearson, wondering whether I'd come in yet. When Buell said I was right there, the General asked him to bring me over—he'd organized a little farewell party for me. Given the puritan that he was, a party with Pearson would be about six minutes (a cup of coffee, a medal, a handshake, and an "I'll see you around"), but it was given out of the goodness of his heart, and that's what counted. Buell, immediately humbled that his boss was my patron, awkwardly accompanied me to Pearson's office, and when we emerged a short while later, his secretary called me back into her office to say he'd changed the report again, back to its prelunch status.

Had the same slipup on my part that so raised Buell's ire occurred the first day he was my boss rather than the last, by the time I left it probably would have been forgotten. Instead it was the basis for my beheading, or it would have been had it not been for a concerned secretary. It was a sick system that could allow a man's future to be seriously damaged on the basis of a single, not exactly critical misstep, or let a onetime warrior turned clerk abuse his power as "boss" so thoughtlessly, and worse, so *easily*. It was crazy that the efficiency-report system had become so inflated that there was little room for maneuver if you were found wanting (i.e., scoring anything other than a 1 on a scale of 1 to 5) in any of some twenty-four "personal qualities" from "adaptability" to "understanding" (and including your "nonduty conduct," which meant how well you kept your personal affairs in order). The ER rating situation was so bad that the night Patty and I had a party at our house and the water pump conked out just before the guests arrived, I'd actually worried about my future (if only for a moment): all the "ingenuity" and "adaptability" that I could muster wasn't going to change the fact that Emerson and Zais, my bosses, and other high-ranking guys and their wives were coming over, and all of them were going to have to piss in the bushes behind the house.

The ER system, like body count, had outlived any useful purpose. It was bad enough in peacetime to be judged on how well you could play golf, but it was beyond reason that in the middle of a war these things still counted, and in the same peacetime measure. Like Gib Gibson and the condemnation he received for suggesting that a soldier's job was to fight. Like Gentleman John Howard, brave fighter and reciter of Kipling, whose superb performance with the 1/327 was lost under the faint praise on his ER: "Although extremely popular he needs to discipline himself socially to acquire additional polish." Like Ben Willis, who would receive a 3 in Sociability (which in ERese meant "Participated freely and easily in social and community activities") from an inept rater who would only see him in a hot combat situation with the ARVN Airborne in the jungles of Cambodia. Like Tim Grattan, who had gotten nothing but the best ERs, but knew it was just a question of time before some clerk pulled the plug. In 1927 it was written in the efficiency report of George Patton, Jr., then a captain, that "this man would be invaluable in time of war, but is a disturbing element in time of peace." It was an assessment that could not have been more astute, and time would prove the absolute necessity for the Pattons of the Army. Yet Patton never would have survived that ER in the New Look Army, or in the sixties Army, where clerks like Alexander Haig pushed for the goal of the Army education system *not* to be the production of leaders of men, but rather the development of political scientists, "because these are the officers who will ultimately influence the application of our power in the future."[17] The dancers and prancers would have used Patton's ER to see him passed over and out of the service before the ink was dry on the page. And worst of all, so wrapped up in their self-importance, they would not even recognize the terrible error they had made.

The run-in with Buell was a perfect way to end my Pentagon tour, evoking as it did all that was petty, stupid, political, and wasteful about the place. Getting out was like being released from jail. And despite Buell's effort, the gibes of OPO managers, or all the inbuilt booby traps in Pentagon duty, my career was still on track if I decided to stay in after my tour at Fort Lewis. At that point, though, I didn't really care—all I ever wanted was to be with soldiers, and whatever happened afterwards, at least that's what I'd be doing now, in a new battalion command.

18 DEATH ROW

Hack had the knack of being able to size up people very quickly.
Almost instantaneously. And I'd say 99 percent of the time he was
right. He could look at a person, and in his vernacular the guy was
either a stud or he wasn't. There was no in between. If he was a
stud, Hack would find a way to get him. And he would not take
no from people if he wanted them. Because he wanted a winning
team. And if a person didn't want to go with him, then
immediately the guy wasn't a stud, you see. Because anybody who
knew Hack or came in contact with him really wanted to be with
him, after he'd known him for a while.

> Brigadier General James H. Mukoyama
> Company Commander, 4/39 Infantry
> Republic of Vietnam, 1969

THE job of a training battalion commander at Fort Lewis entailed
absolutely everything relating to a battalion *except* its training. That was the
responsibility of a centralized Training Committee, a separate entity under
the auspices of Fort Lewis' U.S. Army Training Center (ATC), one of
eleven such operations in the U.S. It was little wonder the people at OPO
couldn't believe I'd wanted this assignment, or that acquaintances wondered
what I'd done to deserve such an end-of-the-line posting. Despite the
strongly held views of a soldier as wise as General Bruce Clarke, who
believed that a training-center assignment should be of critical importance
to an officer's career development, the thinking in the sixties Army was that
good men, especially Regulars on the make, must avoid such duty at all
costs. It was true, the job was totally without the potential for glory, and the
officers who got assigned to Lewis in jobs like mine were all too often
passed-over majors or colonels just marking time until retirement. The work
was mainly administrative, and after you'd made sure your troops had a
place to sleep, food to eat, and chaperones (in the form of your cadre) to get

them to all the Training Committee's classes at the right times, you had little to do but sit in your office all day waiting for the five-o'clock quitting bell to ring.

A training battalion's cadre—its company commanders and NCOs—had as little to do with their days as their battalion commander. The vast majority at Lewis were straight out of the Infantry School (experienced junior officers and NCOs were close to nonexistent), but it was a tremendous waste of potential talent to relegate them to what was essentially a baby-sitting role. I was particularly appalled to see the graduates of the instant NCO program spending their all-important OJT period marching trainees from class to class and otherwise sitting in their offices doing paperwork or writing letters. It defeated the entire purpose of the program, which was to give the shake and bakes hands-on experience dealing with soldiers in a real leadership role.

It quickly became evident to me that all at the Army Training Center at Fort Lewis was not as it had appeared when I'd visited the place from the Pentagon in my role as Chief of Individual Training and then of SED-DIT's Schools Branch. Things I'd accepted unquestioningly then were now, on closer and sustained view, actually quite disturbing. First on the list was the fact that few people outside the Training Committee were checking the quality of the training. I wanted to know what actually happened to the soldiers after their cadres dropped them off at individual classes. It was obvious that visiting the classrooms in uniform in my role as battalion commander was no way to find out (in the face of higher authority, no doubt the instruction would be first rate—it always had been, when I'd come out for a look from the Pentagon), so I decided that the only foolproof alternative was to don the fatigues of a recruit myself and infiltrate the training.

I did this with the blessings of my boss, a wonderfully perceptive officer named Colonel Lewington Ponder. But because I also had to run my battalion, it was obvious I couldn't go through the nine-week AIT "Vietnam-oriented Army Subject Schedule" continuously with the same group. Instead I went block by training block, falling out in 0500 darkness (amidst the inevitable Tacoma rain and fog) with whatever unit was scheduled and, if asked, telling the squad I joined that I was a recycle from another company who'd missed this particular block of instruction. Despite the fact that I was about a million years older than they were, none of the trainees questioned this; the only guy who took any special interest in me at all was a black Regular Army drill sergeant during the very last block of instruction. The company I'd joined was boarding trucks for the field when he came up to me with very suspicious eyes. "Take off your helmet," he snapped, and after I'd complied he bobbed and weaved and crouched like a middleweight as he examined my "whitewalls" no-hair haircut, my dog tags (which I'd borrowed from my Fort Lewis Tom Martin, otherwise known as Private Robert Cena, who stayed in the office keeping me from drowning in paperwork while I played trainee), and checked Cena's name against the company roster. "You a trainee, trooper?" the sergeant finally asked.

"Yes, sir," I replied from my position of attention. "Korean retread, sir."

"Don't you 'sir' me, man!" the sergeant sang in his wonderful jive. "I'm a *sergeant*, a Regular U-S-Army sergeant. So I guess maybe you are a trainee. But you sure are an *old* fuckin' trainee!"

As impossible as it seemed, I didn't get caught throughout the entire masquerade, except the time one instructor was so incompetent and the instruction so bad that I blew my lid *and* my cover and took over the class myself rather than have the trainees lose valuable time and critical information. But the experience was mind-boggling, and unlike anything I could have imagined. Far from the prying eyes of superiors and non-Training Committee personnel, the AIT training I witnessed was criminal. Virtually everything these trainees got was wrong in terms of its applicability to the war in Vietnam. Meanwhile the essential things were ignored completely, or given so little attention as to render them meaningless. During the instruction block on the M-60 machine gun, for example, I sat as dumbstruck as the befuddled trainee beside me while a young instructor who'd never been to Vietnam covered in exceptional detail the making of range cards and the walking of the final protective line—both pretty useless in the jungle, where dense foliage limited vision to a few feet. When we got to the hands-on part where the trainees actually fired the M-60, I noticed most of them didn't react correctly to a misfire. Later, when I asked about twenty-five of these soldiers what the first step was in dealing with a misfire, not one of them had any idea. It should have been as second nature as throwing on the brakes to stop a car.

The four-hour block of instruction dealing with the "starlight scope" night-vision device was so technical and boring that when it was over I couldn't remember even 2 percent of what was covered. Neither could my classmates. The impression the instructor gave was that it was so complicated it was well beyond most of the trainees' grasp; in fact, what the average soldier needed to know to operate this superb battlefield tool was so simple it could have been taught in no more than thirty easy minutes.

With mines and booby traps responsible for probably 50 percent of all U.S. casualties in Vietnam, one would have thought mines and booby-trap training would be a top priority in the Vietnam-oriented AIT—maybe thirty hours' minimum, with the subject integrated into every other aspect of the training. On the contrary, exactly *five hours* of the entire nine-week course were devoted to these lethal devices: four hours on booby traps, which barely scratched the "need to know" surface for the soldiers who would confront them daily in Vietnam, and one hour on mines, and on the World War II M-21 *antitank* mine at that. It was unbelievable. Three years after the first U.S. doughboys learned about these devices the hard way, there wasn't even a Vietnam-oriented mines and booby-trap training film. There was no decent mines and booby-trap training aid, something like what I'd heard the Marine Corps had developed, a device that when "exploded" propelled a red substance that clung to the trainee like blood. As I wrote to General Pearson at DIT during this period of total shock, "almost every U.S. full colonel in Vietnam has an air-conditioned trailer, but we don't have a training aid that could save legs and lives?" I simply couldn't understand it.

Exactly one hour of instruction was devoted to the subject of "Why Vietnam?" which was not nearly enough ammo to counter the "Why *not* Vietnam" message being preached day after day at the antiwar, antidraft "coffeehouses" that were springing up near Army bases all over the country, including Fort Lewis (and it couldn't touch the amount of time the NVA's individual training schedule devoted to this vital and basic question—about 50 percent of its instruction). Our recruits were getting little from their training to change their angry minds about the Army, the government, or the war itself, and a huge part of the problem, I quickly found, was that the average instructor had an even worse attitude than the trainees. These were not the pink-cheeked second lieutenants who'd never left the States, but the (usually) draftee buck sergeant trainers who gave most of the classes, the short-timers fresh out of Vietnam who hadn't wanted to go in the first place and had chips on their shoulders the size of a Soviet RPG-7 rocket launcher. They hated the Army, they hated the system, they hadn't been trained properly themselves, but because they'd been in Vietnam for a year, had the CIB, and wore a couple of rows of "having been there" ribbons, they were considered "veterans," suited for preparing young tenderfeet for battle. This was a problem firmly rooted in the Pentagon, in the DCSPER logic that had a guy being inducted into the service, given eight weeks' basic training, eight to twelve more weeks' AIT, then a short leave before being jetted over to Vietnam for a year, and then brought back with six months left on his mandatory two-year hitch. Instead of training these soldiers—badly—for twenty-odd weeks, only to have them return to train others—just as badly—while marking time as "snowbirds" (the Army slang for a temporary assignment) until they could get out, why weren't they given forty-odd, even *fifty*, weeks' good training up front, then a year in Vietnam, with the last two to four weeks of their hitches back in the U.S. reserved for deprogramming and getting ready for civilian street? It was an unending mystery to me, which, when I experienced the ramifications of it firsthand, became a very serious concern.

The trainees looked at their "veteran" trainers as freshmen do the senior class. The "veteran" trainers knew it, too, and milked their positions for all they were worth. If I saw it once while wearing Bob Cena's soldier suit, I saw it a dozen times: "Gentlemen," a training NCO might start, moments after a couple of cadre members turned the unit over to him and began to walk briskly away, "today we're going to have a four-hour block of instruction on scouting and patrolling. The basic reference for this is Field Manual 21-75. If you know this book it will keep you alive on the battlefield. . . ." The trainer's monologue would continue in this vein until he saw the company cadre getting into their vehicle and driving away. Then he would pause, maybe, until the vehicle was well down the road, and then: "Okay, guys, light up and relax! We're not gonna do much this afternoon. We're just gonna shoot the shit. I'm gonna tell you how it *really* is in the 'Nam. Been there. 4th Div. Bad, bad. Charles is one mean mother—hell, he'll tear your heart right out of your chest!" And for the balance of the class this idiot would tell these hair-raising, superexaggerated war stories that bore little or no relation to what was happening in Vietnam (or, for that matter, to what could possibly have happened to the storyteller). So if a kid was sensitive, and most trainees were, by the end of the session he was scared to death. If he wasn't sensitive, he was totally bored and switched off. And since in either case nobody was better trained for it, the whole thing was a complete waste of everybody's time.

Meanwhile, soldiers just weeks from completing the AIT course were poorly grounded in the basics. As a "trainee" I observed one squad in the attack problem in which my fellow participants, all of them in their sixth week of training, did not know how to crawl, hit the ground, spring from the prone and move, properly camouflage, find or use cover, change M-16 mags in the prone, or deal with a weapon jam. Two weeks after that, theoretically having gotten the hang of these basics and everything else dealing with Vietnam fighting, these same trainees (myself included) loaded onto trucks to begin a forty-eight-hour field-training exercise (FTX) designed to simulate a U.S. patrol base in Vietnam and the activities that might take place around it. Theoretically, this would give the trainees—all of them just days from graduation, a short leave, and a jet ride to the sultry tropics of Vietnam—a chance to test their newly acquired skills.

But the simulated patrol base was covered in snow. And I wouldn't need anything more, for ever and ever, to understand the bitching about poorly trained replacements I'd heard day after day throughout my tour with Slam. It was no wonder each major U.S. unit in Vietnam set up its own one-to-two-week incountry training course, of necessity taking its cadre from among the best in its own line units (even if, in turn, this further shrank its frontline combat strength and effectiveness). I could not believe what I was seeing and hearing. There was little discipline—the trainees shuffled off the trucks and stood in small, shivering, disorganized mobs. There was no training value—with no apparent supervision from above, the decision among the Training Committee sergeants was that it was too cold to train, so they spent their time telling hairy war stories. Soon fires were roaring and the trainees were standing around smoking cigarettes and warming them-selves. When we did finally move out for some little problem, I found myself mesmerized by the little reflectors—only the size of a quarter—each trainee had attached to the back of his helmet. The history of these reflectors was that once upon a time on an early, not unusually (but very) foggy Fort Lewis morning, a car drove into the back of a company that was marching up the road to a training area. A number of trainees were seriously injured, and a new regulation soon came down from on high: henceforth all soldiers would wear reflectors on the backs of their helmets at all times. Yet there we were on this FTX, up in the mountains in the middle of nowhere (not a car around for miles), pretending to fight the Viet Cong (in the snow), and no one had considered telling the troops those reflectors were both unnecessary and inappropriate on patrol. There was absolutely no attention to detail, and it was the details that kept guys alive.

As the training horrors at Lewis unfolded before my eyes, the biggest shock for me was the knowledge that I, too, had been taken in by the impressive statistics and zero-defect appearance of the place for a very long time. I'd visited Fort Lewis several times from the Pentagon for the express purpose of checking up on the training. Was it possible that *every single time* I'd been taken in by a well-rehearsed display of the shiniest pairs of boots on post? And if I'd been taken in at Lewis, no doubt I'd been taken in when I'd visited the other Army Training Centers and service schools around the United States, too. I'd read the sanitized, best-foot-forward training reports and somehow believed them, in much the same way the one-year tourists at division and corps level in Vietnam (whom I condemned so strongly) believed the inflated reports they got from the battlefield and passed the "good" word up the chain of command. After my visits to these centers and schools, again and again I, too, had confidently advised my general, the Director of Training, that things "looked good" at these establishments, and believed it, when in fact things could not have been much worse. And yet recommendations and decisions were made based on these inaccurate "They're really STRAC, sir" reports.

Though belatedly, fortunately I recognized the truth, and from then on it was a different story. The Training Committee was not in my chain of command, so regardless of what I discovered, I really couldn't touch it. What I could do, though, was use my connections with the men who could: General William Beverly, the CG at Fort Lewis whom I'd known since he was Chief of OPO; General Pearson, who as director of DIT had the Army's top job for influencing training; General Sid Berry, now the Assistant Commandant at Benning, who'd been my boss when I was Chief of Individual Training at the Pentagon; and Colonel Gib Gibson at CONARC.

While I kept Pearson, Berry, and Gibson informed through the informal "old buddy" net on a general basis, the very minute I finished a block of training I wrote a critique of it for Colonel Ponder, who passed it on to General Beverly. Much to Ponder's credit for not being afraid to tell the boss things were not right, and to General Beverly's for using his position to do something about it, immediate steps were taken to correct some of the grosser deficiencies my reports uncovered. And I was actually quite pleased with the progress being made, until I went through that snowbound "graduation" FTX. It was only then that the futility of it all struck me: that whatever quick fix or serious and lasting alteration to the training Ponder or Beverly or I could effect at Fort Lewis, we'd never make a dent in what could only be considered a profound lack of concern for the basic requirements and welfare of the fighting man at the highest levels of the Army, *if they could sanction training for the tropical jungles of Vietnam in the snow.*

Ideally all the training for Vietnam should have taken place in Hawaii or Panama or the Philippines, where the Vietnam-bound soldiers could at the very least clear the difficult acclimatization hurdle. It would have worked well, too, to have each training center geared for a specific region in Vietnam, given that the diversity of battlefields (the Highlands, the Delta, I Corps, and around Saigon) made the conflict more like four or five different wars. Fort Lewis, for example, for three out of four seasons greatly resembled the Highlands. But to train men there in the winter months was a cruel joke. Yet no Pentagonian would dare try to close the place, even for those few months. Why? Because Fort Lewis was like any other Army camp on Army real estate in the U.S.A.: it provided jobs and income for the civilian constituents of senators and congressmen who were invariably running for reelection. Fort Lewis was big business to northwest Washington. Politicians demanded it be used in exchange for their nod on continued military appropriations, and the pussyfooting new breed of statesmen-generals didn't have the balls, the *moral courage*, to stand up and say that some things were more urgent, that it was insane to train jungle fighters in the snow. Instead, it was somehow more acceptable to allow badly prepared

Willie Lump Lumps to die all over the battlefield, and just go on answering the letters from brokenhearted parents asking "Why?" that cascaded down to DCSPER desks *through the offices of the very politicians whose ambitions partially held the answers.* Only now did I realize these parents deserved more, much more, in reply than a few pat, randomly chosen paragraphs strung together on a page, or that the real explanation was that, other than criminal negligence, there was no explanation at all. And meanwhile, the training system just kept chugging along—impersonal, inept, and yet terribly efficient—every nine weeks churning out young men with one of three frontline infantryman's MOSs (11B, C or D) stamped on their foreheads, and then channeling these kids into a sister machine, the death disposal of Vietnam, which churned out body bags and little white crosses with equal facility.

Whatever the job description said, it was beyond my capability as a training battalion commander to keep away from the training of my own battalion, the 3d Battalion, 3d Brigade (3/3). I was motivated by the challenge (I'd always said if I had five green soldiers or five thousand, in six weeks I could make all of them pros), and the horror that half these kids could be dead in three months if someone didn't teach them how to stay alive. If there was one thing I knew, it was how to keep men alive on the battlefield, and in the months I was at Fort Lewis, I tried with every fiber of my being to pass that knowledge on. To begin with, though I couldn't change the etched-in-stone Army Training Center training system, at least I could neutralize it. First I took all real responsibility for the potential combat readiness of my troops out of the hands of the Committee (whose centralized system ensured that no one up there was really responsible for anything anyway). I couldn't say, "Hey, what the Committee's teaching you is wrong," but by having my company cadres stay with their units all the time, sitting in on the classes rather than going away, and reporting back to me the deficiencies of the instruction, it put the pressure on the trainers to start doing their jobs right. Simultaneously I increased the 3/3's training requirements overall. Training began at reveille with the men barking the Standing Orders of Rogers' Rangers from memory (the knowledge of which was basic to survival on the guerrilla battlefield), and continued well into the evening and at night, long after the Training Committee personnel had knocked off and gone home. The battalion trained on Saturdays, too, their time too short to be spent shining shoes and readying footlockers for the traditional (though meaningless in Vietnam terms) Saturday-morning inspections. I had volunteer training for the gung-ho guys on Sundays, and made Recondo training available as well, with the successful graduates receiving the coveted black badge.

I wrote a seventeen-page training memorandum that made a priority of the most basic of the basics, all of which the Army Subject Schedule gave short shrift to: how to whisper, sneeze, cough, or even just walk in the bush, day and night. Most country boys learned these things before they were ten, but the Army of the day was not composed of country boys. Crawling, cover and concealment, security procedures, weapons maintenance—these, too, were at the top of the basics list, and when they were mastered, they replaced in the men their feeling of floundering with one of real confidence. Other new SOPs included the troops carrying their M-16s at all times, loaded with blanks to get used to living in an armed environment, and the rifles routinely carried "at the ready," even when marching from class to class. For all training outside the classroom or battalion area, the rule was full camouflage—black cork for faces and hands, tree branches in packs and helmets. Fort Lewis had never seen anything like this, and at first the 3/3 was held up to a lot of ridicule. But while the system was laughing, my men were thinking Vietnam *now*, and after all, at this critical time of their lives, what else mattered?

The troops responded well to the hard, hands-on, repetitive, but still interesting work. They may not have wanted to go to Vietnam, but they sure as hell didn't want to die there, so they even flocked to the off-duty volunteer classes like Recondo. Meanwhile I established the requirement that all officers and NCOs in the battalion read and carry on their person General Bruce Clarke's *Guidelines for the Leader and the Commander* (as far as I was concerned the finest little handbook on leadership and training ever written), and adopt as their own philosophy the one that I'd learned from a 5" × 7" card (which I still had) issued to me in Clarke's Seventh Army in Germany: "An organization does well only those things the boss checks." That, and a constant reminder to the cadre to keep reminding their troops that "the more sweat on the training field, the less blood on the battlefield," provided the foundation for a damn good, almost STRAC battalion.

Another major plank in the 3/3's success was that while all the other training battalions at Fort Lewis (and at the rest of the Army Training Centers) were geared for the individual replacement system being used in Vietnam to keep units as close to strength as possible, from the very first day I viewed my battalion as a TOE regular unit and trained it as such. More than anything, this was an issue of *spirit*.

I had long been an advocate of the unit replacement system, which the Australians used and had proved the worth of brilliantly in both Korea and Vietnam. The unit replacement system entailed troopers living, eating, sweating, and training *as a team* for a solid year before deploying *together*, as a unit, to the war zone, complete with the experienced cadre of regulars who'd trained them. This made the unit a family; the men loved one another and looked after one another, and as they took their lumps they absorbed replacements from within the family as well, through their own replacement package, perhaps an extra detachment brought along expressly for that purpose. In the unit replacement system, unit pride and devotion naturally resulted in pride and motivation among the individual soldiers who were part of the team; the resulting spirit was the key to getting things done and never giving in. (According to its commander, when Hal Moore's 1/7 Air Cav hung on against impossible odds during the battle of Ia Drang, for example, the very thing that saved them was the bond of brotherhood the men shared. "We were victorious," Moore said, "a very small band of American soldiers who had trained, lived, and partied *together* for two years, because we were *determined* to survive as a unit . . . we were disciplined as men and as a fighting team, and we knew that second place on that ground meant death for *all* of us and the battalion reputation; we could not accept that and we won.")

As the U.S. war in Vietnam expanded and units like the instant 196th Brigade began to be deployed not on the basis of combat readiness but on Westmoreland's need for more troops, any emphasis there might have been on a unit orientation quickly changed to an individual one, i.e., replacements for units already in the field. By the time I hit Fort Lewis, three years into the piece, bodies were everything, and the object of the training had first and foremost become to get the new kids, like little plastic replacement parts, off the assembly line and into the action as fast as possible with minimum attrition. In the individual replacement system, the troops' complete bewilderment upon arrival in Vietnam had to be dealt with by complete strangers whose "teams" they joined, despite having no connection with their new teammates or understanding of the nature of the game being played.*

---

* All the replacements suffered for this, but none worse than those inducted under the Project 100,000 program, which was nothing if not the most blatant example of the use and misuse of the poor and disadvantaged in America's wars. The theory was that each year 100,000 young men who had failed, or would fail if put to the test, the armed services' physical or mental requirements be given a chance to be soldiers. Standards were lowered to close to nothing, and the mostly black or lower-class white volunteers, seduced by recruiters' promises of training in skills to help them get along in the world outside the slums or the backwaters, soon found themselves stumbling along in the jungles of Vietnam. "These men proceed through the Army," Ward Just would soon write in *Military Men*, "as they proceed through life, walking wounded in the center of a monstrous joke, forced to struggle with basic training as they are forced to struggle with everything else. . . ."[1] At the same time, the presence of these Project 100,000 soldiers, many of whom were uneducated and more than a few totally illiterate, could create quite significant problems within their units. In the infantry you have to be able to think fast, communicate, and have confidence in your own judgment, none of which were easy tasks for these men who'd grown up as second-class citizens in the U.S.A. And there were certain jobs they simply couldn't do. A soldier who could not read or write, for example, would make a very dangerous mortarman.

At Lewis, I couldn't change the fact that my battalion would be together for only nine weeks before being cast out individually to units all over Vietnam. But while I had them, I was determined that each nine-week cycle of men would be trained in the *spirit* of the unit replacement system, with all the pride, stability, and values this entailed. Just one step in that direction was to nickname the 3/3 the "Always Alert" Battalion, and implement an "Airborne/All the way"–type drill for greetings between the soldiers and their officers ("Always Alert!" the battalion trooper would salute; "Stay Alive," the battalion officer would respond). "Stay alert and stay alive!" became the catchcry of the unit, with the men shouting it in unison at the beginning and end of every class they participated in. It wasn't anything new (though to someone who'd never trained troops the whole drill no doubt seemed very boy scoutish), but it was a gimmick that worked, because it was a continuous reminder about how to survive on the battlefield, and it continually reinforced the Always Alert Battalion's collective identity, until its men were a cocky and spirited team.

In the middle of my unit's transformation, I was called back to Fort Benning at the invitation of General Berry to attend the Dynamic Infantry Conference, a forum sponsored by the Army's Combat Development Command. There were maybe two hundred people in attendance, both military and civilian, and the conference was designed to look at the infantry in terms of both the present and what the future (ten and twenty years down the track) might bring. A significant portion of the program entailed the participants being broken down into panels of perhaps twelve men to work through given subjects or problems, with any findings and/or conclusions presented to the whole group at the end of the week's meetings. One panel I was on concerned the force structure of the Army of the future. From the outset of the meeting the civilians were on the offensive. There was much evidence among them of long study at the Herman Kahn school of instant expertise as they pontificated on the Army's short- and long-term organization and equipment requirements, but because they spoke so glibly and knowingly, few military men objected or even questioned what was being said. (The result, no doubt, of their own long-term attendance at the Herman Kahn school of bowing to overdeveloped civilian brains.) Not so with me, however, or with bird colonel (subsequently two star) Michael J. Healy, whose 173d "Geronimo" Battalion, trained and deployed *as a unit* under Healy's command, was reputed to have been one of the most successful in Vietnam.* The two of us got into a very violent argument with

---

* The distinction was shared with John P. Geraci's 1/506th "Centurion" Battalion, which was similarly unit-trained.

a civilian Ph.D. about machine guns—what their purpose should be, how many there should be in a platoon, and so on. The thing began when everyone on the panel, civilian and military alike, started nodding his head and agreeing with whatever this other civilian said. But the civilian was totally unqualified in the subject. He simply did not know what he was talking about. Healy and I, on the other hand, were more than qualified to talk about machine guns. Between us we probably had thirty years' infantry command experience on the squad, platoon, and company levels, and we had been handling machine guns since we were little more than kids. Yet even after the civilian as good as admitted knowing very little about his subject at all (in answer to our pointed questions), Healy and I were singularly unsuccessful in swaying even our fellow military men to our combat-grounded point of view. To me, it was damn scary, and did not bode well for a "dynamic" infantry future.

On the plus side, the Dynamic Infantry Conference gave a lot of people a chance to catch up with old friends. I ran into old buddies there whom I hadn't seen in years; when the conference was over for the day, it was one big party for the rest of the night. At one of the more formal gatherings early in the week I had a truly great thrill. I walked into a reception room only to hear a delighted, "*That* man, twenty years ago, woke me out of a sound sleep with a big grin and a .45-caliber pistol pointed in my face—and in my own battalion area!" It was Colonel James "The Helmet" Muir from my TRUST days, now a school department head, who had never forgotten my face or the morning my I&R squad plucked him, the aggressor commander, right out of his battalion area in full view of his own troops and taken him back to our HQ as the prize of the maneuver.

Back at Fort Lewis, I turned my attention to my instant NCOs, who did not have the luxury I'd had in Italy of almost three years in which to find my footing as a leader of men. While it would have been unfair to expect the shake and bakes to develop in a few months the leadership skills old NCOs took years and years to perfect, the extra support now at least got them going in the right direction as individual leaders, or out of the program before they got someone killed. I tried to give the instant NCOs as much responsibility and training as possible within the battalion, as squad leaders and platoon sergeants. One of the more frequent problems I saw was that of the "good guy" instant NCOs, who were afraid not to be "liked" by their men. These were the ones who really had to be jumped on, before they completely gave up all claim to a leadership role in their units. Often all this required was to explain to them that when they got to Vietnam they would have a lot more friends in their squad or platoon if they just did their jobs and prevented their ill-prepared and generally poorly led "buddies" from getting themselves wasted the minute they left the base camp. The fledgling noncoms of the 3/3 responded well to the responsibility thrust upon them, and all in all I wasn't unhappy with the progress they were making. So it wasn't until the morning Captain James Mukoyama, acting battalion commander of the 4th Battalion, 3d Brigade, rang me at my office with a little problem that I realized how far the instant NCOs really were from the real thing.

Mukoyama said there'd been an incident the night before in which one of my drill sergeants—"black, about six feet one or six feet two, wearing a 101st patch on the right," Mukoyama said—beat up one of his trainees. It was something you always had to be looking out for, but from the description I knew exactly who the offender was and I was very surprised. Sergeant Martin was a Regular Army paratrooper NCO (one of very few at Lewis), from the 101st no less, and a damn good man. After telling Mukoyama to come right over, I sent word I wanted to see Martin pronto.

"Sir, you've known me for a long time and I don't brutalize nobody," the drill sergeant began when he arrived a short while later. "This is what happened. About 2100 hours last night, it was dark and I was driving home. But then I saw this soldier at the edge of the battalion area, and he was wearing Air Force gloves. . . ."

"Air Force gloves" were hands in your pockets. I had a real thing about soldiers putting their hands in their pockets, and I'd told all my people if they saw anyone doing it to really smoke their asses. Which is exactly what Martin had done. "Hey, trooper, get those hands out of your pockets!" he'd said. "If you're that cold, get yourself some proper gloves, but you don't go stumbling around this battalion area wearing Air Force gloves!" Unfortunately, the trooper was not too cooperative. In fact, he said, "Fuck you, Sergeant, I ain't in your battalion! I can do whatever I want."

Understandably, this got Martin's attention, and he'd bolted out of his car. "You're talking to a sergeant in the U.S. Army, boy," he said to the trainee, "and you don't talk to me that way, you understand?"

"Fuck you, U.S. Army sergeant!" the kid retorted, which was a serious step too far. Martin grabbed the trooper and dragged him to the trainee's company Orderly Room, where a shake and bake NCO was Charge of Quarters. "Sergeant," Martin said to the CQ, "you got a room around here where I can talk to this boy in private?"

The CQ pointed to the company commander's office. Martin dragged the kid in there and proceeded to administer some close and sustained NCO justice.

As the story unfolded, as far as I was concerned I couldn't see what the sergeant had done wrong. It was one of those things. You couldn't have sadists like Sergeant Keen in Berlin beating on kids trapped in cardboard boxes, but you couldn't have your sergeants without any authority either. The fundamental issue here was discipline, the final word in the life-and-death business of infantry. In the line of duty Martin had told the kid to get his hands out of his pockets, and the kid had mouthed off to him. It was a clear breach of discipline. Martin could have turned him over to the CQ and pressed charges under the Uniform Code of Military Justice, but he chose instead to do it the Old Army way, which I not only condoned but would have done myself had I been in his shoes. The sergeant's mistake was he hadn't realized he was behaving Old Army in front of an ultra-New-Army NCO, a shake and bake who hadn't wanted to be in the Army in the first place and whose sympathies lay with the kid. So instead of looking the other way (as an Old Army noncom would have), the instant sergeant CQ wrote in the battalion journal how my man had savagely beaten one of the trainees. Now the kid was pressing charges, and the shake and bake was a witness.

The only two bright spots in the affair were that both Martin and the trainee were black (which closed the door on charges of racism), and that Mukoyama, who'd been called at home by his duty officer soon after the incident, had gotten in touch with me as soon as I got to work at 0500. As it was, there was still very little time. The problem was that there'd been a number of similar incidents around the post lately and a crackdown had been ordered. If the matter wasn't settled by the time the brigade people arrived for work at 0800, they would undoubtedly want Martin's head. But the Army could not afford to lose the few Martins it had left. So if I could just administer some sort of punishment before the brigade staff arrived, the process could be thwarted—to court-martial the man would be double jeopardy. I dismissed the drill sergeant and told him to both "trust me" and stand by. Meanwhile Mukoyama arrived, and together we devised a scheme to save my man's career.

James "the Mook" Mukoyama was a good man. I'd met him months before at Lewis' Training Center HQ when he was Secretary to the General Staff, and for me it had been almost love at first sight: instinctively he'd reminded me of Jimmie Mayamura from the Raider days so long ago. As time passed, that instinct proved correct. Mook was a first-generation American of Japanese descent, whose sense of duty, honor, and country without benefit of a West Point ring was that of someone who had not yet taken it all for granted. On top of that, like Jimmie Mayamura, the Mook was a stud. When we'd met I couldn't understand why he, a Regular Army infantry captain, was wasting his time behind a desk in a flunky HQ. I'd immediately offered him a company command in the 3/3, and it was just my bad luck he'd been about to take a similar job in the 4/3 Battalion. Events were proving, however, that that may have been all for the best. At least for Sergeant Martin.

After rehearsing the plan, Mook and I called in the trainee, the drill sergeant, and the shake and bake. The trainee was, in my judgment, nothing more than a weak, whining punk. He was barely banged up, much less savagely beaten; my guess was Martin had bumped him up against the wall a few times and just scared the shit out of him. Mukoyama explained to the trainee that I had reviewed the situation, that I'd decided the trainee was definitely in the right, and I was going to invoke a general court-martial against my drill sergeant if that's what the trainee still wanted. (Yes, that's what he wanted.) The only problem, Mook went on, was that both the trainee and the shake and bake would have to be confined to Fort Lewis as material witnesses until the court-martial, which could be weeks away given that it was almost Christmas.

"You mean I can't go home for Christmas?" asked the trainee.

"That's right," said the Mook.

"But I'm going to 'Nam right after my leave, Captain," a worried shake and bake chimed in. "I gotta see my mother. I gotta see my girl."

"My hands are tied," Mukoyama said sorrowfully. "You want justice to be done, don't you?"

"Yes, but—" the trainee whimpered.

"Wait a minute," I said on cue. "There *is* another way I could do this. I could give my man a nonjudicial punishment. An Article 15 instead of the court-martial."

"Could we go home if you gave him that?" asked the trainee.

"Yes, you could," I replied. "Of course I couldn't hurt him as much as I'd like to . . . I could only take one stripe, fine him about five hundred bucks, and restrict him for thirty days, which isn't all that severe—"

"Oh, I think that's severe enough, sir," the trainee jumped in.

"You really think it's adequate?"

"Yes, sir," agreed the shake and bake, nodding his head vigorously, "more than adequate, sir."

I turned to Martin. "Sergeant, would you accept an Article 15? I assure you, you're getting away lightly."

"Yes, sir," he replied, "I will."

"Fine," I said. "I'll administer that punishment now." I dismissed the two younger soldiers, who couldn't have been happier to split the scene. When Martin and I were alone and all the paperwork was being typed up, I said to the sergeant, "I'm giving you an Article 15 and I'm fining you five hundred dollars. But unless there's another incident, you won't be out a cent and there'll be no black mark on your record, because the paperwork will never leave my desk."

"Airborne, sir," he said.

"But, Sergeant, if you ever have to do that kind of thing again, for chrissake, choose your witnesses a little more carefully!"

"Sir, he was a noncom!"

"The Army's changed, Martin, the Army's changed."

By 0800 my desk was clear, with the Article 15 safely filed away. So when Lieutenant Colonel Moody, the by-the-book brigade XO, called (*precisely* at 0800) wanting explanations for the damaging log entry and demanding a court-martial, I was able to say, "It's been taken care of, sir," bear his momentary wrath for not consulting him or Colonel Ponder before passing judgment, and then let the whole thing blow over, which it did. I did, however, call the shake and bake into my office to remind him he was now a noncommissioned officer in the U.S. Army. "So stop thinking like a private," I said. "It's a luxury you won't be able to afford on the battlefield, when the real privates turn to you to keep them alive." I don't know whether the guy understood, but even if he did I came out feeling as though I were swimming against the tide. If this kid was the quality—on an attitude level alone—of the instant NCOs coming through the system, combat forces in Vietnam could well be, at best, only marginally the better for them.

And time would prove there *were* some damn lousy instant NCOs in Vietnam. But there were some damn good ones, too. The program wasn't perfect, but it was far better than nothing, and many men did respond to the philosophy at the root of it: *Make men believe they are leaders and they will become leaders.* It had worked for me in Korea in F Company, 223d, when Hudson, Smith, and Allison grew right into the stripes I'd given them out of desperation and a gutted NCO corps; the big problem that arose with the instant NCOs in Vietnam was that the schools system quickly made the measure of the program's success the same measure it used for everything else: a low attrition rate. Real motivation or basic leadership potential, which had been the basis of our success in Fighter Company, became virtually incidental to the output. This bored a huge hole in the whole concept of the program and the reason it had been conceived, but there wasn't a damn thing I could do about it. I had no authority to hire or fire, so all I could do was write letters about the problem to my influential friends, give my own men the best I could, and just hope for the best for the rest.

And that included the kids who didn't want to go. For all my people who went to Vietnam, I was going to be damn sure they got the very best training available in the U.S. Army. But for those who didn't want to, I did what I could to help them stay out. At the beginning of a new training cycle, I had each of my company commanders ask if anyone in his unit was a conscientious objector (CO)—there was no point in training these guys in infantry if they could be gotten out early and trained in something else. (And besides, many a CO went on to Vietnam to become a brave and competent combat medic, making the infantry's loss now the infantry's gain when it counted.) When I interviewed the potential COs I tried to help them get their stories straight: "I agree with you that it's a bad war," I'd say, "but that doesn't qualify you to be a CO. What religion are you?"

"I don't have a religion."

"Well, you better get one," I'd counsel, and send him to the local padre or coffeehouse to make sure he knew the right words. When he came back to see me the next day, I'd pretend I'd never met him; after he said the right words, I'd make my recommendation that he be given CO status.

I don't know what my motivation was. Twenty years before, even ten years before, I would have dealt with COs with extreme prejudice—*Cowards, every damn one of them*, I would have thought. But it was a different world now, and a different war, a war that just months earlier I'd sworn I'd take my son to Canada before I'd let him fight in, a war without a villain—nationalists fighting for a better deal were not exactly Hitler or Tojo. So if a guy didn't want to fight, why should he fight? There were plenty who wanted to, or were programmed by fathers or family histories to *think* they wanted to, to prove their manhood or as a point of honor and hang the cause. The interesting twist about my conscientious-objector policy at Fort Lewis, though, was that with the option available in the 3/3, I actually had fewer guys bucking for CO status than in other battalions in the brigade.

In mid-December I was selected early for the Army War College. I was very proud: first, because I was picked up in the very first year of eligibility (my fourteenth year of Regular service), while most guys might wait six or eight more years after that; and second, because despite the fact I'd been told so often by men in the know that I was viewed as a "comer" and a "shoo-in" for War College and an early star, I'd learned when I was not selected for major in Germany never to count on anything. And after all, "not too many people who start off a buck private in the rear ranks at age 15 make the big league," as I wrote to Ward Just with the news. The personnel people were not in the least impressed with the good word. In fact, they were indignant. I'd escaped my Pentagon jail term early. I'd purposely, even eagerly, taken the "retrograde" and "disastrous" career step of a training battalion at Fort Lewis. I'd ignored the personnel guys' advice *entirely*, and I'd still made the War College list below the zone. It pissed them off royally—and only added to my joy.

I took leave over the Christmas holidays and drove the family to L.A. to spend Christmas with Roy and his new bride, Helen. With three crumb snatchers less than nine years old cooped up in a station wagon for three days, the drive was worse than combat. Fortunately everyone survived, and there was even time to relax for a few days until just before New Year's

(1969) when I received an 0500 call from OPO at the Pentagon. (The time of the call was significant; it was 0800 in Washington, D.C., and my caller's lack of respect for the three-hour time difference to the West Coast was typical of the no-think, can-do attitude that characterized the Army bureaucracy of the day.) "General Ewell wants you to take a battalion in his division," the OPO voice informed me now. "He's requested you by name. We don't recommend it. You've had two battalions—you have nothing to gain, and there's a long line of others who've never had a battalion and are still waiting. You would have to defer War College, and if you go you'll only get in trouble and ruin your chances for a star. We recommend you stay at Lewis until War College in August."

"When do I leave?" I replied.

Patty could have killed me. Even I was surprised at how easily I made the decision, particularly given the intensity of the inner struggle that had been going on since my tour with Slam, which had me always wanting to go back to the fray even as all I wanted to do was quit and disappear before the anger over the senselessness of it all blew up inside me. When I'd read USMC Lieutenant Colonel William Corson's *The Betrayal*, then recently published, about the folly of the U.S. "pacification" effort in Vietnam, I'd recognized that as another drop of water on the rock—after Doc Benjamin, after Ward Just—toward a truer way of seeing, and for the first time had begun to see myself very comfortably removed from both the conflict and the inept managers responsible for it. Meanwhile, in the personal realm, I was very happy at Fort Lewis. I wasn't bored. Patty and I got along fine and I enjoyed being with the kids. We had beautiful quarters, a big, modern, western-style four-bedroom house in a well-forested, secluded part of the post. Tim Grattan, my closest friend, lived in Bellevue, where he was already making big bucks in land development. We got together frequently and, really, until the moment the opportunity came to go back to Vietnam, at least a part of me had planned to give even War College a miss, retire right there, and go to work with Tim. But the opportunity did arise, and though I knew the war was a totally senseless exercise, I took it. It was almost as if the decision had been made for me. But when I wrote to Ward Just to tell him my change of plans, I tried to explain, despite my close and sustained criticism of it all, *why*. "I am a professional," I wrote:

> A "pro" doesn't sit on the bench simply because he has played out his quota of time. He wants to get in there, mix it up and contribute towards moving the ball toward his goal line. Regardless of what the chances of winning are.
> —I know my job. Through my skill, developed through long experience and hard study, I can get the job done at the least possible costs to the young citizen soldiers who make up the "thin red line."

—I have many tactical ideas and theories concerning how to fight the guerrilla which I have been mulling over since my last tour . . . I would like to prove to the traditionalists that there is another way to fight the "G" rather than, "High Diddle Diddle, Right Down the Middle." If I am overwhelmingly successful, I might possibly influence the proponents of the unsuccessful search and destroy operations. At least my credentials will back up my arguments a little better. . . .

—I cannot think of a profession that is more demanding, deadly and where the responsibility is more awesome. As you well know, mistakes that are made on the battlefield cannot be covered up, they always clearly show themselves— on the casualty lists. Thus, I think that our units in Vietnam should have the finest leaders possible . . . at the expense of these leaders' (who are Regulars and goddamnit should be prepared to pay the price) personal discomforts, family, and career development such as attending War College. Christ, we didn't send commanders home during WW II for schooling. Why Vietnam?

Why indeed. Over the next two weeks, while good soldier Patty got the house and the family squared away for the twelfth move in eleven years, I got on the phone to begin assembling my team. The word was the battalion I was about to take over was very sick. I figured if I had about ten good studs we could easily knock it into shape. It really was my dream to mold a combat battalion into a perfect fighting force—"Can always go to War College, but cannot always fight a battalion," as I wrote in less than lofty terms to ex-327 Tiger Major Nev Bumstead, who'd become a good friend, whose judgment and attention to detail I respected, and whom I wanted for my S-3. My only regret was that Hank Emerson would not be my brigade commander. He was actually out of the 9th Div entirely, having been shot down in a chopper in September and evacuated back to the States with severe burns.* Still, I knew I'd have no trouble from above. Because Hank was one of General Ewell's "boys" and I was one of Hank's, General Ewell, who'd asked for me by name as per Hank's recommendation, would respect me as per same to get the job done. That was the way it worked, and as the reality of my imminent return to Vietnam sank in, I couldn't wait to get back in the game.

---

* Hank Emerson did not have good luck with helicopters. In just one of a number of previous instances, once with the 1/101st at Lai Khe, he'd been so focused on a particular action that he insisted on landing in a mushy rice paddy despite his pilot's warning. The chopper landed and Hank jumped out, but because the skids kind of sank down into the paddy, when Hank (who was exceptionally tall) went to step up on a nearby paddy dike, the chopper's rotor blade knocked him right in the head. He went sailing twenty feet. Incredibly, when he got up he was more or less unscathed: as it turned out, the rotor blade had missed him completely even as it crushed in the top inch of his helmet. In the 9th Div case he was not quite as fortunate. He suffered some bad, bad burns when he was trapped inside his downed chopper by a ruptured safety belt. Colonel Ira A. Hunt, the division Chief of Staff (who'd been flying with Hank), braved the fire licking through the aircraft to cut Hank free and drag him out. Some ten seconds later, the helicopter erupted in a ball of flame and disintegrated before their eyes. Fortunately the Gunfighter healed up beautifully, and continued on with his fine career.

✻   ✻   ✻

I'd been at Lewis for four and a half months, able to put my mark on just two full cycles of AIT trainees. It was but a tiny drop in a huge ocean, even though I did get very real satisfaction from the cheery "Always Alert!"s and snappy salutes I got from occasional 3/3 graduates who recognized or served under me in subsequent years in Vietnam. In the end, my only lasting contribution to the AIT program was in thwarting the Army bureaucracy in one tiny way when one of my cycles somehow finished a few days early, but because of some Army regulation, the soldiers weren't allowed to leave Fort Lewis until the originally scheduled date. It was crazy to expect a thousand men on their way to Vietnam to sit on their asses at Fort Lewis for two or three days doing nothing when they could be home with their families or their girlfriends, so I raised hell and yelled and screamed all the way up to General Beverly to let them go. But regs were regs and no one would budge. Fortunately, by now I knew how to manipulate the system on almost every level and I had contacts everywhere; in this case I called General Pearson at the Pentagon, and before the day was out he'd sent a cable to Lewis stating that not only were these men to be allowed to go home immediately, but that the same would apply in any cases like this at any of the other training centers. It was a small victory.

I left Fort Lewis wondering if it would have been better if I'd gone there before my Pentagon stint, rather than after. While the Pentagon statistics and all outward appearances pointed to max efficiency, my eyes had now told me the training system was in shambles. The curriculum was myopic and rigid—a million unbridgeable miles from the present battlefield when there should have been a direct line. By the time the product of these training centers was tested and proved deficient, it was too late to make adjustments or corrections. Had I known this at the Pentagon, I might have made a project of getting every U.S. Army Training Center to have a stud who really understood the war as a liaison on the ground in Vietnam. These guys' entire jobs would be to bop around the country, looking at the units and looking at the war. They'd check in with graduates of their particular training centers, find out how they were and what training areas the now-battle-wise soldiers believed needed expanding. Then the liaisons would report their findings back to their training centers, along with their thoughts on the direction the training should be going.

Had I known at the Pentagon the terrible plight of trainees under the tutelage of short-timer, snowbird instructors, I might have pushed to have the training schedule lengthened up front, to eliminate the short-timers entirely and, in the process, double (at the very least) the training value for everybody.

And why were passed-over, washed-out officers vegetating and waiting for their final parades in one of the most important jobs in the U.S. Army? Training centers and Army service schools should have been manned by the Steve Prazenkas and the Glover Johnses—why not Prazenka and Johns themselves? Had I still been at the Pentagon I might have pushed to have these warriors and others like them recalled from retirement. We were in a war. We didn't need any more dancing-prancing chief of staff material, complete with master's degrees from Harvard. We needed experienced men who could train soldiers for combat. These men wouldn't leave the United States—they'd just make sure the ones who did came back. As (now retired) Colonel Johns wrote to me on the subject: "We now are thrown out on our ass at fifty-five if we have not been touched by the magic finger of fate and come up with a star, regardless of how good we might be at something. . . . Do you think that maybe I, without my star, could not have done a better job of teaching tactics at Benning than a lot of the young kids were doing [if I had] been sent to Vietnam for a few months to see how it was, free to move around and go and do what I wanted—like go on a patrol or b.s. with the GIs?" Yes, Johns could have, and for the sake of the students, he should have been given the chance. "I feel strongly," he continued, "that the more efficient and experienced older officers, even if they know they will not be promoted, should at least be given the opportunity to stay on in the capacity of a permanent instructor, complete with refresher courses in the field themselves. . . . There are so many jobs that young officers on the way up neither want nor need that could be filled by older officers that the Army would do well to seek a special category for such officers, that would in no way interfere with the rapid promotion of the others, and at the same time keep happy and healthy and useful a lot of men who had devoted their lives to their country, knew no other bag, and could do a magnificent job for their country still."

It was a solution that could have worked if someone had been in the right place at the right time, with enough gelignite to upend Mount Everest. But no one was moving mountains, and having done my time in the Pentagon (where, far from the cutting edge, it was so easy to be fooled by the completely institutionalized appearance of total perfection), and then down on the ground level at Fort Lewis (where attention to detail was virtually a mortal sin), I doubted such a sensible idea was even broachable without dismantling the Army's training apparatus and starting from scratch. But since that wasn't going to happen either, it seemed as if the machine would just keep on cranking out young men who were not prepared for the ordeal ahead; who would survive (*if* they survived) by hook or by crook, but with little thanks to the U.S. Army. It was no way to run a war.

19 HARDCORE

Hackworth was essentially a legend. Just before he arrived I recall going to the G-1 and asking who the new battalion commander was going to be. The deputy G-1 said, "Can't tell you"—you know how personnel people are, they like to hip-pocket everything—"but he's 'Mr. Infantry.' " I thought, *Who the hell is Mr. Infantry?* Of course, I'd read about David H. Hackworth . . .

Colonel George Mergner, USA
Executive Officer
4/39 Infantry Battalion
Republic of Vietnam, 1969

Doc Holley and I were sitting in the aid station drinking beer and saying, "God, this is going to be hell—we've got some GI Joe lifer out here who's going to just ruin us." That was probably the lowest point of morale in the battalion. Not only had we been taking a lot of casualties, but now it looked as if somebody was going to come in and kick ass and make career soldiers out of us.

Charles Wintzer
Medic, HQ Company, 4/39 Infantry Battalion
Republic of Vietnam, 1969

One of the guys who talked to me was an E-6 or E-7 in charge of communications. He said, "Look, Captain, there's a price out on Hackworth's head—you gotta stay away from him, because someone's going to shoot him." I said, "My job is to stay in his hip pocket." He said, "Somebody's going to kill him here. Within the next week he's going to be a dead man, so I'm telling you to stay away from him."

Well, what do you do with information like this?

Colonel Emile Robert, USA, Ret.
4/39 Artillery Liaison Officer
Republic of Vietnam, 1969

As for the bounty, I heard it was eight hundred dollars no questions asked. I only heard of someone taking a few shots at a helicopter he was flying in. I also remember somebody giving that person hell for shooting at the helicopter, because there were other innocent people in there who may be killed accidentally.

> Daniel E. Evans, Jr., DVM
> Medic (DSC winner), B Company
> 4/39 Infantry Battalion
> Republic of Vietnam, 1968–69

I might not be able to write for a week or so. The new commander is a little crazy and I think he will be relieved of command shortly. He is pushing the men too hard. I'll explain later.

> Dan Evans
> Letter home dated
> 4 February 1969

We were rotten 'fore we started—we was never disciplined:
We made it out a favour if an order was obeyed.
Yes, every little drummer 'ad 'is rights an' wrongs to mind,
So we had to pay for teachin'—an' we did!

> Rudyard Kipling

THERE was no sense in showing this sorry outfit I was in a state of shock. It wasn't just that the CP group slept on cots inside tents, that they had folding chairs and stateside footlockers, portable radios, and plastic coolers filled with beer and Coke at their fire base out in the field. More than that, it was that they had portable toilets, too (the result, I was told, of my predecessor's philosophy that "for a penny more you can go first-class"), and apparently were blissfully unaware that just nearby their troops were crapping on the ground and not even covering it up. In the sanitation department, the fire base was even worse than the ROK defensive position we took over at the Punch Bowl in Korea in 1953.

"It's a pussy battalion," General Ewell had explained when I first arrived in-country, "and I want tigers, not pussies," he'd gone on to say in his characteristic Oklahoma drawl. But he'd gotten it wrong. With the 4th Battalion, 39th Infantry it was not a question of feline degree. As far as I could see, this unit was not even a military organization.

It was total disintegration. Throughout the fire base, amid the shit and the toilet paper and the machine-gun ammo laying in the mud, were troops who wore love beads and peace symbols and looked more like something out of Haight-Asbury than soldiers in the U.S. Army. All were low on spirit and a few were high, openly, on marijuana. There was minimum security. Few men carried or cared for their weapons—most had let them go red with rust as they strolled around without them. Grenades weren't taped, and when a unit moved out, most of the gunners wore their ammo Pancho Villa–style, the ideal way to guarantee a weapon jam sometime down the track, when dirty, dented cartridges were inserted into their M-60s.

The 4/39's fire base was located in the Wagon Wheel, an AO so named for the five canals that converged there, which, from the air, looked like the hub and spokes of a wheel. The night before I took over the battalion I sat up all night in the center of the base, back-to-back with Nev Bumstead, who'd come along as my handpicked S-3. Neither of us was game to sleep (if the VC attacked, the battle would be over before it even began, with the position safely in enemy hands), so I spent the time discussing with Nev the things we'd have to do to turn the lackluster unit around and ruminating on how such disintegration ever could have occurred. It would be fair to say that my own on-the-ground observations did not exactly reflect the "spirit, morale, and devotion to duty" among the personnel in Vietnam that CONARC CG, now four-star general James Woolnough, observed and wrote about to Chief of Staff Westmoreland less than a month before, during his whirlwind nine-day trip to the war zone.[1] Woolnough told the Chief that the almost universal opinion among those he'd spoken with was that the young officers and EM being sent to Vietnam were indeed "properly prepared for combat, both by training and mental conditioning." One would have thought that Woolnough, who as DCSPER had been so shocked by the results of our friendly fire study and so helpful in implementing change, would have been somewhat more discerning; though his memo to Westy was unknown to me at the time, I wonder how that January 1969 finding would have gone over with the parents of the draftee replacement in my battalion who, about four days after I arrived, set up a (clearly marked) claymore mine backwards in front of his position, heard something in the night, and blew his own head off. What a mistake it was to listen to the generals of corporate HQ, who were briefed only in zero defect terms and, so far from the cutting edge, expected nothing less. It was among the biggest mistakes of the war: the politicians only listened to these generals and these generals to themselves. Few people asked the frontline soldiers, the only ones who really knew. After nine days on the ground in Vietnam, Woolnough had been able to offer Westmoreland the informed opinion that the war had already been won militarily and "what is left appears . . . to be a mopping-up operation. . . . I do not believe," Woolnough continued, "that, in the current situation, the enemy has the capability to more than harass us. I did not find a division commander who disagreed with this conclusion with respect to his own TAO [Tactical Area of Operation]."

As I waited for dawn at the 4/39 fire base, I considered the "harassment" my new command had been on the wrong end of for the past six months. Whatever the name one ascribed to it, it had gutted the unit both physically and emotionally. According to the old-timers, they had not met the enemy at all, yet they had taken tremendous casualties. When I arrived, the "dich board" (dich, pronounced "dick," was one of many names that had evolved for the enemy), a tally board Battalion Operations Sergeant Jerry Slater had been tasked to set up to keep track of casualties, read: "(Dichs) O KIA, O WIA, O POW; (Friendly) 24 KIA, 485 WIA." Rockets, mortars, booby traps, and friendly fire were responsible for these tragic figures, and with the rifle companies usually operating at 50 percent of TOE strength, over six months those faceless menaces accounted for the equivalent of 100 percent casualties in the unit. No wonder morale was lower than whaleshit.

The following day, I took over the battalion from Lieutenant Colonel Franklin A. Hart in a parade-field change of command in the middle of the Mekong Delta. *What kind of war have I gotten myself into?* I wondered. A perfectly starched General Ewell was there, having flown in for the occasion in his polished chopper; there were other brass, too, and photographers, the American flag, the battalion colors, which were ceremoniously passed to me, and all this before the scroungiest, most spiritless assembly of soldiers I'd ever seen. Incredibly, none of the generals or colonels seemed to notice the slack condition of my new charges or their positions. And despite Ewell's earlier remarks to me or those of the 1st Brigade CO, Colonel John P. Geraci (who'd told me the 4/39 was the worst battalion he had), Frank Hart would still receive a Legion of Merit for his job "well done" with the battalion.

It was hard to believe that as late as 1968 "the Army was still bringing in lieutenant colonels looking for their first CIB," as one battle-wise battalion officer and friend put it, but that was the story with Hart. While men like Gib Gibson, so eminently qualified for command (and who cared to do nothing else), couldn't get in the troop-leading door, it seemed to me as if "waterwalkers" like this guy—twenty-first in his West Point class, he'd been General Westmoreland's aide and would be again—could transparently get their first and only combat-command ticket punched and even win three Silver Stars and a Legion of Merit while their dich boards remained blank and their soldiers' morale wasted away.

Finally General Ewell and the other guests flew off and the battalion was mine. I thought of Colonel (later Major General) Numa A. Watson, my TRUST regimental commander, and of the time when I was a corporal and my squad was acting as a battalion CP for a command-post exercise. Our job was simply to feed canned information via radio to Regiment in the troopless maneuver designed to train the regimental staff, but in the middle of it Watson came by and said to me, "You're running a fine battalion here, Colonel." He was just playing with me, of course, but being called "Colonel" was such a thrill I never forgot the words. It was hard to believe that now, two decades later, I really was a colonel (a light colonel anyway), and I had the battalion I'd been preparing for for all those years. Little could I have guessed that whipping it into shape would require every bit of knowledge I'd gained in the interim.

From the outset I realized that to make this unit an effective military force I'd have to implement about a thousand changes. So I figured we'd start with five a day—little things, *basic* things like "wear your steel pot" and "clean and carry your rifle at all times," and "ammunition will not be worn Pancho Villa–style." My first order was that come darkness the fire-support base perimeter would pull back three hundred meters. The troops instantly began to grumble at this, but it was the next order that really began the mutinous feeling within my hard-luck outfit. "Anything you can't carry twenty-four hours a day," I intoned, "is gone on the next chopper." Good-bye tents and cots and rucksacks and footlockers. The bitching and moaning began in earnest as piles and piles of junk mounted at the LZ to be whisked away by Chinook. But I didn't care. I wasn't there to have them like me.

By midnight, as per my instructions, the battalion was dug in in new positions, with security out. A short time later, we were hit with a barrage of rocket and recoilless-rifle fire, but most of it fell on the *old* positions. When I got on the horn and called for artillery, I was surprised to find that I was very nervous. Command is not like hopping back onto a bicycle, and after two and a half years away from it I was rusty, and actually scared I'd screw up. But then I heard a guy, later to be identified as Lieutenant Larry Tahler, who worked in the S-3 section, running behind me to his defensive position. "He's a mean son of a bitch but he knows what he's doing," Tahler said as he ran, and I knew I was back. The following morning Bob Press, the Abus' first sergeant in our shared 1/101 days whom I'd nabbed for my sergeant major in the 4/39, reported he'd already noted a big decrease in the bitching as he toured around the perimeter. It hadn't gone unnoticed by the troops that there'd been no casualties the night before, where in Press's estimation "at least twenty would have been headed for hospitals or zipped up in body bags" had they been sleeping on cots or even just above ground. So I won a few hearts and minds the first night.

But none too many. For the first month I was with the unit I refused to crack a smile. And by constantly demanding professionalism from everyone, just about everything I did pissed somebody off. I did some wholesale firing of personnel (all told throughout the tour, some fifty-nine lieutenants, eight captains, and two majors, following the "there are no bad units, only bad officers" philosophy of General Cleland), and after a few days I heard petitions had started going around the companies stating that in protest the men weren't going to go out on missions anymore. Fortunately I was cut some slack in at least one quarter. The CO of A Company, whom I'll call Captain Billy Winston, had served in the 1/101 in '65–'66 and we'd known each other well, so he brought his guys together, told them I might not be perfect but I wasn't that bad, and they ought to give me a chance. The bounty Bravo Company put on my head, which ranged from eight hundred dollars to thirty-five hundred, depending on whom you talked to, was also fairly easily dismissed. The first I heard of it was when General Ewell (of all people) got the word and came to warn me. He said he was going to infiltrate some CID people into the company to ferret out the ringleaders of the plot. Meanwhile, he strongly suggested I ease up on the troops. I wasn't going to ease up and told the General so; besides, there was a simpler way to call Bravo's bluff. Before long we were conducting operations, and on one of them I found myself with fractious B Company, all of us approaching in a skirmish line a small enemy force in a clump of the Delta's ubiquitous nipa palm. A fight seemed imminent, and since my experience told me that soldiers in a firefight are generally too busy, too scared, and place far too much faith in their leader's ability to get them out safely to knock him off, I felt it was a perfectly unperilous (for me) opportunity to make Bravo shit or get off the pot. So I moved up well in front of the advancing skirmish line, with my back an easy target for even the sorriest rifleman in Vietnam. And I was right. Thoughts of wasting the battalion commander were forgotten as the little fight heated up; working together with a common purpose, we killed a few VC in exchange for not a single B Company casualty, and I don't think I heard much about a price on my head ever again.

The men of the 4/39 had no unit identity, and no pride in themselves. As a first step toward rectifying this I decided to call my hard-luck battalion "the Hardcore," and the troops "Recondos" (the latter being the nickname of the 1st Brigade, 9th Div, of which the 4/39 was a part). Just as I had in the 3/3 at Fort Lewis, I insisted on an "Airborne/All the way" greeting between the 4/39's soldiers and their officers: when a soldier saluted an officer he said, "Hardcore Recondo, sir!" and when the officer responded it was with a heartfelt "No fucking slack!" At first my cynical hippie troops sniggered over what they considered "GI Joe bullshit," but it didn't matter—I knew the time would come when it would mean one hell of a lot to each and every one of them.

Simultaneously, I started establishing SOPs that would not only keep the troops alive, but also give them, for the first time, the feeling that they were in charge of their situation, not at the mercy of the VC or their insidious booby traps. (The battalion overall was composed mostly of draftees, and many had actually assumed that the way they lived and got blown away under my predecessor without ever meeting the enemy was how it was supposed to be.) The SOPs included such things as every officer having to read Mao's *Little Red Book* (how could we beat an enemy if we made no attempt to know what made him tick?) and 100 percent stand to's prior to dawn, dusk, and sometimes in the middle of the night, any of which might occasionally be augmented with a Mad Minute. I was vastly assisted in the implementation of these procedures by both Bumstead and my XO, a superb officer named George Mergner. In that Mergner was not part of the "team" I brought with me, and I hadn't known him before, his thoroughly competent presence in the battalion came as a wonderful surprise. Besides being a fine soldier with a couple of years' Delta combat experience as an adviser under his belt, George was the perfect foil for me, and it was for good reason I dubbed us "the animal and the intellect" (and no big mystery who was who).

While Bumstead, Mergner, and I worked twenty hours a day in an effort to get the officers and troops in the field up to scratch, Sergeant Major Press went back to Dong Tam, home of the six-hundred-acre 9th Division base camp, to sort out the battalion rear area. It was a hell of a mess. The unit had turned over dozens of times throughout the past two years on virtually an individual basis, and the absence of continuity during that period had permitted metal shipping containers (known as conexes) to be left unopened and gathering dust for God only knew how long. Also, the longtime absence of discipline and attention to detail among the leadership of the battalion had allowed some 150 lame and lazy, not-so-Hardcore 4/39 troopers to get permanently lost inside the sprawling division facility, which more than anything was like a war-zone country club, complete with virtually every amenity known to man, including a miniature golf course.

The first thing Press did was open up the conexes. Inside, besides the beer and Coke and personal belongings of guys who'd died, been evacuated, or rotated home long before, he found hundreds of thousands of dollars' worth of brand-new, totally forgotten equipment—rifles, starlight scopes, machine guns, you name it. The find was a perfect example of the waste, inefficiency, and complete disorganization inherent in the individual rather than unit replacement system, but it was also a windfall, so it was no time to bitch. Out in the field we were short on most all of these things. The following day, Press rounded up all the Hardcore personnel who'd gotten used to luxuriating in the battalion rear, and leaving just twenty-five men behind to begin sorting through the mounds of new loot, he brought the rest of the little lost soldiers back to the battalion fire base at the Wagon Wheel, where they rejoined their rifle units. Those who considered themselves lucky enough to remain behind were in for a rude shock. Press dubbed this element "F Troop," even bestowing upon them a green guidon on which was painted a crossed pick and shovel, and within a week most were more than eager to get back to what they figured *had* to be an easier life than they were suddenly finding in the rear. Meanwhile I started smoking the company commanders to get with it on their field strengths ("Captain, you show on your morning report that you're assigned a hundred eighty-five men. I've just done a physical count and you've only got ninety-one men here in the field. Where the hell are all your people?") until they realized that they had to *take charge* of their units. This sort of problem wouldn't have occurred had there been even a small Old Army NCO base within the units, keeping tabs on the men who'd take a mile if you gave an inch. But company commanders in the 4/39 were lucky if they even had an instant lieutenant, much less an Old Army NCO. In shades of Fighter, 1952, in at least one company, junior-grade enlisted men—corporals—were being made platoon leaders.

Despite the multitude of obstacles, the 4/39 quickly began to shape up. Just days after I arrived, Brigade CO Geraci gave us an invaluable push when he made the Hardcore the base of an independent task force and assigned us to the Plain of Reeds, a sprawling AO that in WW II would have been assigned to an entire field army. Our mission was to deny Viet Cong infiltration from nearby Cambodia through the Delta by picking off the VC at (and between) their many way stations in the area.

With few exceptions, we didn't make much contact in the three weeks we were there, but the Plain of Reeds mission gave me a unique opportunity to shake down the battalion and mold it into a fighting force with no interference from above. It was like a big ATT. We moved our fire-support base every three days, each time digging in, filling sandbags, the complete drill. Each morning we were joined by an Air Cav troop from the "Black Hawk" Squadron (7/1 Cav), and with these pros, we methodically searched the wide expanses of tall elephant grass that particularly characterized the Plain of Reeds. While the rifle companies generally worked over large areas in a loose recon screen (saturating the AO in the hope of stirring up a contact), based on intelligence, we also "jitterbugged" (a series of predesignated helicopter insertions made one by one until a contact was made) and conducted "eagle flights" (helicopter raids in which we went right to a suspected target). Both jitterbugging and eagle flights were Hank Emerson's innovations. They were ideal for the Delta, terrain so flat it was just one big landing zone. While employing them my fledgling battalion was hunting Charlie, but perhaps more important for the moment, the troops were getting damn good training along the way. And the Black Hawks, without whom it would not have been possible, were the best Air Cav I could have asked for. Theirs was a unit filled with bold and gutsy crews who knew their jobs and had little fear. They were a colorful bunch who wore blue Civil War campaign hats, had yellow crossed Cav swords painted on the noses of their choppers, and actively employed a bugler. They were characters—the real stuff of Hollywood, as *Apocalypse Now* would prove a decade later.

The best way I knew to shape up the 4/39 was by day-to-day personal example, by slowly but constantly tightening the screw. I had a lot of fun playing squad and platoon leader again for those few weeks in the Plain of Reeds, getting to know all the troops, checking out the leaders, teaching the men not only how to soldier but also teaching them my style. For example, I sacked on the spot the D Company commander who let a group of VC slip past his unit one night because he didn't want to give his position away. That kind of behavior bred cowardice and fear. On the other hand, if my people were maneuvering for three VC in the trees and the unit commander said there were a lot of mines in there, I'd tell him to pull back. I might bring in artillery or mortar fire or even an air strike, but I wasn't going to lose any legs for a couple of VC. I was into fighting hard, but not at the expense of bleeding troops; the fact that I walked with the platoons put me in the good graces of a lot of the men, but my stock rose even faster when word got around that I wasn't a butcher.

It was important for me, too, to learn the terrain, the enemy, and the situation on the ground on this battlefield so different from any I'd ever fought on. I'd learned how little I really knew on the very first day I had the helicopter assets (a C&C bird, two gunships, and four troop-carrying slicks). We'd been flying along and my pilot said, "Hey, look . . . there're eight gooks running into those trees. Request permission to paint them red."

But my brain was still in the Highlands where you took a little more time. You really looked things over. And you couldn't just paint people red, especially in the Mekong Delta, where 35 percent of South Vietnam's population lived and hospitals all over the region were already filled with civilian casualties. So I said, "They look like eight little kids to me. Let's go down and have a really good look."

We went down to about one hundred feet. The suspects were still running, but this closer inspection confirmed my initial feeling: they were just eight kids, no older than thirteen or fourteen, simply scared shitless as they ran looking for cover, carrying neither weapons nor military equipment. "No," I told the pilot. "I don't give you permission to fire. I'll put an infantry insert on them." I instructed the platoon leader whose men were aboard the four slicks where to land. With gunships covering, the platoon hit the ground. They immediately received small-arms fire and took a couple of wounded. The little kids were, as my savvy pilot had said from the outset, Viet Cong.

It was a major lesson learned for me, but one impossible to etch in stone. I had a couple of men wounded who would not have been if I'd just said to blow those kids away, but I couldn't say "blow 'em away" because they appeared unarmed. Yes, they were VC, but they could just as well have been kids ditching school who happened to get caught in the cross fire. Anything was possible. And I suddenly realized it would not be easy, this Delta war. It wasn't easy to tell the good guys from the bad guys anywhere in South Vietnam, but here in the Delta it was damn near impossible.

The AR-15, the precursor of the M-16 I'd given the thumbs down to back at Campbell, was still the Air Force's survival weapon. It was a light, small, kind of "prestige" item; Frank Hart had carried one in the 4/39, and when I took over the battalion he'd offered it to me. It was a nice gesture on his part (he was going on to a staff job), and I took the weapon. Five years after I'd first tested it in prototype, however, on the battlefield the thing performed as predictably as it had at Fort Campbell. In the very first firefight I got into, it jammed on me. I ended up having to throw the worthless piece of junk away and scrounge a weapon from one of our wounded. In the course of the same fight I also got hit in the leg when the trooper next to me tripped a booby trap. Fortunately it was a minor wound; in fact, since we were operating in waist-deep water that day, I didn't even realize I'd been hit until I got back that evening and found my boot was filled with blood.

All the 4/39 had really needed was a good kick in the ass, which included creating or bringing in leaders who cared for their men, and giving the men some sense of real purpose. Just prior to my arrival, the battalion's assignment had been the morale-busting exercise of base-camp security at Dong Tam ("Other than being made fools of by the local VC, there wasn't much to it," explained Bob Lacey, a fine shake-and-bake squad leader in A Company who represented the best of the NCO Candidate Course and all I had hoped it could produce); now, as early as two weeks into my tenure, the troops were getting into the spirit of the hunt (though not without some bitching and moaning along the way), rising to the challenges that daily confronted them, and even beginning to see themselves as warriors. The growing regard the men had for themselves and their battalion did not, however, translate into gratitude or appreciation for being drafted or having to wear the uniform. If I'd thought that for even a minute, it was dashed the day I noticed one of the RTOs in Slater's Operations shop had the letters "FTA" printed boldly on his helmet cover in two-inch-high letters. Historically, members of the battalions of the 39th painted "AAA-O" on their helmets, the legacy of Colonel Paddy Flint, legendary World War II regimental commander of the 39th who'd coined the unit motto "Anything, Anywhere, Anytime, Bar Nothing," but "FTA" I'd never seen before. So I asked the RTO what it meant. He looked down at his boots and started shuffling around, and finally, very reluctantly and in a very small voice, said, "It means Fuck the Army, sir."

Instantly I felt the fire licking my face. The guy could have said anything he wanted about the Vietnam War, because I probably would have agreed with him. But he was talking about *the Army.* I was red-hot. Besides, that kind of crap was lousy for unit discipline and team spirit. I wasn't going to have a bar of it, and I fired him on the spot. The next day, Sergeant Slater, who'd been on R&R and thus unable to plead the case of his favorite RTO, tried to convince me it was all a joke, and that FTA meant "Fun, Travel, and Adventure." I had to hand it to that fine old soldier for his creativity, but it wasn't going to, nor did it, wash.

Even when they pissed me off, I had to admit there was something I liked about the draftees who didn't want to be there and made no bones about it. I liked draftees in general, even with the attendant problems. Historically draftees have kept the military on the straight and narrow. By calling a spade a spade, they keep it clean. Without their "careers" to think about, they can't be as easily bullied or intimidated as Regulars; their presence prevents the elitism that otherwise might allow a Regular army to become isolated from the values of the country it serves. Draftees are not concerned for the reputation of their employer, the Army (in Vietnam they happily blew the whistle on everything from phony valor awards to the secret bombings of Laos and Cambodia); a draftee, citizens' army, so much a part of the history of America, is an essential part of a healthy democracy, one in which everyone pays the price of admission.

"Hardcore 6, this is Apache 6. We've sighted damn near a naval convoy headed south! About forty sampans loaded with troops and supplies. We're taking them under fire."

It was good news. A short time before, as I'd released the Air Cav troop for the night, I'd told the troop commander I wanted him to sweep down the

Mekong River from the Cambodian border on his way back to his base, in case Charlie was hoping to get a head start on his nocturnal wanderings. The commander hadn't been too happy about it—it had already been a long day—but my hunch was correct, and now he had a good fight on his hands.

It was dark by the time I coordinated air assets with Brigade and headed by chopper toward the contact area. By then the Cav had broken off, having exhausted both fuel and ammo. But they'd done some serious damage in the meantime, with Apache 6 reporting numerous rocket hits, several secondary explosions, and a number of sampans sunk. The remaining sampans had gone to ground, and all I had to go on to find the contact area in the pitch-black night were the grid coordinates the Cav had given me. I studied my map under a red light in the chopper, cursing the Delta, which looked the same wherever you went, and myself for never having mastered map reading at two and a half miles per hour let alone at a hundred mph. Then I looked out the door, and there, suddenly, right below me was an exact replica of the objective area I was looking at on my map—just the right crisscross of canals, the same curve in the Mekong River. "This is it!" I told the pilot, who was naturally awestruck by my great nighttime navigational sense, unaware that it was blind luck. It was an ongoing joke among my old friends that the only reason I was so successful at finding and fighting the VC was that I was always lost and stumbling into Charlie in the most unlikely places.

"Good map reading, stud," radioed Geraci, who was over the target area above me in his C&C. "You're a real Ranger. Now, pile on!" he said, and we did, with two companies blocking the banks of the river. At first light the VC had flown the coop, but they'd left behind their large sunken sampans complete with probably thirty tons of resupply—enough goodies to keep a VC regiment going for a month. In a period where contact was infrequent, this was a bonanza. "Your lash-up's beginning to act like a parachute battalion, Hack," Geraci radioed his congratulations. "Tell 'em I think they're STRAC!"

I loved working for Geraci. He was a fine commander who gave me max support, not just with assets but also in my efforts to get the Hardcore trained up and fighting well. Geraci was a real leader and soldier's soldier who knew how to tap the spirit of men. He knew how to prepare them for combat, too —the performance of his 1/506 Airborne "Centurion" Battalion in Tet of '68 (1,294 VC KIA for 11 dead of his own) well reflected the fine grounding Geraci had insisted upon for the 1/506 when he'd trained them *as a unit* in the U.S., before their Vietnam deployment. (Geraci's pre-Vietnam training schedule included jungle-swamp training, mountain training, and Ranger techniques, as well as innumerable training raids, ambushes, and recon patrols, all of which were conducted at night.) In Geraci's own history lay the key to his training savvy. A Marine private in World War II, he'd climbed the hard battlefield promotion ladder from private to master sergeant as he island-hopped through the Pacific. After the war he went through ROTC training at college to become a lieutenant. He served with distinction in Korea, and had since commanded Ranger, Special Forces, and Airborne units. In a nutshell, he was one of the greatest combat soldiers who ever stepped into a pair of jungle boots.

He was also an animal, a rough, profane, grizzly bear of a guy who ate staff officers uncooked for breakfast but whom the troops idolized and who loved them in return. Some described him as a bull in a china shop; to me he was a Damon Runyon diamond-in-the-rough kind of character. His radio call sign was "Mal Hombre," which I translated as "one mean mother," because that's what he was, and the two of us couldn't have gotten along better. We were cut from the same bolt of cloth, so he trusted me enough to give me a free hand. "All right, stud, here's what I've got for you," he'd say and then present the facts—intelligence, mission, assets available, coordinating details. All muscle, no fat. "Any questions?" he'd wind up, and then, "All right, tiger, go out there and knock their cocks stiff." Geraci was so easy to get along with and so decentralized in his approach that when our Plain of Reeds mission ended I hardly minded the battalion's next move, to Fire Support Base Moore, where we were to co-locate with the brigade CP.

About this time the stud battalion commander of the 2/39, Don Schroeder, was killed in action. The story was he'd been flying along in his C&C when he saw an enemy soldier running across the ground below. Schroeder, an old 2/502 man whom Hank Emerson had brought with him to the 9th Div, was a daring, superconfident, seemingly indestructible kind of guy, and it was only natural for him to decide to dive down there and scoop this VC up. The only problem was that he was so intent on his prey that he didn't check out the area first. He just went down, jumped out of his chopper, chased the guy into a tree line where he thought he'd nab him, and ran into a couple of squads of VC waiting in ambush. And he died. I'd known Schroeder since the 101, and I'd spent a week with him in his battalion doing OJT before I took over the Hardcore. He was a great soldier and leader, and his death kind of took the fire away for a few days. The two of us were a lot alike. What he did was something I, too, could easily have done. It's easy to forget you can get overdaring.

1 May 1969

Dear Ward . . . Recently had an absolute screwball for a brigade commander. An engineer. He was not in the least concerned with reducing casualties and doing things the right way. He wanted only instant glory. He threw troops all over the battlefield without concern for the contingency of getting into deep shit. I fought him vigorously and would not allow him to jeopardize my units. Luckily, he was not here long enough to rate me or I'd be washed up. His name is Ira A. Hunt. Watch for him. He is another "inevitable general" and, in my judgment, twice the phony.

A few days after the Hardcore moved to FSB Moore, a strange voice using Mal Hombre's call sign started issuing orders directly to my engaged companies on my battalion command net. This was something that just wasn't done, and he actually sounded so strange that at first I thought it was a VC playing games. "I don't know who you are, but you sure as hell ain't Mal Hombre," I said, "so I advise you to get off my net. It's seriously obstructing my command and control."

The voice immediately informed me that Geraci had been evacuated, and that I was, in fact, speaking to the new commander of the 1st Brigade, Ira Augustus Hunt, Jr. Hunt also happened to be the division Chief of Staff. "All right, Mal Hombre," I said, "but if you have instructions for me, give them to me on your brigade command net, which I am monitoring, and get off my internal net so I can fight my units."

"Pop a smoke. I'm coming to see you," he responded (now on the brigade net at least). I did, and before long a spit-polished chopper landed and out stepped my new CO. Ira Hunt was a tall man, handsome, but turning to fat. He looked very much a soldier, all fitted out with a rappeling rope, trench knife, and grenades (like John Wayne in *The Green Berets*), with the only perfumed-prince touches being the starch in his perfectly faded fatigues, his spit-shined shoes, and the sleeves of his shirt, each rolled up exactly five times and ending in a precise, two-and-a-half-inch roll. "Hackworth," he said, "Colonel Geraci's gone back to the States on emergency leave. I'm the interim brigade commander until a replacement comes in. Meanwhile you will do what I say and when I say it."

"Just stay off my battalion command net," I replied. "I will not allow you or anyone else to deal directly with my companies."

Fortunately someone came along and ambushed the conversation before it could heat up to shoot-out proportions. *Of all the bad luck,* I thought. This was the second time this colonel of engineers—he wasn't even an infantryman—had been given command of the brigade (the first had been when Emerson got shot down), and the scuttlebutt I'd heard from Round One was such that—well, he was no Emerson. As one of my companies was still in contact, I turned my attention to them. Hunt snapped that we'd talk "later," and ran like a real warrior back to his chopper, with a horde of followers/assistants close behind.

The interim brigade commander promptly forgot my warning about speaking directly to my companies on my battalion net. Finally I just told my boys to "skip rope," which was the battalion's informal code for "go to another frequency," and we got on with the fight while Hunt presumably was kept busy playing with the dials on his radio.

It didn't take a sixth sense to realize serious trouble was brewing. And the potentially disastrous situation between Hunt and me was made even worse by our presence at FSB Moore. As Brigade HQ, this was Hunt's home, so we were under his continuous supervision. When intelligence indicated that the fire-support base might be mortared, for example, I put the word out to my commanders to make sure everyone slept under cover. But one element apparently didn't get the message, and when the fire base was hit, this unit took three WIA. The minute the news got to Brigade (some two inches away from the battalion concern), Colonel Hunt came roaring into my CP. "Why weren't those men under cover?" he demanded.

"Well, the company commander said there was a breakdown in communications, Colonel Hunt. A couple of guys just didn't get the word."

"This is your responsibility, Hackworth!" Hunt shrieked, and proceeded to dress me down as if I were a plebe at West Point during Beast Barracks and he were a first classman. The basic gist of his rant was that I was incompetent and should be relieved. Though no one *in the world* got away with talking to me the way he was, I held my temper by concentrating on his mouth and calculating at what point it would begin foaming. I wasn't going to fight him and give him a reason to relieve me. At least not yet.

The east side of Dinh Tuong Province was serious booby-trap country, and a hell of a place to fight. Two days after the mortar incident, as we went into the field, I reminded my commanders not to allow their units to be lured into a wood line by a fleeing Viet Cong only to find themselves knee-deep in mines. The 4/39 had the chopper assets that day (the assets were shared among the brigade's four battalions, so we generally had them every fourth day) and we began methodically searching the AO. Throughout the exercise Hunt was up above in his chopper playing Great Squad Leader in the Sky, overflying, oversupervising, and proving beyond any of my doubts that he didn't have any idea about infantry combat. As one of my company commanders later put it, "He had no concept of reality on the ground. He was the kind of person who'd be telling me to move much faster when I was waist-deep in mud and it was physically impossible to do what he wanted me to do. He was aggressive, but he was aggressive from his seat in his helicopter."

The whole morning passed with no contact, and Hunt met me on the ground where my chopper was refueling. "You're not making enough inserts," he said. To Hunt, who was actually quite a genius in the Mc-Namara/Enthoven just-give-me-the-figures-don't-give-a-shit-what-makes-soldiers-tick mold, the whole thing was only a numbers game (in this case, the more inserts, the more contacts), and he actually went on to warn me to get with the program or else. I was insulted. "I don't tell you how to build bridges," I replied, "so you don't tell me how to fight my battalion." Engineer Hunt didn't have a hell of a lot to say to that, and as I got back into my chopper I couldn't help but marvel that this was the same guy who had saved Hank Emerson's life.

In the afternoon, elements of D Company were inserted into both ends of a canal. With the help of gunships they flushed out and killed a dozen VC and captured one prisoner. It was a good start for the new D Company commander, ex-1/327 Tiger Dennis Foley, whom I'd recruited for the Hardcore team and who'd taken over his command just a few days before. Now Dennis reported mines and booby traps in the contact area as thick as fleas. I told him to break off and head for a pickup zone while Captain Emile "Chum" Robert, my magnificent artillery LNO (as well as my de facto deputy CO, S-2/S-3, expediter of all things operational, and all-around right-hand man), peppered the trees with artillery and organized the Air Force to put in a napalm strike. But then Hunt piped up on the radio. "I want the area swept," he ordered.

At this time, I had only just begun to make progress getting the powers that be to recognize that a field full of VC mines and booby traps, however primitive the devices, was just as deadly to life and limb as the minefields of WW II and Korea. In wars past, you didn't go headlong romping and stomping around in minefields if you valued your life, or order your men to if you valued theirs, and certainly not just to look for bodies to count. So there was no way I was going to send my infantry into this minefield now. But I couldn't tell Hunt that—my intuition was he'd use my refusal as an excuse to relieve me. (*He refused to fight the enemy, General. Killed twelve, captured one, and ran. No fighting spirit, sir . . . no fighting spirit.*) So instead I just said, "Roger, on that. I'll go down and brief the commander myself while I pick up the prisoner."

I told Foley to squat right where he was, but to dummy radio traffic as though he were moving, because I knew Hunt would be monitoring our net. With that I took the POW back to my forward CP. All too soon Hunt landed as well, lumbered over to me, and launched into another of his incredible tongue-lashings. Hunt was a real bully—abusive and de-meaning—and I was getting it as if I were a brand-new shavetail right off the boat. "Pursuit! Pursuit!" he screamed. "That's what war is all about! You don't win by bugging out!"

"Colonel Hunt," I said, as pleasantly as I knew how, "I'd like you to look at this prisoner D Company picked up. You know, sir, I think he's top brass. Just look. He's got smooth hands and feet. Look at his neck muscles. He probably hasn't carried a thing for the last ten years. And look at those intelligent eyes. You know, sir, I wouldn't be surprised if this bastard were a *general!*"

In an instant, Hunt forgot about inserts. He forgot about monitoring my radio. He forgot about sweeps. There, before his eyes, was ninety-eight pounds of instant glory. Imagine, the first Viet Cong general captured in the war, captured in the command of Ira Augustus Hunt, Jr., West Point engineer. "You know, you might have something there, Hack," Hunt said warmly, newly friendly, like a used-car salesman about to close a deal, and he eagerly disappeared with his spoil of war. Interrogation would prove that the "general" was in fact a lieutenant with no intelligence or career-enhancing value for Hunt at all, but the ruse at least let my men keep their legs, and it got the Great Squad Leader off my back for the rest of the day.

By day's end, D Company had killed some thirty VC and captured one general. Before releasing the assets, I put the battalion in three company-size ambush positions, which, over the next three days (while the choppers were rotated to the other battalions and we were foot mobile), would serve as the nuclei for small recon, combat, and ambush patrols. Bone-tired, I got back into my chopper and headed off to FSB Moore.

As soon as I landed, Nev Bumstead ran onto the helipad. "Thought you should know, boss, Colonel Hunt ordered me to dispatch some ambush patrols along the MSR. He thinks the VC will be hot and heavy tonight." It was Tet of '69, and Hunt had already told me he expected a replay of the previous year.

The rage started building. "Did you do it?" I asked.

"Had to," Nev replied. "You weren't there and he wasn't going to wait around."

I was livid. Hunt probably thought since I'd obediently eaten shit all day he could now start issuing orders to my squads—and through my S-3, a *staff officer* yet. In the Army *I* came from, senior officers did not break the chain of command, and staff officers never issued an order unless it was first approved by their immediate CO. These were cardinal rules in a unit, ones that preserved its command and control.

I stormed past Nev into the TOC. I canceled the patrols, and then had Nev so inform the brigade S-3, a good man named Major James Mussel-man. Within minutes a raging bull in the form of Colonel Hunt came barreling in. "Hackworth—" he bellowed.

I interrupted. "Colonel, I think we should step outside." I wasn't going to talk to him in front of my men, particularly not if I ended up punching him out, a scenario I would have dearly loved.

We stood by the heavily sandbagged entrance of the TOC. "Colonel," I began, "you've been on my ass all day, just generally fucking me around and fucking things up. You don't issue orders directly to my subordinates, and I'll be damned if you think I'm going to take your shit."

"Let me remind you, Hackworth, that I am your brigade commander and you are being insubordinate."

"You can pull rank all you want, Colonel, because no matter what you are, you're not a soldier, even if you do stick your nose into everything as if you know what you're doing."

"I could relieve you, Hackworth!"

"Yeah? Well, go ahead. Because before the sun sets tomorrow night I'll be commanding another battalion in another brigade in another division right here in Vietnam. But if I leave this battalion, I promise I'll take you with me, Colonel. I'll only be pushed and bullied so far!"

I was so angry I could have killed Hunt then without a moment's regret. He must have read my thoughts, because he soon retreated to more secure territory. Only after he'd gone did I discover a more concrete reason for his withdrawal: throughout my tirade I'd unconsciously been pounding my fist again and again into a rock-hard sandbag on the edge of the TOC, until the rugged nylon cover had ripped and the bag caved in.

Dusk came and time passed. Little by little my rage began to settle. Then I was informed I was wanted at Brigade. I felt an inner stab. I knew Hunt was going to relieve me, but on his own turf and with his own witnesses.

With heavy heart, I walked over to the brigade CP. Most unexpectedly, the first thing I saw was Hunt pacing back and forth in front of a bank of radios. From the sounds of the radio transmissions I knew someone was in a hell of a fight, and from the worried look on Hunt's face I knew who was getting the raw end of the deal. "Colonel Hackworth reporting, sir," I said, snapping a rigid salute as I came to an even more rigid attention, using the formality—most uncommon on the battlefield—as a form of insubordination. Unfortunately, on this occasion it went unnoticed, because Hunt had troubles on his mind. "Colonel," he said as he pointed to a map, with what seemed to me barely controlled hysteria, "we put a LRRP team in here. They're in real trouble. Their insert chopper has been shot down, they're on the ground, surrounded, and they've taken heavy casualties—sixteen WIA out of eighteen men."

So what? I thought to myself. *It's your problem. I ain't your own personal Houdini.* "I want you to take my loach,"* Hunt continued, "and go up and see what we can do."

"What do you mean, 'we'?" I demanded, snapping out of my internal rebellion. It seemed to me the reason those LRRPs (pronounced "lurps") were in trouble was that Hunt hadn't followed proper deployment procedures. Normally a division LRRP team was attached to the battalion in whose AO it was to be employed. Then the battalion commander controlled its insertions, and took care of the team with, say, a backup reaction force ready to launch if the LRRPs ran into the slightest difficulty. At the very least, Hunt's LRRPs should have had a pair of supporting gunships from the beginning, which might have taken a little heat off while the soldiers were sorting themselves out. But no. And no surprise the result. "Get me all the choppers you can spring loose," I said. "Get all the gunships to report over the contact area, and all the slicks here to pick up my C Company. Tell them we'll operate on my battalion command freq." I turned and started for the bunker door. Hunt followed me.

"Colonel, do everything you can to extract them."

"Colonel Hunt," I replied, "if I get those people out I never want you to fuck with my battalion again. You just tell me what you want done and when you want it done, but keep off my ass while I'm doing it. Do you understand?" Hunt gravely nodded his head. He knew as well as I did that if that LRRP team was eaten up by the Viet Cong his chances of becoming boy general wouldn't be red-hot.

While Nev alerted Gordie DeRoos' C Company to prepare to move to a pickup zone to conduct a night air assault, I met Chum Robert at the helipad. A LOH was waiting. Once airborne and over the contact area, I switched the helicopter's radio to the LRRP patrol frequency. "Mayday! Mayday! Mayday!" was all I could hear amidst the background chatter of automatic weapons and exploding grenades, whose fires I could see on the ground below, silhouetting the downed chopper in the middle of a mangrove swamp. I figured the LRRP RTO was so rattled he had a death grip on his "push to talk" button (although later I would discover this was not the case; the handset had actually been broken or shot in half and could not receive). "Work up a wall of steel around those cats," I yelled to Chum. "Start way out and walk it in till it's right around the chopper. Then keep it up until I tell you to lift it." The shells would keep Charlie from doing anything too provocative for a while and buy us a little time, because that's what I needed—just then Nev called to say that the choppers had not shown up yet at the pickup zone.

* Light observation helicopter (LOH).

Chum was putting in his artillery fire six rounds at a time in a precise circle around the downed chopper. It was a technique we'd used many times in the Highlands with the 101; not exactly the safest procedure in the world, but it was better to run the risk of stray shrapnel skipping into the position than to allow the VC to overrun the outnumbered, crippled force. I tried to contact the LRRP RTO again. "Mayday! Mayday! Christ, someone help us! Mayday!" was all I could hear.

"Hardcore 6, this is Blue Jay 6. I'm twenty minutes out with your insert. Got eight gunships with me. Request sitrep."

"Not good," I replied. And it wasn't good, if for no other reason than I didn't know what the situation really *was*. If I could only talk to someone on the ground. As it was, I couldn't send Gordie's men in there. To send troops in without knowing the situation on the ground would be cold-blooded murder.

"Red light, sir," said my pilot. "I'm running out of fuel. I'd like to break off."

"How much have you got?"

"Twenty minutes, sir."

"Stay on station. There's a fifty-five-gallon drum stashed five minutes from here." We had drums hidden all over the battlefield for such contingencies, but in this case I didn't know what good it would do. Maybe it would keep us airborne, but what I needed was someone on the ground to run the show. I didn't know what to do. DeRoos' people would be on station in no time. *You've got an excuse to break off,* I told myself. *You're running out of fuel. They're not your LRRPs anyway . . .* By this time my pilot was squirming and moaning about having only minutes left of flying time and here we were out in the middle of the Delta with bandits all around us. I appreciated the problem. "Look, I'll tell you what," I said. "It'll solve all your problems. Land."

"No way, sir! I'm not gonna land. I *refuse* to land."

"Chum, get your shit together, 'cause we're going down there," I yelled. "Just get us as close as you can to that downed chopper and drop us off," I said to the pilot.

"I'm not going to land," he replied.

I took my .38 out and thumped it up against his head. "Land or you're dead."

He decided to land.

We got a lot of fire as we came in, straight down like an elevator beside the crippled chopper. Some of the LRRP people saw us coming and raced through the waist-high water to grab the LOH's skids, trying, as the pilot hovered some six feet over the scene, to claw their way into our bird. They were going to pull us right out of the sky. Chum and I literally had to kick them off just to be able to get out ourselves. These were LRRPs all right—self-proclaimed superfighters but in reality just badly led phonies who couldn't hack it in the field. Their track record (in the 9th Division at least) was a pathetic litany of extractions from hardly hot situations, a record that had earned them among the real warriors the derisive motto "Stay a LRRP and Stay Alive." And while there was no question that they were in a bad situation now, nine-tenths of the problem was simply that they had not kept their cool.

As my pilot (the soon-to-be recipient of the Distinguished Flying Cross for his part in the mission) flew away, Chum and I waded through the mangrove swamp. The LRRPs and the downed chopper crew were bunched up and in a state of panic near the broken bird. As Chum got artillery erupting all around us, I just started grabbing people and literally threw them into the fight. "Get your ass over here and fire in that direction!" I said again and again until we'd formed a loose perimeter and word came that DeRoos' C Company was overheard and ready to come in. Then it was just a question of getting those men on the ground, a drill complicated both by the downed bird splayed across the two-chopper LZ and the fact that the VC must have decided they better do whatever they planned to do while they still had a chance to do it, and mounted an attack from one quarter. Chum turned off his artillery as I directed Blue Jay 6 to make a couple of runs over the bad guys; the gunships hosed the area down well with rockets blazing, and the VC attack ceased.

DeRoos was still hovering overhead. With a strobe light in a steel pot (so it couldn't be seen except from above), I stood near the downed helicopter and directed the first slick in. Having fought in the Highlands where LZs were usually even smaller than this one, the procedure was old hat to me but hard on these 9th Div pilots who were more accustomed to the wide, pool-table-flat expanses of the Delta plains. Soon Chum took over the job of bringing in the slicks. One by one each discharged its troops, and while I put the new arrivals in position on the ground, Chum backloaded the wounded LRRP troops and chopper crew and got them out of the contact area. Finally, when C Company was all in and the LRRPs were all out, Chum and I jumped into the last outgoing chopper (leaving DeRoos' very competent force to knock off the VC and secure the downed bird until it could be pulled out the next morning) and returned to FSB Moore.

The LRRP extraction was without a doubt the biggest risk I took in my life, and probably in Chum Robert's life as well. Never before or after that night did I go into a situation totally blind, without even one clue to help me calculate the odds of my success, or even my survival. And though I liked to think it was dedication to duty that forced my hand, it might just as well have been ego—the ego of a guy who (everybody knew) always made touchdowns and just refused to fumble now. The legend dictating to the man. Part of it, too, was surely to prove to Ira Hunt that I was a thousand times the soldier he could ever dream of being. And despite the fact that he probably would have had to kiss his stars good-bye if I had failed, I never got over the feeling that a big part of him would have been very pleased if I had. As it was, he didn't utter a peep throughout the affair, and afterwards generally left me alone, tactically speaking, for the rest of his twenty-day tenure as brigade CO. (His sense of urgency, however, which according to one of the brigade staff was "excellent, except that everything was an emergency to him and everything was top priority, therefore crisis management was a way of life," had him on one occasion taking the air assets away from me to send to the scene of another battalion's action when I was midway through extracting one of my companies from a minefield, and another case saw him bursting into the battalion aid station demanding to interrogate a seriously wounded prisoner whom Doc Byron Holley, the 4/39's infinitely capable battalion surgeon, was operating on at that very moment. When Holley, a draftee doc who took shit from no man, myself included, refused, Hunt tried to pull rank—apparently ignorant of the fact that Holley wasn't even in his chain of command—and even threatened a court-martial. "Help yourself. Maybe I'll get out of here early," Holley retorted, and the POW was soon evacuated to MASH without a bout in Hunt's hot seat.)

I always felt the only thing that kept complete mutiny against Hunt at bay in the 1st Brigade (and in the 9th Div HQ, for that matter) was that he was very much the boy of the division CG, Julian Ewell. They were a real pair, those two—Hunt with his red-faced rages and Ewell with his quirky way of pointing at you accusingly, with thumb extended out the side while revolving his whole hand by the wrist. Ewell himself was Maxwell Taylor's boy, and, since Normandy, had followed him wherever he went. All the way to the White House, actually, when Taylor was recalled to active duty as Chairman of the Joint Chiefs of Staff and Ewell became his aide-de-camp. With such credentials, Ewell really had it made careerwise (even if the Airborne connection was losing its value now, with Westy as good as gone and Abrams, a tanker, in the saddle).

Julian Ewell was a very effective division commander for the war in Vietnam, because whatever else might be said about him (like my feeling that he had no heart, which to me was the bottom line of soldiering, competence notwithstanding), he brought home the bodies. Pressure from Division was actually most phenomenal in this regard. All the battalion commanders had to carry a 3″ × 5″ card with an up-to-date, day-to-day, week-to-week, and month-to-month body-count tally, just in case General Ewell happened to show up wanting to know. And woe to the commander who did not have a consistently high count, even if the quest too often led to unnecessary American casualties or to what could be called "passive atrocities." With the main motivator being body count, in my view the powers that be didn't give a damn whose body was counted, and a great many—too many—civilians in the Delta were part of the scores. The old Army axiom "If it moves, shoot it; if it doesn't, paint it" could have been given a new lease on life in the 9th Div, with a twist: "If it moves, shoot it; if it doesn't, count it" would have been the perfect division motto.

The emphasis on cold statistics in the 9th Division was not confined to body count, however. Thanks to Ira Hunt and his computerlike brain, in the 9th Div there was an obsession with analyzing every aspect of the war in terms of easily manageable numbers. Blade Time (how long could/did a chopper stay in the air), Reliability of Intelligence, Location of Enemy Devices—all these and all else, it seemed, could be, and were, turned into percentages, indices, or ratios. (Significantly, one ratio that was thoroughly disregarded at Division HQ was the one hashed out by Napoleon 150 years before: "The spirit is to the matériel as three is to one.") But save for body count, there didn't seem to be any priority among these varied statistics. At Division briefings, the emphasis on, say, the number of troops down with immersion foot would be no greater or less than the emphasis on the number of U.S. Savings Bonds sold to the troops, or the amount of U.S. labor used on civic action projects in the AO. It was all the same. This did not make the whole picture look any less impressive, however, and I always thought that was a big reason Ewell was so enraptured by Hunt and so eager to advance his career. Hunt was just *so* smart. He could dazzle you with his figures, and you only realized they added up to nothing or were obtained at too high a price if you understood what the hell he was talking about in the first place. Statistically, he made the division look unbeatable, which made Ewell look pretty damn good himself.

On 1 March 1969, the Hardcore left FSB Moore for digs of its own. Our mission was to establish Fire Support Base Dickey from scratch on the western edge of Dinh Tuong Province, an area known to be teeming with Viet Cong. I told Division there was just no way my Hardcore troops could operate out of a base called "Dickey," and finally got them to agree to change the name to Fire Support Base Danger.

The site for FSB Danger was just one of many flat, muddy rice paddies on a wide, characterless plain just off Highway 4. The division engineers brought in a couple of bulldozers, and, with one of my rifle companies providing security, began to push the earth up to produce a four-sided sodden mud fort. At one stage of this work, one of the dozers uncovered the decomposed body of an enemy soldier, complete with AK47. I happened to be standing right there, looking on with a number of my troops. I jumped down into the hole and pulled the AK out of the bog. "Watch this, guys," I said, "and I'll show you how a real infantry weapon works." I pulled the bolt back and fired thirty rounds—the AK could have been cleaned that day rather than buried in glug for a year or so. *That* was the kind of weapon our soldiers needed, not the confidence-sapping M-16. The demonstration over, in good 9th Division tradition we reported to Brigade a body count of one, complete with weapon.

In no time at all FSB Danger was combat-ready. In the center of the mini-fort was an artillery battery (six 105s), which, in the best Westmoreland (and French) tradition, the fire base was designed to protect. At each corner of the base was a manned observation post (another wrinkle inherited from the French) on which personnel radars were mounted, and fighting bunkers were cut into the berm walls all the way around. Cyclone wire covered the apertures of every bunker to detonate incoming rocket-propelled grenade (RPG) rounds before they hit their mark. Concertina wire laced with booby traps and flares ran out five hundred yards and ringed the entire position. I had a well-organized command post with good communications. Everyone else had an assigned battle position (the rifle company that was standing down and drying out provided the fire base's security, augmented by the HQ and arty people), and with regular stand to's to bring it all together, Danger was locked and cocked, and set to command and support by fire any Hardcore unit in an eleven-kilometer radius.

We had contacts right away. No American unit had ever operated in the area and the VC had long considered it home turf and safe haven. It was a regular infiltration route dotted with way stations and permanent VC unit base camps; in my heart I hoped that the Hardcore was really ready for the hardball no doubt soon to come.

A few days after we set up, an intelligence intercept indicated the presence of a VC force with a number of recoilless rifles. The closest unit to the village the intercept pinpointed (at just a few hours' hike) was Foley and his D Company; I told him to turn around and go for it. But Foley didn't want to. His men were tired, he said, and ready to lay up.

"I know," I said, "but there are no air assets, you're the closest, and it's top priority. So get cracking."

"But, sir—" Dennis tried again, but I didn't have the time or the patience to fight the problem. I exploded.

"Look, Dennis, if the goddamn kitchen's too hot, man, get out of it. If you can't run the outfit, I'll find somebody around here who can!"

I am convinced that no American soldier has ever suffered more than the infantrymen who fought in the Mekong Delta during the Vietnam War, and that includes those at Valley Forge, the Bulge of Christmas '44, and Korea the winter of '50. It was a horrible place. An alluvial plain less than six feet above sea level wherever you were, your feet were always wet, and for a large majority of the time so was the rest of you. At low tide the rice paddies were a foot deep, at least six inches of which was thick mud; you had little choice but to wade through them, though, because the dikes were generally booby-trapped. When the tides were out, the myriads of crisscrossing canals were often mud up to your neck; you couldn't avoid them and you'd emerge exhausted, with leeches clinging to your body. One time, a staff sergeant named Onisk actually got stuck in the middle of a muddy canal. Mergner and I came to the rescue in our little LOH, only to find we still needed two tries *and* Mergner holding the sergeant's pack while Onisk held the skids. The suction was such that the chopper shivered and shook from the strain, and when Onisk finally came out with a huge, slurpy POP! he had a cubic foot of mud clinging to his feet.

Red ants were another Delta villain (they actually jumped on you with a bite so painful "you'd stand up in the middle of a firefight," as one of the squad leaders put it), and mosquitoes treated themselves to the unlimited smorgasbord of your flesh each night as you froze in your wet clothes. But it was immersion foot, the Vietnam version of the trench foot of WW I, that was the worst of all. The skin turned soft and wrinkly from extended time in the water, and then the slightest friction—a foot rubbing against the inside of a boot—caused an abrasion. If the affected guy didn't get out of the water at that point, this abrasion became ulcerated, and soon the ulcer grew to become as deep and painful as a bullet hole. Whole chunks of skin would just peel off a man's feet in serious cases. The only reliable treatment was to get the sufferer out of the water and into the sunlight to let his feet dry out. Not surprisingly, immersion foot took a tremendous toll on field strength in the Delta: if the victim was dried out early enough, he could return to his unit, but if he had the full-blown disease, generally he had to be reassigned out of the AO to some drier spot in South Vietnam. In the 4/39 we fought the problem with a rule that a company could stay in the field for a maximum of five days, but even that was probably stretching it a bit—three or four days would have been better. And it was this as much as anything that was behind Foley's reluctance to take D Company on the unscheduled mission. His men had been out in the field for four days already. If he didn't bring them in soon he could lose them all for a few weeks. I was as aware of this as he was, but the mission had to come first.

"Wilco, out," Dennis snapped angrily in response to my threat to relieve him, and began the trek to the village. I called Brigade and scrounged a chopper so I could meet D Company there. Airborne, I got word that the unit was in the middle of a minefield and Dennis had been hit. My pilot landed as close to the scene as possible, in the rubble of a bombed-out house. Fortunately no booby traps or mines had been laid there, but they were everywhere else, and no one could get to Foley. But he was bleeding like crazy, and I was afraid he'd bleed to death. So I held my breath and took off at a broken run through the field. I grabbed my injured friend and ran with him back to the chopper. My pilot immediately flew him on to MASH, and in the absence of any other officers, I took command of D Company. We slogged on through a couple of klicks of knee-high water and mud, and finally encircled the suspected hamlet. Ironically, the result of the thing was zero: the intercept had been a false alarm.

I felt damn guilty about Dennis' getting hit, particularly because it had been a bad mission, but also because of the flap we'd had just before. My hot head and stinging words had probably caused him to move recklessly, and I actually felt so bad about it that the next day I broke my private rule and went to the hospital to see him. I always went out of my way to avoid hospital visits. I just couldn't stand seeing what I, as a result of my direct orders, was responsible for. Dennis would be okay (his wound was very serious, though, destined to get him all the way back to Walter Reed and nearly costing him his leg), but I didn't believe, nor would I ever, that a commander can send his men into battle day after day, then review the results and still remain sane. You always did the best you could to preserve the lives and limbs of your men, but the mission had to come first. Visions of broken bodies and amputated limbs, past *or* potential, would eventually paralyze you. And besides, what do you say to the boy whose world has been ruined by your orders? Only empty words of comfort—he knows as well as you do that the next day you will send someone else out in his place.

At last it looked as though the 1st Brigade's interim commander was on his way out. Colonel John Hayes, whom I'd last seen in Nha Trang when Slam and I examined the SF Delta Force (Hayes's then command), was set as the new brigade CO, and for me he couldn't come a moment too soon. Hunt's continuing modus operandi was kind of a malevolent version of the Dodo's caucus race in *Alice in Wonderland* (everyone runs in circles, no one really gets anywhere, and when it's over everyone gets a medal); the problem was that the Beast of Delta Tango,* as Hunt had been dubbed by many of us living through his reign, had yet to call the race, and the entire brigade was running on empty. No one had had even a minute's rest, in large part due to Hunt's other job as the division Chief of Staff, which all along added enormously to his power as a brigade commander. What division staff member would not honor the requests of his soon-to-be-returning boss, who in fact controlled all the assets and resources of the division anyway?

On 11 March, just a few days before Hayes was to take over the brigade, the 4/39 was alerted to move to the area of a CIDG camp at My Phouc Tay: an element of Lieutenant Colonel Robert Sullivan's 2/39 Battalion had gotten into some serious trouble at nearby Thanh Phu village on an east-west running canal. Colonel Hunt was having lunch in a restaurant in the provincial capital of My Tho at the time, but when he returned and took the reins of the hotting-up battle from Brigade S-3 Jim Musselman, he decided that Sullivan's people had stirred up a large-sized enemy force, and determined that we would effect a perfect brigade seal around them.

The 2/39 was on the south side of the canal to be sealed. I was directed to insert my units (two Hardcore companies and a third attached from the 6/31st) to the north. It was a damned difficult situation: the canal—the boundary between the two units—was not very wide, so the men had to be especially careful not to fire "across the blue" (as the troops in the Delta called any canal, stream, or river) into friendlies. Even worse was the smoke that virtually engulfed the battlefield. At times you could barely see a thing, on the ground or from the air, the result of brushfires that had begun early in the piece when HE rounds hit the tinderbox-dry grass of fallow rice paddies. For me, the exercise was particularly frustrating because I'd lost my right hand—the 1/11 Artillery CO, Lieutenant Colonel William Hauser, had replaced my brave and thoroughly competent LNO, Chum Robert, with an inexperienced captain I didn't know and thus couldn't trust.

It was almost dark by the time my force was in place. Simultaneously, A Company, 2/39 was attempting to close on the riverbank directly opposite my A Company (essential to effect the seal), only to be stopped by heavy machine-gun fire. Over the radio I heard Hunt screaming at the 2/39 company commander to keep moving, berating him in the interim brigade CO's inimitable style. But it would have been madness for the young commander to follow the ill-conceived order. To continue on would have meant attacking across wide-open rice paddies right into the enemy's lethal grazing fire. Finally the young CO had enough of Hunt's tirade, and told his almost-hysterical superior that if Hunt wanted to make the attack he ought

---

* Delta Tango was the military phonetic code name for the 9th Div's base camp at Dong Tam.

to come down and lead the soldiers himself because the company commander sure as hell wasn't going to do it, or words to that effect.

Throughout the fight it was nothing short of a miracle that we lost no
gunships to artillery fire or air strikes. In a situation where centralized
control over fire support was essential, Hunt refused to relinquish any
control over the assets, and Bill Hauser soon found his job to be not just
ordering artillery, but playing traffic cop for Cobra gunships that popped out
of the smoke right through the trajectory of friendly incoming artillery fire.

For much of the battle, Hunt flew around the battlefield well above the
action—at "oxygen-starvation altitude" as one officer who accompanied
him put it—yelling and screaming and asking for the latest body count, or
making his own by directing fire onto enemy no one else in his chopper
could see (the figures for all kills he personally made sure were reported back
to the brigade TOC during the battle). At one stage he called me in my
LOH to say he was going to bring some gunships in by the canal at the inside
edge of my battalion's positions. I told him negative, it was too dangerous,
and went back to fighting my battalion. Gunships at the best of times were
lousy for close-in support; to even contemplate using them that way in the
dark with all that smoke and confusion on the ground was insane. Hell, if
I didn't know exactly where my boundaries were, how could the gunship
pilots?

I'd barely finished the thought when I saw it: a Cobra making a run right
at my A Company, miniguns and rockets blazing. I got on the air-to-air freq
to tell the pilot to break off, only to see him turn around and come back for
a second run. I couldn't stop him; he hosed down the company again.
("Those rockets and miniguns were scorching the earth," A Company squad
leader Bob Lacey later described those moments on the wrong end of this
savage U.S. firepower, "and all I could think of was I was glad I wasn't a
VC.") When I saw the Cobra coming around for a third pass, I was wild. I
told my LOH pilot to switch on all his navigational lights and hover over my
people so the gunship couldn't get in. It worked. Then I called the acting
company commander, Lieutenant John Roberson III. Roberson was a
South Carolinian Citadel stud of the highest caliber. He actually belonged
to D Company, but whenever I was short a commander I turned to him to
fill in. Now I asked him if his unit was okay.

"Yes, sir," he replied. "We've got four, maybe five wounded."

I noticed a crack in Roberson's voice. "How about you?" I asked.

"Just a scratch, sir," he said.

Roberson's "scratch" had actually been losing a finger on one hand to a
piece of flying shrapnel while he was talking on the radio trying to call off
the gunship fire. Charlie Wintzer, the 4/39's HQ Company medic who

always seemed to be thrown into the breach when a problem arose in the field, patched Roberson up that night, and said the lieutenant refused morphine until just before he was evacuated rather than leave his company in the lurch. Now *that* was hardcore. What a good man.

I called Hunt on the brigade net. "Okay, you've done your bit, Colonel. Your gunships wounded five of my men. Are you satisfied now?"

Hunt had nothing to say to me, but I heard later he immediately turned to another officer in the chopper and asked, panicking, "Don't you think I did right there?"

Throughout the battle, Hunt's insistence on controlling just about everything and everyone led to confusion and frustration on the ground and in the air. It came as no surprise to most of us, then, when upon the ultimate completion of the seal in the still-dark early hours of the morning, the enemy had long split the scene—if he had even been there in any big numbers in the first place.

When daylight came the battlefield was swept. My units on the north side of the canal had killed twenty-seven VC during the entire fight (mostly small groups of stragglers fleeing the impact area). Sullivan's men, on the south, had gotten a dozen or so more, and though tac air and gunships may have killed more still, there were no bodies or weapons to be counted. So there were about forty enemy dead. Yet Hunt was convinced that we'd annihilated a large force. In fact, when he returned to the brigade TOC after the height of the fighting, apparently he was very upset to see the dich board had recorded a lower body count than he remembered reporting. So he called Division, said there'd been a mistake, and gave them a higher figure.

The next morning, two choppers arrived from Division at Dong Tam with a bevy of journalists whom Hunt wanted to brief personally at the site of his great battle. The fact that said battle had actually started out as a screwup in one of the 2/39 companies (for which its CO was later relieved) and barely improved from there went unmentioned. Fifteen reporters came, and went home believing, first, that we'd engaged and demolished a VC battalion of some 430 men (questionable at best), and second, that fifty-seven enemy bodies had been found on the battlefield (an outright lie).[2]

In any event, Hunt's caucus race was drawing to a close, and it was time to give out the medals. The 9th Div had quite a system organized for this task. The first time I'd walked into the battalion's Awards and Decorations section at Dong Tam I'd been amazed to see nearly a dozen guys madly churning out citations. "Sir, it's General Ewell's policy that every man in this division get two awards before he goes home," one of them had explained. This was the end result of Ewell's determination (according to Major Edwin A. Deagle, Jr., who had been the division's Special Assistant to the Chief of Staff for Combat Research and Analysis) that the enlisted men of the 9th get their "fair share" of awards vis-à-vis the officers, and that was fair enough. But another part of Ewell's policy required Silver Stars, Bronze Stars, Distinguished Flying Crosses, and other such mid-level valor decorations be awarded to the 9th Div's combat leaders "at the same rate," according to Deagle, "as was done in other divisions—even if inflated—so as not to penalize them professionally." This was a typical example of the prostitution of the awards system in Vietnam, which in turn rendered individual decorations virtually meaningless. (The blind enthusiasm of the Awards and Decorations machine actually netted me a Silver Star in the 9th Div for an act I did not perform, during an action that occurred *after* I left the 4/39. I had to go to Saigon to MACV AG [Adjutant General] to have the order rescinded and the award removed from my records.) According to Hank Emerson, one good part of Ewell's awards policy was the General's adamant refusal to give himself as CG or the other general officers in the division these same valor decorations. This was a far cry from, say, the 1st Div under DePuy, where it seemed most field-grade officers and above, to include Commanding General Depuy himself, received at least one Distinguished Service Cross, Distinguished Flying Cross, Silver Star, and Bronze Star "V" during his tour (not to mention a Legion of Merit and countless Air Medals, the latter of which, according to MACV policy, were automatic issue for every twenty-five hours a man spent flying over a combat area). It was almost like an awards "package" in the Big Red One, which you received if you performed in any way admirably while with the unit. *

At least the 9th Division didn't stretch that far to look after its own: after My Phuoc Tay, when I got a call from Division saying I was to prepare a statement about the battle for a Distinguished Service Cross for Ira Hunt and I refused (about the same time a Spec 4 from Division walked into Jim Musselman's Brigade S-3 office and informed him, "I'm here to assist you to write a DSC for Colonel Hunt" and Musselman threw him out of his office), I was left alone, and to my knowledge Hunt went without a valor award for the operation.

Six weeks later, I was told to report to Hunt at Division—the Chief of

---

* Bernard Rogers, for example, received a DFC for relaying "vital information" obtained by making "repeated low passes over the [battle] area to determine the strength and battle formation of hostile forces" to ground commanders of an engaged ARVN unit, and for flying "at a dangerously low altitude to ensure the maximum effectiveness of the friendly supporting fires" he was at the time both calling and adjusting. For a brigadier general/assistant division commander, it was hardly a remarkable, DFC-winning achievement, any more than the action that resulted in Rogers being awarded an Air Medal with the "Valor" device: apparently the general, "with complete disregard for his personal safety . . . leaned precariously out of his aircraft to maintain visual contact with the friendly forces and to search for enemy troop concentrations." Also mentioned favorably in the Air Medal "V" citation was Rogers' "ability to operate the console radio of the aircraft under severely adverse conditions."

Staff even sent his personal chopper to pick me up from Danger. When we met, it was alone with no witnesses, and it was all "let bygones be bygones" stuff. The many head-on confrontations we'd had throughout his stint were, to Hunt at least, forgotten. He handed me a draft paper he called "The History of the Battle of Thanh Phu," a "historical report" that he, members of his staff, and a POW taken by ARVN subsequent to the events of 11–12 March (but who had been at My Phouc Tay) had put together. I really couldn't believe what I was being asked to read. With Slam I'd seen my share of false reports. In the Pentagon I'd experienced my share of snow jobs. But to me, this was the *quintessential* false report. The absolute, *ultimate* snow job. A flawless description of a perfect seal operation that bore little resemblance to what actually happened on the ground at Thanh Phu/My Phouc Tay under Hunt's command. The already inflated body-count figure of fifty-seven was inexplicably raised to seventy-two in Hunt's account of the battle in this report; the prisoner Hunt had assisting him corroborated most of what Hunt had to say *except* the body-count figures—according to the POW, his battalion had actually been gutted, with 203 KIA.

Hunt wanted me, of all people, to endorse this load of self-serving bullshit. Naturally I refused, as he must have thought I would, for he immediately sweetened the pot by insinuating that if I endorsed it he would make sure the Hardcore was considered for a Valorous Unit Citation. I refused again (though what commander wouldn't want a Valorous Unit Citation for his unit?), and unsurprisingly, the 4/39 didn't get a VUC for this or any other action while I was in command, well deserved as it would have been. Ira Hunt, on the other hand, hadn't needed my endorsement anyway, as things turned out. His "History of the Battle of Thanh Phu, 11–12 March 1969," in its final, For Official Use Only, elaborate but no more accurate form, was given wide distribution throughout Vietnam (I for one saw it two years later just as I was about to speak at the Vietnamese War College). It hit General Abrams' desk, and I heard it made it back to the States, too, to be used at Benning as an example of a perfect seal. George Mergner even found a copy of it on a subsequent tour to Panama ('71–'74), translated into Spanish. To me, it was the perfect hoax; the faker outfaking the fakers, even making a point in the process of absolving himself of any responsibility for personally ordering gunships into my battalion position and blowing John Roberson's finger off as well as wounding four more of my men (a "mishap," Hunt wrote in the "history," which occurred when a flare caught some VC out in the open and "the Cobra pilot, with instant reflexes, cut loose with his miniguns."). Hunt's narrative continues, "It looked to me as if he cut down at least ten VC. Shortly thereafter A/4-39, north of the canal, complained that they were being shot up." The prisoner who validated so many of Hunt's claims, and whose own account made Hunt's report (in Hunt's own words) "an historical document of some significance, because the opportunity did not arise too often for such an exercise,"[3] was nothing if not an eager accessory to Hunt's deception. I'd been too busy fighting my battalion to pay much attention when word filtered down from Dong Tam that a Viet Cong had been taken who'd been at My Phouc Tay, so I didn't know that the method of interrogation this prisoner (derisively nicknamed "Super P" by members of the division staff) underwent had him "sitting around the Chief of Staff's office at division headquarters . . . being treated like a million bucks,"[4] and being wined and dined on ice cream from the generals' mess. It sure beat being shot at, and little wonder the POW knew just the right things to say.

But to me, probably the saddest part of the Battle of My Phouc Tay and the historical report that came out of it was the conclusion of the powers that be, when the opportunity arose two years later to reexamine the fight and the bogus, zero-defect report that was being used as a bona fide teaching aid in Vietnam, in the U.S., and God only knew where else, that "the account of the Battle of Thanh Phu [My Phouc Tay], while perhaps not entirely accurate, cannot be considered a false report."[5] Such understanding of the less than perfect/candid/honest, particularly in a West Pointer and a general officer (which Hunt was at the time), was a first in my Army experience.*

In any event, in the middle of March 1969, Hunt went back to Division, and the brigade he left behind collapsed from exhaustion, immersion foot, overexposure, and abuse. Then we got up, gingerly licked our wounds, and tried to regroup. It was the second time this had proved necessary— old-timers of the brigade said Hunt had crippled the unit when he'd been put in charge after Hank Emerson was hit, too, in the month until Geraci arrived. Now, as then, maintenance of soldiers and equipment had become nonexistent; the brigade was shot and it took weeks before anyone was really operating at full speed again.

As a result, these were not the happiest weeks for the new brigade commander, John Hayes. When he'd first arrived to OJT with Hunt for a few days before taking over, apparently both Hunt and Ewell had told him that if he didn't get as high a body count as Hunt was achieving he wouldn't be with the division long. Now, as the brigade limped along, not making a lot of great contacts as it tried to heal itself, Hunt was riding Hayes, saying shit like when he was skipper the brigade was really performing and asking

---

* The reexamination of the Battle of My Phouc Tay occurred in connection with my speaking out publicly about the Army's performance in Vietnam, and the ticket punchers, typified by Ira A. Hunt, who were too often in control. Unfortunately, the Army was far more concerned with denying my credibility than anything else at that time, and the truth of the My Phouc Tay battle was just another casualty in the campaign.

what was wrong with Hayes, that under him the unit wasn't doing a damn thing.

Fortunately, throughout this period the Hardcore was still providing Hayes with a good, solid body count every day, through our well-established, highly successful sniper program. The sniper capability in Vietnam had been Hank Emerson's idea, born when we were in the Pentagon together. Hank had gone to Fort Benning and gotten half the Army Marksmanship Detachment assigned TDY to the 9th Div in Vietnam, to have them train selected "Old Reliable" troops as the division snipers (who would then be farmed out to units in the field). When Hank got shot down, the program basically collapsed, so when I got to the 4/39 it was just a good idea waiting to be exploited.

I wanted to develop a strong sniper capability on the battalion level. So I brought my guys back after their training at the excellent division sniper school, outfitted them with sniper rifles and starlight scopes, and put them up in the four observation towers of the fire base. A good sniper could drill your teeth with one of those scopes if you were unfortunate enough to be picked up walking along on a night patrol, and in conjunction with the small infantry radar system Geraci had brought into the brigade (which could locate by "blip" any and all personnel approaching the concern still outside the starlight scope's range), we began to get good numbers on the old dich board. The only problem was that once Charlie realized we'd learned to pierce the night somehow, he didn't come around anymore. It was the way he was with everything. Whatever magic formula for winning the Americans came up with, be it APCs or choppers, people sniffers, hydrofoils, or electronic fences, the minute Charlie figured out that whatever we were up to was bad for his health, he just stopped playing the game, at least until he came up with a countermeasure. McNamara's fence across the DMZ, as just one example, was (a billion dollars later) about to be more or less abandoned because the enemy now scooted around it (as any professional soldier knew he would) through Laos and Cambodia. And when, soon down the track, the 4/39 started doing tremendous damage to the Viet Cong outfits in our AO, and no matter how they tried to outfox us, we were too organized and too alert to fall for it, they simply rethought their situation and returned to a *very* old practice. They packed about three hundred pounds of explosives into a box, put it on a catapult not unlike the ones used in medieval times to crash into an opponent's fortress, and in the middle of the night flung the damn thing over our berm. I was sleeping in the corner of the conex we used as our battalion TOC when the device exploded. I was hurled to the top of that tin box, bounced off it a couple of times, and was then kind of propelled through the door. It would have

leveled the CP, killing me as well as a number of the snipers (who were
wounded as they slept in a bunker nearby), but for a two-and-a-half-ton
water tanker that was fortuitously parked between my CP complex and the
outer berm, and which took the brunt of the blast. But I had to hand it to
the Viet Cong. They were like little ants struggling with a crust of bread.
They never gave up, and nothing wore them out.

So meanwhile, they'd stopped playing ball with our snipers in the
observation towers. We needed a new gimmick. I called in Larry Tahler, an
OCS draftee lieutenant and nice Jewish boy from New York who'd found
his niche as the snipers' boss. I told him my problem, and asked him to have
a think about this idea I had, to put snipers on choppers. In short order,
"Night Hunter" was born.

Two snipers and three helicopters—a slick and two gunships—made up
each Night Hunter team. The choppers flew in blackout, the slick just a
couple of hundred meters off the deck, its sniper passengers lying prone in
the back, checking out the crisscrossing Delta canals and trails with starlight
scopes. The gunships, meanwhile, hovered maybe five hundred meters
overhead. If through their scopes the snipers saw enemy below, they and the
slick's door gunners would take them under fire, with weapons loaded with
tracer rounds. This showed the gunships exactly where in the pitch-black
night the target was, and in turn, the gunships would hose the area down.
The slick could also drop Air Force flares to light up the contact area, and
a reaction force was always ready and waiting at the fire base if a target
justified "piling on."

From the outset, Night Hunter was incredibly successful, with scores of
dead VC and no friendly casualties at all. Geraci, who was still in command
when the program began, loved the idea and loved the result, and made sure
Tahler (who as "Night Hunter 6" was in charge) got the assets every night.
After one particularly fruitful nighttime outing, Geraci even ordered
everyone who'd participated to his office at 0700, to give each one an award.
And while it was true that most of our greatest successes were in the first few
weeks (before Charlie realized we had something magic in the sky and began
to be more careful how he moved), for me Night Hunter was the first step
in my quest to turn off the Americans' stage lights. We would no longer be
the counterinsurgents who, like actors on a well-lit stage, gave all their
secrets away to an unseen, silent, and ever-watchful (insurgent) audience in
a darkened theater. Instead we would approach the battlefield and the war
as our enemy approached it, and in so doing begin to outguerrilla the
guerrilla—"out-G the G," as I hammered it again and again into the men
of the Hardcore—and *win*.

To this end, from Night Hunter evolved another role for the snipers, this one in daylight. In the early hours of the morning, two-man sniper teams, armed with sniper rifles with silencers and smokeless ammo, an M-79, and a radio, would be inserted around the battle area by unescorted slicks. Under a hessian camouflage cloth, positioned feet-to-feet on their bellies, these guys would just lie on the ground in the middle of bandit country waiting for something to happen. If they saw a half dozen VC coming toward their ambush they'd start with the last guy and pop them all off one by one. If the enemy were spotted nearby but going in the wrong direction, i.e., away from the ambush, the snipers would just call for artillery or air strikes to drive them into range.

As with Night Hunter, the daytime sniper program was tremendously successful. The result of it all was that the snipers, like the Tigers before them in the 1/327, became my pets. I called them "my little babies," and showered them with attention and recognition for their contribution to the battalion's effort. I even gave them their own uniforms (camouflage, à la Tigers) with the added touch of black berets with a red Recondo patch sewed on. In many respects the snipers' job was "easier" than the average trooper's sorry lot in a line company (the snipers didn't have to slog through the chest-deep mud of the paddies for days on end, or constantly be on the lookout for killer booby traps), but what they did, especially on the daylight operations, took an incredible amount of balls, and I admired them for it. The psychological element of the job couldn't be dismissed either. The high-powered sniper scopes brought the enemy (visually) within arm's reach, a connection between the hunter and the hunted that most infantrymen were spared. A certain constitution was thus required in a sniper, especially when among your targets could well be women or young girls. This was the case for Larry Tahler one morning as he surveyed a group of six dead VC he and another sniper had taken at a creek bend. "And I turned my scope on this one," he told me upon his return, "and it was a girl. And all I could think was how beautiful she was." It was just another strange element in a strange and difficult war.

The snipers were just one among many ideas I was experimenting with to make the 4/39 a real guerrilla battalion. Even before Hunt left I'd implemented some changes, and by the time Hayes was firmly in the saddle, the reorganization was almost complete. The basic concepts behind my changes were that men, not helicopters or mechanical gimmicks, won battles, and that the only way to defeat the present enemy in the present war at a low cost in friendly casualties was through adopting the enemy's own tactics, i.e., "out G-ing the G" through surprise, deception, cunning, mobility (which was where helicopters came in handy, not as a magic panacea but as a vehicle to move men quickly into battle), imagination, and familiarity with the terrain. In the end (and in an otherwise even match), our unbeatable firepower would always turn the tide of battle in our favor, but to use that hammer least wastefully and to its fullest effect first required the basic skills of men.

Each Hardcore company specialized in a particular facet of guerrilla warfare as tailored to our needs. Alert and Claymore companies (formerly Alpha and Charlie) were my ambush elements, long range and short range respectively. Both Battle and Dagger (Bravo and Delta) were Ranger-like (Korean War vintage) guerrilla units, though Battle had the Vietnam-era luxury of airmobile assets when they were available to the battalion, while Dagger moved almost solely on foot once in its AO. The new configuration offered maximum flexibility for me as a commander, and the specialization of roles well compensated for my soldiers' overall low skill level. It stood to reason that if a company did just one thing all the time, be it ambushes or eagle flights or whatever, it wouldn't take long to become truly professional at it. And not only did the changes improve the overall success of the battalion, they also did wonders for individual and team morale. For the first time the soldiers really knew *what* they were doing, *where* they were doing it, and *why*.

John Hayes was behind the "new" Hardcore 100 percent, despite the fact that I delivered it to him more or less as a fait accompli. Hayes was a great officer (and an old friend from as far back as Germany, when he was a captain in the 10th Special Forces Group at Bad Toltz and I was trying like hell to get out of the hotel business and into his organization), and he had four attributes that made him a perfect CO for this particular war, not to mention for me. First, he had a great appreciation for the cutting edge, having fought in Korea for three years as a recon platoon leader and a rifle-company commander and been wounded four times. Second, he'd already spent four years or so in Vietnam, so he had a basic understanding of the Viets and the war itself. Third, having been commissioned as an Armor officer, his tactical orientation from the earliest days of his career was for shock action and flexibility, which is what I was into and what guerrilla warfare was all about. And finally, in addition to having formed and trained the first Ranger battalion in the Vietnamese Army in 1962, Hayes had had a lot of G experience of his own in Southeast Asia, with the Special Forces Apache and Project Delta teams. Unlike Geraci, who was a dynamic, charge-Charge-CHARGE Airborne kind of guy, John Hayes was a quiet, careful, methodical, and introspective soldier, just like the guerrilla enemy we were tasked to fight, and had, as an added bonus, a keen understanding of the Oriental mind. He was a good man whose belief in his country and his duty as a soldier would, ironically, guarantee he wouldn't make general.

Though promoted below the zone to colonel in 1968, when he turned down attendance to War College two years in a row, he was told by the chief of the Colonels' Division that he'd reached the end of the line careerwise. Apparently general officers, this guy said, didn't take kindly to people who considered continued involvement in a combat position in Vietnam more important than going to War College.

But that was still in the future. In March 1969, Hayes and John Paul Vann, two men I respected enormously (and Vann being without doubt *the* most knowledgeable American, military or civilian, in and about the war in Vietnam), both agreed that my guerrilla battalion configuration was the best innovation that could have been effected at that stage of the Delta war. That kind of confidence behind me certainly added to my own, which itself grew daily as the Hardcore moved from strength to strength. One tremendous blow in the middle of it all, though, was the night two platoons of D Company were attacked in their own ambush position by a VC element that (we conjectured later) had been watching them all day. The company was completely asleep at the switch, and its casualties were close to a score dead and wounded, including the new company commander (KIA). I was both heartsick and totally humiliated that this had happened to one of my units, and just thankful that my boss was Hayes, a warrior, who accepted probably better than I did that this sort of thing happened in war. I turned the remains of Dagger Company over to Captain Ed Clark, whose cherubic face belied his guts and nerves of steel, and in the days to come he brought the unit back to strength, both physically *and* in their heads (which was even more important).

The rest of the Hardcore, meanwhile, though sobered by word of D Company's debacle, picked it up as a "lesson learned" and didn't look back. The esprit of the unit was growing stronger every day, a combination of a number of factors not least of which were the battalion's steady kill rate and the fact that the *Old Reliable* 9th Div newspaper and *Stars and Stripes* were beginning to write up some of the Hardcore's exploits. Such recognition did wonders for morale (and for producing cocky wiseasses en masse), and as I started giving back to the men many of the privileges I'd stripped away so savagely at the outset of my tour in order to bend them to my will, I couldn't help but get the feeling the 4th Battalion, 39th Infantry was on the verge of something big.

Ed Clark, new commander of Dagger Company, ran one fine guerrilla outfit. They were "up tight" (in the vernacular of Vietnam) and ready for anything when, in the early-morning hours of 23 March, their listening posts spotted enemy troops slipping into attack positions. With the memory of his predecessor's last fight still fresh, Clark felt the VC knew all too well where his people were. He immediately moved his unit back a couple of hundred meters. Minutes later, two companies from the Main Force VC 261 Alpha Battalion launched an attack on Clark's old position, rocket launchers and light machine guns blazing. When they realized their prey had flown the coop, the VC moved slowly forward. I wanted to send in some artillery when Clark radioed his sitrep, but Dagger's CO said no, not yet; he wanted Charlie to get a little closer in. Then a VC tripped a claymore and it was on: the enemy's attack formations were gutted as U.S. machine guns and individual weapons tore into their ranks. In the light of popping flares, gunships placed effective fire on Charlie and his probable escape routes. Artillery crashed down, too, and the enemy broke off their attack before it had really begun, making for safety as best they could.

It was a good, good contact, and as dawn broke I had tracker dogs flown in to follow the blood trails of the fleeing VC. Based on the confession of a Dagger prisoner taken during a sweep of the battle area (who'd said his battalion's base camp was not far away), the pursuit began in earnest, with Troop C of the Black Hawks tracking down the enemy in LOHs flown barely above grass level. We could see foot tracks trampled into the young rice in the paddies, and trails where sampans had slipped through the water. From time to time we'd find an isolated group of Viet Cong and a platoon would be dropped off to deal with them. Then, about two miles along, we lost both the tracks and the trails. They just disappeared in the shimmering plain of water-soaked rice paddies and mangroves. After long years in the infantry, I prided myself on having phenomenal eyes for spotting the enemy from the ground or the air (using the simplest rules like, Where would I move? Where would I hide?), so I was a little pissed off by the sudden hiccup. But then, out of the corner of my eye, I saw a black silhouette leaning against a tree. And somehow, in that instant, Charlie's entire configuration became clear to me. I could see his perimeter, I knew what he was thinking and how he was going to move. "Swing it around," I told the pilot of my C&C, and as the chopper whirled I saw this Viet Cong slip into a hole. Then we saw other enemy soldiers moving to prepared defensive positions. The Air Cav CO sent his scout ships in. One of them blew away some foliage only to uncover a .50-caliber U.S. machine gun. The gutsy LOH pilot whose bird uncovered it immediately dived down and pulled that gun right out of the enemy's hole.

I put four companies in a loose net around the VC positions and called in tac air to pummel the center and blast any escape routes that couldn't be blocked by my infantry. In the middle of the inferno that followed, my pilot told the two door gunners on our chopper to spray down the lily pads floating along the canal we were flying over. I couldn't imagine why, but the guy had done a lot of flying in the Delta so I figured he must have a reason. As the gunners opened up, the tactic became quite clear: one by one the lily pads bled red, and soon bodies began popping to the surface. It was another Delta trick I hadn't known before. To evade capture the VC would go underwater, grab a lily pad and, using reeds to breathe, just float along until they were out of harm's way.

Thirteen air strikes later the enemy gave up the fight. I'd put Clark's troops on the most likely escape route, figuring Dagger deserved the honor of delivering the final blows to an enemy who'd made the lethal error of tangling with them in the first place. Sure enough, as Charlie broke out of the charred foliage that had once so adeptly concealed his base camp, he ran right into Dagger Company's waiting guns. That night, Alert and Dagger made some forty more kills as VC stragglers attempted to steal away in the dark, and when dawn came and a final count was made, the Hardcore had utterly demolished the 261 Alpha's base camp, killed 143 men, and captured the battalion colors. Our own casualties were eight WIA, none of whom needed immediate medical evacuation.

I was so proud. D Company had out-Ged the G, no question about it, proving themselves to be guerrillas as dangerous and savvy as their opponents. My reaction force, Alert and Claymore companies (4/39) and Alpha of the 6/31, had performed like total pros. There was much cause for rejoicing at FSB Danger that day. It had been a guerrilla battle like Hank Emerson's 2/502 had fought at Bu Gia Mop (i.e., recognizing we were on to something big and consolidating our forces around the enemy); it was a battle fought as the 1/327's My Canh battle *should* have been fought three years before. And it was a battle that most likely would not have been fought the way it was had I not been in charge, or someone like me who had had his My Canh, who had learned how high the price was (regardless of what Benning continued to teach) of "closing" with our guerrilla enemy when our superior firepower could be used not just to destroy our foe but actually to preserve American lives. This time around, not one life was wasted, because I'd been there before and I'd learned. How different the war would have been in 1969 if all of us who'd fought and learned in those early days had stayed through the years as our brothers and fathers did in WW II, rather than being rotated out to make way for the ticket punchers or to advance our own careers with assignments we didn't even want. If the mostly draftee Hardcore, with me about the only one who'd experienced anything like this battle before, could capture the battalion colors of a unit that had moved relatively freely through the Delta for years—the 261 had been the heroes of Ap Bac, the momentous 1962 battle that became Ho Chi Minh's "rallying cry of the revolution in the South"—and deal that force a stinging defeat, imagine the long-term success an *experienced* battalion of men would have had.[6]

After the fight, I sent Dagger Company back to Dong Tam, ostensibly to train but more so to stand down, drink beer, and savor their victory. Besides, I knew word of the action would quickly make the rounds at Division, and I wanted the REMFs back there collecting combat pay to know what real warriors looked like. The following day Hayes informed me an awards ceremony had been scheduled for the men of Dagger. I was happy to hear about it, but I didn't want to attend. The battalion had the assets and I had a feeling of unease about going off to Dong Tam and leaving them on their own. Hayes insisted, however, so I briefed Nev Bumstead on what I had in mind for the day, which was to go back to the previous day's battlefield to get the VC I felt sure would return to pick up their dead. But, I told him, under no circumstances was he to get decisively engaged. Then Hayes and I flew off to Dong Tam.

The whole time I was away I was worried. Worry bordering on panic—I was *not* where I should have been, I could feel it. By the time the awards ceremony was over, I was frantic. Finally, finally we headed home, and the minute we got within radio range I called the Hardcore. Nev sounded downright exhilarated as he reported we had a great contact going and everything was just fine. Hayes took me to the scene in his C&C, and immediately I knew why I'd been so concerned. All the while we'd been at Dong Tam, my B Company was having the shit shot out of it.

The unit was in the middle of a three-hundred-meter paddy devoid of cover and concealment. Two men were lying on their backs, which meant they were dead. (A guy seldom lay on his back on the battlefield if he was alive. There was a psychological thing about keeping your belly close to the ground. Guys about to die, on the other hand, frequently flipped over on their backs, because they didn't care about protecting their bellies anymore.) I couldn't believe my eyes. Hayes dropped me off immediately, and Nev, whom I probably would have punched out if I hadn't had a higher priority, swooped down in my C&C to pick me up. Battle Company was being pinned down by four machine guns, a bastard of a sniper, and a continuous stream of RPG rounds. They couldn't effectively return fire for fear of hitting their own men, and each time Lieutenant William Torpie, the young B Company XO and acting company commander (standing in for Bob Knapp, who was on R&R), tried to get them low-crawling to the safety of a ditch, they drew more fire. It wasn't that the men could not get out; it was just that they were seriously hampered by a simultaneous effort to extract a number of their severely wounded.

I took charge of the battle, but no matter what I did, I couldn't bust

Charlie's ass hard enough to allow those kids to come up for air. I used tear gas, napalm, artillery, white phosphorus, air strikes, the works; I drew on all the combat experience and knowledge I'd ever collected—my entire bag of tricks—and nothing helped. When I finally ran out of options, I decided to go in and get the wounded out myself. It was the only way I could think of to give Torpie room to maneuver. I asked the pilot and his crew if they'd volunteer, because I knew it was going to be a hell of a mess on the ground. I told the gunship commander to keep fire going on the wood line where the machine guns were blazing, hoping to persuade Charlie to keep his head down. My chopper crew were good men and with me all the way, and we soon landed, right under a machine gun, within thirty feet of the wounded men. The gunships, meanwhile, began to hose down the enemy positions that were in very close proximity to our ship. One by one they swooped down and blasted those positions, and they continued to do so the whole time we were on the ground. They were our saving grace.

Bullets punched through the chopper as Nev and I jumped out. Together we ran over to the farthest wounded guy, grabbed him, ran back, and tossed him into the bird where he was attended to by Captain Schwartz, an Air Force doc who'd replaced Holley. We picked up a second WIA the same way, and then a third (amazingly, without becoming casualties ourselves), but by the time everyone was loaded onto the helicopter there was no room inside for me. I stood on the skids and put my crash helmet on so I could tell the pilot to take off (at the time he was just where he should have been given the circumstances, i.e., as close to the floor of the chopper as possible, using its console as cover). But I found I couldn't talk. I was so dried out my tongue had welded itself to the roof of my mouth out of pure fear. I had to open my canteen and drink some water before I could even gasp, "Let's get this mother out of here!"

We took the wounded back to Danger and returned to the fight. Without anything to hold him up now, I couldn't figure out why Torpie didn't do something about getting his men consolidated outside of that paddy. He still kept saying he was pinned down. Finally I lost my temper. I really chewed his ass over the radio, demanding he get cracking and get those men out of that paddy, like NOW. Apparently the next thing he did was put down the radio, stand straight up, and begin running from man to man to get them to move back. He got mowed down right away, and died a short time later.

Maybe I hadn't learned a damn thing at My Canh. Or from Dennis Foley's near-miss in that minefield. I hadn't asked Torpie to stand up (he didn't need to in order to extricate himself, and it hadn't occurred to me that he would). But I had been playing the game as if Knapp, a natural and more-seasoned leader, was in charge. It was due to the force of my word as his commander that this inexperienced young lieutenant was sent to his death. Like Jim Gardner's, Torpie's death was a big guilt thing for me, and has remained so all my life.

Dark was coming. With the exception of one lieutenant, all of B Company's officers had been killed or wounded. I sent Nev in to get the unit organized and withdrawn from the paddy. As night fell all the wounded were evacuated and the unit was safely out of the machine guns' reach. But it had been a defeat. A stinging defeat and a waste of good men's lives damn hard for me to accept, especially after our brilliant victory just two days before. But before I had a chance to figure out how to reverse our fortunes, my chopper, flying low over the now mostly quiet battle area, took a serious spray of machine-gun slugs in the belly. My artillery LNO got hit in the gut, and I took one in the leg. At first glance my wound didn't seem so bad, but the LNO needed immediate medical attention so I called Hayes and told him I was going in. Hayes put Mergner in charge of the battalion, and Chum Robert, now the brigade liaison officer, came down to help until a replacement for the wounded LNO was found. In the subsequent hours the two tried to get something going with the enemy, but the goal would prove elusive: on the one hand, Billy Winston, the company commander of Alert Company (which had been sent in to take the pressure off Battle and to salvage the fight), was about to go tilt in a bona fide nervous breakdown, and on the other, Nev Bumstead, though courageous by day, had had his bottle fill up and overflow three years previously during the 1/101's fight at Dak To and, as a result, he seemed to become almost paralytic, operationally speaking, in the dark. Consequently there was no seal and no sweep of the area. The morale-shattered remnants of B Company (which had taken six dead and about eighteen wounded) and the leaderless men of A basically squatted in their holes until morning, during which time the VC ran away. To make matters worse, one of our ammo resupply choppers, trying to negotiate an ill-thought-out, too-small LZ in the darkness, hit a tree and crashed to the ground, killing one of the door gunners who was pinned in the wreck and burned alive, and tossing exploding ammo all over the perimeter. Talk about a bad night.

My C&C was still operational after it got hit, so we bypassed Danger and flew directly to the 3d Surgical Hospital at Dong Tam to get my LNO looked at. There I found I wasn't walking too well myself, so two guys carried me in. At the door I ran into gutsy Charlie Wintzer, the HQ Company medic. He saluted smartly and said, "Hardcore Recondo, sir," and immediately a chorus of "Hardcore Recondo, sir"s rang out from within the emergency room. The unwavering Hardcore spirit among these guys who'd just paid the price themselves was a huge boost for my morale, and I certainly needed it, because I was steaming. There was no excuse for what had happened on that battlefield, I was mad as hell that I didn't know what was happening there now, and one place I knew I didn't want to be was in the hospital. Especially *this* hospital, which, as I lay on a stretcher waiting to go into surgery, happened to be under a heavy mortar attack, as was the rest of the Dong Tam installation.

Fortunately the little room where I was waiting was, in fact, an underground, reinforced bunker. For the moment at least it kept out the debris of the mortar fire, but did nothing to prevent most of D Company, under Captain Clark, from storming in to see me. Still on their short vacation, the guys had heard I was hit and thought I could use a lift. They brought beer and war stories and we swilled both down, talking loudly and just ignoring the mortar rounds crashing down outside. When we were all there together, it might as well have been rain.

The verdict on my wound was "serious," but it could have been a lot worse. The bullet entered my leg just below the calf and came out four inches higher up. It missed the shinbone by millimeters (without which I probably would have lost the leg), and only a small amount of leg muscle was damaged. Still, the decision was made that I would be evacuated to Long Binh and then to Japan. It was the worst word I could get. If I went to Japan, I'd be dropped from the theater rolls of Vietnam and I'd lose the Hardcore. I immediately set to work figuring out a way to thwart this eventuality, but soon realized it could well be an irrelevant concern: the way things looked, I was never even going to get out of Dong Tam. Alive, that is. Just as the chopper full of wounded I was on took off, enemy mortar rounds scored a direct hit on a huge, World War II–style (totally inappropriate for a guerrilla war) ammo dump nearby. The dump exploded like something I'd never seen—hundreds and thousands of rounds setting one another off like a world-premiere Fourth of July. It was really quite beautiful, save for the whizzing shrapnel and the fact that our medevac helicopter actually leaped into the sky from the concussion and was being buffeted in all directions. Throughout, I found myself laughing out of pure fear, and I greeted our ultimate arrival at Long Binh with great relief.

There I was looked at by a light colonel Regular Army doc who was most understanding of my desire to stay in-country. Since I couldn't stay at Long Binh until my wound healed, he suggested reverse evacuating me back to MASH at Dong Tam. This is exactly what happened, and though I didn't get back to the battalion on a full-time basis for some time, at least I didn't lose it. Meanwhile, it was more than ably commanded by XO George Mergner. Without too much to do during the three weeks I was recuperating, I had plenty of time to think. And what I thought about most was Nev

Bumstead, my S-3, whom I'd personally chosen and brought with me to the 4/39. It was the first time in my career that I had to say I'd truly blown it in the judgment department.

Nev Bumstead was, in appearance, almost a caricature of a soldier. He was a small, slender, intense guy who took his soldiering *very* seriously (and himself as well), and who had or carried all the warrior gimmicks: a folding stock shotgun, a bone-handled knife which he hung upside down in a shoulder strap (for quick draw), jungle boots with Velcro fasteners so he could get in and out of them fast, and web gear and load-bearing equipment almost invisible under the myriads of grenades and ammo pouches he always had hanging around his waist. As weird as Nev looked, however, was as erudite as he was, particularly in the ways of the military. He was also incredibly meticulous and thorough, attributes I came to appreciate in the years after he served with me in the 101, during which time he was an enormous help getting photographs together for the *Vietnam Primer* and some articles I'd written, and keeping me informed throughout those dry Pentagon days on how went the war from the on-the-ground perspective of his next Vietnam assignment. So when the 4/39 came up, it was only natural that I'd want him on my team.

I made him my Operations officer because it was the perfect staff job for this perfect staff officer. I was basically my own S-3 on an operational level; what I needed Nev for was to take care of the details, write the never-ending reports, and read my maps so I always knew where I was. Unfortunately, Nev wanted to be (and from the first acted as if he were) my deputy commander rather than the S-3 staff officer I hired. It was bad enough that part of his new act was a curt, sometimes downright rude manner toward his subordinates, but much worse was that he began giving orders that were not his as a staff officer to give. In this way, he quickly became more of a liability than an asset on the battlefield, and I soon began to leave him back at the base camp to take care of the hundreds and hundreds of little operational things that had to be attended to (due to the nature of our many movements and varied missions), and let Chum Robert do whatever I couldn't on the battlefield.

What I hadn't realized was that Nev Bumstead, after four tours, had been in Vietnam too long. He was burned-out. He no longer had the capacity for the job, even back at the base camp. It was soon apparent that the admittedly cracking pace I set battle-rattled him, the priorities eluded him, and my impatient demand for perfection had him quaking. And as I watched him begin to slip, and then to make more and more mistakes (like falling asleep in meetings or in the middle of radio transmissions), I became even more impatient, and then angry and unforgiving.

Meanwhile, since all Nev really wanted was to be a warrior (not unlike a little kid might want to be a clown after his first visit to the circus), the only time he really came alive was during big fights, even when he was the whole way back at the fire base. When Chum and I were in the middle of that Hunt-organized LRRP exercise, for example, trying to bring in reinforcements, evacuate wounded, and chase away the Viet Cong, Nev called me on the radio from FSB Moore to say, "Sounds like you're really doing a job in there, *King David*," and again later to say, "Hey, *King David*, there's a cold beer back here just waiting for you." I didn't know what the "King David" crap was all about, but besides the fact that it was really embarrassing, the guy was tying up the net with bullshit when he shouldn't have been saying *anything*. He just wanted to be part of the action. And it was through this sort of thing I came to conclude that for Nev, combat was cops and robbers, and all his Batman gear—which I'd always chosen to ignore—was part of some make-believe toy soldiers' game. Which, translated into the real world with real soldiers, had the potential for being the deadliest game of all. And then had come the B Company disaster, after I'd told him specifically not to get decisively engaged (and after I'd told myself I'd be damned before I'd let him play his games with the lives of the men in my command). I held him fully responsible for every single death that occurred that day, and for the entire mess. And that was irrespective of his bravery on the ground with me in picking up those wounded. As one participant in the battle put it, "It is said that there is a fine line between heroism and a court-martial. In this case, I feel Major Bumstead qualified for both."

For so long I'd contemplated relieving Nev, always trying to figure out a way to do it that would ease him out yet save my pride at the same time. (It just wasn't done for a new battalion commander to bring his own S-3 into a unit. So having done that *and* having sung Nev's praises to everyone from the first day because I believed in him, to then turn around and fire the man would have made me look pretty stupid.) But I'd let it all go on too long, and now six men were dead as a direct result. So I couldn't wait any longer. I decided to relieve Nev, and not only that, to make sure he never had the chance to command combat troops again, never had a chance to kill six men, or six hundred, or six thousand, to be another Mark Clark at San Pietro just because war to him was nothing more than a big game of cops and robbers.

And the way I did it was by zeroing him out on his ER. It was a completely calculated effort on my part, and never before or after did I use the terrible rating system I despised so much so completely in the very manner for which I despised it. ERs were so inflated by now that careers could be ruined by a percentile score of eighty-five (i.e., the "ranking of this officer in comparison with all Army officers of this grade and branch I know well enough to rate"); I gave Nev a 25 percent. I said he should not be promoted, and I did not recommend him for further military schooling.

Bumstead never did command troops again. But years would pass before I would realize I could have accomplished the same result without being so extreme, without destroying a man's dignity. I was angry at the time, overemotional because of the unnecessary casualties, smarting, too, from the embarrassment Nev had caused me, and, most of all, disturbed by my own lack of balls earlier in the piece: I should have gotten rid of him right away, not covered my ass for weeks and weeks just to save face. But probably even worse, in the long run, was that while I knew for certain that Bumstead had to go and used the system to make sure he did, I did nothing about Billy Winston, the A Company commander who went flat crazy after I was evacuated. At the time, no one understood why I described Winston's abrupt departure as a "change of command," how I could say that his crack-up was a "combat casualty," no different from being hit in the arm or leg. It was only years later that I understood why they were so puzzled. I always thought I spared Winston because I knew he had great potential as a staff officer, even if he should no longer command troops. Somehow it never occurred to me that by not addressing his breakdown in the field I'd done nothing to *prevent* him from again commanding troops; one day, as commander of a division, a corps, or an army he could just as easily lose it all over again. His bottle had filled, just as Nev's had at Dak To, and I should have let that be known.

On the other hand, perhaps the reason Winston was spared and Nev was not was that I didn't see Winston spinning out over the edge (as I did see Nev), working too hard, getting no sleep, and screwing everything up. While as a rule I tried to ensure that the troops got enough rest (or at least rested at the right times, like between 1600 hours and darkness, a time when tired soldiers had a tendency to become careless and take the preponderance of booby-trap casualties), I had different standards for the officers. My reasoning was that if I could get along with little to no sleep (and I was a good ten to twelve years older) then so should my officers. And if that was unrealistic, if you'd asked me then I'd have said *too bad*—war is a serious business, and with the lives of men at stake you can't wait around for the second-string players.

The most striking thing about Winston and Bumstead was that both were truly dedicated, superconscientious, overly bright graduates of the Military Academy. They were the typical West Point product, skilled in good manners and the social sciences, but not cut out for warriorhood. It was a failing of the Academy that the fighters among its graduates—the Pattons, the Gavins, the Emersons, the Willises, the Howards, and the Browns—were increasingly becoming the exceptions, not the rule, and it was a disservice to both the officers who came out of the school and the nation they pledged to serve, that getting down on the ground was among the last things the students were prepared for when they graduated from West Point.

As soon as I got off my crutches and on to a cane, I went back to the Hardcore. In my absence our guerrilla battalion tactics had continued to strike at the heart of the enemy: because we made a point of never establishing a routine; for the first time the VC were the ones kept guessing. And with the generous contribution of the snipers, our body counts (calculated in 9th Div arithmetic, i.e., $2 + 2 = 8$) were consistently high.

As their confidence and pride grew, the men of the Hardcore started talking about ways to let the VC know what unit was dishing out the relentless punishment they were receiving. Until now the men had made do just flipping the 1st Brigade's calling card on the enemy dead (the Recondo symbol printed on a small piece of cardboard, with a little message in Vietnamese explaining to the living how and why the deceased exited Planet Earth). But now that wasn't good enough. My men didn't see themselves as Recondos, just one of four battalions. My guys were *Hardcore* Recondos, which made all the difference in the world. So the search began for a new, unique way of letting Charlie know. Soon one of our sergeants came up with the ultimate of identifiers—a branding iron that read HARDCORE. Talk about dehumanization of the enemy. Still, it was a novel idea, and damned potent psychologically; logistically, though, the minute the sergeant presented the device to me I knew we would never use it—not only would someone have to lug the thing, but there was the added problem of how we would heat it up. So we went back to flipping Recondo cards. But we did keep the branding iron around for its value as representative battlefield humor.

At night at FSB Danger, I often walked the berm and talked to the troops on guard duty. Along with some of the snipers and HQ personnel, guard was pulled by whichever rifle company was in from the field resting up and drying out, so these late-night chats gave me the chance to get to know the individual men (and vice versa), the personalities of the individual outfits, and an up-to-date measure of the overall proficiency, discipline, and spirit of the battalion. One evening, just at dusk as I made my rounds I must have been somewhat preoccupied, because one of the sniper sergeants stopped me. "Why do you look so sad, sir?" he asked. "Have we had a low body count today?"

"Yeah," I replied, playing along, "six dichs. That's it, all day."

"Well, how 'bout if I get you three more, sir?" he asked, and, leaning against the sandbagged top of the berm, he aimed his powerful sniper rifle at three ARVN soldiers guarding a bridge about four hundred meters away. "That'll make it nine."

I knocked the barrel of the weapon up in the air as I saw the sergeant taking the slack up on the trigger. "Hold it, man!" I said. "They're South Vietnamese."

"A gook's a gook," the sergeant replied, shrugging.

"Look, we'll get some dichs tonight, okay? Tahler will bring 'em in. So just cool it."

"Yes, sir."

A *gook's a gook*, he said. Otherwise known in the 9th Division as the *mere gook rule*. I couldn't even chew the guy's ass. He was wrong, but I knew why he thought he was right, and I knew he was not alone in his feelings. Most everybody in the Hardcore hated ARVN (just as most everyone in the 1/101st had hated ARVN, and for the same reasons). In particular, the battalion from ARVN's 7th Infantry Division that shared our AO. Day after day these Viet troops went out and never found the Viet Cong. Yet, if we followed in their tracks, we had to fight it out every step of the way. The ARVN unit had reached a "you don't shoot us, we won't shoot you" accommodation with the enemy. If they saw a contact brewing, they just walked around it. My guys saw this, and when they saw the medevac ships carrying away their buddies who'd been wounded or killed while ARVN sat back and let us fight their war, it bred tremendous resentment. The kind of resentment that made "a gook a gook."

ARVN's stock didn't go up much higher when a civilian bus was mistakenly blown up by a VC mine, and one ARVN soldier, instead of helping the docs patch up his countrymen, stole the bandages. The civilian population also played a role in outraging the troops (in the bus incident, MPs had to fire shots in the air to keep the unhurt civilians from robbing the wounded) and confounding the entire U.S. effort, the latter something the American draftee soldier found incomprehensible, since we were there to *help* them. Just one example was the 1st Brigade truck driver bringing supplies to us at Danger who got into a hassle on the road with a jeep driven by a South Vietnamese troop. The Viet got so pissed off that he hopped out of his vehicle, walked right up to the truck driver, pulled out his pistol, and shot the driver dead as a doornail.

At Danger itself, I allowed no Viet inside, civilian or military, regardless of rank. I didn't trust a single one of them not to be a potential VC spy or collaborator, and the fact that not once while we were there was FSB Danger attacked by enemy infantry or sappers proved the validity of the "No

Viet" rule. I did let one local civilian set himself up as the battalion barber near the front gate. He was good at his job and very punctual, and I always thought it was just a bit of paranoia on my part that I felt a little queasy when, after he'd cut my hair, he pulled out a flashing straight-edged razor to apply the finishing touches. Then, one day he did not show up for work. The next night he was recognized among a pile of VC killed in a Hardcore ambush. My throat tingled for a week.

There were just so many incidents—seemingly hundreds of them—that involved civilian VC sympathizers. A particularly bad one in the 4/39 occurred before I arrived, when three VC sympathizers in the form of teenage girls selling Coca-Cola were responsible for an ambush that led to serious casualties. In the words of Dan Evans, DSC-winning medic (for his outstanding performance during the Battle Company fiasco) who made regular Medical Civic Action Program (MEDCAP) visits to the villages as part of the U.S. "win the hearts and minds" campaign: "Most of the time I enjoyed helping the people. But on days like [that] I just felt like shooting them all."

It really was a wonder there were not more My Lais.

I always found the "mere gook rule" very ironic, because whatever one thought of ARVN or of the South Vietnamese, the one thing I never would have accused the *Viet Cong* of being (and certainly not the Main Force VC) were mere gooks. On the contrary, Charlie was a most worthy opponent, and my own run-ins with him in the Delta only increased my respect for him.

In the Delta, the VC generally hid all day to avoid our air surveillance and ground operations, and moved at dusk when the Americans traditionally weren't paying any attention, having stopped the war to eat dinner. So whenever I saw a chopper flying anywhere near Danger at the end of the day, I flagged the pilot down for a quick overfly of our area in the hope of catching Charlie on the move. A lot of times I personally knew the pilots I asked to perform this extra duty, but even when I didn't they were usually eager to oblige. It was well known that at Danger we made a point of providing such volunteers with souvenirs (like captured Soviet weapons) and other tokens of appreciation. One evening, a brigade LOH came into Danger flown by Warrant Officer Kenneth Carroll, one of the three pilots who flew for the brigade command regularly. Carroll was also one of the best pilots I'd ever known, and I loved to fly with him because whenever we got together (especially for these sundown hunting parties) something exciting seemed to happen. One reason for this was probably that Carroll had long before chosen to ignore the word younger pilots got before they were assigned to me, that "whatever Hackworth says," they were not to fly me one inch below fifteen hundred feet; another was that he had great courage and a sense of adventure. He was a good pal and we made a great team—Carroll was even adept at flying his bird and simultaneously passing me M-79 rounds when we got into our aerial end-of-the-day High Noons. So on this particular evening, we took off and, as usual, started our visual recon from the outer strand of defensive wire that wrapped around Danger. Carroll flew along about twenty feet off the ground as I checked the wire for cuts and the surrounding area for tracks, bent grass, or other signs indicating enemy presence. As we slowly circled, I saw nothing unusual at first. Then, to my complete surprise, I saw a guy in a green uniform studying our position, lying motionless near the last strand of wire but exposed thanks to the blast of air created by the chopper's rotor blades, which flattened the grass all around him.

The first order of business was to find out if he was alone. I wanted this joker, but not bad enough to go down there and get Carroll and myself blown away if there were more VC concealed in the high grass nearby. We hovered right over him and I leveled my M-79 (so he knew the game was over). Then Carroll swung the chopper around and we did a quick but thorough search of the area. We found nothing, so we went back to the guy, landed, and I motioned with my weapon for him to get into the chopper. Not surprisingly, he didn't want to, so I got out and hoisted him into the backseat. I got in the front and poked my .38 Smith and Wesson through the cables between the front and back seats as a gentle reminder for the guy to stay put. I hoped he would. If I actually had to shoot him, the bullet would probably go right through his body and into the helicopter's transmission.

Our plan was to take him back to the fire base, but as the chopper lifted off, the VC started to panic. It was obviously his first helicopter ride. In the rush of things I hadn't buckled him in; now he got up and started moving toward the door. We were up about thirty feet when he turned paratrooper and bailed out for his cherry jump. Fortunately, his chuteless self landed in a rice paddy, so he splashed rather than splattered on impact. We went down again and hovered over him as I motioned with my M-79 for him to get back into the chopper. Once again, the VC refused to comply, but this time he grabbed a skid of the helicopter and began to shake it. And he shook it and shook it as if he really thought he could pull that bird out of the sky. Carroll took the aircraft up fifty feet or so, but the guy hung on, still shaking and kicking up a storm. Carroll took the bird down a little and finally the VC fell off, only to make for a clump of bushes. I didn't know what was back there (and I wasn't going to let us get zapped as Don Schroeder had been the day his number came up), so Carroll spun the chopper around between the

VC and the bushes, and I shot the enemy soldier at point-blank range. It was getting dark, so we only had time for a very quick look around the area to find out what the guy had been up to. We soon discovered a number of wooden arrows on the ground pointing toward Danger, which indicated to us that this VC had been a recon man, with the mission of designating enemy weapons emplacements for an imminent attack on our fire base. Well, the attack was not so imminent anymore.

Still, part of me didn't feel very good about killing that VC. Besides the fact that I'd rather have taken him back as a prisoner, our one-on-one encounter had somehow connected us, and I admired his guts. Unfortunately for him, my job was not to admire his guts. I knew, too, that if he could have wasted me instead, he'd have done so in a second.

Some time later, I got involved in a true David and Goliath drama with another, even more gutsy VC, this time in broad daylight. Clark's company was in contact, and as I flew around the battle area I saw a squad of VC hightailing it away from Clark's maneuvering forces. We followed them in my LOH, only to discover an entire *platoon*, all looking good in pith helmets and neat uniforms, wearing load-bearing equipment and carrying AK47s. It was one of the few times in the Delta I saw such a large group congregated together in daylight. I called for gunships and told Clark to move an ambush force in that direction. Meanwhile, to buy some time and to pin them down until the guns were on station and Clark made his move, we took the VC force under fire from the LOH. Instantly they scattered in every direction—all, that is, except one guy. Far from running away, every time we made a pass in the chopper (with my M-79 blazing) this character would adopt the most perfect firing position Fort Benning ever dreamed of, and shoot at us with his AK47. On one knee, foot pointed toward the target and elbow under his weapon, this guy didn't even flinch as the chopper barreled at him. He was absolutely determined to get us, and his only problem was that I was just as determined as he was. But neither of us could manage a direct hit. The VC's slugs would come straight toward us, but then they seemed to hit the chopper's airstream and veer off at the last moment. On my end, I had to aim well in front of my opponent (using the wildest Kentucky windage imaginable), fire, and hope the airstream did the rest. And while the current did pick up the rounds and whip them around toward the guy, I could never get right on target. And no matter how close I *did* get, that VC just knelt there with his perfect bearing, firing his weapon at my chopper. Finally a close hit on my part knocked him over, and after a moment he took off. I didn't go after him, though. In fact, I wished him well. He was one courageous dude— probably the platoon commander of the unit I'd surprised—willing to take me on against near-impossible odds so the rest of his platoon could escape.

Perhaps the studliest Viet Cong of all that I encountered in Vietnam was the POW Gordie DeRoos' company took from the 261 Alpha Battalion, the unit Dagger had battered and the Hardcore had creamed in March. Despite being warned he was a belligerent, mean little bastard who wouldn't give me a word more than his name, rank, and serial number, I wanted to talk to the guy. I'd been tracking the 261A as it rebuilt (both because there was little doubt they were the best in Dinh Tuong Province, and I had a feeling they had plans for my battalion), and I thought I could get some information out of him.

The S-2 brought him to me just as I was eating at the end of a long day. The prisoner was a first lieutenant, a recon-company commander in his late twenties, as defiant as I'd been warned and even more banged up. The worst of his many battle scars was a leg that had a depression in it almost as deep and wide as my fist. A huge chunk of flesh had been blown out and never sewn up. It would have been a bad, bad wound even if medical attention *had* been available. Still, it had healed, and the guy had gone back to duty. This was one hardcore stud.

He didn't want to talk to me, so I pointed to the old wound in his leg and through an interpreter asked if he had been hit. He said he had. "No hospital?" I asked. The prisoner shook his head almost scornfully. Then I showed him some of my wounds, which provoked the first bit of interest from the guy. He asked if they were from Vietnam. "No, no." I replied. "Before. Korea. But this one," I continued, showing him my leg wound, "this one came from the VC here in the Delta." The wound was still red and raw, with big, vicious-looking stitch marks.

"Maybe I did it," said the VC lieutenant, and he roared with a huge belly laugh.

"Yeah, maybe you did," I replied.

The warrior-to-warrior exchange broke the ice. It was a common bond that transcended patriotism or nationalism or causes. We laid down our flags and allowed ourselves to be friends.

"Look," I said, "I know you're a hardcore son of a bitch. I know you'd like to grab a weapon or a hand grenade and blow us all up. Let's not do it that way. Let's be honorable. I know you're not going to tell me anything about your unit's disposition, because I know you wouldn't get anything from me about my outfit. So I'm not going to ask. But I'm a soldier. I admire your army's skill, and your fighting spirit. So I want to know more about your army and your cause. Why you're fighting and why you believe as you do."

For the next three nights, I'd come in from the field and the prisoner and

I would get together for chow and a talk. For all my talk of honor, in the back of my mind I still hoped to break him down. I wanted to know where the 261 Alpha was and how it operated. But while we talked of many things, that subject was one he didn't say a word about. Meanwhile, the Intelligence people at higher headquarters were starting to yell for him. I'd initially said I was hanging on to him because he was giving me hot stuff on the 261A, but after a couple of days, patience up above was wearing thin. "Look, my friend," I told the POW, "the word is I've got to evacuate you. Since I can't get any decent intelligence from you, I'm going to have to send you to my division HQ, where you will be interrogated further, and then they'll turn you over to the 7th ARVN Division. Now, the first thing ARVN is going to ask you is to *chieu hoi.** If you do, they'll send you to a reeducation center, and when you come out you'll get a South Vietnamese uniform, a new M-16, and be assigned to a South Vietnamese unit. Maybe you'll even come back here as a Tiger Scout so we can work together. So when you go to the 7th Division, tell them you're going to *chieu hoi.*"

"I'll never do that," the prisoner replied.

"But you've *got* to do it," I said. "Do you know what they do to people who don't *chieu hoi?* They shoot them!"

"Then I will be dead. I expect to die anyway, fighting for my cause, the freedom of my country Vietnam."

"My friend, you've put me in a very bad position. I like you. I respect you as a warrior. I know we're not going to convert you, but I do not want to see you get blown away. So do me one favor. Lie. *Chieu hoi.* I'll see if you can come back to my unit."

"No. I believe in my cause," he said, and began pointing to his mangled leg and his many other raggedly healed wounds. "I believed in it through all of these. I will never surrender. I will fight until I'm dead. If they ask me to *chieu hoi* I will spit in their faces."

I thought of Duk, one of my Tiger Scouts, an ex-VC company commander (now he was my main adviser), who had *chieu hoi*-ed because as a South Vietnamese nationalist he'd become convinced that the Communists from the North were just using his people, that what they really planned to do was gobble up all of Vietnam for themselves. Who was wiser, I wondered: Duk, or the prisoner before me now? Who was right? And then I realized it didn't matter. Because I knew that if the Viet Cong was composed of soldiers such as the VC lieutenant with the gouged-out leg, then right, wrong, wise, or simply gullible, they would prevail. Unless we could duplicate their will and dedication, all the cannons, all the helicop-

---

* *Chieu hoi,* or Open Arms, was a program designed to encourage VC defections.

ters, all the high technology we could invent and employ, enough even to send men to the moon, would never beat them.

Since I couldn't get the guy to *chieu hoi* I turned to Plan B, which meant organizing for him to be flown back to Saigon to be turned over to an American POW camp. That way not only would he be spared ARVN's final solution (and the bamboo splinters under the fingernails, tiger cages, and electric shocks along the way), but he would not have to *chieu hoi*, and he would be allowed to live. And though I never saw him again, I have little doubt that he did.

Throughout this latter stage of my tour, I couldn't have asked for a better brigade commander than John Hayes, who supported the Hardcore in all the things I felt were necessary to keep the battalion in fighting shape. He knew I sneaked each of the companies back to Dong Tam for regular two-to-three-day winddowns and training (so did Assistant Division Commander Brigadier General Frank Gunn, but they kept it from General Ewell and his statistic-crazy chief of staff, both of whom actively frowned on anything that brought down "paddy strength," which might, in turn, bring down the division's overall, all-important body count). Hayes knew as well that I sent Hardcore company commanders to train with the Australians, as I had with the young 1/327 leaders, so that they could pick up the skills of those well-trained and careful jungle fighters. Professionally, Hayes and I were of one mind, which invariably saved a lot of time (not to mention preventing frayed nerves), but it also led to a keen competitive spirit between us, not unlike Hank Emerson and I had shared in the 1/101st. Fortunately, Hayes and I were also very good friends, which took the edge off some of the one-upmanship games we played.

John, for example, had a thing about snakes. He loved them. He kept a boa constrictor in his quarters, and always had some new variety around as well, to show off to his friends. I, too, had a thing about snakes. I hated them. If the truth be known, they were about the only thing in the world I was truly and consistently afraid of. So John used them to try to get under my skin. One time he radioed me from his chopper that he was coming into Danger and he wanted me to meet him at the helipad. When I did, he said he'd bought me a present at the PX (which I thought was a really nice thing to do), and handed me a bag. But when I opened it up, inside I found a live cobra. With no mongoose in sight, without even thinking I flung the bag and contents into the air, snapped my .38 out of the spring holster under my arm, and put six slugs through that snake before it splashed down into a water-filled bomb crater nearby. "You killed the little darling!" John cried.

"And I'll do it again if you bring any more of those things around here,"

I replied gruffly, reholstering my still-smoking pistol. (I didn't get him back for that one until two years later, just before I left Vietnam, when he took me for a farewell lunch at the My Canh floating restaurant in Saigon. As we walked down the gangplank leading into the place, I asked him what he was doing wearing a pistol. "You don't need a side arm here in Saigon!" I exclaimed, and grabbed Hayes's Luger right out of his holster and tossed it into the canal. Hayes was aghast. A Luger was not just a side arm, it was the *ultimate* side arm, and John was extremely proud of his. He immediately flagged down a little kid and paid him to retrieve the Luger from the water. The kid did, and all was well that ended well. But more important, I'd evened the score.)

At this point in the war most of the VC activity had gone back to hit-and-run, small-unit stuff. Although the real reason for this was to evade our firepower, it allowed the American command to form the mistaken impression that the enemy was down and on his way out. The truth was, despite the efforts of the Accelerated Pacification Campaign (the latest hype), which, according to the U.S. command in March of '69, showed 79.2 percent of the South Vietnamese population living under relatively secure non-Communist control, the pacification "hold" was really only as strong and as long as the light of day. Generally speaking, the VC still owned 100 percent of the night, at least in the Delta.

When I got hit on the twenty-fifth of March, I'd been just about to launch an attack on an area not far from Danger that was seeing a tremendous amount of VC traffic. At first I'd thought it was just a way station, but the more I watched the more I'd felt a large enemy force was using it as a base camp. Why not? Each day we operated far and wide throughout our huge AO looking for Main Force units, and very seldom ventured into the relatively secure areas right on our doorstep at FSB Danger. Wasn't the safest place for a crook to hide on top of the police station? But when I got hit, my hunches had to go on the back burner. I told Mergner (who more and more was finding himself the battalion CO, XO, *and* S-3) I didn't want anyone to go in there—I'd been watching the area for too long, and I knew the time was not yet ripe. I told Hayes the same thing when he came to visit me in the hospital at Long Binh: "It's not ready yet. I'm letting it cook. So don't touch it!"

But as Hayes later admitted, he couldn't resist. In the interests of one-upmanship—after all, he knew there were VC in there, too, and the possibility existed for a big victory and a chance to shove it amicably up my nose—he launched a 1st Brigade attack on "my" target. And the whole thing backfired. First of all, he went in with three complete battalions—an overkill tactic that surprised me, given Hayes's undeniably guerrilla mind.

Second, part of the airmobile assault went off prematurely (not Hayes's fault), which would have tipped his hand for sure even if, third, John hadn't used ARVN troops as part of the plan. In my judgment that was Hayes's biggest weakness in general, trusting the Vietnamese, and about the only place we disagreed about anything. I was convinced that ARVN was infiltrated from top to bottom with VC, and as far as I was concerned, giving them a piece of the plan was about the same as giving the complete operations order to the enemy. In any case, the net result of the operation was zero—the VC had cleared out.

I was so pissed off I could barely talk to Hayes, commanding officer or not. "That was a rotten goddamn thing to do," I told him. "That's treachery, John Hayes." But when I got out of the hospital and back to the Hardcore, and the intelligence profile on the area started developing again—the same activity, the same movement of people and supplies—I lost my anger and called on my guerrilla's patience to tide me over. And for almost six weeks, I waited.

Life did not stop throughout this period, of course. While the battalion had no big battles, the men continued to rack up a body count daily all over our AO—an ambush netting six VC here, the snipers getting eight there, eagle flights scarfing up another dozen somewhere else. On the third of May, a platoon in Clark's Dagger Company ambushed a couple of sampans, killing four VC and capturing several weapons not far from my "pet" target area. When a couple of enemy troops got away across the canal, the platoon leader, Lieutenant Dave Crittenden, grabbed a few of his men and dashed across as well, in hot pursuit. Unaware that they were virtually walking into the headquarters of the 261A Battalion, Crittenden's force came under fire from a well-defended VC bunker. Crittenden destroyed the bunker, and in the subsequent search came away with vital enemy documents, including the 261A's Order of Battle and attack plans.

It was a true windfall, giving focus to the picture my intelligence was piecing together, and shape to the enemy's intention. Among the documents was an attack plan against a nearby Regional Forces camp. If the VC were going for an RF camp their objective was obviously not military. Instead, it was psychological, and targeted at the local villagers, i.e., if an RF company could be destroyed under the nose of a U.S. battalion, how secure was the average peasant? Fortunately for us, the attack plan came complete with the locations of all the 261A companies' assembly areas, so as I watched enemy activity heat up on my profile, I knew we were one up on our foe whenever they decided to launch.

Our target was perishable, but not so perishable that it was appropriate to bombard the VC positions with artillery or tac air immediately, or grab every chopper I could find for a hasty airmobile assault. If I intended to get a complete harvest of these jokers, the only way to do it was to out-G them, and for the moment I was content reinforcing the RF camp with a U.S. rifle platoon and two M-41 "dusters"* with twin 40-mm cannons. After that I was prepared to wait.

By the twenty-first of May the enemy activity we'd been monitoring was at frenzy level. There was no question that their attack on the RF camp was imminent, and time for us to make our move. I got my companies in the field turned around, all tasked to move at dark, by stealth, toward the objective area to set up ambushes along all the enemy's probable withdrawal routes. Meanwhile, still in daylight, we made false helicopter insertions (the same as real helicopter insertions only no one got out of the birds, and upon lifting off, the doors were closed and the troops lay down on the floor) along these same routes, to make the VC think twice in case they got wind of our plan and had a mind to bug out. When dark came, more forces left Danger bound for other critical ambush positions, and by 0600, 22 May, the stage was set.

At 0700 Battle Company conducted an airmobile assault into the heart of the VC encampment. Their job was not to get decisively engaged, but simply to act as a beater. It proved one easy mission, for the VC, who only stood and fought when there was nowhere to go, immediately ran away through what looked like an easy escape route. Their only problem was that we had chosen that route for them: at the end of it, and every other escape route they tried, the Hardcore had an ambush ready and waiting.

The scene on the ground was mass panic among the VC. From the air it was like watching a game of pinball. Forced out into the open by U.S. air strikes, artillery, and gunship fire, Charlie bounced off one ambush right into the next, recoiling from one blocked escape route only to hit another and then yet another as he tried frantically to get away, each time leaving seven or nine dead behind. Besides swooping down and picking up each of my company commanders during the fight to let them see the scene from the air before the VC hit their units (which was very effective in helping them plan their next moves, even if it did result in a couple of serious ass chewings from John Hayes, which I yes-sirred), all I did during the battle was sit in my chopper and call down to my leaders when the time came: "Heads up, Clark, they're coming your way, let 'em have it," followed by "All right, DeRoos, they'll be in your position in about twenty minutes," as I watched the VC reel back from Clark's people and dash on to their next "avenue of escape."

---

* A full-track vehicle, kind of a cross between a light tank and a Korea-vintage quad-50, designed for antiaircraft but used in Vietnam in a direct support role.

It was the most satisfying operation of my career. It was the way I'd instinctively wanted to fight Operation Gibraltar four years before. Four years later I knew *it was how the war should be fought.* Synthesizing guerrilla tactics with our enormous firepower, we'd beaten them at their own game. We'd used *their* book of tricks to fight them on the ground and at the time that was to *our* advantage. The VC could not be destroyed by conventional tactics employed by the average U.S. battalion in Vietnam. Only guerrilla tactics augmented by U.S. firepower (and our tremendous air mobility when required) could defeat the enemy at a low cost in men and material. In this battle, for example, when the VC realized they were trapped, many resorted to hiding in bunkers. But there they were only further pummeled by the seven air strikes, five hundred rounds of artillery, and wall-to-wall chopper, minigun, and rocket fire we laid on them, until they either got up and fled to the ambushes or went to ground until dark when they could try to steal away. In the latter case, they had no better luck. At the end of the day, when the rest of the battalion vacated the battlefield, Gordie DeRoos' C Company went into a hide position (after a false helicopter pickup) to police up any stragglers, and their nighttime ambushes added 17 to the final tally of 113 enemy dead. In exchange for that number, the Hardcore took exactly four casualties, all just slightly wounded.

The next day Louis B. Mayer would have been impressed by the number of stars we had visit us at FSB Danger: the Deputy COMUSMACV, the USARV CG (who, incredibly, had actually radioed me during the battle the day before and ordered me to meet him at Danger *immediately*, to brief him on the ongoing fight), the IIFFV CG, the division CG and his ADCs. All were there to congratulate us on our job well done. And it *was* a job well done—like a graduation exercise for the 4/39, after being transformed from a hard-luck battalion into the Hardcore, after months of becoming more and more skillful and sophisticated in fighting Charlie, after taking his initiative away and chasing his sweet ass ragged around the province. Now he was reacting to us, and so busy doing it there was no time to overrun district and province outposts or to intimidate the people. In our corner of the Delta, that birthplace of the Viet Cong and their longest and strongest of strongholds, we were cleaning their clocks. During the months I commanded the 4/39, our body-count figures were more than twenty-five hundred VC KIA in exchange for twenty-five battalion lives. 100:1. Even with a hefty rate of inflation taken into account, these were damn good numbers. And if such numbers could have been obtained within other free-world forces fighting in Vietnam as well, the cost of the conflict could have been brought down to a level acceptable to allow us to fight a protracted war. And if we could have fought a protracted war, then ultimately the VC could have been forced *to the very limits* of DePuy's much vaunted but heretofore impossible to achieve "threshold of pain." And in this way, the war could have been won, at least from a military standpoint.

And yet no one tried to copy us. The Hardcore had come up with a brand-new (albeit four-thousand-year-old), low-cost way to fight the war, and yet not one of those fourteen stars patting us on the backs on 23 May 1969, asked, "How'd you do it?" or suggested, "Let's get this Hackworth and a few people from his outfit to go around and train everyone." Even General Abrams said that all his battalions should fight like the 4/39, but no effort was made to make sure they did. I wrote a couple of articles for military publications in the next two years explaining our tactics and describing our fights, and while there seemed to be widespread agreement on the principles, no one seemed willing or able to try them out. So in the end, yet again, there were no lessons learned, and the same mistakes were allowed to be made, day after day after day.

If that was not disappointment enough, worse yet was the fact that, after only four and a half months in command, I was about to lose the battalion. The problem was that I'd been hit four times since February, and after the last one General Abrams himself had stepped in and said, "Enough's enough," that I was too great an asset, and if I got wasted it would be a great psychological victory for the VC. All my protests on the subject fell on deaf ears, but the part that disgusted me most was that it was really my own damn fault. I could have prevented Abrams even knowing about the last wound.

I'd gotten it on one of my personal hunting expeditions. I'd just blown up two VC and a sampan with my M-79 when our LOH took a number of hits, shrapnel from which got me in the leg just a few inches below the wound I'd taken in late March. It was the kind of thing I definitely would have been evacuated for, but I was afraid I'd lose my command, so I thought of my VC friend with the huge hole in his leg whose many wounds had healed very well unattended, and went to the battalion aid station. I told Wintzer I didn't want to be evacuated and was leaving it to him to pull the shrapnel out. He probed around, feeling but not quite being able to reach it, until the pain for me was just too great and I told him to forget it. So he just pumped me with penicillin and wrapped up the leg. I swore him to secrecy and over time I healed up just fine. No one noticed anyway because I was still limping from the last wound, and that might have been the end of it, except I really wanted that Purple Heart. To a warrior it was the only award that meant anything (particularly since the rest had become so completely degraded), and it was my eighth one. I was proud of that, and I wanted it on my record. So I asked Mergner to see if he could slip the paperwork through.

He warned me that because I was a light colonel it would go directly to COMUSMACV and he felt sure I'd lose the battalion. I insisted, however, betting that the clerks would never notice. As usual, Mergner was right.

I was told I could have any assignment I wanted in the theater commensurate with my grade, as long as it wasn't in a direct combat role. I elected to go with General Timothy, who had recently called to ask if I wanted to be his G-3 adviser up at II Corps Headquarters at Pleiku. Besides being an essential part of my education for Latin America in the eighties, I thought it was time I learned about the advisory side of the war, and with Nixon and Kissinger now talking about turning the conflict over to the Vietnamese, I was sure my services could be of some use in an advisory role. In the process, maybe I'd even be able to answer the $64,000 question and find out why the little buggers from the South wouldn't fight. In any event it was better than the job I would have had in August—G-3 of the 9th Div—had I not been pulled from the battalion prematurely. In general terms, the "3" of a division was a plum assignment, but in this case I could think of nothing worse. Defying all logic (given that the Delta was where a third of the South Vietnamese population lived, where most of the VC were, where most of the fighting was taking place these days and the 9th was doing the bulk of it), the 9th Division was about to be the first unit pulled out of Vietnam.* As G-3, I would have been part of the transition team whose job it would be to turn these combat soldiers fresh off the battlefield into peacetime shoeshiners in Hawaii. Not exactly my style.

Because I knew the division was soon going home, it was possible to leave the 4/39 without feeling too badly about it. Harris Hollis, the division commander (a tanker) who'd replaced Ewell, bade me good-bye at my exit interview by suggesting I had a death wish (it was a rumor he'd heard *and was it true?*). I assured him if I'd had any such thing I would have been able to bring it to fruition long before now, a response that seemed to satisfy his impolite soul.

The Hardcore Battalion proved to me everything I'd ruminated on throughout the two years that went before—all those ideas and theories on how to fight the G. If there was satisfaction in that, there was much less in the fact that my success didn't make a dent in the way the war was prosecuted. Ironically, what did was the debacle of Hamburger Hill, where Screaming Eagle CG Melvin Zais ordered eleven assaults up an extremely well-fortified, totally useless piece of real estate, as if he thought he was in

---

* This did not even address the tactical absurdity of having the 9th Div in the Delta in the first place. The Marine Corps was the Defense Department's amphibious arm. Yet throughout this period, when the Army was stumbling and splashing like ducks through the waterways of the Mekong Delta, the Marines, configured, trained, and equipped as amphibious shock troops (perfect for Delta combat), were fighting an infantry footslogging war up in I Corps, the most rugged terrain in Vietnam.

Korea or storming Kraut positions at Normandy. Almost four hundred American men dead or wounded later, the 101 unit *was* King of the Mountain, but within a week the objective was abandoned. The ensuing, horrified uproar among the American people and in Washington made sure Hamburger Hill was the last huge and costly battle fought by American troops in Vietnam. So I guess if no one learned how to fight the war from me and the men of the Hardcore, at least from General Zais they finally learned how *not* to.

But we were already four years into the war. And there were almost four more to go.

20 BORN TO LOSE

> Communist insurgents cannot be handled effectively by large "conventional" military forces . . . our assistance to ARVN has revolved around the development of a large conventional force . . . with the dual purpose of protecting South Vietnam from a conventional attack by North Vietnam while at the same time serving as an instrument in the counterinsurgency program.
>
> I think it is quite obvious to all who have looked at the situation that ARVN carries within it a number of brakes in its effective use in counterinsurgency. These include
>
> (1) the organization and training tend to channel the thoughts and reactions of its senior commanders toward conventional rather than guerrilla tactics;
>
> (2) the various layers of command from Corps through Division to Regiment to Battalion and finally to Company tend to make it extremely slow in reacting to Viet Cong small-unit activities and overly cautious in striking out at the Viet Cong in an offensive role.
>
> Memo from David G. Nes
> Deputy Chief of Mission (Vietnam)
> to Ambassador Henry Cabot Lodge
> 10 March 1964

JOHN Hayes had a neat "safe house" in Saigon, which he gave me to wind down in for a few days before I headed north to Pleiku. My Linh, my lovely, longtime Vietnamese pal and I were having a fine old time there when we were interrupted by a phone call from Karl Beach, onetime XO of Company A, 2/502 who, in Ronnie Brown's absence, had skippered his unit during the 1/101's first night's action at Dak To three years before. Now Karl was aide-de-camp to General Ewell, who'd gone from the 9th Div up to II Field Force as CG, and he was calling to tell me Ewell had a job for me.

"You've got to be kidding," I said. "He's the last person I'd ever work for again."

"Well, I can't tell him that, sir," Karl replied. "I'll pick you up at General Abrams' chopper pad tonight at 1730. General Ewell would like you to have dinner with him."

Ewell's gleaming chopper touched down on time that evening as I dutifully waited at COMUSMACV Abrams' MACV I helicopter pad. I was *not* going to work for that man, but I knew it wasn't in my best interests to ignore his invitation to dinner. It was obviously very serious: what with Ewell's own bird and personal aide-de-camp as escort officer, I was getting the full treatment.

The IIFFV generals' mess was the most lavish I'd ever seen; the division messes at the 1st Air Cav and the Big Red One were like Salvation Army soup kitchens by comparison. Ewell certainly had hit the big time. As a three-star he had a very large general staff, all of whom, when I arrived, were in the middle of their cocktail hour, mingling with martinis in perfectly starched jungle fatigues and camouflage scarves, a million miles away from the war of the grunt, which ran along unabated just beyond the berm of Long Binh's enormous base camp.

I sat next to General Ewell at dinner. Throughout the meal he treated me like a long-lost friend, and somewhere in the middle of it he made his pitch. "Hack, I want you in my G-3 section. I'm going to set up a team to do after-action interviewing of the type Slam Marshall does, and I want you to run it."

"Sir, I'm going to Pleiku to work for General Timothy."

"That's a dead-end assignment, and you know it."

"I'm not going there to advance my career."

"You know, Colonel," Ewell pressed, "I can pick up the telephone and get you assigned to my shop whether you like it or not."

"No, you can't, General. General Abrams said I could go anywhere in Vietnam I wanted, as long as it wasn't a direct combat assignment. I chose Pleiku, and that's where I'm going."

The meal ended in a stalemate. Afterwards, Ewell invited me back to his quarters, as if in a private tête-à-tête I'd give ground I'd refused to in the very public mess. "Hack, I really want you here," he urged.

"Sir, I would much prefer to work for General Timothy than for you. I do not want to be part of your command. Whatever you say, I'm not coming." There was no point in telling him it was a question of heart, because I didn't think he'd understand. In fact, he got the message loud and clear. Just *how* loud and clear I didn't learn until later, though, when I was picked up below the zone for bird colonel and my name was nominated throughout USARV as being available for a brigade command. General Ewell actually went out of his way to write me a letter telling me "we reap the harvest from the seeds we sow," and that when my name had come up in his command, he'd said I was unacceptable. (General Zais, who was now a three-star as well and ran the U.S. units in I Corps, had a long memory, too. He'd not forgotten that I'd refused to go back to the 101st with him as G-3, a move I still had no regrets over except that maybe I could have prevented the disaster on Hamburger Hill. But in tandem with the Ewell situation, what this meant was that my big mouth and stubbornness had cost me the chance to command a brigade in combat in Vietnam.)

Still, at the time I left Ewell, I had the impression he was going to get me assigned to his headquarters come hell or high water. In the morning I called Timothy to ask him to make sure Abrams knew I wanted to go with him, and then hotfooted it up to Pleiku still three or four days early, just to be on the safe side. There, I took my place among the thousands of U.S. advisers all over Vietnam who were tasked with the difficult job of turning the war back to the Vietnamese. How prescient Colonel (later Brigadier General) Ted Mataxis's fear had been, expressed as a warning as early as his advisory days in 1962, of the war becoming "Americanized." It had indeed become that over the last four years, so much so that now, from President Nixon down through the multilayered American command, the act of "Vietnamizing" it was as deathly serious as it was basically absurd. In the months ahead, I would also find it was coming much too late.

The six months I spent at II Corps were noteworthy only in that they were a complete waste of time. My job was to assist ARVN's II Corps in the area of operations and training, through my "rapport" (the magic word in the advisory effort) with my II Corps G-3 counterpart, Colonel Binh, and the forty U.S. personnel in my G-3 advisory shop (each of whom had his own ARVN counterpart to advise in some G-3 area, be it air, artillery, signal, chemical, operations, training, plans, etc.). But very little was actually accomplished. For one thing, at corps level we were too remote from the action to make much difference. For another, we on the advisory team were so inordinately busy shuffling paper and managing ourselves that many times the advisory part felt almost like an afterthought.

More than half my time was spent writing reports that were little more than collations of the written reports coming up from the battalions. (As I wrote to my brother after three months in the job, "Busy as hell moving rolls of red tape. This advisory duty is one big reporting task. Everyone is interested in how ARVN is doing. But advisers cannot assist because they are too busy writing reports.") Most of the other half of my time was spent on matters dealing strictly with the Americans in my section—personnel

problems, rotation, and the like—and in my subsequent advisory assignments, the amount of time required in this area only increased. It was easy
to believe the experience related to me by one AID adviser I knew who'd
worked in the same province from 1964 to 1968 and watched the adviser
numbers therein swell from twelve people to some two hundred. Far more
good was accomplished with the first dozen men, this AID guy said, than
ever was with the next 188.

On the other hand, whatever the advisory effort's bureaucratic hurdles did
to impede a concentrated, effective push toward Vietnamization, at Pleiku
I concluded pretty quickly that the South Vietnamese at corps level did not
particularly *care* about Vietnamizing the war, much less about our advice to
that end. The main reason for this, as far as I could guess, was that they
really didn't think the Americans were going to leave. Over the past four
years the U.S. had fought the big-unit war for the Vietnamese, and allowed
them to sit back in a passive/defensive role (guarding towns, defending
fire-support bases, and, on paper at least, securing the people under the
guise of pacification). While we'd built our own empires in Vietnam, those
mammoth U.S. base camps and overstaffed American advisory HQs, we'd
allowed the Viets to grow fat and complacent and to turn the war into a
business venture. We'd even allowed them to become the best VC recruiters
in the country by not stopping them from acting out the role of occupier—
raping women, stealing livestock and rice—rather than protector of the
people. Over the past four years, few Americans had pushed ARVN to
perform, and few had pushed them to train. The Viets had gotten used to
the musical-chairs game of second-string and/or unqualified advisers—
artillerymen, tankers, air defense, and military intelligence personnel—
rotating through infantry battalion and regimental advisory slots one after
another, all with bright ideas that (after three or four advisers) the Viets had
learned how to stall until the adviser inevitably went on to a new job and the
Viets could maintain the status quo. The Americans had never put their foot
down before, and MACV's sudden tough talk now was so antithetical to the
"blank check" attitude of the last fourteen years of advisory assistance that for
many of the Viets it didn't even register.

My counterpart, for example, was a shrewd entrepreneur who owned
houses all over South Vietnam (which he rented to the Americans at
exorbitant prices). Wherever we went—to Hue, Nha Trang, Qui Nhon,
wherever—Colonel Binh owned a house. He'd say, "Oh, I bought this one
two years ago" (or "five years ago" or "six months ago"), and in each one I
found the same permanent fixtures: two Rangers from II Corps' 22d Ranger
Battalion. "I borrow soldiers and they guard my houses," Binh would
explain, smiling brightly, leaving me not just to wonder what kind of IOUs

this corps G-3 must have had over the 22d Rangers' battalion commander that he could usurp perhaps twenty of his men to secure his real-estate empire, but also to marvel at the fact that it truly did not occur (or matter) to Binh that those Rangers might have a more critical role to play in the ever-Vietnamizing war effort and beyond.

The II Corps G-2 was another character, who had a tendency to ignore any and all intelligence his counterpart, my good friend Colonel Wyatt "Jim" Mitchell, passed on to him. Much of this information came through radio intercepts and other high-tech means, and it was accurate, often red-hot stuff. But this guy went out of his way to avoid anything that could possibly involve fighting or pursuing the enemy. It was not unusual at this time for an American adviser to discuss a planned operation with his Viet counterpart in exceptional depth, making sure the latter understood exactly where it was to happen, when it was to happen, how it was to happen and *why*, only to turn around and find the operation had been killed. No reasons given—it was just killed. In II Corps we also had a special problem with the stars. The Vietnamese II Corps commander, Lieutenant General Lu Lan (who, like most of the Viet corps commanders, generally acted more like a feudal baron in medieval Europe than a tactical leader), did nothing without first consulting his astrologer (a ritual, it might be added, that would be taken up and practiced in the White House throughout most of the 1980s). On one occasion, the General refused to conduct an operation, despite reliable intelligence that it was a fat, soft target, because his astrologer told him he'd have bad fortune if he ran such a mission during that particular period. There was no point in arguing with him. I recommended a B-52 arc-light strike instead. The way I looked at it was the astrologer was probably VC (why not? Hitler's was a British agent), and we probably got more kills with the B-52s than we would have had with ARVN's typical "search and avoid" the enemy anyway. (That was not being harsh. Over one three-month period at the weekly Review and Forecast Briefings for IIFFV CG and II Corps senior adviser, Lieutenant General Charles Corcoran, the total result I had to report from eighteen hundred ARVN ambushes was six dead Viet Cong. On one occasion, when I was able to say that one of our ARVN units had engaged an enemy unit and actually cleaned them up, with a body count of twenty-two *with* weapons, General Corcoran had been damn near elated: "It's reports like these," he said, "that help a fellow get through the day.")

The tremendous shortcomings of ARVN, which Vietnamization was "suddenly" highlighting, were nothing that hadn't been identified years before. The big difference was that last time around, the Pentagon and the White House had had the option of using U.S. ground troops to keep

ARVN from being swallowed up, an option now of steadily decreasing availability. David G. Nes, who served as deputy to Ambassador Lodge in 1963–64, was one who had warned early of the likelihood of the eventual disintegration of ARVN as a fighting force. But his bleak assessment and realistic suggestions regarding the war were considered nothing short of heretical by Generals Harkins and Taylor, and he was removed from his post the minute Taylor replaced Lodge as ambassador. Five years later, however, little in Nes's accurate assessment had changed, and this fact alone made the outcome of the first major test of Vietnamization, the Battle of Ben Het, fought in the Highlands of II Corps in May–June 1969, as predictable as it was a complete mess.

Not unlike Tou Morong, Ben Het was a CIDG outpost that came under enemy siege. Only this time, the allied troops coming to the rescue were all Vietnamese, with the U.S. providing only support (air, artillery, and choppers) and limited engineer assistance. The operation was doomed from the start, because ARVN in II Corps was not properly trained, motivated, or led for success. One of the major problems was that most of the soldiers in the regular ARVN units up there were city boys. They were homesick, they hated and feared the Highlands, and considered assignment there the worst of all possible hardship duties. Their junior officers felt the same way, and did little or nothing to raise morale or foster the will to win. In addition, the heavily forested Highlands terrain was not conducive to the conventional infantry tactics the troops' superiors and advisers had been calling on them to use since 1956. While ARVN stumbled along, trying to maneuver in impossibly thick bush, the enemy just set up ambushes that the South Vietnamese walked into again and again. In the Highlands, ARVN was always reacting to the enemy's moves, and almost always coming out with a bloody nose. The result was units suffering heavy desertion rates (20 to 30 percent per year), and those who remained behind fighting exactly as they might have been expected to, given their low morale and bad leadership in this hostile terrain.

During the seven-week siege on Ben Het, the ARVN elements tasked to relieve the outpost moved toward their objective in halfhearted, torturously slow, battalion-size formations. They dragged their heels and called for U.S. air and artillery, and bugged out in the face of any tough opposition, leaving the U.S. arty and engineers supporting them to fend for themselves on the battlefield. This desertion under fire created an explosive situation between U.S. and ARVN units because of the high U.S. casualties that resulted. General Timothy was at his very best during the battle, defusing the acrimony between these "allies" and flying to Kontum to push and prod the lethargic 24th Special Tactical Zone command structure into taking charge of the fight. The General also flew into Ben Het under heavy fire to set the example for the U.S. Special Forces–led Montagnards within. It was a gesture much appreciated by those tenacious fighters, who held on despite the constant battering and repeated attacks on their outpost.

In the end, the defenders at Ben Het did remain King of the Mountain, and this result compelled MACV to proclaim the battle as yet another "great victory" for our side, and proof for all the doubters that Vietnamization was working. But even the most cursory examination of the facts revealed a different story. First of all, the men who held their ground at Ben Het were CIDG troops, not ARVN. And second, while these irregular forces were temporarily able to hold their ground, what had caused the NVA to run away was U.S. air power: tac air and B-52s, tons of bombs and napalm clobbering down and inflicting an estimated three thousand enemy battle casualties. ARVN had nothing to do with the "victory" at Ben Het, and anyone who doubted it need only have looked at the ARVN relief force sent to the outpost's aid. It didn't even arrive at Ben Het until *three days after the last shots were fired*. Whatever the hype, the truth was that ARVN had failed dismally in its first real test.

Some four months later the South Vietnamese Army showed its stuff again, during the Battle of Bu Prang. It was another case of a CIDG camp under siege, another case of ARVN leadership showing no offensive spirit, another case of U.S. firepower (twenty thousand tons' worth) saving the day. And another victory was proclaimed.

It seemed almost incredible that at this critical time in the war the truth of ARVN's inadequacies was not being acknowledged, much less addressed. Despite the billions of dollars spent and the number of American lives lost on the Viets' behalf, it was as if nothing had changed since the early sixties, when the silencing of David Nes and other bearers of bad tidings like John Paul Vann had sent a clear message to those who also recognized the truth but valued their careers more. Criticism of our ally was forbidden. Wave making and boat rocking were distinctly frowned upon. *Especially* in the advisory effort. Diplomacy was the key, a "be-polite-we're-guests-and-remember-it's-their-war" philosophy, which after 1965 was patently untrue, but which, once adopted (and in the years since), had allowed South Vietnam to hustle the United States as adeptly as the smoothest carnival barker.

It was a fundamental flaw in American policy toward South Vietnam. While all along we paid the bills for the war effort and kept our toys and boys coming, we had little real control—indeed, took little real control—over the Viet leaders on the receiving end. And we never would, a fact the Viets probably knew better than we did (and a reason why they probably thought we'd never really pull out and go home). While the American advisers should have been—particularly in this period of Vietnamization—romping, stomping, asskicking Emerson- and Willis–like sons of bitches growling, "You want a blank check? Okay, I'll give you the check, but I expect 'x' amount back in dividends. No return, no more dough, you got the picture?" in fact the advisory effort, at least what I saw of it at II Corps HQ and its subordinate units, was overloaded with "go along to get along" yes-men. There were a few good studs here and there, but not enough to win any ball games;* the problem was that advising, like training, was a job almost totally without glory, and since the full-scale U.S. involvement in the war, generally the only infantry types who got shunted off to the advisory effort were second-stringers who more than likely would not get a U.S. combat command slot.

Whether or not ARVN recognized this situation per se I didn't know. But it was easy to see they knew who had the upper hand *and* how they got it. As the years had passed with the always diplomatic and polite U.S. advisory effort never establishing procedures to keep its ARVN counterparts in line (i.e., preventing them from buying and selling Army commissions, promotions, or U.S. service-school assignments, preventing them from taking bribes and demanding payoffs, from stealing their troops' meal allowances, from being promoted and put into better jobs mere weeks after being found guilty of corruption), ARVN had developed exceedingly effective methods to keep their advisers in their place. This was really just a matter of our arrogance: we assumed we understood the Viet mind and therefore didn't try to; the Viets, meanwhile, watched us carefully until they found out where we lived, and then they went right for it. "Keep Your Mouth Shut" medals—colorful, plentiful, and totally meaningless Vietnamese awards and decorations that the Americans had no business getting anyway—were a prime example. The Viets dangled these things before their adviser counterparts like a carrot before a horse's eyes. Such pieces of plastic and gaudy ribbon were eagerly sought after by the careerist ticket punchers among us, to fill out their fruit salads and give the impression of being warriors to those not in the know. In fact, the awards were "automatic issue," the basic criterion being nothing more than "having been there" in

---

* One very good man was a young Military Intelligence captain named Harry Riley, who arrived at II Corps' 22d ARVN Division expecting to be assigned somewhere as an Intelligence adviser and instead, despite his having had no experience in infantry since he went through OCS seven years before, was assigned as an infantry battalion adviser. Riley had never called artillery, controlled tac air, or requested medevac; the next day, when his new unit got clobbered on a hot LZ, he learned all three real quick while his counterpart, the Viet battalion commander, lay shaking in the foxhole his batman had dug for him the minute the first enemy shots rang out. But it was just the luck of that outfit that Harry Riley was the man he was, able to pick up the pieces of a bad situation rather than fall apart himself; and in the advisory stakes he was unquestionably the exception, not the rule.

a job or on a mission. The Viets quickly discovered, too, that their adviser counterparts were loath to be brought to the attention of their superiors in anything less than a glowing light. The very idea that "Major Hardass does not understand our country or our people. He has such an embarrassing way . . . it is disrupting my unit's performance . . ." might be passed up the advisory chain of command sent shivers up many an adviser's spine, and most felt it easier just to play like The Three Monkeys than run the risk of being singled out in this way. (It didn't help either that every adviser knew his career could suffer if the Viets in his charge did not show progress. As such, it was a widespread procedure among the advisers just to inflate the ARVN outfits' unit-readiness reports—just as U.S. units did their own—to reflect progress rather than strive and possibly fail to really achieve it.)

The U.S. command's inexplicable policy that made American advisers one to three grades lower in rank than their Vietnamese counterparts (*and* without any command experience in units the size they were advising) was another block to a successful advisory effort. Again, at root was our arrogance: was it reasonable to expect a Viet major general division commander who had been involved in the war for twenty years to listen to an American colonel with six months' brigade command experience now just passing through the advisory chain for another six months or a year? Hank Emerson had the best idea for rectifying this problem. He believed that not only should U.S. advisers be assigned grade for grade with their counterparts, but that a successful battalion, brigade, or division commander in a U.S. unit should become a battalion, brigade, or division adviser *in his very next assignment*. Then, since we would have had the experience *and* paid the bills, instead of pandering to our counterparts, we could have *told* the Viets what was to be and damn well expected them to listen. One of our most critical failures in Vietnam was in not properly training and motivating ARVN, and Emerson's idea would have gone a long way in the right direction.

While still at II Corps I received a back channel from the Secretary of the Army, Stanley Resor, who wanted to talk to me when he came to Pleiku. My superiors the whole way up to General Corcoran were beside themselves, thinking I must be really tight with the Main Man. And while it was true I'd had a number of dealings, all of them good, with Resor when I was at the Pentagon, the essence of our relationship was he was a man who liked the straight skinny, and he knew he could get it from guys like me or Emerson or Vann—the warriors—with no bullshit. Resor himself had been an Army captain and rifle-company commander in Europe during WW II. His philosophy as Secretary stemmed in part from

this period of his life: he knew how hard it was for men at the cutting edge
to get their feelings up through channels undiluted, so he made a point of
consulting them directly.

So, when we met in Pleiku and I told him we were losing the war this year
much faster than we had the last, Resor didn't get shook up or try to prove
me wrong. Instead, he asked me for my recommendations. Top on my list
was my belief that if Vietnamization was to have even the smallest chance
of working, the advisory effort was going to have to really smarten up its act,
and put an end to its musical-chairs game of allowing essentially unqualified
American officers to pose as advisers for short stints and then go home. In
what would sow the seeds for the senior adviser Handclasp program that
came into being the following year, I suggested that besides being chosen for
their competence, combat savvy, and ability to kick ass and get the job done
for a change, advisers should have much longer tours, and that as an
incentive to stay on in Vietnam, their families should be moved nearby, to
the Philippines, Hong Kong, or Thailand, with the advisers getting a
three-day leave every month to be with them.

At the end of November 1969, General Timothy and his principal staff
went to Nha Trang to brief COMUSMACV Abrams, who was visiting
IIFFV. Grayish in complexion, pudgy, and smoking an incredibly long
cigar, Abrams already looked like a beaten man (after all, he had the most
unenviable job in Vietnam, as promoter of Vietnamization and overseer of
our defeat), but with it all he was still a warrior, and during a coffee break
he called me over. "How's it feel being on ice, Hack?" he asked.

"Pretty terrible, General. I'd really like to go back to the field. And I'd be
damn careful, General, believe me."

"Well, the Airborne Division will soon be needing an adviser," he
replied, springing a most welcome hidden agenda. "See Smith and tell him
to cut your orders. But I don't want to see you getting hurt, understand?
Because if you do," this great old soldier warned, "you'll be right back on
ice."

"Yes, sir!"

I went to see General Albert Smith, Abrams' J-1, knowing that with
Abrams' blessing already in my pocket the new assignment was a fait
accompli. I was right, but my orders didn't come without a price: an
incredibly cynical lecture from the J-1. "Go home, Colonel," Smith said.
"The war for the U.S. Army is over in Vietnam. You've got all the right
credentials—there's nothing more to be gained here for your career. So go
home. Go to War College now. Prepare yourself for bigger things."

Smith's words were actually heartbreaking. *I'm not over here to prepare myself for bigger things!* I wanted to shout at him. *We're fighting a war! I want us to win! What bigger things are there?*

I went home between assignments for what proved to be a watershed leave. I'd been away a year; just off the plane at LAX I found myself immediately wanting to change into civilian gear—every step I took in uniform seemed to evoke some snide comment or insult or glare from total strangers. *Who's the enemy here?* I wondered. I'd never experienced this before.

There was a message when I got to the house that Ward Just had called. I rang him back and he flew out from Washington to discuss *Military Men*, his work in progress (and another eye-opener for me).

During this leave, too, after almost twelve years, I realized that it was time to call it a day with Patty. The Army life had finally won out, as it was probably destined to: I liked adventure, I liked the bachelor life, I wasn't cut out for family life or fatherhood as much as I loved my children (and I did). I felt pretty well vindicated in my decision to leave by the fact that I'd been little more than an absentee husband and father anyway, and since I'd encouraged and supported Patty as the kids got a little older in her long-deferred nurse's training, it wasn't as if she was helpless now—she had a career. In keeping with my totally self-centered logic, this meant she didn't need me, so I was free to go. But I didn't tell her much of this. I just went back to Vietnam, and for all intents and purposes never came home again.

7 April 1970

Dear Ward. . . . Regarding ARVN . . . I am convinced that they will never make it. The individual soldier has the potential to be great. But to be great he needs leadership and that is the rub. The Vietnamese just don't produce leaders. It is something in their sociological makeup. As a young officer they are afraid to make a decision; as they grow older and develop and gain rank, they acquire the minimum creature comforts—neat apartment, Rolex, several wives, the little leaguers a Honda and big boys a Toyota. To have these goodies they must wheel, and wheel they do. Virtually everyone has a gimmick going for him . . . designed to produce loot. Now producing loot leaves little time for fighting a war. And after a fellow has his fair share of goodies who really wants to fight? So as I see it the gut issue is the Viets do not have the will to fight. Helicopters, modern equipment, and the endless search for the magic panacea . . . that will replace the well-led soldier is not the answer. Leadership is the only answer. And I just do not think that the Viets can produce the type of leadership that is required. The fuckers are too corrupt, too lazy, too stratified (classwise), too indifferent, and too blasé to care. So we can continue to pour in the dollars and our nation's blood. But it will all go into a bottomless pit that will eat and eat and eat and then finally collapse. I say the red, blue, and gold [the flag of North Vietnam] will fly over Saigon within three years after the last U.S. unit embarks for home.

For an infantryman, an ARVN Airborne advisory assignment was the top adviser job in Vietnam, because the ARVN Airborne Division was the elite unit in the South Vietnamese Army. The overall quality of the ARVN Airborne advisers was first-class. There was a long waiting list among U.S. personnel to get in; guys fought for a place because it was great duty: you got a good punch on your ticket, combat was quick in-and-out raids (not months in the boonies), you got to wear a cut-down, very sexy, French camouflage parachute uniform complete with a red beret (which, when augmented with big sunglasses and highly polished jump or jungle boots, made us all look like young Errol Flynns), and when in Saigon you had your own billet with every possible creature comfort.

The Airborne Division, elements of which had been formed by the French and fought as early as 1951 in the Indochina war, had been the nation's Palace Guard since 1955. Throughout this period the Airborne also had acted as ARVN's theater reserve, playing "fire brigade" a brigade or two at a time as required, but always being pulled out and sent back to Saigon as quickly as possible to guard the palace and reconstitute the reserve. As the war progressed and Vietnamization became the rage, more and more Airborne battalions found themselves in the field more and more of the time, until, shortly after I joined the unit, only one battalion was left in Saigon at any one time while the rest of the ARVN Airborne began joint operations with the U.S. 1st Air Cav Division. The Cav provided some training and the helicopter lift while the Airborne provided the bodies. The hope was that the Cav's great fighting spirit would rub off on the Airborne's leadership, and the ARVN unit would pick up the ball and run with it.

Although technically I'd been an adviser for the previous six months, the switch from II Corps to the Airborne Division was, for me, a big one. At Pleiku I'd learned almost nothing about ARVN or the Viets who made up its ranks. I'd been so busy writing reports up there that the only close contact I'd had with the Vietnamese at all was when Colonel Binh had held my hand. (Apparently it was just a Vietnamese sign of endearment, but for me, a big, badass paratrooper, it had been truly agonizing to be at a meeting or at some lower-level command CP, pretending along with General Timothy and the rest of the II Corps advisory staff to be influencing the course of events, and feel Binh's soft, tiny hand creep into mine and hold on tight.) In Saigon with the Airborne, initially as a brigade adviser and then as the division's deputy senior adviser, for the first time I really had to deal in a concentrated way with the Vietnamese character, and with how the Vietnamese war machine functioned at the cutting edge. The experience was mind-blowing, and if it could be rationalized at all, it was only in terms of its being a real miracle that there even *was* a Vietnamese war machine.

Fifteen years before, the French had pulled out, leaving a Viet force of fewer than 100,000 men. There were very few leaders. The French had left the Vietnamese completely unprepared for self-management, government, or defense, and though the United States quickly came in to take care of training and rearming ARVN (in the image of its own armed forces), in the late fifties the Viet Army, specifically its officer corps, was also the pool from which the country's civil service cadre and province and district chiefs (governors and mayors) were drawn. All things considered, these men were the only ones with sufficient managerial skills to turn on the power, control the water board, and keep things running on the political and economic levels. But the constant drain of officers spread ARVN very thin during those formative years, and the situation was only exacerbated by the fact that even the best of ARVN's officers weren't so great in the first place: most senior leaders had not truly earned their rank, having advanced thanks to the patronage of Emperor Bao Dai and then President Diem, and succeeding generations of officers' appointments were not due to any particular qualifications for the job, but came about through the influence of family, friends, or cold hard cash. Furthermore, since under Diem the system was so completely centralized that any military operation of battalion size or larger had to be approved by the president himself, there was no room for growth among those in leadership roles, even those who might have started out with genuine ability.

Meanwhile, thanks to the American advisers' conventional mind-set (which from the outset foresaw the shape of North Vietnamese aggression to be a blitzkrieg attack across the border à la Korea 1950), from the first, ARVN was not trained for the guerrilla war burgeoning within its own boundaries. In fact, in 1961, 80 percent of ARVN's 170,000 troops were posted along the DMZ in blocking positions or garrisoning Saigon, leaving only some 34,000 ARVN soldiers to actually go out, beat the bush, and fight the incipient war in South Vietnam. Yet now, just nine years later, ARVN numbered over a million men, an instant army zipping all over South Vietnam in helicopters, employing all the latest, complicated equipment of a modern Western army. It seemed to me that the level of their effectiveness notwithstanding, and whatever criticism might be justifiably laid on them, the fact that ARVN had been able to adapt to the mammoth changes within the last decade *at all* was no mean feat. On the other hand, I soon learned that adaptability was probably the Viets' strongest point, when it suited their ends

The more I was with the Vietnamese, the less I knew what to expect from them next. Most of the ARVN officers I dealt with exhibited traditional Vietnamese behavior patterns (which included the inability to rock the boat or kick ass), but many of the more senior officers had also gone to top

French schools, and so had developed a decidedly French "air" as well. They were real smoothies who seemed to have retained only the faults of the French military establishment from their educations during the French occupation. As a rule, these officers were arrogant, blasé, careless, and unpunctual; they often showed an open disdain for efficiency, hard work, and organization, and, among the many who were Northerner-Catholics, there was a singular lack of interest in the welfare of their mainly Buddhist, peasant-class troops. When the Americans came, these traits cultivated under the French didn't disappear; instead they were layered over, as the remarkably flexible Vietnamese began to metamorphose into what, in the Airborne at least, was a casting director's absolute model of an American paratroop officer. Good-bye, Charles Boyer; hello, Charles Bronson. The new look was a cigar and sunglasses, whitewalls and crew cut, excellent military bearing and perfect U.S. Airborne slang like "Hey, babe, how's it hanging?"

They could have been Hayeses or Emersons if they weren't Oriental and it wasn't all an act, an act with the specific purpose of impressing their American counterparts. For as much as the Viets had many a career-oriented adviser by the balls with the promise of medals and the unspoken threat of a critical word to his superior, the advisers had one big thing over the opportunistic Vietnamese that the Viets never forgot: the power to recommend (or not) a Viet for a service school in the U.S.A. It was a number-one goal, an assignment to the Big PX in the Sky, where a Viet officer got paid what a U.S. officer of equal rank received, and a small fortune could be amassed while living on the sniff of a rag. (At the Career Course and C&GS I'd seen it: the Viet students cooked their meals in their rooms, hung their laundry all over the BOQ, and all in all adopted a do-it-yourself approach that, according to my Special Forces buddies freshly back from advisory tours, saved bucks to buy goodies to send home to friends, families, and all-powerful patrons, who could resell them for many times the price on the black market.) So to reap this reward the chameleonlike Vietnamese officers watched and listened and studiously took on all the trappings and habits of the all-American trooper; their unenlightened, tourist advisers would look at them as Narcissus might his reflection in the pool, and be delighted with what (they thought) they saw. The Viets' adept mimicry was their secret weapon in an ongoing game of keeping their advisers at bay (a game seemingly taken far more seriously than the war). The mirror-image approach masked all too well that they in fact had little leadership ability, no initiative to act in the absence of orders (after twenty-five years of fighting, most everyone who exhibited such traits had long ago been wasted in battle), and no will to win.

There was one great battalion commander in the Airborne Division by any army's standards. A former corporal who'd reportedly fought with the 6th Battalion of the French Army under Major Bigeard at Dien Bien Phu, this CO had worked his way up through the ranks, been battlefield commissioned, and, without French or American training, attained the rank of lieutenant colonel. Thanks to his gutsy leadership, the battalion he commanded was the best in the entire division. Due to his modest, Buddhist background, he was known to all as "the Peasant Colonel." The day came that the division needed a brigade commander and the division CG (Northerner-Catholic) Major General Du Quoc Dong, asked for an adviser recommendation as to who should get the job. To me, the only man with the goods was the Peasant Colonel. As far as I was concerned, he was the ideal choice for any senior leadership position in the Airborne, perfect for the cocky, street-wise, similarly backgrounded peasant kids who made up the division, who were proud of their outfit, and with the right leadership could have rivaled any unit in the world. But when I made my suggestion to General Dong, he rejected the idea outright. "He's not politically acceptable. He doesn't even speak English," Dong snapped. "He has no contacts, and he could not be trusted." As an adviser I had no power to make my advice a demand, so the Peasant Colonel stayed right where he was. Another arrogant, mainstream smoothie got the job, and the war went on being lost.

The most frustrating thing about this episode was that in all likelihood General Dong could have given the brigade CO's job to the Peasant Colonel despite the latter's political "unacceptability" and few in the government would have said a word. The government needed Dong, Commanding General of the Palace Guard, as protection against any threat, real or potential, to the present military regime. He was the ace in the hole in any attempted coup (in the numerous coups that had occurred in South Vietnam after Diem's death, it was the fidelity of the Airborne Division that each time sealed the outcome), and his continued allegiance gave Dong an automatic IOU with President Thieu and tremendous power overall. And power was very much what Dong was in to. He was an explosive guy with a violent temper; whenever he got angry (which was often), he beat the object of his wrath with his swagger stick or whatever else he had in his hand at the time. Once I was in his helicopter with him when his signal officer, a captain, couldn't raise a unit on the radio whom the General wanted to speak with. The captain was a well-connected mandarin prince whose family had looked after him and made sure he was kept away from direct combat (he'd done the full rounds at Benning—Ranger, U.S. Airborne, Pathfinder, and Infantry courses as well as commo school), but he was also a nice boy and a totally competent signal officer. Unfortunately Dong couldn't see this. All he saw was his will being thwarted, and he immediately began walloping this officer with his swagger stick. The General was in what I considered a truly insane rage, and I could see him beating the kid to death at fifteen hundred feet without a second thought. Fortunately I was sitting next to Dong, on the same side as his beating arm, so when he raised it for another swing, I just grabbed it and held it down on the seat between us. The General gave me a daggerlike glare with those cold, beady eyes of his that always reminded me of a dead fish; I didn't bother to look back. I just held that shaking arm down until I felt Dong had controlled his rage. I never said a word to him about it, then or ever, and neither did he.

When he wasn't busy beating his subordinates, Dong lived like a king. A wealthy man by Vietnamese standards, he had two Vietnamese chefs, one trained for Chinese and the other for French cuisine, and his field generals' mess put out five-star gourmet spreads. From time to time the chefs would serve up some very exotic Chinese or Vietnamese delicacy like fresh monkey brains or aged raw duck eggs (which were purple and yellow with veins popping out and a smell that would drop a skunk); on those occasions I'd tell Dong I was going to eat C rations with my boys. It took me months to deprogram myself from the basic advisory word, that you had to learn the customs of the guy you advised and live by them down the line. The idea was sound, but like so much else in the U.S. Army, it had gone to an extreme. Besides, General Dong's feelings weren't hurt when I left him to his pickled, veiny duck eggs. He didn't expect me to parrot his ways; the only people who did, I found, were the Army academics who wrote the book, and many of the tourist advisers. It seemed to me that my boss, Colonel Charles Greer, was among this group. "It is incumbent on the adviser," he would counsel me when I behaved like myself rather than a stupid, submissive toady, "to establish an effective relationship with his ARVN counterpart." To Greer, who as ARVN Airborne's senior adviser advised General Dong, that meant making no waves and playing it Dong's way; the "effective relationship" that resulted was more a case of Dong, who'd been with the Airborne since he was a second lieutenant in 1951, running circles around the American. Or so it appeared from my point of view as deputy. And ironically, while Greer worked overtime at cultivating his "effective rela- tionship" with his counterpart, from the first day he seemed to go out of his way to alienate his own command. In his first advisers' meeting as senior adviser, for example, he announced policy changes to include our having to get rid of the wrist compasses most all of us wore. "What is this," he snarled, "some kind of CHEAP FAD?" I tried to explain that wrist compasses were essential when conducting airmobile operations and suggested, since he'd been in-country only a few days, he reconsider. The net result of that was not only did we still have to get rid of the wrist compasses, but we had to prove we'd done so by putting them all on Greer's desk, like dutiful fifth graders.

My view of the advisory effort was that whatever the politics, the facts were that we were leaving and the Viets were staying; we were paying the bills and we were going to see something for our money *if it was the last thing the Viets did*. The minute I took over as the Airborne's deputy senior adviser, I put out the word that if Vietnamese commanders refused to run their own shows, then the shows just wouldn't go on. The Viets had come to believe (and to date had had no reason to think otherwise) that their advisers would do anything and everything necessary to assure their missions were accomplished successfully. Now they were going to learn that advisers weren't supposed to (nor were they going to) "do" anything *but* advise. It was up to the commanders to make things happen, to call and adjust artillery, to control tac air, to handle medevac, and to pick up their own chips when things got sticky. The new policy was not well received, to say the least. Fortunately, besides having inherited such great warriors as Old Army First Sergeant Leo B. Smith (1/327) with the Airborne advisers, I'd been assembling my team since my earliest days at Pleiku and now I had a lot of my boys at battalion level to override all objections and get the thing implemented. Among these guys were Peeping Tom Hancock, who hadn't changed a lick since we were together in the 1/327 (and whose latest gimmick was pretending to speak Vietnamese to impress his tourist superiors; whenever any American colonel, general, or visiting fireman came around, he'd count from one to ten and back again very quickly in the language to the nearest polite but oh-so-puzzled Viet), and Ben Willis, whom I'd snatched from behind a desk at IIFFV by trading him for two majors (and whose opinion was that ARVN was no better in 1969 than they'd been during his last advisory tour in '64 and '65).

The new, no-bullshit approach to the advisory effort worked. Once General Dong even told me he knew we Airborne advisers were doing a good job because so many of his commanders were complaining that they wanted one or another of my boys at brigade or battalion level relieved for being abrasive and demanding. But while it made me feel great to know we were making a dent, I never questioned that it wouldn't last, and that when the Americans had gone, the only thing the ARVN would have any hope of winning would be volleyball, a game the South Vietnamese were absolutely brilliant at, showed far more interest in than the war, and in the Airborne played most afternoons at Division Headquarters.

*   *   *

The automatic ambush was a brilliant concept pioneered by the 1st Air Cav Division that was just beginning to be implemented in the Airborne at the time of my arrival. The device was basically any number of claymore mines, camouflaged and attached together by a wire, which itself was attached to PRC-25 battery some fifty meters away. Usually an automatic ambush was set up along a trail, and the beauty of it was that long after friendly troops had split the scene, if the trip wire of the device was disturbed, the trigger mechanism at the battery would be set off and an electric current would shoot down through the wire, detonating all the claymores. *Look, Ma, no hands.* It was a devastating weapons system.

I loved it. The automatic ambush did not run away or search and avoid or play possum. The automatic ambush could inflict max punishment on the enemy at virtually no cost to the Vietnamese. It was just perfect. So I made it my personal campaign to make sure the word got around. I convinced General Dong and Colonel Hau (the Airborne's Assistant Division Commander and my counterpart) of its usefulness. I got an automatic-ambush training team from the 1st Air Cav to really get the Airborne troops turned on to the thing. I made sure all the advisers knew how it worked, taught their counterparts, and pushed its use. I wrote a fact sheet on it that I sent to scores of colleagues all over Vietnam, and wrote an article about it as well that was published in *Infantry*. In the first five or six weeks of widespread use in the Airborne, automatic ambushes claimed more enemy dead than the human elements of the entire division did during the same period.

But then—no more. As usual, the enemy got the message that we had something new out there that hurt, so they stopped using the trails we targeted that they'd almost invariably taken before. From then on, the automatic ambush worked only when we moved into a new battlefield where the enemy wasn't familiar with it, and even then it was good for only three or four days, until he wised up. Yet General Dong kept pushing it to his brigade commanders. I'd listen to him telling them to set these things and I just couldn't understand it. It was so out of the Vietnamese character to expend energy on something that wasn't netting any return. So finally I asked him. "I'm all for the automatic ambush, General Dong, but you know the enemy's on to it. We haven't had a kill in the last month. Is there any reason why you're still advocating it so strongly?"

"Haven't you noticed?" Dong replied.

"Noticed what?"

"The great amount of venison and boar and other fresh meat we've been eating recently in our mess."

"So?"

"The animals were killed by the automatic ambush. It is a fine hunting device."

In the ER Colonel Greer rendered on me before I left the Airborne, he wrote that my "extended service in Vietnam" caused me "to be impatient with ARVN counterparts," which in turn "reduce[d] my effectiveness in an advisory role." Naturally I disagreed. I didn't hit the roof when Dong told me of his new use for the automatic ambush, even if it cost the U.S. perhaps a thousand dollars for every boar he ate for dinner or sent via chopper to a Saigon friend. I didn't even blink when Colonel Hau took me on his rounds to the province chiefs in our AO to collect his share of the chiefs' "takes" collected as tax from all the Viet businesses in the individual provinces (though I think in Hau's case my reasoning was that at least he was up-front with his corruption and never tried to bullshit me about it, and because when he wasn't drinking—an admittedly rare situation—he was a brilliant tactician and one of the only decent things in the leadership chain the Airborne had going for it). And though I almost cried when I heard that down in the Delta Fire Support Base Schroeder—a Siegfried Line–like position manned by ARVN since the 9th Div's departure and named after fine warrior Don Schroeder, who'd been killed there—had been overrun, I did not lash out (even if only apathy could have allowed the VC that success, and it was just *such an insult* to Schroeder's memory). No, the only times I really got angry were when I saw ARVN officers at District or Province, particularly officers I'd met when they were in STRAC Airborne/Special Forces assignments, who'd gone into a total mandarin scene. Because these types epitomized the worst of ARVN's middle-level leadership, the reason why the FSB Schroeders could be overrun, and why ARVN just didn't stand a chance.

You could always tell when a Viet had quit being a soldier and become a businessman by the fingernail on the little finger of his left hand, which he'd grow very long, and by the hair he'd start growing on his face, wispy strands that could hardly be called a beard but which said it all about where the guy was coming from. In these cases, what my ER rater called impatience I preferred to see as a veteran's attitude of cutting through the bullshit. Whenever I ran into one of those ex-stud mandarin types, I always greeted him with a big smile, and only after I'd shook his hand and told him how good it was to see him did I bend that long little fingernail the whole way back until it broke. And only after I'd complimented him on his beard did I grab hold of those few little strands and yank them out. "Don't you think it's time you go back to a unit, Major?" I always said. Sometimes it worked, sometimes it didn't, but at least they knew someone was on to their game.

Corruption was a way of life in the ARVN and it wasn't going to go away. But it took an enormous toll on the leadership chain. As hard as so many of the advisers tried, and even with the help of (the few) gung-ho, caring Viet leaders in the Airborne, I saw little progress, or hope, in getting these guys off their asses on a full-time basis. And if the Airborne—ARVN's best-equipped, best-supported, best-advised, most elite division—couldn't hack it in the long term, what could possibly be expected from the average Viet unit? Too many of the officers, from platoon level to division HQ, were the sons, brothers, and friends of bankers, generals, and politicians— extremely well-connected individuals who had allowed the business of war to take a backseat to the business of business. Many of them had their own very successful enterprises going full bore on the side, generally operated by their wives, and their subordinates had but two options: to mill around like lost sheep or get their own piece of the action, even if on a smaller scale. It was not difficult to understand which option they'd choose.

Probably the most striking aspect of my tour with the ARVN Airborne was the chance it gave me to look at what the Americans' war had done to the economy of South Vietnam, and how money was made and lost by so many in this unharnessed, war-torn land of opportunity. In the big leagues there were people like the woman I called Dragon Lady, whom I played blackjack with whenever I was in Saigon, along with John Westmoreland, other longtime American advisers or civilians working for the U.S. in and out of the military, and a number of well-monied Vietnamese and Chinese.

While most Viets were addicted to gambling, the women often had the biggest habits. Dragon Lady was hardcore. She could drop throusands of dollars in a game and still be back at the table the next night. A sensuous, beautiful, very feminine woman who'd had an "eye job" to become as round-eyed as her Western sisters, Dragon Lady was an unlikely-looking gambler. But she well fit the mold of most women in Vietnam: while on the outside you got the impression they were all soft, pliant creatures subservient to their men, behind the scenes they actually ran most shows, and with an iron hand. From the infamous Madame Nhu on down, the women in this matriarchal society were the brains and guts of the nation; as one unusually frank Vietnamese officer told me, "If the women were in command of our army, the war would be over in a year." Dragon Lady was also very well connected (she was the wife of a Viet three-star general) and not hesitant to take advantage of it. Just one of her setups was to pay Colonel Bao, Chief of Staff of the ARVN Airborne Division, five hundred dollars (American) a month to keep her brother in Saigon as a training officer rather than ever sending him into the field.

Over time Dragon Lady and I became good friends. So good that if I was winning big at the table and she was getting short, I'd lend her whatever she needed. Lending money in a blackjack game isn't exactly wise, but the woman always paid me back; the reason money was no object for her was that her and her husband's main business was laundries, and their company did most of the laundry for the U.S. Marines in I Corps. Dragon Lady also owned a couple of bars on Tu Do Street, which were real money spinners and licenses to steal, and another among her very successful deals was trading in gold. She told me she'd met some Laotian pilots who were smuggling stolen gold into Saigon direct from the Laotian treasury at Vientiane. The way the scheme worked was they'd come to her with fifty thousand dollars' worth of gold bullion that, because it was "hot," they'd sell to her for half its value, and which, in turn, she'd make a killing on by turning it around in Saigon. The very lucrative routine had been repeated four times before I knew about it; Dragon Lady was a shrewd woman, and I'm sure I wouldn't have known about it at all if she hadn't come to me one day asking for a short-term loan. As her story went, the pilots had told her the Laotian authorities were closing in on the scam, and since they could risk only one more haul, they were going to make it a big one—a million dollars' worth of gold, which they'd sell to her for a mere five hundred thousand. Now Dragon Lady was going around trying to raise the cash.

I didn't loan her any. In fact I told her to be careful—the whole thing sounded too easy. But she got the money in loans from her well-heeled friends, and soon handed over half a million bucks in exchange for a million in gold. Of course (as these stories have to end) she was screwed: the Chinese gold broker who assayed the gold found she'd bought a footlocker of lead bars coated with, at most, ten thousand dollars' worth of the real stuff. "You warned me," she said when we next met, "but I was too greedy to see. I am very sad that it happened, and I am very sad for my friends who lent me money. But I will pay them all back." And she did, with her laundries and her bars and her other schemes, all directly or indirectly bankrolled by Uncle Sam through our own naïveté.*

Among the smaller-time operators, the protection racket was a big money-maker. On one occasion a few Saigon "cowboys" (a.k.a. "slicky boys," and easily recognized by their Honda motorcycles and Seiko watches, the gold Buddhas hanging from gold chains around their necks, and the chunky gold bracelets on their wrists) decided John Westmoreland's bars needed their protection, and that Westy would pay them for the privilege.

---

* Some estimates had it that one-fifth of Vietnam's annual budget was scooped off the top in Saigon, and either sent to overseas banks or used to finance businesses not unlike the Dragon Lady's in all the major cities.[1]

To cinch the deal they paid a visit to the New York Bar on an evening Airborne advisor Tom Hancock (whose battalion was the current Palace Guard) happened to be there drinking with John. As Westy told me the story later, the cowboys separated the Americans, and while two of them sat down with Westy, discreetly training their pistols on him under the table as they made him an offer he couldn't refuse, a third cowboy covered Hancock with a pistol at the bar. It was almost a replay in reverse of my run-in with the crazy captain from George Company in the 223d, who was only prevented from blowing my brains out by the quick thinking and boldness of John Westmoreland. Being the brave, cool old warrior that he was, this time around Westy grabbed the two guns trained on him under the table and pointed them (still in the hands of their owners) toward the floor. Then he flashed Hancock the same "do something" look I'd given to Westy seventeen years before. All Hancock had to do was disarm the guy covering him (easy at such close range), knock him on his ninety-pound ass, and then go help John. But he didn't. Instead, he froze. Meanwhile the guy covering him quickly got over his surprise at Westy's bold move, rapped Hancock hard across the face, and as blood flowed out of his cheek, warned him not to move or he was dead. So Hancock didn't move. And while the two cowboys with Westy were still struggling under the table to get their pistols back into action, the third hood left Hancock, broke a beer bottle, and went for Westmoreland's face. The result required some forty stitches.

The following morning, Hancock's Vietnamese counterpart sent a number of Airborne troopers to beat up the cowboys who beat up Westy and Hancock. For the next few days he also stationed members of his battalion at the New York Bar, day and night, in full gear. It wasn't exactly a subtle way to say nobody messed with the ARVN Airborne or their advisers, but it worked, and there was no further trouble at the New York Bar. As time passed, most of Westy's scars disappeared into his already well-weathered face, and while Hancock's did not, at least he got some character into his movie star's mug. Why Peeping Tom hadn't been up for the game when Westy needed him in the bar was something that initially struck me as odd, but for some reason I never gave it further thought. It was my mistake, however, because it might have taught me some things about the guy that, in future, I would have done well to know.

So there was money in gambling and money in protection, but there was also money in money, specifically greenback (U.S. dollars) and scrip (U.S. Military Payment Certificates). MACV had extremely strict currency regulations to prevent abuses of the monetary system. (On the other hand, MACV had extremely strict regulations about everything, and I doubted there were many MACV personnel in Vietnam who hadn't broken one or two of them within their first month in-country.) It was totally against regs, for example, to even have greenback on you, and woe be to the soldier, officer, U.S. civilian adviser, or journalist caught shopping among the money changers to get the best price for his dollars, rather than putting up with the always depressed legal rate of exchange. When Slam Marshall paid our hotel bill in greenback, he'd committed an offense punishable (at the very least) by expulsion from South Vietnam, yet green was used in this way every day, all over the country, by mostly everybody who'd been in Vietnam long enough to know the score. While no doubt the regulations kept money changing from becoming a widespread industry during this time, the general consensus among the old-timers was that currency manipulation was a fact of life in Vietnam, and only a fool would *not* take advantage of the system to get a better price for his scrip or that little leftover greenback he had after R&R.

For the Vietnamese, the currency manipulation game was far more serious because it often involved people's life savings. Thanks to the Americans, inflation in South Vietnam was so outrageous that the piaster was not worth the paper it was printed on. As such, despite another currency regulation which stated that Vietnamese were not authorized to hold U.S. Military Payment Certificates, many times Viet officers would convert their pay or their savings from piaster into MPC and have their counterparts hold it in the advisers' safe. Of course, holding MPC for the Viets was also in violation of the currency regulations, but since getting your Vietnamese counterpart to do *anything* positive toward the war effort was often as hard and painful as pulling teeth, what better leverage could you have than his life savings locked in your safe? The practice worked fine unless or until the safe was knocked off, a calamity that befell the ARVN Airborne advisers' safe and, by extension, one of my majors who'd stashed a thousand dollars in MPC in there for his Viet counterpart. It was a bad situation for the young adviser, a straight-arrow guy and a real comer in the Army: if he took responsibility and paid the guy back himself he'd be out several months' pay; if he told his counterpart the truth and didn't make good the dough, he would lose face and thus his effectiveness; and if word of what happened got to Colonel By-the-Book Greer, the major would be in serious trouble separate and distinct from his dilemma over getting his counterpart his money back. So he came to me. Besides never having been in to court-martials, it seemed to me to be a hell of a lot easier (and fairer) just to find a grand to replace the one lost than to prosecute this guy and ruin his career. So I organized a truckload of beer at the PX through a good Airborne sergeant, and sold it to John Westmoreland for the cost of the beer and a thousand dollars neat. Westy would have paid ten times that price on the black market, so naturally he snapped up the offer; strictly speaking the transaction made me a black marketeer, too, but my conscience was clear. I was helping out a subordinate in a jam and a good friend in the deal. The major got the dough back and his Viet counterpart was never the wiser. I did, however, put a stop then and there to the practice of stashing counterparts' fortunes in the advisers' safe.

At the end of April 1970, a warning order came down from MACV: "Prepare a task force from the Vietnamese Airborne Division to launch an attack into Cambodia. Highest priority." The cable said that ARVN Airborne forces would enter Cambodia as part of a theater Cambodian operation, with the mission of finding and destroying Hanoi's Central Office for South Vietnam (COSVN). Throughout the war, COSVN had been, in the minds of the U.S. command, the Communist equivalent of MACV Headquarters in Saigon. The powers that be figured if it took such a mammoth apparatus as "Disneyland East," as MACV was known, to conduct the war on our side, surely the North Vietnamese would have a similar structure to command the forces on theirs. No one seemed able to grasp that COSVN was more than likely just a few guys on bicycles, and as I reread the mission statement I concluded I was having some sort of mild, mad fantasy. *After all these years*, I thought, no one truly believed that COSVN existed in such a convenient or conventional way. *And no way*, I thought, would the Airborne or anyone else be invading Cambodia— certainly not after all these years—without a declaration of war. Invading Cambodia meant violating the sovereignty of a neutral (albeit nominally so) nation, something I was sure America would never do. But just then Colonel Hau came into my tent waving a parallel order. "I know, Colonel," I told him, "but don't worry about it."

"But we've been told to develop plans!"

"Fine," I replied. We went over to the Operations tent and in about fifteen minutes we'd laid out the general concept. It was just a quick Fort Benning exercise; as far as I was concerned, I'd left fantasyland.

But two days later we received instructions that the operation was a go. General Dong had conveniently made himself absent from the division, so Colonel Hau was to lead the Airborne task force. I, as his adviser, would go along.

Colonel Hau was most excited. "We must go to Saigon to brief the President on the plan!" he enthused. I accompanied him as far as the Presidential Palace, but when Hau went in to talk with Thieu, I went out on the Saigon streets to hunt down Don Baker, my good friend who shared my birthday and was the electronic Ernie Pyle of the Vietnam War, as ABC television's top war correspondent. I had to tell him we were going into Cambodia. I didn't care if the plan was top secret, or that to discuss it with him would be a serious security violation. I wanted Don to be there with his camera and his tape recorder, because somehow I thought that would stop it. Somehow I believed that if he scooped the story we wouldn't go. But I didn't find him, and he didn't get my message in time, and the next time I saw him was on D+3 or so, when a helicopter full of correspondents, the victims of a total press blackout for the first few days of the operation, spilled out onto Cambodian soil. And by then, of course, it was too late.

The Cambodian exercise was the straw that broke the camel's back for me about the war in Vietnam and the direction America was heading. Militarily the operation was correct: a basic rule of counterinsurgency is to deny the insurgent a sanctuary (and as David Nes had warned Ambassador Lodge six years before in his memo of 10 March 1964, "A Communist insurgency having access to an active sanctuary has always prevailed."). But what was wrong with it, besides the fact that it came five years too late (five years in which our Army lost the lion's share of its great NCOs and stud officers, and the American people lost their stomach for the conflict), was that the way it was done violated all the principles the United States of America, the country I loved and I soldiered for, was built on. Cambodia was a *neutral* country. Our incursion, at this time in the war, with no prior notice to the fledgling Lon Nol government or even to our ambassador to Cambodia, was not, to my mind, any different from the Japanese bombing Pearl Harbor. In my estimation the exercise was an immoral, ill-thought-out venture, and one that would prove to be both an expensive tactical donnybrook and an irreparable strategic defeat.

The basic thrust of the attack consisted of the Airborne task force (using U.S. 1st Air Cav choppers) conducting airmobile assaults onto multiple LZs inside Cambodia, with armored columns linking up with us. I thought the armored bit was most appropriate: the essentially German blitzkrieg technique was not unlike that the Nazis used to invade Poland. We jumped off and encountered little more than token resistance. According to the caught-in-the-middle Cambodians, the enemy had abandoned the area the night before by vehicle, bicycle, or foot and headed west. The mission had been compromised, but it was little wonder; though most of the task-force elements had had less than twenty-four hours' notice of the plan, the South Vietnamese command structure was so heavily infiltrated with VC that news of the impending attack may as well have been broadcast over psyops loudspeakers. (This was not to say we didn't have any contacts, but for the main it was hit-and-run stuff—mines, booby traps, and snipers left behind in a deadly screen to draw blood. And draw blood they did. Just one example was Hancock's battalion, which went into Cambodia with 425 troops, got 100 replacements during the sixty-day mission, and though they never even saw one good fight, they still came out with only 200 combat-effective men.)

On the second day of the operation, one of our fighter aircraft got hit while conducting an air strike. The pilot ejected, but as he came down, his parachute became entangled in a tall tree, leaving him dangling in midair. We saw this from my chopper and flew to the rescue. The only way to get the guy was to hover just at treetop level (some sixty feet off the ground) and pull him up into our bird by his chute. The pilot himself couldn't help: the emergency eject system in his jet had catapulted him out but left his legs, from just above the knees down, inside, under the instrument panel. Not an unusual accident, just a small design flaw. So the guy was unconscious, if not dead already, gushing blood straight down, with no chance of survival unless we got tourniquets on what was left of his thighs and got him some medical attention. Then I saw on the ground North Vietnamese troops, complete with camouflaged pith helmets, running toward the scene from all directions. Both door gunners of our chopper took them under fire, but they kept coming, and a wave of despair washed through me. Not just for the pilot, but for the whole damn show. *How can we win?* I asked myself. On the ground we had a brigade-plus of Vietnamese paratroopers who couldn't find a sizable organization to do battle with. Yet the minute a worthwhile target appeared (and bringing home a jet pilot was obviously a big deal—gold-watch material maybe—in the people's hero awards department of the North Vietnamese Army), the enemy magically appeared. They used their tunnels and their camouflage and they sat out our game year after year; just as quickly as they appeared now was as fast as they would disappear again—and again and again—and it just all seemed so futile. Or at least the way we were going about it.

We continued pulling the injured pilot up by his tangled chute, until we started taking hits from enemy fire (bringing home a helicopter was probably an even bigger deal than a jet pilot). By this point we almost had the guy in the bird, but with one slug being too many for a thin-skinned chopper (and we took a bunch), it was clear we weren't going to get the injured flier out before the NVA got us. So we had to let him go. In truth, he was probably dead, and had been throughout our attempted rescue. But it didn't make any of us feel any better as we flew away, to see him dangling lifelessly and leglessly among the trees, like an abandoned marionette, with the enemy swarming below.

The invasion was characterized by heavy, heavy bombing and wholesale destruction of Cambodian towns and villages. Snoul, the only place any real NVA resistance was felt, was positively leveled. The centuries-old hatred between Cambodia and Vietnam led to bloodshed of its own, and the looting was almost unimaginable. As the days passed, whenever I looked into the sky I saw furniture, motorcycles, and luxury automobiles (Mercedes, Peugeots, Citroëns) flying along, suspended from Vietnamese Air Force (VNAF) choppers bound for some senior ARVN or VNAF officer's home, garage, or other stash point. Another big item was livestock, and it was quite a sight watching cows zoom along in midair on their way back to Saigon's slaughterhouses.

On the third day of the operation the Airborne captured a huge cache of medical supplies from West Germany, Britain, and the Quakers in America. The lot, according to one of our medics, was worth at least half a million dollars. That evening, as I watched it being loaded onto VNAF choppers en route to Saigon, I decided to send one of our medical advisory sergeants along on one of the flights, to find out the final destination of the supplies. My suspicions were well founded. Instead of being recycled to ARVN medical units or impounded by the government, the valuable cargo was taken to big commercial warehouses controlled, I was told later, by the overall commander of the Cambodian show, Lieutenant General Do Cao Tri, the III Corps CG. Tri's reputation as a remarkably corrupt figure was well known, and there seemed little doubt his windfall of medical supplies would be sold to drugstores and doctors and whomever else was willing to pay Tri's price. Meanwhile one of my adviser sergeants had his portable radio stolen, and when I suggested in response to his grumbling on the subject that maybe it was because in the eyes of the Vietnamese he must be a rich man to even own a radio, he said, "Oh, I'm not bitching because they stole my radio. All I'm saying is these bastards are so slick they could steal the radio and still leave the music." Which about said it all.

Within the first three days of the Cambodian operation, U.S. officialdom Humpty-Dumptied their definition of "success" for our mission. Realizing that COSVN wasn't to be found in Cambodia's "Fishhook" or the neighboring "Parrot's Beak" or anywhere else, for that matter, the U.S. command decided just to change the objective. Now the highest priority (and the mark of our success) was to be in uncovering enemy caches. Fortunately this worked out just fine for U.S. spokesmen: we found great quantities of ammo, weapons, rice, and other supplies in masterfully concealed depots, and either ferried them out or destroyed them in place. Romping, stomping Green Beret paratrooper Lee Mize, my Medal of Honor–winning friend from Germany and C&GS, commanded a Mike Force battalion (composed entirely of Cambode troops) that uncovered a substantial cache of beautiful Soviet SKS rifles; I flew in to his position to see him and he gave me a few dozen for trading purposes.

In all, Cambodia was mines and booby traps, snipers and small hit-and-run attacks on our units, which pretty well eroded whatever fighting spirit our ARVN charges had had. Cambodia was red dust, churned up from rich volcanic earth by bombs and choppers, that settled on hair and clothes and skin not unlike that mosquito repellent that had turned my guys' faces black when they used it as fuel for lights back in the hill people/bunker rat days of Korea. Cambodia was more of the same superior, condescending bullshit from ARVN officers toward the men they led, like the soldiers of one paratroop company who sat in the darkness along their perimeter eating cold rice, while, protected within, their company commander hosted all his platoon leaders to a lantern-lit, laughter-filled party at his CP that began with a beautiful meal (hot chicken, rice, and vegetables, all of which had been looted from a village they'd just gone through) and ended with a big gambling session that went on well into the night. If an American CO had tried this he probably would have been fragged.* But since that particular response was outside the Vietnamese character, officers went on thinking nothing of flaunting the privilege they felt they deserved, never realizing that the day might come when their men said, "No more."

Cambodia was just waste on a colossal scale, irrespective of the temporary closure of NVA logistic facilities and their significant losses in war matériel. It was an old story repeated many times of an ARVN unit reporting contact with a large enemy force, and rather than hammering away at their foe with machine guns and infantry fire as they'd been trained, they would use it as an excuse to go to ground and take a siesta while calling for U.S. air support. On one occasion a 1st Air Cav aerial rocket artillery (ARA) battalion put more than ten thousand rounds on one of these reported "large enemy forces." At $107 per round, that was more than a million dollars in rocket ammunition; the final result in body count was seven enemy dead.

But few advisers ever told this or any other ARVN battalion commander that $153,000 worth of ammo for one enemy KIA was an unacceptable price. Our own rich ways had totally corrupted them. And since it was allowed to go on, the Vietnamese had grown up little different from the spoiled children of very rich and doting parents. Unlike the Viet Cong and the NVA, they didn't have to believe in anything. They didn't have to have a cause. It was as if we'd taken over that responsibility when we'd taken over the war. We would always be around, they thought, and they never doubted that every gift and every goodie they could possibly want or need would always be there for the asking. So they never felt the need to try for themselves or take care of what they had. I saw it all the time. Once I saw

---

* "Fragging," an all too common occurrence in the latter half of U.S. involvement in the Vietnam War, entailed a troop killing, or attempting to kill, his leader with a fragmentation grenade.

a brand-new VNAF helicopter land near my CP. Had the bird had an American crew, immediately upon landing, everyone—the crew chief, gunner, pilots—would have hopped out and begun checking, tightening, lubricating, and cleaning that chopper, making sure it was in virtually mint condition before it took off again. But in the case of this VNAF aircraft, the South Vietnamese crew hopped out, had lunch, hung their hammocks up, and went to sleep, refusing even to respond to the tactical emergency of a fellow ARVN unit (it was having the shit shot out of it) on the grounds that they'd just started their lunch break. A couple of hours and no maintenance later, the Viets folded up their hammocks and got back into their bird. As they took off, the pilot allowed the skids of the chopper to get caught between the strips of perforated steel plate (PSP) that made up the helipad, and the bird flipped right over, killing the pilot and crew chief and badly banging up the other two inside. In less time than it took to say "*Sing loi*" ("Sorry about that"), a Vietnamese favorite and the most overused and insincere cliché in Vietnam, a $250,000 helicopter had been destroyed and a million dollars' worth of training was down the tubes. On another occasion, when a brand-new chopper being used for medevac went down through sheer recklessness on the part of the Viet crew, I told Colonel Hau, "The crews must learn to be careful. These helicopters are very expensive. We cannot afford to make these mistakes."

Colonel Hau shrugged. "We will just get another one," he said.

Should it have been any surprise that the war was busting the United States financially? Or that the Viets would not have a hope in hell when the fateful day came that they could *not* "get another one," when our horn of plenty dried up, when we took away our tremendous air power that ARVN had grown all too accustomed to hunkering down and calling for instead of fighting it out themselves? And in the meantime, was there any appreciation on the Viets' part for what we had done for them to date and what we were trying to do for them now? If I'd ever thought there was, the belief vanished the night on the ground in Cambodia when I had a long drinking session with Colonel Hau. Freshly "liberated" cognac flowed, and as Hau got progressively drunker, the discussion turned to the American Airborne advisers. "You're no different from the Nazis," he said, with his rich French accent. "Look at you. Blue eyes, blond hair, all of you. The Super Race. For you it is a game of power and killing and glory. You killed President Diem. Your Provincial Reconnaissance Units are now killing our people with abandon. Look at what your bombs and gunships did to Snoul. Look what they do to my country. You make our villages just disappear as you please. You're just like the Nazis."

My anger rose up immediately. It burned my face as I struggled not to say anything, to remember *He's just drunk, he won't even remember it tomorrow*. He did, though, and from his inability to look me in the eye the following morning, it was obvious he regretted his words. But by then I'd recognized some truth in them. The Provincial Reconnaissance Units (PRU) alone bore Hau out. Soon to be renamed (and infamously remembered as) the Phoenix program, PRU was a CIA-trained and -led organization made up of the rougher VC *chieu hois*. Their mission was to go into the villages and one by one knock off the VC infrastructure (VCI). The idea was good and it was the only way to outterror the terrorists, but the execution was bad news. There was little accountability among the individual PRU forces, and already stories were emerging that the Viet participants used their positions as license to indiscriminately steal, torture, and murder, irrespective of their victims' real VCI complicity.

Many of us were blond-haired and blue-eyed. And the ARVN Airborne advisers were particularly STRAC—precise, professional Regular soldiers, probably the best U.S. advisers ever brought together on one team. The invasion into Cambodia had shown our Nazi side, there was no question about that, but what I should have told Hau was that if we were Nazis, we were monsters, and who the hell wasn't a monster in this war? American democratic monsters fighting Communist monsters while supporting Saigon monsters and corrupt military-official monsters who didn't give a damn about the people in the first place. The analysis didn't make Hau's close-to-the-bone charge any easier to take, but at least it gave it a little perspective.

Not long after the Cambodian invasion, a postoperational briefing was held at the 1st Cav CP. Among those in attendance was a young brigadier general with brand-new, rumpled green fatigues and the pasty-white face of someone who's been sitting at a desk too long. It was Army bureaucrat Alexander Haig, visiting from Washington as the President's representative, taking a breather from his job as Kissinger's National Security Council aide on his totally inexplicable, meteoric rise to power in the Nixon Administration. During the briefing, everyone talked about the operation enthusiastically, as if it were the greatest military feat since the Inchon invasion. By the time I was asked to comment on the Viet Airborne's performance, I'd had enough. In what was no doubt my typically abrasive style, I disagreed with just about everything that had been said, and after voicing my opinion that the entire operation was a disaster, tactically and strategically, I said that the U.S. had violated everything it stood for by even attempting it. "It's not the American way," I wound up. When I'd finished, I had a roomful of people glaring at me. Then one of the generals locked my heels together and told me to shut up and sit down.

Cambodia broke my spirit, though I'm not sure I knew it at the time. Unconsciously, I believe I made my decision to quit the U.S. Army then and there, and to leave America, because I couldn't cope with us becoming Nazis or killing students on college campuses simply because they wanted the country out of a bad war. On the conscious level, however, while as an American I was sick in my heart over what we'd done, as a soldier, I was just angry. The Cambodia exercise *was* a disaster. Five years too late in coming and then no COSVN, no destruction of large enemy formations, no victory of any description, just the galvanizing of people all over the world against our presence there. How different it would have been had Generals Harkins and Taylor listened to David Nes rather than firing him to shut him up in '64. How different it would have been had Swede Larsen and all the other generals who knew the truth stood in the door in '66, when Larsen was made to "stand corrected" by Defense Secretary McNamara in his indisputable statement that the NVA were using Cambodia as a sanctuary. How different it would have been had Westmoreland just remembered Napoleon—

A commander in chief cannot take as an excuse for his mistakes in warfare an order given by his sovereign or his minister, when the person giving the order is absent from the field of operations and is imperfectly aware or wholly unaware of the latest state of affairs. It follows that any commander in chief who undertakes to carry out a plan which he considers defective is at fault; he must put forward his reasons, insist on the plan being changed, and finally tender his resignation rather than be the instrument of his army's downfall.

—and told LBJ in '65–'66 that he wanted permission to knock out all sanctuaries and simultaneously close the Ho Chi Minh trail or else Johnson could find himself another boy. But Westmoreland didn't stand up and speak out, and neither did any of the other generals, then or at any time during the war, who saw even from the earliest days that ARVN was a spent force that would never win, and that it was not possible for us to do it for them given the political constraints. So what followed instead was deception built on deception, a lot of money, a lot of death, and *to what end?*

In June I left the Airborne Division to take the job as senior adviser to the 44th Special Tactical Zone (STZ), despite Colonel Greer's ER suggestion that I not be given any more advisory assignments due to my impatience with the Vietnamese. I was able to arrange to take a lot of my team with me, so I couldn't say I had any regrets; I had to admit, though, I felt a bit bad about having to leave behind the ARVN Airborne's volleyball team, which really was the best volleyball team in the history of mankind. *The Best Volleyball Team in the History of Mankind.* On more than one occasion during this tour I'd wondered if Ho Chi Minh's successors had any plan for volleyball in their new order. Now, as I was leaving, I realized it didn't really matter: when the time came, at least the Airborne would have a pretty catchy epitaph.

21 A LAW UNTO HIMSELF

I never worried about him getting killed. He might get wounded,
but in my mind he was incapable of dying in war. He wore golden
armor. He was invincible.
  I did worry about him getting in trouble.

B. Tim Grattan
Platoon Leader, Company Commander
1st Battlegroup, 18th Infantry
Germany, 1961

THE escort convoy of gleaming MP jeeps roared through Cao Lanh
at max speed, sirens blowing, flags flying, machine guns trained menacingly
on both sides of the road. God help anyone or anything in this Delta village
that got in the way: be they oxcarts, bicycles, chickens, or foot-mobile
peasants carrying heavy loads, all were splashed with mud flying up from the
rain-soaked road or sent scurrying out of the way. Some were even flattened.
It could have been a scene from a movie, or a mechanized version of the
great mandarin prince returning to his palace; what it was, in fact, was
Colonel Hanh, my counterpart and commander of the 44th Special
Tactical Zone, making a routine journey back to his plush Cao Lanh villa
from the Zone HQ helipad, and alienating all the people whose hearts and
minds he had to win if we were to win.
  The first time I saw this procession I would have laughed if it hadn't been
so sickening. Hanh was extremely fat (by any standard, much less a
Vietnamese one), with Barney Google eyes, an arrogant manner, and no
concern at all about the people he hurt or the hatred that burned in their
eyes. As his new adviser, I told him the warlord crap had to stop; he couldn't
have been less concerned about what I had to say either, and as he waddled
away I knew it was just the beginning of a long struggle between us, one that
would end only when one of us got fired.
  At the time I arrived in the Zone, the Viet command I was tasked to
advise was like a one-year no-wind clock at the end of the 365th day—i.e.,

on its last tick. There was little sense of urgency; when President Thieu came to visit the day after I got there and I saw rocks being lined up and duly painted, equipment that hadn't been maintained since it left the depot suddenly becoming the very focus of attention as the Viets dashed around their seedy compound in frantic preparation for Thieu's arrival, I marveled at what might have been achieved if only we could have captured all that energy, will, and can-doism and converted it from facade building to fighting the enemy.

Team 50, the U.S. advisory command I took over, was also in pretty poor condition, in large part the result of three months of nonstop Cambodian operations, which had stretched people and assets beyond the breaking point. But that was not all. The men of Team 50 were also suffering from long-term isolation. Cao Lanh village, home of the 44th STZ Headquarters, was located in the boonies smack-dab in the middle of the Delta, which itself was in the middle of nowhere. The team compound, a rectangular fort abutting another rectangular fort that belonged to Colonel Hanh and our counterpart Vietnamese command, was in a terribly run-down state, its security tenuous at best, and it had virtually no recreation facilities. There was simply nothing to do there. My first thought was that jail couldn't have been much worse than the conditions the men of Team 50 were enduring, and while I well understood the widespread lethargy and apathy among the team, what amazed me was that guys hadn't gone truly crazy there, within what was nothing but an endless circle of unsatisfying work and unshakable tedium.

As was my SOP, right away I started bringing in my own team to breathe a little life into the outfit. Milt Menjivar and Tom Hancock joined from the Airborne Division, and guerrilla commander Ed Clark came from the 4/39. First Sergeant Joseph Dayoc (B1/327's first sergeant in '65–'66) and Lieutenant Colonel Burt Walrath signed on from the 1/101, the former as Team 50's new Sergeant Major, and the latter, most recently G-4 of the 25th Division, as my deputy when his outfit went home. Walrath brought with him a windfall of Lightning Division supplies and equipment (including a complete Military Affiliate Radio Station [MARS]) that went a long way toward sprucing up my new command. Jack "Frenchie" Frye, my wayward private in D Company/18th Infantry, now a STRAC master sergeant with three years' hard combat duty in Vietnam under his belt, was another welcome addition to the team, and many others were in the pipeline, including levelheaded warrior Ben Willis, who joined as soon as he got released from the Vietnamese Airborne Division.

Concurrent with the advisory side of things, my first order of business in the Zone was to build esprit into my tired command. Fortunately, in so doing, I was able to attend to my second order of business as well, which was to get our moribund living situation squared away. Operational conditions permitting, every afternoon around 1600 the whole listless group met at the volleyball court. We then divvied up details that, as scrounged materials became available, would ultimately result in one rebuilt compound. No one wore jackets during these sessions so there was no rank; as majors, captains, lieutenants, sergeants, PFCs, and two light colonels all worked, sweated, and got in shape together, we also forged a team.

The overall purpose of the 44th STZ was to interdict enemy infiltration of both personnel and supplies from Cambodia through the Delta. The mission of Team 50 was to advise and assist the Vietnamese Zone commander—a division-level command—and his subordinate units to that end. At this time in the war (July 1970), the Zone did not have many fixed regular units to accomplish the task. Other than three Viet Ranger battalions and Company D, 5th Special Forces Group (and its Viet counterpart organization), which commanded a number of predominantly Cambodian Airborne-trained Mike Force battalions, the Zone's units consisted solely of all the Regional Forces and Popular Forces (RF/PF) in the area. Any other regular ARVN units we might need—Airborne, Marines, armored cav, or straight leg infantry—were attached to us on a mission basis from all over Vietnam.

Our AO was about the size of Luxembourg. It was a huge battlefield, which ran through the Mekong Delta from An Giang Province in the west, along the Cambodian border, to the III Corps boundary in the east. It encompassed three provinces (and parts of two more), and sat astride the major infiltration routes that led to War Zones C and D near Saigon. I was very familiar with the eastern part of the area at least, from my 9th Div experience. The Hardcore had conducted many an operation in the Kien Tuong and Dinh Tuong provinces.

It had been a year since my last view of the Delta, and had I been a casual observer or a one-year tourist, things would have looked just great. VC activity seemed to be at a minimum: there were almost no big fights, roads were not being cut, VC tax collection didn't appear significant, and there were few terrorist tricks. All in all it was a quiet battlefield (unquestionably, the recent attacks into Cambodia had knocked the enemy off balance and torn deeply into the VC supply setup), and the tourists were once again crowing "we've got them on the ropes," as they took the enemy's lack of aggressiveness as a sure sign of defeat. Anyone who'd been in Vietnam for any decent length of time, however, or had any understanding at all of the nature of the war, knew that that was too simple an analysis. The VC were not on the ropes. They'd just shifted down to a lower gear, as they had after they were hit so hard in Tet of '68. They'd gone back to Phase I insurgent warfare: educating, getting to the people, rebuilding their infrastructure, solving the complex logistics problems that the joint U.S.–ARVN forays into Cambodia and the closure of the port at Sihanoukville had dealt them—in short, doing all the things necessary to maintain their ability to fight a protracted war. Always a step behind, the U.S. strategists were measuring the VC's Phase I activity in the Delta on a Phase III (WW II) scale and delighting themselves with the result. But even worse for the war effort during this critical period of Vietnamization was these strategists' accepting, without examination, an untenable corollary to their (incorrect) assessment: that if the VC were down and out, then ARVN must be up and running.

Nothing could have been further from the truth, and the Zone was a perfect example of why. Under Colonel Hanh, the South Vietnamese forces in the Zone had reached a complete accommodation with the enemy. While the U.S. 7/1 (Black Hawk) Air Cav Squadron (who'd worked with us in the 9th Div and now were OPCON to the Zone) went out day after day, finding the enemy and stirring up fights with scout and gunships, whenever they got something decent going and relayed the word back to Hanh's CP, they'd be told that no troops were available for commitment that day, or that it was "too late," even when their call came early in the morning. When Black Hawk CO Lieutenant Colonel John "Jack" Woodmansee alerted me to this routine, I immediately made plans for it to stop. No way was the Air Cav going to fight the war for Colonel Hanh. So the next time Zone G-3 Adviser Tom Hancock got word from the Black Hawks that the Viets were "unavailable" to pile on a contact the Air Cav had stirred up, I played my card.

I called Woodmansee and told him to give his men the next day off—I didn't want any choppers sent to the Zone. The next day came, and with it a very perplexed, soon-to-be-irate Colonel Hanh. "Where is my Air Cav?" he asked.

"It's not your Air Cav," I said, "it's mine. And you're not getting it anymore."

"Why not, Colonel?" Hanh demanded.

"Because every day you and your troops sit on your asses and let the Air Cav fight the war for you. You're not pulling your weight. And if you don't pull your weight, you don't get shit from me. Ever. So no choppers. Not today, tomorrow—not *ever*."

Hanh couldn't believe his ears. He stormed through the door between our offices in our little command building on the Vietnamese side of the compound, threatening to call my superiors all the way up to the President, and assuring me I'd soon be out of a job.

Two more days passed. Hanh complained to anyone who would listen. I remained immovable, though I did have to explain what I was doing to my boss, Major General Hal D. McCown, the CG of Delta Military Advisory Command (DMAC, soon to be renamed Delta Regional Advisory Command or DRAC), who supported me 100 percent. Meanwhile I took the time to try to figure out why, besides the accommodation factor, the Viets so obstinately refused to make helicopter insertions in the first place. (Woodmansee had done a study and discovered they made pitifully few in relation to the number of times they used Air Cav assets.) It soon occurred to me that perhaps part of the problem was that after all this time they still didn't really know how. So on the fourth day, I wandered into Colonel Hanh's office. My counterpart was sulking. "You know, Colonel Hanh," I said, ignoring the fact that he didn't acknowledge my presence, "you could be a hero."

Hanh was immediately all ears. "A hero?" he repeated, his Barney Google eyes popping, already envisioning himself in an even bigger convoy of jeeps, with more flags and louder sirens.

"Yup. You could be *the* Air Cav expert in Vietnam."

Our tiff was suddenly forgotten as Hanh eagerly embraced the idea. "But how do I do this?" he sputtered excitedly in his French-accented English.

"Colonel Woodmansee will brief you on the plan. And I think it is very important for all your commanders to learn all they can about employing helicopters on the battlefield, too."

Jack Woodmansee, meanwhile, didn't have any particular "plan" to brief Hanh on, but he used the opportunity to introduce the Viet colonel to all the things he'd been unable to get through anyone's head in the past. The net result was a fine program in which the 7/1's ground troop gave the Zone's units a week's training each, after which the Cav's choppers came in and gave the Viets a chance to *practice* inserts and extractions and to get acquainted with the birds, with a U.S. sergeant advising.

I soon realized that the only leverage I had over my counterpart were my assets and his greed. As soon as we got the first Drama of the Choppers out of the way, another began when I told Hanh I wanted operations seven days a week. Because the war under Hanh was a nine-to-five, five-days-a-week, business-as-usual affair, the VC in the Zone were extremely loose, security-wise, on the weekends. So I wanted to take advantage of their vulnerability at this time. "But Colonel Hackworth," Hanh protested, "my soldiers have been fighting for twenty-four years. They need to rest on weekends. It is different for you advisers. You only stay for one year."

After reminding him that many of my guys were on their third and fourth tours, and that most of his commanders had been *avoiding* battle for twenty-four years, thereby rendering his entire argument null and void, I said, "A key principle of war is surprise. The VC would never expect us to launch an operation on a Saturday or a Sunday, so if we did, we would achieve surprise. Now, my job is to get you off your ass and start you fighting this war yourself in the most effective way possible. If you don't want to do it, okay. If you don't want to take my advice, fine. But if you don't, I promise you're not gonna get a thing from me, Colonel Hanh. Not even the time of day."

As was par for the course, Hanh immediately tested me on this. At the next morning's briefing, while I was being briefed by Captain B. J. Jensen, our Black Hawk LNO, on the allocation of all the assets (three choppers to move ammunition to a fire base here, twenty choppers to operate with the Rangers there, etc.), I was told Colonel Hanh had a chopper going from Cao Lanh to Saigon. "What's that one for?" I asked.

"His wife, sir."

"Scratch it," I said.

After the briefing I went back to my office on the Viet side of the compound. Within minutes the phone rang. It was Colonel Hanh, next door. "And how are you, Colonel Hanh?" I asked.

"Oh, not very happy today, Colonel," he replied.

"I'm sorry to hear that. It makes me sad that you aren't happy," I said. "Why aren't you happy?"

"Well, there has somehow been a bad mistake made."

"A mistake? Where?"

"Within your headquarters, Colonel. The helicopter I ordered for my wife is not available, and she is ready to go to Saigon today with her friends to shop."

"There's not going to be any helicopter for your wife, Colonel Hanh. I cannot afford that kind of blade time. It's a wasted asset."

"Oh, that makes me very sad," Hanh sighed.

"Yes, I am sad, too," I said. "Why don't you tell her to take a jeep? I'd be happy to give her one of our jeeps. It's only 150 klicks through safe country, according to ARVN and MACV reports, and she'll enjoy the ride. She could visit the people and tell you what's happening with them, the ones we're fighting for."

"Oh, Colonel, she would not like that at all. May I come to see you?"

"No, I'll come to see you." I put down the phone and walked through the door into Hanh's office. I sat down. "This is a very difficult problem," I began, "but I do believe we could work it out if you agreed to kick off that operation we discussed for Sunday, Monday, and Tuesday."

"Oh, you are a very difficult man, Colonel."

"I know that, Colonel Hanh, but we are involved in a great war. We must all make sacrifices."

"Yes, Colonel, you are right. I will call my Chief of Staff at once and tell him to alert the units you request."

"Thank you," I said. "And I will find a chopper for your wife to go to Saigon."

Over time Hanh and I understood each other. For a long time he hated my guts (I never stopped hating his); I took great satisfaction on those occasions when word came down that his boss, the IV Corps CG (and a great general by any army's standards), General Truong, thought I was doing a good job because Hanh called him all the time, complaining that I was arrogant, pushy, and abrasive (all absolutely true), and recommending that I be relieved. Meanwhile, General McCown urged me to keep a running book on Hanh's numerous shenanigans even as I kept on the pressure for him to perform. McCown was a good man, an Old Soldier from Abrams' tanker club who knew Hanh was worthless and the sooner we were rid of him the better. Unfortunately, to remove him was no small chore. For Hanh even to have the job he had he was most likely a friend or business associate of President Thieu's or one of his top cronies. Even the word of a soldier as well respected as Truong couldn't stand up against that kind of firepower.

Yet there was no question that Hanh was a corrupt, lazy bum. With his overstuffed physique, his French accent and droopy mustache, his FDR cigarette holder dangling between his teeth, and his aviator shades, he was an unabashed warlord who got a percentage from every activity that went on in the Zone. He controlled all GI laundry and bar activities in Cao Lanh, and very likely in the other district and province towns as well. A Vietnamese could not open any business at all without Hanh's approval, a nod that invariably cost an ongoing, fixed percentage of the profit. When I went with him on his rounds of all the provinces, Hanh didn't hide the fact that each province chief paid him off; anyone who might have objected to the extortion had been relieved on some ginned-up charge of incompetence long before, and been replaced with one of Hanh's own men. Meanwhile, back at the war, under Hanh every major operation we had was compromised; the VC found out what we were doing faster than our subordinate units did. I felt sure they were getting copies of our operations orders, which could only mean there was at least one high-ranking VC in our camp; we tried many tricks to catch him, but never did. As a countermeasure, I pushed for minimum warning orders and fake OPORDs whenever possible. Of course, Colonel Hanh fought me all the way on this and virtually everything else, but I just kept blackmailing and bribing him until he realized that by making an effort to fight the war he could do even better for himself than he had to date.

From Hanh's point of view, our problems as good as disappeared when, a few months into my tenure, the tiny clapped-out trailer that had masqueraded as Team 50's toothpaste- and cigarette-vending PX was replaced by a small building filled to overflowing with the best in the way of booze, stereo equipment, tape recorders, and so on. From then on, when I really wanted something done that Hanh would not cooperate with, I'd just take him for a walk through the PX. "Come over to my compound," I'd say, "I want you to see the progress we're making." I'd show him around, and on our way to the mess to have a cup of coffee we'd swing by the PX. On these occasions the place was generally closed, but I'd make sure my PX sergeant, the redoubtable, Sergeant Bilko–like Master Sergeant Frank Schuette was on hand to open up for my counterpart. Schuette, a good friend of John Westmoreland's, had managed the two-million-dollar-a-month Saigon PX before taking up my offer to come back to the Zone to start ours from scratch. "Whatever you want, Colonel," I'd say to Hanh, watching my counterpart virtually froth at the mouth with excitement as he looked at the mountains of goodies stacked shelf upon shelf. "You want a case of scotch? Schuette, get the Colonel a case of scotch! A dozen cartons of Salem cigarettes? Schuette, a dozen cartons of Salems for the Colonel! Oh, and a radio, too? Schuette, why don't you just get a list? We'll get some coffee and Colonel Hanh's aide will come over later to pay for the stuff and pick it up. Right, Colonel?"

At this point Colonel Hanh would only be able to nod his head vigorously—he'd be beside himself. The grand or two of (unauthorized) MPC he'd spend at the PX that morning he could double before sunset on the black market. "But just one thing, Colonel," I'd say as we walked toward the door, Hanh having left his precious list in Schuette's care, "before you pick this stuff up. Remember that operation we were talking about earlier, the one you said was impossible at such short notice?"

"Oh, no, Colonel!" Hanh would enthuse. "It is very possible! It is an excellent idea!"

Time after time we went through this routine. I blatantly bought Hanh's cooperation, and he sold it to me as shamelessly as the village whore. And while it was true that letting him have free rein through the PX was a very serious violation of MACV regulations, not only did I not care, but I encouraged all my officers and senior NCOs to offer the same service to their counterparts. What the hell. The U.S. was spending billions of dollars to Vietnamize and win this war, and yet just a few unauthorized PX goodies grabbed the Viet brass right where they lived.

I had less luck with the Cambodian officers whom Premier and Defense Minister Lon Nol sent across the border for a crash course in battalion and brigade operations. We were directed to set up an instant infantry school for these men (now that the war had moved decisively into their backyard), but it quickly became clear the Cambodes were much more interested in Vietnamese women and having a good time than in learning skills to defend their country. These "officers" were all soft, fat, rich playboys who, by comparison, made the South Vietnamese look like storm troopers. They arrived in Cao Lanh from Cambodia in a convoy of old Mercedes-Benzes. They had scads of U.S. greenback; one guy threw around hundred-dollar bills like peanut shells, claiming he'd gotten them from the CIA. When one very corpulent full colonel was found, drunk out of his brain, running and dancing around the parade field (which happened to be a stone's throw from my quarters) stark naked in the middle of the night, I just shook my head. The whole affair gave new meaning to the term "pissing in the wind."

And yet, even I could get a whole different picture of how things were going if I talked to the right people, and time and again find every reason to believe it. The starched briefers at DRAC in Can Tho or MACV in Saigon snapped their pointers onto precise graphs and charts and invariably cited impressive statistics of Vietnamization's ever-widening success; the relevant information was always presented so logically and persuasively that I'd walk out of those briefings thinking I must be crazy. I'd seriously begin to question my own absolutely certain, on-the-ground observations and those of my team, in deference to those seemingly airtight official reports. Fortunately I'd only have to be back in the Zone for a few hours to recognize I'd been seduced, that what I'd heard was the same meaningless statistics, the same old artfully sanitized shit.* But it just showed the incredible power those briefings and reports had. If after all my years in Vietnam, I could still be taken in, at least momentarily, should it have been a surprise how easily and eagerly fooled the tourists still were, and those with a desperate, vested interest in Vietnamization?

Many years later, a civilian adviser I knew told me of his experience in the mid-sixties providing Hamlet Evaluation System (HES) data to result-hungry superiors in his corps. While in fact the HES statistics were supposed to reflect the real progress of the pacification effort, according to this adviser (who had worked with the program for four years, both before and after U.S. ground troops were deployed), "HES was a night once a month when all the

---

* Not unlike a page out of one of Ward Just's articles, "Notes on Losing a War," in which a MACV official gushed to Ward about a newly developed "miracle rice" that would revolutionize farming in Southeast Asia; "There's only one problem," the official said. "The Vietnamese don't like the rice much . . . they don't like the taste of it."[1]

guys got together, had a party, got drunk, and tried to figure out what figures would make higher headquarters happy." In 1970–71, I could see that same sort of calculated deception going on, only now it was beginning *at the highest headquarters*, the Oval Office. Like Johnson before him, Nixon said he was not going to be the first President to lose a war; since he couldn't win it, he and Kissinger had created Vietnamization, so they could "honorably" walk away and in the meantime keep the restive American people at bay. This was a perfect situation for the war managers who had done Lyndon Johnson such a terrible disservice with the sanitized, zero-defect reports that had kept him in the dark as he wrestled with how to prosecute the war and had ultimately cost him the presidency. It was as if the system had come full circle: these same reports, which had been in large part responsible for *escalating* the war, were now eagerly sought after by the Nixon Administration as the ultimate smoke screen for their abandonment of the effort.

When I first arrived at Team 50, my men were living in wide-open, WW II–style Army barracks. The buildings had seen their share of only the most basic maintenance, and little effort at all had gone into trying to make them comfortable. It was the same sad story all over the compound; the mess was terrible, the food was terrible, there weren't even any clubs (there had been, both officer and EM, but like virtually everything else in the compound, they'd been allowed to fall apart and turn to dust). In truth, when I arrived at Team 50, the only exception to the overall run-down condition of my command were the quarters I moved into. While the troops lived in rotting barns, the senior adviser had a fully air-conditioned little house—two bedrooms, a bathroom, a kitchenette, a living room complete with bar, and a full-time Viet maid. Very plush. The only problem with it was that every time I walked in the door I felt guilty. After a month, I had to give it up. I moved myself lock, stock, and barrel into my office on the Vietnamese side of the compound (it had four rooms, and after a few modifications and a good cleanup was totally livable), and gave my senior-adviser quarters on the U.S. side to the carpenters, to be renovated into the new Officers' and Senior NCO Club. The move proved to be a very significant gesture, not only for my men but for the Vietnamese. Due to habitually light Vietnamese fingers, at night the gate between the American and Viet sides of the compound was locked, and the Viets alone secured their side. By living there with them, I, the American senior adviser, proved I trusted them not only not to steal me blind, but also with my very life.

The only real deficiency in my new quarters was the wall-to-wall mouse problem. I bought a bunch of mousetraps, explained their use to the Viet woman who cleaned up the place, and told her that as part of her SOP each evening she was to set these "ambushes," and in the morning report the mouse "body count" to me. The first morning, the maid excitedly reported a body count of four. The second morning, she reported a body count of three. The next morning's figure was the same, and then there was a body count of one and then a body count of none. The next day there was another body count of none, and then every day for the next week there was no body count. I couldn't understand this, because at night I heard mice scurrying all over the place. Finally, one evening I did a little investigation, only to discover that the reason for no body count was no mousetraps had been set. The next day I asked the maid why she wasn't setting ambushes anymore. "No more mice," she said.

"How do you know that?" I asked.

"No body count," she replied. "We killed them all."

It was Vietnamese logic at its most eloquent, and just the way the South Vietnamese were fighting the war: if you couldn't see it, it wasn't there; and if it wasn't there, there was no reason to try to find it. And what could you say to that?

During the renovation of the Officers' Club, we also began building an EM club, and in addition I lit a torch under the mess sergeant's ass to get him fired up and producing good, wholesome food with a lot of variety. These acts alone did wonders to boost spirit, but in the first three months I also got a good number of other programs off the ground that were designed for the health, welfare, and morale of the team, from a "Fat Man" program complete with diet for those who tipped the scales in the wrong direction through boredom or laziness to an in-country R&R program that gave every man on the team a three-day vacation in Saigon or Vung Tau every month. Though we already had two daily briefings for the operational team, I organized weekly update briefings for the support personnel, too, who, generally stuck in the compound every day, otherwise had no idea where they fit into the picture. Every Saturday afternoon we had an awards ceremony and a traditional TRUST-like retreat; this was followed by Hail and Farewell, a routine I'd learned from General Timothy at II Corps (which always turned into one hell of a fun party), designed to introduce new members to the team and say good-bye to any guys who were leaving.

And every afternoon, the building program continued. The hardest part was finding the construction materials we needed to accomplish the task at hand. Going through channels was a guarantee that little would ever get done, so I had an ongoing, all-points alert out for building supplies. My first break was a report that a U.S. Navy-owned commercial cement mixer was sitting abandoned in the middle of bandit country, apparently all that was left of a convoy that had been ambushed. After I'd checked the machine out myself by chopper to make sure it was salvageable, we organized an airmobile assault into the area with Lieutenant Jack Howett's security platoon and pulled the thing out. Only then did we find it needed a few parts that were next to impossible to come by in South Vietnam; my only recourse then was to organize an extra R&R for one of the men, who took a kitful of money to Hong Kong to get them. Soon the cement mixer was churning out as much concrete as we could have asked for. We poured bucket after bucket into metal forms to make cinder blocks, and they in turn became the basic stuff of all our construction.

The rest of the building supplies I also got thanks to the U.S. Navy, from a hitchhiking construction battalion (Seabee) commander whom I picked up one day at the helipad of one of my units I'd been visiting. The guy's basic job was to visit and oversee the Seabee teams he had building things all over the Delta. But as we got to talking, it turned out he had no way to get around on his own. His job entailed constant travel, yet hitchhiking—by chopper, airplane, jeep, truck, or sampan—was his only means of transportation. That didn't seem very fair to me, particularly since some, like myself, had virtually unlimited transport available. So by the time the ride back to Cao Lanh was over, I'd promised the Seabee the use of one of the Zone's choppers every day if, in return, every week a landing craft, mechanized (LCM) arrived at my dock at Cao Lanh crammed from stem to stern with pallets of building materials from this guy's own Delta depot.

From there, in terms of our construction, the sky was the limit. We started with a new cinder-block wall around the compound, which included bunkers and firing positions. Just beyond that we laid a concrete strip studded with broken glass, to stop enemy sappers in the event that one managed to get through the barbed wire we'd set up in front of the concrete strip and (even more difficult) past the ducks that patrolled in between, keeping the grass down and quacking out warnings of intruders. When the security requirement was squared away, we built a library. Over the next nine months came a gym, too, and a steam bath/massage parlor (immediately dubbed the Steam and Cream), which was staffed with reliable, trustworthy, and above all *clean* females from Saigon, whom the team's doc checked out on a regular basis. Here a guy could have a massage or whatever else he arranged with the girls to keep himself from climbing the walls; though highly irregular, this amenity was the least I could do for the troops (besides the readily available heroin in Cao Lanh proper, a tough strain of syphilis was running rampant there, and among my first orders to the team had been that Cao Lanh was completely off-limits). I figured if the French had their *Bordel Mobile de Campagnes*—mobile field brothels—which, as Bernard Fall wrote in *Street Without Joy*, cut down on desertions, rapes of innocent civilian women, and venereal disease during the Indochina war, there was no reason why we shouldn't. It was the regulations that were wrong, and proof of that was in the fact that until the steam bath opened we were averaging several cases of VD a week on the team, whereas afterward, when the place was in full swing, we had almost none at all. This was particularly fortunate for Tom Hancock, whose dubious taste in women coupled with his obsession with being the world's greatest, or at least most-serviced, lover had to date landed him with more cases of clap than Audie Murphy had medals. At Pleiku he'd ended up with one case too many for a normal dose of penicillin, and Doc Holley, the Hardcore's miracle worker, then running a small Saigon hospital, had had to lay him down and administer the antibiotic intravenously, over a couple of days. (Hancock was no less a handful than he'd been five years before in the 1/327. On one occasion in the Zone he overstayed his extension leave in Germany by two weeks, sending me two cables while he was there, not to explain or apologize for his absence but to ask me to deposit a thousand dollars in his checking account in Saigon. Another time, when he hadn't been seen for a few days, couldn't be found anywhere, and I was just starting to believe he'd been kidnapped by the VC, one of our Vietnamese workers found him passed out between the huge blocks of ice in the icehouse. No doubt it was only the alcohol in his blood that prevented him from freezing to death.)

Besides contributing enormously to the morale of Team 50, the Steam and Cream served two other vital functions. First, in that the actual steam room there was strictly for team personnel—no Viets allowed under any circumstances—it was totally spyproof. As such, the plans for many an operation were sweated out there in total secrecy, the participants keeping their cool throughout with a few cold bottles of beer. The second vital function of the steam bath was its contribution to the Team 50 Compound Improvement Fund, an unauthorized bank that had been established early to cope with the ever-burgeoning expenses that went along with our continued construction work, the improved food, the magazine subscriptions, and anything else we couldn't scrounge in our quest for improved conditions. Specific guidelines covered how much and what kind of money could be collected from our various concessions (for example, a flat 30 percent of the gross was collected from the unauthorized but very convenient barber and tailor shops we set up in the compound, but while the Steam and Cream gave Team 50 the same 30 percent, in its case "gross income" was only that derived from the entrance fees for a straightforward steam bath and massage). We could have made a fortune out of the Steam and Cream, but I wasn't in to running a whorehouse. Instead, 70 percent of the steam bath's gross plus the revenue from all the "extras" went to Mr. Ko, the Korean guy who ran the place and paid the girls, and the bulk of our unauthorized funds was generated by another Team 50 institution: the highly successful monthly Monte Carlo night.

Monte Carlo began when we got a gambling "kit" from a Las Vegas hotel. The kit basically consisted of printed velvet sheets that converted ordinary tables to craps and blackjack venues, and green visors for the dealers. It was Las Vegas' contribution to the war effort, and the hotel gladly filled Team 50's subsequent order for more dice, chips, and hundreds of decks of playing cards. The straightest guys on the team would always be appointed to run the games, and on the first Saturday evening after payday, the Team 50 mess hall became Monte Carlo of the Delta. Besides generating a lot of money, the occasion was a great one for fun and excitement, with friends and friends of friends coming from all over the Delta to participate. The officers' and EM clubs would be closed for the night so the club girls could act as waitresses and hostesses, and with low- and high-stake tables for each game, we made sure nobody got carried away by the booze or the broads and lost his life savings. The entire thing was closely monitored; the proceeds, which, over time, came to thousands and thousands of dollars, were accounted for and held by my XO, slow-drawling Iowa Captain Thomas O. Cooney (otherwise known as "Judge," because of his pre-Vietnam legal training), and under his watchful eye, no money ever went south.

Our Compound Improvement Fund was further enriched by the outdoor snack bar we built (which adjoined our outdoor movie theater, which showed a different movie virtually every night), where a guy could buy a beautiful steak sandwich or a hamburger if he didn't want to eat in the mess. The snack bar was another real money spinner; between it and Monte Carlo, and later augmented by the Steam and Cream and the other concessions, before long we didn't have to pass the hat (a practice I'd hated since Trieste) for anything. Farewell presents for departing team members, Red Cross contributions, quarterly parties complete with presents for the Vietnamese who worked in our compound as carpenters and cooks, and many other programs designed to improve both our lot and the lot of the Vietnamese, all came out of the Compound Improvement Fund. In the end, we actually had enough money to redo not just our own side of the compound but the Viet side as well. Over there, thanks to a long line of indifferent commanders, both soldiers and their dependents lived together in crowded, appalling squalor—straw huts with pigs running through them, no electricity, the only water around that from a communal well. When we were finished, just weeks before my tour in the Zone was over, there were twenty-four units for Viet soldiers and their families, complete with electricity and running water, and a compound school for thirty to sixty kids with a teacher whose salary our unauthorized fund paid. Lieutenant Marc Cradduck, the real construction man of the team, estimated the materials alone cost fifty thousand dollars. In the entire year I spent in the Zone, this was the accomplishment I was most proud of. "This house and the school [will] live in the hearts of all Vietnamese in the 44th Zone as a constant reminder of Colonel Hackworth's and Team 50's genuine concern for the people, long after Team 50 [has] parted," proclaimed General Hai, by then the Zone's CG. [2] "This project," I wrote to Jennifer Bates, a woman who was to have as profound an influence on my life as, in their ways, Raphiel Benjamin and Ward Just did, "proves if there's a will there's a way."

It would be fair to say I operated in the Zone with minimal supervision. The deputy DMAC and my closest superior, Major General John H. Cushman, worked out of IV Corps Headquarters at Can Tho, seventy-five kilometers away. Since I'd never liked being too near the flagpole anyway, this suited me just fine, and I gradually slipped into the habit of doing whatever I wanted, or whatever I felt needed to be done. After a while, for example, I noticed that while the guys on the team who came from Airborne or Special Forces were STRAC in their tailored camouflage gear, the rest of the men looked like GP medium tents in their regulation, baggy-assed OD uniforms. They looked terrible, and I got the feeling they *knew* they looked terrible. So I decided everyone would wear camouflage gear. It didn't matter if a guy wasn't Airborne or SF; I knew that once he was suited up as if he were he'd *feel* he was, and that was the object. I had to do a little wheeling and dealing with old friends in the Viet Airborne Division to get the uniforms (the path was cleared by a small cache of SKS rifles we had stashed), but before too long everybody on the team was strutting, with a couple of fine-looking, cut-down parachute uniforms of their own.

It would have been a happily-ever-after story except that on one of General Cushman's visits to the compound he mentioned that a hell of a lot more of my men were wearing parachute uniforms than the team had Airborne slots. I explained to him how the uniforms had been part of the deal I'd had to make with studs like Hancock and Menjivar to get them to come to the Zone (and as for the rest of the men, "Well, sir, it just kind of happened."). Cushman said he understood, but that there were Army regulations to consider, and bearing them in mind, he wanted those uniforms off all non-Airborne personnel immediately. "I can't do that, sir," I said. "I told the men they could wear them. They've spent their money cutting them down, and they take a lot of pride in those uniforms. So if you insist on this, I'll have no recourse but to request relief." It was only a partial bluff. I didn't want to quit the Zone, but I had to stand in the door—if I gave in, I'd lose so much face in my command it'd be even *worse* than quitting.

Cushman immediately suggested a compromise: from that moment, as my old people rotated home their replacements would go back to Army-issued olive drab, and within a certain number of weeks, everybody else (less Airborne) would return to OD, too. I agreed in principle, but after the General went away I formulated what ended up being a much better arrangement. After the deadline, when everyone was supposed to be phased back into leg jungle fatigues, the Team rule was you could wear your camouflage uniform wherever and whenever you wanted except if you went to Can Tho. Then non-Airborne guys had to wear their regulation baggy-assed fatigues. If anyone wearing his parachute uniform accidentally ran into General Cushman outside of Can Tho, the rule was to play it cool, escape, and evade; we soon learned that in this situation, in public, Cushman's tack was to actively ignore the evidence of the breached regulation anyway. *But,* if the General came to the compound, it had to appear as if we were playing by his rules. (Fortunately for all concerned, it was SOP for all inbound helicopters to request permission to land on our pad, so we always had warning of Cushman's impending arrival. As such, when the TOC dispatched a jeep to pick him up, simultaneously they activated the compound's ground-attack siren. The camouflage fatigue-clad team knew the alarm screaming in the middle of the day did not indicate a VC attack; instead, it was their signal to drop whatever they were doing and change into their OD outfits. The guard at the front gate even had his regulation uniform hanging up in his guard box, to slip into in time to salute Cushman as he drove up to the compound some ten minutes after the first warning his chopper was inbound.)

General Cushman and I hit another snag in our relations when I decided to change the name of the compound. When I first arrived, it was called something like the Major Orville C. Snodgrass Compound. I logically asked who this fellow of the unfortunate name was, and was told he'd been a Military Intelligence major or something who, just as the Zone was being established, was standing in the middle of the compound in broad daylight when a Viet Cong 82-mm mortar round slammed in and blew him to pieces. Since he was the first guy killed in the Zone, the place was named after him. "Well, that's just not going to do," I said. "We aren't going to have this compound named after some dead wimp! We're going to name it after a live hero!" and promptly dubbed my new home the John P. Geraci Compound. This met with unanimous approval from the Airborne/Ranger mafia, who all knew and admired Geraci as a great warrior, and it was no less appropriate in that Geraci had been the Zone's first senior adviser. We made a beautiful sign in Ranger colors (also in Geraci's honor) and hoisted it up on the arch at the front gate where Major Snodgrass' memorial had previously resided. Cushman noticed it on his next visit, the very minute he drove through the gate. "What is that sign?" he asked me.

"John P. Geraci Compound, sir," I replied. "It's the new name of the compound."

"Who authorized it?"

"I did, General."

"You didn't go through the Department of Heraldry?"

"No, sir."

"Hackworth, you can't do that! And you *know* you can't do that! And I want that sign changed back, right NOW!"

A few words about General Cushman. He was an energetic, even overzealous man, a very articulate, intelligent, academic/philosopher type and a West Point engineer. He was also an instant Army aviator (the latest punch on the old ticket for senior officers, ever since Chief of Staff Westmoreland went through ridiculously abbreviated flight training and "qualified"), and well lived up to the warning my predecessor, Special Forces Colonel Bob Hassinger, had given me about him: "If his motor's not running his mouth is." Cushman struck me as very much the same type of soldier as William Childs Westmoreland: hard-charging and ambitious, superstraight and without one street-wise bone in his body. A cheerleader for the war effort. And since he didn't understand the Viets, or so it seemed to me, or recognize their total exhaustion with the war or their endemic corruption, through it all he was able to maintain his superoptimistic views. Cushman was as conventional in his thinking as 99 percent of the U.S. generals in Vietnam, and while he, like Westy, may have been a great commander in a conventional war somewhere, he didn't have a clue when it came to the present, guerrilla battlefield. Generally speaking, I had to admit his ignorance worked in my favor. Except for his once-a-month visits, when he came around full of praise for my guys and for everything we were doing (he used Team 50 as an example to get his other three division-level advisory teams cracking), Cushman generally left us alone as, little by little, my men turned the screws and got the Viets producing.

But Cushman was mad as hell about that sign. And he left me no room to maneuver. I wasn't going to quit over it, and this time he was the one standing in the door. So I took the sign down. Still, I thought it was a raw deal and so did my boys, so after discussing it we decided we'd just have two signs: Geraci for general purposes and Snodgrass for General purposes. The only person at all inconvenienced by this was the guy on guard at the front gate. Now when he heard the ground-attack siren announcing Cushman's arrival, not only did he have to change his uniform, but he also had to set up and climb the long ladder we permanently stationed behind the guard position for this contingency, change the sign, climb down, put the ladder away, and be the very model of smiling military precision when the General drove through the front gate a few minutes later.

We got away with that one, but there was always something else I'd come up with that Cushman would lock my heels together and counsel me about. Often he got so pissed off he'd just yell, like the time he got word that I'd told my guard at the front gate to shoot two U.S. Navy guys who'd come to the compound to retrieve "their" cement mixer if they moved the machine so much as one inch outside the compound. (I mean, *we* found it, *we* dragged it back, *we* repaired it and paid for it out of our own pockets. As far as I was concerned, the only way the Navy was going to get that cement mixer back was if I hooked it under a chopper, dropped it from five thousand feet over the exact spot we found it, and they picked it up from where *they* abandoned it. Unless, of course, they came up with something great to swap for it, like a battleship.) I explained all this to General Cushman, but he was unimpressed, and launched into what had become a familiar tirade. "Hackworth, let me remind you that you are a member of the United States Army! You are not down here with your own separate army! You do not make the rules. You are not the law. You belong to a higher command, and you are responsible and reportable to that command! DO YOU UNDER-STAND ME?"

"Roger, sir," I responded (as I usually responded), "I'm sorry. I must have gotten carried away." In the case of the cement mixer, however, I did add that the Navy would take it over my dead body—and they never did get it as long as I was in the Zone. So as far as Cushman went, I generally ended up doing exactly what I'd planned to do anyway, and though the General sometimes got mad, he usually looked the other way, because in the final analysis he was interested in only one thing—results—and Team 50 was giving him results. So when it all shook out, General Cushman was wrong about me and my command. I *did* have my own separate army in the Zone. And I *was* the law.

It would be untrue to say that I wasn't myself in my last command. But I was not the man I'd been nine years before when Colonel Johns led the Vanguards into Berlin, or even five years before when Tim's Traveling Trouble began its whistle-stop tour of battle areas all around South Vietnam. I was forty years old, and I'd suddenly realized that the Army, this rotten whore I'd been madly in love with for the last twenty-five years, wasn't going to mend her ways. It was as if I knew that no matter what I did or what I said, I was always going to find her cheating, find somebody else in our bed (as it were), and while in the past I'd always swallowed the disappointment and the hurt, and backed away, saying, "Sorry, honey, I'll come back in an hour," thinking that everything would be okay then, in the Zone it occurred to me that maybe I was wasting my time. "The Army isn't what it used to be," I lamented to General Cushman one day.

"It never was," he replied.

I didn't want to admit it, but I knew he was right. After all, *Once an Eagle*, that extraordinary, epic Army novel, had recently been published, and in it author Anton Myror had well expressed how the Hunts of the Army world, the callous, career-first ticket punchers (exemplified in the butchering character of Courtney Massengale), had been gliding past the Geracis and Hayeses and Johnses (in Myror's world epitomized in the character of decent warrior Sam Damon) for generations, and always would. So it was just unfortunate that I, who'd set my sights on being a buck sergeant in the marvelous Trieste days that molded me as a soldier and began my love affair with the Army, had somehow never gotten the word.

In mid-November, Brigadier General Jack Hemingway, my battalion commander from the 223d in Korea, now CG of the Aviation Brigade, flew into the Zone to say that the War College list had just been announced and my name was on it. Because I'd deferred the previous two years, the news wasn't a surprise, but it was wonderful to see General Hemingway again and I appreciated his hearty congratulations. I didn't have the courage to tell him I wasn't going to attend, however; other than Ward Just and Jenny Bates, the first to know that were the Army personnel managers, to whom I wrote as soon as I got the official word: "Request that I be removed from the Senior Service School list permanently. My reason for this is I have no aspiration to be a general officer and I have no desire to work in positions where this education is required. Hence it would be selfish of me to use a much-sought-after quota when more ambitious types are available."

Or, as I wrote less loftily to Jim Mitchell, my buddy from the II Corps days, "Have no aspirations to be a general because I have known only a few good ones, and besides, I would have to buy new uniforms and become a phony. Want to be a bird who doesn't give a fuck and who everyone is afraid of because his shit is straight [and] he cannot be intimidated because he doesn't care."

Effectively I was ending my career. I knew I'd soon be promoted to full colonel, and without a star to aspire to from there—and no War College meant no stars for sure—I had nowhere to go. But, as I wrote to Jenny Bates, "I no longer have a burning dedication towards the Army (or for that matter, America as it exists today) so I refuse to serve it just because of the attainments which appear to be certain." I was glad I was going to make bird (the prestige and retirement pay were better), but now that the decision to quit had sneaked up on me and been made, I had to rethink some plans. My first decision was, after the Zone, to get myself a nontroop, fat-cat Army job outside of the United States to ride out the mandatory two years' service the promotion cost me. My second decision, after that, was to just fade away.

There was a tremendous amount of heartbreak involved in all this. I felt the Army had failed me, and through its ineptitude it had inexcusably failed the nation every American soldier was tasked to defend—that nation being the United States of America, *not* South Vietnam. And twenty years after Korea, I now understood the anger of Bill Smith's father over the death of his Raider son. Back then I'd condemned him for not understanding there was a price of admission to the American Way, a price the immigrant Mayamuras had borne without complaint. But now I could see, through the Vietnam debacle, that while there was a price to be paid, it was only correct to pay it if the product—democracy—was sound. And it was not sound in the corrupt ranks of South Vietnam's government and military, nor had it ever been, *nor would it ever be*, regardless of how many of America's sons threw their lives into the pot. As a nation, we had to get out of there.

I'd always been one to speak my mind, but my hurt during this period (added to the fact that I knew I was getting out) made me *too* frank, *too* candid about how the war and Vietnamization were going. Old friends like Joe Love would attend briefings I was tasked to give and later comment to me about my cynicism; after a while, I was not asked to do such briefings anymore. The endless stream of visitors who'd characterized my previous tours, who came to me for the straight skinny on the war, dried up; it was not because I was getting out (no one knew), but because of my "attitude," as a reliable source put it, which had potential guests being dissuaded from visiting the Zone. The word was I was a little "battle-rattled" and maybe I was, I'd never know. All I knew was that Barney K. Neil had been killed at Pleiku on 11 September of that year, 1970, bringing home probably more painfully than any of the other drops on the stone of my consciousness the terrible, *wrongful* waste of it all.

In any event, we in the Zone were effectively cut off from making positive comment to correct the ills that beset the system. My recourse was in my writing—articles that were more and more truthful (and consequently more and more abrasive) yet which continued to be published in military publications—and my press friends, most of whom I'd met and played poker with at the Pleiku press camp when I was at II Corps. These guys gladly accepted my leaks and nonattributable statements, which assisted them in telling the truth of the Vietnamization farce.

Meanwhile, in my command, I gave in to the urge to hurt my too well loved whore as badly as she'd hurt me. First and foremost, my aim was to make her look foolish. Consequently, while I'd never been one for regulations, as time passed in the Zone I went out of my way to break every one I could. I took immense joy in screwing the system, joy that was only matched by the fact that in the process my men had some of the best damn times of their lives. Every day I sent one of my bird-dog reconnaissance aircraft to Saigon to get the latest movie for my troops to see that night, or to bring in steaks for the outdoor snack bar. Experience had shown me the Viets didn't exactly pounce on the intelligence such planes provided, so I knew one aircraft would never be missed. Through our unauthorized fund we kept a safe house in Saigon, and installed Frenchie Frye there, designating him Team 50's unauthorized liaison officer at MACV. His principal job was to cut through the mountains of red tape that accompanied all promotions, awards, orders, and getting good replacements for the team. Often all this required was giving just the right little souvenir to just the right person, and Frenchie quickly proved a master at knowing which button to push. VC weapons were always in, but the best bribe these days was the Vietnamese jump badge, which had to be authorized by the Viets. Every glory-hungry desk jockey wanted to wear that one, and Frenchie had an inside line into getting them on short notice. Frye was also in charge of all major scrounging efforts (although he preferred to call it "relocating government property") in Saigon, and, as required, could even switch gears to play mother hen to fellow team members when they visited the big city on their in-country R&Rs.

Every day we had morning and evening briefings (the war and my responsibilities as a "Vietnamizing" senior adviser didn't stop just because my heart was broken) to allocate and coordinate assets, organize and follow up on operations, thrash out what was being done right and wrong, and how and what things could be improved, etc. Though these were always damned effective working sessions, that did not mean they had to be deadly serious. For one thing, I insisted that all participants feel free to question and to challenge me, to *think* rather than yes-sirring their way into my good books. This brought new vitality to the proceedings and fresh ideas to our operations, not to mention keeping me on my toes. (In the almost quarter of a century since my stern disciplinarian days as a TRUST corporal, my command style had evolved significantly. Now it was closer than anything to the Israeli way of doing things: I was still the boss and the final decisions were mine—and everyone knew it—but all in all there was less emphasis on the Mickey Mouse, more on listening to subordinates and being open to good recommendations.) We adopted as our briefing battle cry "Fuck Ho Chi Minh" (who was dead by now, but what the hell), which was sung out in unison and kept us mission-oriented. I also implemented a Word and Thought for the Day program to open each morning's proceedings. The program was run by Captain Howard E. Cecil, our erudite G-2 adviser and resident military-history whiz. The Word for the Day could be any word in the world, and the Thought from anyone, living or dead; my own favorite Word for the Day was "telesis," which was defined at the briefing as "to make progress," because it appeared again a few days later in the morning's Thought: "To the South Vietnamese," the joker explained, "telesis is a disease to be avoided like the plague." Right on, brother, right on.

Briefing officers were encouraged to let their hair down and have fun during the proceedings. They had to have their shit together—if they didn't, they knew I'd nail them—but as long as aviation LNO "BJ" Jensen gave me an accurate report, I didn't mind if he appeared wearing his blue Black Hawk Civil War hat, or even better, his little cap with a propeller sticking out of the top, which he twirled around as he spoke. In fact, I encouraged it. I thought it was just fine if a briefer came out (as one did) with his hair parted in the middle and plastered down with Brylcreem, wearing granny glasses and a little red paper heart stuck on his uniform over his own heart—anything to eliminate the routine in the routine. And the rule was I was not allowed to crack even the slightest hint of a smile. This, of course, was a great motivator for the men, and from time to time they did catch me out with skits and costumes that were just hilarious. Once I got them all back, however, with a little act I cooked up with Captain Stephen Bates, our Adjutant, who was the last briefer of the evening. While Bates gave his normal report, I sank down in the high-backed leather armchair I always sat in in the front of the room for the briefings, so that none of the other guys, who all sat behind me, could see what I was doing. I put on a long-haired hippie wig that balding Frank Schuette's sister had sent him as a joke, and a spare pair of granny glasses. When I was ready, I gave Bates the signal to launch into our prearranged routine. "Sir, I've noticed that a number of the men are growing sideburns," he said.

At this time in the Army, Chief of Staff Westmoreland's magic panacea for all the screwed-up and/or angry draftees and the problems they caused across the board was to let these men have beer in the barracks, no KP, long hair, and sideburns. It didn't work, because while the Army got rid of the "offending" military traditions, it did not replace these traditions with anything that fulfilled their basic and essential function, i.e., to instill and maintain discipline. Sure, the changes helped keep outright rebellion at bay in various quarters of the Army. But if the Army expected its men to be effective on the battlefield, even to *stay alive* on the battlefield, discipline had to be the number-one priority.

So Bates said some of the men were growing sideburns. "Yes, I know!" I responded sharply, staying low in my seat and ranting in the best tradition of Captain Queeg. "And it's going to *stop*! Today I saw a man with *an inch and a half of hair* on the top of his head! I saw a man with hair on the *sides* of his head, and another man with hair *on the back of his neck*! These men will have *whitewalls*! *Nothing* on the sides! *Nothing* on the back! A half inch ONLY on the top! *Airborne* haircuts, do you men understand?" There was no response behind me. *The Old Man's done it now*, the silence screamed. *He's flipped right out of his head.* "DO YOU MEN UNDERSTAND?" I bellowed, and popped up over my chair to face them. The silence continued for another second as the men looked at my straggly wig and granny glasses in complete disbelief. Then they started to laugh. Bates and my trick brought down the house. It was a good way to end the day.

About a week before Thanksgiving, the senior adviser to the 7th ARVN Division was fired, and Cushman selected me to go "straighten out" that unit. I didn't want to go. I'd worked hard in the Zone, and I'd brought together a damn good team that I was very unhappy about leaving behind. And, as I wrote to Ward about the move, I was "really tired of trouble-shooting. Haven't got the spirit because I know that I'll squeeze ARVN and he will shape up. Week after I leave he's back to his old tricks. So why go through the frustration of squeezing the little bastard?" But I couldn't refuse the assignment, because I hadn't told, nor did I want to tell, Cushman I was getting out of the Army. I felt if he or McCown knew I was quitting, they would think I'd no longer care about doing a good job, and be all over Team 50 like molasses. As it was, Cushman's once-a-month visits were almost too much.

Thanksgiving came, and with it what I thought would be my last big bash with the men of Team 50: a proper "dining-in" in honor of Major General Bill Henderson, my Australian friend (now CG of the Australian Task Force in Vietnam) who had helped get me in hot water, albeit unintentionally, on my last day at the Pentagon. The dining-in was an eighteenth-century British battlefield invention. Historically, its purpose was "to preserve the amenities of civilization and normality in circumstances far from civilized or normal" (as our Letter of Instruction [LOI] for the proceedings explained); it always took place in the field, and its participants were all the officers of the regiment who came together expressly for this formal dinner, which began with drinks and ended with toasts to the reigning monarch. When I was at II Corps, I'd been invited to a dining-in at General Corcoran's IIFFV mess in Nha Trang. The invitation had actually been engraved, with a three-star flag at the top and writing in gold ink. I did not attend. For one thing, it had seemed incredible to me that such a waste of time and assets would be condoned, much less encouraged (in my case alone it was a two-hundred-kilometer chopper ride just to get to Nha Trang, and there were people coming from all over the place). For another, since the vast majority of the participants in this war sat at desk jobs and the like in the huge, plush base camps, their "circumstances" were completely civilized and normal in the first place, the "amenities of civilization and normality" just part of the Vietnam tour package. To me, a dining-in in such "circumstances" was little more than a slightly regimented dinner party, and a wasteful, completely self-indulgent exercise.

My point of view had not changed on this subject in the Zone, but when Henderson said he'd be visiting from Nui Dat at Thanksgiving, the dining-in concept seemed like a fun change for the team (outsiders, besides Henderson, were not invited) and an appropriate tribute to a fine Aussie general. To put everyone in the spirit of things, star scrounger Hancock managed to acquire a dozen cases of VB, General Henderson's favorite Australian beer, and from the moment we cracked the first ones open upon Henderson's arrival, the somewhat irreverent Team 50 Thanksgiving dining-in was destined to be a great success.

A few days later, just before I was to make the move to the 7th Div, my orders were canceled when I landed in the hospital with excruciating stomach pains. After a lot of puzzlement and a lot of tests, it was discovered one of my kidneys had an extra tube, and it had become blocked. That's what a dining-in will get you. It was not a serious affliction, and the flare-up could not have come at a more opportune time.. Not only was I spared the transfer to the 7th Div, but I was out of the hospital and feeling fine in plenty of time for the highlights of the holiday season: the Christmas party Team 50 gave for the (mostly Buddhist) Viets who worked in the compound (our slush fund allowed for a six-piece Viet band, tons of Vietnamese food, free drinks, a gift of ten American dollars converted to piaster—at the best black-market rate of exchange we could get—and a couple of cartons of cigarettes for each worker), and the first annual "Rice Bowl" football game, which was played on New Year's Day, 1971.

The action officers in charge of the Rice Bowl operation had magically transformed Tan Tich airfield into a perfect one-hundred-yard American football field, complete with plywood goal posts on each end, regulation markers, and umpires in black-and-white-striped shirts. They'd also organized sideline activities, including hot-dog stands and enthusiastic Vietnamese cheerleaders (our club girls) in short little skirts. The two teams for the game were the Team 50 "Studs" and the 52d Signal Battalion (a communications platoon of which was attached to us) "Lightning Bolts." I had three hundred dollars riding on my Studs; what the commo sergeant whom I'd drunkenly made the bet with at the New Year's Eve party the night before didn't know was that while his people were all high-school amateurs from way back, I had a team of eleven football stars from various universities. The Studs had it made in the shade.

The game began. Surprisingly, the communicators made the first touchdown. Then they got the second. And the third. By the end of the first half, it was 21–0. We were getting our asses thumped, and the commo sergeant was singing. (In a display of New Year's cheer and with just a speck of guilt for stacking my team with ringers, I'd even spotted him fourteen points.) I couldn't understand it. I sought the advice of Frank Schuette, who'd been a great football player in his day. "I'll tell you what's wrong," he informed me. "You've got eleven stars out there. They all think they're in charge. I think you better go out there and tell them there can only be *one* quarterback. Because if all of 'em keep on showboating like they're doing, not only are they gonna lose, but they're gonna have their asses wiped all over the field."

I went over to the team. "Listen, boys, this shit's serious. Not only are we losing the game, but we're losing it to *legs*. We've got to turn it around. Q" —I turned to Captain Q. (for Quewanncoli) Stephens—"you're the quarterback. You call the plays. Everybody else, just listen and do what Q says, you follow? Okay. So let's get with it!" And they did. In the second half everything clicked. The Signal guys never scored again, and not only did we win, but we beat them by something like forty points.

At the next night's Hail and Farewell, a dispatch was delivered to me from the Zone message center.

> FROM: The President of the United States. TO: Senior Advisor, Team 50. SUBJECT: The Rice Bowl 1971. 1 (S) The fantastic game played in the Rice Bowl totally out shattered other Bowl games and made them look like the minors. I, as well as all of the American People, take great pride in saluting the courage, boldness, and skill of "Cpt Q" 's Studs and Stagg's Bolts. 2 (S) If you brave men in Vietnam will all just extend for one year, I and all the other Republican leaders will personally attend the next Rice Bowl game. Your admiring fan, "Dicky" Nixon.

The dispatch, in the best Team 50 one-upmanship tradition, was a great joke that had most of us going for a few minutes anyway, and while everyone had a good laugh over it, something in me knew that 1971 was going to be one hell of a year.

And it was. First, Patty and the kids were programmed to come out to the Philippines through the Handclasp senior adviser program, but as the time approached I realized I couldn't deal with it and wrote her a letter telling her not to come. After all those years, however, she was not about to be dismissed with a letter, and took the next plane over. And while we only got together once, to organize a legal separation, her presence in the Philippines was brought to my attention on a regular basis by General Cushman, who, along with his Catholic wife, thought I was terrible for doing what I was doing to *my* Catholic wife. Once Cushman even called me into his office to tell me a divorce would jeopardize my career. I blew up and told him it was none of his damned business in the first place, and in the second, since when was there a block on the U.S. Army Officer Efficiency Report that measured how well a man and his wife got along. I wound up by saying I didn't recall the careers of Generals MacArthur, Ridgway, or Gavin being stunted by having been married two or three times, and not surprisingly, Cushman backed off.

When excerpts from Ward Just's soon-to-be-released *Military Men* were published in the *Atlantic Monthly,* however, Cushman jumped right back on. Rumors were rife that I was "The Colonel" of the second installment, and indeed I was. Ward had changed the physical characteristics and a few little details to keep the Army off course, but the outspoken, highly critical opinions expressed by the unnamed officer in the piece were still laid by some at my feet, and a shade more tarnish began to appear on the "battle-weary" golden-haired boy.

At the end of January, finally, finally Colonel Hanh was relieved of command of the Zone. His downfall ultimately came less as a result of the little book I kept on him than of Hanh's own abiding greed: when word got around that during an operation he had used fifteen hundred of his soldiers to drive four hundred head of cattle from Cambodia to Can Tho for his own personal disposal, it was a bit much even by Vietnamese standards. (This did not, however, prevent Hanh from later being promoted to brigadier general and given yet another command.) The Colonel was replaced by one General Hai, a graduate of Benning's Career Course and Leavenworth's C&GS, who, besides being a Northerner-Catholic, had absolutely nothing in common with his corrupt predecessor. Hai was a hardworking, no-nonsense, exacting man, with a refreshing sense of purpose: he was hell-bent on winning the war. He was a damn good leader who set the example and demanded the total commitment of his subordinates. He respected the role of the adviser, so there was no game playing between us (a remarkable feat given that I was his *thirty-second* adviser and he could have had every routine down cold), and he did not require bribery or coercion to get the job done. Hai was my kind of man, and as well as slipping right into an ideal commander/adviser, hand-in-glove relationship, we quickly became good friends.

Hai agreed with me that ARVN's problems were bordering on terminal, and that the key to winning was to be found in the Regional and Popular territorial forces. Together we implemented a program of Territorial (or Mobile) Training Teams, an idea I'd gotten from the Australians, using underworked personnel from my overstaffed HQ to train RF/PF units to provide reliable security at the hamlet/village level. There seemed no question that the people could be won to our side if they knew they were really secure; then they would not be afraid to ban the VC from their villages, an act that would deny the enemy recruits, food, intelligence, and support. Mao's fish would be without water, and their effort would, of necessity, dry up.

Colonel Hanh had been totally against the concept, so until General Hai arrived, this kind of training in the Zone had been virtually the one-man effort of Team 50's Captain "Che" Menjivar (whose real name was Milton, but the short, baby-faced eternally insubordinate El Salvadorean-by-birth acted far more like the recently deceased revolutionary Guevara than some guy named Milton, so we just changed it), who had gone from RF unit to RF unit teaching night-ambush patrols with two Ranger NCOs. Under General Hai, now the Mobile Training Team program was expanded to five teams (each consisting of an American captain, two NCOs, and a Viet interpreter), which were sent to the various districts for up to three weeks each, to train the individual units therein. At the end of these training sessions, the teams would move on and let the Viet units fend for themselves rather than, as was standard procedure, continue to lean on their advisers to make things turn out right. That was the part Colonel Hanh hadn't liked—that we'd pull out and leave his units on their own. But of course, that was the whole idea. The war would soon again belong to the Vietnamese, and after almost a decade of lip service about getting them to fight it, it was my intention in the Zone, as it had been in the Airborne, that that was exactly what they'd do, and do well. As Mao said (and as Team 50 picked up as its motto), *Give a man a fish and he'll have one meal: teach a man to fish, he can eat forever.*

Under General Hai we also initiated an "Ambush Academy" to train RF/PF officers in this most effective tactic for fighting the guerrillas. We put tremendous emphasis on artillery training, too; the use of artillery, once the "big stick" of the South Vietnamese Army until U.S. helicopter gunships superseded it, had to be relearned by the Viets urgently as the wind down of the U.S. effort slashed the number of American gunships available to the Zone. The program was well worth the effort. With a lot of hard work, as well as "spot inspection" teams whose jobs were to swoop unexpectedly into fire bases and have a look at the individual guns and crews, after a few months we were able to see marked improvement in the readiness and accuracy of the Zone's artillery units, and in the confidence of the Viet infantry who had to depend on that artillery in a close support role.

One area Hai was unable to make inroads in was the attitude and performance of our attached Vietnamese Air Force helicopter units, without a doubt the most dangerous collection of amateur fliers I'd ever seen (and only matched, I assumed, by 99 percent of the other VNAF units in the war). For myself, I'd reached the point of categorically refusing to fly in any Viet-maintained or -flown aircraft. Among the final straws that led to this decision was a single moment one day when I was sitting in a VNAF chopper as the only American amidst a Vietnamese pilot and copilot, a Vietnamese crew chief and gunner and General Hai and his all-Vietnamese staff. As we were about to get under way, the pilot, who'd been chatting away in Vietnamese to his passengers and crew, looked to his crew chief and said, in English, "Coming hot." The crew chief responded, "All clear." When I heard that, I knew we were in serious trouble. *The more mechanical become the weapons with which we fight, the less mechanical must be the spirit which controls them,* Field Marshal Wavell wrote—yet here were these Viets, parroting like robots the words of their Fort Rucker, U.S.A. instructors, not relating to them enough even to translate them into their own language.

While VNAF's striking limitations were well known to those whose operations and lives depended on them, it was only when General Tri of the Cambodian invasion was killed (along with, tragically, *Newsweek*'s twenty-four-year Indochina veteran journalist François Sully), in a characteristically neglected bird that burst into flames midair, that the cheerleaders for Vietnamization began to investigate and "discover" they had a problem on the airmobile side of things. Only then did they recognize that the Viets who'd been sent to America, at America's expense, for up to thirty-two weeks of helicopter training (plus six weeks of instruction in the English language), were coming back not with new levels of proficiency, but with vague concepts in disjointed English that they were unable to explain much less perform, and that those tasked with maintenance felt that as long as the chopper logs, which they doctored daily as necessary, reflected that maintenance *had* taken place, that they'd done their jobs.

Meanwhile, back at the 44th STZ, our Viet allies were stealing fuel and equipment from our Tan Tich and Muc Hoa staging fields at a remarkable rate. At Tan Tich alone, in one seven-week period enough fuel was stolen to sustain an entire Air Cav "package" of thirteen choppers (a C&C plus four each of slicks, Cobras, and LOHs) for six days of normal combat operations in the Zone. The scroungers regularly stole flares and ammo as well; they also had a thing about ammo *crates*, which they generally took empty (after uncrating the contents and leaving them—rockets, minigun ammo, what-ever was going—scattered all over the airfield for the rains to destroy). This did little to foster goodwill between our men and the Vietnamese, and in fact there was an increasing number of xenophobic incidents in the Zone, where comments or criticisms, usually warranted but often snidely delivered by American personnel to Vietnamese, resulted in fistfights or weapon brandishings.

And throughout this period, while my honeymoon with Hai continued, the quiet hope his arrival had brought faded away. We did everything in our power to get the Viet troops off their asses, but the bottom line was they did not have the in-depth leadership to bring them up for the long-term game. The NCOs were tired and burned-out—they'd seen far too much combat. The junior officers (lieutenants and captains) were just not motivated to win the war, and the majors, light colonels, and colonels, their bosses, who should have provided that drive to win, served only as role models and inspiration for corruption. The only way to infuse ARVN with strong leadership immediately would have been by taking the top U.S. studs out of U.S. units or advisory jobs and giving *them* command of ARVN companies, battalions, regiments, and divisions. They in turn could have selected the best men—based on ability, not connections—who would then OJT under the American officers until they got it right, at which point the Americans would go home. The process might have taken four to six years, so all the studs would have to be "combat bums" (that generic, derogatory term, generally used by the tourists to describe officers who "copped out" by volunteering for repeated tours in Vietnam rather than returning to stateside duty and the multitudinous career-related activities that were expected of a modern Army officer), but that was all right—what we needed, what we'd *always* needed, to win this war were combat bums.* And volunteers would have queued up for the long-term command/advisory jobs. The technique itself was a proven one, having worked time and again for the British in their

---

* Combat bums came in two main (albeit overlapping) varieties: those who would have marched to the sound of guns wherever they were blazing (and/or had become, as I had, obsessed with figuring out a way to win this particular conflict) and/or those who'd gone native. The natives were most easily identifiable. These were guys, many from Special Forces, who'd been there so long that the place had become a way of life for them. They loved the food, they spoke the language, many owned digs in Saigon or one of the other cities, and had Viet girlfriends to go "home" to when they weren't playing war. Most proudly wore brass bracelets that looked as if they were made of welding rods; besides the occasional gold Buddha a guy wore around his neck, this was the one real outward display of combat-bum status, and proudly signified nothing less than honorary membership in a Montagnard tribe. As a body, almost by definition, the Special Forces in Vietnam were combat bums *and* the best guys to fight the G in this war. But the Special Forces were also animals, which offended all the prancers, and they considered themselves an elite force, which offended most everybody else. General Abrams *hated* them. Yet, if these Green Berets had been allowed to run the show, there's little doubt in my mind that the outcome of the war would have been quite different.

Gurkha and other colonial units; even at this late stage, the plan here in Vietnam would have been well worth the effort. For my money, it was really the only viable option left: I truly believed that if Hai, a great, great general for the Zone, in tandem with the even greater general, Corps CG Truong, could not turn ARVN's fortunes around in our area, then it just wasn't going to happen at all.

This belief was only reinforced when President Nixon expanded the war yet again in February 1971 by launching Operation Lam Son 719, an invasion into Laos designed to sever the Ho Chi Minh trail. All the U.S. advisers were left behind, and besides some U.S. Special Forces Pathfinders, this time it really was an all-ARVN show on the ground, using the very best troops in South Vietnam. And the Viets just blew it. They made a conventional attack, then immediately fell back on American air support to save their asses. And immediately we obliged, with aircraft brought in from throughout Vietnam, Thailand, and the Pacific. (Nixon and Co., while respecting their own rhetoric not to expand the ground war, had no hesitation about the use of air in as large quantities as possible: "There is no limit . . . and we don't see any reason why there should be any limit on the use of that air power," declared Secretary of State William Rogers just before the Laotian operation began.)[3] Unfortunately, the NVA were well ready for the attack, with battle-ready troops backed up with tanks, antiaircraft guns, and surface-to-air missiles. In the two months of fighting that followed, more than a hundred U.S. helicopters were destroyed (and more than six hundred hit, many badly) and 102 American aircrewmen's lives taken. Again the NVA proved willing to take terrific casualties themselves during Lam Son 719, but they also took a hell of a lot of ARVN troops with them when they went (ARVN casualties were between 25 to 50 percent of the total troops involved), and in the end, despite U.S. fighter aircraft, choppers, gunships, artillery, and B-52 strikes, it was ARVN that scurried frantically across the border back into South Vietnam, in undeniable defeat. Three cheers for Vietnamization.

I'd met Jennifer Bates on my first R&R to Australia, which I'd taken with John Westmoreland just before I took over the Zone. Jenny was a Deborah Kerr look-alike, and I fell in love with her at breakfast, the minute I saw her across the dining room of the Chevron Hotel on the Gold Coast. I didn't actually meet her until that evening, a meeting that began with a half-assed argument between us about the American involvement in Vietnam. British-born Jenny had seen her share of gung-ho Yankee soldiers in her job as a stewardess for Australia's Ansett Airlines, and I think she expected me to fit the mold. She was not a little surprised when our "first fight" quickly petered out, with me agreeing with almost everything she had to say. When I went back to Vietnam, we began to exchange letters. Soon we were getting together about once a month as well, thanks to the regular three-day leaves I got as a senior adviser, as part of the Handclasp program. Over time Jenny also became an honorary member of Team 50, kind of playing the Frenchie Frye liaison role for my guys who took their R&Rs in Sydney (telling them where to eat, where the parties were, etc.), and when her annual vacation came up in mid-March, I thought the least we could do was return all her favors and have her as our guest in the Zone. (As a British subject Jenny was free to visit Vietnam at will, and could simply fly into Tan Son Nhut commercially). Ben Willis thought the idea was crazy and tried to dissuade me from going ahead with the plan. I told him I was the boss and I could do anything I damn well wanted to (Ben's voice of reason was often too much for me to take during this period of my rebellion, leading to many bitter fights between us), and I even organized for Judge Cooney's journalist wife, Catherine, to get accreditation from MACV so she could come over as a reporter during the same period, in case I ended up having to be away for four or five days on some big operation and Jenny would otherwise be left alone.

Just before the visit, I was promoted to full colonel. It was a proud, proud day, and one made all the more special by Hank Emerson, now a brigadier general and commander of the Special Warfare Center at Fort Bragg. Hank sent me a gift of the colonel's insignia he had worn until his promotion, the silver eagle which, before that, had belonged to his father before *he* made general. What a good friend Hank was, writing me encouraging letters as my spirits flagged more and more, and trying again and again to turn my mind away from getting out. The team gave me a big, raucous promotion party, organized with love by old soldier and fine NCO Larry Portman. When it was all over and I was alone in my quarters, I marveled at the singular event that had made it all possible. Whatever its outcome, the Vietnam War had made me a colonel, and paved the way for one or maybe two or three stars if I stayed in. Yet, the Vietnam War, through what it had shown me, had destroyed my great love affair with the Army, and made me decide to hang up my suit. *Or had it?* I wondered. The day I made colonel, the choice had never seemed so hard.

Then Jenny arrived, and for two weeks I thought of nothing else. We were together every night, and during the days when we could be. She came along in the chopper when I went visiting individual units and border Ranger camps, and well proved her mettle, too, not losing her cool even when one compound we were visiting came under mortar attack, or when we took a Special Forces airboat ride up the Mekong River and had sniper slugs snapping over our heads. She was the greatest morale booster my advisers out in the boonies could ever have dreamed of seeing, and the same had to be said for the guys at the Team 50 compound. Jenny and Catherine were the first round-eyed women most had seen in months, and the men hovered around them like lovesick kids. I couldn't blame them.

I'd organized an R&R to Hong Kong to coincide with the end of Jenny's tour of the war zone. She flew commercial and I met her there; we had a ball even if I did spend a small fortune on uniforms for my next and last Army assignment, at NATO in Brussels, as Chief of the U.S. Army Section. The job was a far cry from the first one DA offered me, a hush-hush Special Forces assignment in which I would have controlled all covert operations in northern Thailand. It was hard for me to believe I'd actually refused a hot SF job and held out to work in the make-believe world of NATO, but then again, a decade before, I never would have believed it if someone had told me I'd be checking out of the Army any way but feetfirst.

As soon as I got back from Hong Kong, Team 50 received its annual Inspector General (IG) inspection. The purpose of these inspections was to make sure everything was aboveboard and conforming to Army regulations. Since the team was just one big broken reg, we had quite a bit of cleaning up to do to prepare. To be on the safe side, I organized for the IG and his team to be quartered with one of my subordinate units just down the road, rather than have them stay with us at Team 50. I shipped the few malcontents I had on the team off to distant outposts, and put the rest of the men back in their OD fatigues. We folded up the outdoor snack bar and for the purposes of the inspection deemed it a "kitchen annex." We told Mr. Ko to give the Steam and Cream girls a few days off, and made sure no Vietnamese went anywhere near the PX. We put all our hot vehicles—save one—in an area fenced off and guarded by a Viet, with a sign above it in Vietnamese so the IG would leave it alone (thinking it belonged to the Viet unit next door); the one hot jeep we kept out was the one we gave the IG to drive around in throughout his visit. That was my own little joke to have a silent laugh over each morning when the IG pulled up to the compound. Most of the team knew the vehicle was hot, too, and when in the end we came through the inspection with flying colors and had the IG gushing with praise in his exit interview, one of his most favorable comments regarded the team's morale, citing the smiles that greeted him each morning when he drove through our gate in his jeep.

In January of 1971, an ABC journalist by the name of Howard Tuckner came to see me in the Zone. He'd read Ward Just's *Military Men*, had heard I was "The Colonel," and now wanted to do kind of a television version of the chapter for his network. I told him to go home. In the first place, he struck me as a phony, and in the second, while his eight-part, ten-minute-segment series would be great for his career, it would certainly do little for mine. Even if I was going to quit, in the meantime I still had two years' NATO duty to go, and going on national television to tell the American people how badly we'd botched the war did not seem a particularly smart thing to do. But Tuckner was undeterred. I heard from him regularly in the subsequent months, months that saw the debacle in Laos, the disintegration of our own battlefield in the Zone (despite all of Hai's efforts, RF outposts were being gobbled up at an alarming rate), and me finally saying "Enough!" to those MACV briefings that persuasively reported victory was at hand and left me feeling crazy because I knew what I saw on the ground was exactly the opposite. These events, coupled with Tuckner's doggedness, began to wear me down. We had bullshitted ourselves, and the American people, long enough. And it was too late for me to start playing the old "go along to get along" game just because it would serve me the best. So I began seriously to contemplate blowing the whistle in this most public of ways, on national television.

Whether or not to do the show became a number-one concern for me. I probably asked my own advisers—Willis, Hancock, Frank Schuette, Ed Clark, Steve Bates, Jack Howett, G-3 adviser Doug Randles, and Judge Cooney—every single day what they thought I should do. And while old soldier (and NCO) realist Schuette said not to touch it, my young, idealistic officers were behind the thing 100 percent. There were truths that had to be told, they encouraged. But I remained tied up in knots inside. There were few things as taboo in the military as criticizing it outside the fold. And as I wrote to Jenny, I'd been in the Army so long I was like one of Pavlov's dogs: to speak out was against everything I'd been trained for. It was also against everything I'd believed in, against something I'd loved for so long and still did. After all, despite the times I'd felt the Army had failed me, it had also upheld me for most of my life.

But what other avenue was left? I'd written memos and letters to my superiors, those generals who'd become friends, and articles for the Army at large, on every germane issue I thought confronted the American fighting man and adviser in Vietnam. I'd convinced Slam of the need for the *Vietnam Primer*; we wrote it and now two million copies were in print. I'd proved, on the ground with the men of the 4/39, how to fight the war on the cheap, in a way suitable for a protracted, guerrilla conflict, which was the only hope for success. I'd talked to General Johnson, the Army Chief of Staff. I'd talked to Stanley Resor, the Secretary of the Army. I'd contributed as honestly and pointedly as I could to that paper General Westmoreland requested in 1968 when he became Chief of Staff, on where the war had taken us and where we were to go from there. I'd talked to anyone who was anyone who came to visit my commands because *I*, they'd been told, was "someone," until I got tired of standing there politely as I watched my words go in one ear and out the other of my guest, and began to talk even more bluntly. I'd leaked information and stories to trusted pals in the press, thinking they could make a dent in the mind-set of the Army hierarchy. In a word, I'd *tried*. But that fact didn't make the decision to go public any easier.

Then, two things happened, and the decision made itself. First was a promotion list that showed Ira Augustus Hunt, Jr., already a one-star, on the 5 percent list to major general. Second was the conclusion of the Calley trial, which had the recycled OCS lieutenant found guilty of premeditated murder, only to have President Nixon step in and declare that he would personally review the case. And while the two events, on one level, had nothing in common, on another, to me they said it all about what was happening to the Army—and inasmuch as I could possibly do something about it, I just couldn't let it go on unremarked.

In and of itself, the Calley case was a microcosm of everything that was wrong with the Army. I'd first heard the rumor about My Lai when I was in the Delta with the 4/39, and I'd strongly denied even the possibility of it having happened. I'd fought a lot of years as an infantryman and seen my share of what could be called atrocities, but *never* had I seen, nor could I ever imagine it occurring, American soldiers involved in such a massacre of women and children. In my experience, it just wasn't in the American soldier's mentality. (Obviously this was before I studied Sand Creek and other infamous moments in our Army's Indian-fighting days.) Nonetheless, when the truth came out—despite the determined effort of Calley's battalion, brigade, and division commanders to cover it up from the Army, *and* the Army's determined effort to cover it up from the press—what the facts revealed made the crime only too believable. My Lai reflected the horrific inadequacies in the training system, which, rather than coming to terms with the fact that attrition in the schools was a fact of life, pushed proven incompetent misfits through the system and allowed them to lead platoons in combat. The events at My Lai reflected the inadequacy, to the point of total absence, of senior leadership all the way up Calley's chain of command. (As Colonel Lucian K. Truscott III, son of WW II's fighting General Truscott, wrote, "Would My Lai have happened if Koster [division CG] and Henderson [brigade CO] and Barker [battalion CO]—all of whom have claimed that they saw and heard nothing—had been down on the ground where the killing was going on?") And in that the men whose careers stood to be least enhanced by the events at My Lai actively suppressed information or, even worse, simply closed their eyes to cover their own asses instead of immediately and severely punishing the participants in the massacre, My Lai reflected a tragic bankruptcy of moral fiber in the Army's senior officer corps, a direct result of rampant careerism. To me, all this was bad enough. But then, when the Army actually had the balls to stand in the door and convict Calley for murder, to have Richard Nixon come along and for purely political ends interfere with military justice and essentially nullify the result was too much for me. The kid was guilty as hell. Having judged him so, the Army had to start addressing its own inadequacies, to find out how it could have allowed such a "leader" to get through the system in the first place. But Nixon's action was an out—as good as excusing the Army from even *beginning* that self-examination. Fundamentally, it was the worst thing that could have happened since My Lai itself.

So that was one thing that pushed me in the direction of going public. As for the second, the attendant rumor to Hunt's being picked up below the zone to major general was that he was going "all the way," that this man would one day be Chief of Staff. It was *Once an Eagle* all over again, and I was horrified. It was as if I'd climbed to the highest rung of the ladder only to find the ladder was leaning against the wrong wall. If Hunt was what the Army now considered a stud—the kind of man to lead it into the eighties—then as far as I was concerned the Army had been lying to itself for so long about so much that it had totally lost perspective of reality.

So I got in touch with Howard Tuckner. Two days later he and his ABC boss, Nick George, were in Cao Lanh, and for some sixteen hours we discussed the content of the interview, which was to be filmed the following day and aired on ABC-TV's "Issues and Answers" in early July, after my tour was over and I was out of Vietnam. It was almost midnight when we finished up, and I found myself all alone and scared to death. I wrote to Jenny, "That TV camera will be worse than facing a platoon of machine guns. . . . Will try not to be too abrasive but I want to speak the truth of what is happening in Vietnam. If my efforts save one life, then it will be worthwhile."

In the morning the crew arrived. Howett was there, and Willis and Tuckner, who chatted with me while the crew set up and I tried to hold my apprehension at bay. Just as everything was ready, and I was about to sit down in front of that television camera, one of my commo men brought in a back-channel message for me. It was from Hank Emerson in the United States, and it was an invitation to be his deputy for a new leadership study group designed to find out what the hell was wrong with the U.S. Army. Westmoreland had already approved my appointment.

The timing of Hank's offer was most incredible. If that back channel had arrived the day before, I would have canceled the show, no question about it. As it was, I was at a complete loss. Was it fate? God's eleventh-hour way of saying I was making a mistake, that I should stay and fight from within, and not thumb my nose at my lifeblood, especially this way, by speaking out, *in* Vietnam, *in* uniform? I told Tuckner I needed some time to think.

But when I thought, all I could think of—despite Hank and despite his exceptional way of making things happen when everyone else was letting them slide—was Westy's study in '68. In good faith I'd contributed to that report, as one of sixteen of the supposedly sharpest studs in the Army. Three years later, it had changed nothing. After that experience, why I believed that as an *individual* I somehow had the authority to bring those in power to their senses, I didn't know. But I *did* believe it. I truly believed that by going outside channels directly to the American people, I could make these guys think, and bring about change. So in the end, despite Hank's offer, there was not much of a decision to be made. And so the camera began to roll.

22 "ISSUES AND ANSWERS"

SUNDAY, 27 JUNE 1971*

GUEST:

Colonel David H. Hackworth, U.S. Army

INTERVIEWED BY:

Howard Tuckner, ABC News Saigon Correspondent

MR. TUCKNER: You have served in Korea, you have served in Vietnam for a long time, you have served back at the Pentagon. How do you rate the training of U.S. Army troops who came to Vietnam?

COLONEL HACKWORTH: I think in the main the training for Vietnam from the standpoint of the individual soldier, the young officer, and even the battalion, brigade, and division staff officers and senior commanders has been totally inadequate.

I think that our training was geared to the individual replacement system of World War II. The curriculum was wrong, the quality of the instructors and the leaders was—in my judgment we didn't have the type people that should have been there. The commanders there should have been—the battalion commanders should have commanded battalions in Vietnam. The company commanders should have commanded companies, here, and leaders should have been the finest leaders our country could have mustered to provide the young soldiers with the type training, the realistic training that they needed to confront a guerrilla enemy in Vietnam.

And I'd like to just make the point that when my well-trained, STRAC, one of the finest units in the U.S. Army arrived in Vietnam in June and July of 1965, the mistakes they made were criminal. The number of dead that they have killed among themselves, men that were shot by their comrades, artillery that had fallen on them. Great mistakes were made because of improper training, being not prepared for the war, even though we had from 1953 to 1965 to prepare for the war.

---

* This is a direct transcript of the ABC "Issues and Answers" interview aired nationwide in the United States on Sunday, 27 June 1971. No editing or corrections in grammar have been made in the text.

MR. TUCKNER: In your view did poor training lead to higher casualties in Vietnam?

COLONEL HACKWORTH: I am convinced of it. I think that our casualties were at least thirty percent higher because of—or even higher than that, but I'd say, just safely, thirty percent higher because of troops that were not properly trained.

I participated in a study group in the Pentagon in '67 and early '68 which considered U.S. casualties caused by friendly fires and the group was composed of highly experienced personnel that had served in Vietnam and it was our conclusion that fifteen to twenty percent of the casualties caused in Vietnam were the result of friendly fire—one man shooting another man; artillery, friendly artillery firing on a friendly element; friendly helicopters firing on a friendly unit; tac air striking a friendly unit; and I could count you, in my own case, countless personal examples. For example, during the battle of Dak To, June the seventeenth, a rocket ship came into my A Company's position by mistake and released its rockets right on top of the company killing the executive officer and wounding twenty-nine other troopers.

I can recall in September of 1965 as my battalion was deployed, artillery was fired in the wrong place killing seven men in one of my platoons.

MR. TUCKNER: Can it be said that the generals in the U.S. Army, many of them, did not really adjust to the tactics of this war?

COLONEL HACKWORTH: I think the average general that came to Vietnam did not have a good concept, good appreciation of the nature of guerrilla warfare. In most cases because of their lack of even reading in depth about guerrilla warfare, they were not prepared for the war and they had to fall back on Korea and World War II and they used the thought process and the techniques that worked successfully there, moving in large formations, making battalion and brigade airmobile assaults on a small LZ and having everything very tidy, artillery in position and fighting much as we did on the plains of Europe.

I don't feel that too many division commanders, or even separate brigade commanders, really understood the name of the game.

MR. TUCKNER: Did this mean more U.S. casualties, this misunderstanding of the name of the game, as you put it?

COLONEL HACKWORTH: Absolutely. Absolutely. I think probably one of the most classic examples is Hamburger Hill. Here was a hill that had to be taken. Hundreds and hundreds of casualties occurred taking this hill. They had the hill for a few days, the Americans did, and pulled off. So what was the point of taking the hill? Why not stand back if the enemy is on it and bomb, but why use infantry to take the hill?

MR. TUCKNER: Did the upper echelon of the Army really ever become changed on this war? Did they learn from their mistakes?

COLONEL HACKWORTH: I don't think so. I don't think that the top level ever developed a realistic strategic plan nor did they ever have tactics to support that strategic plan.

MR. TUCKNER: Why?

COLONEL HACKWORTH: I think that the top managers of the Army—and there is a big difference between a leader, a combat leader and a manager, the top managers were so involved in systems analysis, in the normal bureaucracy of it all that they were fighting from day to day just to move the paper that crossed their desk and they couldn't see the forest for the trees.

In February when we went into Laos, we went into Laos conventionally. The idea was to block the enemy's supply routes. So we dropped in there. We paid a horrible—the Vietnamese paid a horrible price. Tremendous mistakes were made. Again, conventional thinking. Conventional thinking put us in that operation rather than having a light, mobile guerrilla force, but a guerrilla force that belonged to the Government of Vietnam, or the American Army operating in there like guerrillas. It takes a thief to catch a thief. What we need is a thief. We don't need a conventionally trained FBI agent dashing through the woods with a large force behind him.

We need small people, well trained, highly motivated, and this is what we have not had, because what we have now among the Army is a bunch of shallow dilettantes who run from pillar to post trying to punch their card, serving minimum time at company level because the exposure—you are very close to the heat of the furnace there, meaning you can get in trouble easily.

MR. TUCKNER: Have you found that many other U.S. Army officers who have been here in Vietnam feel the way you do?

COLONEL HACKWORTH: Most of my young friends—that would be captains, majors, and lieutenant colonels—who have a considerable amount of experience in Vietnam, feel as I do. A number of very highly qualified full colonels whom I know feel as I do, and I suppose there are a few generals who feel as I do, but in the main this group unfortunately—I suppose it is because of the nature of the beast—is not highly vocal regarding their views because if one would become highly vocal you might become a Billy Mitchell. It might be the end of your career.

MR. TUCKNER: Hasn't this silence meant that some who have died in this war might have been saved?

COLONEL HACKWORTH: That is right, and that is why perhaps we who have not been vocal should be charged for just criminal neglect, because it is our obligation, it is our responsibility, not only to train our soldiers well, to lead our soldiers well, but to make sure that there are no mistakes made, that they are protected as well as possible from mistakes and error and once you make mistakes they must be surfaced, critiqued, identified, and remedial action taken.

MR. TUCKNER: Colonel, I understand that because of the fact that you are considered one of the best infantry officers in the Army you have been asked a number of times to go to the War College, which is preparation for becoming general one day.

COLONEL HACKWORTH: Yes, I have been asked to go to War College for three years straight, and my reason for refusing is that I just simply felt that we were on the battlefield, we were engaged in a critical battle, and I didn't need to go to school at the time to learn anything. I was learning it on the battlefield and I was transferring the skills that I had to my men and probably saving lives.

I can recall in November of 1969 a major general here in Vietnam told me that, when I asked him, should I extend again, he said, "Hack, get out. The war for the U.S. Army is over with in Vietnam."

He said, "You've got all the right tickets and all the right credentials. Go on to War College now and prepare yourself for bigger things."

MR. TUCKNER: Colonel, we have heard a lot about body count in this war. What about it?

COLONEL HACKWORTH: Well, it has been used as a rule of measurement of success. The body count has cost us a lot. It has cost us unnecessary casualties because always in the chain of command one commander is pressuring the other commander for what is the success, what is the body count and it ends up you are calling the platoon leader, "How many have you killed?"

The platoon leader is in a firefight and he hasn't a clue of how many he has killed, but he may have to stop the fight. He may have to expose a few soldiers to go out and count the bodies during the fight. He may lose the momentum of the attack to stay on the enemy and pursue him while he is counting bodies. He may have to squat on the enemy and count the bodies.

It has also really weakened the moral fiber of the officer corps because it has taught them to lie; it has taught them to exaggerate because, again, it is a form of success. It is "How many touchdowns do you have? What is the final score of the game?" And the body count has been greatly exaggerated as a result of this and I would say it has been exaggerated to the tune of twenty to twenty-five percent.

MR. TUCKNER: Do you know of any example specifically where you were involved in trying to substantiate body count that you didn't think was accurate?

COLONEL HACKWORTH: Yes. I could give several good examples. One which comes to mind is a battle which was fought with a great number of friendly maneuver elements, found—reputedly found—an enemy force; we encircled the enemy force. All night long artillery, rockets, fighter bombers were placed on the enemy for us, and came the dawn when we swept the enemy positions there was a total of enemy dead on the battlefield of not more than twenty.

When I crossed over to the other side of the canal that we were fighting on to talk to the commander of the other battalion which was the other half of the encirclement force, the brigade commander came in and started talking about such a brilliant victory we had and that we killed something like two hundred seventy-five or two hundred eighty enemy dead, and this was a classic battle. It illustrated the techniques of mobile warfare, how we could drop on an enemy force, find them, fix them, surround them, and then destroy them, and I pointed out to the brigade commander, the acting brigade commander, I should say, that there wasn't that many dead on the battlefield. We had only killed, I would say, no more than twelve or fifteen and the colonel on the other side had told me he had six or seven, so there couldn't have been twenty or twenty-two or so and I was told there were two hundred eighty killed. *

This is what had been reported to Division. I said, "Well, it is not right. We only had— This battalion is reported to have a strength of three hundred and if we killed two hundred eighty that would leave less than twenty able-bodied men, able to remove the bodies from the battlefield," which is a normal VC technique, which was his excuse for why the bodies weren't on the battlefield.

He said, "Well, that night the survivors carried them off."

I said, "Look, we had the enemy completely surrounded; there was no corridor in which he could escape. If there were a small path that he could have gained escape through our lines that would have meant that every survivor would have had to carry seven or eight bodies plus all their individual weapons." I think there were five total individual weapons found on the battlefield, and this complete battle was a total lie in my judgment.

I was called in by the commander at the time to endorse his after-action report, this report which had all of these bodies in it, and great other irregularities and falsehood, I think designed to make this individual look like Rommel or look like some great tactician and very, very effective

* Clearly, during the interview my chronology as pertaining to the subject of body count at the Battle of My Phouc Tay (Thanh Phu) was confused. Though the count was inflated by almost one-third by acting Brigade CO Hunt the morning after the battle, the figure of (approximately) 280 did not come to my attention until six weeks later, when Hunt showed me the draft copy of his "History of the Battle of Thanh Phu" and attempted to get my endorsement of it. Similarly, no prolonged discussion about the battle took place between Hunt and myself until that time.

combat leader. And I refused to do it. And he and I had somewhat of a major confrontation.

Also during this time I was asked to sign a statement, a narrative statement to support an award for the Distinguished Service Cross for this individual who didn't even get out of his helicopter during the "battle," and I refused to do that.

It was insinuated if I would sign one or two of these documents that I would be—my unit would be considered, possibly, for a unit citation as a result of this action, which I, of course, refused to go along with.

MR. TUCKNER: Did you sign it?

COLONEL HACKWORTH: Absolutely not.

MR. TUCKNER: When leading U.S. government officials, people like former Secretary of Defense McNamara, come to Vietnam for a visit, do they get the clear, straight picture?

COLONEL HACKWORTH: I think what we do for a presentation for a senior official such as Mr. McNamara is put on a razzle-dazzle briefing, complete with charts and extremely well rehearsed briefing officers, and we try to put our best foot forward to try to look as good as possible. Perhaps a scenario would go kind of like this:

After the briefing Mr. McNamara turned to General Wheeler, who was with him, or to General Westmoreland, who I would think accompanied him, and said, "What do you think about that?" And General Wheeler said, "Great battle! We are knockin' 'em dead." And General Westmoreland would have said, "We really got 'em that time! This is a typical action in Vietnam of your U.S. modern Army in action! We have really nailed them and that is the way we are nailing them and that is why we are winning this war. Just give us a few more troops, a few more resources, and we will have 'em on the run. There's light at the end of the tunnel."

He didn't say the VC was holding the candle but he said the end is in sight.

So as a consequence, Mr. McNamara, believing this, perhaps—because it looked real enough to believe—went back and he is sitting—again part of the scenario with the President, and Mr. Johnson says, "How's it going in Vietnam?" and McNamara says, "We are winning."

MR. TUCKNER: Colonel, in 1968 you were so highly thought of that you were selected from a group of a few officers to contribute to a report to General Westmoreland. What did you say in that report?

COLONEL HACKWORTH: Well, my comments were very exciting insofar as the Army staff was concerned. I felt they were truthful and I said that in my judgment at the time this paper was written in 1968, the U.S. Army had badly botched the war in Vietnam and I had considered from a tactical standpoint we had lost the war.

And now my experience three years later only confirms those comments to General Westmoreland.

MR. TUCKNER: What's happened since then? Has there been any change? Have your comments helped anything?

COLONEL HACKWORTH: No, I don't think so. I said that I felt there have been no viable reforms. I felt that the corruption that exists in Vietnam, the graft, the failure to produce continues to exist. I felt that the military had not established any strategic goals, nor had there been any tactical concept developed to support the strategic goals which were not developed and announced.

I felt that we sent an Army to Vietnam that was not prepared to fight the war. We sent an Army that was top-heavy in administrators and logisticians and bloody thin on fighters, not trained for the war. I felt that we didn't understand the nature of the war in the military. I felt that just everything we had done in Vietnam had been done wrong.

MR. TUCKNER: Do you think it is possible, Colonel, that past United States Presidents who have been involved during the Vietnam War, the present Administration, do you think it is possible they may feel they are getting the straight truth, but that it might not be?

COLONEL HACKWORTH: Well, my thing is infantry, which I am very familiar with, and I don't know what happens at the higher echelons. I know the nature of the beast in the military is to sanitize a report to look good. I have seen what has happened at brigade level where the whole situation has been distorted.

I think it is highly probable that all of these beautiful briefings and excellent reports were so production-line Hollywoodized that by the time they got to the President and they got to the people who were making decisions, they didn't have the real facts; they didn't understand what was happening.

MR. TUCKNER: Colonel, what do you think of the Vietnamization program? Is it viable now?

COLONEL HACKWORTH: Well, my view of Vietnamization is, it is a nice word. I think that it has been glamorized; I think that it has been Madison Avenued; I think that it is perhaps a PR's dream. It is a public-relations gimmick.

I have been with the Vietnamese a long time and I have seen great improvements, significant improvement, but I haven't seen the improvements that I read about in many papers, and different magazines, and I hear leading statesmen of our nation say. I don't think the Vietnamese are that good. I don't think the whole Vietnamization thing is real.

MR. TUCKNER: If the enemy chose to react and if American troops were not here, what do you think would happen to the Vietnamese Army?

COLONEL HACKWORTH: I think if the enemy had the capability of launching a concerted attack I would think we would find ourselves in a situation as we were in in '63, '64, and early '65, really, because of the American involvement here, was to save the shattered Vietnamese Army. We were losing on the average of, as I recall, almost a battalion of Vietnamese a week in '65 and I think we would find the same situation developing. If the North Vietnamese, who I feel have the capability—they certainly proved they were pretty dangerous and tough up in Laos—and we find that we recently made a foray into Cambodia, and the enemy is much harder in Cambodia. Last April the targets we were striking along my zone in Cambodia were like taking candy from a baby. Now you go to Cambodia and you find the enemy with his stuff together. He is tough; he is moving back into the areas we used to raid with ease. I think we are going to find it more and more difficult of making these raids into Cambodia.

MR. TUCKNER: Do you think that the programs that the U.S. military and perhaps the U.S. mission had here did not fit the situation for Vietnamization?

COLONEL HACKWORTH: Exactly. We gave them a sheet of music designed by the military and that is what they had to dance by, and the whole organization of the Vietnamese Army in my judgment has been wrong; it has not been tailored or designed to fight the guerrilla in this type of warfare and we have given them a lot of sophisticated equipment, helicopters, sensor devices, radars, complicated vehicles, other complicated equipment that the Vietnamese are just incapable of using, incapable of maintaining, so we have given them now all kinds of sophisticated junk and asked them to use this. Vietnamization now will suddenly win the war because the Vietnamese have helicopters. We will suddenly win the war because the Vietnamese have the M-16 rifle, but it takes a lot more than a piece of equipment or a complicated piece of equipment such as radar and sensors and so on for them to win the war.

Instead of saying, "What you need is well-trained soldiers, what you need is highly motivated soldiers, what you need is soldiers who are similar to the Viet Cong soldiers who are fighting for an ideal, who are fighting for something—similar to Christianity; who are fighting for a cause, a crusade, not fighting to get a Honda or get a new watch or get a portable radio or to have a nice house, but fighting for a cause, and this is what has not been inculcated in the whole army of Vietnam.

MR. TUCKNER: Colonel, do you feel it is possible you have become too emotionally involved in Vietnam?

COLONEL HACKWORTH: I have become emotionally involved in Vietnam. One couldn't have spent the number of years I have spent in Vietnam without becoming emotionally involved. One couldn't see the number of young studs die or be terribly wounded without becoming emotionally involved.

I just have seen the American nation spend so much of its wonderful, great young men in this country. I have seen our national wealth being drained away. I see the nation being split apart and almost being split asunder because of this war, and I am wondering to what end it is all going to lead to.

23 A HANDFUL OF ASHES

What can we do to him?

Notation on DCSPER routing slip
from the Office of the Deputy Chief
of Staff, Personnel, 23 June 1971

ALMOST two months would pass between the filming and the airing of my "Issues and Answers" interview. Even so, within a week of the filming I'd put in for retirement immediately upon completion of my Zone tour, asking that the two-year mandatory promotion requirement be waived.

There was hardly anything I said to Howard Tuckner that I hadn't said before in my published articles or in discussions with or input to the Army's top brass. But when I played the unedited, three-hour tape of the interview for my team brain trust, their verdict was that there was no way the Army would let me get away with this most public of public airings. Not only would my orders to NATO be rescinded before the credits rolled on the television screen, suggested my friends and advisers, but no stone would go unturned in an effort to make my life as unpleasant as possible. So I applied for retirement.

On one hand, the move took a great weight off my shoulders. "Really feel good inside about my decision," I wrote to Jenny Bates. "It is right because I feel that if you don't like something, don't snivel and whimper about it. Sound off—express your views—be prepared for the consequences." On the other hand, I was devastated. Despite my outward bravado, I went on a bender not unlike the one that had followed my not being selected for major in Germany. Yes, I'd planned all along to get out, but *not yet*. I'd looked forward to those two years in Belgium, not only to prepare myself for civilian life, but because somehow deep inside I'd thought maybe something remarkable would happen during that period to cause me to stay in. And even though I'd said I didn't want a star (or stars) to join the ranks of the Hunts and the Ewells and the Massengales, I'd still thought of those stars, which I would have been proud to wear in the company of the Emersons and the Moores and the Damons. Whatever I'd said, in my head I'd never ruled out making general (on top of anything else, it would have been a hell of a good ending to the story of an orphaned kid from Santa Monica, California), and now that I most definitely would not, I actually mourned.

> It seems to me that Hackworth's impact on military matters would have been more significant *in* the military than standing outside it and criticizing. I think that his suggestions for improving the country's military preparedness would have been heeded much more if he had gone on to be a general officer. I've thought about this many times. I'm not sure his friends were his best advice and counsel back then, and he was truly *asking*. He hadn't made up his mind. . . . I really think we did him and the country a disservice with our advice.
>
> Thomas O. Cooney
> G-4 Adviser, Executive Officer
> 44th Special Tactical Zone
> Republic of Vietnam 1970–71

Having always considered money an easy come, easy go commodity, I'd never saved a cent. Now, the most worrisome thing about my abrupt change of plans was that with more than half my retirement pay going to child support, I was about to start a new life with an empty wallet. It wouldn't have mattered had I had a transferable skill, but what civilian jobs were designed for a forty-year-old ex-infantry colonel? I needed a grubstake and I needed it fast. My only real talent in this area was gambling, and though I'd never actually stopped playing poker and blackjack, in my final weeks in Vietnam I made damn sure that whenever the dealer called "ante up" I was there. I relied on a number of team members to help me get my winnings out of the country. This was against MACV currency regulations (you were allowed to take out of the country, on your own behalf, only what you earned), but over the past two years, I'd never sent money home on my own behalf, earned *or* won. I'd always asked whoever on the team was going on R&R if they could just send it to Patty or Grattan (who was managing my financial affairs in the States) for me. At this point it was virtually an SOP.

Meanwhile, the war went on, with the Viet Cong seeming to be bursting with renewed life. Their main targets in the Delta were the little mud forts of the Regional Forces. These installations were being hit hard and on a regular basis, and for reasons unknown, were simply not hitting back. One evening, a very serious attack on an RF outpost in the Zone kept me up all night trying to bring relief to the besieged position. Fortunately, we had excellent U.S. tac-air and gunship support, and Americans on the ground who were able to prevent the outpost from being overrun. The final "victory" was bitter, however, in that two of my men, members of Major Allen Gezelman's Mobile Training Team who took charge and saved the day when the Viet leaders went to ground, were hit, and one of them, a fine sergeant named Meadows, died from his wounds. Regardless of the number of men I'd had die under my command—and Meadows was the last—it still got to me. And the pain was only eclipsed by the anger I felt, not just at Meadows' death but at every American death in this war that was not our own, that had nothing to do with the security of America, and in which our sacrifices were totally unappreciated: throughout this action, not one key Vietnamese had shown up at the joint U.S./Viet TOC, to play a role or even just to find out what was happening.

DRAC and MACV knew full well the extent of the deteriorating RF scene, but tried their best to cover it up. The Saigon press never grabbed on to the story because RF losses were not highlighted at the "Five-o'clock Follies" (as the MACV and other high-level press briefings were known) and were of too small a scale to be headline grabbers. I got so angry over the continuing deception that I sent Ward Just a study I'd recently received that laid out the sorry truth of Vietnamization in the Delta. Its contents were soon made public in an article Ward wrote for the The Washington Post, and the people of America could read with their own eyes that between January and April 1971 fifty-four Viet bases and outposts—double the figure from the previous year—had been overrun, with the attendant loss of 570 rifles, 79 radios, and enough ammo to supply a division.[1]

The reasons for the losses were many, all of which had as their root bad Viet leadership. Reading between the lines, however, all that was really happening was that the situation was reverting back to the way it had been before the Americans came in 1965. Then, if we hadn't come in, the South Vietnamese forces would have collapsed. Now that U.S. units were pulling out, it was only a question of time before that fate greeted our allies. And whatever the South Vietnamese Army or the South Vietnamese government thought about that, the South Vietnamese people were ready for the inevitable. In 1965 they'd been tired, their faces etched with sorrow and fear. In 1971, the lines were only deeper, the spirits heavy with the futility of it all. Just days before I was to leave the Zone for good, I visited a hamlet that had been clobbered the night before. The village chief and I sat down together to discuss what had happened, but the chief had something more on his mind. "Many years ago, I lost all my sons," he began. "That was when the French fought here. Last night I lost my only grandson. I am the only man of my family who is still alive. Go home, Dai Ta [Colonel]. At least then we will live."

Though the words stung, the chief's statement was only eloquent confirmation of something John Paul Vann had told me almost a year before. "This is a funny war," he'd said. "When the U.S. 9th Division operated in Dinh Tuong and Kien Hoa provinces, they killed more VC than any other unit has ever done in Vietnam. But no progress was made in pacification. When the 9th left, everyone said, 'The VC will take over now.' But it hasn't happened. Just the reverse. The government now controls more. Accommodation. It's a way of life. When the Americans leave, there will be a coalition among the Vietnamese at the grass-roots level. There won't be any idealism. There won't be democracy. But the people will have full bellies. The one thing both sides have going for them is they're both Vietnamese."

Or, as I'd written to Raphiel Benjamin while I was wrestling over whether or not to speak out, "The fight here should not be an international struggle. It is a nationalistic, regional conflict and it is unfortunate that one of the opponents is waving the red flag because this automatically made that side the bogeyman which old Uncle Sam has apparently sworn to contain. And contain for reasons that are unclear to me, except as a kid I was told that the bogeyman was bad and if I didn't come home by a certain time he would eat me up. Think someone like Churchill convinced 'Sam' of the same thing. So as Ward Just said, 'To What End.' "

> The last time I saw David was in Saigon. He called me and asked if I would meet him. But then he brought two or three friends of his with him. I didn't like them. It seemed to me they were influencing him, or had influenced him. Their presence was an imposition. And I didn't really like the way David was handling it, frankly. He'd always been kind of chipper. Happy-go-lucky. Now he was being a little smart-ass. . . .
>
> But the thing that impressed me about that saying good-bye was that I got the feeling he was asking me to understand. He knew I was part of the establishment. So was he, except he was rejecting it. And I got the feeling he was trying to make me understand.
>
> Colonel Harold "Ace" Elliott, USA, Ret.
> Commander, 16th MP Group, 1971

I flew to Can Tho on my last day in the 44th Zone. With veteran pilot Warrant Officer Phillips in the driver's seat, we were zipping along in a brand-new 7/1 Cav C&C chopper when the bird's instrument panel suddenly lit up like a pinball machine. It was definitely a four-alarm emergency, but with Phillips in charge and a fair number of chopper and airplane crashes under my belt, I wasn't too concerned. That is, until I glanced at Phillips. The pilot, who was among the coolest, most skillful aviators I knew, was absolutely ashen. We'd lost our hydraulic oil. "Mayday! Mayday!" Phillips called into his radio mike as he turned off the chopper's engine. "Mayday! Mayday!" as we plummeted down, down, down, like a lead anchor, right into bandit country. *What an inglorious way to go,* I thought, after all I'd been through. I really didn't want to die, and especially the day before I was going home for good. Just as we were about to crash, Phillips threw on all power. The engine caught at once, which broke our fall; still, the bird crashed to the ground, the skids splaying in every direction as we tumbled out, grabbing the door guns, and went into a little perimeter to await the Viet Cong. We didn't have long to wait. Within seconds of the crash, the sky, which had been empty when Phillips first called "Mayday!" was filled with U.S. helicopters and airplanes coming to the rescue. They circled us, spraying holy hell out of the area, and then a chopper swooped in and scooped us up. Within five minutes our broken bird was also saved, hooked out by a CH-47. Whatever else might be said about the U.S. performance in Vietnam, the Americans sure got their aviation trip together there. These guys were *good.*

I said good-bye to General Cushman at Can Tho and received from him a max efficiency report, complete with all the requisite adjectives. "This Officer has applied for retirement," the General explained in his ER comments:

> This is an unfortunate loss to the Army. Colonel Hackworth is a brilliant officer, of impressive reputation as a combat unit commander, extraordinarily innovative, and with exceptional insight into the nature of insurgency. He is a natural leader of soldiers. He attracts outstanding people, especially those of his own "tiger" type. He is tremendously able in a troop situation. He is an excellent organizer, writes very well, and is very widely read in his profession. He has a magnetic, driving personality. His many achievements in this current assignment include the imaginative development of effective mobile training teams for territorial forces, innovations in airmobile tactics, and major upgrading of advisory team administration and the team compound. He works very well with the Vietnamese. Colonel Hackworth is a real standout. If he were to stay in the Army, he should be given a broadening assignment outside a troop situation, working for someone he respects and could emulate, where he could further develop the maturity, tolerance, patience, and breadth that are essential characteristics of a general officer.

In Saigon I found that someone at ABC had let on that I'd talked, and a number of old acquaintances in the press corps came by to get interviews of their own. I hadn't planned to go further than the "Issues and Answers" thing, but now I figured if I was going to stand in the door I might as well go all the way. Besides, in a manner of speaking, some of these correspondents, among them Dan Southerland of *The Christian Science Monitor*, Kevin Buckley of *Newsweek*, and Rick Merron of the Associated Press, were old war buddies. In the case of Rick Merron, he'd actually been a 1/101st trooper when we came over in 1965, took his discharge in Vietnam, and stayed on as a reporter. On the job, he'd received eight separate wounds. So I gave a few more interviews, with the assurance from all that their release would be no earlier than the beginning of July, after I'd left Vietnam for the last time. Then I spent a couple of wild days gambling and partying with John Westmoreland, and then hopped onto a plane to Australia for a two-week leave before I came back to Vietnam for my final outprocessing.

But I hadn't been in Sydney a week when there was a knock on the door of Jenny's apartment. It was a uniformed U.S. Navy officer. "Someone is mad at you, Colonel," he said, and handed me a cable that his commander had received. "REQUEST THAT YOU CONTACT COLONEL DAVID H. HACKWORTH . . . AND INFORM HIM THAT UPON TERMINATION OF HIS LEAVE . . . HE IS TO RETURN TO SAIGON. UPON HIS ARRIVAL HE IS TO REPORT TO INSPECTOR GENERAL, MACV TO PROVIDE INFORMATION IN CONNECTION WITH AN INVESTIGATION OF FACTS AND CIRCUMSTANCES REGARDING HIS ALLEGATIONS."

Obviously someone had jumped the gun and published my comments. Even so, what the Army was calling allegations I knew were facts, and the Army couldn't hang me for telling the truth. I'd even had Judge Cooney check with four MACV JAG lawyers, including one from JUSPAO (the public affairs and information office at MACV), who, having been briefed on the basic thrust of what I had to say, all maintained I was well within my constitutional rights to say it. Still, the tone of the cable was pretty serious, and I figured whatever was going to happen, I might as well get it over with. So I didn't wait until the end of my leave. Instead, I caught the first plane back to Vietnam.

> At the morning briefing on the day following Hack's TV appearance, the ACSI [Assistant Chief of Staff, Intelligence] asked, "Where did this guy get his commission?" I replied, "He received a battlefield commission in Korea." Another officer stated, "He has abandoned his family, you know." Another general officer remarked, "They should take away his retirement pension."
>
> All this left me with a very sick, sick feeling.
>
> Colonel Wyatt J. Mitchell, USA, Ret.
> Staff Officer, Office of the
> Assistant Chief of Staff,
> Intelligence, 1971

I think many people felt the same way I did about the interview.
We didn't feel that it was necessarily wrong for him to do it, but
we felt kind of tainted by some of the things he said about our
behavior in Vietnam. . . . We recognized enough truth, but we
felt at the same time he was painting everyone with the same
brush. He was using a shotgun when he should have been using
a rifle.

> Colonel Henrik D. Lunde, USA, Ret.
> Battalion Commander, Special Forces
> Fort Bragg, 1971

The view here is that Colonel Hackworth represents a unique case
for which there are very few precedents in the Army's long history.
I don't think we have had his like since George A. Custer.

> Back channel from Lieutenant General William McCaffrey
> Deputy Commanding General, USARV, to
> General Bruce Palmer, Jr., Vice Chief
> of Staff, September 1971

A "distinguished visitor" on a military aircraft was anyone of the rank of
full colonel or above. Being a distinguished visitor gave you the right to be
the first to board an aircraft as well as the first to deplane; having never been
into protocol, however, when we arrived at Tan Son Nhut I waited in line
inside the cabin for my turn to get off the aircraft. This also allowed me to
postpone meeting the crowd of reporters waiting outside, whom I could hear
repeatedly calling my name. It was a good move. By the time I finally made
my way down the ramp, they'd either decided Hackworth wasn't on the
aircraft, or left me alone because they didn't know what Hackworth looked
like and I looked too young to be a bird colonel. In any event, I only had
eyes for my old friend Frenchie Frye, who stood on the side of the ramp
halfway down. "The three guys in khaki at the bottom of the ramp are IG,"
he said carefully, without moving his lips, like a convict in the yard.
"They're waiting for you. Do not identify yourself. Go directly to our jeep.
The shit has hit the fan." My heart froze. I saw the 44th Zone jeep parked
a short distance away. When I hit the bottom of the ramp I walked purposely
to it, as did Frye. It was a clean getaway.

Back at the Saigon safe house, Frenchie gave me all the facts that were
available from his MACV contacts. It seemed that the first article (Dan
Southerland's piece) had been published even as I'd gotten onto the plane
to Australia. The others, less Kevin Buckley and Nick Proffitt's *Newsweek*
item, followed within days. The same day Southerland's article appeared,

ABC had begun broadcasting excerpts of the Tuckner interview to plug the upcoming "Issues and Answers" program, and "Issues and Answers" itself had played in the U.S. this very day. Frenchie had called the team at Cao Lanh just before I arrived and was told things weren't too good. Apparently the Inspector General's office had descended upon Team 50 en masse. Mere weeks after we'd been given a clean IG bill of health, now the word was they were digging, looking for something wrong, something irregular, so they could throw the book at me, keep me in Vietnam, hold up my retirement, even court-martial me.

The calm, cool way Frenchie presented all the information he'd collected did little to quell my growing anxiety. Before long I had an overwhelming fear, one that covered all possible contingencies from the IG people abducting me forever and ever to an "enemy" sniper taking a single, lethal shot at me in a Saigon street. So I called Nick George over at ABC and asked for some flank security. The bureau chief, an ex-WW II infantryman, was totally supportive. He said he would assign a camera team to me, whose entire mission would be to go everywhere I went and, if necessary, film whatever happened. Feeling a little safer, I rang the IG office at MACV. "I understand you guys have been looking for me. I just got off the plane—must have missed you. What's up?"

They wanted to see me right away, but by then it was dark and after curfew, so I convinced them to wait until the next day. "General Abrams wants to see you at 0800 at MACV headquarters," they intoned. "Be there."

I was, and so was my film crew. But even with them, I was terrified, and the clusters of soldiers I saw hanging out the windows of Disneyland East, smiling, calling "Right on," and flashing me the peace sign did little to assuage my fear. The ABC crew went as far with me as they could, but they could not go farther than MACV's front door. Inside, I was informed General Abrams no longer wanted to see me, and that I was to leave my phone number and go back to my quarters—I would be contacted. The last thing I was told was that I was not to give any more statements until I returned to the United States. I went outside and gave that statement to ABC (which duly filmed it) and then I went back to the safe house. Later that day I received a call to come back to MACV for a talk with the IG. By then I'd managed to put the cap on my worst-case scenarios, and did not take the ABC crew along.

My "talk" with the IG men would prove to be four days and nights of on-and-off interrogation. I had to go through transcripts of the "Issues and Answers" program and each of the published articles with a pencil, initialing what I'd said or indicating "No, these are not my words" (or "Yes, they are, but they're out of context") as appropriate. I also had to give specifics for each of my allegations, including those concerning the body-count system's encouraging false reporting, and the fact that the Vietnamese had been lousy in 1965 and there'd been little improvement since. (Fifteen years later these and other of my "allegations" would be accepted as among the basic facts of the Vietnam War, but this was no help at the time.) My comments about the disaster on Hamburger Hill and the sorry ARVN attack into Laos were dismissed on the basis that I had no "direct knowledge" of them (i.e., I hadn't been on the ground). This was despite my having read after-action reports and/or having talked to the participants soon afterwards in both cases, in the Slam Marshall vein, which had been thoroughly legitimized in our Chief of Staff–backed *Vietnam Primer*, which was now considered part of Army literature for Vietnam.

Once I got into the swing of the questioning and realized I was dealing with a kangaroo court, I began to take it all a little easier. The only time I got scared was on the second day, when, off the record, the IG told me a little story about a major general in the German Army who'd been paid twenty-five thousand dollars to blow the whistle on his organization. Then the IG said he had information that I'd deposited five thousand dollars in my Pentagon bank account in late May, and asked if I had been paid by *Newsweek* or the newspapers to speak out. I had not, but I also had no idea where all that money in my account came from. My initial thought was I'd been framed. It was not until I got out of there and called Tim Grattan that I found out the money had been deposited by a realtor who'd sold my house in Bellevue, Washington.

I knew I had to get the hell out of Vietnam. If these guys knew what was happening in my bank account in the United States (though the fact that they did was totally illegal),* it wasn't going to take them long to uncover the shallowly buried irregularities in the Zone. One hot jeep would be enough to allow them to whack a criminal charge on me, and then they could keep me in-country as long as they damn well pleased. And besides worrying about that, and about being court-martialed sometime down the track, I was worried about becoming a terrorist statistic right now. Film crew or no film crew, how easy it would be for there to be an "accident," not unlike (in kind) the one I'd had with WO Phillips in my chopper the day before I left Cao Lanh.

After four days it became too much. I told the MACV IG people to shit or get off the pot: they could let me go home as scheduled or they could press charges, but no way were they going to keep me in limbo, virtually under house arrest, forever. I told them I'd already spoken to the press, that I would have no problem doing it again, and anyway, how would it look to the

* Later the president of the bank would explain in a letter of apology that an inexperienced teller had mistakenly released the information to an Army investigator (on the same day Dan Southerland's *Christian Science Monitor* article was published) who'd stated he was acting on orders from the top.

American public if, after four years of serving my country in Vietnam, now, as a result of my beliefs, and of my telling *the truth*, the Army was not allowing me to go home? Shortly thereafter, word came from General Abrams to let me go.

And the word couldn't have come a moment too soon. Late that afternoon, just as I was leaving for the airport, John Westmoreland and I did a routine check of my jeep (which was parked in front of his house) and we found a frag grenade lodged under the front seat. The cotter pin was pulled, and only the way it was wedged under the seat kept the firing pin held back. Had we not found it, the slightest bounce or sudden stop as we drove the vehicle to the airport would have jarred the grenade and caused it to fire. *Good-bye, troublemaker,* sang my paranoid brain. Of course, incidents like this, generally the random work of South Vietnamese cowboys and VC terrorists, were not uncommon occurrences in Saigon, and in all likelihood the grenade under my jeep seat was a coincidental event to my predicament. But it got my complete attention. We safed the grenade and hauled ass to the airport, where I met up with Hancock, Willis, Schuette, and Frenchie Frye, who were going home, too, on the same plane. (All of us but Hancock were overdue, but it was Frenchie Frye, the master organizer who had coordinated our simultaneous flight from the cuckoo's nest.) Frenchie had also organized a much-appreciated order that allowed me to wear civilian clothes for the trip home, and as we got onto the airplane, I was sure I'd never been so relieved in my life. But just as the hostess was closing the door, I saw a light colonel dashing up the ramp holding a thick folder. I froze. They'd found something at Cao Lanh they could really nail me for, and it would be worth all the bad press they'd take. I could feel myself getting ready to bolt when the guy raced up to my seat. "Colonel Hackworth?" he asked breathlessly.

"Yeah," I responded. (*Get off this plane, you're under arrest,* my mind heard him say.)

"Here are your records," he replied, and then lowered his voice to a whisper, "you'll be needing them." It was nice, the way he said it, and his look was one of admiration. Friends like that I was going to need, too.

> Dear Colonel Hackworth, . . . I want to tell you . . . that we
> have received a greater volume of mail concerning your appear-
> ance than for any other guest whom we have presented this year.
> All of the letters were highly complimentary . . .
>
> Letter from Peggy Whedon
> Producer, "Issues and Answers"
> 6 July 1971

Dear "Issues and Answers" . . . The interview with Colonel
Hackworth is, I think, the most important thing you have done
this year. His "emotional involvement" with the soldiers and his
country is akin to that of a mother who has sweated out the draft
with three sons. His patriotism is, I fear, about to be misunderstood by the flag wavers. He deserves our gratitude and our
prayers!

Letter from Mrs. H. E.
Rice Lake, Wisconsin, 27 June 1971

Dear Gentlemen . . . I can't tell you how happy I am to hear just
"one voice in the wilderness" crying out the truth. As a former
combat veteran of Okinawa, I appreciate it even more! However,
Gentlemen, please don't let the Pentagon hurt this man. We need
men like him desperately.

Letter from Dr. R. F.
Glen Cove, L.I., New York, to
"Issues and Answers," 27 June 1971

The plane stopped in Japan and no one pulled me off. We stopped in
Anchorage, too, and no one pulled me off there either, even though that
very day an article I'd written called "The Army's Leadership Failure in
Vietnam" had been published in the *Washington Post* and syndicated
around the country, making angry people just a whole lot angrier. Finally
we got to San Francisco, where Jenny Bates (who'd flown in from Sydney
to meet me) and the press were waiting. My civilian gear allowed me to
escape the media, and Jenny and I headed straight up to Tim Grattan's, so
that the next morning I could zip over to Fort Lewis and sign out of the
Army.

Little did I know that by the time I arrived at Lewis my records had been
flagged and my terminal leave canceled. Fortunately for me, Fort Lewis
didn't know it either, because when the telex bearing this information came
through, it just so happened that all the luck in the world had converged on
the Fort Lewis message center on my behalf. In what had to have been a
one-in-ten-million chance, the Duty Officer that night was none other than
Captain B. J. Jensen, late of the 7/1 Cav, my beanie-propellered aviation
liaison officer in the Zone. When BJ saw the message, he just disappeared
it, and no one was the wiser.

Even with the reprieve, my brief visit to Lewis was plenty tense. Yes, the
young studs in the administration building were flashing the V sign and
saying stuff like "Right on, sir" and "Thanks for telling the truth," just as

they had at MACV in Saigon. But as I waited to see the G-1 colonel who'd be signing me out, a smiling clerk sidled up beside me and whispered, "Watch out for the Colonel, sir. He's working for the establishment against you."

"Thanks," I said, truly surprised. It hadn't occurred to me. I'd known this colonel for years, and I wouldn't have thought he'd be less than friendly. And I was right. The G-1 was all smiles as he ushered me into his office. "Just sign out here, Hack," he said. So I signed the papers that began my two months of terminal leave, after which, I hoped, would come retirement. With the formalities out of the way, the colonel, still as friendly as could be, asked (with the height of casualness), "So where are you going from here?"

I looked at his smiling face and remembered the smiling face of the clerk outside: *He's working for the establishment against you.* "Well," I said, "a good friend of mine has this yacht in San Francisco and he's going to sail down around the Caribbean for four or five months. I thought that was a pretty good way of working the war out of my system, so I'm going along."

"Sounds good."

"Should be."

It was a whopper, but a good one. I could see it now: the U.S. Navy and Coast Guard checking every pleasure yacht and military installation all over the Caribbean in an effort to track me down, while I was up with Tim in Seattle, or bopping around the U.S.A. It was not that I really believed I'd survive the two full months of terminal leave without getting caught. But I needed to delay it as long as possible. I had to know first what the Army had on me and what they planned to do, so I could develop a counterplan.

The evidence against me was mounting all too quickly. At the end of my last interrogation in Vietnam, Colonel Robert M. Cook, the MACV IG, had said, "The object of the IG business is to get things in perspective. If we wanted to get vindictive we could go down and go through your files [at Cao Lanh], and if we were after your ass, we could find all those petty things, but that's not the name of the game."[2] A less accurate statement I was never to hear. They'd already violated my constitutional rights by going into my bank account in the United States. They went to American Express, too, I soon found out, which gave Army investigators my complete files after the investigators promised not to release the source. And down in the Delta, they were digging up every damn thing they could. Pressure on team members was applied, at times lightly, at other times with a constitutionally unsound sledgehammer. Word got back to me that one young trooper in the Zone was told by an overzealous investigator that "the next time you see Hackworth will be at his court-martial." In another case, a proven warrior and friend of mine, called in to testify on the events of the Battle of My

Phouc Tay, was told (off the record) before his interview that if he said anything negative about any other participants in the battle he could very well be sued for slander. In yet another case, the IG handed team member Major Steve Yedinak a sealed letter addressed to Yedinak from me (which had been intercepted by the IG) and asked him to open it and reveal to the IG whether the contents were personal in nature. The major, a bright, honest, and dedicated officer, wrote in a Memo for Record of the incident, ". . . I seriously questioned the authority of the IG to exploit the contents of a personal letter. I asked what my alternatives were . . . the reply, authoritative in nature and tone, was, 'You don't have any alternatives— that's a direct order.' "[3] But all the pressure had the desired effect. It was like the one loose thread that once pulled, unravels the whole rug. People panicked, and one by one the irregularities, many of which the guys hadn't even known were irregular, came out. Their boss, whom they'd loved and respected, had left in his wake unanswered and unanswerable questions, which they were now stuck with: *Do you know of any criminal activities on the part of Colonel Hackworth? Do you have any information on Colonel Hackworth's gambling activities? Was Hackworth a good poker player and a consistent winner? Were you ever approached by Colonel Hackworth to send dollar instruments out of Vietnam? Did Jenny Bates stay in Colonel Hackworth's quarters when she came to visit? Do you know what the sleeping arrangements were? Did Colonel Hackworth use the steam bath? Have you ever seen Colonel Hackworth smoke marijuana?* Then there were the personal questions, asked of virtually every team member, officer and EM, of every grade, under oath: *Have you ever used the Team 50 steam bath? Have you ever engaged in any sexual activities at the steam bath? Have you ever smoked marijuana? Did you ever smoke marijuana during your time in this command?*

Confusion bred resentment, even among some of the most loyal of my friends. The few real malcontents eagerly seized the opportunity to Get Hackworth. One captain, for example, who'd hated me ever since I refused him permission to marry a Viet girl he'd fallen for (because her background check turned up mighty shady), happily passed on the extraordinary word that he'd heard I was involved in a white slavery/prostitution ring in Saigon. And as if that were not enough to send the IG guys leaping with joy over the grave they thought they were digging for me, they actually went to a remote acquaintance of mine whose girlfriend had recently shot him three times with a .45 when she found him in bed with another woman, and suggested to him he'd been shot because he "was not buying booze from the Hackworth mafia" for a Tu Do Street bar he had an interest in.

From what I could gather, the investigators' determination to nail me for smoking marijuana was based on the statement of a PFC who said he'd seen me smoking a joint with several other officers and senior NCOs in front of the Officers' Club late the night of my going-away party in the Zone. What he saw was what he saw, but without any perspective. I was on my way out of the Officers' Club on my way back to my quarters when I ran into the smokers that night.* I was also absolutely knee-knocking drunk at the time, and when that joint was passed to me, I probably would have taken it if it had been cow dung. So I had a few puffs, said good-bye to the guys, and lurched over to my quarters where I promptly threw up.

While the team in Cao Lanh was being raked over the coals, back in Seattle, Army agents conducted a twenty-four-hour-a-day stakeout of the Grattan residence. The CID guys went to see Tim at his office and questioned Darlene in the yard; the two Grattan kids, Lisa and Brad, were well rehearsed in what to say if they were approached going to or from elementary school, and for all of them it was the same drill: "Yeah, we know Hack . . . last we heard from him he was in Australia." In fact, Jenny and I were living in the basement apartment of their house. It was an incredible burden to put on my friends—for Tim, who could tell *no one* I was there (his business associates, whom I'd met in simpler times, were real "establishment" types who'd been outraged by the "Issues and Answers" interview, considered me a traitor, and, according to Tim, would only too gladly have broadcast my presence to the authorities), and for Darlene, who was, after all, only a war buddy by marriage (and in truth was only barely getting over thinking of me as the enemy from the Germany days, when the wives came in a poor last). Fortunately, just as it was all becoming too much, Tim organized a little cabin in the woods for Jenny and me near Spokane, which we slipped up to and stayed in for a couple of weeks before we began what I hoped would be a leisurely drive across America. That had been the plan all along: to show Jenny the sights of the U.S.A. until my terminal leave ended, and then to head for Europe to start a new life.

While we were at the cabin, back in Seattle, Grattan continued to process the information coming in from my personal "underground" (guys in the Zone, and others who were on my side at Fort Lewis and other Army installations across the country as well as the Pentagon), and at prearranged times passed "the latest" on to me from a pay phone near his house to a pay phone near our hideout. The word was never good, and it only got worse. A couple of my closer Zone cohorts were recalled to Vietnam for

---

* Marijuana was something I'd accommodated myself to in the Zone. It was to these late sixties draftees what booze was to the old Regulars, and though I did not smoke it myself (nor had I ever, throughout my career), as long as those who indulged did so in their off-hours, and did not jeopardize their own safety or the safety of the team, I felt comfortable looking the other way. And, if it kept the men who were smoking it from seeking the hard stuff just outside the compound gates, it had its place.

interrogation, and then Hancock (for reasons I would never know) gave blow-by-blow accounts during his interview of every possible indiscretion I and every friend of mine (besides him) in the Zone had ever committed, pausing only to exaggerate each tenfold. Simultaneously, he portrayed himself as the embodiment of Regular Army purity and honor, sullied only by his association with me. He even told the IG he hadn't seen me since we'd flown home from Vietnam together, when, in fact, we'd met in San Francisco just days before he met the IG, when I briefed him on all Zone intelligence I'd collected to that time (he was preparing to return to Vietnam to finish his tour, and we knew he would no doubt face the interrogators). I was flabbergasted by Hancock's treachery, and very, very hurt. But then I realized how typical this behavior really was, and how much of it was, in a sense, my fault. Despite all of Hancock's wild trespasses, in all the years I'd known him I'd remained blind to the exceptional weakness of his character. Even his performance during the run-in with the cowboys at John Westmoreland's bar had not wised me up. And by never recognizing his weakness and reining him in, I'd encouraged him in all his games and gimmicks, if only, sometimes, through benign neglect. So it really shouldn't have been any wonder that when it came to standing in the door, Hancock would only do it for himself. But that didn't make me feel any better. It was bad enough that his bogus testimony opened a whole new can of worms for the IG to chomp on. But what really got me was that I, who prided myself so much as a judge of character, had been so wrong about this human being.

Before I left Cao Lanh I'd worked out the itinerary for Jenny's and my trip across the States. I'd had it typed up and I'd given it to a number of guys on the team; just as we were about to take off on that journey, one of my informants suggested that in all likelihood our schedule had been compromised. We decided to go anyway, as planned, except that we left a few days early, bypassed my hometown, and from time to time juggled the stops in order to stay a few jumps ahead of the Army's posse. From Las Vegas I called Ward Just to tell him I thought I was going to need some help but had so far managed to avoid detection; Ward said, "Hack, you can't out-G the whole goddamn Army," and told me to make my way to Washington, D.C. He had a friend there, a lawyer named Joe Califano, who he thought would be able to help.

For the next month, Army agents were on our tail, but always a few days behind. In a pattern that was repeated again and again, we'd leave one location only to have our host there called or visited by the agents a couple of days later. For me, visiting and introducing Jenny to old friends like Larry Tahler, Raphiel Benjamin, and Doc Holley was a wonderful thing, but all the warm, safe havens these friends provided were just momentary relief in what was the most difficult time I'd ever had. Every little bit of information I received I analyzed a thousand different ways. Despite some very heavy drinking (by the end, almost a fifth of good old Kentucky bourbon every night), my predicament was the last thing on my mind as I went to sleep, the only thing I dreamed about at night, and the first thing I thought of when I woke up. Meanwhile, I was not exactly the knight in shining armor for whom Jenny had given up her home and career in Australia. I confided nothing in her, and all she really knew throughout was that I was in trouble. It actually made me feel guilty that no matter how distracted or secretive I was, or how many times I went out to make my phone calls or into the bathroom to read my mail, she remained unwavering in her support; unquestionably Jennifer Bates was my anchor during a terrible, terrible period, and she was a good woman, too.

Finally we arrived in Washington, D.C. On the outskirts of the city, I called Ward from a telephone booth and he gave me Califano's number. I called the lawyer's office immediately and made an appointment for two days down the track. I would have preferred it sooner, but Califano was still very much a rising star in law and politics, and a damn busy man. Still, he sounded so confident and unconcerned on the phone as he said, "Lay low until then—we'll surface you after we talk," that for the first time I thought maybe things weren't going to be so bad after all.

That overconfident feeling proved to be my downfall. We picked a motel in the very shadow of the Pentagon and got settled in. Later that evening, I decided to call Team 50 member Jack Howett (who was now out of the Army and going to law school in Pennsylvania) on the motel-room phone. Without thinking, I violated the cardinal rule when you're on the lam about using only pay phones, and sure enough, early the following morning— *knock, knock, knock*—two CID agents appeared at our motel-room door. In the land of the free and the home of the brave, the Army had monitored Jack Howett's phone and traced me down. "Your leave has been canceled. Your records are flagged and your application for retirement has been disapproved," one of the agents said sternly, and after directing me to contact Major General Alexander Bolling, Jr., the CG of Fort Lewis, soonest, they both went away. When I called Lewis, I was told to report back there immediately. "Why?" I asked.

"Because you're going back to Vietnam. General Abrams wants to talk to you," Bolling said.

"He does not want to talk to me. The IG told me he was so pissed off at me that he *never* wants to talk to me. Besides, I just drove the whole damn way across the country *from* Fort Lewis. I'll be damned if you think I'm going to drive the whole way back."

"All right, Colonel. Stand by and I'll get back to you."

A short time later the phone rang. This time it was a major general from the Pentagon who, I later found, was particularly interested in seeing me hang. "You are to report to Fort Lewis, Hackworth."

"No, sir, I will not," I replied. "I just got here. Also, I'm not feeling too good." (The words just popped out of my mouth.) "All eight Purple Hearts are hurting."

"Fine," the general said in a flash, "report to Walter Reed Hospital. You'll be assigned there."

Great. I called Califano immediately and told him what had transpired. He was not impressed with the phone-interception business, and assured me he'd have it and any other surveillance stopped. Then I gave him the good news that I'd swung it so I could go to Walter Reed. "For God's sake, man," he exploded, "you don't want to go there! They'll give you a frontal lobotomy!"

His reaction was so immediate and so impassioned that for a second my blood ran cold. This was serious shit. "Call him back," he continued. "Tell him you're feeling fine, you don't want to go to Walter Reed, and he should assign you somewhere else. And as for going to Vietnam, tell them I'm your counsel and I have said to you that if you go to Vietnam you'll be taking me with you." I called the major general. He accepted Califano's judgment and told me I would be assigned to Fort Meade in a few days. It was a convenient choice if they were determined to have my head: Meade was Court-martial Center, U.S.A. and with the Henderson and Medina (My Lai massacre) trials happening there even as we spoke, the wheels of the Army judicial system were already greased and rolling. Meanwhile I was to sign in at Fort Myer, which would officially cancel my terminal leave.

As Jenny and I walked through the motel lobby on our way out that morning, the motel operator stole over to tell me to be careful whom I called from the room. An agent was monitoring my phone, he said. I wasn't surprised, but I knew Califano would put an end to that, too. Then, as we walked out of the motel, I saw two men (one of whom had been to my room) sitting in an old green Army sedan in the parking lot. When I started my car, they started theirs, but their ancient Ford was no match for my 1971 Olds Cutlass, and after they pulled out onto the street behind me, I just screeched out into the traffic, leaving them for dust. "Due to traffic conditions," a CID wrap-up of the exciting day that followed would relate, "contact with Colonel Hackworth was broken."

When we returned to the motel later in the day, from down the block I could see the same green Army sedan now sitting in front of the building. I turned around, circled the block, and, undetected, pulled into a gas station just across the street. I went to the pay phone and called the motel operator. "Hello, this is Colonel Swift from the Pentagon," I said in my most efficient voice. "Is my man still there monitoring the phone calls of your guest Hackworth?"

"Yes, sir," said the cheerful telephone operator, "would you like to talk to him?"

"Thank you," I replied. Immediately the agent came on the line. "Scott," I began, "are you still monitoring Hackworth's phone?" The agent replied affirmatively. "Good," I said. "Now, I want you to look out the front window of the motel. Do you see the fellow in the phone booth at the gas station?"

"Yes, sir," the agent replied.

"What's he doing?"

"He's looking at the motel and smiling and waving at me."

"Right," I said. "And do you know who that is? That's me, Colonel Hackworth. You're doing a great job there, pal." I hung up the phone and got back into my car. As Jenny and I tore away down the street, the green sedan pulled out behind us in an old Ford version of hot pursuit. It followed us for a while, until we both got stopped at a traffic light. There I played the oldest game in the book, one I hadn't played since the mid-fifties with my Austin-Healey. With the agents in the vehicle behind us, when the light turned green, I pretended my car was stalled out at the intersection. When the light turned yellow, I revved the engine, and when the light turned red, I burned rubber across the intersection, leaving the Ford behind as the cars that now had the right-of-way honked and braked and barely missed wiping my Olds off the map. As the CID wrap-up would so charitably put it, the agents' second attempt at a "loose surveillance" of my car was also broken "due to traffic conditions." What the report didn't say was what I saw in my rearview mirror as we sped away: one of the agents smiling and holding his hand up in a V.

For all the fun and games of it, I was now very pissed off. I called the major general who'd rung me earlier from the Pentagon, and told him I wanted the tailing stopped, like *now*, and if it wasn't, I hoped he was ready to read about it in the papers the following day. He told me to report in to Fort Myer, implying that that would be the only way to get these guys off my ass. So I did. Signed in and was back in the Army. The same agent who had tossed me the V earlier in the day was on hand to witness my arrival at Myer. After I signed in he actually came up to me to say, for what it was worth, that he was sorry and ashamed to have been part of the dragnet.

It had been a long day. I parked the car on the street, and as dusk fell Jenny and I took a walk around Capitol Hill. On our way to the Washington

Monument we backtracked by the car, only to see two dark, long-haired, hippielike individuals looking at it. We walked on without a word, but our passing by didn't go unnoticed. The thugs started following us, talking to each other in Spanish. Jenny was terrified, and I was only slightly less so. These were not by-the-book, all-American, white-collar Army agents—these were very heavy guys. They *were* agents, however; it registered in my brain that I'd seen them earlier, near or in an Army green sedan, and I'd thought then how unlikely they seemed to be part of the Army establishment. Still, it wasn't a simple case of me turning around and saying, "Look, guys, ten percent never get the word, so maybe you didn't hear they've called off the dogs." These men appeared to have a mission far less benign than the jokers who'd been on my tail all day. When Jenny and I reached the Washington Monument, we scooted in the entrance as if we were going to take the stairs to the top. But we ducked around a corner instead, and the thugs ran by us. We dashed out again and ran down the street, not stopping until we got to a well-lit hotel, from whose lobby I called Joe Califano at home. "I'll have it stopped or I'll have Westmoreland's head," he vowed. "In the meantime, don't go back to your motel. I'll see you tomorrow as scheduled."

The tailing did stop the next day, and was not resumed. The apartment Jenny and I moved into to wait out my fate, however (the name on the mailbox was "Omar Khayyam," which I thought was pretty great and didn't change), was carefully searched on a regular basis. Besides the bugs that I occasionally found and had to remove from the phone, proof of this came through tiny pieces of wood (broken off a matchstick) or strands of Jenny's hair, one or the other of which I always placed on top of drawers, suitcases, or files before we left the apartment, and which all too often I'd find on the apartment floor when we returned, as telltale signs that our gear had been disturbed.

When I reported in to Fort Meade, I received an ice-cold reception. Officers I'd known for twenty years wouldn't even give me a nod of recognition. "Oh, yes, Colonel Hackworth," said the Adjutant General officer who signed me in but refused to raise his head and look me in the eyes as I stood before his desk, "you're to report to the Chief of Staff, First Army. Just up those stairs." I thought my luck was picking up when I looked at the First Army roster and saw that my new boss was Major General Richard Ciccolella. "The Chick," as many of us had called him when, years before, he'd taken over from Pat Cassidy as assistant division commander of the 101st, was a good, fair man, a hell of a fighting soldier in his day, and someone I'd always had a lot of time for. But the question now was, did he have time for me?

He did. Little did I know that when word came down I was to report to

Meade, he had personally made sure I was assigned to his office. We talked for a good while when I reported in. Ciccolella wanted to know what was happening and I told him—about the Steam and Cream, the snack bar, the gambling, the scrounging, the using recon aircraft to get steaks and movies for the troops, and the Compound Improvement Fund, which made all things possible.

"Hack, you haven't done anything that good combat leaders have not been doing for years," Ciccolella said as my litany of trespasses went on. "Maybe your way was a little extreme, but if they court-martialed you they'd have to court-martial dozens of other commanders for similar violations. You were looking after your troops."

As we continued to talk, it was a hell of a relief to know that even if he didn't agree with everything I'd done or had to say, General Ciccolella was on my side. "What are my duties, sir?" I asked him as the conversation wound down.

"You're working for me. Relax. Leave your phone number with my secretary and I'll call you when I need you."

"Thank you, sir."

"In the meantime, I'm taking you to lunch," he said, and soon I forgot all my troubles, caught up in the camaraderie of the moment: as the Chick and I walked along, salutes were snapped, "Good afternoon, General!"'s rang out, and I felt as if I was back in the Army I loved. At lunch I was treated as I might have been three months before. Suddenly I was a comer again, not the leprous pariah I'd been greeted as a scant hour earlier. It was an amazing transformation, made possible only because I was with the Chick, and I would be forever grateful to General Ciccolella for having the guts to offer up the magic power of his stars to let me come home again, if only for a little while.

And besides, the General was right: I looked after my troops. Yes, I broke regulations, but I'd been breaking regulations since I got busted in basic training for letting my recon squad go swimming rather than patrol. But what had Napoleon said? *Insubordination may only be the evidence of a strong mind.* Yes, I had a slush fund in the Zone (and in the months and years that passed, rumors about the size of that fund, how it was acquired, and how much I personally got out of it—which was nothing—would grow to immense proportions). But how different was it from the fund I'd had in Germany, acquired through proceeds of D Company's mobile mess (which we'd rented to other companies when they were in the field) and used to fund an after-hours club where the guys could go for a sandwich and a beer? Yes, I used the Zone slush fund to better the living standards of the men of Team 50. But was that any worse than the midnight raids we'd made at Manhattan Beach and Fort Mac on nearby civilian construction sites in order to steal the necessary materials to build decent squad rooms for the men? And without our slush fund in the Zone, was there any chance the Viets living next to Team 50 would have had decent quarters or a school?

Yes, I gambled with senior NCOs on the team (another "lead" the IG was following up). But at Team 50, where fewer than two hundred advisers of all ranks (though mostly sergeant and above) were thrown together in a small compound in a combat zone in the middle of the Mekong Delta, was it really necessary to follow strict Army protocol? And besides, if you got down to brass tacks, according to Army regulation, gambling of any kind was prohibited on any U.S. government-owned or leased property *anywhere*, which would have sent about half the brass in the U.S. Army, including COMUSMACV Abrams, to jail. Yes, I had a steam bath (which DRAC knew all about) that doubled as a whorehouse. But if the guys were going to get laid anyway, wasn't it in everyone's best interests to make sure the women were syphilis-free? As it happened, I also had a heroin amnesty program in the Zone. The Army's solution to the (only recently acknowledged) smack problem among the ranks was to make everyone piss into a bottle during outprocessing, single out the addicts, and throw them into the clanger to be court-martialed. The Zone program allowed hooked guys to be brought down and weaned off the stuff under the supervision of Zone Doc Joseph McAuley, with the help of an assigned "buddy" on the team. Not only did the buddy help the addict during bad times as he came down, but he also did the honors in Saigon when it came to the now-*ex*-addict's DEROS and piss test. The problem was that since heroin stayed in the system for a long time, even after a guy was off the stuff he could still be found out in Saigon. So we solved this by having both buddy and ex-addict piss in the bottles at the overcrowded depot, and then just exchange bottles. The buddy would then disappear with the "smoking gun"; the ex-addict would come out clean, go home, and hopefully start a better life.

The real question was, did discipline on Team 50 break down as a result of these command irregularities? No. Did the IG inspection in April uncover gross inadequacies in the running and maintenance of the team? No, just the contrary. Did morale improve with the implementation of these irregular activities? No one could deny it. Did Generals McCown or Cushman come down to see me after these irregularities had been institutionalized, full of praise for the morale of Team 50 and the good work we were accomplishing with the Vietnamese? Yes, on a regular basis, and my end-of-tour ER reflected it. And through it all, did I keep my guys alive? With one tragic exception, yes. So what was the problem?

The problem was twofold. One was that they—the Army's top brass—

intended to get Hackworth *at all costs*. The other was a little matter of twelve thousand dollars' worth of poker winnings that I'd left in Vietnam for some members of my team to send home for me, but which, instead, the CID intercepted. Still, Brendan Sullivan, Califano's assistant, whom the latter turned me over to after our first meeting to prepare the case, said if we went to court I'd win: in most instances my "crimes" were routine, and we would just have to bring in witnesses to establish this fact and prove I was being singled out for special treatment; in others, like the marijuana smoking, without the joint as material evidence there was no case at all; and in the case of the money, the discovery had only added new zest to the investigation into my affairs, and the IG and CID's repeated violations of the First Amendment in their enthusiasm to nail me for violating currency regulations totally compromised any case the Army may have had.* *But*, Sullivan explained, even if I won, I'd lose, because of the incredibly high cost of my defense. To afford Califano's services if the thing went to court could require bucks in six figures.

> I thought he had a cause, something worthwhile that needed saying. But I don't think it had nearly the impact he would have liked it to have had. Because the Army couldn't get it swept under the rug fast enough. First, one of the most decorated colonels in the Army—a future general, a superstar—turns renegade. Then he turns around and blows the whistle on the powers that be. So for the Army it was a double embarrassment. They couldn't get it hushed up fast enough.
>
> Colonel Benjamin L. Willis, USA, Ret.
> Company Commander, A1/327, 1966;
> G-3 Adviser, 44th STZ, Republic of Vietnam, 1971

> Undoubtedly the case would be a long, hard one to prosecute. Although the *Washington Post* and the *Christian Science Monitor* have at least some of the details . . . they have agreed not to run the story. As far as the media are concerned, for the present at least, the Hackworth case is a dead issue.
>
> Memo for Record, Office of the
> Chief of Staff, 28 September 1971

---

* By all means the currency-related allegations were the most serious made against me, and, in hindsight, why I didn't just go into Saigon from time to time, get traveler's checks or money orders, and send them home myself rather than have my men do it for me is something that defies explanation. Unfortunately, a lot of people were hurt when the IG and CID moved in, and in the end, for me, the whole business was unquestionably *the* black spot in a very honorable—Hackworth-honorable—career.

A buck general once told me he had the job at the Pentagon to collect information on Hack. He said he had file cabinets full of stories of improprieties and allegations of wrongdoing. One night he told me Hack was into drug dealing. And I said, "No way. You can tell me that the guy ran a poker game and you can tell me he stole some booze for the troops. but you're not going to tell me he was buying and selling drugs on the international market."

I've heard other rumors from other people, and I've always said I don't want to hear it. It won't make any difference in my life tomorrow except how I feel about the guy. But I don't want any of that to be diminished, because if it is, so many other people and so many things are also diminished. It won't do me any good to know that he is any less of a guy than I thought he was . . . I spent too long, working too hard, being too scared for him because I believed in him, not to believe in him now.

Lieutenant Colonel Dennis Foley, USA, Ret.
Platoon Leader, 1/327 Tigers, 1966
Company Commander, D4/39
Republic of Vietnam, 1969

I've heard he was into dope. I've heard he was running guns. There has been a lot of innuendo—I suspect half-truth and falsehood—that has maligned his integrity. But I have never listened. I didn't want to listen. It's like, I don't want my vision ever, ever spoiled, because I don't know whether I could live with it. It's like your old girlfriend. You want to remember how she looked twenty years ago when she had that buxom figure and that pretty long hair. You don't want to see her now because in your mind's eye she's forever young.

It has been said that David Hackworth "died" in the service of his country in 1971.

Brigadier General John Howard, USA
Platoon Leader, 1/327 Tigers
Republic of Vietnam, 1965–66

While I knew the uproar my sounding off had caused in the Zone, it was not for many years that I discovered the full extent of the furor it caused in the Pentagon. The top Army generals from Westmoreland on down launched a mammoth damage-control mission from the day the first article appeared. The White House, Congress, and the media wanted the Army's answers to what I had to say; many a Pentagon staff officer was kept up nights justifying facts and figures to make sure every single point I made could be countered, on everything from the "success" of Vietnamization to the precise number of jeeps in the South Vietnamese Army.

The readers of the Chief of Staff's "Weekly Summary" (i.e., all general officers in the U.S. Army) were told that my comments "reflect[ed] a lack of understanding about the tactics and strategy employed in RVN [Republic of Vietnam] as well as the implemented improvements being made in the Army to enhance leadership and professionalism." While a related memo stated that Chief of Staff Westmoreland "did not intend for the Army to engage in a debate with Colonel Hackworth in the news media," he did order that a comprehensive in-house program be developed through the Army's Command Information Program to let Army personnel in on these purportedly implemented leadership- and professionalism-enhancing improvements. "Such a program will have the effect of countering the Hackworth statements, although not specifically designed to do so," the memo explained.[4]

"The Hackworth case" generated dozens of letters, memoranda, cables, and long meetings among the top brass of the Army. No top official in the Pentagon asked or sought to determine if my comments had any substance; the main thrust of the frenzied activity was first, to discredit me, and second, to determine what action could be taken to punish me for breaking the sacred taboo and speaking outside the fold.

The in-house discrediting took the form of such things as the Chief of Staff's "Weekly Summary" (it was easy to say I didn't understand the tactics of the war and just ignore the *Vietnam Primer*, whose very existence belied the statement; it was easy to criticize me by saying I did not understand the strategy of the war, because what general reading that statement would admit he didn't understand it himself?*). My public discrediting (tit for tat) was left to the Army's chief apologist, Slam Marshall. Though he had not spoken with or laid eyes on me in three years, Slam wrote with great authority in his syndicated newspaper column that I was battle-rattled ("When a man has been overlong in battle—and that is Hackworth . . ."), damned me with faint praise ("I found him to be fairly steady and always companionable, brilliant in occasional flashes, tending to be resentful of association with higher authority, otherwise generous in spirit . . .") and then lied through his teeth to imply I was a coward ("One year later, we tried the same thing again—at his request—but he simply vanished."). One reader who immediately got Slam's number was one Helen Lord MacNiven

---

* Only three years later would a survey reveal that of the Army generals who had "managed the war" in Vietnam almost 70 percent "were uncertain of its objectives."[5]

of San Pedro, California. Mrs. MacNiven wrote to Slam in an open letter, "May I suggest to you, sir, that . . . your column was designed to belittle, denigrate and demean a Colonel of the United States Army who has already proven himself to be a capable, forthright and courageous man . . . [and] that your petty sniping and carpings are those of an old man who has a dirty hatchet job to do."

Chief of Staff Westmoreland was very much involved with the Hackworth case, even obsessively so. In the earliest days he was just puzzled, calling in men who knew me, like John Hayes, to ask why I'd spoken out (particularly because he'd felt sure, so he told Hayes, that I was going to be one of the next brigadier generals). According to Jack Woodmansee, who was called to his meeting with the Chief while Westy was getting his hair cut, the General felt personally betrayed by my performance, declaring that I wouldn't have done it if I were a good soldier. Woodmansee told him I'd made a great contribution to the 44th Zone, which apparently calmed the Chief down a bit. But then MACV IG began sending word back from Saigon of its Team 50 discoveries, and then Westy got mad. The Inevitable General from South Carolina, who as COMUSMACV had ordered his staff to submit doctored reports on enemy strength in Vietnam to keep the politicians on board his "victory"-bound war train (or so it was proved fifteen years later), still unsullied as Chief, was determined I be punished out of his "concern for the Army's professional standards and ethics" and "the long-range impact . . . on the integrity of the Army, if no action of any kind [were] taken."[6] And even after he was informed by no less than Robert F. Froehlke, the new Secretary of the Army, that the investigation was not going to uncover evidence of "serious criminal misconduct" on my part, Westmoreland was determined that the case remain open. He made sure the Internal Revenue Service was apprised of the situation, and a commitment made by that organization to pursue me outside Army channels. He strongly urged the Secretary of the Army to sign a shattering Letter of Censure to go into my permanent file. In the end he had less luck with the Secretary than he did with the IRS: while I did get a seven-year tax audit (which uncovered nothing, as there was nothing to uncover), not only did I not receive a Letter of Censure for my permanent file, but any other Get Hackworth plans on Westy's part were nipped in the bud on the very day I was to get out. As Secretary of the Army Froehlke wrote in his close-hold Memo for Record on the subject:

> During the course of an investigation instituted by certain allegations made by Colonel David H. Hackworth, testimony was received which indicated possible serious shortcomings in his personal conduct. This investigation of

Colonel Hackworth's personal conduct is not completed. Nevertheless, I am directing that the investigation be closed and retiring him as of this date.

My decision is based on advice of the General Counsel that significant evidence of serious criminal misconduct is unlikely to be developed by the ongoing investigation. Of equal importance is the consideration I gave to Colonel Hackworth's magnificent combat record, lengthy service in Vietnam, and multiple wounds, awards and decorations.

I, of course, knew nothing of all this as day after day I sweated out word that I would be allowed to retire. So when it was over, I could hardly believe my ears. On Tuesday, 28 September 1971, at 1900 hours, Joe Califano called. "Report to Fort Meade on Thursday," he said, "for your discharge." As he went on to explain how he'd persuaded the Secretary of the Army to let the case drop, and how the Secretary had given the hard word to Westmoreland, who'd had to give in, I barely comprehended the words. I was too stunned.

Two days later I reported to the Adjutant General section at Fort Meade. An old, very sympathetic colonel named Webb outprocessed me; it was quite a formal procedure, in which I had to sign papers, collect back pay, and close out this part of my life forever. In the middle of it, Webb received a phone call. He was sitting at his desk when he took it, but when the caller identified himself, the Colonel, a real southern-gentleman type, leaped to his feet. "Yes, sir!" he said with the utmost urgency, and stood at attention as the conversation continued, his side of which went something like, "Yes, sir . . . No, sir . . . No, sir, he hasn't," which I read as *Yes, sir, he's here . . . No, sir, he hasn't left yet . . . No, sir, he hasn't signed out.* "Very well, sir," Webb wound up the call, and I did a quick scope of the area to see how I was going to bust out. In my mind the Colonel had been told: *Don't let him go. We're arresting him and he's going to jail.* But I wasn't going to jail. No way were they going to get me, not after all this.

The Colonel got off the phone. "That was General Westmoreland," he said. He might have said, "That was General Westmoreland's office," but I wasn't sure—I wasn't receiving too well, my heart was pounding too loud and too fast. The Colonel started looking through the pile of documents and certificates that made up my discharge papers. He extracted one and showed it to me: it was a certificate, signed by Westmoreland, thanking me, Colonel David H. Hackworth, for my twenty-five years of honorable and dedicated service to the Army. The personalized certificate, a gimmick instituted by Westmoreland when he became Chief of Staff, was an automatic issue for guys who retired while Westy held the top job. But, "The General doesn't want you to have this," Colonel Webb explained, and deep-sixed it on the spot. And I thought, here is the Chief of Staff of the Army, running an organization of almost two million men, with troops all over the world and a war being lost in South Vietnam, and he has the time—he makes the time—to call, or direct someone to call, the AG at Fort Meade to make sure I, David Hackworth, didn't think he was glad I'd been on his team. As the troops used to say, *So it goes.* . . .

EPILOGUE

A few days after the *Newsweek* article with Hack's interview in it hit the streets of Saigon, I got a call from MACV informing me that my request for an interview with General Abrams had been approved. I thought that it was a bit odd, since I had put in the request six months earlier with no results. When I sat down with him he told me that in exchange for the interview he wanted a favor. He wanted to talk about Hackworth. I agreed and he asked me about Hack's mood during our interview, anything else he had said that did not get into the piece, how deep his bitterness with the Army ran, questions of that sort. When I told him what I knew he said in a sad voice: "Colonel Hackworth is the best battalion commander I ever saw in the United States Army. We cannot afford to lose men of his caliber. If it continues, the damage to the Army will be irreparable."

Nick Proffitt
Newsweek Correspondent
Republic of Vietnam, July 1971

ALMOST eighteen years have passed since I hung up my soldier suit. If I was left with a handful of ashes at the end of my Army career, I was also left with a heartful of memories—profound, wonderful memories that more than offset the ones I would have preferred to forget. I have brothers all around the globe, comrades-in-arms for whom distance and time have meant nothing in terms of the love and friendship we share to this day, forged in conditions I pray our sons and grandsons never have to experience themselves.

Judge Tom Cooney was probably right when he suggested that I could have had a greater impact on military reform and preparedness had I stayed in the Army rather than standing outside it and criticizing. On the other hand, fine warriors like Hank Emerson and Hal Moore, who did stay in and fought from the inside, were both turfed out as three-stars by the clerks at the top when they still had plenty more to offer—Emerson, for criticizing the priorities of the Army's weapons procurement system, and Moore, for taking issue with having women in the combat arms and in certain Engineer and Artillery jobs with high combat vulnerability, as well as for opposing the Army's lowering of recruiting standards (IQ and education) to meet recruitment goals. Many other talented warriors lost the day in similar circumstances; no doubt had I stayed in, a similar fate would have been mine.

But having been thrown out for them did not make Emerson's or Moore's or other fine warriors' criticisms, then or now, any less valid, and similarly, my decision to get out when I did—even my journey partway around the bend in my last command (though some may argue the point)—does not invalidate my own present-day observations, concerns, and suggestions for the future of the Army, an institution I loved for too long not to still love, above almost all else. Though I am no longer in the Army, and for so many years have not lived in the United States, my continued and very real desire to serve both if I possibly can was the basic reason for this book and for the pages that follow.

As I go on, it will be difficult to discuss what have become very political issues in an apolitical way, very difficult to tread the thin line between Left and Right. If my own politics show through as being slightly left of center, it would not be unfair to ask that it be remembered they were once far to the right of John Birch. If my "warts and all" description of my last command (which in the manuscript stage made a number of good friends cringe and beg me to be a little less forthcoming) offends, or in some minds calls my credibility into question, may I say that to tell all was a choice I made: I did not believe I had a right to discuss what happened to my Army if I did not honestly discuss what happened to me as well. And if it appears odd that a self-professed warrior is now pushing the line for peace (or at least a better way to resolve conflict), in fact I am only joining the ranks of MacArthur, Montgomery, Mountbatten, and scores of other retired soldiers who, with no vested interest in the *industry* of war, and with plenty of time to put their feet up and think, recognize that the stakes of war have grown too high to be a viable problem solver.

But first:

Soon after I was allowed to retire, Jenny and I moved to Spain. I planned to write an exposé of the Army, but as the input began rolling in from friends both in uniform or retired and those who had quit in disillusionment, the words of Stanley Resor during our last, chance encounter kept running through my mind. I'd just gotten out of the Army; I'd been walking down the street in Washington looking distinctly unmilitary in jeans and a T-shirt, sandals, and a three-day beard when I saw him standing in front of the Brookings Institute. Deciding the best course of action was to escape and evade, I picked up the pace, looked the other way, and prayed this fine man wouldn't recognize me. But he did, and twenty-five years of military conditioning compelled me to snap a correct "Yes, sir" rather than keep walking when he tentatively called my name. The former Secretary of the Army had heard all about my difficulties. But he was sympathetic, not critical, and told me he was sorry it had ended this way. Resor asked what I planned to do, and when I said I was going to write a book, he said, "Make sure it's constructive, and not just another vindictive attack on a system already suffering mighty blows. Think it out. You could make a great contribution."

I rogered the transmission as a sedan pulled up, which, after shaking my hand, Resor got into and was driven away. Even so, I still had every intention of proceeding with my project. Once settled in Spain, however, I realized that Resor was right, that whatever I would write would be angry, bitter, vindictive, and ultimately valueless. That belief was reinforced with the news that John Paul Vann's chopper had gone down in the Highlands of Vietnam, and that renegade soldier, the first to stand in the door over the U.S. conduct of the war in the early sixties, who retired from the Army but could not turn his back on South Vietnam and returned as a civilian to do what he could, had been killed. Radio Hanoi took credit for the death of Vann, by then the senior adviser of II Corps—a two-star general's billet— and unquestionably the most knowledgeable American on the war ever to serve in Vietnam; while Vann, not unlike Bernard Fall, had been rolling the dice for so long that his fate seemed almost inevitable, the death of this old friend knocked me to my knees.

Jenny continued to be a tremendous source of strength throughout this period. But the pressure that had been building from the moment I'd decided to speak out was not easily dissipated, and it took a tremendous toll on our relationship. We tried to recapture the early magic on a leisurely drive around Europe, but it proved impossible: within a year we parted, though at least as friends.

I migrated to Australia—the farthest place from the United States I could find and still speak English—with little money, the wrong accent, and no obviously transferable skills from the life I'd left behind. I concluded that the only two things I knew anything about were mess halls and motor pools, so over the first couple of years in Australia I dabbled in both, owning a diner and a couple of gas station/garages on Queensland's fast-growing Gold Coast. All were very successful, great money spinners that kept me too busy to feel sorry for myself, but I got tired of the life and sold it all to buy a

160-acre property in the lush rain forests of northern New South Wales. There I entered my hippie phase, and, with a special woman named Christine Hudson as a guiding spirit, was finally able to work the war out of my system and wash most of the pain away. I wrote occasional articles for American and Australian publications, and in April of '75 watched with no satisfaction as my prediction of four years before came true, when the North Vietnamese flag was hoisted to fly triumphantly over Saigon.

Two years later, through John Rowe, a former Australian Army major who'd been with the 1/RAR during my 1/101 days, I met Peter Margaret Cox. Peter was a longtime Brisbane restaurateur, and her establishment at that time, Scaramouche, was the "in" spot in Brisbane. The place was also being hounded by creditors and on the verge of going broke—its owner had incredible flair but absolutely no business sense. It didn't take much to see that the restaurant had everything going for it except organization, and when Peter asked for a hand, I found it a challenge I couldn't resist.

Once I got my SOPs in place, business began to boom. Within a few years the permanent staff of Scaramouche had grown from ten to eighty people, and the weekly gross from two thousand dollars to fifty thousand. Five years after I walked in the door and started paying the bills I'd found stuffed and long forgotten in the backs of drawers, Peter and I walked out, after selling the place for one million dollars. We were also married at this point, and the proud parents of my fourth child, Ben, whom I prayed I'd be a better father to than I had been all those years to Laura, Leslie, and Joel.

The time was 1981, the first year of the Reagan Administration. If I'd thought the sale of Scaramouche would be the beginning of a life of leisure for me, it was a thought soon wiped from my mind as the new rumblings in Washington filled me with alarm I hadn't felt since the height of the Vietnam War. The new President had surrounded himself with Nuke the Pukers for whom the concept of nuclear war between the U.S. and the Soviet Union was not only imaginable but "inevitable," who talked about U.S. losses being kept at a "compatible level of 20 million dead," who said "nuclear war would be a terrible mess, but it would not be unmanageable" . . . "like an amputation: traumatic, but not necessarily fatal." I was stunned. These men, most of them academics who had never been on a battlefield (and many of whom, it would later be discovered, had actively avoided service in Vietnam), who wouldn't have had the slightest idea about death, dying, destruction, and the wholesale suffering attendant on even conventional war, were talking about, conceivably, the end of life on earth as we know it, as if it were a back-lot baseball game.

The more I read about what was happening in Washington, the more concerned I became. It seemed like Vietnam all over again, only the stakes were infinitely higher and the key players understood the game even less. We had killed tens of thousands of people in Southeast Asia to save the region from the Communists. Was the new Administration ready to kill most of humankind to save the West from the same ubiquitous bogeyman? From Australia it seemed as if Reagan's "window of vulnerability" had been opened solely to blow in bitter winds that would fuel the Cold War and whip up nationwide anti-Soviet hysteria: only after the American people were sufficiently scared would they permit the trillion-and-a-half-dollar expenditure the Administration deemed necessary to establish and maintain its noble "Peace Through Strength."

I decided to stick my head in the sand. I figured in Australia my family was moderately safe (though, to hedge my bets, I did begin to "dig in" at my farm, stockpiling food and water just in case an accident, a miscalculation, or the act of a mad zealot brought forth the first salvo of World War III), and I might have played ostrich for the rest of my life but for a telephone conversation with my daughter Leslie, and a visit to my farm by the Hardcore's Night Hunter 6, Larry Tahler.

Leslie at that time was in choppers in the U.S. Coast Guard. We were talking about radioactive fallout and life in general after a Soviet/U.S. nuclear exchange, and she just laughed it off with "I don't worry about that, Dad. It'll be over in a few seconds. We'll be fried and that's it." I was amazed; it had never occurred to me that my daughter took it for granted that one day she'd be vaporized. I was yet to know that that was the price she and her generation paid for being born under the Sign of the Bomb.

When Larry Tahler came to Australia, he told me I had no right to bury my head in the sand. If I believed the nuclear party line coming out of government and military circles in Washington was insane, he said, then as a natural leader and a soldier with my credentials I was *obliged* to speak out. His argument was compelling; the only problem was that I didn't have enough facts to stand upright on my soapbox. Thus began long months of study followed by three years as an active participant in the nuclear debate in Australia. My goal was to educate, to use my knowledge and credentials as a warrior to persuade the Australian people—from members of Parliament to the average man and woman on the street—to also become active participants in the debate, to add their voices to those around the globe protesting the absurd concept of a winnable nuclear war as well as the stockpiling of nuclear weapons, which, rather than adding to the defense of the Western world, only destabilized it. After three years of radio, television, and public-speaking engagements on the subject, when I felt I'd said everything I could possibly say to everyone I could possibly imagine finding to say it to, *twice*, I put my soapbox away. And I had the satisfaction of knowing I'd helped illumine a nation to the most critical issue humankind has faced to this day.

Which brings us to the present.

Besides relating a "life story" in these pages, I have tried to portray what I saw with my eyes of what happened to the U.S. Army through two unwinnable wars, themselves fought under the omnipresent umbrella of *the* unwinnable war—the Cold War. That that war is now discussed and/or recognized in many circles as being over (not through winning or losing or either side changing its global objectives, but through the superpowers acknowledging that they have all but spent themselves broke preparing to fight it) is something to be heralded as a step in the right direction for global stability and East/West economic reconstruction. It does not mean, however, that *war* is over and will never be fought again, or that either superpower has suddenly been exempted from examining its past performances. While the need for such scrutiny should be self-evident, historically the U.S. military as quickly and efficiently as humanly possible sweeps under the rug the reality of its less sterling accomplishments, and there is little evidence to suggest there will be any change now. (It is, of course, impossible for me to conjecture when or how the Soviet military will treat its debacle in Afghanistan.)

Korea, for example, did not become "the forgotten war," as Clay Blair's fine book on the subject is titled, by accident. The absence of a glorious victory in this pretelevision war is no doubt a main factor in the American public's vague recall of the event today; in that generation, however, that absence of victory was tantamount to defeat—unthinkable in the wake of WW II and the trouncing of Germany and Japan—and the first seeds of national self-doubt took root. In the military, the Korea result was even more profound. Never had American arms performed so badly in a time of war as the American military did in the first months of the Korean conflict. Clay Blair's book catalogs the remarkable failings in training, logistics support, and leadership (men arrived in Korea in the summer of 1950 who had never fired their weapons; M-24 tanks whose 75-mm guns had not been fired because their units hadn't received the recoil oil they'd had on order for two years led to the tanks' turrets being blown off the vehicles when the guns were fired for the first time; battalion, regiment, and division commanders arrived too old for the job, whose inappropriate tactics led to the misuse and sacrifice, often in sheer bloodbaths, of the green garrison units at their disposal).[1] The senior brass were so humiliated by their overall ineptitude in the early prosecution of the war and then the stagnation of the later phases that the minute the war was over they hid the truth away, even from themselves. The result was the military learned nothing from the

Korean experience, only to carry the same nonlessons into the next war to blow it all over again.

And Vietnam was all the more humiliating for being exposed on the six-o'clock news every night. But when that war was over, while the first instinct on the part of the generals who managed it was to file it, like Korea, under O for Oblivion, instead, over the last few years it has become clear that another tack has been taken. Now, the war managers are working overtime to *rewrite* the truth of what happened in that war. A score of years later, retired three-star general Robert Schweitzer's suggestion (made as a light colonel in 1968) that ". . . the Army must lead the way in conducting a 'Psyops campaign' that American Arms accomplished their mission in Vietnam" has become an unwritten but vigorously maintained policy.

The major treatise on the American Army's failings in Vietnam is a book titled *On Strategy*, by retired colonel Harry Summers, Jr. *On Strategy* is an important work, correctly analyzing many of the major mistakes and lessons learned from the Vietnam War. The book's basic premise, however, plays right into the bloodied hands of the war managers, and in fact, does a tragic disservice to the American military today, which might well turn to the work as a guide for the future.

Summers contends that the U.S. Army was "unbeatable" on the battlefield in Vietnam, and that the United States won the war *tactically* even as it lost the war *strategically*. In his introduction to *On Strategy*, he backs this up by quoting a conversation that took place between himself and one NVA Colonel Nguyen dôn Tu in Hanoi in April of 1975. ("You know you never defeated us on the battlefield," said Summers. "That may be so," replied Tu, "but it is also irrelevant.") From reading the works of General Giap and my own experience talking to more than one hundred NVA POWs, when I read this in Summers' book I could not believe a North Vietnamese soldier would make such a statement as that attributed to Tu. At the very least, I thought Summers' interpreter must have misunderstood the North Vietnamese colonel. So we contacted Tu, who, ten years after the event, was now Vietnam's military attaché in the U.S.S.R. Tu replied, "As I have not yet read the book, I am afraid that I may not have a full grasp of the author's intention when he made a point which is fully at variance with my point of view. . . . If any sort of question, similar to the one mentioned by the U.S. officer in the book, was asked, any Vietnamese [except the U.S. henchmen in the puppet army and administration] could affirm that the Vietnamese army and people had routed militarily the U.S.A. in both North and South Vietnam and this is the main cause that led to the tragic U.S. defeat in Vietnam."[2]

The catchcry of those rewriting American history in Vietnam is "We won all the battles but we lost the war." But as many of the "war stories" in this book have proved, this is just not true—unless an entirely inappropriate, WW II measure for success is used. *Of course* our opponent in Vietnam could never have won the WW II–style pitched battles our forces employed. But what is not being addressed on the rewritten scorecard is that, with few exceptions, they didn't try.

In Vietnam, America spent more than $141 billion, had more than 300,000 men wounded, and lost some 58,000 men killed. Almost fifteen years since the tragic, inevitable fall of Saigon, there has been no major, *honest* postmortem of the war. There have been critiques dealing with the big picture, examining inarguably profound mistakes like not mobilizing the Reserves and not having an objective. But none has addressed the lessons learned the hard way, at the fighting level, where people died and the war was, in fact, lost.

The people running the Army today were the majors and lieutenant colonels in the Vietnam period. Many ticket-punched their way through Vietnam, learning little from their experience except the wrong way to fight. In the seventies and early eighties they did not want "to look back to learn," as Hank Lunde, who, in 1985, then recently retired after a professorship at the Army War College, reported: "For two years, the voluntary elective on Vietnam at the Army War College had to be canceled because a minimum of four students did not sign up. It was not until the instructor, Colonel Harry Summers, published his book that enough students became interested to make it a go. In the meantime, the touch-and-feel computer classes and management theory and philosophy classes were so oversubscribed that some had to move to large auditoriums."

From the time, early in his presidency, that Ronald Reagan called Vietnam a "noble war," the whitewash has flowed fast from Army brushes to cover the more ignoble truth. This is a dangerous, dangerous trend, because it can only doom the Army, and the country, to repeat the mistakes of Vietnam down to the last death on the next battlefield, and much sooner than many might think.

The next war for the U.S.A. will not be fought in Europe with large armored formations. It will be a war of insurgency; it will be fought— initially—in Latin America, and then quite possibly within the boundaries of the United States, most likely within the next twenty years. Our military leaders must face this reality and take priority steps to prepare for such a mission. The first step must be an honest examination of what went wrong in Vietnam at the tactical level. The ineffectiveness of the Contras in Nicaragua and the sad performance of the El Salvadorean military in their counterinsurgency effort provide ample evidence that little good has been passed on to today's American advisers from our country's tragic experience in Vietnam.

As of this writing, since America's withdrawal from Vietnam the U.S. Army has been involved in two overt combat operations: the Iran raid in 1980 and the Grenada invasion in 1983. Both essentially conventional operations were seriously flawed, and demonstrated disturbing shortcomings in the Army's ability to plan, command, and control operations, and to fight. Both operations were excessively complex and grossly overcontrolled. Both suffered from bad intelligence, critical equipment breakdowns, ponderous and complicated command and control systems, and, in the case of Grenada, grave tactical errors—both the Rangers and the Airborne units attacked Cuban defensive positions frontally in slow, tedious, WW II–like set-piece fashion rather than by employing maneuver designed to get to the enemy's rear and thereby keep casualties to a minimum.

The overall ground force used during the Grenada invasion (including the U.S. Marine Corps elements) was seven infantry battalions plus elements of two additional battalions. These forces were opposed by fewer than two hundred lightly armed Cuban soldiers and a militia of five hundred Cuban construction workers. Yet, despite the Americans' vast numerical superiority, their unmatchable firepower, and their complete control of the air and sea, it took three days to defeat the Cuban defenders. It is reported that the Chairman of the Joint Chiefs of Staff was so disturbed by the Army's slowness that he told Major General Edward L. Trobaugh, the CG, 82d Airborne Division, "We have two companies of Marines running all over the island and thousands of Army troops doing nothing. What the hell is going on?"[3]

Tactically, both the Iran and Grenada operations were total fiascos. Yet, like Vietnam, little has been learned from either because of the "no-fault" mentality of the eighties "Army of Excellence" (itself a descendant of our sixties zero-defect organization), which refuses even to accept that errors can be (and were) made, much less identify where on the ground and/or in the chain of command they occurred. The CG, 82d Airborne, during the Grenada operation for example, left the division before the end of his normal tour, and while evidence does indeed point to his unit's not being up for the Caribbean game, his abrupt reassignment (which from this soldier's perspective could only be read as relief of command) evades the real question of who put him in the slot in the first place. Historically this position has gone to a real fighter and longtime paratrooper. Trobaugh had no Airborne experience at all, yet he was given command of *the* number-one ready force in the U.S. Army.[4] Interestingly, a colonel who served in the 82nd with Trobaugh told me the very reason this general was assigned to the division was to shake up the Airborne clique. Apparently he did bring many needed changes to the 82nd, but was unable to make a dent in the entrenched, half-century old Airborne brotherhood. According to the colonel, as well as the 82nd's plodding performance in Grenada and the awards giveaway program that followed, it was Trobaugh's running battle with the Airborne club that brought him down. When West German teenager Mathias Rust flew his little airplane from Helsinki, Finland, through four hundred miles of Soviet airspace to land right in the middle of Red Square, some two-star Soviet general was not relieved in his wake; the heads that rolled were those of the Soviet Defense Minister and the commander of all Soviet air-defense forces. It would seem that rather than having Trobaugh bear the full weight of responsibility for his unit's performance at Grenada, the four-star general who chose this prodigy for such a critical assignment should have been unceremoniously booted out as well. In Hank Emerson's words, *"That* would get everyone's attention," and in future these high-ranking careerists might start appreciating that there's a hell of a lot more at stake in the business of soldiering than jobs for the boys.

And more at stake than decorations, too. In what could only be seen as a continued debasement of an awards system already thoroughly prostituted in Vietnam, for the Grenada operation 8,612 medals (almost 200 for bravery) were awarded when there were no more than seven thousand U.S. personnel on the tiny island at any time during the three days of sputtering combat against a few Cuban troops. Somehow I don't think that's what Napoleon had in mind when he suggested if he had enough ribbon he could conquer the world. The awards system in the U.S. Army needs a *major overhaul* if it is to have any meaning. The gross inflation of the system during the Vietnam War, particularly regarding high decorations for bravery for division CGs, ADCs, brigade and battalion commanders, had an incredibly negative impact on morale at the fighting level then, and surely cannot go over much better now or in the future. There is a big difference between bravery and good management. When a warrior risks his life and is awarded a medal, a commander/manager must not get that same medal for fighting his unit well or for just being there. Instead, there should be a combat commander's award, which would recognize a CO's "job well done" without making a joke out of the combat awards that real fighters should have the right to wear as badges of honor.

It must be stressed that my criticisms here are *not* of the American fighting man, either in Grenada, specifically, or generally. The American soldier historically has it in him to be tough, resourceful, brave, and hard-charging, and to hang in there when things get grim. But today, the quality of both his leadership, particularly his senior leadership, and his training are letting him down; he is not being given the opportunity or grounding to exploit his abilities to the maximum.

Tim Grattan always described my teaching methods as those of the Kentucky preacher who explained: "You tell 'em what you're going to tell 'em; then you tell 'em; then you tell 'em what you told 'em." At the risk of overstating my case (although I have to say, it worked in training), I am compelled now to tell what I've already told about the absolute necessity for hard, realistic training, strong, caring, *tactically proficient* leaders, and reliable, GI-proof weapons with inexpensive munitions so soldiers can actually *fire* them in training (rather than practice on penny-arcade simulators as is regularly the case today), if the Army's goal is to be combat-ready and capable of defending the United States.

A couple of years ago, I dropped in on a brigade commander whom I'd known when he was a young lieutenant. The previous day, one of his troops had been killed during a chemical-biological-radiological (CBR)* training exercise, and this stud colonel was scared. It wasn't so much that his career was involved; it was that word had immediately come down from Division that put an end to all CBR training until further notice. This, he told me, was the routine response to training casualties on posts around the country. Yet that sort of reaction can hardly be in the Army's best interest. Training for war must be realistic *at all costs*. We can't just discontinue a curriculum when something bad happens, provided that something is not the result of misconduct on the parts of sadistic or unqualified instructors (and then the instructors, not the curriculum, should be dealt with, as in the recent case of Navy petty officer Michael Combe, who was tried and sentenced for the negligent homicide of a recruit whose head had been forced under water in a training pool after the recruit panicked). Training casualties, tragic as they may be, must be accepted as an occupational hazard in the tough and dangerous business of soldiering. The emphasis on safety at the expense of realism may keep Congress and Mrs. Lump Lump at bay (on one post I visited, I learned that the ratio of safety personnel to actual participants in live-fire training exercises was almost 1:1), but it sets up the soldiers it presumably is protecting for failure by stunting their growth and inhibiting their confidence in themselves and their supporting weapons. It's like a fledgling football team learning blocking and tackling by sitting in a room watching video tapes. It is unimaginable that these men would be sent into their first game against seasoned competitors with such training, which could only have them feeling alien and removed from the basics that must be second nature in order to survive, much less to win. And because "wars

* Now known as NBC—nuclear-biological-chemical.

are not fought in grassy meadows on sunny afternoons," as Wellington correctly said, today's training must be scheduled to last extended periods of time in conditions as close to the battlefield as possible. Training exercises must not be controlled, but instead be completely free play with platoons aggressing against platoons, companies against companies, and battalions against battalions in a simulated combat environment in which soldiers can discover for themselves that war is not a series of canned problems with a limited range of responses, but a human encounter where the unexpected always happens and flexibility is the key.

The preparedness of today's soldiers is also being stunted in the leadership department. On the senior levels, the Army's peacetime penchant for neutralizing (if not retiring as early as possible) its warrior leaders leaves no one who *knows* to yell, scream, stand up for, *and lead* the troops who will compose the thin red line in the next war. History has shown that the mavericks—the Jacksons, Grants, Pattons—whom peacetime shunted aside, were the ones who could wage and win the wars the dancers and prancers had bungled in the opening rounds; it is high time this wartime cycle of lost opportunity and waste, which invariably is measured in the lives of young men, be broken. After all, Lee Iacocca, management hero of the eighties, has the keeping of mavericks around as one of his eight commandments of good management. Today's Army bureaucrats would do well to look at Iacocca's example, and if not nurture the mavericks, then at least maintain them in the system in troop-leading positions, which the managers are not interested in (except as a ticket-punching exercise) in the first place. As Jean Larteguy wrote:

> I'd like to have two armies:
> One for display with lovely guns, tanks, little soldiers, staffs, distinguished and doddering generals and dear little regimental officers who would be deeply concerned over their general's bowel movements or their colonel's piles, an Army that would be shown for a modest fee on every fairground in the country.
> The other would be the real one, composed entirely of young enthusiasts in camouflaged uniforms, who would not be put on display but from whom impossible efforts would be demanded and to whom all sorts of tricks would be taught. That's the Army in which I should like to fight.[5]

On the junior levels of leadership, both soldiers and taxpayers are being shortchanged by what has been a gradual but significant transformation of the United States Military Academy from producer of fighter-leaders to manufacturer of corporate whiz kids. West Point's academic requirements today make it one of the hardest schools in the nation to get into. To many this is a state of affairs in which to take great pride, but to a real soldier or to anyone who recognizes you don't have to be an academic genius to be a solid combat commander, it is a serious case of mistaken priorities. Further, with a West Point education an excellent stepping-stone to a high-paying job in the civilian world, far too many USMA alumni go through the motions for the five years their appointments require and then opt for the bucks without looking back (a recent study revealed that 30 percent of cadets who graduated from West Point between 1970 and 1980 left the military after six years, and by the ten-year mark that figure had risen to 48 percent).[6] Given this trend, it would hardly be surprising if the Army's leaders of the future begin to be selected foremost from among OCS and ROTC-trained officers rather than USMA graduates. While the alternate programs do not have the historical and academic prestige of West Point, they are producing leaders with hands-on experience and concrete leadership skills, and, especially among OCS graduates, the desire to apply both in the United States Army. It is time West Point reexamine some of its policies to achieve similar results. For example, what if, instead of jockeying to admit only the cream of America's high schools, West Point made a policy of taking half its input from enlisted personnel already in the Army. Colonel Ken Eggleston has suggested that a man should not be allowed to become an officer without three years of enlisted service first; at the very least, General Hank Emerson believes, the age limit to enter the Point should be raised to allow more mature, experience-rich EM a shot at the officer world. The value of such a move is obvious. These students would already have demonstrated leadership ability, they would already know the Army and love it, so they wouldn't quit—they'd stay in, make a *life* of it, make it better. If the U.S. Military Academy can take the remarkable step of admitting women, surely it can begin to look into the Army's ranks for its combat leaders of the future.

Today's soldiers (and, in turn, the country's defense) are being placed in great jeopardy by the weapons and equipment now being issued from on high. Given the scandals and the resulting publicity that have rocked the Pentagon in recent times, it is not difficult to see why: the U.S. military's procurement system is out of control. Still, the bottom line of the whole business is simply this: the United States buys too many weapons it doesn't need, pays too much for what it gets, what it gets does not do the right job where it counts—on the battlefield—and men's lives are being risked unnecessarily.

The military-industrial complex has a great deal to answer for. Since my retirement, this "organization" has exploded. Between 1975 and 1985 the number of military officials hired by defense contractors increased almost 500 percent, with ex-military men trading off their many contacts still in the service for huge salaries, and active-duty high-ranking officers singing the praises of (at times) hopelessly defective products to ensure that they, too, have lucrative jobs when they retire.[7] The country's coffers are being milked dry by these individuals for whom Duty, Honor, and Country are vague recollections or ideals of yesteryear: while these ex-military people receive huge salaries from defense contractors, who get much of *their* money from the government, they also continue to receive retirement pensions from their services, which, at the four-star level, are in the vicinity of fifty-five thousand dollars per year.*

And what are we getting for all this money and all this apparent expertise of military men in and on the edge of the defense industry? What we're *not* getting is rugged, reliable, easy-to-produce-and-maintain gear that has undergone tough, realistic tests under simulated battle conditions to make sure it works before money is spent putting it into mass production. Instead, we're getting rigged weapons tests. Instead, we're getting enthusiastic, glowing reports on second-rate weapons written in full knowledge of the rigged tests, from a Pentagon office that was set up by Congress *specifically to ensure that all weapons testing was honest and the reporting accurate.*[9] In the Army, at least, we're getting such items as the Abrams tank and the Bradley "fighting vehicle," both designed for war against the Soviets in Europe, the least likely war the United States will ever fight.

At $2.2 million a copy, the M-1 Abrams was pushed into production in 1982 well before all its bugs were ironed out, and, not unlike the M-16 rifle, whose shoddy performance was responsible for the deaths of many of our own men in Vietnam, was deployed in the field with serious teething problems. Modifications were made, but the newer-model M1-A1 is still battle-ready far less frequently and costs as much as three times more to repair than the M60 tank it was designed to replace. It is also already outgunned by the deployed Soviet T-80 tank. The M-1 can travel, on average, only forty-eight miles before requiring essential service maintenance (a not insignificant percentage of which must be done by civilians), and, being an 8.6-*gallon*-per-*mile* (as opposed to mile per gallon) gas-

---

* United Technologies, for example, one of the top U.S. defense contractors, in 1980 hired newly retired General Alexander Haig as its president. In the year Haig spent there before becoming Secretary of State, he earned more than $800,000 in salary and bonuses. Between 1985 and 1987, Haig received, along with his Army pension, more than $3 million from lecturing, writing, and consulting, the latter with companies such as United Technologies, Sperry Electronic Systems (Unisys), Boeing, and ISC Technologies, a manufacturer of cluster bombs.[8] By contrast, one might consider the case of William Westmoreland, who, whatever his limitations as a commander in an unconventional war, has not spent his retirement years chasing the Almighty Dollar that his position could have well afforded him, but instead has chosen to stay close to the cause of Vietnam veterans. General Fred Weyand, that fine soldier who took up the reins of Army Chief of Staff upon Creighton Abrams' death, is another refreshing example of a man who, even in retirement, considers the welfare of his men before himself.

guzzler, has an operational range of just fifty-six miles per fill-up. On average, the tank needs twenty-one dollars' worth of replacement parts for every mile it travels, yet according to one 1983 CBS News report, in 1981 the Department of Defense budgeted for only 13 percent of the $3 billion in spare parts the M-1 would need to fight a sixty-day war, and had no intention, even over the next ten years, of building a solid stockpile of same. The reason? The CBS report cited one senior Army official who said the Army was gambling that there wouldn't be a war, so "would rather commit its resources elsewhere."[10] It's a far cry from the days of the old reliable Sherman: back in the tank company, we'd go days and weeks without a breakdown, and when we had one, Chief Ventura could fix the damn thing himself. We got good gas mileage, too, a decided plus when you consider the vulnerability of a fleet of gas tankers on the modern battlefield, let alone when they're following formations of tanks. Meanwhile, as of this writing, with close to $2 trillion injected into American defense over the last eight years, the Army is quietly pulling every M-1 tank it has out of Europe, and even the M1-A1s that will replace them have to be given new armor first (in light of the now-known destructive capabilities of the far superior Soviet T-80) at a cost of almost $1 billion. Concurrently, in an effort to save money, the tank drivers at Fort Riley, Kansas, train to drive their Abrams tanks in golf carts—a $15,000 to $20,000 tank maneuver costs only $289 in golf carts on the Custer Hill Golf Course.[11] As the old saying goes, you get what you pay for, and we are paying for self-delusion and incompetence. Generals Abrams and Patton must be rolling in their graves.

The M-2 Bradley fighting vehicle, costing $1.5 million a copy, is produced by the Food Machinery Corporation (FMC). One of its champions in the Pentagon was Army Chief of Staff Edward Meyer, who, since his retirement, has been on FMC's board of directors.[12] One of the Bradley's detractors was noted WW II tank commander General Bruce Clarke, who said "most anything on the battlefield can blow a hole through it,"[13] and in 1977, when Hank Emerson, then an outspoken lieutenant general and commander of the elite XVIII Airborne Corps, suggested that there was much more urgently needed equipment and the Army's budget could be better spent for overall combat readiness, he was unceremoniously eased out (read *fired*) at the age of fifty-two.

Emerson was not the only casualty of the Bradley story, a story of a cross between a light tank and an armored personnel carrier that doesn't function even marginally well as either. The Bradley was designed to swim and can't; it was designed to carry a TOE infantry squad and doesn't have the room. Its cannon tends to jam and/or misfeed, and just one missile or tank or RPG round could destroy the high-profile vehicle instantly, not to mention the soldiers buttoned up inside. The Bradley is a high-tech vehicle and a maintenance man's nightmare—too big, too complicated ("gold-plated" as one serving colonel describes the R&D people's overall penchant for trying to make every item capable of doing everything, with the result that many can barely do anything well), with a long record of breakdowns and failures in many areas, including its transmission and electrical systems. And this is the same machine that the top brass of the Army vigorously maintains "with it we win, without it we'll lose" the next war. It's a strange thing, how systems proved to be second- or third-rate are defended so vigorously—even as a matter of our nation's survival—by men who should know better. Where is the moral courage of these men? *Where is their concern for the lives of their soldiers?* Probably in about the same place as that of the Pentagon joker who, in 1968, told me to stop fighting the M-16 rifle and start buying stock in Colt Industries instead.

Another monumental mistake for the Army (which, not unlike the other services, seems all too often all too ready to sacrifice the true readiness of its force rather than have a precious project, worthless or not, taken away) was the "Sergeant York" Division Air Defense (DIVAD) system, designed to replace the Vulcan AD system of the sixties. This high-priority program was undertaken in the late seventies to quickly field a mobile, all-weather air-defense system that could maneuver and fight alongside the brand-new Bradley and Abrams while simultaneously providing air defense over the battle area. Almost $2 billion later, Secretary of Defense Caspar Weinberger canceled the program amidst allegations of military ineptitude, rigged tests, watered-down and/or sanitized test results, inflated costs, and conflicts of interest, after the system, eighty of which had already been fielded at a cost of $6.8 million a copy, failed to live up to even the most modest expectations. On the rare occasions when all the bug-ridden subsystems of the Sergeant York worked correctly, the system itself still could not hit an aircraft flying an evasive course or kill a missile-carrying helicopter standing

---

* As of this printing, most of the mechanical bugs in both the Bradley and the Abrams have been ironed out, and the organizational and training deficiencies have been resolved. But the point is that both vehicles were rushed into production well before the major teething problems were corrected, and deemed operational long before they were combat-ready, simply so the Army could get its bite out of the defense dollar. The M60 tank and the M113 APC then in place could have done the job just fine until the Bradley and Abrams were truly ready. This would have saved billions of dollars in major and minor modifications to these two new vehicles and, more importantly, would not have placed our warriors on a potential battlefield with unreliable gear. In all events, I stongly believe that both the Abrams and the Bradley are too expensive to produce and maintain, too complicated, with, particularly in the case of the Bradley, serious design flaws that make both vehicles losers for everyone but the people who make and sell them.

off at a range of more than four kilometers. Meanwhile, the Abrams and the Bradley are now without an adequate air-defense system and will remain so until well into the 1990s, and the only heads that have rolled or careers that have suffered in the wake of it all have been those of men who screamed all along that the Sergeant York was no good. It is not insignificant to note that among the personnel who either worked directly for Ford Aerospace (the Sergeant York's principal defense contractor) or were highly paid consultants on this air-defense system were four retired lieutenant generals: two who were former deputy CGs of the Army's Weapons Procurement Branch, one who had been the deputy chief of staff for Research and Development when the initial request for the Sergeant York was made, and one who'd been the CG of the Army's Air Defense Center, then director of plans and policy for the Joint Chiefs of Staff.[14] In addition to these men, there was a platoon of recently retired colonels and other officers who'd worked on the Sergeant York while on active duty only to go to work for Ford on the same project immediately after leaving the Army. It is worthy of mention too that at this writing retired general Donn Starry, also a big backer of the M-1 Abrams who, with Chief of Staff Meyer, was a major architect of the new battle concept for the European Theater (which then required a new generation of hardware to include the Abrams, Bradley, and Sergeant York), is working at Ford Aerospace as well, as a vice president.[15]

This incestuous relationship between the military and industry has got to stop. While these ex-military guys go on making deals and personal fortunes, and the procurement of defense contracts goes on being an end in itself, the United States remains fundamentally underdefended. It cannot be denied that the politicians have quite a bit to answer for in this area, too (the defense contractors will go to bed with anyone, and individual politicians have found them no less seductive than military men on the verge of retirement, especially when the contractors pay for the privilege in the form of campaign contributions and jobs in home states), but even as it cleans up its own act, Congress must also pass a law forbidding any retired military man of field grade or above, or any former top Pentagon civilian, to go anywhere near the defense industry as a "second career," or as a paid consultant or lobbyist. And if that proves impossible to achieve, then another law should be passed instead, allowing retired military men to do whatever they damn well please—but if they should take a job in any defense-related industry, they would no longer be entitled to their service pensions. Given that greed is a prime motivator for many people, I truly believe such a law would substantially cut down the numbers of ex-military personnel racing for the defense jobs: without a pension, a guy would have to *work* for a living again, rather than just throw his weight and ribbons around; he could get *fired*, just as normal people are, and not be able to shrug that it was all a game anyway, and retire to his home until some other defense contractor comes along to buy his influence.

While it is at it, Congress might finally and forever heed a call that's been made for decades: to unify the armed services, as the Canadian and Israeli governments did so successfully some years ago. The unification would result in (among many things) all services sharing in the fruits of successful military research and development *as dictated by the strategic interests of the country*. The historical scramble among the services for their share of the defense dollar would be over, preventing the duplication among them in force structure, armament, R&D, command and control, and logistics that has allowed America's defense budget to blow out and set the country on the road to bankruptcy. The Marine Corps and Army must be merged into one ground service (though each would retain its heritage and traditions, i.e., once a 1st Marine, always a 1st Marine, just as the 27th Wolfhounds would always be the Wolfhounds), and while the air arm of this unified service would still be very strong to provide lift, air defense, bombers, and tac air, the naval arm would be greatly reduced from the recent, much-talked-about pie-in-the-sky figure of six hundred ships. The point is, America's force structure must be tailored for the year 2000 and beyond. It must be tailored for the country's strategic needs, *not* based on political consideration or whims or on the dreams and schemes of Buck Rogers designers. No longer can the tail wag the dog as it has for altogether too long in America, with weapons dictating strategy when our country's strategic requirements demand the reverse. The self-serving services today would be dragged kicking and screaming into a structure like that being proposed (and the military-industrial complex would be apoplectic), but for the first time in a long, long time, the nation would be well served.

But that is still the future. In the Army today, the problem of self-serving soldiers who go through the "revolving door" into the defense industry could also be addressed from within by beginning to whittle away at the tremendously bloated senior-officer corps from whom the military-industrial complex presently gets its uniformed, and ex-uniformed, membership. Today's Army, with an active-duty strength of fewer than 800,000, has comparatively more generals than George Catlett Marshall had in 1945 when the U.S. Army's troop strength was 8,000,000.* And even as the Pentagon has recently gone cap in hand to Congress to request another 363 generals and admirals to run today's military (the Army's share would be an

---

* In 1945 the Army had fourteen generals for each active division; in 1982, the Army had twenty-four generals per division.[16]

extra 78 flag officers, totaling 393), it isn't beyond reason to suggest that in the Army at least, a lot of people have been underworked and a lot of others oversupervised in the years since 1981 when general officer slots were frozen at 315. Just two examples are the corps headquarters in Japan, which has no maneuver units yet boasts a three-star CG and staff, and the armored corps collecting dust at Fort Hood, Texas, designed to augment NATO forces in Europe when the balloon goes up, but which will never be used because the U.S. military is incapable, logistically, of getting it where it would have to go in any timely fashion.

It is interesting to note that the glut at the tip in the general officers' ranks has today also reached down into the field grades (major to colonel). In 1945, there were 710 soldiers for each Army colonel. By 1988, this ratio had shrunk to just 146 troops to one bird. The Army's rationale for a fat officer corps is to have a trained cadre available in case of a rapid WW II-like mobilization (a scenario that died with the bayonet attack). In warfare of the future, the Army will go with what it has got. There will not be months and years to prepare to fight on some distant battlefield. And in the meantime, this bloated excess exacerbates the centralization problem, necessitates the many otherwise superfluous headquarters and staff positions (i.e., to give the unneeded officers something to do), and drives the ticket-punching sickness that creates the high turnover of officers down at the fighting level. At this time in history, a 40 percent cut in the Army officer corps would not be unwarranted. It would stabilize the excessive turnover of officers at troop-level, which would mean getting the officers back with troops for longer periods so that they can learn their primary function: how to lead warriors into battle. As of this writing, a RIF program is ongoing in the U.S. Army, but let us also hope that while the deadwood is being cleared away the budding warriors within aren't snipped off the vine: it was with great concern that I recently read a statement from Brigadier General Roy Flint, academic dean of West Point, that "you don't find officers making major now, much less colonel, without advanced education and blue chip credentials."[17] And yet the question remains, as it has since the days of Maxwell D. Taylor when all this sheepskin hysteria began: *Why?*

In at least one respect, the eight years of the Reagan Administration bore a striking resemblance to the Eisenhower years of the late fifties. The huge-budget Strategic Defense "Star Wars" Initiative (SDI) is just a logical progression in the Cold War mania that accompanied Sputnik and egged on the Soviet/U.S. missile race; in both the fifties and the eighties the military's fascination with Buck Rogers wonder gear was very detrimental to the human forces far more likely to be employed. At the same time, the first term of the Reagan Administration had an early-sixties feel about it, too: the

President seemed determined to get a war going (and the military stood poised, chomping at the bit, for the order to move), all in the name of democracy. The public outcry that accompanied the early eighties U.S. posturing in Central America suggested that the American people had learned from Vietnam even if those in power had not: many could see that in Nicaragua and El Salvador we were heading down another Street Without Joy, about to get caught all over again trying to cure the symptoms and not the disease; many wondered whether the Administration's passionate hatred of Communism was blinding it to the legitimate concerns of some truly oppressed people, concerns that historically have pushed societies into the Communist camp, such as hunger and poverty, health, education, employment, and justice for all.

It is all part of America's ingrained Cold War policy—severely warped in the forty-one years since George Catlett Marshall declared in a speech at Harvard, "Our policy is directed not against any country or doctrine, but against hunger, poverty, despotism and chaos . . . to permit the emergence of political and social conditions in which free institutions exist"—of fighting Communism for the sake of fighting Communism wherever the red flag waves around the world. Militarily speaking, that is an extremely vague objective, which can do nothing but leave our armed services floundering; besides, as George Kennan, one of the authors of America's containment policy (which started the whole thing off), has reappraised his position: "The lessons of Vietnam are few and plain: not to be hypnotized by the word communism, and not to mess in other people's civil wars where there is no substantial American strategic interest at stake."[18]

Of course, unlike Vietnam, Latin America is of "substantial strategic interest" to the United States. But the U.S. has made its job of keeping the area within the Western sphere of influence harder every day through its insane policy of economically and militarily supporting repressive regimes with leaders like Somoza, Pinochet, or Duvalier—regimes that are or were as bad if not worse than the worst found among the Soviets' satellite countries or the U.S.S.R. itself—simply because the dictators/crooks at the top have thrown their hats in with the U.S. against the Soviet bloc. Historically this attitude has backfired on the U.S. (recent history shows us Diem in Vietnam, the Shah in Iran, Marcos in the Philippines, to name a few), when the people finally cried, "Enough!" After all, it was *American policy* that sent Castro into the Soviet camp. *American policy* is what has turned Central America into a killing field. *American policy* has allowed that gangster Noriega to poison our children with his drugs on our streets. Ernest Hemingway warned of these sad times in his introduction to *Men at War* in 1942—"We must win it [WW II] never forgetting what we are fighting for, in order that while we are fighting Fascism we do not slip into the ideas and ideals of Fascism"—but his message has gone unheeded in succeeding U.S. administrations, which, on top of all else, have allowed the CIA to run riot in Third World nations, with excesses that rival the Nazis in their heyday.

So developing a humane, empathetic ear for the real problems of our neighbors is a primary goal if the United States truly wants to make Latin America a friend and strategic ally. But another factor must also be considered and dealt with, and that is Castro's Cuba.

Cuba is for the revolutionary nations and people of Latin America what China was for the North Koreans in the Korean War, and what Laos and Cambodia were for the Vietnam War: sanctuaries for our enemies and supply depots for their cause. Yet, as David S. Nes, deputy to U.S. ambassador to South Vietnam Henry Cabot Lodge, wrote so succinctly to his boss in 1964, one of the "two basic lessons which the past twenty years of Communist conquest through 'wars of national liberation' have taught us [is] that . . . [a] Communist insurgency having access to an active sanctuary has always prevailed. The insurgencies in Greece, the Philippines and Malaya were defeated because there was no active sanctuary or because they were deprived of the sanctuary."[19] It is time the United States actively takes issue with Cuba's role as supply depot/middleman for the Soviets in providing equipment to Communist regimes and insurgents in Latin America. Only when the sanctuary is deprived them is there even a remote possibility that the insurgents' arms will be laid down for good. How to do it? If solely diplomatic means don't work, a naval and air blockade would: the Soviets aren't going to fight in Cuba, so far from their shores and so close to ours, and, militarily, it is America's only chance of getting on top of a situation otherwise deteriorating day by day.

And yet . . .

Almost fourteen years after the fall of Saigon, a young, serving brigadier general explained to me that in today's Army the problem is *not* the system's being unable to recognize the lessons of the past—that, he assured, it can do. Instead, he said, the Army's problem is its inability to extrapolate from these lessons so they can be "judiciously applied" in the future. Despite the continued heavy emphasis on armor and potential war in Europe, he went on (and being prepared to fight that war is the crux of deterrence, he said, and in principle I agree), he was encouraged by the Army's move toward the establishment of light infantry divisions to deal with smaller and/or unconventional conflicts as well. So am I. But what the Army (and the military overall) must never forget as it surveys the world's trouble spots and plans for and dreams of its next moment of glory is that neither it nor the country it serves can ever afford—in Central or Latin America, in the

Middle East or anywhere—another "only war we've got." That, too, is one of the legacies of Vietnam.

For years there was a popular belief that the Vietnam War destroyed the U.S. Army, but it didn't. Our Vietnam experience simply cut away the facade and exposed a cancer-riddled interior. Now the Army has fought back from the edge it teetered on in the early seventies when dope raged through the new, all-volunteer force and disillusionment led to the resignations of many of the young Regulars—the Pat Graveses, the Jim Mukoyamas, the Ed Clarks—who were among the best of the Army's future. But it still has a long way to go when an Army Professionalism Study in 1984 yielded almost identical results to a similar study conducted in 1970, which pinpointed faked reports, shoddy leadership, and self-promotion as responsible for eroding the basic values of the Army of the day. [20] The 1984 study actually gave senior officers even lower marks for "competence" and "looking out for their subordinates," than had the report of fourteen years before, and half the officers questioned said that "the bold, original, creative officer cannot survive in today's Army." The 1984 study concluded that "the officer corps is focused on personal gain rather than selflessness," and while this well mirrors what is happening in the world outside the military, it cannot foster and sustain high morale within. Meanwhile, in 1988, as the Marine Corps, under Commandant General Alfred M. Gray, and the Air Force, under Chief of Staff Larry D. Welch, publicly announced a campaign to rid themselves of ticket punchers and the ticket-punching mentality, the Army still maintains that it solved this problem way back in the seventies. As Army Chief of Staff Vuono explained, "We hold our officers to standards of selfless service and bedrock integrity. They must then compete within our officer evaluation, promotion and assignment systems, which are designed to reinforce these concepts and advance those who best meet these standards."[21] The theory is great, but the problem remains: the "standards of selfless service and bedrock integrity" are set by the men at the top, and if the men at the top are careerists, they will make room only for their ilk among those coming up through the officer ranks. Besides recalling an officer of the caliber of Fred Weyand, Hal Moore, or Hank Emerson to be Chief of Staff in these times *when change is possible*, Army policy should require a retired heroic soldier of the likes of Jim Gavin or Jim Hollingsworth to be president of all flag-rank promotions boards, to ensure that the ticket punchers, *not* the warriors, are the ones weeded out in the selection process.

The Army must insist that its leaders be taught how to *think* from the moment they step on the first rung of the leadership ladder. They should be encouraged to become students of war, with independent histories, biographies, and autobiographies of men such as Montgomery, Ridgway, Patton, and Rommel made required reading. Combat now and in the future will require leaders who are able to act independently, and who are not afraid of taking risks. A knowledge of history and the ability to think and synthesize are the tools a warrior needs to confidently weigh up the odds while working out the best course of action.

The Army's current system of "up and out" must be abandoned. Not every man can be a general, nor does he want to be, and there is no reason why a good man cannot skipper a rifle company at the age of forty-five or fifty (First Sergeant Walter Sabalauski, who provided veteran NCO leadership in Bill Carpenter's company during the Battle of Dak To in 1966, was fifty-six years old at the time). The Army needs a flexible personnel system that concentrates on the man, not the computer printout, and it is time the Army seriously consider adopting the British system, which has a major commanding at the company level.

Meanwhile, the draft should be reintroduced to return the Army to a *citizens'* army and to make every American aware and prepared to pay the price of admission to life in a land of freedom. At a savings of literally billions of dollars, a draft would also ensure well-educated, high caliber troops, not unlike the draftee-whiz kids who appeared in force in the late fifties post-Sputnik missile age, to understand and operate the high tech, complicated gear the eighties Army had saddled itself with.

The Army must look deeply into itself and make incisive reforms, to include, for example, establishing an Inspector General specifically for training. The imperative for this is that as nuclear weapons are phased down and, I hope, less and less regarded as a viable means of waging war, the Army must be strong enough to pick up any chips that may fall. A *truly* well-trained, *truly* well-led Army is essential, now, as never before. (It should be added here that the Intermediate Nuclear Force [INF] treaty is a giant step back from the nuclear abyss. But it is still only a first step: the destruction of Iran Air's commercial 747 by the U.S. cruiser *Vincennes* during the Gulf conflict well illustrates the potential for human error among anxious, overtired personnel in stressful situations, and is a somber reminder of the need for the superpowers to drastically cut back, perhaps by 90 percent, their strategic missile arsenals to vastly reduce the risk of an *accidental* triggering of global nuclear war.)

The United States must look deeply into itself, too, to see what we as a nation have become. It seems to me that the values that would make someone a patriot—the values that compelled me to join the Army, and to believe that I had a vital role to play in the preservation of those values—have been bled out of America. The Cold War mantle of the free world's policeman (which, if not really a fact, was at least widely accepted as one for many, many years), though perhaps once a great source of pride to our nation, has proved to be a wellspring of arrogance, not unreasonably making us disliked even among many of our friends around the globe, and perhaps even sowing the seeds that have made greed the major growth industry in our land of opportunity. The last eight years have seen America strutting its stuff on the world stage and spending its citizens' hard-earned wages on billions and billions of dollars' worth of military hardware *that can never be used*; meanwhile its industries have closed down in big numbers, many of its families have gone homeless and its children unfed, and we have become the biggest debtor nation in the world.

The United States must *shape up*. It is a great country with a great heritage; it has set a good example in the past and it can do so in the future, if only it begins to choose its battles carefully and makes sure its causes are right. It is time to reduce the military machine that has broken the back of the nation's economy, and begin to rebuild the industrial plant that made us great. While Americans shrink at the thought of the lost war in Vietnam, they forget that even now Japan is celebrating a belated wartime victory: without the constant drain of resources into wasteful military projects, there is no reason that the United States could not be competitive with, perhaps even outshine, its erstwhile foe, and at the same time maintain the very finest military force, one "from whom impossible efforts would be demanded and to whom all sorts of tricks would be taught."

That's the kind of Army in which I should like to fight.

Forty years ago, when Captain Eggleston told eighteen-year-old me that I would one day make a great contribution to my country, I didn't know what he meant. Maybe he didn't either; maybe he just recognized a boy who believed and, good leader that he was, wanted to give me something to aspire to. Whatever his reasoning, I know it worked. If I left the Army and America with anger in my heart, it was no doubt in large part because I did feel I'd given both my all, including speaking out when too many others were silent, an act not all that far removed from the one of the little boy in Italy who told General Eisenhower he didn't think we should have to eat Spam every day. Maybe that was my contribution. In any event, all these years later the anger is gone, and in its place is the belief that I still have a contribution left to make.

This book is a beginning.

APPENDIX

Standing Orders, Rogers' Rangers
(Major Robert Rogers, 1759)

1. Don't forget nothing.
2. Have your musket clean as a whistle, hatchet scoured, sixty rounds powder and ball, and be ready to march at a minute's warning.
3. When you're on the march, act the way you would if you was sneaking up on a deer. See the enemy first.
4. Tell the truth about what you see and what you do. There is an army depending on us for correct information. You can lie all you please when you tell other folks about the Rangers, but don't never lie to a Ranger or officer.
5. Don't never take a chance you don't have to.
6. When we're on the march we march single file, far enough apart so one shot can't go through two men.
7. If we strike swamps, or soft ground, we spread out abreast, so it's hard to track us.
8. When we march, we keep moving till dark, so as to give the enemy the least possible chance at us.
9. When we camp, half the party stays awake while the other half sleeps.
10. If we take prisoners, we keep 'em separate till we have had time to examine them, so they can't cook up a story between 'em.
11. Don't ever march home the same way. Take a different route so you won't be ambushed.
12. No matter whether we travel in big parties or little ones, each party has to keep a scout 20 yards ahead, twenty yards on each flank and twenty yards in the rear, so the main body can't be surprised and wiped out.
13. Every night you'll be told where to meet if surrounded by a superior force.
14. Don't sit down to eat without posting sentries.
15. Don't sleep beyond dawn. Dawn's when the French and Indians attack.
16. Don't cross a river by a regular ford.

17. If somebody's trailing you, make a circle, come back onto your own tracks, and ambush the folks that aim to ambush you.
18. Don't stand up when the enemy's coming against you. Kneel down. Hide behind a tree.
19. Let the enemy come till he's almost close enough to touch. Then let him have it and jump out and finish him up with your hatchet.

NOTES

CHAPTER THREE   HIT AND RUN
1. Omar Bradley and Clay Blair, A *General's Life* (New York: Simon and Schuster, 1983), 543.

CHAPTER FOUR   THE WOLFHOUNDS
1. Robert Leckie, *Conflict: The History of the Korean War, 1950–53* (New York: G. P. Putnam's Sons, 1962), 239–40.
2. *The New York Times*, 28 December 1950.
3. Ross S. Carter, *Those Devils in Baggy Pants* (New York: Bantam, 1985), Dedication.

CHAPTER SIX   THE ONLY GAME IN TOWN
1. *Time*, 3 September 1951.
2. *Time*, 8 October 1951.
3. Bradley and Blair, A *General's Life*, 651.

CHAPTER NINE   DON'T LOOK BACK
1. *Time*, 1 December 1952.

CHAPTER TEN   BLACK SHOES
1. *Time*, 3 August 1953, quoted from Colonel Melvin Voorhees' *Korean Tales*.
2. Leckie, *Conflict*, 387; *Time*, 3 August 1953.
3. Leckie, *Conflict*, 387.
4. *Time*, 3 August 1953.
5. *Newsweek*, 5 January 1959.
6. *Newsweek*, 22 July 1957.
7. *Newsweek*, 7 October 1957.

CHAPTER ELEVEN   THIS AIN'T THE ARMY, MR. JONES
1. *Newsweek*, 19 December 1960.
2. *New York Times*, 23 March 1969.
3. *Newsweek*, 27 March 1961.
4. *Newsweek*, 10 April 1961.
5. *Newsweek*, 10 April 1961.
6. *Newsweek*, 4 August 1958, quoted from General James Gavin's *War and Peace in the Space Age*.

CHAPTER TWELVE   THE VANGUARDS
1. "Battle Indoctrination and Survival, Evasion and Escape," U.S. Army Infantry School, 17 December 1962.
2. *Newsweek*, 24 April 1961.
3. *Newsweek*, 18 September 1961.
4. *Newsweek*, 31 July 1961.
5. *Newsweek*, 31 July 1961.
6. *Stars and Stripes*, 21 August 1961.
7. *Stars and Stripes*, 21 August 1961.

8. *Newsweek*, 18 September 1961.
9. *The New York Times*, 8 May 1962.
10. *Newsweek*, 7 June 1965.
11. *The New York Times*, 20 December 1957.
12. *Newsweek*, 22 May 1961.
13. David Halberstam, *The Best and the Brightest* (New York: Random House, 1972), 76.
14. *Newsweek*, 31 July 1961.

CHAPTER THIRTEEN SCREAMING EAGLES
1. *Newsweek*, 27 April 1964.
2. *Newsweek*, 17 August 1964.
3. *Newsweek*, 15 July 1963.
4. David Halberstam, *The Best and the Brightest* (New York: Penguin, 1985), 562.
5. *Newsweek*, 14 January 1963
6. *Newsweek*, 11 January 1965.

CHAPTER FOURTEEN TIM'S TRAVELING TROUBLE
1. Dennis Parker, as quoted in the personal Vietnam diary of Patrick Graves, Jr., 14 September 1965.
2. *The New York Times*, 30 July 1965.

CHAPTER FIFTEEN THE YEAR OF THE HORSE
1. The history of the Ibus was provided by Sergeant Major Leo B. Smith (Ret.), with additional information from Colonel Robert Channon (Ret.), and Master Sergeant Lyland "Ole" Baumann's 1963 "Origin of the Abu," published in the Fort Campbell newspaper and reprinted in the Abu/Ibu newsletter No. 1, 25 March 1986.
2. *Newsweek*, 11 March 1966.
3. 101st Airborne Division Association, *Vietnam Odyssey, the Story of the 1st Brigade, 101st Airborne Division, in Vietnam* (Texarkana, Ark.: Southwest Printer and Publishers, Inc., 1967).

CHAPTER SIXTEEN BOX SEAT
1. Bernard Fall, *Street Without Joy* (Harrisburg, Pa.: Stackpole Press, 1967), 62.
2. Vo Nguyen Giap, *"Big Victory Great Task"* (New York: Frederick A. Praeger, 1968), 11–12.
3. S. L. A. Marshall, *Bringing Up the Rear* (Novato, Ca.: Presidio Press, 1979), 286.
4. The running firefight between S. L. A. Marshall and the press is well illustrated in Marshall's "Press Failure in Vietnam" (*The New Leader*, 10 October 1966), and "Reporting Vietnam, Eight Correspondents Rebut S. L. A. Marshall's 'Press Failure in Vietnam' " (*The New Leader*, 21 November 1966).
5. Commander's Combat Note No. 82, 173d Airborne Brigade (Separate), 16 October 1965.
6. Bernard B. Fall, *Last Reflections on a War* (New York: Doubleday, 1967), 231.
7. Fall, *Last Reflections on a War*, 271.
8. Marshall, *Bringing Up the Rear*, 287.

CHAPTER SEVENTEEN CORPORATE HEADQUARTERS
1. Dina Rasor, *The Pentagon Underground* (New York: Times Books, 1985), 73–74.
2. "A Brief Survey of the U.S. Army Experience in Mobilization and Training: Remarks Prepared for Members of the Army Training Study Group, Fort Belvoir, Virginia," Historical Office, U.S. Army Training and Doctrine Command, Fort Monroe, Va.
3. Roger Trinquier, *Modern Warfare* (New York: Frederick A. Praeger, 1964), 65.
4. Ward Just, *Military Men* (New York: Knopf, 1970), 248.
5. *Newsweek*, 16 October 1967.
6. Combat Operations After-action Report, Battle of Dak To, HQ, 4th Infantry Division, 3 January 1968.

7. *The New York Times*, 23 November 1967.
8. *The New York Times*, 22 November 1967.
9. *The New York Times*, 22 November 1967.
10. David Halberstam, "Their Call to Duty," *Parade*, 7 July 1985.
11. *Newsweek*, 18 March 1968.
12. *Newsweek*, 12 February 1968.
13. *Newsweek*, 19 February 1968.
14. *Newsweek*, 19 February 1968.
15. David Halberstam, *The Best and the Brightest* (New York: Random House, 1972), 561.
16. *The New York Times*, 23 March 1969.
17. *Problems Facing the United States Army, a Compendium of Comments from Selected Officers*, 1968.

CHAPTER EIGHTEEN   DEATH ROW
1. Just, *Military Men*, 62.

CHAPTER NINETEEN   HARDCORE
1. Memorandum from General Woolnough to General Westmoreland, 9 January 1969.
2. *The New York Times*, 13 March 1969.
3. Inspector General (IG) Investigation MIV-67–71, Exhibit B-41, p. 1414.
4. Inspector General (IG) Investigation MIV-67–71, Exhibit B-49, p. 1751.
5. MACIG-INV Report of Investigation MIV-67–71, p. 9.
6. Neil Sheehan, "Annals of War, An American Soldier in Vietnam," *The New Yorker*, 27 June 1988.

CHAPTER TWENTY   BORN TO LOSE
1. Peter Arnett, "Profits from Corruption in South Vietnam Being Measured in Millions of Dollars," *Daily Press*, Newport News, Va., 5 May 1967.

CHAPTER TWENTY-ONE   A LAW UNTO HIMSELF
1. *The Atlantic*, December 1969.
2. CID Report of Investigation No. 71-CID248-41126, Exhibit Q, p. 2.
3. *Newsweek*, 8 February 1971.

CHAPTER TWENTY-THREE   A HANDFUL OF ASHES
1. *The Washington Post*, 6 June 1971.
2. Inspector General Investigation MIV-67–71, Exhibit B-33, p. 1290.
3. CID Report No. 71-CID248-41126, Exhibit DDDDDDD.
4. Memo for Record, Office of the Chief of Staff, 12 July 1971.
5. Douglas Kinnard, *The War Managers* (Hanover, N.H.: University Press of New England, 1977), 25.
6. Memorandum for the Secretary of the Army from Chief of Staff Westmoreland, 29 September 1971.

EPILOGUE
1. Clay Blair, *The Forgotten War: America in Korea* (New York: Times Books, 1987), 113.
2. Letter to the authors (in translation) from Colonel Nguyen dôn Tu, 1 November 1985. Colonel Harry Summers, when asked to comment on Tu's 1985 recall, stood by the accuracy of his translator, Master Sergeant Garrett Bell, at the original meeting. Summers added that the present government in Vietnam has never registered an official protest over Tu's words as recorded in Summers's book *On Strategy*.
3. William S. Lind (Military Reform Institute), Report to the Congressional Military Reform Caucus, 5 April 1984.
4. *1982 Register of Graduates and Former Cadets of the United States Military Academy* (Association of Graduates, USMA, West Point, N.Y., 1982), 595.
5. Jean Larteguy, *The Centurions* (New York: E. P. Dutton, 1961).

6. "West Point: Worth the Cost?" *Army Times*, 9 May 1988.
7. "Pentagon 'Revolving Door' Turning Faster," *Cleveland Plain Dealer*, 17 August 1986.
8. *The Washington Post*, 25 May 1987.
9. "GAO: Pentagon Rigs Weapons Tests," *Philadelphia Inquirer*, 26 July 1988.
10. Memorandum from Dina Rasor of the Project on Military Procurement, Washington D.C., 5 June 1988.
11. *Newsweek*, 27 June 1988.
12. "Expensive Army Vehicle Under Scrutiny," *Tampa Tribune Times*, 3 May 1987.
13. *San Jose Mercury News*, 28 April 1987.
14. Gregg Easterbrook, "DIVAD," *Atlantic Monthly*, October 1982.
15. *Army Times*, 18 April 1988. Anyone desiring more information on the Abrams, Bradley, or Sergeant York weapons systems, or on any other dubious products of the military-industrial complex, is referred to the Project on Military Procurement and the Center for Defense Information, both watchdogs of the United States defense industry that are based in Washington, D.C.
16. Rasor, *The Pentagon Underground*, 146.
17. *U.S. News & World Report*, 18 April 1988.
18. *New York Review of Books*, 12 June 1975, quoted in "Lessons of Vietnam and the Future of American Foreign Policy," *Australian Outlook: Journal of the Australian Institute of International Affairs*, August 1976.
19. Memorandum from David Nes to Ambassador Lodge, 10 March 1964.
20. "Can We Fight a Modern War?" *Newsweek*, 9 July 1984.
21. *The New York Times*, 25 April 1988.

GLOSSARY

AAOC Anti-aircraft operations center

ADC Assistant Division Commander

AG Adjutant General

AID Agency for International Development

AIT Advanced Individual Training

Airborne The term used to describe a parachute-trained soldier, a parachute unit, or an operation in which parachutes are employed to drop personnel and equipment.

Airmobile An operation in which personnel and equipment are moved by helicopter.

AK47 A Soviet assault rifle that is the standard individual weapon in Eastern bloc countries.

AO Area of operation

APC Armored personnel carrier; a thin-skinned vehicle used to transport infantry to and around the battlefield.

Arc-light B-52 strike

Arty Artillery

ARVN Pronounced "Arvin," the Army of the Republic of Vietnam (i.e., the South Vietnamese).

Assets Available helicopter and other fixed-wing aviation support.

BAR Browning Automatic Rifle. The standard U.S. infantry assault rifle during World War II and the Korean War; considered by many to be the most rugged, reliable, and effective weapon the U.S. military ever fielded.

Battalion A military unit traditionally composed of 1,000 men.

Battlegroup Under the Pentomic scheme, a unit composed of five maneuver companies as well as support units; basically, a reinforced infantry battalion.

Bird Slang for helicopter or airplane. The term is also used to describe a full colonel (see below).

Bird colonel A full colonel. The term "bird" refers to a full colonel's insignia, which is a silver eagle.

Blue Max Slang for the Medal of Honor

Booby trap An explosive device normally employed in an antipersonnel role.

BOQ Bachelor officers' quarters.

Brigade A military unit that normally controls three maneuver battalions as well as supporting units such as artillery, armor, engineer, medical, maintenance, etc.

C-4 A plastic explosive; its most popular use on the battlefield in Vietnam was to heat water and C rations.

C&C Command and control helicopter

CG Commanding general

Charlie Slang for Viet Cong or NVA personnel.

Chieu hoi Meaning "open arms," a program designed to encourage Viet Cong and NVA surrender or defection. Individual enemy soldiers who came in under the program were also called "Chieu hois."

Chopper Slang for helicopter

CIB Combat Infantryman's Badge

CIC Counterintelligence Corps

CID Criminal Investigation Division

CIDG Civilian Irregular Defense Group; Cambodes, Laotians, and natives (Montagnards, Nungs) trained and employed in Vietnam under the aegis of U.S. Special Forces.

CINCPAC Commander in Chief, Pacific

Claymore An antipersonnel land mine

CO Commanding officer; conscientious objector

Commo Slang for communications

Company A military unit traditionally composed of 200 men.

COMUSMACV Commander, U.S. Military Assistance Command, Vietnam.

CONARC Continental Army Command

Conex A large metal shipping container

COPL Combat outpost line

Corps A military unit traditionally composed of three divisions as well as tactical supporting units such as artillery, armor, communications, engineer, signal, etc.

COSVN Central Office for South Vietnam; the control headquarters for all communist activity, political and military, in South Vietnam.

Counterinsurgency Military operations conducted against insurgents (guerrillas).

CP Command post

CPX Command post exercise

CQ Charge of quarters

DA Department of the Army

DEROS Date eligible return from overseas

Dich Pronounced "dick," one of many slang terms for enemy dead used during the Vietnam War.

DIT Directorate of Individual Training

Division A military unit traditionally composed of three regiments/brigades as well as supporting units.

DMAC Delta Military Assistance Command

DMG Distinguished Military Graduate (ROTC).

DMZ Demilitarized zone

DRAC Delta Regional Assistance Command (formerly DMAC)

DSC Distinguished Service Cross; the U.S. Army's second-highest award.

Dust-off Slang for medical evacuation by helicopter

E-1 (recruit)–E-9 (sergeant major) Enlisted pay grades

EE8 World War II and Korea-vintage field telephone

ER Efficiency Report, also called OER, Officer Efficiency Report

FAC Forward air controller

Fart Sack Sleeping bag

Field first An unauthorized NCO position; the "field first" of a company is the unit's tactical first sergeant in the field when a company's assigned first sergeant is weak or prefers life in the company rear.

FO Forward observer. The FO accompanies infantry in the field, and adjusts artillery and mortar fires.

Frag Slang for a fragmentation grenade; in Vietnam, the term also referred to a mutinous soldier's killing, or attempting to kill, a strong leader with a frag grenade.

Fruit salad A soldier's awards and decorations, displayed as ribbons and badges worn over the left breast.

FSB Fire support base. A permanent or semipermanent installation that houses artillery, infantry, command and control, and supporting facilities; its purpose is to provide indirect artillery support to infantry units within its AO.

FTX Field training exercise

Guerrilla Also referred to as an "insurgent"; a member of an irregular (paramilitary) unit that employs unconventional tactics, usually in fighting a war of resistance.

Guerrilla warfare Low-cost, economy-of-force, unconventional military operations conducted by irregular (guerrilla) and/or regular military personnel, generally against an established government or order.

Gunship A helicopter designed as a firing platform to place supporting fires (machine gun and rocket) on the enemy.

GVN Government of South Vietnam

Half-track The M16, a lightly armored vehicle with front wheels and back tanklike treads; used in World War II as C&C and to transport infantry, and in the Korean War as an infantry support system employing four .50-caliber machine guns.

H&I Harassment and interdictory fire

HE High explosives

HES Hamlet Evaluation System

Huey Slang for any of the UH-series helicopters.

I&R Intelligence and Reconnaissance platoon, also known as the eyes and ears of the regiment.

INCOC Infantry Noncommissioned Officer Course; an accelerated program designed to produce NCOs during the Vietnam War.

Incoming Indirect enemy artillery and mortar fire that falls on friendly positions.

Insert Deployment of any maneuver element by helicopter.

Instant NCO Slang for a graduate of the INCOC.

Insurgency Armed activity directed against a constituted government.

JUSPAO Joint U.S. Public Affairs Office

KATUSA Korean Augmentation Troops, U.S. Army

KIA Killed in action

Klick Slang for kilometer

KMAG Korea Military Advisory Group

KP Kitchen police

LAW M-72 light antitank weapon

LD Line of departure

Leg A non-Airborne soldier

List A term pertaining to helicopter assets and/or inserts.

LMG Light machine gun; in World War II and the Korean War, the .30-caliber, and in Vietnam, the M-60.

LNO Liaison officer

Lock and load To place a weapon on safety, and then ready it to fire by placing a round in the chamber.

LOH Light observation helicopter, also called a "loach."

LP Listening post; an early warning element deployed in front of the main lines.

LRRP Pronounced "lurp," long-range reconnaisance patrol. Members of LRRP teams are also called LRRPs (lurps).

LZ Landing zone

M-1 U.S. .30-caliber semiautomatic rifle used during World War II and the Korean war.

M4 The Sherman medium tank. Thirty-six tons, with a 76-mm main gun, the Sherman is the best tank the U.S. Army has ever fielded.

M-16 Unquestionably the worst infantry weapon ever forced upon America's fighting men; the standard U.S. infantry rifle employed in Vietnam.

M24 A U.S. light tank with a 75-mm gun, used during World War II and the Korean War.

M46 A U.S. medium tank with a 90-mm gun, used during the Korean War.

M-60 A U.S. light machine gun used during the Vietnam War.

M-79 A U.S. infantry direct-fire weapon, commonly called a grenade launcher but which in fact fired 40-mm HE and buckshot rounds; without doubt the most effective U.S. infantry weapon employed during the Vietnam War.

MACV Military Assistance Command, Vietnam

MASH Mobile army surgical hospital

MEDCAP Medical civic action program

Medevac Medical evacuation by helicopter. Also known as "dust-off."

MIA Missing in action

MLR Main line of resistance

Montagnards The indigenous mountain people of Vietnam

MOS Military occupational speciality

MPC Military payment certificate; also known as "scrip" or "funny money" and used instead of U.S. dollars for currency control purposes.

MSR Main supply route

NCO Noncommissioned officer

No-man's-land The contested zone between the main battle areas of two antagonists.

Noncom Slang for noncommissioned officer

NVA North Vietnamese Army

OCS Officer Candidate School; an accelerated program designed to produce officers from within the enlisted ranks.

OJT On-the-job training

OP Outpost or observation post

OPCON A term used to designate the operational control of a unit over a subordinate unit.

OPLAN Operations plan (a contingency plan)

OPORD Operations order

P-38 An infantryman's best friend: his inch-and-a-half long metal can opener. The P-38 was also a World War II reconnaissance aircraft.

P-51 A World War II and Korean War vintage tactical fighter aircraft.

Pacification A MACV program in Vietnam designed to win the hearts and minds of the local populace to our side.

PAVN People's Army of Vietnam, known as the NVA after American forces were engaged.

PCS Permanent change of station

Pentomic The first major reorganization of the U.S. Army in the nuclear age, in which the battalion was disbanded and five battlegroups replaced the traditional regiment. The Pentomic scheme was the Edsel of U.S. Army reorganization.

PF Popular Forces; the village-level South Vietnamese militia.

PFC Private, first class

Platoon A military unit traditionally composed of 40 soldiers.

PLF Parachute landing fall

PRC-25 Pronounced "prick twenty-five," the standard U.S. infantry FM radio used in Vietnam.

Punji stake The ultimate in low-cost antipersonnel weapons: a sharpened bamboo stake, partially buried by the VC in wait for unsuspecting counterinsurgents.

Purple Heart A military decoration awarded for any wound sustained in combat.

PX Post exchange

PZ Pick-up zone (used in connection with helicopter operations).

Quad-50 Four .50-caliber machine guns mounted on an M16 half-track.

RA Regular Army

R&R Rest and recreation

Range card A card used by infantry that shows a position's sector of fire and primary direction of fire.

RCT Regimental combat team

Recon Reconnaissance

Regiment A military unit traditionally composed of three infantry battalions.

REMF Rear echelon motherfucker. A soldier who keeps as far from the fighting as possible; generically speaking, anyone and everyone in the rear or at higher headquarters who is (or appears to be) out of touch with the realities of the battlefield or with the field soldier's lot.

RF Regional Forces; the district- and province-level South Vietnamese militia.

RIF Reduction in Forces; a U.S. Army program designed to shrink the size of its forces. RIF can also mean "reconnaissance in force."

ROAD Reorganization Objectives Army Division, the second major reorganization of the U.S. Army in the nuclear age (replacing the Pentomic scheme). In this very flexible scheme, under the division umbrella were three control headquarters (called brigades), each of which could have atttached to it any number of the division's battalions and support units as required by the mission.

ROK Republic of Korea (i.e., South Korea). ROK also referred to the South Korean Army, members of which were called ROKs.

ROTC Reserve Officers Training Course

RPG Rocket-propelled grenade; specifically, the Soviet B-40 antitank, antipersonnel weapon.

RTO Radiotelephone operator

RVN Republic of Vietnam (i.e., South Vietnam)

S-1 Personnel and administration at brigade/regiment/group or below. In general, the *-1* designation always refers to personnel, whether it is preceded by an "S," a "G," or "J." (The "S" indicates Special Staff, which is always found at brigade/regiment/group and below; a "G" indicates General Staff, which is found at division level and above; a "J" indicates Joint Staff, which is the integrated Army/Air Force/Marine/Navy staff.)

S-2 Intelligence (see S-1 for more details)

S-3 Operations (see S-1 for more details)

S-4 Logistics (see S-1 for more details)

S-5 Civil affairs (see S-1 for more details)

Sapper A soldier specially trained in infiltration and demolition. In the British forces, a sapper is an engineer.

SCR-300 The standard U.S. infantry FM radio used in World War II and Korea.

Scrip see *MPC*.

Search and destroy A military operation designed to destroy enemy formations and facilities, but not to hold ground.

Second balloon Slang for second lieutenant

SED-DIT Schools and Education Division, Directorate of Individual Training

Shake and bake Slang for graduate of INCOC

Sitrep (SITRPT) Situation report

Six Originally the radio identification for unit commander; popularly used as shorthand when referring to the CO, as in "The Six wants it done right now."

SKS A Soviet semiautomatic carbine

Slick A troop-carrying helicopter

Snowbird An interim assignment

SOP Standing Operating Procedure

SPAT A full track, self-propelled antitank vehicle

Spec Specialist; a technical rank that begins at the E-4 pay level (Spec-4) and ends at the E-7 pay level (Spec-7).

Squad The basic infantry fighting unit, traditionally composed of approximately twelve men.

Stand in the door An Airborne term referring to the moment before one steps out of the door of an aircraft; used in popular jargon to signal a total commitment on one's part to a belief, or one's determination to stand by one's word or commitment.

Steel pot A soldier's steel helmet with plastic liner

STRAC Strategic Army Command; in the early sixties, a headquarters that controlled all of the U.S. Army's ready reaction forces. In Army jargon, STRAC has come to mean military perfection and readiness.

Tac air Tactical air support

TAOR Tactical area of responsibility

TDY Temporary duty

Tet The Vietnamese lunar New Year holiday period

TOC Tactical operations center

TOE Table of Organization and Equipment

Top, Topkick First sergeant

UCMJ Uniform Code of Military Justice

USARPAC U.S. Army, Pacific

USARV U.S. Army, Vietnam

VC Viet Cong

VCI Viet Cong infrastructure

Viet Cong Vietnamese Communist

Vietnamization The American program under Richard Nixon to turn the war over to the South Vietnamese so that America could withdraw from the conflict "with honor."

VNAF South Vietnamese Air Force

War of attrition The destruction of enemy forces and matériel at a rate that the enemy cannot sustain.

Waste To kill

Whitewalls An Airborne haircut: shaved on both sides and the back of the head, and no more than about half an inch of hair on top.

WIA Wounded in action

Willie Peter, WP White phosphorous

XO Executive officer

Zap To kill

4-F A World War II medical classification; 4-F meant not fit for military service because of physical or mental impairment or deficiency.

INDEX